CANADA
Lake Superior
MINNESOTA
St. Paul
Minneapolis
WISCONSIN
Green Bay
Madison
Lake Michigan
MICHIGAN
Lake Huron
Lansing
Flint
Detroit
Lake Ontario
Lake Erie
NEW HAMPSHIRE
VERMONT
MAINE
Bangor
Augusta
Montpelier
Concord
NEW YORK
Albany
Buffalo
Boston
MASSACHUSETTS
Providence
RHODE ISLAND
Hartford
CONNECTICUT
New York
Trenton
NEW JERSEY
Philadelphia
PENNSYLVANIA
Harrisburg
Pittsburgh
IOWA
Cedar Rapids
Des Moines
Chicago
Peoria
ILLINOIS
Springfield
Fort Wayne
INDIANA
Indianapolis
Toledo
Cleveland
OHIO
Columbus
Cincinnati
Baltimore
Annapolis
Dover
DELAWARE
Washington, D.C.
MARYLAND
WEST VIRGINIA
Charleston
Richmond
VIRGINIA
Kansas City
Jefferson City
St. Louis
MISSOURI
Springfield
Louisville
Frankfort
KENTUCKY
NORTH CAROLINA
Raleigh
Charlotte
Wilmington
Tulsa
Nashville
Knoxville
TENNESSEE
Memphis
Fort Smith
Little Rock
ARKANSAS
El Dorado
Tupelo
MISSISSIPPI
Jackson
Biloxi
Birmingham
ALABAMA
Montgomery
Mobile
Columbia
SOUTH CAROLINA
Charleston
Atlanta
Augusta
GEORGIA
Savannah
Valdosta
Jacksonville
Tallahassee
Pensacola
Shreveport
LOUISIANA
Baton Rouge
New Orleans
ATLANTIC OCEAN
Orlando
Tampa
FLORIDA
Miami
Gulf of Mexico
BAHAMAS
CUBA

PUERTO RICO
0 20 40 miles
0 20 40 kilometers
San Juan
Bayamón
Carolina
Ponce

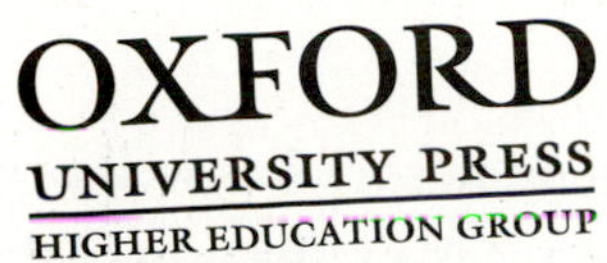

Oxford University Press makes history—again.

Dear Professor,

Oxford University Press has a long tradition of publishing titles by some of the foremost scholars in American history, including five Pulitzer Prize winners in the past ten years. Continuing this tradition of excellence, we are very pleased to announce the publication of our first American history survey textbook in nearly eighty years, *Of the People: A History of the United States*, by James Oakes, Michael McGerr, Jan Ellen Lewis, Nick Cullather, and Jeanne Boydston.

Of the People offers a comprehensive and balanced account of American history and provides a fresh new way of looking at people, places, and power as told through the story of American democracy.

Professor Lloyd Ray Gunn at the University of Utah believes that "*Of the People* promises to emerge as one of the leading American history textbooks on the market," while Professor Melissa Estes Blair at the University of Georgia comments, "It's basically all of the good things about my current textbook, but with better writing and far more useful features."

We invite you to take a guided tour of this text. We believe you will find the authors' commitment to narrating a history "of the people"—of their struggles to shape their lives and their land—apparent on every page.

Like us, you may have noticed the dramatic rise in the cost of textbooks over the past few years. As one of the top publishers in the world and a not-for-profit company in the United States, **we are uniquely situated to produce high-quality scholarship at the lowest possible price for you and your students.**

We invite you to compare the price and quality of *Of the People* to other textbooks published for your course. You'll find that the price of *Of the People*—at $79.95 for each split—is on average 15–40% less expensive than other publishers' comprehensive textbooks.

We know that you can't put a price on a great education, but we can put a price on a textbook. Oxford University Press is committed to publishing the best resources at the lowest possible price.

Furthermore, Oxford University Press publishes a vast array of titles in American history, and most of these titles can be packaged with *Of the People* at no additional cost or at a significant discount to your students. See this insert for a listing of packages.

We hope you will take the time to consider this exciting new textbook. We believe you will find it comprehensive and balanced and a reflection of the authors' belief that all aspects of human existence are the stuff of history.

Sincerely,

Brian Wheel
Executive Editor
Oxford University Press

Of the People offers a comprehensive and balanced account of American History . . .

. . . encompassing the different spheres of human life—cultural as well as governmental, social as well as economic, environmental as well as military. This commitment to comprehensiveness and balance is a reflection of the authors' belief that all aspects of human existence are the stuff of history.

Of the People is a well-rounded and carefully considered synthesis of American history that challenge readers on their conventional views of the material. Well-written and laid out, I would recommend this text for any survey course.

—Tim Garvin, *University of California–Long Beach*

AMERICAN LANDSCAPE

>> The "Crusade" Against Alcohol

A few days before Christmas in 1873, Dr. Dioclelian Lewis arrived in Hillsboro, Ohio, to speak on the evils of alcohol. He had given the speech many times before, but on this occasion the women who came proved unusually responsive. Lewis told them how, when he was a boy, his mother saved his father from drink by persuading a local saloonkeeper to stop selling liquor. The next morning a group of Hillsboro women met for prayer and then marched through the town urging local merchants to stop selling liquor. Inspired by their success, the women kept up the pressure through the winter of 1873/1874.

The Crusade, as it came to be called, quickly spread to more than 900 towns and cities in 31 states and territories. The women closed down thousands of liquor stores and saloons and secured written pledges from hundreds of druggists and hotel keepers not to sell alcohol. With the dramatic success of the Crusade of 1873/1874, temperance was reborn as a movement dominated by women.

From these humble, almost accidental, beginnings, there grew one of the late nineteenth century's largest outlets for women's political activism. Under the auspices of the Woman's Christian Temperance Union, women took up causes that stretched well beyond the suppression of alcohol. Voting and office holding were restricted to men, but the WCTU expanded democratic participation to include tens of thousands of women.

The Politics of Slavery

In 1817 a Boston reporter, observing the absence of the invidious politics that had plagued the first three decades of nationhood, declared that America had at last achieved "an era of good feeling." That sentiment seemed confirmed three years later when President James Monroe was reelected with all but one electoral vote—and that one withheld not in opposition to Monroe but in deference to Washington, the only unanimously elected president.

But all was not right with the new republic. Among the festering problems, becoming more and more apparent even as the nation entered a time of seeming prosperity, was slavery. Its continued existence had become more and more controversial. In 1820 the U.S. Congress defined the slave trade as piracy. Five years later a U.S. patrol seized the slave ship *Antelope*, sailing under a Venezuelan flag with a cargo of 281 Africans. Declaring the slave trade contrary to natural law, the U.S. Supreme Court freed most of the slaves. Because the justices found that the United States had no jurisdiction over the laws of other nations, and that slavery was legal in Spain and Venezuela, the Court returned the ship and the 39 captives held to be owned by Spaniards.

> "This momentous question, like a fire bell in the night, awakened and filled me with terror. I considered it at once the knell of the union. It is hushed, indeed, for the moment. But this is a reprieve only, not a final sentence. . . . I regret that I am now to die in the belief, that the useless sacrifice of themselves by the generation of 1776, to acquire self-government and happiness to their own country, is to be thrown away by the unwise and unworthy passions of their sons, and that my only consolation is to be, that I live not to weep over it."
>
> THOMAS JEFFERSON,
> commenting on the Missouri Crisis, April 22, 1820

Free blacks and a significant number of whites continued to attack slavery as im-

Arctic Circle, where Native Americans began to build the boats, weapons, and tools necessary to hunt whales and seals. Out of these regional environments—Eastern Woodlands, Plains, Great Basin and Southwest, California and Pacific Coast, and Subarctic—developed the distinctive Indian cultures that European explorers later encountered. By the time of Columbus's voyage, these Indian peoples were as different from one another as the peoples of Europe.

Pacific Northwest Indian Mask

The Indians of the Eastern Woodlands

The woodlands east of the Mississippi River gave rise to several distinctive Native American cultures, including the Mississippian mound builders, whose center was at Cahokia (near present-day East St. Louis, Missouri). By 700 BCE, Indians in this area had begun to cultivate crops, and by the twelfth century, agriculture had spread over much of the region east of the Mississippi and into the Southwest. These Mississippian societies were distinguished by the increasing complexity of their crafts, the extent of their trade networks, and their increasing capacity to support large populations from their agriculture. One estimate suggests that maize accounted for half of the Mississipians' diet. All of them built mounds in which to bury their dead and as platforms for temples and other public structures. The mounds can still be seen today at Cahokia, although the structures themselves and the people who worshiped in them have long since disappeared.

These Indian societies were increasingly hierarchical in their political and social

AMERICAN PORTRAIT

>> Tituba Shapes Her World and Saves Herself

Her name was Tituba. Some say she was African, a Yoruba, others that she was an Arawak Indian from Guyana. Had she not been accused of practicing witchcraft in Salem, Massachusetts, in 1692, she surely would have been forgotten by history. Whether she came from South America or Africa, she had been torn away from her home and sent to work on a sugar plantation on the Caribbean island of Barbados, which the English had colonized almost 50 years before. Whatever her origins, Tituba lived in an African-majority society and absorbed African customs.

Tituba was probably a teenager when she was taken, once again as a slave, to Massachusetts in 1680. She had been purchased by a young, Harvard-educated Barbadian, Samuel Parris. Parris's father had failed as a planter, and named only two names—Sarah Good and Sarah Osborne. She talked about a tall, white-haired man in Boston who made her sign a mysterious book, and about conspiring with other, unnamed witches.

Responding to the hints of her Puritan interrogators, Tituba confirmed that she had made a covenant with the devil, the tall man in Boston. But she also added elements that came from African and Indian cultures, such as a "thing all over hairy, all the face harye

Our theme of American democracy unfolds in the story of people and their struggles to shape every dimension of their lives.

Of the People presents American h
tory as both an art, a narrative st
of great interest—and as a science,
enterprise that comes from questi
and the search for answers in the do
ments of the past. Students, in ot
words, might actually enjoy read
for class and come prepared with t
own questions. . . . I think this
approaches the material in a way t
will encourage such an outcome.

–Suzanne Cooper Gua
Queens University of Char

It's About PEOPLE. . . .

Every chapter opens with a biographical vignette, focusing on one person (ordinary or not) whose individual experiences helped to shape our common history.

AMERICAN PORTRAIT

>> "The Queen of the Waves"

On August 6, 1926, Gertrude Ederle walked across the beach at Cape Gris-Nez on the French coastline. Her body and her bright red swimsuit were heavily greased. At 7:00 A.M., the 19-year-old from New York City plunged into the water and began to swim toward the coast of England.

"Trudy," the daughter of a German immigrant butcher, was a champion distance swimmer who had won medals at the 1924 Olympics, but no woman had ever completed the long, hazardous swim across the English Channel. In fact, only five men had accomplished the feat. Ederle herself had tried and failed the year before. Exhausted, she had been pulled from the water by her coach, who rebuked her for playing the ukulele instead of practicing hard in the preceding weeks.

This time was different. Despite the tides, the chill water, and the threat of sharks, Ederle persevered.

namic industrial economy seemed effortlessly to produce plenty of roadsters, movies, and prosperity.

Ederle herself exemplified a new national culture, rooted in the needs of the booming consumer economy, that broke sharply with the forms and conventions of the past. Emphasizing the importance of pleasure, this modern culture celebrated leisure activities such as dancing, channel swimming, ukulele playing, and other diversions. The ukulele-playing Ederle loved "all normal pleasures, including a jazzy dance now and then." The new culture glorified the purchase and consumption

QUEEN OF the WAVES

The chapter openers are wonderful! I would use them as a way to get students to frame the issues and questions that are developed in the chapter. Of the three I read—Rolfe, Maclay and Ruffin—all were very well done. I applaud those choices because they bring to life individuals whose actions exemplify the larger issues unders consideration. The portraits breathe life into these figures and make them more human.

—Vincent L. Toscano, *Nova Southeastern University*

Every chapter contains voices from the people, boxed quotations and retyped letters that remind us that our words also make history.

I like both the fact of having an overarching theme and of having American democracy be that theme. Students tend to have a simplistic view of what American democracy means, and the presentation of it in this text will complicate it. The authors treat the theme more implicitly and subtly than explicitly, which will be fine either in the case that the professor does not wish to highlight it, or if the professor will choose to assist students in identifying how the theme functions in each chapter.

—Anne Foster, *Indiana State University*

South and most did agricultural labor on the lands of t
worked farmland in New Jersey and New York and t

I was about four years old. My mother had several children, and they were sold upon master's death to separate purchasers. She was sold . . . to a Georgia trader. . . . After [my new master] had purchased me . . . he took me before him on his horse, and started home; but my poor mother, when she saw me leaving her for the last time, ran after me, took me down from the horse, clasped me in her arms, and wept loudly and bitterly over me. My master seemed to pity her, and endeavored to soothe her distress by telling her that he would be a good master to me, and that I should not want anything. She then . . . besought my master to buy her and the rest of her children, and not permit them to be carried away by the negro buyers; but whilst thus entreating him to save her and her family, the slave-driver, who had [already] bought her came running in pursuit of her with a raw-hide in his hand. When he overtook us, he told her he was her master now, and ordered her to give that little negro to its owner. . . . he gave her two or three heavy blows on the shoulders . . . , snatched me from her arms, handed me to my master . . . and dragged her back towards the place of sale. My master then quickened the pace of his horse; and . . . the cries of my poor parent became more and more indistinct—at length they died away in the distance, and I never again heard the voice of my poor mother.

Charles Ball,
describing the last time he saw his mother

made it more difficult for owners to emancipate slave
emancipated were often old and deemed of little econ

It's About PLACES. . . .

"American Landscape" features appear in every chapter, brief essays designed to illuminate the diversity of people living their lives in various places and contexts (work life, home life, government life, cultural life, etc.). By focusing on one essential space, building, locale, town, encampment, community, or region in time, **American Landscapes** examine the dynamic of people and power, helping students to appreciate individual differences while drawing upon larger themes of life across American history.

AMERICAN LANDSCAPE

>> The Slave Ship

We do not usually think of a ship as part of a landscape, but the slave ship was one of the most important locations in the eighteenth century. It was at once a floating factory, prison, and fortress. It was there that Africans were transformed into slaves.

Any ship, small or large, could be made into a slave ship. Because the cost of transporting slaves across the Atlantic was so high, accounting for three-quarters of the price of a slave, slave merchants tried to crowd as many Africans as possible into each ship—300, 400, or even 600. The English were particularly efficient, carrying twice as many slaves per crew member and half again as many slaves per ship as the other nations, thereby increasing the profits.

In order to maximize the number of Africans who could be transported on each ... platforms were built be- ... the decks of the ship, ... ubling the surface area ... which the slaves could ... ed. With perhaps only ... nd a half feet between ... tform and the ceiling, ... ricans could not stand ... , because they were ... so tightly, could they ... from side to side. En- ... ing captains made use ... the smallest spaces by ... them with children. ... king so many human ... into such tight quar- ... eated the risk of suffo- ... But if the hatches were ... en, the Africans might ... confinement and over- ... the crew. Hence, grates ... laced over the hatches, ... mall air scuttles were ... the sides of the ship. ... end of the eighteenth century, some ships used large funnel tubes made out of canvas and hoops to carry air below decks.

Men and women were kept separate, their portions of the decks divided by partitions. Male slaves were shackled and confined below deck for most of each day. Chained together and without enough room to stand up, many

continued

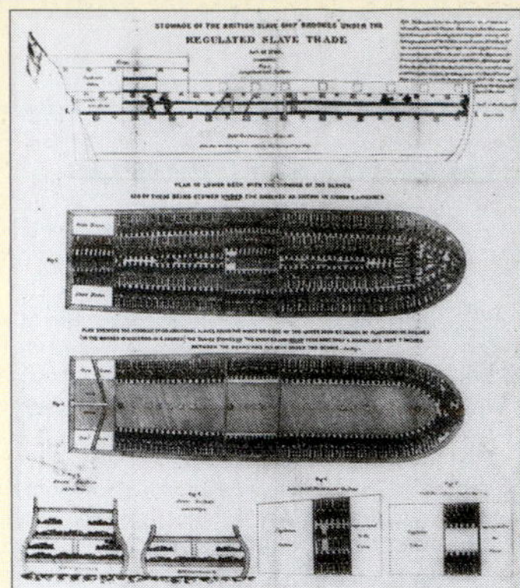

AMERICAN LANDSCAPE

>> Levittown, New York

For many Americans, the first Levittown epitomized the virtues and defects of suburbia, consumerism, and democracy in post–World War II America. The new community seemed to be a democratic triumph, a visual reminder of upward mobility and equality of condition. The male heads of Levittown households tended to be prosperous blue-collar workers, veterans of World War II reaching for middle-class status for their growing, baby boom families. As an observer noted, Levittown was a "one-class community." Most households had an annual income of about $3,500 to $4,000, just enough to afford a place in the suburb.

From another angle, Levittown seemed less democratic. The suburb was notable for who didn't live there. Amid all the young families, there were few teenagers or senior citizens. There were hardly any African Americans, either.

The homogeneity of Levittown was no accident. The developer, William Levitt, had planned it that way. Levittown's first four-room Cape Cod houses came in only five models that differed very little from each other. To observers, the houses and streets of the new development all appeared to be the same. In fact, William Levitt even admitted that he had once gotten lost in all the look-alike streets of his suburb. The uniform style and cost of the houses ensured that the new development would attract only one class of residents. So-called restrictive covenants—special clauses in housing deeds—ensured that only whites bought property in Levittown.

Levitt also tried to impose uniform behavior on his residents. Community rules forbade putting up fences or hanging out the wash on weekends. Some of the residents themselves promoted conformity in Levittown. They wrote the local newspaper to attack neighbors who broke the rules. A nonconformist could expect to be labeled a "commie" or a "Russkie."

In Levittown, as in the rest of America, there was a heavy emphasis on domesticity. The design of the community and its houses reflected the domestic values of the period. The small Cape Cod homes encouraged family "togetherness." With so little private space, family members congregated around the kitchen table or in front of the TV in the living room. The wives of Levittown were expected to spend weekdays doing domestic tasks at home, rather than working at a paying job. That was how Levitt could assume these women would not need to hang out laundry on the weekends. Because the kitchen was supposed to be the center of women's lives, that room was placed at the front of the Cape Cod houses in Levittown.

The design of Levittown also supported men's domestic role. Former apartment dwellers found they had to spend time at home mowing their new lawns. Moreover, Levittown had few traditionally masculine public places—bars, firehouses, ball fields, and the like. Instead, the community promoted family togetherness away from home with plenty of playgrounds and swimming pools for children and their parents. As the local property owners association concluded, "Levittown is a child-centered community."

Despite the power of conformity, Levittown also revealed the survival of individuality in America. In time, the suburb became less homogeneous. With each succeeding year, the Levitts offered houses with a bit more variety. In 1949, they replaced the Cape Cod model with new ranch-style houses. The following years saw new features, including car-

The Suburban Dream. A young family stands proudly in front of a typical house in 1950s Levittown.

AMERICAN LANDSCAPE

>> Tenochtitlán

When the Spanish reached Tenochtitlán, they found a city so beautiful that it "seemed like an enchanted vision." It may have been the largest city in the world at that time. In the center were Moctezuma's palaces, the public buildings, and huge temples sitting atop high platforms. All of these buildings were made of a glistening white stone, decorated in gold and surrounded by magnificent gardens, and all kept immaculately clean except for the blood from human sacrifices. The rest of the city was divided into four regions, which in turn were divided into smaller residential districts, each of which had its own temple, school, administrative buildings, and vegetable gardens.

The society was arranged hierarchically, and the higher the status of the family, the better the housing. Aztec society was no more egalitarian than Spain at the time. Nobles lived in well-decorated two-story stucco homes, while ordinary people inhabited more modest dwellings, with the poorest constructed of wood and straw. Such houses were without any furnishings beyond reed mats for sleeping, a few cooking pots, and the stones on which the women in the family ground maize. Each home had several L-shaped rooms, opening onto a courtyard. Family activities took place in the courtyard, rather than on the street. Most people lived in family groupings—one or two families together—of ten to fifteen people. Married children often lived with the parents of either the bride or groom.

Work was assigned by gender. Every woman, whatever her age or class, spent much of the day weaving. From an early age, girls were taught by their mothers how to spin and weave, and how to grind corn and prepare meals. At the same time, fathers taught their sons how to bring firewood and water back to the home and how to fish.

The heart of Tenochtitlán's economic life was the market at Tlatelolco, on the outskirts of town. It served 25,000 people daily, selling not only food, clothing, and household goods, but also luxuries such as feathers, gold, and precious stones. People sold their services, too, as barbers, fortunetellers, scribes, and even prostitutes. Each kind of good and service was assigned its own section of the market, making it easier for customers to compare quality and price. The state regulated the market, setting an upper limit on prices and taxing each transaction. The state also assigned each group of artisans their own residential neighborhood, with separate districts for featherworkers, stoneworkers, gold- and silversmiths, and so on.

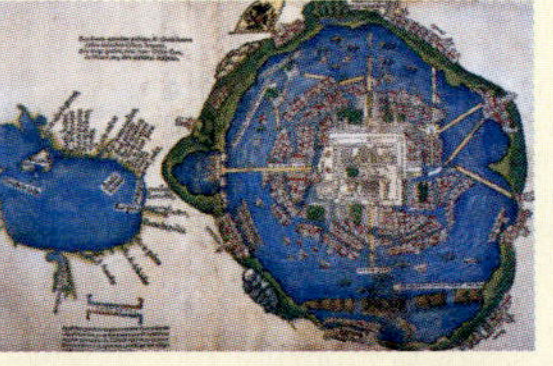

Of the People is similar to the book I am currently using, but the vignettes are vastly superior in this book, and the prose is generally more readable and has a much better flow. It's basically all of the good things about [my current textbook], but with better writing and far more useful features.

—Melissa Estes Blair,
University of Georgia

"America and the World" vignettes also appear in every chapter, setting America's history within a global context.

AMERICA AND THE WORLD

>> The Influenza Pandemic of 1918

The 57th Vermont Pioneer Infantry marched for hours through the rain on the night of September 29, 1918, from Camp Merritt, New Jersey, to open ferries that carried them down the Hudson to Hoboken, where they boarded the U.S.S. *Leviathan* for the trip to France. The 9,000 tired and wet soldiers and 200 nurses aboard the country's largest and fastest troop transport were nervous about U-boats they might encounter in the Atlantic, but they had a deadlier enemy, one that came on board with the men of the 57th.

Within hours of embarkation, every bed in the ship's infirmary was full, and every patient had symptoms that were all too familiar to military doctors: aches in the legs and back, nosebleed, and, in extreme cases, the blue lips and ears, the thin, gasping breaths that indicated advanced pneumonia. But though doctors recognized the signs, they knew nothing about how to treat or prevent Spanish influenza. They could only comfort patients and try, futilely, to separate the sick from the well on the overloaded ship. By the time it arrived in France, 1,700 passengers were down with "the flu." Ninety had died during the passage and 200 more would perish within days of landing.

The 1918 pandemic affected nearly every spot on the globe, killing over 30 million people, far more than died in the world war. Called Spanish because the king of Spain was the first well-known figure to die, the flu was first observed at Fort Riley, Kansas, where the virus may have jumped from pigs to humans. War and commerce accelerated its spread. Men from all of Europe and colonial nations in Asia and Africa came together in the trenches and then carried the disease by steam- ship and locomotive to every continent. In Augus- ... flu mutated into an exceptionally lethal strain. Pat- ... showed signs of massive pneumonia and usually ... within three days.

It spread westward across North America, fo- ... ing the path of the railroads, and within weeks enci- ... the world in a fatal embrace, killing 6 million in I ... 200,000 in Japan, and 675,000 in the United State- ... Cincinnati, Ohio, and Harbin, China, farmers no- ... that the disease killed hogs in the same proportion t- ... killed humans, roughly one in ten. A steamer from ... Francisco put in at Tahiti on November 16, and w- ... the next three weeks 10 percent of the population ... Isolated habitations newly tied to global conduits of ... and communications were hit hardest. The virus ar- ... in Eskimo villages on postal dogsleds and by camel ... van to Arabian towns. Australia closed its ports in a- ... effort to shut out the disease.

At the Paris Peace Conference, delegate and P- ... burg veteran Willard Straight died, and President ... son, Walter Lippmann, Edward House, and the e- ... American delegation were sick. When Wilson s- ... of war and revolution as contagions spreading a- ... the world, it was a terror his audience knew wel- ... the height of the pandemic in Philadelphia, chur- ... schools, saloons, and theaters were shut; San Fran- ... required everyone to wear su- ... masks in public. Trolley cars ... used as hearses, and the dead ... interred in mass graves. Kath- ... Anne Porter, who nearly died ... scribed the "noiseless houses ... the shades drawn, empty streets ... dead cold light of tomorrow."

World war aroused a fervi- ... tionalism, but the pandemic reve- ... that parliaments and autocrats ... equally powerless in the face o- ... tastrophe on this scale. Citizen- ... cused their governments of ap- ... The British Raj was in "a sta- ... coma," the Bombay *Chronicle* ... plained. At Cartwright, on Can- ... Labrador Coast, a minister wrot-

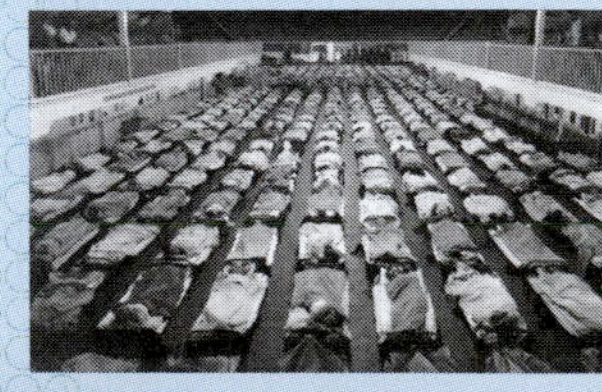

AMERICA AND THE WORLD

>> Slavery as a Foreign Policy

The Pierce administration's disastrous support for the Kansas-Nebraska Act undermined its ability to pursue the expansionist policies of its Democratic predecessors. To be sure, Pierce packed his presidential addresses with bluster about America's right to more Mexican territory and to various parts of the Caribbean, particularly Cuba. But all of Pierce's expansionist efforts were southward, and that meant they all promised the expansion of slavery. This was hardly an accident. Southerners dominated Pierce's cabinet and he appointed slaveholders to crucial diplomatic posts.

Pierce sent a South Carolinian, James Gadsden, to Mexico with instructions to spend up to $50 million to acquire a substantial portion of northern Mexico. Mexico's leader resisted Gadsden's extravagant offer. The American returned to Washington, DC, with a treaty giving the United States just enough territory to build a transcontinental railroad across the southern tier of the nation. But even this was too much for most northern senators. For the first time in American history, Congress rejected land ceded to the United States. The Gadsden Purchase ended up securing only a small piece of land for $10 million to even out the southern border of the United States.

Pierce's expansionist designs fared even worse in Cuba. The president appointed Pierre Soulé, a Louisianan, as minister to Spain. Soulé was instructed to negotiate the purchase of Cuba, with the understanding that if Spain refused to sell he should encourage the Cubans to rise in rebellion. To Soulé's presumptuous behavior the Spanish government offered an extraordinary response. It proposed to free millions of Cuban slaves and arm them for the defense of the island against a possible American invasion.

The United States responded with the Ostend Manifesto, which declared that Cuba was "naturally" a part of the United States and urged Spain to accept an offer of $120 million for the island. If Spain refused, the United States would use all of its power to "wrest" the island of Cuba by force.

The Ostend Manifesto was issued in 1854 at the height of northern reaction against the Kansas-Nebraska Act and was immediately denounced as yet another example of slavery's insatiable hunger for expansion. Expansionism was now hopelessly tainted by its association with slavery. As Pierce's secretary of state, William L. Marcy, admitted, "the Nebraska question" had shattered the Democratic Party in the North "and deprived it of that strength which was needed and could have been more profitably used for the acquisition of Cuba."

AMERICA AND THE WORLD

>> Debating the Morality of Conquest

In 1550, Carlos V, the king of Spain, summoned two of the most important Catholic clerics in the nation, Bartolomé de las Casas and Juan Ginés de Sepúlveda, to debate the morality of conquest before the Council of the Indies. These two priests were the leading spokesmen for two sharply different points of ... Las Casas, whose father sailed with Columbus on ... ond voyage and who himself later became an *en- ... dero*, was convinced by personal experience that ... thing which has been done to the Indians is un- ... d tyrannical." Sepúlveda was an eminent scholar ... mmitted nationalist whose defense of conquest ... eady won him the thanks of the municipal coun- ... Mexico City.

... two adversaries did not meet face-to-face. ... eda appeared first, resting his case on the innate ... ism of the Indians. Some people, he said, were born ... masters and others, slaves. Sepúlveda ridiculed the ... ent that the Aztecs were "civilized" because they ... ities and engaged in commerce. So what if they ... ouses? This "merely proves that they are neither ... nor monkeys and that they are not totally irratio- ... War against such people could be justified "not only ... basis of their paganism but even more so because ... abominable licentiousness, their prodigious sac- ... f human victims . . . their horrible banquets of ... flesh." Subjecting them to Spanish rule would be ... st "beneficial" thing that could be ... or them.

... en Las Casas was summoned for ... uttal. He spoke for five days—in ... until the exhausted Council told ... ey had heard enough. Warfare ... the Indians was not justified, ... sas argued. Instead, they could ... over by peaceful means, for they ... prudent and rational beings, of as ... bility and judgment as other men ... ore able, discreet, and of better ... standing than the people of many ... nations." Las Casas denounced ... eda's "deadly poison" and the ... of the Spanish, which "has led to ... crimes . . . as have never been ... tted by any other nation, no matter how fierce ... have been." He feared that Sepúlveda's course ... in the end, provoke God to "pour forth the fury of his anger and lay hold of all of Spain sooner than he had decreed." The Spanish must convert the Indians, not conquer them.

Although the judges who heard these presentations departed without rendering a verdict, Las Casas's ideas prevailed. Las Casas had already helped shape the Laws of Burgos (1513) and the New Laws of 1542, which attempted to regulate the working conditions of the Indians and finally forbade any further enslavement of the native population. His influence can be seen in the next set of regulations, issued in 1573, written to govern Spain's future colonial ventures, which were to be called "pacifications" rather than "conquests." Henceforth, Indians were to be treated gently "so as not to scandalize them or prejudice them against Christianity." But by that time, Spain's New World empire was essentially complete; there were relatively few Indians left to conquer or to pacify.

Sepúlveda argued for unlimited governmental power, but it was actually Las Casas's views that were most useful to the powerful monarchy. When Spain commenced its overseas ventures, it was not even a nation itself. The century that would witness Spanish expansion into most of present South and Central America also saw the growth of state power in Spain. Las Casas's efforts on behalf of the Indians meshed nicely with the political plans of the Spanish monarchy, which aimed at centralized state power. Like the *hidalgos*, who had claimed as their own the land they wrested away from the Moors, the *conquistadores* attempted to set themselves up as feudal lords, with almost unlimited control over the land in their possession and the Indians who inhabited it, and with only limited obligations to the monarch. In insisting upon humane treatment of the Indians, the Spanish monarchs were undercutting the authority of the local *encomenderos*. In this way, as well as by forbidding the establishment of local representative governments, the Spanish monarchs prevented the development not only of a New World feudal aristocracy, which might challenge its power, but also democratic habits of self-government and local autonomy—all in the name of humanity.

. . . And It's About POWER.

Of the People grapples with questions of power, which necessarily take us to political processes, to the ways in which people work separately and collectively to enforce their will. Politics is defined quite broadly in this book. With the feminists of the 1960s, the authors believe that "the personal is the political," that power relations shape people's lives in private as well as in public. *Of the People* looks for democracy in the living room as well as the legislature, and in the bedroom as well as the business office

The Pursuit of Pleasure

The consumer society depended on Americans' eagerness to pursue pleasure. Businesses made sure that nothing would prevent Americans from buying goods and services. If their wages and salaries were not enough, consumers could borrow. Along with federally guaranteed mortgage loans, people could now get credit cards. In 1950, the Diners Club introduced the credit card for well-to-do New Yorkers. By the end of the decade, Sears Roebuck credit cards allowed more than 10 million Americans to spend borrowed money. In 1945, Americans owed only $5.7 billion for consumer goods other than houses. By 1960, they owed $56.1 billion.

In the 1950s, discount stores such as Korvettes made shopping seem simpler and more attractive, and so did another new creation, the shopping mall. In 1956, Southdale, the nation's first enclosed suburban shopping mall, opened outside Minneapolis, Minnesota. Consumers bought meals more easily, too. The first McDonald's fast-food restaurant opened in San Bernardino, California, in 1948. Taken over by businessman Ray Kroc, McDonald's began to grow into a national chain in the mid-1950s.

To get to McDonald's, the Southdale Mall, Korvettes, and Levittown, Americans needed cars. In the 1950s, automobiles reflected Americans' new sense of affluence and self-indulgence. Big, high-compression engines burning high-octane gasoline powered ever-bigger cars stuffed with new accessories—power steering, power brakes, power windows, and air-conditioning. Unlike the drab autos of the Great Depression, the new models featured "Passion Pink" and "Horizon Blue" interiors and two-tone and even three-tone exteriors studded with shiny chrome.

Automakers used that chrome to solve one of the main problems of a consumer society—getting people who already had plenty to want to buy even more. How could

Icons of the Consumer Society The first enclosed mall in the United States—Southdale, outside Minneapolis, Minnesota.

Gender and Conquest

Every society has its own notion of the proper relationship between the sexes, and this is one of the ways it establishes order. Hence, when one society conquers another, not only do different gender orders come into conflict, but gender is one of the instruments of conquest. For Christopher Columbus, indigenous women were curiosities, objects of conversion, and commodities. On one island, the women "went around as naked as their mothers bore them"; on another, they "wore in front of their bodies a little thing of cotton that scarcely covers their genitals." Such women were "very respectful," and Columbus thought that with proper instruction in their own language, "soon all of them would become Christian."

Yet Columbus thought nothing of seizing friendly native women to bring back

Of the People centers its narrative of U.S. history on competing and multiple notions of American democracy. It is an exciting and innovative approach that will be a welcome option for me and, I imagine, many others who teach the survey.

–**Luis Alvarez**, *University of California–San Diego*

Of the People also devotes much attention to economic life, to the ways in which Americans have worked and saved and spent. Economic power, the authors believe, is basic to democracy. Americans' power to shape their lives and their country has been greatly affected by whether they were farmers or hunters, plantation owners or slaves, wageworkers or capitalists, domestic servants or bureaucrats. The authors do not see economics as an impersonal, all-conquering force; instead, they show how the values and actions of ordinary people, as well as the laws and regulations of government, have formed economic life.

Taino Customs (Left) A young man introducing himself to the family of the young woman he wants to marry. (Right) The Tainos raising their crops in small, carefully kept gardens. These illustrations come ... a Frenchman who ... he 16th century.

The Politics of Slavery

In 1817 a Boston reporter, observing the absence of the invidious politics that had plagued the first three decades of nationhood, declared that America had at last achieved "an era of good feeling." That sentiment seemed confirmed three years later when President James Monroe was reelected with all but one electoral vote—and that one withheld not in opposition to Monroe but in deference

...panish, like all the Europeans who followed them into the Ameri-
...selves as civilized and the Indians as either gentle but primitive
...uman, the differences between Europeans and natives were not
...enturies of warfare with the Moors had made the Spanish a fierce
...believed that practices that later generations would condemn as
...l for people at war. Once the Spanish decided that the Caribs were
...gan to treat them harshly.

The Origins of a New World Political Economy

As early as Columbus's second voyage of 1493, it became clear that the vast treasures he had anticipated were not readily at hand. His crew, however, expected to be rewarded for their services, and the queen and king who had financed his expedition expected profits. Therefore, Columbus packed off more than 500 Indians to be sold as slaves and distributed another 600 or so among the Spanish settlers on the island of Hispaniola.

Once again a pattern of New World development had been established. The European quest for wealth led to the subjugation of native peoples. Each European nation reacted somewhat differently to this movement toward enslavement. Generally, the Spanish rulers tried to restrain their New World colonizers and protect their new Indian subjects. In 1493, Pope Alexander VI confirmed Spanish dominion over all the lands that Columbus had explored, and he commanded the Spanish "to lead the peoples dwelling in those islands and countries to embrace the Christian religion." A papal bull (or proclamation) also established the church's interest in the spiritual welfare of the Native Americans. A subsequent treaty between Spain and Portugal, the Treaty of Tordesillas of 1494, divided between those two countries all lands already discovered or to be discovered, along an imaginary line 370 leagues west of the Azores. This treaty formed the basis for Portugal's subsequent claim to Brazil, which her explorers reached in 1500.

Of the People offers strong pedagogical features . . .

To help students follow the larger narratives of U.S. History, the authors have written "Common Threads" that appear at the beginning of every chapter, prompting readers to draw connections and identify patterns among the events and people found in each chapter.

Common Threads 

>> In previous chapters you read about the development of the American economy and the expansion of slavery. Notice the ways in which these developments became sources of tension between the North and South during the 1850s.

>> The conflict between Whigs and Democrats during the 1830s and 1840s is sometimes called "the first party system." How did this change in the 1850s?

>> Do you think that by 1860 the Civil War was "irrepressible?"

I was very impressed by the quality of that material, as well as the other review material at the end of the chapter. I liked the "Common Threads" feature very much. I ask my students fairly broad questions on my exams; I think these questions would be very useful to students in preparing for that kind of exam.

–Melissa Estes Blair, ***University of Georgia***

Common Threads 

>> How did the Industrial Revolution continue to affect culture and politics, as well as the economy?

>> What differentiated the modern culture of the 1920s from the popular culture of the Gilded Age and the Progressive Era?

>> Why did individualism continue to be such an important force in American life?

>> How did the Republican New Era of the 1920s mark a break from the progressive politics of the 1900s–1910s?

>> What were the long-term implications of a political and cultural order so dependent on material prosperity?

End of Chapter review material includes names and events for students to recall, critical thinking questions, suggestions for further reading, and an inclusive timeline that draws together events from the chapter with events found in the adjacent chapters.

Further Readings

Nancy K. Bristow, *Making Men Moral: Social Engineering During the Great War* (1996). Reformers and women's groups used military training to mold men into model citizens.

John Eisenhower, *Intervention! The United States and the Mexican Revolution, 1913–1917* (1993). The story of the U.S. occupation of Veracruz and Pershing's search for Pancho Villa.

Meirion Harries, *The Last Days of Innocence: America at War, 1917–1918* (1997). Lively anecdotal history of the war years.

David M. Kennedy, *Over Here: The First World War and American Society* (1980). An examination of the home front during World War I.

Edward G. Lengel, *To Conquer Hell: The Meuse-Argonne, 1918* (2008). The experience of combat in the American sector of the Western Front.

N. Gordon Levin Jr., *Woodrow Wilson and World Politics* (1968). Levin analyzes progressive president's response to the disorder of world politics.

Erez Manela, *The Wilsonian Moment: Self-Determination and the International Origins of Anticolonial Nationalism* (2007). The global reaction to Wilson's revolutionary doctrine of self-determination.

H. C. Peterson and Gilbert C. Fite, *Opponents of War, 1917–1918* (1957). On wartime peace movements and the Wilson administration's attempts to suppress dissent.

Linda R. Robertson, *The Dream of Civilized Warfare: World War I Flying Aces and the American Imagination* (2003). While infantrymen died by the thousands for a few yards of mud, Americans dreamed of soaring above the Western Front and winning the war in the skies.

Ronald Steel, *Walter Lippmann and the American Century* (1980). More than any other journalist, Lippmann shaped American foreign policy in the twentieth century.

Who, What?

Porifirio Díaz 729
George Creel 738
Bernard Baruch 739
Langston Hughes 741
Carrie Chapman Catt 742
John J. Pershing 747
Neutrality 731
Propaganda 737
Cost-plus contract 740
Suffrage 742
Red Scare 754

Review Questions

1. Did the war help or hurt the progressive movement?
2. Allied commanders wanted to use American troops as a reserve, but Pershing wanted his soldiers to enter the battle as an army. Why was that so important to him?
3. Did Senate Republicans reject the League of Nations because they wanted the United States to withdraw from the world, or because they wanted to deal with the world in a different way?
4. Managing the pace of change posed a tricky problem for leaders in the early twentieth century. How did Wilson try to control the dynamic of social and political change? What methods of change was he unwilling to accept?
5. Why were American leaders so much more concerned about sedition and dissent during World War I than they were during the Civil War or World War II?
6. How did mobilization for war advance the progressive agenda? In what ways did it set progressives back?

Websites

Carrie Chapman Catt. From American National Biography Online. A powerful advocate for peace and women's suffrage, she and Alice Paul orchestrated the state-by-state campaign for the nineteenth amendment.

From the Home Front and the Front Lines. Library of Congress online exhibit. The Veterans History Project draws together diaries, oral histories, photographs and other artifacts from America's twentieth century wars. http://www.loc.gov/exhibits/treasures/homefront-home.html

For further review materials and resource information, please visit www.oup.com/us/ofthepeople

>> Timeline >>

▼ 1911
Mexican Revolution begins

▼ 1912
Woodrow Wilson elected president

▼ 1914
U.S. troops occupy Veracruz, Mexico
World War I begins

▼ 1915
U.S. troops occupy Haiti (until 1934)
Lusitania sunk

▼ 1916
U.S. forces invade Mexico in search of Pancho Villa
U.S. forces enter the Dominican Republic
Woodrow Wilson reelected.

▼ 1917
Russian czar abdicates; parliamentary regime takes power
U.S. declares war on Germany
East St. Louis riot
Houston riot
October Revolution overthrows Russian government; Lenin takes power

▼ 1918
Wilson announces U.S. war aims: the Fourteen Points
Wilson nationalizes railroads
Sedition Act outlaws criticism of the U.S. government
U.S. troops stop German advance
Wilson sends troops to Siberia
Armistice ends fighting on the Western Front
Influenza pandemic peaks in September  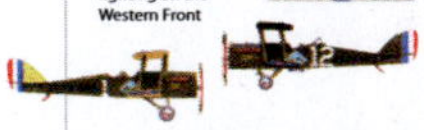

▼ 1919
Eighteenth Amendment outlaws manufacture, sale, and transport of alcoholic beverages
Versailles Treaty signed in Paris
Mail bombs target prominent government and business figures
Gary, Indiana, steel strike
U.S. Senate rejects Versailles Treaty

▼ 1920
Nineteenth Amendment secures the vote for women
Palmer raids arrest thousands of suspected Communists
Sacco and Vanzetti arrested on charges of robbery and murder

The Value of Oxford: The Best Textbook Package at the Best Price . . .

Of the People: A History of the United States **is available both as a complete volume and as two volumes for both halves of the American history survey course:**

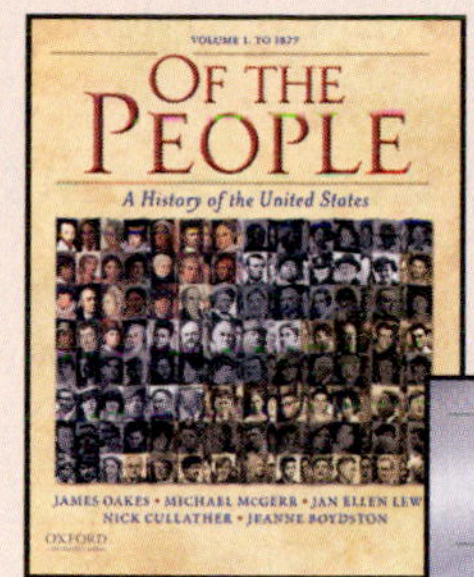

(9780195370942)
Of the People: A History of the United States,
Volume I (to 1877)

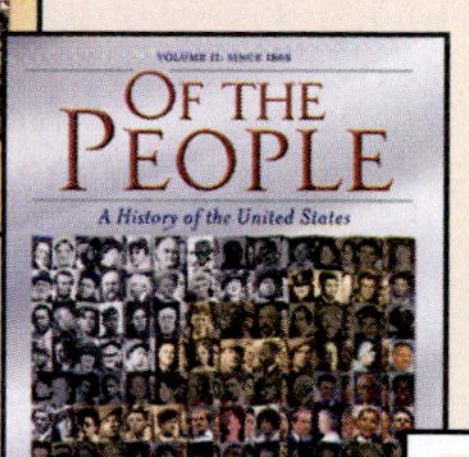

(9780195370959)
Of the People: A History of the United States,
Volume II (Since 1865)

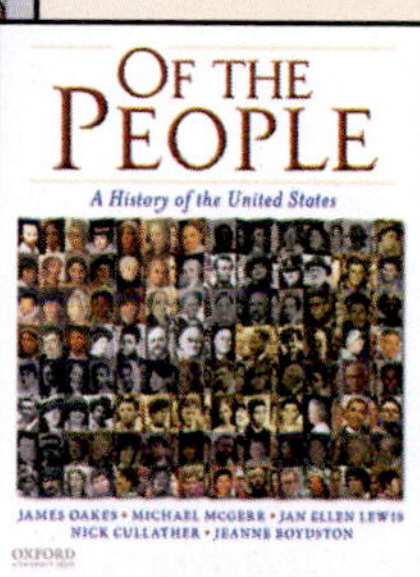

(9780195371031)
Of the People: A History of the United States,
Complete

And *Of the People* offers a complete supplements package . . .

For decades American History professors have turned to Oxford University Press as the leading source for high quality readings and reference materials. Now, when you adopt Oakes's *Of the People: A History of the United States*, **the Press will partner with you** and make available its best supplemental materials and resources for your classroom. Listed here are several supplements of high interest, but you will want to talk with your Oxford Sales Representative to learn more about what can be made available for your course. **Turn to page xl of the Preface inside for more information on the supplements, and see the following page for more OUP titles of interest.**

"*Of the People* promises to emerge as one of the leading American history textbooks on the market. The authors have succeeded admirably in providing students with a well-written and comprehensive overview of American history, integrating the theme of 'American democracy' throughout the text and incorporating such innovative features as 'American Landscapes' and 'America and the World.'"

—Lloyd Ray Gunn, *University of Utah*

for Students

- **Student Companion Website** at www.oup.com/us/ofthepeople (free)
- ***American National Biography* Online** www.anb.org (free subscription with purchase of a new copy)
- ***Writing History*** Third edition, by William Kelleher Storey (free when packaged)
- ***Our Documents: 100 Milestone Documents from the National Archives*** (free when packaged)

for Instructors

Instructor's Manual and Testbank, and Instructor's Resource CD, including Sample Syllabi, Chapter Outlines, In-Class Discussion Questions, Lecture Ideas, Oxford's Further Reading Lists, Quizzes

Other Oxford Titles of Interest for the U.S. History Classroom

Oxford University Press publishes a vast array of highly respected titles in American history. Listed below is just a small selection of books that pair particularly well with *Of the People: A History of the United States*. Any of the books in these series can be packaged with *Of the People* at a significant discount to students. Please visit **www.oup.com/us** for a full listing of Oxford titles.

NEW NARRATIVES IN AMERICAN HISTORY

Intensely personal and highly relevant, these succinct texts are innovative teaching tools that provide a springboard for incisive class discussion as they immerse students in a particular historical moment.

Escaping Salem: The Other Witch Hunt of 1692, by Richard Godbeer

Sleuthing the Alamo: Davy Crockett's Last Stand and Other Mysteries of the Texas Revolution, by James E. Crisp

In Search of the Promised Land: A Slave Family in the Old South, by John Hope Franklin and Loren Schweninger

The Making of a Confederate: Walter Lenoir's Civil War, by William L. Barney

"They Say": Ida B. Wells and the Reconstruction of Race, by James West Davidson

Wild Men: Ishi and Kroeber in the Wilderness of Modern America, by Douglas Cazaux Sackman

The Gentle Subversive: Rachel Carson, Silent Spring, *and the Rise of the Environmental Movement*, by Mark Hamilton Lytle

"To Everything There is a Season": Pete Seeger and the Power of Song, by Allan Winkler

PAGES FROM HISTORY

Textbooks may interpret history, but these books are history. Each title, compiled and edited by a prominent historian, is a collection of primary sources relating to a particular topic of historical significance.

Encounters in the New World (Jill Lepore)

Colonial America (Edward G. Gray)

The American Revolution (Stephen C. Bullock)

The Bill of Rights (John J. Patrick)

The Struggle Against Slavery (David Waldstreicher)

The Civil War (Rachel Filene Seidman)

The Gilded Age (Janette Thomas Greenwood)

The Industrial Revolution (Laura Levine Frader)

Imperialism (Bonnie G. Smith)

World War I (Frans Coetzee and Marilyn Shevin-Coetzee)

The Depression and the New Deal (Robert McElvaine)

World War II (James H. Madison)

The Cold War (Allan M. Winkler)

The Vietnam War (Marilyn B. Young)

PIVOTAL MOMENTS IN AMERICAN HISTORY

For anyone interested in discovering which important junctures in U.S. history shaped our thoughts, actions, and ideals, these books are the definitive resources.

The Scratch of a Pen: 1763 and the Transformation of North America (Colin Calloway)

As If an Enemy's Country: The British Occupation of Boston and the Origins of the Revolution (Richard Archer)

Washington's Crossing (David Hackett Fischer)

James Madison and the Struggle for the Bill of Rights (Richard Labunski)

Adams vs. Jefferson: The Tumultuous Election of 1800 (John Ferling)

The Birth of Modern Politics: Andrew Jackson, John Quincy Adams, and the Election of 1828 (Lynn Parsons)

Storm over Texas: The Annexation Controversy and the Road to Civil War (Joel H. Silbey)

Crossroads of Freedom: Antietam (James M. McPherson)

The Last Indian War: The Nez Perce Story (Elliot West)

Seneca Falls and the Origins of the Women's Rights Movement (Sally McMillen)

Rainbow's End: The Crash of 1929 (Maury Klein)

Brown v. Board of Education and the Civil Rights Movement (Michael J. Klarman)

The Bay of Pigs (Howard Jones)

Freedom Riders: 1961 and the Struggle for Racial Justice (Raymond Arsenault)

VIEWPOINTS ON AMERICAN CULTURE

This series targets topics where debates have flourished and brings together the voices of established and emerging writers to share their own points of view in compact and compelling format.

Votes for Women: The Struggle for Suffrage Revisited (Jean H. Baker)

Long Time Gone: Sixties America Then and Now (Alexander Bloom)

Living in the Eighties (Edited by Gil Troy and Vincent J. Cannato)

Race on Trial: Law and Justice in American History (Annette Gordon-Reed)

Sifters: Native American Women's Lives (Theda Perdue)

Latina Legacies: Identity, Biography, and Community (Vicki L. Ruiz)

OXFORD WORLD'S CLASSICS

For more than 100 years Oxford World's Classics has made available a broad spectrum of literature from around the globe. With well over 600 titles available and a continuously growing list, this is the finest and most comprehensive classics series in print. Any volume in the series can be packaged for free with *Of the People*. Relevant titles include Benjamin Franklin's *Autobiography and Other Writings*, J. Hector St. John de Crèvecoeur's *Letters from an American Farmer*, Booker T. Washington's *Up from Slavery*, and many others. For a complete listing of Oxford World's Classics, please visit **www.oup.com/us/owc.**

Please contact your Oxford University Press Sales Representative at 800-280-0280 for specific pricing information or for additional packaging suggestions.

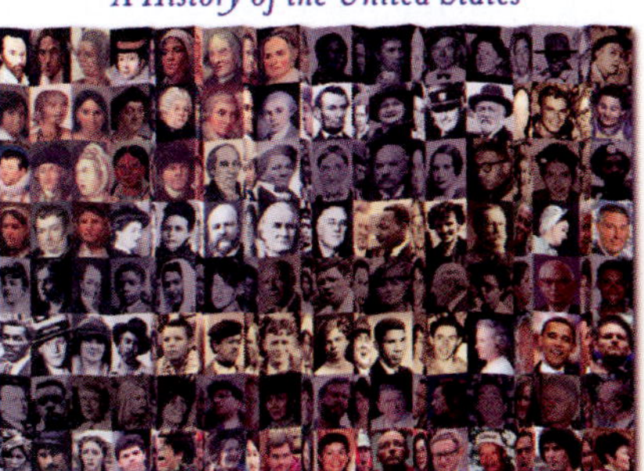

A History of the United States
JAMES OAKES • MICHAEL MCGERR • JAN ELLEN LEWIS
NICK CULLATHER • JEANNE BOYDSTON
OXFORD

Of the People

the People

A HISTORY OF THE UNITED STATES

James Oakes
City University of New York Graduate Center

Michael McGerr
Indiana University–Bloomington

Jan Ellen Lewis
Rutgers University, Newark

Nick Cullather
Indiana University–Bloomington

Jeanne Boydston
University of Wisconsin–Madison

New York Oxford
Oxford University Press
2010

Oxford University Press, Inc., publishes works that further Oxford University's objective of excellence in research, scholarship, and education.

Oxford New York
Auckland Cape Town Dar es Salaam Hong Kong Karachi
Kuala Lumpur Madrid Melbourne Mexico City Nairobi
New Delhi Shanghai Taipei Toronto

With offices in
Argentina Austria Brazil Chile Czech Republic France Greece
Guatemala Hungary Italy Japan Poland Portugal Singapore
South Korea Switzerland Thailand Turkey Ukraine Vietnam

Published by Oxford University Press, Inc.
198 Madison Avenue, New York, New York 10016
http://www.oup.com

Library of Congress Cataloging-in-Publication Data

Of the people: a history of the United States/James Oakes . . . [et al.]—1st ed.
p. cm.
Includes index.
ISBN 978-0-19-537103-1 (cloth)—ISBN 978-0-19-537094-2 (v. 1)—ISBN 978-0-19-537095-9 (v. 2) 1. United States—History. 2. Democracy—United States—History. I. Oakes, James.
E178.037 2009
973—dc22
2009021953

Printing number: 9 8 7 6 5 4 3 2 1

Printed in the United States of America
on acid-free paper

Jeanne Boydston
1944–2008
Historian, Teacher, Friend

ABOUT THE COVER

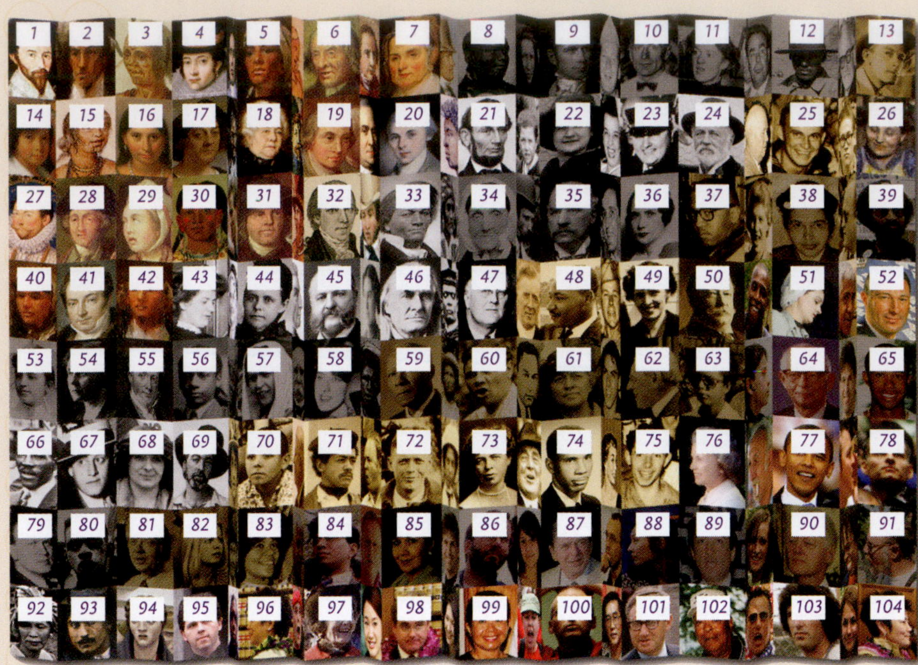

1. Sir Walter Raleigh
2. Judge William Stoughton
3. Paquiquineo
4. Pocahontas
5. Tituba
6. Unknown
7. Lucretia Mott
8. Anthony Burns
9. Henry Clay
10. Unknown
11. Unknown
12. Unknown
13. Hoagy Carmichael
14. Supposed child of Pocahontas and John Rolfe
15. Unknown
16. Pocahontas
17. Christopher Columbus
18. Elizabeth Cady Stanton
19. Unknown
20. James Madison
21. Abraham Lincoln
22. Unknown
23. Unknown
24. Unknown
25. Unknown
26. Unknown

The cover art for *Of the People* was inspired by *The American Flag of Faces*, an interactive exhibit on Ellis Island.

Learn more at www.flagoffaces.org

In keeping with the democratic spirit of this book, we have included portraits of various people—well known and unknown—from across America's history.

27. Sir Francis Drake
28. Unknown
29. Unknown
30. Mah-i-ti-wo-nee-ni
31. Unknown
32. William Maclay
33. Frederick Douglass
34. Unknown
35. J. P. Morgan
36. Margaret Mitchell
37. Unknown
38. Rosa Parks
39. Unknown
40. Unknown
41. Washington Irving
42. Unknown
43. Unknown
44. Luna Kellie
45. Anthony Comstock
46. Edmund Ruffiin
47. Franklin Delano Roosevelt
48. Martin Luther King, Jr.
49. Unknown
50. William Taft
51. Unknown
52. Gene Ferkauf
53. Mary Church Terrell
54. Jane Addams
55. Martin Van Buren
56. Son of Ida Wells Barnett
57. Unknown
58. Unknown
59. A. Philip Randolph
60. Babe Ruth
61. Unknown
62. Woodrow Wilson
63. Elizabeth Eckford
64. Carl Gerstacker
65. Tiger Woods
66. Unknown
67. Unknown
68. Unknown
69. Walt Whitman
70. Unknown
71. Huey Newton
72. Charles Lindbergh
73. Eleanor Roosevelt
74. Medgar Evers
75. Unknown U.S. sailor
76. Sandra Day O'Connor
77. Barack Hussein Obama
78. Unknown
79. Unknown
80. Unknown
81. James Earl Carter, Jr.
82. Sally Struthers
83. Unknown
84. Unknown
85. Linda Chavez
86. Unknown
87. Ronald Reagan
88. Unknown
89. Henry Cisneros
90. William Jefferson Clinton
91. Unknown
92. Unknown
93. Unknown
94. Unknown
95. Michael Milken
96. Unknown
97. Pat Nixon
98. Unknown
99. Kultida (Tida) Woods
100. Unknown
101. Henry Kissinger
102. Earl Woods
103. Unknown
104. Unknown

Brief Contents

Contents

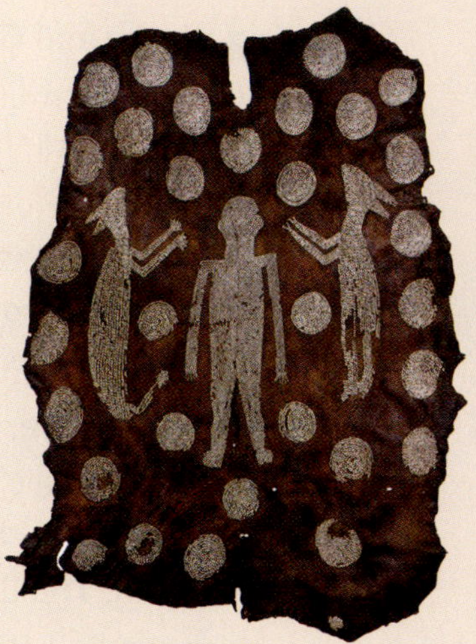

Chapter 5 The Eighteenth-Century World, 1700–1775 140

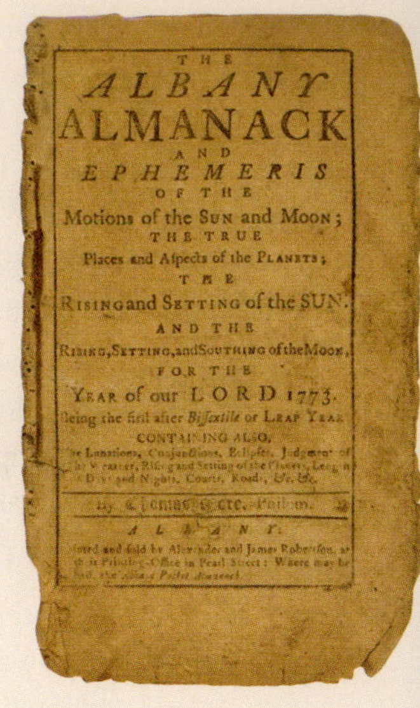

THE
ALBANY
ALMANACK
AND
EPHEMERIS
OF THE
Motions of the SUN and MOON;
THE TRUE
Places and Aspects of the PLANETS;
THE
RISING and SETTING of the SUN.
AND THE
RISING, SETTING, and SOUTHING of the MOON,
FOR THE
YEAR of our LORD 1773.
Being the first after Bissextile or LEAP YEAR
CONTAINING ALSO,
The Lunations, Conjunctions, Eclipses, Judgment of the Weather, Rising and Setting of the Planets, Length of Days and Nights, Courts, Roads, &c. &c.
ALBANY:
Printed and sold by Alexander and James Robertson, at their Printing-Office in Pearl Street: Where may be had the Albany Pocket Almanack.

Chapter 6 Conflict on the Edge of the Empire, 1713–1774 176

Chapter 7 Creating a New Nation, 1775–1788 212

Chapter 8 Contested Republic, 1789–1800 254

Chapter 9 A Republic in Transition, 1800–1819 290

Chapter 13 Manifest Destiny, 1836–1848 432

Chapter 14 The Politics of Slavery, 1848–1860 464

Chapter 15 A War for Union and Emancipation, 1861–1865 496

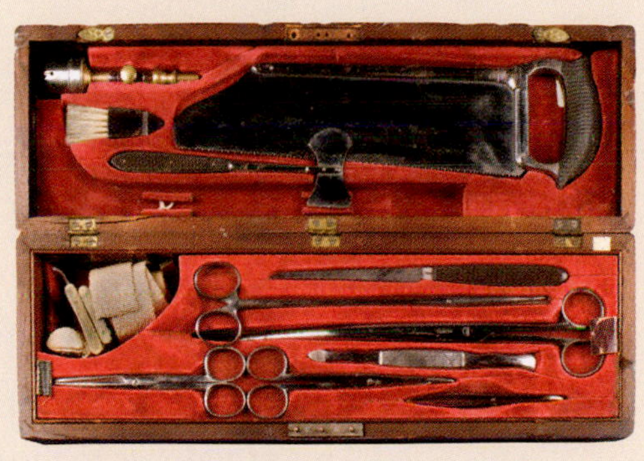

Chapter 16 Reconstructing a Nation, 1865–1877 538

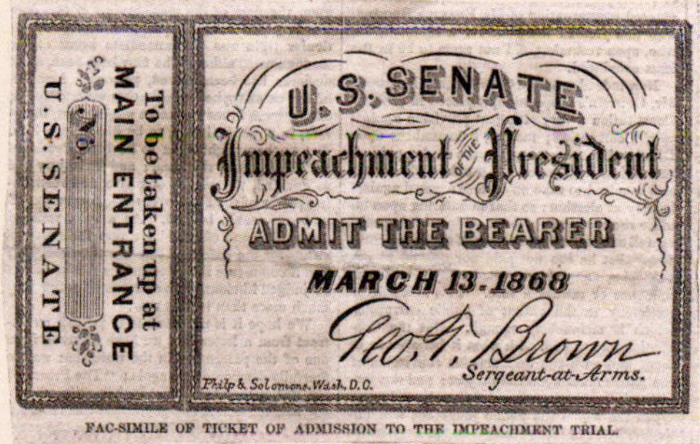

Chapter 17 The Triumph of Industrial Capitalism, 1850–1890 570

Chapter 18 Cultural Struggles of Industrial America, 1850–1895 602

Chapter 19 The Politics of Industrial America, 1870–1892 632

TREASURY NOTE
United States of America
A104454★
100
ONE HUNDRED DOLLARS

THE NEW YORK HERALD.

THE LUSITANIA IS SUNK; 1,000 PROBABLY ARE LOST

GERMANS TORPEDO THE GIANT STEAMSHIP AND SHE FOUNDERS EIGHT MILES FROM IRISH COAST

RESCUE VESSELS SPEED TO THE SCENE TO PICK UP SURVIVORS; ONLY 500 ARE ACCOUNTED FOR

George A. Kessler One of Those Saved, Cable Message to Cunard Office Says

THE MAN OF THE HOUR
WOODROW WILSON

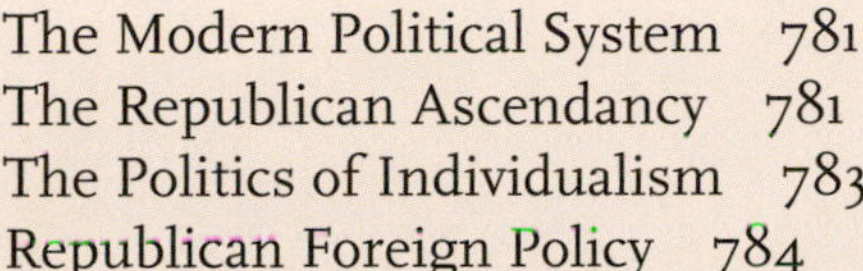

NRA
MEMBER
U.S.
WE DO OUR PART

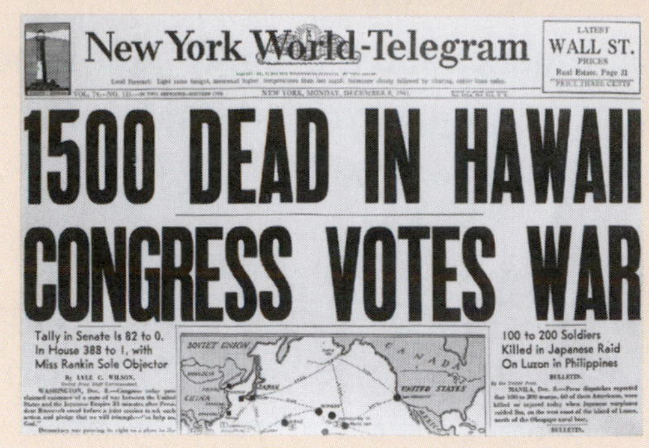

New York World-Telegram

LATEST WALL ST. PRICES

1500 DEAD IN HAWAII

CONGRESS VOTES WAR

Tally in Senate Is 82 to 0. In House 388 to 1, with Miss Rankin Sole Objector

100 to 200 Soldiers Killed in Japanese Raid On Luzon in Philippines

Chapter 26 The Cold War, 1945–1952 858

Whatever the weather
We only reach welfare
together

Chapter 27 The Consumer Society, 1945–1961 890

YOUTH FOR
KENNEDY

Chapter 29 Living with Less, 1968–1980 960

Chapter 30 The Triumph of Conservatism, 1980–1991 996

Chapter 31 "A Nation Transformed," 1989–2008 1032

Appendixes

Maps

Features

American Portraits

American Landscapes

America and the World

Preface

At Gettysburg, Pennsylvania, on November 19, 1863, President Abraham Lincoln dedicated a memorial to the more than 3,000 Union soldiers who had died turning back a Confederate invasion in the first days of July. There were at least a few ways that the president could have justified the sad loss of life in the third year of a brutal war dividing North and South. He could have said it was necessary to destroy the Confederacy's cherished institution of slavery, to punish southerners for seceding from the United States, or to preserve the nation intact. Instead, at this crucial moment in American history, Lincoln gave a short, stunning speech about democracy. The president did not use the word, but he offered its essence. To honor the dead of Gettysburg, he called on northerners to ensure "that government of the people, by the people, for the people, shall not perish from the earth."

With these words, Lincoln put democracy at the center of the Civil War and at the center of American history. The authors of this book share his belief in the centrality of democracy; his words, "of the people," give our book its title and its main theme. We see American history as a story "of the people," of their struggles to shape their lives and their land.

Our choice of theme does not mean we believe that America has always been a democracy. Clearly, it has not. As Lincoln gave the Gettysburg Address, most African Americans still lived in slavery. American women, north and south, lacked rights that many men enjoyed; for all their disagreements, white southerners and northerners viewed Native Americans as enemies. Neither do we believe that there is only a single definition of democracy, either in the narrow sense of a particular form of government or in the larger one of a society whose members participate equally in its creation. Although Lincoln defined the northern cause as a struggle for democracy, southerners believed it was anything but democratic to force them to remain in the Union at gunpoint. As bloody draft riots in New York City in July 1863 made clear, many northern men thought it was anything but democratic to force them to fight in Lincoln's armies. Such disagreements have been typical of American history. For more than 500 years, people have struggled over whose vision of life in the New World would prevail.

It is precisely such struggles that offer the best angle of vision for seeing and understanding the most important developments in the nation's history. In particular, the democratic theme concentrates attention on the most fundamental concerns of history: people and power.

Lincoln's words serve as a reminder of the basic truth that history is about people. Across the 31 chapters of this book, we write extensively about complex events, such as the five-year savagery of the Civil War, and long-term transformations, such as the slow, halting evolution of democratic political institutions. But we write in the awareness that these developments are only abstractions unless they are grounded in the lives of people. The test of a historical narrative, we believe, is whether its characters are fully rounded, believable human beings.

We hope that our commitment to a history "of the people" is apparent on every page of this book. To underscore it, we open each chapter with an **"American Portrait"** feature, a story of someone whose life in one way or another embodies the basic theme of the pages to follow. So, we begin Chapter 8 on the United States in the 1790s with William Maclay, a senator from rural Pennsylvania, who feared that arrogant northeasterners and "pandering" Virginians would quickly turn the new nation into an aristocracy. In Chapter 23, we encounter 19-year-old Gertrude Ederle, whose solo swim across the English Channel and taste for cars and dancing epitomized the individualistic, consumer culture emerging in the 1920s.

The choice of Lincoln's words also reflects our belief that history is about power. To ask whether America was democratic at some point in the past is to ask whether all people had equal power to make their lives and their nation. Such questions of power necessarily take us to political processes, to the ways in which people work separately and collectively to enforce their will. We define politics quite broadly in this book. With the feminists of the 1960s, we believe that "the personal is the political," that power relations shape people's lives in private as well as in public. *Of the People* looks for democracy in the living room as well as the legislature, and in the bedroom as well as the business office.

To underscore our broad view of the political, each chapter presents an **"American Landscape"** feature, a particular place in time where issues of power appeared in especially sharp relief. So, Chapter 2 describes the sixteenth-century Native American villages of Huronia, whose social spaces and sexual relations reflected distinctive ideas about individual freedom and female power. Chapter 21 details the contrasting understandings of democracy at the heart of the early twentieth-century battle over creating a new water supply for San Francisco by building a dam in the Hetch Hetchy Valley of California.

Focusing on democracy, on people and power, we have necessarily written as wide-ranging a history as possible. In the features and in the main text, *Of the People* conveys both the unity and the great diversity of the American people across time and place. Lincoln's "people" have shared a common identity as Americans; but at the same time they have been many distinctive "peoples." So, we chronicle the racial and ethnic groups who have shaped America. We explore differences of religious and regional identity. We trace the changing nature of social classes. We examine the different ways that gender identities have been constructed and reconstructed over the centuries.

While treating different groups in their distinctiveness, we have integrated them into the broader narrative as much as possible. A true history "of the people" means not only acknowledging their individuality and diversity but also showing their interrelationships and their roles in the larger narrative.

Of the People also offers comprehensive coverage of the different spheres of human life—cultural as well as governmental, social as well as economic, environmental as well as military. This commitment to comprehensiveness is a reflection of our belief that all aspects of human existence are the stuff of history. It is also an expression of the fundamental theme of the book: the focus on democracy leads naturally to the study of people's struggles for power in every dimension of their lives. Moreover, the democratic approach emphasizes the interconnections between the different aspects of Americans' lives; we cannot understand politics and government without tracing their connection to economics, religion, culture, art, sexuality, and so on.

The economic connection is especially important. *Of the People* devotes much attention to economic life, to the ways in which Americans have worked and saved and spent. Economic power, the authors believe, is basic to democracy. Americans' power to shape their lives and their country has been greatly affected by whether they were farmers or hunters, plantation owners or slaves, wageworkers or capitalists, domestic servants or bureaucrats. The authors do not see economics as an impersonal, all-conquering force: instead, we try to show how the values and actions of ordinary people, as well as the laws and regulations of government, have made economic life.

We have also tried especially to place America in global context. The story of individual nation-states such as the United States remains a critically important kind of history. But the history of America, or any nation, cannot be adequately explained without understanding its relationship to transnational events and global developments. That is true for the first chapter of the book, which shows how America began to emerge from the collision of Native Americans, West Africans, and Europeans in the fifteenth and sixteenth centuries. It is just as true for the last chapter of the book, which demonstrates how globalization and the war on terror transformed the United States at the turn of the twenty-first century. In the chapters in between these two, the authors detail how the world has changed America and how America has changed the world. Reflecting the concerns of the rest of the book, we focus particularly on the movement of people, the evolution of power, and the attempt to spread democracy abroad.

To underscore the fundamental importance of global relationships, each chapter includes a feature on **"America and the World."** So, Chapter 15 reveals how ordinary Europeans' support for the abolition of slavery made it impossible for their governments to recognize the southern Confederacy. Chapter 20 shows how Singer, a pioneering American multinational company, began to export an economic vision of a consumer democracy along with its sewing machines in the nineteenth and early twentieth centuries.

In a sense, Singer had arrived at Abraham Lincoln's conclusion about the central importance of democracy in American life. The company wanted to sell sewing machines; the president wanted to sell a war. But both believed their audience would see democracy as quintessentially American. Whether they were right is the burden of this book.

Supplements

For Students

Oxford University Press is proud to offer a complete and authoritative supplements package for students—including print and new media resources designed for chapter review, for primary source reading, for essay writing, for test-preparation and for further research.

Student Companion Website at **www.oup.com/us/ofthepeople**

The open-access Online Study Center designed specifically for *Of the People: A History of the United States* helps students to review what they have learned from the

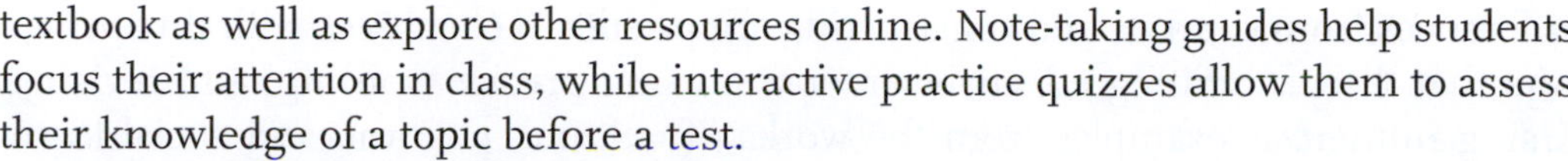

textbook as well as explore other resources online. Note-taking guides help students focus their attention in class, while interactive practice quizzes allow them to assess their knowledge of a topic before a test.

- **Online Study Guide**, including
  - Note-taking outlines
  - Multiple-choice and identification quizzes, (two quizzes per chapter, thirty question quizzes—*different* from those found in the Instructor's Manual/Testbank)
- **Primary Source Companion & Research Guide**, a brief online Research Primer, with a library of annotated links to primary and secondary sources in U.S. history.
- **Interactive Flashcards**, using key terms and people listed at the end of each chapter, help students remember who's who and what's what.

American National Biography Online **www.anb.org**

Students who purchase a **new** copy of Oakes's *Of the People: A History of the United States* will find an access code for a six-month (Volume 1 or 2) or a one-year **free subscription** to this powerful online resource published by Oxford University Press.

American National Biography Online offers **portraits of more than 17,400 women and men**—from all eras and walks of life—whose lives have shaped the nation. More than a decade in preparation, the *American National Biography* is the first biographical resource of this scope to be published in more than sixty years. Originally published in 24 volumes in 1999, the *American National Biography* won instant acclaim as the new authority in American biographies. **Winner of the American Library Association's Dartmouth Medal** as the best reference work of the year, the *ANB* now serves readers in thousands of school, public, and academic libraries around the world. The publication of the online edition makes the *ANB* even more useful as a dynamic source of information—updated semi-annually, with hundreds of new entries each year and revisions of previously published entries to enhance their accuracy and currency. The *ANB Online* features **thousands of illustrations**, more than **80,000 hyperlinked cross-references**, links to select websites, and powerful search capabilities.

ANB Online **is also a great teaching resource, since it can be actively incorporated into classroom lessons.** To assist teachers in fully utilizing *ANB Online*, we have prepared a Teacher's Guide to Using *ANB Online*. Developed with the participation of librarians and teachers, the Teacher's Guide offers six lessons that highlight the importance and value of studying biography as an end in itself and as a starting point for doing further research into the lives of those who shaped the American experience.

Writing History: A Guide for Students Third edition, by William Kelleher Storey, Associate Professor at Millsaps College.

Bringing together practical methods from both history and composition, *Writing History* provides a wealth of tips and advice to help students research and write essays for history classes. The book covers all aspects of writing about history, including **finding topics** and **researching** them, **interpreting source materials**, **drawing**

inferences from sources, and constructing arguments. It concludes with three chapters that discuss writing effective sentences, using precise wording, and revising. Using numerous examples from the works of cultural, political, and social historians, *Writing History* serves as an ideal supplement to history courses that require students to conduct research. The third edition includes expanded sections on **peer editing** and **topic selection**, as well as new sections on searching and using the Internet. *Writing History* can be packaged for free with Oakes's *Of the People: A History of the United States*. Contact your Oxford University Press Sales Representative for more information.

The Information-Literate Historian: A Guide to Research for History Students by Jenny Presnell, *Information Services Library and History, American Studies,* and *Women's Studies Bibliographer, Miami University of Ohio*

This is the only book specifically designed to teach today's history student how to most successfully select and use sources—primary, secondary, and electronic—to carry out and present their research. Written by a college librarian, *The Information-Literate Historian* is an indispensable reference for historians, students, and other readers doing history research. *The Information-Literate Historian* can be packaged for free with Oakes's *Of the People: A History of the United States*. Contact your Oxford University Press Sales Representative for more information.

Primary Source Documents

Our Documents: 100 Milestone Documents from the National Archives brings documents to life, including facsimiles side-by-side with transcripts for students to explore, explanations, and a foreword provided by Michael Beschloss. This primary source book can be **packaged for free** with Oakes's *Of the People: A History of the United States*. Among the documents it contains are: Declaration of Independence; U.S. Constitution; Bill of Rights; Louisiana Purchase Treaty; Missouri Compromise; The Dred Scott decision; Emancipation Proclamation; Gettysburg Address; Fourteenth Amendment to the U.S. Constitution; Thomas Edison's lightbulb patent; Sherman Anti-Trust Act; Executive order for the Japanese relocation during wartime; Manhattan Project notebook; press release announcing U.S. recognition of Israel; President John F. Kennedy's inaugural address, as well as many more.

Other primary source books that can be packaged with Oakes's *Of the People: A History of the United States* include Chafe's ***History of Our Time*** and Bloom's ***Takin' It to the Streets***, as well as ***The Boisterous Sea of Liberty: A Documentary History of America from Discovery through the Civil War***; and ***Documenting American Violence: A Sourcebook.***

For Professors

For decades American History professors have turned to Oxford University Press as the leading source for high quality readings and reference materials. Now, when you adopt Oakes's *Of the People: A History of the United States*, the Press will partner with you and make available its best supplemental materials and resources for your classroom. Listed here are several series of high interest, but you will want to talk with your Sales Representative to learn more about what can be made available, and about what would suit your course best.

Instructor's Manual and Testbank. This useful guide contains helpful teaching tools for experienced and first-time teachers alike. It can be made available to adopters upon request, and is also available electronically on the Instructor's Resource CD. This extensive manual and testbank contains:

- **Sample Syllabi**
- **Chapter Outlines**
- **In-Class Discussion Questions**
- **Lecture Ideas**
- **Oxford's Further Reading List**
- **Quizzes** (two per chapter, one per half of the chapter, content divided somewhat evenly down the middle of the chapter: 30 multiple choice questions each)
- **Tests** (two per chapter, each covering the entire chapter contents: each offering 10 identification/matching; 10 multiple-choice; five short-answer, two essay)

Instructor's Resource CD. This handy CD-ROM contains everything you need in an electronic format—the Instructor's Manual (PDF), PowerPoint Slides (fully customizable), Image Library with PDF versions of *all* 120 maps from the textbook, and a Computerized Testbank.

A complete **Course Management cartridge** is also available to qualified adopters. Instructor's resources are also available for download directly to your computer through a secure connection via the instructor's side of the companion website. Contact your Oxford University Press Sales Representative for more information.

Other Oxford Titles of Interest for the U.S. History Classroom

Oxford University Press publishes a vast array of titles in American history. Listed below is just a small selection of books that pair particularly well with Oakes's *Of the People: A History of the United States.* Any of the books in these series can be packaged with Oakes at a significant discount to students. Please contact your Oxford University Press Sales Representative for specific pricing information, or for additional packaging suggestions. Please visit www.oup.com/us for a full listing of Oxford titles.

NEW NARRATIVES IN AMERICAN HISTORY

At Oxford University Press, we believe that good history begins with a good story. Each volume in this series features a compelling tale that draws on a sustained narrative to illuminate a greater historical theme or controversy. Then, in a thoughtful Afterword, the authors place their narratives within larger historical contexts, discuss their sources and narrative strategies, and describe their personal involvement with the work. Intensely personal and highly relevant, these succinct texts are innovative teaching tools that provide a springboard for incisive class discussion as they immerse students in a particular historical moment.

Escaping Salem: The Other Witch Hunt of 1692, by Richard Godbeer
Sleuthing the Alamo: Davy Crockett's Last Stand and Other Mysteries of the Texas Revolution, by James E. Crisp

In Search of the Promised Land: A Slave Family in the Old South, by John Hope Franklin and Loren Schweninger
The Making of a Confederate: Walter Lenoir's Civil War, by William L. Barney
"They Say": Ida B. Wells and the Reconstruction of Race, by James West Davidson
Wild Men: Ishi and Kroeber in the Wilderness of Modern America, by Douglas Cazaux Sackman
The Gentle Subversive: Rachel Carson, Silent Spring, *and the Rise of the Environmental Movement*, by Mark Hamilton Lytle
"To Everything There is a Season": Pete Seeger and the Power of Song, by Allan Winkler

PAGES FROM HISTORY

Textbooks may interpret and recall history, but these books **are** history. Each title, compiled and edited by a prominent historian, is a collection of primary sources relating to a particular topic of historical significance. Documentary evidence includes news articles, government documents, memoirs, letters, diaries, fiction, photographs, advertisements, posters, and political cartoons. Headnotes, extended captions, sidebars, and introductory essays provide the essential context that frames the documents. All the books are amply illustrated and each includes a documentary picture essay, chronology, further reading, source notes, and index.

Encounters in the New World (Jill Lepore)
Colonial America (Edward G. Gray)
The American Revolution (Stephen C. Bullock)
The Bill of Rights (John J. Patrick)
The Struggle Against Slavery (David Waldstreicher)
The Civil War (Rachel Filene Seidman)
The Gilded Age (Janette Thomas Greenwood)
The Industrial Revolution (Laura Levine Frader)
Imperialism (Bonnie G. Smith)
World War I (Frans Coetzee and Marilyn Shevin-Coetzee)
The Depression and the New Deal (Robert McElvaine)
World War II (James H. Madison)
The Cold War (Allan M. Winkler)
The Vietnam War (Marilyn B. Young)

PIVOTAL MOMENTS IN AMERICAN HISTORY

Oxford's *Pivotal Moments in American History Series* explores the turning points that forever changed the course of American history. Each book is written by an expert on the subject and provides a fascinating narrative on a significant instance that stands out in our nation's past. For anyone interested in discovering which important junctures in U.S. history shaped our thoughts, actions, and ideals, these books are the definitive resources.

The Scratch of a Pen: 1763 and the Transformation of North America (Colin Calloway)
As if an Enemy's Country: The British Occupation of Boston and the Origins of the Revolution (Richard Archer)
Washington's Crossing (David Hackett Fischer)
James Madison and the Struggle for the Bill of Rights (Richard Labunski)
Adams vs. Jefferson: The Tumultuous Election of 1800 (John Ferling)

The Birth of Modern Politics: Andrew Jackson, John Quincy Adams, and the Election of 1828 (Lynn Parsons)
Storm over Texas: The Annexation Controversy and the Road to Civil War (Joel H. Silbey)
Crossroads of Freedom: Antietam (James M. McPherson)
The Last Indian War: The Nez Perce Story (Elliot West)
Seneca Falls and the Origins of the Women's Rights Movement (Sally McMillen)
Rainbow's End: The Crash of 1929 (Maury Klein)
Brown v. Board of Education *and the Civil Rights Movement* (Michael J. Klarman)
The Bay of Pigs (Howard Jones)
Freedom Riders: 1961 and the Struggle for Racial Justice (Raymond Arsenault)

VIEWPOINTS ON AMERICAN CULTURE

Oxford's *Viewpoints on American Culture Series* offers timely reflections for twenty-first century readers. The series targets topics where debates have flourished and brings together the voices of established and emerging writers to share their own points of view in compact and compelling format.

Votes for Women: The Struggle for Suffrage Revisited (Jean H. Baker)
Long Time Gone: Sixties America Then and Now (Alexander Bloom)
Living in the Eighties (Edited by Gil Troy and Vincent J. Cannato)
Race on Trial: Law and Justice in American History (Annette Gordon-Reed)
Sifters: Native American Women's Lives (Theda Perdue)
Latina Legacies: Identity, Biography, and Community (Vicki L. Ruiz)

OXFORD WORLD'S CLASSICS

For over 100 years Oxford World's Classics has made available a broad spectrum of literature from around the globe. With well over 600 titles available and a continuously growing list, this is the finest and most comprehensive classics series in print. Any volume in the series can be **packaged for free** with Oakes's *Of the People: A History of the United States*. Relevant titles include Benjamin Franklin's *Autobiography and Other Writings*, J. Hector St. John de Crèvecœur's *Letters from an American Farmer*, Booker T. Washington's *Up from Slavery*, and many others. **For a complete listing of Oxford World's Classics, please visit www.oup.com/us/owc.**

Acknowledgments

The authors are grateful to our families, friends, and colleagues who encouraged us during the planning and writing of this book.

Nick Cullather: To Isabel and Joey, for (occasionally) allowing me to work, and to Melanie for the 16 best years.

Jan Lewis: I want to express special thanks to Andy Achenbaum, James Grimmelmann, Warren F. Kimball, Ken Lockridge, and Peter Onuf, who either read portions of the manuscript or discussed it with me. And I am grateful to Barry Bienstock for his enormous library, his vast knowledge, and his endless patience.

The authors would like once again to thank Bruce Nichols for helping launch this book years ago. We are grateful to the editors and staff at Oxford University

Press, especially our acquisitions editor, Brian Wheel, and our development editors, Angela Kao and Frederick Speers. Brian's commitment made this edition possible; Fred's vision helped us give the book a new direction. Thanks also to our talented production team, Barbara Mathieu, senior production editor, and Paula Schlosser, art director, who helped to fulfill the book's vision. And special thanks go to Linda Sykes, who managed the photo research; to Teresa Nemeth, our copyeditor; and to Mike Powers and Martha Bostwick, cartographers, and Deane Plaister, editor, at Maps.com, who created the maps; and to the many other people behind the scenes at Oxford for helping this complex project happen.

The authors and editors would also like to thank the following people, whose time and insights have contributed to this edition:

Supplement Authors

Laura Graves,
South Plains College
Instructor's Manual

Andrew McMichael,
Western Kentucky University
Student Companion Website

Jim Jeffries,
Clemson University
PowerPoint slides

Archie McDonald,
Stephen F. Austin State University
Test Bank

Expert Reviewers

Thomas L. Altherr
Metropolitan State College of Denver

Luis Alvarez
University of California–San Diego

Adam Arenson
University of Texas–El Paso

Melissa Estes Blair
University of Georgia

Susan Roth Breitzer
Fayetteville State University

Margaret Lynn Brown
Brevard College

W. Fitzhugh Brundage
University of North Carolina–Chapel Hill

Lawrence Bowdish
Ohio State University

Gregory Bush
University of Miami

Brian Casserly
University of Washington

Ann Chirhart
Indiana State University

Bradley R. Clampitt
East Central University

Cheryll Ann Cody
Houston Community College

William W. Cobb Jr.
Utah Valley University

Sondra Cosgrove
College of Southern Nevada

Thomas H. Cox
Sam Houston State University

Carl Creasman
Valencia Community College

Christine Daniels
Michigan State University

Brian J. Daugherity
Virginia Commonwealth University

Mark Elliott
University of North Carolina–Greensboro

Katherine Carté Engel
Texas A&M University

Michael Faubion
University of Texas–Pan American

John Fea
Messiah College

Anne L. Foster
Indiana State University

Matthew Garrett
Arizona State University

Tim Garvin
California State University–Long Beach

Lloyd Ray Gunn
University of Utah

Suzanne Cooper Guasco
Queens University of Charlotte

Richard Hall
Columbus State University

Marsha Hamilton
University of South Alabama

Mark Hanna
University of California–San Diego

Joseph M. Hawes
University of Memphis

Melissa Hovsepian
University of Houston–Downtown

David K. Johnson
University of South Florida

Lloyd Johnson
Campbell University

Jorge Iber
Texas Tech University

Michael Kramer
Northwestern University

Catherine O'Donnell Kaplan
Arizona State University

Rebecca M. Kluchin
California State University–Sacramento

Louis M. Kyriakoudes
University of Southern Mississippi

Jason S. Lantzer
Butler University

Shelly Lemons
St. Louis Community College

Charlie Levine
Mesa Community College

Denise Lynn
University of Southern Indiana

Lillian Marrujo-Duck
City College of San Francisco

Noeleen McIlvenna
Wright State University

Michael McCoy
Orange County Community College

Elizabeth Brand Monroe
Indiana University–Purdue University, Indianapolis

Kevin C. Motl
Ouachita Baptist University

Todd Moye
University of North Texas

Julie Nicoletta
University of Washington–Tacoma

Charlotte Negrete
Mt. San Antonio College

David M. Parker
California State University–Northridge

Jason Parker
Texas A&M University

Burton W. Peretti
Western Connecticut State University

Jim Piecuch
Kennesaw State University

John Putman
San Diego State University

R. J. Rockefeller
Loyola College of Maryland

Herbert Sloan
Barnard College, Columbia University

Vincent L. Toscano
Nova Southeastern University

William E. Weeks
San Diego State University

Timothy L. Wood
Southwest Baptist University

Jason Young
SUNY–Buffalo

About the Authors

James Oakes has published several books and numerous articles on slavery and antislavery in the nineteenth century, including *The Radical and the Republican: Frederick Douglass, Abraham Lincoln, and the Triumph of Antislavery Politics* (2007), winner of the Lincoln Prize in 2008. Professor Oakes has previously taught at Princeton and Northwestern Universities, and he is now Distinguished Professor of History and Graduate School Humanities Professor at the City University of New York Graduate Center. In 2008 he was a fellow at the Cullman Center at the New York Public Library. His current writing involves a history of emancipation during the Civil War.

Michael McGerr is Paul V. McNutt Professor of History in the College of Arts and Sciences at Indiana University–Bloomington. He is the author of *The Decline of Popular Politics: The American North, 1865–1928* (1986) and *A Fierce Discontent: The Rise and Fall of the Progressive Movement, 1870–1920* (2003). He is writing *"The Public Be Damned": The Vanderbilts and the Unmaking of the Ruling Class.* The recipient of a yearlong fellowship from the National Endowment for the Humanities, Professor McGerr has won numerous teaching awards at Indiana, where his courses include the U.S. Survey, Race and Gender in American Business, War in Modern American History, The Politics of American Popular Music, The Sixties, and American Pleasure Wars. He has previously taught at Yale University and the Massachusetts Institute of Technology. He received the BA, MA, and PhD from Yale.

Jan Ellen Lewis is Professor of History and Associate Dean of the Faculty of Arts and Sciences, Rutgers University, Newark. She also teaches in the history PhD program at Rutgers, New Brunswick, and was a visiting professor of history at Princeton. A specialist in colonial and early national history, she is the author of *The Pursuit of Happiness: Family and Values in Jefferson's Virginia* (1983) as well as numerous articles and reviews. She has coedited *An Emotional History of the United States* (1998), *Sally Hemings and Thomas Jefferson: History, Memory, and Civic Culture* (1999), and *The Revolution of 1800: Democracy, Race, and the New Republic* (2002). She has served on the editorial board of the *American Historical Review* and as chair of the New Jersey Historical Commission. She received her AB from Bryn Mawr College and MAs and PhD from the University of Michigan.

Nick Cullather is a historian of U.S. foreign relations at Indiana University–Bloomington. He is author of two books on nation building: *Illusions of Influence* (1994), a study of U.S.-Philippines relations, and *Secret History* (1999 and 2006), a history of the CIA's overthrow of the Guatemalan government in 1954. His current work includes *Calories and Cold War: America's Quest to Feed the World.* He received his PhD from the University of Virginia.

Jeanne Boydston was Robinson-Edwards Professor of American History at the University of Wisconsin–Madison. A specialist in the histories of gender and labor, she was the author of *Home and Work: Housework, Wages, and the Ideology of Labor in the Early American Republic* (1990); coauthor of *The Limits of Sisterhood: The Beecher Sisters on Women's Rights and Woman's Sphere* (1988), and coeditor of *Root of Bitterness: Documents in the Social History of American Women,* second edition (1996). Her most recent article is "Gender as a Category of Historical Analysis," *Gender History* (2008). She taught courses in women's and gender history, the histories of the early republic and the antebellum United States, and global and comparative history, and she was the recipient of numerous awards for teaching and mentoring. Her BA and MA were from the University of Tennessee, and her PhD was from Yale University.

Of the People

CHAPTER

1

Common Threads

>> In which ways might the Native American societies before the arrival of Europeans be considered egalitarian? What forces shaped their societies?

>> How did Europeans' preconceptions affect their actions in the New World? In which ways did they adapt to new circumstances?

>> What role did gender play in organizing Native American, African, and European societies? What role did gender play in conquest?

>> What were the unintended consequences of conquest?

Worlds in Motion

1450–1550

AMERICAN PORTRAIT

>> Malinche, Cultural Translator

Even her name was a mistranslation. We do not know what name her parents gave her. She was born to a noble family in a Nahuatl-speaking state on the eastern edge of the great Aztec Empire in Mexico. Her widowed mother gave the girl away, to people in another kingdom, who in turn gave her to another people, the Chontal Mayas. Then, in 1519, when the Spanish conquerors arrived, the Chontals gave them twenty women, in the hopes that this gift would induce the Spanish to move on to the west. When Indian peoples first encountered the European invaders, they used every stratagem they could think of simply to get the foreigners to move on.

A priest soon baptized her and gave her the name of Marina. She was turned over to a Spanish captain to serve as his mistress, and then to the Spanish conqueror Hernán Cortés to serve as his translator. In her world and that of the conquerors, women could be handed from one man to another, little more than property. The Spanish had noticed that she could speak not only the Mayan language, but Nahuatl, too, the language of the Aztec Empire they intended to conquer. In time, she learned Spanish also, making all other translators unnecessary. From that moment, she was at Cortés's side until he had conquered all of Mexico. And that is when the Spanish started calling her Doña—or Lady—Marina, in honor of her importance. In Nahuatl, her name became Malintzin (with the *-tzin* signifying her noble status), which the Spanish heard as Malinche, the name we know her by today: a Spanish translation of a Nahuatl translation of a Spanish name given to a Mexican girl.

Cortés never learned the Indian languages. Malinche was the one who translated his words to the Aztec king Moctezuma. Both came from highly developed cultures with elaborate rules for politeness. Neither understood the other's rules, however, and consequently, Cortés and his men had to be held back physically when they breached Aztec custom by touching the king with their hands. Yet when Malinche spoke Cortés's words to Moctezuma, she did not coat them in the honeyed words the king expected of all his subjects, nor did she cast her eyes down. Instead, she looked him in the eye, something not even his own lords would dare to do. What courage this must have taken for the young woman, assuming for herself the arrogance of the Spanish conqueror.

The first meeting of Malinche, called Marina by the Spanish, and Cortés.

Malinche survived the great battle for the Aztec capital, Tenochtitlán, and she saw the Spanish level the once-great city. It was only after the Aztecs had been defeated that Cortés took Malinche as his mistress. Soon she was pregnant, later bearing a son, Don Martín, named for Cortés's own father. Cortés raised the boy as a son, although he soon married Malinche off to one of his friends. Before long, she gave birth to a second child, a daughter. Both of her children lived out their lives in the world of the conquerors, her son in Spain, her daughter married to a Spanish settler in Mexico.

Cortés needed Malinche's translating services for one more venture, however. One of his lieutenants had gone off on his own, conquering Honduras. Cortés, his soldiers, and his trusted translator set out to subjugate the renegade. The path to Honduras took the war party through the province where Malinche had been born. There they encountered Malinche's mother. The older woman was terrified, certain that the daughter she had once given away would now have her executed. Instead, Malinche forgave her and showered her with jewels and gold and fine clothing. She said that she was grateful to God for making her a Christian, or this is what the Spanish thought they heard. She spoke in Nahuatl, a language the Spanish did not understand.

In the long period of encounter and conquest initiated by the Spanish arrival in the Americas, cultural translators, women and men such as Malinche who understood the languages and customs of the different worlds, would possess unique power. In translating one world to the other, they helped create a new world, one very different from any that had ever existed before. ●

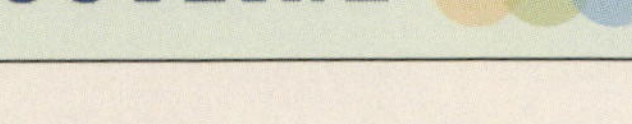

The World of the Indian Peoples

When Europeans arrived in the New World at the end of the fifteenth century, several large and powerful states, such as the Aztec and Inca, had emerged, as well as a number of peoples who lived in less complex social organizations, each with different traditions, cultures, and languages. This diversity had its origins at least 12,000 years earlier when people known as the Archaic or Paleo-Indians crossed from Siberia into Alaska. By the time of Christopher Columbus's voyage, there were hundreds of separate Indian cultures, speaking 375 different languages (see Map 1–1). The total native population of America north of the Rio Grande may have been as high as 18 million (with that of Europe perhaps five or six times higher).

This diversity can be misleading, however. In fact, as early as the first century CE, distinctive regional groups, held together by exchange relations, had begun to emerge. By the twelfth century, there were several centers of exchange north of the Rio Grande (one at Cahokia and the other at Chaco Canyon), although both had begun to decline before the arrival of the Europeans. When Europeans arrived in North America, they encountered a continent that already had a rich and complex history.

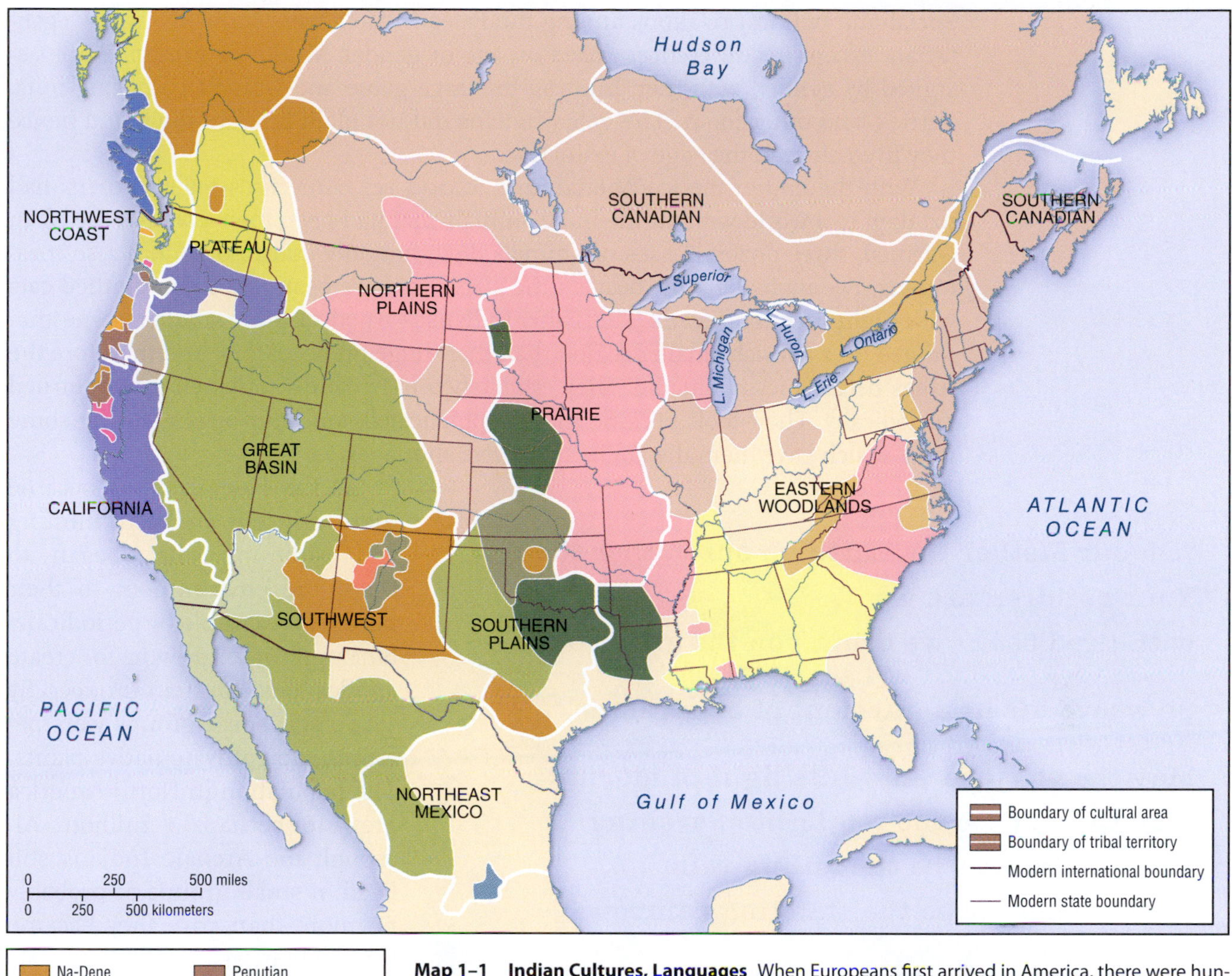

Na-Dene
Algonquian-Ritwan
Iroquoian
Siouan
Caddoan
Muskogean
Kiowa-Tanoan
Keresan
Uto-Aztecan
Hokan
Yukian
Penutian
Sahaptin
Lutuamian
Oregon Penutian
Chinookan
Salishan
Wakashan
Chimakuan
Otomanguean
Area of unknown or complex classification

Map 1–1 Indian Cultures, Languages When Europeans first arrived in America, there were hundreds of separate cultures, speaking 375 different languages. Boundaries between the groups were constantly shifting, as disease, conflict, and environmental changes caused some groups to prosper and others to decline. Much of the Eastern Woodlands region had lost its population to epidemics and emigration. *Michael Coe et al.,* Atlas of Ancient North America *(New York: Facts on File, 1986), pp. 44–45.*

The Archaic Indians

The first Americans were hunter-gatherers who followed the mammoth and other huge animals as they migrated across the land bridge from Asia. These people were modern human beings who stood erect, wore clothing, and made tools. Once they had dispersed throughout America, they lived in small bands of perhaps two dozen people who occasionally interacted with other bands. There were strict bans on incest, so men selected their marriage partners from the women in other local bands.

Social and political relations among the Paleo-Indians were probably highly egalitarian, except for differences based on age or gender. Work, for example, was assigned by gender, with men hunting the large game and women gathering nuts, berries, and other foods. The Paleo-Indians did not plant or store food, and hence they lived close to the edge of extinction.

With the end of the Ice Age, around 10,000 BCE, America's Paleo-Indians had to adapt to a world without the huge animals that had been their prey. As the earth warmed, three dozen classes of animals died, not only mammoths, but also mastodons, twenty-foot sloths, beavers the size of today's bear, and saber-toothed cats with eight-inch-long teeth. The Paleo-Indians learned to hunt smaller game that ranged over a much smaller region than their huge predecessors, and therefore the tribes became less nomadic. They established base camps to which they returned periodically. Their tools became more sophisticated, and they began storing some food, which gave them the ability to survive shortages.

> "Oh our Mother the Earth oh our Father the Sky
> Your children are we
> with tired backs we bring you the gifts you love.
>
> So weave for us a garment of brightness
>
> May the warp be the white light of morning
> May the weft be the red light of evening
> May the fringes be the falling rain
> May the border be the standing rainbow
>
> Weave for us this bright garment
> That we may walk where birds sing
> where grass is green
>
> Oh our Mother the Earth oh our Father the Sky"
>
> A PUEBLO SONG OF THE SKY LOOM, n.d.

As the Paleo-Indians became more efficient in their hunting and gathering, they began to adapt the environment to their needs, for example by periodically burning undergrowth to create an ideal environment for deer. By 3,000 BCE, some groups were beginning to cultivate native plants. The population in North America grew to perhaps 1 million. Although the Archaic Indians still lived in small groups of probably no more than 500, they became less egalitarian.

Changes in the North American climate during the Archaic period led to other, more significant differences among Native American societies. While the Eastern Woodlands area (generally, east of the Mississippi River) was moist and hence hospitable to agriculture, the Plains region (between the Mississippi River and the Rocky Mountains) was arid. Plains Indians lived in small, highly mobile bands and pursued big game such as bison, elk, bear, and deer.

Further west, in the desert regions of the Great Basin and Southwest, Indians subsisted on small game and seeds. These peoples learned how to use the little moisture available to them, and domesticated several crops, including maize (corn) and chiles. Some groups became sedentary, building pueblos and cliff dwellings as permanent homes.

On the California coast and in the Pacific Northwest, Archaic hunter-gatherers made use of the abundant natural resources, particularly fish. They also began to develop striking artwork. Another regional culture began to develop south of the

Arctic Circle, where Native Americans began to build the boats, weapons, and tools necessary to hunt whales and seals. Out of these regional environments—Eastern Woodlands, Plains, Great Basin and Southwest, California and Pacific Coast, and Subarctic—developed the distinctive Indian cultures that European explorers later encountered. By the time of Columbus's voyage, these Indian peoples were as different from one another as the peoples of Europe.

Pacific Northwest Indian Mask

The Indians of the Eastern Woodlands

The woodlands east of the Mississippi River gave rise to several distinctive Native American cultures, including the Mississippian mound builders, whose center was at Cahokia (near present-day East St. Louis, Missouri). By 700 BCE, Indians in this area had begun to cultivate crops, and by the twelfth century, agriculture had spread over much of the region east of the Mississippi and into the Southwest. These Mississippian societies were distinguished by the increasing complexity of their crafts, the extent of their trade networks, and their increasing capacity to support large populations from their agriculture. One estimate suggests that maize accounted for half of the Mississipians' diet. All of them built mounds in which to bury their dead and as platforms for temples and other public structures. The mounds can still be seen today at Cahokia, although the structures themselves and the people who worshiped in them have long since disappeared.

These Indian societies were increasingly hierarchical in their political and social organizations. Some offices were probably hereditary, and large cities such as Cahokia (with a population of between 10,000 and 30,000) dominated smaller ones. When powerful people died, they were buried with huge stores of luxury goods gathered through trade routes that stretched throughout the continent. (Cahokians of lesser rank were buried in mass graves, however.) Because mound builders buried these goods with the dead, rather than passing them on from generation to generation, they had to keep trading for new supplies. They also crafted exquisite objects out of metal and stone to bury with their dead and to trade to distant tribes.

Before the arrival of Europeans, Indian cultures flourished and also disappeared for reasons that are not fully known. Spanish explorers encountered mound-building Indians in the Southeast in the sixteenth century, but by the time the English arrived a century later, the mound builders had disappeared from the Ohio and Mississippi river valleys. Archaeologists have theories about the disappearance of the Mississippians. Although these tribes were aggressive, their collapse does not seem to have been caused by warfare. Instead, preindustrial cities were probably "population sinks," that is, areas where densely packed populations without effective sanitation systems became breeding grounds for lethal diseases. Preindustrial peoples in all parts of the world always lived close to the edge of extinction, and a serious drought or epidemic disease could wipe out an entire population.

At about the time the Mississippian cities were collapsing, other Indian cultures were rising to prominence in the Eastern Woodlands. The Iroquois occupied the

Image of Community of Cahokia The community at Cahokia, at eye level, as envisioned by a modern-day graphic artist. The town was surrounded by a stockade, which enclosed the mounds, plazas, temples, and homes.

southern Great Lakes region, and the Algonquians covered much of eastern Canada and the northeastern United States, as far south as Virginia. These two groups spoke different languages, and the Iroquois were matrilineal (tracing descent through the woman) and matrilocal (with husbands moving into their wives' clans), but in many other ways, the two cultures were similar. The Iroquois and Algonquians south of Canada practiced a slash-and-burn method of agriculture: clearing and burning forests for corn and other vegetables, planting them intensively, exhausting the soil, and then moving on to more fertile regions, where clearings once again were burned. This method of agriculture could not sustain as large a population as the fertile river valley cultivation of the mound builders; nonetheless, farming became increasingly efficient, making hunting less important. Because almost all agriculture was the work of women, their prestige in their villages increased.

Iroquois and Algonquian societies were more warlike than the Mississippians, although scholars are not certain why. One theory suggests that as agriculture became more efficient and women's prestige increased, men resorted to warfare to maintain their own prestige. By the eve of European settlement, many Iroquois tribes had banded together in a confederacy to limit infighting and to strengthen them against external enemies. Political influence within these cultures depended almost entirely on persuasion rather than force. Requiring the consent of all concerned, women included, made the Iroquois particularly cohesive: by the time the Europeans arrived, the Iroquois were able to subdue internal violence, direct it outward at the interlopers, and keep them at bay for more than two centuries.

The Indians of the Plains

The popular image of the Plains Indian comes from Westerns: the warrior on horseback, hunting bison. Plains Indians, however, did not have horses until after the Spanish reintroduced horses to the Great Plains in the sixteenth century (they had died out at the end of the Pleistocene epoch). Like Indians east of the Mississippi, Plains Indians became agriculturalists after the end of the Archaic period. Women were responsible for raising maize and other crops, while men traveled periodically to hunt buffalo. Hunters stampeded buffalo into enclosures, where they ambushed them or forced them to jump over steep cliffs to their death.

After the Spanish brought horses to the Plains, these Indians became nomadic, abandoning their multifamily lodges for tipis that could be carried from one campsite to the next. Buffalo then became a more important part of their diet. With this shift, women's prestige decreased and men's grew.

The Indians of the Deserts

The arid landscape of the desert in the West and Southwest shaped the Indian cultures in those regions. Over the centuries, Indians learned to make maximum use of native plants such as the piñon and to cultivate increasingly productive strains of maize. The population remained relatively small, but by about 200 CE, villages began to appear. At that time, Southwestern Indians began to construct pit houses, round dwellings carved about a foot and a half into the ground with walls and roofs constructed out of mud-covered wooden frameworks.

After 700 CE, as the population grew, Southwestern Indians moved out of these pit houses into adobe pueblos, such as the ones built on the surface at Chaco Canyon (in present-day New Mexico) and those carved into the cliffs at Mesa Verde (in present-day Colorado). Similar to Cahokia, Chaco Canyon was the center of a large population and a vast trade network. These huge complexes must have required the labor of well-organized work forces. Abandoned pit houses were turned into kivas, chambers for the practice of religious ceremonies, sometimes reserved exclusively for men. Pueblo Bonito, the largest town at Chaco Canyon, contained more than 800 rooms and required 30,000 sandstone blocks to build. The surrounding area included 70 towns and 5,300 villages, with a total population of perhaps 15,000. The trade network of Anasazis, as they were called, reached as far south as Mexico (the source of copper bells) and as far west as the Gulf of California, from which seashells were obtained.

Like the cities of the eastern mound builders, the Anasazi Indian communities at Chaco Canyon, Mesa Verde, and several other sites simply disappeared, Chaco sometime after 1100 CE and Mesa Verde in the last quarter of the thirteenth century. Archeologists are not certain why, but recent theories for the abandonment of Mesa Verde suggest a combination of prolonged drought, the need to fight off outsiders, and a new and attractive religion that pulled people to the south and east, away from the dry climate and hostile neighbors. There they would build the Acoma, Hopi, and Zuni pueblos.

The Indians of the Pacific Coast

Along the California and Northwest Pacific coast, plentiful fish, game, and edible plants permitted the population to grow even in the absence of agriculture. In California, the variety of local environments meant that each of 500 local cultures could concentrate on its own specialties, which it traded with its neighbors. The Northwest coastal environment was more uniform, but no less lush, and its inhabitants enjoyed a surplus of food. With so little work needed to supply the food needs of the community, Northwest Coast Indians were able to build up surpluses and create magnificent works of art such as totem poles and masks. Periodically, these Indians held potlatch ceremonies in which they gave away or even destroyed all their possessions. When Europeans first encountered this practice, they found it bizarre and even dangerous, so contrary was it to their own customs of accumulating wealth.

The Great Civilizations of the Americas

Although the Indian peoples north of the Rio Grande River were primarily agriculturalists or hunter-gatherers, several of those to the south developed much more complex political economies, technologies, and urban cultures. The splendid Maya civilization, which had developed both a writing system and mathematics, had dominated southern Mexico and Central America from the fourth to the tenth centuries. Historians do not know for certain why the Maya cultural centers declined, but the causes may have been a change in climate or ecology that made it impossible for Maya agriculture to support so large a population.

Another great empire in the region was that of the Toltecs, whose influence extended from central Mexico as far north perhaps as the cliff-dwelling Anasazis of the American Southwest. After the Toltec Empire was destroyed in the middle of the twelfth century by invaders from the north, the Aztec people dominated the region until their own defeat at the hands of a Spanish and Indian alliance. Elsewhere in the Americas, other peoples were on the move, sometimes engaging in peaceful trade and other times attempting to wrest control of a region from those who inhabited it. The powerful and complex Inca Empire in Peru had just reached its high point when the Spanish arrived.

The Worlds of Christopher Columbus

Imagine a world in which most people live in small villages, where they eat the food that they hunt or raise themselves and never travel more than a few miles from home. At the same time, other people are on the move, especially traders, warriors, and men and women displaced by war and famine. The traders push at the boundaries of the known world, looking for better goods and new markets. The warriors aim at conquest. They seize land that others inhabit, pushing them aside, so that their own people can move in. The traders and the warriors set the world in motion and the population of the world shifts.

Columbus came to the Americas as a trader and became a conqueror. In the process he introduced the ways of the Old World into the New World, changing both of them forever. The modern history of America begins in 1492 with the movement of all of these peoples, from the Old World and the New, on American terrain.

European Nations in the Age of Discovery

In 1492, Europe as we now know it did not yet exist. Many of what later became major European nations—Spain, Italy, Germany—were merely collections of small principalities, each owing its allegiance to a local ruler. Indeed, Spain and Portugal had only recently been liberated from the Moors, a North African people who practiced the Muslim religion and who had invaded the Iberian Peninsula in 711. France and England were led by a single ruler, but the power of that leader was still limited, as the ruler struggled with local feudal lords for control of the nation. It was at this time in history that European nation-states were being consolidated, each under the rule of a single leader, a hereditary monarch. In fact, not until a nation was unified under a strong leader could it turn away from internal struggles and focus on the world beyond. As the first nations to be unified, Portugal and Spain were the first also to begin to explore and conquer foreign lands. The Netherlands, France, and England, unified about a century later, then followed the Spanish and Portuguese lead. Germany and Italy, not unified until the nineteenth century, lagged far behind in the race for foreign territory. The consolidation of European nations unleashed enormous energy, which put the peoples of Europe in motion. The traders charted a way, first to China by an overland route, and then to Africa by sea.

> **"This has been a marvelous thing and the most honorable in the world. . . . The dead weigh on me heavily, but they could not have gone better employed."**
>
> ISABEL
> in a letter to Fernando, who was with the army, fighting in the *reconquista*, May 30, 1486

The Political Economy of Europe

The world's peoples have always traded with one another. However, the period between 1450 and 1750 witnessed the establishment of new trade patterns that changed the face of the world. In the preceding centuries, powerful empires had dominated trade in their regions (see Map 1–2). In the middle of the fifteenth century, Islamic traders, for example, linked parts of Europe, Africa, and Asia. Because trade was a relatively minor part of the world economy compared to agriculture, however, trade had a correspondingly minor effect upon the political and social structure of the world.

Once western Europe began to dominate world trade, after 1450, it began to shape not only the world economy, but global social and political structures as well. The nations of western Europe established global trade networks, linking Europe, Africa, Asia, and the Americas. The inequalities between nations were heightened as wealth flowed first to Spain and Portugal and then to England, France, and Holland. As western European nations became wealthier and their economies more complex, those areas of America, Africa, and (to a lesser extent) Asia that were conquered or colonized became economically dependent on western trade. They supplied the raw materials that made Europe wealthy. Increasingly, their own populations were exploited and even enslaved, to turn out gold, silver, sugar, and tobacco to feed the insatiable appetites of Europe.

When Christopher Columbus sailed west looking for Asia, he was trying to reestablish a European trade that had been disrupted by the Black Death; the bubonic plague had arrived in Europe in 1347, brought by a trade caravan from Asia. Until that time, the Italians in particular had engaged in commerce as far east as the Mongol Empire in China. Marco Polo, the son of an Italian merchant, had written a book that described his stay in China and India between 1275 and 1292. In the middle of the fifteenth century, as Europe began to recover from the plague, its population began to grow, the economy began to expand, and merchants, especially along the Mediterranean, began to look for new markets.

The vast majority of Europeans were peasants, many living close to destitution. Still, an increasingly prosperous elite (both the nobility and the affluent members of the urban middle classes) developed a taste for luxury items such as sugar, spices, fabrics, and precious metals. Marco Polo's descriptions of Asian temples roofed in gold had dazzled Italian readers since the end of the thirteenth century. The desire for luxury goods sent European explorers off in search of new routes to Asia.

By the middle of the fifteenth century, new technologies made it possible for Europeans to travel far from home. Some of these innovations were adapted from other regions of the world—for example, gunpowder from China and the navigational compass from the Arabs. Others came from Europe, including better maps; stronger metal that could be turned into guns and cannons; and the caravel, a light, swift ship that was well suited for navigating along the coast of Africa.

Europe was on the move by the end of the fifteenth century. The Portuguese had begun exploring the Atlantic coast of Africa, searching for a water route to Asia. Portugal had recently driven out its Muslim conquerors. It was a small nation (about 1.5 million inhabitants, compared to almost 10 million for Spain), but it had achieved political unification under a strong king almost a century earlier. The combination of political unity, a strong monarchy interested in extending its power and wealth, and an aggressive merchant class looking for new markets enabled Portugal to become the first of the modern European imperial nations. By 1475, Portuguese explorers had reached the thriving kingdom of Benin on the lower Guinea coast (the modern country of Nigeria) and had established trading posts along the northwestern coast of the continent. In exchange for European goods such as horses, cloth, and wheat, the Portuguese received African luxury products such as ivory, and especially gold, that could be sold in Europe (Map 1–2).

Map 1–2 World Trade on the Eve of Discovery For a thousand years, world trade centered on the Mediterranean. European, Arab, and Asian traders crisscrossed much of the Eastern Hemisphere, carrying spices, silks, and cottons from Asia; linens, woolens, and wine from Europe; and gold and slaves from Africa.

Earlier in the fifteenth century, the Portuguese had begun raiding the Sahara coast for slaves. Once they opened up the new trade with sub-Saharan Africa, however, they discovered that they could exchange European goods directly with African kings and be provided with slaves. The Portuguese then resold the slaves, primarily for use as servants, in Africa or Europe. Until 1500, in fact, the Portuguese were shipping only between 500 and 1,000 slaves a year, most of whom were resold in Africa. However, with the opening of plantations (first in the Canary Islands, which the Spanish had completed conquering in 1496), the slave trade became an important part of the Portuguese economy.

The World of the West African Peoples

Starting with the Portuguese, European traders reached the west coast of Africa in the fifteenth century. There they found much of the population living in powerful and well-organized kingdoms, much like the European states. Some of those states, especially those just south of the Sahara such as Mali and Songhay, had been deeply influenced by Islam and had adopted its written language. Others, such as the central African Yoruba kingdoms, were complex city-states that produced glorious works of art in bronze and ivory. The population density in the Lower Guinea region was higher than that of Europe.

Not all African peoples lived in states, however. Many were members of villages or family groupings without rulers or bureaucracies. Despite this political diversity, religious beliefs were similar among the African cultures, all recognizing a supreme creator and numerous lesser deities. Gender relations among the African peoples were similar, too, with most people living in extended, male-led families and clans, which were the basis for the social order. Although men performed most of the heavy labor and women attended to domestic chores and childrearing, both men and women engaged in farming. Men dominated government and commerce, but on occasion women from prominent families exercised power. Women were active as merchants as well.

Powerful kingdoms dominated commerce and welcomed trade with Europe, which supplied them with prestigious goods. Although Africans themselves manufactured cloth, for example, European textiles found a ready market in Africa. In fact, it was precisely those regions of Africa that already had thriving markets that were most eager to trade with Europeans. Soon African nations willingly entered an international market.

As in Europe, at any given moment in Africa some kingdoms were increasing their dominance while others were in eclipse. But such normal political developments took on new meaning after the appearance of Europeans. In 1591 the defeat of the Songhay Empire by Moroccan invaders created instability in West Africa that offered unique opportunities for Europeans to profit.

Slavery Before 1500

The institution of slavery had a long history in both Europe and Africa. In general, slavery had been of limited importance in Europe, except in ancient Rome. The Roman Empire enslaved a number of the peoples it conquered, using them to raise food for the densely populated center of the empire in Italy. At the height of the

Map 1–3 Africa in the Age of Discovery Before 1450, Europeans knew little of Africa. Until that time, trade between Africa and Europe was controlled by Islamic traders whose empire extended across North Africa. In the middle of the 15th century, the Portuguese reached the western coast of Africa and began importing both trade goods and a small number of slaves. *Mark Kishlansky et al.,* Societies and Culture in World History *(New York: Harper Collins, 1995), p. 414.*

Roman Empire, as many as 35 or 40 percent of its people were enslaved, a total of 2 or 3 million men and women. Unlike modern slavery, Roman slavery was not based on race, and Roman slaves came from a great variety of ethnic groups.

By the time Portugal opened its trade with West Africa, slavery had disappeared from northwestern Europe, although some slaves were being used in parts of Christian Europe along the Mediterranean. The Muslims who invaded Spain and other regions along the Mediterranean in the eighth century had brought their form of slavery with them. In addition to working as domestic servants, these slaves were used in the production of sugar.

Several centuries later, when European merchants expanded their trade into regions controlled by the Muslims, they also began plying the trade in human beings. Slavery had been a relatively minor institution in Portugal, Spain, Sicily, Cyprus, and other regions of Europe that touched the Mediterranean. However, once Portugal took over the Atlantic island of Madeira and Spain controlled the Canary Islands, the cultivation of sugar brought into being the much larger systems of plantation slavery. At first the Europeans enslaved native islanders, and soon after, they imported Africans. Hence Europeans such as Columbus who lived and sailed along the Mediterranean would have been familiar with the slave trade and would have associated slavery with plantation agriculture.

As in Europe, slavery had been practiced in Africa from ancient times, although its character was different because of Africa's different political economy. In Europe, land was the primary form of private, wealth-creating property. In Africa, however, land and cattle were owned collectively, and the primary form of private, wealth-creating property was slaves. European law entitled the landowner to everything that was produced on the land, while African law entitled the slave owner to everything that the slave produced. The way to wealth in Africa was to acquire slaves, and in Europe, to acquire land.

In other ways, however, European and African slavery were similar. African slaves generally worked as domestic laborers, both in Africa and in other regions of the world where they were sold. Similar to European slavery, the status of the slave was not fixed securely by law, and the children of slaves might move into freedom. The African continent was divided among a number of different states that sustained a vigorous internal slave trade. In addition, as the Islamic empire spread in the eighth century, Muslim merchants bought slaves in Africa, usually women and children, for export to other regions of the empire. The African slave trade thus had two components: an internal trade within the continent and an external trade, run primarily by the Muslims. When the Portuguese entered the slave trade, they participated in both components.

Western and central Africans were accustomed to selling slaves, and they entered willingly into the global slave trade. By the seventeenth century, the high prices that Europeans were willing to pay for slaves stimulated the African slave trade and stripped the continent of much of its population.

The Golden Age of Spain

Portugal was the first nation in western Europe to achieve political unity, and hence it was the first to embark on exploration in search of trade. Spain was the second. Until the end of the fifteenth century, the Iberian Peninsula was divided into five independent kingdoms. At one time, the entire Iberian Peninsula had been dominated by Muslims, who had invaded the region from North Africa in 711. Islamic culture exerted a powerful influence in the region. Many Spanish people intermarried with the Muslims, adopting their religion and customs, such as the seclusion of women.

At the time of the invasion, Arab civilization was more sophisticated than the one it conquered. Through the Muslims, Greek science was reintroduced into a

Mosque-Cathedral of Córdoba, Spain The interior of the Mosque-Cathedral reveals a curious mixture of Moorish architecture (begun in the 8th century) and Christian art (in the statues above the arch) of the 16th century.

region that had lost touch with much ancient learning. Muslim, Christian, and Jewish communities generally were able to coexist. Local leaders, however, for reasons that were political and economic as well as cultural and religious, contested the rule of the Muslims and entered into a 700-year period of intermittent warfare known as the *reconquista* or "reconquest."

Warfare became a normal and expected part of life on the Iberian Peninsula, and it shaped society accordingly. The priests who proclaimed the *reconquista* a holy war against the Moorish infidel and the soldiers who carried on the conflict were elevated to positions of prestige. The surest path to wealth and honor lay in plunder and conquest, and an *hidalgo*'s (gentleman's) honor was defined by his capacity to vanquish the Muslims and seize their land and wealth. The Spanish hoped that the *reconquista* would be able to evict from their country those they considered infidels. Ordinary people participated with enthusiasm in what they believed was another crusade against non-Christians.

By the time Christopher Columbus arrived in Spain in 1485, the Muslims had been ousted from all of Spain except Granada. Castile and Aragon had recently been joined by the marriage of Isabel, princess of Castile, and her cousin Fernando, prince of Aragon. Although Isabel was only 18 at the time of her marriage (and her husband a year younger), she had already demonstrated herself to be a woman of boldness and determination. Because the match was more in Aragon's interest than

in Castile's, Isabel was able to dictate the terms of the marriage contract, making it clear that she would play the leading role in governing. Having consolidated their power and asserted their authority over their territories, Isabel and Fernando turned their attention to the final stage of the *reconquista*.

By focusing the attention and energy of their nobles against a non-Christian opponent, Isabel and Fernando were able to forge a Christian Spanish national identity that transcended regional loyalties. Herself an exceedingly devout Christian, Isabel had earlier inaugurated an Inquisition, a church tribunal authorized by the pope, to root out converted Jews and others who seemed insufficiently sincere Christians. By the time the Inquisition was complete, several hundred Spanish people had been burned at the stake and several thousand more imprisoned. Spain finally conquered the Moorish province of Granada in the spring of 1492. Militant Christians soon insisted on a forcible conversion and baptism of those Moors who chose to remain in the region. The Christian conquest of the Moors led swiftly to the eviction of another religious minority, the Jews. Less than three months after the fall of Granada, Isabel and Fernando signed an edict calling for the expulsion of the approximately 150,000 Jews who resided in their kingdom. The Spanish colonization of the Americas and the subjugation of their native peoples were simply the next chapters in the reign of Isabel and Fernando, whose nation defined its identity by its ability to vanquish those labeled infidels.

Painting of Christopher Columbus No one knows exactly what Christopher Columbus looked like. Some thought he had prematurely white hair and a long face, others thought he had a broad face without a beard. Here is one artist's way of imagining him.

It would be a mistake, however, to conclude that Spain was shaped by militarism and intolerance alone: In 1492, Spain was in the middle of its golden age. It was the most dynamic nation in Europe, and it soon became the most powerful. It welcomed and absorbed foreign influences, including Moorish art, science, and customs; Flemish art and architecture; and the Renaissance intellectual movement known as humanism, which was imported from Italy. Indeed, under the patronage of Queen Isabel, Spain became a center of humanism.

Spain's foray into the New World was both a commercial venture and a religious crusade. It was also fueled by the humanist spirit of discovery. In establishing colonies in the New World, Spain spread her religion, her language, and her culture, creating a new political economy in the process.

Worlds in Collision

Christopher Columbus's voyages to the Americas marked the beginning of a new era. The world was made immeasurably smaller, and peoples who had lived in isolation from one another were brought into close contact. In this great age of European exploration, Bartolomeo Dias rounded the African cape in 1488, Vasco da Gama reached India in 1498, and an expedition led by Ferdinand Magellan (Fernão Magalhães, in Portuguese) sailed around the world between 1519 and 1522. These explorers were seeking not to discover new lands but to find faster routes to old ones. They were propelled by an expanding Europe's desire for trade and for spreading the Christian religion. For the first time in human history, all of the world's great urban civilizations, from Tenochtitlán to Cathay, knew of one another's existence. Moreover, despite the obvious differences in language, dress, architecture, art, and customs, Europeans, Africans, and Native Americans lived in political and economic organizations similar enough to make trade and diplomacy possible. Europeans drew the entire world into their trade network, and the Christian religion was spread by both force and persuasion.

"... it seemed to me that they were a people very poor in everything. All of them go around as naked as their mothers bore them; and the women also, ... They are very well formed, with handsome bodies and good faces."

CHRISTOPHER COLUMBUS'S first impression of the Taino he encountered at Guanahani on October 12, 1492

Christopher Columbus Finds a Patron

Between 1492 and 1504, Columbus made four voyages to the New World sailing for Queen Isabel and King Fernando of Spain. Born in 1451 in the Italian city-state of Genoa, Columbus first went to sea on merchant ships that sailed the Mediterranean. In the 1470s, he began sailing to Portuguese outposts such as the Madeiras. Within a decade, Columbus had decided to seek support for a voyage to China and Japan, which he had read about in Marco Polo's book.

Columbus's ambitions were shaped by his reading and his extensive experience as a mariner, which had already taken him thousands of miles from the place of his birth. By Columbus's time, it was generally known that the world was round, but its precise dimensions had not been determined, nor were Europeans certain about the size and configuration of the lands to the east. There was, however, great curiosity about them, fueled by the search for wealth and national power. It was only a matter of time until Europeans headed west and bumped into America while attempting to circumnavigate the globe. Perhaps Columbus was the first (since the Norse planted a short-lived colony at Vinland 500 years earlier) simply because he made a serious mistake in his calculations: his optimism was based upon the mistaken belief that Japan was only 2,400 miles away from the Canary Islands, when in fact it is more than four times that distance away.

No private individual had the resources to finance such an expedition, so Columbus sought royal backing from the king of Portugal; when he turned him down, Columbus departed for Spain, where he sought patronage from Isabel and Fernando. Even though two scientific commissions cast doubt on his geographical assumptions and calculations, the monarchs were intrigued by his vision of a western route to Asia.

The monarchy agreed to finance most of Columbus's trip (paying for it not, as legend has it, by pawning Isabel's jewels, but by the much more modern method of deficit spending) and granted him a number of powers and privileges. Columbus would realize his lifelong ambition of being made a member of the nobility. Columbus was to be named admiral, viceroy, and governor-general of all the lands that he might find. After deducting for expenses, Columbus would get to keep one-tenth of the income from the enterprise, with the monarchy retaining the rest. The small amount spent on Columbus's voyages proved in time to be one of the shrewdest investments in the history of nations.

Columbus Finds a New World

The quest for wealth took Columbus back and forth across the Atlantic four times in 12 years. In those voyages he planted the Spanish flag throughout the Caribbean region, on the modern islands of Cuba, Hispaniola, and Puerto Rico, as well as on the mainland at Honduras and Venezuela. Ten years later Columbus was still as obsessed by gold as ever: "O, most excellent gold! Who has gold has a treasure with which he gets what he wants, imposes his will on the world, and even helps souls to paradise." The Spaniards who followed him onto the mainland eventually found among the Aztecs of Mexico and the Incas of Peru riches to match their most fantastic dreams. By then the patterns that shaped the next century of Spanish-Indian interaction in the Americas had been established.

Late-medieval Europeans tended to view the world in terms of opposites, which led them to exaggerate differences rather than see similarities or complexities. Columbus and subsequent explorers typically described the lands they visited as an earthly paradise, even in the face of contrary evidence. By the time Columbus returned to Hispaniola on his second voyage, accompanied by 1,500 Spaniards, it was clear that his hopes of easy wealth and harmonious relations with the natives were not to be realized. Columbus had left 39 men on the island among the Taino Indian inhabitants and returned to find them all dead, the first of many casualties to the European colonial experience. According to the Taino chieftain, the sailors set off on a spree of gold seeking and debauchery, each of them "taking as many women and as much gold as he could," until they were fighting among themselves and became easy victims for a rival Indian chieftain.

The Spanish could not see the death of their sailors as a predictable response to their behavior. Instead, they fit it into the Europeans' growing perception that all Indians could be divided into two groups: friendly, peace-loving, unsophisticated, "good" Indians, such as the Tainos, and fierce, savage, man-eating, "bad" Indians, for whom they used the Taino term "Caribs."

Historians and anthropologists have identified the Tainos and Caribs as two separate tribes, each with different histories and customs. The Tainos, who inhabited the islands of Cuba and Hispaniola, were sedentary farmers whose agriculture could sustain a population as dense as that of Spain. Taino farmers were accustomed to taking direction from their cacique; hence it was not long before the Spanish coerced the Tainos into working for them. Although the Tainos sometimes fought among themselves, they were generally peace-loving people.

The Caribs were more aggressive. At the time of Columbus's arrival, the Caribs were moving north from the South American coast into the island chains of the Atlantic. If the energies of the Tainos were directed toward agriculture and the practice of religion, the Caribs focused on trade and warfare. Men and women lived separately, and because Carib men often obtained their wives by raiding other villages, over time they came to treat their own women as if they were captives of war. Because the Caribs were a maritime people whose men were skilled warriors, it is not surprising that they came into conflict with another maritime people practiced in the arts of war, the Spanish.

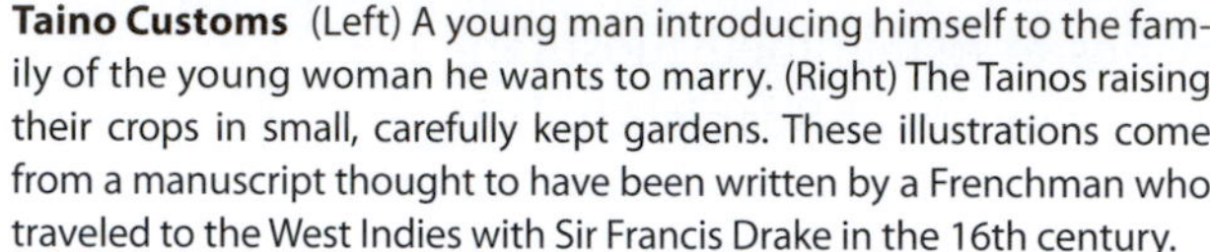

Taino Customs (Left) A young man introducing himself to the family of the young woman he wants to marry. (Right) The Tainos raising their crops in small, carefully kept gardens. These illustrations come from a manuscript thought to have been written by a Frenchman who traveled to the West Indies with Sir Francis Drake in the 16th century.

Although the Spanish, like all the Europeans who followed them into the Americas, depicted themselves as civilized and the Indians as either gentle but primitive or savage and inhuman, the differences between Europeans and natives were not that great. Seven centuries of warfare with the Moors had made the Spanish a fierce people, and they believed that practices that later generations would condemn as cruel were justified for people at war. Once the Spanish decided that the Caribs were an enemy, they began to treat them harshly.

The Origins of a New World Political Economy

As early as Columbus's second voyage of 1493, it became clear that the vast treasures he had anticipated were not readily at hand. His crew, however, expected to be rewarded for their services, and the queen and king who had financed his expedition expected profits. Therefore, Columbus packed off more than 500 Indians to be sold as slaves and distributed another 600 or so among the Spanish settlers on the island of Hispaniola.

Once again a pattern of New World development had been established. The European quest for wealth led to the subjugation of native peoples. Each European nation reacted somewhat differently to this movement toward enslavement. Generally, the Spanish rulers tried to restrain their New World colonizers and protect their new Indian subjects. In 1493, Pope Alexander VI confirmed Spanish dominion over all the lands that Columbus had explored, and he commanded the Spanish "to lead the peoples dwelling in those islands and countries to embrace the Christian religion." A papal bull (or proclamation) also established the church's interest in the spiritual welfare of the Native Americans. A subsequent treaty between Spain and Portugal, the Treaty of Tordesillas of 1494, divided between those two countries all lands already discovered or to be discovered, along an imaginary line 370 leagues west of the Azores. This treaty formed the basis for Portugal's subsequent claim to Brazil, which her explorers reached in 1500.

As the monarch who had driven the Muslims out of Spain, Isabel took seriously her responsibilities to evangelize her Indian subjects. Isabel and her successors also had political and economic goals, all of which they attempted to reconcile by insisting that the Indians who inhabited the islands seized by the Spanish were vassals, subjects of the Spanish Crown. In this way, Isabel attempted to fit the Indians into the Spanish political economy.

Like other vassals in Spain and its growing empire, the Indians were technically free, although they could be required to both work and pay tribute to the Crown. Isabel instructed the governor to impose on them a European-style civilization. They were to be "made to serve us through work, and be paid a just salary," and in order to assure their salvation, "they must live in villages, each in a house with a wife, a family, and possessions, as do the people of our kingdoms, and dress and behave like reasonable beings." Humane treatment, and with it freedom from slavery, thus would be dependent on the Indians' willingness to abandon their religion and customs and adopt those of the Spanish. It is easy to be cynical about Isabel's motives, but her approach was considerably more benevolent than that of most of those who were engaged in the colonizing process.

With the Spanish monarchy refusing to sanction the enslavement of friendly Indians, settlers had to devise an alternate means of getting labor from the Native Americans. Out of this struggle a New World political economy emerged. For the first several years, the Spanish simply demanded tribute from the Tainos. Many of the Spanish found this arrangement insufficiently lucrative, and they began to spread across the island of Hispaniola, subduing individual caciques and compelling their villages to work for the Spanish. The Spanish settlers owned neither the land, which had to be obtained through separate grants from Spanish officials, nor the Indians who worked for them. They possessed only the right to compel a particular group of Indians to work. This system, called the *encomienda,* was unique to the New World. Technically it complied with Isabel's insistence that friendly Indians be made vassals of the Crown rather than slaves.

We do not know precisely how the system developed, although there is some evidence that Spanish men first seized native women as their concubines, and that the village men subsequently worked for the Spanish, perhaps to remain close to their women. We often picture the encounter between Indians and Europeans as armed conflict between groups of men. In truth, women often played a critical role in establishing the shape of a biracial society, whether as captives or as willing participants in a European way of life.

Columbus appears to have sanctioned this new system of labor, and it eventually received begrudging support from the monarchs in Spain. Although the system appeared to give due regard to the Indians' legal rights and spiritual requirements, Native Americans were subjected to overwork and abuse, even if they could not legally be bought and sold as slaves. Spanish settlers' desire to realize a profit in the New World led to a form of exploitation unknown in Europe.

The *Requerimiento* and the Morality of Conquest

Throughout the period that Spain maintained a New World empire, there were tensions between the colonizers, who wished to increase their wealth and enhance their power, and the Crown, which wanted to limit the settlers' autonomy. Moreover, both

AMERICA AND THE WORLD

>> Debating the Morality of Conquest

In 1550, Carlos V, the king of Spain, summoned two of the most important Catholic clerics in the nation, Bartolomé de las Casas and Juan Ginés de Sepúlveda, to debate the morality of conquest before the Council of the Indies. These two priests were the leading spokesmen for two sharply different points of view. Las Casas, whose father sailed with Columbus on his second voyage and who himself later became an *encomendero*, was convinced by personal experience that "everything which has been done to the Indians is unjust and tyrannical." Sepúlveda was an eminent scholar and committed nationalist whose defense of conquest had already won him the thanks of the municipal council of Mexico City.

The two adversaries did not meet face-to-face. Sepúlveda appeared first, resting his case on the innate barbarism of the Indians. Some people, he said, were born to be masters and others, slaves. Sepúlveda ridiculed the argument that the Aztecs were "civilized" because they built cities and engaged in commerce. So what if they built houses? This "merely proves that they are neither bears nor monkeys and that they are not totally irrational." War against such people could be justified "not only on the basis of their paganism but even more so because of their abominable licentiousness, their prodigious sacrifice of human victims . . . their horrible banquets of human flesh." Subjecting them to Spanish rule would be the most "beneficial" thing that could be done for them.

Then Las Casas was summoned for his rebuttal. He spoke for five days—in Latin—until the exhausted Council told him they had heard enough. Warfare against the Indians was not justified, Las Casas argued. Instead, they could be won over by peaceful means, for they were "prudent and rational beings, of as good ability and judgment as other men and more able, discreet, and of better understanding than the people of many other nations." Las Casas denounced Sepúlveda's "deadly poison" and the greed of the Spanish, which "has led to such crimes . . . as have never been committed by any other nation, no matter how fierce it may have been." He feared that Sepúlveda's course would, in the end, provoke God to "pour forth the fury of his anger and lay hold of all of Spain sooner than he had decreed." The Spanish must convert the Indians, not conquer them.

Although the judges who heard these presentations departed without rendering a verdict, Las Casas's ideas prevailed. Las Casas had already helped shape the Laws of Burgos (1513) and the New Laws of 1542, which attempted to regulate the working conditions of the Indians and finally forbade any further enslavement of the native population. His influence can be seen in the next set of regulations, issued in 1573, written to govern Spain's future colonial ventures, which were to be called "pacifications" rather than "conquests." Henceforth, Indians were to be treated gently "so as not to scandalize them or prejudice them against Christianity." But by that time, Spain's New World empire was essentially complete; there were relatively few Indians left to conquer or to pacify.

Sepúlveda argued for unlimited governmental power, but it was actually Las Casas's views that were most useful to the powerful monarchy. When Spain commenced its overseas ventures, it was not even a nation itself. The century that would witness Spanish expansion into most of present South and Central America also saw the growth of state power in Spain. Las Casas's efforts on behalf of the Indians meshed nicely with the political plans of the Spanish monarchy, which aimed at centralized state power. Like the *hidalgos*, who had claimed as their own the land they wrested away from the Moors, the *conquistadores* attempted to set themselves up as feudal lords, with almost unlimited control over the land in their possession and the Indians who inhabited it, and with only limited obligations to the monarch. In insisting upon humane treatment of the Indians, the Spanish monarchs were undercutting the authority of the local *encomenderos*. In this way, as well as by forbidding the establishment of local representative governments, the Spanish monarchs prevented the development not only of a New World feudal aristocracy, which might challenge its power, but also democratic habits of self-government and local autonomy—all in the name of humanity.

the Spanish Crown and the clergy continued to be troubled by the treatment of the Indians. To clarify the legal basis for the enslavement of hostile Indians, in 1513 the Spanish Crown issued the *Requerimiento*, or "Requirement," a document drafted by legal scholars and theologians. The *Requerimiento* promised the Indians that if they accepted the authority of Christianity, the pope, and the monarchs of Spain, the *conquistadores* (conquerors) would leave them in peace. If, however, the Indians resisted the peaceful imposition of Spanish rule, the *conquistadores* would make war against them and enslave them. Henceforth, each *conquistador* was required to carry a copy of this document with him and to read it to every new group of Indians he encountered.

As with the *encomienda*, there is evidence that the *conquistadores* complied with the letter, but not the spirit, of the *Requerimiento*, by mumbling it in Spanish to groups of uncomprehending Indians or reading it from the decks of ships, far from hearing distance. Moreover, the Crown provided no means of enforcement other than the good faith of the *conquistador* or *encomendero* (owner of an *encomienda*). Considering the profits that might be reaped by the subjugation of the population, perhaps what is most surprising is not the failure of the Spanish Crown to protect the Indians, but that it kept trying.

> **"If you do . . . that which you are obliged to do to their Highnesses . . . we . . . shall receive you in all love and charity, and shall leave you, your wives, and your children, and your lands, free without servitude . . . and they shall not compel you to turn Christians, unless you yourselves, when informed of the truth, should wish to be converted to our Holy Catholic Faith, as almost all the inhabitants of the rest of the islands have done. . . .**
>
> **But, if you do not do this . . . we shall powerfully enter into your country, and shall make war against you in all ways and manners that we can, and shall subject you to the yoke and obedience of the Church and of their Highnesses; we shall take you and your wives and your children, and shall make slaves of them . . . and we shall take away your goods, and shall do you all the mischief and damage that we can, as to vassals who do not obey, and refuse to receive their lord, and resist and contradict him."**
>
> THE *REQUERIMIENTO*

The Biological Consequences of Conquest

Some of the most important changes produced by contact between Europeans and Native Americans were wholly unintentional. Each continent had its own diseases, its own plants, and its own animals. The arrival of Europeans tipped a delicate preindustrial balance in which everyone's effort was often needed to provide a food supply. The Europeans also introduced new diseases that spread like wildfire. If the biological effects of human contact were felt immediately, however, the consequences of plant and animal exchange took much longer. New breeds of animals were introduced from Europe into the Americas, and plants were exchanged between the continents. The face of the American landscape was changed, as domestic animals trampled grasslands and increasing acreage was turned over to the cultivation of Old World crops. This environmental transformation ultimately made possible the dramatic growth of the world's population, as new crops were cultivated.

Demographic Decline

Although the *encomienda* system satisfied Spanish settlers, it proved a disaster for the Indians. The agricultural methods of sedentary Indians such as the Taino could not produce the surplus that was necessary to support the Spanish. As soon happened to Indian communities throughout the Americas, the dislocation of their normal way of life proved deeply demoralizing, and the birthrate began to fall.

Within a few years after the appearance of Europeans, the Native American population began to decline, and with the introduction of the smallpox virus to Hispaniola in 1518, the process was hastened: soon no more than a thousand of the island's original half million or so inhabitants survived. Disease worked the same terrible destruction on the nearby islands of Cuba, Puerto Rico, and Jamaica. Disease followed the Spanish and other Europeans every place they went in the Americas, making the work of conquest that much easier.

Europeans did not set out to kill off the native inhabitants of the Americas, but that is exactly what the diseases they brought with them did. Isolation had protected the native peoples from the diseases of the Old World, whereas several centuries of trade among Europe, Asia, and Africa had enabled people from the three continents to share and acquire some natural biological defenses. Without such natural immunities, Indians were overcome by wave after wave of European disease. After smallpox came typhus and influenza, which destroyed entire communities and left the survivors weak and demoralized.

These terrible European diseases challenged Native American belief systems. The Cakchiquel Indian Hernández Arana described the spread of a plague in his native Guatemala in 1521 that killed a substantial proportion of the community: "After our fathers and grandfathers succumbed, half of the people fled to the fields. The dogs and the vultures devoured the bodies. . . . Your grandfathers died, and with them died the son of the king and his brothers and kinsmen. So it was that we became orphans, oh, my sons! . . . We were born to die!" The shock turned Indians against their traditional gods and prepared them to accept the god of the Spaniards.

The transmission of disease was by no means one-way, although most diseases seemed to spread from the Old World to the New World. Because syphilis, or at least a particularly virulent strain, first appeared in Europe shortly after Columbus and his crew made their first return voyage in 1493, historians have suggested that Europeans carried this disease back to the Old World. The disease spread rapidly through the world in the late fifteenth and early sixteenth centuries, from Spain to India, China, and Japan. Syphilis, which killed millions and incapacitated many more, became a legacy of the European age of exploration as it followed traders and armies throughout the world.

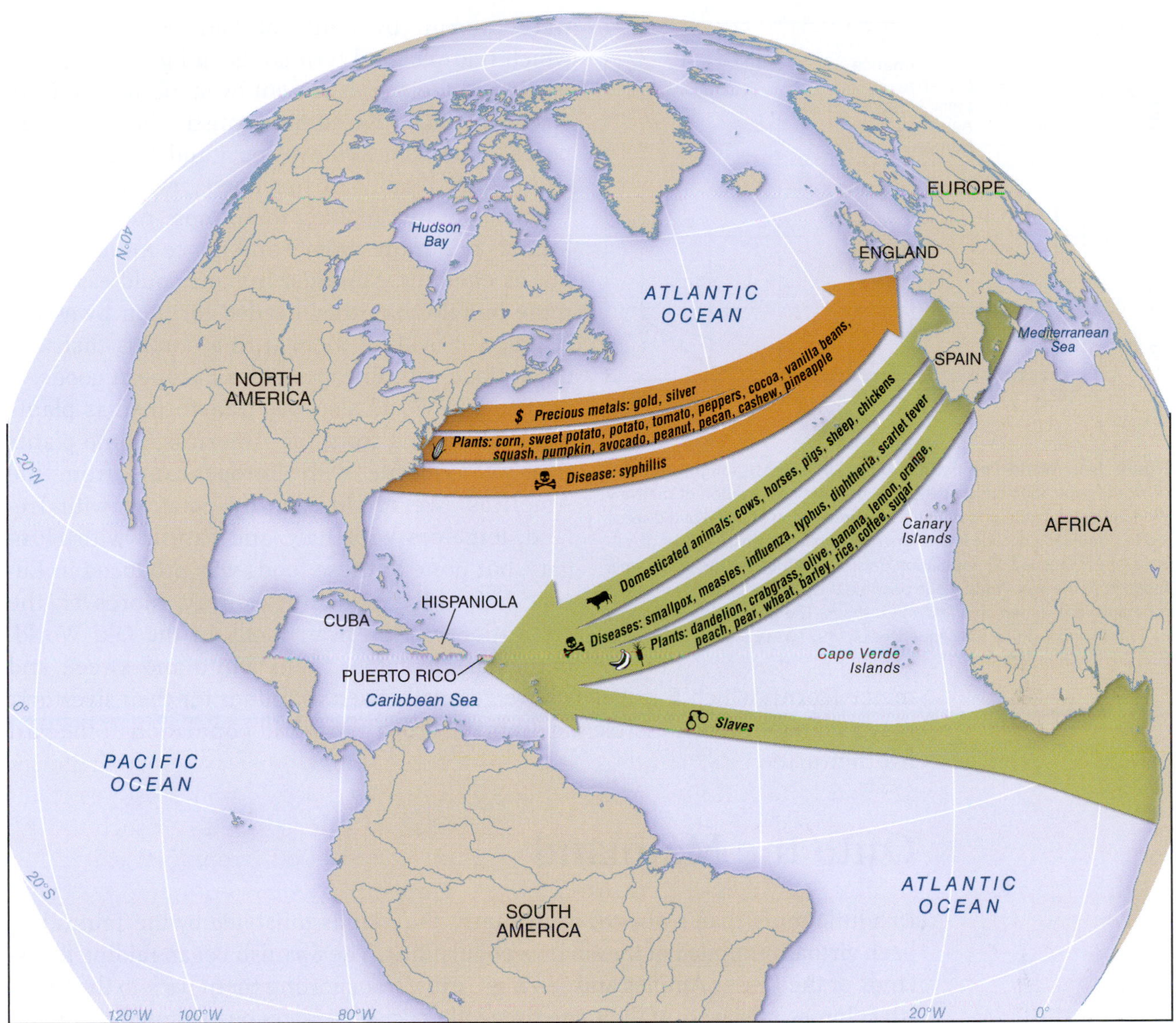

Map 1–4 The Columbian Exchange The exchanges of plants, animals, and diseases dramatically changed both the Old World and the New.

The Columbian Exchange

In what historians have called the Columbian exchange, plants and animals, as well as human beings and their diseases, were shared between the two worlds that were connected in 1492, eventually transforming the environments of the Old World and the New. Along with the 1,500 Spaniards that Columbus brought with him on his second voyage, he also carried pigs, cattle, horses, sheep, and goats, as well as sugarcane, wheat, and seeds for fruits and vegetables (see Map 1–4). European animals reproduced rapidly, overrunning the lands that had once been farmed by Indians.

The introduction of these new plants and animals also dramatically transformed the American landscape. Lands once farmed by native agriculturalists

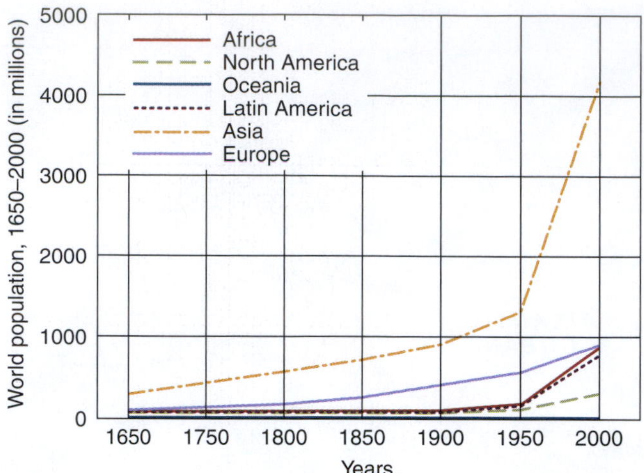

Figure 1-1 World Population, 1650–2000 These rough estimates of world population suggest the way that the colonization of the New World affected world population. The introduction of Old World disease led to population decline in the Americas, while the enslavement of millions of Africans led to population decline in Africa. At the same time, foods from the New World made possible the population increase of Europe and Asia. *Based on Alfred W. Crosby Jr.,* The Columbian Exchange: Biological and Cultural Consequences of 1492 *(Westport, CT: Greenwood Pub. Co., 1972), p. 166.*

were overrun by herds of Old World animals, which trampled old farmlands and grassy regions, leading to their replacement by scrub plants. Indians adapted Old World life forms to their own purposes. American Southwestern and Plains Indian tribes took readily to the horse, which changed their way of life, making them more productive as hunters and more mobile and hence more dangerous as enemies. Mounted Indians could easily kill more buffalo than they needed for their own subsistence, providing them with a surplus that they could trade with Europeans for European goods.

The Old World also was transformed as plants were introduced from the Americas. Some plants that we associate with Europe came from the Americas. We might identify potatoes with Ireland, tomatoes with Italy, and paprika with Hungary, but none of these foods was produced in Europe before the sixteenth century. Moreover, the cultivation of American foods in the Old World, particularly potatoes, both white and sweet, and maize (corn), which Europeans have generally used as fodder for their livestock, may well have made possible the dramatic growth in world population of the past five centuries.

Onto the Mainland

In a little more than a quarter of a century, the islands inhabited by the Tainos had been virtually emptied of their native populations. The Spanish began raiding the islands of the Lesser Antilles and seizing Caribs, transporting them back to the Spanish colonies as slaves. At the same time, other *conquistadores* pushed onto the mainland of America in search of treasure. Indians learned to tantalize the Spanish with accounts of glittering empires just a little further down the trail or up the river, just far enough away to get the Spanish out of their territories. Eventually, the Spanish found the Aztec empire in Mexico and the Inca empire in Peru, which rivaled the most fantastic images from literature and legend.

The First Florida Ventures

Ambitious Spaniards continued the search for paths to East Asia and cities of gold (see Map 1–5). The early expeditions served as a training ground for a generation of young *conquistadores*. Indians who resisted were treated brutally. As the Spanish moved rapidly through a region in the quest for wealth, they disrupted local societies by purposefully spreading disease and undermining their political structures.

Juan Ponce de León was the first European explorer to set foot on the mainland that would later be called the United States. In March 1513 he reached the Atlantic

> "When we saw all those cities and villages built in the water, and the other great towns on dry land, and that straight and level causeway leading to Mexico, we were astounded. These great towns and cues [pyramid temples] and buildings rising from the water, all made of stone, seemed like an enchanted vision. . . . Indeed, some of our soldiers asked if it were not all a dream."
>
> BERNAL DÍAZ DEL CASTILLO, on first seeing Tenochtitlán

shore of the land he named Florida, which he mistakenly thought was an island. He and his men sailed around Florida to its gulf coast, encountering hostile Indians who already knew about Spanish slave traders. On the west coast of Florida, he met the Calusas, the most powerful tribe in the region. When Ponce de León returned to Florida in 1521 to attempt to establish a village, the Calusas attacked. Ponce de León was wounded by an arrow, and he returned to Cuba to die.

As the Spanish entered Florida, the diseases that they brought with them struck the densely settled agriculturalists particularly hard. Subsequent explorers routinely pillaged local villages and enslaved male Indians to carry their goods and females to serve as sexual partners, thereby destroying native populations in another way. There were hundreds of small tribes, each with its own history, culture, and political and economic relationships with its neighbors. All that remains of them are the names that the Spanish recorded.

The Conquest of Mexico

Although the Spanish had continued to believe that vast and wealthy civilizations were to be found in the New World, until 1519 the only peoples they had encountered were small sedentary or semisedentary tribes, who lived in villages of what the Spanish described as huts. They heard tales, however, of the glittering Aztec empire of central Mexico.

The Aztec people had moved into the valley of Mexico only two centuries earlier, but by the time the Spanish appeared, their empire encompassed perhaps 10 or 20 million people, making its population possibly twice as large as Spain's. In several ways, the Aztecs resembled the Spanish: they were fierce and warlike and at the same time deeply religious. Despite many differences in culture, the Spanish recognized in the Aztecs signs of a complex civilization. The Aztecs had built as many as 40,000 temples, and many of these buildings, like the palaces of the nobility, were quite splendid. Aztec society was rigidly hierarchical, with a nobility of warriors and priests at the top and slaves (usually captives of war or debtors) at the bottom. Sex roles were rigid as well, with women of all classes expected to remain in the home. Boys and girls attended separate schools, with the boys learning the arts of war and the girls practicing the skills of the homemaker. The Aztecs were literate, writing in a form of hieroglyphics on folded animal hide. Only a few of these codices, as the inscribed hides are called, survived the conquest.

The capital city of Tenochtitlán was built on a lake, and it was traversed with canals; well-traveled Spaniards said that it reminded them of Venice. With a population of 200,000, it was more than three times the size of Spain's largest city of Seville. Its

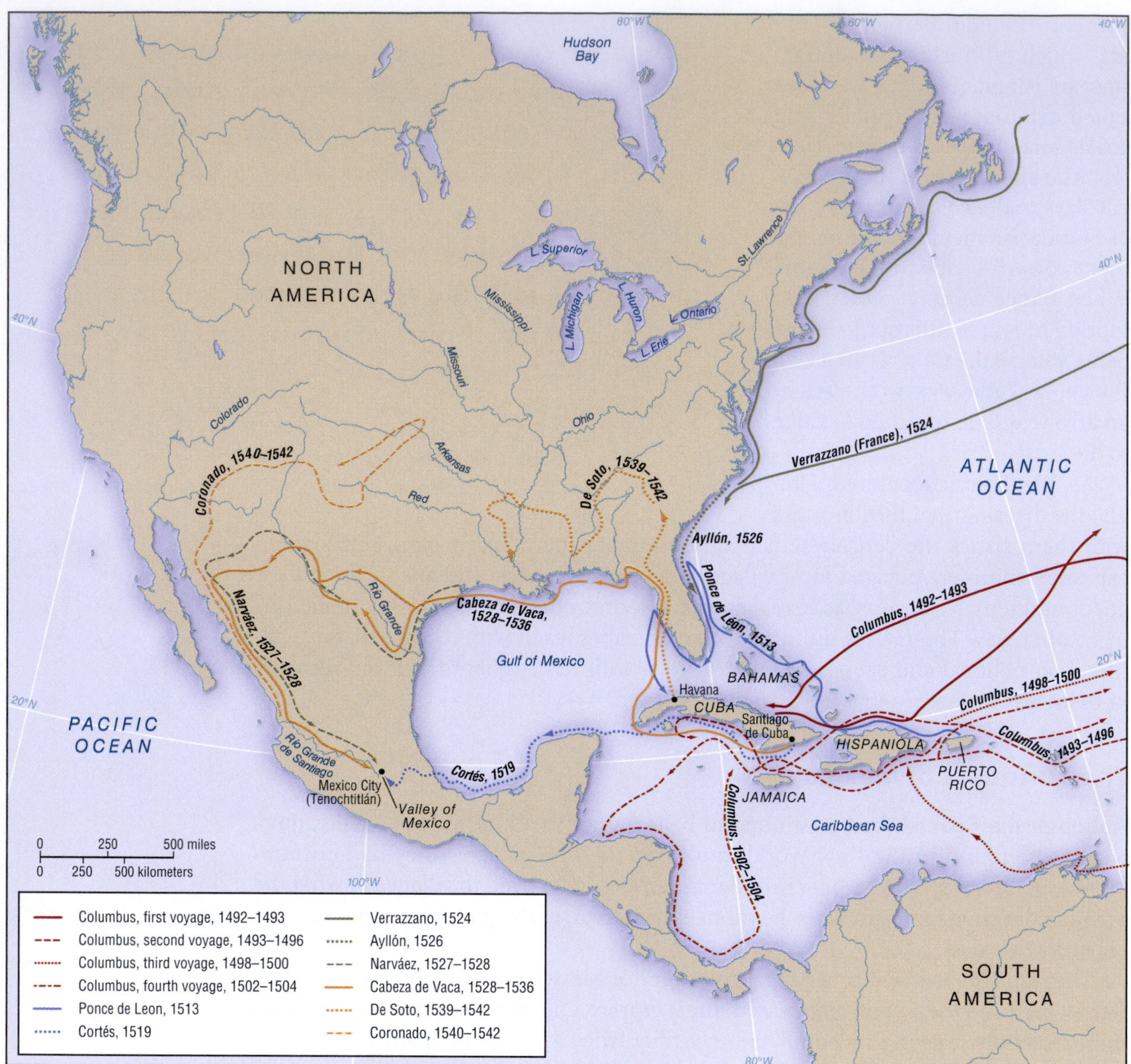

Map 1–5 The Spanish Exploration In the 50 years after Columbus's first voyage, Spanish explorers traveled across most of the southern half of the United States.

whitewashed stone pyramids, temples glittering in the sunlight and reflected water, and clean straight avenues stood in stark contrast to the cramped and dirty streets of a typical Spanish town.

The Aztecs believed that the universe was dangerous and unpredictable and that their gods must always be appeased. In the midst of a serious drought about 1450, the Aztecs feared that their god Huitzilopochtli was angry with them. When they offered him human hearts, cut out of the living with obsidian knives, the drought lifted. From that point on, the pace of human sacrifice quickened; the more victims the Aztecs sacrificed, the greater their empire seemed to become, and the more they

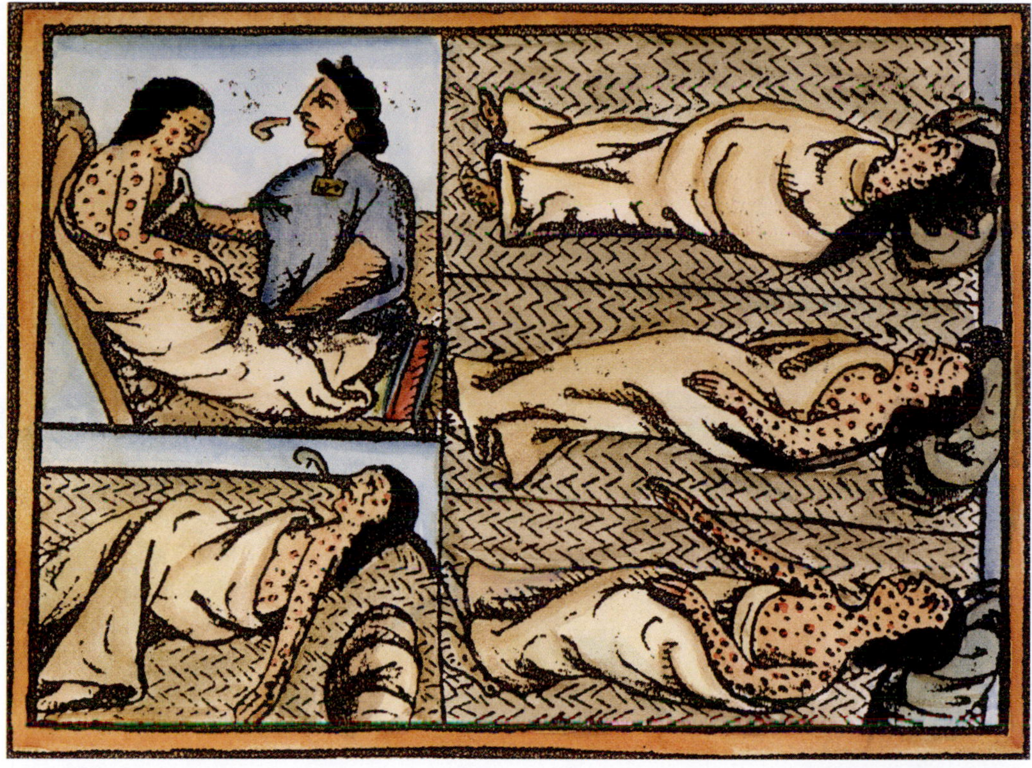

Aztecs Dying of Smallpox These images, from the mid-16th century, clearly depict the ravages of smallpox.

made war against neighboring peoples. The Aztecs demanded tribute from conquered peoples, who both feared and resented the Aztecs, making them eager allies for the Spanish.

Hernán Cortés came with conquest in mind. He landed on the Yucatán coast with 500 men in February of 1519. After the Tabasco Indians were defeated, they gave him all their gold and 20 slave women, one of whom was Malinche, Cortés's translator. As Cortés marched toward Tenochtitlán, he picked up so many Indian allies that they greatly outnumbered his own troops. When they reached the Aztec capital, the ruler, Moctezuma, welcomed them, probably because it was the Aztec custom to offer hospitality to visiting emissaries. The foreigners soon placed Moctezuma under house arrest and laid Tenochtitlán under siege. After three months, in August 1521, the victorious Spanish entered the city, but the proud Aztecs refused either to fight or to submit to the Spanish who had starved them. Frustrated, angry, and unable to understand these now-gaunt people, Cortés and his troops killed 12,000 and let their Indian allies slaughter 40,000 more. Then Cortés turned his cannons on the remaining huddled masses of starving Aztecs. By the time they surrendered, the once-glittering city was in ruins.

The Establishment of a Spanish Empire

The ruined city became the center of a Spanish empire, with a new political economy based on the extraction of silver and gold and the production of plantation crops. In the next decades, the Spanish defeated another rich and complex civilization, the

AMERICAN LANDSCAPE

>> Tenochtitlán

When the Spanish reached Tenochtitlán, they found a city so beautiful that it "seemed like an enchanted vision." It may have been the largest city in the world at that time. In the center were Moctezuma's palaces, the public buildings, and huge temples sitting atop high platforms. All of these buildings were made of a glistening white stone, decorated in gold and surrounded by magnificent gardens, and all kept immaculately clean except for the blood from human sacrifices. The rest of the city was divided into four regions, which in turn were divided into smaller residential districts, each of which had its own temple, school, administrative buildings, and vegetable gardens.

The society was arranged hierarchically, and the higher the status of the family, the better the housing. Aztec society was no more egalitarian than Spain at the time. Nobles lived in well-decorated two-story stucco homes, while ordinary people inhabited more modest dwellings, with the poorest constructed of wood and straw. Such houses were without any furnishings beyond reed mats for sleeping, a few cooking pots, and the stones on which the women in the family ground maize. Each home had several L-shaped rooms, opening onto a courtyard. Family activities took place in the courtyard, rather than on the street. Most people lived in family groupings—one or two families together—of ten to fifteen people. Married children often lived with the parents of either the bride or groom.

Work was assigned by gender. Every woman, whatever her age or class, spent much of the day weaving. From an early age, girls were taught by their mothers how to spin and weave, and how to grind corn and prepare meals. At the same time, fathers taught their sons how to bring firewood and water back to the home and how to fish.

The heart of Tenochtitlán's economic life was the market at Tlatelolco, on the outskirts of town. It served 25,000 people daily, selling not only food, clothing, and household goods, but also luxuries such as feathers, gold, and precious stones. People sold their services, too, as barbers, fortunetellers, scribes, and even prostitutes. Each kind of good and service was assigned its own section of the market, making it easier for customers to compare quality and price. The state regulated the market, setting an upper limit on prices and taxing each transaction. The state also assigned each group of artisans their own residential neighborhood, with separate districts for featherworkers, stoneworkers, gold- and silversmiths, and so on. ●

Incas of Peru, as well as many other tribes of Indians. Spanish rule now extended from the southern tip of South America to halfway up what is now the United States, excepting only the Portuguese colony of Brazil and some of the Caribbean islands. Finally the Spanish had found the precious metals they craved, and when the Indians' stores ran out, the Spanish began using slave labor to mine more.

After silver and gold, sugar was the next most important product of the New World, and as its cultivation spread, so did the demand for labor. By the second half of the sixteenth century, Indian laborers were replaced by African slaves. In this way, Africans became yet another commodity to be transported across the seas, transforming the New World, robbing Africa of its population, and making the Old World rich. Once other European nations saw the great wealth the Spanish were extracting from their colonies, they too were attracted to the New World, where they established their own colonies that came into conflict with the Spanish.

In this context, the Spanish outposts in the present-day United States were simply borderlands, a frontier of much greater importance to Spain from a military standpoint than an economic one. The permanent settlements that the Spanish established in the north (e.g., St. Augustine, San Antonio, Santa Fe, and San Francisco) were relatively small communities. In 1522, as the Spanish completed the conquest of Mexico, this territory was still unexplored, and no European knew whether another awe-inspiring civilization might yet be found.

Gender and Conquest

Every society has its own notion of the proper relationship between the sexes, and this is one of the ways it establishes order. Hence, when one society conquers another, not only do different gender orders come into conflict, but gender is one of the instruments of conquest. For Christopher Columbus, indigenous women were curiosities, objects of conversion, and commodities. On one island, the women "went around as naked as their mothers bore them"; on another, they "wore in front of their bodies a little thing of cotton that scarcely covers their genitals." Such women were "very respectful," and Columbus thought that with proper instruction in their own language, "soon all of them would become Christian."

Yet Columbus thought nothing of seizing friendly native women to bring back to Spain, believing that their presence would assure the good behavior of captive male relatives. As for hostile women, they could be seized as the spoils of war. After a skirmish with some Caribs, Columbus gave a trusted lieutenant "a most beautiful cannibal woman." When she resisted his advances by scratching him fiercely with her fingernails, he whipped her with a leather strap until, finally, she was quiet and submitted. Elsewhere, Columbus's men seized native women on their own. Raping subjugated women is one of the ways that conquerors demonstrate their dominance.

Not all encounters between European men and native women were so violent, however. In more complex Indian societies, such as those Cortés encountered in Mexico, indigenous people were accustomed to using marriage to cement alliances between prominent families. Such was the practice among the European nobility as well. For example, the marriage of Isabel and Fernando had united the provinces of Castile and Aragon. Thus, after Cortés defeated the Tlaxcalans, whose kingdom stood on the path to the Aztec city of Tenochtitlán, they handed over a number of their women as part of the peace offering. A page from a Tlaxcalan codex (a pictorial account painted on a folding piece of bark or paper) illustrates the ceremony. At the top of the picture, Cortés sits in a chair, with his officers behind him. In front of him is the Tlaxcalan leader, also backed up by his nobles. Malinche stands next to Cortés,

Defeat of the Tlaxcalans Here, Malinche stands next to Cortés, receiving the Tlaxcalan women who have been presented to them as gifts by their defeated people.

speaking to three rows of Tlaxcalan women. At the top are a tier of elegantly dressed princesses, intended as wives for the Spanish leaders. Years later, someone added the words, "Here are painted the noblewomen who were the children of kings who were given to the captain," that is, Cortés. Next is a tier of daughters of lesser nobles, less magnificently dressed. And at the bottom are commoners, intended as slaves.

Several decades after the transaction, the names and fates of some of the elite women could still be remembered. Tleucuiluatzin, for example, was the daughter of Xicotencatl the Elder, and she was renamed Doña Luisa and given to Pedro de Alvarado, Cortés' second-in-command. Although, like many of the conquistadores, he had a Spanish wife, he took Luisa as his mistress. She bore him three children. Their daughter herself married another conquistador, and one of their sons died fighting in Peru.

The offspring of the Spanish conquerors and their noble Indian consorts created a New World *mestizo* (mixed-race) elite in which rank was more important than ethnic origin. In fact, the Crown encouraged intermarriage in order to speed the conversion of the Indians and to assist the Spanish in ruling a conquered people. The first generation of elite *mestizo* sons, including Malinche's son Don Martín Cortés, were brought up in their fathers' households and sent to Spain for their education.

The necessity of forging alliances with conquered rulers insured that Indian daughters who were given to the conquerors continued to hold high status, although sometimes at great personal cost. After the defeat of the Aztecs, Moctezuma's daughter Isabel was forced to become the mistress of Cortés, the man who was responsible for the deaths of her father and husband. When he was finished with her, he passed her on to one of his lieutenants.

Conquest enhanced the power of the conquerors, including power over subjugated women. After the fall of Tenochtitlán, Spanish soldiers were so abusive to native women that some of their colleagues complained to the king of Spain. When accused of raping a captive woman, Pedro de Alvarado asked why he would have to force an Indian woman when there were so many poor women who would give themselves voluntarily. Such was the power of the conquerors that they assumed they could have all the native women they wanted, princesses turned over by their fathers and common women seized by force.

Aztecs Performing Human Sacrifice Aztecs perform a human sacrifice atop a pyramid at Tenochtitlán.

The Return to Florida

When the Spanish resumed their exploration of Florida, it was with heightened expectations. There were several ventures, but the most significant were led by Lucas Vázquez de Ayllón, Pánfilo de Narváez, and Hernando de Soto. Ayllón sailed from Hispaniola in 1526. He explored the South Carolina coast and established a short-lived town on the coast of Georgia. Two years later, Pánfilo de Narváez landed near modern-day Tampa Bay with 400 men and the king's commission to explore, conquer, and colonize Florida. Eight years later, a Spanish slaving expedition working in northwest Mexico found the only four survivors of the failed expedition.

The Spaniard who left the greatest mark on the southeastern part of the United States was a classic *conquistador*. Hernando de Soto had participated in the assault on the Inca empire in Peru, which provided him with a small fortune and the belief that more wealth could be found in Florida. He and his forces landed near Tampa Bay in 1539 to explore and settle the region. His party spent four years exploring the southeastern part of the continent, which was densely populated by Mississippian tribes. (De Soto and his company were the first Europeans to see the Mississippi River.)

Hernando de Soto came equipped for conquest. He brought with him 600 young soldiers, a few women and priests, horses, mules, attack dogs, and a walking food supply of hundreds of pigs. He took whatever food, treasure, and people he wanted as he proceeded on his journey. Some Indian communities fought the Spanish fiercely, while others attempted to placate the invaders. In this way de Soto made his way through the Southeast, plundering and battling, his forces slowly diminishing. In May 1542, de Soto himself took sick and died. It was almost a year and a half, however, before the remnants of the expedition, 300 men and one female servant, made their way back to Mexico.

The Spanish never found the great sought-after treasure, and because the land did not seem suitable for the large-scale agriculture of the *encomienda,* Spain never colonized most of the territory that de Soto had explored. Instead, military

Timucua Indians, 1591 Here they celebrate the defeat of the enemy.

outposts, such as St. Augustine, were established to protect the more valuable Spanish territories to the south. To prevent rival nations from claiming the northern reaches of its empire, Spain did not disclose the geographical information it had secured from expeditions like de Soto's. This withholding of information ultimately weakened Spain's claim to the region, because such claims traditionally depended on the right of prior exploration.

The impact of the expedition on the Mississippian Indians is difficult to determine. The Mississippian towns had begun to decline in the middle of the fifteenth century, before the arrival of Europeans. European diseases certainly hastened the process. Perhaps as significant, the Spanish seriously disrupted the Mississippian political economy. Hernando de Soto's custom of capturing chieftains effectively undermined their leadership, and the losses incurred in battles made it impossible for the rulers to command lower-status tribe members to produce the food surplus and build the huge mounds that sustained the social order. After the appearance of the Spanish, no Indian civilizations would be able to match the power and sophistication of the Mississippians.

Coronado and the Pueblo Indians

At the same time that de Soto was attempting to conquer the Southeast, another group of Spaniards was setting out for the Southwest. They had heard tales of a city of Cíbola, supposedly larger than Tenochtitlán, where temples were decorated with gems. In May 1539, a party led by the Moorish slave Estevanico, one of four survivors of the Narváez expedition, reached the city, which was actually the pueblo of Zuni in New Mexico. The inhabitants recognized him as hostile and killed him. The survivors of the party did not contradict the popular belief that Cíbola was filled with treasure, however, and a year later, another aspiring *conquistador*, Francisco Vázquez de Coronado, arrived at Zuni, with 300 Spanish, 1,000 Indian allies from Mexico, and 1,500 horses and pack animals. They took the pueblo by force, and later traveled as far west as the Grand Canyon and as far east as Wichita, Kansas, coming within 300 miles of de Soto's expedition. One unfortunate Indian woman escaped enslavement by Coronado only to fall captive to de Soto.

Unprepared for the cold winter of 1540–1541, Coronado's men and animals depleted the food supplies of the Indians in the region of the winter camp near Bernalillo. Some Spaniards literally took the clothes off the backs of their Indian hosts; when one Spaniard raped an Indian woman, the Pueblos rebelled. By the time the uprising was put down, 100 Indians had been burned at the stake, and 13 or so villages had been destroyed. This was the first of a number of revolts among the Indians of the region; they continued intermittently until the Apache leader Geronimo surrendered to the United States Army in 1886.

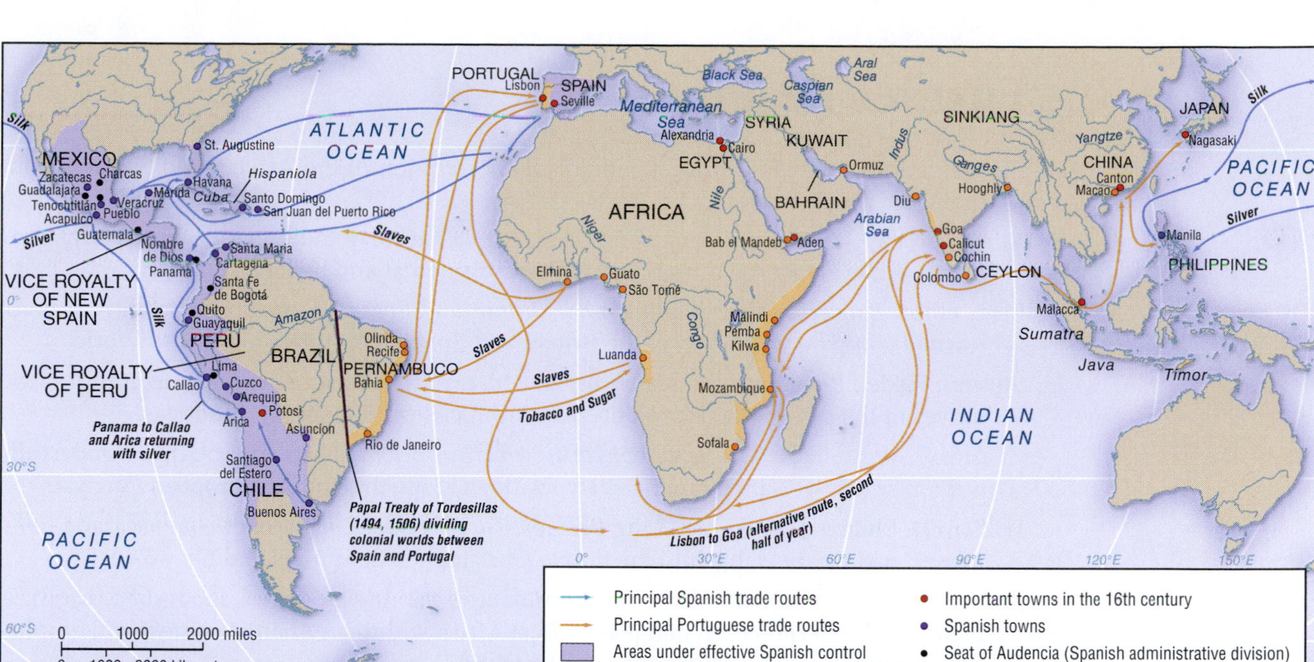

Map 1–6 A New Global Economy By 1600, both Spain and Portugal had established empires that reached from one end of the globe to the other.

Conclusion

Within a half century after Columbus's arrival in the New World, both the world he had come from and the one he had reached had been transformed, as both were drawn into a new, global political economy (see Map 1–6). Spain, the first of the major European states to achieve unity, dominated exploration, colonization, and exploitation of the New World during this period. The wealth that Spain extracted from her New World colonies encouraged rival nations to enter into overseas ventures as well. Eventually France, England, the Netherlands, Sweden, and Russia also established New World colonies, but because Spain (along with Portugal, which claimed Brazil) had such a head start, rival nations, if they did not want to challenge Spain directly, would have to settle for the lands she left unclaimed. Spain and Portugal had demonstrated that great wealth could be obtained from the New World.

In the shadow of this dream of great and unprecedented wealth, a new global economy was established, linking the Old and the New Worlds. The gold and silver extracted from the Spanish empire sustained that nation's rise to power, and the plantation crops of the New World would make many Europeans wealthy. From the beginning, the Spanish enslaved Indians to work the mines, farms, and plantations. As the native populations were depleted and the morality of enslaving native populations was questioned, the Spanish turned to African slaves.

Further Readings

Inga Clendinnen, *Aztecs* (1991). A remarkable description of the Aztec world, written from the Aztec point of view.

Alfred Crosby Jr., *The Columbian Exchange: Biological and Cultural Consequences of 1492* (1972). An eye-opening introduction to environmental and biological history.

J. H. Elliot, *Empires of the Atlantic World: Britain and Spain in America* (2006). A superb, learned comparative history of the British and Spanish empires in the New World.

Stuart J. Fiedel, *Prehistory of the Americas,* 2nd ed. (1992). A comprehensive and authoritative survey of the development of Native American civilizations in the Americas.

Charles C. Mann, *1491: New Revelations of the Americas Before Columbus* (2005). A wonderfully written survey of Native American civilizations at the time of the Europeans' arrival.

William D. Phillips Jr. and Carla Rahn Phillips, *The Worlds of Christopher Columbus, 1400–1680* (1992). A short, readable introduction to Christopher Columbus and his world.

John Thornton, *Africa and Africans in the Making of the Atlantic World, 1400–1680* (1998). A provocative interpretation that places West Africa within an Atlantic context and emphasizes its active participation in the Atlantic world.

Camilla Townsend, *Malintzin's Choices* (2006). A beautifully written biography that shows how the Indian translator was able to shape her world.

David Weber, *The Spanish Frontier in North America* (1992). Both a comprehensive survey of the history of Spanish North America and an interpretation, which shifts the focus of colonial history to the Spanish frontier.

Who, What

Malinche (Malintzin, Doña Marina) 3
Hernán Cortés 3
Ponce de León 26
Hernando de Soto 33
Francisco Vázquez de Coronado 34
Humanism 17
Encomienda 21
The *Requerimiento* 23
Tenochtitlán 27

>> Timeline >>

▼ c. 12,000 BCE
Indian peoples arrive in North America

▼ 711 CE
Moors invade Iberian Peninsula

▼ 1275–1292
Marco Polo travels in Asia

▼ 1347
Black Death (bubonic plague) arrives in Europe

▼ 1434
Portuguese arrive at West Coast of Africa

▼ 1488
Bartolomeo Dias rounds Cape Horn

▼ 1492
Spanish complete the *reconquista*, evicting Moors from Spain
Jews expelled from Spain
Columbus's first voyage to America

▼ 1493
Columbus's second voyage

▼ 1494
Treaty of Tordesillas divides New World between Spain and Portugal

▼ 1496
Spanish complete conquest of Canary Islands

▼ 1497
John Cabot arrives in North America

▼ 1498
Vasco da Gama reaches India
Columbus's third voyage to America, reaches South American coast

▼ 1500
Portuguese arrive in Brazil

▼ 1504
Columbus's fourth voyage to America ends

▼ 1508
Spanish conquer Puerto Rico

▼ 1513
Spanish *Requerimiento* promises freedom to all Indians who accept Spanish authority

Review Questions

1. Describe the development of Indian civilizations in North America from Archaic times until 1500. What were the major forces of change within these early American populations?
2. What were the major similarities among European, Native American, and African societies? The major differences?
3. What were the forces that led Europeans to explore the New World?
4. What did the Spanish expect to find in the New World? How did their experiences alter their expectations?
5. What was the impact of European conquest on the population and environment of the New World?

Websites

The Aztec Empire. A superb website with text and images, ranging from artifacts to pages from the codices produced in the sixteenth century. www.latinamericanstudies.org/aztecs.htm

1492:An Ongoing Voyage. An online version of a memorable exhibit at the Library of Congress commemorating the 500th anniversary of Columbus's first voyage. http://www.loc.gov/exhibits/1492/

Francisco Vázquez de Coronado. From the PBS *New Perspectives on the West* website, excerpts from his chronicles. Follow links from the website home page to learn more about other important figures, both Native and European, in the history of the West. http://www.pbs.org/weta/thewest/people/a_c/coronado.htm

For further review materials and resource information, please visit www.oup.com/us/ofthepeople

Spanish conquer Cuba
Ponce de Léon reaches Florida
The Laws of Burgos attempt to regulate working conditions of Indians

▼ 1518
Spanish introduce smallpox to New World

▼ 1521
Ponce de León returns to Florida
Cortés lands on Yucatán coast

▼ 1519–1522
Ferdinand Magellan's crew sails around the world

▼ 1521
Tenochtitlán falls to the Spanish

▼ 1526
Ayllón explores South Carolina coast and establishes fort in Georgia

▼ 1528
Narváez explores Florida

▼ 1534–42
Jacques Cartier makes three trips to Canada for France

▼ 1539
Estevanico arrives at Zuni

▼ 1539–1543
De Soto and his party explore Southeast, arriving at Mississippi, devastating the Indians and their land

▼ 1540–1542
Coronado explores Southwest

▼ 1542
The New Laws ban further enslavement of Indians

▼ 1565
Spanish establish settlement at St. Augustine
Spanish destroy French settlement at Fort Caroline

▼ 1565–1580
The English conquer Ireland

CHAPTER 2

Common Threads

>> Although they were all European nations, the empires of Spain, France, Holland, and England all developed in different ways. Why?

>> Why did each nation have a somewhat different relationship with Native Americans?

>> What did it mean for the English in North America that they came late to the business of establishing an overseas empire?

>> Chart the paths that each nation took toward offering greater freedom for some groups and less freedom for others.

Colonial Outposts

1550–1650

AMERICAN PORTRAIT

>> Don Luís de Velasco Finds His Way Home

The Spanish gave him the name of Don Luís de Velasco. His own people, the Powhatan Indians of the Virginia coast, knew him as Paquiquineo. The son of a chieftain, he was a young man, perhaps still a teenager, when the Spanish picked him up in 1561 somewhere south of his home. The Europeans often abducted young Indians and took them back to their own nations so that they could serve as translators and guides on subsequent expeditions. Sometimes the process worked the other way around, and Europeans who were members of trading or exploring expeditions were accidentally left behind. In order to survive, they learned the Native Americans' language and customs. If and when they were ever reunited with their countrymen, they were valuable as interpreters. In the early years of colonization, those men and women who had learned the ways of another culture gained influence far out of proportion to their actual numbers.

Don Luís did not see his own people again for 10 years. First the Spanish took him to Mexico, where Dominican friars baptized and educated him. Later, Jesuit priests in Havana pronounced Don Luís "well educated," quite a compliment coming from a religious order known for its intellectual achievements. The young convert was taken to Spain, where he was received royally by King Felipe II, becoming one of his favorites, and then back across the Atlantic to Havana, where he persuaded the priests to let him establish a Christian mission among his own people on the North American mainland. In 1566 Don Luís set sail on a Spanish ship with 2 priests and 37 soldiers, but he was unable to find the Chesapeake. Four years later, when there were only priests and no soldiers on the voyage, Don Luís had no trouble locating his homeland.

Less than a week after the Jesuits and their Indian convert had settled in Virginia, Don Luís returned to his own people and resumed their customs. He scandalized the Jesuits by taking several wives, a privilege of Indian men of high rank. The Jesuits had expected Don Luís to act as an intermediary with his people, securing them supplies and favorable treatment, but they had misjudged him. Soon they exhausted their supply of food and had to beg from Don Luís. But Don Luís was being pressured by his own people to prove his loyalty. They were suspicious of someone who had been away so long and returned with arrogant foreigners who demanded food during a drought.

Don Luís had to make a choice, and he chose his native people. Powhatans killed eight of the nine missionaries. According to Indian custom, one of the victims, a young Spaniard named Alonso, was spared, although Don Luís argued for his death also. Knowing that the Spanish would someday return, he wanted no witnesses. As Don Luís predicted, the Spanish came back a year and a half later. They retrieved Alonso, ordered Don Luís to appear for an inquest, and began trying and executing other Indians when he failed to appear. Don Luís never returned to the Spanish. At these proceedings, Alonso acted as an interpreter.

In 1607 the English planted their first permanent colony on the mainland at Jamestown among Don Luís's people. Don Luís, who was very young when he had been abducted by the Spanish, might well have been alive to greet these new foreigners. Throughout the seventeenth century, the English heard rumors about a Powhatan Indian who had spent time in the Spanish colonies.

Whether or not Don Luís lived to see the English take the place of the Spanish, it is clear that the memory of the Europeans lived on among the Powhatans. Before they established settlements, the English, French, and Spanish all explored the North American coastline. In the process, Indians and Europeans learned each other's languages and customs. During this period of American history, no sharp geographic or cultural line separated the Indians and Europeans. Indians such as Don Luís lived among the Europeans, and Europeans such as Alonso spent time with the Indians. As a result, even before permanent colonies were established each group knew the other moderately well. Although the customs and practices of the other group often seemed odd and even ungodly, they were never fully foreign.

OUTLINE

Pursuing Wealth and Glory Along the North American Shore

The search for wealth and national prestige soon propelled other European nations across the Atlantic. In the minds of European leaders, wealth, glory, and power were almost inseparable. As the English explorer Sir Walter Raleigh explained the principles of political economy, "Whosoever commands the sea commands the trade; whosoever commands the trade of the world commands the riches of the world, and consequently the world itself." Most of the North American colonies established by European nations in the first half of the seventeenth century were outposts in the global economy. There were significant differences among these colonies, but all shared certain factors: First, they were intended to bring in the greatest amount of revenue at the lowest cost. Second, success depended on harmonious relations with—or elimination of—local Indians. Third, colonial societies slowly developed their own distinctive patterns, depending on which route they followed to prosperity.

European Objectives

At first Europeans believed that Columbus had reached Asia by an Atlantic route. By the time they understood that he had discovered a new land, the Spanish were well on their way to conquering native peoples and stripping them of their wealth.

Their success inspired other European nations to search for new sources of gold and silver in the regions Spain had not yet claimed. They also continued to seek a path through the Americas to Asia. Colonization was not a goal for almost a century, and even then colonies were designed to provide a quick return on investment, not to transplant Europeans onto foreign soil.

For many years the nations of northern Europe were unwilling to invest in permanent settlements. A foreign colony was costly. It involved procuring a ship, provisioning it, providing a settlement with food and equipment—and resupplying it until it could turn a profit. Spain had been lucky: Isabel and Fernando had been willing to take a considerable risk, which paid off relatively quickly. The northern European nations could not afford such expeditions, however, and, except for the most adventurous souls, exploration for its own sake had little appeal.

> **"It is of no value, and if the French take it, necessity will require them to abandon it."**
>
> SPANISH EMPEROR CHARLES V, 1541, speaking of France's expedition up the St. Lawrence

Tales of wealth and adventure in New Spain spread throughout Europe, nonetheless. Would-be explorers and *conquistadores* began to sell their services to the highest bidder. John Cabot, who sailed for England, was, like Columbus, born in Genoa, Italy. Before coming to England, he had spent time in Muslim Arabia, Spain, and Portugal, apparently looking for sponsors for a voyage to Asia. He found them in the English port city of Bristol, from whence he sailed in 1497. He landed somewhere in North America, possibly at Newfoundland, and claimed the territory for England.

Although England was slow to follow up this claim to American territory, soon both England and France sent fishing expeditions to the waters off Newfoundland (see Map 2–1). The population of northwestern Europe exploded in the sixteenth and seventeenth centuries, creating an increased demand for fish. Fishing expeditions to the Newfoundland coast came in the spring and left before winter and were relatively inexpensive to sustain.

The French colony of New France, planted in the St. Lawrence River region of Canada, grew out of the French fishing venture off Newfoundland. Early French explorers discovered neither gold nor a Northwest Passage to Asia. French fishermen, however, found that the Indians were willing to trade beaver pelts at prices so low that a man could make a fortune in a few months' time.

The Huge Geographical Barrier

At first, North America had seemed little more than an obstacle on the way to Asia. In 1522 Ferdinand Magellan's expedition had completed the first round-the-world voyage for Spain, proving finally that one could get to the East by heading west. Other nations then became interested in finding a way through, rather than around, North America. Two years after Magellan's voyage, the Italian Giovanni da Verrazano, sailed for France. He explored the North American coast from South Carolina to Maine, and he and his crew were the first Europeans to see the New York harbor. As far as Europeans were concerned, however, all that Verrazano had discovered was that North America was a huge barrier between Europe and Asia (see Map 2–2).

That "huge barrier" of the North American continent was populated by Indians, some wary and some friendly. Unfamiliar with Indian customs, Europeans often could not distinguish hospitality from malice. When Algonquian Indians

Map 2–1 North Atlantic Trade Routes at the End of the 16th Century Hundreds of entrepreneurs from England, France, and Portugal sent ships to fish off the coast of Newfoundland to feed the growing population of Europe. The fur trade grew out of the Newfoundland fishing enterprise when fishermen who built winter shelters on the shore began trading with local Algonquian Indians (green lines). At the same time, European cities sent foods, cloth, and manufactured goods to New Spain, in return for gold and silver (red lines). After 1580, the Portuguese began transporting slaves from Africa to sell in Brazil and New Spain (yellow lines). *D. W. Meinig,* The Shaping of America *(New Haven, CT: Yale University Press, 1986), vol. 1, p. 56.*

attempted to dry out one of Verrazano's sailors, who had almost drowned, by setting him near a campfire, Verrazano feared that they "wanted to roast him for food." In the early years of exploration, the survival of a venture often depended on local Indians, yet because the French were looking either for treasure or a Northwest Passage, they tended to focus on cultural differences rather than similarities. Europeans noticed similarities only when objectives such as trade or alliance were in the forefront.

Between 1534 and 1542, King François I of France financed Jacques Cartier to make three expeditions to seek a route through North America and to look out for any riches along the way. All three came to naught. On the first trip, the French only explored the coastline, but on their second, they sailed up the St. Lawrence River as far as the town of Hochelaga (near present-day Montréal). The Iroquois who lived there spoke of a wealthy land to the west. Although the Iroquois may well have been trying to deceive the French, it is possible that the shiny metal they spoke of was the copper that the Hurons to the west mined and traded. The winter was brutal. Even with food and attentive nursing from the Indians, at the end of the winter almost a quarter of the party was dead. The French found that their survival depended on the native peoples.

The subsequent expeditions failed as badly. The French quarreled with their Indian hosts and fought among themselves. Moreover, the region was so remote that no one could yet fathom why they were even bothering. Although all these early attempts at colonization failed, the French were demonstrating that European claims to the Americas would rest on exploration, conquest of the natives, and colonization. Needless to say, this principle of European colonialism was established without the consent of the Indians who inhabited the land.

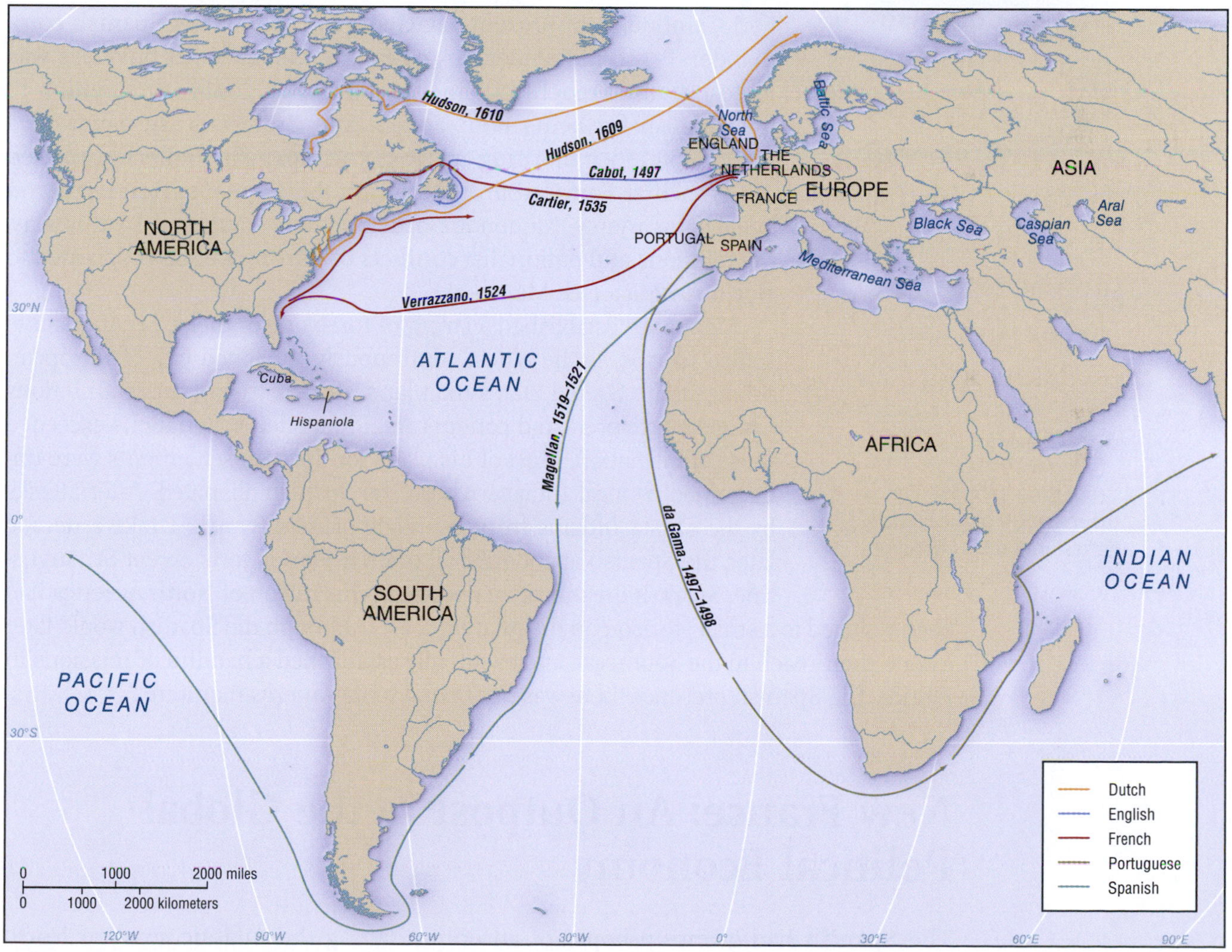

Map 2–2 Voyages of Exploration In a little over a century after Columbus's first voyage, European explorers had circled the world and charted most of the North American coastline.

Spanish Outposts

Throughout the sixteenth century, European nations jockeyed for power on the continent. Because most of these nations were at war with each other, North America was often a low priority. But when the fighting in Europe abated, the Europeans looked across the Atlantic in hopes of gaining an advantage over a rival nation or finding a new source of wealth.

Soon the French and English, who found no gold or jewels when they explored along the coastline, discovered an easier source of wealth—stealing from the Spanish. Every season, Spanish ships laden with treasure that they had seized in Mexico and South America made their way through the Caribbean, into the Atlantic south of Florida, and along the coast until they caught the trade winds to take them east across the Atlantic. By the middle of the sixteenth century, French ships were lying in wait off Florida or the Carolinas. Because it was cheaper than exploration, preying on Spanish ships became a national policy.

> "It seemed to me that to chastise them in this way would serve God Our Lord, as well as Your Majesty, and that we should thus be left more free from this wicked sect."
>
> PEDRO MENÉNDEZ DE AVILÉS
> reporting to his king on the massacre of the French Protestants at Fort Caroline

To put a stop to these costly acts of piracy, King Felipe II established a series of forts along both coasts of Florida. At the same time, a group of Huguenots (French Protestants) established a colony, Fort Caroline, near present-day Georgia. For the new Spanish commander, Pedro Menéndez de Avilés, the first order of business was to destroy the French settlement, which was doubly threatening to the Spanish for being both French and Protestant. At dawn on a rainy September morning in 1565, 500 Spanish soldiers surprised the French at Fort Caroline. Although the French surrendered and begged for mercy, Menéndez ordered their slaughter. In this way, the religious and nationalist conflicts of Europe were transplanted to North America (see Map 2–3).

Menéndez established a string of forts; one of them, St. Augustine, settled in 1565, is the oldest continuously inhabited city of European origin on the United States mainland. As was true of many ambitious European explorers and conquerors, Menéndez's aspirations exceeded those of his nation. Most of his plans for Spanish settlements were undermined by local Indians whom the Spanish alienated. After attacks by the Orista Indians in 1576 and England's Francis Drake a decade later, the Spanish abandoned all of their Florida forts except St. Augustine. Spanish dreams of an empire in this region of North America had been reduced to a small garrison on the Atlantic coast. Although the Spanish would later extend their reach in the Southeast, and eventually established a handful of missions in Florida, the Spanish presence there was peripheral to its American empire.

New France: An Outpost in the Global Political Economy

The Spanish had given up hopes of an empire along the Atlantic coast of North America, but they had succeeded in scaring off the French. After the massacre at Fort Caroline, the French focused their interest on the St. Lawrence region. By the

Map 2–3 European Colonization of the Southeast Beginning in the second half of the 16th century, the French, Spanish, and English established settlements in the Southeast. *Charles Hudson,* The Southeastern Indians *(Knoxville: University of Tennessee Press, 1976), pp. 430–431.*

beginning of the seventeenth century the French had discovered a new way to make a profit in North America. French fishing crews, working off the coast of Newfoundland, traded for beaver pelts with the coastal Abenaki Indians. These pelts found a ready market in Europe, where they were turned into felt hats. A trade that began almost as an accident soon became the basis for the French empire in modern-day Canada. The French were drawing the Indians into a global economy, a process that dramatically changed not only the political economy of the North Americans, but that of the Europeans as well.

The Indian Background to French Settlement

The French intruded on a region where warfare among Indian tribes had been widespread and prevalent, although limited in scope. In the region, Iroquois culture groups were almost always at war, but the total casualties, unlike those in the European wars, were generally light. These fights were blood feuds called mourning wars. When a member of a clan was lost in battle, his tribesmen, encouraged by his tribeswomen, sought revenge on the enemy clan, either killing or seizing a warrior, who was adopted into the tribe to replace the dead clan member. The mourning war sought to fill the space in tribal society that was caused by the loss, either actual or emotional, of a member. If the clan's grief was particularly great, many captives might be necessary to repair the loss. Such warfare was accompanied by rituals that mourned the loss of the clan member, prepared warriors for battle, and integrated captives into their new clan. It also focused violence outward. The cruelty that Indians practiced on their enemies shocked Europeans, whose own societies were quite brutal. Unlike in European society, violence and even crime *within* the clan was almost unknown.

By the fifteenth century, the mourning war was taking too great a toll among the Iroquois of northern New York. Sometime after 1400 (and perhaps as late as 1600), the five tribes that lived south of the St. Lawrence River and east of Lake Ontario, primarily in what is now upper New York State, created an alliance called the Five Nations or Great League of Peace (see Map 2–4). The league strengthened the Iroquois when they encountered their traditional enemies such as the Algonquians and Hurons, a powerful Iroquoian tribe that was not a member of the league, and their new adversary, the French.

Champlain Encounters the Hurons

After Cartier's last voyage in 1541, the French waited more than half a century before again attempting to plant a settlement in Canada because they were preoccupied with a brutal civil war. In 1594, Henry of Navarre, a Huguenot, emerged the victor, converted to Catholicism, and in 1598 issued the Edict of Nantes, which granted limited religious toleration to the Huguenots. The bloodshed over, France could once again look outward to North America.

The French had continued to fish off Newfoundland, and entrepreneurs began sending ships to the mainland to trade for beaver pelts. The French Crown now realized that commerce with the Indians could increase its power and wealth. Several early ventures to establish a permanent settlement failed, but in 1608, Samuel de Champlain and a small band retraced Cartier's route up the St. Lawrence River and established a post at Quebec (see Map 2–5). Champlain, who made several voyages to New France over the next decades, finally established the first French foothold in Canada, created a trading network along the St. Lawrence River and learned how to live among people with a culture different from his own.

The French government provided little support for Champlain's expedition to New France beyond a temporary monopoly on trade with the Indians. Without significant support from France, Champlain's party depended on their Montagnais Indian (an Algonquian tribe) hosts. The price they had to pay to survive in New France was adapting to Indian customs and assisting their Indian benefactors in wars against their enemy. Some of these accommodations were easier to make than others. Killing the enemy in warfare was relatively easy for an experienced soldier such as Champlain. Indian forms of torture, however, seemed barbaric, not because Europeans did not engage in torture, but because Europeans did not practice it against other soldiers, one's supposed equals.

Over the next several years, Champlain established a fur trade in the St. Lawrence region, linking the French and the Indians in a transformed transatlantic economy.

Map 2–4 The Iroquois Region in the Middle of the 17th Century By the middle of the 17th century, the French, Dutch, and English had all established trading posts on the fringe of the Iroquois homeland. In the Beaver Wars (ca. 1648–1660), discussed later in the chapter, the Iroquois lashed out at their neighbors, dispersing several Huron tribes. *Matthew Dennis,* Cultivating a Landscape of Peace *(New York: Cornell University Press, 1993), p. 16.*

Peasants were transplanted to New France in 1614 to raise food for the traders; Catholic priests were sent to convert the Native Americans. The missionaries were more successful than the peasants. The persistence of the Catholic missionaries, their willingness to adapt to a strange environment, and their ability to translate their religion into terms that were meaningful to Native Americans eventually gained them numerous converts.

After Champlain's original monopoly expired, his group competed with other Frenchmen in the fur trade. The French government was too busy with conflicts at home and abroad to support any of these outposts. To maintain a competitive edge, each summer Champlain pushed farther up the St. Lawrence River from his base at Quebec to intercept the Indian tribes who were bringing pelts to the east. Each winter he also sent some of his men to live among the western Hurons and Algonquians, to learn their languages and customs and to strengthen the trading partnerships that had been established. These Indians already engaged in an extensive trade in corn, fish, nets, wampum, and other items. As French traders and Huron and Algonquian hunters created a trade network, each group became dependent on the other.

AMERICAN LANDSCAPE

>> Huronia

In the middle of the sixteenth century, over 20,000 Huron Indians lived in Huronia, a huge region bounded by Georgian Bay and Lakes Huron, Erie, Ontario, and Simcoe. Most Hurons inhabited triple-palisaded villages of 2,000 or so people. The palisades were sometimes as tall as 20 feet high, in order to protect the Hurons from their Iroquois enemy.

The Hurons, like most of the Northern Woodlands tribes, lived in longhouses constructed out of bent tree branches covered with bark. These houses, sometimes as large as 25 by 100 feet, housed several families, all members of the same clan. Inside the longhouse, two sets of racks extended along each side, upon which members of the clan slept at night: children slept in the upper "bunks," and adults in the lower ones. Fires for cooking and warmth were built in the middle of the floor. Europeans found the thick smoke oppressive, but it drove the insects away. With each clan sharing a longhouse, there was no privacy; nor was there a concept of private property.

There were other structures in a Huron village: sweat houses, where one went in the hope of sweating out an illness; small huts in which meat and fish were dried; and elevated racks upon which the dead were placed prior to burial. The ground between the longhouses and other village structures was covered with garbage, including the carcasses of dead animals. The stench must have been familiar to Europeans who came from crowded cities, where offal and human waste were likewise tossed onto the streets. On the perimeter of each village were the fields where the women raised vegetables, primarily corn, squash, and beans.

The Hurons, like the other Northern Woodlands tribes, were matrilineal and matrilocal. Shortly after puberty, Huron men and women entered into sexual relations, which either party might initiate. The relationship might lead to marriage, or either party might move on to another partner. When a couple married, the man moved in with his wife's clan, in her family's longhouse, but when the marriage dissolved, which was commonly the case, he would return to the longhouse of his mother and sisters. Thereupon, his wife's brothers assumed the role of male teachers of the children. Each longhouse was supervised by a clan matron, who saw to the domestic and economic needs of her group; she also chose two men to lead the clan. Because the men of the clan spent much of their time away from the village, hunting, trading, or engaging in warfare, most of the day-to-day responsibilities, including raising crops, making clothing, and rearing the children, were performed by the women of the clan.

Huron children were brought up to participate in the world of the mourning war. Their parents trained them for "autonomous responsibility," to be independent men and women who were loyal to their clan. Babies were indulged by their parents, breastfed by their mothers until the age of three or four, and allowed to "toilet train" themselves. These parents did not believe in punishing their children and instead attempted reason or teasing when their children's behavior got out of hand. One Frenchman observed, "There is nothing for which these peoples have a greater horror than restraint. The very children cannot endure it, and live as they please in the houses of their parents, without fear of reprimand or chastisement." Another observed, "The

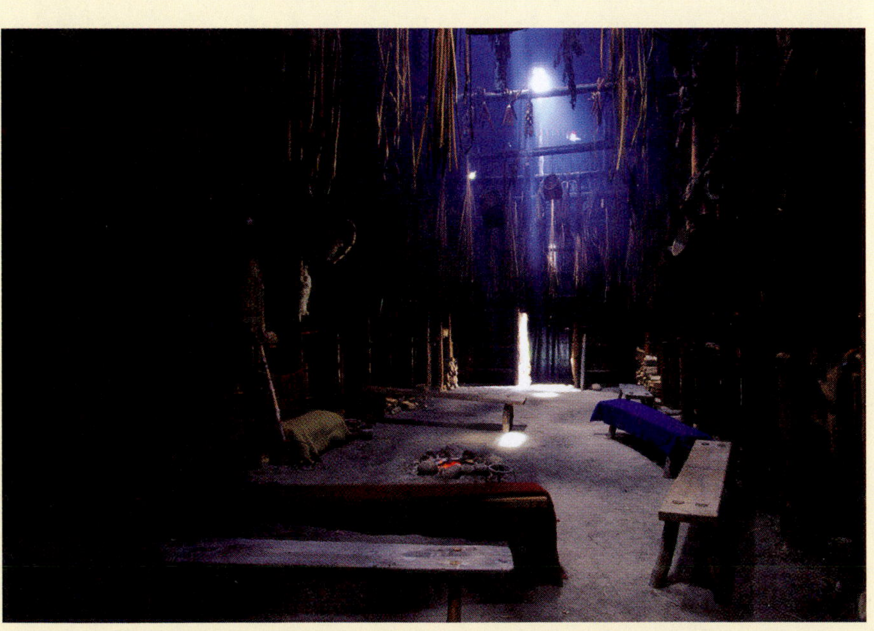

mothers love their children with an extreme passion." Brought up in such a way, Indian children prized their liberty and felt great loyalty to the group that had nurtured them.

Parents taught their children skills that they would need as adults. The girls stayed close to their mothers, performing the easier household tasks, while the boys formed gangs that played competitive games and learned to hunt and make war. Sometimes the boys' gang went off on its own, leaving the village for days at a time. In this way, the boys learned to be independent of their parents and loyal to their group. Huronia taught its children to love both liberty and the group. ●

Creating a Middle Ground in New France

Indians and French traders on the frontier proved able to accommodate each other's cultural practices. Together they created a middle ground that was neither fully European nor fully Indian, but rather a new world created out of two different traditions. The middle ground came into being every time Europeans and Indians met, needed each other, and could not (or would not) achieve what they wanted through the use of force.

As the French drew the Native Americans into a global trade network, the Indians began to hunt more beaver than they needed for their own purposes, depleting the beaver population. Some historians believe that the introduction of European

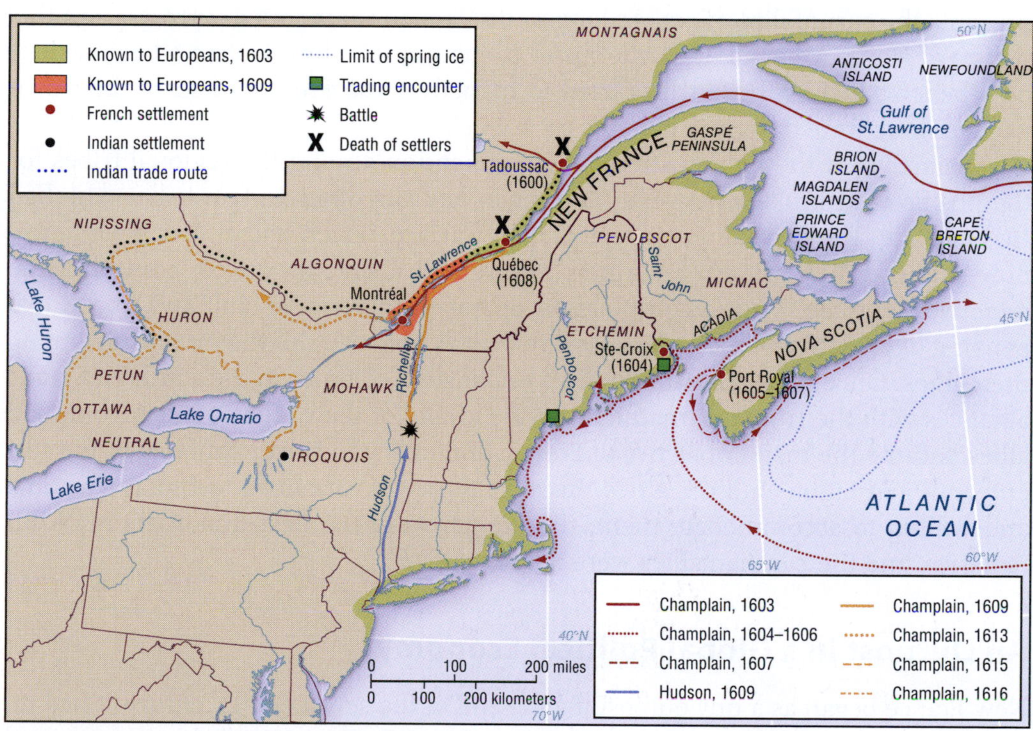

Map 2-5 French Exploration and Settlement, 1603–1616 Between 1603 and 1616, Samuel de Champlain and other French explorers made numerous trips up the St. Lawrence River and along the New England coast as far south as Cape Cod. They established several settlements, and they traded with local Indians and fought with them as well.

goods and commerce into Native American cultures destroyed them from within by making them dependent on those goods and inducing them to abandon their own crafts. Others have pointed out that the trade had different meanings for the French and for the Indians. For the French, trade was important for its cash value; for the Indians, trade goods were important both for the uses to which they could be put and for their symbolic value in religious ceremonies.

Indians integrated European goods into their traditional practices, breaking up brass pots, for example, into small pieces that could be made into jewelry. Iron tools enabled Indian craftspeople to create more detail in their decorative arts. Just as the Indians were pulled into an international trade network centered in Europe, the French were drawn into the Indians' style of life. Traders and priests learned to sleep on the cold ground without complaint and to eat Indian foods such as sagamité, a sort of cornmeal mush in which a small bird or animal was often boiled whole, with only the fur or feathers seared off. Many French traders found Indian wives. Indians such as the Hurons accepted *polygyny*, that is, taking more than one wife, so they were not troubled if the French men who moved in to trade with them had French wives at home. Moreover, the Hurons were accustomed to adopting members of different ethnic groups and the French did not seem to have any aversion to racial mixing. Both the Indians and the French believed that mixed marriages provided a strong foundation for trading and military alliances.

The French were drawn into their Huron and Algonquian allies' world as well. To keep the furs flowing east, they had to take part in war parties (usually against the Iroquois), finance their allies' battles, and purchase their loyalty with annual payments, which the Indians considered "presents." The French considered these presents the cost of diplomacy. As long as the French maintained a presence in this region of North America, they attempted to manipulate their Indian allies for their own benefit, just as those tribes tried to maneuver the French to serve their own needs. There were costs and benefits on both sides.

The arrival of the French stimulated competition among the regional tribes for the positions of brokers between the French and the other Indian tribes who had furs to trade. The pace and nature of Indian warfare, which had always been fierce, now changed dramatically, for a new motive had been introduced: control of the lucrative fur trade. With a combination of honed diplomatic skill and liberal dispensing of presents, French officials were usually able to quell the infighting among their allies. Once the Dutch and English established colonies to the south and made alliances with the Iroquois, maintaining the loyalty of their Huron and Algonquian allies became the major objective of French diplomacy in North America in the seventeenth and eighteenth centuries. Because they were attentive to Indian customs and willing to accommodate them, the French were the best diplomats in North America, and their Indian allies were the most loyal.

An Outpost in a Global Political Economy

New France began as a tiny outpost. By the end of the seventeenth century, it had increased in both size and importance. The French population in North America reached 2,000 in 1650 and 19,000 in 1714, and the primary focus of New France remained the fur trade. In the 1630s, missionaries began to arrive in significant numbers, making the conversion of Indians to Catholicism the second-most important endeavor in the colony. At the same time, the Huron population decreased dramatically. A series of epidemics cut the population in half, carrying off many of Huronia's leaders. The result was internal conflict and political instability that left the Hurons vulnerable to their Indian enemies and increasingly dependent on their French allies. At the same time, the French depended on the Hurons and Algonquians to keep bringing them furs. The Hurons, in fact, operated as middlemen, not trapping beaver themselves, but acquiring beaver pelts from other tribes.

By the middle of the seventeenth century, the supply of beaver in the regions closest to European settlements began to diminish. Before the arrival of the French, the Indians had trapped only enough for their own use. The huge European demand for beaver, however, led Indians to kill more beaver than could be replaced by natural reproduction. As a result, Europeans (or to be more precise, the Indians who acted as middlemen) extended their trade routes farther and farther north and west. This expansion drew increasing numbers of Indians into the emerging global economy.

The European demand for warm beaver coats and stylish beaver hats was insatiable. To provide more trade goods, the French increased domestic manufacturing of cloth, metal implements, guns, and other goods that were attractive to the Indians. This pattern, in which the mother country produced goods to be sold or traded in foreign colonies for raw materials, was replicated in England and Holland. None of these nations found the treasures in the Americas that Spain had located in Mexico and Peru. Instead, they found new products, such as beaver pelts, for which there was a growing demand in Europe.

A new economic theory called mercantilism developed to guide the growth of European nation-states and their New World colonies. Mercantilism's objective was to strengthen the nation-state by making the economy serve its interests. According to the theory, the world's wealth, measured in gold and silver, could never be increased. As a result, each nation's economic objective must be to secure as much of the world's wealth as possible. One nation's gain was necessarily another's loss. The role of colonies was to provide raw materials and markets for manufactured goods for the mother country. Hence national competition for colonies and markets was not only about economics, but about politics and diplomacy as well. The strength of the nation was thought to depend on its ability to dominate international trade.

New Netherland: The Empire of a Trading Nation

In many ways, the Dutch venture into North America resembled that of France. It began with an intrepid explorer in quest of a Northwest Passage and a government that was unwilling to make a significant investment in a North American colony. Unlike the French and Spanish, however, the Dutch government assigned the task of establishing a trading settlement almost entirely to a private company. And because Holland was a Protestant nation, there were no activist Catholic priests in New Netherland to spread their religion and oppose the excesses of a commercial economy. Even more than the French and Spanish colonies, then, New Netherland was shaped by the forces of commerce.

Colonization by a Private Company

Much like England, the other major commercial power at the time, the Netherlands was rising to power as a merchant nation. The nation had secured its independence from Spain after a long and bloody war, which ended in 1648. Also like England, the Netherlands was Protestant, committed to a market economy, and sustained by a thriving middle class. Indeed, Amsterdam was the center of the world's economy. The Netherlands had a distinctive political economy, with neither a powerful aristocracy nor an oppressed peasantry. Its government and economy were dominated by prosperous merchants.

> "The Dutch say we are brothers and that we are joined together with chains, but that lasts only as long as we have beavers. After that we are no longer thought of."
>
> IROQUOIS SPOKESMAN, 1659

Holland was the home of the Renaissance humanist Erasmus, and his values of toleration and moderation permeated society. Jews who had been expelled from Spain found a home in the Netherlands alongside strict Calvinists (Protestants who believed in predestination). The spirit of tolerance enabled the Dutch to put aside religious and political conflict and turn their attentions to trade.

It was an accident that the Dutch and not the British claimed the Hudson River valley. Henry Hudson, an English explorer, sailed several times for the English, testing his theory that a Northwest Passage could be found by sailing over the North Pole. On his final voyage in 1610, Hudson and his crew were frozen into Hudson Bay for the winter. When spring came, the crew mutinied, casting Hudson and the weakest members of the party onto a small boat. They probably did not survive long. But it was an expedition for the Dutch that provided them a claim to the Hudson River valley. In 1609 Hudson persuaded a group of Dutch merchants who traded in Asia, the Dutch East India Company, to finance a venture. Sailing on the *Halve Maen* (*Half Moon,* in English), Hudson and his crew headed toward the Chesapeake Bay, which he believed offered a passage to the Pacific. He sailed along the coast, anchoring in New York Harbor and trading with the local Algonquian Indians. He pushed up the Hudson as far as Albany, where he discovered that the river narrowed, apparently disproving his theory about a water passage through North America.

The opportunity to profit from the fur trade soon drew investors and traders to New Netherland. Within two years of Hudson's "discovery" of the river that still bears his name, Dutch merchants returned to the region, and in 1614 a group who called themselves the New Netherland Company secured a temporary monopoly for trade between the Delaware and Connecticut rivers. The trade was so profitable that other merchant groups were attracted to the region. In 1621 the Dutch West India Company obtained a monopoly for trade with both the Americas and Africa that also entitled it to establish colonies in "fruitful and unsettled parts." In theory, the Company was supposed to operate in the public interest. But both the wealthy merchants who were appointed its commissioners and the more ordinary Netherlanders they enticed to migrate pursued their private interest above all else. The only way investors or settlers could be attracted to a remote colony, however, was by the promise of profits. Within a few years, the Dutch West India Company established settlements at Fort Orange (present-day Albany) and New Amsterdam (present-day New York City) and purchased the entire island of Manhattan from local Algonquian Indians for a meager 60 florins' worth of merchandise. The first 30 families arrived in 1624. Settlers were supposed to serve the fur trade, either by trading with the regional Indians (the Iroquois to the north and the Delawares to the south) or by providing support for the traders. All the profits were reserved for the Company, with the settlers given small salaries.

Until the Company was willing to offer better terms to settlers, the colony grew very slowly. There were 270 inhabitants in 1628, 500 in 1640, and fewer than 9,000 in 1664. It was difficult to attract settlers from a prosperous nation that, while by no means a modern democracy, permitted its people greater religious and political freedom than was customary in most European countries.

The Company experimented with a number of policies to draw colonists to New Netherland. In 1629, it offered huge plots of land (18 miles along the Hudson River) and extensive governing powers to *patroons,* men who would bring 50 settlers to the new colony. It also offered smaller grants of land to individuals who would farm the land and return to the Company one-tenth of what they produced. Both approaches placed restrictions on land ownership and self-government, and neither was successful. In 1640, the Company offered greater rights of self-government and 200 acres to anyone who brought over five adult immigrants. This policy worked better, although the religious and ethnic diversity of New Netherland suggests that the "pull" of relative toleration was greater than the limited "push" of immigrants out of the prosperous Netherlands. Only a few decades into its existence New Netherland had become a magnet for peoples from a wide variety of cultures and nations. As the colony grew in population, it expanded up the Hudson, out from the island of Manhattan into New Jersey and Long Island, and as far south as the Delaware River.

The ethnic diversity of the colony was increased even further when in 1655 it absorbed the small colony of New Sweden, which had been established on the Delaware less than 20 years earlier. In some ways the history of New Sweden was like that of New Netherland writ small. It was a privately financed but government-encouraged trading outpost that failed when it was unable to return a quick profit on minimal investment. The diverse population of New Netherland was united by no single religion or culture that could have established social order. In most European nations at the time, social order was maintained by a combination of state authority and cohesive religious structures and values. Where the religious or government order was fractured, as in France, bloody civil war was the result. In New Netherland, however, not only religious structure, but also the force of government were relatively weak. The governors were caught between the Company, which expected to earn a profit, and the settlers, who wanted to prosper themselves. Peter Stuyvesant, governor from 1647 until the English takeover in 1664, was the most successful of the governors, but even he could not fully control New Netherland's disorder.

In one year alone, at a time when the population numbered less than 1,000, there were 50 civil suits and almost as many criminal prosecutions. The rate of alcohol consumption seems to have been higher in New Netherland than in any other colony on the North American mainland. In 1645, there were between 150 and 200 houses in New Amsterdam—and 35 taverns! As a consequence, one of Stuyvesant's first acts as governor was to shut the bars at nine o'clock at night. There were also complaints of sexual promiscuity, especially between European men and Indian women, bar brawls, and mischief caused by sailors on shore leave.

Stuyvesant met with no more success in regulating the economy. He attempted to set prices on such commodities as beer and bread, but he was overruled by the Company, which feared that controls on economic activity would thwart further immigration. In a pattern that would eventually prevail in all of the North American colonies settled by the Netherlands and England, commerce triumphed.

Slavery and Freedom in New Netherland

The colony, the Company, and the nation all wanted to make themselves wealthy through commerce. This desire led to the introduction of African slavery into New Netherland. The fur trade did not prove as lucrative as investors had hoped, and the Company found that European agricultural workers "sooner or later appl[ied] themselves to trade, and neglect[ed] agriculture altogether." The Company decided that the primary function of New Netherland should be to provide food for its more lucrative plantation colonies in Brazil and the Caribbean. Earlier in the century, the Dutch had seized a portion of northern Brazil from Portugal, introduced a sugar-plantation slave economy, and transplanted that economy to islands in the Caribbean. By that time they had also entered the transatlantic slave trade. In fact, a Dutch warship dropped off the first 20 Africans at the English colony of Jamestown in 1619 in return for food. With its own plantation colonies to supply with slave labor, the Netherlands became a major player in the slave trade, ultimately transporting Africans to the colonies of other nations as well.

In the context of the Netherlands' lucrative trade in sugar and slaves, the colony at New Netherland was only a sideshow. Hoping to make the colony profitable, the Company turned to enslaved Africans. By 1664, there were perhaps 700 slaves in the colony, a minuscule portion of the more than half million Africans the Dutch ultimately seized from their homelands, but a considerable portion (about 8 percent) of New Netherland's population.

The Netherlands was perhaps the most tolerant nation of its day, and the Dutch Reformed Church accepted Africans as well as Indians as converts, provided they could demonstrate their knowledge of the Dutch religion. The Dutch Reformed Church did not oppose the institution of slavery, however. Moreover, the strict nature of Dutch Calvinism, appealing more to the mind than to the heart, placed limits on the Church's tolerance. It insisted that its followers be able to read and understand the Bible and the doctrines of the Church.

The primary force for tolerance in New Netherland was, in fact, the Dutch West India Company, which saw religious toleration as necessary to commercial prosperity. When the head of the Dutch Reformed Church in New Netherland and Governor Stuyvesant attempted to prevent the entry of 23 Dutch Jews whom the Portuguese had expelled from northern Brazil, they were reversed by the Company. The directors, some of whom were Jews, clarified the relationship between religious tolerance and commercial prosperity: They did not know how to keep religious "sectarians" out "without diminishing the population and stopping immigration. . . . You may . . . allow everyone to have his own belief, as long as he behaves quietly and legally, gives no offence to his neighbors and does not oppose the government."

The Company also advocated a policy of fairness to the local Indian tribes. They insisted that land must be purchased from its original owners before Europeans could settle on it. Because some individual settlers were coercing Indians to sell their land cheap, in 1652 Stuyvesant forbade purchases of land without government approval.

It might appear puzzling that the Dutch officials and merchants whose policies encouraged toleration of religious minorities and justice toward Native Americans would also introduce and encourage slavery in North America. The Dutch were not motivated, however, by abstract ideals of tolerance or equality. The primary goal of the founders of New Netherland was profit through trade: toleration of religious and cultural diversity, amicable relations with local Indians, and African slavery all served that end.

The Dutch-Indian Trading Partnership

In the 40 years that the Dutch maintained their colony of New Netherland, its most profitable activity was the fur trade. As the French had done to the north, the Dutch disrupted the balance among regional Indian tribes. The arrival of the Europeans, rather than uniting the Indians, heightened long-standing local animosities. Tribes came to rely on their European allies not only for goods but also for weapons and even soldiers to fight their enemies.

Both the Indians and the Europeans were playing a dangerous game, one that required a constant low level of violence to prevent outsiders from encroaching on an established trade. Yet if the violence escalated into full-fledged warfare, it disrupted the very trade it was designed to protect. As a result, the trade frontier between Indians and Europeans was always filled with peril.

The Dutch began trading in the Albany region around 1614 and built Fort Orange there a decade later. This small outpost was in the middle of a region inhabited by the Mahican tribe, an Algonquian people who gave the Dutch access to the furs trapped by other Algonquian tribes to the north. The Dutch began assisting the Mahicans in their trade rivalry with the Mohawks (an Iroquois nation) only to find themselves attacked—and defeated—by the Mohawks. The Mohawks however asked for peace: their objective was not to eliminate the Dutch, but to secure them as trade partners.

By 1628 the Mohawks had defeated the Mahicans and forced them to move east, into Connecticut, establishing the Mohawks as the most powerful force in the region. Kiliaen van Rensselaer, the *patroon* of a vast estate next to Fort Orange, complained that "the savages, who are now stronger than ourselves, will not allow others who are hostile and live farther away and have many furs to pass through their territory." The Dutch and the Mohawks abandoned their former hostility for a generally peaceful trading partnership.

The Dutch did what was necessary to maintain their lucrative trade. Sometimes that meant giving the Indians gifts, including liquor. At other times, it meant cutting off enterprising individuals who set out on their own, attempting to intercept Indian traders. Despite such efforts, by the 1660s New Netherland was in serious economic trouble. The underlying problem was an oversupply of wampum, beads made from the shells of clams (see Map 2–6). Indians had placed a high value on wampum well before the arrival of Europeans, and the Dutch introduced iron tools to their Indian trading partners and taught them how to mass-produce wampum in small, uniform beads that could be strung together into ropes and belts. They also helped the Indians establish a trade in wampum itself, in which southern New

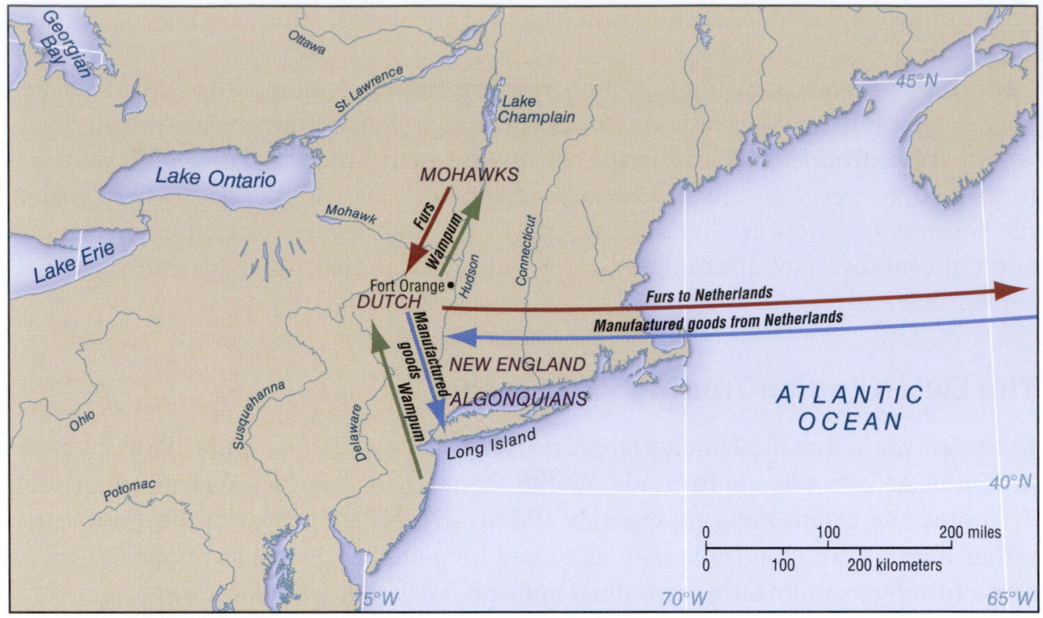

Map 2–6 The Wampum Trade In the wampum trade, southern New England Algonquians manufactured wampum, which they traded to the Dutch for European goods. The Dutch then exchanged the wampum for furs from the Mohawks and other Indian trade partners near Fort Orange. The Dutch conveyed the furs to the Netherlands for more European goods, which they traded to New England Algonquians for more wampum.

England Algonquians manufactured wampum and traded it to the Dutch for European goods. The Dutch then exchanged the wampum for furs from the Mohawks and other Indians near Fort Orange and conveyed the furs to the Netherlands for more European goods. By the middle of the seventeenth century, perhaps as many as 3 million pieces of wampum were in circulation in the area dominated by the Iroquois.

By the 1640s English traders in New England had cornered the market in the beads, just when New Englanders were ceasing to use them as money. The traders then dumped them into the Dutch market by buying up huge quantities of European goods. Almost instantly the price of trade goods skyrocketed and the value of wampum fell, leaving the Dutch with too few of the former and too much of the latter. Competition among Dutch traders increased, the pressure on Iroquois trade partners mounted, and profits fell. The economic crisis tipped the delicate balance of violence on the frontier and precipitated a major war with serious consequences.

The Beaver Wars

As the economic position of the Dutch faltered, the balance of power among many northeastern tribes collapsed. The Iroquois, who depended on the Dutch for a steady supply of guns, were now vulnerable. The Iroquois tribes in the west came under assault from the Susquehannocks, a tribe to the south, while the Mohawks faced renewed pressure from the Mahicans to the east. Simultaneously, the Hurons had cut the Iroquois off from trade with the French to the north. Faced with these pressures, the Iroquois lashed out in hostilities, known as the Beaver Wars, which raged between 1648 and the 1660s. In these conflicts, the Iroquois attacked almost all of their Indian neighbors and succeeded in pushing the few surviving French-allied Hurons to the west.

This warfare was horrendous, not only for the enemies of the Iroquois, but also for the Iroquois themselves. So many had died in battle and been replaced by enemy captives that the tribes were as much collections of adopted enemy tribespeople as they were native Iroquois. As Indian fought Indian, Europeans gained the upper hand. The Iroquois were the technical winners in the Beaver Wars, but their victory was only temporary. Although the Hurons had been pushed west and dispersed, the Iroquois could not secure the French as trade partners. Once the Hurons were gone, the French began trading with other Algonquian tribes to the east. Although the Iroquois remained a powerful force until almost the end of the eighteenth century, the Beaver Wars marked an important turning point. The Indians were never able to replace the population they lost to warfare, even by raiding other tribes. By the middle of the seventeenth century, however, the pace of European colonization was increasing. Waves of Europeans came to North America to fill the land once hunted by Indians.

Even before the English conquered New Netherland in 1664, the Iroquois were looking for new trade partners. They found them in the English. The transition in New Netherland from Dutch to English rule was relatively quiet. The Dutch had established the colony hoping to make money through trade. Having failed in that objective, they had little incentive to fight for control of the North American colony.

England Attempts an Empire

England came late to the business of empire building, but by the time the process was completed, that nation dominated not only North America but also much of the world. Although England's search for an overseas empire was motivated primarily by a search for wealth and power, it is impossible to separate these drives from the religious impulse. All of the great imperial nations of this era—Portugal, Spain, France, and England—believed that they conquered for God and country; hence nationalism was always tinged with religious fervor.

The Origins of English Nationalism

England did not achieve the political unity necessary for empire building until the second half of the sixteenth century. Between 1455 and 1485, England was torn by a dynastic struggle, the Wars of the Roses. King Henry VII and his son, Henry VIII, spent their reigns consolidating the power of the state by crushing recalcitrant nobles. When the pope refused to let Henry VIII terminate his sonless marriage to Catherine of Aragon, the king made Protestantism the official religion of the nation, banned Catholicism, and confiscated the land and wealth of the Catholic Church. Henry's daughter Mary, who reigned from 1553 through 1558, took the nation back to the Catholic religion, burning Protestants at the stake and throwing the nation into turmoil. Order was finally established under the rule of Henry's other daughter, Elizabeth I (reigning from 1558 to 1603),

> "Wee found the people most gentle, loving, and faithfull, void of all guile, and treason, and such as lived after the manner of the golden age."
>
> ARTHUR BARLOWE, reporting from the first English voyage to Roanoke

who reestablished the Anglican Church, subdued internal dissent, and built on the strong state that her grandfather and father had consolidated.

Queen Elizabeth, although the most ardent of nationalists, was unwilling to risk her treasury on North American adventures. Other English nationalists, however, were convinced that a New World empire could lead to wealth and glory for the nation. By the end of the sixteenth century nationalist propagandists, such as two cousins both named Richard Hakluyt, were setting out the case for an overseas empire. The Hakluyts united nationalism, mercantilism, and militant Protestantism. They argued that if England had colonies to supply it with raw materials and provide markets for manufactured goods, it could free itself from economic dependency on France and Spain. Moreover, colonies could drain off the growing numbers of the unemployed. The Hakluyts also believed that North American Indians could be relatively easily converted to English trade and religion, which they would much prefer to Spanish "pride and tyranie." The English could simultaneously strike a blow against the Spanish and advance "the glory of God." Although the Hakluyts's dream of converting the Indians was never realized, their plans for an English mercantile empire eventually provided a blueprint for overseas colonization.

Raiding Other Empires

England's first move was not to establish colonies but to try stealing from the Spanish. The English government had neither the wealth nor the vision to found a colonial empire, and Elizabeth I was unconvinced by the arguments of the Hakluyts and other colonial propagandists. Like most European monarchs, Elizabeth was most concerned about international power politics in Europe, so she was willing to let individual Englishmen try to poach on the Spanish. Her goal was to weaken Spain more than to establish a North American empire.

As early as 1562, John Hawkins tried to break into the slave trade, but the Spanish forced him out. The English moved on to privateering, that is, state-sanctioned piracy. In 1570 Sir Francis Drake set off for the Isthmus of Panama on a raiding expedition. Drake was motivated equally by dreams of glory and a conviction that his Protestant religion was superior to all others. He had his start in one of Hawkins's slaving expeditions, from which he had acquired a hatred of the Spanish.

In years to come, Drake led the second expedition ever to sail around the world, crossed the Atlantic many times, helped defeat a huge Spanish fleet, the Armada, and became an architect of England's colonial strategies. Personally brave and militantly Protestant, Drake was the English version of the *conquistador*. His venture into Panama failed to produce the hoped-for treasure, but it inspired a group of professional seamen, aggressive Protestants and members of Elizabeth's court, to formulate plans for an English colonial empire. This group successfully pressured the cautious queen for support. The success of Drake's round-the-world expedition (1577–1580) spurred further privateering ventures. He brought back to England not only enough treasure to pay for the voyage, but also proof that the Spanish empire was vulnerable. From 1585 to 1604, the English government

Sir Francis Drake One of England's greatest adventurers, Sir Francis Drake sailed around the globe, defeated the Spanish Armada, and made a fortune stealing from the Spanish.

AMERICA AND THE WORLD

>> The English on the Edge of Empire

Just as England came late to the business of exploring North America, so it came late to the exploration of Africa. At the middle of the sixteenth century, England lacked the wealth and technical expertise of Portugal, Spain, or France. Indeed, the most powerful empire in the region at that time was the Ottoman one; it reached from Algiers in the west to the Persian Gulf in the east, covering almost all of North Africa, most of the Mediterranean, and much of southeastern Europe and the Middle East. Its trade routes extended even farther, south across the Sahara into much of Africa. The Ottoman Empire was not only wealthy and powerful, but it was, for its time, relatively tolerant. In fact, many Jews who had been expelled from Spain found a new home in the Islamic empire to the east.

So dominant was the Ottoman Empire that the rest of Europe was, in important ways, peripheral to it. And if the European nations were on the margin of the Ottoman Empire, England was on the margin of Europe. Hence, when it sought to expand, it would have to look to other marginal regions—for example, the venture into Ireland, where the English had to subdue only the Irish themselves. In the middle of the sixteenth century, England sought out trade on the edges of the Ottoman Empire—the Muscovy region of Russia, Morocco, and Guinea, a West African nation where the Portuguese had already established a monopoly.

In fact, the English were latecomers to Africa, just as they were latecomers to North America. The Portuguese had been trading in West Africa for more than a century, and at first the English had trouble finding a foothold. In 1553, English traders made contact with an African leader in the city of Benin. He was gracious, speaking to them in Portuguese, and although he told them that their trade goods were not up to the standard that he expected, he gave them a cargo of pepper on credit, until they could bring back payment. Like the Native Americans the Europeans encountered in North America, Africans welcomed trade with Europeans and competition among them for the best price. The African environment, however, was not nearly as welcoming. Only a month after their arrival in Benin, the English were in such a rush to escape the tropical fevers that had felled much of the crew that they left several merchants behind when they lifted anchor.

In North America, Europeans brought lethal diseases that killed millions of natives. In Africa, however, the situation was reversed: Europeans fell victim to tropical diseases. Not until the nineteenth century, when quinine came into use as a treatment for malaria, were Europeans able to colonize Africa. Until then, the continent was known as "the white man's grave." Europeans could not have established colonies even had they wanted to. Instead, they relied upon their African trading partners.

So unfamiliar were the English with Africa that when, two years later, another merchant returned from West Africa, he had to explain what an elephant looked like. Within a century, however, the English had extracted so much gold from Africa that the new one-pound gold coin was called a guinea, from the region in Africa from which the gold came, and it was adorned with an image of an elephant, right below the bust of the king.

Because of the dominance of the Portuguese in West Africa, however, the English were slow to make inroads. On one early voyage, the English clashed with the Portuguese on the Guinea coast. They had to turn over one of their crew, a 15-year-old boy named Martin Frobisher, as a kind of living security deposit. The Portuguese let Frobisher do some local trading for them, and they eventually sent him back to Portugal, from which he was able to return to England—and embark on a career as a privateer. Later, he explored North America, looking for gold.

At about the same time, another Englishman, John Hawkins, who was backed by English investors, attempted to break into the Portuguese slave trade by force. On his first voyage, he simply seized a cargo of 400 Africans as well as valuable trade goods from a Portuguese fleet and took them to the Spanish colony of Santo Domingo to sell. Even after bribing the Spanish official—trade with England was illegal–the profits were enormous. On his next voyage, Hawkins went directly to the Guinea coast. Rather than working through

continued

>> **AMERICA AND THE WORLD** *continued*

local African rulers, who were happy to sell other Africans as slaves, Hawkins tried to take slaves by himself. He seized ten Africans—and lost seven members of his own crew in the process. Still, by raiding Africans and Portuguese, Hawkins was able to amass another cargo to take to the Spanish colonies. This one he forced upon Venezuelans, threatening to burn their town if they did not purchase from him. Not until his third voyage did Hawkins come to understand that Africans could be allies in the slave trade. While Hawkins and his men were looking for Africans they could seize, an emissary from a local king approached him with a proposition: help the king defeat his enemies and share in the slaves taken as booty. Hawkins agreed, and helped his new allies set fire to a town with 8000 inhabitants. His reward was 250 captives. This voyage ended badly, however. This time the Spanish refused to purchase Hawkins's slaves, and instead destroyed his fleet and killed 300 of his 400 sailors in a battle at San Juan de Ulúa (near Veracruz, Mexico).

In the middle of the sixteenth century, the English were outsiders, trying everywhere they could to force themselves into the empires that more powerful nations had established.

issued licenses to privateers, sometimes as many as 100 per year. Each venture was financed by a joint-stock company, a relatively new form of business organization that was the forerunner to the modern corporation. These companies brought together merchants who saw privateering as a way to broaden their trade and gentlemen who saw it as a way to increase their incomes. Increasingly, the merchants played a dominant role, running privateering as much like a business as possible.

Rehearsal in Ireland

At the end of the sixteenth century, England embarked on a campaign to bring Ireland, which had long been in its possession, under its full control. The conquest of Ireland between 1565 and 1576 became the model for England's subsequent colonial ventures. Ireland presented the English monarchy with the same sort of political problem that all early-modern rulers faced, that is, a set of powerful nobles who put their own interests ahead of those of the nation. Consolidation of the nation meant bringing these nobles into line.

England not only subdued the Irish leaders and their people, but also forcibly removed some of them to make way for loyal Englishmen, who were given land as a reward for their service to the queen. By paying her followers with someone else's land and financing military expeditions from joint-stock companies, England made the conquest of Ireland relatively cheap. These methods provided useful precedents to a queen who was never convinced that the establishment of colonies on the edge of the known world was in England's national interest. If, however, these ventures could be paid for privately, by privateering, charters to individuals, or joint-stock companies, the queen was willing to permit them.

The English conquest of Ireland provided not only practical experience in how to organize and finance a colonial venture, but also a set of attitudes about cultural difference that were applied to the Indians. Although the Irish were Catholics and hence Christians, the English thought that people who behaved as the Irish did must be barbarians. According to the English, the Irish "blaspheme, they murder, commit whoredome, hold no wedlocke, ravish, steal, and commit all abomination without scruple of conscience." Without a shred of evidence, the English also accused the Irish of cannibalism, a mark of the barbarian.

These attitudes became the justification for an official English policy of terrorism. In two grisly massacres, one in the middle of a Christmas feast, hundreds of people—men, women, and children—were slaughtered. The English governor, Sir Humphrey Gilbert, ordered that the heads of all those killed resisting the conquest be chopped off and placed along the path leading to his tent so that anyone coming to see him "must pass through a lane of heads." According to Gilbert, the dead would feel "nothing," but it would bring "terror to the people when they saw the heads of their dead fathers, brothers, children, kinsfolk, and friends." The English justified such harsh policies by the supposed barbarism of the Irish people. These ideas, which were quite similar to early Spanish depictions of the Indians of the Americas, were carried to the New World, England's next stop in the expansion of its empire.

The Roanoke Venture

Roanoke, England's first colony in what became the United States, was a military venture, intended as a resupply base for privateers raiding in the Caribbean. With such a base, the ships would not have to recross the Atlantic each time they completed a raid. In 1584 Walter Raleigh received a charter to establish a colony in North America. Only 30 years old at the time, Raleigh was the half-brother of the late Sir Humphrey Gilbert. Hot-tempered and arrogant, Raleigh had been a soldier since the age of 14. Elizabeth agreed to let Raleigh establish a combination colony and privateering base north of Spain's northernmost settlement at St. Augustine. Raleigh's scouting party had already found a potential site, at Roanoke Island, on the Outer Banks of North Carolina, and brought back to England two Indians, Manteo and Wanchese. Elizabeth gave the enterprise some modest support, even investing in it herself. She knighted Raleigh but refused to let the hotheaded young soldier lead the expedition himself.

The Roanoke expedition left Plymouth in early April 1585, under the command of Sir Richard Grenville, an aristocrat and soldier who had fought in wars in Hungary and Ireland. Half of the crew of 600 were probably recruited or impressed (i.e., forcibly seized) from the unemployed poor of Britain. Little value was attached to the lives of such poor men. When one of the ships in the original expedition became separated from the fleet and found its supplies running low, 20 men were dropped off at Jamaica, only 2 of whom were ever heard from again, and another 32

The arrival of the English at Roanoke, from a 1585 sketch by the artist John White.

John White's Watercolor of an Algonquian Village Much of what we know about Algonquian life at the time of the Roanoke expedition comes from the paintings of John White, who was a member of the expedition. Here we see a small village, surrounded by a tall stockade.

were deposited at an island in the Outer Banks. Such men were expendable—and, ultimately, so would be the entire population of Roanoke.

It turned out that Roanoke was a poor port, dangerous for small ships and totally inadequate for larger ones. When the primary ship in the fleet was almost wrecked and a major portion of the food supply lost, Grenville and the fleet departed for England and fresh supplies. Colonel Ralph Lane, another veteran of the war in Ireland, was left in charge as governor. He was supposed to look for a better port, build a fort, and find food for the 100 men who were left under his command.

Roanoke was established to gain an advantage over the treasure-filled Spanish ships traveling back to Spain. The men who were left on the island prepared for war—with Spain. When the fort was complete, its guns pointed out to sea, toward any Spanish ships that might approach. Raleigh intended to send another supply ship that summer, but the queen insisted that he sail instead to Newfoundland to warn the English there about the beginnings of a sea war with Spain. The first settlers of Roanoke were ill-equipped to build a self-sustaining colony. Half soldiers and gentlemen, and half undisciplined and impoverished young men, no one knew how to work. The aristocrats searched halfheartedly for gold and silver and, when none was found, spent the remainder of their time complaining about the lack of "their old accustomed dainty food" and "soft beds of down or feathers." Unable to provide for themselves, the colonists turned to the local Roanoke Indians (an Algonquian tribe), whom they soon alienated.

The Roanokes were familiar with Europeans and ready to trade with them. The English tendency to resort to force and their need for more food than the natives could easily supply, however, led to conflict. Thinking that one of the Indians had stolen a silver cup, the English retaliated by burning an empty village and the surrounding cornfields, which were necessary to feed both Indians and English. In the light of such actions, the Indians had to balance the benefits brought by trade against the costs of English hostility. After an attempted ambush failed, the Roanokes decided to withdraw from Roanoke Island, leaving the English to starve. When Lane learned of this plan, he attacked the Roanokes, beheading their chieftain Wingina. Thomas Hariot, one of the colonists, later placed most of the blame for the deterioration of Indian-English relations on his countrymen. Such was the result of leaving colonization in the hands of military men such as Lane.

Not all the colonists, however, treated the Roanokes as an enemy to be conquered. Much of what we know about the Roanoke Colony and its Indian neighbors is due to the work of two sympathetic colonists. John White, a painter, and Thomas Hariot, who later became the greatest mathematician of his age, were sent to survey the region and describe its inhabitants and natural features. Their illustrations, maps, and descriptions provide the most accurate information about this region and its inhabitants before the arrival of large numbers of Europeans.

By June 1585, it was clear that Roanoke had failed in its mission. When Sir Francis Drake and his fleet appeared on their way back from a yearlong looting party in the Caribbean, the colonists decided to return to England. So great was their haste to clear out that they left behind three men who were on an expedition into the interior. They were never heard from again. Apparently, Drake also dropped off several hundred Caribbean Indian and African slaves that he had liberated while picking up booty. Freeing slaves was one of his ways to hurt the Spanish. For the same reason, he had burned the outpost at St. Augustine as he passed by on his way up the East Coast. All of these abandoned people (the three Englishmen and Drake's liberated Indians and Africans) probably melted into the Native Indian population, according to the Indian tradition of adoption. When Raleigh's supply ship arrived at Roanoke shortly thereafter, and then Grenville two weeks after that, the colonists had sailed with Drake and the others had disappeared. Grenville dropped off 15 men and returned to England.

Portrait of an Algonquian Mother and Child by John White This beautiful picture illustrates the indulgence of Algonquian mothers and the sensitivity of the English artist who painted this one.

The English advocates of colonization were not yet ready to give up. The original plan for a military-style base had failed and a new vision of colonization would now be tried. Raleigh's commitment to the colony was only lukewarm by this point, for Roanoke had already cost £30,000 without returning a cent. John White, the painter, remained enthusiastic and assembled a group of settlers that was the forerunner of all future successful English colonies. It included 110 people—men, women, and children who were prepared to raise their own crops—and one loyal Roanoke Indian, Manteo. (Wanchese had remained with his own people and was now an enemy to the English.) In return for their investment in the enterprise, Raleigh granted each man 500 acres of land. The new expedition arrived at Roanoke in July 1587. The plan was to pick up the men Grenville had left and proceed north to the Chesapeake, for a superior harbor. The pilot of the fleet, who was more interested in privateering than colony making, refused to take the colonists any farther, however.

The second attempt to establish a colony at Roanoke was probably doomed by the poisoned relations with the Indians. White soon found that Grenville's men had been attacked by Roanokes. The colonists found themselves estranged from their Indian hosts. The survival of the colony now depended on continued support from England. Hence the colonists, who included White's own daughter and granddaughter, sent White back to act as their agent in England. No European ever saw any of these colonists again.

The Abandoned Colony

No one had planned to abandon the little colony. It was mostly a matter of priorities. Raleigh assembled a supply fleet the next spring. A sea war with the Spanish Armada was looming, however, and Elizabeth did not let the ships leave. Raleigh himself became busy with the war against the Spanish and with sending colonists to his plantations in Ireland. In 1588, White secured two ships, but the crews set off in search of treasure instead of Roanoke. In 1589, the supply mission never got beyond the planning stage. In 1590, White arranged with a privateering fleet to drop him at Roanoke. He arrived in mid-August, only to find that everyone was gone. There were signs of an orderly departure, and the word CROATOAN, Manteo's home island, was carved in a post. White assumed that was where the entire group had gone. Short of water and with a storm brewing, the fleet decided to return to the Caribbean for the winter and not to proceed on to Croatoan until the next spring. They never got there.

The colony of Roanoke was not "lost," as legend usually puts it; it was abandoned. Serving no useful economic or military purpose, the men and women of Roanoke were entirely expendable. Because Raleigh's claim to the land depended upon his sustaining a colony, he was better off maintaining the fiction that the colonists were alive than discovering that in fact they were dead or missing. In 1602, Raleigh finally sent out a search party that never quite made it to Roanoke. A year later Queen Elizabeth was dead, and her successor, James I, had Raleigh arrested as a traitor.

What happened to the abandoned colonists? Twenty years after White had last seen them, the English returned to the region, this time establishing a permanent colony at Jamestown, on the Chesapeake. In 1608, Englishmen heard that Roanoke colonists had made their way up to Virginia and settled among the friendly Chesapeake Indians. Indeed, the main body of colonists at Roanoke had intended to seek out the Chesapeake. Perhaps the remainder went to Croatoan, leaving White the message carved into the post.

Those who moved north seem to have become victims of the Powhatans, a powerful and expansionist tribe. At just about the time that the English were arriving, their chief, also named Powhatan, ordered the slaughter of the Chesapeakes and the English who lived among them. There were reports that seven English people had escaped, and for years local Indians told tales about people who lived in two-story stone houses with domesticated turkeys. At one point, a 10-year-old boy with "perfect yellow hair" and "white skin" was sighted among one tribe. The English at Jamestown eventually came to believe that the survivors of Roanoke were living 50 miles away, but no effort was made to find them.

Almost 20 years after the abandonment of Roanoke, the English finally established a permanent North American colony at Jamestown. By that time the Spanish empire was sinking into its slow decline. In theory at least, the English would be able to provide better support for subsequent New World colonies. As their willingness to abandon the colonists at Roanoke demonstrated, however, they had limited interest in colonies that did not return a fast and reliable profit. Moreover, because the English settlers, with few exceptions, antagonized their Indian hosts, the English could not rely on the Indians for food. As a result, the success of the English colonies would depend on their capacity to grow their own food. In addition, the architects of English imperial policy concentrated more on trade with the English inhabitants of the New World than with Native Americans. Consequently, the history of the English in North America is by and large that of the growth of the English population (augmented by immigrants from other European nations and of course Africa) and the steady decline of the original Indian inhabitants.

Conclusion

European nations established colonies to achieve a political or economic advantage over their rivals. Most of the nations that established colonies had only recently been unified by force. This experience gave them both the energy to establish colonies in the rest of the world and a military model that they could use for colonization. The distinctive experience of each nation, however, shaped its relations with the Indians it encountered, just as the distinctive experience of the Indian nations shaped their interactions with Europeans. The Spanish came prepared for a new *reconquista* and poured huge and well-armed forces into the New World. The French sent small numbers of military officers who quickly found Indian allies and became entangled in the Indians' own conflicts. The English used another military model, that of the pacification of Ireland. Some nations, in particular France and Spain, were comparatively willing to reach out to alien cultures by sending missionaries to convert the Indians. Though more ethnocentric than the French or Spanish, the Dutch also recognized that the goodwill of the Indians was vital if a flourishing trade were to be maintained. The English proved the least interested in accommodating Indian cultures and the most interested in transplanting their own. Out of these different experiences, a North Atlantic political economy began to emerge, shaped by the forces of trade and the quest for national power, as Europeans, Indians, and Africans were drawn into a global economy in which the nations of the world competed for advantage. The early years of American colonial history were shaped by vast impersonal forces that built empires and subjugated peoples. But they were also given a lasting imprint by individuals, many of them world travelers. Some set out to find new worlds, while others were forced into them by those with imperial ambitions. Captives such as Don Luís de Velasco, Wanchese, and Manteo; intrepid explorers such as Jacques Cartier and Henry Hudson; ruthless soldiers such as Sir Francis Drake and Samuel de Champlain; the poor who were dragooned into sailing for Roanoke and left there to die; Africans liberated from the Spanish only to be abandoned on the North Carolina shore, perhaps melting into the Indian population; and Huron women who took French traders as their husbands: all of them left their mark on the New World, even before the English planted their first permanent colonies in North America.

Further Readings

W. J. Eccles, *France in America* (1990). The standard introduction to the history of New France, succinct and authoritative.

David Hackett Fischer, *Champlain's Dream: The European Founding of North America* (2008). A comprehensive and readable new account of the life of the French explorer.

Michael Kammen, *Colonial New York: A History* (1975). A readable survey of colonial New York's history.

Karen Ordahl Kupperman, *Roanoke: The Abandoned Colony* (1984), and David Beers Quinn, *Set Fair for Roanoke: Voyages and Colonies, 1584–1606* (1985). Two excellent histories of the Roanoke Colony. Kupperman expertly places the colony in its fullest context, while Quinn offers a more comprehensive narrative.

Donna Merwick, *The Shame and the Sorrow: Dutch-Amerindian Encounters in New Netherland* (2006). An elegant new interpretation that argues that the Dutch betrayed their own ideals.

David Beers Quinn, ed., *New American World: A Documentary History of North America to 1612* (1979). A five-volume collection of documents, indispensable for the study of early explorations of North America.

Daniel K. Richter, *The Ordeal of the Longhouse: The Peoples of the Iroquois League in the Era of European Colonization* (1992). An extraordinary introduction to the history of the Iroquois peoples that shows what early American history looks like when the focus is shifted from European settlers to the original inhabitants.

Helen C. Rountree, *Pocahontas's People: The Powhatan Indians of Virginia Through Four Centuries* (1990). A superb introduction to the history of this southeastern tribe, written by an anthropologist.

Who, What

Jacques Cartier 42
Samuel de Champlain 46
Sir Francis Drake 58
Walter Raleigh 61
Mourning war 45
Polygyny 50
Mercantilism 51
Privateering 58
Joint-stock company 60

>> Timeline >>

▼ 1275–1292
Marco Polo travels in Asia

▼ 1400–1600
Five Iroquois nations create the Great League of Peace

▼ 1455–1485
War of the Roses in England

▼ 1497
John Cabot arrives in North America

▼ 1519–1522
Magellan expedition sails around the world for Spain

▼ 1522
Giovanni da Verrazano explores North American coast for France

▼ 1534–1542
Jacques Cartier makes three trips to Canada for France

▼ 1561
Spanish abduct Don Luís de Velasco

▼ 1562
John Hawkins tries to break into the slave trade

▼ 1565
Spanish establish settlement at St. Augustine
Spanish destroy French settlement at Fort Caroline

▼ 1565–1576
The English conquer Ireland

▼ 1570
Don Luís de Velasco returns home to Virginia

▼ 1577–1580
Francis Drake sails around the world for England

Review Questions

1. What were the key European objectives for exploring North America in this period? To what extent did England, Spain, France, and the Netherlands achieve their objectives?
2. What was the "mourning war"? What function did it serve in Iroquois culture? How was it adapted to new circumstances in the seventeenth century?
3. Compare the early encounters with Native Americans of the English, French, and Dutch.
4. Compare the approaches to colonization of the English, French, and Dutch governments.
5. What was the "middle ground," and how was it created?
6. Why was the colony at Roanoke established, and why was it abandoned?

Websites

John White's Watercolors. Images of John White's beautiful paintings of Indian life at Roanoke, compared to the later engravings by Theodore De Bry. http://www.virtualjamestown.org/images/white_debry_html/jamestown.html

Roanoke Revisited. The National Park Service's Roanoke website, including a link to Thomas Hariot's "A Brief and True Report." http://www.nps.gov/archive/fora/roanokerev.htm

Voyages of Samuel de Champlain. The three-volume collection of Samuel de Champlain's account of his travels, digitized by Project Gutenberg. http://www.gutenberg.org/etext/6653

For further review materials and resource information, please visit www.oup.com/us/ofthepeople

▼ 1584
Walter Raleigh receives charter to establish colony at Roanoke

▼ 1585
First settlement at Roanoke established

▼ 1587
Second attempt to found colony at Roanoke

▼ 1590
English settlers at Roanoke have disappeared

▼ 1607
English establish permanent colony at Jamestown

▼ 1608
Samuel de Champlain establishes a fort at Quebec

▼ 1609
Henry Hudson arrives at New York, sailing for the Netherlands

▼ 1614
Dutch begin trading in Albany region
French settlers arrive in New France

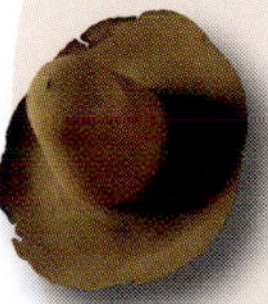

▼ 1621
Dutch West India Company established

▼ 1624
First Dutch families arrive at Manhattan

▼ 1648–1660s
Beaver Wars fought

▼ 1664
English take over New Amsterdam

CHAPTER 3

Common Threads 

>> After the failure at Roanoke, how were the English finally able to plant successful colonies?

>> Why did the Jamestown Colony almost fail, and why did the New England ones succeed almost immediately? Can the Chesapeake or New England experience be considered more "typical" of what would become the United States?

>> How did the gender and family orders differ in the Chesapeake and in New England, and what impact did gender and family have in shaping these societies?

>> What were the similarities and differences in each region's relations with Native Americans?

>> What role did religion play in shaping the Puritan colonies?

The English Come to Stay

1600–1660

AMERICAN PORTRAIT

>> The Adventures of John Rolfe

John Rolfe was an adventurer. In 1609, when Rolfe was 25, he and his wife set sail for the two-year-old English colony at Jamestown. Their ship was blown off course and wrecked off the island of Bermuda. It was not until a year later that Rolfe reached Virginia, having survived a mutiny and the death of his infant daughter. Rolfe's wife herself died shortly after their arrival at Jamestown (not only were the date and cause of her death lost to history but so was her name). Soon Rolfe was experimenting with tobacco, trying to find a strain that would produce a fragrant leaf in Virginia's soil. Walter Raleigh's men had introduced tobacco to England, where the addictive pleasures of smoking soon created a market. The English imported their tobacco from the Spanish West Indies, but with the founding of their colony at Jamestown, they hoped for their own source. Unfortunately, the variety grown by Virginia's Indians was "poore, weake, and of a byting taste." Rolfe tried planting West Indian tobacco seeds and, using a process of trial and error, produced a successful crop. By 1617, Virginians were exporting Rolfe's variety of tobacco to England. It was not as sweet as the West Indian product, but it was a great deal cheaper. Tobacco proved the economic salvation of Virginia, making many men and women rich and robbing others of their freedom. Like other foreign colonies, Virginia achieved prosperity by feeding European cravings. Tobacco was no more a necessity than other plantation crops such as sugar, coffee, and tea. Like them, it was merely a pleasurable and habit-forming taste.

Relations with the local Powhatan Indians were tense from the moment of the colonists' arrival. In the spring of 1613, the English captured Pocahontas, the favorite daughter of the chieftain Powhatan, and brought her to Jamestown. By summer, John Rolfe had fallen deeply in love with the 18-year-old princess. He asked permission of the English authorities to marry her, realizing that his countrymen would disapprove of his attachment to "one whose education hath been rude, her manners barbarous, her generation accursed." He thought people would gossip that he was marrying her just to satisfy his lust, but if that were the case, he reasoned, he "might satisfy such desire . . . with Christians more pleasing to the eye." He even feared that his love for Pocahontas was the work of the devil, and so he resolved to convert her to Christianity. In John Rolfe, the traditional ethnocentrism of the English was at war with love. Love won out. Yet the marriage was more than a triumph of two people in love: it also established an alliance between two peoples that brought an end to warfare.

In 1616, Rolfe took his wife and their young son to England, where Pocahontas adopted the dress of an English lady and even met the king and queen. The Virginia Company used her as a sort of walking advertisement for their colony. Her transformation suggested to the English that Indians could easily be "civilized." Before the ship that would take Rolfe and his wife back to Virginia could set sail, Pocahontas took ill and died. Only 31, John Rolfe had already buried two wives. By the time that Rolfe returned to Virginia, tobacco dominated the economy and tobacco-planting settlers encroached on the Powhatans' land. On the morning of March 22, 1622, the new leader of the Powhatan Confederacy, Opechancanough, orchestrated attacks on all the plantations along the James River. By the time they were finished, nearly one-third of all the Virginia colonists—women and children as well as men—had been killed. John Rolfe was one of the victims.

No images of John Rolfe exist. His wife Pocahontas and their son Thomas are depicted in this late-18th century portrait (whose authenticity, however, cannot be established).

John Rolfe had imagined that English and Indians could live together in harmony. He was wrong. Once he developed a marketable strain of tobacco, the English could not be stopped from turning Powhatan lands into tobacco fields. European demand for tobacco doomed not only the Indians who were driven from their homeland but also generations of European indentured servants and, eventually, African slaves. A new kind of society based on plantation slavery took shape. Rarely in history is one person so directly responsible for the demise of his own dreams.

OUTLINE

The First Chesapeake Colonies

In 1607, 20 years after the abandonment of the Roanoke Colony, the English returned to North America. Their nation was strong and unified, at the beginning of a rise to wealth and power that would carry it well into the twentieth century. The English, however, had learned little from their failure in Roanoke, and although their colony at Jamestown was better financed, it was poorly planned. A combination of unrealistic expectations, flawed leadership, troubled relations with the local Powhatan Indians, and lack of economic viability almost doomed the colony. The difference between survival and extinction was tobacco. With the development of this cash crop, for which there was demand in Europe, Virginia began to prosper. Once John Rolfe had developed a palatable strain of tobacco, the primary requirements were land and labor. The English settlers' desire for land led them into warfare with the Powhatans; their desire for cheap labor led them to import indentured servants, white and black, and African slaves.

Planning Virginia

When Queen Elizabeth died in 1603, she was succeeded by King James I, who signed a treaty with Spain, ending decades of warfare. With peace established between the English and Spanish, all those who had lived off privateering and warfare had to look for another source of income, from legitimate trade. They joined with old advocates of colonization such as Richard Hakluyt to establish new colonies in North America. In 1606, James granted charters to two groups of English merchants and military men, one in London and the other in Plymouth. The Plymouth group was permitted to colonize New England, and the Londoners the Chesapeake region. Each operation was chartered as a private company, which would raise money from shareholders and finance, populate, and regulate each charter colony that it established. The Virginia Company used this structure to finance its colony, raising more money from wealthy London merchants than for any other colonial venture. Although both the Virginia and Plymouth companies reported to a Royal Council, these ventures were fundamentally private operations, subject to little governmental control.

Both the Virginia and Plymouth companies eventually founded North American colonies, but the Virginia Company (named in honor of the nation's recently deceased unmarried queen) met with success first. Just before Christmas 1606, the Virginia Company of London sent out three ships under the leadership of Captain Christopher Newport, a one-legged veteran Atlantic explorer. When the ships arrived at Virginia on April 26, 1607, and the company's sealed orders were opened, the 104 colonists learned that they were to be governed by a council of seven men. Unfortunately, two of them, Edward Maria Wingfield, an original investor in the company but "an arrogant man of no special capacity," and Captain John Smith, a 27-year-old

The Fort at Jamestown, as It May Have Appeared in 1607 The settlement at Jamestown was surrounded by a palisade, a high wooden fence.

equally arrogant but considerably more capable soldier of fortune, already despised each other, and Smith had been put under arrest early in the voyage. By the end of the summer, another council member had been executed because he was a double agent, working simultaneously for the Spanish. The early years of the new colony at Jamestown were marked by internal wrangling. Soon external conflict developed as well, as the colonists antagonized their Indian hosts. Indeed, almost everything that could go wrong did.

The English hoped to find a land like Mexico that would provide them with gold and less glamorous raw materials. Whatever limited manufacturing was needed could be performed either by English criminals, who were sent over to work as their punishment, or by indentured servants, English men and women drawn from the lowest ranks of society who agreed to work for a set period of time to pay their transportation expenses. The colonists expected to strike up a trade with the local Indians, who would be the primary suppliers of food.

The Company planned to get the colony up and running within seven years. During that period all the colonists would work for the Company, which would give them food and shelter. At the end of that period, all of the colonists would receive grants of land. The Company evidently thought that such a colony would need a great deal of direction, for more than one-third of the original settlers were gentlemen, that is, members of the elite. In its first years, the proportion of elite in Jamestown's population was six times higher than it was in England.

The Company also sent skilled laborers, many with skills for which there was little use in the new colony, such as tailors, goldsmiths, and a perfumer. Some were thought necessary for the upkeep of the gentlemen. Others were supposed to work with the gold and precious gems the colonists hoped to find. Farmers and ordinary laborers, on the other hand, were in short supply.

> **"This was that time, which still to this day we called the starving time; it were too vile to say, and scarce to be beleeved, what we endured: but the occasion was our owne, for want of providence, industrie and government, and not the barrennesse and defect of the Countrie, . . ."**
>
> CAPTAIN JOHN SMITH

Starving Times

Poor planning and bad luck placed the colonists on swampy ground with bad water. The concentrations of salt in the James River were high enough to poison those who drank the water. In addition, in summer the water became a breeding ground for the microorganisms that cause typhoid and dysentery. Some historians have argued that these diseases left the survivors too weak to plant food, while others note that many of the healthy seemed to prefer prospecting for gold. Whatever the reason, the colonists depended on the resentful Powhatans for food. Malnutrition and even starvation made the effects of disease worse. This combination of factors, along with conflicts with the Powhatan Indians, led to appallingly high mortality rates. By September 1607, half of the 104 Jamestown colonists were dead, and by the next spring only 38 were still alive. Recent archeological excavations at Jamestown have uncovered the graves of four gentlemen who died that first summer,

buried within the fort so that the Powhatans would not see how many of the English had died.

Although the Company sent over more colonists, they continued to die off at extraordinary rates. As late as 1616, the English population was only 350, although more than five times that number had emigrated from England (see Table 3–1).

Most who died were victims of malnutrition and disease. The lack of food was so great that over the winter of 1609–1610, the inhabitants were reduced to eating roots, acorns, and even human excrement. Archeological evidence shows that men and women butchered their own dogs and cats. One man killed his pregnant wife,

 **Table 3–1** English Population of Virginia, 1607–1640

Population in Virginia Colony	Immigration to Virginia Colony
104 (April 1607)	104 (April 1607)
38 (Jan. 1608)	
	120 (Jan. 1608, 1st supply)
130 (Sept. 1608)	
	70 (Sept. 1608, 2nd supply)
200 (late Sept. 1608)	
100 (spring 1609)	
	300 (Fall 1609, 3rd supply)
	540 (1610)
450 (April 1611)	
	660 (1611)
682 (Jan. 1612)	
350 (Jan. 1613)	
	45 (1613–1616)
351 (1616)	
600 (Dec. 1618)	
	900 (1618–1620)
887 (Mar. 1620)	
	1051 (1620–1621)
943 (Mar. 1621)	
	1580 (1621–1622)
1240 (Mar. 1622)	
	1935 (1622–1623)
1241 (April 1623)	
	1646 (1623–1624)
1275 (Feb. 1624)	
1210 (1625)	
	9000 (1625–1634)
4914 (1634)	
	6000 (1635–1640)
8100 (1640)	total: 23,951

Source: Data from Carville Earle, *Geographical Inquiry and American Historical Problems* (Stanford: Stanford University Press, 1992) and Virginia Bernhard, "Men, Women, and Children at Jamestown: Population and Gender in Early Virginia, 1607–1610," *Journal of Southern History*, LVIII (1992).

Note: Although about 24,000 men and women immigrated to Virginia between 1607 and 1640, in 1640 the population stood at only 8,100. Most of the inhabitants fell victim to disease, although the Indian uprising of 1622 took 347 lives.

ripped the fetus from her womb, then salted his wife's corpse and had it half eaten before his crime was discovered.

For centuries this starvation has perplexed historians. The land was fertile and abounded with game, and the James River was teeming with fish. The colonists should have been able to raise enough to keep themselves alive. Captain John Smith blamed the starvation on the laziness of the colonists, who preferred searching for riches to planting grain. When he served as president of the council from 1608 to 1609, only a handful of colonists died. He moved some of the colonists away from Jamestown's lethal water supply, and he bullied the Powhatans into giving the English some food, leaving the women who had raised it weeping as they contemplated their own families' hunger. He imposed military-style discipline and required all the colonists to work four hours a day. Drought, disease, and malnutrition, however, were probably more to blame than laziness. Moreover, seeing so many die around them only increased survivors' sense of despair. They probably suffered from depression.

Decisions by the leadership made the plight worse. John Smith, an effective but hated disciplinarian, returned to England in 1609 after a gunpowder injury. The new rulers unwisely split up the settlement, sending a group of men down the James River to establish a fort and two other parties to establish settlements in spots already inhabited by Indians. In both cases the English were attacked and suffered heavy losses. The colonists who survived were "distracted and forlorn," in many ways resembling modern prisoners of war. They had begun to abandon the colony when they were stopped by the arrival of Lord De La Warr, the new governor who came to impose harsh martial law.

Troubled Relations with the Powhatans

In Virginia, the English encountered one of the most powerful Indian tribes on the continent, the Powhatans, a confederacy of Algonquian tribes who, under their chieftain Powhatan, were bringing less powerful Algonquians under their control. The English described him as an emperor who "ruleth over many kings." At the time Powhatan's confederacy included about 20,000 Indians, divided into about three dozen tribes. Each group, English and Indian, tried at first to get the other to accept the status of an allied but subordinate tribe. At one point, the English pushed the aging Powhatan down to the ground and put a fake crown on his head, imitating the ceremonies in which feudal princes pledged allegiance to a king. For his part, Powhatan held John Smith captive and tried to bully him and other English leaders into acknowledging his supremacy. In the context of these political maneuverings, English bullying sometimes yielded food from the Indians, but it also led to increased animosity, as did English settlement on Indian land.

Powhatan's Mantle This deerskin mantle, decorated with seashells, is supposed to have belonged to the great leader of the Powhatan confederacy.

English leadership also made the tensions between the two peoples worse. Some of the early English leaders had hoped for a biracial society in which the Native Americans would become loyal subjects and trading

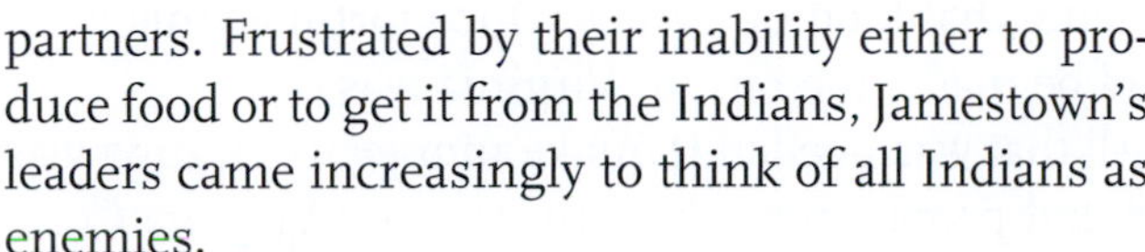

Powhatan and English Dwellings These are reconstructions of typical Powhatan Indian and English homes, ca. 1607. Both are dark and small.

partners. Frustrated by their inability either to produce food or to get it from the Indians, Jamestown's leaders came increasingly to think of all Indians as enemies.

No sooner had Lord De La Warr arrived than he set out to subjugate the Indians. He ordered Powhatan to return English captives. When Powhatan refused, De La Warr ordered an attack on an Indian village. The English killed about 75 of the inhabitants, burned the town and its cornfields, and took as captives the wife of a chieftain and her children. As the English sailed back to Jamestown, they threw the children overboard and shot them as they swam in the water. This was the opening battle of the First Anglo-Powhatan War, the first in a series of three conflicts between 1610 and 1646. The first ended in 1614, when the marriage between Pocahontas and John Rolfe cemented a truce. In permitting his daughter to marry an Englishman, Powhatan was adapting a means he had used to establish his powerful confederacy. He himself had an unusually large number of wives, selected from throughout his realm, as a means of tightening his dominion. Each of Powhatan's wives represented an important link between Powhatan's tribe and her own. After each of his wives had borne him a child, she and the child were sent back to her home village, allowing Powhatan to maintain a presence there. Sometimes, Powhatan also appointed his own son or son-in-law as chief of a village, bringing the village more tightly under his control and undermining the customary right of Algonquian women to participate in the selection of leaders. By tradition, chiefs, or *werowances,* were the kinsmen of *werowansqua* (tribal queens). At the same time that Powhatan was consolidating his personal leadership, he was enhancing patriarchal authority in the tribes he controlled.

The marriage of John Rolfe and Pocahontas ushered in a brief period of peace. The English were so pleased with the new alliance that they soon asked for another one of Powhatan's daughters as a bride for one of their councilors. Powhatan refused, fearing that, as with Pocahontas, he would lose a daughter rather than gain a powerful and loyal English son-in-law. Powhatan had failed in his objective of turning the English into his vassals.

Pocahontas Pocahontas, also known to the Powhatans as Matoaka and to the English as Rebecca, wore English dress when she accompanied her English husband John Rolfe to England.

Toward a New Political Economy

The tide finally turned against the Powhatans, not so much because of diplomacy or the politics of marriage but because the English finally found a way to make money in Virginia. John Rolfe's improved strain of tobacco found a ready market in England, which stimulated the Virginia economy, transforming the colony almost overnight into a different sort of society than the one the Virginia Company had planned. Within three years of Rolfe's first cargo, Virginia was shipping 50,000 pounds of tobacco to England per year. Suddenly Virginia experienced an economic boom. By 1619, a man working by himself was making £200 in one crop, and a man with six indentured servants could make £1,000. Only the nobility was accustomed to seeing that kind of money. Once fortunes this large could be made, the race to Virginia was on.

All that was needed to make money in Virginia was land and people to work it. In 1616 the Virginia Company, which had plenty of land but no money, offered land as dividends to its stockholders. Moreover, those already living in Virginia were given land, and anyone who came over (or brought another person over) was to be granted 50 acres a head (called a headright). The Company was taking an important step in the direction of private enterprise, away from the corporate, company-directed economy of the early years. The leadership of the colony was also generous in its grants to itself, laying the basis for its own wealth and power. It became far easier to obtain land in Virginia than in England.

As another means of attracting settlers, the Company replaced martial law with English common law, which guaranteed the colonists all the rights of the English people. The colonists were also granted greater rights to self-government than were enjoyed by those who lived in England at the time. The first elected representative government in the New World, the Virginia House of Burgesses (renamed the General Assembly after the American Revolution), met in Jamestown on July 30, 1619.

These inducements attracted 3,500 settlers to Virginia in three years, three times as many as had come in the past ten years. By accident more than planning, Virginia had found the formula for a successful English colony. It was a model that all the other colonies generally followed: colonists would have to be offered greater opportunities to make money and greater rights of self-government than they had at home. These changes came too late, however, to rescue the Virginia Company, which went bankrupt in 1624. King James I dissolved the Company and turned Virginia into a royal colony under direct royal control.

Toward the Destruction of the Powhatans

As the new colonists spread out, establishing private plantations, English settlers claimed all the Indians' prime farmland on both sides of the James River and began to move up the river's tributaries (see Map 3–1). At the same time, the Powhatans became increasingly dependent on English goods such as metal tools. Moreover, as the English population began to grow its own food, it had less need of Indian food, the only commodity the Indians had to trade. The Indians slowly accumulated a debt to the English and lost their economic independence.

After Powhatan died, his more militant brother, Opechancanough, decided to get rid of the English interlopers. On the morning of March 22, 1622, the Indians struck at all the plantations along the James River. By the time they were finished, one-third of the colonists had been killed, including John Rolfe. The Second Anglo-Powhatan War, which continued for another ten years, had begun. This war marked a turning point in English policy. Although some of the English recognized that the Indian attack had been caused by "our own perfidiouse dealing," most decided that the Indians were untrustworthy and incapable of being converted to the English way of life. Therefore, a policy of extermination was justified. Some were almost happy that the Indians had attacked; John Smith concluded that the massacre "will be good for the Plantation, because now we have just cause to destroy them by all meanes possible." Until this point, the English had claimed only land the Indians were not farming. Now they seized territory the Indians had cleared and planted. In only 15 years' time, the English and Indians in Virginia had become implacable enemies.

Map 3–1 English Encroachments on Indian Land, 1613–1652 After John Rolfe's development of a marketable strain of tobacco, the English spread out through the Chesapeake region, encroaching steadily on Indian land. Tobacco planters preferred land along the rivers, for casks filled with tobacco bound for England were more easily transported by ship. *Frederic Gleach,* Powhatan's World and Colonial Virginia *(Lincoln: University of Nebraska Press, 1997), and James Horn,* Adapting to a New World: English Society in the Seventeenth-Century Chesapeake *(Chapel Hill: University of North Carolina Press, 1994).*

Indian resistance made the English more determined to stay, and with the tobacco economy booming, settlers continued to pour into Virginia. They spread across the Chesapeake to the Eastern Shore and as far north as the Potomac River. The aged Opechancanough, determined to make one final push, struck again on April 18, 1644, killing 400 English people and taking many prisoners.

The Third Anglo-Powhatan War ended, however, in the Indians' total defeat two years later. Opechancanough was seized and killed. The English took complete possession of the land between the James and York rivers. Henceforth, no Indian was allowed to enter this territory without wearing a special jacket indicating that he was bringing a message from the chief *werowance*. Any English person who gave shelter to an Indian without permission was put to death. The land north of the York River was to be reserved for the Indians, making it the first American Indian reservation. In a few years' time, English settlers moved into that region, too. It was not the last time that the English settlers would break a treaty with the Indians.

A New Colony in Maryland

Virginia's original plan to make money from trading with the local Indians was not entirely forgotten. When tobacco prices dipped in the 1620s trade became attractive once again. By the late 1620s, an outpost had been established at the northern end of Chesapeake Bay to obtain beaver furs from the Susquehannocks. Sir George Calvert, the first Lord Baltimore and a Catholic, saw the commercial potential of this region and in 1632 persuaded King Charles I, a Catholic sympathizer, to grant him the land north of the Potomac and south of the Delaware that was "not yet cultivated and planted." This territory became Maryland, the first proprietary colony, that is, a colony that was owned literally by an individual and his heirs. (Virginia was originally a charter colony, one that was held by a group of private shareholders. Unlike royal colonies, in charter and proprietary colonies, the English Crown turned over both financing and management to the shareholders or proprietors.) Maryland, named after the Catholic queen of England, remained the hereditary possession of the Calvert family until 1689.

As the first proprietary colony, Maryland established a pattern for subsequent proprietorships. The proprietor had extensive powers to grant land and make laws by himself, but perhaps because Calvert knew he would have to compete for settlers with Virginia, which already had a representative government, he agreed to the establishment of a representative assembly. In 1649 that assembly passed the Act of Toleration, which said that no one would be "compelled to the beliefe or exercise of any other Religion against his or her consent." Even though religious toleration was extended only to those who professed a belief in Jesus Christ, Maryland was among the most tolerant places in the world at that time. Moreover, this right was explicitly extended to women as well as men. (This experiment in religious toleration came to an end, however, in 1689, when Coode's Rebellion overthrew the proprietor, making Maryland a royal colony and, in 1702, establishing the Anglican Church. See Chapter 4.)

Although it would be a number of decades before Maryland's population increased substantially, the familiar political economy emerged early. As in Virginia, attracting colonists to the New World required greater opportunities and freedoms—of self-government and of religion—than they enjoyed in England. Throughout the period of conflict with the Powhatan Confederacy, the booming tobacco economy drew settlers to Virginia and, after about 1650, to Maryland as well. Although they had separate governments, Virginia and Maryland had similar political economies, based on tobacco. The defeat of the Indians made more land in the Chesapeake region available for cultivation; the colonies needed only people to work it.

The Political Economy of Slavery Emerges

Chesapeake society in the first half of the seventeenth century was shaped by four forces: weak government, the market for tobacco, the availability of land, and the need for labor. Because government was weak, the forces of plantation agriculture were unchecked, and the profit motive operated without restraint. Those who could take advantage of these opportunities—male and female both—profited wildly, while the poor, both white and African, were without defense. Artificial distinctions such as social status counted for little in comparison to willpower, physical strength, and ruthlessness. Even gender roles were undermined as women worked in the fields and wealthy widows controlled large estates. In this environment the political economy of slavery took root.

> "And I have nothing to comfort me, nor is there nothing to be gotten here but sickness and death. . . . I have nothing at all—no, not a shirt to my back but two rags, nor clothes but one poor suit, nor but one pair of shoes, but one pair of stockings, but one cap. . . ."
>
> RICHARD FRETHORNE,
> letter to his parents in England, 1623

The Problem of a Labor Supply

Once the crises of the early years had passed, the Chesapeake's greatest problem was securing laborers to produce tobacco. As soon as John Rolfe brought in his first successful crop, the Virginia governor began pressing England to send him its poor. The Virginia Company also encouraged the emigration of women, for the young colony was primarily male. No matter how many colonists came, however, the demand for labor always outstripped the supply. By 1660, 50,000 Britons, mostly single men in their 20s, had migrated to the Chesapeake, but the population was still only a little over 35,000. Because of the poor water supply and disease, the death rate remained extraordinarily high.

The profits from tobacco were so great and the risk of death so high that landowners squeezed out every penny of profit as quickly as they could. Those who obtained land and servants to work it could become rich overnight. Colonial officials, including members of the legislature, took advantage of their positions and discovered a variety of ways to make themselves wealthy, from claiming vast tracts of land to assessing high fees for all sorts of transactions. Great wealth, however, could be achieved only by the labor of others. The demand for labor was almost insatiable. Perhaps 90 percent of those who migrated to the Chesapeake in the seventeenth century came as servants, and half died before completing their term of service. Servants were worked to the point of death. In England, custom and law both afforded servants some basic protections, but in Virginia, working conditions were brutal. In 1623, Richard Frethorne, a young servant, wrote back to his parents in England complaining about life in Virginia. "With weeping tears," he begged them to send food. "We must work early and late for a mess of water gruel and a mouthful of bread and beef."

Servants might be beaten so severely that they died, or they might find their indentures (the contract that bound them to service for a period of usually seven years) sold from one master to another. Their treatment was brutal, and they found little protection from the Virginia or Maryland courts. They were not, in fact, slaves. They would become free if they outlived their period of indenture; they retained all of the rights of English people, and their servitude was not hereditary. But, they were far worse off than servants in England.

The Origins of Slavery in the Chesapeake

Other New World plantation societies where labor was in short supply had already turned to slavery, so it was probably only a matter of time until the Chesapeake did so as well. Historians do not know precisely when slavery was first practiced

AMERICA AND THE WORLD

>> Christian Slaves in Muslim Africa

At the same time that Europeans were enslaving Africans and transporting them to the New World to labor on plantations, North Africans were carrying on a vigorous trade in European slaves. Between 1500 and 1800, the North African Barbary States, which were part of the Ottoman Empire, captured and sold as many as 1.25 million Europeans and sold them as slaves to other North Africans. This slave trade was an extension of the near-constant state of war between the Ottoman and Hapsburg empires. International law held that enemies captured in war could be enslaved, and that enslavement was preferable to death. This was the rationale used to justify enslavement, even when the objective of the war itself was to obtain slaves.

Indeed, most of the European slaves captured by North Africans were used as galley slaves in corsairs, pirate ships that preyed upon commercial traffic in the Mediterranean and that raided the coastal regions of southern Europe. In other words, North Africans needed slaves in order to obtain more slaves. The mortality rate was so high—one scholar has estimated that it was as high as 20 percent a year—that the demand for fresh slaves was almost insatiable.

The treatment of slaves, particularly in the galleys, was brutal. There, as many as five men would be chained together at each oar of the corsair. They would row night and day, for days on end, always chained, and half-naked and with no protection from the elements, so that their "flesh is burned off their backs." There was enough slack in the chain that each oarsman could stumble over his neighbors to make it to the end of the bench, where there was an opening in the hull of the ship where they could relieve themselves. But often the galley slaves were too exhausted or depressed even to do that, and as a result, the stench in the galleys—from sweat and human waste—was unimaginable.

The corsairs preyed not only on ships at sea but also along the coastlines. The Mediterranean islands such as Sardinia and Sicily were particularly vulnerable, but so also were coastal Italy and Spain. In some regions, whole villages were abandoned. Such was the case in large por-

tions of the Italian peninsula, where the governments were too weak to protect their citizens and instead ordered them to move to the interior. Although most of the Christian slaves came from southern Europe, North African slaving expeditions ranged as far as the North Atlantic too, not only seizing British ships but also raiding along the coasts of Ireland, Cornwall, and Devon, ultimately seizing perhaps 7,000–9,000 British men, women, and children.

Almost all the captives seized from ships were male, but when raiders descended upon European communities, they took women and children as well. Still, the vast majority of European slaves—perhaps 95 percent—were male. In addition to serving as galley slaves, they worked primarily in heavy construction. Some few became house servants. Europeans believed that some of the men, particularly young ones, were turned into male prostitutes and sexual slaves. While it is true that, unlike Europe at the same time, North African cities had vibrant homosexual cultures, it is hard to know how widespread the practice of sexual enslavement was. In fact, some of the best-known homosexual men in North Africa were Europeans; quite possibly, they had voluntarily migrated to North Africa, attracted by a culture they found more hospitable.

While the number of Europeans enslaved by North Africans is just a fraction of the number of Africans transported to the Americas, the Muslim trade in Europeans provides a context for the African slave trade. First, both slave trades developed at the same time, in an era in which captives of war were often enslaved. Second, the basis for both slave trades was ethnic and religious, not racial. Only later was the African slave trade justified in racial terms. And the African slave trade developed differently in another way: North Africans were willing to ransom back Europeans to their families or nations and, in fact, often seized wealthy Europeans in the hope of selling them back for huge sums. Europeans, however, never ransomed Africans. Once Africans were seized by European slave traders, they lost any hope of ever returning to their native lands. Finally, the trade in Europeans was essentially a premodern economic enterprise, neither requiring much capital nor producing much wealth. The trade in Africans, however, required significant capital investment and consequently required, as well, efficient organization. Plantation slavery was a modern business enterprise, which developed new methods of turning human beings into property.

in the Chesapeake colonies, but Africans first arrived in Virginia in 1619, when a Dutch ship sailing off course sold its cargo of "twenty Negars" to the Virginians. It is not clear, however, if these Africans were indentured servants or lifelong slaves. As long as life expectancy was low, it was more profitable for a planter to purchase an indentured servant for a period of seven years than a slave for life. Not until life expectancy improved toward the end of the seventeenth century were significant numbers of African slaves imported into the Chesapeake.

All of the English plantation colonies followed the same pattern in making the transition from white servitude to African slavery. The shift toward African slavery was quick in some places and slow in others; in Virginia, it took about three-quarters of a century. This transition was made everywhere without debate. The primary factors dictating how quickly English colonists adopted African slavery were the need for plantation laborers and the availability of African slaves at a good price. By the time the English began to import African slaves into their colonies in the seventeenth century, the Spanish and Portuguese had been using enslaved Africans as plantation laborers for well over a century. The English were entering into a global economy that had already come to rely upon slave labor.

To the extent that there was any discussion at all about the justice of slavery, the English claimed that slavery was an appropriate punishment for certain crimes and for prisoners taken in just wars. No white people were ever enslaved in the English colonies, however. It was a practice reserved for "strangers," primarily foreigners of a non-Christian religion. Still, all the British colonies eventually practiced slavery, and it became critical to plantation economies. African slaves were even brought back to the British Islands, and by the middle of the eighteenth century, 2 percent of London's population was African.

Even before they had substantial contact with African people, the English and other northern Europeans probably harbored prejudice against dark-skinned people. By the second half of the sixteenth century, the English were depicting Africans in derogatory terms. They said that Africans were unattractive, with "dispositions most savage and brutish," a "people of beastly living" who "contract no matrimonie, neither have respect to chastity." Northern Europeans considered African women particularly monstrous, sexually promiscuous, and neglectful of their children. One sixteenth-century traveler to Guinea thought that African men and women were almost indistinguishable. They "goe so alike, that one cannot know a man from a woman but by their breastes, which in the most part be very foule and long, hanging down like the udder of a goate." Although these views were not used to justify slavery, they formed the basis for the racism that would develop along with the slave system.

During the seventeenth century, African slavery and white and African servitude existed side by side, and laws to enforce slavery appeared piecemeal. The Chesapeake was a society with slaves, but it was still not a slave society. The first clear evidence of enslavement of Africans in the Chesapeake dates to 1639, when the Maryland Assembly passed a law guaranteeing "all the Inhabitants of this Province being Christians (Slaves excepted)" all the rights and liberties of "any natural born subject of England." The first Virginia law recognizing slavery, passed in 1661, said that any English servant who ran away with an African would have to serve additional time not only for himself but for the African as well. Historians presume that such Africans were already slaves for life and hence were incapable of serving any additional time.

Such laws and legal proceedings show the great familiarity that existed between white and black servants. Slaves and white servants worked together, enjoyed their leisure together, had sexual relations with each other, and ran away together. As late as 1680, most of the labor on plantations was still being performed by white indentured servants. There is no evidence that they were kept separate from Africans by law or inclination.

As long as the black population remained small, the color line was blurry. Not until late in the seventeenth century were laws passed that restricted free African Americans. In fact, in 1660, Anthony Johnson, an African who had arrived in Virginia as a servant in 1621, owned both land and African slaves. In the 40 years that he had been in Virginia, slavery had become institutionalized and recognized by the law, but laws separating the races had yet to be enacted.

Gender and the Social Order in the Chesapeake

The founders of England's New World colonies hoped to replicate the social order they had known at home. For that reason, as early as 1619, the Virginia Company began to bring single women to the colony to become brides of the unmarried planters. As in England, it was expected that men would perform all the "outside" labor, including planting, farming, and tending large farm animals. Women would do all the "inside" work, including preserving and preparing food, spinning and weaving, making and repairing clothing, and gardening. In English society, a farmer's wife was not simply a man's sexual partner and companion; she was also the mistress of the household economy, performing work vital to its success. Both men and women were vital to the social and economic order that the English wanted to create in the Chesapeake.

However, the powerful tobacco economy transformed both the economy and society of the New World. With profits from tobacco so high, women went directly into the tobacco fields instead of the kitchen. When children were born, as soon as they could work, they were in the fields, too. Only when a man became wealthy did he hire a servant—often a woman—to replace his wife in the fields. As a result, for many years, Virginia society lacked the "comforts of home" that women produced, such as prepared food, homemade clothing, and even soap. Tobacco was everything.

The circumstances of colonial society weakened patriarchal controls. Chesapeake governments tried—but failed—to control immigrant women, insisting, for example, that a woman receive government permission before marrying, and prosecuting for slander women who spoke out against the government or their neighbors. But government in the Chesapeake was relatively weak, and, far from their own fathers, women in the Chesapeake found themselves unexpectedly liberated from traditional restrictions.

Although women without the protection of fathers were certainly vulnerable to exploitation in seventeenth-century plantation societies, where men outnumbered women three or four to one, women often found themselves in a position of relative power. Local governments struggled to impose order by prosecuting women for adultery, fornication, and giving birth to bastard children. The public, however, was more tolerant of sexual misconduct than government officials. When the widow Alice Boise and Captain William Epes kept a roomful of drunken partygoers awake most of the night with their "great bussleing and juggling" on the bed, they were not prosecuted for fornication. Instead, the man who gossiped about their nighttime activities was tried for slander. Similarly, when a ship's captain was executed for having sex with a boy on his ship (one of five recorded executions for homosexual activity in the colonial period), the protests were so widespread that the protesters themselves were punished.

The first generation of women to immigrate to the Chesapeake region married relatively late—in their mid-20s. Many had to wait out their periods of service until they could marry. As a result, they had relatively few children, and it was many decades before Chesapeake society reproduced itself naturally. With disease taking a huge toll, perhaps half of all children born in the colony died in infancy, and one marriage partner was also likely to die within seven years of marriage. At least until 1680 or so, to be a widow, widower, or orphan was the normal state of affairs. In such a society, widows who inherited their husbands' possessions were powerful and in demand on the marriage market. Children, however, were especially vulnerable, often losing their inheritances to a stepparent.

A Bible Commonwealth in the New England Wilderness

In 1620, 13 years after the founding of the Virginia Colony, England planted another permanent North American colony at Plymouth, and nine years after that, one at Massachusetts Bay. In many ways the Virginia and Massachusetts colonies could not have been more different. The primary impetus behind the Massachusetts settlement was religious. Both the Pilgrims at Plymouth and the much more numerous Puritans at Massachusetts Bay moved to New England to escape persecution and to establish new communities based on God's law as they understood it. The Puritans and Pilgrims were middle class, and their ventures were well financed and capably planned. The environment was much healthier than that of the Chesapeake, and the population reproduced itself rapidly. In addition, relations with the Indians were better than in the Chesapeake. Nonetheless, the Puritan movement was a product of the same consolidation and growth of national states in Europe and the expansion of commerce that led to the European exploration of the New World.

> **"I shall . . . begin with a combination made by them before they came ashore; being the first foundation of their government in this place. Occasioned partly by the discontented and mutinous speeches that some of the strangers amongst them had let fall from them in the ship: That when they came ashore they would use their own liberty, for none had power to command them, the patent they had being for Virginia and not for New England, which belonged to another government, with which the Virginia Company had nothing to do. And partly that such an act by them done, this their condition considered, might be as firm as any patent and in some respects more sure."**
>
> WILLIAM BRADFORD,
> writing about the origins of the Mayflower Compact in *Of Plymouth Plantation*

The English Origins of the Puritan Movement

In Europe during the sixteenth century, ordinary people and powerful monarchs had vastly different reasons for abandoning the Roman Catholic Church in favor of one of the new Protestant churches. In England, these differing motives led to 130 years of conflict, including a revolution and massive religious persecution. In the 1530s, Henry VIII established his own state religion in England, the Church of England, for political rather than for pious reasons. After many years of marriage to Catherine of Aragon, the daughter of Isabel and Fernando, Henry still did not have a male heir. With one of Catherine's ladies-in-waiting, Anne Boleyn, already pregnant, Henry pressed the pope for an annulment of his marriage to Catherine. In 1533, the pope refused the annulment, and Henry removed the Catholic Church as the established religion of England, replacing it with his own Church of England. An added bonus for Henry came from the confiscation of Catholic Church lands, which he redistributed to members of the English nobility in return for their loyalty. In one move, Henry eliminated a powerful political rival, the Roman Catholic Church, from his domain, and he consolidated his rule over his nobility. Henry's replacement of the Catholic Church did not bring stability, however. His successors alternated between adherence to Protestantism and persecution of Catholics, and support of Catholicism and persecution of Protestants. Under the reign of Catherine's daughter Mary, hundreds of Protestants left the country to avoid being burned at the stake.

When Mary's Protestant sister, Elizabeth I, ascended the throne, these exiles returned, having picked up the Calvinist doctrine of predestination on the continent. John Calvin, the Swiss Protestant reformer, insisted that even before people were born, God foreordained "to some eternal life and to some eternal damnation." Although the Church of England adopted Calvin's doctrine of predestination, it never held to it thoroughly enough or followed through on other reforms well enough to please the Puritans, those who desired further reforms. And because the monarchs viewed challenges to the state religion as challenges to the state itself, religious dissenters were frequently persecuted for their beliefs.

What Did the Puritans Believe?

Like all Christians, Puritans believed that humanity was guilty of the original sin committed by Adam and Eve when they disobeyed God in the Garden of Eden. They believed that God's son, Jesus Christ, had given his life to pay (or atone) for the original sin, and that as a consequence, all faithful Christians would be forgiven their sins and admitted to heaven after they died. Calvinism differed from other Christian religions primarily in insisting that there was nothing that men or women could do to guarantee that God would give them the faith, by an act of "grace," that would save them from eternal punishment in hell.

Protestants rejected the hierarchy of the Catholic Church, maintaining that the relationship between God and humanity was direct, "unmediated." Because every person had direct access to the inspired word of God through the Bible, Protestants promoted literacy and translating the Bible into modern languages. As Calvinists, Puritans wanted to "purify" the Church of England of all remnants of Catholicism. Anglicans had reduced the number of sacraments; Puritans wanted to eliminate them all. Anglicans retained some church rituals and a church hierarchy (but not the pope); Puritans rejected all rituals and all priestly hierarchy.

Finally, Anglicans had increasingly come to think that believing Christians could earn their way to heaven by good works, a doctrine that the Puritans labeled Arminianism. Puritans, in contrast, believed that salvation was the free gift of God and that human beings could not force his hand. All that individuals could do was to prepare for grace, by reading and studying the Bible, so that they understood God's plan, and by attempting to live as good a life as they could in the meantime. Because they could never know for certain whether they had been saved, Puritans always lived with anxiety.

Puritanism contained a powerful tension between intellect and emotion. On the one hand, Puritanism was a highly rational religion. It required all of its followers to read and study the Bible, as well as to listen to long sermons that explored fine points of theology. As a result, Puritanism led to high rates of literacy among its followers, both male and female. On the other hand, Puritans believed that no amount of book learning could get a person into heaven and that saving grace was as much a matter of the heart as of the mind. Throughout its history, the Puritan movement struggled to contain this tension, as some of its believers moved toward a more fully rational religion and others abandoned book learning for emotion.

Puritans believed that church membership was only for those who could demonstrate that they were saved. As they were persecuted for their faith, they came to believe that, like the Israelites of old, they were God's chosen people, that they had a covenant or agreement with God, and that if they did his will, he would make them prosper.

The Puritans first attempted to reform the Church of England. Once it became evident to them that the Church of England would resist further reformation and would continue moving away from the Calvinist principle of predestination, some Puritans began to make other plans.

The Pilgrim Colony at Plymouth

The first Puritan colony in North America was established in 1620 at Plymouth, by a group of Puritans known as the Pilgrims, Separatists who had given up all hope of reforming the Church of England. The Pilgrims had already moved to Holland, thinking its Calvinist religion would offer them a better home. It was hard for the Pilgrims to fit themselves into Holland's highly structured economy, however, and they found their children seduced from strict religion by "the manifold temptations of the place."

By 1620 the Pilgrims were ready to accept the Virginia Company of London's offer of land in America for any English people who would pay their own way. With the colony at Jamestown floundering, the Company was looking for other opportunities for profit. To that end, the Company filled the two ships in the expedition, the *Mayflower* and the *Speedwell,* with non-Pilgrims (known as the "Strangers") who were willing to pay their own way, Separatists who had not gone to Holland, as well as Pilgrims.

The *Speedwell* leaked so badly it turned back, but the *Mayflower* arrived at Plymouth, Massachusetts, in November 1620, far north of its destination and outside the jurisdiction of the Virginia Company. Because the Pilgrims had landed in territory that had no legal claim and no lawful government, 41 of the adult men on board signed a document known as the Mayflower Compact before disembarking. The men bound themselves into a "Civil Body Politic" to make laws and govern the colony and also to recognize the authority of the governor. While the Compact provided a legal basis for government until the colony was annexed by Massachusetts Bay in 1691, it would be a mistake to see the document as wholly democratic. Some of the Strangers had been talking about mutiny, so the Pilgrims wanted to make their government secure.

Only one of the 102 passengers had died en route, but only half of the party survived the harsh first winter. Years later the second governor, William Bradford, remembered the Pilgrims' arrival in a strange land and their early ordeals. The Indians, he claimed, were "savage barbarians . . . readier to fill their sides full of arrows than otherwise." And their new home was "a hideous and desolate wilderness, full of wild beasts and wild men."

In fact, the Plymouth Colony would never have survived had it not been for the assistance of friendly Indians. Like the French in New France and in contrast to the English at Jamestown, the Pilgrims were able to establish diplomatic relations both because they were better diplomats and because the local Indians needed foreign allies. Until shortly before the Pilgrims' arrival, Plymouth Bay had been inhabited by as many as 2,000 Indians, with ten times as many in the surrounding region. Then European fishermen and traders introduced some fatal disease—a recent theory suggests it was viral hepatitis, spread by spoiled food—which was carried as far as the trading network reached and carried off 90 percent of the population. Indians "died in heapes as they lay in their houses." Former villages were filled with the skulls and bones of the unburied dead. So recently had Patuxet and Pokanoket Indians inhabited the region that the Pilgrims were able to supplement their meager supplies by rummaging Indian graves, homes, and hidden stores of grain.

The world was vastly changed for those Native Americans who survived. Squanto, a Patuxet warrior, had spent the plague years in Europe, having been kidnapped by an English ship's captain. In London, Squanto praised the virtues of his native land in the hopes that the English would take him home. Much like Don Luís de Velasco (see Chapter 2), once back in Massachusetts, Squanto abandoned the English exploring party that had returned him. He found that his own tribe, the Patuxet, had almost entirely disappeared. The once-powerful Pokanokets, led by Massasoit, were now paying tribute to the Narragansetts, who had escaped the deadly disease. Squanto persuaded him that the English might prove effective allies against the Narragansetts. Thus in the spring of 1621, Squanto and Samoset, a member of another local band, offered the Pilgrims their assistance and showed them how to grow corn.

From the Indian perspective, this assistance was not so much an act of charity as a diplomatic initiative. The two Indians helped negotiate a treaty between the Pokanokets and the Pilgrims. By the time Squanto died of a fever in 1622, he had helped secure the future of the Plymouth Colony. The Pilgrim colony at Plymouth grew slowly and proved a disappointment to its investors, who eventually sold their shares to the Pilgrims. Plymouth remained a separate colony until 1691, when it was absorbed into Massachusetts, which was larger and more influential. Socially and religiously similar to the Massachusetts Bay Colony, Plymouth was economically somewhat less diverse. Plymouth demonstrated that New England could be inhabited by Europeans and that effective diplomatic relations with local Indians were critical for a colony's survival.

The Puritan Colony at Massachusetts Bay

Throughout the 1620s, other groups of English people attempted to found colonies in the region around Massachusetts. Most of them failed on their own, although one, Thomas Morton's community at Merry Mount, was actually crushed by other Englishmen, the Pilgrims at Plymouth. Morton and a handful of English servants had adopted Indian customs, drinking and "dancing and frisking" with the local Indian men and women.

In 1629, the Massachusetts Bay Company, a group of London merchants, received a charter from King Charles I to establish a colony. The plan was similar to that on which Virginia had been founded. The investors in the joint-stock company would have full rights to a swath of land reaching from Massachusetts Bay west across the entire continent. Along with a number of Puritans who were looking for a new home, the company included some who still hoped, in the face of abundant evidence that it was impossible, to turn a profit from trade. The Puritans' objective was to make the colony entirely self-governing, with the directors of the Company and the governors of the colony being one and the same.

The expedition began in 1630, and by the end of that year Boston and 10 other towns had been founded. By the early 1640s, between 20,000 and 25,000 Britons had migrated to the Puritan colonies of Plymouth, Massachusetts Bay, Connecticut, Rhode Island, and New Hampshire. Although fewer than half as many people migrated to New England as to the Chesapeake region, by 1660 both had populations of a similar size—around 35,000 (see Map 3–2).

New England was able to catch up and keep pace with the Chesapeake for two reasons. First, New England was a much healthier region than the Chesapeake. The long, cold winters killed the mosquitoes that carried fatal diseases, the water supply was good, and food was plentiful. Second, Puritans migrated as families. Ninety percent came as part of a family group. This pattern was almost exactly the reverse of that in the Chesapeake. In the healthy environment of New England, the population soon reproduced itself.

The Puritans came to stay. Before leaving England, they sold their property. Most were prosperous members of the middle range of society. Many of the men were

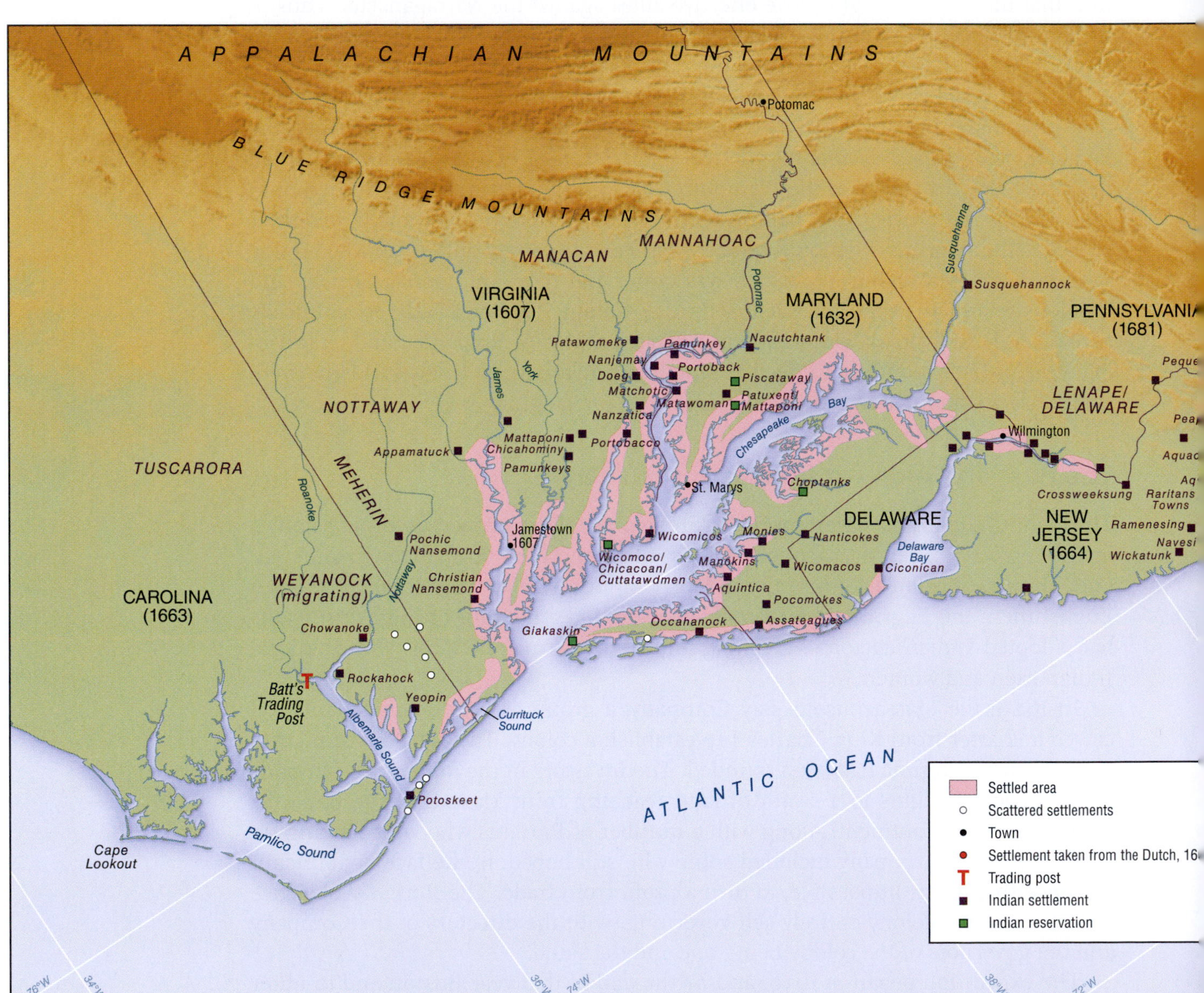

Map 3–2 The English Colonies, 1660 By 1660, English settlements dotted the East Coast, but most of the population was concentrated in two regions: New England and the Chesapeake. *Helen Hombeck Tanner, ed.,* Settling North America *(New York: Macmillan, 1995), pp. 46–47.*

professionals—doctors, lawyers, and an extraordinary number of ministers. Others were craftsmen. By and large, these people were profiting from the changes in the English economy of the late sixteenth and early seventeenth centuries. Once again, the contrast with the Chesapeake was dramatic. There, the vast majority of migrants were people with few skills and dim prospects.

The New England Way

The Puritans were men and women with a mission. Their first governor, John Winthrop, set out the vision of a Bible commonwealth in a sermon he preached aboard the *Arbella* in the spring of 1630, even before the ship docked at Boston. God, Winthrop said, had entered into a covenant with the Puritans, just as they had entered into a covenant with one another. Together they had taken enormous risks and begun an extraordinary experiment to see whether they could establish a society based on the word of God: "We shall be as a city upon a hill, the eyes of all people are upon us. So that if we shall deal falsely with our God in this work we have undertaken, and so cause Him to withdraw his present help from us, we shall be made a story and a by-word through the world." Although not all those who migrated to New England were Puritans, and there were significant variations among the Puritans themselves, this vision shaped the development of New England's society.

This communal vision made early New Englanders relatively cohesive. Each town was created by a grant of land by the Massachusetts General Court (the name given to the legislature) to a group of citizens. The settlers in turn entered into a covenant with one another to establish a government and distribute the land they held collectively. This was by no means a democracy, for Puritans believed in hierarchy, and their vision was more communal than individualist. Nonetheless, there was considerably more economic equality and cohesion than there would be in the next centuries.

At first, the newly established towns divided up only a portion of the land that they held, reserving the rest for newcomers and the children of the original founders. The land was distributed unequally, according to social status and family size (see Table 3–2). Although in absolute terms New England society was relatively egalitarian, with only a small gap between the richest and poorest, the Puritans set out to create a social hierarchy. As Winthrop explained, "God Almighty . . . hath so disposed of the condition of mankind as in all times some must be rich, some poor; some high and eminent in power and dignity, others mean and in subjection." The rich and powerful were supposed to take care of the poor, and, indeed, Puritan towns developed mechanisms for assisting all those who could not care for themselves. Each town administered itself through a town meeting, a periodic gathering of the adult male property owners to attend to the town's business. In the past, historians pointed to the democratic elements in the town meeting, finding in it the source of American democracy. More recently, historians have emphasized undemocratic elements. Participation was restricted to adult male property holders, who were perhaps 70 percent of the men, but only 35 percent of the adult residents, once women are considered. In addition, the habit of deference to those who were powerful, prosperous, and educated was so strong that a small group of influential men tended to govern each town. Moreover, Puritans abhorred conflict, so great social pressure was used to ensure harmony and limit dissent. If democracy means the right to disagree and majority rule in open elections, then the New England town meeting was not fully democratic, for it squelched dissent in order to achieve harmony. However, even with

Table 3–2 Distribution of Land in Rowley, Massachusetts, 1639–1642

Rowley, 1639–c. 1642	
Acres	**No. of Grants**
over 400	
351–400	
301–350	
251–300	
201–250	1
151–200	1
101–150	
51–100	7
21–50	22
20 or less	63
no record	1
Total	95

Source: David Grayson Allen, *In English Ways: The Movement of Societies and the Transferal of English Local Law and Custom to Massachusetts Bay in the Seventeenth Century* (Chapel Hill University of North Carolina Press, 1981), p. 32.

Note: Between 1639 and 1642, the town of Rowley, Massachusetts, distributed a little over 2,000 acres to 95 families—an average of just 23 acres per family—even though the grant to the town was for many thousand acres. Although most grants were for less than 20 acres, some families received considerably more. The founders of Rowley wanted to re-create the hierarchical social order they had known in England.

all these restrictions, the New England town meeting was far more democratic than any form of government in England at the time, where the vast majority of men, not to mention women, were excluded from political participation.

Changing the Land to Fit the Political Economy

The Puritans' corporate social vision was generally compatible with a capitalist political economy. Although land was distributed to towns, once those towns transferred parcels of the land to individual farmers, the farmers were free to leave it to their heirs, to sell it to whomever they pleased, and to buy more land from others. Any improvements that people made on their land (from clearing away trees to building homes, fences, dams, or mills) remained the property of the owners. These practices followed English law.

The contrast with Indian patterns of land use was dramatic. Indians held their land communally, not individually. When it was sold, the entire group had to consent to its transfer. Moreover, when Indians "sold" land to the Puritans, they thought that they were giving them the right to use the land only and to share the land with them. Hence they might allow the Puritans to build a village, to plant, and to hunt, while they retained similar rights over the same parcel of land. Therefore, Indians believed that they could sell the right to use the land to several groups of Europeans at once.

The Puritans' notion of exclusive land rights was a cornerstone of their political economy. Because a man could profit from the improvements he and his family made on his land and pass those improvements on to his heirs, he had incentives to make such improvements. Moreover, not only the land but its products became commodities to be sold. In addition, like other European colonists, the Puritans turned their Indian neighbors into commercial hunters. For centuries, the Indians had taken only as many beaver as they needed, but soon they were overhunting, which led to the disappearance of beaver in the region. The Puritans themselves cleared the forests of trees. They found a ready market for timber in England, as New England's trees were much taller and straighter than any known in Europe at the time. The English navy came to depend on New England for its masts (see Figure 3–7). Although the bounty of the land had seemed limitless, by 1800 much of southern New England had been stripped of its forests and native wildlife.

Prosperity did not come to Massachusetts immediately. For the first decade, the colony maintained a favorable balance of trade with England only by sending back the money that new immigrants brought with them in return for goods imported from the mother country. New England's rocky soil meant that it would never develop a cash crop such as tobacco. In the 1640s and 1650s, the government encouraged local manufacturing (to cut down on imports) and export of raw materials. Through a combination of government policy and individual initiative, New Englanders eventually profited from selling timber, wood products, and fish, and by acting as merchants.

The Puritan Family

Like most early-modern western Europeans, Puritans thought of the family as the society in microcosm. As they put it, "a family is a little Church, and a little commonwealth." There was no sharp distinction between home and the wider world.

AMERICAN LANDSCAPE

>> New England Settlements

When we picture a New England town, we think of a cluster of two-story, white-clapboard colonial homes with black shutters, arrayed around the town green, at one end of which sits a little church, its steeple rising above the village. We can find many such villages dotting the New England countryside, but in fact, they date not from the colonial period but the early nineteenth-century instead.

When the Pilgrims and the Puritans after them moved to New England, they had to adapt to a new environment. Many of their preachers hoped that they would settle in small villages in which the houses were close to each other. In 1635, the Massachusetts General Court instructed that "noe dwelling howse shalbe builte above half a myle from the meeting howse." This law, however, was an after-the-fact attempt to keep the population from dispersing. From the earliest years of the Plymouth settlement, the settlers spread out, seeking pastures for their cattle. William Bradford complained that "no man now thought he could live except he had cattle and a great deal of ground to keep them. . . . By which means they were scattered all over the Bay quickly and the town in which they lived compactly till now was left very thin and in short time almost desolate." It was too late, however, to pull the New Englanders back into clustered villages.

The only places in New England where settlers built their houses close to each other and to the church were market and commercial towns, where the economy could sustain this kind of development. Many of the first New England settlers had lived in market towns in England, and they would have practiced their crafts and trades in the New World if they could have earned a living in that way. In New England, most of them turned to farming, and in particular raising cattle, which required large expanses of pastureland. Fortunately, New England's coastal marshes proved ideal for this purpose, and New Englanders spread themselves and their cattle out along the marshes and meadows, taking advantage

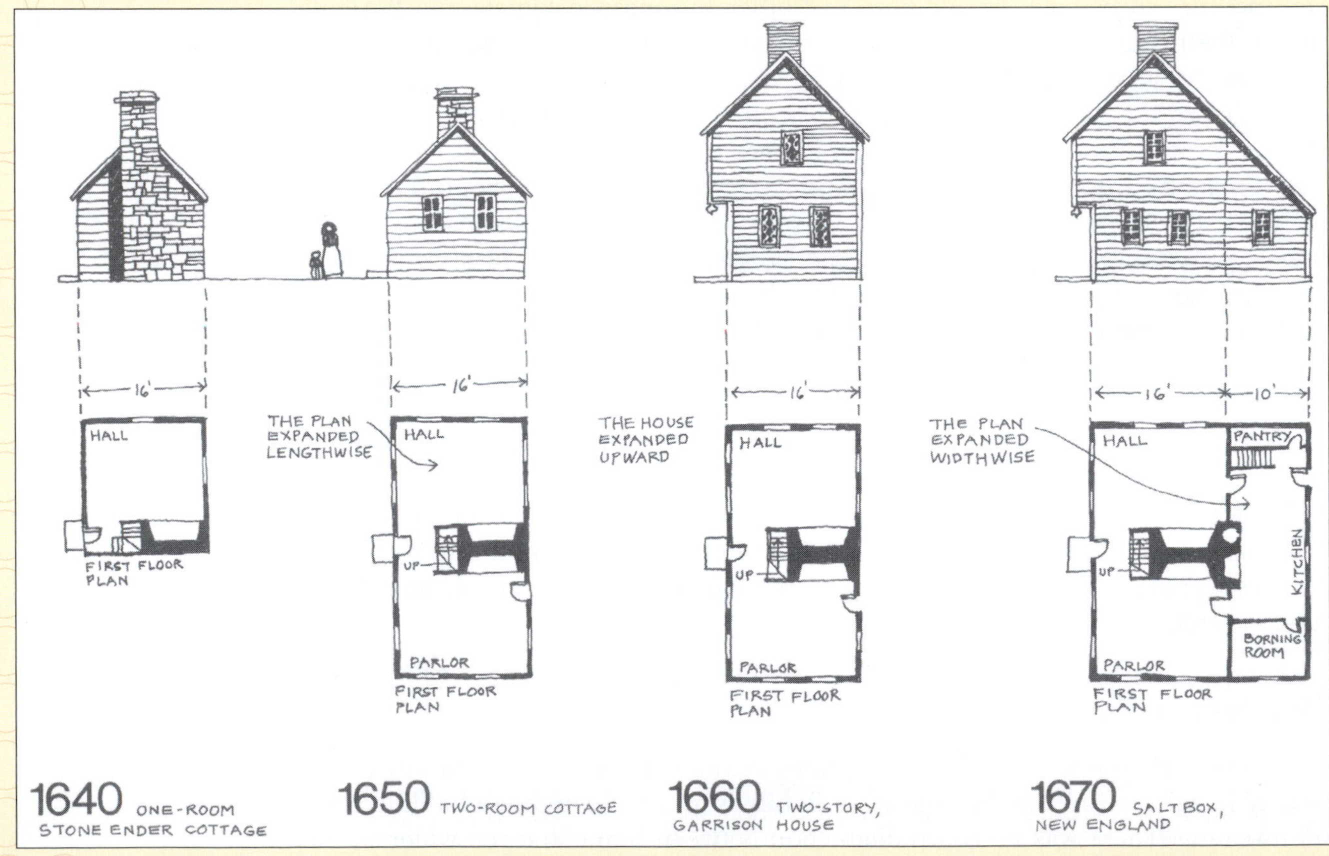

of the environment. Even in Boston, the region's largest settlement, the farming population soon spread out. Boston's site was chosen because of its harbor, its water supply, and its capacity to be defended, rather than its farmlands. The original settlers sent their sons and servants to outlying areas to farm for them, and they eventually broke away to create new towns. The environment and the drive to earn a living were more powerful forces than religion or community. Over time, this impulse toward economic independence would undermine the forces of cohesion.

The first houses the settlers built were little more than huts, little one-room windowless cottages with chimneys made out of clay-covered logs. But even the homes that replaced these first, temporary shelters were modest one-and-a-half-story, unpainted houses with low ceilings and very few windows. Although affluent people such as Governor John Winthrop began to build larger and more elegant homes—his had a hall, parlor, bedrooms, kitchen, and garrets—as late as the end of the eighteenth century, most New England homes were still very small by modern standards. The typical house was just over 800 square feet, perhaps 40 feet long by 20 feet wide, with many only half that size, or even smaller. Considering that eight or nine people typically lived in such homes, living conditions could be quite crowded.

Only when the scale of economic development changed, so that town centers could sustain a variety of stores and shops, did New Englanders build their homes around the village green, and begin painting them white. The classic New England village is in fact the creation of the nineteenth century. Until then, most New Englanders lived in small dark homes, scattered across the countryside, closer to their farmlands than their neighbors.

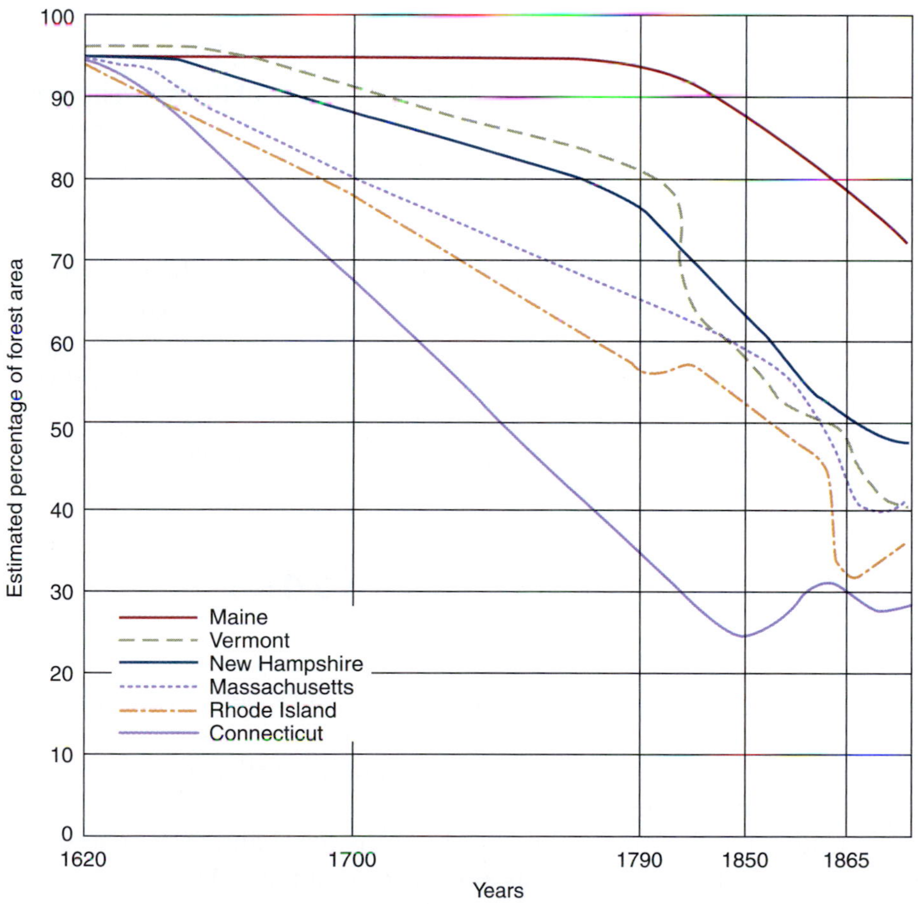

Figure 3–1 Disappearance of New England's Forests As the rate of settlement increased, the percentage of the land that was forested decreased. *Carolyn Merchant,* Ecological Revolutions: Nature, Gender, and Science in New England *(Chapel Hill: University of North Carolina Press, 1989), p. 225.*

Although Harvard College was founded in 1636 (to train ministers) and the Massachusetts General Court established a system of public education in 1647, most early instruction and virtually all vocational teaching took place at home. Indeed, parents were required to teach their children to read the Bible.

The family was also a place of business, the center of the Puritans' economy. Farmers, of course, worked at home, as did almost all craftsmen. Women also performed tasks critical to the economic survival of the family. Although tasks were assigned by gender, in the absence of her husband a woman could assume his responsibilities, selling the products he had made or even picking up a gun to fight off Indians. The family, like society, was a hierarchy, with the husband at the top and his wife as his "deputy."

Puritans lived in fear of lawlessness, and they used the family as an instrument of order. Even Puritans who could afford to care for their own children sometimes sent them into other homes, perhaps because they believed that other parents might be better disciplinarians than they could be. Puritans considered excessive affection and particularly excessive maternal love a danger. Those children who remained in their parents' household were subjected to strict discipline not out of cruelty, but from the deepest and most sincere religious convictions. Considering that Puritan women bore on average eight or nine children and that families were confined in small houses over long New England winters, this harmony was probably necessary for survival.

Despite the premium placed on control, Puritan households were hardly prisons. If Puritans believed that men were the natural heads of the household and that women bore particular responsibility for Eve's original sin, they also believed that both men and women were equally capable of preparing for and receiving God's grace. Puritans distrusted the passion of love, because they thought it could lead to impulsiveness and disorder. They had great respect, however, for the natural affection that grew between a man and a woman over the course of their marriage.

So successful were the early Puritans in establishing tight-knit communities that only two years after the great migration to America had begun, the Reverend Thomas Welde could write proudly back to England that "here I find three great blessings, peace, plenty, and health. . . . I profess if I might have my wish in what part of the world to dwell I know no other place on the whole globe of the earth where I would be rather than here."

Dissension in the Puritan Ranks

The Puritan movement embodied tensions that inevitably made for individual and social turmoil. Puritans had difficulty finding a balance between emotion and intellect, between the individual and the community, between spiritual equality and social hierarchy, between anxiety over salvation and the self-satisfaction of thinking yourself one of a chosen people.

Furthermore, the Puritans had no mechanisms for channeling or accommodating dissent, which they interpreted as a replay of Adam and Eve's original sin. The migration to a new and strange land, populated by people they thought of as savages, as well as the pressure of thinking that the whole world was watching them, only increased the Puritans' desire to maintain a strict order.

Roger Williams and Toleration

> Gov. John Winthrop:
>
> Mrs. Hutchinson, you are called here as one of those that have troubled the peace of the commonwealth and the churches here; you are known to be a woman that hath had a great share in the promoting . . . those opinions that are the cause of this trouble, and to be nearly joined not only in affinity and affection with some of those the court had taken notice of and passed censure upon, but you have spoken divers thing . . . very prejudicial to the honour of the churches and ministers thereof, and you have maintained a meeting and an assembly in your house that hath been condemned by the general assembly as a thing not tolerable nor comely in the sight of God nor fitting for your sex, and notwithstanding that was cried down you have continued the same. Therefore we have thought good to send for you to understand how things are, that if you be in an erroneous way we may reduce you that so you may become a profitable member here among us. Otherwise if you be obstinate in your course that then the court may take such course that you may trouble us no further. Therefore I would intreat you to express whether you do assent and hold in practice to those opinions and factions that have been handled in court already, that is to say, whether you do not justify Mr. Wheelwright's sermon and the petition.
>
> Mrs. Anne Hutchinson:
>
> I am called here to answer before you but I hear no things laid to my charge.
>
> From the transcript of the trial of Anne Hutchinson

The Massachusetts Bay Colony was only a year old when trouble appeared in the person of Roger Williams, a brilliant and obstinate young minister. No sooner had he landed than he announced that he was really a Separatist and would not accept appointment at a church unless it repudiated its ties to the Church of England. Massachusetts Bay was already walking a fine line between outward obedience to the laws of England and inner rejection of the English way of life. The leadership considered an explicit repudiation of England's established church an act of political suicide.

Without a church of his own, Williams began preaching to those who would listen. Saying that the king had no right to grant land owned by the Indians, he questioned the validity of the Massachusetts charter and argued for strict separation of church and state as well as strict separation of the regenerate (those who had had a conversion experience) and the unconverted. Williams went so far as to advocate religious toleration, with each congregation or sect governing itself completely free from state interference.

These doctrines were heresy to the Puritan church and state both. In 1635 when Williams violated an order to stop preaching his unorthodox views, the magistrates decided to ship him immediately to England, where he might be imprisoned or even executed for his religious notions. John Winthrop warned Williams of his impending fate, giving him time to sneak away to Narragansett Bay, outside the jurisdiction of Massachusetts Bay. Some of Williams's followers joined him, and they established the new colony of Rhode Island, which received a charter in 1644. The colony soon became a refuge for dissenters of all sorts, although the Puritans of Massachusetts referred to it as "the sewer of New England."

Anne Hutchinson and the Equality of Believers

One of Puritanism's many tensions concerned the position of women. By insisting on the equality of all true believers before God and the importance of marriage, Protestantism and especially its Puritan branch undermined the starkly negative image of women that prevailed in sixteenth-century Europe. When Puritan ministers preached that women and men were both "joynt Heirs of salvation" and that women, rather than being a "necessary evil," were in fact "a necessary good," they were directly criticizing both the Catholic legacy and common folk belief.

At the same time that Puritanism extended women respect, it also insisted that they be subordinate to men. In the hierarchical Puritan society, woman's position was clearly beneath that of man. "Though she be . . . a Mistress, yet she owns that she has a Master." It was never easy, however, for Puritanism to find the balance between women's spiritual equality and their earthly subordination: although most Puritan women were deferential to male authority, others took advantage of the opportunity that Puritanism seemed to offer. Without exception, the Puritan authorities put them back in their place.

Anne Hutchinson was just over 40 when she, her husband, and their 12 children followed the Reverend John Cotton to Massachusetts Bay. Cotton was a popular preacher who placed particular emphasis on the doctrine of predestination. Hutchinson pushed that doctrine to its logical, if unsettling, conclusion. She claimed that she had experienced several direct revelations, one telling her to follow Cotton to Boston. At informal Bible discussion meetings at her Boston home, which even the new governor attended, Hutchinson challenged the Puritan doctrine of "preparation": if God had truly chosen those whom he would save, it was unnecessary for Puritans to prepare themselves for saving grace by leading sin-free lives. Nor was good behavior a reliable sign that a person had been saved. It was not that Hutchinson favored sin; she simply thought that her neighbors were deluding themselves into thinking that good works would save them. Hence, she accused them of the heresy of Arminianism. For her part, by claiming that the Holy Spirit spoke directly to her, Hutchinson opened herself to charges of another heresy, *antinomianism*.

Hutchinson's views were so popular that perhaps a majority of the colony's residents became her followers. Once she accused certain ministers of being unconverted, the colony leaders mounted a campaign against her and her allies. In 1637 they moved the site of the election for governor outside Boston, where her strength was greatest, so that John Winthrop could win. Then, after her most prominent ally among the ministers had been banished, Hutchinson was put on trial for slandering the ministry. She almost surely would have been acquitted had she not asserted that God had revealed to her that he would punish her persecutors. This was a dangerous heresy: the Puritans believed divine revelations had stopped in biblical times. Hutchinson was convicted and ordered to leave the colony. Followed by 80 other families, she and her family found temporary refuge in Roger Williams's Rhode Island. (Eventually, she moved to New Netherland, where she was killed in an Indian war.) The fact that Hutchinson's ideas came from a woman made them even more dangerous to the Massachusetts leadership. John Winthrop suggested that she might be a witch. Without any evidence at all of sexual misconduct, ministers asserted that Hutchinson and her female followers were driven by lust and that unless they were punished, it would lead to communal living, open sex, and the repudiation of marriage.

It is sometimes asserted that Puritans came to New England in search of religious freedom, but they never would have made that claim. They wanted the liberty to follow their own religion but actively denied that opportunity to others. Puritans insisted on their right to keep out nonbelievers. "No man hath right to come into us," John Winthrop wrote, "without our consent."

Puritan Indian Policy and the Pequot War

The Puritan dissidents, despite the diversity of their beliefs, were all critical of the Puritans' Indian policy. Thomas Morton had been "frisking" with the Indians, Roger Williams insisted on purchasing land from the Indians instead of simply seizing it, and the men in the Hutchinson family refused to fight in the Pequot War of 1637. The Puritans had been fortunate in beginning their settlement in a region where the Indian population had recently been decimated and in having the English-speaking Squanto's diplomatic services. The Puritan communities expanded so rapidly, however, that they soon intruded on land populated by Indians who had no intention of giving New Englanders exclusive rights to it.

Within a few years of the founding of the Massachusetts Bay Colony, small groups of Puritans were spreading out in all directions (see Map 3–3). The Reverend John Wheelwright, Anne Hutchinson's brother-in-law and most ardent supporter, took a party into what is now New Hampshire. Others settled in Maine. In 1638, New Haven, Connecticut, was founded by the Reverend John Davenport and a London merchant, Theophilus Eaton, who purchased land from the local Indians. Four years earlier, the first Puritan settlers had reached the banks of the Connecticut River in western Massachusetts. In 1636 the Reverend Thomas Hooker led his followers to the site of Hartford, Connecticut. Many were drawn by the fertile soil of the region, although religious differences played a role too. Puritan Congregationalism encouraged individual ministers and their followers to interpret church teachings in a variety of ways.

The Pequot War grew out of conflicts among Europeans about who would govern the Connecticut River valley and among Native Americans about who would trade with the Europeans. Until the arrival of the English, the Dutch had controlled trade along the Connecticut River. They had granted trading privileges to the Pequots, which frustrated other tribes, who could trade only through these middlemen. When the English arrived, the Pequots' enemies attempted to attract them to the valley as trading rivals to the Dutch. The Pequots, afraid of losing their trade monopoly, made the mistake of inviting Massachusetts Bay to establish a trading post in the region. They were playing a dangerous game, counting on their ability to control not only their Indian enemies but the Dutch and English as well. As hundreds of settlers led by Thomas Hooker poured in, the Pequots

Map 3–3 New England in the 1640s This map shows the land settled by each of the New England colonies, the regions inhabited by Indian tribes, and the region of Dutch settlement. *John Murrin et al.,* Liberty, Equality, Power *(Orlando, FL: Harcourt College Publishers, 1995), p. 73.*

became alarmed. They appealed to their one-time enemies, the Narragansetts, to join with them to get rid of the English. The Narragansetts, however, had already been approached by the Puritans to join them in fighting the Pequots. That is where the Narragansetts calculated that their long-term advantage lay.

The Pequots were caught in a rivalry between the parent colony at Massachusetts and the new offshoot in Connecticut, both of which wanted to dominate the Pequots' land. The Connecticut group struck first, avenging an attack by the Pequots, which in itself was in revenge for an attack upon their allies. At dawn on May 26, 1637, a party of 90 Connecticut men accompanied by 500 Narragansett allies attacked a Pequot village at Mystic filled with women, children, and old men. As the raiders knew, most of the warriors were away from home. As his men encircled the village, the commander, Captain John Mason, set a torch to the wigwams, shouting, "We must burn them." Those Pequots who escaped the fire ran into the ring of waiting Englishmen. Mason's party killed between 300 and 700 Indians, while losing only two of their own men. The Narragansetts' allies were so horrified by the brutality of the attack that they refused to participate in it.

Deeply demoralized, the remainder of the Pequot tribe was easily defeated. By 1638, the Puritans could declare the Pequot tribe dissolved, and in 1639 Connecticut established its dominance over the Pequots' land. In that year Connecticut established its own government, modeled after that of Massachusetts. In 1662 it became a royal colony.

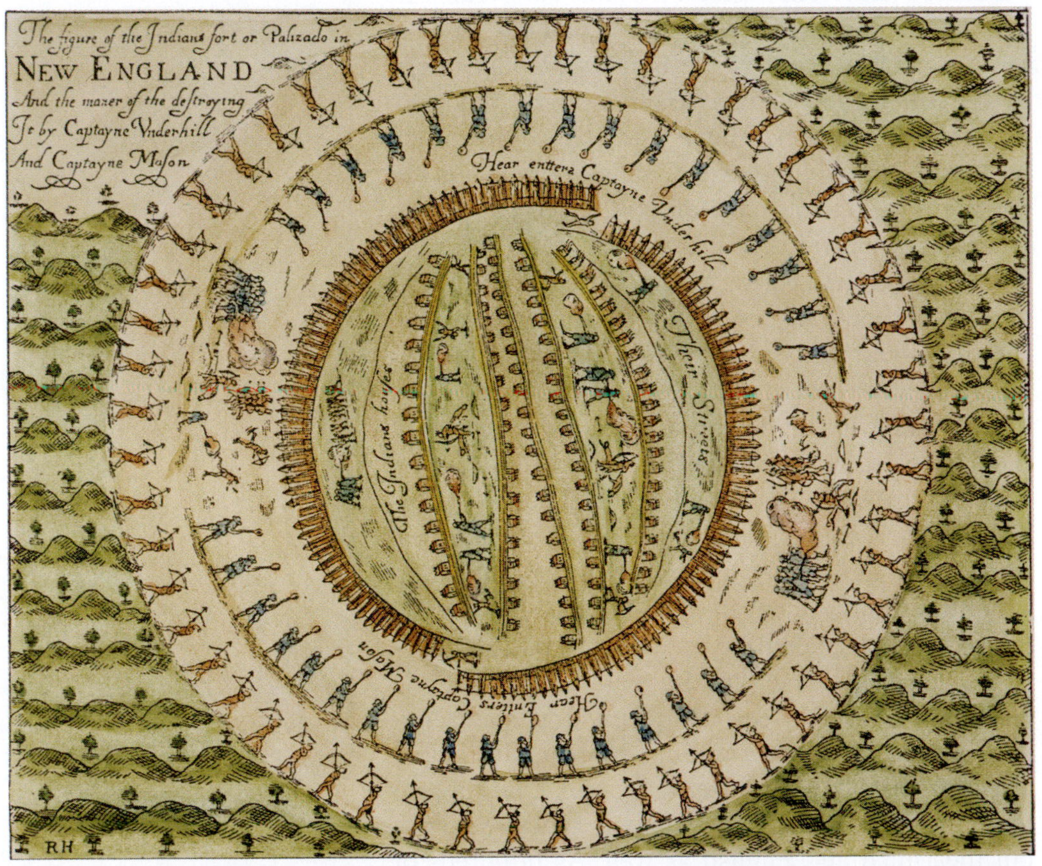

The Attack on Mystic Fort On the inner ring are the New Englanders, attacking the palisaded Indian village.

Conclusion

At the middle of the seventeenth century, the New England and Chesapeake colonies could hardly have appeared more different. Although the forces of capitalism shaped each region, other factors—disease, demographic patterns, relations with the Indians, and, especially, the objectives of the founders—left their distinctive imprints. The early history of New England was shaped by the extraordinary energy and cohesiveness of the Puritans, which made them uniquely successful in the history of colonial ventures. If New England achieved settlement within a few years, unsettlement was the norm. That surely was the case in New Spain, New France, and New Netherland, which all bore the marks of rough, frontier societies for many decades, and it was particularly true of the Chesapeake colonies, which were still raw colonial outposts long after New England had achieved a secure order.

All of the North American colonies except those of New England were outposts in the transatlantic political economy, created to enrich their mother countries and enhance those countries' power. Indeed, had the Virginia Company known that the Puritans wanted to create a religious refuge rather than a money-making venture, it probably would not have given them a charter. So successful was New England in achieving a stable society that we sometimes forget that it was the exception and not the rule.

Further Readings

Francis J. Bremer, *John Winthrop: America's Forgotten Founding Father* (2003). A deeply researched new biography of the important Puritan leader.

Kathleen M. Brown, *Good Wives, Nasty Wenches, and Anxious Patriarchs* (1996). A provocative interpretation of colonial Virginia that puts gender at the center.

William Cronon, *Changes in the Land: Indians, Colonists, and the Ecology of New England* (1983). A comparison of the ways that Indians and New Englanders used, lived off, and changed the land.

John Demos, *A Little Commonwealth: Family Life in Plymouth Colony* (1970). Brief and beautifully written, this book helped revolutionize the writing of American social history by showing how much could be learned about ordinary people from a sensitive reading of a wide variety of sources.

Jack P. Greene, *Pursuits of Happiness: The Social Development of Early Modern British Colonies and the Formation of American Culture* (1988). An interpretive overview of colonial development that argues that the Chesapeake was the most American region of all.

Stephen Innes, *Creating the Commonwealth: The Economic Culture of Puritan New England* (1995). Argues that the Puritans were capitalists.

Francis Jennings, *The Invasion of America: Indians, Colonialism, and the Cant of Conquest* (1975). A highly critical history of Puritan Indian policy that may be read along with Alden T. Vaughan, *New England Frontier: Puritans and Indians, 1620–1675* (1979), which is more sympathetic to the Puritans.

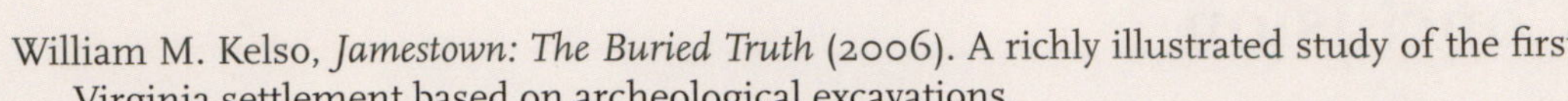

William M. Kelso, *Jamestown: The Buried Truth* (2006). A richly illustrated study of the first Virginia settlement based on archeological excavations.

Karen Ordahl Kupperman, *The Jamestown Project* (2007). A new and provocative account that argues that, through trial and error at Jamestown, the English learned how to make colonies succeed.

Edmund S. Morgan, *American Slavery, American Freedom: The Ordeal of Colonial Virginia* (1975). A powerful and magnificently written history of Virginia that argues that racism was intentionally cultivated by elites to keep poor blacks and whites from uniting.

Edmund S. Morgan, *Visible Saints: The History of a Puritan Idea* (1963). A brilliant explanation of one of Puritanism's key ideas.

Cynthia J. Van Zandt, *Brothers Among Nations: The Pursuit of Intercultural Alliances in Early America, 1580–1660* (2008). Focuses on Native Americans' strategic use of alliances with Europeans.

Sarah Vowell, *The Wordy Shipmates* (2008). Although not a scholarly book, this appreciation of the Puritans by a leading humorist is sympathetic and insightful.

Who, What

Pocahontas 69
Captain John Smith 71
Powhatan 74
Squanto 87
John Winthrop 89
Roger Williams 95
Anne Hutchinson 96
Charter colony 71
Indentured servants 72
Anglo-Powhatan Wars 75
Headright 76
Royal colony 76
Proprietary colony 78
Calvinism 85
Arminianism 85
Antinomianism 96
Pequot War 97

>> Timeline >>

▼ 1533
Henry VIII breaks with Roman Catholic Church, establishes Church of England

▼ 1603
Queen Elizabeth I dies, succeeded by King James I

▼ 1606
James I grants two charters for North American settlement to Virginia Company

▼ 1607
English found Jamestown

▼ 1608
John Smith named president of Virginia's council

▼ 1609
John Smith returns to England

▼ 1610–1614
First Anglo-Powhatan War

▼ 1612–1617
John Rolfe develops a marketable strain of tobacco

▼ 1614
John Rolfe and Pocahontas marry

▼ 1616
Virginia Company offers a 50-acre headright to each immigrant

▼ 1619
First meeting of Virginia General Assembly
First Africans arrive in Virginia
Virginia Company pays for transportation of women to Virginia

▼ 1620
Pilgrims found colony at Plymouth; Mayflower Compact signed

▼ 1622–1632
Second Anglo-Powhatan War

▼ 1624
Virginia Company dissolved; Virginia becomes a royal colony

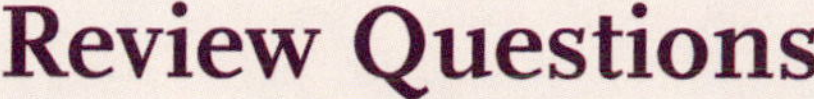

Review Questions

1. What were the objectives of the founders of Virginia? Why did the colony survive, in spite of poor planning?
2. What were the objectives of the founders of the Puritan colonies at Plymouth and Massachusetts Bay? Compare the early years of these colonies to those of the Virginia Colony.
3. What role did gender play in the social order of the Chesapeake and New England colonies? Compare and contrast family life in the two regions.
4. Compare and contrast relations with the Indians in the Chesapeake and New England.

Websites

Anne Hutchinson: A transcript of her trial. http://www.annehutchinson.com/anne_hutchinson_trial_001.htm

The Avalon Project. This terrific collection includes charters for all the colonies. http://avalon.law.yale.edu/subject_menus/17th.asp

The Plymouth Colony Archive Project. An excellent digital archive, with primary sources and images. http://www.histarch.uiuc.edu/plymouth/index.html

Virtual Jamestown. A superb digital archive of primary sources combined with an extraordinary recreation of the first European settlements, as well as contemporary Native American sites. http://www.virtualjamestown.org/

For further review materials and resource information, please visit www.oup.com/us/ofthepeople

▼ 1625
James I dies, succeeded by King Charles I

▼ 1629
Massachusetts Bay Company receives charter to establish colony in North America

▼ 1630
Massachusetts Bay Colony founded

▼ 1632
George Calvert receives charter for Maryland

▼ 1636
Harvard College founded
Roger Williams exiled from Massachusetts

▼ 1637
Anne Hutchinson and her followers exiled
Pequot War

▼ 1638
New Haven founded

▼ 1639
First law mentioning slavery, in Maryland
Connecticut establishes its government

▼ 1644
Rhode Island receives charter

▼ 1644–1646
Third Anglo-Powhatan War

▼ 1647
Massachusetts establishes system of public education

▼ 1649
Act of Toleration passed in Maryland

▼ 1661
First Virginia law mentioning slavery

▼ 1691
Plymouth Colony absorbed into Massachusetts

CHAPTER 4

Common Threads

>> What forces—political, economic, military, social, cultural—gave shape to the English empire? Which of these forces figured in the conscious plan of empire, and which shaped the empire nonetheless?

>> How did imperial politics—in particular the contest between England and France and England's larger geopolitical objectives—affect the lives of ordinary men and women in the colonies?

>> What is a slave society, and how did Virginia become one?

>> Which European institutions transplanted easily to North America and which did not?

Continental Empires

1660–1720

AMERICAN PORTRAIT

>> Tituba Shapes Her World and Saves Herself

Her name was Tituba. Some say she was African, a Yoruba, others that she was an Arawak Indian from Guyana. Had she not been accused of practicing witchcraft in Salem, Massachusetts, in 1692, she surely would have been forgotten by history. Whether she came from South America or Africa, she had been torn away from her home and sent to work on a sugar plantation on the Caribbean island of Barbados, which the English had colonized almost 50 years before. Whatever her origins, Tituba lived in an African-majority society and absorbed African customs.

Tituba was probably a teenager when she was taken, once again as a slave, to Massachusetts in 1680. She had been purchased by a young, Harvard-educated Barbadian, Samuel Parris. Parris's father had failed as a planter, and now he himself had failed as a merchant. In 1689 Parris moved his wife, their three children, Tituba, and her slave husband John Indian to Salem Village, where he had taken up a new profession, the ministry.

Three years later, all of their lives changed forever when one of Parris's daughters, Betty, and her cousin Abigail followed the folk custom of trying to see their futures in the white of an egg dropped into a glass of water. Soon several girls and young women were playing with magic. Then Betty began to experience strange and seemingly inexplicable pains, which spread to other young women. When neither doctors nor ministers could cure them, a neighbor asked Tituba to bake a "witchcake" out of rye flour and the girls' urine. This was "white magic," intended to uncover the identity of the witch who was thought to be bewitching Betty and the others. Their suffering, however, only got worse. Parris now questioned the girls: Who was bewitching them? This time the girls had an answer: two older, rather marginal white women—and Tituba.

The three women were charged with the capital offense of witchcraft. Under duress, the first woman, Sarah Good, implicated the second, Sarah Osborne. Osborne steadfastly denied her guilt—and was returned to jail. Finally, Tituba was summoned. As a slave, she was particularly vulnerable. Perhaps calculating the odds carefully, Tituba slowly began to embroider a story. She named only two names—Sarah Good and Sarah Osborne. She talked about a tall, white-haired man in Boston who made her sign a mysterious book, and about conspiring with other, unnamed witches.

Responding to the hints of her Puritan interrogators, Tituba confirmed that she had made a covenant with the devil, the tall man in Boston. But she also added elements that came from African and Indian cultures, such as a "thing all over hairy, all the face harye & a long nose . . ." Tituba's tales of witches' meetings, flying to Boston on a broomstick, and wolves and birds and hairy imps persuaded her interrogators that their colony was beset by witches. A children's game spiraled into panic, but Tituba escaped with her life. Having spent her life as a prisoner in other people's lands, she had combined their cultures with her own, crafting them into a strategy for survival.

Colonial America in the second half of the seventeenth century was remarkably unstable. Without secure colonial governments, colonial societies were torn by conflicting cultures and economic currents. In some ways, Tituba was a victim of these crosscurrents. She was in Salem because Samuel Parris failed as a merchant, unable to succeed in the world's economy. Tituba's freedom was sacrificed so that other, more powerful people could become prosperous. Instability, however, creates opportunity at the same time that it creates danger. By melding her own culture and that of her captors, Tituba became a cultural shape-shifter, and she was able to save herself when the dislocations of the late seventeenth century brought her to face accusations of witchcraft. Though more dramatic, Tituba's story is like that of many Americans of the late seventeenth century. Caught in the crosscurrents of cultural and economic transformation, they adapted their cultural inheritances to new circumstances.

OUTLINE

The Plan of Empire

Trying to make sense out of the haphazard development of Britain's American colonies, the English political theorist Edmund Burke explained in 1757, "The settlement of *our* colonies was never pursued upon any regular plan; but they were formed, grew, and flourished, as accidents, the nature of the climate, or the dispositions of private men happened to operate." In comparison, the Spanish and French governments played a more active role in directing their colonies, but even then, the portions of their empires that would one day become the United States were so marginal politically and economically that they, too, received relatively little attention. The British colonies were all private ventures by individuals or groups, chartered by the British government but given little supervision or material support. So long as the mainland colonies contributed little to the national wealth and cost the government less, the government was willing to exercise only the loosest of controls and permit each of the colonial societies to develop in its own way.

The result was a period of significant instability at the end of the seventeenth century, as local colonial governments struggled to control their own inhabitants, police their borders, and establish successful economies. In many of the colonies,

elites vied for control, while in others poor people rose up against insecure local leadership. As expanding populations and aggressive traders pushed against native populations, violence exploded. Elsewhere, the British, French, and Dutch—and their Indian allies—collided. Everywhere, Europeans attempted to control Indians, their own countrymen, and the growing population of African slaves. In the midst of these struggles, colonists like Tituba found themselves caught in—and taking advantage of—the crosscurrents.

Turmoil in England

In the middle decades of the seventeenth century, the British government was thrown into turmoil as Parliament and the king struggled over the future direction of the nation. Two fundamental and overlapping issues were at stake: religion and royal power. The uneasy balance that Elizabeth I had established between Puritans and the Church of England collapsed under her successors, James I (1603–1625) and Charles I (1625–1649). Archbishop of Canterbury William Laud moved the Church of England away from the Calvinist belief in predestination, brought back worship ceremonies that smacked of Catholicism, and persecuted Puritans, prompting Presbyterian Scotland to revolt.

Parliament refused to appropriate the funds that King Charles requested to quash the revolt. Instead, in 1628, Parliament passed the Petition of Right, which reasserted those freedoms that Britons held dear, including no taxation except by act of Parliament, no arbitrary arrest or imprisonment, and no quartering of soldiers in private homes. After years of stalemate, in 1642 Charles raised an army and moved against the recalcitrant Parliament, beginning the English Civil War, which concluded in 1647 with Parliament's victory. Two years later, Charles was beheaded. Oliver Cromwell, a Puritan, ruled as Lord Protector until his death in 1658. When Cromwell's son and successor proved an inept leader, Charles II was invited to reclaim the crown in 1660.

Execution of King Charles I This eyewitness picture was painted by John Weesop, a visiting Flemish artist.

Although the monarchy had been restored, its authority had been diminished. Britain had been transformed into a constitutional monarchy in which the power of the Crown was balanced by that of Parliament. In addition, Britain once again found a middle way between a Calvinist Protestantism and Catholicism. When the Catholic King James II (1685–1688) tried to fill the government with Catholics and to rule without the consent of Parliament, he was removed in a bloodless revolution, known as the Glorious Revolution (1688). It brought Mary, James's Protestant daughter, and her equally Protestant husband, William of Orange (Holland), to the throne.

The Political Economy of Mercantilism

After the reassertion of Parliament's authority in 1688, the British state became increasingly strong and centralized. Britain then embarked on a course that would make it the world's most powerful nation by the early nineteenth century.

Throughout the political turmoil of the seventeenth century, Britain's economic policies were guided by a theory called mercantilism, which held that the chief object of a nation's economic policies was to serve the state. Mercantilism developed just at the time that the European nation-states were consolidating, and it was designed to facilitate that process. The new nations required vast amounts of money to support their growing bureaucracies and the armies and navies. Mercantilism's theorists considered the economy and politics both as zero-sum games; one side's gain could come only by another's loss. Mercantilism defined wealth exclusively as hard money, that is, gold and silver. Since there was only a finite amount of gold and silver in the world, a nation could best improve its position by capturing a share of other nations' money. Mercantilism thus led to rivalry between nations. Between 1651 and 1696, the British government, following mercantilist theories, passed a series of trade regulations, the Navigation Acts, requiring that all goods shipped to England and her colonies be carried in ships owned and manned by the English (including colonists). In addition, all foreign goods going to the colonies had to be shipped via Britain, where they could be taxed. Certain colonial products (tobacco, sugar, indigo, and cotton, with others added later) had to be sent first to England before they could be shipped elsewhere. According to mercantilist doctrine, the mother country was to produce finished products, and the colonies, raw materials. Hence, when the colonies began to manufacture items such as woolen cloth and hats, Parliament passed legislation to restrict those industries.

New Colonies, New Patterns

In the absence of tight control by the English government, each colony developed in a different direction. In the second half of the seventeenth century, two important new English colonies, Pennsylvania and South Carolina, were established, and New Netherland was seized from the Dutch. As a rule, the most successful colonies offered the most opportunity to free white people and the greatest amount of religious toleration.

New Netherland Becomes New York

By the middle of the seventeenth century, the British were ready to challenge their chief trade rival, the Dutch. The two nations fought three wars between 1652 and 1674, and the English emerged victorious. The Navigation Acts cut the Dutch out of international trade, and Britain began to challenge Dutch dominance of the slave trade. In 1663 King Charles II chartered the Royal Africa Company to carry slaves out of Africa to the British West Indies. At the same time, Britain made a move for New Netherland.

James, the Duke of York and King Charles II's younger brother, persuaded Charles to grant him the territory between the Connecticut and Delaware rivers (present-day Pennsylvania, New Jersey, New York, and part of Connecticut), which was occupied by the Netherlands. In 1664 James sent over a governor, 400 troops, and several warships that easily conquered the small colony of New Amsterdam. In 1665 James gave away what is now New Jersey to two of his royal cronies, Lords John Berkeley and George Carteret, and in 1667 New York's governor gave the territory on the western side of the Connecticut River to Connecticut. New Netherland had become New York.

The new colony was part Dutch (in New York City and along the Hudson) and part English (on Long Island, where New England Puritans had migrated). The first governors attempted to satisfy both groups. On the one hand, the governors confirmed Dutch landholdings, including the huge estates along the Hudson, and guaranteed the Dutch the freedom to follow their own religion. On the other, the governors distributed 2 million more acres of land, most of it in enormous chunks called manors. The owners of these manors, like feudal lords, rented out land to tenants and set up courts on their estates.

If religious toleration attracted diverse peoples to the region, feudal land policies and England's failure to restore self-government kept others away. Without an elective legislature to raise taxes, the governors, following English mercantilist policy, used customs duties to raise the revenue necessary to run the colony and send back a profit to James. These attempts to regulate trade and direct the economy angered local merchants and harmed the economy. For example, New York's fur production declined between 1660 and 1700. Eventually, James gave in to popular discontent, and in 1683 he allowed New York to have an elective assembly.

Deed Blandina Kierstede Bayard's purchase of land from Lenape Indians in 1700.

At its first meeting, this small group of English and Dutch men passed a "Charter of Libertyes and Priviledges," which, had the king approved it, would have guaranteed New Yorkers both a number of civil liberties and the continuing right to self-government by their elected assembly. The charter was an expression of the principles of liberalism that were beginning to spread through both Britain and the Netherlands. (Liberalism places an emphasis on individual liberty and holds that all human beings are equally entitled to enjoy the freedom and fulfillment to be found in their social lives—their work, their families, their churches.) The charter would have guaranteed all freemen the right to

AMERICAN LANDSCAPE

>> New Amsterdam/New York

Today it is called Wall Street, and it represents the center of world finance, but in 1660, it was literally a wall that marked the northernmost edge of settlement on the island of Manhattan. Although some of the street grid remains—and today's Broad Street was once a huge canal—most of the other traces of the Dutch settlement of New Amsterdam have disappeared.

Lower Manhattan did not become a business and commercial center until the nineteenth century, however. Until then, it was a little urban village, first Dutch and then English. Even after the English takeover in 1664, the town retained its Dutch character and distinctive Dutch architectural styles. The original New Amsterdam was home to a variety of crafts- and tradespeople: not only the merchants, brokers, lawyers, and shipmasters one would expect in a commercial port, but also druggists, painters, printers, tailors, and boardinghouse keepers. The homes and workshops were built in the Dutch style, out of red and yellow brick, with leaded-glass casement windows, and terracotta tiles on the roofs. The interiors were decorated with blue and white delft tiles and the floors covered with glazed tiles in rust and green. The feel of such homes was comfortably bourgeois, not unlike a middle-class home in Amsterdam.

Because, in fact, buildings often functioned as both homes and workshops, any household might contain not only the nuclear family, but also the employees who worked in the family business, and slaves, both Indian and African. (In 1703, 40 percent of New York's households contained African slaves.) If the architecture and furnishings made New Amsterdam and its successor, New York, look like a European town, the presence of large numbers of Africans and Indians gave the little settlement a distinctive New World character.

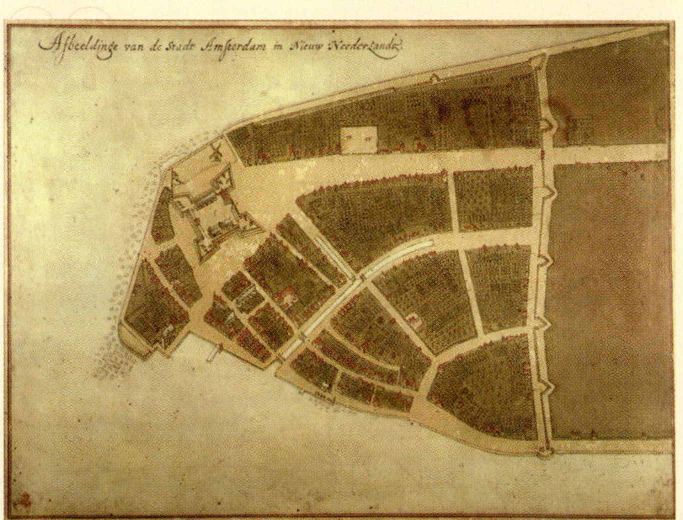

From its earliest years, New Amsterdam was an urban village in a global economy, home to immigrants and natives, all buying and selling in a global market. The Kierstede family built their house at the corner of what today are Pearl and Whitehall Streets, looking out on the East River. Hans Kierstede was a German, born in Saxony, a refugee from the religious warfare that devastated the region. He came to New Amsterdam as a surgeon, the first in the region. His wife, Sara Roelofs, had been born in Amsterdam, and as a child, she lived in Rensselaerswyck, near present-day Albany. There, she and her sister played with the local Indians and learned their languages. After she moved to New Amsterdam and married Kierstede, she built a shed in their backyard where Indian women crafted goods to sell in the market just across the street from the Kierstedes' home. In 1664, Sara Roelofs Kierstede had another opportunity to put her language skills to use, serving as a translator when Peter Stuyvesant negotiated a treaty with the local Indians. The Lenape Indian sachem Oratam was so pleased with her translating abilities that he gave her a little over two thousand acres of land on the Hackensack River, in present-day Bergen County, New Jersey. Some years later, one of Sara's daughters, Blandina Bayard (who was, by that time, a widow), herself purchased land from the Lenape in Mahwah, New Jersey, and built a trading post on it.

When archeologists excavated the Kierstede-Bayard home late in the twentieth century, they found bits and pieces of the variety of material cultures that mixed on the island of Manhattan: pipes made in Holland and imported even after the English takeover; a wineglass made in Silesia, Germany, early in the eighteenth century; a piece of a sword; hair curlers, for curling wigs; whistles carved from clay pipes and traded to the Indians for furs; and ceramic gambling tokens, similar to ones that have been found at plantations in the South and the West Indies.

New Amsterdam was a crossroads of empire. There people—and goods—from both sides of the Atlantic, Europeans, Indians, and Africans, met and traded with each other, creating a new world made out of bits and pieces from each of their cultures. ●

vote and to be taxed only by their elective representatives. It also provided for trial by jury, due process, freedom of conscience for Christians, and certain property rights for women, the latter two items reflecting Dutch practices. However, the king refused to approve the charter on two grounds: it would give New Yorkers more rights than any other colonists, and the New York Assembly might undermine the power of Parliament. Without a secure form of self-government, New Yorkers fell to fighting among themselves, and political instability in combination with feudal landholdings slowed New York's population growth.

Diversity and Prosperity in Pennsylvania

Pennsylvania demonstrated the potential of a colony that offered both religious toleration and economic opportunity. Its founder, William Penn, was a Quaker and the son of one of King Charles II's leading supporters. After his restoration to the throne, Charles had a number of political debts to repay, and giving away vast chunks of North America was a cheap way of doing it. As a Quaker, Penn was eager to get out of England. In 1661 alone, 4,000 English Quakers were jailed, and Penn himself was imprisoned four times. The Quakers were a radical sect of Protestants who believed that God offered salvation to all and placed an "inner light" inside each man and woman. A hardworking, serious, and moral people, Quakers rejected violence as a means of resolving disputes and hence refused to serve in the military or pay taxes for its support.

Penn received his charter in 1681. To raise money for his venture, Penn sold land to a group of wealthy Quaker merchants. In return for their investment, he gave them government positions and economic concessions. Penn also sought to attract ordinary settlers. He promised self-government (although stacked in favor of the merchant elite), freedom of religion, and reasonably priced land.

In 1682, when Penn arrived at Philadelphia (Greek for the "city of brotherly love"), the colony already had 4,000 inhabitants. Penn had clear ideas about how he wanted his colony to develop. He expected the orderly growth of farming villages, neatly laid out along Pennsylvania's rivers and creeks. He mapped out the settlement of Philadelphia along a grid pattern, with each house set far enough from its neighbors to prevent the spread of fires. He sought and achieved orderly and harmonious relations with the local Indians.

Penn's policies attracted a wide variety of Europeans to his colony. Soon Pennsylvania was populated by self-contained communities, each speaking a different language

> **"Now you might perhaps ask whether I with a pure and undisturbed conscience could advise one and another of you to come over to this place. . . . I would be heartily glad of your dear presence; yet unless you (1) find yourselves freedom of conscience to go, (2) can submit to the difficulties and dangers of a long journey, and (3) can resolve to go without most of the comforts to which you have been accustomed in Germany, such as stone houses, luxurious food and drink, for a year or two, then . . . stay where you are for some time yet."**
>
> N. N.,
> German immigrant, writing home from Philadelphia, March 7, 1684

William Penn Concluding a Treaty with the Delaware Indians, as Depicted by Benjamin West In this exchange, Penn presents the Indians with cloth, one of the European trade goods most in demand by Indians.

or practicing a different religion. Pennsylvania's early history was characterized by rapid growth and widespread prosperity. However, this growth and prosperity undermined Penn's plans for a cohesive, hierarchical society. People lived where and how they wanted, pursuing the economic activities they found most profitable.

While moving away from the inequalities of the Old World, Pennsylvania replicated those of the New World. A high proportion of the Europeans who came to the colony were indentured servants or *redemptioners,* people who worked for a brief period to pay back the ship's captain for the cost of transportation to the colony. And by 1700, the Pennsylvania Assembly had passed laws recognizing slavery, although not without opposition. That the institution could take root in a colony where some questioned its morality suggests both the force of its power in shaping early America and the weakness of the opposition.

Indians and Africans in the Political Economy of Carolina

Like Pennsylvania and Maryland, South Carolina was a proprietary colony. One of the proprietors, Anthony Ashley Cooper, the Earl of Shaftesbury, and his secretary

John Locke drafted the Fundamental Constitutions for the new colony. Locke later became a leading political philosopher, and the Constitutions reflect the liberal, rights-guaranteeing principles that he later developed more fully.

The Constitutions made provisions for a representative government and widespread toleration of religion. At the same time, the document embodied the traditional assumption that liberty could be guaranteed only in a hierarchical society. Shaftesbury and Locke attempted to set up a complex hierarchy of nobles at the top and hereditary serfs at the bottom. The Fundamental Constitutions also recognized African slavery. Carolina was the first colony that introduced slavery at the outset. The Constitutions never went into full effect, for the first Carolina representative assembly rejected many of the provisions. As might have been predicted, the attempt to transplant a British-style nobility failed. The only aristocracy that the Carolinas developed was one of wealth, supported by the labor of slaves.

The first settlers arrived at Charles Town (later moved and renamed Charleston) in 1670. The area had a semitropical climate with wonderfully fertile soil, 50 inches of rain a year, and a growing season of up to 295 days. The region had once been explored by the Spanish, who still claimed it. It was inhabited by mission Indians, that is, Indians who had converted to Catholicism.

As happened so often when Europeans entered a region, Indian tribes competed to trade with them, and rival groups of Europeans struggled to dominate the trade. In the colonial period, Indian wars usually pitted one group of Europeans and their Indian allies against another group of Europeans and their native allies, with the Indians doing most of the fighting. Such wars were an extension

Trial of John Lawson In 1711, while exploring present-day western North Carolina for South Carolina, John Lawson and his party were captured by Tuscarora Indians. Lawson was put on trial and then executed. Notice his African slave, also bound and facing the Tuscarora tribunal.

of Europe's market economy: Indians fought for access to European goods, and Europeans fought to achieve a monopoly over Indian products. The English were particularly successful in achieving dominance because of their sophisticated market economy. London's banks had perfected the mechanisms of credit, which financed a fur trade in the forests half a world away.

At the same time that Carolina traders were exchanging European goods for southeastern deerskins, they had found an even more valuable commodity on the southeastern frontier, Indian slaves. In fact, until about 1690, slaves were the most valuable commodity produced by the Carolina Colony. One raid against Spanish mission Indians brought back 5,000 captives, comparable in size to a slaving foray in Africa.

Carolina Indian traders quickly established their control over the entire Southeast (see Map 4–1), pushing out the Spanish, the French, and even the Virginians. In 1680, in the Westo War, the Carolina traders sent their allies, the Savannah Indians,

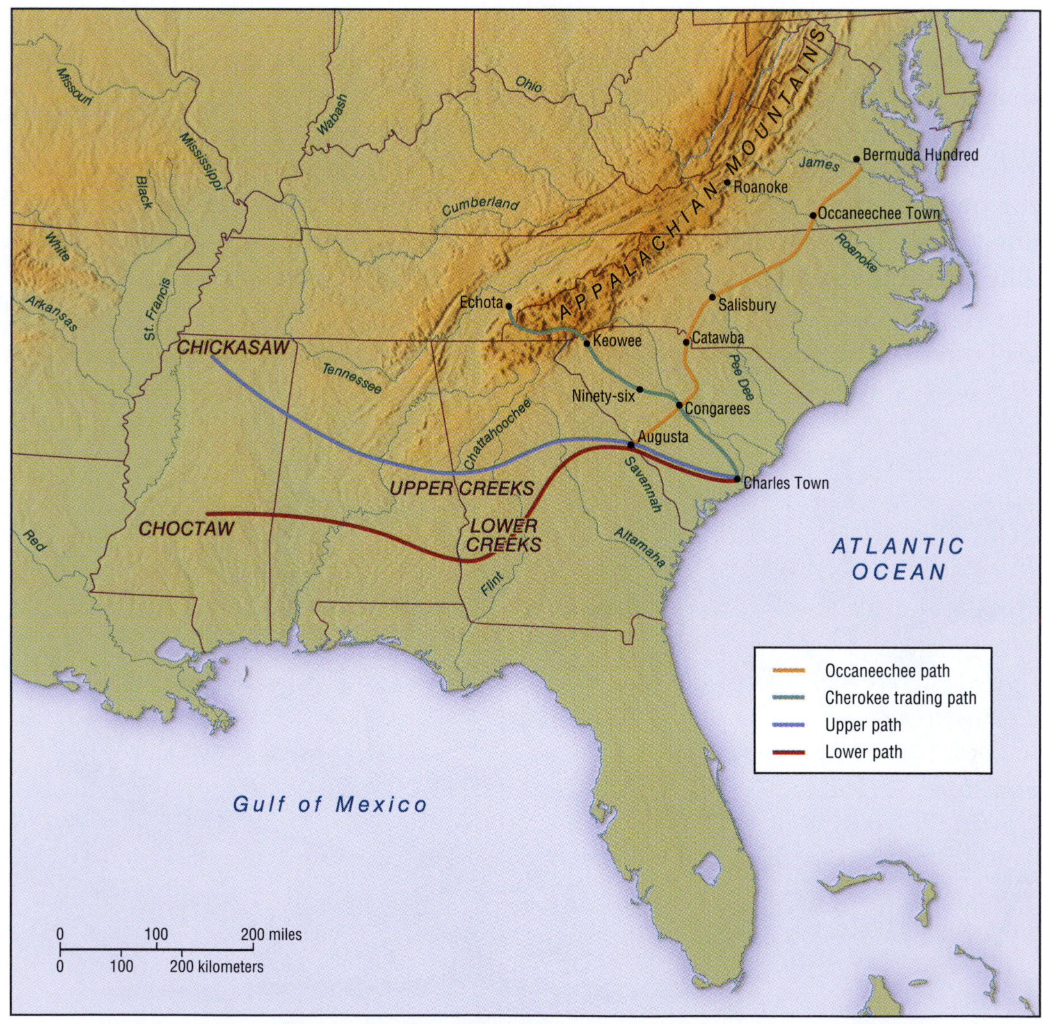

Map 4–1 Trade Routes in the Southeast Beginning in the 17th century, English traders from Virginia and later Carolina followed several paths to trade with Southeastern Indians as far west as the Mississippi. *Adapted from W. Stitt Robinson,* The Southern Colonial Frontier *(Albuquerque: University of New Mexico Press, 1979), p. 103.*

out to destroy the Westos, who were the Virginians' link to the Native American trade of the Southeast. The Carolinians vanquished the Spanish by sending in other Indian allies to destroy the mission towns. In this way, the Carolina traders eliminated their European rivals and established their dominance over all the regional Indians.

Peaceful relations did not last. In 1711, the Tuscarora Indians attacked settlers in western North Carolina. The short and brutal war ended in the defeat of the Tuscaroras. The survivors made their way north, where they joined the Iroquois Confederacy. Although the Yamasees had been reliable trading partners for 40 years and had fought with the British in Queen Anne's War (see later in the chapter), South Carolina traders cheated them out of their land and enslaved their women and children. In retaliation, the Yamasees attacked, picking up Indian allies along the way and getting within 12 miles of Charleston, before they were stopped by the crumbling of the Indian alliance. The Yamasee War (1715–1716) claimed the lives of 400 white South Carolinians (a higher proportion of the population than was lost in King Philip's War in New England), forced South Carolina to abandon frontier settlements, and revealed the precariousness of the entire South Carolina settlement. When international war commenced again in 1739, the frontier regions were, as they had been a quarter of a century earlier, dangerous and unstable for settlers, traders, and Indians alike.

The Barbados Connection

Carolina was part of a far-flung Atlantic political economy based on trade, plantation agriculture, and slavery. Many of the early Carolina settlers had substantial experience with African slavery in Barbados, a small island in the Caribbean that was settled in 1627 and within a decade became a major source of the world's sugar. By that time, it had an African majority, making it Britain's first slave society. By the end of the seventeenth century, Barbados was the most productive of all Britain's colonies. As a result, per-person income was much higher in Barbados than in England.

This income was not shared equally among the inhabitants of the island, however. Those who owned the largest plantations became fabulously wealthy, and even lesser planters enjoyed a high standard of living. Conditions for African slaves, however, were brutal. As in their other slave societies, the British magnified the differences between Europeans and Africans to enhance the distinction between landowners and slaves. Barbadians were the first to portray Africans as beasts. The racism of Caribbean planters was intense, and the slave codes were the harshest of any in the Atlantic world. The laws prescribed that male slaves convicted of crimes could be burned at the stake, beheaded, starved, or castrated. When Caribbean slavery was imported into Carolina, these attitudes came with it. The Carolina slave code, enacted in the 1690s, was the harshest on the North American continent. At the same time that laws and attitudes separated whites from blacks, differences among Europeans were minimized. Despite early restrictions against Irish Catholics and Jews, after Barbados became a slave society, some of those restrictions were lifted. In 1650, the council in Barbados allowed the immigration of Jews and other religious minorities, six years before similar legislation was passed in England. As

Table 4–1 Population of British Colonies in America, 1660 and 1710

Colony		1660			1710	
	White	**Black**	**Total**	**White**	**Black**	**Total**
Virginia	26,070	950	27,020	55,163	23,118	78,281
Maryland	7,668	758	8,426	34,796	7,945	42,741
Chesapeake	33,738	1,708	35,446	89,959	31,063	121,022
Massachusetts	22,062	422	22,484	61,080	1,310	62,390
Connecticut	7,955	25	7,980	38,700	750	39,450
Rhode Island	1,474	65	1,539	7,198	375	7,573
New Hampshire	1,515	50	1,565	5,531	150	5,681
New England	33,006	562	33,568	112,509	2,585	115,094
Bermuda	3,500	200	3,700	4,268	2,845	7,113
Barbados	26,200	27,100	53,300	13,000	52,300	65,300
Antigua	1,539	1,448	2,987	2,892	12,960	15,852
Montserrat	1,788	661	2,449	1,545	3,570	5,115
Nevis	2,347	2,566	4,913	1,104	3,676	4,780
St. Kitts	1,265	957	2,222	1,670	3,294	4,964
Jamaica				7,250	58,000	65,250
Caribbean	36,639	32,932	69,571	31,729	136,645	168,374
New York	4,336	600	4,936	18,814	2,811	21,625
New Jersey				18,540	1,332	19,872
Pennsylvania				22,875	1,575	24,450
Delaware	510	30	540	3,145	500	3,645
Middle Colonies	4,846	630	5,476	63,374	6,218	69,592
North Carolina	980	20	1,000	14,220	900	15,150
South Carolina				6,783	4,100	10,883
Lower South	980	20	1,000	21,003	5,000	26,003
Totals	109,209	35,852	145,061	318,574	181,511	500,085

Source: Jack P. Greene, *Pursuits of Happiness* (Chapel Hill: University of North Carolina, 1988), pp. 178–9.

in the Chesapeake, increasing freedom for Europeans developed in tandem with the enslavement of Africans.

The sugar plantations of Barbados, and later Britain's other Caribbean islands, made their extraordinary profits from the labor of African slaves. British planters worked Africans harder than they would work European indentured servants. Profits came from keeping labor costs down, as well as from the growing demand for sugar. It is important to remember that the New World slave system would not have grown as it did without European demand for plantation crops. African slaves were imported into Carolina at the outset of the colony's existence, but only after 1690 did the colony develop a staple crop—rice—that increased the demand for slave labor. It soon became the region's major cash crop, and African slaves became more valuable. By 1720, Africans comprised more than 70 percent of Carolina's population. With a black majority, a lethal environment, and wealth concentrated in the hands of an elite, Carolina resembled the Caribbean islands more than it did the other English colonies on the mainland. In only a few decades, Carolina had become a slave society, not simply a society with slaves: slavery stood at the center of the political economy and gave shape to society.

The Transformation of Virginia

At the same time that a newly invigorated England was planting new colonies, those established earlier were reshaped. In the final quarter of the seventeenth century, the older colonies experienced political and sometimes social instability, followed by the establishment of a lasting order. In Virginia, the transition was marked by a violent insurrection known as Bacon's Rebellion. Significantly, the rebels sought not to overthrow the social and political order but to secure economic opportunity and a legitimate government that protected that opportunity. In its aftermath, Virginia became a slave society.

Social Change in Virginia

As Virginia entered its second half-century, the health of its population finally began to improve. Apple orchards had matured, so Virginians could drink cider instead of impure water. Ships bringing new servants arrived in the fall, a healthy time of year. Increasingly, these men and women lived to serve out their period of indenture and set out on their own to plant tobacco. However, most of the best land in eastern Virginia had already been claimed, and the land to the west was occupied by Indian tribes that had entered into peace treaties with the English. In addition, the government was in the hands of a small clique of men who were using it as a means of getting rich. For example, Virginia's legislators voted themselves payments 200 times as high as representatives in New England were getting. Taxes, assessed in tobacco, were extraordinarily high, and as taxes rose, the price of tobacco began to fall. Ordinary planters were caught in a squeeze. Many went to work for others as tenants or overseers.

Despite these circumstances, servants kept coming to the colony, most from the low ranks of society. A restless and unhappy set of men and women, these servants participated in a series of disturbances beginning in the middle of the century. The elite responded by lengthening the time of service and stiffening the penalties for running away.

Bacon's Rebellion and the Abandonment of the Middle Ground

When the revolt came, it was led not by one of the poor or landless but by a member of the elite. Nathaniel Bacon was young, well educated, wealthy, and a member of a prominent family. Bacon made an immediate impression on Virginia's ruling clique, and Governor Berkeley invited him to join the colony's Council of State. For reasons that are unclear, however, Bacon cast his lot with Berkeley's enemies among the elite. At that time, the instability of colonial elites gave rise to political factions in a number of colonies. When ruling elites, such as Berkeley's in Virginia, levied exorbitant taxes and ignored the needs of their constituents, they left themselves vulnerable to challenge.

The contest between Bacon and Berkeley might have remained an ordinary faction fight had not Bacon capitalized on the discontent of the colony's freedmen (men who had served out their indentures). In 1676, the conflict known as Bacon's

Rebellion was triggered by a routine episode of violence on the middle ground inhabited by Indians and Europeans. Seeking payment for goods they had delivered to a frontier planter, a band of Doeg Indians killed the planter's overseer and tried to steal his hogs. Over the years, Europeans and Indians who shared the middle ground had adapted the Indian custom of providing restitution for crimes committed by one side or the other. Although this practice resulted in sporadic violence, it also helped maintain order. But this time, the conflict escalated, as Virginians sought revenge, prompting further Indian retaliation.

Soon an isolated incident had escalated into a militia expedition with 1,000 men, an extraordinarily large force at the time. For six weeks the war party laid siege to the reservation of the Susquehannocks, a tribe drawn unwillingly into the conflict, who in turn avenged themselves on settlers on the frontier.

When Berkeley refused to commission an expedition against the Susquehannocks, the frontier planters were infuriated. They complained that their taxes went into the pockets of Berkeley's clique instead of being used to police the frontier. Planter women were particularly upset, and they used their gossip networks to tell "hundreds" that Berkeley was "a greater friend to the Indians than to the English."

With his wife's encouragement, Nathaniel Bacon agreed to become the leader in a wholesale war on "all Indians whatsoever." Bacon's rebels massacred some hitherto friendly Occaneecchees. Bacon then marched on the government at Jamestown with 400 armed men, demanding an immediate commission to fight "all Indians in general, for that they were all Enemies." Berkeley consented, then changed his mind, but it was too late. Bacon was effectively in control, and Berkeley fled to the eastern shore.

By the time a royal commission and 1,000 soldiers arrived in January 1677 to put down the disorder, Bacon had died and Berkeley had regained control. Twenty-three leaders of the rebellion were executed, and the king removed Berkeley from office. Support for Bacon's Rebellion had been broad but shallow. Berkeley estimated that upwards of 14,000 Virginians had backed Bacon, but after his death, that support quickly dissipated.

After Bacon's Rebellion, the government remained in the hands of the planter elite, but the rebels had achieved their primary objective. The frontier Indians had been dispersed and their land was now free for settlement. Those in power became more responsive to the needs of white members of society. Other factors, not directly related to the revolt, also improved economic conditions. Tobacco prices began a slow climb, and planters replaced indentured servants with slaves.

Virginia Becomes a Slave Society

No one had planned for Virginia to become a slave society. With the new colonies like New York and Pennsylvania offering greater opportunity to poor whites, the supply of European indentured servants to the Chesapeake dried up just when more Africans were becoming available. Britain entered the slave trade at the end of the seventeenth century, authorizing private merchants to carry slaves from Africa to North America in 1698. Planters could not get enough slaves to meet their needs.

In 1680, only 7 percent of Virginia's population was African in origin, but by 1700 the proportion had increased to 28 percent, and half the labor force was enslaved (Table 4–1). Within two decades, Virginia had become a slave society, in which slavery was central to the political economy and the social structure. With the bottom tier of the social order enslaved and hence unable to compete for land or wealth, opportunity for all whites necessarily improved.

As the composition of Virginia's labor force changed, so did the laws to control it. Although all slave societies had certain features in common, the specifics varied from place to place, as governments enacted slave codes to maintain and define the institution. By 1705, Virginia had a thorough slave code in place.

All forms of slavery have certain elements in common: perpetuity, kinlessness, violence, and the master's access to the slave's sexuality. First, slavery is a lifelong condition. Second, a slave has no legally recognized family relationships. Because kinship is the basis of most social and political relationships in society, a slave is socially "dead," outside the bounds of the larger society. Third, slavery rests on violence or its threat, including the master's sexual access to the slave.

American slavery added several other elements. First, slavery in all the Americas was hereditary, passed on from a mother to her children. Second, compared to other slave systems, including that of Latin America, *manumissions*—the freeing of slaves—in the American South were quite rare. Finally, slavery in the South was racial. Slavery was reserved for Africans, some Indians, and their children, even if the father was white. The line between slavery and freedom was one of color, and it was this line that the slave codes defined.

Slave codes also defined gender roles. Two of the earliest pieces of legislation denied African women the privileges of European women (Table 4–2). A 1643 statute made all adult men and African women taxable, assuming that they (and not white women) were performing productive labor in the fields. Nineteen years later, another law specified that children were to inherit the status of their mother.

"A white woman is rarely or never put to work in the ground, if she be good for anything else . . . whereas it is a common thing for to work a woman slave out of doors."

VIRGINIA PLANTER ROBERT BEVERLEY

The same set of laws that created and sustained racial slavery also increased the freedom of whites. New World plantation slavery was developed in a world in which the freedom of most Europeans also was limited in various ways. In fact, two-thirds of the Europeans who migrated to British America before the American Revolution were unfree—servants or redemptioners. (When Africans are added, virtually all of whom were enslaved, the total increases to 90 percent.) The increase in freedom for whites was the product of several sorts of policies. First, it depended on the widespread availability of cheap land. As we have already seen, whites could obtain this land only by dispossessing the Indians who inhabited it. Second, it depended on policies of the British government, such as permitting self-government in the colonies. As we have seen, colonies offered this right as a means of attracting immigrants. Third, it depended on specific laws that improved the conditions of whites, often at the same time limiting the freedom of blacks. For example, in 1705 Virginia made it illegal for white servants to be whipped without an order from a justice of the peace.

Table 4–2 Codifying Race and Slavery

1640—Masters are required to arm everyone in their households except Africans (Virginia)

1643—All adult men and African women are taxable, on the assumption that they were working in the fields (Virginia)

1662—Children follow the condition of their mother (Virginia)

1662—Double fine charged for any Christian who commits fornication with an African (Virginia)

1664—All slaves serve for life; that is, slavery is defined as a lifelong condition (Maryland)

1664—Interracal marriage banned; any free woman who marries a slave will serve that slave's master until her husband dies, and their children will be enslaved (Maryland)

1667—Baptism as a Christian does not make a slave free (Virginia)

1669—No punishment is given if punished slave dies (Virginia)

1670—Free Blacks and Indians are not allowed to purchase Christian indentured servants (Virginia)

1670—Indians captured elsewhere and sold as slaves to Virginia are to serve for life; those captured inVirginia, until she age of 30, if children, or for 12 years, if grown (Virginia)

1680—In order to prevent "Negroes Insurrections": no slave may carry arms or weapons; no slave may leave his or her master without written permission; any slave who "lifts up his hand" against a Christian will receive 30 lashes; any slave who runs away and resists arrest may be killed lawfully (Virginia)

1682—Slaves may not gather for more than 4 hours at other than owner's plantation (Virginia)

1682—All servants who were "Negroes, Moors, Mollattoes or Indians" were to be considered slaves at the time of their purchase if neither their parents nor country were Christian (Virginia)

1691—Owners are to be compensated if "negroes, mulattoes or other slaves" are killed while resisting arrest (Virginia)

1691—Forbidden is all miscegenation as "that abominable mixture"; any English or "other white man or woman" who marries a "negroe, mulatto, or Indian" is to be banished; any free English woman who bears a "bastard child by any negro or mulatto" will be fined, and if she can't pay the fine, she will be indentured for five years and the child will be indentured until the age of 30 (Virginia)

1691—All slaves who are freed by their masters must be transported out of the state (Virginia)

1692—Special courts of "over and terminer" are established for trying slaves accused of crimes, creating a separate system of justice (Virginia)

1705—Mulatto is defined as "the child of an Indian, the child, grandchild, or great grandchild of a negro" (Virginia)

1705—Africans, mulattoes, and Indians are prohibited from holding office or giving grand jury testimony (Virginia)

1705—Slaves are forbidden to own livestock (Virginia)

1705—"Christian white" servants cannot be whipped naked (Virginia)

1723—Free Blacks explicitly excluded from militia (Virginia)

1723—Free Blacks explicitly denied the right to vote (Virginia)

Note: Slavery is a creation of law, which defines what it means to be a slave and protects the master's rights in his slave property. Slave codes developed piecemeal in the Chesapeake, over the course of the 17th century. Legislators in the Chesapeake colonies defined slavery as a racial institution, appropriate only for Africans, and protected it with a series of laws, which, in the process, also created a privileged position for whites.

New England Under Assault

As the New England colonies prospered, their prosperity led to problems, both internal and external. How would a religion that had been born in adversity cope with good fortune? A combination of conflicts among the New England colonies and a growing population that encroached on Indian lands led to the region's deadliest Indian war in 1675. At almost the same time as Bacon's Rebellion, the New England colonies were thrown into turmoil.

Social Prosperity and the Fear of Religious Decline

In many ways, the Puritan founders of the New England colonies saw their dreams come true. Although immigration came to a virtual halt as the English

Revolution broke out, natural increase kept the population growing, from about 23,000 in 1650 to more than 93,000 in 1700. Life expectancy was higher than in England, and families were larger.

> "Thou English man hath provoked us to anger & wrath & we care not though we have war with you this 21 years for there are many of us 300 of which hath fought with you at this town. We hauve nothing but our lives to loose but thou hast many fair houses cattell & much good things."
>
> A NIPMUCK INDIAN,
> in a note attached to a tree near Medfield, Massachusetts, February 1676

Most New Englanders enjoyed a comfortable, if modest, standard of living. By the end of the century, the simple shacks erected by the first settlers had been replaced by two-story frame homes. Fireplaces were more efficient, making homes warmer in winter, and glass windows replaced oiled paper, letting light into rooms on sunny days. By our standards, these homes would still have been almost unbearably cold in the winter, when indoor temperatures routinely dropped into the 40s. Still, by the end of the century New Englanders were beginning to enjoy the sort of prosperous village life their ancestors had once known in England.

For Puritans, such good fortune presented a problem. Prosperity became a cause for worry, as people turned their minds away from God to more worldly things. In the 1660s and 1670s, New England's ministers preached a series of *jeremiads,* lamentations about spiritual decline. They criticized problems ranging from public drunkenness and sexual license to land speculation and excessively high prices and wages. If New Englanders did not repent and change their ways, the ministers predicted, "Ruine upon Ruine, Destruction upon Destruction would come, until one stone were not left upon another."

Most of the churches were embroiled in controversy in the 1660s concerning who could be members. The founders had assumed that most people, sooner or later, would have the conversion experience that entitled them to full church membership. By the third generation, however, many children and grandchildren of full church members had not had the deeply emotional experience of spiritual rebirth. In 1662 a group of New England ministers adopted the Half-Way Covenant, which set out terms for church membership and participation. Full church membership was reserved for those who could demonstrate a conversion experience. Their offspring could still be "half-way" members of the church, receiving its discipline and having their children baptized. The ministers were resisted by those who wanted to maintain the purity and exclusivity of the church. Rather than settling this question, the Half-Way Covenant aggravated tensions that were always present in the Puritan religion.

Turmoil broke out as well in the continuing persecution of Quakers, despite Charles II's having issued an order to stop their persecution. Only two years earlier, in 1660, Massachusetts had executed the Quaker Mary Dyer, who had returned to Boston after her banishment. The Quakers had been brazen in their defiance of authority, not only returning to the colony when they knew it meant certain death, but even running naked through the streets or in church.

King Philip's War

Although New England's colonies developed along a common path, conflicts among them were intense. In fact, the region's deadliest Indian war grew out of one of these conflicts. As in Bacon's Rebellion, the underlying cause of the war was the steady encroachment of English settlers on land inhabited by Native Americans. In the 1660s, Rhode Island, Massachusetts, and Plymouth all claimed the land occupied by the Wampanoags, Massasoit's tribe, now ruled by his son Metacom, known by the colonists as King Philip. By 1671, the colonies had resolved their dispute and ordered King Philip and his people to submit to the rule of Plymouth. No longer able to play one colony against another, King Philip prepared for war, as did the colonists of all the colonies except Rhode Island, which attempted to mediate. In June 1675 King Philip's men attacked the Plymouth village of Swansea.

Over the course of the next year, New Englanders attacked entire villages of noncombatants, and the Indians retaliated in kind. At the beginning of the war, New Englanders looked down on their opponents' traditional methods as evidence of Indian depravity, saying they fought "more like wolves than men." By the end of the war, however, they too were practicing "the skulking way of war." Both sides committed brutalities, including scalpings and putting their victims' heads on stakes. That was the fate of King Philip himself. His wife and nine-year-old son were sold into slavery, along with hundreds of captives.

The New Englanders won King Philip's War, but the cost was enormous. The casualty rate was the highest for any American war, before or since. About 4,000 Indians died, many of starvation, after the New Englanders destroyed their cornfields. The war eliminated any significant Native American presence in southeastern New England and killed 2,000 English settlers (one out of every 25). The Indians pushed to within 20 miles of Boston, attacked more than half of New England's towns, and burned 1,200 homes. It took the region decades to rebuild.

Moreover, the Puritans owed their victory to the Anglican colony of New York, its governor Edmund Andros, and his Mohawk allies. Andros worked effectively with local Indians, not because of any natural sympathy, but because he kept his eye on the big picture. In the long run, he believed, the British Empire would be best served by maintaining peace among its various colonies and the regional Indians, putting the British in a better position to fight their true enemies, the French and the Dutch. Over the protest of New England, Andros encouraged the Mohawk to attack King Philip's forces. Once the Mohawk entered the war, the tide was turned.

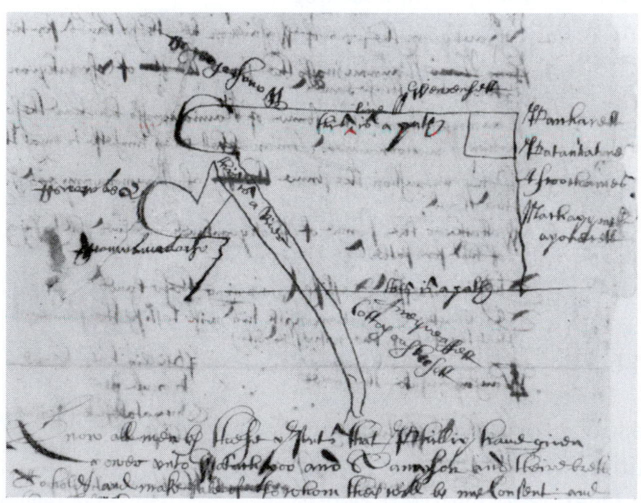

King Philip's (Metacom's) Map, 1668 A map of the lands that Metacom (known by New Englanders as King Philip) sold in 1668. Note that Metacom's understanding of what it meant to "sell" land differed from English conceptions of property ownership. He insisted that the Indians who were living on the land could continue to do so.

Indians and the Empire

New England's relations with Indian tribes were not simply a local concern. They were of deep interest to the British Empire, as Andros's participation demonstrated. The British government had to balance the desires of its colonists against the empire's larger objectives. As the French expanded their presence in North America, using friendly Indians to check their advance became one of those objectives. In 1673 the French explorers Jacques Marquette and Louis Joliet had traveled down the Mississippi River as far south as the Arkansas River, and nine years later Réne-Robert Cavelier, Sieur de LaSalle reached the mouth of the river and named the surrounding territory Louisiana, in honor of King Louis XIV. Biloxi was founded in 1699, New Orleans in 1718, and the forts at Cahokia and Kaskaskia several years later. Through their trade partnerships, the French and their Indian allies controlled the Great Lakes region and the eastern shore of the Mississippi all the way to its mouth, while the British were confined to the East Coast.

Sir Edmund Andros Andros, Royal Governor of New York, was named by James II as "Governor of the Dominion of New England."

This geopolitical reality dictated Britain's Indian policy. Andros saw a role for Native Americans as trade partners and allies in Britain's continuing conflict with the French. His role in achieving victory enabled him to dictate the terms of the peace at the end of King Philip's War. He welcomed the Indian survivors of the conflict into New York and refused to send them back to New England for execution and enslavement, thus becoming the "father" who offered protection to his Indian "children." The British and the Iroquois, who dominated all the other tribes in the region, joined in a strong alliance known as the Covenant Chain, which enhanced the positions of both New York and the Iroquois. The Iroquois became the middlemen between other tribes in the area and the merchants at Albany and were allowed to push as far north and west against French-allied tribes as they could (see Chapter 3.)

With New York exercising the dominant role in the British-Indian alliance, the New England colonies were effectively hemmed in. New York used the Mohawk to make a claim to Maine and blocked New England's movement to the west. Moreover, Albany became the undisputed center of the Indian trade. In every way, King Philip's War proved exceedingly costly for the New England colonies.

The Empire Strikes

As Britain regained political stability at the end of the seventeenth century, it tried to bring more order to its "accidental empire," not so much by interfering in colonial affairs as by making the colonies play a larger role in its empire. While the Glorious Revolution that removed King James II from the British throne secured constitutional government for Britain's subjects on both sides of the Atlantic, it also made Britain strong and stable enough to challenge France for world supremacy. Between 1689 and 1763, the Anglo-French rivalry drew the colonies into four international wars that shaped them in important ways.

The Dominion of New England

When James II ascended the throne, he decided to punish New England for its disloyalty to the Crown during the Puritan Revolution. Moreover, there were continuing reports that New Englanders were defying the Navigation Acts by smuggling. Across the English Channel in France, Louis XIV had centralized his administration and brought both his nation and his empire under firm control, and James decided to try similar tactics. In North America, he began unilaterally to revoke the charters of the colonies. By 1688, Massachusetts, Plymouth, Connecticut, New York, New Jersey, New Hampshire, and Rhode Island had been joined together into the Dominion of New England, and Edmund Andros was named its governor.

Before James II and Andros were deposed by the Glorious Revolution of 1688, they wreaked considerable havoc in New England, and Massachusetts, New York, and Maryland had all suffered revolts. James's attempt to centralize administration of the empire and tighten control over the colonies failed, but it marked a turning point: the colonies' last period of significant political instability before the eve of the Revolution.

James's attempt to tighten control over the colonies affected Massachusetts most seriously. He ordered it to tolerate religious dissenters; some feared that he would impose Catholicism on the colony. He took away liberties that residents had enjoyed for over half a century: Juries were to be appointed by sheriffs, town meetings were limited to once a year, and town selectmen could serve no more than two two-year terms. All titles to land had to be reconfirmed, with the holder paying Andros a small fee for the privilege. Andros claimed the right to levy taxes on his own and began seizing all common lands. Some Boston merchants allied themselves with Andros, hoping to win his favor. This alliance revealed a growing rift in New England between those who welcomed commerce and a more secular way of life and those who wished to preserve the old ways. By and large, however, most people in Massachusetts despised Andros and feared the road he was leading them down.

The Glorious Revolution in Britain and America

The Glorious Revolution made it clear that Parliament, not an autocratic monarch, would henceforth play the leading role in government. It also determined, after almost a century and a half of conflict, that the Anglican religion would prevail. The Glorious Revolution ushered in a period of remarkable political stability that enabled Britain to become the world's most powerful nation.

In the next century Britain's North American colonies looked to this moment in British history as a model of constitutional government. Their understanding of events in Britain was shaped by political philosopher John Locke's *Two Treatises of Government* (1690). Since the time that he and Shaftesbury had written Carolina's Fundamental Constitutions more than 20 years earlier, Locke had become increasingly radical. The *Treatises* boldly asserted fundamental human equality and universal rights and provided the political theories that would justify a revolution.

The *Treatises* have become the founding documents of political liberalism and its theory of human rights. Locke argued that governments were created by people, not

by God. Man was born "with a Title to perfect Freedom," or "natural rights." When people created governments, they gave up some of that freedom in exchange for the rights that they enjoyed in society. The purpose of government was to protect the "Lives, Liberties," and "Fortunes" of the people who created it, not to achieve glory or power for the nation or to serve God. Moreover, should a government take away the civil rights of its citizens, they had a "right to resume their original Liberty." This right of revolution was Locke's boldest and most radical assertion. Once news of the Glorious Revolution reached Massachusetts, its inhabitants poured into the streets, seized the government, and threw the despised Andros in jail. They proclaimed loyalty to the new king and lobbied for the return of their charter. Rhode Island and Connecticut soon got their charters back, but Massachusetts, which was perceived as too independent, in 1691 was made a royal colony with a royal governor. Although Massachusetts lost some of its autonomy and was forced to tolerate dissenters, the town meeting was restored. At the same time, New Hampshire became a royal colony.

The citizens of Maryland and New York also took the opportunity presented by the Glorious Revolution to evict their royal governors. In Maryland, tensions between the tobacco planters and the increasingly dictatorial proprietor, Charles Calvert, Lord Baltimore, had been building for several decades. Although the price of tobacco had fallen, Baltimore refused to lower the export duty. Four-fifths of the population was Protestant, but the colony's government was dominated by Catholics, who allocated to themselves the best land. When Protestant planters protested, Baltimore imposed a property qualification for voting and appointed increasingly dictatorial governors. When news of the Glorious Revolution reached Maryland in 1689, a group led by John Coode, a militia officer, took over the government in a bloodless coup (known as Coode's Rebellion), proclaimed loyalty to William and Mary, and got the new government in Britain to take away Baltimore's proprietorship. In 1691, Maryland also became a royal colony, and in 1702, the Anglican Church was established as the official state church, bringing to an end Maryland's experiment with religious toleration.

> **"The Province of Maryland is in a deplorable condition, for want of an established ministry. Here are ten or twelve counties, and in them at least twenty thousand souls, and but three Protestant ministers of the Church of England. The priests are provided for; the Quakers take care of those that are speakers; but no care is taken to build up churches in the Protestant religion. The Lord's day is profaned; religion is despised and all notorious vices are committed; so that it is become a Sodom of uncleanness and a pest-house of iniquity."**
>
> THE REVEREND JOHN YEO,
> writing the Archbishop of Canterbury in support of Coode's Rebellion

New York's rebels were less successful in achieving their aims. There, a group of prosperous Dutch traders led by Jacob Leisler took over the government. Unlike Coode in Maryland, Leisler was not willing to turn the reins of government over to the new king's appointees. As a result, once the new governor assumed power, he put the rebel leaders on trial, and Leisler and his son-in-law were executed, their bodies decapitated and quartered.

This brutal conclusion to a bloodless revolt did not bring political stability to New York, however. The ethnic and regional divisions ran too deep. In the other colonies, by the end of the seventeenth century the elite had consolidated their position by accepting British authority, on the one hand, and providing opportunity and self-government for their fellow colonists, on the other. In New York, however, the top tier of the English elite competed for leadership with the second, Dutch, tier, keeping the colony in political turmoil.

The Rights of Englishmen

Although the Glorious Revolution restored self-government to Britain's North American colonies, the colonists and their British governors interpreted that event somewhat differently. In the minds of the colonists, it gave them all the rights of Englishmen. These rights were of two sorts. First came civil rights, from trial by jury to freedom from unreasonable searches. Equally important were the fundamental rights of self-government: taxation only by their own elected representatives, self-rule, and civilian rather than military rule. The colonists believed that their own legislatures were the local equivalent of Parliament, and that just as the citizens of Britain were governed by Parliament, so they should be governed by their own elective legislatures.

The British government held a different set of assumptions. First, it believed that the colonies were children of the mother country, dependents who needed a parent's protection and who owed that parent obedience. Second, the good of the empire as a whole was more important than that of any one of its parts. The worth of a colony was established, as one British official put it, by how much it contributed to "the gain or loss of *this* Kingdom." Third, just as the colonies were subordinate to the empire, the colonial governments were subordinate to the British government. Finally, the British government had complete jurisdiction over every aspect of colonial life. Even if the government chose not to exercise this power, it could still do so if it wished. Later, when events required the colonists to compare their idea of how the empire should operate with Britain's, they discovered how radically their viewpoints had diverged.

Conflict in the Empire

Between 1689 and 1713, Britain fought two wars against France and her allies, King William's War (1689–1697) and Queen Anne's War (1702–1713). At the same time, competition for the allegiance of Indian tribes and the struggle among individual colonies over trade and territory made the borders between European and Indian settlements uncertain and dangerous.

King William's War and Queen Anne's War followed a similar pattern in North America. Each was produced by a European struggle for power, and each resulted in a stalemate. The North American phase of each war began with a Canadian-Indian assault on isolated British settlements on the northern frontier (see Map

4–2). King William's War commenced with the capture of the British fort at Pemaquid, Maine, and the burning of Schenectady, New York, and Falmouth, Maine. Queen Anne's War began in North America in 1704 with a horrific raid on Deerfield, Massachusetts. Half the town was torched, almost one-fifth of its population of 300 was killed, and another third were carried north as captives.

The British colonies responded with massive retaliation. They sent out their own raiding parties and poured resources into ambitious and ultimately unsuccessful attacks on Quebec. In May 1690 Massachusetts governor Sir William Phips conquered the French privateering base at Port Royal, Acadia, then determined to seize Quebec in a two-pronged attack by land and sea. The failed expedition cost 1,000 lives and £40,000. Unable to defeat the French, the American colonies remained vulnerable on the northern frontier, and settlers retreated.

Map 4–2 Frontier Warfare During King William's and Queen Anne's Wars During these international conflicts, the New England frontier was exposed to attack by French Canadians and their Indian allies. *Adapted from Alan Gallay, ed.,* Colonial Wars of North America, 1512–1763 *(New York: Garland, 1996), p. 247.*

Queen Anne's War followed much the same course. Canadian-Indian attacks on frontier villages were met with raids on Indian villages. Once again, New England attempted a two-pronged attack on Quebec. When 900 troops (and 35 female camp followers) were killed as their ships ran aground in the foggy St. Lawrence River, the commander canceled the expedition. Like King William's War, Queen Anne's War ended in disillusionment for New Englanders who had been eager to remove the twin threats of Catholicism and French-backed Indians to the north.

The imperial wars merged with and were survived by long-standing conflicts with Indian tribes. In North America, rival European powers almost never confronted each other directly but instead mobilized their Indian allies and made war on those of their adversaries. These tactics, in addition to the expansion of the colonial population and the attempt of Native American tribes to secure trade monopolies, made conflict on the frontiers endemic.

Massachusetts in Crisis

If the imperial wars provide a window onto international tensions, the Salem witchcraft trials provide a window onto a society in crisis, one coping with economic development; the conflict between old and new ways of understanding the world; and the threats presented by political instability, imperial war, and conflict with the Indians. In 1692 Massachusetts executed 20 people who had been convicted of witchcraft in Salem. Even in a society that believed in witchcraft, the execution of so many people at once was an aberration that revealed deep tensions.

The Social and Cultural Contexts of Witchcraft

Although the majority of New England's colonists were Puritan, many probably believed in magic. At the same time that they subscribed to such tenets of Puritanism as predestination, they also believed that they could make use of supernatural powers to predict the future, protect themselves from harm, and hurt their enemies. Although the ministry identified the use of magic with the devil, Tituba's folk religion and that of New Englanders were not incompatible. Before the development of scientific modes of explanation for such catastrophes as epidemics, droughts, and sudden death, people looked for supernatural causes.

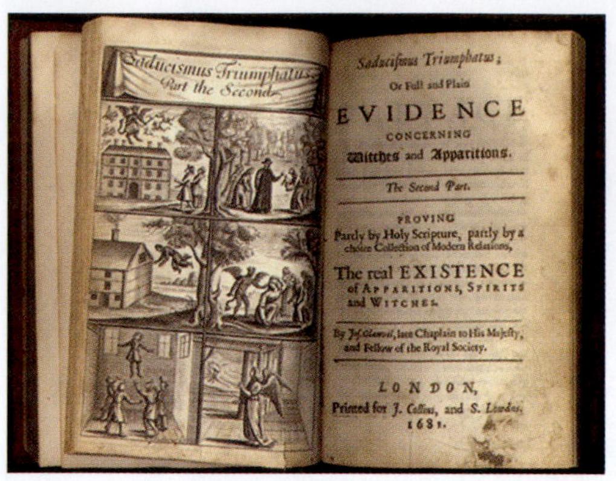

Frontispiece to Joseph Glanvill, *Saducismus Triumphatus; or, Full and Plain Evidence Concerning Witches* (1689) Books such as this combined folklore and Christian theology, providing graphic representations of Satan and witches alongside standard religious doctrine.

In 1692, the inhabitants of Massachusetts were unusually anxious. They were without an effective government because they had not yet received their new charter. The opening battles of King William's War had just begun, with the French Catholics of Canada and their Algonquian Indian allies raiding settlements on the northern and eastern frontiers. Slaves reported that the French were planning to recruit New England's Africans to join a force of Indians and French soldiers. These immediate sources of stress increased underlying tensions, many of which concerned gender. Although men and women both attempted to use magic, the vast majority of those who were accused of witchcraft in seventeenth-century New England were women. Almost 80 percent of the 355 persons officially accused of practicing witchcraft were women, as were an even higher proportion of the 103 persons actually put on trial. Most of these women had neither sons nor other male heirs. They were thus an anomaly in Puritan society, women who controlled property. By the end of the seventeenth century, land was an increasingly scarce commodity in New England, and any woman who controlled it could be perceived as threatening to the men who wanted it.

> "I desire to be humbled before God. It was a great delusion of Satan that deceived me in that sad time. I did not do it out of anger, malice, or ill-will."
>
> ANN PUTNAM JR., in 1706, making public apology for the accusations of witchcraft she had made in Salem when she was twelve

In addition, declining opportunity also disrupted the social order that the Puritans had worked so hard to maintain. Because land was scarce, it became difficult for young couples to start out. Consequently the age of marriage increased, and the number of women who were pregnant on their wedding day began to climb. The number of women who gave birth without marrying at all began to grow, but courts less frequently insisted that fathers pay for the support of their babies. Instead, courts increasingly shifted responsibility to the young mothers. By the end of the seventeenth century, New Englanders were even more inclined than previously to hold women responsible for sin.

Witchcraft at Salem

In this context of social strain and political anxiety, on February 29, 1692, magistrates John Hathorne and Jonathan Corwin went to Salem to investigate accusations of witchcraft. By the time the

AMERICA AND THE WORLD

>> Witchcraft in Global Perspective

In the context of the witchcraft panic that swept Europe in the sixteenth and seventeenth centuries, the trials at Salem appear relatively insignificant. In the European panic, approximately 110,000 people were put on trial; more than half were convicted and subsequently executed, typically by hanging or burning at the stake. In comparison, fewer than 2 percent of those tried by the notorious Spanish Inquisition were put to death.

Yet even these numbers do not give a full sense of the dimensions of the hysteria. Thousands more fell under suspicion, and at some times and in some places, entire communities were paralyzed—900 executed in Würzberg during one seven-year period, 133 one day in 1589 in Quedlingberg.

Although witchcraft trials took place in every country in Europe during the early modern period, they were much more common in some places than in others. About half the prosecutions took place in the German states, and many of the others took place in adjacent regions—Poland, Switzerland, and France. What those places had in common was religious and political instability. Waves of Reformation and Counter-Reformation left pockets of Protestants or Catholics in states or territories dominated by the other religion. In such regions, the majority often feared that their society was being undermined from within.

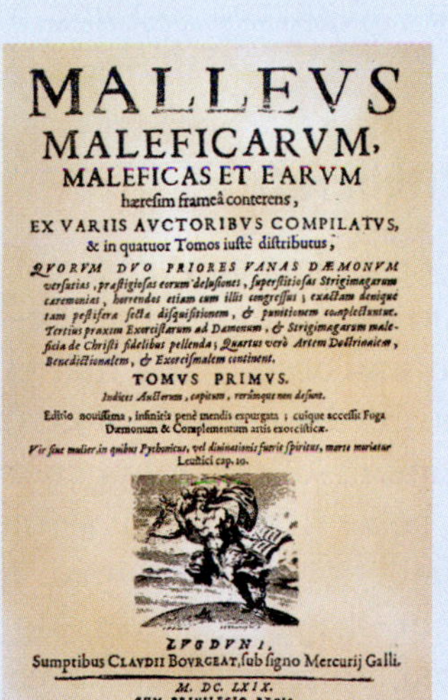
MALLEVS MALEFICARVM, MALEFICAS ET EARVM hæresim frameâ conterens, EX VARIIS AVCTORIBVS COMPILATVS, & in quatuor Tomos iustè distributus;

QVORVM DVO PRIORES VANAS DÆMONVM versutias, præstigiosas eorum delusiones, superstitiosas Strigimagarum cæremonias, horrendos etiam cum illis congressus; exactam denique tam pestiferæ sectæ disquisitionem, & punitionem complectuntur. Tertius praxim Exorcistarum ad Dæmonum, & Strigimagarum maleficia de Christi fidelibus pellenda; Quartus verò Artem Doctrinalem, Benedictionalem, & Exorcismalem continent.

TOMVS PRIMVS.

Indices Auctorum, capitum, rerúmque non desunt.

Editio nouissima, infinitis penè mendis expurgata; cuique accessit Fuga Dæmonum & Complementum artis exorcisticæ.

Vir siue mulier, in quibus Pythonicus, vel diuinationis fuerit spiritus, morte moriatur Leuitici cap. 20.

LVGDVNI, Sumptibus CLAVDII BOVRGEAT, sub signo Mercurij Galli.

M. DC. LXIX.

CVM PRIVILEGIO REGIS.

This was also the period in which modern nation-states emerged. As kings tried to consolidate their rule over church and state, they inspired witch hunts in order to impose conformity. Witchcraft trials were also common in politically unstable regions, ones where the local prince was relatively weak. In such places, local magistrates could drum up a fear of witchcraft and conduct prosecutions with a free hand. Moreover, once a populace was agitated, it might go off in search of more witches, widening the scope of the original hunt. When such hysteria was unchecked by political authorities, it threatened to continue without end. In 1685, officials in the German town of Rottenburg worried that every woman in the town ultimately would be executed. In that same year, two other German villages had been reduced to one woman apiece.

Almost everywhere in Europe, women constituted the majority of accused—and executed—witches. To be sure, the disproportionate number of women accused—as high as 90 percent in some regions—reflects an underlying misogyny in western European culture at the time. The *Malleus Maleficarum (The Witch Hammer)*, the guidebook for witch hunting, first published in 1486 but reprinted many times over the next several decades, claimed that women were by their nature passionate and gullible and hence particularly vulnerable to the devil's wiles. Female witches were thought to engage in "carnal copulation" with Satan and to procure him children to eat. "Blessed be the most high who has so far preserved the male sex from such crime," the book concluded.

Such views found a ready audience in western Europe at that time. Some historians suggest that the witchcraft trials strengthened patriarchal controls over women. The typical accused witch was unmarried and hence not under the direct control of a husband or father. Moreover, the dislocations of the early modern period, including warfare and the plague, had left an increasing number of women without husbands. By the seventeenth century, as many as 20 percent of the women in some regions never married.

Early-modern Europe suffered from many forms of dislocation: warfare, religious upheaval, economic depression, epidemic disease. Witchcraft prosecutions sought to restore order to society by rooting out a subversion that seemed to come from within. In societies that were organized by gender—rather than other forms of hierarchy—women became the focus. Russia is the exception that proves the rule. There, the majority of the prosecutions were of men. But Russia remained a society organized by rank and place, and there the focus of anxiety was vagabonds and itinerants, men who had stepped out of their communities or their positions in society.

The witch hunts in New England, though much less sweeping than those of Europe, reveal the same pattern: a period of political instability that made people anxious to establish control, particularly of vulnerable women.

investigation and trials ended, 156 people had been jailed and 20 executed. As in previous witchcraft scares, most of the accused were women past the age of 40, and most of the accusers were women in their late teens and 20s.

Most of the accused fell into several categories that revealed the stresses in Puritan society. Many, like Sarah Good, were the sort of disagreeable women who had always attracted accusations of witchcraft. Others had ties to Quakers or Baptists. Several were suspiciously friendly with the Indians. Indeed, a significant number of the accusers had been orphaned or displaced by the recent Indian wars, and it is not surprising that they described the devil as "a Tawney, or an Indian color." As a dark-skinned woman from an alien culture, Tituba was also vulnerable. In addition, most of the accusers lived in Salem Village, an economic backwater, while most of the accused lived in or had ties to Salem Town, a more prosperous merchant community several miles to the east. The pattern of accusations suggested resentment, perhaps unconscious, about the increasing commercialization of New England's economy.

By late September, accusations were falling on wealthy and well-connected men and women such as the wife of the governor. The original accusers were taken from town to town to root out local witchcraft, while other people were drawn to Salem like medieval pilgrims, looking for explanations for their problems. At that point, the leading ministers of Boston, most of whom believed in witchcraft but had been skeptical of the Salem trials, stepped in, and the governor ordered the court adjourned. No one was ever convicted of witchcraft in New England again.

The End of Witchcraft

Although New Englanders and other colonists continued to believe in witchcraft, magic, and the occult, by the end of the seventeenth century they came to believe that the universe was orderly and that events were caused by natural, and hence knowable, forces. By the eighteenth century, educated people took pride in their rational understanding of natural phenomena, such as weather and diseases, and they disdained a belief in the occult as mere superstition. This change in thinking reflected a new faith not only in human reason but also in the capacity of ordinary men and women to shape their lives. More and more people, especially those who were well educated, prosperous, and lived in cities, believed that they could control their destinies and were not at the mercy of invisible evil forces. The seed of individualism had been planted in New England's rocky soil.

As individualism slowly spread (it would not triumph for more than another century) and communities became larger, the cohesion of Puritan communities necessarily waned. The eighteenth century also brought new attitudes toward women that stripped them of their symbolic power to do harm.

The witchcraft trials also marked the conclusion of New England's belief in itself as a covenanted society with a collective future. Because Puritans had believed that God had chosen them for a special mission, they read a providential meaning into every event, from a sudden snowstorm to an Indian attack. By the eighteenth century, however, people began to evaluate events separately, rather than as part of God's master plan.

Empires in Collision

As late as the middle of the eighteenth century, Native Americans still outnumbered Europeans on the North American continent. At the end of the seventeenth century in the territory that became the United States, Britain was the only European power that had established a substantial presence (see Map 4–3). The French and Spanish both had outposts on the American mainland north of the Rio Grande, but these European nations concentrated their resources on more valuable colonies: for the Spanish, Mexico and Latin America, and for the French, the West Indies. Nonetheless, the imperial

Map 4–3 Colonial North America, East of the Mississippi, 1720 This map shows the expansion of European settlement. English settlement was concentrated in a strip down the East Coast from Maine to North Carolina, with pockets of settlement in Canada and Carolina. French settlements formed a ring along the St. Lawrence River, from the Great Lakes south along the Mississippi, and along the Gulf Coast. The Spanish had outposts along the Gulf and in Florida. *Adapted from Geoffrey Barraclough, ed.,* The *Times* Concise Atlas of World History *(Maplewood, NJ: Hammond, 1994), p. 67.*

ambitions of the European powers brought them into conflict on the North American continent, where they jostled against each other and the Native Americans, affecting the lives of natives and Europeans both.

France Attempts an Empire

France's civil wars of religion ended early in the seventeenth century, leaving France free to establish foreign colonies. Until the middle of the century, its efforts were haphazard, but after 1664, France's minister Jean Baptiste Colbert tried to establish a coherent imperial policy, directed from Paris. He envisioned a series of settlements, each, in accordance with mercantilist principles, contributing to the wealth of the nation, through the fur trade and fishing in North America and plantation agriculture in the West Indies. France tried to direct the development of its New World empire, but it lacked the resources and capacity to control small settlements so far away. The difference between the British and the French, then, was primarily intent.

Colbert attempted to control every aspect of life in the colony of Quebec. He subsidized emigration and had the backgrounds of female migrants investigated to make sure that they were healthy and morally sound. To encourage reproduction, dowries were offered to all men who married by the age of 20. Agriculture developed and the population grew, more from natural increase than immigration. Colbert's attempt to make Quebec a hierarchical society on the Old World model failed, however. First, very few French men and women were willing to settle in the New World. Between 1670 and 1730, perhaps fewer than 3000 of them moved to the mainland of North America (and only a few thousand more to the West Indies). Second, those who did move resisted being controlled from Paris. Colbert, for example, instructed the Quebec governor to "crowd [settlers] together, and group them and settle them in towns and villages," but the settlers preferred to spread out along the river bank.

Under these circumstances, Native Americans were more successful in shaping the fur trade, the mainstay of the Quebec economy, than was Colbert. The French depended on their Indian trading partners to supply them with furs and serve as military allies. When Indians tried to trade their furs to the British, the French established—at considerable cost—forts to intercept them. At the same time, French traders smuggled furs to the British in return for British-made fabrics that the Indians preferred to inferior French goods. Moreover, to maintain the allegiance of their Algonquian allies, the French supplied them with gifts of ammunition, knives, cloth, tobacco, and brandy. When the declining revenues from the fur trade are balanced against the cost of these presents and the maintenance of forts and a military, it is questionable whether Canada was of any economic benefit to France. In fact, France maintained the fur trade more for political than for economic reasons.

It was for political reasons as well that France established a series of outposts in present-day Louisiana and Mississippi, including Fort Biloxi (1699), Fort Toulouse (1717), and New Orleans (1718), all in the territory named Louisiana. (At the same time France built a number of forts in the north—Louisburg [1720], Fort Niagara [1720], and Fort St. Frédéric [1731]—to guard against English encroachments there.) When the French explorer LaSalle reached the mouth of the Mississippi River in 1682 and claimed it for France, the Spanish mainland empire was cut in two and the British faced a western rival. British traders in Carolina had pushed into the lower

Mississippi region looking for deerskins and Indian slaves. By the time the French arrived, tribes such as the Choctaws and Mobilians were looking for allies to protect them from the British and their allies. In return for the customary "presents," even the Chickasaws, who had recently lost 800 men in warfare, were willing to ally themselves with the French. Within several decades, the French had established trading posts as far north as the Illinois Territory. Farther west, French settlement of the lower Mississippi Valley led to conflict with the Natchez Indians, whom they conquered and sold into slavery.

The early history of the Louisiana colony resembled that of the British settlement at Jamestown. The French shifted authority back and forth between the state and private investors. As in Virginia, the first settlers were ill-suited to the venture, top heavy with military personnel and Caribbean pirates. Louisiana was so unattractive a destination that it could not attract colonists wanting to better their lives, so France began deporting criminals to the colony. Debilitated by the unhealthy environment, colonists could not even grow their own food. Caught up in wars on the continent, the French could not or would not provide adequate support for the colony, so its survival depended on the generosity of local Indians. Without a secure economic base, the leaders of the Louisiana colony began clamoring for African slaves. As early as 1699, one of the founders of the colony asked for permission to import slaves from Africa. A few years later, another suggested trading Indian slaves, who routinely deserted back to their tribes, for Africans. When these requests were rejected, they began smuggling slaves in from the Caribbean. In 1719, France permitted the importation of African slaves, but even as the African population grew, the colony still floundered.

Unlike the Chesapeake, colonial Louisiana never developed a significant cash crop. Because the colony was not important to French economic interests, French mercantilist policies protected Caribbean plantations at the expense of those in Louisiana. Deerskins purchased from the Indians often rotted in the steamy weather. Although the colony had a slave majority by 1727, the settlement was not a slave society. Louisiana's economy was one of frontier exchange among Europeans, Indians, and Africans, rather than one of commercial agriculture. As it was marginal to France's empire, Louisiana was largely left to itself. Europeans, Indians, and Africans all depended on each other for survival. They intermarried and worked together to maintain an exchange economy. As late as 1730, Native Americans still made up more than 90 percent of Louisiana's population. Despite Louisiana's leaders' hopes of creating a hierarchical order based on plantation agriculture, social and economic relations in the colony remained fluid.

The situation could not have been more different in France's Caribbean empire. There, by the end of the eighteenth century, most of the native population had been killed by disease or war. It was soon replaced by African slaves. By 1670, the islands of Martinique and Guadeloupe were producing significant amounts of sugar with African slave labor. Between 1680 and 1730, 380,000 Africans were imported into those islands and the French colonies of Saint-Domingue, on the western half of the island of Santo Domingo. By 1730, Africans on Saint-Domingue outnumbered Europeans by an astonishing ratio of 7.6 to 1. By the middle of the eighteenth century, Saint-Domingue was producing more sugar than any colony in America and was soon to become the world's greatest producer of coffee as well. In a few decades'

Drawing of the *Savages of Several Nations, New Orleans, 1735,* by Alexandre de Batz Notice the array of foods, products, and crops produced by the Indians in the New Orleans area.

time, the French West Indies had been transformed into slave societies, where slavery shaped every aspect of the economy and the society. The French West Indies were by far the most valuable part of France's New World empire.

The Spanish Outpost in Florida

Like France's colony at Louisiana, Spain's settlement at St. Augustine, Florida, was intended to be a self-supporting military outpost. Unable to attract settlers and costly to maintain, Florida too grew slowly and unsteadily. At the beginning of the seventeenth century, the Spanish considered abandoning the colony and moving the population to the West Indies.

When the British established their colony at Carolina, however, Florida once again became important to Spain—and it gained a new source of settlers in runaway slaves. The British and Spanish began attacking each other, usually using Indian and African surrogates. Spanish raiders seized slaves from Carolina plantations. The Spanish paid these Africans wages and introduced them to Catholicism. Soon, as Carolina's governor complained, slaves were "running dayly" to Florida. In 1693, Spain's king offered liberty to all British slaves who escaped to Florida.

The border between the two colonies was a place of violence—and also, for Africans, a place of opportunity. Africans gained valuable military experience and,

in 1738, about 100 former slaves established the free black town of Gracia Real de Santa Teresa de Mose, two miles from St. Augustine. Mose's leader was the Mandinga captain of the free black militia, Francisco Menéndez. A former slave who had been reenslaved, he persisted in petitioning for his freedom. Spain freed Menéndez and other Africans like him and reiterated the policy that all British slaves who escaped to Florida should be free. Thus, the persistence of Menéndez and the other escaped slaves led to the establishment of the first free black community on the North American continent.

Conquest, Revolt, and Reconquest in New Mexico

In the western half of the continent, New Mexico developed into a colonial outpost on the edge of a world empire, far from centers of power and irrelevant to Spain's economy or political power. Early in the seventeenth century, the Spanish considered abandoning the settlement, but Franciscan missionaries persuaded Spain to stay so the priests could minister to the Native Americans. In the eastern half of the continent, regional Indians could play the European powers against each other, but in the western part, Spain was the only European nation with a presence, reducing the Pueblo Indians' leverage. When the Pueblo Indians rose up against the Spanish at the end of the seventeenth century, the survival of New Mexico was in doubt.

Spain had established its colony in New Mexico by conquest. Although Coronado's party had explored the Southwest from Arizona to Kansas (1541–1542), it had not planted a permanent settlement. In 1598, Juan de Oñate was appointed governor and authorized to establish a colony. Much like his great-grandfather Cortés, in some places Oñate persuaded the local Pueblos to accept him as their ruler. In other places, he overcame them by force. His harsh means proved effective, and the Spanish soon dominated the entire Southwest. In 1610 they established their capital at Santa Fe, and the colony, called New Mexico, began to grow slowly. The primary purpose of the New Mexico Colony was to serve as an outpost of the Spanish Empire in North America, protecting its northern border from the French, just as St. Augustine was established to defend against the English. The most important "business" in the colony was to convert the Pueblo Indians to Catholicism.

Franciscan priests established a series of missions in New Mexico. Although there were never more than 50 or so Franciscans in New Mexico at any time, they claimed to have converted about 80,000 Indians in less than a century. Most of these conversions, however, were in name only. In hindsight it is clear that the Indians deeply resented the priests' attempts to change their customs and beliefs. By forcing the Indians to adopt European sex roles and sexual mores, even dictating the acceptable positions for sexual intercourse, the Franciscans undermined not only Pueblo religion, but also their society.

Spanish rule fell harshly on the Pueblos. Although Spanish law forbade enslavement of conquered Indians, some Spanish settlers openly defied that law. More common was the *encomienda* system. Oñate rewarded a number of his lieutenants by naming them *encomenderos,* which entitled them to tribute from the Indians who lived on the land they had been awarded. Some *encomenderos* instead demanded labor or personal service. Women working in Spanish households were vulnerable to sexual abuse by their masters. Suffering under such burdens, the Indian population declined from about 40,000 in 1638 to only 17,000 in 1670.

A combination of Spanish demands for labor and tribute and a long period of drought that began around 1660 left the Pueblos without the food surpluses that they had been selling to the nomadic Apaches and Navajos to the west. As a consequence, those tribes began to raid the Pueblos, taking by force that which they could no longer get by trade. Under these pressures, Pueblos turned once again to their own tribal gods and religious leaders.

> "Who shall kill a Spaniard will get an Indian woman for a wife, and who kills four will get four women."
>
> POPÉ

When the Spanish punished the Indians who returned to their traditional religion, they pushed the Pueblos into revolt. A medicine man named Popé united the leaders of most of the region's Pueblos and sent messengers out to carry his message, promising that if the Indians threw out the Spanish and prayed once again to their ancient gods, food would be plentiful once more. Nor would the Indians ever have to work for the Spanish again, he said, and Indian customs would be restored.

Popé's revolt began on August 10, 1680, just before the resupply caravan from Mexico arrived, and when the Spanish were low on supplies. First, the Indians seized all the horses and mules, preventing the Spanish from notifying other settlements quickly or engaging in mounted warfare. Next, they blocked the roads to Santa Fe. Then they systematically destroyed all the Spanish settlements, one at a time. By the end of the day, more than 400 Spanish had been killed, about a fifth of the Spanish population. The Pueblos laid siege to Santa Fe,

The Pueblo at Acoma The Acoma Pueblo sits atop a mesa that rises 400 feet aboveground. In January 1699, Spanish soldiers destroyed the pueblo and killed 800 of its inhabitants, in retaliation for the killing of a dozen soldiers. All the male survivors over the age of 12 and all female survivors were sentenced to 20 years of servitude to the Spanish, and the men over the age of 25 each had a foot cut off as well. The pueblo was rebuilt after its destruction.

eventually forcing the Spanish survivors to abandon the town and retreat to El Paso. In the most successful Indian revolt that North America would ever see, the Spanish had been driven from New Mexico.

The Pueblos held off the Spanish for 13 years, until 1696, but the ongoing struggles took a heavy toll. Contrary to Popé's promise, the drought continued. Warfare took additional lives, and the population continued to drop.

The revolt taught the Spanish several lessons. The new Franciscans who came to minister to the Indians were far less zealous than their predecessors. The *encomienda* was not reestablished, and levels of exploitation were significantly lower. Slowly the Spanish colony began rebuilding (see Map 4–4).

The population was divided into four social groupings, ranging from a small nobility at the top to enslaved Indians at the bottom. The nobility, a hereditary aristocracy of 20 or so families, included government officials. In all societies with hereditary aristocracies, those groups develop codes of honor to distinguish themselves from the lower orders. This group prided itself on its racial purity, considering whiteness of skin a clear sign of superiority, and scorned those of mixed blood, many of whom, of course, were the illegitimate children of elite Spanish men and the Indian women they raped or seduced. Aristocratic men placed a high value on the personal qualities of courage, honesty, and loyalty, as well as sexual virility. Female honor consisted of extreme modesty and sexual purity.

The second group in the Spanish society in New Mexico were landed peasants, most of them *mestizos,* half-Spanish and half-Indian. In this highly color-conscious society, the *mestizos* prized the Spanish part of their heritage and scorned the Indian. Next came the Pueblo Indians, living in their own communities. At the bottom were the *genízaros,* conquered Indians who had been enslaved. This lower class of slaves was joined by Indians who left their tribes and moved to Spanish settlements. Often these immigrants were outcasts from their own tribe, such as women who had been raped by Spanish men and were now shunned by their own society. A century after their first conquest, the Pueblo Indians had begun to adopt the values of their conquerors.

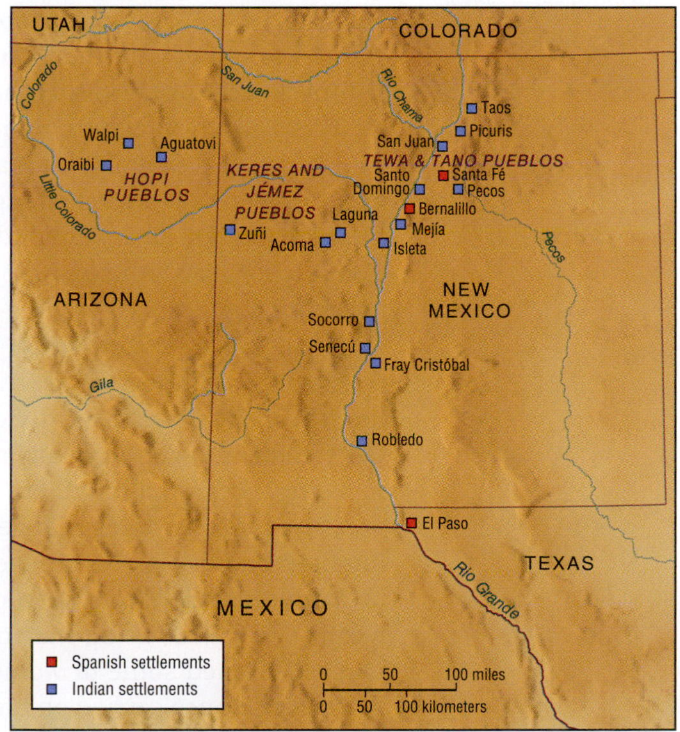

Map 4–4 Region of Spanish Reconquest of New Mexico, 1692–1696 This map includes the pueblos reconquered by the Spanish, as well as Spanish settlements. *Adapted from Oakah L. Jones Jr.,* Pueblo Warriors and Spanish Conquest *(Norman, OK: University of Oklahoma Press, 1966) p. 37.*

Native Americans and the Country Between

Spain paid little attention to its impoverished colonial outposts in New Mexico, leaving them vulnerable to the more numerous Indians to the east. When the French in Louisiana started arming their Comanche, Wichita, and Pawnee trading partners, the New Mexicans—Spanish and Pueblos alike—found themselves challenged.

The Indians of the Great Plains, however, profited from the conflict between France and Spain. Not only did they obtain guns from the French, making them more fearsome as fighters, but they got horses from the Spanish. After the Pueblo revolt, the Spanish left behind hundreds of horses, that Pueblo and Apache Indians claimed and, in turn, passed on to the Plains Indians. By the middle of the eighteenth century, all the Plains Indians were on horseback. Their new access to horses transformed Plains Indian life dramatically. They became more effective buffalo hunters, thus making them better fed, clothed, and housed. Their new mobility gave them an increasing sense of freedom, too. But the horses—and the better living conditions that hunting on horseback made possible—attracted other Indians to the Great Plains from both the east and the west. In fact, most of the Indians we now associate with the Great Plains—Sioux, Arapaho, Cheyenne, Blackfoot, Cree—did not arrive there until the eighteenth century.

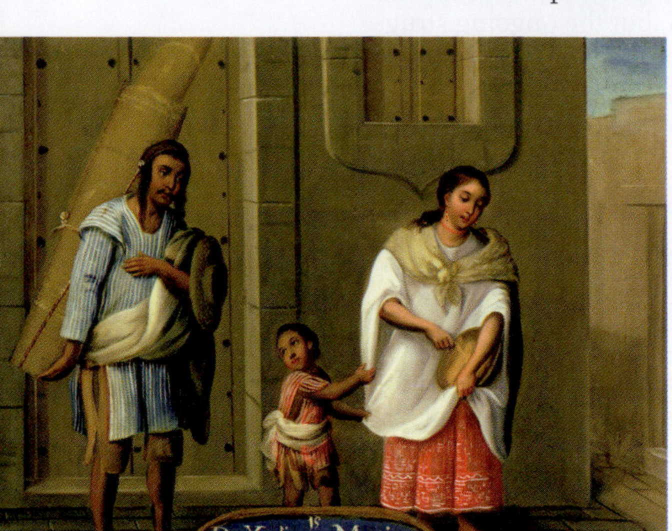

Eighteenth-century Spanish Illustrations of New World Racial Mixture In this case, the union of an Indian ("Yndio") and a "Mestiza" produces a "Coyote" child. The Spanish were much more attentive to color distinction than were the English, and they developed a large vocabulary so that they could make these distinctions with great precision.

The result was increased warfare among the Plains Indians. Those Indians with the best access to horses fared the best. For example, the Comanches came to dominate the southern plains, from western Kansas to New Mexico, where they intruded on both the Apaches and the Spanish. The Comanches raided the Apaches, taking not only their horses, but also their women and children as captives, some of whom they adopted into their tribe and others whom they sold as slaves—*genízaros*—to the Spanish. The Comanches became powerful enough to cut the Apaches off from French traders to the east. The Apaches in turn moved west and south, bringing them into conflict with the Pueblos and the Spanish. In defense, the Spanish built a string of armed settlements in current-day Texas, but they were not strong enough to withstand the Comanches, and even the New Mexican settlements were endangered. By 1777, the governor lamented that the Comanches had reduced New Mexico "to the most deplorable state and greatest poverty."

Eventually, the new horse-centered way of life took its toll on the Indians themselves. Although some tribes grew stronger at the expense of others, all suffered from the increase in violence. European diseases proved deadly, as well. One eighteenth-century smallpox epidemic wiped out two-thirds of the Mandans in a single year, making them an easy target for their Lakota enemy. Under such pressures, gender roles changed. Men sought distinction as warriors, demonstrating their success by the number of scalps or captives they seized. Yet so many fell in battle that they were soon outnumbered by women, which in turn led to polygamy, as the surviving warriors took multiple wives. And although the arrival of horses lessened some of women's burdens—horses now carried the heavy loads that women once carried on their backs—on balance, the effects were negative. As men's status as warriors and hunters rose, that of women—the agriculturalists—fell. Men also increased their status by seizing—and selling—female captives. In a warrior society, women were important markers of male prestige.

Conclusion

After a period of considerable instability, by the beginning of the eighteenth century, almost all of the British North American colonies had developed the societies that they would maintain until the American Revolution. For the most part, the colonies were prosperous, with a large white middle class. The efforts to replicate a European hierarchical order had largely failed. Each region had found a secure economic base: farming and shipping in New England, mixed farming in the middle colonies, and single-crop planting in the southern ones. The southern colonies had become slave societies, although slavery was practiced in every colony. For the most part, the colonies had figured out how to control their own populations, whether by affording them—in the case of Europeans—increased opportunity and political rights, or by exercising tighter control, as was the case with enslaved Africans. These strong economic foundations, when combined with political stability, were the preconditions for the rapid population growth of the eighteenth century, when the British population on the mainland would far surpass that of the French and Spanish colonies. The French and Spanish colonies on the mainland were still little more than frontier outposts, although both nations still maintained imperial visions for North America. Native Americans remained a strong presence, but the competition among the European powers—and even the individual colonies—for the loyalty of the Indian tribes, their trade, and their land, remained a source of conflict.

Further Readings

John Putnam Demos, *Entertaining Satan: Witchcraft and the Culture of Early New England* (1982). A fascinating exploration, from a variety of perspectives, of witchcraft in New England life.

Allan Gallay, *The Indian Slave Trade: The Rise of the English Empire in the American South, 1670–1717* (2002). An important study of a once-neglected topic, the enslavement of Native Americans and its significance in the development of the colonial South.

Richard Godbeer, *The Devil's Dominion: Magic and Religion in Early New England* (1992). Shows the ways in which occult and folk religion were an integral part of New England's culture.

Ramón A. Gutiérrez, *When Jesus Came the Corn Mothers Went Away: Marriage, Sexuality, and Power in New Mexico, 1500–1856* (1991). A brilliant analysis of the role of gender and sexuality in structuring colonial New Mexican society.

James Horn, *Adapting to a New World: English Society in the Seventeenth-Century Chesapeake* (1994). A bold interpretation that argues for the influence of English patterns and values in colonial Chesapeake society.

Winthrop D. Jordan, *White Over Black: American Attitudes Toward the Negro, 1550–1812* (1968). Slightly dated, but still the most comprehensive account of the development of American racism.

Jill Lepore, *The Name of War: King Philip's War and the Origins of American Identity* (1998). A provocative interpretation of King Philip's War that emphasizes the cultural distance between Puritans and Indians.

Jennifer L. Morgan, *Laboring Women: Reproduction and Gender in New World Slavery* (2004). Puts gender at the center of the development of slavery and racism in the New World.

James Pritchard, *In Search of Empire: The French in the Americas, 1670–1730* (2004). An excellent survey of France's efforts to establish an American empire, from Quebec to the Caribbean.

Wilcomb E. Washburn, *The Governor and the Rebel: A History of Bacon's Rebellion in Virginia* (1957). A highly readable account of Bacon's Rebellion.

Who, What

Review Questions

1. What was Britain's plan of empire? What role were the American colonies supposed to play in it?

>> Timeline >>

▼ 1598
Juan de Oñate colonizes New Mexico for Spain

▼ 1610
Santa Fe established

▼ 1627
Barbados settled

▼ 1628
Parliament passes Petition of Right

▼ 1642–1647
English Revolution

▼ 1649
King Charles I beheaded

▼ 1652–1674
Three Anglo-Dutch Wars

▼ 1656
Britain seizes Jamaica from Spain

▼ 1651–1696
Navigation Acts passed to regulate trade

▼ 1660
British monarchy restored, Charles II crowned king

▼ 1662
Half-Way Covenant

▼ 1664
British seize New Netherland, renaming it New York

▼ 1665
New Jersey established

▼ 1669
Fundamental Constitutions written for South Carolina

▼ 1670
Carolina settled

▼ 1673
Marquette and Joliet explore Mississippi for France

▼ 1675–1676
King Philip's War

▼ 1676–1677
Bacon's Rebellion

▼ 1680
Pueblo Revolt in New Mexico reestablishes Indian rule

2. Many of the American colonies experienced a period of political instability in the last quarter of the seventeenth century. Describe the rebellions and other examples of political instability, and explain what caused them.
3. What effect did political turmoil and the change of leadership in Britain have upon the American colonies in the second half of the seventeenth century?
4. Describe Indian-white relations in the American colonies in the second half of the seventeenth century. What was the Covenant Chain, and how did Edmund Andros's vision of Indian-white relations differ from that of settlers in New England?
5. What were the primary causes of the witchcraft trials in Salem in 1692? What were the primary results?
6. Describe the causes and results of Popé's Rebellion of 1680, and describe New Mexican society in the early eighteenth century.

Websites

The Pueblo Revolt. A translation of the account of the revolt written by Governor Don Antonio de Otermin, September 8, 1680. http://www.pbs.org/weta/thewest/resources/archives/one/pueblo.htm

Salem Witchcraft Trials, 1692. A wide array of court records, transcripts, maps, and biographies, with gateways to archives of primary sources. http://www.law.umkc.edu/faculty/projects/ftrials/salem/salem.htm

William Penn's Charter. And other documents from the early history of Pennsylvania, including the statutes enacted by the first legislature and a 1685 map. http://www.docheritage.state.pa.us/secIndex1.asp

For further review materials and resource information, please visit www.oup.com/us/ofthepeople

Westo War, Carolina defeats the Westos

▼ 1681
William Penn granted charter for Pennsylvania

▼ 1683
New York's assembly meets for first time

▼ 1685
King Charles II dies and James, Duke of York, becomes King James II

▼ 1686
Massachusetts, Plymouth, Connecticut, Rhode Island, and New Hampshire combined in Dominion of New England; New York and New Jersey added two years later

▼ 1688
Glorious Revolution

▼ 1689
Leisler's Rebellion in New York, Coode's Rebellion in Maryland
William and Mary become King and Queen of Britain; Dominion of New England overthrown

▼ 1689–1697
King William's War

▼ 1690
Publication of John Locke's *Two Treatises of Government*

▼ 1691
Massachusetts made a royal colony
Maryland made a royal colony
New Hampshire made a royal colony

▼ 1692
Salem witchcraft trials

▼ 1696
Reconquest of New Mexico

▼ 1702–1713
Queen Anne's War

▼ 1706
Spanish establish settlement at Albuquerque

▼ 1715–1716
Yamasee War

▼ 1718
French establish settlement at New Orleans

CHAPTER 5

Common Threads

>> What were some of the choices that individual men and women made in the eighteenth century—for example, about where to live, how to work, what to purchase, what to believe—and how did those choices affect their society?

>> How did such choices make everyday life more democratic? What were the forces that worked against such democratization?

>> How were free Americans able to become wealthier even without significant technological innovations?

>> How did the consumer revolution affect American society and culture?

>> As the colonial population became more diverse and complex, with separate regional cultures and an increasing variety of beliefs and religious practices, were there other experiences that colonial Americans had in common? Is it possible yet, on the eve of the American Revolution, to talk about a common American experience or culture?

The Eighteenth-Century World 1700–1775

AMERICAN PORTRAIT

>> George Whitefield: Evangelist for a Consumer Society

In 1740 there were no more than 16,000 people living in Boston, but on October 12, some 20,000 men and women filled the Common to hear an English minister preach. Everywhere he went, the crowds were unprecedented—8,000 in Philadelphia, 3,000 in the little Pennsylvania village of Neshaminy. Those who could not see the evangelist in person read about him in the newspapers. If there was one binding experience for the American people in the decades before the Revolution, it was George Whitefield's ministry.

When George Whitefield was born in Bristol, England, in 1714, no one would have guessed that he would become not only a leading preacher of the Great Awakening of religion in the American colonies but one of the most influential preachers in the history of Christianity. He had trouble with his studies and preferred the theater, romance novels, and fancy clothes. Because of the growth of the market economy, men and women on both sides of the Atlantic could now participate in a consumer culture that offered many ways to spend money and leisure time. To those schooled in a traditional Calvinist religion, the consumer society was both attractive and frightening. Could one serve God and oneself at the same time?

At the age of 17, when Whitefield discovered that he had no aptitude for trade, the career he had chosen, the boy from a poor family faced a personal crisis. Then, one morning, he blurted out the words that had just come into his mind: ". . . God intends something for me which we know not of." Whitefield then set out to prepare himself for the ministry. He enrolled at Oxford University, paying his way by working as a servant to wealthy students. He became friendly with the Methodists, a group of religious young men who were planning a mission to the new English colony of Georgia. Under their influence, Whitefield turned his back on the attractions of consumer culture. Now, "whatsoever I did, I endeavoured to do all to the glory of God." Whitefield was determined to share what he had learned with all who would hear.

Whitefield helped create a mass public that broke down the boundaries of small communities. Before his ministry, each minister or priest typically addressed only his own congregation. The crowds Whitefield attracted were often too large for any building to hold, so he preached outdoors, with a voice so loud that Benjamin Franklin calculated that it could be heard by 25,000 people at a time. In Philadelphia, he told the crowd, "Did I desire to please natural Men, I need not preach here in the Wilderness." Although Whitefield spoke directly to the heart of each individual, he also drew together entire communities in a way no one had ever done before.

Whitefield embodied the great contradictions of his age without threatening the political or economic order that sustained them. He appealed to men as well as women, to the poor as well as the rich, to slaves as well as their masters, and to those who were suffering from capitalism as well as those who were benefiting from it. Whitefield's strategy was to criticize the individual without attacking the system. In Philadelphia, he preached, "Do not say, you are miserable, and poor, and blind and naked, and therefore ashamed to come, for it is to such that this Invitation is now sent. The Polite, the Rich, the Busy, Self-Righteous Pharisees of this Generation have been bidden already, but they . . . are too deeply engaged in going one to his Country House, another to his Merchandize."

The religious leadership came under his censure, but not the church itself. Cruel slave masters were condemned, but not the institution of slavery. He showed men and women who were adrift in the new political economy how to acquire the self-discipline that would enable them either to succeed in a competitive market

continued

>> AMERICAN PORTRAIT *continued*

or to bear failures with Christian resignation. He helped them experience religion as an intense personal feeling. He showed people how to find meaning for their lives in a time of rapid economic transformation.

A world traveler who came to call Georgia his home, Whitefield died in Newburyport, Massachusetts, in 1770, preaching to the end. Five years later, a band of Continental Army officers, on their way to fight the British in Quebec, dug up his corpse. The evangelist's body had decayed, but his clothing was still intact. The soldiers snipped pieces of it to take with them, to protect them on their perilous mission.

OUTLINE

The Population Explosion of the Eighteenth Century

George Whitefield could speak to the hearts of the American colonists because he understood their world. As the American colonies matured, they were tied into the North Atlantic world, which brought dramatic changes. One of the most important changes was the increase in population, both from immigration and natural increase. This population produced products for the world economy and provided a market for them as well. The population boom was both the product of American prosperity and the precondition for its further growth.

> "I must own, to the shame of my own countrymen, that I was first kidnapped and betrayed by some of my own complexion, who were the first cause of my exile and slavery; but if there were no buyers there would be no sellers."
>
> OTTOBAH CUGOANO,
> describing his enslavement at the age of thirteen

The Dimensions of Population Growth

The population in the American colonies grew at a rate unprecedented in human history. In 1700 there were just over 250,000 people living in the colonies, but by 1750 the population had grown to more than 1 million. The rate of growth was highest in the free population in the prosperous farming regions, but it was rapid everywhere, even among slaves, in spite of their harsh living conditions.

Much of the colonies' population growth was caused by their unquenchable thirst for labor. The colonies attracted an extraordinary number of immigrants, and when free labor did not satisfy the demand, unfree labor (slaves, indentured servants, and redemptioners) filled the gap. In fact, when the number of Africans who came in chains is added to the Europeans who came as indentured servants and redemptioners, 90 percent of the immigrants to the British colonies between 1580 and 1775 were unfree at the time of their arrival.

Increasingly, these immigrants reflected the broad reach of the North Atlantic political world. At the beginning of the eighteenth century, the population of the American colonies was primarily English in origin. By the beginning of the American Revolution, the population in the British colonies had changed significantly. There were small numbers of people with Finnish, Swedish, French, Swiss, and Jewish heritage. There were also large numbers of Welsh, Scotch-Irish, Germans, Dutch, and Africans. The foundation for the subsequent diversity of the American population had been laid.

Bound for America: European Immigrants

A significant portion of the colonies' population increase came from immigration. In the eighteenth century, substantial numbers of people came from Scotland, Northern Ireland, Wales, and Germany. In all, about 425,000 Europeans migrated to the colonies in the eighteenth century.

The largest number of European immigrants were Scotch-Irish, that is, Scottish people who had moved to Northern Ireland to escape famine in their own country. As many as 250,000 came to the British colonies to seek a better life and to escape the religious persecution they experienced as Presbyterians in an Anglican society. At first, Massachusetts invited the Scotch-Irish to settle on its borders, as a buffer between the settled region of the colony and the Indians. Once the Scotch-Irish began to arrive in large numbers, however, the English inhabitants worried that they would have to provide for the impoverished newcomers. In 1729 a Boston mob turned away a shipload of Scotch-Irish immigrants, and in 1738 the Puritan inhabitants of Worcester burned down a Presbyterian church. Thereafter, the vast majority of Scotch-Irish immigrants headed for the middle colonies and the South, where they were more welcome.

Going where land was the cheapest, the Scotch-Irish settled between the English settlements along the seaboard and the Indian communities to the west, from Pennsylvania to Georgia (see Map 5–1). As their numbers increased, the Scotch-Irish pressed against the Indians, seizing, for example, a 15,000-acre tract that the Penn family had set aside for the Conestoga Indians. Like the Scotch-Irish, most German migrants settled in the backcountry from Pennsylvania to the Carolinas. Between 1700 and the start of the Revolution, more than 100,000 Germans moved to the American colonies, and by 1775, a third of the population of Pennsylvania

Map 5–1 Expansion of Settlement, 1720–1760 By 1760, the colonial population made up an almost continuous line of settlement from Maine to Florida and was pushing west over the Appalachian Mountains.

was German. The Germans were diverse, including not only Lutherans and Catholics but also Quakers, Amish, and Mennonites. German immigrants established prosperous farming communities wherever they settled. Indeed, those colonies such as Pennsylvania that welcomed the widest variety of immigrants became not only the most prosperous, but also the ones in which that prosperity was most widely shared. Unlike most seventeenth-century migrants, a large proportion of eighteenth-century migrants were skilled but relatively impoverished artisans drawn to America by the demand for skilled labor. As African slaves began to fill the demand for agricultural workers, especially in the South, the colonies needed skilled workers, especially those who could build anything from houses to bridges and those who could repair whatever was broken.

The majority of European migrants to the colonies were unfree, not only indentured servants and redemptioners but also the 50,000 British convicts whose sentences were commuted to a term of service in the colonies. Most English and Welsh migrants were single men between the ages of 19 and 23 who came as indentured servants. The Scotch-Irish migration included a larger number of families, and three-fourths of the Germans came in family groups. For all immigrants, the passage to America, which could take three months or more, was grueling. Gottlieb Mittelberger described the afflictions of the journey: "The ship is full of pitiful signs of distress—smells, fumes, horrors, vomiting, various kinds of sea sickness, fever, dysentery, headaches, heat, constipation, boils, scurvy, cancer, [and] mouth-rot." Once the migrants arrived, the servants and convicts were sold for terms of service in auctions that resembled those held for African slaves.

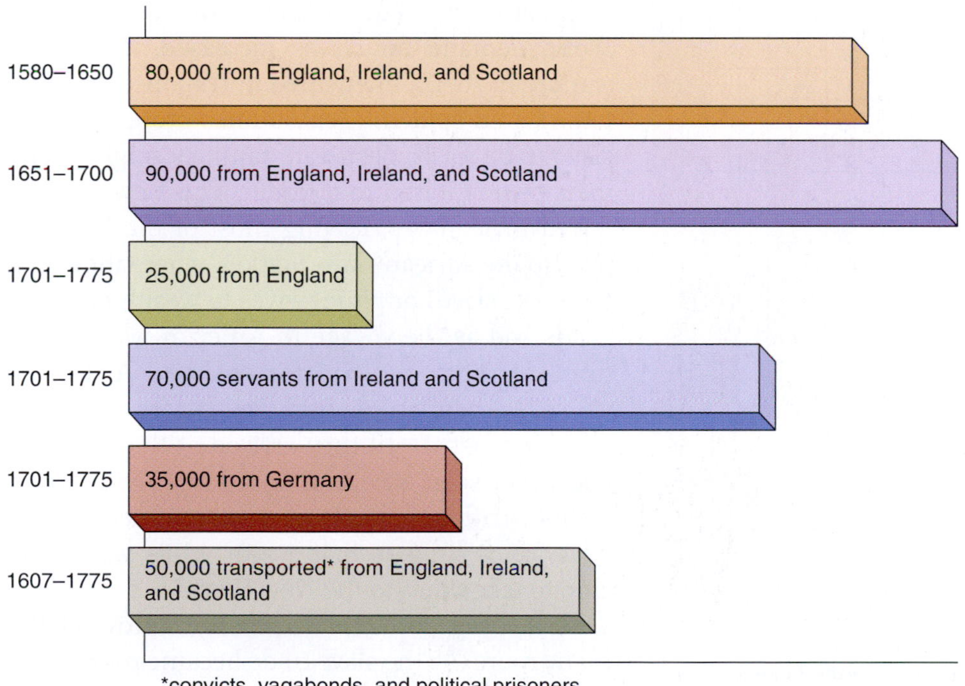

Figure 5-1 The Importation of Servants from Europe into British America, 1580–1775 By the time of the American Revolution, 350,000 servants had been imported into the colonies, most of whom came from the British Isles. *Richard S. Dunn, "Servants and Slaves," in Jack P. Greene and J. R. Pole,* Colonial British America *(Baltimore: Johns Hopkins, 1984), p. 159.*

Bound for America: African Slaves

The increase in the African population was even more dramatic than that of Europeans. In 1660 there were only 2,920 African or African-descended inhabitants of the mainland colonies. A century later they numbered more than 300,000. The proportion of Africans grew most rapidly in the southern colonies, where it stood at almost 40 percent on the eve of the Revolution. By 1720 South Carolina had an African majority. Most of the increase in the African population came from the slave trade. By 1808, when Congress closed off the importation of slaves to the United States, about 523,000 African slaves had been imported into the nation (see Figure 5–2).

The African slave trade was a profitable and well-organized segment of the world economy. Until the eighteenth century, when demand from the New World increased, the transatlantic slave trade was controlled by Africans who set the terms, including the prices, of the trade. Generally, Europeans were not allowed into the interior of Africa, so slaves were brought to the coast for sale. Many African nations taxed the sale of slaves and regulated the trade in other ways. Some nations supplied a steady stream of slaves, while others offered them intermittently, suggesting that participation in the trade was a matter of conscious policy.

Because African slaves were unwilling and sometimes rebellious passengers on the ships that transported them across the Atlantic, European slave ships needed larger crews and heavier weapons than ordinary cargo required. This resistance on the part of the slaves increased the cost of transporting them so much that the higher prices may have spared half a million Africans enslavement.

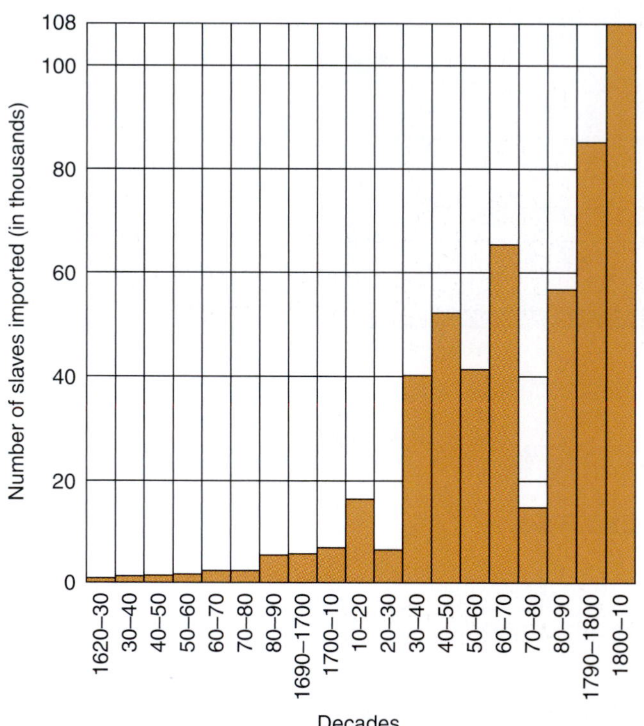

Figure 5–2 The Importation of Slaves into the Colonies, 1620–1810 The number of Africans imported into the colonies increased dramatically in the eighteenth century, and, except for an interruption during the American Revolution, continued until the African slave trade was made illegal in 1808. *Helen Hornbeck Tanner,* The Settling of North America *(New York: Macmillan, 1995), p. 51.*

Most slaves were captives of war, and as the New World demand for slaves increased, the tempo of warfare in Africa intensified in response. In times of famine and epidemic, sometimes brought on by the slave trade itself, desperate families might even sell their own children to a trader. The New World preferred male slaves, leaving most of the female captives to the African slave market, where they became domestic slaves or plural wives to wealthier Africans.

As bad as the voyage to America was for indentured servants, the trip for enslaved Africans was worse. Perhaps 10 percent died before reaching the African coast. Until they arrived at the coast, many had never seen an ocean or a white man, and both sights terrified them. They were confined in pens or forts for as long as half a year while waiting for a ship to take them to the New World.

The voyage, or "middle passage," proved lethal to many more. As the slave trade became more efficient in the eighteenth century, the mortality rate dropped, from perhaps 20 percent to half that amount. Those who survived were ready to begin their lives as New World slaves.

AMERICAN LANDSCAPE

>> The Slave Ship

We do not usually think of a ship as part of a landscape, but the slave ship was one of the most important locations in the eighteenth century. It was at once a floating factory, prison, and fortress. It was there that Africans were transformed into slaves.

Any ship, small or large, could be made into a slave ship. Because the cost of transporting slaves across the Atlantic was so high, accounting for three-quarters of the price of a slave, slave merchants tried to crowd as many Africans as possible into each ship—300, 400, or even 600. The English were particularly efficient, carrying twice as many slaves per crew member and half again as many slaves per ship as the other nations, thereby increasing the profits.

In order to maximize the number of Africans who could be transported on each ship, platforms were built between the decks of the ship, thus doubling the surface area upon which the slaves could be placed. With perhaps only four and a half feet between the platform and the ceiling, the Africans could not stand up. Nor, because they were packed so tightly, could they move from side to side. Enterprising captains made use of even the smallest spaces by filling them with children.

Packing so many human beings into such tight quarters created the risk of suffocation. But if the hatches were kept open, the Africans might escape confinement and overpower the crew. Hence, grates were placed over the hatches, and small air scuttles were cut into the sides of the ship. By the end of the eighteenth century, some ships used large funnel tubes made out of canvas and hoops to carry air below decks.

Men and women were kept separate, their portions of the decks divided by partitions. Male slaves were shackled and confined below deck for most of each day. Chained together and without enough room to stand up, many

continued

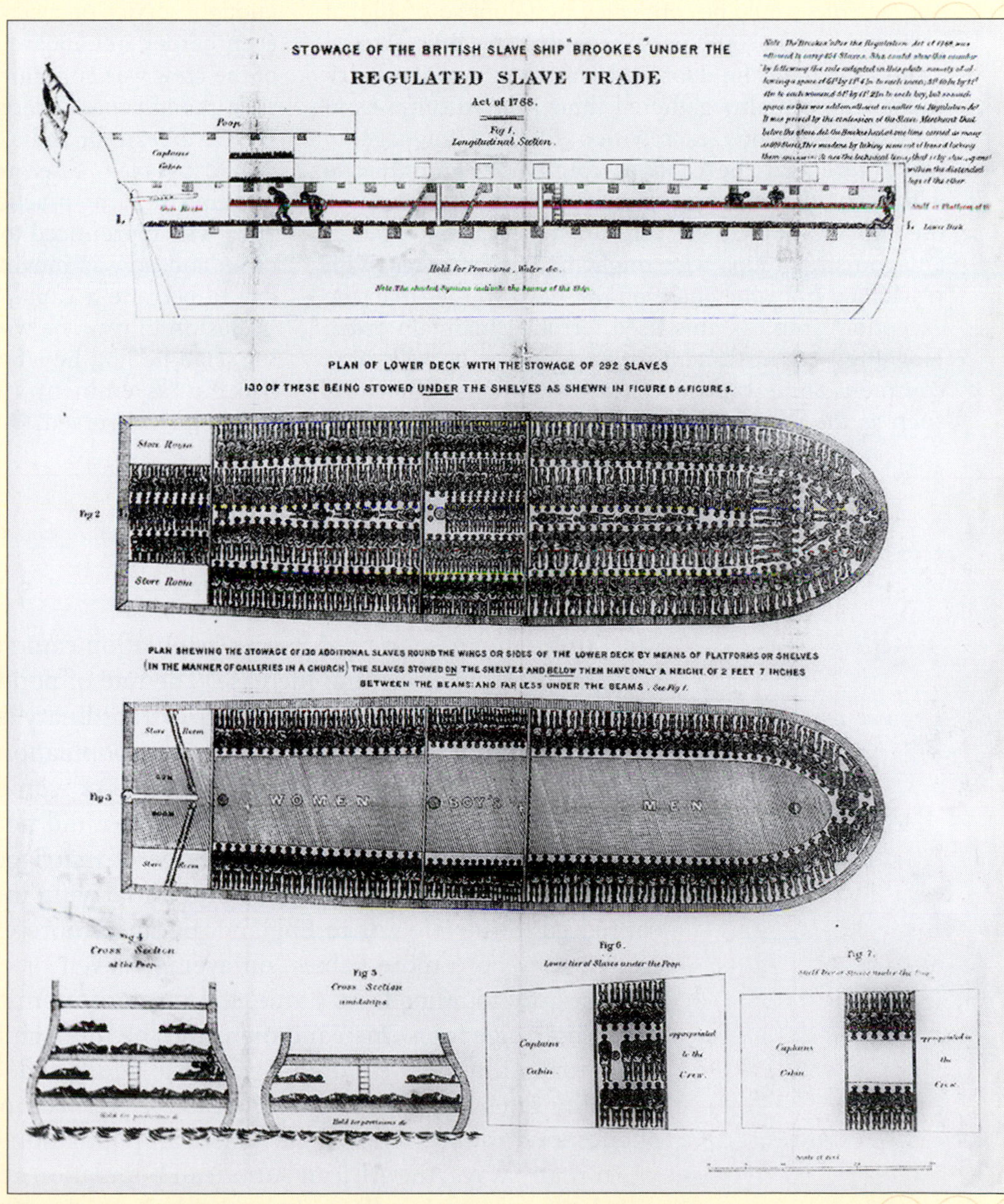

>> **AMERICAN LANDSCAPE** *continued*

were unable to reach the large buckets that served as latrines. Some captains let the slaves lie in their own filth until the voyage's end. Heat and disease compounded the misery. One ship's doctor reported that the slaves' deck "was so covered with the blood and mucus which had proceeded from them in consequence of the flux, that it resembled a slaughterhouse." The women were left unshackled, but their relative freedom left them prey to the sailors' lust. When slaves were brought above deck, some would jump overboard. Captains stretched netting around their ships to prevent such suicides.

In order to protect the crew in case of insurrection, slave ships often had thick, ten-foot-high walls—barricados—to separate the crew from the human cargo. The two sections would be connected by a door so small that only one person could pass through it at a time. Armed sailors guarded the door and patrolled atop the barricado. Ship captains gathered their human cargo from a variety of regions, each with a different language, to make sure that the captives could not communicate with each other and foment rebellion. At the same time, the captains had to be careful not to bring together antagonistic groups who might fight each other. With resistance from the enslaved the norm rather than the exception, ship captains used terror to maintain order. Flogging—a punishment used on sailors, as well—was common. Some captains used instruments of torture, such as the thumbscrew, "a dreadful engine, which, if the screw be turned by an unrelenting hand, can give intolerable anguish." The object was not only to punish the disobedient but to cast fear into the hearts of their shipmates. That was surely the result after some of the Africans aboard the *Brownlow* rebelled. The captain dismembered the rebels with an axe "till their bodies remained only like a trunk of a tree when all the branches are lopped away," and he threw the severed heads and limbs at the other slaves, who were chained together on the deck of the ship.

Such terror hardened the captain and crew as well. Few sailors signed onto a slave ship if they had better options. One captain described his crew as the "very dregs of the community." The life of a sailor was hard enough; service on a slave ship—a floating prison—was even harder. Yet aboard ship, even the lowest member of the crew was superior to the enslaved. Consequently, even though many were dark-skinned men from Asia, the Caribbean, or India, at sea, they were all known as "white people." After repeated voyages, both captain and crew became practiced in the ways of cruelty. Silas Todd was apprenticed to a slave ship captain at the age of 14, and he was moving up in the ranks, hoping one day to become a captain himself. Then, while ashore in Boston in 1734, he was "saved" in the Great Awakening. Had he not, he later reflected, he might later have become "as eminent a savage" as the captains under whom he had served. ●

The Great Increase of Offspring

Most of the increase in the colonies' population came not from immigration or the slave trade but from natural increase. The rate of population growth for both Europeans and Africans in the colonies was extraordinary (see Fig. 5–3).

For Euro-Americans the main source of population increase was a lower age of marriage for women and a higher proportion of women who married. In England, for example, as many as 20 percent of women did not marry by age 45, compared to only 5 percent in the colonies. The age of marriage for women in the colonies was also considerably lower, with women marrying in their late teens or early 20s, compared to the late 20s in England. Because more women married, and married earlier, they bore more babies, on average seven or eight each, with six or seven surviving to adulthood. As a rule, the more economic opportunity, the earlier the age of marriage for women and men, and the more children. Likewise, the healthier the climate, the more children survived to adulthood, but compared to today, child mortality rates were high. Still, the rate of population growth in the colonies was phenomenal, and as a result the American population was exceptionally young.

In many ways, the African American population resembled the Euro-American population, for both suffered from the dislocations of moving to a new land. Those

This group is being force marched by an African slave trader from the interior of Africa to a European trading post on the coast.

slaves who were born in the colonies married young and established families as stable as slavery permitted. By the time they were 18, most slave women usually had their first child. As was customary in Africa, they might not form a lasting union with the father, but within a few years many settled into long-lasting relationships with the men who would father the rest of their children. Slave women bore between six and eight children, on average. With child mortality even higher for African Americans than for Euro-Americans, between 25 percent and 50 percent of these slave children died before reaching adulthood. Even so, the slave population more than reproduced itself. By the middle of the eighteenth century the African American population was growing more from natural increase than from the importation of slaves. Only a tiny fraction of the Africans sold into slavery ended up in mainland British colonies. Nonetheless, when slavery was abolished after the Civil War, the United States had the largest population of African descent in the New World.

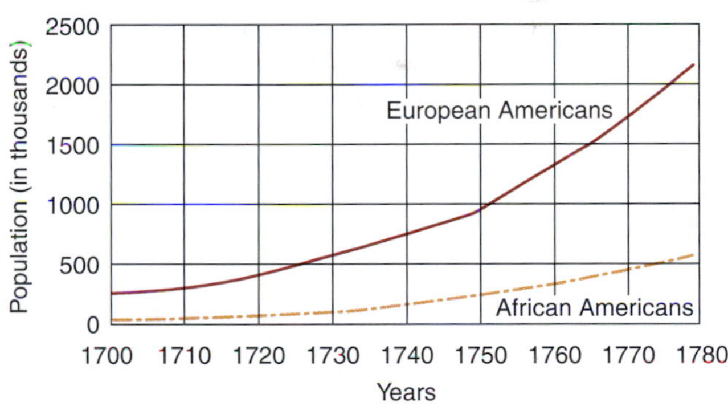

Figure 5–3 Population of the Thirteen Colonies, 1610–1780 Because of natural increase and immigration, the European population in the colonies grew even more rapidly than the African one. *Jacob Cooke, ed.,* Encyclopedia of North American Colonies *(New York: Scribner's, 1993), pp. 1, 470.*

The Transatlantic Economy: Producing and Consuming

In the eighteenth century, as the colonies matured, they became capitalist societies, tied increasingly in to an Atlantic trade network. More and more, people produced for the market, so that they could buy the goods the market had to offer.

Throughout the Atlantic world, ordinary people reoriented their economic lives so they could buy more goods. Historians talk about two economic revolutions in this period: a consumer revolution—a slow and steady increase in the demand for, and purchase of, consumer goods—and an industrious revolution (not industri*al* but industri*ous* revolution), in which people worked harder and organized their households (their families, servants, and slaves) to produce goods for sale, so that they would have money to pay for items they wanted. Income went up only slightly in the eighteenth century, yet people were buying more. In the process, they created a consumer society, one in which most people eagerly purchased consumer goods.

"It seems indelicate, at least new, to strip, surrounded by different Ages & Sexes, & Rise in the Morning, in the Blaze of Day, with the Eyes of, at least, one blinking Irish Female searching out Subjects for Remark."

PHILIP VICKERS FITHIAN,
a young Presbyterian minister, who was lodged one night with an entire family in a single room in their small cabin on the Pennsylvania frontier

The Nature of Colonial Economic Growth

Throughout human history, population growth has usually led to a decline in standard of living as more people compete for fewer resources. In the American colonies, however, population growth led to an expansion of the economy, as more of the continent's abundant natural resources were brought under human control. The standard of living for most free Americans probably improved, although not dramatically. As the economy matured, a small segment of the economy—urban merchants and owners of large plantations—became wealthy. At the same time, the urban poor and tenant farmers began to slip toward poverty.

All of these changes took place, however, without any significant changes in technology (such as the power looms that would be invented later in the century or the system of interchangeable parts that would make mass production possible). Most wealth was made from shipping and agriculture. Eighty percent of the colonies' population worked on farms or plantations, areas with no major technological innovations. Virtually all gains in productivity came instead from labor: quite simply, more people were working, and they were working more efficiently.

The economy of colonial America was shaped by three factors: abundance of land and shortages of labor and capital. The plantation regions of the South and the West Indies were best situated to take advantage of these circumstances, and the small-farm areas of New England were the least suited. Tobacco planters in the Chesapeake and rice and indigo planters in South Carolina sold their products on a huge world market. Their large profits enabled them to purchase more land and more slaves to work it.

Because northern farmers raised crops and animals that were also produced in Europe, profits from agriculture alone were too low to permit them to acquire large tracts of land or additional labor (see Table 5–1). Northerners who hoped to become wealthy had to look for other opportunities. They found them in trade, exchanging American raw goods for European manufactured ones and selling them to American consumers.

The Transformation of the Family Economy

In colonial America, the family was the basic economic unit. From the time they were able, all family members contributed to the family economy. Work was organized by gender. On farms, women were responsible for the preparation of food and clothing, child care, and care of the home. Women grew vegetables and herbs, provided dairy products, and transformed flax and wool into clothing. The daughters in the family worked under their mother's supervision, perhaps spinning extra yarn to be sold for a profit.

Men performed the work on the rest of the farm. They raised grain and maintained the pastures. They cleared the land, chopped wood for fuel, and built and maintained the house, barn, and other structures. They took their harvested crops to market. Men's and women's work were complementary, and both were necessary for the family's economic survival. For example, men planted apple trees, children picked apples, and women made them into cider. Men herded the sheep whose wool women sheared, carded, spun, and dyed. When a husband was disabled, ill, or away from home, his wife could fill in for him, performing virtually all of his tasks as a sort of "deputy husband." Men almost never performed women's work, however, and men whose wives died remarried quickly to have someone to take care of the household and children.

The eighteenth century's industrious revolution transformed the family economy: when people decided to produce goods to sell, they changed their family economies. Historians believe that increased production in this period came primarily from the labor of women and children, who worked harder and longer than they had before.

 **Table 5–1** How Wealthy Were Colonial Americans?

Property-owning Class	New England	Mid-Atlantic Colonies	Southern Colonies	Thirteen Colonies
Men	£169	£ 194	£ 410	£260
Women	£ 42	£ 103	£ 215	£132
Adults 45 and older	£252	£ 274	£ 595	£361
Adults 44 and younger	£129	£ 185	£ 399	£237
Urban	£191	£ 287	£ 641	£233
Rural	£151	£ 173	£ 392	£255
Esquires, gentlemen	£313	£1,223	£1,281	£572
Merchants	£563	£ 858	£ 314	£497
Professions, sea captains	£271	£ 241	£ 512	£341
Farmers only, planters	£155	£ 180	£ 396	£263
Farmer-artisans, ship owners, fishermen	£144	£ 257	£ 801	£410
Shop and tavern keepers	£219	£ 222	£ 195	£204
Artisans, chandlers	£114	£ 144	£ 138	£122
Miners, laborers	£ 52	£ 67	£ 383	£ 62

Source: Alice Hanson Jones, *Wealth of a Nation to Be: The American Colonies on the Eve of the Revolution* (New York: Columbia University Press, 1980), p. 224.

Sources of Regional Prosperity

The South, the most productive region, accounted for more than 60 percent of colonial exports (see Map 5–2). Tobacco remained the region's chief cash crop. Next came cereals such as rice, wheat, corn, and flour, and then indigo, a plant used to dye fabric.

Slave labor accounted for most of the southern agricultural output, and the slave labor force was organized to produce for the market. When profits from tobacco began to slip because of falling prices and the depletion of the soil, planters worked their slaves harder and, in the Chesapeake, began to plant corn and wheat. By diversifying their crops, planters were also able to keep their slaves busy throughout the year. Successful planters made maximum use of their slave labor force.

The work routine of slaves depended on the crops that they tended. On tobacco plantations, where careful attention to the plants was necessary to ensure high quality, planters or white overseers worked the slaves in small gangs. Each gang was carefully selected and arranged to maximize productivity. The strongest field hand, for example, would be put at the head of a row of hoers, and all the other slaves would be made to work at his pace.

In the rice-growing regions of the lower South, however, slaves were usually assigned specific tasks, which they would work at until the job was completed. Rice growing required far less supervision than did tobacco planting. Because many Africans had grown rice in Africa, it is likely that they taught Europeans how to

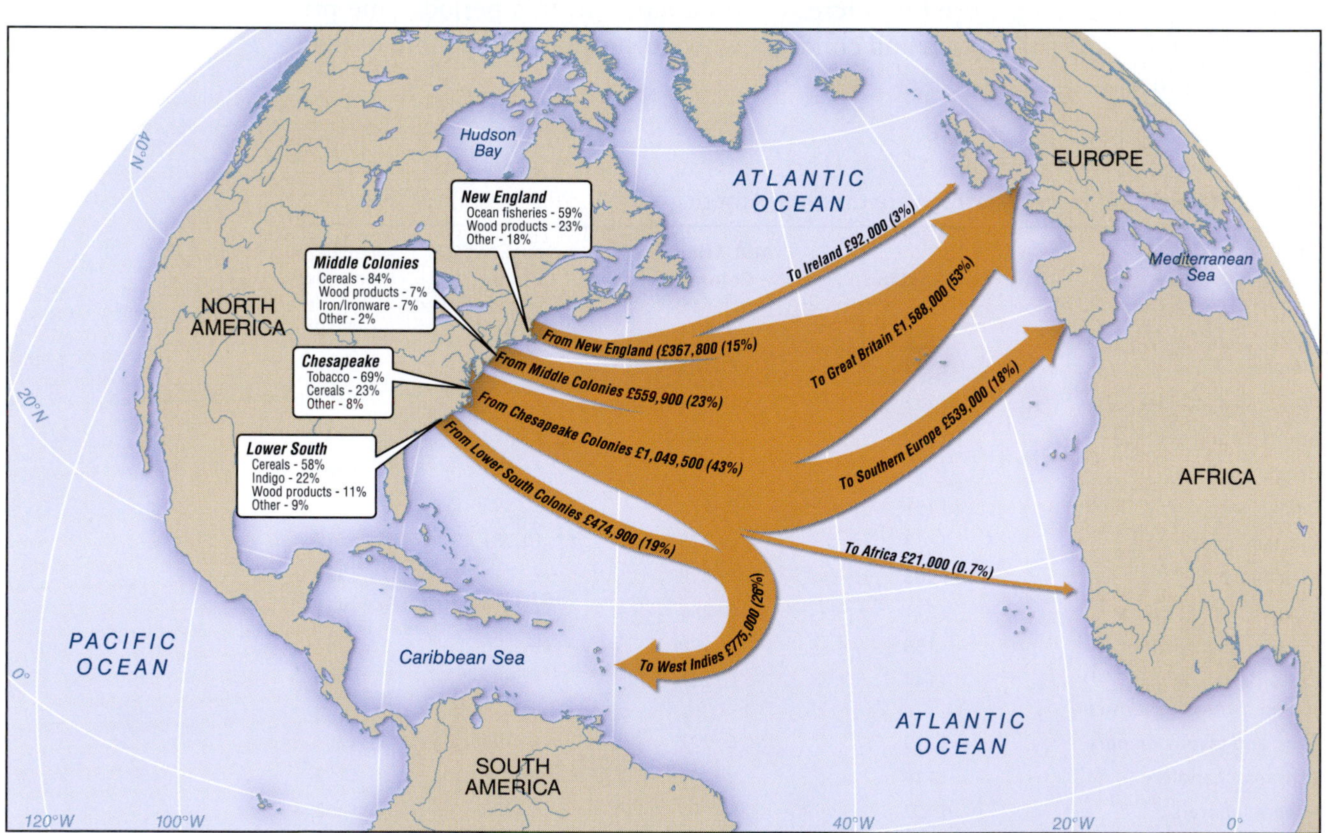

Map 5–2 Exports of the Thirteen Colonies, ca. 1770 Almost two-thirds of the exports from the colonies came from the South, and more than one-half went to Great Britain alone. Tobacco and grains were the most important exports of all. *Jacob Cooke, ed.,* Encyclopedia of North American Colonies *(New York: Scribner's, 1993), pp. 1, 514.*

grow it in America. Under these circumstances, rice planters let the slaves set their own pace. Once the slaves had finished their task for the day, they could use their time as they pleased. Many planted gardens to supplement their own diets or to earn a small income. Slaves trafficked in a wide range of products, not only rice, corn, chickens, hogs, and catfish, but also canoes, baskets, and wax.

The inhabitants of the middle colonies grew prosperous by raising wheat and other grains to sell on the market. The ports of Baltimore, Philadelphia, Wilmington, and New York became thriving commercial centers that collected grain from regional farmers, milled it into flour, and shipped it to the West Indies, southern Europe, and other American colonies. Farmers relied on indentured servants, cottagers, and slaves to supplement the labor of family members. *Cottagers* were families who rented out part of a farmer's land, which they worked for wages.

As long as land was cheap and easy to obtain, the middle colonies enjoyed the most evenly shared prosperity on the continent. Most inhabitants fell into the comfortable middle class, with the gap between the richest and the poorest relatively small. Pennsylvania, which offered both religious toleration and relatively simple procedures for the purchase of land, was particularly prosperous. The energy that elsewhere went into religious conflict here was freed for work and material accumulation. Gottlieb Mittelberger, who endured a horrendous journey to Pennsylvania, described his new home as a sort of paradise: "Our Americans live more quietly and peacefully than the Europeans; and all this is the result of the liberty which they enjoy and which makes them all equal."

When land became expensive or difficult to obtain, however, conflict might ensue. In the 1740s and 1750s, both New Jersey and New York experienced land riots when conflicting claims made land titles uncertain. In other regions, such as the Chesapeake and southeastern Pennsylvania, increasing land prices drove the poorest inhabitants into tenancy or to the urban centers. The widespread prosperity of the eighteenth century led Americans to expect that every family who wanted a farm would be able to own one. Unlike in Europe, land ownership was the rule, not the exception, and any deviation from this norm produced tension and anger.

Like the middle colonies, New England was primarily a farming region. However, indentured servants, cottagers, and slaves were far less common there. Instead, most farm labor was provided by male family members. Although farms in some regions, such as the Connecticut River valley, produced surpluses for the market, most New England farm families had to look for other sources of income to pay for consumer goods.

Town governments in New England encouraged enterprise, sometimes providing their inhabitants with gristmills, sawmills, and fields on which cattle could graze. As a result the region prospered, and New Englanders came to expect that government should act to enhance the economy. Agricultural exports from the region were relatively slight, although New Englanders sent both grain and livestock to the slave plantations of the West Indies. In fact, more than 25 percent of the American colonies' exports (and more than 70 percent of New England's exports) went to the West Indies.

The other major exports of the American colonies in the eighteenth century were fur and hides. By the eve of the Revolution, 95 percent of the furs imported into England came from North America. As in the previous century, most of the furs were provided by Indians, who traded them to European middlemen.

Drying Cod Men landing and drying cod in Newfoundland. Increasingly, fishing became a form of dependent wage labor, as merchants supplied boats and equipment and hired other men to fish for them.

Merchants and Dependent Laborers in the Transatlantic Economy

Almost all regions of the colonies participated in a transatlantic economy. In each region, those who were most involved in the market were those with the most resources: large planters in the southern colonies, owners of the biggest farms in the middle colonies, and urban merchants in the northern colonies. The wealthiest colonists never made their fortunes from farming or planting alone but always supplemented their incomes from activities such as speculating in land, practicing law, or lending money.

If some economic development was spurred from above, by enterprising individuals or by governments, much also developed from the aspirations of ordinary men and women. New England's mixed economy of grain, grazing, fishing, and lumbering required substantial capital improvements such as gristmills, sawmills, and tanneries if the inhabitants were to turn a profit. By the beginning of the eighteenth century, shipbuilding was a substantial part of the economy. In fact, by 1775, one-third of the English merchant fleet had been built in the colonies.

The shipbuilding industry, in turn, spurred further economic development. In a process called linked economic development (because it ties together a variety of enterprises), shipbuilding stimulated other activities, such as lumbering. In addition, the availability of ships made possible a flourishing trade. The profits generated by shipbuilding and trade were reinvested in sawmills to produce more lumber, in gristmills to grind grain into flour, and, of course, in more trading voyages. The growth of shipping in port cities such as Boston, Newport, New York, Philadelphia, and Charleston led to the emergence of an affluent merchant class. Trading was a risky business, and although many tried it, few rose to the top. One ship lost to a storm could ruin a merchant, as could a sudden turn in the market. In 1759 two enterprising Philadelphians, Daniel Wister and Owen Jones, with just over £4,000 between them, persuaded English merchants to send them £94,000 worth of goods. For two years the partnership prospered, but when the market went sour in 1761, Wister was left bankrupt while Jones struggled to pick up the pieces. With an average of 10 times the capital of colonial merchants, English merchants could weather such reverses. Because capital was scarce in the colonies, merchants took great risks, seeking to turn a quick profit during wartime (see Chapter 6) or gambling on a sudden spurt in the price of wheat. Bad choices or bad luck could ruin any merchant.

The seafaring trades were at the forefront of capitalist development. A wealthy, risk-taking merchant class emerged, as well as that other distinguishing mark of a capitalist economy, a wage-earning class. As long as there was a labor shortage in the colonies, workers had an advantage. By the beginning of the eighteenth century, however, rapid population increase led to a growing supply of labor in towns such as Salem and Marblehead in Massachusetts. Although they were free to shop around for the best wages, workers became part of a wage-earning working class, dependent on others for their employment and income. Only a small portion of the

"Commerce Moves All," According to This Certificate of Membership in a Sailmakers' Society. Here we see not only linked economic activities such as sailmaking (lower right-hand corner) and trade but also the moral benefits that were imagined to flow from commerce—charity (upper right-hand corner) and abolition of slavery (upper left-hand corner).

American population was working for wages on the eve of the Revolution, but was a sign of things to come.

Consumer Choices and the Creation of Gentility

Under the British mercantilist system (see Chapter 4, "Continental Empires"), the colonies were supposed to export raw materials to the empire and import finished products from the empire. Thus the colonies sent sugar (from the West Indies), tobacco, wheat, lumber, fish, and animal pelts to Britain and imported cloth and iron. Yet within this general pattern, individual men and women made choices about what to buy.

On both sides of the Atlantic, demand for both plantation products and consumer goods was insatiable. At first only the wealthy could afford such luxuries as sugar and tobacco. But as more and more labor was organized to produce for the market, ordinary men and women found themselves with added income, which they used to purchase luxury products. Tea, imported into both Britain and the colonies from Asia, became, like tobacco and sugar, a mass-consumed luxury. By the time of the Revolution, annual sugar consumption in England had skyrocketed to 23 pounds

AMERICA AND THE WORLD

>> Consumer Tastes in Global Perspective

It is no surprise that Europeans got hooked on the products of colonial plantations: many of them were mildly, if not highly, addictive. The addictive properties of tobacco are well known today, but many of the other products raised on colonial plantations also were habit forming: coffee, cocoa, tea, and sugar (and its by-product rum). As consumer demand for such products grew in Europe, colonial plantation agriculture expanded.

Consider the case of coffee. It originated in Ethiopia but was introduced into the Middle East by Arab traders around 1000 CE. The drink had made its way to the Ottoman Empire by the middle of the sixteenth century, and although some Muslim theologians disapproved of the drink, it soon became popular. European travelers to the major Muslim cities—Constantinople, Cairo, Alexandria, Aleppo—picked up a taste for coffee and began importing it into Europe. The first coffeehouse in London was built in 1652; 60 years later, there were at least 500. Coffeehouses in Europe quickly became what they were in the Middle East: places of male sociability.

By 1700, the prime coffee-growing region of Yemen could no longer meet the growing demand, so Muslim traders introduced coffee cultivation to India. Then, Europeans expanded cultivation to their colonies in Jamaica, Barbados, and Indonesia. Here, the Dutch East India Company played a leading role, introducing both coffee planting and slavery to Indonesia. The French brought coffee cultivation to Martinique in the West Indies, and the Portuguese took it to Brazil.

The history of tea drinking in Europe is similar; tea was introduced to Britain in the seventeenth century and eventually became more popular even than coffee. By the middle of the eighteenth century, tea was an item of mass consumption, with everyone in London and the major cities drinking it regularly. Most of it was imported—legally and illegally both—from China or India.

Europeans liked their coffee and tea very sweet, so sugar consumption skyrocketed too. The plantations of the New World, particularly the French West Indies, supplied this demand. The demand for sugar also created a demand for people to grow it: slaves imported from Africa. In fact, New World slavery came into being to satisfy Europeans' craving for tobacco and sugar, which were luxuries, rather than the necessities of life.

The history of opium, the highly addictive drug that also became popular in the eighteenth century, is somewhat different. Here, the British East India Company—the firm that sold tea to the American colonies—pushed the drug into China, in order to help rectify an imbalance in trade. As British imports of tea from China increased, the British needed products to sell to China, ones that would be as popular as tea. The Chinese were not terribly interested in any of the British manufactures, but they developed a taste first for Indian fabrics and then for Indian opium. The East India Company secured a monopoly over Indian opium in 1773 and exported it to China, even though the Chinese had officially banned the drug.

The trade in addictive substances tied the continents of the world together in the eighteenth century. A global trade network, organized by state-supported companies and in many cases by slave labor, supplied the world's consumers with the addictive substances that they craved.

The port of Mocha in Yemen, here depicted in 1692, was the center of the global trade in coffee.

per person, and tobacco consumption was about 2 pounds per person—enough for a pipeful a day. Demand for these plantation products led directly to the traffic in African slaves.

As plantation products flowed east across the Atlantic, so manufactured goods came back to the colonies. Consumer behavior on both sides of the Atlantic was similar: people were smoking tobacco; sweetening their tea with sugar; and buying more clothing, more household items, more books, and more of every sort of manufactured goods.

This consumer revolution was not a product of higher wages. Instead, people made choices about how hard they would work—they chose to work harder. They made choices about what kind of work they would do—they chose work that brought in money. They decided what they would do with that money—they chose to buy particular items. Increasingly, people bought items that their friends and neighbors could see and that they could use in entertaining them. In seventeenth-century America, extra income was spent on items of lasting value, such as tablecloths and bed linens kept folded away in a chest, to pass on to one's children. In the eighteenth century, men and women bought more clothing made out of cheaper and less durable fabrics. Until this time, most people had only a few outfits. What they were not wearing at the time, they hung on pegs in the wall. The wealthy, of course, always had large wardrobes made from fine fabrics. In the eighteenth

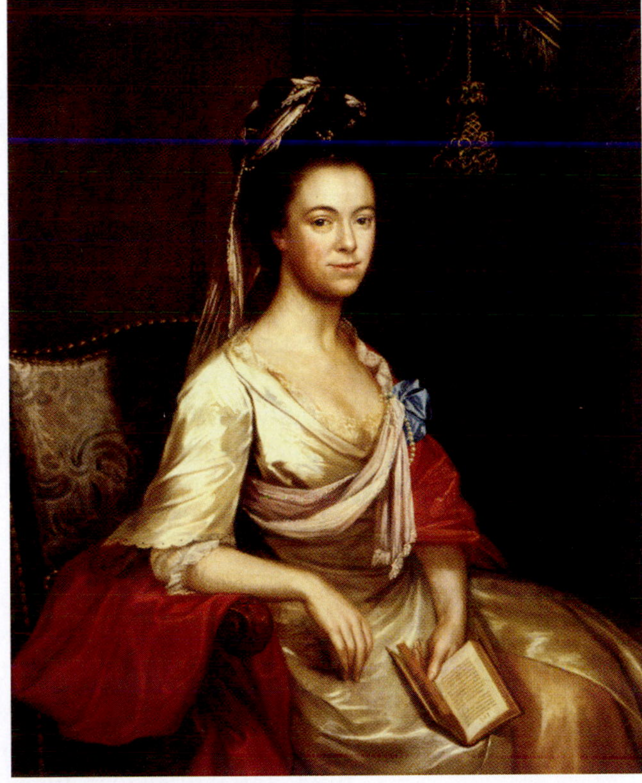

James Balfour and His Wife Jemima James Balfour, the representative of an English mercantile firm, and his wife Jemima moved to Virginia, where they assumed the roles of proper members of the merchant elite. James is depicted with his business papers and his son, illustrating the two aspects of a gentleman's character: his acumen for business and his affection for his family. His wife is pictured holding a book, demonstrating that she is a woman of education, with the leisure to pursue it.

century, however, fabric prices fell, and new, cheaper fabrics were manufactured to satisfy growing consumer demand. Then people needed new pieces of furniture in which to store their garments. Chests of drawers, or dressers, first became available to wealthy Britons and Americans in the 1630s and 1640s. By 1760, they had become a standard item of furniture for the middle class.

People became increasingly interested in how they appeared to others. Ordinary people began to pay attention to the latest fashions, which had once been a concern only of the wealthy. By 1700, two new items made it easier for those who had the time and money to attend to their appearance: the dressing table and the full-length mirror. For the first time, people could see how they looked, head to toe. Washing oneself and styling one's hair or periwig became standard rituals for all who hoped to appear "genteel."

In the eighteenth century, prospering people on both sides of the Atlantic created and tried to follow the standards of a new style of life, gentility. Gentility represented all that was polite, civilized, refined, and fashionable. It was everything that vulgarity, its opposite, was not. Gentility meant not only certain sorts of objects, such as a dressing table or a bone china teapot, but also the manners needed to use such objects properly. Standards of gentility established boundaries between the genteel and the vulgar. Those who considered themselves genteel looked down on those whose style of living seemed unrefined, and they became uncomfortable when circumstances required them to associate with their social inferiors.

Yet if gentility erected a barrier between the genteel and the vulgar, it also showed the vulgar how to become genteel. All they needed to do was acquire the right goods and learn how to use them. Throughout the colonies, ordinary people began to purchase consumer goods that established their gentility. Even relatively poor people often owned a mirror, a few pieces of china, or a teapot. The slaves who were executed in New York City in 1741 were probably conspiring not to burn the city down, but to steal clothing and other fancy goods that could be resold to poor people in the underground economy. This mass consumption and widespread distribution of consumer goods created and sustained the consumer revolution.

The consumer revolution had another egalitarian dimension: it encouraged sociability. Throughout the Atlantic world, men and women, particularly those with a little leisure and money (perhaps half the white population) began to cultivate social life. Many believed that the purpose of life was the sort of society that men and women created in their parlors when they met with friends and family for an evening of dining and conversation.

To put all of their guests on an equal footing, men and women began to purchase matching sets of dinner plates, silverware, glasses, and chairs. Until the eighteenth century, the most important people at the table—the man of the house, his wife, and high-ranking men—got the best chairs. Children, servants, and those of lower social standing sat on stools, benches, or boxes, or they stood. Dishes, utensils, and mugs rarely matched. Matched sets of tableware and chairs underscored the symbolic equality of all dinner guests.

The newest and most popular consumer goods made their way quickly to America—forks, drinking glasses, and teapots. Each new implement and style had its own etiquette. Such rules were daunting for the uneducated, but once they were mastered, a person could enter polite society anywhere in the Atlantic world and be accepted. The eighteenth-century capitalist economy created a trade not only in goods and raw materials, but one in styles of life as well.

Historians debate the effects of the consumer revolution, but on balance it was a democratic force. Ordinary men and women and even slaves came to think it was their right to spend their money as they pleased. As one Bostonian put it in 1754, the poor should be allowed to buy "the Conveniencies, and Comforts, as well as Necessaries of Life . . . as freely as the Rich." After all, "I am sure we Work as hard as they do . . .; therefore, I cannot see why we have not as good a natural Right to them as they have."

The New Gentility In 1750 in Charleston, South Carolina, Mr. Peter Manigault and his friends toasted each other, demonstrating their civility and their knowledge of the rules of polite behavior, including how to drink punch from a stem glass.

At the same time, the consumer revolution rested on new systems of production that eventually led to the Industrial Revolution and the creation of a working class. Even before that time, men and women were working harder so that they could buy the new goods. Some worked harder voluntarily, but many did not. In the southern colonies, slavery expanded in order to produce the luxury goods that new consumers wanted to buy.

The Varieties of Colonial Experience

Although the eighteenth-century industrial and consumer revolutions tied the peoples of the North Atlantic world together, climate, geography, immigration, patterns of economic development, and population density made for considerable variety. Although the vast majority of Americans lived in small communities or on farms, an increasing number lived in cities that played a critical role in shaping colonial life. At the same time, farming regions, both slave and free, were maturing, changing the character of rural life, and the growing population continued to push at the frontiers, leading to the founding of Georgia.

Creating an Urban Public Sphere

At the end of the seventeenth century, none of the colonial towns—except Boston, with 7,000 people—was much more than a rural village. By 1720, Boston's population had grown to 12,000, Philadelphia had 10,000 inhabitants, New York had 7,000, and Newport and Charleston were home to almost 4,000 each. Forty years later, a number of other urban centers had sprung up, each with populations around 3,000—Salem, Marblehead, and Newburyport in Massachusetts; Portsmouth, New Hampshire; Providence, Rhode Island; New Haven and Hartford, Connecticut; Albany, New York; Lancaster, Pennsylvania; Baltimore, Maryland; Norfolk, Virginia;

and Savannah, Georgia. By the eve of the Revolution, the largest cities were even larger. Philadelphia had 30,000 residents, New York had 25,000, and Boston had 16,000 (see Map 5–3). All of these cities were either ports or centers for the fur trade. Colonial cities were centers of commerce; that was their reason for being.

Social life in colonial cities was characterized by two somewhat contradictory trends. On the one hand, nowhere in the colonies was social stratification among free people more pronounced. By the eve of the American Revolution, each city had an affluent elite, made up of merchants, professionals, and government officials, who established a refined style of life. Each city also had a class of indigent poor.

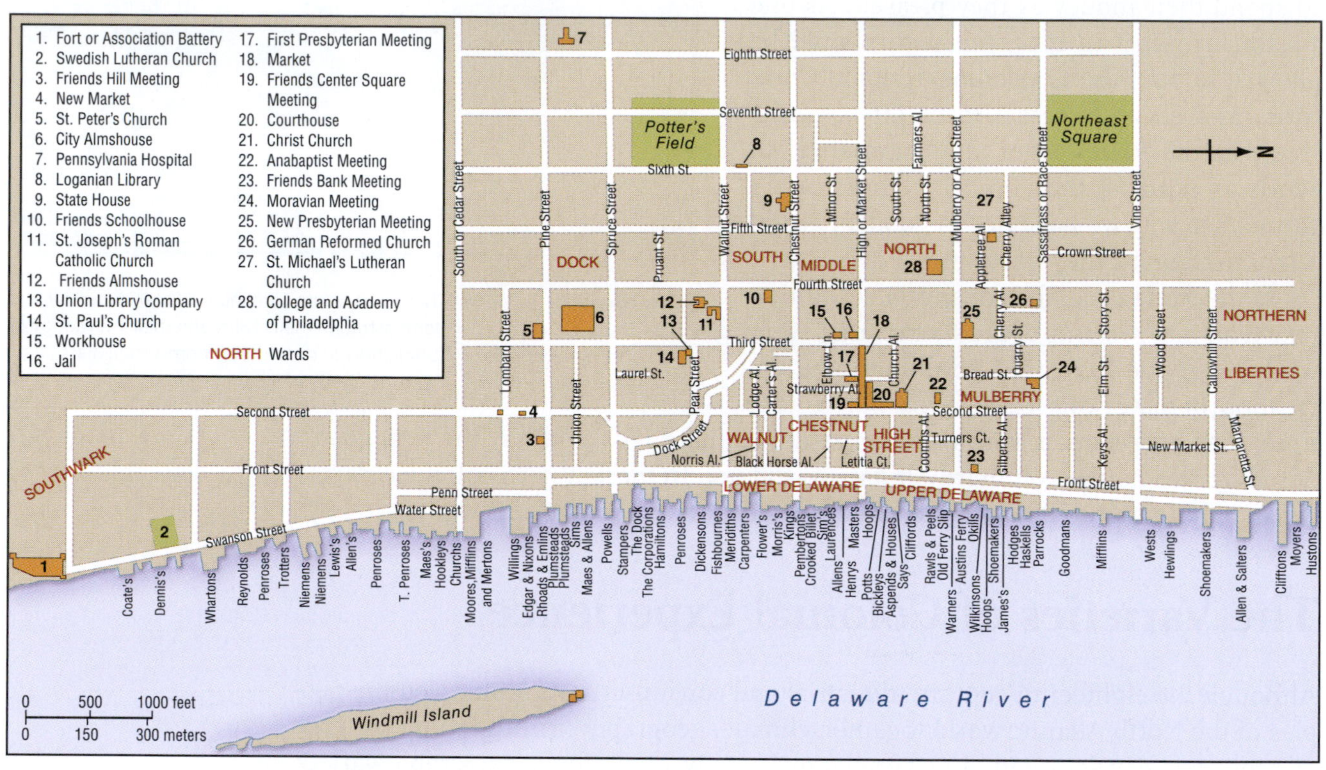

Map 5–3 Commerce and Culture in Philadelphia, ca. 1760 This map illustrates the close connection between commerce—note how many docks there are along the Delaware River—and culture. By 1760, Philadelphia was home to churches of many different denominations, as well as an array of enlightened institutions—a hospital, a college, and two libraries. *Lester Cappon, ed.,* The Atlas of Early American History *(Princeton, NJ: Princeton University Press,1976), p. 10.*

Philadelphia seen from the southeast, looking across the harbor.

On the other hand, urban life brought all classes of society together at theaters, in taverns, and at religious revivals such as the one led by George Whitefield. This civic life became one of the seedbeds of the Revolution because it provided a forum for the exchange of ideas.

Affluent city dwellers created a life as much like that of London as they could. They imported European finery and established English-style institutions. Urban elites founded social clubs, dancing assemblies, and fishing and hunting clubs. Although many of these associations were for men only, some brought men and women together. Such organizations helped the elite function as a class. By the middle of the eighteenth century, half of Philadelphia's merchant families belonged to the Dancing Assembly.

Urban associations reflected the ideals of the Enlightenment (see "The Ideas of the Enlightenment," p. 167). Some, such as the Masons, a European fraternal order that had branches in all the major colonial cities, espoused the ideal of universalism, that all people were by their nature fundamentally the same. Other institutions advocated self-improvement. Whereas some urban institutions separated out the elite and others challenged the ruling hierarchy, still others brought together all members of society in a "public sphere." City dwellers could see stage plays in Williamsburg by 1716, in Charleston and New York by the 1730s, and in Philadelphia and Boston by the 1740s. Taverns brought all ranks into even closer proximity. By 1737, Boston had 177 taverns, one for every 99 inhabitants of the city. (Between 30 and 40 percent were owned by women, usually widows.) Taverns not only served food and drink but also became true public institutions where people could meet and discuss the issues of the day.

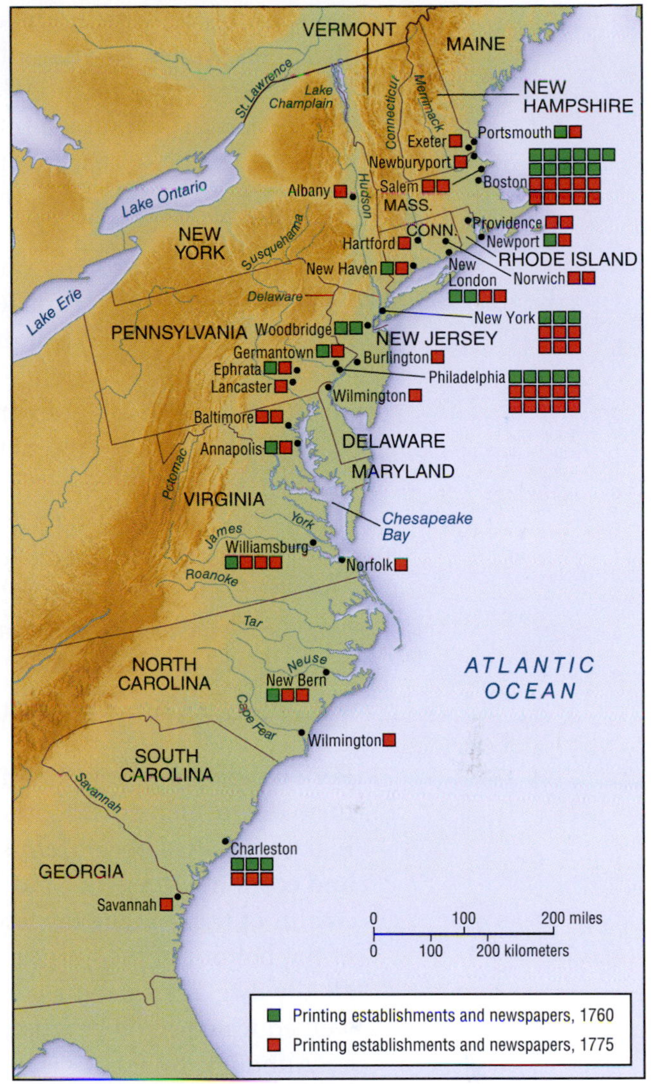

Map 5–4 Printing Presses and Newspapers, 1760–1775 Between 1760 and 1775, the number of printing presses and newspapers in the colonies grew dramatically, as new cities acquired presses, and major cities such as Boston, New York, and Philadelphia gained additional ones. *Lester Cappon, ed.,* The Atlas of Early American History *(Princeton, NJ: Princeton University Press, 1976).*

Newspapers also played a critical role in creating a public sphere and extending it beyond the cities. The first newspaper was the *Boston News-Letter,* which appeared in 1704. By the time of the Revolution, 39 newspapers were being published, and the chief town in each colony except Delaware had at least one newspaper (see Map 5–4).

Strict libel laws prohibited the printing of opinions critical of public officials, or even the truth if it cast them in a bad light. John Peter Zenger, editor of the *New-York Weekly Journal,* was tried in 1735 for criticizing the governor. Zenger's flamboyant attorney, Andrew Hamilton, persuaded the jury that they should rule not simply on the facts of the case (Zenger *had* criticized the governor) but on whether the law itself was just. When the jury ruled in Zenger's favor, cheers went up in the courtroom. Although it would be many years before freedom of the press would be guaranteed by law, the Zenger case was a milestone in the developing relationship between the public and government officials. The verdict expressed the belief that in the contest between the two, the press spoke for the people, and hence it was the people themselves, not government, that would hold the press accountable.

Coffee pot by Paul Revere.

City dwellers came to think of themselves as a "public." Not only successful artisans such as Benjamin Franklin and Paul Revere but less affluent craftsmen and mechanics all thought of themselves as part of a public that had certain rights or liberties, such as making their views known and enjoying a fair price for their goods. At times, working people, acting as a public, and sometimes with support from the elite, used mob action to assert their political views. Mobs in both New York and Boston reacted violently to press gangs that scoured the waterfront for additional hands for the Royal Navy. By the time of the Revolution, city dwellers had a long history of asserting their rights in public.

The Diversity of Urban Life

Periodic downturns in the urban economy, especially after the middle of the century, led to increased activism on the part of workers and the urban poor. Colonial politics had been premised on the deference of the less powerful to their social and economic "betters," but by the middle of the eighteenth century, the increasing wealth of those at the top and the appearance of a small class of permanently poor at the bottom of the economic hierarchy began to undermine the assumption that all city dwellers shared a common interest and that, consequently, the wealthy and well-educated could be trusted to govern for the benefit of everyone.

Although by today's standards the colonial population, even in the cities, was remarkably equal economically, in the eighteenth century it became more stratified than it had been. At the beginning of the eighteenth century, none of the cities had a substantial number of poor people. In New York, in 1700, there were only 35 paupers, almost all of whom were aged or disabled. Over the course of the eighteenth century, however, colonial wars sent men home disabled and left many women widowed and children orphaned. Each city responded to the growth in poverty by building almshouses for the poor who could not support themselves and workhouses for those, including women and children, who could. In Philadelphia and New York about 25 percent of the population was at or below the poverty level for the time, and in Boston perhaps as much as 40 percent of the population was living at or near subsistence. Many colonists feared that colonial cities were coming to resemble London, with its mass of impoverished and desperate poor.

All the major cities had slaves, and in some cities the black population was considerable. By 1746, 30 percent of New York City's working class consisted of slaves. After a serious slave revolt in 1712 and a rumored revolt in 1741, the white population responded with harsh punishments (but without halting the slave trade). In the wake of the 1712 revolt, which had left nine white men dead, city officials executed eighteen convicted rebels, burned three at the stake, let one starve to death in chains, and broke one on the wheel, a medieval instrument of torture. Six more committed suicide. The response to a rumored slave insurrection in 1741 resembled Salem's witchcraft trials: eighteen slaves and four whites were hanged, and thirteen slaves were burned at the stake.

New York enacted a stringent slave code after the 1712 revolt, and Boston and Pennsylvania imposed significant import duties on slaves. Nonetheless, the importation of slaves continued into all the port cities, where they were in demand as house servants and artisans. Almost all of Boston's elite owned at least one slave, as did many members of the middle class. Wealthy white artisans often purchased slaves instead of enlisting free whites as apprentices.

In Charleston, where more than half the population was enslaved, many masters let their slaves hire themselves out in return for a portion of their earnings. Such slaves set their own hours, chose their own recreational and religious activities, and participated in the consumer economy by selling their products and making purchases with the profits. Some whites complained about the fancy dresses of the black women at biracial dances attended by "many of the first gentlemen" of Charleston. Interracial sex in Charleston seems to have been common. Although white city dwellers were troubled by the impudence and relative freedom of urban slaves, urban slavery flourished.

The Maturing of Rural Society

Population increases had a different impact in rural areas than in cities. During the eighteenth century, some long-settled regions became relatively overcrowded. Land that had once seemed abundant had been carelessly farmed and had lost some of its fertility. This relative overcrowding, which historians call *land pressure,* led to a number of changes in colonial society, felt most acutely in New England. Population density increased, and with no additional farmland available, migration from farms to newly settled areas and cities increased. Both the concentration of wealth and social differentiation increased, dividing the farm community into rich and poor.

Such broad economic changes had a direct impact on individual men and women. Families with numerous children to provide for were hard pressed if the original plot of land could not be divided into homesteads large enough for each son. (Daughters were given movable property such as farm animals, household equipment, and slaves.) Some sons migrated to cities, looking for employment. Others worked on other men's farms for wages or, in the South in particular, became tenant farmers. Daughters became servants in other women's households. In

> **"Concord plains are sandy, Concord soil is poor; you have miserable farms there, and no fruit. There is little hope you will ever do better than your father. . . . Lucy had better marry her cousin John. His father will give him one of the best farms in the town, and Lucy shall match his land acre for acre. You must marry a Concord girl, who cannot tell good land from poor. As for Lucy, you must forget her."**
>
> JONATHAN BARNES,
> refusing to let Joseph Hosmer marry his daughter Lucy. Then, Lucy became pregnant, and Barnes consented to their marriage.

such older settled regions, the average age of marriage crept upward. In Middlesex County, Virginia, by 1740, women were marrying at age 22, two years older than before. By the time of the Revolution, women in Andover, Massachusetts, were, on average, 24 before they married, a year or two older than in the previous century.

As young men and women in long-settled regions had to defer marriage, increasing numbers had sexual relations before marriage. In some towns, by the middle of the eighteenth century, between 30 percent and 50 percent of brides bore their first child within eight months of their wedding day. The growing belief that marriage should be based primarily on love probably encouraged some couples to become intimate before they married, especially if poverty required them to postpone marriage. Young women who engaged in sexual relations before marriage took a huge risk, however. If their lovers declined to marry them they would be disgraced and their future would be bleak.

The World That Slavery Made

The rural economy of the South depended on slave labor. Whites and their black slaves formed two distinctive cultures, one in the black-majority lower South and the other in the Chesapeake region. In both regions, the most affluent slave masters sold their crops on the international market and used the profits to buy elegant furniture and the latest London fashions. Like their affluent English counterparts, wealthy planters aimed for moderation in all things—from the measured cadences of the minuets they liked to dance and the highly stylized language of their love letters, to restrained mourning on the death of a loved one.

Chesapeake planters modeled themselves after English country gentlemen, while low-country planters imitated the elite of London. Chesapeake planters designed their plantations to be self-sufficient villages, like English country estates. Because slaves produced most of the goods and services the plantation needed, planters such as William Byrd II imagined themselves living "in a kind of independence on everyone but Providence." But unlike English country gentlemen, southern slave owners were wholly dependent on both slave labor and the vagaries of the market for their fortunes. South Carolina planters used their wealth to build elegant homes in Charleston and other coastal cities, where they spent as much time as possible and established a flourishing urban culture. By the eve of the Revolution, the area around Charleston was the most affluent in the mainland colonies. In spite of their affluence, the southern planter elite never achieved the secure political power enjoyed by their English counterparts. In England the social elite dominated the government: not only the hereditary positions, but the appointive and elective ones as well. With noble rank inherited and voting rights limited to male property owners, the English government was remarkably stable. The colonial elite, however (in the northern colonies as well as the southern ones), were cut off from the top levels of political power, which remained in England. The colonists were at the mercy of whichever officials the Crown happened to appoint.

Unable to count on support from above, the colonial elite needed to guarantee the loyalty of those below them. In Virginia, the elite acted as middlemen for lesser planters, advancing them credit—in the form of a line written in the merchant's ledger—and marketing their tobacco. In general, they wielded their authority with a light hand,

and punishments for crimes committed by whites were light. In addition, the elite enhanced their authority by the use of ritual. Actions were calculated for the effect they would produce on both peers and social inferiors. Sitting astride his horse, dressed elegantly, and wearing a wig, a planter was an imposing figure on the landscape.

Although members of the Virginia gentry tried to distance themselves from their slaves, whom they considered "vulgar," some whites crossed the color line in a dramatic way, eighteenth-century racial views notwithstanding. Some historians believe that sexual relations between whites and blacks were common. Several prominent Virginians acknowledged and supported their mixed-race children. Some interracial relationships were affectionate; others were coerced. All the resulting offspring were in a vulnerable position; like all slaves they were dependent on the will of whites.

In the low country, the absenteeism of the planters combined with the task system to give plantation slaves an unusual degree of autonomy. Living in a region where they were in the majority, slaves were better able to retain their own religions, languages, and customs than were those in the Chesapeake. For example, the Gullah language, still spoken today on the Sea Islands off the coast of South Carolina and Georgia, combined English, Spanish, Portuguese, and African languages.

The mainland colonies' bloodiest slave revolt, the Stono Rebellion, took place in 1739, only a year after the founding of the Spanish free black outpost of Mose in Florida. The uprising was led by about 20 slaves born in Kongo (present-day Angola). The rebels were probably Catholics, for the king of Kongo had accepted conversion from the Portuguese and made Catholicism his nation's religion. Early in the morning of September 9, the rebels broke into a store near the Stono Bridge, taking weapons and ammunition and killing the storekeepers. The rebels moved south toward St. Augustine, killing whites and gathering blacks into their fold. Although the main body of the rebels was dispersed that evening, and many were executed on the spot, skirmishes took place for another week, and the last of the ringleaders was not captured for three years.

The authorities reacted with predictable severity, putting dozens of slave rebels "to the most cruel Death" and revoking many liberties the slaves had enjoyed. A prohibitive duty was placed on the importation of slaves, and attempts were made to encourage the immigration of white Europeans. Although slave imports dropped significantly in the 1740s, by 1750 they rose to pre-Stono levels because slave owners had neither the heart nor the inclination for the sort of systematic policing of their slaves that would have kept them completely under their control.

Georgia: From Frontier Outpost to Plantation Society

Nowhere was the white determination to create and maintain a slave society stronger than in the colony of Georgia. It is sometimes said that the introduction of slavery in North America was an unthinking decision, that the colonies became slave societies slowly, as individual planters purchased Africans who were already enslaved, and without the society as a whole ever committing itself to slavery. Although there is some truth to this analysis, it is not accurate for Georgia, where the introduction of slavery was a purposeful decision.

The establishment of the English colony at South Carolina had, of course, made the Spanish nervous because of its proximity to their settlement at St. Augustine, Florida.

With the French founding of New Orleans (1718) and Fort Toulouse (1717), Carolinians felt increasingly threatened. They were therefore eager for the English to establish a colony to the south, which would both serve as a buffer between Florida and South Carolina and, if extended far enough west, cut the French colonial empire in two.

The British Crown issued a 21-year charter to a group of trustees led by James Oglethorpe, who had achieved prominence by bringing about reforms in England's debtors' prisons. The colony, Georgia, was designed as a combination philanthropic venture and military-commercial outpost. Its colonists, who were to be drawn from Britain's "deserving poor," were supposed to protect South Carolina's borders and to make the new colony a sort of Italy-on-the-Atlantic, producing wine, olives, and silk.

Unfortunately, Oglethorpe's humanitarianism was not coupled with an understanding of the world political economy. By that time it was well known that excessive indulgence in alcohol was undermining the cohesion of many Indian tribes. Consequently, Oglethorpe had banned liquor from the colony. However, without a product to sell, the colony could not prosper. South Carolina's wharves, merchants, and willingness to sell rum enabled it to dominate the trade with local Indians. Oglethorpe had also banned slavery for humanitarian reasons (making it the only colony expressly to prohibit slavery). As a result, Georgia farmers looked enviously across the Savannah River at South Carolinians growing rich off slave labor. The settlers were angry too that, contrary to common practice in the colonies, women were not allowed to inherit property. Finally, contrary to common practice in the colonies, the trustees made no provision for self-government. Georgia, despite its founders' noble intentions, lacked everything that the thriving colonies enjoyed: a cash crop or product, large plots of land, slaves to work the land, and laws of its own devising.

Never able to realize their dream of a colony populated by small and contented farmers, the trustees surrendered Georgia back to the Crown a year early, in 1752. With Oglethorpe's laws repealed and slavery introduced, the colony soon resembled the plantation society of South Carolina. Savannah became a little Charleston, with its robust civic and cultural life, and its slave markets as well.

The Head and the Heart in America: The Enlightenment and Religious Awakening

American life in the eighteenth century was shaped by two movements, the Enlightenment and a series of religious revivals known as the Great Awakening. In many ways, these movements were separate, even opposite, appealing to different groups of people. The Enlightenment was a transatlantic intellectual movement that held that the universe could be understood and improved by the human mind. The Great Awakening was a transatlantic religious movement that held that all people were born sinners, that all could feel their own depravity without the assistance of ministers, and that all were equal in the eyes of God. Although the movements might seem fundamentally opposite, with one emphasizing the power of the human mind and the other disparaging it, both criticized established authority and valued the experience of the individual. Both contributed to the humanitarianism that emerged at the end of the century, and both were products of capitalism.

The Ideas of the Enlightenment

The roots of the Enlightenment can be traced to the Renaissance and the spirit of inquiry and faith in science that led explorers like Columbus halfway around the globe. But the gloomy mysticism of Columbus and the belief in the supernatural held by virtually all the early explorers and colonists disappeared in the bright light of the Renaissance. Men and women of the Enlightenment, on both sides of the Atlantic, contrasted the ignorance, oppression, and suffering of the Middle or "Dark" Ages, as they called them, and their own enlightened time. Thomas Jefferson described the earlier period as "the times of Vandalism, when ignorance put everything in the hands of power and priestcraft." Enlightened thinkers believed fervently in the power of rational thinking and scoffed at superstition.

> "The rapid Progress true Science now makes, occasions my regretting sometimes that I was born so soon. It is impossible to imagine the Height to which may be carried, in a thousand years, the Power of Man over Matter. . . . all Diseases may by sure means be prevented or cured. . . . O that moral Science were in as fair a way of Improvement, that Men would cease to be Wolves to one another, and that human Beings would at length learn what they now improperly call Humanity!"
>
> BENJAMIN FRANKLIN

People of the Enlightenment believed that God and his world were knowable. "Your own reason," Jefferson told his nephew, "is the only oracle given you by heaven." Rejecting revelation as a guide, the Enlightenment looked instead to reason. Jefferson's "trinity of the three greatest men the world had ever produced" included not Jesus Christ but Isaac Newton, the scientist responsible for modern mathematics and physics; Francis Bacon, the philosopher who outlined the scientific method; and John Locke, the political philosopher of democracy. The Enlightenment was interested in knowledge not for its own sake but for the improvements it could make in human happiness.

Enlightenment thinkers were more interested in what all people had in common than in what differentiated them. No passage in the Bible was more important to the Enlightenment than Genesis 1:27: "So God created man in his own image." It was the basis not only for overcoming Calvinism's belief in humanity's innate depravity but also for asserting the principle of human equality.

Humanity's duties were both clear and simple. Chief among them, according to Benjamin Franklin, was "doing good to [God's] other children." In fact, people served God best not by praying, which, as Thomas Paine put it, "can add nothing to eternity," but "by endeavouring to make his creatures happy." Scientific inquiry and experiments such as Franklin's with electricity all had as their object the improvement of human life.

Although the eighteenth century had seen a number of improvements in the quality of life, the world was still violent and filled with pain. The Enlightenment responded to the pain and violence of its world in two ways. First, it attempted to alleviate and curtail them. Scientists eagerly sought cures for diseases. The Reverend Cotton Mather of Boston learned about the procedure of inoculating against smallpox (using a small amount of the deadly virus) from a scientific article and from his African slave Onesimus, who knew of its practice in Africa. An epidemic that began in 1721 gave him an opportunity to try out the technique. The revulsion against pain and suffering also encouraged humanitarian reform, such as James Oglethorpe's reform of English debtors' prisons and, eventually, the antislavery movement.

Men and women of the Enlightenment also cultivated a stoic resignation to the evils that they could not change, and a personal ideal of moderation, so that they would neither give nor receive pain. The gentility and politeness of the urban elite was an expression of this ideal of moderation. In fact, both gentility and the Enlightenment were espoused by the same set of people, the urban elite: professionals, merchants, and prosperous planters tied into the global economy.

The Enlightenment and the Study of Political Economy

Enlightenment thinkers began to study the connections among society, politics, and the economy. John Locke, the English philosopher, was the first to link these in a theory of political economy. He argued that there was a systematic connection between social institutions (such as the family), political institutions, and property rights. He began with the claim that each person has the right to life and the right to preserve that life. To sustain their lives, people form families, and to support themselves and their families, they labor. The basic right to life thus gives people the right to the product of their labor—property. To protect their lives and their property, people create governments. They give up some of their liberty, but receive protection of their lives and property in return.

Locke also developed a new economic theory. He said that money has no intrinsic value. His idea was a departure from mercantilism, which said that the value of money was fixed. In the second half of the eighteenth century, Scottish philosophers such as Francis Hutcheson and Adam Smith carried Locke's ideas even further, arguing that human beings should be free to value the things that made them happy. They developed a full-scale defense of consumerism.

Using happiness as their standard for human life, the Scots argued that people should be free to produce. Adam Smith's influential *The Wealth of Nations* (1776) was both a critique of mercantilism and a defense of free markets and free labor. According to Smith, "Every man is rich or poor according to the degree in which he can afford to enjoy the necessaries." For Smith and other Enlightenment theorists, the best incentive to hard work was the increased wealth and comforts it would bring. Human beings were happiest, they said, when they lived under free governments, which protected private property but left the market largely unregulated. These ideas became increasingly popular around the time of the Revolution.

Enlightened Institutions

The Enlightenment spurred the creation of institutions that embodied its principles. Humanitarianism led to the building of the Pennsylvania Hospital in 1751 and the Eastern State Mental Hospital at Williamsburg in 1773. Benjamin Franklin played a central role in organizing a number of institutions. In 1743 he proposed a society of learned men, modeled after the Royal Society of London, to study and share information about science and technology. He also helped establish the Library Company of Philadelphia in 1731, the first lending library in the colonies. Philadelphia acquired a second library in 1751 when the Quaker philosopher and book collector James Logan bequeathed his library, books and building both, to the city. By the time of the Revolution, Newport, New York, Charleston, and Savannah all had libraries.

The Enlightenment had a significant effect on organized religion as well. The Anglicans, in particular, were receptive to its ideals of moderation and rationalism. In England, John Tillotson, the Archbishop of Canterbury, preached a comforting and simple Christianity: God was "good and just" and required nothing "that is either unsuitable to our reason or prejudicial to our interest . . . nothing but what is easy to be understood, and is as easy to be practiced by an honest and willing mind."

This message became popular in the colonies, even among Congregationalist ministers, who abandoned the Calvinism of their forefathers. John Wise, the minister of Ipswich, Massachusetts, insisted that "to follow God and to obey Reason is the same thing." Arminianism, the belief that salvation was partly a matter of individual effort rather than entirely God's will, enjoyed a new popularity. Harvard University became a hotbed of liberal theology, and in response, religious conservatives founded Yale in New Haven, Connecticut, in 1701, to guarantee that New England's ministers could get a proper Calvinist education.

Origins of the Great Awakening

The problem with rational religion was that it was not emotionally fulfilling. In addition, rapid population growth had left the colonies without enough churches and ministers. Popular demand for more and better religion led to a series of revivals, known as the Great Awakening, that swept through the colonies between 1734 and 1745. At first, church leaders looked with pleasure on the stirrings of spiritual renewal. In the winter of 1734/1735, some of the rowdiest young people in Northampton, Massachusetts, men and women who carried on parties for "the greater part of the night," began seeking religion at the church of a brilliant young minister, Jonathan Edwards. Everyone rejoiced at such signs of spiritual awakening.

The Grand Itinerant

When George Whitefield arrived in Philadelphia in 1739, the local ministers, including officials of Whitefield's own Anglican church, welcomed him. Whitefield drew audiences in the thousands everywhere he spoke. In the 15 months of his grand tour, he visited every colony from Maine to Georgia, met all the important ministers, and was heard at least once by most of the inhabitants of Massachusetts and Connecticut (see Map 5–5). He spoke to the entire community—rich, poor, slave, free, old, young, male, and female—acting out simple scripts based on biblical stories. The message was always the same, the sinfulness of man and the mercy of God.

Map 5–5 George Whitefield's Itinerary In the 15 months between October 30, 1739, and January 18, 1741, Whitefield covered thousands of miles, visiting every colony from New Hampshire to Georgia, and stopping in some states such as Pennsylvania, South Carolina, and Georgia several times.

In a calculated move, perhaps intended to increase his audiences, Whitefield began speaking out against some in the ministry, accusing them of being unconverted. He started with the deceased Archbishop of Canterbury, John Tillotson, and went on to criticize some of the clergymen who were alive and preaching. Following his lead, Gilbert Tennent, who was now on a preaching tour of New England, warned about "The Danger of an Unconverted Ministry." Tennent compared some of the region's ministers to the "Pharisees" of biblical times, who "look'd upon others that differed from them, and the common People with an Air of Disdain; and especially any who had a Respect for JESUS." He implied that such ministers were in it for the money and that true Christians should leave their churches for those of honest preachers.

Even ministers sympathetic to the revival were shocked by these accusations, which turned their congregations against them and split their churches. Ministers such as Charleston's Anglican commissary Alexander Garden and Boston's Congregationalist minister Charles Chauncy, who already had reservations about the revivalists because of their emotional style, now condemned the revival. That only made the revivalists more popular and attracted larger crowds.

Cultural Conflict and Challenges to Authority

The Great Awakening walked a fine line between challenging authority and supporting it, which no doubt explains its widespread appeal. It antagonized the top tier of the elite, those with the most power and arrogance, but did not challenge the fundamental structures of colonial society. By attacking the ministers, but not government officials, the revivalists criticized authority without suffering any real consequences.

The Great Awakening appealed to all classes of people throughout the colonies. Its greatest impact, however, was in areas that had experienced the greatest change—in particular, cities (especially among the lower orders), the frontier, and older towns that were beginning to suffer from overcrowding. In these places lived the people whose lives were most disrupted by economic changes. Disturbed by the increasing competitiveness of society, men and women were attracted to the democratic fellowship of the revivalist congregation.

While criticizing the materialism and competitiveness of eighteenth-century society, the revival told men and women to look inside themselves for change, not to the structures of society. For example, a woman named Sarah Osborn, who heard Whitefield preach at Newport, Rhode Island, blamed herself for her woes, which she thought were punishment for her sinful singing and dancing. After her spiritual rebirth, she trusted in God and reconciled herself to her poverty. Spiritual rebirth provided such men and women with joy and fulfillment that their competitive and changing world had been unable to supply.

The revival also walked a fine line in its treatment of slavery. Early in his travels to the colonies, Whitefield spoke out against the cruelties of slavery and harangued slaveholders. At the same time, however, Whitefield maintained a slave plantation in South Carolina and pestered the trustees to permit the institution in Georgia. Like many slave owners after him, Whitefield argued that it was immoral to enslave Africans, but not to own them, provided that one treated them well and Christianized them. By linking humanitarianism, Christianity, and slavery, the Great Awakening anchored slavery in the South, at least for the time being.

Although it is hard to say if slaves were treated more humanely on the plantations of evangelicals, beginning in the 1740s large numbers of slaves were converted to Christianity, and by some point in the nineteenth century virtually all slaves had become Christians. Although some may have converted to please their masters and to get Sundays off, blacks were attracted to evangelical religion for the same reason that whites were. It offered them a way to order their lives and believe that their lives were meaningful.

To a great extent, poor whites and slaves, especially in the South, had been left out of the society that more prosperous people had created. Evangelical religion placed the individual in a community of believers. It offered slaves the opportunity for church discipline and personal responsibility on almost the same terms as whites and gave some blacks the possibility of leadership in a biracial community. Africans grafted some of their religious practices, such as shouting and ecstatic visions, onto the Christian revival, so that worship in southern Baptist and Methodist churches became a truly African-American phenomenon.

What the Awakening Wrought

The opponents of the Great Awakening feared that it would turn the world upside down, but the leaders of the revival disciplined their own wildest members, such as New London's James Davenport. Davenport had led his flock through the streets late at night, singing at the tops of their lungs. They also made a bonfire so that they could rid themselves of heresy by burning the books of their opponents and idolatry by burning the clothes they were wearing. The stripping party was stopped by several evangelicals in the crowd, and Davenport was brought back to his senses by his fellow revivalist ministers. In general, the Great Awakening took colonial society in the direction in which it was already heading: toward individualism. Church after church split into evangelical and traditional factions, and new denominations appeared. Which religion to follow became a matter of personal choice, and colonies with established churches tolerated dissenters. Religion itself, as a general force, was strengthened, making the colonies simultaneously the most Protestant and the most religiously diverse culture in the world.

The Great Awakening also spurred the establishment of educational institutions. Princeton, chartered in 1748 as the College of New Jersey, grew out of an evangelical seminary. Next came Dartmouth, Brown, and Rutgers, chartered in 1766, to advance "true religion and useful knowledge." Columbia, chartered in 1754, represented the Anglicans' response. The focus of higher education was slowly shifting from the preparation for the ministry to the training of leaders more generally. The Great Awakening diminished the power of ministers while increasing the influence of personal religion.

At the height of the Awakening, opponents lined up on either side, defending and attacking religious enthusiasm. Yet it was hardly a battle of the pious against the godless or the well-educated against the uninformed. Jonathan Edwards, one of the greatest minds of his age, drew from the Enlightenment as well as from Calvinist ideas. He praised both Locke and "the incomparable Mr. Newton." For Edwards, however, reason and good habits were not enough. Reason must be supplemented by emotion, in particular the emotion of God's grace. By insisting that religious salvation and virtue were more matters of the heart than of the head, Edwards opened the way for a popular religion that was democratic, intensely personal, and humanitarian.

Conclusion

Eighteenth-century America was part of an expanding world market and a capitalist political economy. A growing population sustained a vigorous economy, one that produced for and purchased from the world market. As participants in an "industrious revolution," white Americans worked themselves and their slaves harder to purchase consumer goods. These new goods enabled people to live more genteelly and to cultivate a social life. Especially in the cities, this new emphasis on social life spawned an array of institutions where people could acquire and display learning and gentility. The benefits of the economy were not shared equally, however. Slaves produced for the market economy but were denied its rewards. The increasing stratification of urban society and land pressures in rural regions meant that a growing segment of the population was too poor to profit from the expanding economy.

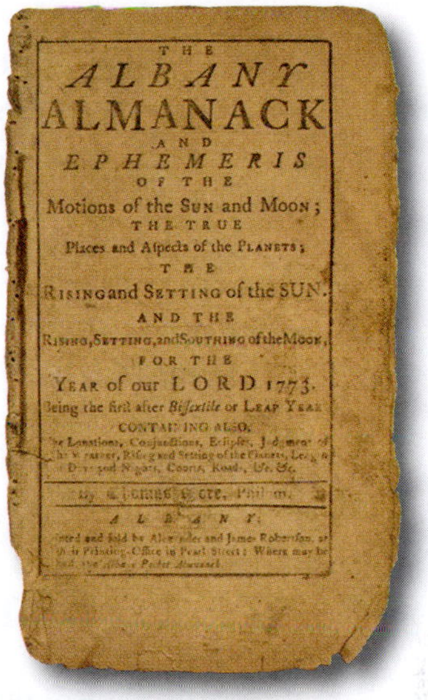

The eighteenth-century world spawned two different but related intellectual responses, the Enlightenment and the Great Awakening. Both were critical in shaping the eighteenth-century colonial world, and both paved the way for the Revolution. The Enlightenment led some to believe that rational thought and the scientific method would conquer human ills. At the same time, the Great Awakening reminded men and women that life was short and ultimately beyond their control. In different ways, then, the Enlightenment and the Great Awakening both encouraged the individualism that would become a distinguishing characteristic of American life.

Further Readings

Richard Bushman, ed., *The Great Awakening: Documents on the Revival of Religion, 1740–1745* (1989). There is no better introduction to the Great Awakening than this collection of sermons and first-person accounts.

Cary Carson, et al., *Of Consuming Interests: The Style of Life in the Eighteenth Century* (1994). An important introduction to the material culture of eighteenth-century consumer culture.

Cornelia Hughes Dayton, *Women Before the Bar: Gender, Law, and Society in Connecticut, 1639–1789* (1995). Uses court records to reveal the lives of ordinary women and their deteriorating position in the eighteenth century.

Thomas M. Doeflinger, *A Vigorous Spirit of Enterprise: Merchants and Economic Development in Revolutionary Philadelphia* (1986). Describes the lives and aspirations of this important segment of the colonial population while providing an excellent introduction to the period's economic history.

David Eltis, *The Rise of African Slavery in the Americas* (2000). A bold interpretation of the development of slavery that places it in a global context and emphasizes the role of Africans in shaping the slave trade.

Rhys Isaac, *The Transformation of Virginia, 1740–1790* (1982). A magnificent description of the different cultures of Virginia's elite and poor, showing how religious revivals changed them forever.

Ann Smart Martin, *Buying into the World of Goods: Early Consumers in Backcountry Virginia* (2009). Shows how even poorer people in rural areas were tied in to the world of goods.

Philip D. Morgan, *Slave Counterpoint: Black Culture in the Eighteenth-Century Chesapeake and Low Country* (1998). A learned and comprehensive study of slave life in the colonial South.

Gary B. Nash, *The Urban Crucible: Social Change, Political Consciousness, and the Origins of the American Revolution* (1979). Detailed, comprehensive, and indispensable for understanding the social and political world of urban working men.

Stephanie E. Smallwood, *Saltwater Slavery: A Middle Passage from Africa to American Diaspora* (2007). An evocative book that charts the passage of Africans from their homeland to their new lives as American slaves.

David Waldstreicher, *Runaway America: Benjamin Franklin, Slavery, and the American Revolution* (2004). A provocative book that situates Benjamin Franklin in his society.

Serena Zabin, *Dangerous Economies: Status and Commerce in Imperial New York* (2009), a dazzling new portrait of life in mid-eighteenth-century New York with a focus on gender and race.

Who, What

George Whitefield 141
Cottagers 153
James Oglethorpe 166
Jonathan Edwards 172
Consumer revolution 150
Industrious revolution 150
Linked economic development 154
The Great Awakening 166
The Enlightenment 166
The Wealth of Nations 168

Review Questions

1. What were the primary sources of population increase in the eighteenth century? Compare the patterns of population growth of Europeans and Africans in the colonies.

>> Timeline >>

▼ 1693
College of William and Mary founded

▼ 1701
Yale founded

▼ 1704
First newspaper, *Boston News-Letter*, published in colonies

▼ 1712
Slave revolt in New York City

▼ 1717
French build Fort Toulouse

▼ 1718
French found New Orleans

▼ 1731
Library Company, first lending library in colonies, erected in Philadelphia

▼ 1733
Georgia founded
King of Spain guarantees freedom to English slaves who escape to Spanish territory

▼ 1734
Great Awakening begins

▼ 1735
John Peter Zenger acquitted of libeling New York's governor

2. What was the “industrious revolution”? How did it shape the development of the colonial economy? What were the other key factors shaping the development of the colonial economy? What effect did this development have on the lives of ordinary men and women?
3. What were the primary changes in urban and rural life in the eighteenth century?
4. Describe the development of the eighteenth-century consumer culture and discuss how it affected everyday life.
5. What were the chief ideas of the Enlightenment? Why did some men and women find them attractive?
6. What were the sources of the Great Awakening? Why were some men and women drawn to it?

Websites

The Franklin Papers. A digital and searchable version of the papers of Benjamin Franklin http://www.franklinpapers.org/franklin/

The Grosvenor-Sessions Abortion Case, Pomfret, Connecticut, 1742. Documents about a fascinating trial in which a young man and a doctor were prosecuted for murder after the young man's beloved died from an abortion. http://facultystaff.richmond.edu/~aholton/Dayton/index.html

Sermons of George Whitefield. Digital versions of the evangelist's sermons. http://www.anglicanlibrary.org/whitefield/sermons/index.htm

The Trans-Atlantic Slave Trade Database. An extraordinary resource with information on 67,000 Africans who were transported to the Americas. It also includes images, graphs, and maps. http://www.slavevoyages.org/tast/index.faces

For further review materials and resource information, please visit www.oup.com/us/ofthepeople

▼ 1739
Stono Rebellion
George Whitefield begins his American tour

▼ 1741
35 executed in New York City after slave-revolt scare

▼ 1748
College of New Jersey (Princeton) founded

▼ 1751
Pennsylvania Hospital built in Philadelphia

▼ 1752
Georgia becomes a Crown colony

▼ 1754
Columbia College founded

▼ 1755
Philadelphia College (University of Pennsylvania) founded

▼ 1766
Queens College (Rutgers) founded

▼ 1773
Eastern State Mental Hospital built in Williamsburg

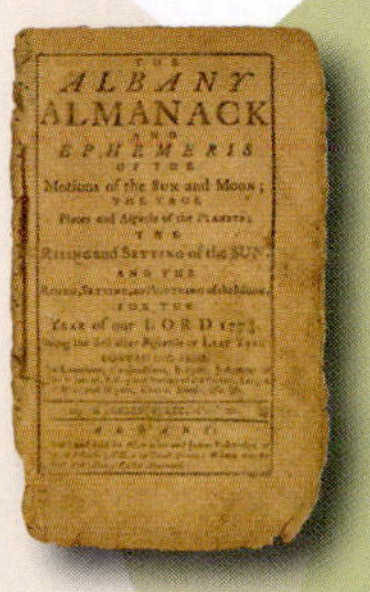

CHAPTER 6

Common Threads

>> What role did the colonies play in imperial conflict? That is, how did they shape that conflict and how were they shaped by it?

>> How were Native Americans drawn into imperial conflict? To what extent were they able to shape it for their own purposes?

>> What did it mean for the American colonies to be peripheral—literally—to the British Empire?

>> How did the colonists adapt the available political theories to their purposes? What in the American experience made those theories attractive to the colonists?

Conflict on the Edge of the Empire 1713–1774

AMERICAN PORTRAIT

>> Susannah Willard Johnson Experiences the Empire

Today the town is Charlestown, New Hampshire, but then it was "No. 4," a small farming village on the northern frontier of Massachusetts. In 1754 Susannah Willard Johnson and her husband James lived there, having taken advantage of a break in the near-constant struggle between Britain and France for North America by moving up to the frontier. At 24, Susannah had been married for seven years and already had three children, with another due any day. James, a native of Ireland, had commenced his life in America as a servant indentured to Susannah's uncle. After working for him for ten years, James purchased the remainder of his time, married Susannah, and made his way by a combination of farming and shopkeeping. He also became a lieutenant in the militia.

The region's Abenaki Indians—Algonquians who were allied with the French and had their own grievances against the encroaching settlers—presented both danger and opportunity. At first the settlers at No. 4 were so frightened that they stayed in the fort. However, Susannah later reported, "hostility at length vanished—the Indians expressed a wish to traffic, the inhabitants laid by their fears. . . ." James Johnson was part of the consumer revolution, selling goods to his fellow settlers and to the Abenakis, who gave him furs in return.

A NARRATIVE OF THE CAPTIVITY OF MRS. JOHNSON. CONTAINING An ACCOUNT of her SUFFERINGS, during *Four Years* with the INDIANS and FRENCH. *Published according to Act of Congress.* PRINTED AT WALPOLE, NEWHAMPSHIRE, BY DAVID CARLISLE, jun. 1796.

Susannah Johnson described her family's life as "harmony and safety," and "boasted with exultation that I should, with husband, friends, and luxuries, live happy in spite of the fear of savages." By the summer of 1754, however, there were rumors of impending warfare with France, which would make the frontier village a target of France's Abenaki allies.

On August 30, 1754, just before daybreak, a neighbor who was coming to work for the Johnsons appeared at the door. As the Johnsons opened the door for him, the neighbor rushed in, 11 Abenaki men following him. Soon, Susannah said, they were "all over the house, some upstairs, some hauling my sister out of bed, another had hold of me, and one was approaching Mr. Johnson, who stood in the middle of the floor to deliver himself up."

The Abenakis tied up the men and gathered the women and children around them and marched the party to the north. They marched hard, even though Susannah, who had lost her shoes, had bloody feet. On the second day of her captivity, Susannah went into labor. Attended by her sister and husband, Susannah gave birth to a daughter, whom she named Captive. Before they returned home five years later, Susannah and her family were held captive in Canada and sent to England as part of a prisoner exchange.

The French and Indian War had begun on the northern frontier, and the Indians were manipulating it to their advantage. In peacetime they traded furs for manufactured goods, but in wartime they seized British settlers, took them to Canada, and sold them to the French, who either ransomed them back to the British or traded

continued

>> **AMERICAN PORTRAIT** *continued*

them for prisoners of war. What to others might look like an imperial struggle, Susannah Johnson experienced as a terrifying assault at dawn that took her from her home and eventually her family. The consumer revolution that gave settlers such as the Johnsons the opportunity to live a good life on the frontier was rooted in a struggle between France and England, two empires competing over both the markets the consumer revolution was creating and the lands it was populating. As families such as the Johnsons pushed at the frontiers, they became actors on a global stage.

OUTLINE 

The Victory of the British Empire

From 1689 to 1763, Britain and France were at war more than half of the time. These wars gave shape to the eighteenth century and created the international context for the American Revolution in several ways: First, the Revolution grew out of Britain's ineffective efforts to govern the enlarged empire it gained after its victory over France in 1763. Second, France's support for the colonies in their war against her enemy Britain helped secure the colonies' victory. Third, once the colonies secured their independence, they entered a world still torn by the conflict between Britain and France.

All of these wars had their roots in a struggle for world dominance between the two powerful empires. To a great extent, colonial and imperial objectives coincided. Both Britain and the colonies would benefit from securing the empire's borders and from expanding British markets. Yet the imperial wars also exposed the growing divergence between the political economy of the colonies and that of the mother country. When the growing empire and its wars threatened to increase the British government's power over the colonists, raise their taxes to pay for the empire, and station among them a permanent army, the colonists resisted and finally rebelled.

New War, Old Pattern

> **"Jaghte oghte."**
>
> EUNICE WILLIAMS,
> responding in Mohawk ("maybe not") to an offer to be ransomed back to her family in Massachusetts eight years after she had been captured at the age of seven. By this time, she had been adopted by the Mohawks, converted to Catholicism, taken a new name—Marguerite—and married a Mohawk man named Arosen, with whom she would live until his death fifty years later.

After the conclusion of Queen Anne's War in 1713 (see Chapter 4, "Continental Empires"), England and France were at peace until 1739. It was an uneasy peace for the British North American colonies, however. On the north, New Englanders continued to fight with the Abenakis, in what is now Maine, forcing that tribe into a closer alliance with the French. At the same time, the French attempted to stabilize alliances with their Algonquian allies. The most common method was by providing "gifts" of trade goods.

Another round of international warfare broke out in 1739 and continued for nine years. In the first phase, the War of Jenkins's Ear (1739–1744), Britain attempted to expand into Spanish territories and markets in the Americas. Urged on by the merchants, and with the approval of colonists who wanted to eliminate Spain as a rival, Britain found an excuse for declaring war against Spain: a ship's captain, Robert Jenkins, turned up in Parliament in 1738 with an ugly stump on one side of his head, holding in his hand what he claimed was his ear, severed by the Spanish seven years earlier in the Caribbean. Once again, colonists joined in what they hoped would be a glorious international endeavor, only to meet disillusionment. In 1741, 3,600 colonists, mostly poor young men lured by the promise that they could share Spanish plunder, joined 5,000 Britons in a failed attack on Cartagena, Colombia. More than half the colonial contingent died.

Another ambitious attempt to seize part of the Spanish empire failed in 1740: James Oglethorpe and settlers hired by South Carolina, accompanied by Cherokee and Creek allies, failed to seize the Spanish outpost at St. Augustine and left the southern border vulnerable. When Oglethorpe and his troops repulsed a Spanish attack in 1742, however, Spain's plan to demolish Georgia and South Carolina and arm their slaves was thwarted.

Just as the War of Jenkins's Ear ended in stalemate, so did King George's War (1744–1748), a conflict between Britain and Austria, on one side, and France and Prussia on the other, over succession to the Austrian throne. In North America, a French raid on a fishing village in Nova Scotia met with a huge retaliation by the British. Troops from Massachusetts, subsidized by Pennsylvania and New York and supported by the British navy, captured the French fort at Louisbourg. Finally, a joint British-colonial venture had succeeded. But, true to the old form, a planned two-pronged attack on Quebec was called off when the British fleet failed to arrive. At the end of the war, Britain returned Louisbourg to France and warned the colonists that they had to maintain the peace. Events in North America, however, were out of European control. The British blockade of French ports cut off trade to Canada, including the all-important presents to Indian allies and trade partners. Without these gifts, the French-Indian empire began to crumble.

The Local Impact of Global War

Successive rounds of warfare had a significant impact on politics and society in British North America. Although the colonists identified strongly with the British cause, decades of warfare were a constant drain on the colonial treasury and population.

Wars are expensive. Generally, rates of taxation in colonial America were low, except when wars had to be financed (see Figure 6–1). In a rehearsal for the conflicts that would lead to the American Revolution, the British government complained that the colonists were unwilling to contribute their fair share to the imperial wars. As a rule, colonial legislatures were willing to go only so far in raising taxes to pay for imperial wars or expeditions against Indians. Then they simply issued paper money. Inevitably, the currency depreciated, making even worse the boom-and-bust cycles that war economies always produce.

No colony did more to support the imperial war efforts than Massachusetts, but the result was heightened political conflict at home. Royal governors, eager to ingratiate themselves with officials in London, pushed the colony to contribute to the imperial wars. As many as one-fifth of the men of that colony may have served in the military in the middle of the eighteenth century. In 1747 Boston mobs rioted for three days to resist the Royal Navy's attempt to "impress" (force) men into service, and the local militia refused to restore order. For the first time, Bostonians began to speak about a right to resist tyranny.

Much more than in Europe, civilians in America became victims of war. By the eighteenth century, conventions of "civilized" warfare held that civilians should be spared, but this belief broke down in America for two reasons. First, without a transportation system to bring supplies to the army, troops often relied on plunder. As New England soldiers marched north through Canada to Louisbourg in 1745, they stole chickens, wine, and livestock from French farmers along the way. Second, frontier Indians, adapting their traditional mourning war (see Chapter 2, "Colonial Outposts"), routinely attacked villages, seizing captives to replenish their populations and to ransom to the French. Between 1675 and 1763, with war more common than peace, frontier settlers such as Susannah Johnson were often at risk. During that period, Indians took more than 1,600 New England settlers as captives, more than 90 percent during times of war (see Figure 6–2).

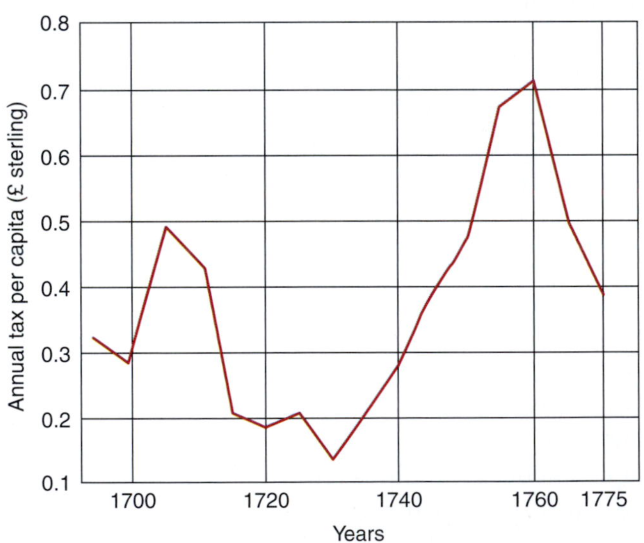

Figure 6–1 Tax Rates in Boston, 1645–1774 The per capita tax rate in Boston followed the course of imperial war in 1713, increasing during the War of Jenkins's Ear (1739–1744) and rising to unprecedented heights to support the French and Indian War (1754–1763). *Data from Gary B. Nash,* The Urban Crucible *(Cambridge, MA: Harvard University Press, 1974), p. 403.*

Almost half the colonists who were seized eventually returned home, but, as with Susannah Johnson's son Sylvanus, who had forgotten English entirely, Indian customs "wore off" only "by degree." Other captives died during the arduous march north to Canada. Sometimes Indians killed those they thought were too weak to survive the journey. Many died of disease, and a few, typically girls between 7 and 15, remained with their captors voluntarily. Historians debate why this was so. Perhaps it was because Puritan culture trained girls to be espe-

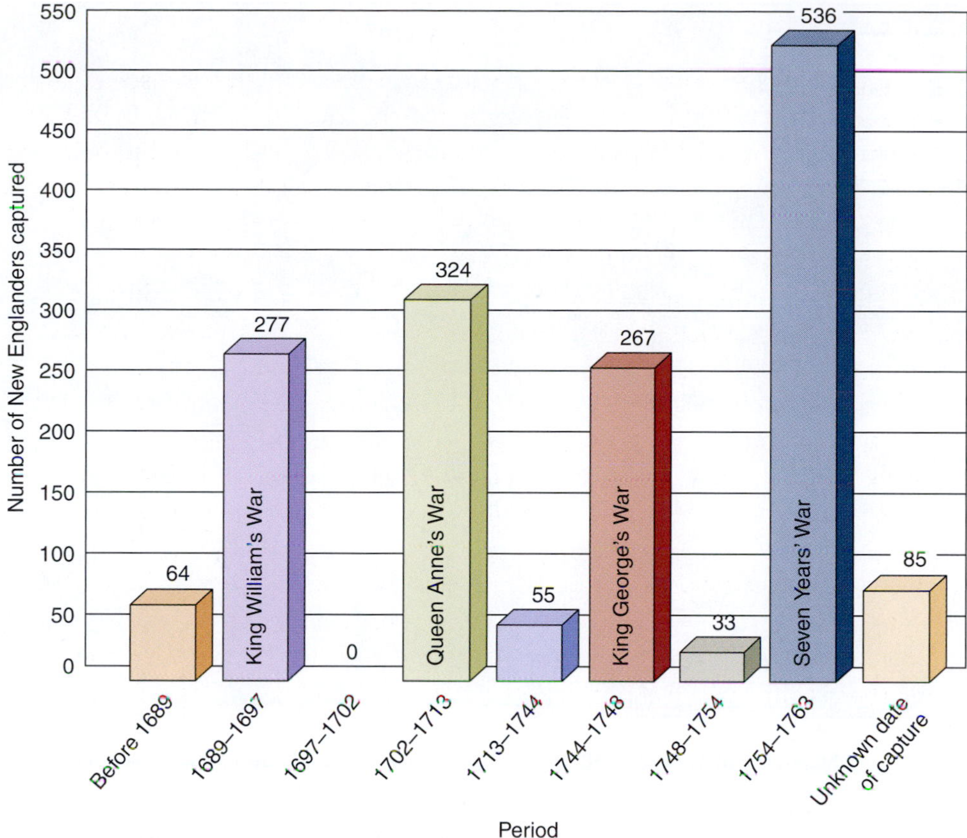

Figure 6–2 New England Captives, 1675–1763 During periods of war, the number of New Englanders taken captive by northern Indians and the French increased dramatically, with more than 90 percent of the captives being taken during times of war. *Alden Vaughan,* Roots of American Racism *(New York: Oxford University Press, 1990), p. 31.*

cially pliant, responding without question to those in authority. Or perhaps it was because, after the rigors of a Puritan upbringing, the relative freedom of Indian culture was inviting.

The French Empire Crumbles from Within

In the years after King George's War, a change in French policy offered a small band of Miami Indians the chance to gain an advantage over rivals. In the process, they started a chain of events that led to the French and Indian War.

Although King George's War had ended in a stalemate, the French position in North America was weaker at the war's conclusion than at the beginning. The costs of war had forced the French to cut back on their presents to allied Algonquian tribes, especially in the Ohio River valley. In addition, to raise revenue, the French sharply increased their charges for the lease of trading posts; in turn, traders raised the prices that they charged the Indians for trade goods. These changes significantly weakened the French hold over their Indian allies, creating political instability that was the underlying North American cause of the French and Indian War.

The Ohio River valley was inhabited by a number of small, refugee tribes (see Map 6–1). As long as the French could provide liberal presents and cheap trade

Map 6–1 The Ohio River Valley, 1747–1758 This territory, inhabited by a number of small bands of Indians, was coveted by both the French and the British, not to mention several competing groups of colonial land speculators. The rivalries between the imperial powers, among the Indian bands, and between rival groups of speculators made this region a powder keg. *Adapted from Michael McConnell,* A Country Between *(Lincoln: University of Nebraska, 1992), pp. 116–117.*

goods, they maintained a loose control. Once that control ended, however, each tribe sought to increase its advantage over the others. Moreover, at just this moment the British recognized the strategic and economic importance of the region.

The temporary power vacuum afforded a small group of Miamis, led by a chieftain called Memeskia, an opportunity to play one group of colonists off another. The chain of events that led to the French and Indian War began in 1748 when Memeskia's group moved east from their home to establish a new village, Pickawillany, near the head of the Miami River. Memeskia welcomed English traders from Pennsylvania, because their trade goods were better and cheaper, and their terms less demanding, than those of the French. He hoped to trade with the British unencumbered by political or military obligations.

Memeskia's move threatened not only the balance of power between Britain and France but also that between the colonies of Pennsylvania and Virginia. The Pennsylvanians welcomed trade with the Miamis, for it gave them a claim to western lands that Virginians sought. At the same time, Memeskia used his access to British traders to attract small bands to his village, and within a year his following had grown substantially. Alarmed, the French shifted their policy away from trade to force. In 1749, they sent a small expedition to cow their former Indian allies back into submission. When it failed, they began to raid dissident Indian encampments and planned to establish a fort in the Ohio River valley. With this change in French policy, Indians in the region seemed to have two options: to gather Indian allies (Memeskia's tactic), or to make alliances with the British (the strategy of a refugee

Iroquois chieftain named Tanacharison). Neither route offered the Indians any real security, but the chaos these bids for advantage created drew the French and British into war.

In 1752, Tanacharison agreed to cede to Virginia not only the 200,000 acres claimed by the Ohio Company, a group of Virginia speculators, but also all the land between the Susquehanna and Allegheny rivers (that is, present-day Kentucky, West Virginia, and the western half of Pennsylvania). In return, Virginia promised Tanacharison's people trade and protection from their enemies. Memeskia was left out in the cold. With no European or Indian power dominant in the region, conflicts broke out, and the French were able to pry off some of Memeskia's alliance and conquer what was left. In a raid on Pickawillany, 250 pro-French Ottawas and Chippewas killed Memeskia. The village was destroyed, and the demoralized Miamis returned to the French fold, asking for protection. For the moment, the French regained the ascendancy, but by shifting their policy from trade to force, they put themselves on a course that would lead to the loss of their North American empire.

The Virginians Ignite a War

Both France and Virginia now claimed the Ohio River valley, and they raced to establish forts that would secure their claims. Virginia entrusted the job to a well-connected 21-year-old with almost no qualifications for the post: George Washington. Washington was tied to the powerful Fairfax clan, a British family that owned 5 million acres in Virginia and held a share in the Ohio Company. In the Anglo-American political and social world, advancement came through such interlocking ties of family and patronage. As Washington himself recognized, "It was deemed by some an extraordinary circumstance that so young and inexperienced a person should have been employed on a negotiation with which subjects of the greatest importance were involved."

In the spring of 1754, the French and Virginians scrambled to see who could build a fort first at the forks of the Ohio (present-day Pittsburgh). The force that Virginia sent to the region, with Washington as second in command, was pathetically small. Although the French army—numbering 1,000—was only 50 miles away, a combined Virginia-Indian band led by Washington recklessly attacked and defeated a small French reconnaissance party. The French and Indian War (known in Europe as the Seven Years' War) had begun.

The Virginians had bitten off more than they could chew. The small fort that Washington and his men built was reinforced by British regulars but quickly deserted by the Indian allies, who recognized it as indefensible. The French overwhelmed the fort, sending Washington and his troops scrambling back to Virginia. Although war was not officially declared in Europe until May 1756, fighting soon spread throughout the frontier.

From Local to Imperial War

At the beginning of the war, the advantage was with the French. Although the population in the British colonies greatly outnumbered that of New France, France's population was three times larger than Britain's, and its army was ten times the size. Even more important, the French state was more centralized and hence better prepared to coordinate the massive effort that an international war required. The British government knew that lack of coordination among its North American colonies could cripple the war effort. Hence, as early as the summer of 1754, it instructed all the colonies north of Virginia to plan for a collective defense and to shore up the alliance with the Six (Iroquois) Nations. Pennsylvania's Benjamin Franklin offered the delegates, who met in Albany, a plan, known as the Albany Plan of Union, which every colony rejected.

The characteristic localism of the American colonies made cooperation difficult if not impossible. This localism was a deeply ingrained value, one that was profoundly suspicious of the centralized European state and its army of professionals.

Britain was now engaged in its fourth war with the French in less than a century. It had authorized Virginia's foray into the Ohio River valley and now sent two regiments, under the command of General Edward Braddock, to Virginia in late 1754, hoping that the colonists could fight the war with only a little British assistance. But the disarray at Albany continued: colonial soldiers were reluctant to obey an officer from another colony, let alone one from the British army.

With four times as many troops as the British had in North America, superior leadership, and the lack of intercolonial rivalries, the French dominated the first phase of the war, from 1754 through 1757. The British and colonial governments, with armies made up of British regulars and colonials, planned to besiege four French forts: Fort Duquesne (Pittsburgh), Fort Niagara (Niagara Falls), Fort St. Frédéric (Crown Point, at the southern end of Lake Champlain), and Fort Beauséjour (Nova Scotia).

George Washington This painting is from 1772, but depicts Washington in his uniform from the French and Indian War.

Braddock was to lead the attack on Fort Duquesne, with a combined force of British regulars and colonial troops. No Indians, however, accompanied the expedition. Braddock had alienated the regional Indians, who moved back into the French alliance. After a grueling two-month march in which they built their own roads ahead of them, on July 9, 1755, Braddock's forces were surprised just a few miles from their objective by a French and Indian force. Almost 1,000 British and colonial troops were killed or wounded, including Braddock himself, who was hastily buried. One of the survivors was George Washington, who had been serving as an unsalaried adjutant to Braddock to learn the art of war.

Two of the other three planned assaults ended in disappointment as well. William Shirley, who became commander in chief of the British forces, decided to lead the attack on Fort Niagara himself, and he assigned leadership of the attack on Fort St. Frédéric to William Johnson, a Mohawk Valley Indian trader who was soon made superintendent of Indian affairs for the northern colonies. Johnson was well suited for leading Iroquois forays against the French, and Shirley sent him to besiege Fort St. Frédéric, a four-story stone tower surrounded by thick limestone walls. Johnson led a force of about 3,500, including 300 Iroquois, building their road ahead of them. Their advance was stopped by an ambush from the French and their Native American allies, but with equal casualties on both sides and the capture of the French commander, the British declared it a victory and elevated Johnson to the nobility. The British settled in for the winter of 1755–1756 to build Fort William Henry, and the French, Fort Carillon (which the British renamed Ticonderoga).

Hampered by a rough terrain and intercolonial political wrangling, Shirley's force never made it to Fort Niagara. The only outright success was at Fort Beauséjour, across an isthmus from the British colony at Nova Scotia. It was the only one of the four campaigns that did not require an arduous wilderness march. A British-financed expedition of New England volunteers easily seized the fort, and the British evicted 10,000 Acadians (French residents of Nova Scotia) who would not take an oath of loyalty. About 300 ended up in French Louisiana, where their name was abbreviated into "Cajuns."

Braddock's Defeat This detail depicting Braddock's defeat is from a drawing by an engineer with the British army.

Like the British, the French had reluctantly increased their expenditures on the war, but both nations still expected their colonists to carry most of the load. The British defeats and continued intercolonial rivalries left the British vulnerable and the frontier exposed. The French began a cautious but highly successful offensive. First, they encouraged Indian raids along the frontier from Maine to South Carolina. Indians swung back to the French because the French appeared less dangerous than the land-hungry British. The price for French friendship, however, was participation in the war against the British. Indians attacked all along the frontier. By the fall of 1756, some 3,000 settlers had been killed, and the line of settlement had been pushed back 150 miles in some places.

In the more conventional part of their offensive, the French and their Indian allies seized Fort Bull in March 1756 and Fort Oswego several months later. A little over a year later, the French assembled a massive force to attack Fort William Henry. This loosely organized army of 8,000 included 1,000 Indian warriors from as far as 1,500 miles away and another 800 converted Algonquians accompanied by their Catholic priests. After a seven-day siege and heavy bombardment, the British commander surrendered on August 9, 1757. Louis-Joseph de Montcalm, the French commander, offered them European-style terms: The British were to return their French and Indian prisoners, keep their personal weapons, and march back to Fort Edward, on the lower Hudson River, promising not to fight the French for 18 months. Historians still debate whether Montcalm knew what was about to take place. The Indians had expected, as was their custom, to be allowed to take plunder and captives. Denied this opportunity by Montcalm, they fell on the British, including the sick, women, and children, as they were evacuating the fort the next morning. Montcalm later commented that "what would be an infraction in Europe, cannot be so regarded in America."

> "I make war for plunder, scalps, and prisoners. You are satisfied with a fort, and you let your enemy and mine live. I do not want to keep such bad meat for tomorrow. When I kill it, it can no longer attack me."
>
> ANONYMOUS WESTERN INDIAN,
> explaining why he refused the French governor's offer of two gallons of rum instead of being allowed to attack the British prisoners

The massacre at Fort William Henry had significant repercussions. Still angry at being denied the spoils of war, Montcalm's Indian allies returned home, taking smallpox with them. The French would never again have the assistance of such a significant number of Indian allies; the British were outraged. The new British commander, Lord Jeffrey Amherst, declared the surrender terms null and void. Later, under his order, Delaware Indians who had been invited to a peace talk were given, ostensibly as presents, blankets that had been infected with smallpox. Historians are not certain whether these blankets

Johnson's Home Iroquois Indians were frequent guests at the home of trader and British official William Johnson. He took an Iroquois woman, Molly Brant, as his common-law wife. Johnson's Iroquois allies followed him into battle in the French and Indian War.

were responsible for the outbreak of the disease among local Indians, but that was certainly Amherst's intent.

Lord Amherst The new British commander, Lord Jeffrey Amherst, authorized germ warfare against the Delaware Indians who were fighting with the French. He invited them to a "peace talk" where they were given blankets infected with smallpox.

Problems with British-Colonial Cooperation

The British and the colonists blamed each other for their collective defeats. There was some truth in each side's accusations: unwillingness to sacrifice and disastrous infighting among the colonists, and arrogance among the British. These recriminations, more than any failing on either side, created problems. The colonists and the British had different expectations about how each should contribute to the war effort. The colonists were not prepared for the high taxes or sacrifice of liberty that waging an international war required.

The British were dismayed by what they perceived as the colonists' selfishness. Colonists engaged in profiteering and trading with the enemy. In Albany, colonists were selling boards to the army at prices inflated 66 percent. Colonial governments were no more generous. Braddock's expedition to Fort Duquesne was delayed by the colonies' unwillingness to provision his army.

After Braddock's defeat, it was not only supplies the army needed; it was troops, too, as colonials deserted in droves. The British began recruiting servants and apprentices, angering their masters. Another serious problem was that of quartering soldiers over the winter. Under English law, which did not extend specifically to the colonies, troops in England could be lodged in public buildings rather than private homes. In the colonies, however, there weren't enough buildings in which to house soldiers without resorting to private homes. The residents of Albany took in soldiers only under threat of force. Philadelphians faced the same threats but were rescued by the ever-resourceful Franklin, who opened a newly built hospital to the troops. In Charleston, soldiers had to camp outdoors, where they fell victim to disease.

A second set of problems arose from joint operations. The British army was a trained and disciplined professional fighting force, led by members of the upper classes; service in it was a career. In contrast, colonial soldiers were primarily civilian amateurs, led by members of the middle class from their hometowns. Colonial soldiers believed that they were fighting under contracts, limiting them to service under a particular officer, for a set period of time, for a specific objective, and a set rate of pay. If any of the terms were violated, the soldier considered himself free to go home.

The British, however, expected the same adherence to military discipline from the colonists as they did from their professional army. All colonial soldiers operating with regular forces were subject to British martial law, which was cruel and uncompromising. One regular soldier, for example, was sentenced to 1,000 lashes for stealing a keg of beer, which a merciful officer reduced to a mere 900! The British officers neither understood nor forgave the colonists' different expectations and were almost unanimous in their condemnation of the colonial soldiers. According to Brigadier General James Wolfe, "The Americans are in general the dirtiest most contemptible cowardly dogs that you can conceive."

Yet the colonists certainly believed that they were doing their share. Taxes were raised dramatically. In Virginia, the tax rate tripled in three years, while in Massachusetts it went up to about £20 per adult man, a considerable sum when the average wealth was £38 per capita. The human contribution was even more impressive. At the height of the war, Massachusetts was raising 7,000 soldiers a year, out of a colony with only 50,000 men. Perhaps as many as three out of ten adult men served in the military at some point during the war, and only the Civil War and the Revolution had higher casualty rates.

The British Gain the Advantage

Montcalm's victory at Fort William Henry marked the French high-water mark. With a change of British government in 1757 came a new resolve to win the war, as William Pitt became head of the cabinet. His rise to power represented the triumph of the commercial classes and their vision of the empire. Pitt was the first British leader who was as committed to a victory in the Americas as in Europe, believing that the future of the British Empire lay in the extended empire and its trade. Consequently, Britain's aim in North America shifted from simply regaining territory to seizing New France itself. Pitt sent 2,000 additional troops, promised 6,000 more, and asked the colonies to raise 20,000 of their own. To support so large an army, Pitt raised taxes on the already heavily taxed British and he borrowed heavily, doubling the size of the British debt. He won the cooperation of the colonies by promising their legislatures that Britain would pay up to half of their costs for fighting the war. As all of this money poured into the colonies, it improved their economies dramatically.

Now the British were prepared to take the offensive (see Map 6–2). In a series of great victories, they won Louisbourg on Cape Breton Island in July 1758; then Fort Frontenac in August; and finally, in November, Fort Duquesne, which the British renamed Fort Pitt. The only defeat was at Fort Carillon (called Ticonderoga by the British). There, Susannah Johnson's husband James was one of the casualties. Once the British seized Fort Frontenac, disrupting the supply lines from the French to the Ohio Valley Indians, those Indians shifted their allegiance. At the same time, the British moved from a policy of confrontation to one of accommodation, partly under the influence of Sir William Johnson. In the Treaty of Easton (1758), more than 500 representatives of 13 Ohio Valley tribes agreed to remain neutral in return for a promise to keep the territory west of the Alleghenies free of settlers. At the same time, gifts to the Iroquois brought them back into the fold.

The British were now ready for the final offensive. Historians always argue about when and why a war is "lost": unless an army has been annihilated and the population entirely subjugated, which is rare, when to surrender is always a subjective

Map 6–2 The Second Phase of the French and Indian War, 1758–1763 This map shows British advances in Pennsylvania, New York, and Canada.

decision. Those who wield political and military power must decide when the loss in lives and resources can no longer be justified, and the population must agree that further fighting is pointless. By 1759, some of the French believed that the war was essentially over. Casualties were extremely high, food was in short supply, and inflation was rampant. Most of the Indian allies had deserted the cause, and the French government was unable to match Pitt's spending on the war. It would take two more years of fighting and the loss of thousands more lives before the French surrendered, however.

In the summer of 1759, General James Wolfe took the struggle for North America into the heart of Canada, laying siege to Quebec. Quebec's position on a bluff high above the St. Lawrence made the city almost impregnable, so for months Wolfe bombarded the city and tried to wear down its citizens, terrorizing those who lived on its outskirts by burning crops and houses. In mid-September, Wolfe ordered an assault up the 175-foot cliff below the city. Hauling two cannons up with them, Wolfe's well-trained soldiers reached the top and, in a battle that lasted only half an hour, claimed victory on the Plains of Abraham. Each side suffered casualties of 15 percent, and both Wolfe and his French opponent, Montcalm, were killed. Four days later, New France's oldest permanent settlement surrendered to the British. By the time the British reached Montréal, the French army numbered fewer than 3,000 men.

Map 6–3 The North American Colonies Before and After the French and Indian War In the Treaty of Paris in 1763, more American territory was transferred than at any time before or since. *Helen Hornbeck Tanner,* Atlas of Great Lakes Indian History *(Norman: University of Oklahoma Press, 1987), p. 54.*

The Treaty of Paris, which concluded the war, was signed in 1763. By that time, Britain had also seized the French sugar islands in the Caribbean and, after Spain entered the war on the French side, Havana and the Philippines. Pitt would have continued to fight, but the British public was unwilling to pay more to increase the size of the empire. The French too were thoroughly tired of war. They surrendered all of Canada except for two small fishing islands in return for the right to hold on to the most valuable sugar islands, which were the most important part of their American empire. France even gave New Orleans and all of its territory west of the Mississippi to Spain as compensation for losing Florida, which the British claimed (see Map 6–3). (Britain let Spain keep Havana and the Philippines.) Britain staked its future on the mainland of North America, believing correctly that it would ultimately be more valuable than the sugar islands of the Caribbean.

Enforcing the Empire

Even before the French and Indian War began, some members of the British government believed that tighter control had to be exercised over the American colonies. What British officials stationed in the colonies saw during the war only reinforced that view. Colonists smuggled and even traded with the enemy throughout the war, while the colonial assemblies sometimes impeded the war effort. Pitt had increased Britain's national debt to pay for the war, rather than waiting for the colonial assemblies. Now, with the war over, Britain faced a staggering debt of £122,603,336. Moreover, there was a huge new territory to govern, a territory that was coveted by speculators and settlers and inhabited by Indian tribes determined to resist encroachment.

Painted Caribou Skin Coat Innu, ca. 1783–1805. Quebec-Labrador Peninsula. Courtesy Innu Nation and The Rooms Corporation of Newfoundland and Labrador, Provincial Museum Division. Photo: Shane Kelly

The American Revolution grew out of Britain's attempts to draw its American colonies more closely into the imperial system. Although from time to time various master plans for reorganizing the empire had been circulated, there was never an overarching design or a clear set of guidelines. What was new in 1763 was a resolve to enforce a set of assumptions about how an empire should function and what the role of colonies in it should be. In 1760 a new king, the 22-year-old George III, ascended to the throne upon the death of his grandfather. Reasonably well-educated, although lacking in genius, the young king was determined to play a role in government. He changed ministers frequently, which made the British government chaotic. It is not clear, however, that more enlightened leadership would have prevented the war, for George's ministers pursued a consistent, if imperfectly executed, policy toward the colonies. In resisting that policy, the American colonists developed a new and different idea of the purpose of government, one that propelled them to revolution.

> **"What had little Boys and Girls done; what could Children of a Year old, Babes at the Breast, what could they do, that they too must be shot and hatcheted?—Horrid to relate!—and in their Parents Arms! This is done by no civilized Nation in Europe. Do we come to America to learn and practise the Manners of Barbarians? But this, Barbarians as they are, they practise against their Enemies only, not against their Friends."**
>
> BENJAMIN FRANKLIN,
> condemning the Paxton Boys

Pontiac's Rebellion and Its Aftermath

Because the British had defeated the French in war and had entered into alliances with the Iroquois and the Ohio Valley Indians, peace in the West should have been easy to secure. The British, however, soon made the same mistake that the French had made when they discontinued presents to their Indian allies 15 years earlier. Thinking that they could impose their will on the Indians, the British instead found themselves embroiled in another war.

At the conclusion of the French and Indian War, the western Algonquian tribes hoped that the British would follow the practices of the middle ground by mediating their disputes, trading with them at advantageous prices, and giving them presents. Lord Jeffrey Amherst, who commanded the British forces in North America, cut off the presents, believing them too expensive. He thought that threats of an Indian revolt were exaggerated, and he was willing to take the risk of war.

The war that resulted in 1763 is commonly known as Pontiac's Rebellion, named after the Ottawa chieftain who played a prominent role. It was the first battle in a long, and ultimately unsuccessful, attempt by Indians to keep the region between the Mississippi River and the Alleghenies free of European settlers. The Indians seized every fort except for Pitt, Niagara, and Detroit, and Detroit was under siege for six months (see Map 6–4). The war spawned violence all along the frontier. Casualties were high: about 2,000 civilians, 400 soldiers, and an unknown number of Indians. Tortures by both sides were horrific, and American colonists took out their aggressions on peaceful or defenseless Indians living in their midst. In December 1763, a party of 50 armed men from the Pennsylvania village of Paxton descended on a tiny community of Christian Indians living at Conestoga Manor, eight miles west of Lancaster. They killed and scalped the six people they found—2 men, 3 women, and a child—and burned their houses. Two weeks later, another group of these "Paxton Boys" broke into the county workhouse, where the remainder of the small tribe had been put for their own protection, and killed them too.

Although colonial leaders decried acts of violence, they did little to prevent or punish them. British officials saw the inability of the colonists to maintain order on the frontier and protect innocent Indians from violence as further evidence of the fecklessness of colonial governments. Even before Pontiac's Rebellion ended in a draw, the British had decided that peace with the western Indians could be preserved only by keeping colonial settlers and speculators away. The Proclamation of 1763

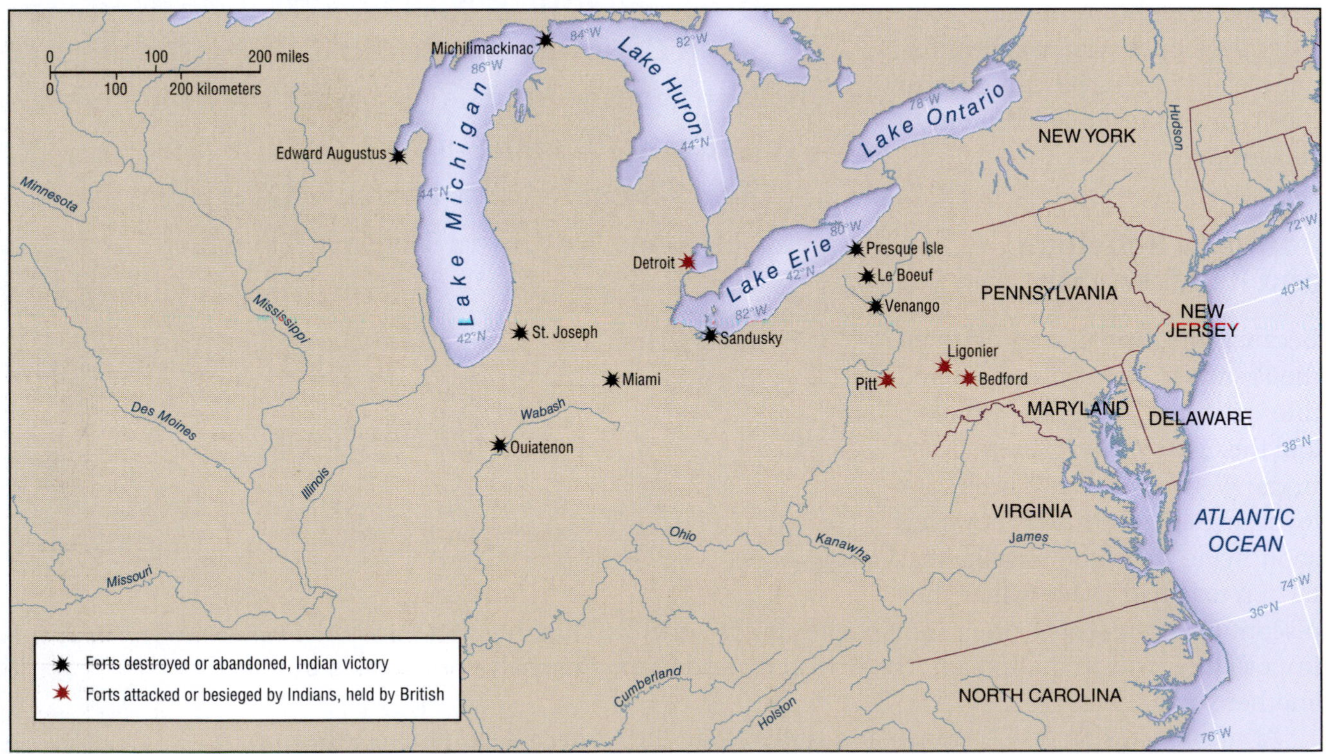

Map 6–4 Pontiac's Rebellion, 1763 The war began when the British abandoned the policy of the middle ground and cut off presents to the western Indians. In their uprising, the Indians destroyed nine British forts and attacked another four before the war ended in a draw. *Tanner,* Atlas of Great Lakes Indian History, *p. 49.*

attempted to confine the colonists to the east of an imaginary line running down the spine of the Alleghenies. George Washington called the proclamation "a temporary expedient to quiet the minds of the Indians" and ignored it. Other Virginia speculators looked for a pretext for taking the territory by force. It came in 1774 when several settlers killed several Indians, and John Logan, a Mingo Indian, sought vengeance for his slain relatives. Rather than resolving this conflict in the time-tested ways of the middle ground, Virginia's royal governor, Lord Dunmore, did the bidding of the colony's speculators and sent a force of 2,000 Virginians to vanquish the Indians. Although the Virginians' success in Lord Dunmore's War extinguished Indian claims to Kentucky, Britain was still not ready to permit speculators or settlers to claim the land.

Negotiating the Conclusion of Pontiac's Rebellion Colonel Henry Bouquet in council with Shawnee, Seneca, and Delaware Indians on the banks of the Muskingum River in October 1764.

Paying for the Empire: Sugar and Stamps

On the edge of the British Empire, the colonies were important, but not nearly as important as Britain's domestic concerns. One of George III's highest priorities was to maintain the size of the army. During the French and Indian War, the size of the British army had doubled, and it was filled with officers who were loyal to the king. Responding to the king's wishes, Parliament in 1763 voted to maintain a huge peacetime army, part of which would be stationed in the colonies and West Indies. Colonists feared that the British intended to use the army to enforce customs regulations rather than to police the Indians.

This large army, of course, was going to strain the British budget, already burdened by a huge war debt. George Grenville, the new prime minister, believed that the colonists should pay a portion of the £225,000 a year that the standing army would cost.

Under Grenville's leadership, Parliament passed four pieces of legislation to force the colonies to contribute to their own upkeep. The Molasses Act of 1733 had established a duty of six cents per gallon, but smugglers paid off customs officials at the rate of one and a half cents a gallon. At Grenville's urging, Parliament passed

AMERICA AND THE WORLD

>> Paying for War

For most of human history, the costs of war have worked as a check on war making: a country could not spend any more on warfare than it could pay for at the time. Some countries, such as Prussia, plundered their neighbors. Others taxed their own people, but there are always absolute limits to how much money can be extracted from one's own people at any one time. Other countries borrowed from foreigners, but that put them at the mercy of their foreign creditors.

In the seventeenth century, the Dutch figured out a new method of financing government: borrowing money from its own citizens by selling them interest-paying bonds. The government then taxed its own people to pay off the bonds and the interest, which enabled it to spread out the costs of war over a long period. The result was higher taxes in peacetime—but no excessive burden during times of war. At the same time, those who bought government bonds were literally making an investment in their nation and profiting from its success.

This was the method that the British used to pay for their rise to power beginning in the eighteenth century. It allowed the nation to raise astronomical sums of money: £31 million for King William's War, £51 million for Queen Anne's War, £73 million for the Seven Years' War. And with each war, the government borrowed an increasing portion of the costs. King William's War was paid for entirely by taxation, but by the time of the Seven Years' War, the English government had borrowed—from its own citizens—78 percent of its cost.

As Britain's war debt increased—it was up to £122,603,336 at the end of the Seven Years' War—the country had to raise taxes to pay for it. The English were paying higher taxes than any other nation in the world except for the Dutch. In fact, at the time of the French Revolution—brought on in part by unacceptably high taxes—the British were taxed at a higher rate than the French. Yet the mechanisms of taxation were so efficient and the political processes by which they were levied so finely tuned, that the government was able to collect tax revenues with relatively little resistance.

This achievement is all the more remarkable when one considers the relative unfairness of the English tax system. The burden fell upon the middle classes, while by a combination of intent and political accommodation, both the poor and the affluent were relatively lightly taxed. With the poor, it was mostly a matter of design. There was widespread agreement that the wages and necessities of the poor should be taxed lightly or not at all. Instead, the burden should fall, in theory, upon the wealthy. Indeed, in 1690, 47 percent of England's revenues came from taxes on land and other property of the rich, but the powerful landowners refused to pay higher rates of taxation and so, as the nation's need for revenue increased, the proportion of taxes paid by the wealthy fell. By 1763, it was down to 23 percent.

In search of revenue, the English government levied excise and stamp taxes, which fell most heavily on the middle classes. By the end of the Seven Years' War, the public had come close to reaching its limit. It was already unhappy with the tax on beer, and it objected when the ministry proposed one on cider too, to help pay the interest on the loan for the final year of war.

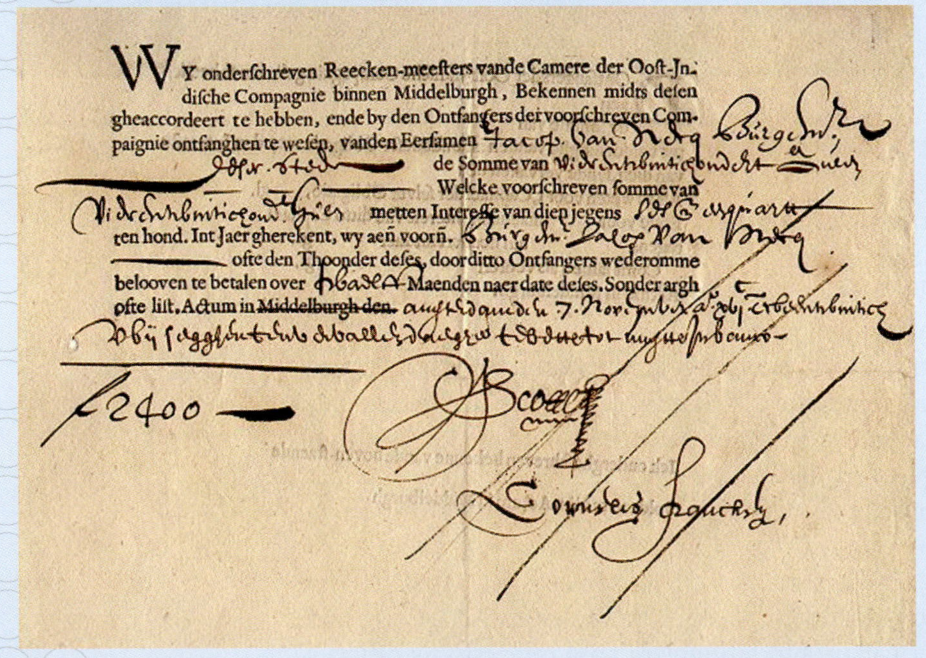

WY onderſchreven Reecken-meeſters vande Camere der Ooſt-Indiſche Compagnie binnen Middelburgh, Bekennen midts deſen gheaccordeert te hebben, ende by den Ontfangers der voorſchreven Compaignie ontfanghen te weſen, vanden Eerſamen … de Somme van … Welcke voorſchreven ſomme van … metten Intereſſe van dien jegens … ten hond. Int Jaer gherekent, wy aen voorn. … ofte den Thoonder deſes, door ditto Ontfangers wederomme belooven te betalen over … Maenden naer date deſes. Sonder argh ofte liſt. Actum in ~~Middelburgh den.~~ …

f 2400

A Dutch bond, issued in 1623.

This was the context for Britain's attempt to collect more money from its colonies. Parliament worried that it could not increase taxes on its own people any further, and so it looked for other sources of revenue, in other parts of its empire. At just the time that Parliament tried to tax the American colonies to pay for the troops that were stationed there, it was also stationing more forces in Ireland—and trying, unsuccessfully, to get the Irish parliament to pay for them. When the East India Company conquered the huge Indian state of Bengal, King George III imagined that the wealth of India was "the only safe method of extracting this country out of its . . . load of debt." In return for letting the East India Company continue to govern Bengal, the government extracted a fee of £400,000 a year, which the Company demanded from the Bengalis. This crushing burden of tax, which fell at the same time as a serious drought, plunged Bengal into a famine that killed 10 million people, a third of the population. With strong traditions of local government, the American colonists and the Irish were better able to resist England's attempts to tax them.

the Sugar Act (1764), which dropped the duty to three cents but established procedures to make certain it was collected. To discourage smuggling, all shippers were required to file elaborate papers each time an item was loaded onto a ship. In addition, accused violators were to be tried in admiralty courts, the closest of which was in Nova Scotia. There, the burden of proof would be on the defendant, and the judgment would be rendered by judges rather than a jury.

To regulate the colonial economies so that they served the interest of British creditors, the Currency Act (1764) forbade the issuing of any colonial currency. The immediate cause was the complaint of British merchants that colonists were discharging their debts in depreciated paper money. Moreover, the Sugar Act and the Stamp Act (passed the following year) required that duties and taxes both be paid in specie, that is, silver and gold. The colonists complained, however, that there was not anywhere near as much specie in the colonies as they needed.

The third and most important piece of imperial legislation enacted in this flurry was the Stamp Act (1765). Its objective was to raise revenue. Unarguably the first direct tax on the American people, the Stamp Act placed a tax on documents used in court proceedings; papers used in clearing ships from harbors; college diplomas; appointments to public office; bonds, grants, and deeds for land mortgages; indentures, leases, contracts, and bills of sale; articles of apprenticeship and liquor licenses; playing cards and dice; and pamphlets, newspapers (and the ads in them), and almanacs.

The final piece of legislation, the Quartering Act (1765), required the colonies to provide housing for troops in public buildings and to provide them with firewood, candles, and drink.

Although the colonists objected to all of these pieces of legislation, the Stamp Act was the most troubling. By taxing newspapers and pamphlets, it angered printers and editors. This was a foolish group to alienate at a time when newspapers were taking the lead in criticizing the government and were perhaps the most significant public institution in the colonies. In addition, by taxing legal documents, the Stamp Act angered lawyers, for every time a lawyer performed the simplest task of his trade, he would have to buy a stamp. Collectively, these laws fell hardest on the most affluent and politically active colonists, the merchants, lawyers, and printers. In contrast, when Parliament wanted to raise money in Britain to pay for the army and the national debt, it levied a tax on cider, the drink of the common man. All of these pieces of legislation were an attempt to tie the colonies into a modern, centralized state. As the colonists framed their response to the new laws, they struggled with a question that has been central to American history: Could the people share in the benefits of the modern state—in particular a trade protected by its navy and borders secured by its army—without the state itself?

Rejecting the Empire

Colonial resistance to the imperial legislation of 1763 to 1765 was swift and forceful. A coalition of elite leaders and common people, primarily in the cities, worked to overturn the most objectionable aspects of the new regulations. In 1765, there was almost no thought of revolution, nor would there be for almost 10 years. Instead, the colonists rested their case on the British Constitution. All they wanted, they claimed, were the rights of Englishmen. Although in theory the colonists, as British subjects, were entitled to all of those rights, precisely *how* the British Constitution applied to colonists had never been clarified. The first phase of opposition, then, took the form of a debate about the British Constitution, with the colonists insisting on their rights and the British government focusing on the colonists' obligations.

An Argument About Rights and Obligations

All along, Britain had maintained its right to regulate the colonies. Precisely what this meant became a matter of dispute after 1763. Did it mean regulation of trade? Taxation? Legislation? When Parliament passed these pieces of legislation, it represented a change in British *practices,* not in how Britons thought about the colonies or the empire. The empire was a whole, the parts existed for the benefit of the whole, and Parliament had the authority to govern for the whole.

Britons were justifiably proud of their Parliament, which was one of the premier institutions of self-government in the world at the time. In principle Parliament represented all the elements in society: the king, the aristocrats (in the House of Lords), and the common people (in the House of Commons). Applying the terms used by the Greek philosopher Aristotle, this was a mixed or balanced form of government. It mixed and balanced these three elements of society, which also represented the three possible forms of government—monarchy, rule by the king; aristocracy, rule by the hereditary aristocrats; and democracy, rule by the people—thus preventing both tyranny and anarchy and preserving liberty.

The British believed, and American colonists agreed, that their superb government was the product of centuries of struggle. First the aristocrats struggled with the king for more freedom for themselves, gaining it in the Magna Carta of 1215, and then the people struggled and won liberty, most recently in the Glorious Revolution of 1688. In this view, liberty was a collective right held by the people against the rulers. Liberty thus was thought of as a limitation on the power of the monarch. A chief example of public or civil liberty was the right to be taxed only by one's own representatives. Taxes were a free gift of the people that they might yield up but that no monarch could demand.

These ideas about the British government can be described as *constitutionalism*. Constitutionalism comprised two elements: the rule of law and the principle

of consent, that one could not be subjected to laws or taxation except by duly elected representatives. Both were rights that had been won through struggle with the monarch. In the decade between 1765 and the outbreak of the American Revolution, the colonists worked out their own theory of the place of the colonies in the empire. A consensus formed on exactly these points, the importance of the rule of law and the principle of consent. Those colonists who became revolutionaries never wavered on these two points. What the colonists debated in the decade between the Stamp Act and the beginning of the American Revolution was whether particular pieces of legislation violated these principles and how far the colonists should go in resisting those that did.

British officials never denied that the colonists should enjoy the rights of Englishmen. They merely asserted that the colonists were as well represented in Parliament as the majority of Britons. In fact, only one out of ten British men could vote, compared to about 70 percent of American white men. Yet British officials said that all Britons were represented in Parliament, if not "actually," by choosing their own representatives, then by *virtual representation,* because each member of Parliament was supposed to act on behalf of the entire empire, not only his constituents. In Britons' minds, Parliament was supreme, and it had full authority over the colonists. In the decade between the Stamp Act and the beginning of the American Revolution, the controversy turned on only two questions: How forcefully would the British government insist on the supremacy of Parliament? And could colonial radicals put together a broad enough coalition to resist Britain's force when it came?

The Imperial Crisis in Local Context

While colonial political thinkers were filling newspapers and pamphlets with denunciations of the new imperial legislation, Americans in every colony were taking their protests to the streets and to the colonial legislatures. Everywhere, a remarkable cross-class alliance of prosperous merchants and planters who had been the chief beneficiaries of the consumer revolution, and poor people who had not yet enjoyed its benefits, joined to protect what they perceived as their rights from encroachment by British officials.

By the day that the Stamp Act was to go into effect, November 1, 1765, every colony except Georgia had taken steps to ensure that the tax could not be collected. In Virginia, the House of Burgesses took the lead. A young and barely literate lawyer, Patrick Henry, played a key role in the debate on the Virginia Resolves, the four resolutions protesting the Stamp Act that were passed by the Burgesses. They asserted that the inhabitants of Virginia brought with them from England the rights of Englishmen, that Virginia's royal charters confirmed these rights, that taxation by one's own representatives was the only constitutional policy, and that the people of Virginia had never given up their rights. Henry came close to treason when he asserted that "Tarquin and Jul[i]us had their Brutus, Charles had his Cromwell, and he Did not Doubt but some good American would stand up in favour of his Country." In Boston, as in the other colonies, the protest united the elite with poorer colonists, building on long-standing tensions between colonists and royal officials. Massachusetts was still reeling from the loss of life and extraordinary expense of the French and Indian War. Now that the war was over, imperialists such as Lieutenant Governor Thomas Hutchinson wanted to tie Massachusetts more tightly to the empire. He advocated a consolidation of power, a diminution of popular government (e.g., by reducing the power of the town meeting), making offices that were elective appointive instead, and limiting the freedom of the press.

Boston's public, which had a history of radicalism, was ready for a much stronger response to the Stamp Act than the Massachusetts House of Representatives seemed prepared to make. The *Boston Gazette* criticized the House's resolution as a "tame, pusillanimous, daubed, insipid thing." Once word of the more radical Virginia Resolves arrived, the *Gazette* rebuked the weak political leaders of Massachusetts again. A group of artisans and printers who called themselves the Loyal Nine and later changed their name to the Sons of Liberty began organizing the opposition, probably in concert with more prominent men who would emerge as leaders of the revolutionary movement, such as James Otis, John Adams, and his cousin Sam Adams, the Harvard-educated son of a brewer.

In a carefully orchestrated series of mob actions, Bostonians made certain that the Stamp Act would not be enforced. When the militia refused to protect royal officials, including the collector of the stamp tax, the officials took refuge in Castle William in the harbor. Over a period of several days, the mob slowly and systematically vandalized the homes of several wealthy government loyalists, including Hutchinson. Although the mob consisted mostly of artisans and poor people, it had the support of Boston's merchant elite, for no one was ever punished. The protest succeeded, and the Stamp Act was never enforced.

Samuel Adams This portrait of one of Boston's most effective political agitators in the years leading to the Revolution was painted by John Singleton Copley ca. 1772.

Not only did each colony mount its own protest against the Stamp Act, but a majority of the colonies were now ready to act together. In October 1765, delegates from nine colonies met in New York in the Stamp Act Congress to ratify a series of 14 resolutions protesting the Stamp Act on constitutional grounds. The congress asserted, for example, "that it is inseparably essential to the freedom of a people, and the undoubted rights of Englishmen, that no taxes should be imposed on them, but with their own consent, given personally, or by their representatives." At the same time, activists shut down colonial courts so that no stamps could be used, and merchants agreed not to import any British goods until the act was repealed. With 37 percent of British exports going to the colonies at this time, this was no idle threat (see Figure 6–3).

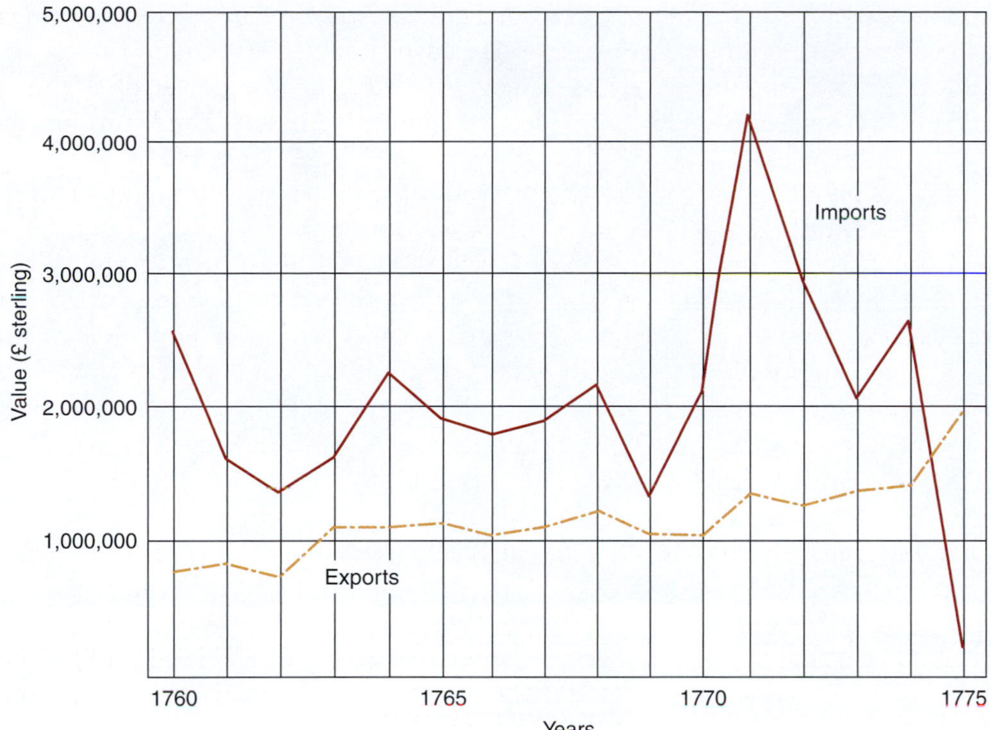

Figure 6–3 Trade Between England and the Colonies In the years between 1760 and 1775, colonial exports to England grew slowly but steadily, only dropping off after the beginning of the Revolution. On the other hand, imports from England—which always exceeded exports—rose and fell in response to political conditions. Colonial nonimportation agreements forced drops in imports after the imposition of the Stamp Act and Townshend Duties. But in both cases, imports increased after repeal, and the growth of imports after repeal of the Townshend Duties was dramatic and unprecedented.

In the face of this opposition, the British partly backed down. George Grenville had been replaced by the 35-year-old Marquess of Rockingham, who preferred racehorses to politics. He remained in office just long enough for Parliament to repeal the Stamp Act. Parliament was not prepared to concede the constitutional point, however, and in the Declaratory Act of 1766 asserted ominously that Parliament "had, hath, and of right ought to have, full power and authority to make laws and statutes . . . to bind the colonies and people of America, subjects of the crown of *Great Britain,* in all cases whatsoever."

Contesting the Townshend Duties

Britain gave up on trying to tax the colonies directly, for even some prominent Britons such as William Pitt sided with the colonists on that point. But between 1767 and 1774, those in power still tried to tighten the bonds of empire by forcing their vision of empire on the colonies. In response, radical activists and thinkers coalesced into a national opposition. Together, these radicals took constitutionalism in new directions. By the time of the American Revolution, they had turned it into a new theory of government.

THE REPEAL, or the Funeral Procession, of MISS AMERIC-STAMP.

Repeal of the Stamp Act, 1766 This cartoon shows the repeal of the Stamp Act, with George Grenville and other British officials carrying a coffin containing the act. In the background, languishing on the dock, is cargo that could not be shipped to America during the colonial boycott.

After a brief return to power by William Pitt, Charles Townshend, a brilliant but erratic man nicknamed "Champagne Charlie," became the third prime minister in as many years. His first act was to punish New York's assembly, which intentionally violated the Quartering Act. The assembly, denied the right to pass any legislation until it complied with the Quartering Act, quickly backed down.

The colonies refused, however, to comply with Parliament's next piece of legislation, the Townshend Revenue Act of 1767, which levied import duties on lead, paint, glass, paper, and tea. Townshend believed that the colonists objected only to taxes within the colonies, "internal taxes," but that they would accept an "external tax," such as an import duty. The revenue would be used to support colonial officials, making them independent of the colonial assemblies that had paid their salaries.

Resistance to the Townshend Act built slowly. Even though standard constitutional arguments were used, it was hard for colonists to make a case against all duties. Merchants were now complying with the new Revenue Act of 1766, which reduced the duty on molasses to one cent per gallon. Those colonists who had been most troubled by the first round of imperial legislation, however, were convinced that the Townshend Duties were part of a pattern of British oppression that would lead to tyranny.

A body of thought known as *republicanism* helped the colonists make sense of British actions. Republicanism was a set of doctrines rooted in the Renaissance that held that power is always dangerous, for "it is natural for Power to be striving to enlarge itself, and to be encroaching upon those that have none." Republicanism supplied constitutionalism with a motive. It explained how a balanced constitution could be transformed into tyranny. Would-be tyrants had at their disposal a variety of tools, one of which was a standing army, whose ultimate purpose was not the protection of the people but their subjection. Tyrants also engaged in corruption, in particular by dispensing patronage positions. So inexorable was the course of power that it took extraordinary virtue for an individual to resist its corruption. Consequently, republican citizens, it was thought, had to be economically independent. The poor were dangerous because they could easily be bought off by would-be tyrants. A secular theory with connections to Puritanism, republicanism asserted that people were naturally weak and that exceptional human effort was required to protect both liberty and virtue.

Not only did people have to keep a close eye on power-hungry tyrants, they also had to look inside themselves. According to republican thought, history demonstrated that republics fell from within, when their citizens lost their virtue. The greatest threat to virtue was luxury, an excessive attachment to the fruits of the consumer revolution. When colonists worried that they saw luxury and corruption everywhere, they were criticizing the world that the consumer revolution had created. Although it is understandable why poor people, who saw others getting rich while they were squeezed, embraced republicanism, it might seem perplexing that wealthy merchants and planters were among the most vocal in their denunciations of "malice, covetousness, and other lusts of man." Yet the legacy of Puritanism was powerful, and even those who were profiting most from the new order felt ambivalent about the direction of change in their society. Joining with poorer people in criticizing British officials, and accusing them of attempting to undermine colonial liberties, helped forge a cross-class alliance.

The colonial legislatures slowly began to protest the duties. Massachusetts's House of Representatives, led by Sam Adams, sent a circular letter to each of the other lower houses in the colonies, asking them to join in resisting "infringements of their natural & constitutional Rights because they are not represented in the British Parliament. . . ." When Lord Hillsborough, a hard-liner recently appointed to the new post of secretary of state for the colonies, received the letter, he instructed the colonial governors to dissolve any colonial assembly that received the petition from Massachusetts. Massachusetts refused to rescind its letter, so Governor Francis Bernard dissolved the legislature. With representative government threatened, those colonial legislatures that had not already approved the Massachusetts circular letter did so now—and were then dissolved. In response, many legislatures met on their own, as extralegal representative bodies.

Not only did legislators assert their own authority, but ordinary people did so as well. In each colony, the radicals who called themselves Sons of Liberty organized a nonimportation movement, using both coercion and patriotic appeal to the entire community. Women were actively recruited into the movement, both to encourage household manufacture (an economic activity redefined as a political one) and to refuse British imports. In 1769 women in little Middletown, Massachusetts, wove 20,522 yards of cloth, and in towns and cities throughout the colonies women added their names to the nonimportation agreements. This politicization of ordinary men and women horrified conservative British observers. Although there were pockets of defiance, the movement succeeded in cutting imports dramatically. By the time that the Townshend Duties were repealed in 1770, Britain had collected only £21,000, and lost £786,000 in trade.

AMERICAN LANDSCAPE

>> Occupied Boston

For a year and a half, Boston was an occupied city. British troops began arriving in October 1768. They were supposed to maintain order and enforce customs regulations in a town that its own officials thought was dangerously out of control.

Republicanism, however, warned that tyrants used standing armies to deprive the people of their liberties. Hence, the appearance of British warships in Boston Harbor and the disembarking of 1700 soldiers in full "Battle Array" only increased Bostonians' anxiety. It was, however, the daily interactions between soldiers and locals that demonstrated why occupying armies so often antagonize just the people they are supposed to calm.

The immediate problem was where to lodge the troops. The Quartering Act required the town to provide housing but Bostonians refused. Governor Bernard sent the soldiers to an old manufactory that had been turned into housing for the poor. The inhabitants refused to move. The army began renting lodgings wherever it could, thus scattering soldiers throughout the city.

But it was not only the Bostonians who needed policing. With the troops dispersed, it proved impossible for their officers to control them. Within two weeks, 70 soldiers had deserted. Policing civilians, especially those who are your own countrymen and countrywomen, was not an attractive assignment. In order to prevent further desertions, the army posted an armed sentry at the narrow isthmus that then was the only connection between Boston and the mainland. But that made the Bostonians feel as if they were prisoners in their own city. The army executed one young deserter in full public view. Such harsh punishment shocked the Bostonians.

Still, in a city as small as Boston, with so many young soldiers stationed in it, conflict between citizens and soldiers was almost inevitable. Because of an economic depression, liquor was cheap, and off-duty soldiers regularly became drunk and offensive. Prostitution increased, and inebriated soldiers assaulted local women. Because sentries could not distinguish between civilians and deserters wearing civilian clothing, every citizen had to be prepared to stop and identify himself or herself, at the point of a bayonet. In addition, moonlighting soldiers were willing to work cheaper than Bostonians.

Some of the officers tried to keep their soldiers under control, but, because of the underlying political conflict that had brought British troops to Boston, there was no mechanism that could keep conflict from spiraling out of control. Patriots controlled the local justice system, and they used it to harass misbehaving soldiers. Any sentry who provoked a civilian could find himself hauled before a patriotic magistrate who would make him post a huge bond, no matter how flimsy the charges. Yet even when the charges were truly serious, the attorney general—loyal to the Crown—would not prosecute. In the absence of effective justice, gangs began to take the law into their own hands.

One of the confrontations was caused by John Mein, the publisher of a Boston newspaper. He printed the names of local merchants, some of them members of the Sons of Liberty, who were violating the nonimpor-

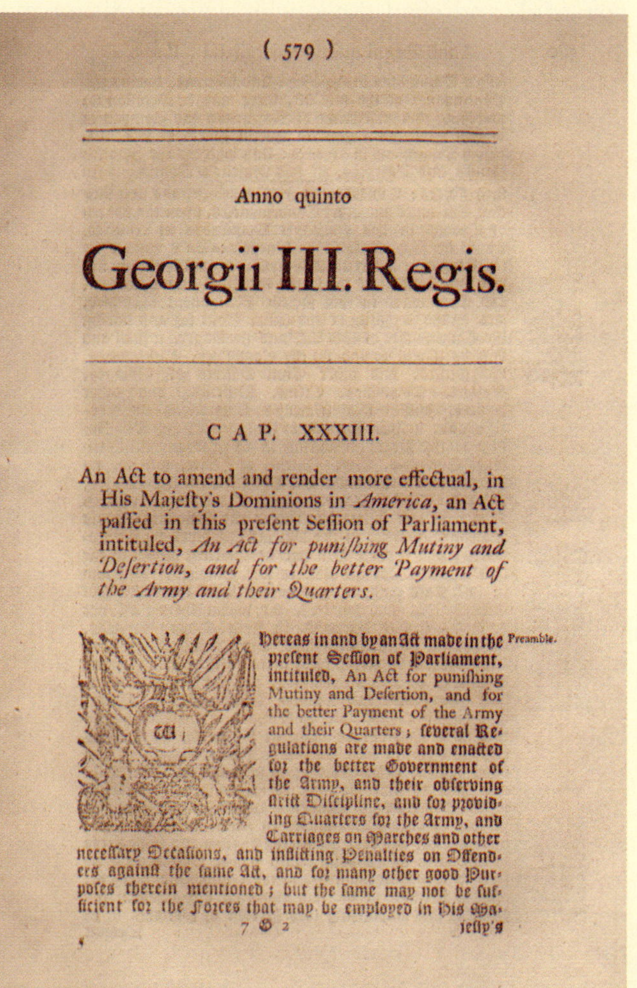

(579)

Anno quinto

Georgii III. Regis.

C A P. XXXIII.

An Act to amend and render more effectual, in His Majesty's Dominions in *America*, an Act passed in this present Session of Parliament, intituled, *An Act for punishing Mutiny and Desertion, and for the better Payment of the Army and their Quarters.*

Whereas in and by an Act made in the present Session of Parliament, intituled, An Act for punishing Mutiny and Desertion, and for the better Payment of the Army and their Quarters; several Regulations are made and enacted for the better Government of the Army, and their observing strict Discipline, and for providing Quarters for the Army, and Carriages on Marches and other necessary Occasions, and inflicting Penalties on Offenders against the same Act, and for many other good Purposes therein mentioned; but the same may not be sufficient for the Forces that may be employed in His Majesty's Preamble.

7 G 2

tation agreements. Cynically, he wanted to demonstrate "that their Patriotism was founded on Self Interest and Malice." When patriots beat up first one man and then another who had the misfortune of resembling him, Mein appealed to Acting Governor Thomas Hutchinson for protection. Hutchinson told him there was nothing he could do until a crime had actually been committed. Mein took to carrying a pistol when he went out.

On the afternoon of October 28, 1769, a band of patriots fell upon Mein and his partner, throwing bricks at him and shouting, "Knock him down! Kill him!" The men took refuge with soldiers in a small guardhouse that was soon surrounded by a mob of 200. When the partner's gun went off accidentally, the patriots assumed that Mein himself had taken a shot. Sam Adams got a friendly magistrate to issue a warrant for Mein's arrest for firing at citizens who were "lawfully and peacefully assembled together." Mein was certain that if he were taken into custody, he would be killed. He sent a desperate appeal to Hutchinson. By now the mob had grown to more than 1000.

Hutchinson knew, however, that if he called out the army to rescue Mein, it would only "have set the whole province in a flame, and maybe spread farther." So Mein remained hidden in the guardhouse until friends could smuggle him onto a ship leaving Boston.

The army that had been summoned to Boston to maintain order learned that it, like many an army of occupation, was close to powerless in the face of a population that resisted its rule. ●

A Revolution in the Empire

The resistance to the Townshend Duties established a pattern that would be repeated again and again in the years before the Revolution. Each attempt to enforce the empire met with organized colonial opposition, to which the British government responded with a punitive measure. Ostensibly economic regulations such as the Sugar Act, the Townshend Duties, and the subsequent Tea Act, when rejected by the colonies, led to clearly political responses from Britain. Economics and politics became inseparable, as two visions of the empire came into conflict. Britain saw the colonies as a small but integral part of a large empire held together by an increasingly centralized and powerful government. The goal of the empire was to enhance its collective wealth and power, albeit under a system of constitutional government. While not rejecting the notion of a larger empire outright, increasingly the colonists equated representative government with prosperity, not just for the empire as a whole, but for its citizens in the colonies as well. Each round of colonial protest mobilized a larger segment of the population.

> "A Subscription Paper was handed about, enumerating a great Variety of Articles not to be imported from England, which they supposed would muster the Manufacturers in England into a national Mob to support their Interests. Among the various prohibited Articles, were Silks, Velvets, Clocks, Watches, Coaches & Chariots; & it was highly diverting, to see the names & marks, to the Subscription, of Porters & Washing Women."
>
> PETER OLIVER,
> a Boston conservative, ridiculing the nonimportation movement and the kinds of people who participated in it

"Massacre" in Boston

Years of conflict with royal officials, combined with a growing population of poor and underemployed, had made Boston the most radical and united spot in the colonies. The political leadership had learned how to win popular favor in their ongoing strife with the governor and those who were loyal to him. The repeated attempts of the British government to enforce its legislation, exerting increasing pressure on Boston, led finally to revolution.

In an attempt to tighten up the collection of customs duties, the British government, now led by Lord North, decided to make an example of John Hancock, Boston's wealthiest merchant and not yet a confirmed radical. In June 1768, Boston's customs commissioners seized Hancock's sloop, the *Liberty*, on a technical violation of the Sugar Act. Hancock and several associates were threatened with fines totaling £54,000 (most of which would go into the pockets of the governor and the informer). All charges were dropped, however, after a riot of 2,000 "sturdy boys and men" sent the customs officials once again scuttling off to Castle William for protection. Now Hancock was a radical.

In the wake of the *Liberty* riot, Governor Bernard called for troops to support the customs commissioners. Rather than restoring order, the arrival of the troops led to further conflict. For a year and a half there was tension, as might be expected with so many soldiers stationed in a city of 15,000. The Boston Massacre grew out of these tensions.

What angry colonists called a "massacre" was the culmination of several months of scuffling between young men and adolescents and soldiers, perhaps in-

British Landing, 1768 This engraving by Paul Revere depicts the landing of British troops at Boston, on October 1, 1768.

evitable in a town with so many men competing for work. Most of the participants knew one another from previous conflicts. On March 5, 1770, a fracas between a young apprentice and an army officer escalated as a crowd surrounded the officer, insulting him and pelting him with snowballs. Someone shouted, "Fire!" and the crowd grew. Seven soldiers came to rescue their terrified colleague, and they too were hit with snowballs and taunts of "Kill them." When one was knocked down, he screamed, "Damn you, fire!" and the soldiers fired on the crowd. Eleven men were wounded, and five were killed. One victim was Crispus Attucks, a 47-year-old free black sailor. Subsequently, the soldiers were tried, but the only two who were convicted were later pardoned. The British withdrew their troops from Boston.

As long as the British were willing to back down, more serious conflicts could be avoided. The Boston Massacre was followed by a three-year period of peace. The Townshend Duties had been repealed—except the one on tea, which the colonists could not manufacture themselves—and the nonimportation movement had collapsed. Colonial trade resumed its previous pace, and in 1772, imports from England and Scotland doubled. Colonists were not prepared to deny themselves consumer goods for long. The Quartering Act had expired and the Currency Act was repealed. As long as Britain allowed the colonists to trade relatively unimpeded, permitted them to govern themselves, and kept the army out of their cities, all could be, if not forgotten, at least silenced by the clink of coins in the shopkeeper's till.

The Empire Comes Apart

Although the British government was under the control of conservatives who believed that sooner or later the colonists would need to acknowledge Parliament's supremacy, the move that led directly to revolution was more accidental than calculated. The North American colonies were only part of Britain's extended empire. There were powerful British interests in India, where the British East India Company was on the verge of bankruptcy. Parliament decided to bail out the company, both to rescue its empire in India and also to help out the influential stockholders. The duty for importing tea into Britain—but not America—was canceled. Moreover, Parliament allowed the company to sell directly to Americans through a small number of agents, cutting out all the middlemen. As a result, the price of tea would drop below that of smuggled Dutch tea. Also, in all of Massachusetts, only five men would be allowed to sell British tea—two sons, a nephew, and two friends of the much-despised Governor Thomas Hutchinson. The agents in the other colonies were also loyalists who gained their appointments by their connections.

Radicals faced a real challenge, for they realized that once the tea was unloaded and the duty paid, colonists would be unable to resist the cheap tea. In each port city, activists warned their fellow colonists that the Tea Act (1773) was a trick to con them into accepting the principle of taxation without representation. According to the New York Sons of Liberty, the purpose of the Tea Act was "to make an important trial of our virtue. If they succeed in the sale of that tea, we shall have no property that we can call our own, and then we may bid adieu to American liberty." In Philadelphia, a mass meeting pronounced anyone who imported the tea "an enemy to his country."

Boston Tea Party Here colonists dressed as Mohawk Indians dump crates of tea into Boston Harbor.

As might be expected, the most spirited resistance came in Boston, where Hutchinson decided the tea would be unloaded and sold—and the duty paid. Sam Adams led extralegal town meetings attended by 5,000 people each (almost one-third of the population of Boston) to pressure Hutchinson to turn the ships away. When Hutchinson refused, Adams reported back to the town meeting, on December 16, 1773, "This meeting can do nothing more to save the country!" (see Table 6–1). Almost as if it were a prearranged signal, the crowd let out a whoop and poured out of the meetinghouse for the wharf. There, about 50 men, their faces darkened and their bodies draped in Indian blankets, boarded three tea-bearing ships, escorted the customs officials ashore, opened 340 chests of tea, and dumped their contents into Boston Harbor: 90,000 pounds, worth £9,000. Perhaps as many as 8,000 Bostonians observed the "tea party." John Adams, never much for riots, was in awe. "There is," he said, "a Dignity, a Majesty, a Sublimity in this last Effort of the Patriots that I greatly admire."

Instead of dignity and patriotism, the British government saw defiance of the law and wanton destruction of property. Parliament passed five bills in the spring of 1774 to punish Boston and Massachusetts collectively for their misdeeds. First, the Boston Port Bill closed the port of Boston to all trade until the East India Company was repaid for the dumped tea. Second, the Massachusetts Government Act changed the Charter of 1691 in several important ways. From then on, the Council (upper house) would be appointed by the king, rather than elected by the House, town meetings were forbidden without approval of the governor, the governor would appoint all the provincial judges and sheriffs, and the sheriffs would select juries, who until then

 **Table 6–1** Major Events Leading to the Revolutionary War, 1763–1774

1763	Proclamation of 1763	Confines colonists to the east of an imaginary line running down the spine of the Allegheny Mountains.
1764	Sugar Act	Drops duty on molasses to 3 cents/gallon, but institutes procedures to make sure it is collected, such as trial at Admiralty Court (closest is in Nova Scotia), where burden of proof is on defendant and verdict is rendered by judge rather than jury.
1764	Currency Act	Forbids issuing of any colonial currency.
1765	Stamp Act	Places a tax on 15 classes of documents, including newspapers and legal documents; clear objective is to raise revenue.
1765	Quartering Act	Requires colonies to provide housing in public buildings and certain provisions for troops.
1766	Declaratory Act	Repeals Stamp Act, but insists that Parliament retains the right to legislate for the colonies "in all cases whatsoever."
1767	Townshend Revenue Act	Places import duty on lead, paint, glass, paper, and tea; objective is to raise money from the colonies.
1770	Boston Massacre	Several citizens killed by British soldiers whom they had pelted with snowballs; grew out of tensions caused by quartering of four army regiments in Boston to enforce customs regulations.
1773	Tea Act	After Townshend Duties on all items other than tea are removed, British East India Company is given a monopoly on the sale of tea, enabling it to drop price—and cut out middlemen.
1773	Boston Tea Party	To protest Tea Act, Bostonians dump 90,000 pounds of tea into Boston Harbor.
1774	Intolerable Acts	To punish Massachusetts in general and Boston in particular for the "Tea Party": 1. Port of Boston closed until East India Company repaid for dumped tea. 2. King to appoint Massachusetts's Council; town meetings to require written permission of governor; governor will appoint judges and sheriffs, and sheriffs will now select juries. 3. Governor can send officials and soldiers accused of capital crimes out of Massachusetts for their trials. 4. Troops may be quartered in private homes.
1774	Quebec Act	Gives Ohio River valley to Quebec; Britain allows Quebec to be governed by French tradition and tolerates Catholic religion there.
1774	First Continental Congress	Representatives of 12 colonies meet in Philadelphia and call for a boycott of trade with Britain, adopt a Declaration of Rights, and agree to meet again in a year.

had been elected by the voters. Third, the Administration of Justice Act empowered the governor to send to Britain or another colony for trial any official or soldier accused of a capital crime who appeared unlikely to get a fair trial in Massachusetts. Fourth, a new Quartering Act permitted the quartering of troops in private homes. Fifth, not directly related, but also odious to Protestant colonists, was the Quebec Act, for the administration of Quebec. It assigned to Quebec the Ohio River region, which the colonists coveted. Moreover, in Quebec, there was to be no representative government, civil cases would be tried without juries, and the Roman Catholic religion would be tolerated. Together, these acts were known in Britain as the Coercive Acts and in the colonies as the Intolerable Acts.

At the same time, General Thomas Gage was appointed governor of Massachusetts and authorized to bring as many troops to Boston as he needed. As regiment after regiment arrived, Boston became an armed camp. The Port Act was easily enforced as Gage deployed troops to close the ports of Boston and Charlestown. The Government Act was another matter. Citizens who were summoned by the sheriff simply refused to serve on juries, and some judges even refused to preside. When Gage called for an election to the legislature, only some towns elected delegates, and a shadow "Massachusetts Provincial Congress" met in Concord in October 1774. The citizens of Massachusetts had taken government into their own hands.

The British had thought that Massachusetts could be isolated. Their chief miscalculation was in underestimating the colonists' attachment to their liberties. The threat to representative government presented by the Intolerable Acts was so clear that the other colonies soon rallied around Massachusetts. In June 1774, the Virginia Burgesses sent out a circular letter suggesting a meeting of all the colonies. At about the same time, Massachusetts had issued a similar call for a meeting in Philadelphia. Spurred by the two most radical colonies, the others agreed to meet in early September.

The First Continental Congress

Every colony except Georgia sent delegates to the First Continental Congress, which convened on September 5, 1774. Only a few of the delegates had ever met any of their counterparts from the other colonies, an indication of just how provincial the colonies were. First impressions, however, were positive. Everyone admired the Virginians. "More sensible, fine fellows you never saw," according to Delaware's Caesar Rodney. For seven weeks these strangers met in formal sessions and social occasions. Together they laid the foundation for the first national government.

With Massachusetts and Virginia almost ready to take up arms, and the middle colonies still favoring conciliation, the greatest challenge was how to achieve unity. Massachusetts needed the support of the other colonies, and hence it was prepared to abandon any discussion of offensive measures against the British. In return, the Congress ratified the Suffolk Resolves, a set of resolutions adopted by Massachusetts's Suffolk County that recommended passive resistance to the Intolerable Acts.

Having addressed Massachusetts's problem, the delegates could now consider national action. Hoping to exert economic pressure on Britain, Congress issued a call for a boycott of all trade, both imports and exports, between the colonies and Britain and the West Indies. Then the delegates adopted a Declaration of Rights that reiterated, refined, and for the first time expressed as the collective determination of every colony (except Georgia) what had become standard constitutional arguments. The colonists were entitled to all the "rights, liberties, and immunities of free and natural-born subjects" of England. Parliament could regulate trade for the colonies only by the "consent" of the colonies. Otherwise, Parliament could neither tax nor legislate for the colonies. Again and again, the Declaration reiterated the twin principles on which resistance to imperial legislation had been based: consent and the rule of law.

Finally, Congress agreed to reconvene in half a year, on March 10, 1775, unless the Intolerable Acts were repealed. Although the Congress was less radical than John Adams and Patrick Henry might have wished, the delegates had achieved consensus on the principles that would shortly form the basis for a new and independent national government.

Conclusion

Within a decade, the British Empire had come apart on its westernmost edge. The ground had been prepared decades earlier when Britain unintentionally allowed the colonies to develop in ways that assured more self-government and personal freedom than in Britain itself, without requiring them to pay a proportionate share of the costs of empire. As a result, the colonies developed their own vision, one that linked democratic government and prosperity. Once Britain decided to knit the colonies more tightly into the empire and impose on them the controls of the centralized state, conflict was inevitable. At the same time, both Britons and Americans revered the same Constitution, and Americans' protests invoked the values and protections of that political system. That those protests would culminate in revolution was by no means a foregone conclusion. Revolution would require two key elements: Britain's unwillingness to compromise on issues of governance, and the ability of colonial radicals to convince moderates that there was no other way. By the end of 1774 that point had almost been reached.

Further Readings

Fred Anderson, *Crucible of War: The Seven Years' War and the Fate of Empire in British North America, 1754–1766* (2000). An engaging narrative that argues that the Seven Years' War was a critical episode in itself and not simply the prelude to the Revolution.

John Brewer, *The Sinews of Power: War, Money and the English State, 1688–1783* (1990). Brewer's book demonstrates how important war and its financing were in shaping the British state in the eighteenth century.

Nicole Eustace, *Passion Is the Gale: Emotion, Power, and the Coming of the American Revolution* (2008). A provocative new interpretation that shows how new ideas about emotions helped pave the way for the Revolution.

Peter Silver, *Our Savage Neighbors: How Indian War Transformed Early America* (2007). A stunning new interpretation that shows how war with the Indians helped to unite European Americans into a single people with a single identity.

Ian K. Steele, *Betrayals: Fort William Henry and the "Massacre"* (1990). A brief but gripping account of the siege at Fort William Henry in 1757, later fictionalized in James Fenimore Cooper's *The Last of the Mohicans.*

Richard White, *The Middle Ground: Indians, Empires, and Republics in the Great Lakes Region, 1650–1815* (1991). A brilliant analysis of the conflict among the French, British, and Great Lakes Indian tribes for control of that region.

Who, What

Memeskia 182
George Washington 183
William Pitt 188
Thomas Hutchinson 198
Sam Adams 198
Albany Plan of Union 184
Pontiac's Rebellion 191
Proclamation of 1763 192
Constitutionalism 196
Republicanism 200

>> Timeline >>

▼ 1715–1716
Yamasee War

▼ 1717
French build Fort Toulouse

▼ 1718
French build New Orleans

▼ 1720
French build Louisbourg and Fort Niagara

▼ 1731
French build Fort St. Frédéric

▼ 1733
Molasses Act

▼ 1739–1744
War of Jenkins's Ear

▼ 1741
Attack upon Cartagena fails

▼ 1744–1748
King George's War

▼ 1748
Village of Pickawillany established by Memeskia and his band of Miamis

▼ 1749
French military expedition fails to win back dissident Indians in Ohio Valley

▼ 1752
Tanacharison cedes huge chunk of Ohio Valley to Virginia

▼ 1753
French build small forts near forks of Ohio River

▼ 1754
Albany Plan of Union

▼ 1754–1763
French and Indian War

▼ 1755
Braddock's forces defeated

▼ 1757
British defeated at Fort William Henry, survivors massacred
William Pitt accedes to power in Britain

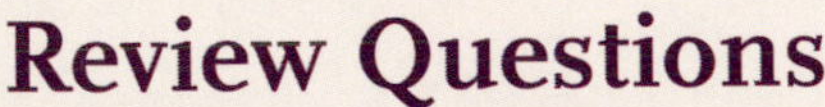

Review Questions

1. What effect did the imperial wars of the eighteenth century have on the American colonies?
2. What were the reasons for the conflicts among the British, French, Spanish, and the various Indian tribes on the North American continent?
3. How and why did Britain attempt to reorganize its North American colonial empire? Why did the colonies resist?
4. What was the series of events that brought Britain and the colonies to the brink of war by 1774? To what extent were they the product of poor leadership? Differing theories of government? Different social experiences?

Websites

The American Revolution: A Documentary History. The Avalon Project at Yale Law School maintains an online collection of documents in law, history, and diplomacy, including the most important documents of the American Revolutionary era. http://avalon.law.yale.edu/subject_menus/amerrev.asp

The Boston Massacre Trials: An Account, by Daniel Linder. A complete set of documents, including eyewitness accounts of the trials at which John Adams defended the soldiers accused of killing Boston civilians. http://www.law.umkc.edu/faculty/projects/FTRIALS/bostonmassacre/bostonmassacre.html

A Narrative of the Captivity of Mrs. Johnson (1796). A scanned version of the first edition of Susannah Willard Johnson's account of her captivity. http://www.canadiana.org/cgi-bin/ECO/mtq?doc=39311

For further review materials and resource information, please visit www.oup.com/us/ofthepeople

▼ 1758
Treaty of Easton secures neutrality of Ohio Valley tribes in return for territory west of Alleghenies

▼ 1759
British seize Quebec

▼ 1763
Treaty of Paris, ending French and Indian War, signed Pontiac's Rebellion
Proclamation of 1763
Parliament increases size of peacetime army to 20 regiments

▼ 1764
Sugar Act
Currency Act

▼ 1765
Stamp Act
Quartering Act
Stamp Act Congress

▼ 1766
Declaratory Act

▼ 1767
Townshend Revenue Act

▼ 1768
Lord Hillsborough's circular letter
John Hancock's sloop *Liberty* seized
Treaty of Fort Stanwix

▼ 1770
Boston Massacre

▼ 1773
Tea Act
Boston Tea Party

▼ 1774
Intolerable Acts (known as Coercive Acts in Britain)
Lord Dunmore's War /TL-TX:

▼ 1775
First Continental Congress

CHAPTER 7

Common Threads 

>> Which political theories did the American colonists use to justify their revolution, and how did they adapt those theories over the course of the next decades in the light of their experiences?

>> What does Britain's failure to defeat the colonies tell us about the limits of empire?

>> How did the doctrine of equality take on a life of its own?

>> To what extent has the conflict between the Federalists and the Antifederalists continued to shape American history?

>> In which ways was the American Revolution democratic? Not democratic?

Creating a New Nation

1775–1788

AMERICAN PORTRAIT

>> James Madison Helps Make a Nation

Why do some people achieve greatness? Perhaps it is not as much a matter of personal qualities as a match between the person and the times, an ability to understand and respond to the needs of the age. There was nothing in James Madison's childhood to suggest that he would become a leader of a revolutionary nation in a revolutionary age.

Madison grew up on the plantation his grandfather and his grandfather's slaves had cleared out of the Virginia Piedmont forest in 1732. Only a few months later, Madison's grandfather was killed by several of those slaves. One of the slaves was executed, but another, a woman named Dido, was given 29 lashes and sent home to work for the widow Madison. Perhaps James had his own grandfather in mind when he wrote later that men are not angels, and that is why government is necessary.

James went north to college, attending Princeton in New Jersey. After his graduation in 1771 at the age of 20, he suffered some sort of breakdown. Back in Virginia, Madison described himself as "too dull and infirm now to look out for any extraordinary things in this world. . . ." Short and slight of build, Madison was convinced that his poor health would lead to an early death. The event that drew this sickly, nervous young man out of his shell was the American Revolution. He became a leader in the nation that he helped create and whose Constitution he helped write. James Madison committed himself to the principles of liberty and order, and he devoted his life to establishing a government that would ensure both. Perhaps more than any other leader at the time, Madison understood how difficult reconciling these two principles would be.

Madison believed that strife and violence were deeply embedded in human nature, and he spent his adult life trying to create a government that would ensure peace without destroying liberty. He helped write the Constitution and then worked for the adoption of the Bill of Rights. His first political battle in Virginia had been on behalf of the Baptists, a dissenting Protestant denomination that demanded religious liberty. Madison was convinced that freedom of conscience was fundamental and that religion must be kept absolutely free from governmental interference. As a political thinker and leader, Madison came to advocate the great liberal principles of his age: the rights of conscience, consent, and property. Believing fervently in both human liberty and the rights of property, he could never reconcile himself either to slavery or its abolition. He put his faith in the new government, hoping that just as he had learned to live with his own mental and physical disabilities, so the nation would rise above its internal conflicts and inconsistencies. ●

OUTLINE

The War Begins

By the end of 1774, conflict between the colonists and Britain seemed unavoidable. The British government, under the leadership of Lord North and King George III, seemed unwilling to make significant concessions. In the colonies, the radical opponents of British rule dominated politics. Despite these signs of impending conflict, no one anticipated eight years of warfare that would make the colonies a single nation under a centralized government.

> "Society is in every state a blessing, but government even in its best state is but a necessary evil; in its worst state an intolerable one. . . . Government, like dress, is the badge of lost innocence; the palaces of kings are built on the ruins of the bowers of paradise."
>
> THOMAS PAINE, *Common Sense*

The First Battles

Before he became governor of Massachusetts in 1774, General Thomas Gage had a long record of advocating force. He had called for the stationing of troops in Boston in 1768, leading to the Boston Massacre. Even before the Boston Tea Party and Britain's retaliation with the Intolerable Acts, he recommended limiting democratic government

in Massachusetts. He believed that the merchants and lawyers of Boston were instigating the poor; hence, his objective always was to isolate the colonial Revolutionary elite, by force if necessary.

In the spring of 1775, Gage received orders from England to take decisive action against the colonists. He was determined to seize the colonists' military supplies, stored at Concord, but the alert Bostonians worked out a system to signal the patriot leaders once British troops began to march. On the night of April 18, the silversmith Paul Revere and the tanner William Dawes slipped out of Boston on horseback to carry the message that British troops were on the move. Militiamen from several towns began to gather.

The British soldiers arrived at Lexington at daybreak and ordered the militia to surrender, which they refused to do. Exactly what happened next remains unclear. The colonists swore that British soldiers opened fire, saying, "Ye villans [sic], ye Rebels, disperse; Damn you, disperse." The British major insisted that the first shot came from behind a tree. British soldiers lost control and fired all about, and the colonists returned fire. When order was restored, eight Americans were dead, most killed while attempting to flee.

At the same time, the Concord militia had assembled. When the British marched up the road toward the North Bridge, the militia pulled back about a mile, allowing the British to enter an almost-deserted town. Fighting broke out when a fire that the British troops had set to the Concord liberty pole spread to the courthouse. Determined to protect their town, the militia began marching on the British. When the Americans drew near, the British fired. In the ensuing exchange, three British soldiers were killed and several more were injured. The British were forced back across the bridge. The entire battle took two or three minutes (see Map 7–1).

Once news of the fighting at Lexington and Concord spread, militias converged on Boston to evict Gage and his troops. More than 20,000 men soon were encamped in Boston. Gage declared that all the inhabitants of Massachusetts who bore arms were rebels and traitors, although he was willing to pardon everyone but John Hancock and Sam Adams, two leaders of the defiant Provincial Congress. Rather than backing down, the colonists fortified Breed's Hill (next to the more famous Bunker Hill) in Charlestown, overlooking Boston. On June 17, Gage sent out 2,400 soldiers to take the hill, but the cost was enormous: 1000 soldiers and 92 officers were killed or wounded (compared to 370 casualties among the colonists). The British learned an important lesson: not to make frontal assaults against fortified positions.

At about the same time, other New Englanders were taking matters into their own hands. A group under the leadership of Benedict Arnold, an ambitious, 34-year-old New Haven merchant, and Ethan Allen, the leader of the Vermont Green Mountain Boys, seized the crumbling fort at Ticonderoga on Lake Champlain as well as several other small posts. In these heady days early in the Revolution, many colonists thought that this would be a quick and painless war.

Congress Takes the Lead

When the Second Continental Congress convened in Philadelphia on May 10, its greatest challenge was to maintain consensus. The most radical leaders, such as Sam and John Adams from Massachusetts and Richard Henry Lee from Virginia,

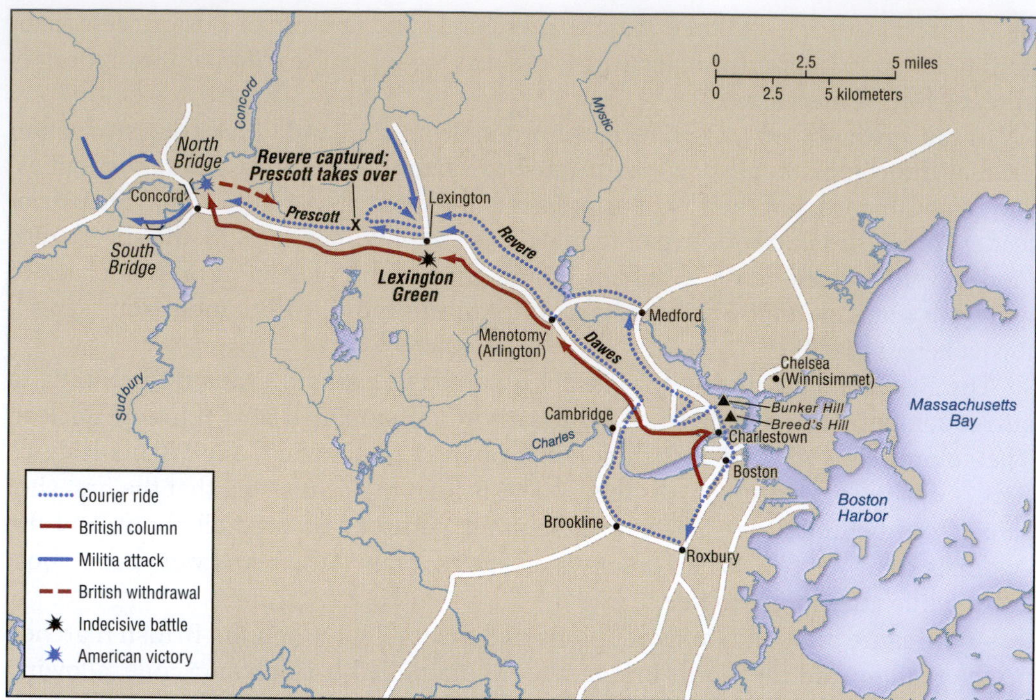

Map 7–1 Battles of Lexington, Concord, and Breed's Hill This map shows the sites of the first battles of the Revolution in and around Boston, along with the routes taken by Paul Revere and William Dawes to warn the colonists of the approach of British troops.

were ready for war. However, many leaders, especially in the middle colonies, still hoped that war could be avoided.

Because Congress was an extralegal body, the duly elected colonial assemblies might easily have rejected its authority. But one after another, they transferred their allegiance from the British government to Congress. Although some moderates in Congress hoped for a negotiated settlement with Britain, they were caught between a public and a British government that both anticipated war. The British ministry refused even to acknowledge the petition sent by the First Continental Congress. That refusal, combined with Gage's attack on Breed's Hill, convinced the moderates that military preparations were necessary. Congress voted to create a Continental army and put it under the leadership of Virginia's George Washington. Not only was Washington experienced in military matters and widely respected, but his selection helped solidify the alliance between New England and the South. Congress decided to attack Canada in the hope that a significant defeat would force the British to accede to American demands. To justify all of these actions, Congress also adopted the Declaration of the Causes and Necessities of Taking Up Arms, a rousing indictment of British "despotism," "perfidy," and "cruel aggression" drafted by Virginia's Thomas Jefferson.

At the same time, to preserve unity with the moderates, the radicals agreed to petition the king one more time. While not making any concessions, the Olive Branch Petition appealed to George's "magnanimity and benevolence." Nevertheless, on August 23, 1775, the king declared the colonists to be in "an open and avowed Rebellion." Although Congress had neither declared war nor asserted independence, the American Revolution had begun.

Military Ardor

Military ardor in the colonies reached its high point in the period between the fall of 1775 and the spring of 1776. Colonists expected war, and they thought it would be quick and glorious. As a consequence, the first enlistments were for a term of only a year. Even if the war was not over by then, Revolutionaries were fearful of creating a permanent standing army.

In the summer of 1775, the Continental army marched on Canada. Victory would have either forced the British to the bargaining table or at least protected New York and New England from assault from the north. The contingent of the Continental army under General Benedict Arnold's command sailed from Newburyport, Massachusetts, to Maine and then marched 350 miles to Quebec. In November, after a grueling march, Arnold's forces prepared to assault Quebec, joined by troops under the leadership of General Richard Montgomery, who had just seized Montréal. The battle was a disaster. Half of the 900 soldiers were killed, captured, or wounded, including Montgomery. By the time the expedition retreated to New York in the spring, 5,000 men had been lost. The suffering was extraordinary, but it only increased American resolve.

Declaring Independence

By the beginning of 1776, moderates in Congress who still hoped for a peaceful settlement found themselves squeezed from both directions. The king and Parliament were unyielding, and popular opinion increasingly favored independence. Word arrived from Britain that all American commerce was to be cut off and the British navy was to seize American ships and their cargoes. Britain also began hiring German mercenaries known as Hessians, and Virginia's Governor Dunmore shelled Norfolk from warships offshore. He had already offered freedom to any slaves who would fight for the British. It seemed that every frightening prediction that the radicals had made was coming true.

Public opinion also pushed Congress toward a declaration of independence. In January 1776, Thomas Paine, an expatriate English radical who had moved to Philadelphia only two years earlier, electrified the public with his pamphlet *Common Sense,* which sold 75,000 copies in a short time. At the age of 39, Paine had failed at almost everything he had ever done. *Common Sense* was his first and greatest success. In it, Paine liberated Americans from their ties to the British past so that they could start their government fresh. The idea of a balanced constitution that combined king, nobles, and the common people in one government was "farcical," and monarchy was "exceedingly ridiculous." Why should Americans have any respect for an aristocracy that traced its origins to William the Conqueror, "a French bastard landing with an armed banditti"? Paine had a message for Congress, too: "The period of debate is closed."

Most members of Congress either desired a declaration of independence or thought it inevitable. Most delegates also agreed that unanimity was more important than speed, so they waited through the spring of 1776 as, one by one, the state delegations received instructions in favor of independence. Then, under instructions from his colony, on June 7, 1776, Virginia's Richard Henry Lee asked Congress

Thomas Paine Paine's *Common Sense* sold more than 75,000 copies in just a few weeks.

to vote on the resolution that "these United Colonies are, and of right ought to be, free and independent States." A committee of five, including Thomas Jefferson, Benjamin Franklin, and John Adams, was appointed to draft a declaration of independence. Adams asked Jefferson, a 33-year-old Virginia radical who had already demonstrated his ability to write stirring prose, to write the first draft. For four days, the delegates debated Jefferson's draft and took preliminary votes. A clause that accused King George of forcing African slaves on the colonies was deleted. On July 2, the delegates voted unanimously to declare independence.

Many years later Thomas Jefferson insisted that there was nothing original about the Declaration of Independence, and he was not entirely wrong. The long list of accusations against King George, which formed the bulk of the Declaration, contained little that was new, and even some of the stirring words in the preamble had been used by the radicals time and again. Moreover, the Revolutionaries borrowed ideas from a number of British and European sources, including constitutionalism, republicanism, Enlightenment thought (see Chapter 6, "Conflict on the Edge of the Empire"), and millennial Christian thought. The millennial strain in evangelical Protestantism suggested that the 1,000-year reign of Christ might begin soon in America if Americans would repent their sins, seek a spiritual rebirth, and defend their liberties.

However, in a different sense the Declaration of Independence was truly original. Jefferson's achievement was to reformulate familiar principles in a way that made them simple, clear, and applicable to the American situation.

The most important of these principles was human equality, that all people were born with certain fundamental rights. Second, and closely related, was the belief in a universal, common human nature. If all people were the same and had the same rights, then the purpose of government was to protect those rights. Just as people created government to protect their rights, they could abolish any government that became despotic. Third, government should represent the people.

It was many years, however, before the radical implications of the Declaration became fully evident to the American people. At the moment, more attention was focused on immediate political struggles. The Revolution succeeded because moderates and radicals were able to create effective alliances, reversing the pre-Revolutionary trend toward class and political conflict. To maintain their positions as leaders of the opposition to Britain, elite Revolutionaries like John Hancock continually appealed to their poorer and often more radical countrymen and countrywomen and looked out for these people's interests as well as their own.

The result was a revolution that was more moderate than it might otherwise have been, not to mention a revolution that succeeded. But it also meant ongoing

Destruction of Statue of King George Here, a small crowd in New York City pulls down the statue of King George on July 9, 1776, a few days after independence had been declared.

struggles between radicals and moderates over the meaning of the Revolution. Just as military fervor reached its high point in the spring of 1776, so did political unity.

Creating a National Government

Although both the public and the state governments acted as if Congress were a legitimate national government, it actually had no more authority over the states than they were willing to give it, and it had none whatsoever over the people. At the same time that Richard Henry Lee presented Congress with his proposal for independence, he also suggested that Congress create a permanent national government, a confederation of the states with a written constitution. John Dickinson, a moderate, was assigned to draft the Articles of Confederation. He sketched out a weak central government with the authority to make treaties, carry out military and foreign affairs, request the states to pay its expenses, and very little else. There was no chief executive, only a Congress in which each state would have one vote. Term limits were imposed on representatives. Any act of Congress would require 9 votes (of 13), and the Articles would not go into effect until all 13 states had approved them.

With Congress functioning adequately and state jealousies strong, it took Congress more than a year to revise and accept a watered-down version of the Articles of Confederation. Not until March 1781, with the end of the war only a few months away, did the final state ratify the Articles of Confederation, thereby putting them into effect. By then, the weaknesses in a national government with no means of enforcing its regulations were becoming evident.

Creating State Governments

In 1776, all attention was focused on state governments, where the new ideas about liberty, equality, and government were put into practice. Americans were exhilarated by the prospect of creating their own governments. Between 1775 and 1780, each of the 13 states adopted a new written constitution.

The new state governments were the products of both theory and experience. Because the Revolutionaries feared concentrations of power, the powers of governors were sharply limited. In two states, Pennsylvania and Georgia, the position of governor was abolished and replaced with a council. Governors were given term limits or required to run for reelection every year. Because the colonists had seen royal governors appoint their cronies to powerful positions, governors also were stripped of their power of appointment.

The new state constitutions made the legislatures more democratic. The number of representatives was doubled in South Carolina and New Hampshire and more than tripled in Massachusetts, to a ratio of about one representative for every 1,000 people. Many constitutions imposed either term limits or frequent elections for representatives, like for governors. As the property qualifications for holding office were lowered, poorer men came to sit in legislatures alongside richer ones. The admission of more ordinary men into government was one of the greatest changes brought about by the Revolution. Now the elite had to learn to share power and to win the votes of men they had once scorned.

Winning the Revolution

The British entered the war with clear advantages in population, wealth, and power, but with a flawed premise about how the war could be won. Britain, arguably the most powerful nation in the world, had the mistaken idea that the colonists could be made to submit by a swift and effective use of force. It also assumed that Americans loyal to the Crown would rally around the British troops. The actions of Britain's troops, however, alienated Americans. Probably no more than one-fifth of the population remained loyal to Britain, but many more shifted loyalties depending on local circumstances. The war ultimately became a struggle for the support of this unpoliticized, local-minded population.

> "We are being left like sheep among wolves, were obliged to give up to them our Arms and take purtection. But no sooner we had yielded to them but [they] set to Rob us taking all our livings, horses, Cows, Sheep, Clothing, of all Sorts, money, pewter, tins, knives, in fine Everything that sooted them. Untill we were Stript Naked."
>
> GEORGE PARK,
> a resident of the South Carolina upcountry, complaining about the depredations of the British army

Competing Strategies

British political objectives shifted during the war. The first goal, based on the belief that resistance was being led by a handful of radical New Englanders, was to punish and isolate Boston. This was the strategy of 1774 and 1775, with the Intolerable Acts and the battles of Lexington, Concord, and Breed's Hill. This strategy failed miserably. The early failures derived from the faulty assumption that well-trained British regular soldiers were necessarily superior to untrained colonial rustics. However, if the British had a misplaced faith in their invincibility, the Americans had a misplaced faith in their moral superiority. Over the course of the war, most people realized that neither British professionalism nor American moral superiority could guarantee victory. The result was a long war, as both sides tried to avoid decisive engagements that might prove fatal.

For seven years, the two armies chased each other across the eastern seaboard. Neither side had masses of men to pour onto the battlefield. Moreover, there was no consensus in Britain about the strategic or economic value of the colonies, and hence there was always opposition to the war and a limit to the investment that the British were prepared to make in it. Consequently, every battle presented a significant risk that troops who were lost could not be replaced.

Manpower was also a serious problem for the Americans. It was difficult to recruit enough soldiers into the Continental army. After a defeat in battle or near the end of the year when terms of enlistment were up, men left the army to return home. Militia strength rose and fell depending on the prospects for success. Hence, one of the goals of the American war effort was to avoid demoralizing the colonists. In other words, there was limited incentive to risk all in battle.

Early in the war, however, both sides hoped for a decisive victory. The Americans failed in their assault on Quebec. The British pursued the Americans back to Ticonderoga on Lake Champlain, but Benedict Arnold's leadership prevented the British from pushing the Americans any farther. The theater of action then shifted to southern New York and the middle colonies. Having given up hopes of crushing New England directly, the British planned to isolate the region and defeat the Continental army under George Washington's leadership.

The British also aimed at seizing all the major American cities. Indeed, at one point or another during the war, the British captured Boston, Newport, New York, Philadelphia, Charleston, and Savannah. The capture of American cities, however, did not bring about an American surrender. With 90 percent of the American population living in the countryside, the British found that the seizure of a major city did not strike the hoped-for psychological or economic blow.

The British on the Offensive: 1776

In preparation for a British offensive in 1776, the new commander, General William Howe, assembled a huge force on Staten Island: 32,000 soldiers and 13,000 seamen. Some of these British soldiers were

George Washington Washington as he appeared at the Battle of Princeton, in a painting by Charles Willson Peale.

AMERICAN LANDSCAPE

>> The Winter at Jockey Hollow

It was the worst winter in a century. It snowed 28 times, and the drifts were so high that they covered the fences in the hollow of land tucked between Long Hill and the Watchung Mountains. It was snowing again on December 1, 1779, the day that General George Washington moved the Continental army into its winter quarters, four miles outside the little New Jersey village of Morristown.

Washington chose Jockey Hollow because the low mountains and surrounding swamps offered it protection from sudden attack. The hilly terrain was covered with trees, which his soldiers, almost 11,000 of them, could chop down to build themselves cabins. The water supply was good, and the many farms in the region could provide food.

The first order of business was to build cabins, but the winter was so harsh that the work proceeded slowly. Until cabins were built, the soldiers and the line officers had to sleep in their tents. The storm that raged for three days in early January was "one of the most tremendous snowstorms ever remembered; no man could endure its violence many minutes without danger of his life," Dr. James Thatcher reported. "Some of the soldiers were actually covered while in their tents and buried like sheep under the snow."

Not until February were most men in the "Log-house city" of more than 1,000 cabins. They were all the same size and design, about 14 feet wide by 15 or 16 feet long, and 61/2 feet high at the eaves. They were constructed out of notched logs, cut from the woods of Jockey Hollow, with the cracks filled in with clay. Each cabin had a fireplace, made out of stones, and twelve bunks for the dozen soldiers who would call it home. Often, the soldiers did not cut windows until the spring.

Both food and clothing were in short supply. Joseph Plumb Martin, a 19-year-old private from Connecticut who had been in the army for three years, complained bitterly, "We were absolutely, literally starved. . . . I did not put a single morsel of victuals into my mouth for four days and as many nights." Some officers gave their soldiers their own small rations of meat. Washington's requests to the Continental Congress for food and supplies had gone unanswered, but local farmers brought their produce to camp to sell at extortionate prices. Hungry soldiers, who had gone unpaid for five months, began foraging for themselves in the neighborhood. Washington threatened that unless the surrounding counties quickly sent supplies (for which he would issue IOUs) to his camp, he would organize a systematic forage of New Jersey. The problem was solved for the moment; but the large army quickly went through the new supplies, and by spring it was hungry again.

Some men began talking mutiny, "venting our spleen at our country and government, then at our officers, and then at ourselves for our imbecility in staying there and starving . . . for an ungrateful people who did not care what became of us, so they could enjoy themselves while we were keeping a cruel enemy from them." Officers were able to appeal to the troops' patriotism, telling them that they had "won immortal honor to yourselves . . . by your perseverance, patience, and bravery. . . ." Cold, hungry, half-naked, most of the soldiers stayed on. "We were unwilling," Private Martin said, "to desert the cause of our country, when in distress . . . we knew her cause involved our own."

The encampment at Jockey Hollow was a laboratory where nationalism was created. The adversity bound soldiers and officers together; their suffering and sacrifice transformed the rage militaire of the early days of revolution into the deep and enduring commitment to a shared destiny that became the foundation of the new nation.

actually German mercenaries, the Hessians. In anticipation of battle and hoping to protect New York, Washington moved his army south to New York (see Map 7–2). He had about 19,000 soldiers, too few to hold up to the British in a pitched battle. Washington kept about half his troops in Manhattan and sent the other half to Brooklyn Heights, where they dug in, in hopes of protecting Long Island. The British sneaked up behind the Americans, inflicting heavy casualties, and on August 27, 1776, Washington pulled the remainder of his Brooklyn forces back into Manhattan. Had the British pursued rapidly, they probably could have crushed Washington's army, but Howe may have been more concerned with winning a peace than a war. After Washington retreated, Howe invited members of the Continental Congress to meet with him privately on Staten Island. He was unable to recognize American independence, which was what the representatives insisted on, so his peace strategy failed.

Still hoping for peace, Howe then began pushing Washington back, first out of lower Manhattan, then out of the northern part of the island. Simultaneously, he offered peace to any colonists in the region who would declare their loyalty, and thousands accepted the offer. On November 16, the British succeeded in forcing the Americans out of Manhattan. Howe pursued them to White Plains and then through New Jersey to New Brunswick. The British almost caught Washington twice in New Jersey, but on December 8 the Americans crossed the Delaware at Trenton, taking every boat in the area with them to prevent pursuit. By Christmas Eve, Washington had only 3,000 soldiers, and General Charles Lee, the commander of the other half of the Continental army, had been captured. As Thomas Paine wrote, "These are the times that try men's souls."

Howe had captured New York, had taken possession of New Jersey, and was poised to seize Philadelphia (which fell in September 1777). At the end of 1776, the British were close to achieving their objective. Then, on Christmas night, with morale in the Continental army dangerously low, Washington took his army across the ice-clogged Delaware and surprised the British garrison at Trenton at dawn, capturing 1,000 Hessian soldiers. About a week later, Washington evaded a British trap and sneaked behind the lines to capture an outpost at Princeton.

These American successes were enough to bring another 1,000 troops into the army. Even more significant, the British decided to concentrate their troops near New Brunswick, fearing the loss of any more garrisons, which were necessary for defending the Loyalists. This strategic decision revealed the weakness in the British position and demonstrated why, at the moment when victory seemed closest, it was very far away. Never able to raise enough troops to overcome the Americans' home advantage, the British needed to make certain that civilians did not aid the Revolutionary War effort. In order to assure the allegiance of Loyalists, the British had to offer them protection from American reprisals. However, the British were seizing the Americans' goods and property for the war effort. Then, once the garrisons were withdrawn, those who had declared loyalty to the British were left alone and vulnerable to the reprisals of the patriots.

The British could control the American countryside only by maintaining troops there, but once the troops were withdrawn, civil warfare would break out. Thus, even though Washington's victories at Trenton and Princeton were small, they exposed the incapacity of the British to defeat the Revolutionaries unless they settled an army of occupation on the Americans, something they were not prepared to do.

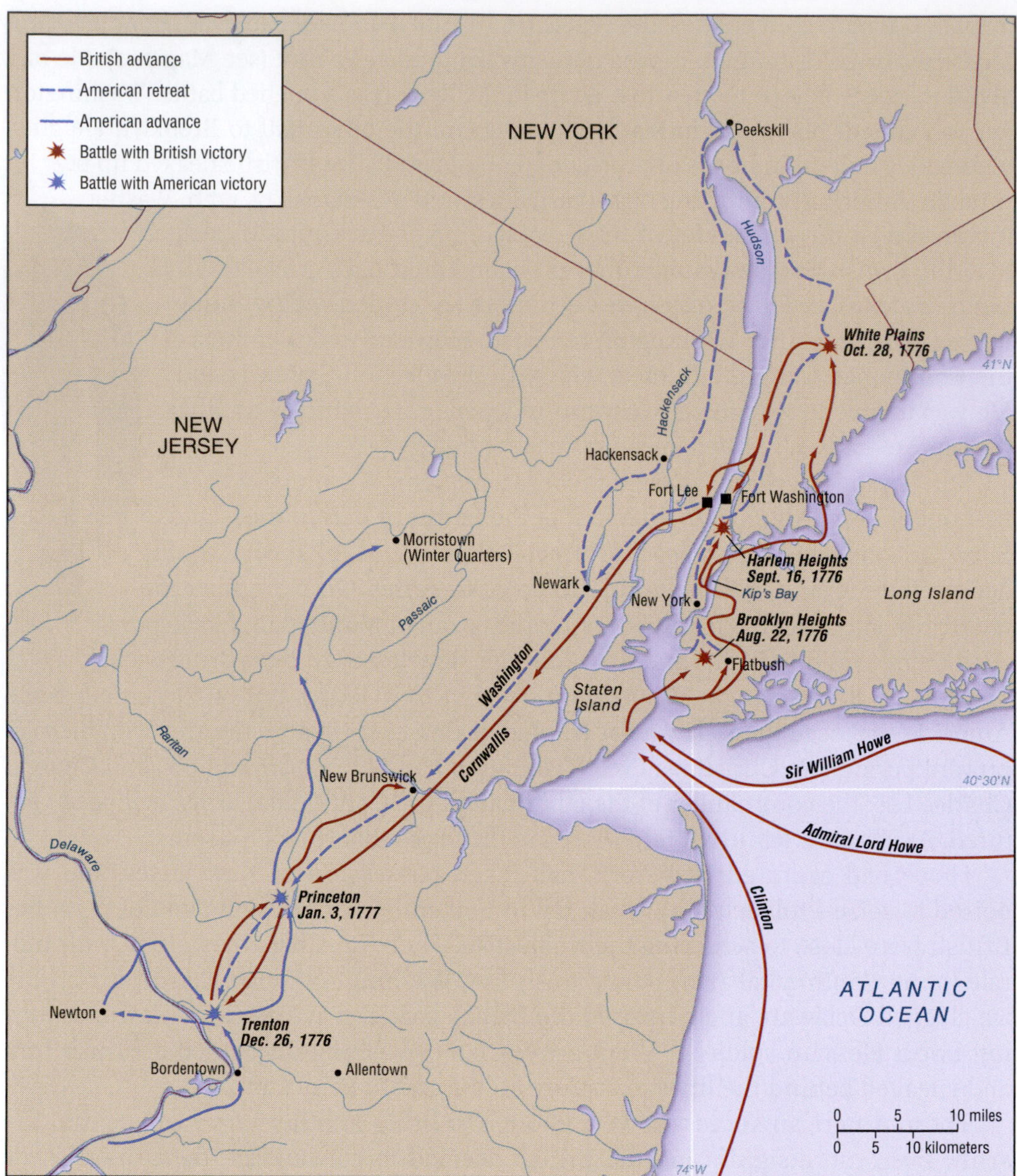

Map 7–2 New York and New Jersey Campaigns, 1776–1777 In the second half of 1776, British troops chased Washington out of New York and across New Jersey. As he would for the remainder of the war, Washington took care never to let the British capture him and his troops, leaving him free to attack at Trenton and Princeton.

A Slow War: 1777–1781

Washington settled in for a long war, enlisting soldiers for an extended period. He never had enough soldiers to confront the British head-on, so he mostly led the British on chases across the countryside. Maintaining such an army year after year was expensive, but the American population was unwilling to be taxed at high rates. Soldiers in the Continental army, who were from the bottom tier of society, suffered grievously; at Jockey Hollow, New Jersey, in the winter of 1779/1780, men roasted their own shoes to eat and even devoured their pet dogs.

AMERICA AND THE WORLD

>> Mercenaries in Global Perspective

In 1776, the Declaration of Independence warned that King George "is, at this time, transporting large armies of foreign mercenaries to complete the works of death, desolation, and tyranny already begun." It charged that the use of such mercenaries was "scarcely parallelled in the most barbarous ages, and totally unworthy the head of a civilized nation." In fact, the use of mercenaries was the norm, rather than the exception, among European nations in the eighteenth century. Some countries, in particular Britain, France, and Prussia, routinely rented soldiers from other countries, while other nations supplied them. Between a fifth and two-thirds of the British, French, and Prussian armies were foreigners, typically Swiss, Dutch, and various Germans. Wealthy nations could buy other countries' soldiers, thereby protecting their own citizens' freedom.

The practice of using mercenaries had developed several hundred years earlier. Under the feudal system, a lord could command service only for defensive wars. Any lord who wanted to embark on a foreign war would have to pay for soldiers. As the pace of foreign wars increased in the seventeenth century (and feudalism died), so also did the practice of hiring foreign soldiers. Under the new system, some nations became major hirers of mercenaries, while other nations became sources. Nations might offer employment to individual soldiers. John Smith, for example, was a mercenary before he joined the Virginia expedition. He fought for the Dutch, as they tried to oust the Spanish from the Netherlands, and later, he fought the Turks in Hungary for the Austrians.

At the same time that professional soldiers fought for whichever nation would pay them, less fortunate men found themselves conscripted into their country's service only to be shipped off to fight another nation's war. This was the standard practice in the little German principality of Hesse-Cassel, which routinely rented soldiers to other nations. In fact, in the middle of the eighteenth century, half of the government's revenues came

continued

>> AMERICA AND THE WORLD *continued*

from this source, and Hesse-Cassel's ruler observed that "these troops are our Peru. In losing them we would forfeit all our resources." The government claimed that it was conscripting only "masterless servants and loafers," men who were not contributing to the family economy, but as Hesse-Cassel became increasingly dependent on the revenue from its mercenaries, it began to reach into peasant families, seizing their servants and younger sons. The law exempted from service men who owned homes. Consequently, parents tried to give all their sons enough property to keep them out of the army. When Hesse-Cassel tightened inheritance laws to keep parents from dividing their estates, parents began giving their daughters' dowries directly to their sons, sacrificing the girls' prospects for a good match to keep the boys out of the army. In this way, relations between the great nations reached deep into families, affecting the most important decisions they made.

Although the use of mercenaries was the norm in European wars, American colonists rejected this practice as "totally unworthy" of a "civilized nation." By the end of the eighteenth century, Enlightenment philosophers had begun to condemn the trade in soldiers—for that is what it was. Under new doctrines of nationalism, men were supposed to fight for patriotism, not for pay, and a nation that hired mercenaries began to seem less than "civilized."

In 1777, the British political objective was still the same: to isolate New England by seizing the middle colonies. American troops had the advantage in upstate New York by three to one, however, and they defeated the British under General John Burgoyne at Saratoga, stopping the British advance (see Map 7–3).

The victory at Saratoga convinced the French to enter into a formal alliance, negotiated by Benjamin Franklin, the American envoy. Winning French support was perhaps the major accomplishment of the middle phase of the war. Not only did the entry of the French tie down the British in other parts of the world, but it also brought America more than $8 million in aid.

The British strategy of isolating New England had failed, and it proved impossible to pacify the countryside of the middle colonies. As a result, the focus shifted away from the least loyal section of America, New England, to the most loyal area, the South. Stated British war aims shifted, too, in response to political realities at home. The new justification was to protect the Loyalists from vengeful patriots.

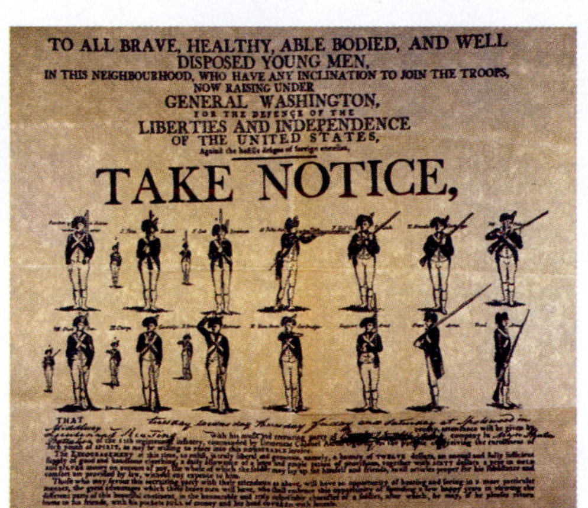

Seeking to capitalize on internal conflicts and to rally southern Loyalists, the British invaded Georgia in 1778 and South Carolina in 1780. After seizing Charleston and trapping the American commander and thousands of troops, the British ranged out into the countryside, trying to rally the Loyalists and live off the land—the same contradictory strategy that had failed in New Jersey.

In the meantime, the Continental army and the militia worked together to wear down the British. The Continental army in the lower South was never large enough to risk a major battle. When the Continental army actually engaged the British, as at Camden, South Carolina, in August 1780, it was defeated. However, as the British marched through South Carolina and North Carolina, they were harassed by bands of irregulars and militia. Each hit depleted the British forces, and each small victory brought more men into the American ranks. This, in fact,

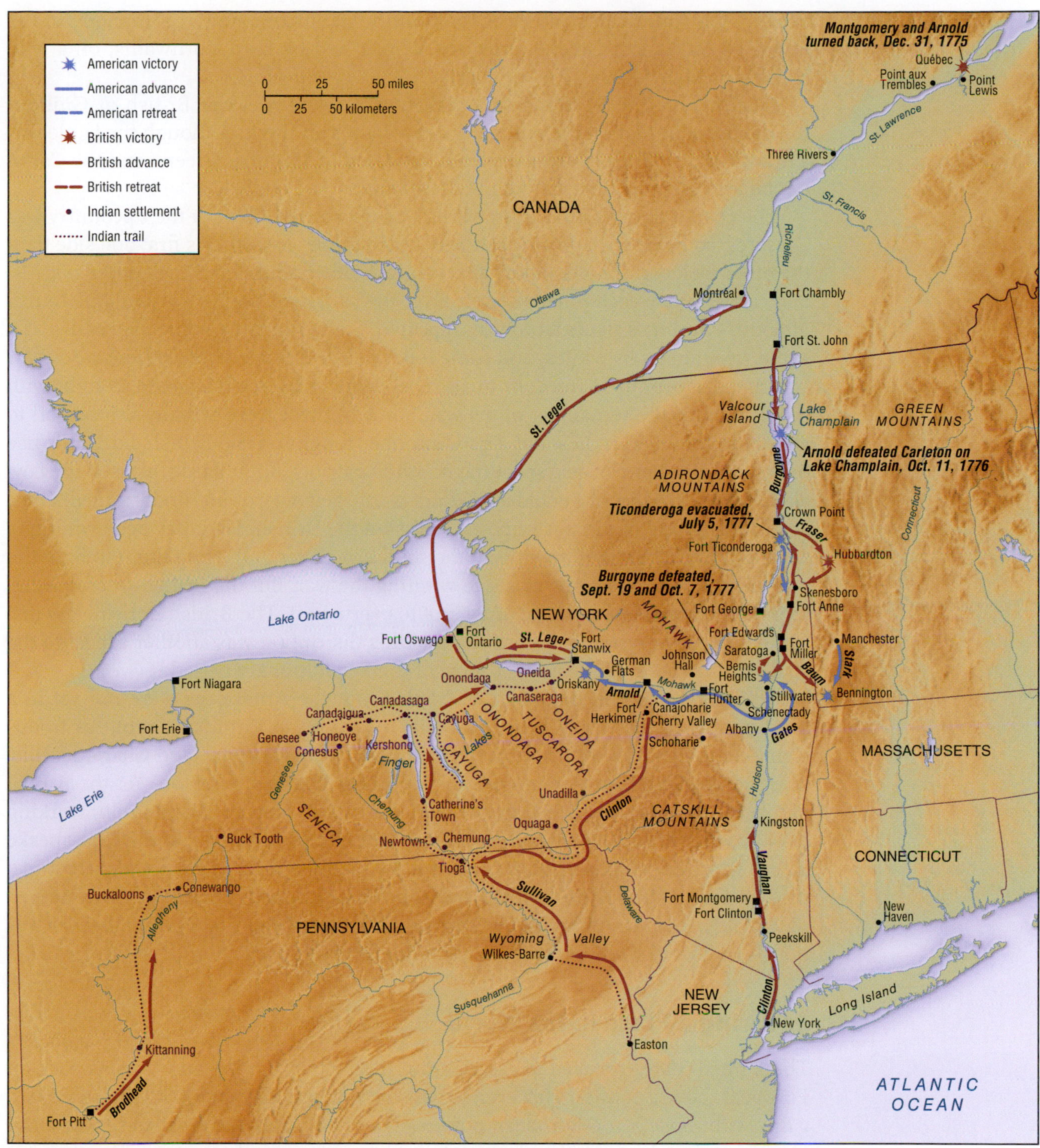

Map 7–3 The Battles for New York The war for New York was waged on two fronts. North of the Hudson River, the Americans failed in their attempt in 1775 to seize Quebec, were forced to abandon Fort Ticonderoga in July 1777, but defeated the British at Saratoga that fall. In 1778 and in 1779, west of the Hudson, General Sullivan and his troops succeeded in their goal of destroying the Iroquois and bringing devastation to their land.

became the American strategy as the Continental forces, now commanded in the South by Nathanael Greene, drew the British, led by Lord Cornwallis, on a wild chase (see Map 7–4).

Finally, with the British near exhaustion, Greene met the British at Guilford Court House in March 1781, inflicting heavy losses on them. Although the battle was a draw, Cornwallis, his forces depleted, retreated to Virginia. Greene and the Continental army retook almost all of the deep South.

The cost to South Carolina, however, was enormous. Most of the upcountry was crisscrossed by troops and stripped bare of anything of worth. As first one side then the other took control, neighbors attacked each other, plundered each other's farms, and carried away each other's slaves. Over the course of the Revolution, one-fourth of South Carolina's slaves simply disappeared. Some ran away, some died of disease, some were stolen by whites, and some followed the British when in June 1780 their commander promised freedom to all rebel-owned slaves who agreed to fight with the British for the remainder of the war. Some of these were actually shipped off to slavery in the West Indies, but a good number fought on the British side. This use of slaves as soldiers, of course, outraged white patriots, but it hardly pleased the Loyalists either. Loyalist slaveholders did not want their way of life undermined. Once again, the nature of the war imposed limits on the British. Had they been willing to wage a war of liberation, freeing all the southern slaves and using them to fight the war, they might have come closer to winning the war. But the British were fighting to preserve social and political order, not to overturn it. The British nonetheless disrupted the slave system significantly, and this disruption was another aspect to the civil war that beset the region for most of the Revolutionary period.

The British southern strategy had failed, but the Americans were not yet in a position to win the war. When Cornwallis moved on to Virginia in 1781, his troops went where they wanted, capturing Richmond, the new capital, and Charlottesville, there coming within a few minutes of capturing Thomas Jefferson. Yet the British had been seriously weakened by the war of attrition. George Washington, working closely with the French—who sent a huge fleet of 28 warships into the Chesapeake across from Cornwallis's quarters at Yorktown—drew most of his forces, accompanied by French troops, to Virginia and laid siege. Trapped, Cornwallis surrendered on October 19, 1781. Although the Treaty of Paris (see Map 7–5) ending the war was not signed for two more years, the war was effectively over.

Securing a Place in the World

The United States revolted to escape from the British Empire and turn its back on European power politics. However, to win the war, the new nation had to strike bargains with those same European powers. These alliances and treaties set the stage for national and international struggle as Americans tried to establish a place for themselves in the world order.

Early in the war the United States called on Britain's continental enemies—France, Spain, and Holland—for support, and it played these new allies off against Britain with as much intrigue and cunning as any Old World diplomat. Benjamin Franklin, Congress's envoy to France, now 70, arrived at court in 1776 dressed like a country rustic instead of wearing the expected silks and powdered wig. His unfashionable appearance was a ruse, intended to make the French think that he

Map 7–4 The War in the South, 1779–1781 In 1779, the theater of action shifted to the South. Washington's objective was to wear the British down, avoiding decisive battles in which his outmanned troops might be defeated. With the help of the French, his strategy succeeded, leading to the British surrender at Yorktown in October 1781.

was innocent and uncalculating. France entered the war in the hope of breaking up the British Empire and reestablishing itself as the world's most powerful nation. France and Spain both wanted the United States to be independent but small and weak.

The United States wanted to secure its own independence, first and foremost, but it had no intention of remaining small or feeble. Americans hoped to obtain the territory between the Appalachians and the Mississippi River and a sizable chunk

Map 7–5 The Treaty of Paris The Treaty of Paris confirmed the boundaries of the new United States, north to the Great Lakes, south to Spanish Florida, and west to the Mississippi. But it left the British in several forts west of the Appalachians, which they did not abandon until 1797. *Walter LaFeber,* The American Age, *2nd ed. (New York: W.W. Norton,1994), p. 29.*

of Canada, as well as the right to navigate the Mississippi. In return for French and Spanish assistance, the United States at first offered only the right to trade, vastly overrating the value of the American trade to European heads of state.

Because America wanted France and Spain to fight for expanded American territory, while those two nations wanted instead to keep the new nation small, it took three years, until 1778, to negotiate formal treaties. Franklin pushed the French along by holding secret truce discussions with a British agent late in 1777 and then leaking reports to well-placed French friends. Although the alliance was an impressive accomplishment for the new nation, it involved several concessions.

The Americans promised not to negotiate separately with Britain and to remain France's ally "forever."

The United States broke both promises, the first within a few years and the second in the 1790s. In April 1782, after Cornwallis's surrender at Yorktown but before France and Spain had gained their military objectives, Franklin began peace negotiations with a British representative. By November, a draft of the treaty had been completed, although Franklin assured the French that nothing would be signed without their consent. It was clear, however, that the agreement primarily served British and American interests. Under the terms of the Treaty of Paris, signed in 1783, Britain recognized American independence, and the United States acquired the territory between the Appalachians and the Mississippi River and south of the Great Lakes (see Map 7–5).

In the long run Britain probably struck the shrewder bargain. The land it ceded was of little use. The Americans failed to press for commercial concessions, and by the mid-1780s, the British had forbidden the Americans to trade directly with either Britain or the West Indies. These restrictions seriously damaged the new nation's economy.

Neither France nor Spain gained much from the war. Although Spain won Florida, neither country achieved its other territorial objectives, and, as was always the case after international wars, France was left with a large debt.

Surrender of British Army Here Cornwallis surrenders to Washington.

If America's allies were relative losers, so also were Britain's allies, the American Loyalists and Indian tribes that fought with them. The best the British could do for the Loyalists was to secure a commitment of no further reprisals against them and Congress's promise to get the states to consider making restitution. Rather than attempting to protect their Indian allies, the British sold them out by transferring their land (the territory between the Appalachians and the Mississippi) to the United States. Although in many ways a stunning achievement, the Treaty of Paris also set the stage for future conflicts.

The Challenge of the Revolution

During the Revolution and in the years that immediately followed, Americans experienced all the upheavals of war: death, profiteering, and inflation followed by economic depression. There were other challenges as well, those presented by the ideology of the Revolution, based on novel ideas about liberty and equality.

Radicals and moderates had compromised to begin and win the Revolution, yet there were significant disagreements between them that resurfaced once the fighting ended. One of the greatest challenges that Americans faced was endeavoring to design political structures that could contain these conflicts. The other great challenge came from the philosophy of revolution itself. Equality implied a transformed society. Followed to its natural conclusion, not only would the transformation lead to widespread prosperity, it would necessarily challenge slavery and the subordination of women.

Braintree March 31 1776

I long to hear that you have declared an independency—and by the way in the new Code of Laws which I suppose it will be necessary for you to make I desire you would Remember the Ladies, and be more generous and favourable to them than your ancestors. Do not put such unlimited power into the hands of the Husbands. Remember all Men would be tyrants if they could. If perticuliar care and attention is not paid to the Laidies we are determined to foment a Rebelion, and will not hold ourselves bound by any Laws in which we have no voice, or Representation.

That your Sex are Naturally Tyrannical is a Truth so thoroughly established as to admit of no dispute, but such of you as wish to be happy willingly give up the harsh title of Master for the more tender and endearing one of Friend. Why then, not put it out of the power of the vicious and the Lawless to use us with cruelty and indignity with impunity. Men of Sense in all Ages abhor those customs which treat us only as the vassals of your Sex. Regard us then as Beings placed by providence under your protection and in immitation of the Supreem Being make use of that power only for our happiness.

Abigail Smith Adams,
to her husband John.

The Departure of the Loyalists

About 15 to 20 percent of the white population had remained loyal to the Crown during the Revolution, along with a majority of the Indians and a minority of slaves. Although this was a sizable number of people (almost half a million whites), the Loyalists were never well-organized enough to present a real danger to the success of the Revolution.

During the war, partisan fighting was fierce in those regions where neither side could maintain control, such as the Carolinas and New Jersey, but there was relatively little retribution after the war. There were no trials for treason, mass executions, or significant mob actions directed against whites. Nor was there any significant resistance from the Loyalists. Perhaps as many as 80,000 left the country for Canada, Great Britain, or the West Indies. Among them were thousands of former slaves who had accepted the British offer of freedom.

The white exiles came disproportionately from the top tier of society, and their departure left a void that less prominent Americans scrambled to fill. Confiscated Loyalist property represented a great deal of wealth to be redistributed. Most often, it was people just below the top rung of society who took the Loyalists' places. The departure of the Loyalists enhanced the democratizing tendencies of the Revolution by removing the most conservative element in American society and creating an opportunity for many Americans to rise to power.

The Challenge of the Economy

Wars disrupt the economy in two ways. First, they interfere with production and exchange, hurting some people and creating opportunity for others. Second, because wars are expensive, they require some combination of increased taxation and deficit spending.

Those who suffered the greatest economic hardships and enjoyed the greatest opportunities from the Revolution were those most deeply involved in the market. During the war, trade with Britain and the British West Indies was cut off, and the British navy seized American ships and destroyed the New England fishing industry. After the war, Britain continued to exclude American ships from the West Indies. Congress, operating under the Articles of Confederation, was too weak to negotiate a more advantageous trade relationship, and merchants who had depended on trade with Britain and the West Indies were ruined.

At the same time, other opportunities opened up. Merchants who were willing to risk seizure of their ships continued the trade with Europe and sold the goods they imported at astronomical prices. Privateering made other merchants rich, as did provisioning the Continental army. In 1779 alone, the army spent $109 million on provisions, fueling a wartime economic boom. In addition, the army's demand for supplies drove prices up. Prices for grain increased 200 to 600 percent in some regions, while those for wheat in Maryland skyrocketed 5,000 percent (see Figure 7–1). Enterprising Americans with a little capital to invest could rise quickly. Not everyone could take advantage of the dislocations of the Revolutionary economy. In fact, although the Revolution eliminated a portion of the ruling elite, it did not level the social classes. Those who could not profit from the war economy had to work harder and struggle with rising prices. To meet the army's demand for cloth and make up for the lack of imports, women increased the pace of home production. Because cities and states set prices for cloth, however, women were unable to reap exorbitant profits for their work.

Skyrocketing prices were hardest on those with limited incomes. While some cities imposed price controls and Congress debated whether setting prices interfered with liberty, aggrieved citizens sometimes took matters into their own hands. In Boston, a mob of at least a hundred women seized a hogshead of coffee from the merchant Thomas Boylston, who was hoarding it. Such conflicts pitted the community against the entrepreneur and raised serious questions about the purpose of the Revolution: Was it to create opportunities for the individual or protect the well-being of the community?

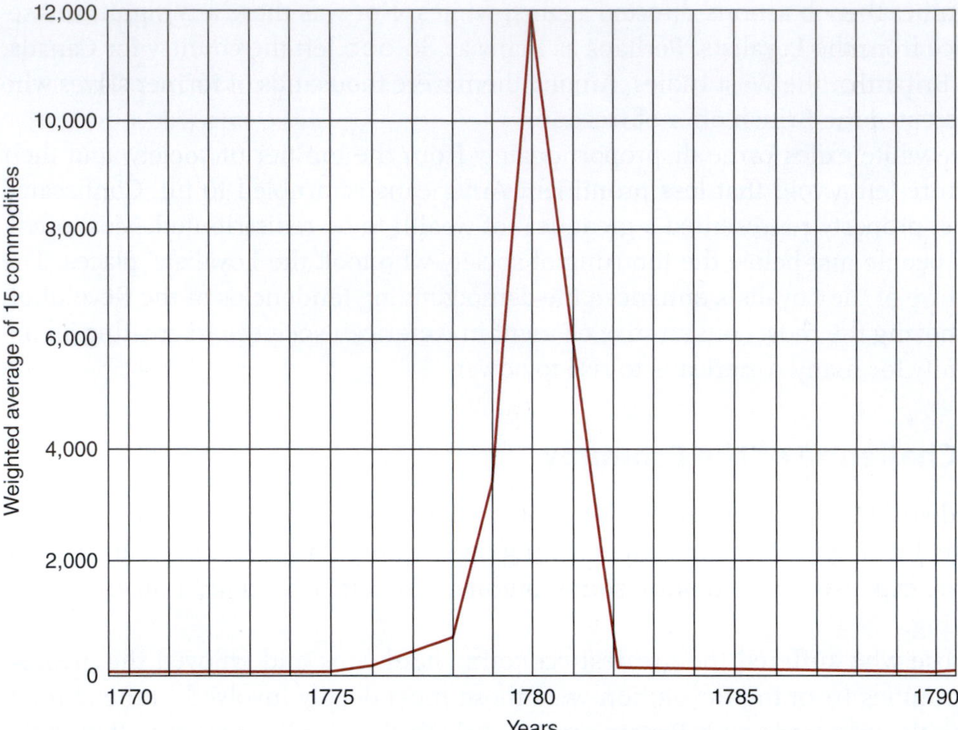

Figure 7–1 Inflation at Philadelphia, 1770–1790 Beginning in 1776, wartime shortages caused prices for basic commodities—beef, chocolate, coffee, corn, flour, molasses, pepper, pork, rum, sugar, tea, wheat, iron, and tar—to skyrocket. By 1781, prices were 12,000 percent higher than a decade earlier. They began to fall the next year, finally reaching prewar levels by late in the decade.

After the war, opportunities for profit and prosperity for some increased, while a postwar deflation pushed others to the brink of misery. Speculation in land and currency offered the fastest ways to become rich. Entrepreneurs bought up paper currency and land patents at a fraction of their worth, counting on the day when they would be redeemed at their face value.

Even before the war ended, America's growing population was clamoring for land. Between 1776 and 1790, America's population grew by almost 70 percent, from 2.3 million to 3.9 million, almost all from natural increase. Since before the Revolution, colonists had been pushing against the Indians to the west. By 1783, the Wilderness Road had taken thousands of settlers into Kentucky; seven years later, 100,000 people were living in Kentucky and Tennessee.

With the demand for land so great, speculators who could corner huge tracts stood to reap extraordinary profits. Before the Revolution, seven men had secured a patent to 29,350 acres in upstate New York; by the time the Revolution was over, three of them were dead, one—a Loyalist—had left the country, and the others were broke or close to it, all victims of the dislocations of the wartime economy. William Cooper, until then a small-scale merchant and speculator, moved in and bought the patent in a possibly rigged auction for the bargain-basement price of £2,700. Yet this investment was worthless unless Cooper could get others to buy portions of the huge patent from him. Within a few months' time, Cooper had sold off thousands of acres not to poor farmers but to groups of speculators who returned to their home villages to sell farm-sized plots to their townsmen, turning a profit by increasing the price.

All along the western frontier, farmers rushed in to take up new lands. This rush into newly opened farming regions reversed the pre-Revolutionary trend, in which the growing population sought employment in the cities. With the opening of new regions to the west, America would remain a farming nation for decades more, rather than industrializing rapidly and displaying the rigid class stratifications of European industrial economies. At the same time, slavery expanded into new territories in the South, ensuring the persistence of inequalities based on race.

Even more than the dislocations of the Revolutionary economy, the financing of the Revolution challenged the American economy. Taxing the population was out of the question, not only because Americans had begun the Revolution precisely to avoid high taxes, but also because Congress had no authority to tax. Instead, it simply printed more money. There was no increase in underlying wealth to back up this currency, and the more Congress printed, the less it was worth. By 1780, Congress had printed more than $241 million. In addition, Congress paid for supplies and soldiers' wages with certificates that circulated like money. These certificates put another $95 million into circulation.

The plan was for each state to raise taxes to buy up the Continental currency and remove it from circulation. However, the states were either unable or unwilling to buy up enough currency to maintain its value. Moreover, the states issued their own paper money. Eventually, the states had to tax their inhabitants at rates far higher than had ever been seen before. Levying taxes was one thing; collecting them was another: people could not pay in hard money, and the Continental currency depreciated so rapidly that it was almost worthless (see Figure 7–2).

By April 1777, Continental currency was worth only half its face value and by April 1781, only half a percent of its face value. By the end of the war, some creditors were refusing to accept paper money for the debts owed to them, insisting on hard money instead. Then, when the war ended and trade with Britain resumed, imports increased sharply (because of pent-up demand for consumer goods), while exports fell (because trade restrictions kept American goods out of British markets). The result was severe deflation, as America was flooded with cheap imports.

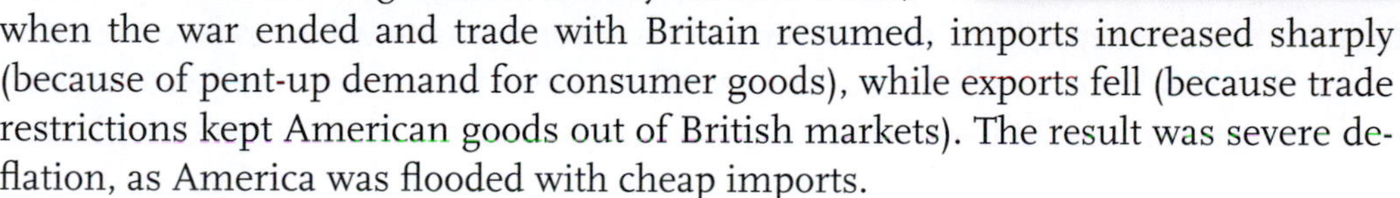

The weak central government was almost powerless to address these economic upheavals. In 1780 it stopped paying the army, which almost led to a mutiny at the encampment at Newburgh, New York. Congress looked to the states, which addressed their economic problems in different ways. Each state had to decide what to do about its debt and which element of its population to serve. Many showed mercy to their debtors. Some states sold confiscated Loyalist property to help pay off their debts, while others tried to seize Indian lands in the west to sell for the same purpose. In states that increased taxes to pay off the state debts (at just the time when the postwar depression hit), hard-pressed debtors clamored for tax relief. In western Massachusetts, a group of farmers led by Revolutionary War captain Daniel

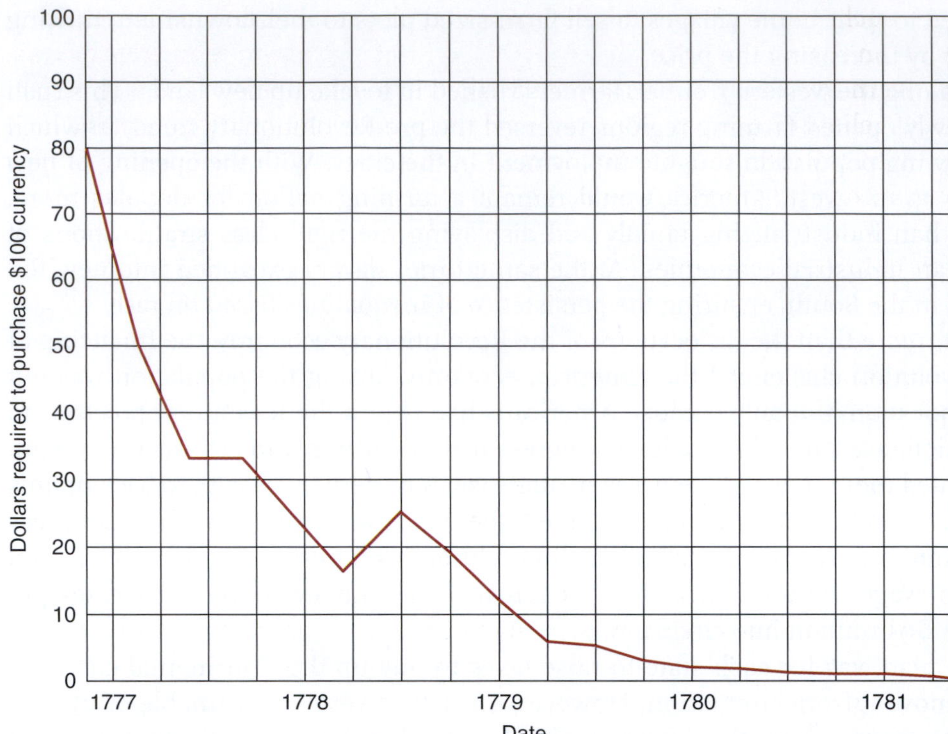

Figure 7–2 Depreciation of Continental Currency, January 1770–April 1781 At the same time that prices were rising, the value of Continental currency was falling dramatically. Between 1777 and 1781, it lost almost all of its value, becoming close to worthless.

Shays shut down the courts to prevent them from collecting debts. This is known as Shays's Rebellion.

Contesting the New Economy

Economic upheaval and popular uprisings against state governments led many Americans to question whether democratic government could survive. The process of rebellion that started in 1765 seemed to be beginning again, this time directed against the new republican state governments. Americans now had to face the same issue that had led to conflict with Britain: Were they willing to pay the costs of waging a huge war? Could they avoid the perils of tyranny, on the one hand, and anarchy, on the other? Could they, in short, maintain democratic forms of government?

Shays's Rebellion was simply an extreme form of the protest that occurred in many states. It was an attempt by debtors from western Massachusetts to force the government to alleviate their economic distress, primarily by shutting down the courts so that their debts could not be collected, but also by passing legislation for the relief of debtors. By 1786, many western Massachusetts farmers had become accustomed to the absence of government. Courts had been shut down in the region since 1774. Those who put down Shays's Rebellion did so in republican terms, faulting the Shaysites for inadequate virtue.

Popular uprisings of this sort raised serious questions about whether the democratic governments created after the Revolution could contain anarchy. Every state that faced such uprisings learned, however, that peace could best be preserved by going easy on the rebels. After Shays's Rebellion was put down, John Hancock was elected governor with the support of the Shaysites on a platform of amnesty for the rebels and relief for debtors. As a rule, popular uprisings by economically independent men (as distinguished from those by dependent laborers or slaves) have been punished very lightly in America, which may be a source of American political stability.

Although the relatively light punishments meted out to debtor insurgents and the generally inflationary policies of state governments quelled popular unrest, the postwar depression and the inability of Congress to negotiate trade agreements with Britain devastated commerce. The huge national debt went unpaid, leaving numerous creditors holding worthless pieces of paper. Popular unrest in the states had helped debtors but hurt those to whom they owed money. The nationalists, a group of commercial-minded political leaders centered in Congress and including James Madison, Gouverneur Morris, Robert Morris, and Alexander Hamilton, began to make a case for a strong national government that would actively advance commerce and protect private property. These nationalists were, in general, the moderates of the Revolutionary era. Radicals envisioned a nation based on a weaker central government, a more localized democracy, and a hands-off approach to the economy. Whether these two visions of America could be reconciled was one of the greatest challenges presented by the Revolution.

Can Women Be Citizens?

The American Revolution raised questions that threatened and in some cases changed the social order. A revolution based on beliefs in human equality and a common human nature brought into question all social relations, including the role of women.

Many women were drawn into the Revolution as consumers. They had been actively recruited into the boycott movements of the 1760s and 1770s, and they had eagerly participated both in boycotts and in increased home production. Many women identified with the goals of the Revolution and often directed one of its engines of enforcement: riots against merchants suspected of unfair dealings. Women could turn their efforts against the Revolutionary governments, as well, when they perceived interference with their rights as consumers and duties as homemakers. Early in the war, the women of Kingston, New York, mobbed the town's Revolutionary committee and threatened that unless the committee turned over the tea it held, "their husbands and sons shall fight no more."

If it was generally agreed that women could extend their traditional economic roles as producers and consumers to support the war effort, there was no consensus on how greatly women's political roles should be expanded. Some women, such as Richard Henry Lee's sister Hannah Lee Corbin, pointed out that the right to be taxed only by one's own representatives should apply to them, too. Under the principle of *coverture*, married women were generally denied the right to own property, but what was the basis for denying the vote to unmarried women who owned property? In 1776, New Jersey extended the vote to unmarried women who met the property qualification (although this right was rescinded in 1807).

Although American Revolutionaries were not prepared to let women vote, except in New Jersey, they began to expand their views about women's intellectual and political capabilities in other ways. The state laws that confiscated Loyalists' property, for example, often presumed that married women were capable of making their own political choices. This notion was a radical break with the past, which had always asserted that married women had no political will separate from their husbands.

The Revolution challenged the idea that women lacked independent minds and could not think for themselves. The Enlightenment belief that all human beings were endowed with the capacity to reason led to significant improvements in women's education after the war. Reformers, many of them women, argued that if women appeared ignorant or incapable, it was only because of their inferior education. Massachusetts writer Judith Sargent (Stevens) Murray asked, "Will it be said that the judgment of a male of two years old, is more sage than that of a female's of the same age?"

Enlightenment ideas about women's intellectual abilities meshed neatly with republican ideas about the need for virtue, and liberal ideas about the necessity of consent. If the fate of the nation depended on the character of its citizens, both men and women should be able to choose intelligent, upright, patriotic partners. Likewise, the Revolution's rejection of arbitrary power accelerated a trend for people to choose their own marriage partners and marry for love rather than for crass

Liberty Displaying Arts and Sciences So powerful was the Revolutionary idea of human equality that many came to believe in the liberating potential of education for both women and blacks.

material interest. If women were to make such choices wisely, then they must be educated well.

Yet once again the Revolutionary impulse had its limits. Discussions about women's citizenship and intellectual capacities implicitly applied only to prosperous white women. Moreover, almost no one advocated professional education or even knowledge for its own sake for women. Overly intellectual women were ridiculed as "women of masculine minds." Women's education was supposed to make them better wives and better mothers and enable them to perform their domestic roles better. Because the family was still the bedrock of the nation no one was willing to answer Abigail Adams's question: What recourse was open to women who found that they were treated with "cruelty and indignity" at home?

The ideas of the Revolution presented a powerful challenge to the subordination of women, one that the Revolutionary generation was only partially prepared to meet. Women were recognized as intelligent beings who could make important choices in the market, about their families, and even about their political loyalties. They were partial citizens, and this revealed the limits of Revolutionary doctrines of equality.

The Challenge of Slavery

No institution in America received a greater challenge from the egalitarian ideals of the Revolution than slavery. While slaves always resisted their enslavement, the world's first organized antislavery movement began before the Revolution with the Pennsylvania Quaker John Woolman, who in 1754 condemned slavery in humanitarian and religious terms. Within a few years, radicals in both the North and the South recognized that the institution was inconsistent with their ideals of freedom.

African American slaves saw immediately that the Revolution offered opportunities for freedom. The combination of egalitarian ideas and wartime disruption enabled thousands of slaves to claim their freedom. Some used a combination of Christian and Revolutionary principles of liberty to petition for "the natural rights and privileges of freeborn men." Others fought for their liberty by joining the Revolutionary forces; by the end of the war, three-fourths of the Rhode Island regiment and perhaps one-fourth of Washington's troops were black. Many more took advantage of British offers of freedom to slaves who deserted their masters. Tens of thousands of slaves ran away, especially in areas occupied by the British or torn by war. This combination of Revolutionary ideals of freedom and African American activism presented a significant challenge to white Americans, and they were able to meet it in part. Every state north of Delaware eliminated slavery, either in their constitutions or through gradual emancipation laws. In addition, the Northwest Ordinance of 1787 prohibited slavery in the Northwest Territory (the future states of Ohio, Indiana, Illinois, Michigan, and Wisconsin). In the states of the upper South (Virginia, Maryland, and Delaware) legislatures passed laws making it easier to emancipate slaves.

If slavery was eliminated—though sometimes slowly—in the North and questioned in the upper South, it still survived in every state south of New Jersey. Revolutionary ideals made slaveholders uncomfortable with the institution. Unwilling to eliminate it, they offered excuses, protesting that abolishing slavery was too difficult or inconvenient. Historians still debate whether the inroads Revolutionary thought made against slavery were one of the Revolution's greatest successes—or whether its inability to curtail the institution was its greatest failure.

A New Policy in the West

The new nation faced a major challenge in the West. It had to devise a policy that would be consistent with its political economy, rejecting the old colonial models of Britain, France, and Spain. But how would the United States organize the new territory acquired through the war? There was at the time no useful model that would enable new territories and their citizens to become equal members of an expanding, democratic nation.

The Indians' Revolution

At the beginning of the American Revolution, most Indians regarded it as a fight among Englishmen that did not concern them. At the end of the war, all Indians were losers, as land-hungry Americans poured into the region beyond the Appalachians.

By 1776, both the British and the Americans were recruiting Indians for their causes. Within a few years, Indians all along the frontier had been drawn into the struggle, most often on the British side. These Indians were fearful of American encroachments onto their land; also, only the British could provide the customary "presents" that cemented alliances. Indians struck at American communities all along the frontier (see Map 7–6).

In retaliation, Washington ordered General John Sullivan to accomplish "the total destruction and devastation" of Iroquois settlements in New York and western Pennsylvania and the capture of "as many prisoners of every age and sex as possible." In the fall of 1778, Sullivan's expedition systematically burned 40 Iroquois towns. One chief complained that the Americans "put to death all the Women and Children, excepting some of the young Women, whom they carried away for the use of their Soldiers & were afterwards put to death in a more shameful manner." Such brutality understandably undermined American efforts to keep Indian allies.

> **"It is also your Business Brothers to exert yourselves in the Defense of this Road by which the King, our Father, so fully supplied our Wants. If this is once stopt we must be a miserable People, and be left exposed to the Resentment of the Rebels, who notwithstanding their fair Speeches, wish for nothing more than to extirpate us from the Earth, that they may possess our Lands, the Desire of attaining which we are convinced is the Cause of the present War between the King and his disobedient Children."**
>
> SAYENQUERAGHTA,
> a Seneca war chief, addressing an Indian council at Niagara, 1779

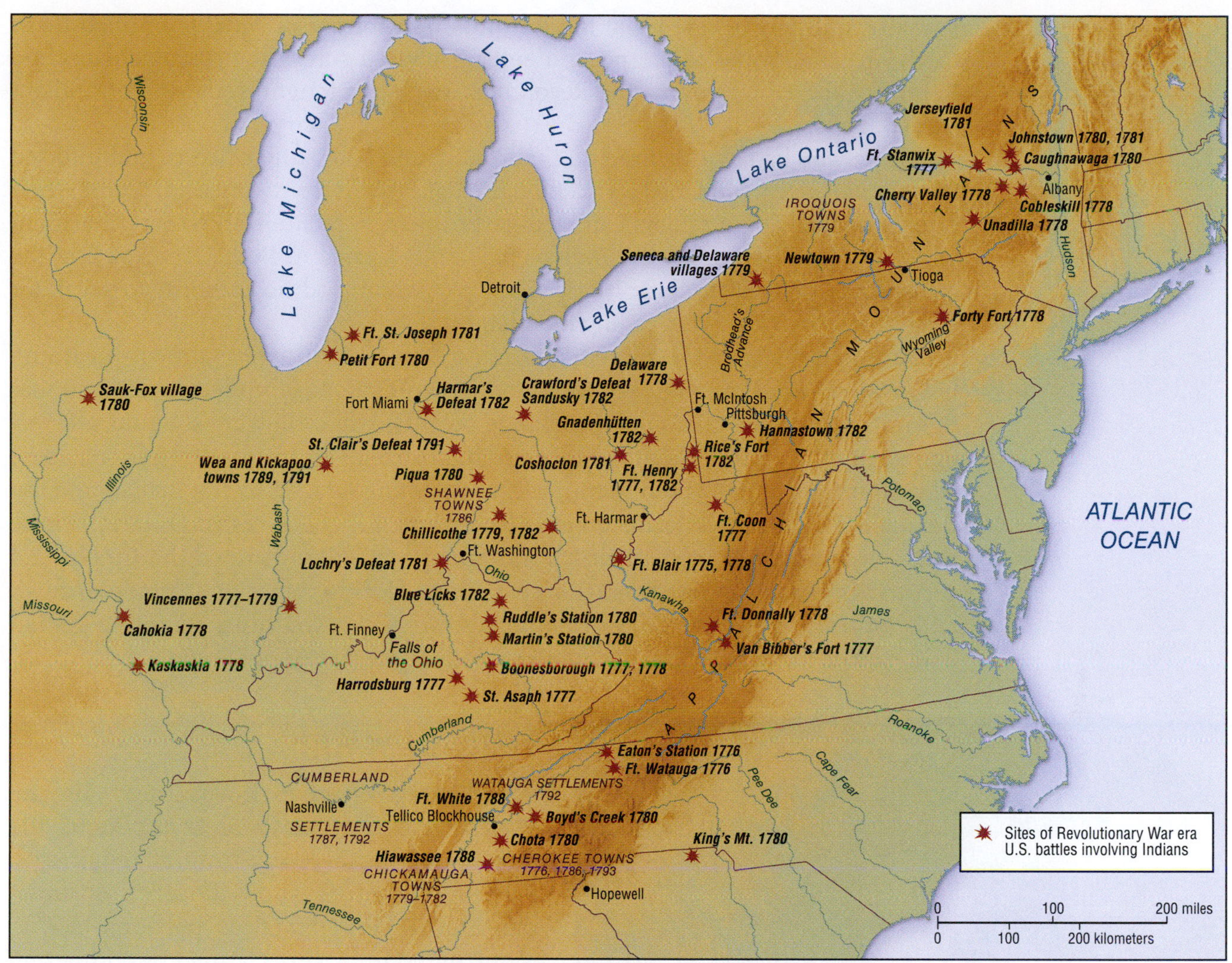

Map 7–6 Sites of Revolutionary War Battles Involving Indians Indians were active participants in the Revolution, fighting on both sides and making the West a significant site of conflict. *Wilcomb Washburn,* Handbook of North American Indians *(Washington, DC: Smithsonian, 1988), p. 115.*

The End of the Middle Ground

The end of the Revolution brought neither peace nor order. The Indians who had won victories on the frontier were amazed when word came that the British had surrendered and turned over all of the Indians' land to the Americans. Needing land for settlers more than it needed diplomatic allies, the United States soon abandoned the middle ground (see Chapter 2). No longer able to play one group of Europeans against another, Indian tribes had little leverage.

Western Indians soon found themselves in the midst of a competition among whites for their land. Congress wanted to establish a national claim to Indian lands so it could sell them to pay off the war debt, while New York, Pennsylvania, North Carolina, and Virginia all attempted to seize land that lay within their borders. Speculators moved in, knowing they could sell land at an immense profit. At the end of the Revolution, one-third of the men in western Pennsylvania were landless and they believed that the Revolution's promise of equality entitled them to cheap land. Some of the poorest settlers poured across the Appalachians into Kentucky and Ohio, even as the Revolution was being fought, squatting on Indian-owned lands.

Those who had already lived on the frontier and both suffered from and inflicted frontier violence maintained a visceral hatred of Indians, sometimes advocating their extermination. These settlers expected government to secure frontier land for them and to protect them from the Indians who still claimed it. Both Congress and the states moved quickly to force Indians, some of whom had no authority to speak for their tribes, to sign treaties ceding their land.

Such treaties (15 were signed between 1784 and 1796) were almost meaningless. Native Americans refused to honor agreements made under duress and that did not include the customary exchange of gifts, while the states would not recognize another state's claims or those of the national government. Indian leaders who attempted to rally their communities were encouraged by the British and the Spanish. The Mohawk leader Joseph Brant took his followers to Ontario, where they were welcomed by the British. Alexander McGillivray united the Creeks and secured military support from the Spanish in Florida. Years of struggle ensued, and not until well into the nineteenth century were American claims to Indian land east of the Mississippi secured and Indian resistance put down.

Joseph Brant After the Revolution, the Mohawk leader Joseph Brant took his followers into exile in Canada.

Settling the West

Establishing effective government in the West was one of the biggest problems the new nation faced. Many frontier regions (in particular Kentucky and the area north of the Ohio River, as well as portions of Vermont and Maine) were claimed by competing groups of speculators from different states. The Articles of Confederation gave Congress limited powers of government in the West, and it soon became clear that a national policy was necessary. In the years just after the Revolution, groups of dissident settlers in New York, Pennsylvania, Kentucky (then part of Virginia), and Tennessee (then part of North Carolina) all hatched plans to create their own states.

Both state governments and nationalists in Congress believed that the Union was in peril. Yet it was difficult to reach a compromise among the competing interests. States with significant western claims wanted Congress to recognize their claims, while states without any western lands wanted all of the western lands to be turned over to Congress. Also at issue was which speculators' land claims would

Map 7–7 Western Land Cessions Between 1782 and 1802, eastern states ceded to the national government the territory they claimed in the West. Under the principle established by the Northwest Ordinance, new states were carved out of this territory. Never before had a nation developed such a procedure for bringing in new regions not as colonies but as fully equal states.

be upheld. In several regions, groups of speculators with dubious claims to the land were selling it to settlers at bargain prices.

The Northwest Ordinance, ratified by Congress on July 13, 1787, was a compromise among these competing interests. Finally realizing that they could not manage vast areas of territory, the large states yielded their claims to Congress. Because Congress validated the claims only of respectable speculators, it made losers not only out of unscrupulous ones but the poor people who had bought land from them at cheap prices.

The Northwest Ordinance set out a model of government for the western territories that reflected the liberal political philosophy of nationalists in Congress and established a process for the admission of new states into the nation. In a clear rejection of Britain's colonial model of territorial expansion, territories would be eligible to apply for statehood once they had 60,000 free inhabitants. There were other important breaks with the past as well. Slavery was now forbidden north of the Ohio River; it was the first time that a line was drawn barring slaves from a particular region. Trial by jury and habeas corpus were guaranteed, as well as the right to bail and freedom of religion. Cruel and unusual punishments were barred. These were important principles that, except for the provision excluding slavery, would all appear again in the Constitution and Bill of Rights.

The Northwest Ordinance was designed to create an orderly world of middle-class farmers who obeyed the law, paid their debts, worshiped as they pleased, and were protected from despotic government and the unruly poor. The ordinance represented the triumph of the moderate Revolutionaries' vision of government.

Creating a New National Government

At the beginning of the Revolution, radicals and moderates had been able to work together to accomplish their common goals. The years of war, however, slowly pulled the radicals and moderates apart. During this period, many moderates, particularly those who served in Congress or as officers in the Continental army, became nationalists. They worked with men from other states on national projects, and they came to think of the states as a threat to the success of the Revolution. Many of the radicals, meanwhile, retained a local perspective. Still influenced by republican political thought, they continued to dread a centralized government, and they feared that the Continental army would become a standing army that might take away their liberties.

> **"If money be the vitals of Congress, is it not precious for those individuals from whom it is to be taken? Must I give my soul—my lungs, to Congress. Congress must have our souls. . . . I tell you, they shall not have the soul of Virginia."**
>
> PATRICK HENRY,
> speaking against the ratification of the Constitution

This split between moderate nationalists and radical localists culminated in the battle over the Constitution, written by the nationalists to create a stronger central government and resisted by the localists, who feared that it would subvert liberty. Almost all the problems that led the nationalists to wish for a stronger national government concerned the economy: paying the war debt, paying the soldiers for their service during the war, improving commerce. The nationalists were deeply involved in the market economy as merchants, financiers, farmers, and planters. The localists, as a rule, were much less involved in the market and suspicious of those who were. As long as taxes were low and their creditors did not harass them, they were satisfied. From their perspective, the Articles of Confederation provided all the national government and economy that was needed.

A Crippled Congress

It soon became evident to nationalists in Congress that the national government was powerless to address the most pressing economic questions. By 1779 Congress had printed $200 million worth of paper money that was dropping in value by the day, and it had shut down its printing presses. It then told the states that it was their responsibility to provision the army. State legislatures dithered while the army went unclothed and unfed, and the unpaid army threatened mutiny. Congress gave up trying to pay its war debt and passed that back to the states as well. Some states refused. States such as Massachusetts that raised taxes to pay off their portion courted armed upheavals such as Shays's Rebellion.

Congress was powerless to alleviate the economic distress. At the end of the war, British goods flooded into a nation that had been starved for them, and consumer demand seemed insatiable. However, there was no comparable British demand for American exports; in fact, Britain closed its ports to American trade. America could not retaliate by closing its ports to British ships, because the Articles of Confederation denied Congress the authority to regulate commerce. Additional foreign loans, which had kept the nation afloat during the Revolution, were out of the question. Congress could not pay back the loans it had already taken out. Even western policy, the area of Congress's greatest triumph, presented problems. The states had ceded western territory to Congress. Yet once those lands came under Congress's jurisdiction (leading to the passage of the Northwest Ordinance), Congress discovered what the British government had learned at the end of the French and Indian War: it takes an army and a great deal of money to police a territory inhabited by Indians and coveted by land-hungry settlers. Congress did not have that money, and it could not even pay the army that it had.

By the early 1780s, nationalists were attempting to strengthen Congress, but these attempts failed without the approval of the states. By the middle of the decade, several of the boldest nationalists had decided that reform was not only impossible but undesirable. They were convinced that a new and stronger form of government should be created. When James Madison returned to Virginia at the end of 1783 (a victim of term limits, having served the maximum of three consecutive years in Congress), he began a study of history to learn the principles of effective government. Other nationalists began talking about calling a constitutional convention. But the challenge they faced was how to effect changes that the states themselves did not seem to want.

The road that led to the Constitutional Convention in Philadelphia in 1787 ran through two earlier meetings. First, in 1785, at Madison's suggestion, commissioners from Virginia and Maryland met at George Washington's home, Mount Vernon, to resolve disputes about navigating the Potomac River. Madison suggested a further meeting of representatives from all the states in Annapolis, Maryland, to build on the accomplishments from Mount Vernon. When only 12 men, representing five states, arrived, they issued a call for another meeting, in Philadelphia, nine months later. In those nine months, Shays's Rebellion and the continued stalemate in Congress persuaded nationalists that strengthening the government should be considered. So, over the summer of 1787, 55 men from twelve states met in Philadelphia to write one of the most influential documents in the history of the world.

Writing a New Constitution

The men who assembled in Philadelphia were primarily moderate nationalists. It is a measure of their commitment to the goals of the Revolution that they sought, in James Madison's words, "republican remedies" for the problems of republican government. The 55 delegates met for almost four months during the summer of 1787, finally ratifying the Constitution on September 17. They conducted their deliberations in secret, which enabled them to talk freely and achieve compromises. Hence, the shutters to the room were closed and nailed shut, and precautions were taken to ensure that the talkative Benjamin Franklin did not spill any secrets. The heat and stench of sweat in the room must have been almost unbearable.

Although there were sharp differences of opinion on specific issues, there were wide areas of agreement. Most of the delegates had considerable experience in state and national government. George Washington, a member of Virginia's delegation, was the most widely respected man in the nation. He was elected the presiding officer of the convention.

Collectively the delegates were young, with most in their 30s and 40s. No one played a more important role in the convention than James Madison, who had just turned 36. Madison came to the Constitutional Convention with a design for the new government already worked out. Known as the Virginia Plan, it became the outline for the Constitution.

The Virginia Plan was a blueprint for substantial change: a strong central government divided into three branches, executive, legislative (itself with two branches), and judicial, that would check and balance one another; a system of federalism that guaranteed every state a republican government; and proposals for admitting new states and amending the Constitution. The only alternative, the New Jersey Plan, offered on June 15, was rejected three days later. It proposed a single-house legislature, with all states having an equal vote, and also a plural executive, chosen by the legislature (see Table 7–1).

The delegates were in basic agreement that the new national government would have to be much stronger: Congress would now have the power to collect taxes and duties, to pay the country's debts, to regulate foreign commerce, and to raise armies and pay for them. Once the delegates compromised on a method for choosing the president (by electors chosen in each state) and the length of his term (four years, eligible for reelection), they readily agreed to grant him considerable power to propose legislation, veto bills of Congress (subject to congressional override), conduct diplomacy, and command the armed forces.

The delegates vested judicial authority in the Supreme Court and inferior federal courts and granted them authority over the state constitutions as well. Although the delegates were able to reach agreement rather easily on the structure and powers of the new government, they argued bitterly any time the interests of their states seemed in jeopardy. The most difficult issues related to representation: Would the numbers of senators and representatives be based on population or wealth, or would each state have equal numbers? If based on population or wealth, would slaves be counted? Large states generally wanted representation to be based on either population or wealth (they had more of both), while northern states did not want slaves to

 **Table 7–1** Key Provisions of the Articles of Confederation, the Virginia Plan, the New Jersey Plan, and the Constitution

	Articles of Confederation	Virginia Plan	New Jersey Plan	Constitution
Executive	None	Chosen by Congress	Plural; chosen by Congress	President chosen by Electoral College
Congress	One house; one vote per state	Two houses	One house	Two houses
Judiciary	None	Yes	Yes	Yes
Federalism	Limited; each state retains full sovereignty	Yes; Congress can veto state laws	Yes; acts of Congress the "supreme law of the states"	Yes; Constitution the "supreme law of the land"; states guaranteed a republican form of government; Supreme Court to adjudicate disputes between states
Powers of Congress	Conduct diplomacy and wage war; cannot levy taxes or raise army	All powers of Articles of Confederation, plus power to make laws for nation	All powers of Articles of Confederation, plus power to regulate commerce and make states pay taxes	Numerous powers, such as levy taxes, declare war, raise army, regulate commerce, and "make all laws which shall be necessary and proper" for carrying out those powers

be counted, either as population or wealth. The conflict between the large and small states was resolved by Roger Sherman's Connecticut (or Great) Compromise: Each state would have an equal number of senators, satisfying the small states. The number of representatives would be based upon either population or wealth, satisfying the large states.

The Connecticut Compromise solved the conflict between small and large states, but only by creating another between slave and free states. The South Carolinians were adamant: whether slavery was called population or wealth, the institution must be protected. The argument was fierce, with several delegates threatening to walk out. Finally, the convention compromised. Representation in the House would be based on the entire free population (including women and children, but not Indians) plus three-fifths of the slaves, thus increasing the South's representation. The delegates recognized that the Three-Fifths Compromise was fundamentally illogical, but only when it had been accepted could the delegates agree to the Connecticut Compromise. The Three-Fifths Compromise made the Connecticut Compromise possible.

The Three-Fifths Compromise, or Clause, became the most notorious provision in the Constitution. Although the delegates were careful not to use the word "slave" (instead using bland phrases such as "other persons"), clearly they were establishing a racial line. The convention made two other concessions to slavery. First, it agreed, over Madison's vehement protest, that Congress could not ban the slave trade until 1808 at the earliest. In addition, the Constitution included a fugitive slave clause, which required states to return runaway slaves. The reopening of the slave trade did more to strengthen slavery than the other compromises on slavery. Madison predicted accurately that "twenty years will produce all the mischief that can be apprehended from the liberty to import slaves." Between 1788 and 1808, thousands and thousands of Africans were sold into slavery in the United States.

The nationalists were determined not to leave Philadelphia until they had a constitution, and they were willing to enter into whatever compromises seemed necessary. Despite occasional impasses and heated debates, those compromises were achieved, and the convention adjourned on September 17. The delegates' work was not over, however. Now the Constitution had to be ratified.

Ratifying the Constitution: Politics

There was nothing inevitable about the nation, the Constitution, or the particular form either took; that the Constitution would be ratified was by no means a given. The Constitution was the creation of a small group of men who thought nationally, the Federalists. They then had the difficult task of getting the Constitution ratified by a nation that still thought about government in almost wholly local terms.

The Philadelphia Convention decided that the Constitution would go into effect once nine states had ratified it. They could not bind any states that had not ratified, but the nine signatories could go ahead. Ironically, after all the small states/big states debate in the convention, small states were the first to ratify, because they were the ones that most needed the union. For example, Georgia, the fourth state to ratify, was still in many ways a frontier region, vulnerable to Indian assault, its capital at Augusta an armed camp. The most serious opposition came from the large, powerful states of Massachusetts, New York, and Virginia.

The convention had concluded on September 17, and by December 7, Delaware had already ratified the Constitution. By January 9, 1788, New Jersey, Georgia, and Connecticut followed, with barely any dispute. The Federalists in Pennsylvania forced ratification by using strong-arm tactics. The Federalists in other states learned from these mistakes and more willingly made concessions to their Antifederalist opponents.

In Massachusetts, as in Pennsylvania, there was considerable opposition from the western part of the state among those sympathetic to Shays's Rebellion. In an inspired move that would be used also in Virginia, the Federalists made certain that the Constitution was debated section by section, enabling them to win point by point. And in another critical strategic decision, the Federalists agreed that the convention in Massachusetts should propose amendments. Equally important was the form that these amendments would take, not as a condition for ratification, but as part of a package that recommended ratification. This concession, which ultimately made the Constitution both stronger and more democratic, was critical in winning ratification.

Only three more states were necessary for the Constitution to go into effect. The more politically adept Federalists postponed or stalled the debate until states that were most favorable to the Constitution had ratified it, since it would go into effect once nine states had ratified it. The Virginia ratifying convention was one of the most dramatic, with leaders of the Revolution divided over the issue. Patrick Henry, who had refused to attend the Philadelphia Convention, saying that he "smelt a rat," spoke in opposition. Each of Henry's impassioned speeches was rebutted by James Madison's careful and knowledgeable remarks. Having worn down the Antifederalists (as the opponents of the Constitution were called) with logic, the Federalists carried the day, and the Constitution was ratified. The Antifederalists agreed to abide by the result, even though there had been threats of armed rebellion. The decision of Antifederalists to accept the Constitution and to participate in the government it created was one of the most important choices made in this era.

In New York, the Federalists stalled the debate until news of Virginia's ratification arrived. Then they posed the inevitable question: Ten states had now voted in favor and the Constitution had been ratified; would New York join in or not? Eventually it was ratified by all the states. As a condition for ratification, several states had insisted that the first Congress consider a number of amendments. These amendments became the Bill of Rights.

Ratifying the Constitution: Ideas

The Constitution was the product of many compromises, and it did not precisely fit anyone's previous ideas. As the Federalists explained the benefits of the Constitution in terms that would make sense to skeptical Americans, and as the Antifederalists tried to explain what they thought was wrong with it, a new understanding of what American government should be evolved. Although there were still significant disagreements, this new understanding, which incorporated the Bill of Rights, was sufficiently broad that Antifederalists could join the new government.

Nonetheless, the differences between the Federalists and Antifederalists were profound. As a rule, the Antifederalists were more rural and less involved in the market, came from the western or backwoods regions, and were more likely to be veterans of the militia than of the Continental army. The Antifederalists were, above all, old-line republicans who continued to use the language of corruption, tyranny, and enslavement, although now it was the Federalists, not the British government, who represented the danger to liberty.

The Antifederalists believed passionately in the local community. They asserted that republics could survive only in homogeneous communities, where all people had the same interests and values. They believed that too much diversity, whether economic, cultural, ethnic, or religious, destroyed a republic. One Massachusetts Antifederalist criticized the Constitution because it would not allow states to cut off the flow of immigration so as "to keep their blood pure." Although Antifederalists generally, like Federalists, supported freedom of religion, they also favored the spread of Protestantism as a means for assuring morality.

At the same time, the Antifederalists were committed to individual rights, and it is to them that the nation is indebted for the Bill of Rights. They retained the republican fear of power, and they did not trust the person they could not see. If government were remote, then it would become oppressive, it would deprive the people of their liberties, and it would tax them. One of the most consistent complaints of the Antifederalists was not so much that taxation would be enacted without representation as that it would be enacted at all. If the national government needed money, let it ask the states for it (although this system had been tried and had failed under the Articles of Confederation). The Antifederalists turned against the new government out of the same fear of centralized government and hatred of taxation that had led them to revolt against Britain. The Antifederalist contribution to American political thought was a continuing critique of government itself.

Federalists shared many of the beliefs of the Antifederalists. They were firmly committed to the rights of individuals, which was why they so readily accepted the Antifederalist proposal to list and protect those rights as amendments to the Constitution. The second area of overlap was a suspicion of government. Most Federalists agreed with Thomas Paine that "government even in its best state is but a necessary evil." The separation of powers and elaborate series of checks and balances that the Constitution created, as well as the system of federalism itself, reflects this fear. The Federalists divided power; unlike the Antifederalists, they did not deny it.

Their experience in the market economy, as officers in the Continental army and as members of the national government, provided the Federalists with a different perspective on political economy. They had come to believe that all people were motivated by self-interest. While the Antifederalists hoped to reform people out of their self-interest, the Federalists were willing to accept self-interest and build a government around it.

The experience of the 1780s had convinced the Federalists that no government could rest entirely on the virtue of its people. The challenge was to construct a government out of imperfect human materials that would preserve liberty instead of destroying it. In *The Federalist* No. 10 (one of a series of 85 essays known as the *Federalist Papers,* written by Madison, Hamilton, and John Jay and published anonymously to influence the ratification debate), Madison explained that the causes of conflict "are sown into the nature of man." The only way of eliminating them would be either by "giving to every citizen the same opinions, the same passions, and the same interests" (the Antifederalist solution) or by destroying liberty itself. But "as long as the reason of man continues fallible, and he is at liberty to exercise it, different opinions will be formed." Toleration was the price of liberty and the necessary result of human imperfection.

In the Philadelphia Convention, the Federalists had been so intent on working out compromises and reconciling their own states' competing interests that they had not had time to develop a philosophy to explain the profound changes they were proposing. That philosophy emerged from the ratification debates, where it was met by the alternative philosophy of the Antifederalists. Both these bodies of thought, sometimes in harmony, sometimes in disagreement, constitute the legacy of the Revolution. This dialogue has continued to frame American government from their day until ours.

Conclusion

In rejecting the increasingly centralized British state, the Revolutionaries were clear about what they did not want. Over the course of the Revolution, they began to envision the kind of society and nation that they hoped to create. It would ensure individual liberty and economic opportunity. But this was a vague vision for the future. As the first modern nation created by revolution, the United States was entering uncharted territory. Winning independence from the world's most powerful nation, ratifying the federal Constitution, and planning for the admission of new territories into the federal union were all extraordinary accomplishments, unique in world history.

Yet there were many problems left unresolved. Not only was Britain still occupying forts in the Northwest Territory, but the European nations were skeptical that the new nation would survive. Although the United States had more than doubled its size, much of the new territory could not be settled because it was inhabited by Indians who refused to recognize America's sovereignty. There were also disagreements among Americans themselves, particularly about the meaning of democracy. How could a nation founded on the principle of liberty practice slavery? How would individual rights be reconciled with the general welfare? Whose economic interests would be served? The American people had begun a great experiment whose outcome was far from assured.

Further Readings

Douglas Bradburn, *The Citizenship Revolution: Politics and the Creation of the American Union, 1774–1804* (2009). A new interpretation of the creation of the new American government that focuses on citizenship.

David Brion Davis, *The Problem of Slavery in the Age of Revolution, 1770–1823* (1975). A brilliant analysis that places the first debates about slavery in America in the context of the first worldwide abolition movement.

Linda K. Kerber, *Women of the Republic: Intellect and Ideology in Revolutionary America* (1980). An older book, but still unsurpassed at demonstrating the centrality of gender to Revolutionary ideology and the importance of Revolutionary ideology in thinking about gender.

Cassandra Pybus, *Epic Journeys of Freedom: Runaway Slaves of the American Revolution and Their Global Quest for Liberty* (2006). A succinct but moving account of the thousands of slaves who took advantage of the Revolution to leave slavery for other parts of the world.

Charles Royster, *A Revolutionary People at War: The Continental Army and American Character, 1775–1783* (1979). A dazzling and beautifully written analysis of conflict between ideology and military necessity in the winning of the Revolution.

John Shy, *A People Numerous and Armed: Reflections on the Military Struggle for American Independence* (1990). A provocative series of essays that places the war for American independence in the wider context of military history.

Alan Taylor, *The Divided Ground: Indians, Settlers, and the Northern Borderland of the American Revolution* (2006). An important book by a gifted storyteller that puts Indians at the center of nation making in the era of the American Revolution.

Gordon S. Wood, *The Creation of the American Republic, 1776–1787* (1969). One of the most important books ever written on the American Revolution, it makes a powerful case describing a profound change in the way some Americans thought about the nature and purpose of government over the course of the Revolution.

Alfred F. Young, *Masquerade: The Life and Times of Deborah Sampson, Continental Soldier* (2004). A remarkable book about a remarkable woman, Deborah Sampson, who disguised herself as a Continental soldier to fight for the American cause in the Revolution, and an excellent example of how history can be written "from the bottom up."

Who, What

Richard Henry Lee 216
Thomas Jefferson 216
Common Sense 218
Loyalists 223
Shays's Rebellion 236
Coverture 237
Northwest Ordinance 243
Federalists 248
Antifederalists 249

Review Questions

1. Why was Revolutionary ardor highest at the beginning of the war?
2. What were American and British strategies for winning the war? What were the chief challenges the Americans faced in mounting the war, and how did they affect military strategy? What were the constraints upon the British in waging a war on American soil?

>> Timeline >>

▼ 1774
Intolerable Acts

▼ 1775
Battles of Lexington and Concord
Fort Ticonderoga seized
Battle of Breed's Hill
Second Continental Congress convenes
Continental army created, with George Washington in charge
Congress adopts "Declaration of the Causes and Necessities of Taking Up Arms"
George III declares colonists in rebellion
Governor Dunmore offers freedom to Virginia slaves who fight for the British
Continental army attacks Canada

▼ 1776
Thomas Paine writes *Common Sense*
Declaration of Independence
Articles of Confederation drafted
British capture Manhattan
Washington captures Trenton and Princeton
New Jersey Constitution allows unmarried, property-owning women to vote
Washington captures Princeton

▼ 1777
British capture Philadelphia
American victory at Saratoga

▼ 1778
French enter into treaty with United States
British conquer Georgia
Sullivan expedition into New York and Pennsylvania

▼ 1779
Continental troops winter at Jockey Hollow

3. What was the effect of the war on American society? How did Americans respond to the challenge presented by their doctrine of equality?

4. Which Americans believed a stronger central government was needed, and why? What were the compromises they made in writing the Constitution?

5. Describe the political philosophies of the Federalists and Antifederalists.

Websites

Common Sense, by Thomas Paine (1776). One of the most influential books ever written, it can be found online at http://www.ushistory.org/paine/commonsense/.

Correspondence Between John and Abigail Adams. From the collections of the Massachusetts Historical Society, transcriptions as well as digital images of the originals. http://www.masshist.org/digitaladams/aea/letter/

The Founders' Constitution, ed. by Philip B. Kurland and Ralph Lerner. An amazing resource for the study of the Constitution and the sources that the Founders drew upon to draft it. Invaluable for studying the origins of the Constitution and early interpretations of it. http://press-pubs.uchicago.edu/founders/help/about.html

Pictorial America. Illustrations of the American Revolution from the Library of Congress's collections of prints and photographs. http://www.loc.gov/rr/print/list/picamer/paRevol.html

The Records of the Federal Convention. The Library of Congress has placed Max Farrand's *The Records of the Federal Convention*, originally published in 1911, online and in searchable form. This is the complete record of the debates in the Constitutional Convention. http://lcweb2.1oc.gov/ammem/amlaw/lwfr.html

For further review materials and resource information, please visit www.oup.com/us/ofthepeople

▼ **1780**
British conquer South Carolina

▼ **1781**
Articles of Confederation ratified
Battle of Guilford Court House
Cornwallis surrenders

▼ **1782**
Franklin begins peace discussions with British

▼ **1783**
Newburgh Conspiracy
Treaty of Paris

▼ **1785**
Land Ordinance of 1785
Virginia and Maryland commissioners meet at Mount Vernon

▼ **1786–1787**
Shays's Rebellion
Meeting at Annapolis

▼ **1787**
Northwest Ordinance
Constitutional Convention

▼ **1787–1788**
Federalist Papers published
Constitution ratified

▼ **1789**
George Washington inaugurated

▼ **1791**
Bill of Rights ratified

CHAPTER 8

Common Threads

>> What were the continuing disagreements about the power of a central government?

>> What were the conflicting values and ideas of citizenship?

>> How did the new nation negotiate with the European powers?

>> What was the status of slavery in the early republic?

Contested Republic

1789–1800

AMERICAN PORTRAIT

>> William Maclay Goes to the Senate

Pennsylvanian William Maclay had supported the ratification of the Constitution, and when the new federal government was launched, he was easily the first person elected to the Senate from his state. But almost from the beginning of his brief service (he drew the initial short term as the Senate staggered its election cycles), Maclay's optimism about the new government began to fade. He recorded that disillusionment in a diary he kept from March 4, 1789, until he left the Senate on March 3, 1791.

Some of Maclay's discontent arose from his own temperament. He had no tolerance for the inefficiency that came with setting up a government. He was impatient with long discussions over the proper wording of the enacting clause of legislation: should it read *be it enacted by the Senate and Representatives*, or simply *be it enacted by the Congress?* He was exasperated when the Senate suspended all its other business while the two houses of the legislature figured out a formal protocol for communicating with one another.

But many of Maclay's irritations with the Senate also suggested deeper and broader disagreements over the nature of a republican government. For example, there were biases of region. Although Maclay was a person of stature at home in central Pennsylvania (he was a wealthy landowner and had served as a state legislator, a judge, and a member of Pennsylvania's executive council), many of Maclay's more cosmopolitan colleagues saw him as something of a country bumpkin. They ignored him in debate and more than once made him the brunt of some demeaning prank. Incapable of taking his revenge on the Senate floor, Maclay nursed his wounded pride in his diary, where he showed his own prejudices: easterners were power hungry, New Englanders were "insolent," Virginians were panderers, especially to the new president.

Maclay also recorded what he saw as an alarming aristocratic bent in the new administration. He thought Washington delivered his inaugural address with too much pretentiousness, and wished "that this first of Men, had read off his address, in the plainest Manner." It was a small irritation, but only 10 days later Vice President John Adams proposed calling the president "His Highness the President of the United States of America and Protector of the rights of the same"—a preposterous title for the executive of a republic, Maclay thought.

Maclay soon found other, more serious signs of antirepublicanism. He was convinced that the executive was trying to encroach on the legislative authority. He considered the Judiciary Act of 1789 "a Vile bill" that gave too much power to the courts. He was appalled by Treasury Secretary Alexander Hamilton's suggestion that the old depreciated Continental currency be redeemed at full face value, a trick to line the purses of speculators, he thought. And he viewed the national bank (proposed by Hamilton in 1790) as "an aristocratic engine . . . operating like a tax in favor of the rich."

On February 12, 1791, just two weeks before Maclay left Congress, the Senate passed a bill leveling an excise tax on certain internal manufactures, including distilled spirits—"a pretty piece of business," Maclay sarcastically dubbed it, a "Box of Pandora with regard to the happiness of America." One of Maclay's colleagues exulted that "we have a Revenue that will support Government." Maclay's response was grim: "I told him perhaps we might undo all. That the high demands we had made, would raise Opposition and That Opposition might endanger the Government."

His worries were well founded. The following July a group of Maclay's fellow Pennsylvanians met in southwestern Pennsylvania to petition for relief from the tax, which fell especially hard on western Pennsylvania distilleries. Their protest was peaceful, but the tax eventually sparked an armed confrontation between citizens and the new federal government. Before it was over, President Washington had marched 30,000 troops into western Pennsylvania against the Republic's own citizens, and the national political scene had dissolved into a battleground of warring parties.

OUTLINE

The United States in 1789

William Maclay was not alone in his reservations about the new federal government. Over the course of the 1790s, differences in style and philosophy would give rise to fierce disagreements among the inhabitants of the new nation and to violent party divisions, until, by the end of the century, some politicians would call for a complete repudiation of the original federal compact. The Constitution had been ratified, but the process of ratification had testified as much to differences among people and groups and states as to shared assumptions. In 1789, the forces toward union and the forces toward fragmentation remained in a powerful tension.

Lands and People

The United States of America had come into formal existence as a republic with the Articles of Confederation in 1781, and its existence had been recognized in the subsequent Paris Peace Treaty with Britain in 1783, and again in the ratification of the federal constitution. Nevertheless, much about the nation remained unclear, unfinished, and highly contested when George Washington took office in 1789.

On the simplest level, the new republic lacked even clear external borders. Although the Treaty of Paris seemed to describe a very specific territory being ceded from Britain to the United States, what seemed clear on the written page was much less clear on the ground. For example, the treaty prescribed a boundary beginning "from the northwest angle of Nova Scotia, viz., that angle which is formed by a line drawn due north from the source of St. Croix River to the highlands; along the said highlands which divide those rivers that empty themselves into the river St. Lawrence, from those which fall into the Atlantic Ocean, to the northwesternmost head of Connecticut River; thence down along the middle of that river to the forty-fifth degree of north latitude . . .," and on across the Great Lakes and roughly down the Mississippi River and across the border of New Spain to the Atlantic. But what exact spot marked "the source of the St. Croix River"? What was the line of the "highlands"? Where was the "middle" of the Connecticut River? These were not abstract problems: Britain and the United States would argue for years over present-day Maine, and Spain claimed a sizable chunk of present-day Mississippi and Alabama that the United States considered its own.

European empires were not the only ones challenging the territorial integrity of the new nation. There were also a hundred thousand or so Native Americans who lived *within* the boundaries of the republic, many of them still crisscrossing large expanses of hunting and growing grounds in seasonal migrations. The United States had acknowledged the sovereignty of Indian nations in eight treaties before the ratification of the Constitution and again in Article I of the Constitution, granting Congress the power "to regulate commerce with . . . the Indian tribes." But the Native Americans rejected both Euro-American ideas of fixed borders and the specific borders delineated in the Treaty of Paris. Most of the "United States of America" was still Indian land to them—the land of the Shawnee, for example, or of the people of the longhouses or of the turtle people. Indian bands made these understandings clear in recurrent raids on poaching settlers in the Carolinas and in the Ohio River valley.

As if all this didn't create enough potential problems for the allegedly sovereign United States, even the states of the new nation disagreed on the division of lands within its borders. Many of the original boundary conflicts had been settled in the 1780s, but Virginia, Georgia, and North Carolina still claimed lands running to the Mississippi River (although North Carolina was looking for a way to cede the land to the United States). And Massachusetts, New Hampshire, and New York still fought over present-day Maine.

The new nation also lacked a clear cultural or ethnic identity. Most of the population was of European descent and most of the Euro-Americans claimed English heritage. But 40 percent—almost half of the white population—were of Scottish, Scots-Irish, Irish, German, Dutch, Swedish, Welsh, or French descent. In Pennsylvania, the English were a minority, their numbers rivaled by the Germans, and they were a bare majority in New York. Being "European" did not necessarily give the white population common cause, or even a common language. The Irish,

Map 8–1 Western Expansion, 1785–1805 Between the Treaty of Paris (1783) and the Louisiana Purchase (1803), Americans flooded into the territories that lay between the Appalachians and the Mississippi River. Then (as later) migration often followed rivers and valleys into the interior of the continent. *Data from Gregory Evans Dowd,* A Spirited Resistance: The North American Indian Struggle for Unity, 1745–1815 *(Baltimore: Johns Hopkins University Press, 1991), p. 92.*

Table 8–1 Americans in 1790

Population 1790: 3,929,000					
Northeast		**Northcentral**		**South**	
Whites	1,901,000	Whites	50,000	Whites	1,271,000
African Americans	67,000	African Americans	1,000	African Americans	690,000
Urban	160,000	Urban	0	Urban	42,000
Rural	1,807,000	Rural	51,000	Rural	1,919,000
Free African Americans	58,000				
African American slaves	700,000				

Welsh, and Scots bore old colonial animosities toward the English (who often returned the sentiment). England and France had just ended a prolonged war with each other (the fourth in a century), much of it fought in North America.

Many Americans, especially middling and wealthy families in cities and villages, were churchgoers, and religion separated them as much as it united them. The English, Welsh, Dutch, Swedish, and many Germans were Protestant—but not the same *sort* of Protestants—while the Irish and most of the French were Catholic, in a century in which Protestant-Catholic differences provided a central justification for European wars. During the Revolutionary War, many of these differences had been submerged in the fight against a common enemy, but they reemerged with independence.

Roughly 18 percent of the total population of 3.9 million consisted of enslaved Africans, African Americans, and Afro-Caribbeans (sometimes with mixed European or Native American heritage)—people or the descendants of people brought to the United States under coercion from hundreds of cultures, speaking hundreds of languages and dialects, and carrying with them the customs of hundreds of different societies. In large areas of Virginia and South Carolina, slaves made up at least half of the population. Moreover, although most enslaved persons lived and worked in the mid-Atlantic or southern states, slavery was not a peculiarly southern institution. In 1789 northerners still owned more than 30,000 slaves. New York City had the second highest concentration of enslaved people in the nation, after Charleston, South Carolina. Northern merchants remained active in the overseas slave trade, and countless shippers, merchants, and artisans in the North relied on business ties to the South. Some Americans spoke out against the institution in the years after the Revolution, but the Constitution implicitly recognized slavery as a part of the United States republic in the Three-Fifths Compromise and explicitly protected the institution for at least 20 years.

Ways of Living

The United States was overwhelmingly a rural nation. Ninety-seven percent of the almost 4 million people ennumerated in the first census lived in the countryside, most of them on family farms of 50–100 acres. These farming families combined self-sufficiency with barter and trade. As Samuel Goodrich later recalled of his rural New England boyhood, "every family lived as much as possible within itself." Men

Map 8–2 Distribution of Black Population, 1775 At the founding of the nation, the overwhelming majority of African Americans lived in the South and were enslaved. In parts of the South Atlantic states, African Americans had long outnumbered whites. (Future states here are identified in parentheses.) *Lester J. Cappon et al., eds.,* Atlas of Early American History: The Revolutionary Era, 1760–1790 *(Princeton, NJ: Princeton University Press)*

and boys grew grain for meal and flour; women and girls put in a family garden for vegetables, tended orchards for fruit, and kept chickens, and a cow or pig or two for milk and meat.

And yet almost no families were entirely self-reliant. Rural households were tied to villages, where they bought, sold, and bartered with small shopkeepers and independent craftspeople for what they could not produce. Even though the Goodriches of Connecticut grew much of their own food and made their "own bread . . . soap, candles, butter, cheese, [and] cloth," they also traded in a general store and hired the services of a butcher, a shoemaker, a carpenter, a seamstress,

A Farmer Plowing His Field Near the Moravian Settlement of Salem, North Carolina In 1789, most Americans lived in the countryside and considered farming the activity most likely to produce political virtue in the new republic. As this illustration suggests, by "farming" Americans meant not simple subsistence, but a division of the land into cultivated, privately owned (and at least partly commercial) property.

and a spinner. Some households combined farming and craftwork: a farm woman might also serve as midwife to her surrounding community, or might do specialized sewing for wages; a man might work as a blacksmith or mason when he wasn't tending his fields.

Not everyone who was technically free owned property. Perhaps as many as one-third of nonenslaved rural Americans lived and worked as indentured servants or as hired farm laborers, paid (often on seasonal contracts) in some combination of wages and their keep. Others became squatters, former servants or hired laborers who moved to the edges of settlements to claim a piece of property simply by their labor, without benefit of legal title.

For white settlers, daily life was a combination of extremes. Constant outdoor hard work through the growing season was punctuated by indoor tedium in the coldest months. Most families saw friends or government officials only rarely. Settlers traveled only rarely to the town centers where elections were held. Their most frequent encounters with government were likely to be run-ins with surveyors (and the sheriffs who protected them), appearances in local courts to fight out boundary disputes, or petitions complaining that state government or the new federal government had not done enough to drive off Native Americans. In New England, the cash-poor economy ran on paper debts to neighbors, that is, notes in account books that said someone owed someone else a certain amount of money. Merchants often sued poor farmers to collect those debts. Theoretically, adult men were liable for militia service, but their participation depended on needs at home, the local prestige of the militia leader, and the immediate aims of the call-up. Some folks—squatters, for example—actively avoided contact with the law altogether.

But this isolation from the rest of the world stood in stark contrast to the crowding of everyday family life. Most families lived in houses with only a couple of rooms. Women cooked in dangerous walk-in hearth fireplaces, in the same small, drafty, earthen-floored rooms where their husbands repaired bridles, their daughters mended clothing or kneaded bread, and their youngest children learned their letters.

The roughly 5 percent of the free population who lived in the coastal port cities lived very different lives—different from the country people and different from each other. At one extreme were the few very wealthy families: southern planter families and northern landed proprietors who kept city houses, and large merchants who lived in the port cities. These groups lived in commodious houses with imported furnishings, foods, and wines, and numerous servants. The landed proprietors and great planters were always attentive to the backcountry, where slave rebellions or squatter revolts might threaten their investments. Still, most very wealthy Americans—and certainly the merchants—identified more strongly with their European counterparts than with their compatriots, many of whom they considered decidedly inferior to themselves.

Below them on the economic and social ladder was the large but amorphous "middling" group—householders who were able to put together a relatively secure livelihood from a combination of household production (including sometimes a small garden and a few chickens or pigs) and the income of a profession, craft, or small shop. Many of these people did not own their own homes, and many, even middling craftsmen, lived in small and fairly crowded dwellings, where household labor and paid labor intermingled with family life and sociability in the same or closely adjacent spaces.

Second Street, Philadelphia As the view of this busy street scene in Philadelphia shows, social, commercial, political, and religious—"public" and "private"—life all commingled on the streets of the the early republic's cities.

The poor made up the biggest segment of urban life, although this group, too, defied easy categorization. These were people, men and women and children, who made their living as indentured or hired servants, as apprentices and shop helpers, as day laborers, piecework seamstresses, or in any one of hundreds of makeshift occupations of the streets—selling salvage coal, for example, or vending food, or begging. Indentured and hired servants, apprentices, and journey craft workers sometimes lived with their masters and employers. But that older model of paternalism was already giving way to the mixed blessings of wage payment. Poor people sometimes packed an entire family into a single rented room, constructed makeshift hovels at the edges of town, or lived in the nooks and crannies of the alleys.

Most of the small but growing free black population must be counted among the poor. Although the disruptions of wartime and postwar emancipations were already nurturing a community of free black Americans, their numbers remained small in 1790—perhaps 60,000 at most, divided fairly evenly between the northern and the southern states. Even in New England, enslaved African Americans outnumbered free African Americans. Lacking the money to purchase land, most free blacks lived in port cities, where they worked in domestic service, the trades, day labor, or in small enterprises that could be launched with little capital, like running a grocery out of their home, cleaning chimneys, or selling soup or coffee in the streets. Free property-owning African American males enjoyed the right to vote in many northern and even some southern states in the first years of the republic, but few black men had sufficient property to activate that right.

Enslaved Americans lived and worked in a variety of settings. Most lived in the South and most did agricultural labor on the lands of their white owners. But slaves worked farmland in New Jersey and New York and throughout New England, as well. The largest of holdings—for example, the rice plantations of Georgia—ranged up to thousands of acres worked by several hundred slaves. But smaller white farmers often owned or rented the services of a slave—commonly throughout the South but also in New Jersey, Delaware, New York, and, in smaller numbers, throughout New England. Not all slaves worked in the fields. Some, like Jupiter Hammon of Long Island, New York, worked as a clerk in his owner's business and traveled back and forth to New York City. Others worked at crafts, or in their owners' homes as servants. Their lives had not been much improved by the Revolution, and in some important ways slaves were far worse off than they had been under British rule. In southern states, the fear of slave rebellion had resulted in tighter controls and harsher treatment during the war. In the postwar period, state legislatures made it more difficult for owners to emancipate slaves, and those slaves who were emancipated were often old and deemed of little economic value by their owners.

> I was about four years old. My mother had several children, and they were sold upon master's death to separate purchasers. She was sold . . . to a Georgia trader. . . . After [my new master] had purchased me . . . he took me before him on his horse, and started home; but my poor mother, when she saw me leaving her for the last time, ran after me, took me down from the horse, clasped me in her arms, and wept loudly and bitterly over me. My master seemed to pity her, and endeavored to soothe her distress by telling her that he would be a good master to me, and that I should not want anything. She then . . . besought my master to buy her and the rest of her children, and not permit them to be carried away by the negro buyers; but whilst thus entreating him to save her and her family, the slave-driver, who had [already] bought her came running in pursuit of her with a raw-hide in his hand. When he overtook us, he told her he was her master now, and ordered her to give that little negro to its owner. . . . he gave her two or three heavy blows on the shoulders . . . , snatched me from her arms, handed me to my master . . . and dragged her back towards the place of sale. My master then quickened the pace of his horse; and . . . the cries of my poor parent became more and more indistinct—at length they died away in the distance, and I never again heard the voice of my poor mother.
>
> Charles Ball,
> describing the last time he saw his mother

Individual and small groups of Native Americans were still common sights even in more settled Euro-American areas—showing up at farmers' homes or village stores to swap goods or beg food. The farther inland one traveled, the more Native Americans visibly claimed the landscape of the new republic, either in their migrations to and from hunting and growing grounds, or in settled communities that functioned as important points of socializing, trade, and diplomacy for French, Spanish, and American traders as well. The town of Kekionga ("Miami Town") illustrated the vibrancy of Indian economies in the late eighteenth century. Kekionga was strategically located east of Lake Erie on the portage of the Maumee and Wabash Rivers, near a British fort. The village was surrounded by huge cornfields and vegetable gardens, supported large herds of cattle, and accommodated guests of all backgrounds and purposes. Residents and visitors bargained furs, tools, quills, beads, animals, food, and services.

Native Americans did live under systematic forms of governance, although those systems were less centralized than the new government of the United States.

Most Indian communities identified their leaders through consensus rather than formal balloting. Councils met as needed and policy was implemented through the personal authority of leaders and the willingness of others to follow them. Over the years, Native Americans had shared land and resources, reconciled differences, sustained elaborate and long-distance trade relations, and supported powerful intertribal confederacies. Where native people differed from Americans of European descent was in their views of what constituted an enlightened way of life. Eastern Woodland and Great Lakes Indians did not share Euro-American views on the importance of privately owned property. Few Indian societies valued material accumulation for its own sake. Instead, they encouraged gift giving as a mark of rank. White American society seemed to native people to be driven by an "insatiable avarice" that clouded the heart and distorted the mind.

In a country of such diversity, its population spread across hundreds of thousands of square miles, divided by mountain ranges and rivers, by languages, cultures, already long-established enmities and by the institution of slavery, where was the glue to make a nation?

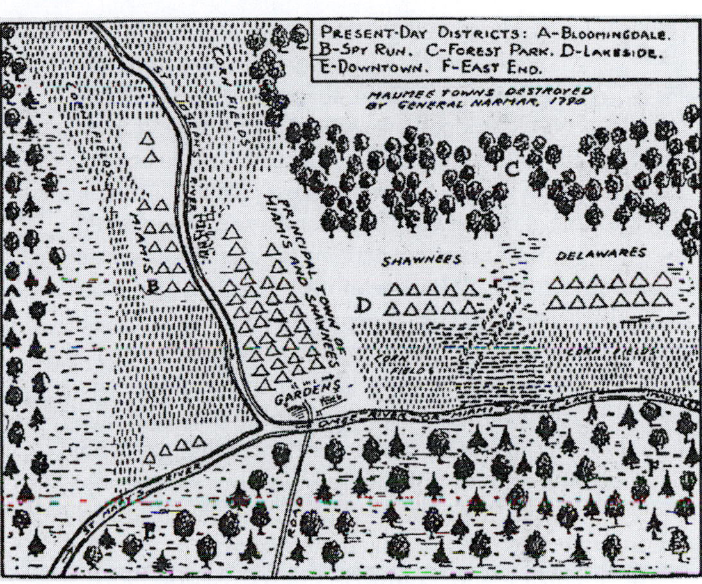

Maumee River Indian Towns This 1790 drawing suggests the complex economic arrangement of the Maumee River Indian towns and the diverse groups that occupied the towns.

The First Emancipation Movements

Although slavery had existed in America for over 150 years by the ratification of the Constitution, its perpetuation into the new republic was not a foregone conclusion. By 1789, many European nations were beginning to reconsider their own involvement in the slave trade. Even England, which led all other nations in slave trafficking by the late eighteenth century, outlawed slavery within its borders and by 1783 was in the early throes of a dedicated 50-year-long drive to abolish both English involvement in the slave trade and the ownership of slaves by English subjects outside of England (including in the British colonies). Although Napoleon would later resurrect slavery in the French colonies, in 1794 revolutionary France abolished slavery in the nation and all of its colonies.

Such moves might have been conceivable in the United States. Whether they were prepared to embrace a racially mixed society or not, many white Americans considered slavery an immoral and antirepublican institution. Numerous Christian denominations (notably including Quakers, Baptists, and Methodists) spoke out against it. None of the first state constitutions specifically recognized slavery, and many central and northern states took steps to outlaw it, either directly in their new state constitutions or in subsequent state supreme court decisions interpreting those constitutions. Vermont, Massachusetts, and New Hampshire enacted state constitutions with broad declarations of rights, although it took a series of court decisions in Massachusetts to make that declaration operable in terms of slavery.

AMERICAN LANDSCAPE

>> Philadelphia

Philadelphia served as the nation's capital in the 1790s. This was the city where the new doctrines of freedom were given shape, in new Congress Hall just west of Independence Hall, in humble homes, and in the president's mansion.

Philadelphia was America's biggest city, and growing bigger by the day. Between 1780 and 1790, the population grew by more than 50 percent, to 42,520. Once the Revolution concluded, European immigrants began to arrive again; at the same time, people from the countryside flocked to the city. The rapid growth in the city's population led to overcrowding, especially for the laboring class. Poor people were renters, living in rooming houses or back alleys, typically in overcrowded wooden buildings. Tailor William Smith and his wife shared their tiny home—550 square feet—with their three children and two boarders. Mrs. Smith cooked their meals in her fireplace.

The financier Robert Morris offered George Washington and his family the use of his home on Market Street. Morris had already expanded the house once. By the standards of the day, it was a mansion, two-thirds the size of the White House, which would be built several years later. It already had at least six bedrooms and four servants' rooms, as well as a detached two-story kitchen, an ice house, a bath house, and a stable for twelve horses, but it was not large enough for Washington's household. Washington added a two-story bow to one side of the house and a number of rooms for his servants. When the Washingtons took up residence in November, they had with them about thirty people, not only the president and his wife Martha, but her grandchildren, his secretary and the secretary's wife, three more male secretaries, eight African slaves from Mount Vernon, and about fifteen white servants.

At this time, Philadelphia was also home to about 1,600 African Americans, two-thirds of whom were free and who created there the nation's first significant free black community. James Oronoko Dexter, one of the leaders of that community, lived only a few blocks from Independence Hall, on the north side of Fifth Street, between Arch and Race, which was then on the periphery of the city. This was a densely populated region of the city, filled with frame-and-brick buildings that served as the homes and workshops of the artisans, laborers, and merchants who lived there. Dexter's house, which he shared with his wife and family, was described in 1791 as a "very plain" two-story house sitting on a 20-by-80-foot lot. Dexter's wife Sarah worked as a washerwoman.

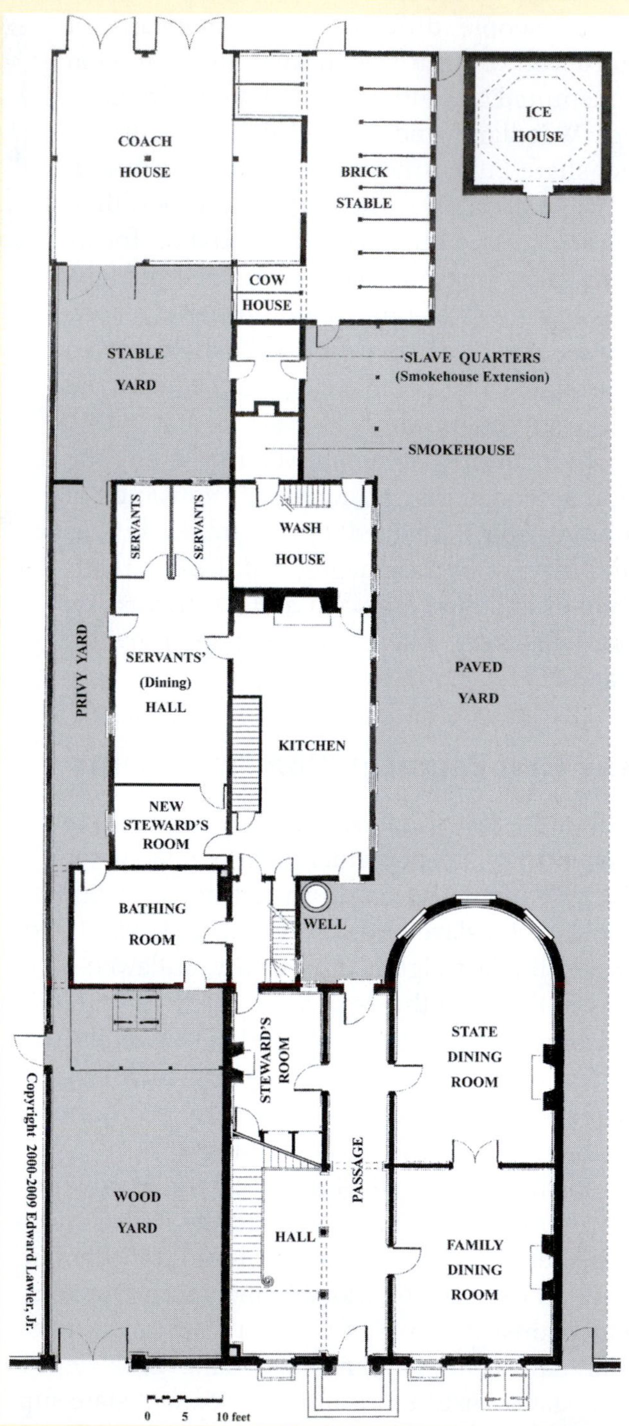

Floor Plan of the President's House in Philadelphia. This is how historians think the first floor of George Washington's house might have looked. The servants' hall and the slave quarters were added by Washington in 1790.

The center of the free black community was only two blocks from the president's house, and it was to that community that Oney Judge, Martha Washington's young chambermaid, turned when she wanted to make her escape from slavery. When Washington's term was coming to an end, and the slaves were told that they would all soon return to Virginia, Judge decided to liberate herself. "Whilst they were packing up to go to Virginia," she later explained, "I was packing to go, I didn't know where; for I knew that if I went back to Virginia, I should never get my liberty. I had friends among the colored people of Philadelphia, had my things carried there beforehand, and left Washington's house while they were eating dinner."

Her friends put her on board a boat bound for Portsmouth, New Hampshire, where, however, it was her bad luck to run into the daughter of the Washingtons' good friend, Senator John Langdon. "*Oney!*" she called out. "Where in the world have you come from?" The young woman could not understand why anyone would run away "from such an excellent place." "Yes—I know," Oney Judge replied. "But I wanted to be free, misses; wanted to learn to read and write."

Informed that his slave was in Portsmouth—where slavery was still legal, although unpopular—Washington asked a government official there to send Judge back. The official did not see how he could do it "without exciting a riot or mob," and so Judge remained in New Hampshire. Several years later, however, one of Martha Washington's nephews turned up at Judge's house, where she told him, "I am free now and choose to remain so." When the nephew told Senator Langdon that he planned to seize Judge by force, the senator passed word to Judge so that she could go into hiding.

As the gospel of liberty spread through the new nation, slaves such as Oney Judge seized their own freedom, and along the way they had help from free blacks and whites both, expanding the landscape of American freedom. ●

Pennsylvania had been home to an active abolition movement since at least 1775, when Anthony Benezet organized the Society for the Relief of Free Negroes Unlawfully held in Bondage. African Americans were important voices in this growing abolition sentiment. In his 1786 Address to the Negroes of the State of New York, Jupiter Hammon, enslaved on Long Island and the first published African American author, called upon slaves to obey their masters, refrain from stealing, and cultivate humility. But he also noted that slaves would be welcomed in heaven (where "we shall find nobody to reproach us for being black, or for being slaves," and advocated gradual emancipation. Phillis Wheatley (1753–1784), the first published African American poet, wrote mainly about religion, not slavery. As she showed in "On Being Brought From Africa To America," the subject of salvation led easily to the subject of slavery: "Some view our sable race with scornful eye, / 'Their colour is a diabolic die.'/ Remember, Christians, Negros, black as Cain, / May be refin'd, and join th' angelic train."

Although the process of emancipation in the North was sometimes slow and, in many places, contested, the first steps toward the elimination of slavery had been taken. By 1804, every state north of Delaware had placed slavery on the road to extinction. In the South, no state constitution specifically recognized slavery in 1789 and no southern political leaders rose publicly as proslavery leaders—but there was no strong abolitionist organization either. With slavery on the path to extinction in the North and it persisting in the South, the distinctions between North and South became more pronounced.

Conflicting Visions of Republican Society

Agreeing on a structure for the new republic had been no easy matter. It had taken free Americans 13 years to frame the government they now set out to live under: a year to propose the Articles of Confederation, four years to pass them, seven more to fight over them and devise an alternative (the Federal Constitution), and then two

AMERICA AND THE WORLD

>> Transatlantic Talk About the Rights of Women

Abigail Adams's famous 1776 request to her husband, John Adams—that "in the new Code of Laws which I suppose it will be necessary for you to make I desire you would Remember the Ladies, and be more generous and favourable to them than your ancestors"—was not unique in the Atlantic world. Throughout much of Europe, as well as in the new United States, the democratic revolutions of the eighteenth century provoked debate on the social status and political rights of women.

In France, in 1791, Olympe de Gouges, a butcher's daughter, published a "Declaration of the Rights of Woman and Female Citizen," a rebuttal of the omission of women from the revolutionary French manifesto, "Declaration of the Rights of Man." So far, de Gouges complained, the French Revolution had yielded women only "a more pronounced scorn, a more marked disdain." In a point-by-point rewriting of the earlier document, which presumably enumerated the claims of all citizens to "liberty, property, security, and resistance to oppression" (but without mentioning women), de Gouges inserted women into the new social and political contract of France. "[T]he only limits on the exercise of the natural rights of woman," she added, "are perpetual male tyranny." De Gouges insisted, "The laws must be the expression of the general will; all female and male citizens must contribute either personally or through their representatives to its formation; it must be the same for all: male and female citizens, being equal in the eyes of the law, must be equally admitted to all honors, positions, and public employment according to their capacity and without other distinctions. . . ."

Although England did not experience an outright revolution in the eighteenth century, there, too, agitation for political reform stirred debate on the proper role of women in democratic governments. In 1790, historian Catherine Macaulay published her *Letters on Education*, arguing that with the proper education women should be capable of competing equally with men in all aspects of social life. Two years later, in 1792, educator and radical journalist Mary Wollstonecraft published *A Vindication of the Rights of Woman*. Wollstonecraft agreed with most of her contemporaries that women as a group tended to be vain and seemed to lack the reasoning ability required of citizens. But these deficiencies were artificial, she argued, the product of "the tyranny of man" in the family, society, and politics—a tyranny that had deliberately kept women in a state of "ignorance and slavish dependence." In fact, she asserted, women were the moral and intellectual equals of men and, if properly educated, were fully as capable as men of reason and of participation in "all political privileges."

These women were connected by historic circumstance: each lived in a society in which turbulent political change was undercutting old assumptions that rank and property earned political power (including for a few women) and prompting new questions about whether females could be citizens of new democratic nations. They were also connected, however, by acquaintance and by expanding forms of international contact. For example, Mary Wollstonecraft, who acknowledged a deep influence from Catherine Macaulay, followed closely in letters and newspaper accounts the growing repression in France that led to the execution of de Gouges. Abigail Adams corresponded with Macaulay (who had visited the United States in 1785), and, like many men and women in the United States, eagerly read Wollstonecraft's *Vindication* as soon as it became available.

As the revolutionary moment peaked and passed in the three countries, however, it became evident that women's status as citizens would remain ambiguous at best in the new democratic regimes. Various explanations for this failure are possible. De Gouges died in 1793, a victim of the French Reign of Terror, and Wollstonecraft in 1797, following childbirth. In all three countries, moreover, the exhilaration of the revolutionary era was followed by a period of conservative retrenchment, during which the discussion of women's rights as *citizens* narrowed to a discussion of women's domestic contributions to the public welfare (as wives and mothers) and of their right to an education—a discussion confined, moreover, to white women from the prosperous classes. Nowhere did the call for rights for women become a wide-ranging call for universal rights, regardless of class or race as well as gender. Meanwhile, in Europe and the United States, white male suffrage steadily expanded through the nineteenth century, but not until more than 100 years passed did women achieve suffrage in Britain, France, or the United States.

years to ratify it. Even then, many Americans had continued to oppose ratification, and two states (North Carolina and Rhode Island) had not yet ratified the Constitution when George Washington was sworn into office. Moreover, as William Maclay's experience in the first Senate showed, those who had supported the Constitution did not necessarily agree on its meanings or on the principles that should drive a republican society.

A core of assumptions did offer a sort of common ground for many white inhabitants of the new republic. Most free Americans believed that the success of the republic depended ultimately on the political virtue of its citizens, by which they meant the cluster of characteristics that would enable citizens to protect themselves against either would-be tyrants or lawless mobs. For many people these included, in some form, industriousness, independence, and an ability to put self-interest aside for the larger good. Very often, Americans associated these qualities with certain types of economic life. When people grew too wealthy and accustomed to luxury, many Americans believed, they grew lazy and were willing to support corrupt governments for their own selfish purposes. Poverty, on the other hand, led to desperation, riots, and anarchy.

This consensus obscured very real disagreements about what a republic looked like in daily life and about who really embodied the key virtues of a republic. In 1790, 97 percent of free Americans lived in nuclear households (parents and children) on farms or in rural villages, where they produced much of their own food, clothes, tools, and furnishings. For this great mass of the people, republican virtue was rooted in the land, and particularly in the working freehold farm. In *Letters From an American Farmer* (1782), J. Hector St. John de Crevecoeur had identified the new nation as "a people of cultivators scattered over an immense territory . . . animated with the spirit of an industry that is unfettered and unrestrained, because each person works for himself." Thomas Jefferson, who actually managed his lands rather than farmed them himself, had nevertheless echoed this view in his *Notes on the State of Virginia* (1785): "Those who labor in the earth are the chosen people of God, if ever he had a chosen people, whose breasts He has made His peculiar deposit for substantial and genuine virtue." Jefferson thought only the independent farmer could achieve true self-reliance, warning that "Dependence begets subservience and venality, suffocates the germ of virtue, and prepares fit tools for the design of ambition."

This emphasis on labor and the private ownership of land did not mean that rural Americans opposed manufacturing and trade. Farms were tied to villages and most of those villages were tied to larger markets in the port cities and overseas. Even Jefferson considered overseas trade essential to rural virtue, because it gave Americans access to manufactured goods without the blight of industrialization. As trade with Britain improved and the demand for American agricultural products grew both in Europe and in the slave colonies of the West Indies (where plantations focused on commodity crops rather than food to feed their workers), rural Americans grew convinced that the success of the new nation required a booming free international trade.

The profits made by large merchants and landowners were another matter, in the eyes of most farmers. Many of these wealthy families had laid the foundations of their fortunes before the Revolution, with the help of the Crown, and they continued to dominate the economy. In Boston, the wealthy merchant families who made up 10 percent of the population controlled 65 percent of the wealth, while the poorest one-third of the population owned less than 1 percent of the wealth. Great proprietors controlled the most precious commodity of the countryside, land. They hired surveyors to stake their claims, refused to sell homesteads in favor of charging high rents, and threw squatters off the land. Both large landowners and merchants tended to support strong governments, which meant higher taxes for common folks.

Farmers, small shopkeepers, landless settlers, and craft workers saw the wealth accumulated and inherited by large merchant families and families with great landed estates as the moral equivalent of theft. "[N]o person can possess property without laboring," farmer and tavern keeper William Manning emphasized, "unless he get it by force or craft, fraud or fortune, out of the earnings of others." Manning viewed this distinction between "those that labor for a living and those who get one without laboring—or, as they are generally termed, the Few and the Many"—as "the great dividing line" of society.

Unsurprisingly, the "independent Lords" saw matters differently. Merchants and landed proprietors agreed that republican virtue resided in labor, but they meant *commercial* labor, which opened markets and expanded trade, nurtured invention, taught discipline, and contributed new wealth to the community as a whole. Alexander Hamilton, the first secretary of the Treasury of the new nation, was a chief proponent of this view. Born in the West Indies, he was raised by his mother, Rachel, a shopkeeper, who died when he was 13. Hamilton then entered the merchant firm of Beekman and Cruger as a clerk, eventually proving himself so valuable that Cruger paid for his college education. These experiences taught Hamilton that the merchant class (traders, investors, and financiers who risked their private means to generate new wealth, new markets, and new ideas) best embodied the qualities needed in republican citizens.

Just as farmers viewed merchants and financiers with distrust, so wealthy merchants and proprietors often regarded Americans of the middling and laboring ranks as their inferiors. The mass of the people were undisciplined and gullible, Hamilton believed. Vulnerable to the deceptions of fanatics and demagogues, they required proper leadership. City elites dismissed their backcountry compatriots as "yahoos" and "clodpoles." To the rich, the rude huts of homesteaders, their barefoot children, and their diets of beans, potatoes, and coarse bread all signaled not the hardships of settlement, but rather the laziness of the settlers. The merchants and proprietors especially disliked the casualness with which country people treated debt. Rural people conducted trade in a combination of barter, cash, and promissory notes, with records kept casually and payments constantly renegotiated in terms of the goods, services, or whatever paper money might be at hand. Working on a national and international scale, merchants and proprietors needed timely payment, preferably in hard currency, to pay off their own debts, make new investments, or arrange long-distance transactions.

Most white Americans denied that hard work produced republican virtue in slaves. They argued that because slaves could not own the property they produced, slaves' labor could never lead to self-reliance or the stake in the public order essential to citizenship. This view was rife with contradictions. As Thomas Jefferson, himself a slave owner, pointed out in *Notes on the State of Virginia,* slavery undermined the ambition of slave owners. "[I]n a warm climate, no man will labor for himself who can make another labor for him," Jefferson wrote. Even more fundamentally, if slaves were incapable of virtue simply because of their status as slaves, then surely the institution of slavery was itself unrepublican.

Nevertheless, the unrepublicanism seemed to attach itself to the person, and to his or her African American descent, rather than to the institution. Although northern states moved to abolish slavery, they did so only gradually, often expressing concern about the ability of former slaves to adjust to freedom and democracy. The anonymous author of the antislavery tract *Tyrannical Libertymen: A Discourse on Negro-Slavery in the United States* (published in New Hampshire in 1795) argued that during the transition to freedom, younger slaves should be held in "a state of dependence and discipline," after which they should be resettled in the territories. Older slaves should be shipped to Africa. All across the northern states, white craftsmen refused to work in shops that employed free African Americans, white passengers refused to ride in stagecoaches alongside them, and landlords refused to rent them any but the worst housing. Meanwhile, the Naturalization Act of 1790 restricted naturalized citizenship to "free white persons."

Although most Americans believed free white women to be citizens of the nation in some very general sense, many did not believe women should be active in policy making, and women labored under severe legal disabilities and social prejudices in the early republic. Under the English common-law principle of coverture, a married woman subsumed her separate legal identity under that of her husband. Although some individual women (usually wealthy women who had access to special legal measures) did own property in their own names, as a category married women could not own property or wages, could not enter into contracts, and were not the legal guardians of their own children. Still, most women lost control of their property when they married and took little property other than their own clothing in divorce.

Social prejudice also made it difficult for most women to earn an independent living. Both wives and unmarried women continued to ply their skills as midwives, seamstresses, hucksters, grocers, milliners, and in a variety of other trades. But the more lucrative male crafts and professions were closed to them, and most working-women struggled to make ends meet.

If anything, women appear to have faced a growing bias against the idea of female autonomy in the final years of the eighteenth century. The earlier years of the century were by no means a golden age of female independence, yet age, wealth, and family appear to have mattered as much as gender in delineating individual status. And for a time it seemed that women (at least wealthy white women) might be among the beneficiaries of the Revolutionary spirit. Indeed, New Jersey granted single, property-owning women the right to vote in its 1776 state constitution (but rescinded it in 1807), and women participated actively in the discussions both of their own new republic and of the French Revolution. In France and in England, women spoke out publicly against restraints on the natural rights of women.

In the wake of the creation of the new republic, however, attitudes toward women grew more conservatively gendered. As the *Apollo Magazine* put it in 1795, the exemplary woman married and asked no more than that "Her good man [was] happy and her Infants clean." Ironically, these hardening attitudes may in some ways have resulted from the experiment in democracy itself. In the face of ongoing social and political disorder, heavy prescriptions on the conduct of females may have seemed reassuring to some Americans.

The Culture of the Republic

Americans discussed and articulated these views, both the agreements and the disagreements, through a variety of practices—written and simply enacted.

Perhaps most important was the circulation of information through newspapers. Fewer than 20 newspapers were published in all the British North American colonies in 1760, but by 1790 the new republic claimed 106 newspapers; by 1800, there were more than 200. Much of the content of these newspapers was strictly local, but editors sought to fill out their pages (and satisfy their readers) by publishing official government documents and reprinting articles from other cities, states, and even countries.

The 1790s also saw the beginnings of an indigenous fictional literature. In 1789, William Hill Brown published *The Power of Sympathy,* often considered the first genuinely American novel because some of its content was based on contemporary events in Boston. Other novelists also tried to develop distinctly American stories and themes. Actress and author Susannah Rowson's historical novel *Rachel and Reuben* (1798) imagined the lives of the fictional heirs of Columbus, and Charles Brockden Brown chose the countryside outside of Philadelphia as the setting for *Weiland* (1798), a tale of religious zealotry and the fallibility of human reason. In Connecticut, a group of poets known collectively as the Hartford Wits (Federalist in sympathy) produced a series of political satires that celebrated New England as the model for national order and self-discipline.

Regional and national news was easiest to come by in the cities, but a variety of information sources linked city to backcountry and region to region. Copies of periodicals and books found their way out into the countryside, and comparatively high literacy rates produced a reading audience that went beyond urban elites. Gathered in shops, taverns, and homes, those who could not read listened as a coworker, family member, or friend read aloud. Where papers did not reach, travelers, itinerant peddlers, and preachers served as additional conduits of information and opinion. Among the peddlers was Mason Locke "Parson" Weems, whose *The Life and Memorable Actions of George Washington* included the fictional account of Washington's chopping down the cherry tree.

In cities, prosperous Americans established salons (where local luminaries, male and female both, gathered to discuss politics and culture), museums, libraries, and specialized societies of learning. Many of these reflected Americans' fascination with their place in the world and their keen sense of themselves as involved in a distinct historical undertaking. The Philadelphia subscription library, founded in 1731 by Benjamin Franklin and others, became the de facto library of the new government until 1800, when the capital moved to Washington, and the Library of Congress was founded.

For every experience or condition or belief that drew American citizens together, however, there seemed to be another that divided them. Especially, strong attachments to place and great disparities of condition often transformed seemingly shared values and ideas into fodder for sharp conflicts.

William Maclay's disorientation when he left central Pennsylvania for New York City reflected the close identification most Americans felt—even most educated and prosperous Americans, like Maclay—with the regions, states, and even sections of states within which they lived, rather than with the nation as a whole. If anything, the process of ratification had underscored just how many differences remained among Americans. Advocates had won approval only by putting together a different coalition of interests in each state, not by drawing on a uniform set of interests across all the states. Even so, a bare nine states had ratified the document and virtually all of these had made qualifications.

The localism that characterized American society in 1789 was evident in daily life as well as in formal political actions. Never traveling far from home, ordinary Americans did not know much about other parts of the country and tended to view them as quite different, with that sense of differentness assuming a more exotic—and frightening—quality the greater the distance. Writing from Massachusetts to Philadelphia in 1776, Abigail Adams had asked John whether it was true that in Virginia the "gentery" were "Lords" and "the common people vassals." Those who did travel often described other parts of the nation as if they were commenting on the life and manners of a foreign country. When he toured New England in 1790, William Loughton Smith, of Charleston, South Carolina, was so unnerved by the quiet of Connecticut towns that he felt like he "had entered a deserted village." The hard economic times of the war and postwar era also nursed a suspicion of strangers, who might end up a drain on town resources.

William Maclay's tendency to describe the differences he experienced as an East-West contrast was also common in the early years of the nation. Local backcountry revolts in the Carolinas in the 1760s and Shays's Rebellion in western Massachusetts in 1786–1787 had underscored the differences of interest between backcountry farmers and eastern commercial elites, differences that settlers experienced as conflicts of interest between "the people" and eastern governments. This sense of division and distrust persisted in the 1790s. Kentuckians objected that Congress intended to sacrifice the backcountry to the interests of eastern merchants.

These disagreements ran deep at the founding of the republic and were not confined to formal politics or to polite discussion and restrained debate. Newspapers were often venues of sharp local bias and became the arena of vituperative debates over the proper direction of republican politics. They were accompanied into the public arena by vitriolic political tracts and single-page "broadsides" that attacked individual politicians. Among these was William Manning's 1798 "Key of Liberty," condemning the predations of the "Few" upon the "Many."

By no means did all of the arguments take place in print. Wealthy city people met in parlors and salons to discuss the concerns of the day, while common Americans held their arguments on the grounds of courthouses and churches, on post office porches, at liveries and craft shops and in taverns like the one run by William Manning. Travelers, itinerant peddlers, and preachers served as conduits of information and opinion. In Virginia, peddlers organized mercantile fairs that brought together large groups of people to swap news as well as make deals.

The early republic was also an era of school building, primarily academies to prepare sons for professions or university training and daughters to participate in the discussions (if not the formal electoral politics) of republican society. More than 350 academies for females opened between 1790 and 1830. The first to be publicly incorporated was the Young Ladies' Academy of Philadelphia (1787). Its goal was to educate young women in "Reading, Writing, Arithmetic, English, Grammar, Composition, and Geography." The school was intended for young women of prosperous families, to be sure, but its curriculum implicitly made the argument that women could flourish in a challenging academic environment.

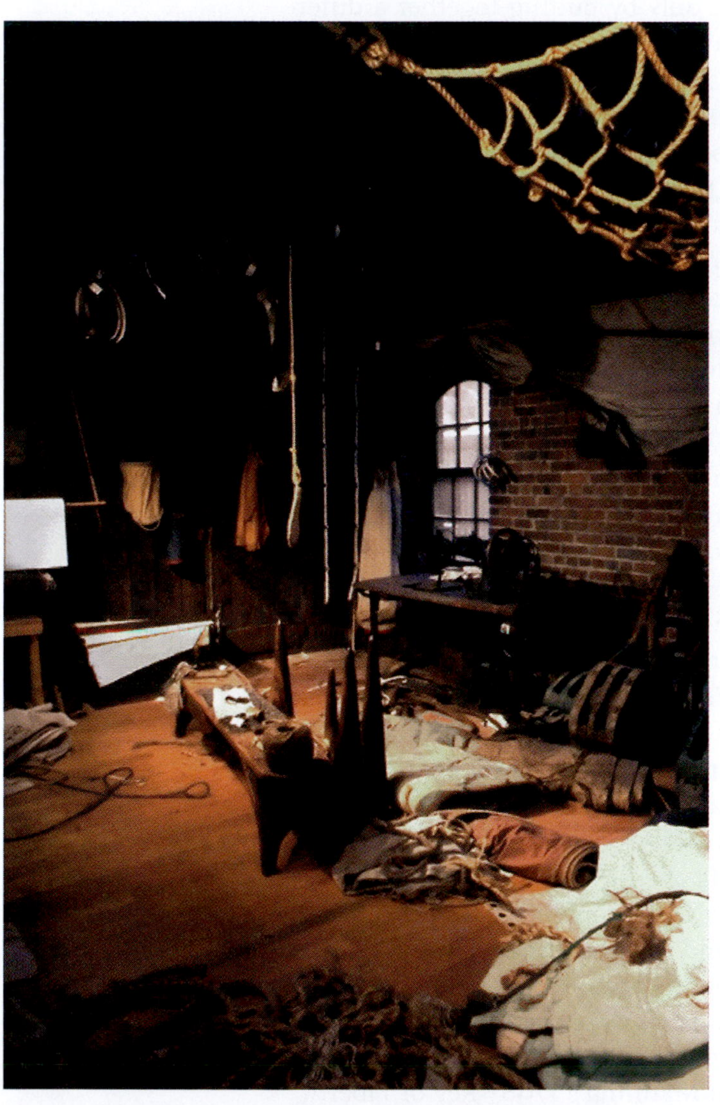

Sailmaker's Shop A reconstruction of the interior of a sailmaker's shop.

Citizens also formed societies intended to provide relief to the needy in their communities. A group of prosperous Philadelphians established an almshouse to improve the care and housing of the poor and to teach them the values of industry, and a penitentiary to reform criminals by isolating them from one another's influence. Jewish organizations founded in New York in the late eighteenth century provided aid for medical care, food, shelter, and burial costs for the city's small Jewish community.

To these associations were added a variety of occupational and manufacturing societies. Masters and journeymen formed craft associations to further their common interests, sometimes against what they perceived as the haughtiness of the merchants. Many of the trades of Philadelphia participated in the Federal Procession of 1789, for example—a visible reminder to the elites that craft workers had their own expectations of the new republic. Promoting a very different vision of political economy, in 1791, in Paterson, New Jersey, Alexander Hamilton and his assistant secretary, Tench Coxe, formed the Society for Establishing Useful Manufacturers, a joint-stock corporation intended to demonstrate the economic virtues of investment cooperation between the private sector and the government.

The Struggle to Form a Government

Concerns about the political economy of the new nation focused not only on the character of citizens, but also on the character and operation of government. Here, too, questions of property loomed large. In *The Federalist* No. 10, James Madison had argued that the most common cause of internal conflict in a nation was "the various and unequal distribution of property," arising from selfish interests on the state and local level. He felt that an important benefit of the new central government would be its capacity "to break and control" provincial interests. Most state ratifying conventions had expressed just the opposite worry, however: they were worried about the self-interests that might control the federal government.

> One of the advantages of manufacturing is "the employment of persons who would otherwise be idle (and in many cases a burthen on the community), either from the byass of temper, habit, infirmity of body, or some other cause, indisposing, or disqualifying them for the toils of the Country. It is worthy of particular remark, that, in general, women and Children are rendered more useful and the latter more early useful by manufacturing establishments, than they would otherwise be. Of the number of persons employed in the Cotton Manufactories of Great Britain, it is computed that 4/7 [4 out of seven] nearly are women and children; of whom the greatest proportion are children and many of them of a very tender age."
>
> ALEXANDER HAMILTON,
> Report on Manufactures, 1791

The States and the Bill of Rights

At the state ratifying conventions, the Federalists had agreed to let the conventions propose amendments to the Constitution, possibly to be added as a bill of rights. Two hundred of these had been suggested (see Chapter 7). A number of Federalists originally opposed the idea of a bill of rights: if the Constitution itself did not protect liberty and property, no appended list of rights would help. At first James Madison had agreed with this view, but by the time he ran for the House of Representatives, he pledged that his first priority would be to secure additional safeguards.

Within a month of Washington's inauguration, Madison set about making good on his promise. By no means did all of the state proposals deal directly with questions of property. For example, the ratifying conventions were adamant about the need for freedom of religion and freedom of the press. The state proposals betrayed a fear that the new federal government would seek to amass power against the interests and freedom of individual citizens. To prevent this, states proposed amendments to limit the power of Congress to levy taxes, and amendments to protect the right to bear arms, and to trial by a jury, as well as the right against unreasonable search and seizure.

Madison never expected to incorporate all 200 of the state proposals in a bill of rights, and he never imagined that he could placate all of the groups critical of the

Constitution. But he did believe that, with a few minor changes, moderate Antifederalists could be brought into sympathy with the new order. This goal guided Madison's selection of proposed amendments. He tended to reject proposals that altered the structure of the central government or strengthened the powers of the states at the expense of the federal government. Instead, he favored amendments that affirmed human rights within the structure already ratified (although the reference to a "well-regulated Militia" in the Second Amendment and the Third Amendment's restrictions on the quartering of soldiers reflected Americans' profound mistrust of standing national armies). The First Amendment protected citizens against congressional interference with freedom of religion, speech, the press, the right of assembly, and the right of petition. The Fourth Amendment protected the rights of citizens "against unreasonable [government] searches and seizures." The Fifth, Sixth, Seventh, and Eighth Amendments laid down the rights of citizens accused of crimes and established protection from "cruel and unusual punishments." The Ninth affirmed that the Constitution's silence on a specific right of the people "shall not be construed" as a denial of that right, and the Tenth ambiguously reserved all rights not delegated to the new government "to the States respectively, or to the people."

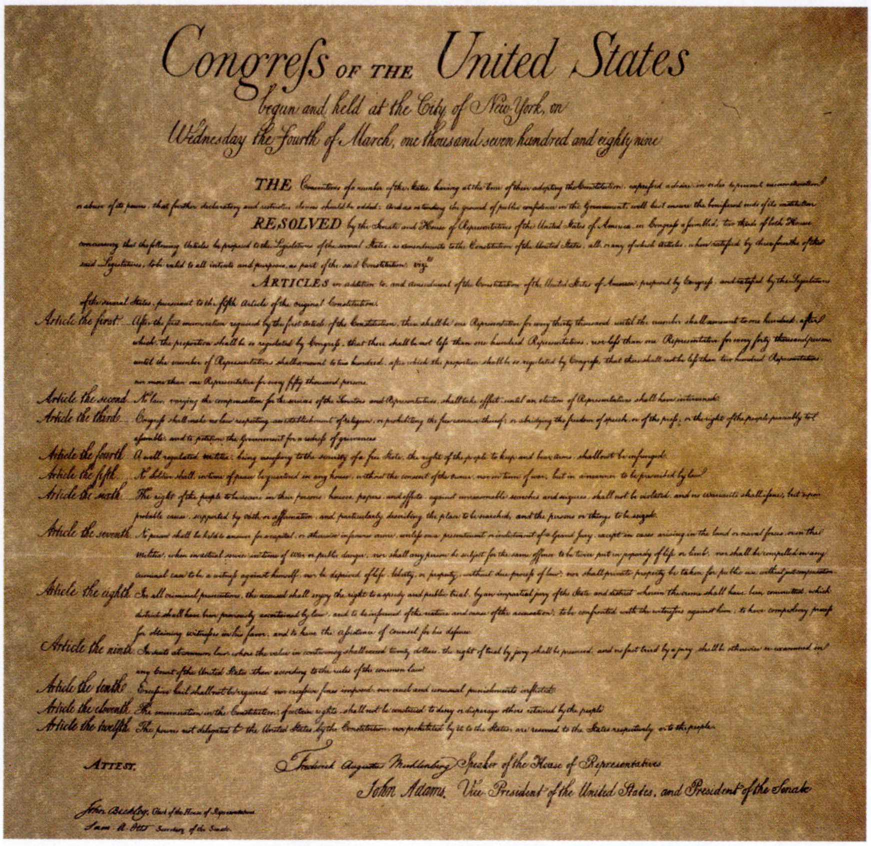
Congress of the United States
begun and held at the City of New-York, on
Wednesday the Fourth of March, one thousand seven hundred and eighty nine

Congress eventually sent twelve amendments to the states for ratification. Of these, two were rejected: one on Congressional compensation (finally adopted in 1992 as the Twenty-seventh Amendment) and one covering representation. The remaining ten amendments were declared in force on December 15, 1791.

Congress Begins Its Work

Although George Washington did not take the oath of office until April 30, his term began on March 4, 1789. By the time Washington was inaugurated, then, Congress was already in session. It had not made a promising start: only 13 members of the House of Representatives and 8 senators were on hand when the first Congress convened.

Among Congress's first tasks was deciding what the president should be called, the task that had so enraged Maclay. Believing that the president of the republic should have an impressive title to demonstrate that the new nation was "civilized," a Senate committee recommended "His Highness the President of the United States of America, and Protector of the Liberties." But the House argued that the Senate's suggestion smacked of aristocratic pretension. In the end, the House insisted simply on "The President of the United States."

Meanwhile, the Congress approved a series of official advisors to the president (the cabinet). Washington's first administration reflected both his own close circle of friends and the political clout of the large states. The president was from Virginia, the most populous state, as were his secretary of state, Thomas Jefferson, and his attorney general, Edmund Randolph. For his secretary of the Treasury he chose former aide-de-camp Alexander Hamilton of New York. Washington's vice president (John Adams), his secretary of war (Henry Knox), and his postmaster general (Samuel Osgood) were from Massachusetts. The Constitution had specified the existence of a third branch of government, a federal judiciary to have power over "all cases, in law and equity, arising under this Constitution, the laws of the United States, and treaties made," but had not offered much of a blueprint for its structure. Congress might have created a federal system that dominated state courts. Recalling the high-handedness of British courts, however, Congress passed the Judiciary Act of 1789, which created a federal court system with limited power. Under its first chief justice, John Jay, the Supreme Court remained a minor branch of government.

Political Economy and Political Parties

As Congress deliberated the structure of government, Secretary of the Treasury Alexander Hamilton turned to the problem of financial solvency. His recommendations to Congress concerning the fiscal operation of the new nation soon polarized views on the political economy.

The first challenge was to raise money for the current expenses of the government. Hamilton proposed that Congress place a tariff on imported goods and the foreign ships carrying them. The Tariff Act of 1789 passed easily. In the coming years the federal government would depend on tariffs for the vast majority of its funds.

Hamilton was also eager for the United States to pay off the enormous debt left over from the American Revolution. He advised that the federal government should guarantee the payment of all remaining state and national debts incurred in the Revolution. Those debts existed in the form of scrip and paper money the states and Continental Congress had used to purchase goods and services during the war. Hamilton suggested that the national government replace all of these obligations dollar-for-dollar with new federal bonds. To fund the plan, he proposed that the government sell additional bonds, the interest from which could be used only to pay off the interest and principal on the debt.

Madison and Jefferson were alarmed. Most southern states had paid their debts by 1790. Federal assumption would force them to help pay northern debts as well, in effect rewarding northern states for being slow to meet their financial obligations. Although many members

 **Table 8–2** Sources of Federal Revenue, 1790–1799

	Tariffs	Internal Taxes	Other (Inc. sale of public lands)
1790–1791	$4,399,000		$ 10,000
1792	3,443,000	$209,000	17,000
1793	4,255,000	338,000	59,000
1794	4,801,000	274,000	356,000
1795	5,588,000	338,000	188,000
1796	6,568,000	475,000	1,334,000
1797	7,550,000	575,000	563,000
1798	7,106,000	644,000	150,000
1799	6,610,000	779,000	157,000

Source: Curtis P. Nettels, *The Emergence of a National Economy, 1775–1815* (White Plains, NY: 1962), p. 221.

of Congress disliked Hamilton's proposal, other issues eventually led to its passage. Southerners were also unhappy about the possibility that the nation's capital (temporarily located in New York) might be moved permanently to Philadelphia. They preferred a site on the Potomac River in Virginia. At last representatives struck a compromise: Hamilton got his debt plan, and southerners got the nation's capital. The following December, Hamilton asked for a series of new taxes, including one on spirits, to generate revenue. This excise tax became law in March 1791.

Hamilton next recommended the creation of a national bank to manage fiscal functions. He saw the bank as ensuring a stable currency and enabling the government to mobilize large amounts of capital for development, two activities he considered essential to an expanding commercial economy. The bank would be chartered by Congress to collect, hold, and pay out government receipts; would hold the new federal bonds and oversee their payment; would issue currency; and would be backed up by government bonds.

The bank proposal passed Congress against the opposition of Madison, Jefferson, and other Virginians, who viewed the bank as an extralegal structure to support the interests of merchants and financiers against "the republican interest." Jefferson advised the president to veto the bill on the grounds that the Constitution gave the federal government no expressed authority to create such an institution, a position known as *strict constructionism*. Hamilton countered that every specified power in the Constitution implied "a right to employ all the means requisite . . . to the attainment" of that power. In granting the federal government the responsibility to coin and regulate money, pass and collect taxes, pay debts, and "make all laws which shall be necessary and proper" to these ends, the Constitution implied the power to create a bank. In the end, Washington accepted Hamilton's position and signed the bank bill.

Hamilton's final major recommendation to Congress was that the federal government subsidize domestic manufacturing. Jefferson and Madison were now convinced that the republic was being sold out to the interests of speculators and financiers. Hamilton had been using a Philadelphia newspaper, John Fenno's *Gazette of the United States* (founded in 1789), to promote his views. In October 1791, Jefferson and Madison prevailed on their friend Philip Freneau to come to Philadelphia to establish a newspaper favorable to their position, and Madison began to use Freneau's *National Gazette* to publish a series of essays in which he framed the rationale for the permanent necessity of political parties in a republic. There would always be schemers who placed self-interest above the good of the whole, and true republicans would always be forced to organize against them. Parties, according to Madison, arose in a struggle of the true "republican interest" against dangerous conspirators, a struggle of "good" against "evil." He identified the two groups as "Republicans" and "Anti-Republicans."

In late 1792 and early 1793, sympathizers with Jefferson and Madison became known as Democratic Republicans, after the Democratic Republican Societies that opposed a strong central government and vowed to maintain vigilance against the "monied interests" who threatened "liberty and equality." The societies included some common people, but most of the known members were from middling and even prosperous families. Washington considered the societies dangerous and blamed them for spreading "suspicions, jealousies and accusations of the whole government."

Hamilton and his supporters were no more tolerant of disagreement than were the Democratic Republicans. In the election of 1792, allies of Hamilton identified themselves as supporters of Washington's administration, advocates of the policies of the secretary of the Treasury, or, increasingly, as Federalists, using the name to suggest their abiding commitment to union and the new government. As late as the election of 1794 most candidates resisted formal party alignment, and congressional voting patterns showed little sense of "party" discipline. There were several reasons for this, including the tendency of most citizens (including many of the partisans themselves) to associate political parties with corruption and a loss of independence. By 1796, however, the lines had become clearly drawn. The jumble of labels had sorted itself out to Democratic Republicans and Federalists, and congressional voting patterns revealed a distinct tendency to vote on one side or the other.

Controlling the Borderlands

For all of its symbolic importance as the reservoir of republican order, the backcountry had so far been a setting for constant conflict among owners and settlers and between Indians and Americans.

Americans fought over land prices and rights of ownership. Seeking quick revenue, the government sold large tracts of land to speculators and large proprietors, some of whom were federal officials. For example, Alexander Hamilton and Secretary of War Henry Knox were both silent partners in the huge Macomb Purchase in New York. Proprietors subdivided their tracts for sale, but the resulting prices were often too high for average settlers, who squatted on lands and claimed the rights of possession and improvement, much to the annoyance of the legal owners.

Despite their differences, squatters, proprietors, and governments shared the assumption that the land was theirs to fight over. The Treaty of Paris had contained no acknowledgment of Indian claims, and treaty promises that Indians would be left in peace in exchange for land cessions proved illusory (see Chapter 7). By the time Washington took office in 1789, the backcountries were in an uproar. Undisciplined federal troops and freebooting state militias crisscrossed western lands in search of a fight, often attacking neutral or sympathetic Indian villages. Betrayed and angry, Indians banded together in loose confederations, retaliating against settlers and striking alliances with the British and Spanish.

By 1789, the lives and cultures of Eastern Woodland and Great Lakes nations had been deeply altered by the westward pressure of white settlement. In the North, a group of Iroquoian villages, the battered remnants of a once-powerful confederation, traded large tracts of land for promises of security and called on the tribes of the Northwest Territory to do the same. However, these peoples refused to compromise with the whites and effectively shut down settlement north of the Ohio River valley. In the South, the Creeks, trapped between oncoming white settlement and the Native American nations of the Mississippi River valley, allied with militant Cherokees to keep the Georgia, Tennessee, and Kentucky frontiers ablaze with war parties.

There were additional reasons for Washington to worry about order in the western territories. By 1789, Spain was actively luring United States settlers into New Spain at the foot of the Mississippi River. It was a strategy designed to weaken the loyalty of the West to the new United States government. In the Great Lakes region, meanwhile, Great Britain hung onto the string of forts it had promised to give up as a part of the Treaty of Paris. Many Americans believed that Britain was biding its time to regain control of the lands south of the Great Lakes.

All of this turmoil took its toll in the East. The inability of the national government to control Native Americans angered states, would-be settlers, and the small-business people who expected to profit from settlement. Landowners complained that their property rights were not being protected, and small settlers complained of favoritism in land distribution. Understanding that not only external relations, but also the domestic authority of the federal government was at stake, Washington turned immediately to the problem of the backcountry. His policy was twofold. On the one hand, working with Secretary of War Henry Knox, Washington sought to bring consistency and a greater degree of fairness to Indian policy. On the other hand, he used the territories to demonstrate the power of the federal government.

Less than a month after assuming office, Washington submitted to Congress a report on Indian affairs authored by Henry Knox. Knox argued that the United States should acknowledge a residual Indian "right in the soil" not affected by a treaty between Britain and the United States. That right could be extinguished, Knox insisted, only by some separate dealing with the Indians, and he recommended that the United States purchase Indian claims to disputed lands. At Knox's suggestion, in 1789, Congress appropriated $20,000 for negotiations.

In part, Knox and Washington saw this policy shift as required by justice, but they were also trying to avoid the costs of having to take the Northwest Territory by war. A change in tactics did not constitute a change in ultimate goals, however. Although Knox undertook to keep white settlers outside treaty boundaries, his policy did not recognize the Native Americans' right to refuse to negotiate. Seeking to bolster the authority of the national government, Knox argued that Indian bands were not communities within state borders, but rather foreign entities, on the level of nations. Indian relations were therefore properly the business of the federal government. Knox in effect declared Indians aliens on their own lands, lending the weight of federal policy to American inclinations to see the Indians as the ultimate outsiders.

By 1790 continuing troubles in the Northwest Territory convinced Washington that the federal government had to project a military presence into that region. His first two efforts were dismal failures. In 1790 a combined Native American force led by the Miami war leader Little Turtle routed the United States Army, led by General Josiah Harmar. The next year a much smaller party crushed the troops of territorial governor general Arthur St. Clair. At last, in 1792, Congress authorized "strong coercive force" (bigger, better paid, and better trained) and Washington turned to a 47-year-old seasoned infantry officer, Pennsylvanian major general Anthony Wayne. By the time Wayne found the Indians in 1794 at Fallen Timbers, near the west end of Lake Erie, his army numbered more than 3,000. Facing a force of only 400 warriors, Wayne claimed a decisive victory.

According to the Treaty of Greenville, signed August 3, 1795, Indians ceded two-thirds of the later state of Ohio and a piece of present-day Indiana. In return, they received annual federal payments ranging from $1,000 to $500 per band. The annuities bought the United States influence within Indian communities and rendered the Indians more economically dependent. In addition, the treaty tried to convert the Indians to white ideas of work and economy by offering to pay the annuities in the form of farm equipment, cows, and pigs.

Indian efforts at confederacy proved less successful in the South, where deep fractures existed within the Cherokee and Creek nations. Older leaders, wearied of constant warfare with settlers, and mixed-heritage populations, more familiar with white economic and social ways, sometimes favored accommodation over battle and entered into agreements they lacked the authority to make. At the Treaty of New York in 1790, Alexander McGillivray and other Creek leaders agreed to exchange lands belonging to the entire Creek nation for annual payments from the federal government and promises of U.S. protection for their remaining lands. A faction of the Cherokee nation entered into a similar pact at Holston in 1791.

These internal disputes weakened Indian military efforts. When the government proved unable to stem the tides of settlers flowing into the future state of Tennessee, younger Creeks, Chickamaugas, Cherokees, and Shawnees repudiated the treaties and attacked the American community at Buchanan's Station, near Nashville, Tennessee, planning to proceed south to Nashville itself. Fearing reprisals, older Cherokee leaders betrayed the plan, and the assault was thrown back. United States Indian commissioners used a series of military victories to coerce new land cessions

Map 8–3 Major Indian Villages and Indian–United States Battle Sites, 1789–1800 During its first decade of existence, the new federal government struggled to assert control over the trans-Appalachian territories, claimed by Native Americans as their homelands and coveted by United States settlers and land speculators.

from the southeastern nations and to insinuate white customs more deeply into Indian cultures, especially that of the Cherokees.

Resistance continued, in both the North and the South, but dreams of a pan-Indian confederation were temporarily stymied. They would be resurrected at the turn of the century by two Shawnees, already young men by the time of Wayne's victory. One, Tenskwatawa, would later become an important prophet. The other, his half-brother, was named Tecumseh.

The West posed a domestic, as well as an external, threat to the federal government. By 1791 western settlers were disenchanted with the seeming inability of the government to protect their interests and had fallen into the practice of disregarding federal policy. They trespassed onto Indian lands, dispatched unorganized militias to enforce their claims, and traded illegally with Indians. In 1791, western Pennsylvanians took the step of repudiating the authority of the federal government explicitly, setting the stage for a direct confrontation.

The trouble began with the passage of Hamilton's excise tax. Living in an area perfectly situated to function as a gateway to the Northwest Territory, residents of western Pennsylvania anticipated an economic bonanza from free-flowing westward migration and were frustrated with the failure of the government to secure safe passage into the Ohio River valley. Hamilton's tax on spirits gave their simmering anger another focus, the question of republican fairness. Many Americans regarded excise taxes (internal taxes on specific goods) as unfair in principle. This particular tax seemed targeted specifically at western farmers, who found it easier to transport their grain in liquid than in bushel form.

Popular protests had begun within months of the tax's passage, and they intensified at each new report of the army's failure in the Northwest Territory (efforts the tax was supposed to fund). Western Pennsylvanians dug in their heels, vowing that they would not pay the tax and calling on citizens to treat the collectors with "contempt." Washington took the challenge seriously, and in August 1794 he sent 13,000 troops into western Pennsylvania. In the face of this show of force, the Whiskey Rebellion fizzled, but the government drove its point (and power) home. Remaining protestors were roughly rounded up and held in open pens; twenty men were returned to Philadelphia to face treason charges, and two were sentenced to death. Washington eventually pardoned both, but he had proven the authority of federal law in the new republic.

The citizens of western Pennsylvania were not without sympathizers, however. The congressional elections of 1792 were fought as contests between the policies of Alexander Hamilton, on the one hand, and the beliefs of the self-named "republican interest," on the other, over what exactly it meant to be a republican nation and society.

America in the Transatlantic Community

The internal turbulence the United States faced during these years was matched by conflict in the larger Atlantic community of which the new nation was inextricably a part, both as a result of its history and as a result of its current trade dependencies. George Washington would later summarize his foreign policy goals: "The great rule of conduct for us, in regard to foreign nations, is, in extending our commercial relations, to have with them as little political connexion as possible." But Washington's own experience, and that of his successor, John Adams, taught that commerce and politics were not so easily separated.

Other Revolutions

Just as the United States was launching its federal republic, France entered the throes of revolution. After years of fiscal mismanagement on the part of the crown, high unemployment, and widespread malnutrition and starvation, the French bourgeoisie initiated a reform of the monarchy that soon led to wholesale grassroots revolution. In July of 1789, just eight weeks after Washington took the oath of office, the people of Paris stormed the Bastille prison in symbolic rejection of the power of the monarchy. The next month the new National Constituent Assembly abolished feudalism and promulgated the Declaration of the Rights of Man and of the Citizen, modeled on the American Declaration of Independence.

Initially, most Americans, including many Federalists, supported the French Revolution. As a part of its long eighteenth-century conflict with Great Britain, France had aided the Americans in their own revolution, and had recognized the nation and its diplomats after the war. Americans now saw the efforts of the French people to overthrow monarchy as a reflection of their own struggle against Britain, and they read events in France as a confirmation that the United States would lead the world into a new era of democracy.

By 1793, however, as the Parisian mob grew more violent and moderate politicians lost power, many Federalists and even some Democratic Republicans lost their enthusiasm for the French republic. Although many Americans, Jefferson and Madison among them, remained avid French partisans, others grew convinced that France was spiraling into chaos.

Part of their alarm may have derived from the fact that the spirit of liberty had spread to the French colony of Saint Domingue in the West Indies. In 1791, the free people of color of Saint Domingue led an insurgency against the white planter class but soon lost control in the face of a full-scale revolution by the island's tens of thousands of slaves. Eventually, under the leadership of former slave François-Dominique Toussaint-Louverture, Saint Domingue would become the first black republic in the Americas.

Haitian Revolution The 1791 slave revolt against plantation owners and their families in the then French colony of Saint Domingue (Haiti). This engraving is from a contemporary German report on the uprising.

Washington's response to the revolution in Saint Domingue was complicated. He did not support the Caribbean revolutionaries, especially after the movement for equality for free blacks turned into a slave rebellion. Like other slave owners, Washington feared that encouraging the Dominguans would encourage slave rebellion in the southern United States. On the other hand, he did not want to enter into an alliance with France (which opposed the revolution on economic grounds) that might seem hostile to the British. His compromise was to direct his administration to provide supplies and ammunition directly to the island's beleaguered white planter ruling class.

Between France and England

Washington's efforts to avoid the appearance of pro-French partiality were soon further tested. On February 1, 1793, France and Spain declared war on Great Britain and Holland. Americans were divided in their sentiments. Many Democratic Republicans (among them Jefferson and Madison) viewed with horror the possibility that America might join with its former colonial master against a fellow republic. Hamiltonians, meanwhile, believed that friendly relations with Great Britain best served American interests. Searching for a middle ground, President Washington endorsed neutrality.

Then, on May 16, Edmond Charles Genêt, citizen of France, arrived in Philadelphia, now the nation's temporary capital. France had several hopes for the Genêt mission. The revolutionary government believed that it was the destiny of the French republic to free the oppressed people of Europe from their tyrannous monarchs. As a part of this undertaking, Genêt was to incite the European colonies in the Americas to revolution. Genêt was also to press the United States for a new commercial treaty allowing French naval forces and privateers to rearm and provision themselves in American ports as they battled Great Britain on the seas. These hopes were not entirely fanciful. Impoverished as it was, the Washington administration had advanced money to help the new French government, and Washington had instructed the U.S. ambassador to France, Gouverneur Morris, to recognize the republic as the legitimate government of France.

But the French overestimated the lengths to which the American government would go to achieve that goal. Preferential treatment for French ships, either warships or commercial ships, could only strain relations between America and England. Barely able to muster a force to the northwest, President Washington was not about to risk a foreign war or to have tensions further inflamed on the nation's western borders. Washington considered Genêt's proposals reckless.

Believing that Washington's views did not represent the sentiments of Americans generally, Genêt put into motion a series of actions that assumed essential American support for French goals. He authorized the refitting of a captured English ship, anchored in Philadelphia, which was intended for duty as a French privateer, and he encouraged efforts to organize American settlers in Kentucky to attack the Spanish.

Washington was furious. "Is the Minister of the French Republic to set the Acts of this Government at defiance, with impunity?" he fumed. Issuing a formal Proclamation of Neutrality, Washington disavowed Genêt and in August 1793 demanded that he be recalled. Disappointed by Washington's growing support of Federalist policies, Jefferson resigned as secretary of state in December.

To the Brink of War

Even without Genêt's provocations, by 1794 tensions with Great Britain were high. To the old issues of unsettled Revolutionary War reparations and the British forts in the Northwest had been added new charges that the British navy was harassing U.S. merchant ships. Still, Washington sought to avoid confrontation. In spite of restrictions on British ports, U.S. shipping had been steadily expanding. Under these conditions, it was hard to argue that British policies were so injurious as to warrant the risk of a trade war. Washington dispatched Chief Justice of the Supreme Court John Jay as a special emissary to England to resolve outstanding issues between the two nations.

Although Great Britain at first had little interest in the mission, the heating up of French-British animosities enabled Jay to negotiate a treaty that reduced tensions between Britain and the United States. Britain agreed to open West Indies ports to some U.S. ships, and both countries agreed that (except for tonnage restrictions) their ships would receive equal treatment in each other's ports. They also agreed to establish boards of arbitration to set the boundary between Canada and the United States, and Britain promised to evacuate its forts in the Northwest by June 1, 1796.

Most Americans knew nothing about the provisions of Jay's Treaty until after it was approved, for the Senate debated it in secret. When Democratic Republicans learned of its contents and its ratification, they protested the concealed character of the deliberations and objected that the treaty would benefit the merchant class while taxing everyone to pay for its provisions. But public protest soon fizzled. News of Anthony Wayne's victory against the Great Lakes tribes cast the treaty's provisions for the evacuation of the British forts in a more positive light. Word followed that Thomas Pinckney had also concluded a treaty with Spain, opening the Mississippi River to U.S. navigation and permitting Americans to store goods duty-free in New Orleans. (Pinckney's Treaty also set the boundary between the United States and Florida at the 31st parallel.) The treaty was a sign of Spanish weakness. Seeing the United States make peace with Britain, and fearful of an Anglo-American alliance, Spain resigned itself to the possibility of increased American encroachment across the river and sought peace with the new republic.

Taken together, Wayne's victory and Jay's and Pinckney's negotiations seemed at last to open the territories to settlement. Western land prices soared and the U.S. export trade boomed. By the time opponents in the House of Representatives tried to scuttle Jay's Treaty by denying the funds necessary to enforce it, popular sentiment had shifted to strong support for the treaty as an element of returning prosperity.

The Administration of John Adams

George Washington had been reluctant to serve a second term in office and had been convinced to do so when Jefferson and Hamilton argued that no one else could bring the young republic's fractious politics together. But Washington refused to run for a third term, and in 1796 the nation faced its first contested presidential election.

In his farewell address, published on September 19, 1796, Washington made clear his own essentially Federalist concern with social order and personal discipline. Having acknowledged the right of the people to alter their Constitution, he stressed the "duty of every individual to obey the established Government," until it was changed "by an explicit and authentic act of the whole people." Sounding themes that would echo through the first half-century of the republic, he warned against unlawful "combinations and associations" with designs on the rightful "power of the people," an image that, 30 years later, would drive the emergence of Jacksonian democracy.

Led by Hamilton (who could not run for the presidency himself, having been born in the West Indies), Federalists put forward vice president John Adams as their candidate. Adams had served in the Continental Congress, been a part of the committee to draft the Declaration of Independence, served as representative to France during the American Revolution, helped negotiate the peace treaty, and served two terms as vice president. Thomas Pinckney of South Carolina was their vice-presidential choice. For president, Democratic Republicans supported former

Map 8–4 Extension of United States National Territories, 1783, and Extension of United States National Territories, 1795 The Treaty of Paris with Great Britain (1783) left the United States' borders with Spain (much of the western and southern boundaries) ambiguous. Those borders were clarified in the Pinckney Treaty with Spain (1795).

secretary of state Thomas Jefferson, along with Madison, the most visible opponent of Hamilton. New Yorker Aaron Burr was intended as vice president.

Although it was contested, the election of 1796 was not decided by popular majority. State legislatures chose two-fifths of the members of the Electoral College. Moreover, procedures in the Electoral College did not permit a distinction between votes for the office of president and vice president. The person who received the most electoral votes became president. The person who received the second highest number of electoral votes became vice president.

This procedure proved dangerously unpredictable in a political climate in which idyllic republican consensus had already yielded to political parties. While the Federalist Adams received a majority of electoral votes (71) and became president, the Democratic Republican Jefferson received the second highest count (68 to Pinckney's 59) and became vice president.

Benjamin Franklin once said of John Adams that he was "always an honest man, often a wise one, but sometimes, and in some things, absolutely out of his senses." Wise he may have been, and honest, but he was also cranky, defensive, and plagued by self-doubt. He was not the man to negotiate growing party rifts successfully. Many Federalists looked to Hamilton, rather than Adams, for direction, but any possibility for alliance between those two was dashed when Adams learned that Hamilton had considered supporting Pinckney for the presidency.

These party resentments formed the background against which Adams confronted an increasingly hostile relationship with France. Unsurprisingly, Franco-American relations had been harmed by the signing of Jay's Treaty—which seemed to France to ally America with England—and by the French practice of plundering American ships. To these tensions would be added the issue of Saint Domingue. By the time John Adams took office, the revolutionaries (now led by former slave Toussaint-Louverture) were seeking the resumption of trade with the United States as a step toward full independence. An abolitionist in sentiment, Adams had no qualms about supporting the revolutionaries and saw a number of advantages in allying with them. A trade deal with Haiti would further isolate the island from French imperial control; it would help the United States economy; and it might prompt Louverture to close his ports to the French privateers attacking U.S. merchant ships. In June 1799, the Adams administration signed a three-way British-U.S.-Saint Dominguan trade agreement. Although that agreement remained unratified when Adams left office, in the last months of his presidency Adams stationed U.S. warships outside Dominguan ports to help quash an internal rebellion of conservative free people of color wishing to reimpose slavery, and members of his administration engaged in informal conversations with Louverture about the form an independent Saint Dominguan republican government might assume. None of this would please France, particularly not after the rise of Napoleon and the resurgence of French imperial ambitions in the late 1790s.

Even before his inauguration on March 4, 1797, Adams began to entertain the possibility of sending a special envoy to France to resolve these issues. When Adams's cabinet objected, the president temporarily abandoned the plan. At the end of March, he learned that newly arrived American ambassador Charles Pinckney had been unceremoniously kicked out of France. The French foreign minister had informed Pinckney that the French government would "no longer recognize or receive" an ambassador from the United States. In this context, Adams returned to the idea of sending a mission to France. In the end, he appointed Elbridge Gerry, John Marshall, and Pinckney, who was still in Europe.

When the American mission arrived, French Foreign Minister Talleyrand let it be known that he expected a bribe for his willingness to talk. Arrangements of this sort were not uncommon in eighteenth-century European politics, but to the starched and circumspect Adams, the idea was abhorrent. He turned over the entire documentation of the affair to Congress, altering the papers only to the extent that he identified Talleyrand's agents by letters: X, Y, and Z.

The news of the so-called XYZ Affair came to a largely Federalist Congress, which immediately suspended commercial ties to France, empowered American ships to seize armed French vessels, and embarked on an expansion of the nation's military. In what became known as the "Quasi-War" (because neither nation formally declared war), between 1798 and 1800 the United States and France skirmished on the seas, with the United States capturing more than 80 French ships. In the Convention of 1800, France and the United States agreed at last to end these hostilities. France agreed to return captured American ships, the United States assumed Americans' claims against the French for damages in shipping, and the earlier Franco-American Alliance was terminated, replaced by mutual most-favored-nation status.

The military expansion necessary for this armed conflict soon created tensions at home. In order to finance the buildup, Adams and Congress needed $2 million, which they found by imposing a tax on houses, land, and slaves. Each state had a specified portion of the cost to pay. The levy on houses, which was assessed according to the size of the house and the number and size of its windows, fell especially hard on residents of states with few or no slaves or huge plantation estates, and it was particularly odious to German immigrants, whom it reminded of harsh hearth taxes exacted by the kings of Germany. When the assessors reached eastern Pennsylvania, settled predominately by German immigrants, unrest became civil disobedience. Rallying around John Fries, men of the area raised a small army to chase the collectors away. Meanwhile, women poured hot water on the assessors as they tried to count and measure the windows. When the governor tried to have the resisters arrested, Fries's supporters surrounded the state militia and freed the prisoners. Hearing of the uprising, Adams sent a militia of 1000 men into the region to capture the leaders. Fries and most of the other leaders were arrested, tried for treason, and sentenced to hang. In the face of strong public sentiment against the executions, Adams eventually pardoned the rebels. (This was the second uprising in less than a decade, and in both cases, the rebels were pardoned.)

> **"There goes the President and they are firing at his arse. . . . I do not care if they fire thro' his arse!"**
>
> LUTHER BALDWIN, Newark, New Jersey, July 1798, as President John Adams passed by. These words would get him tried and convicted of violating the Sedition Act.

Meanwhile, the Federalists had also used the XYZ Affair and growing hostilities with France for domestic political purposes. Insisting that pro-French influence was endangering the nation, in 1798 Congress passed the Alien and Sedition Acts, measures aimed at gagging the Democratic Republican opposition and preventing it from using the war issue to win the 1800 election. The acts required a 14-year naturalization period, the highest at any period in American history, and targeted immigrants, whom the Federalists presumed to be Democratic Republicans. The acts also empowered the president to deport any "suspicious" aliens, and established a broad definition of sedition, intended to stop all Democratic Republican criticism of the administration's policies.

A Brawl in Congress The politics of the early republic were often rough. Here two congressmen (one of them later convicted under the Sedition Act) come to blows on the floor of the House of Representatives.

The Alien and Sedition Acts backfired against the Federalists. Twenty-five prosecutions were eventually brought under the Sedition Act (all against Democratic Republicans) and ten men were convicted. The acts were so transparently partisan that individuals convicted under them became martyrs to the Democratic Republican cause. A Vermont congressman who published criticisms of administration policies was reelected even as he served out his four-month jail term. But by targeting those believed to be "radical," especially newspaper editors, and warning immigrants away, the acts silenced the most outspoken opponents of the government.

Although Democratic Republicans insisted that the acts were

unconstitutional, they hesitated to challenge them in the Supreme Court, both because the Court was dominated by Federalists and because Democratic Republicans did not want to set a precedent for giving the Supreme Court the power to rule on constitutionality. Instead, Madison and Jefferson encouraged the states to pass resolutions denouncing the Alien and Sedition Acts. Madison, who had since retired from Congress, authored a set of resolutions in Virginia affirming the rights of states to judge the constitutionality of federal laws. Jefferson, who was vice president of the United States, framed a more militant set of resolutions for the Kentucky legislature, stating that states might declare federal laws they deemed unconstitutional to be "without force" within their state boundaries.

Jefferson and Madison likely expected that other states would rally to the support of the Virginia and Kentucky resolves, but they did not. Rather, voters simply returned the Democratic Republicans to power in the election of 1800, and the acts expired in 1801.

Before retiring, the Federalist Congress got off one more shot at the Democratic Republicans. In January 1801, just as the session expired, Congress passed the Judiciary Act of 1801, which gave John Adams the power to expand the federal judiciary by appointing new judges, justices of the peace, attorneys, clerks, and marshals. Needless to say, he filled these positions with good Federalists, and then he left office.

Conclusion

William Maclay lived until 1804 and continued to be active in public affairs in his home state of Pennsylvania. From time to time he added notations to his journal, underscoring the accuracy of his early forebodings.

Indeed, the first decade of the federal government's existence had demonstrated that the love of liberty and the love of order sometimes led in different directions, and they gave rise to very different visions of what constituted "good" citizenship. Democratic Republicans fumed at what they saw as the liberties Federalists had taken with the Constitution, and their willingness utterly to abrogate civil rights. Federalists were more convinced than ever that Democratic Republicanism was a dangerous scourge upon the land, tantamount to lawlessness and, itself, the greatest threat to the republic. The 1790s had witnessed a steady escalation of suspicion and distrust, of which the Whiskey Rebellion, the Alien and Sedition Acts, and the Virginia and Kentucky resolves had been only the most striking illustrations. The political parties organized that fractious spirit, but they did little to defuse it. Meanwhile, even as Americans fought over the terms of the new republic's founding, those terms began to change.

Further Readings

Catherine Allgor, *Parlor Politics: In Which the Ladies of Washington Help Build a City and a Government* (2000). The role of elite women in creating a national political culture.

Joanne B. Freeman, *Affairs of Honor: National Politics in the New Republic* (2001). A brilliant analysis of political culture in the new nation.

Frederick Hoxie, Ronald Hoffman, and Peter J. Albert, eds., *Native Americans and the Early Republic* (1999). This collection of essays counters views of Native Americans as passive victims of American westward settlement in the early republic.

Clare Lyons, *Sex Among the Rabble: An Intimate History of Gender and Power in the Age of Revolution, Philadelphia, 1730–1830* (2006). This is a lively and fascinating social and cultural history of class, gender, and street life among the poorer sort in a late eighteenth-century American city.

Gary B. Nash, *The Forgotten Fifth: African Americans in the Age of Revolution* (2006). Brief and highly readable, this book traces the history of race and slavery in the United States from the Revolution to the Missouri Compromise.

Jeffrey Pasley et al., eds., *Beyond the Founders: New Approaches to the Political History of the Early Republic* (2004). Lively new perspectives on the founding era.

Alan Taylor, *Liberty Men and Great Proprietors: The Revolutionary Settlement on the Maine Frontier, 1760–1820* (1990). Using the Maine frontier as a microcosm, Taylor describes the militant and often violent resistance of land-poor white settlers to the legal claims of wealthy proprietors.

David Waldstreicher, *In the Midst of Perpetual Fetes: The Making of American Nationalism, 1776–1820* (1997). The role of the popular celebrations in creating American nationalism.

Philipp Ziesche, *Cosmopolitan Patriots: Americans in Paris in the Age of Revolution* (2009). A very smart discussion of the way in which Americans understood their Revolution to be just like the French Revolution—and profoundly different.

Who, What

>> Timeline >>

▼ 1781
Articles of Confederation ratified

▼ 1787–8
Constitution ratified

▼ 1789
George Washington inaugurated
Judiciary Act of 1789
Tariff Act of 1789
John Fenno founds *Gazette of the United States*
William Hill Brown publishes *The Power of Sympathy*

▼ 1790
Alexander Hamilton's Report on the Public Credit
Assumption Act
Naturalization Act

▼ 1791
Excise tax (including tax on whiskey) passes
First Bank of the United States
Philip Freneau establishes *National Gazette*
Bill of Rights ratified

▼ 1792–94
Whiskey Rebellion

Review Questions

1. What were the key elements of Hamilton's fiscal and economic policies?
2. What were the first two political parties in the federal republic? Who led each and how did the two parties differ?
3. Who were "the Few and the Many"?
4. How did the Whiskey Rebellion reflect larger tensions in the early republic?
5. The Constitution did not define "citizenship." What early laws and policies do you think gave practical meaning to the idea of citizenship? Do you think everyone agreed on who was included and who was not?

Websites

The Alien and Sedition Acts, along with the Virginia and Kentucky resolutions. From the Avalon Project. http://avalon.law.yale.edu/subject_menus/alsedact.asp

Primary Documents in American History: The Bill of Rights. A collection of important documents in the history of the Bill of Rights, from the Library of Congress. http://www.loc.gov/rr/program/bib/ourdocs/billofrights.html

The President's House in Philadelphia. Documents and images about George and Martha Washington's home while he was president, and the slaves who shared it with them, shed light on slavery in Philadelphia. http://www.ushistory.org/presidentshouse/

Slavery in the North. A collection of histories and documents. http://www.slavenorth.com/index.html

For further review materials and resource information, please visit www.oup.com/us/ofthepeople

▼ 1793
Fugitive Slave Act
Edmond Genêt arrives in the United States

▼ 1794
Battle of Fallen Timbers

▼ 1795
Jay's Treaty
Treaty of Greenville
Pinckney's Treaty

▼ 1796
John Adams elected president

▼ 1798–1800
XYZ Affair and Quasi-War

▼ 1798
Alien and Sedition Acts

▼ 1798–1799
Virginia and Kentucky resolves

▼ 1800
Jefferson elected president

▼ 1801
Judiciary Act of 1801

CHAPTER 9

Common Threads

>> Why was overseas trade so important to Washington, Adams, Jefferson, and Madison? To ordinary farmers?

>> How did the way average Americans lived change over the first quarter-century of the republic?

>> How were the political debates of ratification and of the 1790s still playing out during Jefferson's and Madison's administrations?

>> What important changes in context and content occurred in U.S. Indian policy over the period of the first four administrations?

>> What roles did organized religion play in shaping the society of the early republic?

>> Was the market revolution important in the South?

A Republic in Transition

1800–1819

AMERICAN PORTRAIT

>> Washington Irving's America

One of the new republic's first successful writers, Washington Irving was born in New York City in 1783, the eighth surviving child of a fairly prosperous merchant family. It proved especially apt that his mother named him after George Washington, since much of Irving's career as a writer focused on the real and fictional history of his country. But Irving also spent much of his energy and time trying to negotiate the present, as the young nation underwent far-reaching economic, political, and social changes. His tales reflected some of that turbulence.

Although he and his family were of Federalist sympathy, Irving came of age just as Americans elected Thomas Jefferson to the presidency, throwing off the party of Washington, Hamilton, and Adams and ushering in a quarter of a century of Democratic Republican dominance. It was an upheaval in politics that Jefferson later described as "as real a revolution in the principles of our government as that of 1776 was in its form."

Accompanying this change in politics was a profound transformation in the economy and society of the United States. Cash relations began to supercede barter and trade in daily life. Cities grew and prospered but also became more anonymous. More people worked for wages, fewer worked for room and board. Even farmers oriented themselves toward commercial markets.

As a member of the merchant class, Irving benefited from many of these commercial changes. But he also felt their cost. Irving and his family were victims of the constant disruptions of American foreign trade after 1809, and, in 1817, they at last went bankrupt, forcing Irving himself to move to England to try to recoup their fortunes.

Irving had never cared much for business. He had become a lawyer (following a growing number of Americans into that profession), but his real love was always the arts. Irving began publishing when he was only 19, contributing letters and essays to *The Morning Chronicle* under the pseudonym Jonathan Oldstyle. In 1807, he founded his own literary magazine, *Salmagundi*, devoting its pages to ridiculing the provincial smugness of city culture. It was in an issue of *Salmagundi* that Irving coined the nickname "Gotham" for New York City.

In 1809, Irving launched an elaborate hoax to stir up interest in his newly completed satire *A History of New-York from the Beginning of the World to the End of the Dutch Dynasty, by Diedrich Knickerbocker*. Before the book's appearance, he posted a series of advertisements in a New York paper pretending to be a local hotelier who had been swindled out of his fee by a guest, the now-missing (fictitious) historian Diedrich Knickerbocker. The equally fictitious landlord threatened to sell a manuscript Knickerbocker had left behind (the *History of New-York*) to settle accounts. New Yorkers followed the ongoing story in the advertisements and were primed to make the book an instant success when it finally appeared.

But Irving's most lasting literary fame came from the series of stories published in 1819–1820 as *The Sketch Book of Geoffrey Crayon, Gent.*, which included both "The Legend of Sleepy Hollow" and "Rip Van Winkle." In "Sleepy Hollow" Irving poked fun at the clash of two cultures: the educated, scientific (and foolish) worldview of schoolteacher Ichabod Crane (who eventually became a lawyer in Philadelphia) and the old-world, old-fashioned (but in some ways very wise) customs of the townspeople of "Sleepy Hollow."

It was "Rip Van Winkle" that best captured Washington Irving's changing America. A simple fellow with a fondness for liquor and "an insuperable aversion to

continued

>> AMERICAN PORTRAIT *continued*

all kinds of profitable labour," Van Winkle fell asleep in the Catskill Mountains for 20 years and awoke to a world utterly unrecognizable. His village was "larger and more populous. There were rows of houses which he had never seen before, and . . . [s]trange names were over the doors—strange faces at the windows—everything was strange. . . . The very character of the people seemed changed. There was a busy, bustling, disputatious tone about it, instead of the accustomed phlegm and drowsy tranquillity." In the story, Van Winkle eventually understands what has happened, and although he himself slides comfortably back into his old ways, he is welcomed by and in turns welcomes the changes in his world.

Although the story was set in the period of the American Revolution, it could have applied equally to the first two decades of the nineteenth century, and to the profound alterations in American economy, politics, and society that ushered in that century. Ironically, the story appeared just as those changes ushered in the most severe fiscal panic in the republic to date, throwing farmers off their lands and drying up job opportunities in the cities. For many of those people, the story did not end so well as it had for Rip Van Winkle.

OUTLINE

A Politics of Transition

In his inaugural address in 1801, Jefferson strove to put the partisan bitterness of the previous decade behind American politics. He asked Americans to come together "in common efforts for the common good" and assured Federalists that he was committed to the rights of the minority. "Let us, then, fellow-citizens, unite with one heart and one mind," he encouraged. "Let us restore to social intercourse that harmony and affection without which liberty and even life itself are but dreary things." In some ways, Jefferson got his wish: over time many of the policies of the Democratic Republicans would so come to resemble the policies of the Federalists that it would seem as if the two parties had grown closer. In the ongoing battle of daily national politics, however, it was hard to tell that the Democratic Republicans and the Federalists shared any common ground at all.

> "This day I have witnessed one of the most affecting scenes of my life. . . . [Vice president Burr spoke] with so much tenderness, knowledge, and concern that it wrought upon the sympathy of the Senators in a very uncommon manner. . . . the firmness and resolution of many of the Senators gave way, and they burst into tears. There was a solemn and silent weeping for perhaps ten minutes. . . . My colleague, General Smith, stout and manly as he is, wept as profusely as I did. He laid his head upon his table and did not recover from the emotion for a quarter hour or more."
>
> SENATOR SAMUEL MITCHILL,
> telling his wife about Aaron Burr's farewell speech to the Senate

Democratic Republicans in Office

Immediately upon gaining office, Democratic Republicans set about closing the loophole in the Constitution that had almost cost them the election. With 53 percent of the popular vote, Jefferson had clearly defeated Adams. But in the Electoral College, the practice of balloting by party allegiance (rather than by office) had spelled disaster. Both Jefferson and Aaron Burr, the Democratic Republican vice-presidential candidate, received 73 votes. In the House of Representatives, Federalists threatened to support Burr to block Jefferson. Only after 34 ballots was Jefferson elected. Stunned Democratic Republicans rushed to pass the legislation that became the Twelfth Amendment (1804), providing for party tickets in national elections.

Meanwhile, Democratic Republicans turned their attention to revenge. They attempted to reduce the Federalist presence on the Supreme Court by impeaching Associate Supreme Court Justice Samuel Chase.

Chase was notorious for his open partisanship during the Sedition Act prosecutions, but it was unclear whether his behavior met the constitutional standard of "Treason, Bribery, and high Crimes and Misdemeanors." Although Democratic Republicans were suddenly content with a loose reading of the Constitution, Federalists took up strict constructionism, arguing that the power to impeach had been narrowly drawn and should be used only in cases of clear criminal behavior. In the final vote, Chase was acquitted. The Supreme Court remained Federalist, 5 to 1. Jefferson's desire for a Democratic Republican court had to wait for unforced vacancies in 1804 and 1807 and the creation of a new western circuit in 1807.

Before leaving office, the Federalists had tried to pack the courts with Federalists. The Judiciary Act of 1801, passed by the lame-duck Federalist Congress, increased the number of federal judgeships. Adams promptly appointed—and Congress confirmed—loyal Federalists. He also issued commissions for 41 justices of the peace, but they had not yet been acted on when he left office, and Jefferson ordered their appointments withheld. One of those "midnight" appointees, William Marbury, went directly to the Supreme Court, asking it for a "writ of mandamus," a court order to Madison to compel him to issue the commission. In a landmark decision,

Chief Justice John Marshall, speaking for the Federalist-dominated Court, refused—but in a ruling that actually enhanced its power. The provision in the Judiciary Act of 1789 (which Congress had reinstated after repealing the Act of 1801) that gave the Supreme Court the power to issue writs of mandamus was unconstitutional. The Constitution had set out the powers of the Supreme Court, and no act of legislation could change them. Marbury was out of luck, but the principle of judicial review (which itself was nowhere mentioned in the Constitution) had been established, and henceforth, the Supreme Court would decide whether acts of legislation were constitutional or not. Jefferson had won the battle but lost a very big constitutional war.

Jefferson also set out to reduce the size of the federal government. Working with Secretary of the Treasury Albert Gallatin, he slashed the army budget by half and the navy budget by more than two-thirds. He also supported congressional efforts to reduce the $80 million national debt and to repeal internal taxes, including the hated one on whiskey. By 1807 the government had cut the national debt in half.

These efforts at thrift were soon derailed by the politics of overseas commerce. The monarchs of the North African nations of Tunis, Algeria, Morocco, and Tripoli had long sought to dominate shipping on the Mediterranean, exacting tribute as the price of permitting ships to travel the Barbary Coast. As soon as the United States became a separate nation, it became liable for such payments. In 1794 the United States created the navy to protect American shipping in the Mediterranean, the very navy whose budget Jefferson cut.

Renewed demands for tribute in May 1801 brought the crisis to a head. Democratic Republicans opposed war as expensive and tending to enlarge the powers of the federal government. Yet to pay tribute was to abandon the principle of free trade. Concluding that his only hope lay in a small, contained war, Jefferson supported a Congressional appropriation for warships and gunboats "to protect our commerce and chastise their insolence—by sinking, burning or destroying their ships and vessels wherever you shall find them."

Results were mixed. Democratic Republicans did manage to avoid new internal taxes, and they were able to cut the national debt substantially. They were not, however, able to dismantle Hamilton's economic system, which provided the revenue to finance the country's defense. Nevertheless, America's military intervention in the Mediterranean was not particularly successful. The warship *Philadelphia* ran aground off Tripoli and would have become loot of war had a raiding party led by Lieutenant Stephen Decatur not burned it before it could be taken.

The Louisiana Purchase

Many citizens of the republic, including Jefferson himself, had long presumed that white Americans would eventually settle west of the Mississippi River but Pinckney's Treaty of 1795 (which had improved American access to the Mississippi) had removed any need for immediate action.

Napoleon Bonaparte changed all that. By the turn of the century, American-French relations had chilled. Ambitious to establish his own empire in the Americas and determined to prevent further United States expansion, in 1800 Napoleon acquired Louisiana from Spain. Jefferson worried that France would eventually send troops to occupy New Orleans. Hoping to block Napoleon, Jefferson dispatched Robert Livingston and James Monroe to France to purchase New Orleans and West Florida too.

Bonaparte indeed intended to fortify New Orleans, but he first diverted his troops to Saint Domingue in an attempt to reverse the revolution there. Some 30,000 French troops died in the failed attempt. Defeated by a combination of the island's former slaves and infectious disease, Napoleon was ready to unload his American territory. He stunned the American agents by offering to sell not only New Orleans, but the entire Louisiana Territory—883,000 square miles. (The Americans claimed that the purchase included West Florida, but Spain said it had never sold that territory to France. This issue was not resolved until 1819; see Chapter 11.) On April 12, 1803, the deal was struck. The United States paid France $11.25 million and agreed to satisfy American claims against France (from the Revolution) up to a value of an additional $3.75 million. For $15 million, or roughly 3.5 cents an acre, the United States obtained the Louisiana Territory.

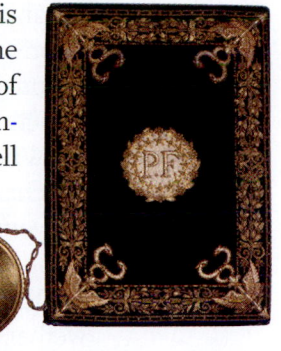

Louisiana Purchase Treaty The P. F. stands for "Peuple Français," or, "the French People."

Jefferson's own "strict" reading of the Constitution indicated that the purchase required a constitutional amendment. But this Democratic Republican belief in explicit powers ran counter to his Democratic Republican belief that the nation required land for expansion. Congress granted citizenship to French and Spanish

Map 9–1 Louisiana Purchase Although Lewis and Clark made the first exploration of the Louisiana Purchase, other explorers quickly followed. Among the most important were Zebulon Pike, who explored the Arkansas and Red rivers, and Steven Long, who explored the Arkansas and Platte rivers. Long described the plains as the "Great American Desert."

inhabitants of the territory, ignored the status of Indians living there, rebuffed an effort to outlaw slavery, and authorized the purchase without further ado. Jefferson rationalized "that the good sense of our country will correct the evil of [loose] construction when it shall produce ill effects."

When the United States had requested a statement of the exact boundaries of its purchase, French minister Talleyrand had declined: "You have made a noble bargain for yourselves, and I suppose you will make the most of it." Indeed, long before Louisiana was in the hands of the United States, Jefferson began to plan its exploration.

To lead the expedition, Jefferson appointed his trusted secretary, Captain Meriwether Lewis, and another officer, William Clark. Lewis was an ambitious soldier with some experience in the Old Northwest. Clark, who had commanded troops on the Mississippi, was a skilled surveyor and mapmaker. Their mission was "to explore the Missouri River, & such principal streams of it, as, by its course and communication with the waters of the Pacific Ocean, whether the Columbia, Oregon, Colorado or any other river may offer the most direct & practicable water communication across this continent for the purposes of commerce." The commerce Jefferson sought was not across the Pacific, but rather with the Indians along the northern Missouri River and its tributaries who traded chiefly with the British.

The expedition set out from St. Louis on May 14, 1804. It included three boats containing 45 men and a dog, firearms, medicines, scientific instruments, tools, flour, and salt. The party traveled first up the Missouri River, closely observed by the Mandans and the Minnetarees and later the Hidatsas, who visited their camps at night and sent ahead stories of these curious people. In early November, the white men made their winter camp. When the expedition broke camp the following spring, a Shoshone woman, Sacagawea, her French-Canadian trapper husband, and their newly born child left with them. As a young girl, Sacagawea had been captured and adopted by the Minnetarees. Now, traveling with Lewis and Clark, she would return home. En route, her foraging and fishing skills supplemented the party's diet and she became an invaluable guide and interpreter. Native women such as Sacagawea and Malinche often served as cultural mediators.

Some of the expedition's encounters with Native Americans were less friendly. Far more dangerous than the Indians, however, were waterfalls and rapids, freezing temperatures and paralyzing snows, accidents, diseases (especially dysentery), and dead-end trails. The final portage across the Rocky Mountains in the fall of 1805 proved longer and more difficult than anticipated. Snow and hail brought the expedition to a standstill. Exhausted and underfed animals wandered off. Supplies ran out. On the verge of slaughtering their pack animals, the expedition members at last cleared the worst of the mountains and came to Indian villages, where they were fed and sheltered. On November 7, 1805, Lewis and Clark reached the Pacific Ocean.

Throughout their journey, Lewis and Clark had represented themselves as the envoys of a great nation with whom the Native Americans should now trade. To cement relations, they presented medals of friendship to Indian leaders. But they also kept an eye out for the prospects of future settlement. What they found, according to Lewis, was "a most delightfull country . . . fertile in the extreem . . . covered with lofty and excellent timber." After their return, in 1806, parts of their journals and letters, including detailed maps and drawings, slowly found their way into print, advertising to the settlers who would soon follow the full extent of what Jefferson called America's new "empire for liberty."

Other Americans had other plans for the territory. In 1805, former vice president Aaron Burr made his way to New Orleans to have a look at the new country. He immediately fell in love with it, and saw, too—or so he later claimed—that the United States might extend its sovereignty to include some of Spanish Mexico, where settlers were unhappy with high taxes and little government attention. Some people thought he intended to lead a breakaway rebellion and establish a separate republic. Whatever his intentions, by 1806 Burr had raised a force of several thousand men. Convinced that Burr intended treason, and wanting to avoid trouble with Spain, Jefferson ordered his arrest. Burr was brought back to Richmond to stand trial before John Marshall, who happened to be presiding over the federal circuit. Prosecution proved difficult. Marshall interpreted treason in the narrowest sense possible, as requiring two witnesses to an overt act of war against the United States. No witnesses were forthcoming. Jefferson's refusal to supply some correspondence requested by the defense and subpoenaed by Marshall further weakened the case. Burr was acquitted, but he was also disgraced.

Embargo

In the fall of 1804, Jefferson's popularity was soaring. Internal taxes had been abolished, the national debt was falling, the United States had (seemingly) stood up to international coercion, and, most amazingly, America had acquired a huge western empire. Choosing George Clinton of New York as his running mate, Jefferson won reelection handily, and the Democratic Republicans took control of both houses of Congress. Faced with the prospect of federal surpluses, Jefferson again abandoned strict constitutionalism and began to contemplate a future role for the federal government encouraging "the great objects of public education, roads, rivers, canals, and such other objects of public improvement as may be thought proper." But Jefferson's second term had barely begun when his attention was riveted to developments in Europe.

A Philosophic Cock This 1804 cartoon caricatured Jefferson as a "philosophic cock" courting his slave Sally Hemings. Jefferson's Federalist opponents tried to tarnish his reputation by publicizing his relationship with his slave, but the voters reelected Jefferson by a decisive margin.

In his first inaugural address, Jefferson had counseled "peace, commerce, and honest friendship with all nations, entangling alliances with none." He remained committed to American neutrality, but by 1805 Napoleon's growing power in France and his expansionistic designs on Europe had considerably complicated this policy. On the one hand, Jefferson knew he might need Napoleon's help to settle the unresolved question of West Florida, still claimed by Spain. On the other hand, France's increasing indifference toward American shipping rights raised the possibility that the United States might need Britain as an ally. Napoleon's victory over Austria in 1805 made France the undisputed master of western Europe. At the same time, English victories over the fleets of France and Spain had made England the undisputed master of the seas. The stalemate had dire consequences for American shipping.

Jefferson's early hopes that Britain might respect the neutrality of American ships were dashed in 1805 when Britain reasserted an old policy to seize ships traveling between enemy ports. The revived practice was announced with the seizure of more than 200 American ships in that year alone. Not to be outdone, Napoleon declared a blockade of England and also began confiscating American ships. In June 1807 the British ship *Leopard* stopped the American frigate *Chesapeake* just as it left the port of Norfolk, Virginia. Insisting that the *Chesapeake* had recruited British deserters for its crew, the captain of the *Leopard* demanded the right to search the American ship. When he was denied, he fired on the ship, boarded it, and took four men prisoner, leaving the *Chesapeake* to limp home.

Jefferson immediately ordered all British ships out of American waters and demanded reparation for the *Chesapeake*. In secret sessions, Congress passed an act that permitted only those American ships with the president's express approval to sail into foreign ports and prohibiting foreign ships from the American export trade. In effect, the United States had embargoed itself.

It was the most disastrous policy of Jefferson's career. Because enforcement was impossible, wealthy merchants who could bear the risks enjoyed the large profits of smuggling. At the same time, small merchants, sailors, and shopkeepers who depended on steady maritime trade were thrown into crisis, and farmers in the South and West, who needed regular markets, had trouble finding overseas trading outlets. As the economy settled into depression in 1808, the remaining Federalists charged that the embargo was helping Napoleon, whose weaker navy was free to concentrate on the British. Adding to American frustration, Napoleon then slyly claimed the right to attack U.S. ships in any continental port, because by Jefferson's own order they could not be legal carriers.

The ironies of the embargo did not end there. As violations mounted, Congress passed, and the president signed, ever more repressive versions of the embargo. The final, fifth Embargo Act (signed January 9, 1809) swept away protections against self-incrimination and the right to due process and trampled on the right to trial by jury. By comparison, even the Alien and Sedition Acts looked tame.

As he himself acknowledged, the Embargo Acts represented the failure of Jefferson's agrarian political economy. His dream of a republic of farmers was dead, the victim of the principles of territorial expansion and free trade on which he had based it. Pinning America's need for manufactured goods solely on "this exuberant commerce," as Jefferson admitted in 1809, "brings us into collision with other powers in every sea, and will force us into every war of the European powers. The converting of this great agricultural country into a . . . mere headquarters for carrying on the commerce of all nations, is too absurd."

The anguish caused by the Embargo Acts brought into the open long-simmering dissension within Democratic Republican ranks. The most serious rupture came in the aftermath of the Louisiana Purchase. Although Jefferson insisted that he had obtained West Florida as a part of the Louisiana Purchase, Spain claimed that it had never ceded that land to France in the first place. Napoleon hedged, but his ministers let it be known that the right price might convince them to lobby the

American cause with Spain. Jefferson approached Congress for the money. To his critics, Jefferson's willingness to bribe France was the last straw. Loosely organized, Jefferson's congressional critics dubbed themselves the *Tertium Quid* (the "third something") to distinguish themselves from both the Federalists and the Democratic Republicans. By 1808, the Quids were threatening open rebellion. Although Secretary of State James Madison seemed the logical heir to Jefferson's presidency, Quids talked of throwing their support to James Monroe of Virginia or even Vice President George Clinton of New York. To avoid the risk of public party brawling, in 1808 party loyalists met in closed caucus to select Jefferson's successor. They chose James Madison. In the election, Madison captured 122 electoral votes to Federalist Charles C. Pinckney's 47. Clinton, who ended up on the ballot, won only 6 electoral votes. The Democratic Republicans again won both houses of Congress.

From 1801 until 1829, the federal government would remain under the control of a single party. In and of itself, that did not challenge Democratic Republican principles. Neither Madison nor Jefferson considered a two-party system a necessary feature of American political life. Both, however, warned against the day when a small cadre of like-minded men would meet together in secret to choose the nation's ruler. Democratic Republican ascendancy itself had now come to rest upon just such a closed institution. Meanwhile, with American hopes for international prestige turned into a joke, commerce deteriorating, and agriculture crying out for relief, on March 1, 1809, Jefferson signed a bill repealing the Embargo Act. Three days later, Jefferson left the office that he now described as a "splendid misery."

The War of 1812

Facing serious enough ruptures in his party to accept nomination by the kind of closed and antirepublican institution he himself had once condemned, James Madison took office on March 4, 1809. Madison had stood side by side with Thomas Jefferson on virtually every important political and ideological issue since the founding of the nation. Now he inherited his friend's presidential woes.

Madison and the War

In 1809, with Madison's approval, Congress replaced the embargo with the Non-Intercourse Act, reopening trade with all of Europe except England and France, but authorizing the president to resume commercial ties with whichever of these countries dropped its restrictions and attacks on American shipping. The act set off a series of diplomatic feints on the part of England and France, both pretending to alter their policies without making actual concessions.

France eventually won the game. In the summer of 1810, Napoleon's ministers officially communicated to Madison that, as of November of that year, France would stop seizing American ships on the condition that Britain would do likewise. Probably correctly, Britain did not believe France would follow through on this policy. But Madison accepted the French declarations, and he altered American Non-Intercourse Act policy to apply to Britain alone.

> "The distinction of Federalists and Republicans will cease; . . . the inquiry will be, are you for your country or against it?"
>
> TENNESSEE CONGRESSMAN AND WAR HAWK FELIX GRUNDY

Still, war might have been averted. A quarter of a century of European wars, and Napoleon's continental policy—which closed continental markets to English goods—had taken its toll on Britain's economy. Although far more powerful militarily than the United States, Britain would have been happy to avoid the cost of an additional war. On June 1, 1812, in light of continuing British attacks on American shipping, Madison requested that Congress declare war on Great Britain. He listed several other reasons, including that the British were "impressing" American seamen into service and instigating Indian attacks in the Northwest. On June 4, the House voted to pass a war bill. On June 18, the Senate concurred. Ironically, unaware of events in the United States, England announced that it was revoking its maritime policy against United States ships.

The war vote in Congress went largely along party and regional lines. New England shippers remained firmly opposed, protesting that shipping was just beginning to recover and that American prosperity was dependent on Britain. Farmers and planters in the West and South were ready to fight to open up the seas. They suspected that the war might prove useful in other ways, too. Western migrants were convinced that Creek and Shawnee resistance was the work of the British, still hanging on to their forts along the Great Lakes. War with England could provide the excuse for an American invasion of Canada, which could both grab more land and wipe out the Indians. Even the Democratic Republicans were not fully unified, however. Led by Henry Clay of Kentucky and John C. Calhoun of South Carolina, the War Hawks (a group of fiercely nationalistic and resolutely expansionist young men who had come of age since the Revolution) were eager to respond to British insults. Moderate Democratic Republicans were more hesitant. They dreaded the cost of the war and doubted that the nation could gear up to take on such a formidable foe.

All of these tensions were reflected in the election of 1812. Maverick Democratic-Republican De Witt Clinton rallied the support of Federalists and ran as Madison's opposition. He did not win, but his 89 electoral votes (to Madison's 128) constituted a higher proportion than the Federalists had enjoyed since the election of 1800.

Doubts about America's war readiness were soon justified. An attempt in the summer of 1812 to invade Canada foundered in confusion and indecision. Two thousand American troops surrendered at Detroit, and two overland advances failed when state militiamen insisted that their military obligations did not include leaving the country to fight. Only Commodore Perry's dramatic victory on Lake Erie saved American honor in the north. On September 10, 1813, Perry forced the surrender of the entire British Great Lakes squadron. "We have met the enemy," he relayed to a relieved General William Henry Harrison, "and they are ours—two ships, two brigs, one schooner, and a sloop."

A comparable victory eluded Americans in the Atlantic. After a few initial successes at sea, the tiny American navy was easily overwhelmed by superior British sea power. Americans turned to private schooners and sloops and by the war's end managed to capture more than 1,300 British vessels. Nevertheless, by 1813 the British navy had succeeded in blockading the American coast from the Chesapeake Bay south through the Gulf of Mexico to New Orleans. The following year the blockade was extended to New England. The British fleet pummeled the cities and villages along the U.S. coast. On August 24, 1814, the British troops invaded Washington;

Fort McHenry Fort McHenry is best known for its role in the War of 1812, when it successfully defended Baltimore Harbor from an attack by the British navy in Chesapeake Bay. It was this bombardment that inspired Francis Scott Key to write "The Star-Spangled Banner."

burned the Capitol, the White House, the Treasury Building, and the Naval Yard; and terrorized the civilian population. The entire cabinet, including President James Madison, had already evacuated.

While Washington lay smoldering, the British turned their attention to Baltimore. Through the night of September 13, the ships fired on Fort McHenry, the island citadel that guarded Baltimore's harbor. Among the anguished observers in the harbor was a Washington lawyer by the name of Francis Scott Key. Elated when the rising sun revealed the United States flag still flying over the fort, Key quickly scribbled the words that would in 1931 be adopted as the lyrics of the national anthem, "The Star-Spangled Banner."

In the South, Andrew Jackson used the war to suppress Indian resistance to U.S. settlement. When news reached Nashville that the militant Creek faction known as the Red Sticks had attacked a U.S. fort and settlers in Mississippi Territory, Jackson assembled a volunteer militia, including free African Americans and Indians, and went in pursuit. In March 1814, Jackson defeated the insurgents at Horseshoe Bend, forcing them to sign a treaty ceding two-thirds of remaining Creek lands to the United States.

Map 9–2 Battles and Campaigns of the War of 1812 The War of 1812 was largely a naval war, fought along the Atlantic coast, in the Gulf of Mexico, and on the Great Lakes. Several land campaigns proved important, however: the British ground attack that ended in the looting and burning of the capital, and Jackson's trek overland to New Orleans.

Federalist Response

For a time the hardships of the war worked in favor of the Federalists. Although they did not win the presidency in 1812, they doubled their numbers in Congress. Perhaps misled by those results, some Federalists grew rash. Angry at declining profits and frustrated by Virginia's domination of the presidency, in October 1814, Massachusetts Federalists called for a convention of the New England states "to lay the foundation for a radical reform in the National compact." They planned to meet on December 15 in Hartford, Connecticut.

The Federalists who convened in Hartford were divided. Extreme Federalists, arguing that the Union could no longer be saved, lobbied for a separate New England confederacy that could immediately seek an end to the war. More moderate voices prevailed, and in the end, the convention sought amendments to the Constitution. The Federalists demanded restrictions on the power of Congress to declare war, an end to the Three-Fifths Compromise that allowed slaves to be counted for purposes of representation, exclusion of naturalized citizens from elective federal office, and restrictions on the admission of new states. They also sought to limit the number of terms a president could serve and the frequency with which the candidate for president could be chosen from a given state. The resolutions expressed a developing identification of the Democratic Republicans as the party of the South.

Federalists misjudged their strength and mistimed their efforts. By 1814, weary of war, Great Britain was ready to end the skirmish with its former colonies. Emerging as the dominant power in Europe, Britain had little incentive to offer the Americans more than simple peace. Signed in Ghent, Belgium, on December 24, 1814, the treaty that ended the War of 1812 was silent on the issues of free trade and impressment that had triggered the war. The Treaty of Ghent also sidestepped boundary disputes between Canada and the United States. On one point the British negotiators gave ground: they agreed to remove British troops from the Old Northwest, in effect acknowledging the failure of Indian resistance to white settlement.

Only Andrew Jackson's ragtag militia saved Americans from outright humiliation in the war. After the victory at Horseshoe Bend, Jackson's troops moved south to Pensacola and west to New Orleans, where a British fleet prepared to attack the city and take control of the mouth of the Mississippi River. Unaware that a peace treaty had been signed, on January 8, 1815, a force of 7,500 British regulars stormed Jackson's position. In 30 minutes the battle was over, and, miraculously, the Americans won. Establishing Jackson as a national hero, the Battle of New Orleans signaled the rise of a new star.

But that day was still a decade away. In 1815, the chief political importance of Jackson's victory was the lift it gave to American nationalism and the light it cast on the Federalist Hartford Convention, still meeting in Connecticut. Threatening secession was one thing in the context of a failing war, but quite another in a moment of national triumph. Suddenly, the proceedings at Hartford seemed downright traitorous.

An Economy in Transition

The period after 1815 is sometimes referred to as the "market revolution" in United States history. Calling the cluster of changes that occurred over the next several decades a "revolution" suggests their eventual scope and magnitude: the decline of paternalistic employment arrangements (apprenticeship, indenturing, and the master shop) and the growth of labor contracts and wage-dependency; the decline of relative self-sufficiency and the growing importance of longer-distance market exchange; and the decline of informal forms of transaction (barter, for example, or accounts held pending for long periods of time simply on the basis of friendship) and the growing importance of formal contracts and book accounting. These changes in American economic life were reflected in every aspect of society, from religion to politics to invention and discovery to family life and everyday values. The term "revolution" slightly misrepresents the pace of this change, which was actually quite gradual. And yet, like Washington Irving's fictitious Rip Van Winkle, a woman or man who fell asleep before the War of 1812 and woke up 30 or 40 years later would have found him- or herself in a startlingly altered world.

International Markets

There were many sources of the economic transformation of the late eighteenth and early nineteenth centuries. One of the most significant in terms of its widespread impact was the gradual revival of overseas commerce at the end of the eighteenth century, much of this supported by the ongoing conflicts in Europe. As Napoleon tried to spread the French Revolution (and his own power) throughout Europe, Europe remained at war—disrupting agriculture on the Continent and impeding European overseas trade of all kinds. American shippers happily filled the gap.

This American shipping was of three kinds: export/import (exporting American wheat, rice, indigo, tobacco, some sugar, and especially cotton to Europe, whose own agricultural capacity was ravaged by the Napoleonic Wars) and importing manufactured goods from Europe to growing United States markets; re-export (carrying goods between two foreign ports with an intermediate stop in the United States, often to appear not to be violating French and English embargoes on each other's Caribbean colonies); and the simple carrying trade between two foreign ports (as England and France continued at war with each other, for example, U.S. ships became the main carriers between the two countries). American ships usually carried farm products and manufactured goods, but they also carried people: political refugees from France and from Ireland's ill-fated rebellion traveling to safety in the new republic, and, before 1808, when the slave trade was officially ended, captives from Africa forced through the middle passage to slavery in the Caribbean and the United States.

Overall, American shipping tonnage tripled between 1780 and 1810, reaching almost 11 million tons annually. American ships increased their share of the traffic between England and the United States from 50 percent in 1790 to 95 percent by 1800. Although American shipping was not entirely free from harassment by European powers (notably the British seizure of American sailors to serve on British ships), the value of the re-export carrying trade increased from about $500,000 a year in the 1790s to about $60 million a year in 1807. By the first decade of the nineteenth century, American ships were in the harbors of India, the East Indies, China, the Philippines, Japan, and Hawaii, and on the Pacific coast of North America and along the eastern coast of South America.

In the short run the return of overseas trade fed an already-rampant inflation (the result of a shortage of gold and silver and a surfeit of local and state-issued currencies of doubtful values). But it also created jobs, in steady ripples moving out from the wharfs all the way into the American backcountry. As it created jobs, it helped alter the way Americans understood the terms of labor.

Merchants contracted for vessels (which shipbuilders turned out at an astonishing rate), captains hired crews, and teamsters hurried goods to port. Some merchants overlapped their investments into aspects of port-city manufacturing. They became shop masters of a sort, gathering tailors, for example, into large central shops to turn out cheap clothing for sailors, or to sell to planters for their slaves—although the merchant-manufacturers seldom recognized the traditional obligations of master to

AMERICA AND THE WORLD

>> The United States in China

Although much of the history of the early republic unfolded in the Atlantic world, in terms of both politics and commerce the Pacific Ocean was also an important stage for American ambitions.

American traders had sent ships to China as early as 1784, when Robert Morris hired the ship *Empress of China* to sail out of New York Harbor and around the cape of Africa to Macao, China. With the end of the Revolutionary War, wealthy Americans were keen to purchase Chinese consumer goods—tea (boycotted during the Revolutionary War), porcelain, silk, and spices—and American merchants (barred from British colonial ports) were eager to find new markets. When the *Empress* returned a year later to realize a $30,000 profit, other American merchants jumped into the China trade.

From the beginning, however, Americans faced several problems. First, although the Chinese were willing to trade with foreigners, they did not want foreigners in the country. Traders were forced to stay in designated areas, called *hongs*, where Chinese traders came to them to discuss possible deals. Fearing the settlement of foreign families, the Chinese insisted that any women on board trading vessels (not entirely uncommon at the time) wait on the Portuguese island outpost of Macao.

The second problem was the lack of interest on the part of the Chinese for most products the United States had to offer. The ginseng market was pretty quickly saturated. From there American traders shifted to fur pelts obtained by sailing around the cape of South America and up the Pacific coast to trade with the Indians of the Pacific Northwest. From there they sailed across the Pacific, often stopping in the Sandwich Islands (now Hawaii) to pick up sandalwood for the Chinese market.

Among the American merchants who eventually realized a fortune from this trade was John Jacob Astor, who migrated from Germany to America just after the Revolutionary War and, with his wife Sarah (a smart businesswoman and an expert in furs), set up shop in New York City, dealing mostly in furs from the Canadian Great Lakes region. But after Astor sent his first ship to China soon after the turn of the century, and made $50,000 from the venture— a staggering sum, for the time—his eyes were also on the China trade, envisioning a route that would carry New England manufactured goods to the Northwest Indians for furs to be traded with China. He established a trading post in present-day Oregon for that purpose in 1811.

In the meantime, the most successful commodity Americans had found to sell in China was silver, which the Chinese were very willing to take in payment. But the United States was a specie-starved nation and had no silver mines, so obtaining the metal required either trading for silver with the Spanish South American colonies or acquiring specie bit by bit in complex trading patterns among European ports before heading off to China.

As early as the late eighteenth century, Americans found another trading medium: opium. Opium had long been chewed in parts of South and Southeast Asia as a general analgesic, but the far more addictive practice of smoking opium became common only with the introduction of tobacco and contact with foreign merchants and sailors (perhaps one reason the Chinese so strictly barred Europeans from their country). England's trade monopoly in India made the sale of opium in China especially attractive to the English, but by the first decade of the nineteenth century Americans were finding ways to horn in on the action. Soon, American ships were being specially designed to carry opium from India to Canton. Eventually, some of the early republic's greatest merchants' fortunes—including those of Stephen Girard of Philadelphia and James and Thomas Perkins of Boston—were amassed in part on the profits of drug trafficking in Southeast Asia.

worker: food, housing, and training. Rather, they tended to hire unattached journey workers or apprentices or jobless young men adrift in the city, and put them to work at some single, specialized aspect of the craft. In turn, some traditional shop masters became merchants, taking investments in ships to carry their goods to southern and Caribbean markets in anticipation of bigger profits.

The growth of overseas shipping also acted as a spur to the development of business services in the early republic, particularly in the port cities. The National Bank of the United States would be reauthorized in 1816. In the meantime, citizens came together to form insurance companies against the risks of loss in trading (weather, piracy, or detention by another nation) and local institutions for pooling capital for investment. By 1810 there were more than 100 banks in the nation. Many of these enterprises—banks, corporations, insurance companies—operated under special state charters that allowed them to function as legal entities. As the businesses mushroomed, so eventually did new middling-level jobs for clerks and lawyers.

Out in the countryside, farming families shifted from a relatively self-sufficient model of agriculture (in which they grew much of their own food or traded locally for what they needed) to more commercially oriented enterprises. Farmers were willing to travel longer distances to sell their goods. When they were able, they expanded the size of their holdings. In Delaware, for example, families used the profit from women's dairying activities to finance new land to grow wheat for sale in the cities or in Europe. As they made these changes, farmers, like merchants and shop masters, tried to hedge their bets by reducing their own costs and liabilities. They ceased using indentured servants, to whom they would have owed year-round room and board and a freedom bonus at the end of their term, in favor of hiring seasonal wage workers, to whom they had no responsibilities in the off-season.

The most significant boost to American commercial agriculture arose from the late eighteenth-century mechanization of the English textile mills and the resulting increased demand for cotton. The colonies had not been an important source of raw cotton, because the only variety that grew well in most parts of North America was extremely laborious and time consuming to clean. Spurred by the new English markets, in 1793 Eli Whitney invented a mechanism that reduced the cleaning time of this short-staple cotton from a pound a day to 50 pounds a day. Almost at a stroke, Whitney's gin made cotton a viable cash crop for much of the South.

The invention occurred at a critical moment. American indigo was losing English market share to indigo from the East Indies. Sales and prices of tobacco were in decline. The market for rice was still strong, but rice cultivation required such large investments of land and labor as to exclude most farmers from production. Cotton gave the South a new commodity crop, and one that, unlike rice, could be grown on small farms, without significant investment. Between 1790 and 1810, American cotton production increased from 3,000 bales to 178,000 bales a year. Increasingly after 1800, cotton was the largest single U.S. export commodity, making the development of the nation, not merely the development of the South, dependent on cotton and its labor system, slavery.

Crossing the Appalachian Mountains

Especially after the Treaty of Greenville opened the Ohio River valley, the expansion of overseas markets fed an already pent-up desire for new lands in Tennessee, Kentucky, and the soon-to-be-state of Ohio (1803). The Land Ordinance of 1785 had provided for sales to private individuals who could afford sections of 640 acres or more at a dollar an acre, but that was far beyond what any ordinary citizen could afford. Sales were effectively restricted to speculators. Hoping to find a source of revenue for the federal government, in 1796 Congress made matters worse by raising the price to two dollars an acre.

Finally, in 1800, settlers got some federal relief. The Land Act of 1800 (passed at the urging of William Henry Harrison, delegate to Congress from the Northwest Territory) reduced the size of the minimum parcel from 640 acres to 320 acres. For the first time, buyers were permitted to spread their payments over time. In 1804, the minimum size was decreased to 160 acres, and the price was reduced from $2.00 to $1.64 an acre. Even though the cost of land and supplies for the journey was still prohibitive for many Americans, and credit provisions sometimes lured desperate families into unmanageable debt, lower prices per acre, lower minimums, and the promise of credit opened the West to tens of thousands of settlers who would not otherwise have been able to go.

The unprecedented fury of migration into the territories set off by the Treaty of Ghent quickly swelled the population of the trans-Appalachian region. Kentucky grew from 220,955 in 1800 to 564,317 in 1820, Tennessee from 105,602 to 422,823, and Ohio from 42,159 to 581,434. Equally important, settlement led to the organization of new states. After Ohio in 1803, nine years passed before the next new state, Louisiana, entered in 1812. But then the admissions came rapid-fire. Indiana became a state in 1816, Mississippi in 1817, Illinois in 1818, and Alabama in 1819. By then both Missouri and Maine were also eager to join the Union.

American westward migration was a remarkably heterogeneous parade. The earliest arrivals were usually hunters, fur traders, explorers, and surveyors. Wealthy speculators (European as well as American) sometimes traveled to the backcountry just long enough to buy up the best parcels of land, then scurried home to sell their tracts to other investors and would-be migrants. Single men (displaced mechanics, youngest sons of poor farmers, husbands sent ahead to purchase land) picked their more humble ways along dusty roads, sometimes on horseback, often on foot. Families soon followed. Experienced and well-off families traveled in small but solid wagons, packing food and seed, a few household items, an axe, and perhaps a gun, and herded a cow or a few pigs alongside. But equally common was the sight of a "man, wife, and five children, with all their household goods thrown in a wheelbarrow . . . walking to Ohio."

The backcountry roiled in "anxiety and confusion," one observer noted, as newcomers raced to claim their share of territorial lands. There were cotton lands in the South and huge expanses for grain in the old Northwest Territory—and (as settlers along the rivers foresaw) favorable possibilities for transportation economies. Speculators were eager to seize the chance for huge returns on land investment, and migrants were eager to escape debt and taxes, oppressive jobs, and overworked soil.

Invention and Exploration

Western lands offered the potential for vastly enlarged markets within the United States. Settlers were eager to get their tobacco, wheat, corn, hemp, and cotton to coastal and European customers, and merchants and manufacturers were impatient to get their buttons, shoes, pots, pans, and farm tools to rural stores. Making that connection was still a backbreaking task, as John Owen's 1818 journey to Alabama illustrated. Owen classified the roads he and his family crossed on a simple scale: "tolerable," "intolerable," and "infernal." The challenge of figuring out how to connect people to land and products to markets more efficiently spurred some of the century's most important inventions.

The first efforts at improving transportation came in a spate of largely locally sponsored toll-road building. Although states generally granted a special charter of incorporation for such projects (and occasionally purchased a few shares), most of the capital came from investors in the immediate neighborhood who expected to benefit from tolls. New York communities, the most aggressive in this respect, increased their road mileage from 1,000 miles in 1810 to more than 4,000 miles in 1820. In an effort to bolster the trade from cities like Cincinnati, Pennsylvania extended an older highway that ran from Philadelphia to Lancaster all the way to Pittsburgh. But the toll roads proved a poor investment. Only one (a short turnpike in Connecticut) paid profits of even 5 percent and many made no money at all.

In the end, the most important consequence of road building in the post–War of 1812 era was the encouragement it gave to bridge building. Erected at critical points of passage, the new bridges (like one constructed over the Hudson River at Newburgh, New York) made a dramatic difference in the time and cost of transport. They were heavily used and usually turned a good profit.

But it was the application of the steam engine to transportation that made the most dramatic difference in travel in this time period. By the time the War of 1812 was over, the steam engine had reached a sufficient level of development to attract investors. A few hardy souls experimented with steam-powered overland rail carriers, but these lines remained fragmentary until the 1850s and conveyed only passengers, not cargo. The use of steam engines to power boats proved more successful. As early as 1787, James Rumsey of Maryland built a boat propelled by a jet stream from the stern, and John Fitch of Connecticut designed a steam-driven paddleboat. By 1790 Fitch was running a passenger ferry on the Delaware River. In 1804 Philadelphian Oliver Evans demonstrated a steam-powered river dredger, fitted with a stern wheel.

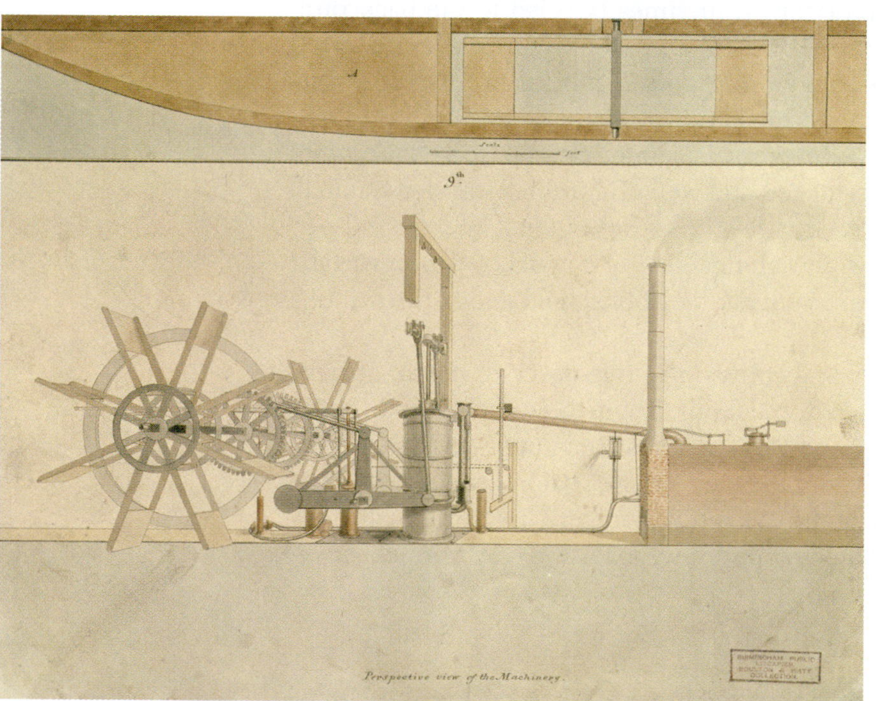

Fulton Steamboat Paddle Wheel The original patent drawing, a perspective view of the machinery drawn for Robert Fulton, 1809.

This technology was at last brought together in August 1807 when Robert Fulton and his patron Robert Livingston (Jefferson's minister to France during the Louisiana negotiations) announced the Hudson River trial run of the *North River Steamboat of Clermont,* a 140-foot-long vessel with two steam-driven paddle wheels. Fulton wryly described the trip, 150 miles from New York City to Albany, as "rather more favorable than I had calculated." "I ran it up in thirty-two hours, and down in thirty," he boasted. "I had a light breeze against me the whole way, both going and coming, and the voyage has been performed wholly under the power of the steam engine. I overtook many sloops and schooners beating to windward, and parted with them as if they had been at anchor."

Although he had not invented the steamboat, Fulton had demonstrated its practical application for the transportation of people and goods. By 1817 steamboats were common in the coastal waters of the East and across the Great Lakes, but their most telling impact on American life occurred on the western rivers: the Ohio, the Wabash, the Monongahela, the Cumberland, and especially the Mississippi. In 1809 Livingston and Fulton hired Nicholas Roosevelt to survey the river waters from Pittsburgh to New Orleans, and in 1811 they sent the steamboat *New Orleans* downriver from Pittsburgh. Pressed into service carrying troops and supplies up and down the river during the War of 1812, in 1815 steamboats began to ply regular private routes upriver on the Mississippi.

The steamboat powered the market development of the Mississippi River valley. Able to travel upstream as well as down, it knitted the northern and southern regions of the river together in an integrated economic system, with eastern manufactured goods and passengers flowing upriver all the way into the Ohio River valley, and northern grain, livestock, and manufactured goods flowing to downstream markets and out through the Gulf of Mexico, joined in Kentucky, Tennessee, and Mississippi by a swelling cargo of cotton. In 1811 the Mississippi River valley produced some 5 million pounds of cotton. Within two decades it produced 40 times that much, virtually all of it carried downstream to market on steamboats. In 1817 the overland route from Cincinnati through Pittsburgh to Philadelphia or New York took nearly two months. On steamboats, freight sent downriver from Cincinnati through New Orleans and on by packet to Philadelphia took about half the time.

The steamboat soon became a conspicuous and controversial symbol of American economic promise. Not only were steamboats fast, trim, and exciting, but they were relatively inexpensive to own and operate, not within the reach of average Americans but well within the means of small investors, who were eager to have a chance at making their fortunes. Citing the importance of orderly and reliable service, however, state lawmakers often encouraged large enterprises, awarding monopoly rights to specific prime routes. In 1798, for example, Robert Livingston had gained exclusive rights for 20 years over the waters of the state of New York by vessels propelled by steam, a monopoly he revived and expanded to include Robert Fulton in 1803. Fulton and Livingston failed to obtain sole rights to the Mississippi, but in 1811 they succeeded temporarily in gaining a monopoly on steamboat transportation at the mouth of the river. Their success provoked a hailstorm of protest from would-be competitors, who saw government aligning itself with wealth at the expense of the small entrepreneur. In 1819 the monopoly was withdrawn, but many small operators remained convinced that the power of the state had been brought to bear in favor of the wealthy and against the average citizen. In fact, few operators got rich running steamboats on the Mississippi. The twists and hidden snags of the shallow river saw to that. Only in the East, where rivers were deeper and where steamboats became the fashionable means of transportation for wealthy travelers, did investors realize large profits.

Even steamboats were limited by the existing waterways. Since the turn of the century, various investors and inventors had sought ways to enlarge those water routes by linking them artificially with canals. As with the first experiments with steamboats, the early history of canals did not portend great success. By the end of the War of 1812, only about 100 miles of canals existed in the United States (the longest ran 27 miles between the Merrimack River and Boston Harbor). None earned much money.

Thus, when, at the end of the war, New York City mayor De Witt Clinton proposed building a canal to connect Albany and Buffalo, most people thought he had taken leave of his senses. The canal would run 364 miles, making it the longest canal in the world. It would require an elaborate system of aqueducts and locks to negotiate a 571-foot rise in elevation and would cost $7 million. It was a far larger investment than anything comparable in the history of America. Opponents derided the idea as "Clinton's Big Ditch."

Clinton argued that the canal would "create the greatest inland trade ever witnessed." It would, he claimed, tie the "most fertile and extensive regions of America" to the city of New York, making that city "the granary of the world, the emporium of commerce, the seat of manufactures, the focus of great moneyed operation." In 1817 he convinced the state legislature not only to authorize the project but also to pay for it entirely in state funds, a gamble that amounted to a $5 per capita levy for the entire population of New York.

Begun on July 4, 1817, the Erie Canal was completed in 1823 and officially opened two years later. At 10:30 on the morning of Wednesday, November 2, 1825, the first boats cleared the final locks and made their way into the Albany basin. Bells pealed, bands played, a huge crowd cheered, and 24 cannons fired successively in a national salute. That night, downtown Albany was lit up in celebration, and from the State

Erie Canal Opening, 1825 New York governor De Witt Clinton pouring water from Lake Erie into the Atlantic Ocean at the Grand Erie Canal Celebration in New York Harbor on Nov. 4, 1825.

Capitol hung a backlighted mural depicting scenes of internal trade and navigation, titled "Peace and Commerce!" Presiding over it all was now-*Governor* De Witt Clinton.

Clinton's gamble paid off spectacularly. Passenger boats and transport barges crowded each section as quickly as it was opened, producing revenues so high that the state was able to pay for later stages of construction from the profits of early ones. Transportation costs from Buffalo to New York City, $100 a ton before construction of the canal, fell to about $10 a ton when the canal opened and dropped even lower later on.

The Erie Canal set off an explosion of canal building that lasted up to the Civil War, but later canals seldom duplicated its success. The federal government granted roughly 4 million acres of public domain to various canal companies, and states put up most of the money for construction. In the East, however, the terrain impeded construction, making canal building dangerous and costly. In the West, projects fell victim to local interests, overran their budgets, and were seldom able to make back their investments.

Early Industrial Society in New England

New Englanders had been experimenting with the idea of water-powered textile mills since the 1780s, when prominent Massachusetts merchant families tried to convince the state legislature to support the creation of textile machinery in the United States (including bribing a few English textile mechanics to show them how, if necessary). In 1790, émigré mechanic Samuel Slater had replicated the English water-powered carding and spinning machines in his mill in Pawtucket, Rhode Island. But Slater lacked the power loom, necessary to turn yarn into finished cloth. It took Eli Whitney's invention of the cotton gin in 1793, some additional industrial sabotage, and the devastating trade losses during the embargo and the War of 1812 itself to finally propel Americans to devise a power loom and invest seriously in a domestic textile industry. Boston merchant Francis Cabot Lowell pioneered the shift.

A graduate of Harvard with a mathematics major and a knack for machine design, Lowell traveled to England to see the loom for himself and surreptitiously to memorize its plan. Back home, he worked with mechanic Paul Moody to duplicate the English model. By 1814 he had succeeded. Armed with a special charter from the Massachusetts legislature, Lowell and his Boston associates (now organized as the Boston Manufacturing Company) opened the United States' first fully mechanized textile mill in Waltham, Massachusetts. Within three years the mill had expanded to two buildings and was paying a whopping 20 percent dividend.

Lowell died in 1817, but under Nathan Appleton's leadership the company (now the Merrimack Manufacturing Corporation) raised more

This daguerreotype of a woman working at a power loom dates from 1850.

than $8 million to finance a second group of mills in East Chelmsford, Massachusetts. The new mills turned out their first finished cloth in 1823. A sleepy rural village of 200 in 1820, by 1826 East Chelmsford had grown to 2,600 and had incorporated as the city of Lowell, America's first industrial town. The mills relied entirely on the South for their raw cotton. Northern domestic purchase of raw

Map 9–3 The Development of Regions and of Roads and Canals By 1830 internal development had fostered a growing transportation infrastructure throughout the United States. That development was regional in character, however. In the southern states, where natural waterways ran from deep in the interior to the coast, citizens saw little need to build additional linkages. In the North, where natural waterways seldom ran directly to coastal outlets, investors were far more willing to spend money on internal development, especially canals.

southern cotton grew from 8 million pounds in 1800 to 31.5 million by the end of the war in 1815.

The Waltham system, as Lowell's approach was called, differed from earlier American manufacturing enterprises in several ways. The Waltham mill was the largest industrial undertaking attempted in America up to that time. It housed the full production process, from fiber to finished cloth. It relied on a new organization plan, in which a professional managerial rank (separate from the owners) oversaw the daily operation of the mill. Finally, to cultivate an appearance of benevolence (in contrast to the plight of workers in the English mills), the Waltham system required that employees live in subsidized and supervised housing at the mill site.

For their workforce, the owners turned to the young women in the surrounding countryside of Vermont, New Hampshire, and western Massachusetts. The decision to hire women was not altogether remarkable. Textiles were traditionally women's work, and power-driven textile machinery was not necessarily identified with either sex. The chief precedent for mechanized textile production, the Rhode Island mills, employed children and whole families. Moreover, female workers were cheaper than men, the result of their long exclusion from customary craft protections and their loss of the right to make contracts if they were married.

In the early years, parents and daughters both saw benefits in mill work for unmarried young women. Presumably, a daughter would leave her family anyway when she married. Having her work in the mills before marriage reduced the number of mouths to be fed at home. The residential system put to rest fears that a young woman was compromising her respectability. Matrons supervised company-owned boardinghouses, where operatives lived together in single-sex settings. Strict rules of behavior guided the workers' leisure time, and factory bells started and ended the workday and announced lunch breaks.

The success of the mills underscored the paradoxes of American slavery and American freedom in the early nineteenth century—not least in the lives of the young female operatives who worked there. In the early years, at least, the mill operatives enjoyed a financial and social independence virtually unknown under the parental roof. They lived, ate, and played together

> **"Whereas we the undersigned residents of Lowell, moved by a love of honest industry and the expectation of a fair and liberal recompence, have left our homes, our relatives and youthful associates and come hither, and subjected ourselves to all of the danger and inconvenience, which necessarily attend young and unprotected females, when among strangers, and in a strange land . . . we firmly and fearlessly (though we trust with a modesty becoming our sex) claim for ourselves, that love of moral and intellectual culture, that admiration of, and desire to attain and preserve pure, elevated, and refined characters, a true reverence for the divine principle which bids us to render to every one his due; a due appreciation of those great and cardinal principles of our government, of justice and humanity, which enjoins us 'to live and let live' . . ."**
>
> CONSTITUTION OF THE LOWELL FACTORY GIRLS ASSOCIATION, 1834

and looked for much of their guidance to a female head-of-household. They returned home largely at their own discretion for periods of vacation. Many of the young women kept all or most of their pay, enjoying (perhaps for the only time in their lives) a separate disposable income. They developed pride in their work and in their community and began to articulate a sense of themselves as part of a long Yankee history of hard work and independence. All of this was made possible by the fact of slavery in the American South.

The final irony of this contradiction would play out only in the later years of the mills, after employers had cut pay and intensified production. In 1834 and again in 1836 the operatives turned out in defiant strikes—condemning the mill owners for reducing them, "the daughters of freemen," to the condition of slaves.

The Rule of Law and Lawyers

Before settling on a writing career, Washington Irving had first trained in the law. He was one of a growing number of young men to do so in the early nineteenth century, as the revival of commerce and the work of state and federal governments converged to make that occupation attractive. The change was apparent in the makeup of Congress: about one-third of the members of the first Congress were lawyers; by 1815 lawyers made up about half of that body.

Americans had long emphasized the importance of the written law to the preservation of the republic, but the law became important in additional ways in the expanding commercial economy of the turn of the century. Overseas trade, internal expansion, the buying and selling of land, new inventions—they all required complex legal documents and lawyers to draw them up and execute them. The power of the legal profession made itself felt even in the territories—as backwoodsman Daniel Boone learned to his chagrin. Well into the 1790s, Boone had been able to turn his knowledge of Kentucky into a thriving business as a land hunter, earning commissions from speculators and accumulating a large landholding of his own. But as more settlers poured into the state, more people filed claims on those lands and hired lawyers to contest successfully Boone's original titles.

The growing importance of lawyers reflected the growing importance of courts and of the judiciary. Again and again, judicial interpretation reinforced and set the course for market development. When the common law tradition clashed with economic development, judges tended to side with the entrepreneurs. For example, as businesses experimented with the use of water power in manufacturing, they sought to erect dams and millraces that altered the flow of streams. English common law assumed the owners and users of waterways had a right to enjoy those waterways undisturbed by alterations upstream. But in 1805, in *Palmer v. Mulligan*, a New York court ruled in favor of the right of development, against customary common law rights. For workers, the social power of judicial interpretation became alarmingly clear in March 1806, when the striking Philadelphia journeyman boot makers and shoemakers were found guilty of common law conspiracy to restrain trade. Conservative Philadelphia newspapers applauded the verdict, but the Jeffersonian *Aurora* protested that there was nothing in the (written) Pennsylvania or U.S. Constitution to support such a decision. The unwritten common law, the *Aurora* insisted, would soon "reduce the laboring whites to a condition still more despicable and abject" than "the unfortunate Africans."

On the federal level, the power of the Democratic Republicans (and, later, the Jacksonian Democrats) in the executive and legislative branches was countered by the power of John Marshall (a Federalist) as the chief justice of the Supreme Court from 1801 until 1835. Between 1805 and 1824, the Marshall Court issued a series of decisions that brought the Constitution to bear in support of the new market-based economy.

The earliest of the three, *Dartmouth v. Woodward* (1819), explicitly reinforced the principle that the rights of people were best protected through the rights of contract. The case concerned an attempt by the state legislature of New Hampshire to alter the original charter of Dartmouth College, given to the college by King George III in 1769, when the nation was still a set of British colonies. New Hampshire argued that the original charter was not binding on the current state government, but Dartmouth insisted that the charter was in fact a contract, protected under Article VI of the U.S. Constitution, which protected debts and engagements entered into before the Revolution. Acting to ensure the stability of contract in the broadest sense, the court ruled in Dartmouth's favor.

The case of *McCulloch v. Maryland,* also decided in 1819, centered on the Second Bank of the United States. The creation of the bank had been one of the successes of the new Democratic-Republicans, who had managed to overpower traditional objections to national banks in their party by attracting Federalist votes. Since its establishment, the Second Bank had created a number of branches, one of which was in Baltimore. Viewing the presence of the federal institution within its borders as a potential threat to its sovereignty, Maryland attempted to assert its authority over the Baltimore branch by taxing it. Acting on behalf of the bank, James W. McCulloch, chief clerk of the branch, refused. Maryland appealed to the Supreme Court, arguing that because the federal government was a creation of the states, its branch institutions could be taxed in the states where they existed. Marshall's court unanimously rejected this position. The federal government was superior to the states, the Supreme Court concluded. Because the power to tax was potentially the power to destroy, the states could not have the power to tax the creations of the federal government, wherever they might be located.

Gibbons v. Ogden (1824), the last in Marshall's long line of landmark decisions, concerned a disputed ferryboat monopoly in New York. Having been awarded exclusive rights to operate steamboats in the state's waters, Robert Fulton and Robert Livingston had, in turn, "contracted" a part of this right out to Aaron Ogden, giving him a ferry monopoly across the Hudson River from New York to New Jersey. At the same time, however, a man by the name of Thomas Gibbons had obtained a federal license to operate a boat line along a coastal route that came into conflict with Ogden's line. The question was: Who controlled these waters and therefore had the right to grant licenses, New York or the federal government? Consistent with its national view of power and development, the Marshall Court found in favor of the federal power. The decision noted that the Constitution had given to Congress (Article I, Section 8) the right "to regulate Commerce with foreign nations, and among the several States." Because the waterways under dispute did not fall clearly within the boundaries of a single state, the state power was in this case in conflict with the federal power. Where an action of a state conflicted with an action of the federal government, the Marshall court found, the federal power took precedence.

Ways of Life in Flux

When Irving's Rip Van Winkle woke up to his new world, he was saddened and confused to discover that all his old friends had either left or died. On the other hand, his wife had also died and Van Winkle was happy to be freed from her company. Unlike Van Winkle, Americans at the turn of the century were not merely passive objects of the political, social, and economic changes affecting their communities. Those changes grew out of choices some Americans made—to invest in an overseas trading venture, for example, or to buy new lands in the West to grow wheat or cotton. Their choices affected their own lives and the lives of others and slowly added up to a far more market-driven way of life.

> "To promote [the Indians'] disposition to exchange lands, which they have to spare and we want, for necessaries, which we have to spare and they want, we shall push our trad[e] . . . and be glad to see the good and influential individuals among them run in debt, because we observe that when these debts get beyond what the individuals can pay, they become willing to lop them off by a cession of lands."
>
> THOMAS JEFFERSON, 1803

Indian Resistance to the Yeoman's Republic

Although he expressed benevolence toward Indians, President Jefferson believed that they must give way to American settlement. Not only did the territories represent the supply of land necessary to nurture republican virtues and stabilize republican institutions; they also provided a buffer against Britain, France, and Spain on the western borders. Preferring that American westward expansion occur peacefully, Jefferson fostered a cycle of growing Indian dependency on American agents which would, he hoped, eventually bring them to sell off their lands.

Nevertheless, by the turn of the century, westward American migration was devastating native life and culture in the region. As settlers occupied new lands, Indians lost their villages and fields. Thrown back on the fur trade, they overhunted dwindling grounds. By 1800 many of the pelts and skins brought to traders in the Northwest Territory had actually been hunted west of the Mississippi River, and the deer were all but gone in the Southeast. Protestant missionaries urged the Indians to adopt Euro-American religious and social practices, including male-headed households and private ownership of property. Unscrupulous agents coaxed and bullied Indian nations into signing away their land. When the Indians resisted, the agents made deals with leaders they knew to be of doubtful legitimacy, promising bounties and annuities for territory.

Native Americans resisted these assaults on their autonomy. Seneca communities accepted some missionary aid but refused to abandon their community holdings, gender division of labor, and matrilineal households. The southern nations declined Jefferson's promise of new lands in the West and focused on constructing internal institutions that Americans might recognize as "civilized." For example, the Cherokees adopted a series of laws that functioned as a constitution, established a congress, and executed individual land titles. Meanwhile, both north and south, resistance to Euro-American culture also took the form of a broad movement for spiritual revitalization. Ganioda'yo (Handsome Lake), who rose to influence among the Senecas after 1799, preached revival through a synthesis of traditional beliefs and Christianity, but among other groups revitalization centered on cleansing themselves of Euro-American practices. In the South, Cherokees revived the Green Corn Ceremony, which celebrated the importance of personal bonds and repudiated material wealth.

Tenskwatawa (known as The Prophet) This is a copy of a portrait of the Indian prophet painted sometime between 1822 and 1832; the original was destroyed by a fire in 1865 at the Smithsonian, where the portrait was displayed.

This crisis of cultural and economic survival virtually ensured armed confrontation. As early as 1807, William Henry Harrison, governor of the Indiana Territory, heard rumors of "a general combination of the Indians for a war against the United States." Two Shawnee leaders, Tecumseh and his half-brother, Tenskwatawa (known as The Prophet), coalesced the diffuse anger into organized resistance. Tecumseh fought against whites both in the Old Northwest and in the South, experiences that helped him build a pan-Indian alliance. Tenskwatawa became influential after 1805 as the leader of a movement that rejected white culture. About 1808, Tecumseh and Tenskwatawa founded a village in present-day Indiana on the banks of the Tippecanoe River. The Prophet remained there while Tecumseh traveled widely, encouraging organized resistance to white settlement.

By 1811, Tecumseh's widespread success alarmed Harrison. That fall, Harrison marched an army toward Tecumseh's village on the Tippecanoe River. Although cautioned by Tecumseh not to be drawn into battle in his absence, on November 7, 1811, The Prophet engaged Harrison's troops and was defeated. The Prophet was discredited, but when war broke out between Britain and the United States the following year, Tecumseh retained sufficient influence to amass a huge force on the side of the British. He played a decisive role in the British victory over United States troops at Detroit but was killed in battle in October 1813. His death marked the end of organized Indian resistance east of the Mississippi.

Winners and Losers in the Market Revolution

For many Americans, the changing, more cash- and contract-based landscape of the turn-of-the-century United States offered both new freedom and new wealth. Large merchants who were able to absorb the risks of war, either wars between European nations, the American "Quasi-War" with France, or the outright War of 1812 with England, might realize enormous profits in transatlantic shipping.

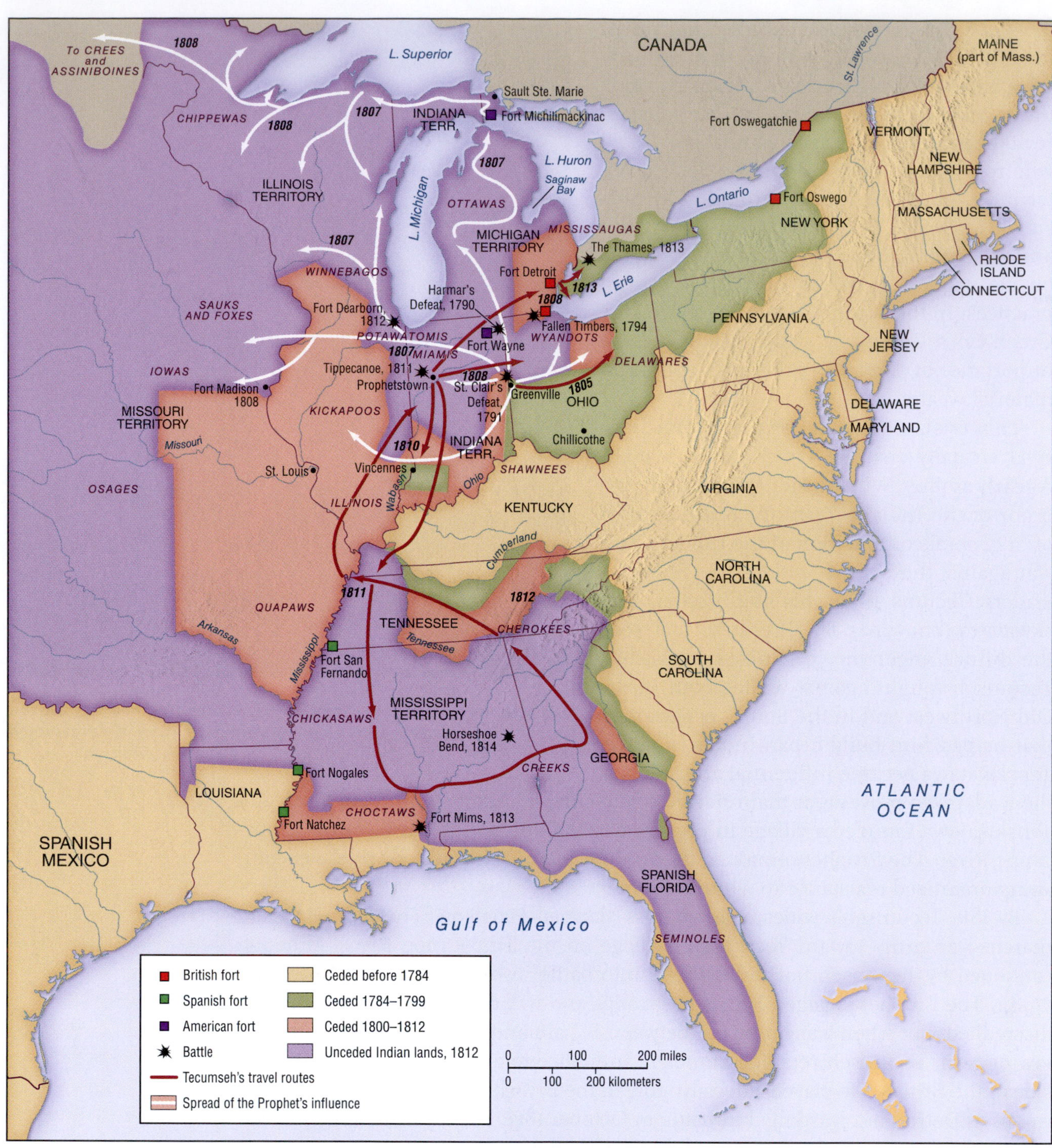

Map 9–4 Mounting Land Pressure, 1784–1812, and the Rise of Tecumseh's Confederation. The pan-Indian movement led by Tecumseh and The Prophet was the culmination of years of United States incursions into Indian lands and pressure, official and unofficial, on Indians to cede territories to the United States. As this map suggests, the influence of Tecumseh and The Prophet was greatest in the regions most recently ceded or where ongoing pressure was greatest in 1800–1810.

Owners of shipbuilding enterprises and of all the subsidiary sectors of that industry benefited from the prolonged boom in American shipping. Farmers who were in a position to expand their holdings and take advantage of commercial networks thrived in the increasingly commercial environment.

The blessings of these new liberties were mixed. New, unskilled workers took jobs away from journeymen, but they were as quickly fired as hired. Wages fell. Pressed to the edge of destitution, journeymen in Philadelphia, New York, and Baltimore began to form mutual aid societies, helping each other in times of need and laying the foundations for trade associations. But when they tried to organize for higher wages, they discovered that they had little power. In the eyes of the law, these assertions of liberty amounted to a conspiracy against the rights of trade. When associated Philadelphia journeyman shoemakers demanded a craftwide bill of higher wages in 1805–1806 (in what was the first strike in United States history), they were arrested, tried, convicted, and required to pay stiff fines.

But masters paid, too. New opportunities in manufacturing lured entrepreneurs and merchants who organized bigger shops, hired cheap workers, and offered small masters cutthroat competition. Initially, the traditional craft masters refused to associate with these new entrepreneurs. By the early 1800s, however, there were signs of erosion in their solidarity. Wanting to take advantage of economic opportunities or to cut their own costs, shop masters began to hire runaway servants with no questions asked or to take on unskilled workers to whom they had fewer lasting obligations.

Throughout the nation, people described these changing relations of labor and society in the language of the Revolution. Elites fretted that the masses were unfit for republican self-government, while workers condemned the older, paternalist structures of authority as repugnant to a free people. However, local conditions were at least as important as national political sentiment in creating the new social instability. Apprentices ran away not to express their allegiance to Jeffersonianism, but to escape cruel masters or to seek higher wages elsewhere. Masters did not hire untrained workers to affirm republican freedom but to protect profits by cutting costs.

Religion

These were years of ongoing religious upheaval, some of it evidence of Americans embracing a new freedom of belief and some of it expressing a sense of profound personal dislocation.

The new demands for personal liberty focused on religion as well as work and family, as a growing number of Americans objected to requirements that they pay taxes to support the state-sponsored Anglican and Congregational churches. Anglicanism had been disestablished in the South in the 1780s, replaced by the Protestant Episcopal Church. Disestablishment of the Congregational Church in New England was not complete until 1834, yet by the turn of the century new denominations were thriving in all regions.

Southerners were drawn especially to new evangelical Christian faiths, principally Methodism and the various forms of Baptist practice. In contrast to the more staid and ritual-based Episcopal Church, these sects stressed the personal, emotional nature of religion and the ability of individuals to struggle actively for

AMERICAN LANDSCAPE

>> Religion in the Backcountry: Cane Ridge, Kentucky

Barton W. Stone was a Presbyterian minister, but a Presbyterian minister with a number of reservations about the church he served. Particularly, Stone doubted the key Presbyterian doctrine of original sin, which directed that all humans were born utterly sinful and were unable to act in any way for their own salvation; salvation, orthodox Presbyterians believed, came completely through the grace of God. To Stone, as to a growing number of dissenting Presbyterian ministers, God had imbued humans with a capacity to yearn toward salvation and required fervent belief and longing as a condition for grace. Religion without that longing seemed to Stone lifeless and cold.

Pastor of the Presbyterian Church of Cane Ridge, Kentucky, Stone worried especially about the deadness to God's grace in the people he saw around him in the backcountry. The year was 1801 and many of Stone's congregants and neighbors were newcomers to the region, transplants from Virginia and Maryland who were busy settling new farms, slaves newly forced from their families in the East, and drifters who had broken free of family and community bonds. Most had few church ties and, in Stone's view, little interest in religion.

But by 1801 something was stirring in the backcountry. Prayer meetings in fairly dispersed locations in eastern and central Kentucky were drawing thousands of participants: 4,000 at Concord, for example, and 6,000 at Lexington. When Stone heard of one to be held in Logan, he went to investigate for himself—and was amazed at what he found: "Many, very many fell down . . . in an apparently breathless and motionless state," Stone recorded in his journal, their trances broken only "by a deep groan, or piercing shriek, or by a prayer for mercy most fervently uttered." When at last they regained their senses, they rose up "shouting deliverance . . . men, women and children declaring the wonderful works of God."

Returning to Cane Ridge, Stone set about organizing a sacramental communion service to be held in August, sending out invitations by word of mouth across the region. Participants began to arrive on August 6. As one observer described the scene: "On the first Sabbath of August, was the Sacrament of Kainridge, the congregation of Mr. Stone.—This was the largest meeting of any that I have ever seen: It continued from Friday till Wednesday. About 12,000 persons, 125 waggons, 8 carriages, 900 communicants. . . ." The prayer meetings continued day after day and deep into the night. News of events at Cane Ridge spread "like fire in dry stubble driven by a strong wind." Soon, the roads were jammed "with wagons, carriages, horsemen, and footmen," as "between twenty and thirty thousand" people (women, men, and children, whites and blacks, Methodists, Baptists, Presbyterians, the churched and the unchurched, anguished sinners, prodding family members, and the merely curious) hastened to the scene. The revival was more than 10 times the size of the population of Lexington, the state's capital.

METHODIST CAMP MEETING.

Cane Ridge was the largest, and the climactic, event of the western revivals of 1800–1801, but it fed waves of revivals that moved back east and north into upstate New York (later dubbed "the burned-over district" for the intensity of its meetings). Throughout the opening decades of the nineteenth century, religious enthusiasm flamed brightly in the republic. In one sense, there is no

surprise in this. Religion had always played an important role in American history. But why this particular outpouring of fervor, and why just at the turn of the century? And why the Kentucky frontier?

Some of the answers lay in the broader rejection of old Calvinist orthodoxies and hierarchical religious styles at the turn of the century. The revival ministers preached a theology of self-striving that was surely welcome to people in the process of gambling everything they owned on their ability to make a better life for themselves in the West. And they preached that message with a directness and intimacy, a spontaneous passion that ran like lightning from one convert to another, that could not have been in starker contrast to the stern and intimidating formality of most Presbyterian and Congregational churches. Ultimately, the Baptists and Methodists were the chief beneficiaries of this shift. Although Stone himself was a Presbyterian, he was dismissed from the Kentucky Synod for his nonconformist beliefs shortly after Cane Ridge and went on to help found the nondenominational Christian Restoration Movement, which had no formal creed.

Some of the answers to why these revivals caught fire on the Kentucky frontier resided in the circumstances of frontier life in 1800 and 1801. The new plain-style sects were more willing than the Presbyterians and Congregationalists to send itinerant ministers into the field, to minister to people wherever they lived. Those preachers often found people newly dislocated from family and friends, excited about the new possibilities of their lives but also isolated and homesick. Christian churches had often supplied sites of solace and community for Americans.

The anxieties of the frontier extended beyond the loss of the familiar. These settlers were part of a torrent of expansion across the Appalachians, advancing into territories still claimed by indigenous people. The settlers were therefore the objects of constant resistance from Cherokees, Chickasaws, Shawnees, and others. For Euro-Americans, Christianity had long served as a boundary of distinction between themselves and Native Americans and as a marker of superiority. And it served that purpose again as migrants grappled with the consequences to others of their new opportunities. ●

their own redemption. Methodists, for example, rejected what they deemed artificial differences among Christians, pronouncing "[o]ne condition, and only one" required for salvation: "a real desire." Their system of itinerant preaching (preachers traveled among congregations, rather than associating with a single church) enabled the clergy "to preach in many places," as minister Jesse Lee put it, and to reach out to the dispersed and the displaced. Emphasizing inner truth, a plain style, and congregational independence, the evangelical denominations offered a relatively egalitarian vision of the community of believers that was especially attractive to the poor, to enslaved and free African Americans, and to white women. Some congregations went so far as to question the morality of slaveholding itself. Among the itinerant preachers were African Americans like Jarena Lee, whose extraordinary gifts as an exhorter had earned her a wide reputation up and down the coast.

Although Congregationalism was not fully disestablished in all states until later, by the turn of the century it was plagued by breakaway movements from within as well as by competition from the evangelical sects. The most important of the splinter groups were the Unitarian and Universalist movements, which held generally positive views of human nature, embraced universal salvation, and appealed especially to educated northerners seeking an alternative to strict Calvinism. Even in New England, however, the far greater threat to established religion came from the Methodists and Baptists, who found willing converts among country folks and city workers.

This widespread religious turmoil was expressed in a series of highly emotional revivals at the turn of the century, sometimes referred to as the Second Great

Awakening. These began in Virginia and western New England and, perhaps fed by the isolation of the backcountry, spread quickly into the newly settled areas of Kentucky and Tennessee. The most famous of these revivals occurred in August of 1801, in the tiny rural community of Cane Ridge, Kentucky, where thousands of men, women, and children, black and white, free and enslaved, came to watch and experience mass conversions. Eventually, the awakening spread to all parts of the country and to virtually all faiths—even, for a time, to the Congregationalists and Presbyterians, who joined in a Plan of Union to extend their influence in the West by settling joint congregations. Yet many members of these older denominations were displeased that revivals were led by unschooled preachers and encouraged unconventional beliefs and extravagant emotionalism. In 1803 to 1805 these misgivings led to schism, as the "Old Light" members of the Kentucky Synod purged "New Light" revivalists. In 1805, the national Presbyterian General Assembly reminded its members that "God is a God of order and not of confusion."

Where Congregationalists and Presbyterians saw confusion, Methodists and Baptists saw converts. In the first years of the nineteenth century, the number of Baptist congregations multiplied from about 400 to about 2,700, and membership in Methodist churches more than doubled, from 87,000 to 196,000. Eager to reach prospective members, Methodists founded the first denominational publishing house in the United States (the Methodist Book Concern). In 1817, they founded the national Sunday School Union.

Federalists often viewed this religious upheaval as a sign of the deterioration of both politics and morality in the new nation. Thomas Robbins, Congregational minister of Danbury, Connecticut, regarded Methodists in New England as dangerous "infestations" encouraged by the growth of the Democratic Republican Party. The linkages were seldom so simple. Neither Jefferson nor Madison, the founding lights of the Democratic Republican Party, embraced evangelical faiths. Moreover, far from signaling a drift toward irreligion, this contentious fragmentation of belief at the turn of the century had the effect of securing the language of religion, especially Protestant Christianity, as an idiom of both identity and exclusion in the new nation. Even as they fought over which form of Christian practice was correct, many Americans formulated their visions of the ideal community, including the ideal political community, in the language of Protestant Christianity and suspected those who disagreed with them not only of bad politics but also of bad faith.

The Problem of Trust in a Changing Society

Rip Van Winkle was not much bothered by awakening to find himself in a land of strangers. But real people often were. As old friends headed for new lands to the west, as young people slipped away from the supervision of parents or masters, as newcomers (from overseas or from the countryside) swelled the populations of port cities, many Americans grew skeptical about whom or what they could trust.

Particularly distressing to middling and wealthy Americans were signs that workers and children were forgetting their proper place. The customary discipline of the craft shop seemed to be crumbling. Apprentices demanded better treatment, refused drudgery work, or just ran away. In the larger port cities, unemployed young men gathered on the streets shouting obscenities at respectable citizens, frightening children, hassling shopkeepers, and sometimes attacking strangers. Journeymen in Philadelphia and New York demanded better pay and threatened to take their skills elsewhere if they weren't satisfied.

Household governance seemed to be falling apart, too. Domestic workers informed masters and mistresses that they would no longer be called "servants," insisting instead on being referred to as "help." Indentured workers balked at having their time and movements closely scrutinized. Even children seemed to have found a new "republican" determination to make their own decisions about whom to marry, where to live, and what work to pursue.

To their parents and masters and mistresses, it seemed that the youth and laboring classes of the nation were out of control. Indeed, in 1820, half the nation's population was under the age of 16 (compared to 26 percent under 18 in 2000). Parents threatened and cajoled. Masters offered rewards for runaway apprentices. Ministers warned against libertinism (especially young women's fashions, cut too daringly, they thought). Meanwhile, municipal and state authorities responded more concretely, with laws intended to control apprentices and regulate public behavior.

For several reasons, these efforts were largely doomed. The Revolution and its aftermath had changed society. Young people coming of age at the turn of the century had been nurtured on the rhetoric of independence. The economic boom of the 1790s and the larger market revolution of the turn of the century offered them numerous practical alternatives to older structures of authority. Why should a young man or woman remain on the family farm when there were jobs to be had in nearby towns? Why remain under the strictures of indentures or an apprenticeship when one could just leave? Why stay in the lagging economy of Philadelphia when New York beckoned?

Rumor and deception thrived in this landscape, both among those who had been displaced by the market revolution and among its beneficiaries. Washington Irving's Knickerbocker hoax in 1807 showed just how easy it was to pull the wool over people's eyes in the anonymity of a large city—and to benefit financially from doing it! Irving was not alone in his ruse. In 1812, just as the nation was reeling on the brink of war, a man by the name of Charles Redheffer presented himself to the Philadelphia city government with the claim that he had invented a perpetual motion machine. In the new era of steam power, Philadelphians were riveted by the possibilities, but the city commissioners who inspected the machine discovered that Redheffer was actually powering it through a hidden cranking device. Rather than simply crying foul, they responded with a hoax of their own, having a local engineer build a similar but even more cleverly deceptive machine. Redheffer fled Philadelphia immediately, moving on to New York City, where he was later exposed by Robert Fulton (who no doubt took a professional interest in debunking the machine).

Redheffer's Perpetual Motion Machine

Meanwhile, the New England countryside was filled with treasure hunters who had heard rumors of long-buried riches and were eager to find them. The stories about the origins of this treasure were legion. Some people said pirates who had once plied the New England coast had buried it. Others said Indian bands—now long dead or departed—had hidden it. Some of these seekers were amateur scientists and historians, drawn by the historical claims that often surrounded the stories. Some were charlatans, trying to make a quick buck off gullible visitors to the region. Some were the down-and-outers of New England's changing economy, honest people who still believed in a mystical landscape and in miracles that might turn their fortunes around.

One of these was the treasure seeker Joseph Smith. Smith was born in 1805 to a family of poor farmers in Vermont and grew up in western New York surrounded by economic and religious uncertainty. Although the family moved constantly and the region was bursting with development, economic security eluded the Smiths. Perhaps in search of some sense of constancy in daily life, Joseph was drawn to the religious revivalism that scorched upstate New York, and he believed in direct spiritual revelation. From time to time Smith and his father used what they claimed were supernatural powers to hire out as guides in what one observer described as "the money digging business." In 1819, however, Joseph Smith's powers of divination took a different turn: he experienced the first of a series of revelations in which he claimed that God had instructed him to found a new church that would teach the true lessons of Jesus Christ. In a second vision a few years later, an angel disclosed to him the location of golden tablets, buried in the ground near his home. They described God's intentions for the "latter days" of creation, now approaching. In 1830 Smith published his translation of the ancient writings on the tablets as the *Book of Mormon*. He formally founded the church that is now known as the Church of Jesus Christ of Latter-day Saints (or the Mormon Church).

The Panic of 1819

In 1819 Americans learned that the market revolution could produce dream-shattering plunges as well as exhilarating rises. Having signed the bill chartering the Second Bank of the United States in 1816, James Madison had promptly appointed an old political ally, Captain William Jones, as its director. Jones proved a poor choice; he speculated in bank stock and was willing to accept bribes to overlook reckless local practices. By the time Jones was replaced, bank stock was at an all-time low, and the state banks had glutted the economy with unsecured paper money.

Jones's successor, Langdon Cheves, moved quickly to cut the supply of paper money (too quickly, given that Great Britain was taking the same measures). Cheves began to call in loans and to redeem the bank's holdings of currency issued by the various state banks. Dangerously overextended, the state banks were forced to respond with their own programs of retrenchment. As credit dried up and the value of paper money plummeted, the nation was thrown into depression. Without credit or sufficient circulating money, commodity prices crashed throughout the Atlantic community. The market in cotton, which had propped up the growing American economy, fell by almost two-thirds. When they could not make their mortgages, farms and businesses failed. As businesses failed, tens of thousands of workers lost their jobs. For three long years, the economy stalled. Visitors to America warned potential immigrants not to come, as their chances of success would be "at best problematical."

Because the branches of the Second Bank of the United States reached far beyond the East Coast, so did the distress of the panic. When the branch in Cincinnati, Ohio, suddenly cashed in the paper money it held from local banks, for example, Cincinnati's booming economy felt the blow, as local banks scurried to collect enough debts to make good on the face value of their paper. In similar fashion, the shock waves rolled through Kentucky and Tennessee and into the states of the lower South.

Cheves had saved the monetary system of the United States, but he had not made many friends for the Second Bank. State legislators, who saw the national bank (not runaway local speculation or wildcat state banks) as the villain, scrambled to reduce its power. Fourteen states passed laws preventing the bank from collecting its debts, Kentucky abolished imprisonment for debt, and six states levied heavy taxes on bank branches (the practice that was soon banned by the Supreme Court in *McCulloch v. Maryland,* discussed earlier). After opening 18 branches in 1817, the Second Bank opened no additional new branches until 1826.

Conclusion

Over the course of his career, Washington Irving proved a keen and amusing observer of American life. He wrote about John Jacob Astor's fur company in the Pacific Northwest, about Native Americans, about the folk customs of various immigrant groups. He wrote a history of Christopher Columbus. He did not write about the American South, or about slavery—except in a piece titled "The Origin of the White, the Red, and the Black Men" to locate blacks at the lowest level of God's human creation. Like most white Americans of his day, Irving seemed neither aware nor concerned that the growth of the nation he so loved to chronicle was being powered by the enslaved labor of black workers, and that his own comfortable life in New York was being sustained, directly and indirectly, by that labor.

Further Readings

Gregory Evans Dowd, *A Spirited Resistance: The North American Indian Struggle for Unity, 1745–1815* (1992). Dowd argues for the emergence, in Jeffersonian America, of a coordinated and militant resistance, led by prophets like Tenskwatawa and his half-brother, Tecumseh, and expressed through a pan-Indian spiritual revival.

Annette Gordon-Reed, *The Hemingses of Monticello: An American Family* (2008). A magnificent biography of the slave family that was closely connected to Jefferson.

Marla R. Miller, *The Needle's Eye: Women and Work in the Age of Revolution* (2006). Miller offers an unusually vivid as well as thorough account of women's labor in the needle trades at the end of the eighteenth century and into the market revolution.

Gary B. Nash, *Forging Freedom: The Formation of Philadelphia's Black Community, 1720–1840* (1988). This study of the struggles of Philadelphia's African American population (both enslaved and free) to build a community in the early republic includes discussions of work, religion, class, and the responses of the African American community to growing white hostility.

Curtis P. Nettels, *The Emergence of a National Economy, 1775–1815* (1962). Although almost 50 years old, this remains one of the clearest and most comprehensive overviews of shipping, farming, business, and manufacturing in Jefferson's America and of the inventors, workers, and settlers who made the changes possible.

Peter S. Onuf, *Jefferson's Empire: The Language of American Nationhood* (2000). Connects Jefferson's ideas about race to his ideas about empire.

Howard B. Rock, *Artisans of the New Republic: The Tradesmen of New York City in the Age of Jefferson* (1984). Rock traces the experience of the craft workers of New York City from 1800 to 1815, examining the legacy of pride and independence that mechanics and tradesmen carried with them from the Revolution, as well as the dislocations and loss of status threatened by the changing marketplace and the expanding commercial economy.

Robert W. Tucker and David C. Hendrickson, *Empire of Liberty: The Statecraft of Thomas Jefferson* (1990). This exploration of Jefferson's political philosophy and foreign policy is an especially useful guide to the circumstances surrounding the Louisiana Purchase and the War of 1812.

Laurel Thatcher Ulrich, *A Midwife's Tale: The Life of Martha Ballard, Based on Her Diary, 1785–1812* (1990). A 20-year-long diary provided the primary source for this careful examination of the work, family events, and daily social interactions of a midwife in rural Maine in the early republic.

>> Timeline >>

▼ 1800
Thomas Jefferson elected president

▼ 1801
Judiciary Act of 1801
Cane Ridge (Kentucky) Revival
Barbary War

▼ 1803
Louisiana Purchase
Marbury v. Madison

▼ 1804
Jefferson reelected
Lewis and Clark begin exploration of Louisiana

▼ 1805
Palmer v. Mulligan (New York)
Essex Decision (British Admiralty Court)

▼ 1806
Conspiracy trial of Philadelphia journeyman shoemakers

▼ 1807
First Embargo Act
Hudson River trial of Fulton's *North River Steamboat of Clermont*

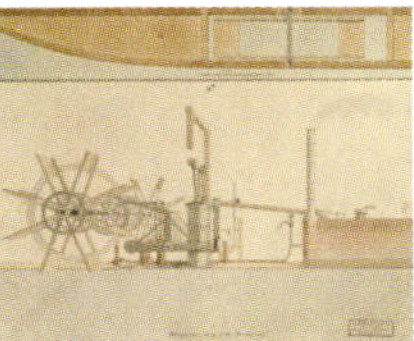

▼ 1808
External slave trade becomes illegal
Madison elected president

▼ 1809
Non-Intercourse Act

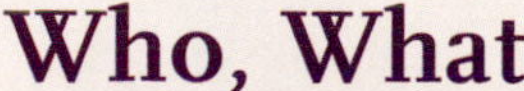

Who, What

Thomas Jefferson 292
John Marshall 294
James Madison 299
De Witt Clinton 300
Robert Fulton 308
Tecumseh 317
Market revolution 303
Revivals 320

Review Questions

1. What was the market revolution? What concrete changes did it make in Americans' daily lives?
2. How would you account for the timing of the many innovations in transportation at the end of the eighteenth century and the beginning of the nineteenth?
3. By 1816, were the differences between the Federalists and the Democratic Republicans matters of politics, or principle, or both?
4. What were the main themes of Jefferson's presidency?

Websites

DoHistory: Martha Ballard's Diary Online. An interactive website based on Laurel Thatcher Ulrich's award-winning book, *A Midwife's Tale,* about the life of a Maine midwife and how one writes history. http://dohistory.org/

Journals of the Lewis and Clark Expedition. The complete journals of the expedition, along with images, maps, and a wealth of other sources. http://lewisandclarkjournals.unl.edu/index.html

Monticello. The website for Jefferson's home, with abundant information not only about Jefferson but also the slaves who lived and worked there. http://www.monticello.org/

For further review materials and resource information, please visit www.oup.com/us/ofthepeople

▼ 1810
American cotton production reaches 178,000 bales

▼ 1811
Tecumseh at peak of influence
Battle of Tippecanoe River

▼ 1812
War of 1812 begins
James Madison reelected

▼ 1814
Federalist Hartford Convention
Treaty of Ghent ends War of 1812
Fully steam-powered textile mills established in Waltham, Massachusetts

▼ 1815
Battle of New Orleans

▼ 1817
Work on Erie Canal begun
Steamboats common on Mississippi River

▼ 1819
Panic of 1819
Dartmouth v. Woodward
McCulloch v. Maryland
Irving publishes "Rip Van Winkle"

▼ 1824
Gibbons v. Ogden

▼ 1825
Erie Canal completed

CHAPTER 10

Common Threads

>> What was the impact of the cotton gin on American overseas trade?

>> How did the economic development of the South affect the economic development of the nation?

>> How did the social and cultural development of the South after 1800 affect the daily lives of northerners?

>> How did the tariff affect the South?

Slavery and the Nation
1790–1828

AMERICAN PORTRAIT

>> Lucretia Coffin Mott and the Free Produce Movement

Lucretia Coffin Mott was born in 1793 on the island of Nantucket in Massachusetts. In her adulthood Mott would become one of the most influential and powerful voices for social justice in the United States, a strong supporter of women's rights and a revered antislavery leader. That commitment was honed early in her life by the conflict between her Quaker ideals and the evidence all around her—including in her own family—of the iron grip of slavery on the young republic in which she lived.

Lucretia Coffin was the child of devout Quaker parents, Thomas and Anna Folger Coffin. By the late eighteenth century the Society of Friends had become one of the most outspoken communities of antislavery sentiment in the United States. Indeed, after 1774 many Quaker meetings had begun expelling members who owned slaves. Coffin spent the first 11 years of her life in the tight Quaker community of Nantucket, imbibing Quaker beliefs about the dignity and equality of all people, female and male, white and black. She was educated in Quaker schools, including the Friends Boarding-School at Poughkeepsie, New York, where she was first a student and then an assistant teacher. It was there, too, that she met James Mott, who shared her Quaker beliefs and became her husband in 1811. When Lucretia joined her parents in Philadelphia in 1809, she moved into the heart of Quaker activism in the United States.

But Lucretia was also the child of a family that was deeply dependent on the northern merchant economy, which by 1809 had numerous ties, direct and indirect, to slavery. Lucretia's father, Thomas, was a sea captain engaged in whaling and in the late eighteenth-century China trade. Although the family neither owned nor directly trafficked in slaves, Thomas almost certainly filled out his cargo with food supplies for the Caribbean slave islands and for the West African slaving ports he passed on his way to the China seas. Lucretia's mother, Anna, maintained a family store on shore, where she sold goods acquired in Thomas's voyages. In 1804 the family had become successful enough to move to the larger commercial entrepôt of Boston, and Thomas had expanded his business to include the trade in cotton. By the time the family moved on to Philadelphia, in 1809, other New England merchant families were already beginning to experiment with the textile mills (using southern cotton) that would soon power the northern industrial economy. In Philadelphia, meanwhile, Thomas operated a hardware business with Lucretia's husband, James, that almost certainly included southern planters as customers.

Lucretia Mott later recalled that her "sympathy was early enlisted for the poor slave, by the class-books read in our schools, and the pictures of the slave-ship," but it may have been in Philadelphia, under the influence of radical Quaker preacher Elias Hicks and others, that she began to contemplate her own personal involvement with slavery. Hicks had long insisted that opposing slavery meant not only refusing to own slaves, helping to emancipate and educate them, and speaking out formally against the institution, but also cleansing one's own life of all of the luxuries made possible by slave labor. Under this influence, and the influence of English Quaker Elizabeth Heyrick, whose *Immediate, Not Gradual Abolition* advocated the same position, Lucretia began to boycott commodities made by slaves, chiefly cotton and sugar. But it wasn't easy to procure substitutes. In 1826 Lucretia and James (who had by this time divorced his business from the slave trade) helped form the Philadelphia Free Produce Society to make alternative choices available to members.

continued

>> AMERICAN PORTRAIT *continued*

Lucretia Mott continued to fight slavery all of her life, but the free produce movement she helped found did not prove a very effective tool in that crusade. The movement suffered from a lack of internal support: some activists simply didn't consider a boycott a strong enough or direct enough measure against the towering crimes of slavery. Although free produce advocates opened additional stores in the middle and northeastern states to sell cotton goods manufactured from cotton grown by free labor, most northerners understood that it would take political action, not consumer boycotts, to abolish slavery in the United States.

OUTLINE

Southern Slavery

Southern slavery took many forms in the antebellum years. Some enslaved laborers worked as hired-out field workers or house servants, some worked in mines and mills, some belonged to small farmers, although most slaves lived on plantations. But what made all of them "slaves," no matter what they did or where they lived, was the fact that they were defined as property, treated as property, and defended as property.

"Property in Man"

By the time the first slaves arrived in colonial Virginia Europeans had been buying and selling African slaves throughout the Atlantic world for more than a century. For most of that time the trade was dominated by the Spanish and the Portuguese, but at the moment the first Africans were sold to Virginians, the Dutch were assuming the dominant position in the transatlantic slave trade. So it was no surprise that the first 20 slaves brought to Jamestown in 1619 had been purchased in Africa a few months earlier and were sold to the English colonists from a Dutch man-of-war.

Those first Africans were already property—slaves—when they arrived, and the English colonists who owned them had a common law of property into which the slaves could be fitted. Within a few years the slaves were showing up in the estate inventories of English settlers as part of the property to be passed on to the relatives of deceased owners. Because slaves were *human* property, masters had to enact slave codes to regulate the slaves' behavior, laws that had no bearing on nonhuman property such as houses and livestock. But the slave codes were the footnotes of slave law, which was at bottom property law.

In most slave societies—ancient Rome, medieval Islam, western Africa, Brazil, Cuba—significant numbers of slaves were individually freed, a process known as manumission. For a few decades after 1620 the Chesapeake followed this familiar pattern: A good number of the African slaves were freed, and some of those who were freed became slaveholders themselves. Anothony Johnson, for example, arrived as a slave, was freed, and ended up owning many slaves on Maryland's eastern shore. But in the second half of the seventeeth century the slave societies of the Anglo-American world began to distinguish themselves by the very low number of slaves who were freed. Nevertheless, even in the earliest decades most Africans were treated as property and remained slaves for their entire lives.

> Charlottesville, Oct. 8, 1852
>
> Dear Husband
>
> I write you a letter to let you know my distress my master has sold albert to a trader on Monday court day and myself and other child is for sale also and I want you to let [me] hear from you very soon before next cort if you can I don't know when I don't want you to wait till Christmas I want you to tell dr. Hamelton and your master if either will buy me they can attend to it know and then I can go afterwards. I don't want a trader to get me they asked me if I had go any person to buy me and I told them no they took me to the court houste too they never put me up a man buy the name of brady bought albert and is gone I don't know where they say he lives in Scottesville my things is in Staunton and if I should be sold I don't know what will become of them I don't expect to meet with the luck to get that way till I am quite heartsick nothing more I am and ever will be your kind wife
>
> Maria Perkins
> To Richard Perkins

The problem for slaveholders was that most property law was written to cover real estate, primarily land and houses. Inherited from the Middle Ages, property law was riddled with restrictions on how the owner could dispose of an estate. But slaves were moveable property and their owners chafed under the ancient feudal restraints on real estate. At first they carved out legal distinctions within the law of "real" property, distinctions that gave masters freedom to dispose of their slave property more easily. But by the end of the eighteenth century the slaveholders had devised a better solution. They rewrote the law entirely, transferring their slaves from the category of "real" property to the much more flexible category of "personal" property. In the nineteenth century only Kentucky continued to define slaves as a special category of real property. Louisiana devised a similar exception within its distinctive civil law tradition. But the effect was the same: in the nineteenth-century South, what made a slave a slave was his or her status as the personal property of the master.

This was important because slave economies need slave trades, and by defining slaves as personal property, the slaveholders who wrote their own laws gave themselves the freedom to buy and sell their slaves virtually without restraint. To be sure, Congress banned the foreign slave trade in the United States as of 1808 (the earliest date permitted by the Constitution). In anticipation of this action, between 1800 and 1808 slave traffickers delivered and southern planters purchased at least 40,000 Africans into American slavery. Lax federal enforcement allowed some smuggling of slaves into the United States until the Civil War, but by then the southern states had become dependent on a flourishing domestic trade in slaves.

The invention of the cotton gin in the 1790s provoked a boom in cotton production and with it the aggressive expansion of the South into the new cotton lands in the West. In response, eastern slave owners whose farms and plantations were no longer able to sustain single-crop production and whose profits were therefore in decline began to orient themselves to the business of supplying slaves—selling their own excess labor "South"—to newer farms in Mississippi, Alabama, and western Tennessee and Kentucky. There is little evidence that slaveholders consciously "bred" slaves to increase profits. But there is abundant evidence that slaveholders were aware of the additional profits to be garnered from slave women who bore many children, and many went out of their way to encourage slave reproduction. Even as the United States withdrew from the Atlantic slave trade, a flourishing domestic slave trade arose to take its place.

The Domestic Slave Trade

Before 1808 most enslaved people who were forced to migrate south and west did so as a part of planter migrations. But by the 1820s, as many as one-third of all migrating slaves (a figure equal to about 15,000 people a year) went west as the property of traders. Although sometimes run by freelancers, the internal slave trade was often a highly organized business, with firms employing 10 or 20 employees (bosses, clerks, guards, agents) in fine offices in Charleston, Richmond, and Baltimore. One of its features was the slave market.

The slave market had long been a southern institution, but its sheer inhumanity was laid visible anew as it became the prime symbol of being "sold South." The market was a ghastly collision of worlds: for potential buyers, sellers, and mere onlookers, it was a social setting (not unlike a club or tavern) where white men might renew friendships and exchange information on their families or their crops or politics—a camaraderie called into being by the difference between the easy sociability of the white people milling around and the terror of the black people about to be offered for sale. Indeed, that amiability helped establish the distinction, so that potential buyers might the more easily understand themselves as rational and well-motivated businessmen, rather than purveyors of misery. And yet the truth of the transaction permeated the place—in the audible sobs of mothers and children, in the harsh calculations and coarse comments of attendees, and in the absence of white females, a powerful silent admission that whatever was occurring at the slave market was so nakedly brutal as to taint the purity of white women.

Some slaves were shipped south on a boat, but they were often driven overland. It was a "singular spectacle," one English visitor to Tennessee remembered. "In the early gray of the morning, [I came upon] a camp of negro slave drivers, just packing up to start. They had about three hundred slaves with them, who had bivouacked the preceding night in chains in the woods." Leading the convoy was "a caravan of nine waggons and single horse carriages, for the purpose of conducting the white people."

American Slave Market A 19th-century painting of a slave auction, the meeting point for internal slave trade within the southern states.

Former slave Frederick Douglass, born in Maryland, later described the terror that the threat of being "sold South" struck in the hearts of enslaved African Americans. His owner died when Douglass was eight years old. The enslaved workers were hustled together to be appraised and allotted—some to be retained by family members, some to be "sold at once to the Georgia traders." "I have no language to express the high excitement and deep anxiety which were felt among us poor slaves during this time," Douglass wrote. "Our fate for life was now to be decided. We had no more voice in that decision than the brutes among whom we were ranked. A single word from the white men was enough—against all our wishes, prayers, and entreaties—to sunder forever the dearest friends, dearest kindred, and strongest ties known to human beings." One in three enslaved children under 14 was separated from at least one parent as a result of westward migration. One in three slave marriages in the upper South was destroyed.

Slave Badge Slaves hired out for wages were often forced to wear badges like this one, identifying them as slaves and indicating their occupation and the place where they worked.

The journeys of 20-year-old Elizabeth Ramsey and her infant daughter, Louisa, were illustrative. Elizabeth and Louisa were sold from South Carolina to a Georgia cotton planter by the name of Cook. When cotton speculation and high living landed Cook in bankruptcy, he fled to Mobile, Alabama, where he hired out both Elizabeth and Louisa as domestic servants. His fortunes still failing, he eventually sold Elizabeth to a new owner in Texas and her daughter to a man in New Orleans.

Plantation Slavery

The symbol of the early nineteenth-century South was the cotton plantation, a large farm owned and operated by a single white family and worked by a large number of enslaved laborers, toiling up and down plowed rows planting the seed in the spring, hoeing the tender young plants in the hot summer sun, moving in slow phalanxes across the fields picking the sticky cotton balls in the autumn. And with good reason did this image seem to capture the way of life of the slave South. Although slavery existed in America long before the cotton boom that began in the late 1790s, that boom vastly increased the demand for slaves. Cotton was a crop highly suitable to slave economies. It could be grown on large plantations tended by gangs of coerced workers who (thanks to the relatively short height of the cotton plant) could be kept under supervision at all times. Of the 1.5 million

Cotton Plantation Overseers and slaves on a cotton plantation in the American South: colored engraving, 19th century.

AMERICAN LANDSCAPE

>> Gowrie: The Story of Profit and Loss on an American Plantation

"Gowrie" was a plantation, 265 acres of fertile rice fields spread across a large island in the middle of the Savannah River, just upstream from Augusta, Georgia, and just over the border from South Carolina.

In 1833, Gowrie's land and enslaved labor force of 50 people became the property of Charles Manigault. Manigault had lost half of his paternal inheritance in merchant ventures in the volatile markets of the early 1820s. By the end of the decade he was eager not simply to restore his earlier wealth, but also to establish his family among the ruling dynasties of the South.

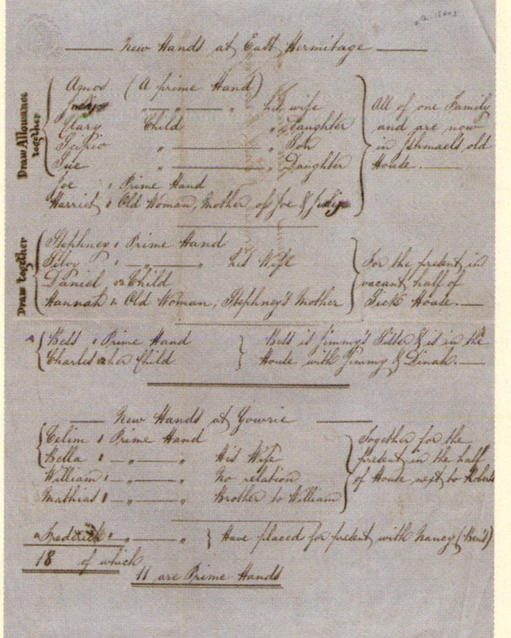

New Hands at East Hermitage

Draw Allowance together:
Amos (A prime Hand)
Judy " " his wife
Mary Child, Daughter
Scipio ", Son
Sue ", Daughter
Joe, Prime Hand
Harriet, Old Woman, mother of Joe & Judy
} All of one Family and are now in Ishmael's old House

Draw together:
Stephney, Prime Hand
Silvy ", his Wife
Daniel, a Child
Hannah, Old Woman, Stephney's mother
} For the present in vacant half of Sick House

Bell, Prime Hand
Charles, her Child
} Bell is Jimmy's Sister & is in the House with Jimmy & Dinah

New Hands at Gowrie

Celim, Prime Hand
Bella ", His Wife
William ", No relation
Mathias ", Brother to William
} Together for the present in the half of House next to [illegible]

Frederick ", } Have placed for present with Nancy ([illegible])

18 of which 11 are Prime Hands

For Manigault, Gowrie was the means to that end—an investment and a profit-center, but never his "home." He never lived full time at Gowrie and never built a family seat there, preferring instead the elaborate mansion at Marshlands, his plantation seven miles outside of Charleston. Manigault ran Gowrie from afar, directing affairs through periodic visits and regular letters of instruction to his resident overseer, while he traveled abroad and enjoyed more cosmopolitan living.

For the enslaved workers who lived there, Gowrie held different meanings. It was, above all, a place of hard, forced labor. Rice cultivation began in the winter months, when slaves burned off the old stubble in Gowrie's 15 fields and leveled and plowed the land. Women seeded the rice between mid-March and early June. As soon as the seed was in, "trunk-minders" (aided by the tides of the Savannah River) opened the elaborate irrigation systems to flood the fields, protecting the seeds from birds and the sprouts from too much sun. As the seeds grew into young plants, the slaves periodically partially drained the fields (to allow for weeding and hoeing) and then reflooded them, until the final flooding in mid-July.

The flooding and draining reduced (but did not eliminate) the work of cultivation. However, it created the additional labor of building, repairing, and cleaning ditches and canals to channel the water, traps to close it off, and drains to carry it away. Men constructed the systems, while women were put to work hauling in the mud to construct earthworks and hauling away the muck that collected in drains and clogged ditches and canals.

But for its laborers, Gowrie was also home. Life at Gowrie offered slaves a few advantages over life on other types of farms. Because rice was most profitably grown on a large scale, rice plantations were among the largest in the South and had unusually large slave populations—119 at Gowrie at its largest in 1849. The size of the workforce created a community of kin and friends unknown to slaves on smaller holdings. Moreover, the complexity of the work led most overseers to employ the task system—which provided slaves with a degree of autonomy in the organization and execution of their labor. The periodic breaks in the rhythms of cultivation (first while the seeds sprouted and then during the main growing season) allowed slaves time to plant their own gardens, yielding produce to improve their diets and perhaps some to sell. The slaves were all but forced to do this. Rice planters like Manigault systematically underfed their workers in the expectation that the slaves themselves would make up for it in their spare time by fishing, raising chickens, tending vegetable gardens, and exchanging their produce among themselves.

So although Gowrie was home to the slaves who lived there, it was a harsh home. Tending the muddy or flooded fields was dangerous as well as exhausting labor, and accidents were common. Because embankments regularly washed away, and ditches filled with silt, rice plantations required colder, wetter winter labor than other kinds of plantations. Constantly wading in the waters, rice workers were particularly subject to snakebites and to malaria. Gowrie's location on a river and near the ocean, which made it easier to flood, made the plantation an especially dangerous place for slaves. Being

continued

>> **AMERICAN LANDSCAPE** *continued*

forced out in the unpredictably high tides, hurricanes, and floods to mend dikes and clear canals was part of everyday labor on rice plantations. Manigault evidently did little to reduce these dangers. Health decisions were often left up to the overseer (who virtually never called in a doctor) and to a single elderly slave woman (who was hard pressed to care for such a large community).

While Manigault grew spectacularly wealthy, the ultimate price of rice production to enslaved workers was a staggeringly high mortality rate, especially among children. None of the six infants present at Gowrie when Manigault purchased the estate lived to see adulthood. By January 1835, only half of the original labor force remained alive.

enslaved inhabitants of the South in 1820, probably three-quarters lived on plantations with 10 or more slaves.

The number of slaves on a given plantation varied widely. Sugar plantations averaged 30 or more workers. Rice plantations were somewhat smaller, but still larger on average than cotton and tobacco farms. The wealthiest families of the South owned hundreds of slaves on several different plantations, often hundreds of miles apart. The size depended partly on the crop and its cultivation, but also on the aspirations of the owner. Owning large tracts of land and large numbers of enslaved workers was the highest symbol of status in the South. Cotton plantations proliferated in the new western lands. Meanwhile, the reopening of international markets gave new life to tobacco plantations in Virginia and North Carolina, rice plantations in South Carolina and Georgia, and sugar plantations in Louisiana.

For a slave, there was nothing worse than the hellish way of life of the sugar plantation. Masters on sugar plantations drove their workers hardest, producing the highest rates of sickness and death in the South. The crop cycle for sugar was 13 months or more, which meant that the planting of a new crop overlapped with the harvesting of the old one—producing weeks of almost unbearably intense labor. Because sugar, unlike cotton or tobacco, had to be processed immediately upon harvesting, sugar plantations had to have the boiling and pressing machinery to rush the cane into production immediately after it was picked. For these reasons sugar planters preferred to buy strong adult men. With fewer women there were fewer slave families on sugar plantations. To top it off, this intense exploitation took place in the hottest, swampiest parts of the South. Higher rates of sickness and death combined with lower rates of reproduction meant that sugar planters had to restock their slave labor force with constant infusions of newly purchased slaves. The cost of the sugar presses, plus the cost of buying the most expensive slaves—strong young men—meant that only the wealthiest owners could afford to set up sugar plantations, and it meant that sugar plantations were only profitable with large numbers of slaves. It is hardly surprising, therefore, that the sugar parishes of southern Louisiana sustained the Old South's largest slave market, in New Orleans.

Rice cultivation was not quite as lethal, but it was also centered in the sickliest low-country regions of the South—not southern Louisiana but the coastal tidewater regions of South Carolina and Georgia. Rice workers stood ankle deep in mud under the blazing sun in snake-infested, swampland fields: it was "by far the most unhealthy work in which slaves are employed." The crop also influenced the organization of labor. Skilled rice cultivators commonly worked by the "task" system, under which workers were assigned a specific objective for the day's work (e.g., repairing a drainage ditch) and were able to exercise some autonomy over their labor.

But sugar and rice were restricted by geography to relatively contained regions of the South. The vast majority of the slaves were set to work cultivating cotton and, to a lesser extent, tobacco, on farms and plantations that flourished in the drier inland regions. With these crops the growing seasons were shorter and the plantations were more self-sufficient in foodstuffs. As a result, cotton and tobacco slaves were relatively healthy. On large cotton plantations, slaves were more likely to be organized in "gangs," set at repetitive tasks (like hoeing or picking) with close supervision. At harvest, cotton workers dragged their load to the gins that pulled the sticky cotton fibers from their bolls, continuing by the light of torches long after sunset. Tobacco workers were especially busy in the spring, carefully transplanting young plants and pruning off extra shoots.

Not all plantation slaves were field workers. On tobacco farms slaves hung and tended the drying leaf. Sugarcane plantations generally included the workshops required to wash, chop, and squash the stalks and reduce their juices to sugar. Jefferson's Monticello included a distillery, a mill, and a nail factory that were as important to his profits as were the crops. On big cotton and tobacco plantations, as much as one-quarter of the workforce was assigned to domestic service or to crafts intended to make the plantation more self-sufficient. Although white observers tended to view household servants as fortunate, the lot of house slaves was not necessarily better than that of field workers. They were constantly on call, so their workday could last even longer than that of field workers. They were also especially vulnerable to the whims and moody outbursts of owners.

More independent than the house slaves were the 5 to 8 percent of the workforce trained for craft work. Men became carpenters, ironworkers, and boatmen. A smaller number of women became spinners, weavers, seamstresses, and dairymaids. Because their work was housed in separate shops, craft workers often enjoyed a degree of autonomy rare for most slaves.

Some plantations were complex economic concerns, with dispersed fields, multiple barns and outbuildings, batteries of craft workers, a village of slave cabins, and an elegantly furnished "big house." Planters like George Washington and Thomas Jefferson devoted years to the design and furnishing of their homes, creating settings of luxury and ease—in Jefferson's case, settings artfully arranged to conceal the slaves whose work created the luxury. But many plantation houses were a good deal less noble. Northerner Emily Burke described the big house of a Georgia plantation as a mere husk of a building with unplastered walls, a plank floor she could see through, and a roof like a sieve.

Other Varieties of Slavery

Although most enslaved African Americans were held on fairly sizeable plantations, some slaves worked in other settings. On large plantations that did not always require the work of all the slaves, and on plantations in the older states, where soil was exhausted, planters made part of their income by renting out slaves, who might go to other plantations or small farmers to help with seasonal tasks. Other enslaved people were hired out to nonagricultural work. By one estimate, a quarter of all Appalachian slaves were hired out, most of those to nonagricultural jobs. Virginian

AMERICA AND THE WORLD

>> The Demand for Raw Cotton

The economic and territorial expansion of the United States in the early nineteenth century was propelled by the cotton boom. And the American cotton boom was propelled by the growing European (primarily English) demand for raw cotton.

Americans were not the only suppliers to the British mills. Britain also imported large amounts of raw cotton from its colonies in India (and then returned the finished cloth to colonial markets for sale). But the voyage from India to England was long and difficult, and India production alone was unable to satisfy the voracious English cotton mills. Moreover, American short staple proved both more durable than India cotton (a result of longer fibers) and cheaper because it was produced by slave labor. By 1800, American planters were producing over 36 million bales of cotton (compared to a mere 1.5 million in 1790, three years before Eli Whitney's invention of the cotton gin). By 1830, that volume had grown by a factor of ten to nearly 366 million. By then, cotton accounted for roughly half of all American exports, a proportion that kept growing.

As the international market grew, and the annual production of cotton increased, so did the number of slaves and the extent of slave territory in the United States. In 1790 there were approximately 700,000 enslaved people in the United States. By 1830 that number had nearly quadrupled, to 2 million. (It would double again in the next 30 years, to almost 4 million.) As the number of slaves increased, so did the price of each person—from an average of about $250 for a field hand in 1790 to $1,500 in 1825—a difference that remained fairly closely correlated with the volume of cotton production. In 1790 most slaves in the United States were held in Virginia, with North and South Carolina and Maryland ranking next in slave populations. By 1830, the number of slaves in Maryland was in decline, but slavery had expanded west and south in Kentucky, Tennessee, Georgia, and Alabama, following the availability of the rich cotton lands in those regions.

Former slave Charles Ball later recalled that the explosion in the British demand for American cotton not only bolstered the internal slave trade but also shaped the qualities that planters looked for in the slaves they purchased. In 1805 Ball overheard another white man advising Ball's master to take his coffle of slaves to Columbia or Augusta. "The landlord assured my master that at this time slaves were much in demand" in those places. "[P]urchasers were numerous and prices good; . . . Cotton, he said, had not been higher for many years, and as a great many persons, especially young men, were moving off to the new purchase in Georgia, prime hands were in high demand, for the purpose of clearing the land in the new country—that the boys and girls, under twenty, would bring almost any price at present, in Columbia for the purpose of picking the growing crop of cotton, which promised to be very heavy; and as most persons had planted more than their hands would be able to pick, young niggers, who would soon learn to pick cotton, were prime articles in the market. As to those more advanced in life, he seemed to think the prospect of selling them at an unusual price, not so good, as they could not so readily become expert cotton-pickers. . . ."

The international cotton market was not stable during these years. Plunges in prices could be triggered by any number of factors far beyond the control of American producers: the War of 1812, the collapse of credit in 1819, the volatility of world markets—any of these could and did catalyze dramatic shifts in the price of cotton. In the two-month period between October and the end of December in 1818, for example, the value of cotton ready for loading in American seaports dropped by 26 percent. As the steady growth of cotton cultivation indicates, however, planters' response to declining prices was not to cut back on cotton cultivation, but to plant even more cotton.

Thomas Prosser allowed his slave Gabriel to hire himself out as a carpenter. Other slaves hired out to work in stores, hotels, blacksmitheries, and cotton gin works. Frederick Douglass hired himself out as a skilled caulker on the Baltimore docks.

Frederick Douglass

A smaller number of slaves worked in extractive industries or mills in the South. In Kentucky, Virginia, and West Virginia, for example, slaves worked in saltworks. White people held virtually all of the supervisory positions, but slaves tended and stirred the boiling kettles of brine and prepared the salt for drying and packing. By 1828 there were 65 salt wells in West Virginia, operated by a workforce of just under 500 slaves and producing a total of almost 800,000 bushels of salt every year. As the industry grew, it supported an expanding economy in lumber, coal mining, boatbuilding, and shipping (down the Ohio and Mississippi rivers), among other commercial sectors. Some of these related jobs (cutting lumber, operating boats and ferries, coal mining) were also done by slaves, and some by free workers whose employment thus depended on the continuation of a slave-based industry. In the southern Appalachian region, the early 1820s saw the beginnings of a gold rush that did not peak until the 1830s. By 1833 some 5,000 slaves (men and women) were at work in gold mines in a single North Carolina county—enough to raise concerns among local white people about the possibilities of rebellion. Slaves also worked as copper and coal miners and in copper smelters and iron forges. By the late 1830s, Ice's Ferry Iron Works in West Virginia (perhaps the largest forge in the country) employed 1,700 workers, both slave and free.

Neither slave owning nor plantation farming typified the experiences of southern whites, most of whom lived on small holdings of several hundred acres or less. These "yeoman" households typically owned no slaves, although they sometimes hired slaves from nearby planters. Living in rough and isolated dwellings, they produced as much of their own food as they could; planted small amounts of cash-crop tobacco, cotton, or grain; and often relied on nearby planters as agents in selling their crops or purchasing seed or new equipment. They also relied on larger estates as a source of labor when they needed to hire a slave for a brief period of time. Beneath the yeoman households, economically and socially, was a white underclass of tenant farmers and day laborers, and a precarious free black population.

Although most white people did not own slaves, the institution of slavery influenced their material lives and personal values. A workforce made up of millions of unpaid laborers meant fewer stores and businesses in the slave states than in the Northeast. A large number of rivers flowing from the inland regions to the coastal ports reduced the need for expensive railroads and canals. All of this meant that the southern economy remained less developed than the North's, and this had important consequences for the lives of southern whites who owned no slaves. By 1820 the South did have mills and factories, but most of the workers were slaves. For those who preferred subsistence to commerce, the relatively underdeveloped slave economy offered some measure of protection. For more ambitious farmers, slavery restricted economic opportunity to the accumulation of land and slaves. Small farmers could hire field slaves from larger planters at rates cheaper than they could hire free labor, and planters could put a slave to craft work for less money than it would cost to hire a free artisan.

Because southern slavery was overwhelmingly agricultural, the South had fewer and smaller cities than the North. Even in the older seacoast states, less than 3 percent of southerners lived in cities. This number included planters taking refuge during the malaria season, slaves hired out to domestic service for the urban professional class, and the South's free African American population. In a long-standing practice, southern planters looked to Philadelphia and New York for services and luxury goods. When planters sought alternatives to this pattern of external dependence, they looked not to local villages or towns but to their own plantations, reassigning field workers to produce the butter, cheese, and tools they might otherwise have purchased locally. With a few exceptions, the economies of southern cities were based narrowly on the commerce of slaves and cotton.

African American Scrubwoman This early 19th-century drawing of an African American scrubwoman is interesting both because it individualizes the subject and because the subject, a worker, is presented in a style of almost classic reflection.

Most white southerners continued to live in rural settings under the authority of fathers. In this environment, white southerners clung to the patterns of domestic patriarchy that had emerged in the eighteenth century. They had long since accepted the modern notion that freedom and human fulfillment were to be found in the private sphere of life, in families and private property. Although they had rejected patriarchy as a form of political organization, they retained it as a form of family organization. In this view of the world the good citizen was the patriarchal father who protected his family, wisely stewarded his human and nonhuman resources, and was generous to his neighbors. Whether the farmer was deeply engaged in the production of cash crops, or concerned primarily with self-sufficiency, his manhood was closely bound up with the economic independence that came with the ownership of land.

In this view of the world the slaves were another part of the master's property, and were fiercely defended as such. But because the accumulation of slaves was a source of wealth in its own right, the economic interests of the master often dovetailed with the benign treatment of his human property. The most consistent calls for reform of the slave system came from efficiency experts who argued that the most profitable plantations were those on which the slaves were well fed, adequately housed, and decently clothed. That was the ideal, of course, but for all too many masters the temptation to provide the slaves with as little as possible was hard to resist. A rational system of incentives was one way to motivate slave labor, but the whip was often easier. And in any case, the proper maintenance of slave property only served to highlight the fact that slaves were, after all, property.

Resistance and Creation Among Southern Slaves

For enslaved people, slavery was not merely a system of enforced and often harsh labor. It was also a system of daily survival, practically and emotionally. It was a struggle against poor food, poor shelter, and the constant threat of brutal treatment and separation; a decision to speak or not speak, a judgment to refuse or not refuse, a choice, usually, between unsatisfactory alternatives.

In all its forms, slavery constituted a steady assault on the selfhood and the family and community life of slaves. The killing of a slave was the most extreme example of this aggression. But maiming and branding were also common practices in the South—so common that inventors devised special instruments for them and owners included descriptions of signs of torture in their advertisements for runaway slaves. For example, in 1802 Virginian John Stevens was very comfortable letting his friends and neighbors know that his runaway slave Toney "has scars on his back [not for his good behavior] and one very noted scar on his breast as large as a man's finger and as long, like unto a gristle; he has been branded on both jaws, he being very crafty, and has laid poison oak on them, and has removed the brand and is now become a scar on each jaw like unto the other."

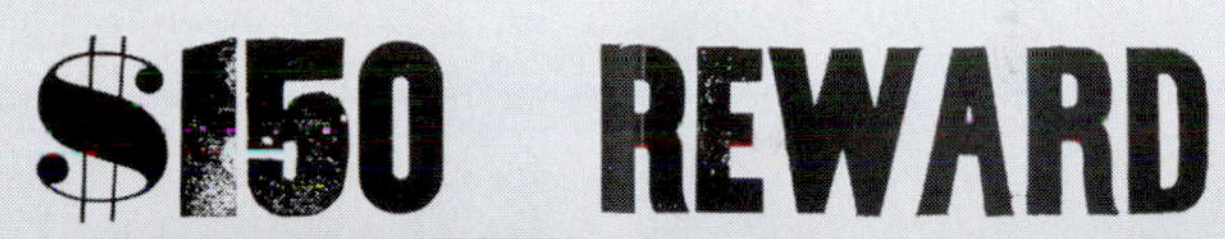

$150 REWARD

RANAWAY from the subscriber, on the night of the 2d instant, a negro man, who calls himself *Henry May*, about 22 years old, 5 feet 6 or 8 inches high, ordinary color, rather chunky built, bushy head, and has it divided mostly on one side, and keeps it very nicely combed; has been raised in the house, and is a first rate dining-room servant, and was in a tavern in Louisville for 18 months. I expect he is now in Louisville trying to make his escape to a free state, (in all probability to Cincinnati, Ohio.) Perhaps he may try to get employment on a steamboat. He is a good cook, and is handy in any capacity as a house servant. Had on when he left, a dark cassinett coatee, and dark striped cassinett pantaloons, new---he had other clothing. I will give $50 reward if taken in Louisvill; 100 dollars if taken one hundred miles from Louisville in this State, and 150 dollars if taken out of this State, and delivered to me, or secured in any jail so that I can get him again.

WILLIAM BURKE.

Bardstown, Ky., September 3d, 1838.

The scarring and chaining and beating were common. So, too, were the casual humiliations and interference with daily life. The early life of Elizabeth Keckley (who later purchased her freedom and founded the Contraband Relief Organization to support freed slaves during the Civil War) illustrated common patterns of dislocation. Born in 1818, Keckley scarcely knew her father, who belonged to a different Virginia planter. When she was 18, Keckley was hired out to a man in North Carolina, by whom, cut off from the protection of family and friends, she conceived a child. She later returned to Virginia, where she lived with her mother, but was then forcibly taken west to St. Louis. There, faced with the threat of having her aging mother hired out for service, Keckley worked for wages as a seamstress, "ke[eping] bread in the mouths of seventeen persons."

It was not unusual for enslaved women to bear children whose fathers were free and white. Undoubtedly, some intimate relations between enslaved women and free men were consensual, but most were not. In *Incidents in the Life of a Slave Girl,* Harriet Jacobs described the limited choices available to female slaves. Jacobs's master began making sexual advances when she was only 15: "[S]hudder[ing] to think of being the mother of children who should be owned by my old tyrant," and hoping to make him so mad that he would sell her, Jacobs entered a sexual relationship with another white man, with whom she eventually bore two children.

In some moments slaves chose rebellion. Although slaves in the colonies and the new republic had not successfully overthrown the institution, by the turn of the century the record of attempted revolts in America was long—and the recent and nearby model of the successful revolution in Saint Domingue powerful enough to nurse constant fear and dread among white southerners. In the first dozen years of the nineteenth century, enslaved Americans made two more dramatic strikes for freedom.

The earlier of the two was in 1800, in Richmond, Virginia. It was led by a 24-year-old young man, a slave named Gabriel. Gabriel grew up on the plantation of his owner, Thomas Prosser, where he was taught to read and was trained as a carpenter. When he wasn't needed on the plantation, however, Gabriel was sometimes allowed to hire out his own labor in the city, turning over most of his wages to his master.

THE ESCAPED SLAVE.—PHOTOGRAPHED BY T. B. BISHOP.—[SEE PAGE 422.]

"The Escaped Slave" An engraving from a photograph published in Harper's Weekly, July 2, 1864. This engraving is from the collection of The Library of Virginia.

There, Gabriel negotiated his own hours, handled his own pay, and worked side by side with free men. He watched as other young men—free men, but men no smarter or more skilled or educated than himself—passed through Richmond on their way to claim new land and new economic opportunities to the west. He may have heard other workers complain about the control of the city's fathers (mainly merchants, and Federalist in sentiment) and vow that one day soon a Democratic Republican victory would wipe away the last vestiges of elite control.

Gabriel's plan was bold: to assemble in the woods outside of Richmond, to advance into the city and take control, and then to spread through the countryside, freeing slaves as they went. By some accounts, the rebels intended to kill all the whites except those "friendly to liberty" and the "poor white women who had no slaves" and then (aided by the French or by Indians) to escape to freedom. By other accounts, Gabriel was willing to make his peace with white southerners, if only they would free African Americans.

The conspiracy was discovered, but not before hundreds of slaves had been recruited to the cause. Twenty-seven African Americans, including Gabriel, were eventually executed. According to white witnesses, all went to their deaths with "a sense of their rights and a contempt of danger." It was a determination, Congressman John Randolph later recorded grimly, "which, if it becomes general, must deluge the Southern country in blood."

Eleven years later, that prediction seemed to be realized in St. John the Baptist Parish, Louisiana, when a force of perhaps 500 slaves marched on New Orleans, burning fields, destroying crops, and gathering weapons as they made their way toward the city. Louisiana had long been a cauldron of slave unrest, probably buttressed by events in revolutionary France and Saint Domingue and by the arrival in New Orleans in 1810 and 1811 of perhaps 10,000 refugees from the Haitian Revolution—whites, free people of color, and slaves. But the 1811 uprising was homegrown, led by a Louisiana-born slave of mixed racial background, Charles, who was owned by the wealthy and established Louisiana Deslondes planter family.

The exact plan of the uprising is unclear. Largely unarmed, the rebels made their way from plantations 30 or 35 miles away down the bank of the Mississippi River toward New Orleans. They were armed chiefly with farm tools but captured some weapons and ammunition as they moved from plantation to plantation, destroying crops, burning buildings, and gathering recruits. Just west of the city, they were met by a planter militia, hastily called together by the governor and reinforced with United States troops. At least 60 slaves were killed in the ensuing struggle. Charles Deslondes and 15 other slaves were captured, tried, and executed, their decapitated heads raised on pikes along the road as a warning to any other slaves who might be thinking of rebellion.

Slave resistance took many forms other than outright rebellion, or attempted rebellion. Although masters and mistresses were ready enough to punish slaves without cause, individual slaves also set boundaries on that punishment. In his later *Narrative of the Life of Frederick Douglass, An American Slave*, Douglass recalled the day he reached his limit. Douglass had been rented out to Edward Covey, a poor farmer with a reputation for "breaking young slaves." Covey whipped Douglass regularly for six months. And then Douglass was done with it. He fought back, brawling with Covey for two hours until finally, exhausted and bleeding, the white man gave up. He never tried to whip Douglass again.

But most forms of resistance were far less dramatic, far more ordinary and daily, than Douglass's act of defiance. Feigned illness or ignorance, carelessness, a slow pace of work—all of these diminished the power of the master or mistress or driver, forcing him or her to recognize and adjust to the distinctive tempo or personality of the laborer. Field workers carved out implicit understandings with their masters about at least some of the terms of their labor. Task groups who finished early expected to be rewarded with free time. Individuals with particular expertise expected deference from drivers, overseers, and even owners. Throughout much of the South, a two-hour lunch break in the hottest part of the summer day was customary, and slaves had Sunday for their own work and families.

Slaves were also able to accumulate a certain status, based on age or expertise or their place in the slave community, that owners found it difficult to ignore altogether. Such a person was Harriet Jacobs's grandmother. In her memoir of her time in slavery, *Incidents in the Life of a Slave Girl*, Jacobs recalled that her grandmother delivered "scorching rebukes" to her master, for which he dared not punish her.

To focus only on their acts of resistance, however, is to see unfree African Americans only in relation to the institution of slavery. Albeit with one eye always on survival, enslaved African Americans also created and nurtured strong familial and community bonds, rich cultures, and a humanity that often outstripped that of their owners. Parenthood often came to slaves unchosen or, if chosen, nevertheless under circumstances choreographed by owners (who often tried to arrange partners). Certainly, some slaves—like some free people—were unable to navigate the responsibilities of parenthood successfully. Separated from spouses and children, many slaves never had the chance to try. All these conditions make the record of strong slave parenting all the more impressive. Douglass recalled that his mother walked 12 miles at day's end to put her son to bed and lie with him until she had to rise to return before dawn the next morning. Parents taught their children to fish and hunt and cook favorite dishes. They praised their children. They told them stories about their grandparents and great-grandparents. White owners flattered themselves that they were the masters of all their chattel, but African American parents made certain their children understood, as Jacobs remembered her father's words, "You are my child, and when I call you, you should come immediately, if you have to pass through fire and water."

Enslaved Americans also created communities of custom, both formally and informally. Market women carried garden produce and handicrafts to county seats, and gossiped and laughed while they traded with local whites. Men fished and trapped small game. Men and women perfected skills at cooking and storytelling, quilt making and wrestling, and gained reputation and status among their friends. Whites denied legal recognition to slave marriages, but slaves sanctioned their own relationships, combining African ceremonies with European wedding rituals.

As slaves built the economy of the South, they also left a lasting imprint on the culture of southern whites as well as blacks. Enslaved African Americans began converting to Christianity in the late eighteenth century, and many embraced the religious revivals of the early nineteenth century. Yet as they accepted Christianity, they made it their own. Slave preachers made selective use of Christian themes, emphasizing the story of Moses and the escape from bondage over homilies on human depravity and the importance of absolute obedience. Newly arrived Africans provided a constant infusion of African religious forms, such as dancing, spiritual singing, chanting, and clapping. They also introduced distinctly African and Afro-Caribbean religions, such as voodoo. Slave religious practice became both the embodiment and the instrument of self-assertion. The call to "cross over Jordan" that constituted the refrain of many slave songs symbolized the harshness of slave life, but it might also signal the singer's intention to escape.

Slavery and National Development

By 1827, when New York finally concluded its long abolition process, few slaves resided in the states and territories of the North and Northwest. But in the North, as in the South, dependency on slavery was not a simple matter of owning or not owning slaves. A free American worker might never see a slave and yet be economically dependent on the shipping business that carried slave-produced goods or the manufacturing or farming enterprises that supplied planters' needs. A patriotic American proud of the country's growth might cherish elaborate shirts and petticoats as evidence of success without ever wondering where the cotton came from. A white American might never have seen a slave and yet believe that there was some natural association of African Americans with servility. As the example of Lucretia Coffin Mott suggested, the dependences were cultural as well as economic, and they ran deep in the North as well as the South.

Detroit, March 23, 1844
Wm. Gatewood
Bedford, Kentucky

Dear Sir:

I am happy to inform you that you are not mistaken in the man whom you sold as property, and received pay for such. But I thank God that I am not property now, but am regarded as a man like yourself, and although I live far north, I am enjoying a comfortable living by my own industry. If you should ever chance to be traveling this way, and will call on me, I will use you better than you did me while you held me as a slave . . .

I think it is very probable that I should have been a toiling slave on your property today, if you had treated me differently.

To be compelled to stand by and see you whip and slash my wife without mercy, when I could afford her no protection, not even by offering myself to suffer the lash in her place, was more than I felt it to be the duty of a husband to endure, while the way was open to Canada. My infant child was also frequently flogged by Mrs. Gatewood, for crying, until its skin was literally purple. This kind of treatment was what drove me from home and family, to seek a better home for them. But I am willing to forget the past. I should be pleased to hear from you again, on the reception of this, and should also be very happy to correspond with you often, if it should be agreeable to yourself. I subscribe myself a friend to the oppressed, and Liberty forever.

Henry Bibb

Slavery and Industrialization in the Northeast

The seagoing economy of the central and northern coast had always been entangled with slavery, carrying food to the slave islands of the Caribbean and carrying slave-produced commodities to European markets. By the late eighteenth century, American merchants were second only to British merchants in the slave traffic itself. But they were a distant second, and in the early nineteenth century the patterns of regional interdependency began to change. The northern economy began to develop robustly on its own, while the slave economy continued to depend upon the northern and European markets for the sale of its cash crops.

In the North, cities like Philadelphia, New York, and, later, Chicago began to stretch their economic tentacles deep into the surrounding countryside, sucking the region's farmers into the urban orbit to feed a growing army of factory workers and other wage laborers within the city itself. Meanwhile, southern cities like Charleston and New Orleans continued to operate chiefly as commercial ports showing few signs of the internal economic development that was beginning to emancipate northern cities from their long-standing commercial dependence on the southern slave economy.

Boosters of the southern slave economy missed the signs of the North's slowly emerging economic independence because their own cotton economy was thriving.

The slaveholders were shipping an ever-larger volume of cash crops to the North, which they saw as evidence of increasing northern commercial dependence on southern slave society. And in many ways the slaveholders were right. The ties that bound the northern and southern economies grew stronger in the first half of the nineteenth century. Merchants in New York and Philadelphia began to specialize in consolidating shiploads of consigned cotton and sending it to England, to agents there who arranged for the local sales to English textile manufacturers. Those same agents then put together shipments of consumer goods to be carried back to the United States for sale, often to southern planters. The importance of this commerce to the economy of the north cannot be measured in voyages alone. Every voyage required a ship and a crew. The ships were made in Boston, Salem, Essex, and other New England towns, where local residents were employed in logging or as carpenters, caulkers, sailmakers, and on the rope walks. The crews came from around the world and included African Americans and Native Americans, but most of the sailors were New England bred. Most of the clothing they wore was made of cotton hand stitched by New England seamstresses, and most of the food they ate was grown by northern farmers, dependent on the merchants to sell their produce. In tandem with the overseas trade came the business services of the seaport cities. Insurance companies and banks in the mid-Atlantic and New England ports catered to the financial needs of the southern planters, providing agents for their sales, protecting their goods against the considerable risks of oceanic trade, and holding their debts.

Northerners also benefited from the consumer patronage of southerners. Planters' annual shopping trips to Philadelphia or New York prompted merchants to import expensive English furniture and Chinese porcelain, and encouraged tailors, seamstresses, milliners, and glove makers to keep up with the latest European fashions. Peddlers carried smaller household goods into the southern countryside and northern bookbinders sought to sell religious tracts and popular prescriptive manuals to southern households. In the early years of the nineteenth century, private northern academies solicited students from the South.

The symbiotic relationship of northern industry and the slave South is nowhere clearer than in the textile mills that sprang up in early nineteenth-century New England, powering the Industrial Revolution in the North. The desire for such mills was an old story in the republic, dating from the symbolic importance of spinning bees as acts of female patriotism during the Revolutionary War. But it took slave-produced southern cotton to make that aspiration viable.

There was probably a time when the idea of water-powered mills existed apart from the idea of water-powered textile mills using southern cotton. There was little reason to expect a southern cotton explosion in 1789, for example, when Massachusetts chartered a mill in Beverly. But even then southern plantations were producing some cotton and various mechanics were working on designs to clean cotton faster.

It is certainly the case that the cotton boom propelled Lowell and his associates to make the large investments they did during and after the War of 1812. Cotton, then, sustained the first major factory workforce in the United States. More than that, it funded purchases of large tracts of land with rivers and falls, and it eventually supported industrial towns across Rhode Island and Massachusetts (and all of the ancillary commercial activities that occurred within those towns). This was more particularly the case early on, when both the Slater and the Waltham methods struc-

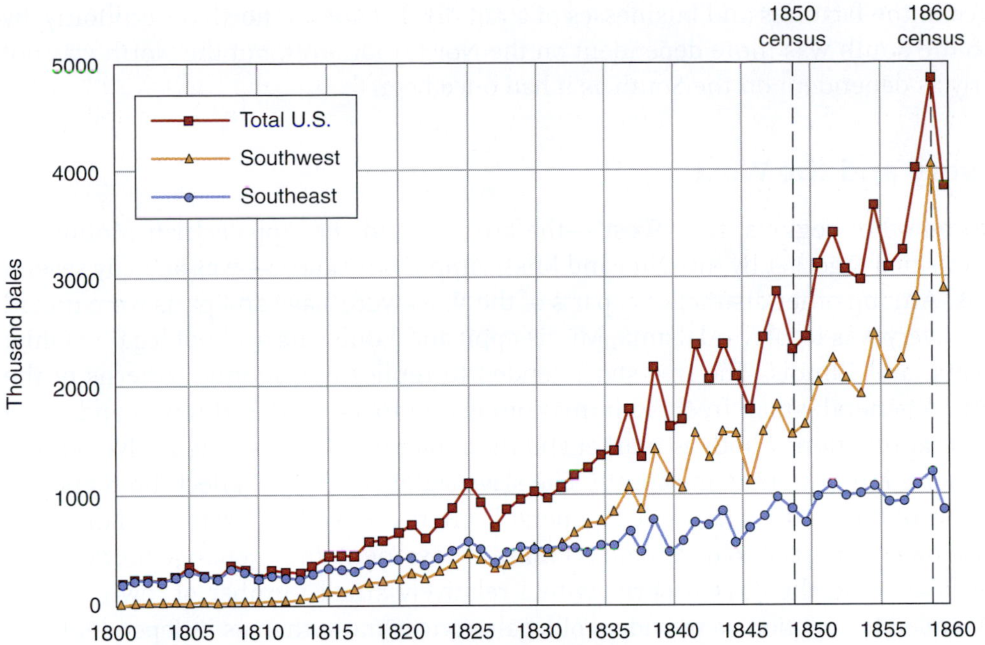

Figure 10-1 Cotton Production by Region, 1800–1 through 1860–1 *Source: James Lawrence Watkins,* King Cotton: A Historical and Statistical Review 1790 to 1908 *(Santa Barbara, CA: Greenwood Press, 1970).*

tured communities that were dependent on the mills for their housing, their food, their shopping, and even their religion. Cotton built those communities.

The textile industry relied on the South not only for its raw material but also for its customers. Especially early on, most of the cloth produced by the New England mills was rough and coarse and considered suitable only for sailors and day laborers—and slaves. To protect this southern trade, in 1816 Lowell lobbied for (and received) a tariff that taxed imported woolen and cotton goods 25 percent, with a minimum rate per yard set at 30 percent.

The reliance was reciprocal. Just as southern cotton underwrote this aspect of northern industrialization, so too did the northern mills at critical moments save the southern cotton industry. The interruption of export trade before and during the War of 1812 was difficult for southern cotton growers, but it might have proven even more harmful had the new northern mills not offered an alternative market for their crops.

The many linkages between the northern and southern economies led some slaveholders to predict defiantly that the Yankees would never dare to wage war on slavery because they were too dependent upon the South to survive without it. But this was an illusion. What the northerners wanted was cotton, whether it came from Egypt or Alabama, whether it was produced by wage laborers or by slaves. No doubt the slaveholders were impressed by export statistics showing the predominance of cotton to America's overseas trade. But what those statistics did not show was the far greater volume of commercial activity within the northern states themselves, a trade that depended on the development of cities and industry at home rather than oceanic commerce. The textile mills depended on the cotton produced by southern slaves, but the mill owners and shoe manufacturers of New England knew that their businesses depended even more on northern customers who made their living off wages in the factories and businesses of a rapidly developing northern economy. By 1860 the South was more dependent on the North than ever, but the North was not nearly as dependent on the South as it had once been.

Slavery and the West

Like the other regions, the "West"—the area beyond the Appalachian Mountains that was tied together by the Ohio and Mississippi river valleys—was actually several Wests. Among other distinctions, parts of the West were slave and parts were not: in 1819 slavery was legal in Alabama, Mississippi, and Louisiana and not legal in Ohio, Indiana, and Illinois. The free states tended to replicate economic patterns of the North in general: small freehold farms connecting to a network of towns and small cities that functioned both as market and manufacturing centers themselves and as transportation centers to the coasts. The slave states tended to reflect the economic patterns of the South: many small general farmers and some very large plantations whose owners tended to dominate economic movement and exchange between the countryside and the coastal ports, with a relatively small number of town centers that tended to function as providers of legal services more than as independent economic units.

In some parts of the western region, these differences and the identities they fostered were quite pronounced, dividing at the Ohio River. But the river valleys also united the economies north and south and merged them into a single region. Farmers in the Northwest had for years been frustrated by their lack of convenient access to eastern markets. The opening of cotton lands along the southern Mississippi resolved that problem, providing new and growing local markets for their grain and pork and lumber products. Northern cities along the Ohio provided transportation, business, and manufacturing services to customers and producers all up and down the river system.

Cincinnati was an example of the interconnections of western development. Like other settlements on the Ohio and Mississippi rivers, Cincinnati's location positioned the town to become a thriving trade center, shipping wheat, corn, rye, and livestock overland to Pittsburgh and downriver to New Orleans, and selling goods and services to local farmers. Even before the War of 1812, Cincinnatians had begun to reorient their trade from overland routes across Pennsylvania to water routes down the Mississippi. The outcome of the war guaranteed the United States access to those routes all the way to the Gulf of Mexico and opened the way for the newly invented steamboat to carry goods upriver as well. By 1819, when it incorporated as a city, Cincinnati had 10,000 residents and had earned the title "Queen of the West."

These economic interdependencies sometimes led to political sympathies. Although technically free, Ohio entered the Union with a draconian "black code" that barred all blacks and persons of mixed race from entering the state unless they could prove that they were free, required that such people purchase certificates of freedom from the clerk of the county where they resided, and required that employers verify their free status before hiring black people. Both Indiana and Illinois abolished slavery in their state constitutions, but both followed Ohio's model in passing harsh restrictions on free blacks. Even as a territory in 1813, Illinois prohib-

Cincinnati Public Landing A gateway to the Northwest and the South, Cincinnati was by 1820 a thriving city. This view of the Ohio River wharf by John Caspar Wild suggests the complex economy that supported the city's prosperity: retail establishments, wagons carrying settlers west and bringing produce from the backcountry, and steamboats transporting goods and people up and down the Mississippi River system as far south as New Orleans.

ited free blacks from entering, under penalty of 39 lashes and expulsion—although the territory was quite willing to allow out-of-state slaveholders to rent their slaves to work in Illinois saltlicks. In 1822 proslavery sentiment was so strong in Illinois that voters tried to legalize slavery in the state. In elections that year voters elected proslavery majorities to both houses of the legislature and just missed electing a proslavery governor. When the matter reappeared as a referendum on the 1824 ballot, proslavery forces lost, but they took 43 percent of the vote.

Slavery and the Laws of the Nation

The men who wrote the Constitution had compromised on the issue of slavery, and it is in the nature of compromises that their implications are ambiguous. After the Constitution was ratified, for example, both New York and New Jersey abolished slavery in their states—completing the process of emancipation in the North. The first federal Congress that assembled under the new Constitution reenacted the Ordinance of 1787, prohibiting the importation of slaves into the Old Northwest. Congress likewise prohibited the importation of slaves in the federal territories of the Old Southwest. And in 1807, at the earliest possible date allowed by the Constitution, Congress prohibited the importation of any more slaves from the Atlantic slave trade. Thus, under the new Constitution, the states were left free to abolish slavery on their own and the federal government assumed the power to regulate and even prohibit slavery in the territories. The Founders' misgivings about slavery were reflected in their deliberate decision to exclude the word "slavery" from the Constitution itself.

At the same time, however, the Constitution recognized and even protected slavery from federal interference in the states where it already existed. The Three-Fifths Clause, for example, insured that white southerners would have disproportionate power in the House of Representatives and the Electoral College (where the number of electors for each state was based on the number of senators and representatives). And although the Constitution implicitly recognized slavery as a matter of *state* law, Article IV nevertheless made the protection of the slave owners' property a *national* obligation: "No person held to service or labour in one state, under the laws thereof, escaping into another, shall, in consequence of any law or regulation therein, be discharged from such service or labour, but shall be delivered up on claim of the party to whom such service or labour may be due." The article studiously avoided the word "slave," but everybody referred to it as the fugitive slave clause of the Constitution.

The Constitution thus produced a patchwork of state and national laws, some of which restricted or abolished slavery and some of which protected it. In 1793, for example, Congress enacted a fugitive slave law that made it a federal crime to aid an escaping slave. But it left enforcement of the law to the states, and in the North that meant that accused runaways were often guaranteed the due process rights of free citizens, much to the dismay of the slaveholders. The slaveholders objected because slaves were, by definition, not citizens. But northerners resented the Three-Fifths Clause for precisely the same reason. In principle, only citizens were supposed to be counted for purposes of representation. By counting three-fifths of the slave population, the Constitution gratuitously rewarded southern states with enough extra representatives and Electoral College votes to help ensure the election of a string of presidents from the South. Those presidents' support for a limited federal government in turn helped protect slavery from federal interference in matters that belonged to southern states.

Local and state laws concerning slavery affected the lives of men and women in all the states. Northern states, for example, passed personal-liberty laws that were designed to protect free blacks from being kidnapped into slavery by bounty hunters in search of fugitive slaves. But northerners clearly understood that the personal-liberty laws made it much harder for masters to enforce the fugitive slave clause of the Constitution. Southern masters deeply resented what they saw as northern-state interference with their rights of property. Conversely, when Charlestonians, fearful of the influence of free black sailors over South Carolina slaves, empowered sheriffs in southern ports to lock up free black sailors while their ships were in port, they affected the lives and the employment of men who hailed from Boston and Nantucket and New York. The law they created not only specified the imprisonment of black sailors but also required a bond from their captains to cover the costs of incarceration. Under pressure from an organization of planters known as the South Carolina Association, the sheriff of Charleston imprisoned free Jamaican sailor Harry Elkinson. When Elkinson's case came to court, lawyers argued that any treaty that interfered with the power of the state to guard against internal revolution must be unconstitutional. The court rejected this position (agreeing with Secretary of State Adams that the law violated international treaties), but South Carolina continued to enforce the act. By this time, black sailors made up roughly a fifth of northern seamen—a proportion far higher than their presence in the free population. Sailing was an important occupation for them and their families. The South Carolina law in effect made hiring them a handicap to any captain intending to go through South Carolina's ports and jeopardized the sailors' employment. The South Carolina act was later copied by Louisiana, North Carolina, Alabama, Georgia, Florida, and Texas.

Free Black People in a Republic of Slavery

By 1815, some 200,000 African Americans lived as free inhabitants of the United States, most of them in urban areas. Whether they were more than inhabitants—whether they were in fact citizens—varied from state to state as well as from North to South.

Free blacks faced formidable discrimination in all parts of the country. In the slave South, their very existence represented a threat to the system, both in the possibilities of freedom they represented and in the avenues of communication they offered enslaved people. Southern and border states responded to this perceived threat by gradually narrowing laws permitting individual emancipation, by tightening surveillance of slaves, and by regulating the movement and occupations of free black people. Southern courts increasingly argued the "taint" of color followed African Americans out of slavery, so that judges in most slave states assumed that free blacks lacked the privileges and immunities of citizens. Free blacks in the South were barred from militias, from the ownership of weapons, and from occupations that might bring them into contact with slaves, like operating groceries or taverns. What's more, they lived in daily danger of being enslaved, especially as the demand for slaves in the new southern territories increased. It was worth a free black person's life to cultivate some ties with the white community, should he or she need authority to ward off the greed of traders. Some border states—including Maryland, New Jersey, and Ohio—barred free blacks from settling within their borders.

Free blacks in the North suffered from many of the same discriminations, but their conditions varied more widely from state to state. In New England, for example, blacks could vote and send their children to public schools alongside white children. In other states, such as New York, free black men could only vote if they met a property qualification that did not apply to white men. Elsewhere blacks were barred from voting altogether. Most northern courts assumed that blacks were citizens and as such were entitled to own property, make contracts, move about freely, and, if accused of a crime, to have a jury trial. But some northern states, particularly along the borders of the South, prohibited free blacks from moving into the state, thus denying them one of the traditional "privileges and immunities" of citizenship. And as in the South, a vast patchwork of private discriminations required the segregation of blacks from whites in schools, churches, theaters, cemeteries, hotels, streetcars, ferries, and railways.

In both the North and the South, however, the laws were not always a reliable measure of social practice. In many communities free blacks and whites interacted every day in ways that defied state statutes. They did business with one another, attended the same church services, and helped one another in times of need. In some southern states the laws restricted free blacks from owning land and houses, but free blacks did so anyway. Periodically, states and localities would clamp down and require free blacks to be licensed for certain forms of employment, or to carry freedom papers with them at all times, but the laws were only erratically enforced. The threat of enforcement, however, was a constant source of pressure on free black communities across the South.

Within this complicated mosaic of formal and informal discriminations, free African Americans found ways to survive, to eke out a living, and, once in a while, to flourish. By the 1820s, the self-help movement founded at the beginning of the republic had yielded a rich harvest of African American mutual-aid and benevolent associations. Organizing was most lively in Philadelphia, where free blacks established more than 40 new societies between 1820 and 1835, but (propelled by the growth of the free black community) the self-help impulse extended south to Baltimore and Charleston and north to New York and Boston. Although some societies were clearly limited in membership to relatively prosperous free blacks, self-help organizing was vigorous across economic lines: coachmen, porters, barbers, brick makers, sailors, cooks, and washerwomen all formed associations.

Although the overwhelming proportion of free blacks lived in cities, a few lived in the countryside. A fraction of those owned their own land, but most worked as farm laborers or as sharecroppers (dividing their produce with the white landowner on a preagreed basis, usually not advantageous to the sharecropping family). Free black farm laborers often did not live on the farms they worked, but rather resided in nearby small towns, where they might find at least a few other free black men and women like themselves and where they were freer from white landowners who might have treated them like slaves had they lived where they worked.

The growing prevalence of white racial prejudice in the nineteenth century was reflected not simply in the spread of laws discriminating against blacks, but also in renewed calls for the abolition of slavery. In 1816, a group including prominent national politicians, northerners, and slave owners formed the American Colonization Society. The Society protested that, in the words of Henry Clay, because of "unconquerable prejudice resulting from their color, they never could amalgamate with the free whites of this country." Styling itself a benevolent society, the association (whose founders included Andrew Jackson, Francis Scott Key, and Daniel Webster, in addition to Clay) determined that African Americans could succeed only in Africa, declared their home (although by 1816 almost all United States slaves had been born in the republic). Made up of wealthy, influential white men, the ACS lobbied Congress for funds. It received $100,000 in 1819 and set out its first emigrant ship in 1820. Dedicated to removing free African Americans from their native land to Liberia, in Africa, the ACS signaled waning white support for a racially integrated republic.

Even the federal government restricted African Americans from certain occupations. For example, as early as 1798 the secretaries of war and the navy had each tried to bar African Americans from the military. In 1810, the federal government excluded African Americans from delivering the mail.

The Politics of Slavery

In 1817 a Boston reporter, observing the absence of the invidious politics that had plagued the first three decades of nationhood, declared that America had at last achieved "an era of good feeling." That sentiment seemed confirmed three years later when President James Monroe was reelected with all but one electoral vote—and that one withheld not in opposition to Monroe but in deference to Washington, the only unanimously elected president.

But all was not right with the new republic. Among the festering problems, becoming more and more apparent even as the nation entered a time of seeming prosperity, was slavery. Its continued existence had become more and more controversial. In 1820 the U.S. Congress defined the slave trade as piracy. Five years later a U.S. patrol seized the slave ship *Antelope,* sailing under a Venezuelan flag with a cargo of 281 Africans. Declaring the slave trade contrary to natural law, the U.S. Supreme Court freed most of the slaves. Because the justices found that the United States had no jurisdiction over the laws of other nations, and that slavery was legal in Spain and Venezuela, the Court returned the ship and the 39 captives held to be owned by Spaniards.

> **"This momentous question, like a fire bell in the night, awakened and filled me with terror. I considered it at once the knell of the union. It is hushed, indeed, for the moment. But this is a reprieve only, not a final sentence. . . . I regret that I am now to die in the belief, that the useless sacrifice of themselves by the generation of 1776, to acquire self-government and happiness to their own country, is to be thrown away by the unwise and unworthy passions of their sons, and that my only consolation is to be, that I live not to weep over it."**
>
> THOMAS JEFFERSON,
> commenting on the Missouri Crisis, April 22, 1820

Free blacks and a significant number of whites continued to attack slavery as immoral and proposed to abolish it. A larger group of white people, though far from being committed abolitionists, felt uncomfortable supporting the institution. Northern churchgoers were uneasy with their denominations' acquiescence to slavery, for example, and northern mill owners and merchants, tied as they were to the institution, nevertheless shied away from acknowledging that linkage publicly. And many northerners who thought very little about slavery at all were nonetheless aware that the Three-Fifths Clause had helped assure southern victories in seven of the first eight presidential contests. Had it not been for that clause, they believed, that single northerner, John Adams, would have been reelected president over Thomas Jefferson in 1800.

Map 10-1 Westward Expansion and Slavery, 1820 As treaties signed with Great Britain and Spain in 1817, 1818, and 1819 began to outline a United States that would stretch from the Atlantic Ocean to the Pacific, Americans worried about the division of that territory into areas open to slavery and areas closed to slavery. Although in 1820 more acres were closed to slavery than not, the Missouri Compromise permitted slavery in territories where it had not existed before, reinforcing northerners' fears that planter interests dominated in national policy.

The Missouri Compromise

Land hunger had fueled the new American economy. By 1819, land had come to represent national as well as individual prosperity for many Americans. For several decades northerners had been trying to block slavery's westward expansion, only to be thwarted by an increasingly aggressive and belligerent block of powerful southern politicians. During the War of 1812, calls for national unity had silenced antislavery advocates. But when peace returned, a spate of proslavery expansionism provoked the most powerful reaction yet among northerners. Before the war, Americans had withdrawn from the despicable Atlantic slave trade, but now that the war was over, there was unmistakable evidence that southern

expansionism was giving rise to an equally despicable domestic slave trade. By 1819, when Missouri applied for permission to organize as a state, antislavery politicians had had enough.

The question of Missouri, though legally framed in terms of national political power on the federal level, was inextricable from the larger dispute over the morality of slavery. Northerners had long been unhappy with what they saw as the unfair advantage awarded to southern states by the Constitution's Three-Fifths Compromise. Admission of Missouri would extend that unfair pattern of representation in the House and create a new imbalance in the Senate, where each state had the same number of representatives regardless of population. In 1819 there were 22 states in the Union, 11 free and 11 slave. Admission of Missouri would give the slave states domination in any purely sectional disputes. (Florida, certain to apply for admission as a slave state at some point in the future, would add to the disparity.) Meanwhile, the South continued to dominate the presidency.

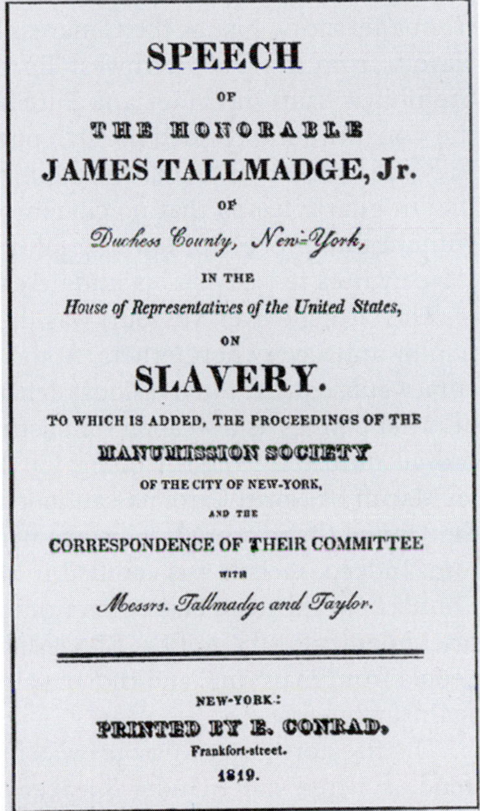
SPEECH
OF
THE HONORABLE
JAMES TALLMADGE, Jr.
OF
Duchess County, New-York,
IN THE
House of Representatives of the United States,
ON
SLAVERY.
TO WHICH IS ADDED, THE PROCEEDINGS OF THE
MANUMISSION SOCIETY
OF THE CITY OF NEW-YORK,
AND THE
CORRESPONDENCE OF THEIR COMMITTEE
WITH
Messrs. Tallmadge and Taylor.

NEW-YORK:
PRINTED BY E. CONRAD,
Frankfort-street.
1819.

Speech Pertaining to the Missouri Compromise The title page of the speech by Rep. James Tallmadge (NY), 1819, which he gave in the House of Representatives, arguing for the gradual abolition of slavery in Missouri. It was the "Tallmadge Amendment" to a bill for Missouri statehood that sparked the first nationwide debate over slavery.

There were other issues. Missouri was the first wholly new state to be organized from the Louisiana Purchase. (Louisiana had already entered as a slave state, but slavery had been established there before the territory became a part of the United States.) Missouri, northerners feared, would set a precedent for extending slavery into additional new states carved out of the territory. Moreover, by 1819 many northerners no longer believed that slavery would simply die out of its own accord. Far from withering away, the institution seemed to be thriving. Americans had imported only about 5 percent of the Africans forced into slavery in the hemisphere, but by 1819 slaves in the United States constituted one-third of all the people of African descent in the Americas. Slavery seemed to be making some headway even in free states. When Illinois had entered the Union in 1818, for example, it had entered as a free state, but with a "black code" that limited the economic and civil rights of free blacks and contained some provisions for the continuation of slavery where it existed in the southern parts of the state.

The trouble over Missouri began almost at once. In the course of the House debate, New York representative James Tallmadge proposed that Missouri be admitted under two conditions. First, no more slaves were to be brought into the state, and second, slavery was to be gradually abolished after the state was admitted to the

Union. Southerners lined up unanimously against the amendment, while northerners voted unanimously in favor of it. The more populous North carried the vote. But when the House bill reached the Senate committee charged with its consideration, the vote was reversed. The Tallmadge amendment died in committee, to be reintroduced in the next session.

By the time Congress reconvened, positions on both sides had hardened. Northern congressmen insisted that Congress had the power to prohibit slavery from a territory. Just as the Congress of the Confederation had earlier prohibited slavery from the Old Northwest Territory, now the federal Congress must act to prohibit it from the Louisiana Purchase. Southern congressmen responded that the Constitution provided no such power to Congress and that the states had carefully preserved their equality in joining the federal pact. In addition, they argued that in guaranteeing that no citizen could be deprived of life, liberty, or property without due process of law, the Fifth Amendment actually protected the right of slave owners to carry slaves into new states.

The struggle over Missouri was the culmination of decades of growing frustration by antislavery northerners. At the same time, it foreshadowed with chilling accuracy subsequent congressional debates over slavery. It also foreshadowed the use of racial politics as a weapon for silencing antislavery politics, a pattern that would prevail until the 1850s. Arguing for the continuation of slavery, Senator Nathaniel Macon of North Carolina cautioned his northern colleagues that in no place in the United States were free people of color truly welcome. No one rose to dispute him. Indeed, racism was codified in many northern state constitutions. Ohio and Connecticut excluded black men from voting. Vermont and New Hampshire barred black men from the militia. Rhode Island and Indiana prohibited black and white people from marrying, and Indiana also barred blacks from appearing as witnesses against whites.

The firestorm over Missouri was finally resolved when Maine applied for statehood as a free state. Under Speaker of the House Clay's guidance, the two bills were linked, preserving the balance in the Senate. The compromise also contained a provision that slavery would be permitted in Arkansas Territory but excluded from the rest of the Louisiana Purchase. The compromise passed narrowly in March of 1820.

Almost immediately, another problem arose when Missouri submitted a state constitution that barred free black people and free persons of mixed heritage from the state. This was a clear violation of Article IV of the Constitution, which provided that citizens of one state should enjoy the rights of citizens in all states. Here was another sign of an emerging sectional division over the issue of black citizenship, a division that was still restricted to the contrasting assumptions of northern and southern state courts but which would explode into national politics with the Supreme Court's Dred Scott decision of 1857. But in 1821, during the second round of the crisis over Missouri, that division was just beginning to show itself. Struggling to put the deal back together, Henry Clay engineered a second compromise. Congress allowed Missouri to enter under the proposed constitution, but it demanded that the new state legislature promise never to interpret the clause to mean what it so obviously meant, that Missouri reserved the right to deny free African Americans their constitutional rights. The Missouri territorial legislature made the promise but added a disclaimer of any power to bind the people of the state to what it said. Finally, in August 1821, President James Monroe greeted Missouri as the 24th state of the Union.

Antislavery in the 1820s

The Missouri Compromise was a devastating defeat for the opponents of slavery. For decades they had struggled to hold back the expansion of slavery and the growing power of the slaveholders in national politics. Disgusted and shocked by the increasing belligerence of proslavery politicians, antislavery northerners had thrown themselves into a campaign to keep slavery out of Missouri and, they hoped, to stop slavery once and for all. But they had failed, and the ominous consequences of their failure soon became apparent. Slavery's defenders had always used racial politics to try and stop antislavery politics, but their successes were limited and local until the 1820s. Impressed by the strength of antislavery sentiment during the Missouri crisis, southerners joined an emerging political coalition that came to be known as the Democratic Party. This coalition started from the premise that slavery would henceforth be excluded from national politics by means of an increasingly effective white racial consensus. It worked. By the late 1820s national antislavery politics was effectively dead.

With the collapse of antislavery politics in the mid-1820s, the leadership of the movement passed to a small group of articulate abolitionists who took up the cause with more fervor than ever. Free black leaders in the North led the way. They began to wonder whether the American Colonization Society had become a cover for slaveholders who wanted to forestall the progress of abolition by insisting that blacks were unfit for self-government. Colonization, which began as a conservative means of supporting abolition, looked more and more like an effort by slaveholders to rid themselves of the troubling presence of free blacks. The transformation of the American Colonization Society was further evidence of the collapse of antislavery politics.

There was another, bigger, problem with colonization. By the 1820s almost all African Americans in the United States were American born. Although some later thought about migration to Haiti or to Canada, most claimed the United States as their own. They rebuffed the American Colonization Society's attempt to recruit them for relocation efforts. (Even in the midst of the economic hardships of 1819, only 22 of Philadelphia's 10,000 free black women and men signed on to the Liberia voyage.)

Many earlier black efforts had focused understandably on self-help and community building. The emphasis on self-help remained and strengthened in the wake of the Missouri debates, the organization of the ACS, and the racism of the early nineteenth century. It was a constant refrain from black abolitionists: "Too long have others spoken for us," John Russwurm and Samuel E. Cornish declared in the first issue of the first independent black newspaper, *Freedom's Journal*. In the 1820s, free blacks began to confront the American Colonization Society directly and to form their own all-black antislavery groups, beginning in 1826 with the General Colored Association of Massachusetts, an all–African American antislavery organization. Their protest was not timid. In 1829 David Walker, an early member of the General Colored Association, published a pamphlet titled *An Appeal to the Colored Citizens of the World,* calling on blacks to take resistance to slavery into their own hands by armed insurrection, if necessary. Like other black antislavery writers in this period, Walker's protest took a new and very direct aim at the hypocrisies of white people. In his first article, for example, he noted a piece he had seen in a South Carolina newspaper a few years earlier that had labeled Turks "'the most barbarous people in the world'" and charged that "'they treat the Greeks more like brutes than human beings.'" In the same paper, however, Walker had also found an advertisement for the sale of "'Eight well built Virginia and Maryland Negro fellows and four wenches [to] positively be sold this day to the highest bidder!'" "And what astonished me still more," Walker added, "was, to see in this same humane paper!! the cuts of three men, with clubs and budgets on their backs, and an advertisement offering a considerable sum of money for their apprehension and delivery." "I declare," he concluded, "it is really so funny to hear the Southerners and Westerners of this country talk about barbarity, that it is positively, enough to make a man smile." Many whites were furious, and southerners put a $3,000 bounty on his head. Walker remained undeterred: "Somebody must die in this cause," he added. "I may be doomed to the stake and the fire, or to the scaffold tree, but it is not in me to falter if I can promote the work of emancipation."

FREEDOM'S JOURNAL.

"RIGHTEOUSNESS EXALTETH A NATION."

CORNISH & RUSSWURM, Editors and Proprietors. NEW-YORK, FRIDAY, JUNE 22, 1827. VOL. I, NO. 16.

The defeat of the antislavery forces in 1820 also helped inspire a new and more radical abolitionist movement among a small but vocal group of white Americans. In 1821 Ohio newspaperman Benjamin Lundy began publication of *The Genius of Universal Emancipation* (which he moved to Jonesboro, Tennessee, in 1823 and on to Baltimore, Maryland, in 1824). A Quaker, Lundy opposed slavery absolutely, but he recommended that emancipation be gradual and that African Americans leave the United States. By the mid-1820s, popular clamor had prompted a few northern states to pass laws divorcing them from the national Fugitive Slave Act. They passed state laws making it more difficult for masters to recapture runaway slaves. An 1820 Ohio law, for example, made it illegal for Ohio aldermen or justices to enforce the federal 1793 Fugitive Slave Act and made kidnapping free people of color in Ohio punishable by fines of up to $2,000 and "seven to twenty-one years' imprisonment at hard labor." When proslavery forces tried to scuttle the act in 1826, antislavery workers—black and white—combined to pass another bill that essentially simply restated the first. Meanwhile, Quakers in Philadelphia and a few other northern cities began to try to wean themselves from dependence on slave goods.

With the defeat of antislavery forces and the triumph of racial politics, radical abolitionism emerged to fill the void in the 1820s. Absent the discipline of party politics, the abolitionists would reveal themselves to be a contentious lot. But through the 1830s and into the 1840s they were the lonely voices of antislavery idealism in America, and from the start they made it their business to break through the racial consensus and put opposition to slavery back on the national political agenda. In the wake of disastrous defeat, and in the face of overwhelming opposition, abolitionists white and black alike never gave up. And in the long run, they would win.

Conclusion

One of the reasons the Founders had compromised with slavery when they produced the Constitution of 1787 is that they thought it was a dying institution. By then most of the northern states had abolished slavery, there were increasingly powerful antislavery movements making headway in the two northern states where it remained, slavery's expansion into the northwestern frontier had been restricted, and the slave economy in the tobacco states seemed to be floundering. But the Founders underestimated slavery's strength in the deep South, and they could not have predicted that within a few years of ratification a new machine—the cotton gin—would revive southern slavery, making it stronger and more aggressive than ever. The result was a lethal paradox: As slavery became stronger, it also became strictly sectional. As northerners stepped up their attempts to thwart slavery's expansion, the slaveholders stepped up their defense of slavery. By 1820 it looked as though the experiment in republican government would collapse over the issue of slavery. But a compromise, followed by a determined effort to keep the slavery issue out of national politics, established an uneasy truce that kept the Union intact for another generation. With slavery shoved to the sidelines, American voters turned to the contentious but less threatening issues of economic development and political democracy.

Further Readings

John Craig Hammond, *Slavery, Freedom, and Expansion in the Early American West* (2007). Hammond's is a forcefully argued and persuasive new account of the politics of slavery in the early republic, demonstrating both the depth of antislavery sentiment and the aggressiveness of proslavery politicians.

Anthony E. Kaye, *Joining Places: Slave Neighborhoods in the Old South* (2007). Kaye expands the study of slave culture beyond families and plantations, and makes one of the most comprehensive efforts to demonstrate the political significance of the slaves.

Matthew Mason, *Slavery and Politics in the Early American Republic* (2006). Mason examines attitudes toward slavery before and after the Missouri Compromise, arguing for that event as a watershed in how Americans viewed the relationship of their republic to the institution of slavery.

Thomas Morris, *Southern Slavery and the Law, 1619–1860* (1996). This is a dense but profoundly important book. Morris does more than anyone else to clarify the slave's basic status as property.

James Oliver and Lois E. Horton, *In Hope of Liberty: Culture, Community and Protest Among Northern Free Blacks, 1700–1860* (1997). This is a broad survey of African American life in the northern states before the Civil War, giving equal attention to cultural, social, and political issues.

Dylan C. Penningroth, *The Claims of Kinfolk: African American Property and Community in the Nineteenth-Century South* (2002). Penningroth's book suggests that the slaves retained African conceptions of property distinct from those of the southern master class.

Gavin Wright, *Slavery and American Economic Development* (2006). The best book on the slave economy, and the only one that takes slaves' status as "property" as the starting point.

>> Timeline >>

▼ 1791
Haitian Revolution

▼ 1793
Eli Whitney invents cotton gin

▼ 1800
Thomas Jefferson elected
Gabriel's rebellion, Richmond, Virginia

▼ 1807
First trip of Robert Fulton's *North River Steamboat of Clermont*

▼ 1808
External slave trade illegal

▼ 1810
American cotton production reaches 178,000 bales

▼ 1811
Slave rebellion in Louisiana

$150 REWARD

RANAWAY from the subscriber, on the night of the 2d instant, a negro man, who calls himself *Henry May*, about 22 years old, 5 feet 6 or 8 inches high, ordinary color, rather chunky built, bushy head, and has it divided mostly on one side, and keeps it very nicely combed; has been raised in the house, and is a first rate dining-room servant, and was in a tavern in Louisville for 18 months. I expect he is now in Louisville trying to [illegible]

▼ 1814
Treaty of Ghent reopens trade with England
Waltham mills open

▼ 1815
Steamboats begin regular two-way trips on the Mississippi

▼ 1816
Tariff provides protection to northern textile mills
James Monroe elected president
American Colonization Society founded

Who, What

Review Questions

1. What were the provisions of the Missouri Compromise?
2. How were the Waltham and Lowell mills linked to the South?
3. How did the 1808 abolition of the foreign slave trade affect slavery in the United States?
4. What assumptions about American society were expressed in the American Colonization Society?

For further review materials and resource information, please visit www.oup.com/us/ofthepeople

▼ 1817
New York begins construction of Erie Canal (opened 1825)

▼ 1819
Missouri applies for statehood
Panic of 1819

▼ 1820
Maine becomes a state

▼ 1821
Missouri becomes a state

Benjamin Lundy founds *The Genius of Universal Emancipation*

▼ 1822
South Carolina Negro Seamen Act

▼ 1823
Merrimack Manufacturing Company mills in Lowell produce first finished cloth

▼ 1824
John Quincy Adams elected president

▼ 1825
Antelope affair

▼ 1826
Lucretia Mott and others form Philadelphia Free Produce Society

▼ 1829
David Walker publishes *An Appeal to the Colored Citizens of the World*

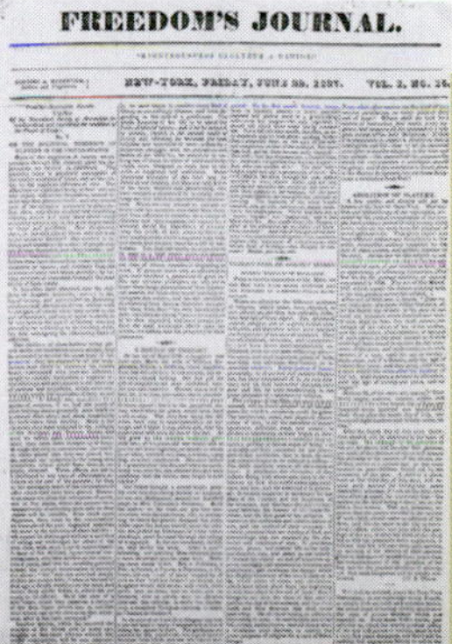

FREEDOM'S JOURNAL.

CHAPTER 11

Common Threads

>> Why was the Bank of the United States so controversial in the early republic?

>> How did the market revolution affect wage labor?

>> What actions and policies of the Democratic Republican presidents, 1800–1824, laid the groundwork for Jackson's breakaway movement?

>> Did the territorial expansion of the republic require the removal of Native Americans?

Jacksonian Democracy

1820–1840

AMERICAN PORTRAIT

>> Harriet Noble

By 1824, the New York backcountry was abuzz with talk of Michigan Territory and the opportunities that lay there for families willing to make the trip. The economy was at last bouncing back from the Panic of 1819. Markets for agriculture, in the east or down the Mississippi River, were reviving. Land prices had declined slightly and families could buy in for smaller parcels.

"My husband," Harriet Noble later wrote, "was seized with the mania," and by September, the Noble family—Harriet, 21, her husband, 23, and their two young daughters—had joined the growing migration of Americans moving west. "Could we have known what it was to be pioneers in a new country, we should never have had the courage to come," Harriet recalled.

Harriet's husband had already made the journey once that year, with his brother, to scout out land for their families. Now the two families embarked on a three-part trip. First came a rough trip by wagon over bad roads to Buffalo. Next, after a four-day wait in Buffalo for a steamship that never showed up, a seven-day trip on a schooner across Lake Erie "so entirely prostrated with seasickness," Noble recalled, "as scarcely to be able to attend to the wants of our little ones." And then, just when Harriet was certain that she would gratefully endure anything if she could only be on land, days of trekking through the Michigan wilderness on foot, through mud and swamps, over fallen trees, through thick brush until "my feet were so swollen I could walk no further." At last they arrived at Ann Arbor: "some six or seven log huts occupied by as many inmates as could be crowded into them." The Nobles jammed in with the others, so packed that they could not move in the night without stepping on someone's hand or foot. They had to cook outside, where the winds whipped up sparks that set their drying clothes on fire.

And so they survived for a month and a half, until the men managed to put up the walls and a roof on separate cabins. But that winter most of the community fell mysteriously ill. Deciding they had chosen an unhealthful place, the following spring the Nobles sold out, packed up, and moved again, this time to Dexter, 10 miles west. They were fortunate enough to be able to take over a shell of a cabin—"the square log pen" without a roof—abandoned by discouraged settlers before them. That summer and fall Harriet and her husband worked together to put a roof over their heads and dig and haul stones to set a fireplace. By the second winter, they had a roof, a floor, a fireplace, and a door. "And but for the want of provisions of almost every kind, we should have enjoyed it much," Harriet later recalled dryly. Waiting 15 days for her husband to return from Detroit with supplies, Harriet ran out of flour. "After being without bread three or four days, my little boy, two years old, looked me in the face and said, 'Ma, why don't you make bread; don't you like it? I do.'"

No pictures of Harriet Noble exist, but this one of Ann Allen, who moved to Michigan at the same time, suggests what Noble might have looked like in her 50s.

The difficulties continued into the next year: first Harriet and her husband were seriously and recurrently ill with fever and barely able to work. Just as they seemed to be recovering, her husband had his hand "blown to pieces" in a gun accident, permanently disabling him and forcing Harriet to do all the field work, the tending of the animals, and the laying by of wood. Not until the following spring, three years after their arrival, did prospects look up, when Harriet's husband was at last able to travel back east to get a nephew to come help with the work.

Harriet Noble and her husband were the kind of Americans Andrew Jackson considered the heart of the democracy—ordinary citizens of modest means willing to

continued

>> AMERICAN PORTRAIT *continued*

risk their resources, even their lives, to gain new opportunities and forge new freedoms. They were the people for whom he and his generation had fought the Revolutionary War and the people for whom the nation should exist. Especially after he lost his first bid for the presidency in what he considered "a corrupt bargain" among the eastern and western elites, Jackson resolved that these Americans must be protected in their strivings. Of course settlers were not the only struggling common Americans by 1824. The port cities were awash with wage laborers trying to support themselves and their families on smaller and smaller paychecks. But Jackson was a man of the pre–market revolution era. He distrusted paper money and wages and banks and most people associated with those economic innovations. His was still a world of early settlers needing to be protected against the rich and well connected. He was convinced that he alone could provide that protection. He would do this even if it meant forcibly dispossessing tens of thousands of indigenous people, ignoring the decisions of the Supreme Court, threatening to send federal militia against state authorities, and, all in all, claiming for the executive branch of government an expanse of powers so unprecedented that his critics would label him "the tyrant."

OUTLINE 

Common People and the Political Economy of Democracy

Americans had long associated republican virtue with labor, particularly with labor that afforded economic independence. In the early years of the republic, that virtue-producing labor was most often represented in the figure of the farmer. In the wake of the market revolution and the madcap dash across the Appalachian Mountains, that image had both changed and been fractured. In place of Jefferson's cherished yeoman farmer were the settlers and the urban workers.

Settlers

The migration into the backcountry, set off by the Treaty of Ghent in 1815, continued apace throughout the 1820s. After Maine in 1820 and Missouri in 1821, no new states entered the Union until Arkansas in 1835. But in the meantime the populations of the new states grew steadily, in some cases doubling and tripling in a single decade: Mississippi grew from 75,448 in 1820 to 136,621 in 1830, Illinois from 55,211 to 157,445, and Indiana from 147,178 to 343,031.

North or South, these migrants wanted land. That meant that they wanted easy credit and low prices—but they weren't always convinced that government was their friend in getting these. To be sure, the price of land per acre and the size of the minimum-permitted individual purchase had fallen steadily over the course of the early nineteenth century (although some people thought it could have fallen faster, if northeastern industrialists hadn't wanted to prevent a loss of labor for their mills). The Land Act of 1820 reduced the price to $1.25 per acre for a minimum purchase of 80 acres. In lowering the minimal outlay to $100, however, Congress also eliminated the 1800 provision that had permitted settlers to buy on credit from the government, and added the requirement that land that wasn't promptly paid for would go back up for sale. This made small buyers even more dependent on easy credit from local or state banks. There were plenty of these institutions (their number had mushroomed to take advantage of revived markets after the war), but state and local bankers were often more interested in putting together big deals with land speculators than in making smaller loans to risky individual settlers. And when Langdon Cheves, the bank's director, called in National Bank monies in 1819, even those local sources dried up for a time. When local banks had tried to foreclose on mortgages in arrears, other settlers had formed vigilante committees to attend the auctions and intimidate potential buyers, trying to convince the banks that foreclosure was not in their financial interest.

> "... our fathers have purchased for us political rights and an equality of privileges which we have not yet had the intelligence to appreciate, nor the courage to protect, nor the wisdom to enjoy. For although it cannot be denied that in this country there can be no advantages, powers, or privileges which everyone has not an equal right to enjoy, yet do we not see everywhere around us, privileges, advantages, monopolies enjoyed by the few which are denied to the many ...?"
>
> FREDERICK ROBINSON,
> Fourth of July speech, Boston, 1834

The obstacles to land purchase for ordinary citizens had kept alive the practice of squatting, of claiming land simply by occupying it, demanding that a person's labor on it over time be recognized as a legal claim. As they had in the late eighteenth century, squatters harassed surveyors and ran off sheriff's deputies. Even when a small settler had a legal claim, if the land was good, or minerals were found there,

Emigrants Crossing the Appalachians This early 19th-century engraving depicts emigrants crossing the Appalachians on their way to Pittsburgh, Pennsylvania. Harriet Noble and her family would have traveled in a similar wagon.

or the area showed promise of development, like Daniel Boone, the settler was likely to have to fight off high-powered lawyers and their well-heeled clients. Backwoodsmen, squatters, and settlers did not always share the same interests, but probably all would have agreed with William Manning that "[N]o person can possess property without laboring, unless he get it by force or craft," and that "those that labor for a living and those who get one without laboring—or, as they are generally termed, the Few and the Many"—was "the great dividing line" of society.

The Political Economy of Free Labor

Settlers were not the only ordinary Americans who sometimes felt abandoned to the wiles of the wealthy. Although farm labor would dominate American occupations for decades to come, by the second decade of the nineteenth century its percentage had peaked, and non-farm waged labor was becoming more common. Especially in the port cities of the coasts, growing numbers of men and women worked for wages in increasingly precarious circumstances. They had been hard hit by the disruptions of the war, and even improved prosperity after the war left many wageworkers with barely enough money to supply their own and their families' needs. Few owned their own residences. In some cases, multiple families crowded into a single apartment. An outhouse offered the only plumbing and an indoor open brazier the only cooking stove.

Like the frustrated settlers, wageworkers and their advocates worried that the new political economy of the nation was functioning to keep common working people dependent on the rich. Workers had stuck with Jefferson and Madison through the embargo and the War of 1812, but their patience grew thin. In 1817 Cornelius Blatchly, a Quaker physician from New Jersey, published a pamphlet titled *Some Causes of Popular Poverty,* arguing that property owners had become tyrants, enabled by law to steal from laborers the value that they produced and that rightfully belonged to them.

The Panic of 1819 strengthened that skepticism and gave rise to the beginnings of organized protest in the 1820s. Workers turned out in huge numbers to hear social critics denounce the growing inequities of American life. Scotswoman Frances Wright, one of the most popular of these speakers, focused on education and religion, charging that the clergy conspired to keep workers shackled to superstition. Wright also inveighed against slavery and advocated for women's rights.

In addition, workers began to form unions and go out on strike. Printers, weavers, carpenters, tailors, cabinetmakers, masons, stevedores, and workers in other crafts turned out on strike throughout the major cities of the nation, protesting poor pay and long hours. Strikers argued that the shorter day was essential if they were to have time to refresh themselves, to spend with their families, and to obtain the education necessary for newly enfranchised voters. Over time, these separate strikes merged into cross-trade citywide and regional labor organizations. The first, the Mechanics' Union, was established in Philadelphia in 1827. Pledged to the ten-hour day, the union protested the mental and spiritual exhaustion associated with industrialization and the "desolating evils which . . . arise from a depreciation of the intrinsic value of human labor."

Suffrage Reform

At the founding of the nation, suffrage was restricted not only by gender and race but even more on the basis of property ownership and tax payment. Urban craft workers, who often owned little more than their tools and clothing, had objected to this state of affairs, demanding the vote on the basis of their military service, loyalty, and economic importance to the nation. Most of all, they had demanded the vote as the emblem of liberty. "Suffrage," as one editor insisted, "is the first right of a free people."

Territorial expansion also raised the question of suffrage. Settlers who owned little more than the mortgages on their land saw themselves as the chief embodiment of the republican spirit. They wanted their votes to count as much as the votes of wealthy speculators and bankers, and of landed proprietors.

The new, less settled states led the way in expanding white male suffrage. Vermont entered the Union in 1791 (the first new state after the original 13) with virtually universal white manhood suffrage. The following year, neighboring New Hampshire dropped its last effective qualification, and Kentucky entered the Union without restrictions on adult white males. Tennessee, which became a state in 1796, required that voters own property but did not set a minimum value. Ohio became a state in

The County Election This famous painting by George Caleb Bingham shows voting as a joyous—and manly—activity. Notice the African American man on the left pouring liquor for a white man who is already tipsy, and notice, too, that men of all classes have come together to vote and enjoy the day.

1803 without property requirements for voting, and every one of the six states admitted between 1812 and 1821 entered with universal white male suffrage (see Map 11–1).

In 1817 Connecticut became the first of the older states to abolish all property qualifications for white men. By 1821 the demand for suffrage reform had reached the proportions of a "passion . . . pervading the union." Three years later, when Jackson made his first run for the presidency, only Virginia, Louisiana, and Rhode Island retained any significant restrictions on white male suffrage and only 6 of the 24 states retained indirect selection of the delegates to the Electoral College.

The struggle for an expanded male suffrage was fought openly on the landscape of race. Opponents of suffrage reform offered lurid visions of politically energized African Americans taking advantage of loosened property restrictions and "rush[ing] to the polls in senseless and unmeaning triumph." As suffrage was extended to all white males, it was withdrawn from African American men in New York, Maryland, Pennsylvania, Connecticut, and New Jersey (where single, propertied women also lost the right to vote). In addition, every new state admitted after 1819 specifically excluded African Americans from the vote. Through suffrage reform, white Americans refashioned the vote as an emblem and right of white citizenship. "The people of this state are for . . . a political community of white persons," one Pennsylvanian asserted bluntly.

The partial exception to this pattern was Rhode Island, where elites blocked universal white male suffrage throughout the 1830s. When, in 1841, white working men called a People's Convention to demand universal white male suffrage, they rejected pleas to include African American men in their demands. Spurned by

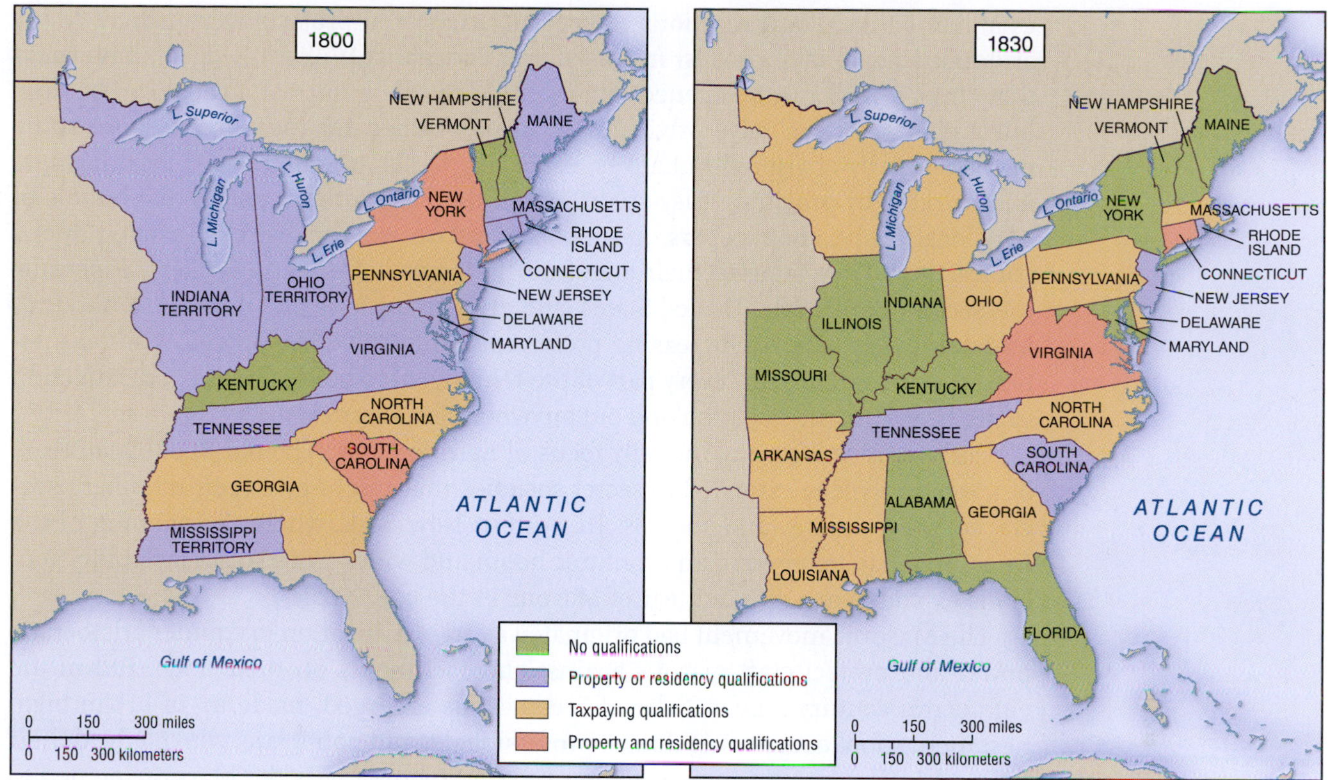

Map 11–1 Toward Universal White Male Suffrage As the western territories organized and entered the Union, they formed a band of states in which there were no property qualifications on white male suffrage, and often minimal taxpaying qualifications. By 1830, Virginia and Connecticut were unusual in the nation for restricting white male suffrage based on both property and tax payment. At the same time, free black males and women lost the vote where they had enjoyed it.

the white working men, African Americans supported the conservative opposition, creating a situation in which the state militia was mobilized against white workers. When Rhode Island conservatives later broadened the franchise, they repaid African American men for their earlier support by including them.

Opposition to Special Privilege and Secret Societies

Since the nation's founding, one strain of American political rhetoric had focused on corrupt insiders who enjoyed opportunities not available to other citizens. In the early nineteenth century, the religious and economic emphasis on personal striving combined with the growing political assertiveness of white working men to reinvigorate those older fears. Politics became a symbolic battle of the virtuous "many" against the corrupt "few."

Early in the century, specially chartered corporations became visible symbols of affluence and the target of these suspicions. Created by special acts of state legislatures, these corporations were, theoretically, open to all Americans. However, the charters were granted on a highly personal basis to people known to individual legislators, people of wealth, power, and reputation.

The movement to use charters to promote development accelerated after the War of 1812. States chartered companies to build roads, provide transportation, and establish banks. Local reactions to specially chartered projects were mixed. Many ambitious persons of modest means shared journalist William Leggett's bitterness that "[n]ot a road can be opened, not a bridge can be built, not a canal can be dug, but a charter of exclusive privileges must be granted for the purpose." Yet some of the specially chartered initiatives, especially banks, seemed to aid local farmers and workers by providing easy credit. When the Panic of 1819 ended that bubble of easy local credit, shopkeepers, farmers, and urban workers were devastated by the contraction. They focused their anger on the power of eastern bankers, especially the Second Bank of the United States, and grew suspicious that the new Republican leadership was bent on increasing preferential rules. By 1820 John C. Calhoun noticed the appearance, in "every part of the Union," of "a general mass of disaffection to the Government . . . looking out anywhere for a leader."

Corporations were not the only focus of hard feelings. The old Republican fears of special privilege extended to secret societies that might give their members special access to money and success. In western New York, where the opening of the Erie Canal had ushered in an economic boom and widespread social instability, tensions exploded in a virulent fear of Masons in the late 1820s.

The Masonic movement had originated as an organization to counter aristocratic power and protect craft masons against encroachments on their trade. But in the eighteenth century a new Order of Freemasons emerged, made up of urban businessmen, shopkeepers, merchants, professionals, and politicians who pledged their political and economic support to one another. By the 1820s the Masons seemed to many working people to embody a dangerous antidemocratic spirit. This vague distrust was galvanized into popular opposition in 1826 by the mysterious disappearance (and presumed murder) of New Yorker William Morgan, who had authored an exposé of the order's purported secret designs on public power. Morgan vanished when he was released from jail after being arrested on a small debt charge. The story spread that Morgan had been ferreted away to Niagara Falls, held for three days, and then drowned. The seriousness of this subversion of justice was magnified, in the popular outcry, by the fact that public officials, including both Andrew Jackson and Henry Clay, were also Masons. By 1827 New Yorkers who opposed the Masons had organized a separate political party and pledged never again to vote for a Mason and to work for the defeat of any Masons already in office.

The Antimason Party spread from New York into other states, doing especially well in local elections in Massachusetts, Pennsylvania, and Vermont. In 1831 Antimasons held the first open presidential nominating convention, choosing William Wirt of Maryland as their candidate. Wirt carried only one state, and the party remained a minor player in national politics. Nevertheless, the battle against cabals illustrated the belief that American party politics amounted to a struggle of common people against the monied aristocracy. This would become a staple of Jacksonian political rhetoric.

Jackson and the National Republicans

By 1816, the party of Jefferson itself was changing. Jefferson had demonstrated that, as need arose, even Democratic Republicans could shift from strict to loose constitutional constructionists. Both Jefferson and party cofounder James Madison had

willingly flexed the muscles of the central government during the War of 1812 and the events leading up to it. Jefferson and Madison had both loathed Hamilton's bank and Madison had happily allowed its charter to expire in 1811. But that was before the war taught him the importance of a central bank for financing war. In 1816 the same James Madison signed the bill to recharter the bank—on the same terms as the first!

Changes in the Democratic Republican Party

In the early nineteenth century the Democratic Republican Party fell increasingly under the influence of a new generation of politicians. Having come of age during the troubled years of the Confederacy, and having witnessed the effects of poor transportation and a weak federal military in the War of 1812, these men did not fear a strong national government. To the contrary, they believed that an activist national government might well be the nation's best protection against localism and dangerous fragmentation. By the election of 1824, they would identify themselves as National Republicans.

> **"Thousands and thousands of people, without distinction of rank, collected in an immense mass round the Capitol, silent, orderly, and tranquil, with their eyes fixed on the front of the edifice, waiting the appearance of the President in the portico. The door from the Rotunda opens. . . . [the] old man with his grey locks, that crown of glory, advances, bows to the people, who greet him with a shout that rends the air, the Cannons, from the heights around, from Alexandra and Fort Warburton proclaim the oath he has taken and all the hills reverberate the sound. It was grand—it was sublime!"**
>
> MARGARET BAYARD SMITH,
> describing Andrew Jackson's inauguration

This new brand of Republicanism was epitomized by four men: Henry Clay of Kentucky, John C. Calhoun of South Carolina, and Daniel Webster and John Quincy Adams of Massachusetts. Henry Clay (1777–1852) entered national politics as the champion of the large planters and merchants of Kentucky. Putting aside possible differences of interest among them, the Kentucky elites had turned to the federal government for support for projects (especially transportation improvements) they could not win at home. John C. Calhoun (1782–1850) was first a representative and then senator and vice president. Although both Calhoun and South Carolina later became symbols of states' rights sentiment, in the postwar years South Carolinians believed that their export economy (based on rice, indigo, and cotton) was best served by a strong federal government able to ensure access to international markets.

Adams and Webster, both New Englanders, illustrated the compatibility of National Republicanism with the old Federalist views. Webster steadfastly promoted the interests of New England's banking classes. He was a strong supporter of protective tariffs after the War of 1812, as Massachusetts merchants shifted from importing to manufacturing. Born in 1767, John Quincy Adams was influenced by his father's Federalist views, and he was first elected to the Senate in 1800 by the Federalist

Henry Clay Henry Clay was 44 when Charles Bird King painted this portrait in 1821, but he looks much younger. He had the power to charm women and men both. Margaret Bayard Smith said that he had a "power of captivation, which no one who was its object could resist."

Massachusetts legislature. Adams broke rank with his party when it opposed the Louisiana Purchase, however.

Led by Clay, the new nationalists fashioned a vision of a Republican political economy based on individual entrepreneurial and market development (including domestic manufacturing), guided by the active involvement of the federal government. Not surprisingly, their platform, loosely called the American System, was a patchwork devised to appeal to local interests and identities. In the West and South, that meant promoting a national subsidy to improve transportation. For the Northeast, this new breed of Republican called for a protective tariff for domestic industries. To protect the federal credit and stabilize currency and internal credit, they supported a national bank.

The various elements of the American System came before Congress as separate bills after the War of 1812, each commanding a different coalition of supporters. The bills to create the Second Bank of the United States and to increase the national tariffs passed with relative ease and were signed by President Madison. Authorized in 1816, the Second Bank of the United States was chartered for 20 years and located in Philadelphia, with the federal government providing one-fifth of its $35 million capitalization and appointing one-fifth of its directors. The tariff bill (with Lowell's relief included) was less aggressively protective than some nationalists wished.

Transportation subsidies fared less well. Madison was skeptical about the constitutionality of this form of federal intervention. In his annual messages of both 1815 and 1816 he urged Congress to initiate a constitutional amendment to clarify federal power in this area. Although deeply torn, Congress eventually passed a bill creating a federal fund for internal improvements. On his last day in office, Madison vetoed it. In 1818, the federal government opened a section of the National Road, a highway that connected Baltimore to Wheeling, Virginia (later West Virginia). Otherwise, federal transportation initiatives fell victim to questions of constitutionality and regional jealousies.

James Monroe and National Republicanism

In 1816, Republican James Monroe ran for the presidency against Rufus King, the last Federalist to vie for that office. In the flush of postwar victory and prosperity and in the aftermath of the Hartford Convention, the returns were lopsided in Monroe's favor: Monroe took every state but Maine, Massachusetts, Rhode Island, and Delaware and

AMERICA AND THE WORLD

>> The Monroe Doctrine

In his annual address to Congress in 1823 (the forerunner of the modern presidential State of the Union address) President James Monroe declared that ". . . the American continents, by the free and independent condition which they have assumed and maintain, are henceforth not to be considered as subjects for future colonization by any European powers. . . ." Seemingly a statement about the United States' commitment to indigenous democratic movements among its neighbors, and a continuation of the young nation's sense of itself as the beacon of democratic hope everywhere, the Monroe Doctrine was actually not about democracy at all. It echoed an equally persistent, but quite different, strain of American foreign policy, the desire to avoid entanglement in European wars.

Equally importantly, the Monroe Doctrine represented the United States' perfect willingness to isolate itself from democratic movements stirring within Europe and being opposed by conservative forces there. In 1820 disgruntled and unpaid Spanish soldiers (needed to fight the breakaway American republics) rebelled against their monarchy. The insurgence soon spread to Naples, Italy. After years of domination by the Ottoman Empire, in 1821 Greek revolutionaries (including many merchants and shippers) had launched a conspiracy against the state that ended in civil war. By 1823 the bourgeoisie and commoners of France were growing angry with the assaults of the restored Bourbon monarchy on the franchise and the freedom of the press. Insurgences also occurred among the Poles, the Hungarians, the Czechs, and others. Even in Great Britain, the fall of Napoleon ushered in a prolonged period of agitation for parliamentary reform and the broadening of the franchise.

In his 1823 statement, Monroe acknowledged these democratic movements and expressed a broad support for them, but he declared that the issues and circumstances in Europe were "eminently and conspicuously different" from those in the Americas: "Our policy in regard to Europe, which was adopted at an early stage of the wars which have so long agitated that quarter of the globe, nevertheless remains the same, which is, not to interfere in the internal concerns of any of its powers; to consider the government de facto as the legitimate government for us."

Even within the Western Hemisphere, the area Monroe specified, the meaning of the doctrine was ambiguous. The Monroe Doctrine applied to the Americas —but within that context, only to Central and South America and, within that context, only to new republics formed by mixed European-American populations. It did not apply to Canada: the United States would make no effort to support revolts against the British government there in the 1830s. And Monroe did not intend his

continued

"The Birth of the Monroe Doctrine" Here, President James Monroe and his cabinet discuss foreign policy, crafting what will later be known as the "Monroe Doctrine." Left to right: John Quincy Adams, William Harris Crawford, William Wirt, Monroe, John C. Calhoun, Daniel D. Tompkins, and John McLean.

>> **AMERICA AND THE WORLD** *continued*

doctrine to apply to the black republic of Haiti. Moreover, even as James Monroe informed Europe that the United States would be the guarantor of the new American republics, some Americans were already coveting northern Mexico.

It was, then, not the abstract principle of democracy that made the new American republics of special interest to the United States. Nor, in fact, was it the specific examples of democracy they represented. They could as well have been insurgent monarchies, as far as Monroe's doctrine was concerned. The "interests" they activated in the United States were a coincidence of politics and geography. They had been European colonies; they had broken away; European efforts to recolonize them might once again bring war to the Americas and to the United States.

won 183 electoral votes to King's 34. He was the third Virginian in a row to hold the office—the fourth Virginian of only five presidents total.

Monroe's inaugural address sounded many of the themes common in those of earlier Republican presidents: he praised the virtue of the American people and warned against corruption, greed, and the usurpation of power by nefarious foes of the republic. But by way of explaining the "principles" that would guide him in office, Monroe seemed almost to sound Federalist themes. Although he emphasized the primary importance of the local and state militias, he suggested the need for a more vigorous national defense and a more aggressive foreign policy toward Europe generally: "Our distance from Europe and the just, moderate, and pacific policy of our Government may form some security against these dangers, but they ought to be anticipated and guarded against." He averred that a constitutional amendment might be required, but he nevertheless recommended federally subsidized internal improvements as necessary to the prosperity and political cohesion of the nation: "Other interests of high importance will claim attention, among which the improvement of our country by roads and canals, proceeding always with a constitutional sanction, holds a distinguished place. By thus facilitating the intercourse between the States we shall add much to the convenience and comfort of our fellow-citizens, much to the ornament of the country, and, what is of greater importance, we shall shorten distances, and, by making each part more accessible to and dependent on the other, we shall bind the Union more closely together."

In office, Monroe governed with the nationalist bent suggested in his inaugural address. Tellingly, although it meant passing up other deserving contenders, he asked former Federalist John Quincy Adams to be secretary of state (the presumed stepping stone to the presidency). Together Monroe and Adams moved toward a new United States assertiveness in the Atlantic world.

The first initiatives in this direction were a series of agreements clarifying details of the country's relations with British colonies in North America. In 1817, Richard Rush (acting secretary of state until Adams was able to return from Europe) and British minister Charles Bagot agreed to limit British and American forces on the Great Lakes. The next year, the Convention of 1818 extended that nonmilitarized border along the 49th parallel to the Rocky Mountains. It also formally acknowledged American fishing rights off the Labrador and Newfoundland coasts.

In 1819, the United States at last fixed definite borders to the Louisiana Purchase. After the purchase, Jefferson had attempted unsuccessfully to buy Florida from Spain. His successor, Madison, had simply declared that West Florida had been a

part of the Louisiana Purchase all along. Taking the Florida peninsula itself had been left for James Monroe. With Spain too weak to prevent Seminole raids into Georgia and South Carolina, Monroe authorized war hero Andrew Jackson to lead a raid into Florida, ostensibly to frighten the Seminoles into leaving white settlers alone. But Jackson wanted more. Without clear authorization, in 1818 Jackson's troops entered Florida, destroying Seminole settlements, capturing a Spanish fort (contrary to explicit orders), and executing two British citizens whom Jackson held responsible for supporting Indian resistance. Jackson did not conquer all of Florida; there was no need. By May 1818 it was plain that the United States could take the territory whenever it chose.

A year later, in the Transcontinental Treaty of 1819, Spain ceded all of Florida to the United States in return for the U.S. government's agreement to assume private American claims against Spain in the amount of about $5 million. The Transcontinental Treaty also clarified the border between the United States and Spanish Mexico. The United States gave up claims not only to California (which few people considered part of the original purchase) but also to Texas (which many people did). In return, the United States gained a boundary that ran in a series of ascending steps from Louisiana to the Pacific. This treaty defined the United States as a nation that spanned the continent.

In the 1820s, under Monroe, the United States began to view itself as American, not quasi-European, and as protector of the Americas against Europe. By 1815 a number of former Spanish colonies, including Argentina, Chile, and Venezuela, had revolted, and an independence movement was under way in Mexico. As these new republics won their independence, they turned to the United States for recognition and support. Against this tide, the absolute monarchies in Europe sought to preserve and extend their territorial empires. France supported the Spanish monarchy against an internal revolt and offered to help Spain regain its colonies in South America. Russia reasserted and strengthened its long-standing claims in the Pacific Northwest.

Disavowing any future new territorial ambitions for itself in the Americas, Great Britain offered to make a joint declaration with the United States warning other nations against intruding in the internal affairs of Western Hemisphere countries. An alliance with Britain would have enhanced U.S. diplomatic credibility, but many Americans suspected that once it established a right to have its navy in the area, Britain would squeeze the United States out of South American markets.

Secretary of State John Quincy Adams convinced Monroe to refuse the British offer and, instead, to issue a unilateral statement of support for the new republics. It would be far better, he argued, to act independently than to seem "to come in as a cockboat in the wake of the British man-of-war." Adams hoped that being identified with this policy would help him shed the pro-British tag that was associated with many New Englanders.

In his annual message to Congress in 1823, Monroe enunciated the policy that has since become known as the Monroe Doctrine. Monroe asserted a special United States relationship with all parts of North and South America, with which, he insisted, "we are of necessity more immediately connected." "We owe it . . . to candor and to the amicable relations existing between the United States and those [European] powers," he continued, "to declare that we should consider any attempt on their part to extend their system to any portion of this hemisphere as dangerous to our peace and safety." The Monroe Doctrine marked an important milestone in the development of American nationalism and internationalism. The United States not only asserted a new relation (as peer) to the European nations, but a new relation to the Americas as well. Surveillance over the nations of North and South America would be the domestic right of the United States.

The Election of 1824 and the "Corrupt Bargain"

In the usual order of custom in the young republic, Secretary of State John Quincy Adams would have been Monroe's presumed successor. But by 1824 the Republican Party housed a host of experienced men who considered themselves next in line for the office. In addition to Adams, there were John C. Calhoun (Monroe's secretary of war), Henry Clay (speaker of the House), and William H. Crawford of Georgia (Monroe's secretary of the Treasury, who suffered a massive stroke in 1823). This group, which called itself the National Republicans, was composed of some of the nation's most experienced and respected leaders.

And then there was the outlier, Andrew Jackson. From his unpromising beginnings as an orphan of backcountry settlers, Andrew Jackson had gradually worked his way to wealth and to public prominence. After the Revolution, Jackson studied law for a time in North Carolina and was admitted to the bar in 1787. That year, he moved west to Jonesboro, later to be part of the new state of Tennessee. There Jackson practiced law and made a reputation for himself representing settlers with disputed land claims. He was a delegate to the Tennessee constitutional convention in 1796 and was elected the state's first congressional representative. In 1797 he was elected senator but resigned within a year to serve as a justice on the Tennessee Supreme Court until 1804. In that year, he bought land near the future city of Nashville, Tennessee.

Jackson became a national figure during the War of 1812, first as commander of the devastating campaign against the Creek nation and then, at war's end, as the hero of the Battle of New Orleans. His controversial but effective campaign against the Seminoles in 1818 and 1819 and his subsequent brief career as governor of the Territory of Florida completed his credentials as an unyielding champion of the western settler.

Still, when the Tennessee legislature nominated Jackson for the presidency in 1822, few politicians took the candidacy seriously, given his competition. But by 1824 voting Americans were beginning to pull back from the new expansive Republican vision. Among the viable candidates in the field, all but Jackson advocated a strong central government—an indication perhaps of how out of step the Republican leadership was with its constituents.

An early indication of the storminess of the election came with the Republican nomination. Because James Monroe had not designated a successor, the selection was thrown to the Republican congressional caucus, a circumstance expected to benefit Crawford. But this time, unlike earlier nominations, the other candidates loudly disowned the caucus as a corrupt and irregular institution. So effective was their repudiation that only 66 of a possible 216 Republican members of Congress even attended. As expected, Crawford got the nod, but its value had been diminished.

When the election was held, no candidate claimed a majority either of the popular vote or of the Electoral College. Equally stunning, the one who came closest was the underdog Andrew Jackson, with 43 percent of the popular vote and 99 electoral votes. Next was Adams, who tallied 31 percent of the popular vote and 84 electoral votes. Crawford managed only 41 electoral votes. Clay came in last with 37 electoral votes. (Calhoun had pulled out of the election.)

The election was thus thrown to the House of Representatives, where members had to select from among the three candidates with the highest electoral count. As the highest vote getter, Jackson was confident at first, but by late December he began to hear rumors "that deep intrigue is on foot." Those rumors were correct. Although Adams did not receive a single popular vote in Kentucky, and although the Kentucky state legislature had directed its delegation to vote for Jackson, Clay used his prestige to override those instructions and to marshal additional support for Adams in other states. With Clay behind him, Adams received the votes of 13 of the 24 state delegations. Jackson received 7 and Crawford received 4.

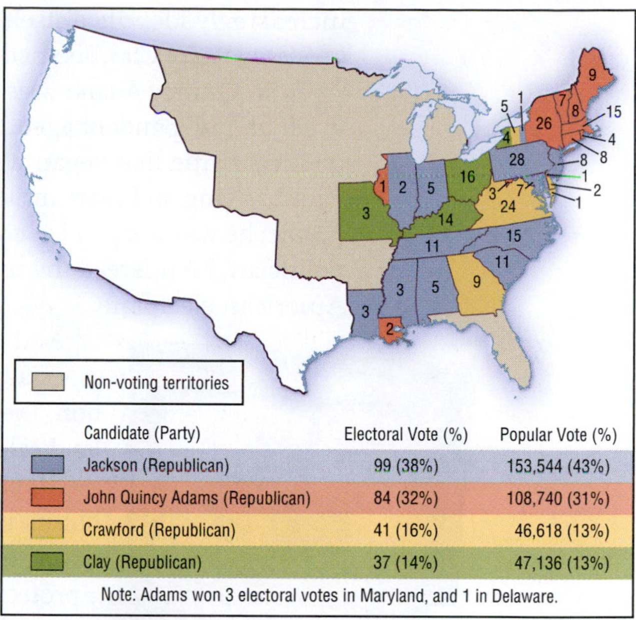

Candidate (Party)	Electoral Vote (%)	Popular Vote (%)
Jackson (Republican)	99 (38%)	153,544 (43%)
John Quincy Adams (Republican)	84 (32%)	108,740 (31%)
Crawford (Republican)	41 (16%)	46,618 (13%)
Clay (Republican)	37 (14%)	47,136 (13%)

Note: Adams won 3 electoral votes in Maryland, and 1 in Delaware.

Map 11–2 The Election of 1824 Almost all of Adams's electoral votes came from the Northeast, while Jackson's were spread through the South, the Midwest, and the Mid-Atlantic.

Jackson later charged that Adams had bought Clay's support with the promise of the post of secretary of state. In fact, Adams did give Clay that job. Even without a reward, however, Clay had good reasons for allying himself with Adams. Clay and Adams shared similar political philosophies. In addition, Jackson and Clay vied for the same regional vote. Supporting Jackson in 1824 would have helped the Tennessean build a stronger western base for 1828.

Jackson was furious. "Intrigue, corruption, and sale of public office is the rumor of the day," he roared. His supporters charged that the election had been stolen in a "corrupt bargain" brokered by insiders who debased the virtue of the republic and flagrantly disregarded the clear will of the electorate.

The Adams Presidency and the Gathering Forces of Democracy

In many respects, Adams's choice of Clay made perfect sense. Since the postwar period both men had advocated a shared commitment to the principles of the "American System": the preservation of a national bank, the levying of a national tariff, and the improvement of infrastructure to make the movement of goods faster and more efficient.

Much to the consternation of fiscal conservatives and even some moderates, Adams continued to support these policies once in office, even using his first annual message to Congress in 1825 to lay out a grand vision for federal involvement in the nation's political economy. He called not only for economic projects, like transportation improvements, but also for the creation of a national university, a national observatory, and a naval academy, as well as an elaborate system of roads and canals supported by federal expenditures. In a particularly ill-chosen phrase, Adams urged Congress not to be "palsied by the will of our constituents." His opponents railed that this was clear evidence of his intention to benefit the wealthy at the expense of the common people, and that this branch of the Republican Party (which increasingly identified itself as the National Republicans), including new Secretary of State Henry Clay, seemed more Federalist than Jeffersonian.

John Quincy Adams was a wise and principled statesman, but he was never able to set an independent agenda for his presidency. His every act was shadowed by the political battle that began with his election and in which his regional identification with banking and mercantile interests constantly hurt him. Defensive and prickly in public, he was not good at creating strong political alliances. Not a particularly canny politician, he misread the times and underestimated the gulf developing within the American electorate.

And Jackson's supporters worked hard to discredit Adams, especially on the issue of the tariff. In the early years of the nation, the federal government had depended on the tariff and on land sales for most of its revenue. By the end of the War of 1812, the importance of the tariff for generating funding had declined, but its importance as a language for addressing the growing regional economic differences had increased. The 1816 tariff was protectionist, but only very mildly so. Its chief achievement was to give some recognition to the importance of domestic manufactures. But the Panic of 1819, brought on in part by the reliance of the United States on world markets, reenergized protectionists: a bill that would have raised tariffs on the entire list of imported products by 5 percent (and even higher for cotton, wool, iron, and glass) failed passage by only one vote. It was broadly supported in the western and middle states and opposed in the South (where it was seen as increasing dependence on high-priced New England products), while New England split on the issue. But by 1824 New England was committed enough to industrial growth to become solidly protariff. That year, when Congress proposed a tariff that included levies of 35 percent on imported cotton, wool, hemp, and iron, passage was a foregone conclusion.

Passage of the 1824 tariff was ominous for several reasons. First, of course, it was vehemently opposed by the South. But just as portentous was the fact that neither the North nor the federal government really needed it. In 1824 the federal government reported a surplus of funds, and by that year manufactures were doing well enough in New England that they did not really require the help. The tariff had become the language of sectionalism. But the underlying issue was the deep conflict over the power of the federal government. This was not a simple question of nationalism versus localism. Jackson was a nationalist who was willing to support some level of protective tariff and had even conceded in the 1824 campaign, "It is time we became a little more Americanized." The difference between Adams and Jackson was the question of the basis of federal legitimacy. In what actions could the federal government claim the authority of the American people? And in what actions did it overstep that authority? That conflict was now infused with the energy of a rising democratic spirit.

The Election of 1828

The campaign that followed was personal and vicious. Adams's supporters tarred Jackson as a liar and a blasphemer incapable of self-restraint. They accused Jackson of having "prevailed upon the wife of Lewis Robards of Mercer County, Kentucky, to desert her husband, and live with himself, in the character of a wife." (Rachel Jackson's divorce may not have been final when she and Jackson married.) Jackson supporters retorted that Adams was a Sabbath breaker, a closet Federalist, and an unprincipled hypocrite whose long residence in Europe had taught him disdain for popular government. To make the point, Jacksonians began to refer to themselves as Jacksonian Democrats (or just the Democrats).

The Democratic campaign of 1828 ushered in a new era of national political campaigning. Whereas earlier campaigns had been fought primarily on the local level and among a far smaller group of potential voters, in 1828 Martin Van Buren coordinated a Democratic national campaign designed to appeal to a mass electorate. Van Buren oversaw the creation of a highly controlled party hierarchy structured like the Benevolent Empire (See Chapter 12), with local societies linked to state societies linked to the national organization. Van Buren pioneered the use of carefully choreographed demonstrations and converted nonpartisan occasions (like Fourth of July celebrations) into Democratic rallies by sending out armies of Jackson supporters armed with American flags and placards. Van Buren also engineered the use of political imagery to evoke campaign themes. Taking advantage of Jackson's nickname, "Old Hickory" (for the hardest wood in the United States), campaign workers handed out hickory canes to crowds at political events. At the same time, supporters used editorials and campaign tracts to describe Jackson as the embodiment of the common man. Turning Jackson's obstinacy and lack of formal education into strengths, they argued that he was nature's product, with a "native strength of mind" and "practical common sense."

Jackson Forever!
The Hero of Two Wars and of Orleans!
The Man of the People!
HE WHO COULD NOT BARTER NOR BARGAIN FOR THE
PRESIDENCY!
Who, although "*A Military Chieftain*," valued the purity of Elections and of the Electors, MORE than the Office of PRESIDENT itself! Although the greatest in the gift of his countrymen, and the highest in point of dignity of any in the world,
BECAUSE
It should be derived from the
PEOPLE!
No Gag Laws! No Black Cockades! No Reign of Terror! No Standing Army or Navy Officers, when under the pay of Government, to browbeat, or
KNOCK DOWN
Old Revolutionary Characters, or our Representatives while in the discharge of their duty. To the Polls then, and vote for those who will support
OLD HICKORY
AND THE ELECTORAL LAW.

This poster, from the 1828 election, sets out the case for Jackson as a man of the people.

When the votes were counted in 1828, Jackson had won a clear majority: 56 percent of the popular vote and 178 electoral votes to Adams's 83 electoral votes. Although Adams had retained New England, New Jersey, Delaware, and northern Maryland, Jackson had solidly taken the South and the West, as well as Pennsylvania, most of New York, and even northern Maine.

Jackson was elected by a strong cross section of voters who identified with his stance as an outsider to, and victim of, eastern elites. He was the candidate of westerners, migrants, settlers, and landowners who opposed eastern banks and congressional land policies, but Jackson also drew support from urban professionals, shopkeepers, laborers, and craftsmen who believed that special privilege was denying them their chance of prosperity. A planter and a southerner, Jackson could claim the mantle of Jeffersonians. Reflecting that older political economy, he favored limited government, feared concentrations of economic and political power, and seemed

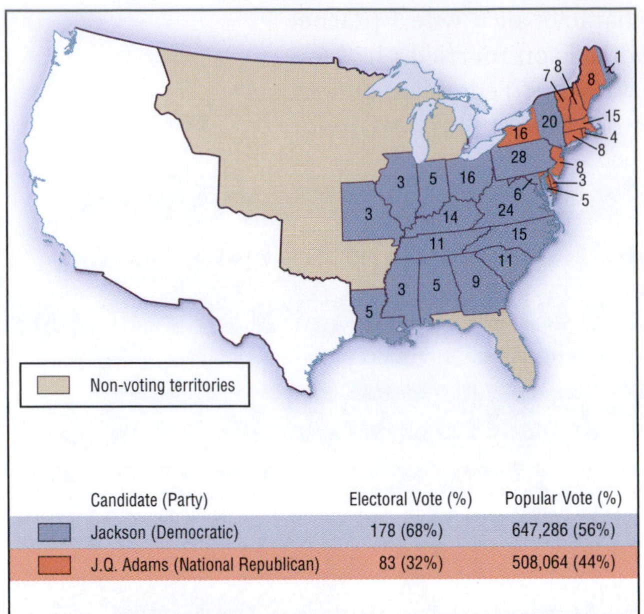

Map 11–3 The Election of 1828 In 1828, Jackson solidified his hold on the South and Midwest and even made inroads in the Northeast.

to share Jefferson's emphasis on the individual common American.

At the same time, the Jacksonians were vague about exactly where the heart of their new democratic movement resided. Structurally, they believed that it evolved from the states. This endorsement of federal restraint was confused, however, by Jackson's equally strong conviction that he *was* the people and his will was indistinguishable from theirs. The ironic result was a continuous migration of power from the states to the executive during the presidency of the man elected to protect the common man.

The tendency to personalize political struggle characterized Jackson's presidency. He never forgave the National Republicans for publicly questioning the legitimacy of his marriage. Later, he viewed his battle against the Second Bank of the United States in the same highly personal terms: "The Bank," he informed Van Buren, "is trying to kill me, but I will kill it."

If Jackson understood himself as the embodiment of the people's will, he understood the new Democratic Party as its direct instrument. After personal loyalty to Jackson, party loyalty became the avenue to appointment and the justification for an unprecedented turnover in appointees. Unfortunately, party loyalty did not guarantee competence or honesty. Jackson's choice for New York customs collector, Samuel Swartwout, used his position to embezzle more than $1 million.

The overall results were mixed. Invigorated by his confidence that he spoke for the nation, Jackson expanded the powers of the presidency, but his conviction that he alone embodied the true virtue of the republic also led to personal pettiness, widespread patronage, and turmoil within his cabinet. His efforts to abolish the Second Bank of the United States wreaked serious material hardship for average Americans, and his hostility to Native Americans resulted in widespread death and impoverishment.

A Policy of Removing Indigenous People

Even in the pandemonium of the inauguration, the message of the new presidency was clear: "As the instrument of the Federal Constitution," Jackson declared in his inaugural address, "I shall keep steadily in view the limitations as well as the extent of the Executive power." He advocated fiscal restraint, an end to government patronage, and a constitutional amendment to remove "all intermediary agency in the election of President and Vice-President." The task of his administration, Jackson announced, must be "the task of reform."

Jackson and Native Peoples

For Andrew Jackson, the quintessential "common man" was the western settler, struggling to bring new lands under cultivation and new institutions to life. Pioneers confronted various obstacles in their migrations west, but none loomed larger than the resistance of Indian peoples. The War of 1812 had brought an end to intertribal resistance east of the Mississippi River. By 1828, most of the Great Lakes nations had been pushed out of Ohio, southern Indiana, and Illinois, but the Ojibwa, Winnebago, Sauk, Mesquakie, Kickapoo, and Menominee tribes retained sizable homelands in the region.. In the South, in spite of repeated forced cessions, the Chickasaws, Choctaws, Creeks, Cherokees, and Seminoles retained ancestral territories.

Jackson's views concerning Native Americans had been settled many years earlier, in the crucible of the Indian wars of the 1790s. "Does not experience teach us that treaties answer no other Purpose than opening an Easy door for the Indians to pass [through to] Butcher our citizens?" he wrote in 1794, from his first home on the Cumberland River. Congress should "Punish the Barbarians."

In these views Jackson was no different from many American settlers—some of whom had directly experienced the violence that arose from white incursions into Indian Country, but many of whom formed their ideas long before they ever saw an Indian, basing their preconceptions on inflamed newspaper accounts in the new mass-produced "penny press" and on unsubstantiated rumors passed around in taverns and parlors. Most American settlers saw Indians only casually and in passing. Some of these encounters were surely unnerving. In her travels west, for example, Harriet Noble was at one time convinced that an Indian woman was following her to take her baby. Several times she found Indians staring in her doorless threshhold, begging for food, she thought. But more often than not, no physical harm came to the settlers from these incidents. The harm that Indians represented was at once more abstract and more material than that: they occupied lands recognized as belonging to them in treaties with the federal government. Despite recurrent wars and land cessions, western settlers were no happier with federal initiatives in the 1820s than they had been in the 1790s.

Tension ran especially high in Georgia. There officials complained that the federal government had not kept its promise to remove all Indians from the state, a condition of Georgia's agreement to cede its western land claims to the federal government in 1802. A few Creeks and most of the Cherokee nation remained. In 1826 the federal government pressured the Creeks to give up all but a small strip of their remaining lands in Georgia, but white Georgians were not satisfied. Georgia governor George Michael Troup sent surveyors onto that last piece of Creek land. When President Adams objected to this encroachment on federal treaty powers, Troup threatened to call up the state militia.

The election of Andrew Jackson emboldened the Georgians to go after Cherokee land. They invalidated the constitution of the Cherokee nation within Georgia and proclaimed that the Cherokees were subject to the authority of the state of Georgia. When discoveries of gold sent white prospectors surging onto Cherokee land, Georgia refused either to stop the trespassers or to protect the Indians. To the contrary, the state passed a series of laws that deprived Cherokees of their rights and stripped them of their land. Jackson quickly made his position clear, notifying the Cherokees that it was his duty, as president, to "sustain the States in the exercise of their rights."

In fact, the states were not exercising their rights. In 1830 the Cherokee nation took the state of Georgia to the Supreme Court, arguing that the Cherokee nation was a "foreign nation in the sense of our constitution and law" and that, as a state, Georgia had no right to pass laws over the inhabitants of a foreign nation. Chief Justice John

Marshall agreed that the Cherokees were a distinct political society—a "denominated domestic dependent nation," as he termed it—but he demurred that they were not a foreign state "in the sense of the constitution, and cannot maintain an action in the courts of the United States." But the following year, *Worcester v. Georgia,* which was *not* brought by the Cherokee nation, gave Marshall the opportunity to say more. He identified the Cherokee nation as "a distinct community, occupying its own territory, with boundaries accurately described in which the laws of Georgia can have no force, and which the citizens of Georgia have no right to enter but with the assent of the Cherokees themselves or in conformity with treaties and with the acts of Congress." Indeed, Marshall concluded, "The whole intercourse between the United States and this nation is, by our Constitution and laws, vested in the government of the United States." Georgia had acted unconstitutionally.

Jackson refused to enforce this decision. He had long believed that the best policy, "not only liberal, but generous," would be to remove the Indians entirely from lands sought by settlers. The place he had in mind was across the Mississippi River. Because full-scale removal of the Indians involved shifting populations across state lines and into federal territories, however, it required congressional consent.

The proposed policy was not unopposed. "[I]f, in pursuance of a narrow and selfish policy, we should at this time, in a time of profound peace and great national prosperity, amidst all our professions of magnanimity and benevolence . . . drive away these remnants of tribes, in such a manner, and under such auspices, as to insure their destruction . . . ," Jeremiah Evarts, secretary of the American Board of Commissioners for Foreign Missions, warned, "then the sentence of an indignant world would be

The Grand National Caravan Moving East In this satirical cartoon, Jackson and Van Buren are on the left, followed by the devil, an army officer, and a group of caged Indians, who represent Indian removal. On the ground, a drunken Jacksonian proclaims, "Hail! Columbia, happy land."

uttered in thunders, which would roll and reverberate for ages after the present actors in human affairs shall have passed away." In Congress the Native Americans found unexpected allies. To the old Adams men, now led by Henry Clay, "removal" was the policy of states, forced on the federal government. For Congress to pass an act authorizing the policy would mean encouraging states to trample on federal powers.

Van Buren responded by forming a counterlobby, the Board for the Emigration, Preservation, and Improvement of the Aborigines of America, which argued that Indians were ill equipped for contact with white civilization and that removing them was humane. Among the proponents of removal was former president John Quincy Adams. In the end, the bill passed by only five votes and only after four months of debate.

The Removal Act

In 1830 Congress passed and President Jackson signed an act "to provide for an exchange of lands with the Indians residing in any of the states or territories, and for their removal west of the river Mississippi." In one sense, the act only made

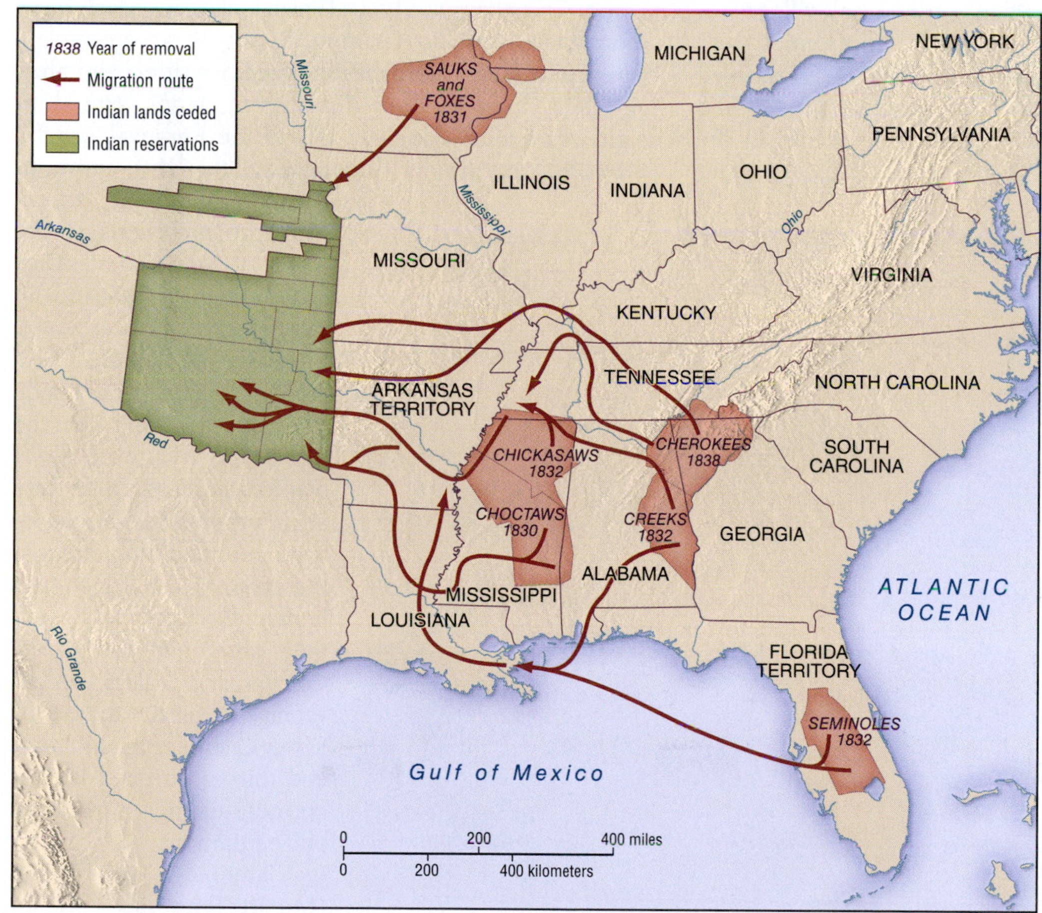

Map 11–4 Indian Removals Jackson's policy of Indian removal required Native American peoples to leave their homelands east of the Mississippi River for government-designated lands west of the Mississippi. Some Indian groups signed treaties ceding their lands, but these groups often lacked authority to do so. Some groups (like the Cherokees) fought removal in court. Others (like the Seminoles, Sauks, and Foxes) fought the policy in open combat.

AMERICAN LANDSCAPE

>> Liberty and the Land: Cherokee Removal

The Cherokees, one of the largest Indian nations the United States sought to displace, had lived on the rocky slopes and in the pocket coves of the southern Appalachians since long before the arrival of the Europeans, and their understanding of themselves as a people was intimately tied to the mountains. Their ancestors, Kana'ti and Selu, the first man and the first woman of the Real People, had migrated into this land when the land itself was newly created. They had been fed from game Kana'ti found in a deep cave and from the corn and beans Selu had produced by rubbing her stomach and armpits.

These beginnings were preserved in the social and economic life of the Cherokees in the early nineteenth century. They lived in settled agricultural villages in the Smoky Mountains, where their communities were anchored by the fields women cultivated. Men traveled long distances and sometimes for years at a time to find game, but they always returned to their homes in the mountains. Although the Cherokee diet included other foods, corn and deer remained at the ceremonial center of the culture. Men and women ritualized marriages by exchanging corn and deer, and each year communities celebrated the Green Corn Festival, when their elders recited the stories of their origin and migration into the mountains. Social and political life were governed by the principle of harmony and balance. Each village had a council hall large enough to hold the entire community, and decisions were achieved by consensus. For the Cherokees, where they lived was who they were. They had become Cherokee by entering the land of the mountains, and they remained Cherokee because they remained in the mountains.

Two centuries of contact altered that way of life. Some Cherokees embraced racial slavery. Most grew more dependent on farming. Trying to accommodate white practices, Cherokees adopted a written alphabet. Yet they clung to their diminishing lands. Not until eight years after Congress passed the Removal Act did the U.S. Army (under General Winfield Scott) arrive, in late spring of 1838, to enforce the provisions of the Treaty of New Echota. They found a settled people unwilling and unprepared to move. They had not gathered their families together or set aside blankets and food for the trip. Their fields were newly planted, and their cattle were at spring pasture. Cherokees were rounded up, often at the point of a bayonet, and herded into stockades, where they were held for weeks. Corrupt land dealers took advantage of the circumstances to buy Cherokee lands cheap, and thieves stripped houses and outbuildings of furniture and equipment.

Gathered at three points (two in Tennessee, one in Alabama) for embarkation, the Cherokees went west in two waves. Under the supervision of the army, three

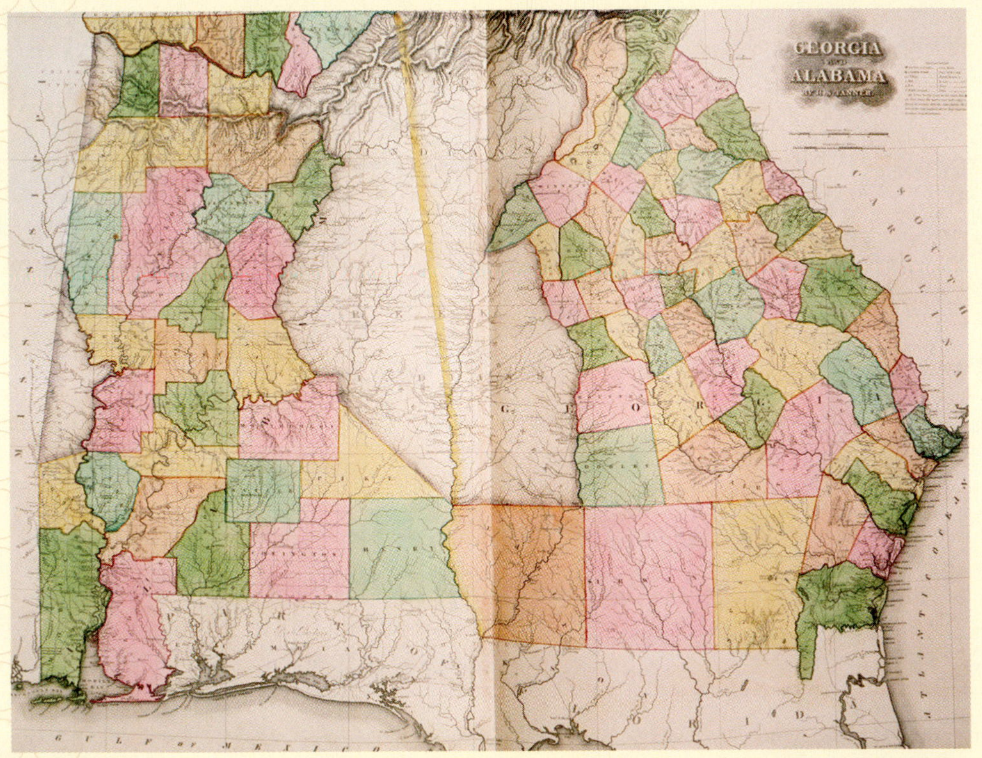

A Map of Georgia and Alabama in 1823 This map shows the two states prior to the Indian Removal Act of 1838.

groups totaling nearly 3,000 Cherokees started almost immediately, in the hottest part of the summer ("the sickly season," the Cherokees called it). According to one missionary present at the events, the agent shipped the Cherokees "by multitudes," "[n]ine hundred in one detachment, and seven hundred in another . . . driven onto boats" to carry them up the Tennessee and Ohio rivers to the Mississippi. "It will be a miracle of mercy if one-fourth escape the exposure to that sickly climate." Hundreds did not.

With the death count mounting, the Cherokees requested authority to manage their own removals and to delay them until the end of summer. After getting this permission, they used every means at their disposal to survive the journey. Those who were permitted to return to their homes before leaving salvaged whatever bedding, food, and equipment remained. By one account, some of the contingents included hundreds of wagons and thousands of horses, but others were far less well supplied. The wagons sometimes began as family vehicles but soon became the equipment of the entire caravan, carrying whoever could not walk, usually the sick and the aged. Those who lacked wagons or ponies and could still walk bundled their goods in blankets on their backs or made pallets.

All of the contingents were escorted by soldiers, sometimes making them look like "the march of an army, regiment after regiment, the wagons in the center, the officers along the line and the horsemen on the flanks and at the rear." At least for the removals they organized, however, the Cherokees established their own internal police, "whose duties are to seize & promptly punish any offences against good order," according to an army lieutenant. To the meager stocks of salt pork and often moldy corn and wheat flour provided them by military suppliers, the Cherokees added whatever they could hunt or forage along the way: turkeys, small game, occasionally deer, and berries. Those who had pots shared them with those who did not.

The later removals avoided the season of greatest disease, summer, but they faced the cold weather, winds, and ice storms of winter. Many of the migrants had only thin clothing and few blankets, and the cold was especially hard on elders, children, and the sick. To protect their members, caravans "sent on a company every morning, to make fires along the road, at short intervals," so their poorly dressed comrades could warm themselves periodically.

Removal did not annihilate the Cherokees, but it did indeed inflict deep gashes in the fabric of their society. The entire process claimed 4,000 (perhaps as many as 8,000) of the roughly 17,000 Cherokees who were initially rounded up. Those who arrived in Indian Territory found a land very different from the one they had known, drier and flatter. The United States government had promised to support the migrants during their first year in the West, but government subcontractors lined their own pockets by supplying insufficient and substandard goods. As deaths mounted and poverty, illness, and alcoholism increased, the hatred between proremoval and antiremoval parties within the Cherokee nation ignited into civil war, leaving Cherokees to begin a long process of rediscovering the principle of harmony that lay at the center of their world. In the meantime, their ancestral lands had been cleared for white settlers and their African American slaves. ●

official a policy that Americans had pursued since the founding of the nation, but official approval accelerated the process. In his State of the Union address that year, Jackson congratulated Congress on the passage of the Removal Act, praising the law as an act of "Philanthropy." He reminded Congress that for generations Euro-Americans had been "leav[ing] the land of their birth to seek new homes in distant regions." New lands meant opportunity and liberty, the chance to "range unconstrained in body or in mind, developing the power and faculties of man in their highest perfection." "Doubtless it will be painful to leave the graves of their fathers," he acknowledged of the eastern Indians, "but what do they more than our ancestors did or than our children are now doing?" In fact, leaving "the land of their birth" was a very different act for Native Americans than it was for the white western settlers—not an act of opportunity, but rather an eviction from their very identity as a people.

In 1830 the Choctaws were forced from their lands in Mississippi to a location in present-day Oklahoma. The Chickasaws and the Creeks followed in 1832.

Then, in 1836, six years after passage of the Removal Act and four years after they had exhausted their judicial options, a small splinter group of the Cherokees (claiming to speak for the whole nation) at last agreed to removal. The Treaty of New Echota provided that within two years the Cherokees would leave the mountains for Indian Territory, in return for safe passage, $5 million, and food, shelter, equipment, and medicine for a year after their arrival. The Senate ratified the treaty in the spring of 1836 and considered that the clock had begun to tick on Cherokee removal. The pro-treaty Cherokees began to leave almost immediately. The overwhelming majority of Cherokees, who considered the treaty fraudulent, remained in the East.

Three years later, after their unsuccessful appeals to the Supreme Court and after several years of continued resistance, the Cherokees were removed from their eastern lands. In a forced march that became known as the Trail of Tears, they were driven off their homelands to Indian Territory in what is now eastern Oklahoma. Most people had delayed leaving until the last moment and had made few preparations for the journey. Many died of disease, malnutrition, dehydration, and exhaustion along the way.

Indians did not accept removal willingly. In 1831, the Sauk and Fox people (descended from Native Americans who had earlier been pushed across the Great Lakes

The Trail of Tears This depiction by 20th century artist Robert Ottokar Lindneux shows Cherokees being forcibly marched from their homelands in eastern states to Indian Territory in what is now Oklahoma.

region) were forced to relocate once again. No sooner did they reach their new lands, however, than they began to hear rumors that whites were desecrating their former burying grounds. When Indians recrossed the Mississippi to rebury their dead and harvest produce from their old fields, white farmers and Illinois militia attacked them. The Sauk and Fox Indians turned for leadership to a revered old fighter, Black Hawk, who raised a band of 500 warriors. Attacked by state militiamen, they spent the summer fighting a series of skirmishes called Black Hawk's War. Finally, on August 2, 1832, low on food and exhausted, the remnants of Black Hawk's band were cornered and massacred by the army.

More successful were the Florida Seminoles, also a diverse community including militant Creek warriors, known as Red Sticks, and runaway slaves. When federal troops arrived to remove the Seminoles in 1832, the Indians resisted with skill and determination. Unfamiliar with the terrain and vulnerable to malaria, the American troops were picked off by both disease and snipers. The war dragged on for seven years. Not until 1842 could President John Tyler proclaim victory.

History, Destiny, and the Disappearing Indian

American territorial expansion implied more than just a positive association between American citizens and the land. It also implied a negative association between the land and its current occupants. In this view, the land and the striving American individual could fulfill their joint destinies only if the Indians and their cultures disappeared.

Drawing on a tradition that extended back at least to Jefferson, proponents of dispossession formulated an argument based on the character of the land itself. They argued that certain environments were *naturally* fitted to certain groups of people, and naturally unsuitable for others. Ensuring maximum progress was a matter of fitting the people to the place. Native American dispossession was inevitable, they insisted—not only because white Americans were perfectly matched to the land, but because Indians were *not*. White Americans had tried again and again to help Native Americans survive, Jackson's secretary of war Lewis Cass claimed, but to no avail. "The cause of this total failure cannot be attributed to the nature of the experiment, nor to the character, qualifications, or conduct, of those who have directed it," he maintained, but to "some insurmountable obstacle in the habits or temperament of the Indians," whom he considered inferior to the challenge of taking full advantage of the land. Jackson himself put the matter more bluntly in his 1833 address to Congress. Native Americans, he declared, had "neither the intelligence, the industry, the moral habits, nor the desire of improvement which are essential" to realizing the potential of the land.

This understanding of manifest destiny as entailing the inevitable disappearance of Native Americans made its way into American literature in the 1820s, just as white Americans were seriously contemplating the pros and cons of Indian removal as an official government policy. Its venue was the historical novel. The depiction of Native Americans in antebellum historical novels represented a departure from earlier Indian captivity narratives, which often described Indians as almost incapable of human feeling and bent on the violent destruction of Euro-American civilization. Although the historical novels of the 1820s did not romanticize all Native Americans, they did identify among the Indians individuals of high character—of integrity, intelligence, and great sensitivity—but who, significantly, were always doomed to extinction.

The most notable of these were James Fenimore Cooper's wildly popular Leatherstocking Tales—a series of novels that follow the life and eventual death of the backwoodsman Natty Bumppo, the son of a Native American father and a white mother. Bumppo was a man of inherent mobility, a true friend of both Indians and whites. But as Cooper made clear, Bumppo was tied to a particular moment in national development. Like the wilderness, his life gave way to the arrival of white settlement.

Bumppo was by no means unique. In *Hobomok: A Tale of Early Times,* published in 1824, Lydia Maria Child (1802–1880) recounted the story of Hobomok, a Native American torn between friendship to the Salem settlers and loyalty to his own people. In the story, Hobomok falls in love with and marries a Puritan woman, who consents to the marriage only after she believes that her fiancé has been killed at sea. Mary and Hobomok have a son, and over time Mary comes to respect Hobomok for his strength of character and courage, if not to love him. But Child makes it clear that Mary's future, and that of her child, is with her own people. When Mary's lover unexpectedly returns, Hobomok graciously withdraws and Mary and the boy return to white society. Carrying Hobomok's name, the mixed-heritage boy grows up to attend Cambridge and become the new American citizen—his name marking the passing of his father's way of life.

Although dispossession was a devastating experience for Native Americans, native cultures survived, both within Euro-American culture and independently. For example, although during the 1820s Euro-Americans made a concerted effort to Christianize the Cherokees (four different denominations established seven schools and sent almost 80 missionaries onto Cherokee lands), at the end of the decade missionaries were able to claim only about 1,300 converts out of a total Cherokee population estimated at almost 16,000. Most of these were wealthy Cherokees who had already accepted Euro-American ways. The remaining vast majority of the Cherokee nation pursued the traditional practices and told and retold the traditional stories of their forebears. Even when they incorporated aspects of Euro-American culture into their lives, most Cherokees appear to have done so as a means for preserving their own heritage. Initially, Cherokees rejected the Euro-American emphasis on literacy, as a tool of cultural obliteration. (One story told that the original book had been given to the Cherokees but stolen by the whites when the first Cherokees were distracted.) When in 1821 Sequoyah invented the Cherokee syllabary (a system of written symbols representing the sounds of the spoken Cherokee language), most Cherokees were indifferent. Only as they came to realize how few whites could read the symbols did ordinary Cherokees begin to take an interest in the syllabary. By the mid-1820s perhaps half of the Cherokee nation had become proficient in Sequoyah's system, using it to communicate privately among themselves and to preserve the sacred stories of their culture.

But most Cherokees, like most Native Americans, preserved their culture simply by withdrawing from the intruding gaze of government officials and missionaries. They dealt with whites when they had to—for trade, for annuity payments, for various jobs that enabled their families to survive—and they adapted to white ways as necessary, but the core of their lives lay elsewhere, in dwellings built apart from white missions and settlements and in practices and rituals from which whites were barred.

The Bank War

Jacksonians saw the Indians as the western barrier to their progress, but when they looked eastward, they saw a different set of obstacles: the special privileges and unfair advantages available to the rich and well connected. In his career, Jackson had associated this obstacle with Henry Clay, John Quincy Adams, John Calhoun, and the Republican caucus. By 1828 Jackson focused his anger on the Second Bank of the United States.

> **"It has all the fury of a chained panther, biting the bars of his cage. It is really a manifesto of anarchy, such as Marat or Robespierre might have issued to the mob of the Faubourg St. Antoine."**
>
> NICHOLAS BIDDLE, reacting to Jackson's veto message. He thought, incorrectly, that Jackson had overreached.

Jackson's Opposition to the National Bank

Jackson hated the bank for all the reasons common among southerners and westerners: it was powerful and privileged, and wealthy easterners and foreign investors controlled its private stock. Also, as much as they liked easy credit, most Americans were suspicious of banknotes of all kinds. They had been stung too often by counterfeiters and deadbeats.

But Jackson also had very personal reasons for opposing this particular bank. Soon after his first election, Jackson heard rumors that the Second Bank of the United States had used its power to buy votes for Adams in 1828. Declaring that the bank threatened "the purity of the right of suffrage," Jackson vowed to oppose it.

Nicholas Biddle, the bank's president, refused to take Jackson's criticisms seriously. Confident that the bank enjoyed the support of most Americans, Biddle decided to force the issue before the next presidential election. Although the bank's authorization ran until 1836, on January 6, 1832, Biddle requested Congress to take up renewal early. Jackson may have felt Biddle's behavior to be a personal challenge, because when the act reached him in July 1832, he vetoed it, with a fiery statement of his political principles. "The rich and powerful," he said, "too often bend the acts of government to their selfish purposes. . . . [W]hen the laws undertake . . . to make the rich richer, . . . the humble members of society . . . have a right to complain of the injustice of their Government."

The Democrats carried the bank veto proudly into the 1832 election. It was, they insisted, a contest of "the Democracy and the people, against a corrupt and abandoned aristocracy." The Republicans responded that Jackson's veto showed his tendency toward despotism. The Supreme Court had ruled the national bank constitutional, and Congress had voted to recharter it. Jackson had trammeled the authority of both of the other branches of government, taking upon himself the sole right to determine the future of the bank.

Dismembering the Bank

Jackson won reelection in 1832, although by a smaller majority than in 1828. By 1833 he was ready to move ahead with his plans to disassemble the Second Bank of the United States. He asked Secretary of the Treasury Louis McLane to select other banks into which the federal government could move its deposits. McLane balked, worried that the selection would be compromised by politics and that the state banks would lose all fiscal restraint. Impatient, Jackson replaced McLane with William J. Duane, and then replaced Duane with Attorney General Roger Taney. On October 1, 1833, the federal government began to distribute its deposits to 22 state banks. By the close of the year, the government deposits had been largely removed.

The deposits in question had been used to make loans to individuals and corporations around the country. To make the funds available, the Second Bank set furiously about calling in loans and foreclosing on debts. In effect, and no doubt with a certain grim relish, Biddle was repeating the process that triggered the Panic of 1819. In six months he took more than $15 million worth of credit out of the economy.

As recession gripped the nation, the Senate passed an unprecedented resolution censuring Jackson for assuming "authority and power not conferred by the constitution and laws." Jackson's response underscored the new "democratic" politics of the times: "The President," he maintained (and no other branch of government), "is the direct representative of the American people." The expansion of white male suffrage (and the spreading practice of electing members of the Electoral College directly) made Jackson the first president who could claim to be elected directly by the voters. Congress, on the other hand, would soon become the power base of transregional elites.

The first recession passed quickly as state banks that received the federal deposits began to churn out loans and wildcat banks sprang up to take advantage of the glut of paper money. Much of the borrowing went for land sales.

The Specie Act

Correctly, Jackson believed that the excess of paper money in circulation had caused the recession. As soon as conditions began to improve, he implemented a hard-money policy. Late in 1833 he had announced that the federal government would no longer accept drafts on the Second Bank in payment of taxes, a move that reduced the value of the bank's notes. In 1834 Jackson declared that the "deposit" banks receiving federal monies could not issue paper drafts for amounts under $5 (later raised to $20), an act that reduced the small-denomination paper in circulation. In July 1836 he had the Treasury Department issue the Specie Circular, which directed land offices to accept only specie in payment for western lands. This effectively shut out actual settlers, who could not get together enough gold or silver for their purchases. Meanwhile, the Deposit Act, passed in June 1836, expanded the number of "pet banks" to nearly 100 and provided for the distribution of a federal surplus of more than $5 million to the states. This money was on top of the more than $22 million already deposited in the state banks from the Second Bank of the United States. Underregulated and susceptible to local pressure, the state banks were incapable of absorbing this flood of funds. They issued loans and printed money that vastly exceeded their assets. When the bubble burst in 1837, the nation was thrown into the worst financial disaster of its young history.

The Growth of Sectional Tension

The growing fiscal strains in Jacksonian America were matched by brewing sectional conflict. Americans had not always viewed the differences in the political economies of the North and South as bad. Those very regional differences had powered northern industrialization during the War of 1812 and had laid the foundation for the National Republican vision of strengthened nationalism in the years after the war. But economic expansion eventually matured old differences into open conflict. The immediate catalyst was the tariff, but by 1832 the question of the tariff had ignited a far broader debate over the institution of slavery.

The Political Economy of Southern Discontent

Although they had apparently won the struggle, many white southerners had felt betrayed by northern criticisms of slavery during the Missouri controversy. A series of economic and political frustrations in the 1820s nurtured that sense of mistreatment, creating the context within which the planter class, which had so far dominated the nation's presidency, began to picture itself as the victim of the federal government.

White southerners read signs of shifting public attitudes toward slavery. Proslavery advocates in Illinois (where many African Americans were already held in indentures comparable to slavery) were unable to elect a proslavery congressman in 1820. In 1824 Ohio asked Congress to consider a plan for the gradual abolition of slavery throughout the United States. On July 4, 1827, New York completed its long process of gradual emancipation, an occasion celebrated by free African Americans as far south as Virginia. On top of this, news from England had it that abolitionist William Wilberforce was likely to succeed in his effort to get slavery outlawed in the British West Indies.

> "I consider then the power to annul the law of the United States, assumed by one State, INCOMPATIBLE WITH THE EXISTENCE OF THE UNION, CONTRADICTED EXPRESSLY BY THE LETTER OF THE CONSTITUTION, UNAUTHORIZED BY ITS SPIRIT, INCONSISTENT WITH EVERY PRINCIPLE ON WHICH IT WAS FOUNDED, AND DESTRUCTIVE OF THE GREAT OBJECT FOR WHICH IT WAS FORMED."
>
> ANDREW JACKSON,
> Proclamation, December 10, 1832

Most important, though, was the economy. By 1828 cotton prices were only about one-third of their 1815 levels. Many planters and farmers tried to compensate for falling profits by planting more acres, but worn-out fields kept production low. Large eastern planters rode out the hard times with difficulty, often having to sell off slaves, lands, and city houses to meet their obligations. Many smaller farmers, dependent on cotton as their cash crop to pay off debts, were forced to sell out. Although the Panic of 1819 hurt northern farms and businesses, too, most of the Northeast bounced back faster than the South, a circumstance that focused planter attention on the 1816 protective tariff as a sign of government favoritism. They complained that the tariff policy was unnaturally driving up the prices of European imports, forcing already strapped southerners to purchase expensive northern-made products and driving down southern export sales. "We have no objection to the North being enriched by our riches," one Charleston *Mercury* reporter wrote sarcastically in 1827, "but not from our poverty."

Among the slaveholding states, South Carolina was particularly insecure. In addition to other anxieties, white South Carolinians were faced with a growing African American majority (the result of white migration west), a demographic condition that heightened their fears of slave insurrection.

South Carolina's Protest

Passage of the Tariff of 1828, the "tariff of abominations," led to nullification talk in South Carolina and created a new leader, John C. Calhoun. Like other South Carolinians, Calhoun had been disenchanted by the experiences of the 1820s and was a far less enthusiastic nationalist than he had once been. Yet he retained enough faith in the Democratic Party to believe that Democrats would lower the tariff, once in office, and could be made to see the injury that such national laws were inflicting upon southern states. Hoping to encourage both results, in 1828 Calhoun wrote the *South Carolina Exposition and Protest,* a justification for the theory of nullification, under which states might declare particular federal laws null and void within their borders. Although Calhoun published the pamphlet anonymously (still aspiring to the presidency, he was reluctant to associate himself too openly with the extreme position), he let his authorship be widely known, hoping thereby to gain the support of radicals in his home state. In the *Exposition,* Calhoun argued that the federal government was the creation of the states. In agreeing to create a federal government, Calhoun argued, the states had ceded some of their powers, but only conditionally. They had always reserved the right to do whatever was necessary to ensure their survival as "distinct political communities." Should the policies of the federal government threaten the distinctive character of a state, that state had the right to assert its sovereignty in defiance of those policies. It was at such a juncture, Calhoun argued, that the states of the South had arrived in 1828. They had become the "minority" culture, their interests and institutions endangered by "the unrestrained will of a majority." The tariff would gradually drain away the money and the independence of the South, subjecting it to northern tyranny.

There was much in America's history to support Calhoun's view. The states had existed before the federal Constitution. Representation at the Constitutional Convention and ratification of the Constitution had been by state, and representation in the federal government continued to be on the basis of states. Moreover, among the defenders of the theory were no less personages than Thomas Jefferson and James Madison, in their resolutions opposing the Alien and Sedition Acts.

On the other hand, the Constitution's status as the supreme law of the land rested on the fact that it had been ratified by the *people,* acting through special conventions, *not* by the state governments, and subsequent suffrage reform had enlarged the popular participation of white men. Moreover, after the debacle of the Hartford Convention, states' rights arguments had the whiff of treason. And the *Exposition* went a good deal further than that convention had: Calhoun argued explicitly what the Federalists had dared only hint, that if all else failed, states retained the right to withdraw from the compact.

Among the Americans who viewed the federal government as properly the creation of "the people," not of the states, and who regarded threats to withdraw from the Union as unforgivable, was President Jackson.

The Nullification Crisis

Other southern states, less economically pressed than South Carolina and more optimistic that the differences in the political economies of the various regions could yet be reconciled, did not rush to endorse the *Exposition*. Perhaps nothing would have come of the matter, had it not been for two events—a seemingly innocuous Senate debate over western land sales that unexpectedly heightened the rhetoric over sectional difference, and a slave rebellion in Virginia that came closer than any other to succeeding.

Eager to attract population, westerners had long lobbied for a reduction in the price of federal lands. Southern representatives offered to support the measure if the western states would join in opposing the tariff. When, in December 1829, Senator Samuel A. Foot of Connecticut advocated limiting land sales in the West, South Carolina Senator Robert Y. Hayne accused him of conspiring to keep labor prices low in the East and insinuated that the government was keeping land prices artificially high to build a slush fund "for corruption—fatal to the sovereignty and independence of the states."

Rising to defend the patriotism of his region, Senator Daniel Webster of Massachusetts countered that it was South Carolina, not the Northeast, that was a hotbed of disloyalty, and he pointed for evidence to the South Carolina *Exposition*. The Revolution had been fought by *the American people,* Webster thundered, and *the American people* had created the federal government. Uncannily foreshadowing, Webster evoked the image of "a once glorious union" "rent with civil feuds, or drenched, it may be, in fraternal blood!" Such a fate must be prevented, Webster roared. "Every true American heart" must recommit itself to the founding spirit of the nation: "Liberty and Union, now and forever, one and inseparable."

Webster's address was widely reported and enthusiastically received in the North, but Calhoun and the South Carolinians persevered. The following April, at a banquet commemorating Jefferson's birthday, they made the mistake of putting that assumption to the test. With President Jackson present, southern congressmen rolled through a series of prepared toasts celebrating the principle of state sovereignty. Called on to propose the first voluntary toast, a mortified Jackson reputedly stared hard at John Calhoun and lifted his glass: "Our federal Union," he declared. "It must be preserved."

Although he supported the federal Union, Jackson did sympathize with southern complaints that tariff levels were unfair to some sections of the country, and he advocated tariff reform. The Tariff of 1832 lowered duties on many goods to 1816 levels, but it did not lower protection on textiles and iron. In this continued protection for the largest northern industries, South Carolinians saw a defiant reaffirmation of a special relationship between northern interests and the federal government.

By then, the South had been the scene of another slave insurrection. In the summer of 1831 an African American driver and preacher by the name of Nat Turner launched a rebellion in Virginia. The rebellion was put down and Turner and other conspirators were executed, but unlike earlier plots, this revolt *had actually taken place*. Inspired by a millennialist fervor, for two days Turner and his followers had effectively controlled parts of the southern Virginia countryside, recruiting new allies, executing whites, and freeing slaves. Although the number of active insurrectionists probably never exceeded 70 or so, before the uprising was over, 57 whites had died. This was higher than the number of white fatalities in any previous slave rebellion. Southern whites took their revenge, instituting a monthlong reign of vigilante terror, yet the insurrection had left its mark. Southern whites lived in a state of constant fear, convinced that northerners and southern slaves were in league against them. In November 1832 South Carolina Radicals called a statewide convention whose delegates voted 136 to 26 to nullify the tariffs of 1828 and 1832 in the state. The acts of the convention forbade the collection of the tariffs within South Carolina.

For Jackson, the act of nullification transformed the crisis from a question of regional interests to a question of national union. "The laws of the United States must be executed," he declared, "I have no discretionary power on the subject; my duty is emphatically pronounced in the Constitution." He soon asked Congress for a law specifically affirming his responsibility to compel the collection of the tax in South Carolina, by force of arms if necessary.

Congress rushed to find a compromise. In early 1833 it passed a tariff that gradually reduced duties over the next decade, but Congress also passed the law Jackson had requested, known as the Force Bill. On March 2, 1833, Jackson signed both the new tariff law and the Force Bill, a pointed reminder to South Carolina that nullification and secession would not be tolerated.

In 1832 South Carolina stood virtually alone even among southern states. The supporters of nullification had no choice but to withdraw their ordinance. At the same time, however, they voted to nullify the Force Bill within the boundaries of the state of South Carolina. Jackson let the gesture pass, and at least for the time being, the constitutional crisis was over.

Conclusion

The political economy of the Jacksonian consensus was forged from belief in the efficacy of the individual, a distrust of unfair privilege, and a commitment to geographic expansionism. Few of these elements were new to the American political economy, but their meanings had undergone important shifts since 1776. The republic was becoming a democracy. But the harmony that seemed to be expressed in the Jacksonian celebration of democracy was misleading. Consensus was always partial, and conflict was always present and growing. African Americans and Native Americans were excluded altogether; workers and women were included only contingently. If Jackson the southerner, the settler, and the son of common parents was able to draw support from across a wide variety of constituencies, he was not without his detractors. These included southerners who hated the tariff, workers who sought urban, not agricultural, utopias, reformers who opposed his policies, and merchants and entrepreneurs who wanted a more stable currency. Within 25 years of Jackson's election, workers were in the streets, hundreds of thousands of Americans were petitioning to end slavery, the political parties had dissolved into chaos, and the nation stood on the brink of civil war.

Further Readings

Daniel Walker Howe, *What Hath God Wrought: The Transformation of America, 1815–1848* (2007). A comprehensive history of the period.

Donald Jackson, ed., *Black Hawk: An Autobiography* (1955). This volume reprints an 1833 publication alleged to be the autobiography of the influential Sauk leader Black Hawk, along with a critical introduction examining the authenticity of the document (which was written down by a French interpreter and edited and published by an American journalist) and raising important questions about how students and historians should read and use such evidence.

Theda Perdue and Michael D. Green, *The Cherokee Nation and the Trail of Tears* (2007). A brief, readable history of a pivotal episode in American history.

Adam Rothman, *Slave Country: American Expansion and the Origins of the Deep South* (2005). Connects the expansion of slavery to the dispossession of Native Americans, in both of which Andrew Jackson played an important role.

John William Ward, *Andrew Jackson—Symbol for an Age* (1953). Half a century old, Ward's study remains highly provocative in suggesting the qualities of background and personality that underlay Jackson's popularity and his ability to embody the broad democratic impulses of his times.

Harry L. Watson, *Liberty and Power: The Politics of Jacksonian America* (2006). Although its primary focus is on politics and parties, *Liberty and Power* grounds the party politics of the Jacksonian era securely in broad social and economic currents of the age, including slavery, westward expansion, and Indian removal.

Who, What

>> Timeline >>

▼ **1816**

American Bible Society founded

▼ **1824**

John Quincy Adams elected president (the "corrupt bargain")

Rappites sell New Harmony to Robert Owen and return to Pennsylvania, establishing third community, Economy

Charles Grandison Finney begins preaching in upstate New York

▼ **1825**

Owen establishes New Harmony labor reform community

▼ **1827**

Antimason Party organized

▼ **1828**

Andrew Jackson elected president

Virtually universal white male suffrage

Philadelphia workers organize the Philadelphia Working Men's Party

Protective Tariff of 1828 passes

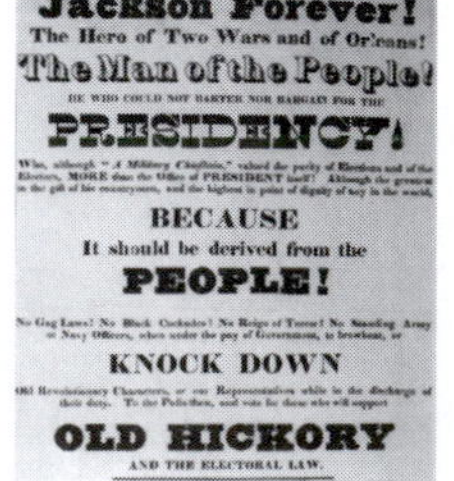

▼ **1830**

Shakers support 60 communities

Removal Act passes

Joseph Smith organizes the Church of Jesus Christ of Latter-day Saints

Review Questions

1. What about Andrew Jackson's life or career would have appealed to voters in 1828?
2. What was so democratic about the Jacksonian Democrats?
3. Why did Jackson, a southerner, oppose the *South Carolina Exposition and Protest*? Why did other southern states not support South Carolina in the nullification crisis?
4. How did Native Americans fight removal?
5. Why might white Americans have found the image of the disappearing Indian comforting? Did it share any cultural attractions with the colonization movement?

Websites

Andrew Jackson: Good, Evil & The Presidency. Companion website to the PBS documentary, with features and images. http://www.pbs.org/kcet/andrewjackson/

A New Nation Votes. A searchable collection of election returns from 1787 to 1825. http://elections.lib.tufts.edu/aas_portal/index.xq

Trail of Tears. The state of Georgia's website on the Trail of Tears includes a number of important documents. http://georgiainfo.galileo.usg.edu/trailtea.htm

For further review materials and resource information, please visit www.oup.com/us/ofthepeople

▼ **1831**

Antimason Party holds first open presidential nominating convention

Cherokee Nation v. Georgia

▼ **1831–1832**

Alexis de Tocqueville visits United States

▼ **1832**

Worcester v. Georgia

Black Hawk's War

Jackson vetoes act rechartering Second Bank of the United States

Jackson reelected

▼ **1834**

Female Moral Reform Society formed

▼ **1836**

Deposit Act expands number of Jackson's "pet banks" and provides for distribution of federal surplus

CHAPTER

12

Common Threads

>> How did African American activism change over time?

>> How did the market revolution shape the Benevolent Empire?

>> How did the conditions of paid labor change 1789–1835?

>> Why did many white northerners oppose abolition?

Reform and Conflict

1820–1840

AMERICAN PORTRAIT

>> Nat Turner

On October 2, 1800, just a week before the slave Gabriel was executed for conspiring to lead a revolt in Richmond, a slave child by the name of Nat was born in nearby Southampton County. Nat was the property of Samuel Turner and was raised to be one of Turner's field hands. But he was a bright child and learned to read and write early. Deeply religious, Nat Turner spent whatever time he could in prayer and fasting and soon matured into a charismatic preacher and prophesier, respected by blacks and whites alike.

According to Thomas Ruffin Gray, who later interviewed him, by the time Nat was in his twenties he understood that he "was ordained for some great purpose in the hands of the Almighty." One day while Nat was working in his master's field, he heard a huge noise in the sky "and the Spirit instantly appeared to me and said the Serpent was loosened, and Christ had laid down the yoke he had borne for the sins of men, and that I should take it on and fight against the Serpent, for the time was fast approaching when the first should be last and the last should be first." The yoke he was to take up was the freeing of the slaves. Three years later, he interpreted a solar eclipse as a black hand covering the power of white people, and he began to plan revolution.

Three months after the eclipse, on August 21, 1831, Nat Turner led one of the largest uprisings against slavery in United States history. Gathering a group of over 50 people, both slaves and free black people, for two days Turner and his followers controlled the Southampton countryside. When it was done, the rebels had killed 57 white men, women, and children.

Turner's success, though fleeting, enraged and terrified the white population of Virginia. The state eventually executed 55 African Americans suspected of taking part in the revolt. Several hundred more were beaten, mutilated, and murdered by white mobs. The legislature passed laws tightening controls on the movement and assembly of blacks and augmenting the power of slave patrols.

But Turner's rebellion catalyzed another, perhaps less predictable response in Virginia in 1831: a prolonged discussion of whether the state should figure out some way of ridding itself of slaves and slavery. The discussion was not altruistic. Whites made up just under 58 percent of Virginia's population. They lived in fear of another rebellion. Moreover, not all whites in Virginia supported slavery. The western part of the state had never been vitally dependent on it economically, and many western Virginians associated slavery with the disproportionate state legislative power of the eastern part of the state. And while the east was deeply proslavery in its plantation culture, its plantation economy had been in slow decline for many years, the result of long-exhausted soil. Maybe it was time to get rid of slavery.

Also, the discussion was not about human dignity. The proposals the Virginia House of Delegates entertained would have had slaves either sold out of state before they reached adulthood or freed in stages and removed "beyond the limits of the United States."

Still, most eastern Virginians remained committed to slavery. After some months of debate (and, probably, the private intervention of Vice President John C. Calhoun), the legislature abandoned the whole idea, concluding by a 67–60 vote that action should "await a more definite development of public opinion."

But if Turner's rebellion seemed to go nowhere in Virginia, it was having profound repercussions elsewhere in the nation. Northern abolitionists were following events in Virginia closely, watching to see whether there was any chance that a southern state would voluntarily act to eliminate slavery, even through colonization. As it became clear that Virginia would not even undertake colonization in a serious and large-scale way, abolitionists prepared for an unprecedented massive and militant propaganda assault on the South. ●

OUTLINE

Perfectionism and the Theology of Human Striving

There was nothing about the depth of Nat Turner's faith, or its centrality to his life and identity, that set him apart from many other Americans in early nineteenth-century America. The profound revivals of the turn of the century were continuing into the 1830s and set the terms in which many people understood themselves and their world. Some Americans looked at the changes of the preceding decades and saw a nation on the verge of losing its moral compass. Convinced that the day of final reckoning grew near, they preached doom and withdrew from society into covenanted communities to prepare themselves for the end of time. Others remained hopeful that the nation could yet be redeemed. These reformers believed that it was the responsibility of each individual to work actively to perfect American society. Where the reformers agreed with separatists, however, was in their conviction that social life should be modeled on the principles of Protestant Christianity.

Millennialism and Communitarians

Separatist communities were not new to the American spiritual landscape in these years, and they never accounted for more than a minority of the American people. Nevertheless, they enjoyed renewed success in the 1820s. As a group, these religious communitarians sought to create more perfect societies on earth, an effort they undertook by withdrawing from daily contact with their neighbors and instituting tightly controlled spiritual, social, and economic regimens.

> **Almost all the religion in the world has been produced by revivals. God has found it necessary to take advantage of the excitability there is in mankind, to produce powerful excitements among them, before he can lead them to obey. Men are so sluggish, there are so many things to lead their minds off from religions, and to oppose the influence of the gospel, that it is necessary to raise an excitement among them, till the tide rises so high as to sweep away the opposing obstacles. They must be so excited that they will break over these counteracting influences, before they will obey God.**
>
> CHARLES GRANDISON FINNEY,
> Lectures on Revivals of Religion, 1835

One of the earliest of these religious communities was the United Society of Believers in Christ's Second Appearing, a radical branch of Quakerism. This group was soon dubbed "Shakers" by its critics, for the "[d]ancing, singing, leaping, clapping . . . , groans and sighs" that characterized its services. Shakerism was rooted in the experiences of Ann Lee, a late-eighteenth-century English factory worker and lay preacher who believed that she was the second, female embodiment of the Messiah. Lee preached that believers should return to the simplicity and purity of the early Christian church, pooling their worldly resources, withdrawing from the vanities of the society, and observing celibacy. The Shakers migrated to North America in 1774 and established their first community near Watervliet, New York. "Mother" Ann died in 1784, but by the turn of the century the Shakers had established a dozen communities in New England. Soon afterward, they began to move west, establishing four settlements in Ohio and Kentucky. By the 1830s, membership approached 4,000.

Shaker beliefs required the establishment of a community on the basis of a "union of faith, of motives, and of interest" of all members. To ensure this perfect unity, Shakers organized their communities into "families" of 30 to 100 members, each of which was supervised by a panel of eight people (two women and two men to oversee spiritual matters, and two men and two women to oversee temporal concerns). The "families" within a community were guided by a ministry (also composed equally of men and women), and the individual communities submitted to the authority of a head ministry at New Lebanon, New York.

Their search for perfection led the Shakers to repudiate the values of the increasingly market-driven American economy. Although Shakers sold goods to outsiders, they rejected materialism and competitive individualism, allocating individual labor according to the needs of the community. This alternative political economy resulted in prosperity and a high level of invention. Shaker gardeners developed the first American seed industry, and Shaker farmers produced bumper crops of grain and bred large and healthy herds of dairy cattle.

Women appear to have been especially drawn to Shakerism, probably because of the Shaker belief in the spiritual equality of women and men. This was reflected in the authority structure of the communities, with "sisters" and "female elders" supervising the women's lives and "brothers" and "male elders" supervising the men's. The Shaker practice of celibacy afforded women freedom from the dangers of childbirth.

Shakers Outsiders labeled members of the United Society of Believers in Christ's Second Appearing "Shakers" after the active twirling and shaking movements that accompanied their services.

Like the Shakers, the followers of German farmer George Rapp rejected the private ownership of property and practiced celibacy. Believing that "the kingdom of Jesus Christ is approaching near," they considered it the responsibility of the truly devout to amass great material wealth to put at the disposal of Jesus Christ upon his return to earth.

Rapp and several hundred followers arrived in North America in 1803 and migrated to western Pennsylvania, where they established the town of Harmony. They moved in 1815 to the banks of the Wabash River in Indiana Territory. By 1824 their membership numbered 800, and their holdings had grown to more than 20,000 acres. There they grew fruit, grain, and cotton; grazed sheep; and erected a cotton and woolen mill and a distillery. Unfortunately, the climate that made the Wabash hospitable to agriculture also made it hospitable to malaria. Weary of yearly scourges, in 1824 the Rappites sold New Harmony to the English social reformer Robert Owen and moved back to western Pennsylvania.

In terms of numbers and longevity, the most important of the millennial communities of the early nineteenth century was the Church of Jesus Christ of Latter-day Saints, also known as the Mormons, founded by Joseph Smith Jr. in 1830. Smith preached that God had made known his intentions for the "latter days" of creation, now approaching, in golden tablets revealed to Smith by the angel Moroni. Essentially Christian in many ways, the Mormon Articles of Faith also included a belief "in the literal gathering of Israel and in the restoration of the Ten Tribes; that Zion (the New Jerusalem) will be built upon the American continent; that Christ will reign personally upon the earth; and, that the earth will be renewed and receive its paradisiacal glory."

Smith's preaching gradually attracted a body of rural followers, most of them people who had been displaced by the changes affecting the antebellum North. To these listeners, Smith preached that it was God's will that they go forth into the wilderness to found the city of Zion, where they would reign over the coming millennium.

The opposition of their neighbors, who considered Mormon beliefs blasphemous, soon forced the Mormons to leave New York. Smith first moved his followers to Ohio, where they organized a communal economy run by the church, and then to Missouri. In 1839 a large group of Mormons moved on to Illinois, where they founded the city of Nauvoo. By the early 1840s, Smith had begun to preach the doctrine of plural marriage. The Mormon community split and anti-Mormon outrage flared anew. Smith was arrested and thrown in jail in Carthage, Illinois, where, on June 27, 1844, he was murdered by a mob (allegedly with the help of a jail guard and the support of leading citizens). In 1847, under the guidance of Brigham Young, the Mormons uprooted once more, this time reaching the Great Salt Lake in the West. By 1850, hard work, irrigation, and careful cultivation had turned the desert into a garden paradise inhabited by more than 11,000 people.

Urban Revivals

Separatist millennialists represented a relatively minor stream in the floods of religious organizing that characterized the 1820s and 1830s. Far more numerous were the Americans who sought to perfect society by carrying the spirit of reform into their own communities. This massive evangelizing of America took many forms. Itinerant Methodists and Baptists continued to minister to newly settled churches in the backcountry. By the 1820s, however, the revivals had also assumed an urban character. Soon even the great metropolises like Boston, Philadelphia, and New York became hothouses of evangelism.

The career of Presbyterian minister Ezra Stiles Ely reflects this shift in mainstream American religious life. From 1811 to 1813, Ely was a chaplain for the Society for Supporting the Gospel, working with men and women who lived in public shelters. He led religious services, distributed Bibles, and prayed at the bedsides of the sick and dying, observing firsthand the growing poverty of American cities. After the War of 1812, he extended his work into the shanties and tenements of New York's poor neighborhoods. He increasingly understood his mission to be not merely providing solace but also converting souls. Ely and other city missionaries did not believe that they could save people who were not chosen by God, but they did believe that the elect could be found even among the poor.

The new urban-based missionary societies soon turned their attention to the boomtowns of the West. The New York Evangelical Missionary Society of Young Men raised money to send missionaries to new settlements of western Pennsylvania, upstate New York, and Georgia. Of these missionaries, none was more successful or controversial than Charles Grandison Finney, who became an influential advocate for a dynamic Protestantism based on personal responsibility.

Finney had originally trained in the law, but in 1821 he experienced a calling to the ministry. Although Finney's rejection of the Presbyterian belief in original sin worried

Salt Lake City The establishment of a Mormon settlement at Salt Lake City quickly became an important stop for westbound migrants, a place where they could rest and resupply their wagons before completing the journey.

his teachers, he soon developed into a charismatic preacher, and in March 1824 he was ordained as a minister and he moved to upstate New York to begin his work.

By the 1820s, construction of the Erie Canal was well advanced, drawing even the most remote farmers closer to the markets of the East Coast and enmeshing them in relations of cash and commerce. Inhabitants of towns and small cities were at the center of the rapidly developing market economy. Some of those people were troubled by the swirl of development around them. Others were more alert to the possibilities for success and were attracted to the way the new economy appeared to reward industry, hard work, and personal ambition.

To this latter audience, Finney preached a message of the power of human spiritual striving. In the place of the stern God of Calvinism, he offered a God of

Justice, who laid his case before a humankind "just as free as a jury" to accept salvation or not. This theology gave great latitude to human effort, but it also placed a new burden on the sinner. If "a man that was praying week after week for the Holy Spirit . . . could get no answer," Finney insisted, it must be that the man "was praying from false motives," not that an indifferent God had abandoned him.

Finney enjoyed immediate success in the Genesee Valley of New York. Especially drawn to his preaching were those most directly benefiting from the economic boom: the families of merchants and bankers, of grain dealers and mill owners, and young, ambitious employees in such businesses. Finneyite Presbyterianism set individual ambition in a new context as part of the process of salvation, a sign of the human potential for good. Eventually, Finney repudiated the older Calvinism, claiming for America a new and optimistic religion based on the power of the individual.

Finney's preaching alarmed the Presbyterian establishment in the East, which feared the emotional style and unorthodoxy of the revivals, and Finney's influence in the new western areas. Among the eastern leaders was Lyman Beecher, pastor of the prestigious Hanover Street Presbyterian Church in Boston. Like many New Englanders of his generation, Beecher was convinced that the future greatness of the United States lay in transferring New England culture, and especially New England orthodoxy, westward. Finney represented a dangerous threat to that orthodoxy. In 1832, Beecher moved his family to the new boomtown of the West, Cincinnati, where he wrote *A Plea for the West,* in which he predicted that the final battle of the Christ and the Antichrist would take place in the American West.

Charles Finney Charles Grandison Finney was one of the most popular revivalist preachers in 19th century America.

The Benevolent Empire

"Every truly converted man turns from selfishness to benevolence," Charles Finney said, "and benevolence surely leads him to do all he can to save the souls of his fellow man." The new evangelical emphasis on personal agency soon assumed the character of a broad impulse for social reform, expressed in religious terms and organized through a loose network of charities and associations, often referred to as the Benevolent Empire.

The Benevolent Empire was grounded in Americans' love of organizing, a tendency observed by Frenchman Alexis de Tocqueville when he visited the United States in 1831–1832. Americans, Tocqueville wrote, "combine to . . . found seminaries, build churches,

AMERICA AND THE WORLD

>> The American Board of Commissioners for Foreign Missions

The soldiers of the Benevolent Empire did not confine their attention to the citizens of the United States. In 1810, in the earliest awakenings of the reform spirit that would characterize antebellum American culture, the General Assembly of Massachusetts (the governing body of the Massachusetts Congregational Church) created the American Board of Commissioners for Foreign Missions, an umbrella organization intended to promote Christian evangelizing in "heathen" lands around the world. The action came at the urging of a group of young Williams College students, who four years earlier had pledged their lives to the project of "send[ing] the Gospel to the Pagans of Asia, and to the disciples of Mohammed."

Modeled on the London Missionary Society, the ABCFM sent out its first company of missionaries to Calcutta, India, in 1812, but other groups soon followed—to Hawaii, Turkey, and Palestine in 1819, to China in 1830, and to Africa in 1833. (By then, a number of other Christian denominations in the United States had founded their own foreign missionary branches.) But "foreign" referred to the non-Christianized condition of the missionized communities, rather than literally to their residence in another country. From very early on the ABCFM identified among its goals "to extend the blessing of civilization and Christianity, in all their variety, to the Indian tribes within the limits of the United States." The most famous of these interventions was among the eastern Cherokees, where ABCFM influence encouraged acculturation and, later, voluntary removal.

As with other benevolent enterprises, the efforts of the ABCFM were funded through the donations of a vast network of local societies that sprang up in communities across the United States (particularly New England). Local supporters sponsored speakers, solicited donations, and began to churn out a stream of pamphlets and letters to the editor on the importance of carrying Christianity to the "ignorant" people of other lands. By mid-century, the foreign missionary movement may well have been the largest of the undertakings of the Benevolent Empire.

The ABCFM, like other Christian missionary enterprises, consistently linked Christianity with United States culture, and its evangelizing efforts focused as much on teaching the mores of western European society as on the Christian gospel. Making the Christian Bible available and accessible to non–English speakers involved ABCFM agents in educational and translation projects, and sometimes in the creation of a written language for a nonliterate culture. ABCFM schools taught American standards of conduct and dress, as well as the English language. Mission hospitals introduced American medicine. The practice of sending married couples meant that missionary communities replicated American norms of domesticity, including food etiquette, dress, and gender relations. In 1817 the Board founded its own school, the Foreign Mission School in Cornwall, Connecticut, for educating converts to return to their own lands as missionaries of Christianity and United States civilization.

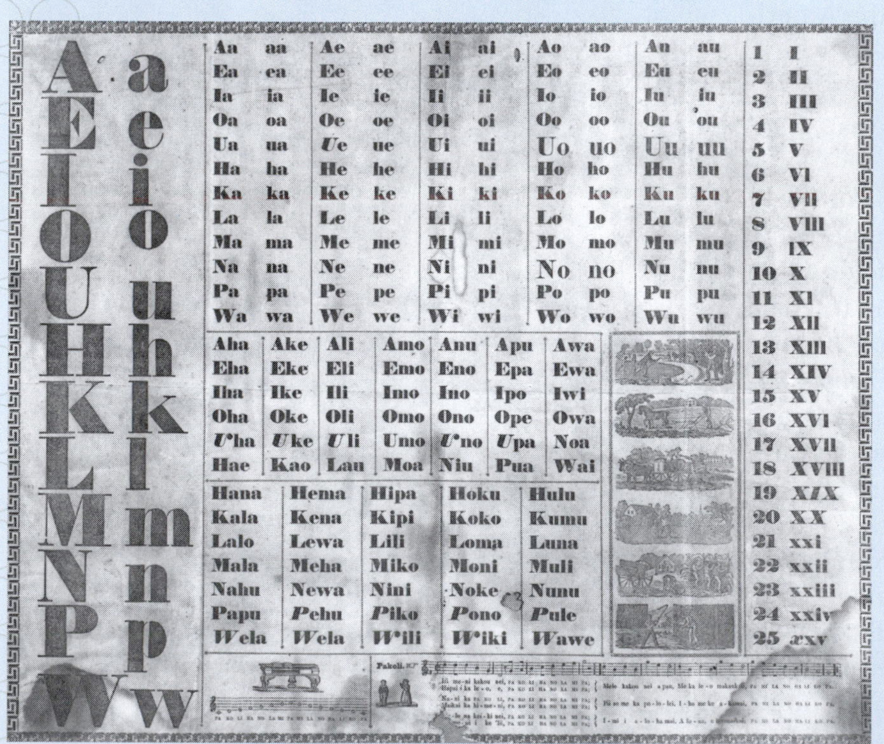

A a E e I i O o U u H h K k L l M m N n P p W w

Aa	aa	Ae	ae	Ai	ai	Ao	ao	Au	au
Ea	ea	Ee	ee	Ei	ei	Eo	eo	Eu	eu
Ia	ia	Ie	ie	Ii	ii	Io	io	Iu	iu
Oa	oa	Oe	oe	Oi	oi	Oo	oo	Ou	ou
Ua	ua	Ue	ue	Ui	ui	Uo	uo	Uu	uu
Ha	ha	He	he	Hi	hi	Ho	ho	Hu	hu
Ka	ka	Ke	ke	Ki	ki	Ko	ko	Ku	ku
La	la	Le	le	Li	li	Lo	lo	Lu	lu
Ma	ma	Me	me	Mi	mi	Mo	mo	Mu	mu
Na	na	Ne	ne	Ni	ni	No	no	Nu	nu
Pa	pa	Pe	pe	Pi	pi	Po	po	Pu	pu
Wa	wa	We	we	Wi	wi	Wo	wo	Wu	wu

Aha	Ake	Ali	Amo	Anu	Apu	Awa
Eha	Eke	Eli	Emo	Eno	Epa	Ewa
Iha	Ike	Ili	Imo	Ino	Ipo	Iwi
Oha	Oke	Oli	Omo	Ono	Ope	Owa
Uha	Uke	Uli	Umo	Uno	Upa	Noa
Hae	Kao	Lau	Moa	Niu	Pua	Wai

Hana	Hema	Hipa	Hoku	Hulu
Kala	Kena	Kipi	Koko	Kumu
Lalo	Lewa	Lili	Loma	Luna
Mala	Meha	Miko	Moni	Muli
Nahu	Newa	Nini	Noke	Nunu
Papu	Pehu	Piko	Pono	Pule
Wela	Wela	Wili	Wiki	Wawe

1	I
2	II
3	III
4	IV
5	V
6	VI
7	VII
8	VIII
9	IX
10	X
11	XI
12	XII
13	XIII
14	XIV
15	XV
16	XVI
17	XVII
18	XVIII
19	XIX
20	XX
21	xxi
22	xxii
23	xxiii
24	xxiv
25	xxv

Even as it intervened in the cultures of other societies, discouraging traditional customs and replacing them with the social and religious norms of the United States, the

ABCFM shaped Americans' views of other parts of the world and their relation to it. Missionaries constantly wrote letters home. In 1821 the ABCFM founded its own magazine, the *Missionary Herald*, where the reports of missionaries were printed for distribution at home, and throughout the nineteenth century the Board encouraged and subsidized the printing of missionaries' recollections of their sojourns abroad. The destinations of missionary activity came alive in these pages as exotic places with strange and dangerous customs, where ignorant people "jabber[ed] in their horrid jargon," worshiped "idol gods," and lived at "the lowest depths of sin and depravity."

American missionaries in Asia sometimes employed their observations there to criticize other imperial nations, especially Great Britain for its role in creating the Chinese opium trade (although rarely did these same writers note the participation of American vessels in that commerce). Occasionally missionaries reflected critically on their own society. Encountering systems of bondage in other cultures, for example, a few ABCFM agents lamented the survival of slavery in the United States.

But for the most part the impact of the American mission movement was to portray the non-European world as a lost paradise, awaiting the arrival of its American rescuers. As one missionary to Hawaii wrote, in the non-Christian world even "the fruits and vegetables . . . taste of *heathenism*."

distribute books, and send missionaries to the antipodes. . . . [I]f they want to proclaim a truth or propagate some feeling by the encouragement of a great example, they form an association."

Local societies linked up into national umbrella groups. Among the largest of these were the American Bible Society (which distributed Bibles in cities and new settlements), the Female Moral Reform Society (devoted to reclaiming women from prostitution), and the American Board of Commissioners for Foreign Missions (which promoted missions in the West). In addition, every major city fostered Bible groups, asylums to help the poor, houses of industry, orphanages, and humane societies, among other charitable organizations. By 1830, evangelical benevolence had also given rise to a Sunday school movement and a movement to prohibit the delivery of mail on the Christian Sabbath.

Benevolent societies represented a curious combination of emotional and rational approaches to reform. The method of the Benevolent Empire was moral suasion. Reformers believed that social change came about not from external rules but rather through the gradual internal awakening of individual moral purpose through personal contact, testimony, and (where needed) exhortation. Yet, increasingly, the structure of benevolence became that of the bureaucratic corporation.

Founded in 1816 in New York by a group of wealthy Christian men, the American Bible Society illustrates this paradox. The society consisted initially of a volunteer board of managers who hired out the printing and binding of Bibles. By 1818, however, the board hired a full-time salaried manager to oversee its business affairs, and before 1832, the society added four more professional staff members and built its own building in Manhattan. However, the society still depended on idealistic young ministers as its traveling agents and local volunteer organizations as its community contacts.

As they pursued their good deeds—whether distributing Bibles, praying with the sick, or handing out religious tracts—evangelicals came into intimate contact with the poor and began to minister to their material needs. They arranged fuel deliveries and medical care, helped homeless families find lodging, and organized soup kitchens to feed the poor.

Both men and women were engaged in the charitable associations of the early nineteenth century, but voluntary reform offered special opportunities for women.

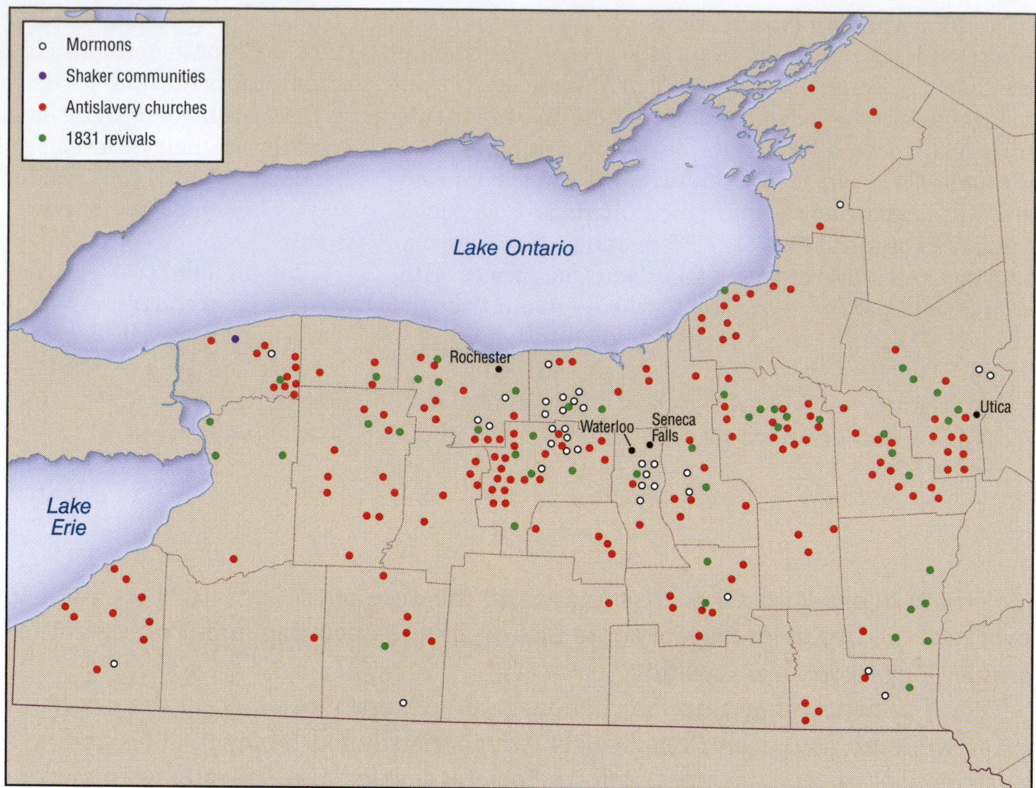

Map 12–1 Revival and Reform Social and economic transformation, religious revival, and social reform movements went hand in hand in the antebellum North. The so-called burned-over district of New York (the region directly served by the Erie Canal) nurtured numerous millennial sects (including Mormons and Shakers), Antimasonry, Finneyite revivals, and antislavery activism, as well as the Seneca Falls Woman's Rights Convention.

Women had already been active in organizing maternal societies to discuss and scrutinize their parenting habits, and Bible societies to discuss their own moral failings. By the second decade of the nineteenth century, women were founding orphan asylums, becoming involved in the Sunday school movement, starting homes for wayward girls, and establishing asylums for "respectable" homeless adults. By the 1830s, women were fast becoming the acknowledged volunteer backbone of the Benevolent Empire.

Reform and the Urban Classes

As well as addressing purely spiritual concerns, the robust religious organizing of the early nineteenth century also reflected worries about secular life. These concerns focused largely on the cities, where the market revolution of the turn of the century and ongoing immigration opened huge rifts between the haves and the have-nots.

Wage Dependency and Labor Protest

By 1830, in response to growing regional and local markets, master craftsmen had subdivided the production process into smaller discrete tasks. When possible, they distributed aspects of the production to outworkers, who worked part of the shoe, or hat, or shirt, returning it to the manufacturer (or a subcontractor) for piece wages. In house, employers relied more and more on the labor of apprentices or poorly trained helpers, whose labor came cheaper than that of journeymen. As work was subdivided, workers became more interchangeable, and their wages dropped.

> **It is a fact, that Popery is opposed in its very nature to Democratic Republicanism; and it is, therefore, as a political system, as well as religious, opposed to civil and religious liberty, and consequently to our form of government. . . .**
>
> SAMUEL F. B. MORSE, 1835

The Panic of 1819 had thrown thousands of people out of work, driving wages down and prices up. The reviving economy of the 1820s did not reverse those trends, which were deepened by depressions in 1829 and 1837. In an 1833 appeal, workers in Manayunk, Pennsylvania, protested 14½-hour days in "overheated" rooms "thick with the dust

Five Points, in New York City Once the site of a thriving community of craft shops and smaller retailers, Five Points had become one of New York City's poorest neighborhoods and, as this drawing suggests, a symbol of urban poverty, immorality, and crime.

AMERICAN LANDSCAPE

>> Freedom and Wage Labor

In the summer of 1832, only months before Andrew Jackson was elected for his second term as president, former Rhode Island carpenter Seth Luther traveled across New England denouncing the political economy of Jacksonian America. Journeying from city to city, through Maine, New Hampshire, and Massachusetts, Luther condemned the "tyranny," "avarice," and "exclusive privilege" that drove "AMERICAN MANUFACTURE" and laid before his sympathetic audiences a chilling catalogue of the havoc wrought in the lives of the "producing classes." He reminded his listeners of the 15-hour days, driven by the despotism of the clock and "the well seasoned strap" of the boss—all for a mere 75 cents a day. He described adults exhausted and brutalized, and children made "pale, sickly, haggard . . . from the worse than slavish confinement of the cotton mill." Luther lingered especially over the stories of the children. He spoke of one 11-year-old girl whose leg was shattered by an impatient supervisor wielding a stick of wood, and another child who had a board split over her head by "a heartless monster in the shape of an overseer of a cotton mill 'paradise.'" Early industrialization was turning out vast quantities of cottons and woolens. But here, in these changes in the lives of workers, was the true product of "the AMERICAN SYSTEM," he jeered. It created a social order in which "manufactures must be sustained by injustice, cruelty, ignorance, vice, and misery," a system in which "the poor must work or starve" while "the rich . . . take care of themselves." It was a bleak description of the political economy of an industrializing democracy.

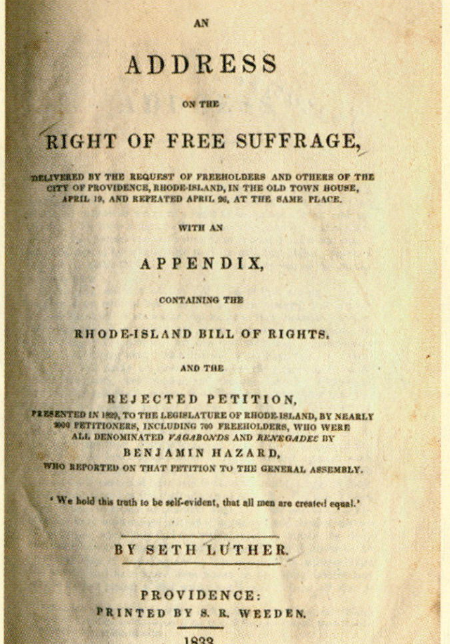
AN
ADDRESS
ON THE
RIGHT OF FREE SUFFRAGE,
DELIVERED BY THE REQUEST OF FREEHOLDERS AND OTHERS OF THE CITY OF PROVIDENCE, RHODE-ISLAND, IN THE OLD TOWN HOUSE, APRIL 19, AND REPEATED APRIL 26, AT THE SAME PLACE.
WITH AN
APPENDIX,
CONTAINING THE
RHODE-ISLAND BILL OF RIGHTS,
AND THE
REJECTED PETITION,
PRESENTED IN 1829, TO THE LEGISLATURE OF RHODE-ISLAND, BY NEARLY 3000 PETITIONERS, INCLUDING 700 FREEHOLDERS, WHO WERE ALL DENOMINATED *VAGABONDS* AND *RENEGADES* BY
BENJAMIN HAZARD,
WHO REPORTED ON THAT PETITION TO THE GENERAL ASSEMBLY.
'We hold this truth to be self-evident, that all men are created equal.'
BY SETH LUTHER.
PROVIDENCE:
PRINTED BY S. R. WEEDEN.
1833.

In some respects, Luther's harangue was simply the labor counterpart of a standard Jacksonian political stump speech. It rang with denunciations of wealth and special privilege, praised the worth and dignity of common people, demanded reform, and flamed with images of the impending Armageddon. However, Luther was speaking in 1832, not 1828, and he was addressing a nation in which the common man had presumably reigned triumphant for four years. Luther's closing exhortation that workers were free men in name only and must now rededicate their lives to "LIVE FREEMEN and DIE FREEMEN" hinted at deep failures in Jacksonian democracy.

In some respects, Luther's indictment seems unaccountable. Jackson's landslide 1828 election had represented the successful coming together of a remarkably diverse coalition, including southern planters and northern manufacturers, wage workers and entrepreneurs, and political pragmatists and at least some social and religious perfectionists. These groups represented very different interests, but in 1824 and 1828 they had found enough common ground to produce a clear majority behind the Jacksonian Democrats. By 1832, moreover, Jackson had done a good deal to reward the expectations of the voters. He had cleaned house of National Republican appointees. He had supported white claims to Indian lands in the West, opening hundreds of thousands of acres to new settlement. He was preparing to take on that behemoth of elite privilege, the Second Bank of the United States. In national presidential politics, the consensus held. Jackson was re-elected in 1832 and his vice president succeeded him to the presidency in 1836.

But Jackson's first four years in office had also revealed disturbing, unreconciled tensions within the new democratic political economy. These tensions arose in part from the very strengths of democracy and economic growth. The expansion of personal liberties created a society in which persisting inequities were all the more obvious, their persistence underscored by Americans' very commitment to perfectibility. Of all groups in the United States, white working men had experienced the most dramatic expansion of their political rights (and, in some respects, their economic independence) in the early nineteenth century. Yet, as Luther's criticisms made clear, by 1832 many American workers (female as well as male) felt threatened by the new industrial order. By the early 1830s, worker protests had become common in the cities and manufacturing centers of the nation, and working men's parties had begun to assume a more

clearly oppositional stance toward the major political parties. "The dignity of common labor" had become the rallying cry of protest.

Rather than turning out into the streets, Americans of more middling means responded to the volatility of industrial society by attempting to withdraw from it. Although this new American middle class continued to insist upon the dignity of labor, it grew less certain that the laboring classes could claim this dignity. If workers were poor, perhaps they lacked ambition, were negligent, drank too much, or were irreligious. Criticisms of workers soon focused especially on Irish immigrants, whose growing numbers brought to the surface the virulent anti-Catholicism of many native-born Americans, middle class and working class alike.

and small particles of cotton, which we are constantly inhaling to the destruction of our health, our appetite, and strength." "Our wages," they declared, "are barely sufficient to supply us with the necessaries of life." They cited the larger system of market relations that gripped them in its vice: "It requires the wages of all the family who are able to work," they explained.

The lives of outwork seamstresses, of whom there were tens of thousands in the eastern cities, were even more harrowing. Philadelphia philanthropist Mathew Carey estimated the wages of Philadelphia seamstresses at $1.25 a week. As it turned out, Carey was overly optimistic. A committee of seamstresses quickly informed him that they were lucky to earn $1.12 a week. After rent, they were left with a little more than a nickel a day for food, clothing, heat, and anything else they needed.

By 1830 the urban Northeast was bearing witness to the damages of wage dependency and the subdivision of labor. In the largest cities, neighborhoods had become stratified by class. The New York neighborhood of Five Points had once been a thriving community of master craftsmen and trade shops. By 1829, it was the home of prostitutes, beggars, public drunks, thieves, and confidence men. In working-class neighborhoods, high rents crowded whole families into single unventilated rooms. Many people went homeless or threw up makeshift shanties.

The organizing that had begun in the 1820s exploded in the 1830s, both among craft workers and in occupations long excluded from craft recognition. When the Philadelphia Mechanics' Union dissolved, leadership passed to the New England Association of Farmers, Mechanics, and Other Workingmen, founded in 1831 by, among others, Seth Luther. The New England Association invited "every citizen whose daily exertions . . . are his means of subsistence" to participate in its efforts. The association also used its newspaper, the *New England Artisan,* for worker self-education and organizing and published Luther's Address to the Workingmen.

In February 1831, protest erupted in an unexpected quarter. With wages in sharp decline, over 1,800 tailoresses (women who worked in specific aspects of the tailoring craft) struck the central shops and retail establishments of the New York garment industry. The tailoresses had been advised not to strike, that striking would only expose them to harsh public censure, that they should wait patiently for times to improve. "We have been told, my friends," declared Sarah Monroe, the secretary of the union, "that it is impossible for us to do anything at present to improve our miserable condition." But, Monroe asked, who would do so, if not the women themselves? She answered her own question: "Long have the poor tailoresses of this city borne their oppression in silence, until patience is no longer a virtue—and in my opinion to be silent longer would be a crime." The women drew up a constitution, elected officers, and stayed out on strike for five months.

Deteriorating labor conditions led to protest even in that industrial paradise, Lowell (see Chapter 10). After a decade of rapid expansion, the market stalled in 1834. In response to falling prices, the owners cut wages by 12.5 percent. Some 800 female operatives walked off their jobs. The protest failed (owners used the break in production to lower their inventories), but two years later, when the owners tried to increase the price of company housing, 2,000 operatives went out on strike, forcing the owners to rescind the increases. The 1836 victory was fleeting, however. Business was booming, and the owners had a vested interest in keeping the mills open. When business was slow or inventories high, workers would have far less power to assert their interests.

Workers attempted to strengthen their position by forming regional and national associations, now a possibility thanks to improved transportation and interdependence of markets. The most successful national association was the National Trades' Union (NTU), formed in 1834. The NTU survived for a number of years, but it was unable to effect the type of statewide coordinated actions its organizers envisioned. In the end, much of the energy of the national union went into lobbying for currency reform, worker access to education, free land for workers, and the ten-hour day.

A New Urban Middle Class

Seth Luther framed his criticisms of American industrial society in terms of a struggle between the "producing classes" and the "rich." However, this bipartite division did not adequately describe American industrial society. The concept of the "producing classes" was ambiguous, encompassing Americans of many different standards of living and levels of wealth. When Luther used the term, he meant primarily urban-based households dependent on wage labor. Luther sometimes fell into a more complex way of analyzing American society, distinguishing among the "poor," the "rich," and the "middling classes." Americans had long taken pride in their great "middling" ranks of solid farmers and artisans. But the composition of the category had changed by the 1830s, as had its relation to the group Luther now called the "working classes."

These new middling classes were difficult to define exactly. Like the new working classes, the middling classes were primarily urban based. Middle-class households tended to receive their income in the form of fees and salaries, rather than wages, and their paid workers were employed in jobs that required mental, rather than physical, labor. These included doctors, lawyers, ministers, middle managers, agents, supervisors, tellers, clerks, shopkeepers, editors, writers, and schoolteachers.

The relationship of these urban households of moderate means to the new industrial economy was complicated. On the one hand, they were not immune to catastrophic economic reversal, in the form of sudden unemployment, business failure, or bad speculation. Popular essayist Lydia Maria Child underscored this point in her 1829 *The American Frugal Housewife*. Addressing "persons of moderate fortune," Child nevertheless concluded the book with a sobering chapter titled "How to Endure Poverty."

At the same time, the new middle class was created by and benefited from the industrial transformation. The paid occupations on which middle-class families depended had expanded enormously as a result of the growth of commerce and industrialization. These jobs brought annual salaries ranging roughly from $1,000 to $1,500, compared to the $300 to $400 an average working man might earn. In addition, middle-class families tended to have access to a variety of other resources, through family, friends, and business connections.

The middle class celebrated the new political economy, commended the expansion of democracy, praised the growth of individual opportunity, and deplored lingering evidence of the special privilege of the wealthy. As a group they were profoundly religiously oriented. Embracing the doctrines of personal agency, they were churchgoers who both donated to and participated in the causes of the Benevolent Empire.

Individuals who aspired to urban middle-class status took far greater pains to distinguish themselves from the urban poor than from the rich. This was especially evident in their understanding of personal responsibility and material success. In sermons and tracts, children's books and novels, members of the new middle class described the industrial economy as a test of personal character. Success demonstrated superior individual industriousness and self-discipline; failure signified the opposite. These beliefs took their toll on the middle class itself, because middle-class families did fail, bringing on themselves social and psychological censure. Nevertheless, middle-class writers continued to hone the broad idiom of the "common man" into the more class-based language of the "self-made man" of business. From this point of view, the middle class saw itself as the repository of moderation in the changing political economy, the heir of Jefferson's idealized "husbandmen."

Meanwhile, middle-class families struggled to distinguish themselves from the working class. Middle-class parents recoiled from the "ungentility" of manual labor and urged their sons to become "a rich merchant, or a popular lawyer, or a broker." They expressed a new value for education, even for their daughters. While workers crowded into smaller and smaller living areas, the emerging middle class expressed itself in terms of increasingly elaborate residential space. The ideal home of the emerging middle class, the "cottage," offered a private sitting room for the family and a separate "public" parlor for receiving guests. The parlor also provided a stage where the family could present tangible evidence of their success through display of costly furnishings and decorations.

To emphasize their desired distance from the industrial world, the new urban middle class insisted on a "natural" division of temperament and capability between men and women. Although men were required to expose themselves to the degradations of labor, women were of a gentler disposition, intended by nature to remain at home to revive the hardened sensibilities of husbands and raise children protected from the ravages of industrialization.

This view of women as the primary influence on children represented a dramatic change from colonial opinions. Moreover, it was largely inaccurate, because many middle-class women pursued paid labor. They took in boarders, did fancy sewing, opened schools, and worked in family-owned businesses. All women of the new middle classes worked unpaid at the daily labor of cooking, cleaning, washing, ironing, preserving food, sewing, and caring for children. Nevertheless, domestic womanhood became the primary symbol of middle-class respectability and a bulwark against the many contradictions of the new industrial political economy.

Immigration and Nativism

Swept up in enormous changes, even those Americans who seemed to be benefiting from early industrial society were alert for sources of potential danger. Many labor leaders and utopians felt that industrialists were posing that danger. More common, however, was the tendency to focus anxieties on the poor, who were deemed incapable of achieving republican virtue. Immigrants became natural targets, and especially the Catholic Irish.

In spite of the difficulties encountered by wage workers, the robust economy of the United States drew increasing numbers of immigrants from Europe. Ninety percent of the immigrants came from England, Germany, or Ireland. The largest group by far was Irish. Plagued by recurrent poverty and harsh British rule, almost 60,000 Irish citizens migrated to the United States in the 1820s, 235,000 in the 1830s, and 845,000 during the potato famines of the 1840s. Through most of the period, Irish immigrants accounted for more than one-third of all immigrants.

Their customs and their poverty made Irish immigrants conspicuous. Unable to afford land, they remained crowded in the seaports where they arrived. Unfamiliar with urban life, they were the prey of con artists. Desperate, they often had to accept jobs and conditions that native-born workers scorned. Because they had no other place to go, one boss observed, the Irish could "be relied on at the mill all year round."

Not all of the Irish went into mills. Many built roadways, dredged river bottoms, and built canals. Irish women cooked and did laundry for the camps or hired out as domestic workers in middle-class households.

Most of all, the Irish were distinguished by their Catholic religion. By 1830, immigration had virtually doubled the number of Catholics in the country. Not all Catholics were Irish, but many were, leaving the Irish particularly visible as targets of long-standing American anti-Catholic prejudices. Anti-Irish sentiment often took the form of stereotypes that represented Catholics as given to superstition and unthinking obedience. Funded by members of the new middle class and supported by Protestant ministers, anti-Catholic newspapers charged the Catholic hierarchy with "tyrannical and unchristian" acts "repugnant to our republican institutions."

By the early 1830s, anti-Catholicism spilled over into street violence. Organizations such as the New York Protestant Association, founded in 1831, sponsored "public discussions" on the immorality of monks, the greed of priests, and the pope's alleged designs on the American West. The debates soon deteriorated into small riots, which Protestant newspaper editors described as papist attacks on "the liberty of free discussion." Anti-Catholicism took an especially dangerous turn in Massachusetts. In 1834, the associated Congregational Clergy of Massachusetts issued a frantic challenge to all Protestants to rescue the republic from "the degrading influence of Popery." Sermons and editorials whipped up a frenzy of anti-Catholic fear. The hysteria was aimed especially at an Ursuline convent in Charlestown, Massachusetts, in which, purportedly, nuns were brainwashing their innocent Protestant students. On the night of August 11, 1834, a mob torched the convent, cheering as it burned to the ground. Anti-Catholicism was beginning to serve as a bond among Americans who otherwise had less and less in common with one another.

Internal Migration

The constant stream of internal migrants also heightened the sense of turmoil in antebellum American society. The swirl of internal migration was evidence of growth and opportunity, but it also produced a steady flow of individuals who seemed to have no settled stake in American society.

Many of these travelers were westward settlers, but many were rural folks losing out in the Industrial Revolution and migrating to the cities in search of employment. There was both a push and a pull to this internal movement. Children were pushed out from farming families whose land could no longer support them. They were pulled to the cities by the same conditions that spelled disaster for the artisan tradition: the breakdown of the apprentice system and the subdivision of skills.

In the cities, these young people often lived in rented rooms, apart from adult guidance. Young men joined neighborhood fire companies that served as gathering places for fun and sport. Young women navigated the city unescorted. Young men and women used their earnings to buy the things unavailable in the countryside: new shoes, clothing of the latest cut, hats, and canes. Perhaps most unsettling of all, these young people moved almost too fast to be counted.

Migrants did not usually move very far in any single trek, traveling the fairly short distances to the nearest large towns and cities. Nonetheless, they swelled the populations of the midsized cities in which most American manufacturing took place. About 50 miles up the Schuylkill River from Philadelphia, Reading, Pennsylvania, was a hub for regional manufacturing, transportation, and trading. In the 1840s, Reading's population doubled to 15,000 people. Nearly half of the unskilled laborers in Reading had come from within 25 miles, mainly from areas with poor land and big families.

The constant, restless migration of Americans westward provoked alarm among the eastern, urban middle class. Moralistic observers worried that this migration was sapping ambitious, upright citizens away from the East Coast, exposing them to the dangers of the wilderness, and leaving the dregs of society behind. Observers like Lyman Beecher (author of *A Plea for the West*) worried about the influence of the West on future American citizens. The West lacked all those institutions that easterners associated with civilization and civic responsibility. There were few schools and churches and too many unattached young men, saloons, and brothels. Moreover, in some respects westward migration canonized the materialism and greed that easterners were beginning to worry about. The desire for money drove some families on and on in an almost endless migration. One family, the Shelbys, had made four moves by 1850, when they ended up in Oregon. The father had been born in Kentucky, the mother in Tennessee, three children in Illinois, three in Iowa, and the youngest in Oregon.

Into this land of apparently unsteady habits were being born more and more of the nation's young. Once the frontier had passed the stage of initial exploration and families had begun to pour in, fertility rates in the newly settled areas became far higher than they were in the older, coastal regions. Easterners were alarmed by the specter of a generation of children growing up in the wilderness, without the proper social constraints. The values of self-reliance, industry, and civic virtues, values that only a decade before had seemed to capture the essence of American nationalism, appeared to be in danger of disappearing. By the 1820s, these observers had begun to focus their fears on the growing waves of European immigrants.

Self-Reform and Social Regulation

In his address to working men in 1832, Seth Luther explained that he would uncover "principles and practices which will, if not immediately eradicated and forsaken, destroy all the rights, benefits, and privileges intended for our enjoyment, as a free people." Earlier reformers had adopted a far more optimistic tone. Faced with deep divisions and seemingly insurmountable obstacles to perfecting industrial society, American reformers began to refocus their efforts away from broad programs of social perfection, to endeavors that centered on self-control and external restraint.

> We must neither feel nor act as if all progress was ended, and man had attained all the perfection of which he is capable. . . . Everywhere one part of our fellow beings are wasting away in luxury, indolence, listlessness, and dissipation; and another part pining in wants and neglect, devoured by discontent and envy; and when we see this can call it neither good nor necessary. We ask that it may be cured, and we turn to the future with full faith that it will be.
>
> ORESTES BROWNSON, 1835

A Culture of Self-Improvement

Answering criticisms from fellow senators that only the rich and well connected enjoyed the benefits of the new American industrial order, in 1832 Henry Clay rose to the defense of the entrepreneurial class. "In Kentucky," he asserted, "almost every manufactory known to me is in the hands of enterprising and self-made men, who have acquired whatever wealth they possess by patient and diligent labor." Clay's emphasis on personal enterprise captured a perspective that was increasingly common among ambitious Americans by the 1830s. Success or failure was less a matter of external injustice and constraint than of individual striving. Those who truly worked hard—who were industrious and clever and frugal—would succeed.

The culture of self-improvement enjoyed a particular popularity among members of the new middle class. The emphasis on self-creation helped to resolve middle-class ambivalence about industrial society: middle-class families had escaped the worst ravages of wage labor not because they were lucky or had some special advantage, but because they worked harder.

The culture of self-improvement was not limited to lessons for the mind and spirit, however. It embraced the body as well. From the 1820s to the 1840s, health reform became a national obsession, as Americans experimented with new diets, clothing, exercise programs, abstinence in various forms, and hydropathy, the cleansing of the body through frequent bathing and drinking of water. Particularly influential among the health reformers was Sylvester Graham, who came to prominence in 1832 as Americans braced themselves for a return of cholera. In a series of lectures, Graham argued that Americans were susceptible to illness because they ate too much meat and spicy food and drank too much alcohol, coffee, and tea. Graham recommended a diet of fruits, vegetables, and coarsely ground wheat (the origin of the graham cracker), combined with regular bathing and loose clothing. By 1834, Graham had extended his regimen of self-discipline to warn that sexual excess (masturbation, but also too-frequent sexual relations between spouses) "cannot fail to produce the most terrible effects."

Men and women of the new middle class crowded lectures and devoured written materials that espoused the philosophy of self-culture. By 1831 the lyceum movement claimed several thousand local organizations and a national umbrella association, and sponsored such speakers as the writer Ralph Waldo Emerson, Daniel Webster, and later Abraham Lincoln himself. Meanwhile, middle-class readers supported a publishing bonanza in novels, periodicals, and tracts devoted to self-improvement.

These publications promoted a variety of images of the self-made American. In his *Leatherstocking Tales,* James Fenimore Cooper celebrated the pioneer. Novels like Catharine Sedgwick's *Rich Man, Poor Man* romanticized urban poverty and

Lyceum Movement Americans' enormous interest in self-improvement in the antebellum years was reflected in their enthusiasm for public lectures, known as the lyceum movement. This cartoon gently spoofed a lecture by James Pollard Espy, a meteorologist. As the drawing suggests, women were prominent in lyceum audiences.

suggested that "true wealth" (virtue) lay within the reach of even the most humble family, if only they worked hard.

Although in most of its manifestations the myth of the self-made American was decidedly male, it also had important implications for women. On the one hand, it highlighted the importance of childrearing. Periodicals like the *Ladies Magazine* and *Godey's Lady's Book* (both edited by popular author Sarah Josepha Hale) and advice books like Lydia Maria Child's *The Mother at Home* and William Alcott's *The Young Mother* instructed women on the development of proper mental and moral habits in the young. On the other hand, a generation of female novelists appropriated the themes of self-culture to emphasize female self-reliance. In her 1827 novel *A New-England Tale,* Sedgwick told the story of a young orphan, left penniless by an improvident wealthy father and a pampered mother. Jane, the protagonist of the tale, learns that hard work builds both economic independence and strength of character and is appropriately rewarded with a prosperous husband, children, and a safe middle-class home.

Some writers mounted a determined assault on the new American political economy. American Transcendentalists like Ralph Waldo Emerson, Margaret Fuller, and William Ellery Channing believed in the power of the independent mind not only to understand the material environment but also to achieve a spiritual wholeness with the world. They saw that, in contemporary America, self-improvement was often cultivated only for immediate material gain. In his essay "Self-Reliance" (1841), Emerson tried to distinguish true independence of mind from slavish rushing after preferment and celebrity. Although Emerson was a professional man, not a laborer, in many respects his attack on the political economy of antebellum America echoed the themes of Seth Luther.

Temperance

Of the many movements for regulating the body, the largest by far—and the longest lived—was the temperance movement. By the 1840s hundreds of thousands of Americans had taken the pledge to swear off demon rum.

Prior to the nineteenth century, liquor played a central role in the work and social lives of Americans. The Puritans (even ministers) had insisted on having their good supply of wine, beer, and hard cider. In craft shops, workers took rum breaks from their labor. Well into the 1840s, advice-manual writers felt they needed to convince mothers that it was safe to forego the occasional dollop of hard spirits to the children.

Some religious groups, especially the Quakers and the Methodists, had opposed the drinking of hard liquor in the eighteenth century, but it was only in 1808, in Saratoga, New York, that the first temperance society was formed. Within the next five years, at least four more temperance societies were established in New England.

In the 1820s, the temperance movement was taken over by evangelicals who understood demon rum as the enemy not just of piety, but of that self-control so central to the broad perfecting of society. Evangelists began to depict drinking as one of the signs of social disorder in democratic America. Propounding this new view, in a series of six sermons preached in 1825, Lyman Beecher effectively changed the debate over alcohol. He did not call for absolute abstinence from hard liquor, and he inveighed on his followers to form voluntary associations to drive

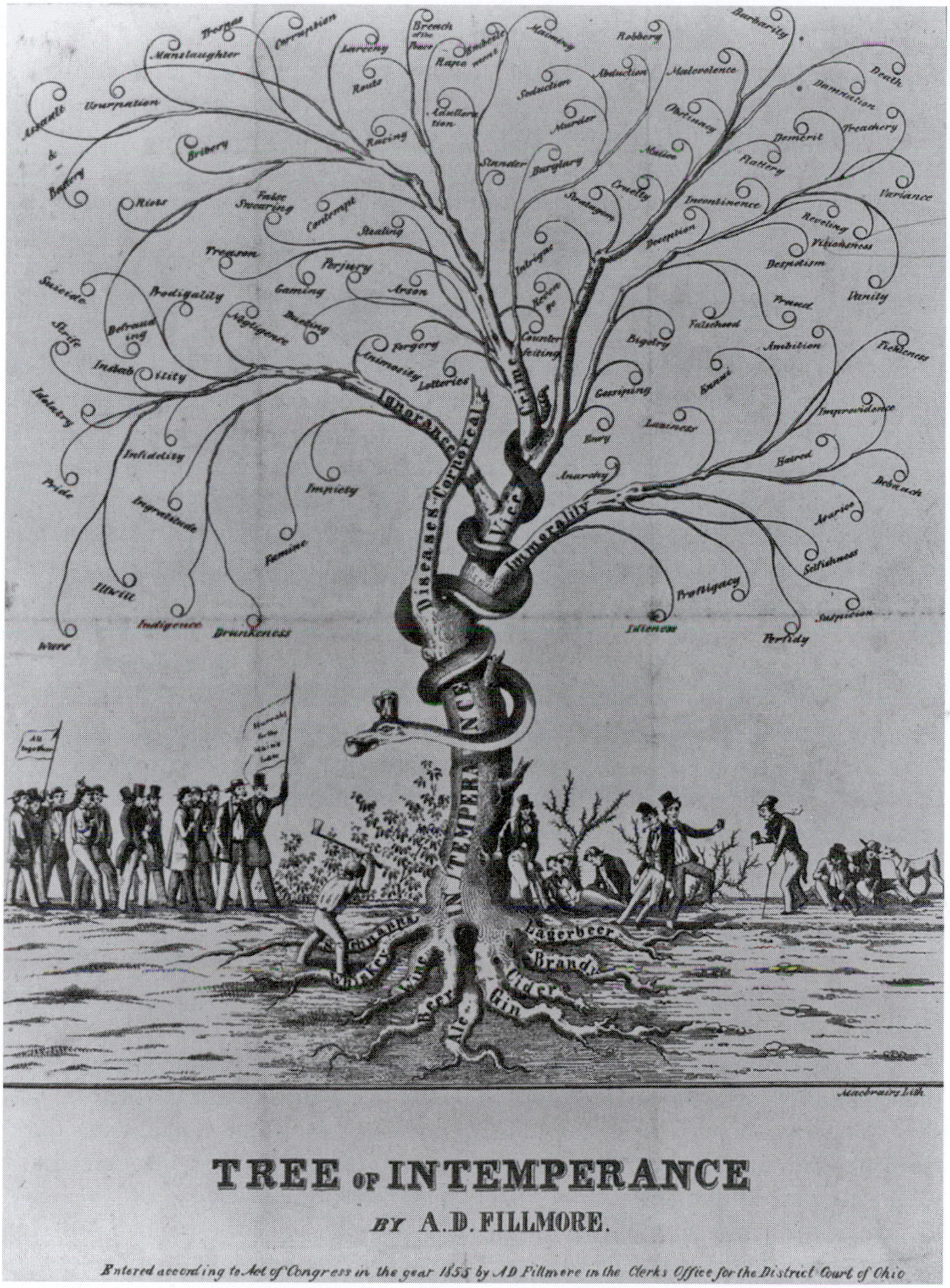

Temperance Movement This antebellum temperance cartoon equated the consumption of alcohol with any number of physical and moral disorders. Even some of those who sympathized with the movement thought it was too moralistic.

the demon rum from American society. The following February saw the formation of the American Society for the Promotion of Temperance (ASPT). Using the structure of the Benevolent Empire, the ASPT quickly set about organizing local chapters across the country. By 1834 there were at least 5,000 state and local temperance societies.

The Common School Movement

By the 1830s, workers, members of the new middle class, and elite philanthropists all identified education as a critical arena for reform. In this as in other reform movements, however, the motives of different groups varied widely.

Since the founding of the nation, educational opportunities for the sons and daughters of prosperous parents had steadily increased. Children from wealthy urban families had private tutors, followed (for boys) by formal training in private seminaries and academies. By the 1820s, young women from prosperous northern families could choose from a growing number of formal seminaries. Meanwhile, subscription schools offered basic education to rural children.

These schools were out of reach for working-class children. Labor reformers linked this lack of schooling directly to the larger process of industrial oppression. In their 1831 constitution, the Working Men's Association of New York placed the demand for "a system of equal, republican education" above every other goal, convinced, as they explained, that education "secures and perpetuates every political right we possess." Seth Luther elaborated on the theme, blasting industrialization as "a cruel system of exaction on the bodies and the minds of the producing classes," preventing them "from a participation in the fountains of knowledge." Benevolent reformers had founded charity schools in many eastern cities, but workers saw these as inferior. Only free public education, workers argued, could defy "the siege of aristocracy."

Many middle-class parents were also unable to afford the costs of private academies. In 1830, worried fathers in Utica, New York, called for a public school system that would permit children to "keep pace with the age in its improvements" and "calculate their own profits in the world."

Middle-class parents were anxious about daughters as well as sons. They worried that traditional housewifery skills would be of little use to daughters who faced increasingly complex market relations and new domestic technologies. Most of all, they worried that their daughters might not marry or might marry into families that would face financial ruin. These conditions suggested that daughters, as well as sons, should be educated.

Reformers often also supported expanded public education out of anxieties that the expanded suffrage would introduce volatility into the American electoral process. "The great bulwark of republican government is the cultivation of education," Governor Clinton urged the New York legislature in 1827. If white workingmen and their sons were to vote, it was important that they first be educated.

This convergence of interests led to a growing demand for expanded common schools. Nevertheless, broad segments of the American public resisted the idea. In Cincinnati, wealthy property owners opposed paying taxes to send poor children to school. Other skeptics considered the whole idea an invasion of their rights as free citizens. States were often reduced to passing simple enabling legislation, like Pennsylvania's 1834 act that made public schools a local option.

In 1837 the Massachusetts legislature at last ventured further, creating a state Board of Education and appointing longtime educational reformer Horace Mann as its first secretary. Mann framed the common school debate in language that reflected the anxieties of more-prosperous Americans. On the one hand, he reassured middle-class parents that relying on an extrafamilial institution was both right and natural, given the vast changes in society. On the other hand, he assured them that nothing else need change about the industrial society on which they depended. Poverty, he later wrote, was not decreed by God or required by American society. Only the lack of education barred the poor from prosperity. "When we have spread competence through all the abodes of poverty," Mann reassured his fellow citizens, then America would realize its long-deferred potential as the treasury of human virtue. Mann provided a comforting vision of a world in which benevolence and education would "disarm the poor of their hostility toward the rich."

Whites were less concerned about the potential hostility of the small free African American community. Until the 1850s, free African American children were excluded from public common schools, and public school tax monies were not used to establish schools for them. Education for free black children came almost entirely from the work of the free African American community. In the North, the efforts bore fruit, but in the South, opposition to the education of slaves hardened. In fact, many enslaved and free African American southerners did learn to read and write, but usually surreptitiously.

Penal Reform

In the first years of the republic, when memories of British injustice were still fresh, Americans tended to think of crime as a problem of bad laws, not flawed individual character. Fair laws would nurture good republican character, and good republican citizens would respect laws they had a hand in passing.

Yet by the 1820s eastern cities were incarcerating thousands of citizens—some for debt (which a growing number of people considered inappropriate in a republican government) but many for robbery, larceny, fraud, vagrancy, and disorderly conduct. To many Americans—especially members of the middle class—it seemed that good laws were not sufficient to create a good citizenry. Like salvation, law-abiding behavior was a function of individual effort. Where individuals failed to obey the law, the community must devise some mechanism for its own protection.

The solution that enjoyed the greatest popularity from the 1820s on was the establishment of state prison systems, where deviant individuals could be kept apart from the striving community but where inmates might also be rehabilitated. State and city prisons soon began to replace older charity institutions. The two primary models, devised by New York and Pennsylvania, were variants on a single principle: The first step in making prisons places of genuine reform was to prevent inmates from influencing one another.

The New York version became most widely associated with the penitentiary at Ossining, New York, known as Sing-Sing. At Sing-Sing, prisoners worked side by side all day but were prevented from talking or even looking at one another. They slept in separate cells. The Pennsylvania model, put into practice in the late 1820s, called for absolute isolation of the prisoners.

Visitors to the United States often toured these prisons and frequently applauded them, but they also commented on the exaggerated hopes that Americans seemed to invest in them. Famous French visitor Alexis de Tocqueville observed of American reformers: "Philanthropy has become for them a kind of profession, and they have caught the *monomanie* of the penitentiary system, which to them seems to remedy for all the evils of society."

Electoral Politics and Moral Reform

As reformers grew frustrated with the seeming resistance of social problems to moral suasion, they turned increasingly to electoral politics for solutions. The effect was to fragment and weaken party organization rather than to consolidate it. The political landscape became littered with specialized and often largely local parties, demonstrating the inability of the major parties to address fundamental areas of social conflict.

Nowhere did possession of the vote assume a more central role than among newly enfranchised white male workers. During the struggles of the 1820s and 1830s, laboring people had concluded that many of their problems would be remedied only through electoral action. As long as the economic power of employers was backed up by laws that oppressed workers (debt laws that imprisoned them, bankruptcy laws that took their property, conspiracy laws that made union organizing illegal), strikes and petitions would never be enough.

By the late 1820s workers had begun to mobilize politically. In 1827 a group of workers in Philadelphia formed the Mechanics' Union of Trade Associations. Within a year they had dissolved that group into the Philadelphia Working Men's Party, a new political party dedicated to promoting "the interests and enlightenment of the working classes." Over the next five years, under various names, the movement spread through most of the nation, becoming strongest in the cities from Philadelphia northward.

That such parties came into existence at all suggests that workers were at a crossroads. On the one hand, the formation of the Working Men's Party implied that workers still remained optimistic that change was possible, and it signaled that workingmen thought of themselves as citizens with the right and power to affect the entire social and cultural makeup of the republic. This was evident in the variety of issues they advocated, including public education, broadened incorporation laws, an end to imprisonment for debt, and banking reform. On the other hand, the organization of a separate political party indicated that workers remained deeply skeptical that the existing parties would be responsive to their concerns. Workers were moving toward a distinct identity within the new political economy.

In the winter of 1835/1836 anger at the legal system came to a head. With inflation and unemployment running high, New York City journeymen tailors went out on strike. The leaders of the union were arrested, tried, convicted on conspiracy charges, and fined. The labor press denounced the courts as "the tool of the aristocracy, against the people!" Nearly 30,000 people (the largest crowd in American history to that date) turned out to protest the convictions. The protesters resolved to meet the following fall in Utica, New York, to organize a "separate and distinct" political party to represent workers' interests. The 93 "workers, farmers, and mechanics" who met in Utica six months later voted to form the Equal Rights Party.

Labor movements in other states also began to focus their efforts on legislative reform. The ten-hour day, a long-standing demand, reemerged in the late 1840s as a central point of labor organizing. Throughout New England, workers supported candidates friendly to the ten-hour day, petitioned legislatures for state laws setting work hours, and testified before legislative committees. Much to the shock of their middle-class detractors, female workers sometimes testified as well, using their life stories to create sympathy for the cause. It was male workers, however, who had the power to vote representatives out of office.

Other reform movements also began to focus their energies on electoral strategies, although their motives for doing so varied. The Female Moral Reform Society, which had long worked to redeem prostitutes from their sins, shifted strategies and began advocating and lobbying for the passage of rent laws and property protections for women. This growing emphasis on legal reform grew out of an enhanced sense of connection between the reformer and the recipient of her aid.

Throughout the 1840s, temperance workers focused their efforts increasingly toward state legislators and the passing of laws. Among some temperance advocates (especially females) the shift was motivated by concern for legal protections for the wives and families of alcoholic men. But an increasing emphasis on legal strategies also expressed a growing belief on the part of middle-class, native-born reformers that alcoholism was a problem of the unruly immigrant working classes. As they identified drinkers as fundamentally different from themselves, temperance workers grew less interested in working directly with drinkers and more willing to take recourse to legal controls.

Abolition and Women's Rights

Many of the reform movements of the antebellum era generated widespread controversy and passionate disagreement. But no others touched the central nerve of antebellum society like the organized abolition movement after 1830 and the women's rights movement. Slavery and patriarchy, it seemed, were the structures upon which many antebellum Americans assumed the identity of their nation and society.

Antislavery Becomes Abolition

Although some whites thought that African Americans had already become too assertive in their own cause, insisting that Nat Turner must have read and been influenced by David Walker's 1829 *Appeal to the Colored Citizens of the World,* black organizing continued to grow more assertive over the 1830s. Most black abolitionists did not counsel armed insurrection, but a growing number wrote and lectured on slavery and the condition of African Americans in the republic. The year 1829 had also seen the publication of Robert Alexander Young's *The Ethiopian Manifesto: Issued in Defense of the Black Man's Rights in the Scale of Universal Freedom,* which had stopped short of that level of militancy but had, like Walker's *Appeal,* argued for a common, transnational black identity. In 1832 Maria Stewart, a free black woman in Boston, urged African Americans gathered at Boston's Franklin Hall to take their destinies into their own hands. "If they kill us," she said of white opponents, "we shall but die."

These entreaties found responsive audiences. From 1830 until 1835 (and less regularly thereafter), free African Americans met in annual conventions intended to coordinate antislavery efforts and secure to free African American men "a voice in the disposition of those public resources which we ourselves have helped to earn." This National Negro Convention movement consistently framed its goals in the idiom of "manhood," calling for "the speedy elevation of ourselves and brethren to

> We hold these truths to be self-evident: that all men and women are created equal; that they are endowed by their Creator with certain inalienable rights; that among these are life, liberty, and the pursuit of happiness. . . .
>
> This history of mankind is a history of repeated injuries and usurpations on the part of man toward woman, having in direct object the establishment of an absolute tyranny over her. To prove this, let facts be submitted to a candid world.
>
> He has never permitted her to exercise her inalienable right to the elective franchise.
>
> He has compelled her to submit to laws, in the formation of which she had no voice.
>
> He has withheld from her rights which are given to the most ignorant and degraded men—both native and foreigner.
>
> Having deprived her of this first right of a citizen, the elective franchise, thereby leaving her without representation in the halls of legislation, he has oppressed her on all sides.
>
> He has made her, if married, in the eye of the law, civilly dead.
>
> He has taken from her all right in property, even to wages she earns.
>
> He has made her, morally, an irresponsible being. . . .
>
> He has endeavored, in every way he could, to destroy her confidence in her own powers, to lessen her self-respect and to make her willing to lead a dependent and abject life.
>
> "Declaration of Sentiments,"
> Seneca Falls Woman's Rights Convention, 1848

the scale and standing of men." Nevertheless, African American women worked to raise funds for the antislavery press and to raise awareness by inviting antislavery speakers to address their societies. In 1832 African American women formed female antislavery societies in Salem, Massachusetts, and Rochester, New York.

Although white opposition and criticism persisted, by the 1840s militant abolitionism had grown common in African American communities. A group of black Americans declared in the pages of the *Colored American:* "The time has come, when to remain inactive in the midst of ruinous forms of oppression with which we are surrounded, is to confirm the gainsaying of our foes, and to convince mankind that we are indifferent as to the recovery of our birthright privileges. . . ." In 1841 escaped slave Frederick Douglass would deliver his first public abolitionist speech in Nantucket, Massachusetts; four years later he would publish his blunt autobiography of the brutalities of slavery, *Narrative of the Life of Frederick Douglass, An American Slave, Written By Himself.* In 1843 former slave and itinerant preacher Isabella Baumfree changed her name to Sojourner Truth. Truth became a powerful and popular antislavery speaker throughout New England. Also in 1843, Henry Highland Garnet delivered "An Address to the Slaves of the United States of America," in which he chided the conventioneers for becoming too preoccupied with their own condition and called 4 million American slaves to open rebellion: "[A]rise, arise!" he cried, "Strike for your lives and liberties. Now is the day and the hour. . . . Rather die freemen than live to be slaves."

Although many whites in the North disliked the institution of slavery, most were reluctant to confront an issue that had such power to ignite violence and political division. It took the growth of the perfectionist impulse to begin to dislodge northern complacency. The most dramatic break came in the person of William Lloyd Garrison, whose commitment to perfectionism led him to found his own abolitionist newspaper, *The Liberator,* in Boston in 1831. In the first issue Garrison announced his absolute break with all forms of antislavery sentiment that compromised with the institution: "I will not equivocate—I will not excuse—I will not retreat a single inch—and I will be heard." Garrison's approach was known as immediatism—by which abolitionists meant not the immediate abolition of slavery, but the immediate beginning of the process that would lead to slavery's ultimate abolition. Immediatists rejected all forms of compromise with slavery, public or personal, wherever they encountered them.

Immediatist white antislavery activism centered in Boston and tended to attract individuals, like Garrison, who had been only peripherally linked to the mainstream Benevolent Empire. Most were urban professionals from liberal Protestant backgrounds, such as the author Lydia Maria Child, wealthy lawyer Samuel Sewall, Wendell Phillips (scion of an old Massachusetts family), and Henry and Maria Weston Chapman (he a merchant, she the principal of a young ladies' high school before her marriage). In 1831, under Garrison's leadership, they formed the New England Anti-Slavery Society.

NARRATIVE

OF THE

LIFE

OF

FREDERICK DOUGLASS,

AN

AMERICAN SLAVE.

WRITTEN BY HIMSELF.

BOSTON:

PUBLISHED AT THE ANTI-SLAVERY OFFICE,

No. 25 Cornhill.

1846.

Other antislavery workers were more willing than the Garrisonians to risk contact with the imperfect world. One of these was Theodore Dwight Weld. Born in Connecticut, Weld was an early supporter of the Colonization Society. After his conversion in the Finneyite revivals of 1825 and 1826, however, he began to doubt that the society would ever risk alienating its southern constituency. By the 1830s Weld was a committed abolitionist. As a student at Lane Seminary in Cincinnati, Ohio, he organized 18 days of antislavery discussions and led a group of students out of Lane to Oberlin College when Lane president Lyman Beecher moved to squelch their activities. In 1834, Weld became a full-time antislavery organizer.

There were some quick converts to the new, energized antislavery movement, especially in urban areas of the Northeast, upstate New York, and Pennsylvania, and in western states heavily settled by New Englanders, especially Ohio. Quakers and liberal Congregationalists were particularly active. Local antislavery societies formed throughout New England by 1832. Although Garrison envisioned an integrated abolition movement in terms of race and gender, local societies were generally segregated both ways. By the end of 1833, local and state organizations had grown strong enough to support a national society, the American Anti-Slavery Society, which included six African Americans on its original board.

Abolitionism and Antiabolition Violence

The American Anti-Slavery Society dedicated itself to the abolition of slavery without compensation for owners, and to the admission of African Americans to full citizenship. Society members pledged to pursue their goals through nonviolent moral suasion, by exhorting individuals to undertake voluntary self-reform and the reform of society.

Although it was nonviolent, moral suasion was not nonconfrontational. In 1835, in the wake of Virginia's disappointing unwillingness to take any action against slavery, the Society ratcheted up its confrontation with American society, and especially the South. The Society dramatically increased its publication of antislavery pamphlets from approximately 100,000 pieces to 1 million pieces. Roughly 20,000 tracts, fliers, and periodicals were mailed to southern destinations. Meanwhile, agents and lecturers spread out across the North.

The response, in the North as well as the South, was immediate and fierce (see Map 12–1). In the South, anger and panic turned violent. With the memory of Nat Turner still fresh, slave owners denounced the campaign as incendiary. Southern communities offered rewards for prominent abolition leaders, dead or alive. Local authorities appointed vigilante committees to police free African American neighborhoods, to patrol coastal boats for runaway slaves, and to search post offices for offending materials. In Charleston, South Carolina, a mob broke into the post office, ransacked the mail, stole abolitionist literature, and burned it publicly.

Even before the 1835 campaign, northerners had begun to express their disapproval of abolitionists. In 1833, whites had boycotted a Connecticut school for young women when its principal, Prudence Crandall, admitted two African American scholars. When Crandall admitted an entirely African American student body, white citizens lobbied for laws to bar black students from the state, threatened Crandall, and burned the school to the ground.

The postal campaign unleashed a new fury in the North. Anti–African American and antiabolitionist riots tore through St. Louis, Pittsburgh, Cincinnati, and Philadelphia. From Boston to Utica, New York, to Granville, Ohio, abolitionist meetings were broken up by mobs. In Boston in 1835, a crowd captured William Lloyd Garrison and dragged him through the streets on a rope.

Responding to the abolitionists' use of the press, antiabolitionist mobs targeted newspapers. In 1836, an antiabolitionist mob in Cincinnati made "the destruction of their Press on the night of the 12th instant" the symbolic warning of greater violence to come. Rioters in Alton, Illinois, destroyed abolitionist newspaper editor Elija Lovejoy's press four times in 1837. In the last attack, they murdered Lovejoy himself.

Many white northerners who opposed slavery were nonetheless distressed by the violence. A few northern state legislatures admonished radical abolitionists for their extreme measures, although none passed laws restricting abolitionist activity. Many antislavery activists chastised what they saw as the extreme fringe of their own movement, criticizing them for a too-zealous approach. Writers for the *Boston Courier* worried that the abolitionists would dangerously "inflame the passions of the multitude, including the women and children."

Abolitionists were undeterred and even began to find a wider range of converts. Antiabolition violence suggested to some moderates that proslavery forces would stop at nothing—even the flagrant violation of civil rights, the destruction of property, and murder. They were alarmed when, in his annual address to Congress in 1835, President Jackson asked for measures curtailing antislavery organizing, including closing the mails to abolitionist literature. Congress refused, but northerners were shocked by the idea that the president would propose to restrict freedom of the mails to protect southern interests.

If antislavery advocates took heart from Congress's refusal to interfere with the mails, they were less happy with other decisions. Opponents of slavery had long petitioned Congress to end slavery in the nation's capital. Seeking to mollify southerners, in June 1836 the House of Representatives resolved that antislavery petitions to Congress be automatically tabled. The resolution, known as the "gag rule," was renewed by succeeding Congresses until 1844.

The American Anti-Slavery Society was quick to capitalize on the passage of the gag rule. In July the society published *An Appeal to the People of the United States,* charging that the gag rule was a flagrant violation of the right of petition. That same summer, female antislavery leaders from all over the North began organizing a systematic, widespread drive to obtain signatures on antislavery petitions. Female abolitionists traveled across the North, speaking in private parlors and in public halls. Within two years, they collected some 2 million signatures, more than two-thirds of which were women's.

The petition campaign called attention to the gag rule, to congressional support of slavery, and to the ability of proslavery forces to abridge the rights of all Americans. It also provided moderate northerners with a nonconfrontational avenue of protest. Benefiting from a growing public discussion of slavery, the American Anti-Slavery Society grew from 225 local auxiliaries in 1835 to more than 1,500 by the end of the decade.

Immediatist sentiment often contained a critique of the North as well as of the South. The critique expressed disillusionment with northern reformers who were willing to compromise with slavery. Perhaps, "besotted by the influence of the institution of slavery," as Garrisonian Samuel J. May would later put it, the North had already lost its moral bearing in the headlong rush to industrial prosperity.

—VOL. I. NO. 5.—

THE AMERICAN ANTI-SLAVERY ALMANAC, FOR 1840,

BEING BISSEXTILE OR LEAP-YEAR, AND THE 64TH OF AMERICAN INDEPENDENCE. CALCULATED FOR NEW YORK; ADAPTED TO THE NORTHERN AND MIDDLE STATES.

Slave State

Free State

NORTHERN HOSPITALITY—NEW YORK NINE MONTHS' LAW.

The slave steps out of the slave-state, and his chains fall. A free state, with another chain, stands ready to re-enslave him.

Thus saith the Lord, Deliver him that is spoiled out of the hands of the oppressor.

NEW YORK:

PUBLISHED BY THE AMERICAN ANTI-SLAVERY SOCIETY, NO. 143 NASSAU STREET.

The new interest in electoral politics created major divisions in abolitionism. Among moderate abolitionists, the passage of the congressional gag rule had raised questions about the effectiveness of Garrison's antipolitical stance. They also flinched at the increasingly aggressive tactics of the Garrisonian-led movement and at the visible participation of women and African Americans.

These tensions were palpable in 1840 as the American Anti-Slavery Society met for its national convention. Participants quickly divided over whether women should participate in deliberations and whether the organization should work to elect abolitionist candidates to office. The Garrisonian branch took control of the convention. When Abby Kelley was elected to the previously all-male business committee of the association, anti-Garrisonians walked out. The exodus freed the renegades, led by philanthropists Arthur and Lewis Tappan, to launch an abolitionist political party. By the end of the year, the new Liberty Party, formed on the platform that the Constitution barred the federal government from creating slavery in any new states or territories, had nominated abolitionist James Birney for the presidency.

By definition, recourse to electoral reform excluded females. Nevertheless, some women were among the earliest advocates of the new electoral strategies. Laboring women worked for bankruptcy reform, ten-hour laws, and an end to conspiracy trials. Middle-class women advocated temperance laws and supported antislavery candidates for office. In the 1830s few of those women intended to claim electoral rights for themselves.

The Gender Limits of Antebellum Activism

Women from all classes and ranks in antebellum society were beginning to chafe under cultural and legal restrictions that rendered them less-than-autonomous members of American society. The young women who had worked and marched at Lowell described themselves as "daughters of freemen," and in that identity edged closer to claiming an independent status as citizens, as did the tailoresses who tired of waiting on chivalry to improve their lot. Educated women, and women who worked as authors, editors, and educators, participated actively in the public discourse and had a profound influence on public opinion. Were they to be regarded as mere subordinates to fathers and husbands?

For many women, the growing importance of suffrage and electoral tactics to reform movements gave rise to a new consciousness of their precarious status. Reform work permitted women to participate actively in shaping the new democratic order and to perfect skills useful in civic culture. They ran meetings, kept track of money, took notes, maintained records, and honed their skills at public speaking. For elite women involved in charities, there were also lessons in making use of the new institutions of the market revolution. Because married women could not hold property or make contracts in their own names, most women would have had trouble accumulating the money to fund asylums and schools. But *these* married women, the wives and daughters of wealthy and influential men, could use their social position to obtain donations, endorsements, and even special charters (comparable to the charters granted to male entrepreneurs) that permitted a group of married women to function legally as males.

Reform women soon learned that there were limits to the authority that religion or domesticity could confer, however. Even those women who were involved in the mildest of reform activities (e.g., as members of the American Bible Society) were rebuked for "acting out of their appropriate sphere." Women engaged in more controversial activities like labor reform or abolition work were often heckled and sometimes hounded by mobs.

In 1837, in her *Essay on Slavery and Abolitionism,* Catharine Beecher attacked female abolitionists for violating the bounds of "rectitude and propriety" and accused them of being motivated by unwomanly "ambition." The same year, the Massachusetts clergy issued a pastoral letter attacking Sarah and Angelina Grimké (members of the southern planter class who were touring the North in the abolitionist cause) for daring to take "the place and tone of man as public reformer."

By the late 1830s women involved in abolition work were subjected to growing criticism from within their own ranks. Although Garrison remained a staunch ally, other leaders, like the Tappan brothers, believed that outspoken, assertive women were embarrassing the movement. For women who had given years of their labor and had endangered their lives in the cause of abolition, these attacks were galling. Disappointing, too, was the willingness of such men to abandon the old moral reform strategies. In moral reform, women were men's peers. The central act of moral suasion, personal conversion, was not limited to either gender. But the turn toward electoral reform reduced women to second-class status in reform. They could still raise money, lobby, and speak, but they could not perform the new essential act of reform, voting.

After the 1840 split of the American Anti-Slavery Society, in which controversies over political strategies and women's rights figured centrally, abolitionist women spearheaded a drive for an organized women's rights movement. Early efforts came to fruition in Seneca Falls, New York, in July 1848. On July 14, five women (including the seasoned Quaker abolitionist Lucretia Mott and the much younger Elizabeth Cady Stanton) placed an advertisement in the *Seneca County Courier* stating, "A convention to discuss the social, civil and religious condition and rights of woman will be held in the Wesleyan Chapel, Seneca Falls, New York, on Wednesday and Thursday, the 19th and 20th of July current, commencing at 10 A.M."

The response was overwhelming. On July 19, 300 people (including perhaps 40 men, among them the famous abolitionist Frederick Douglass) showed up. By the end of the second day, the group had debated, voted on, and passed a Declaration of Sentiments (modeled after the Declaration of Independence) and a list of resolutions. They demanded specific social and legal changes, including a role in lawmaking, improved property rights, equity in divorce, and access to education and the professions. All of the resolutions passed unanimously but one: a demand for the vote. Even as American reform became ever more deeply embedded in electoral strategies, some of the assembled reformers considered suffrage too radical for women.

Conclusion

When Andrew Jackson took office in 1828, he declared his mission to be "reform." Jackson, of course, meant reform of America's political society, and specifically personal revenge on every vestige of the politicians who had earlier denied him the presidency. By the time Jackson left office in 1836, and continuing in the years after, Americans had taken the cause of reform into their own hands. For some, it was a purifying mission, returning the nation to the promises of justice and equality promised at the founding. For others, it had become a fool's errand, tearing apart the fabric of the democracy. In the nation's short history, the West had always functioned as the republic's social and cultural release. Soon that symbol of reconciliation and prosperity would become the site of America's insoluble conflicts.

Further Readings

Frederick J. Blue, *No Taint of Compromise: Crusaders in Antislavery Politics* (2005). Using the lives of several antislavery reformers, Blue reveals the efforts of abolitionists to push slavery back into politics.

Stuart M. Blumin, *The Emergence of the Middle Class: Social Experience in the American City, 1760–1900* (1989). In the most complete examination of the middle class in the nineteenth century, Blumin pays particular attention to the middle-class reform impulse.

Daniel Walker Howe, *What Hath God Wrought: The Transformation of America, 1815–1848* (2007). Howe puts middle-class reform at the center of this monumental history of the period.

Bruce Laurie, *Beyond Garrison: Antislavery and Social Reform* (2005). Laurie's book traces the many links between antislavery radicalism and other forms of social and political activism before the Civil War.

Timothy Patrick McCarthy and John Stauffer, eds., *Prophets of Protest: Reconsidering the History of American Abolitionism* (2006). A sample of some of the latest scholarship by leading historians of American abolitionism.

Richard S. Newman, *The Transformation of American Abolitionism: Fighting Slavery in the Early Republic* (2002). Newman fills in the gap between the antislavery radicalism of the late eighteenth century and the emergence of "immediatism" in the 1830s. He is particularly attentive to the role of African Americans in the antislavery movement.

Who, What

>> Timeline >>

▼ 1822
Denmark Vesey conspiracy

▼ 1826
General Colored Association of Massachusetts formed
American Society for the Promotion of Temperance formed

▼ 1827
Russwurm and Cornish found *Freedom's Journal*

▼ 1828
Andrew Jackson elected president
Tariff of 1828
Calhoun writes *South Carolina Exposition and Protest*

▼ 1829
David Walker publishes *An Appeal to the Colored Citizens of the World*

▼ 1830
National Negro Convention movement begins

▼ 1831
Nat Turner leads rebellion in Virginia
William Lloyd Garrison begins publication of *The Liberator*
New England Anti-Slavery Society founded
New England Association of Farmers, Mechanics, and Other Workingmen founded
New York Protestant Association founded
Lyceum movement begins

Review Questions

1. What conditions gave rise to labor protest in the 1820s and 1830s? What forms did that protest take?
2. What conditions gave rise to the early women's rights movement?
3. Did the rise of perfectionism and the Benevolent Empire reflect a new democratic impulse or a desire for social control?
4. Why did some reformers abandon the tactic of "moral suasion" over time?

For further review materials and resource information, please visit www.oup.com/us/ofthepeople

▼ 1832
Tariff of 1832
Jackson reelected
South Carolina passes Nullification Resolution
Maria Stewart lectures in Boston

▼ 1833
Congress passes Force Bill
American Anti-Slavery Society founded

▼ 1834
Anti–African American riots in major cities
Anti-Catholic mob burns Ursuline Convent in Charleston, Massachusetts
Lowell operatives go on strike
National Trades' Union formed

▼ 1835
American Anti-Slavery Society begins postal campaign
Lyman Beecher publishes *A Plea for the West*

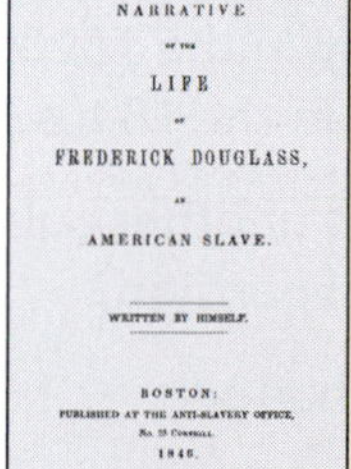
NARRATIVE
LIFE
FREDERICK DOUGLASS,
AMERICAN SLAVE.
WRITTEN BY HIMSELF.
BOSTON:
PUBLISHED AT THE ANTI-SLAVERY OFFICE,
1845.

▼ 1836
Congress passes "gag rule"

▼ 1837
Abolitionist editor Elija Lovejoy murdered in Alton, Illinois
Bread riots in New York City
Massachusetts creates first State Board of Education; Horace Mann appointed secretary

AMERICAN
ANTI-SLAVERY
ALMANAC,
1840,
NEW YORK:

CHAPTER 13

Common Threads 

>> How did the expansion of slavery in the 1820s and 1830s affect U.S. foreign policy in the 1840s?

>> How did settlers' preconceptions of other cultures affect their attitudes toward expansion?

>> How did the Democratic Party change 1828–1848?

>> Was "manifest destiny" consistent with the Monroe Doctrine of 1823 or a repudiation of it?

>> How important were the politics of slavery in the 1840s, compared with the previous decade and the decade following?

Manifest Destiny

1836–1848

AMERICAN PORTRAIT

>> Mah-i-ti-wo-nee-ni Remembers Life on the Great Plains

Mah-i-ti-wo-nee-ni was born in the mid-1830s in the Black Hills. Her father was Cheyenne, and her mother was Lakota (or Sioux). Her homelands had been a part of Jefferson's 1803 Louisiana Purchase and would later become the states of South Dakota and Wyoming. In the 1830s, however, the Great Plains remained Indian country.

By the time Mah-i-ti-wo-nee-ni was born, contact with whites had been reshaping the life of Great Plains Indians for more than two centuries. The Cheyennes had once been a semiagricultural people who "planted corn every year . . . then went hunting all summer," returning in the fall to gather the crops. The reintroduction of the horse by the Spanish in the sixteenth century had enabled Plains Indians to become faster and more efficient hunters, and more effective raiders. Over time, the Cheyennes had given up farming and had organized their economic life around the hunt, foraging other food as they went. Now whole villages migrated to seasonal hunting grounds. Competing for game, they sent out raiding parties to steal horses or take captives for exchange. Individuals and small groups crisscrossed the landscape in search of trade. Mah-i-ti-wo-nee-ni recalled a time in her childhood (probably in 1840) when the Cheyennes and the Arapahoes traveled south to meet in a great peace council with their traditional enemies, the Kiowas, Comanches, and Apaches.

By the 1830s, the proximity of white Americans was beginning to affect the Cheyennes in direct ways. Although Mah-i-ti-wo-nee-ni did not remember much contact with white people during her early childhood, at the time of the great southern peace council, massive U.S. overland migration to the Pacific was already under way. For these settlers, migration was part of a personal search for liberty and opportunity, and of the political process of nation building. In the West, many Americans believed, the nation renewed its virtues and purified the republican model of government. In the mid-1840s, Americans coined a lasting phrase for this association of land and liberty. Taking the continent was their "manifest destiny."

American settlement of the West implied a different destiny for Mah-i-ti-wo-nee-ni and her people, however. First came missionaries, exhorting Indians to convert to Christianity. The settlers soon followed, trampling Indian plantings, destroying villages, spreading disease, and decimating the buffalo. At first the U.S. agents who appeared among the Cheyennes wished merely to trade gifts of kettles, coffeepots, knives, and blankets for Indian promises to permit settlers to cross Cheyenne lands. Soon, the U.S. government wanted the land itself. Although the nomadic Cheyennes long resisted removal, by 1877, after years of struggle and compromise, Mah-i-ti-wo-nee-ni and her people were forcibly displaced from their homelands to the Black Hills and conveyed south into Indian Territory.

Because much of the land Americans sought for settlement lay within the boundaries of the nation of Mexico, the trans-Mississippi manifest destiny of white Americans also implied a distinct destiny for Mexicans. Claiming mistreatment by the Mexican government, white American settlers in the Mexican province of Coahuila y Tejas formed the Republic of Texas and sought entry into the United States. In 1846 the United States provoked a war with Mexico to claim large portions of that nation's northern territories.

That war gained the United States secure access to the Pacific Ocean. But Americans also paid the costs of the manifest destiny. Each stage of geographical expansion reignited controversies over the institution

continued

>> **AMERICAN PORTRAIT** *continued*

of slavery. While many white Southerners claimed a fundamental constitutional right to own slaves, and felt betrayed by growing Northern opposition, Northern reformers inveighed against the immorality of the institution. They flooded the mails with abolitionist tracts, and Congress with antislavery petitions. This collision of interests and ideals flared within a national political system ill equipped to respond to it effectively. American politicians continued to try to forge compromises between slave-owning and non-slave-owning interests, but the party structure was in disarray, and no strong leader arose to hold it together. By 1848, some Americans were prepared to give up on their government altogether.

OUTLINE 

The Decline of Jacksonianism

Andrew Jackson had governed on a philosophy of federalism, in which a strong presidency had been necessary to combat, rather than shore up, the growth of a powerful central government. He had supported territorial expansion, the powers of the individual states, and the claims of settlers, and had opposed federal control of those processes. By 1836, people in new territories sought admission to the Union, settlers were launching the largest sustained westward migration in the history of the nation, and Jackson's Democratic Party seemed to have reduced the old Republican dynasty (now regrouped as Whigs) to whining observers. But there were costs to Jackson's successes: his hatred of strong central government had finally thrown the nation's banking system into chaos, his zeal for territorial expansion had helped nurture a strong abolition movement in the North, and his own Democratic Party had grown too diverse to remain stable. Jackson would be succeeded in 1837 by a Democrat and a man known for his political acumen, Martin Van Buren, but the "Little Magician" would lose reelection by a landslide in 1840 and fail again when he ran on a third-party ticket in 1848.

Political Parties in Crisis

The expansion of white male suffrage and the translation of moral-reform agendas into electoral politics energized American politics in the 1830s and 1840s. In 1840, 66 percent of the electorate voted in Massachusetts, 75 percent in Connecticut, and 77 percent in Pennsylvania. Yet the capacity of major political parties to accommodate a wide range of conflicting interests and beliefs was limited.

> **The inauguration of Martin Van Buren, as President of the United States, took place at the Capitol, in Washington, on Saturday last, at noon. . . . Mr. Van Buren delivered an Inaugural Address on the occasion, which . . . professes to be an avowal of the principles by which the new President intends to be guided in his administration of the government; but with the single exception of the principle of opposition to the abolition of slavery in the District of Columbia, which it expresses with most uncalled for and unbecoming haste and positiveness, he might, with as much propriety, have sung Yankee Doodle or Hail Columbia, and called it "an avowal of his principles." . . . Mr. Van Buren's indecent haste to avow his predeterminations on the subject of slavery has not even the merit of boldness. It is made in a cringing spirit of propitiation to the south, and in the certainty that a majority at the north accord with his views.**
>
> WILLIAM LEGGETT,
> March 11, 1837

Increasingly fractured since the election of 1824, the Republican Party had struggled to reorganize on the basis of opposition to Andrew Jackson. Jackson's war on the national bank had offered the immediate occasion. Although unable to save the bank, Henry Clay and the anti-Jacksonians narrowly passed a Senate resolution in 1834 censuring Jackson for assuming "authority and power not conferred by the Constitution and the laws." (Jackson had refused to turn over a paper on the bank he had read to his cabinet.) In the debate leading up to the censure, Clay identified his own anti-Jackson position as "Whiggish" (meant deliberately to evoke memories of the English "Whigs" who opposed royal tyranny in the eighteenth century). That label stuck as the name of the new political party.

Former National Republicans in the urban Northeast and upper West made up the bulk of the new Whig Party. Some of these were beginning to doubt the wisdom of uncontrolled territorial expansion, which seemed to promote political corruption, economic disorder, sectional conflict, and the extension of slavery. They feared the power of wildcat settlers, wageworkers, the urban poor, and immigrants to subvert orderly economic relations. Whigs supported market expansion, but under stronger guidance from a strong, interventionist central government. Accordingly, they continued to embrace the basic elements of the earlier "American System": a new national bank, a strong protective tariff, and government-sponsored internal improvements.

By 1834, some former Democrats were also disenchanted with the party of Jackson. Prospering shopkeepers and middling merchants began to understand their own interests as distinct from those of the urban laboring classes. They were attracted by the Whig emphasis on personal and political discipline and order. Some southerners were still angry over the tariff and the Nullification Crisis. Some small farmers and shopkeepers who had been wiped out by the Depression of 1837 blamed Jackson for their hard times. Workers, who had little trust for the merchant classes that made up the core of the new Whig Party, tended to form splinter parties or to stay with the Democrats.

Through the 1830s the Whigs remained an amorphous and disorganized opposition. Unable to decide on a single candidate, in 1836 they ran four regional challengers, hoping to deny Van Buren a majority in the Electoral College. The Whig field included William Henry Harrison (best known as governor of Indiana Territory and victor at the Battle of Tippecanoe, but nominated by an Antimason convention in Pennsylvania), Senator Hugh Lawson White (Jackson's replacement in the Senate who had grown disenchanted with the president and was nominated by unhappy Democrats in Tennessee), Senator Daniel Webster (former National Republican and famous orator, nominated by the Massachusetts legislature), and Willie P. Mangum (a protest candidate of the South Carolina Nullifiers).

Jackson's vice president, Martin Van Buren, seemed well positioned for the race. To Van Buren went much of the credit for creating a successful Democratic coalition. Surely he was the one to hold it together. Van Buren had been constantly at Jackson's side, first as secretary of state and then as vice president. Few politicians seemed better situated to inherit Jackson's popularity. What's more, Van Buren seemed perhaps uniquely positioned to bridge the growing gulf between northern antislavery Democrats and southern proslavery Democrats: his popularity in New York appeared broad and solid enough for him to risk alienating some of the antislavery vote in the effort to gain southern support, a risk he took by publicly declaring himself "the inflexible and uncompromising opponent of any attempt on the part of Congress to abolish slavery in the District of Columbia" or to interfere with slavery "in the states where it exists."

Martin Van Buren One of the most powerful politicians of his time, Martin Van Buren was also one of the first to extol the virtues of party competition.

The election was close. Van Buren won part of New England (but not Massachusetts or Vermont). He took the line of states that run down the Appalachian Mountains: his home state of New York, Pennsylvania, Virginia, and North Carolina. And he took a crescent of far-west states, most of them slave states: Michigan, Illinois (technically free but popularly proslavery, especially in the south), Missouri, Arkansas, Louisiana, Mississippi, and Alabama. He won 58 percent of the electoral vote (but that included the weighting of the Three-Fifths Compromise in the South) and a bare majority (51 percent) of the popular vote. A shift of fewer than 2,000 votes in Pennsylvania would have deprived Van Buren of an Electoral College majority and thrown the election to the House of Representatives.

Van Buren and the Legacy of Jackson

In his 1837 inaugural address, Martin Van Buren announced that the nation had arrived at a "singularly happy!" condition. Less optimistic, Missourian Thomas Hart Benton observed that in Van Buren's ascendancy to office "the rising was eclipsed by the setting sun." Benton was closer to the truth. Van Buren's struggle to unite Jackson's party enough to get elected was only the first of the challenges he inherited from his mentor.

The signs of the Panic of 1837 were already visible when Van Buren was inaugurated in March 1837. Jackson's pet banks had ensured that western land speculation would be built on easy credit. His hard-money measures, culminating in the Specie Circular that had effectively drained the nation of specie, did not end the bubble of credit. It simply diverted its source to European financiers, who got higher interest in the United States than in their home countries. When European banks responded to specie shortages in their own countries by increasing interest on deposits and tightening credit, the Europeans called in their American loans. The sudden collapse of credit was exacerbated by crop failures in 1835 and 1837, which not only put farmers at greater risk for defaulting on their loans but also reduced American exports.

As credit evaporated, interest rates rose, paper money depreciated, and debt mounted. The credit-dependent cotton market began to collapse, taking with it several large import-export firms in New York and New Orleans. In the context of years of high inflation, the failures ignited a run on the overextended banks, as depositors tried to hoard their savings before the hard currency was paid out for mercantile debts. "[E]ven during the Embargo, & war that followed," merchant John Perkins Cushing reported to an old friend in China in May of 1837, ". . . there was nothing like the complete prostration of commercial credit & confidence that has taken place within the last two months."

Perhaps a strong federal hand could have stemmed the damage, but Van Buren shared Jackson's view that the federal government should not manage currency. Van Buren's announcement on May 4 that he intended to maintain the Specie Circular in force ensured that the pressure on banks would continue. On May 10, 1837—five days after Cushing wrote his letter—frightened depositors drained $650,000 from their reserves, and New York City banks closed. Only a show of force by the military prevented a riot.

Coinciding with large waves of German and Irish immigration, the depression fell with special severity on the East Coast. Wages declined faster than prices. Unemployment was widespread, and losses touched even the prosperous middle classes. Hard times remained until 1843. While Democrats scrambled to avoid political responsibility and bombarded Van Buren with contradictory advice, the new Whig Party began to look ahead optimistically to 1840.

Although an additional infusion of federal funds to state banks in 1837 might only have fed the frenzy, Van Buren's decision to delay the scheduled distribution (on the grounds that the windfalls had amounted to a federal influence over banking practice) added a new confusion. In an effort to return stability to the nation's monetary system, Van Buren proposed that the Treasury Department establish its own financial institutions to receive, hold, and pay out government funds. The institutions would

Panic of 1837 "The moderen Balaam and his ass." An American cartoon placing the blame for the panic of 1837 and the perilous state of the banking system on outgoing president Andrew Jackson, shown riding a donkey in its cartoon debut as the symbol of the Democratic Party.

exist for the sole purpose of managing government accounts. They would not issue paper currency and would not make loans to business.

The proposal for an independent treasury met with substantial opposition. Predictably, Whigs objected that removing government holdings from circulation in the economy would reduce capital investment. But many Democrats (less antibank than Jackson had been) also thought the new system would retard growth. The independent treasury did not pass until 1840, when it was enacted as an entirely separate, specie-based system, empowered neither to receive nor to pay out paper currency.

Van Buren's challenges spilled over from domestic politics to international crises. Twice, the fears and frustrations of Americans along the Canadian border almost brought the United States and Canada/Great Britain to blows. Americans and Canadians had long argued over who owned the rich timber reserves in the Aroostook Valley on the border of Maine and New Brunswick. When the Americans heard rumors in 1838 that Canadian lumberjacks were infiltrating the region and taking trees at will, they were more than ready to believe it. The Democratic governor of Maine declared that Maine was under invasion, and demanded federal protection. Van Buren could not ignore the request and sent in the army under General Winfield Scott. Aware that the economy was in no condition to support a war, however, he also instructed Scott to offer terms for a truce. If Canada would acknowledge Maine's predominant interest in the valley, the United States would respect existing Canadian settlements pending final disposition of the area.

Meanwhile, Americans along the northern New York border were picking sides in an internal Canadian rebellion against Great Britain, 1837–1838. Although the United States was technically neutral, disgruntled unemployed American workers saw the

rebels as latter-day embodiments of the spirit of the American Revolution and were drawn into alliance with them against wealthy Canadians and the British government. Actively recruited by the rebels, sympathetic New Yorkers raised funds and offered ships to transport men and arms to Canada. On the night of December 29, 1837, Canadian pro-British troops crossed the river into Schlosser, New York, captured the *Caroline* (owned by American William Wells), towed it out into the middle of the river, and set it afire. A few months later, Americans retaliated by seizing and sinking a British ship. There matters stood, with the United States and Britain exchanging diplomatic demands, until 1840, when a Canadian deputy sheriff by the name of Alexander McLeod got a little drunk in a tavern on the United States side and began bragging that he had personally killed an American during the *Caroline* incident. New York authorities immediately arrested him and New York mobs clamored for blood, while Great Britain protested that McLeod's status was an international matter, out of the jurisdiction of the state of New York, and threatened a full break in diplomatic relations. By that time Van Buren was fighting for reelection as the anti-big-government Democratic candidate and was unprepared to intervene. Only with the election of a Whig president and Congress in 1840 was McLeod released.

The Political Economy of the Trans-Mississippi West

Jackson had embodied nothing so much as the restless energy and assumed right of white Americans to settle ever deeper in the North American continent. Manifest destiny, the belief that white Americans had a providential right to as much of North America as they wanted, had been part of the beliefs of citizens and of U.S. policy since the founding of the republic. It was implicit in the Northwest Ordinance, in scores of Indian treaties, in the Louisiana Purchase, in the Transcontinental Treaty, in the 1824 Monroe Doctrine, and in the Removal Act of 1830. But only in 1845 did the phrase enter the American vocabulary, when journalist John O'Sullivan proclaimed grandiosely that it is "[o]ur manifest destiny . . . to overspread the continent allotted by Providence for the free development of our yearly multiplying millions." As the United States' treatment of Native Americans had long made clear, according to many Americans the manifest destiny of the nation was racial as well as territorial and political.

Manifest Destiny in Antebellum Culture

On the simplest level, manifest destiny was a political slogan and a crass claim for property, a way of asserting that Americans wanted the continent all the way to the Pacific and intended to have it. But most Americans resisted such a naked statement of their ambitions, and framed—and deeply understood—their aspirations in the language of democracy and freedom. This particular land was the place intended by Providence as the physical site and the fostering environment of a unique national greatness. In antebellum culture, this understanding of the singularity of North America as a physical place was often articulated through a pair of evocative and linked images: first, the image of the awesome power and natural majesty of the

American wilderness, and second, the image of the primitive wilderness giving way to an even nobler state of cultivation upon the arrival of American settlers.

Both images, and their linkage, were evident in antebellum landscape painting, particularly in the work of a group of painters known as the Hudson River School. Like most Americans of the antebellum era, the Hudson River painters were influenced by the Romantic movement then sweeping Europe, which emphasized among other themes the power and beauty of untouched, untamed nature. For example, the canvasses of Thomas Cole, who was born in England but lived most of his life in the United States and became the leader of the Hudson River School, depicted wilderness bluffs surrounded by ageless forests presumedly never penetrated by American settlers. Ancient trees spiked toward the heavens and wild waterfalls cascaded over crags far above the ground. Cole's *Falls of Kaaterskill* (1826) portrayed such a scene, with a massive storm gathering over the forest to underscore the unchecked power of the American wilderness. In these landscapes, the only human figures are usually Native Americans, who are figured as additional emblems of the primitive beauty of the scene.

> **There are several factories in different parts of North-Adams, along the banks of a stream, a wild highland rivulet, which, however, does vast work of a civilized nature. It is strange to see such a rough and untamed stream as it looks to be, so tamed down to the purposes of man, and making cottons, woolens &c.—sawing boards, marbles, and giving employment to so many men and girls; and there is a sort of picturesqueness in finding these factories, supremely artificial establishments, in the midst of such wild scenery. For now the stream will be flowing through a rude forest, with the trees erect and dark, as when the Indians fished there. . . . And taking a turn in the road, behold the factories and their range of boarding-houses, with the girls looking out of the window as aforesaid. And perhaps the wild scenery is all around the very site of the factory, and mingles its impression strangely with those opposite ones.**
>
> NATHANIEL HAWTHORNE, 1838

Yet Cole and other Hudson River painters often combined these visual celebrations of the power and majesty of the American landscape with images of American settlement. In these latter paintings, the arrival of the Euro-Americans seemed not only to complement, but in some sense to bring to fruition, the innate grandeur of the nature landscape. Cole's *Landscape* (1825) suggested this harmonious blending of destinies, as did *West Rock, New Haven,* painted by Connecticut native Frederick Church in 1849. The Hudson River paintings sometimes suggested a bittersweet sadness at the passing of the wilderness, even as they celebrated the coming of the ordered fields of farming communities.

Antebellum poets and novelists also took up the theme of the land, often envisioning it (as did landscape painters) as a shifting scenery in which the fearsome majesty of the wilderness seemed merely to await transformation at the hands of American pioneers. This was the environmental narrative behind the human stories of James Fenimore Cooper. The Leatherstocking Tales narrated Euro-American

Thomas Cole's *The Hunter's Return* One of the foremost landscape artists of his time, Thomas Cole romanticized nature and the simple life of the independent farmer.

settlement of the New York backcountry as a grand myth of manifest destiny, in which settlement tamed the land even as the land itself became the agent through which the newcomers were forged into a new, ennobled society. In *The Last of the Mohicans,* Cooper described the New York backcountry of 1757 as "an impervious boundary of forests" torn by dangerous rapids and rugged passes, haunted by fitful winds that arose in "the interminable forests of the west." By 1793, the fictional time of *The Pioneers,* that same landscape had become "a succession of hills" and "narrow, rich cultivated dales" dotted by "beautiful and thriving villages" and "neat and comfortable farms." "Only forty years have passed," Cooper wrote at the opening of *The Pioneers,* "since this whole territory was a wilderness." In the same spirit, poet William Cullen Bryant visited the austere Illinois plains in the 1830s and saw not a timberless landscape but the "gardens" and "fields, boundless and beautiful" which he believed American cultivation would create and which would cradle American greatness. The uniting of the national culture and the land was the "manifest destiny" not only of American citizens but also of the land itself.

Jefferson had imagined this relationship of the people to the land chiefly in terms of the yeoman farmer, with the craftsman a secondary "handmaid." In the wake of innovations in travel and machinery design in the early nineteenth century, however, images of trade and manufacturing began to make their way into ideas about the abundance of the land. Americans would unleash the fecundity of the continent not only through farming but also through commercial enterprises. De

Witt Clinton's prediction of the impact of the Erie Canal on New York City—that the city would become the emporium of the world—captured this new vision in the politics of trade: as a result of extensive commerce, Clinton insisted in 1819, "the distinctions of eastern and western, of southern and northern interests, will be entirely prostrated." Commerce would "increas[e] the stock of human happiness—by establishing the perpetuity of free government—and by extending the empire of improvement, of knowledge, of refinement and of religion. . . ." In this view, the American wilderness, first cultivated into a homestead, was further tamed to a huge highway for the transportation of goods and culture.

To this image of North America's natural advantages as a transportation network, Americans soon added the image of North American power harnessed into manufacturing output. In an 1839 article titled "The Great Nation of Futurity," for example, John O'Sullivan (who would later coin the term "manifest destiny") located the distinctively American future not only in the farmers of the nation but also in its "mechanical population" and in the absolute "freedom of trade and business pursuits." Others agreed with him. The proof of America's greatness lay not only in the riches to be coaxed from the land but also in the seemingly endless array of manufactured goods available on the market. Reviewing an exhibit of goods manufactured in Massachusetts in 1839, one magazine correspondent argued that manufacturing "blended harmoniously together" the interests of all Americans. "It is a cavilling spirit, that makes the luxury of life a subject of complaint because its direct enjoyments are necessarily confined to limited numbers," another booster proclaimed. "Indirectly, they extend to all classes. They keep in circulation the vital air of the political system." In fact, those enjoyments did not extend to all people and the "vital air of the political system" too often became fetid with the stench of greed.

Texas

By the terms of the 1819 Transcontinental Treaty, the United States had given up claims to Spanish lands south of the 42nd parallel. Nevertheless, within a few years Americans began to enter the region.

Many of these immigrants were specifically invited; some were not. The Spanish had conceived of their northern region as a buffer zone against the Lipan Apaches and Comanche Indians, on the one hand, and between New Spain and the United States, on the other. After independence, the Mexican government expanded those policies by offering land grants to Americans in return for the promise to bring settlers to bolster the sparse population. The first American to take full advantage of the invitation was Stephen F. Austin, who began settling a colony on the banks of the Brazos and Colorado rivers in 1821. By 1830 there were more than 20,000 Americans (including 1,000 slaves) living in the northeastern province of Mexico, adjacent to Louisiana.

Conflict between immigrant Americans and resident Tejanos was inevitable. Tejanos resented the influx of Americans. The national government often awarded to Americans lands that already belonged to Tejanos or that included Tejano communities. Tejanos complained that the *empresarios* (American landholders) were "nothing more than money-changing speculators" who had no respect for existing claims and made little attempt to control their settlers or illegal squatters who used the American colonies to hide stolen livestock.

In fact, although they were happy to take advantage of the cheap prices Mexico offered, many Americans had never fully acknowledged the right of Mexico to these

AMERICAN LANDSCAPE

>> Culture and Politics in Manifest Destiny: Tejanos in Texas

When white Americans rebelled against Mexico in 1836, they cited among their justifications not only specific policies of the Mexican government but also the culture of the Mexicans among whom they lived and whom they viewed as inferior to the citizens of the United States. They called Tejanos immoral, lazy, and "unmanly" largely because Tejanos were not interested in the aggressive forms of development favored by the immigrants. They were right in at least one respect: Tejano culture was distinctly different from the culture the immigrants brought with them, and most Tejanos neither welcomed nor respected the ways of the newcomers. Chief among those distinctive qualities of Tejano culture were a striking sense of community, an awareness of the collective good that stood in stark contrast to the individualism increasingly valued in American culture, and, even more fundamentally, a racial fluidity that challenged the very premises of southern American expansionism.

By 1836, there were three major regions of Tejano settlement in northern Mexico: the northernmost Nacodoches region (inland and closest to Louisiana) and the Bexar-Goliad and Rio Grande regions farther south and closer to the coast of the Gulf of Mexico. The three bore some differences (the result of different settlement patterns and histories) but they shared a heritage that blended Spanish, Mexican, and native influences, melded together to suit the land and the circumstances of survival in a hard and isolated region.

Settlement of the area had come slowly. Although the earliest Spanish foray was in 1716, Spanish authorities (and most Mexican officials, after the national revolution) concluded that the chief value of the region was as a *frontera*—a boundary land where priests could missionize "heathen" Indians and where soldiers in armed garrisons (*presidios*) could prevent Lipan Apache and Comanche raiding parties from making deeper incursions into the colony. Semiarid, largely void of vegetation, and far removed from the comforts of established society, the land offered few rewards to potential colonists. Mortality rates ran high, especially among males (who were required to serve as *ciudadanos armadas*, a sort of armed civilian reserve, in exchange for land) and children. As late as 1821, the year in which Mexico achieved independence, the region claimed fewer than 2,500 settlers.

As was the case among the settlers, land ownership was a central principle of Tejano culture. By the beginning of the nineteenth century some families, and groups of families, had ventured out from the towns to establish ranches on the banks of the rivers that flowed out to the Gulf of Mexico, and a discernible class system, based on the private ownership of property, began to take shape. At one extreme were a few wealthy families, settled on large ranches in elaborate houses and employing numerous servants and ranch workers. At the other extreme were the mission Indians, technically free but often held in conditions of semibondage.

Yet a strong sense of obligation to the collective continued to characterize Tejano culture, mediating the impulse toward stark individualism and rough Jacksonian entrepreneurialism. This principle of social life may have resulted in part from the influence of the Tlaxcalan Indians (originally part of the Aztec empire), among whom the principle of *calpulli*—the close-knit tribal unit—was particularly strong. It may have been nurtured by the defensive posture of the early settlements and by their distance

continued

>> **AMERICAN LANDSCAPE** *continued*

from central government. Certainly, it was fostered by the semiarid conditions of the land, and was most evident in the treatment of water resources. Water projects were considered the work of the entire community, and ranches were laid out in long thin plots running away from the riverbeds, ensuring each landowner access to water rights.

This sense of collective obligation may also have been a consequence of (and may have supported) the racial fluidity of Tejano society. Most of the settlers came from the northern Coahuila province, where intermarriage among native people, Mexicans, and Spaniards had long been common. Although the Spanish authorities had frowned on it, over time the soldiers in the *presidios* had also intermarried with the colonists and with local Indians. The result was a community in which most people claimed racially mixed heritages and in which race did not directly correspond to status and rights in the way it did in the southern United States.

Most alarming to the white American settlers, locals opposed slavery and repeatedly petitioned their government to end the practice of allowing white Americans to establish the institution in Texas. There had been African American slaves in the region for at least 300 years, but in such small numbers that the institution had little social or economic importance before the early nineteenth century. The number of slaves increased after 1800, when the weakening of the central government made it possible for slave traders to use Texas as an entry to the U.S. market. Especially after Mexico gained its independence, Tejanos condemned the trade as antirepublican.

The clash of white American and Tejano cultures in Texas, then, spoke to both the past and the future of republicanism in the United States. Against the growing competitive individualism of American society, the Tejano community represented a powerful sense of obligation to the commonweal that had once been the very essence of American republicanism. Against the increasingly racialized politics of the United States, Tejanos insisted on a culture in which race would not directly determine status and individual rights. ●

lands. Viewing the region as the natural next frontier for American plantation agriculture, southerners had denounced the 1819 treaty and lobbied first John Quincy Adams and then Andrew Jackson to purchase the tract free and clear. By 1839 some Americans were convinced that Texas was destined to become the "land of refuge for the American slaveholders."

The immigrants themselves framed their criticisms of the Mexican government in the standard language of republicanism. They objected to high taxes, but then so did everybody. They objected to being required to convert to Catholicism in order to intermarry with Mexicans and control their Mexican wives' property, but those laws were not really enforced. They objected to being expected to adopt the Spanish language. But beneath these objections were more fundamental issues, including a deep discontent—which many Mexicans shared—with the autocratic Mexican government.

Southerners who moved to Texas had a particular complaint—the Mexican government's erratic policies on slavery. There had been African American slaves in the region for at least 300 years, but very few. The number of slaves increased after 1800, when slave traders began to use Texas as an entry to the U.S. market. After independence, Mexican critics condemned the trade as antirepublican. But like the young United States, the new and internally unstable Mexican government took an erratic course, now banning slavery altogether, now allowing slaves to enter the nation but providing for mandatory gradual abolition.

By the mid-1820s, however, the immigrants had developed a cotton economy dependent on slave labor and were determined to preserve the institution. They regarded Mexican inconsistency and resistance as evidence of betrayal. In 1824 Stephen Austin, never a devoted supporter of slavery, devised a set of regulations for his colony that included harsh provisions for slaves who tried to escape or free people who abetted runaways. By 1830 Austin had come to the conclusion that "Texas must be a slave country.

Circumstances and unavoidable necessity compels it. It is the wish of the people there. . . ." "The people," in Austin's view, included only white U.S. immigrants and others who agreed with their goals.

But slavery was not the major reason for the increasing tension between Texas and the Mexican government. After 1830 the government took steps to stem immigration and located troops on the United States–Mexican border. Immigrants interpreted these measures as obstructions to their rightful claims. The rise of General Antonio López de Santa Anna provided the occasion for registering their complaints. But when Santa Anna dissolved the Mexican Congress and made himself dictator in 1834, Texans—both Anglo and Tejano—sharpened their criticisms of Mexican government. Casting themselves as the quintessential republicans, they and several other Mexican states joined in the rebellion. Hoping to secure U.S. statehood, Texas first declared itself a sovereign republic on March 2, 1836.

Map 13–1 Republic of Texas After the decisive American victory at San Jacinto that resulted in the independence of Texas, the border dispute between Texas and Mexico continued until it was resolved by the Mexican War a decade later.

Four days later armed conflict broke out when the huge Mexican army, led by Santa Anna, wiped out 187 Texas patriots barricaded in a mission called the Alamo. It was a costly and fleeting victory. Santa Anna's army suffered 1,544 casualties and created martyrs for the rebels' cause. Under the leadership of Sam Houston, the rebels retreated east, gathering recruits as they went. On April 21 they surprised an encampment of Mexican troops on the San Jacinto River and scored a huge victory, crowned by the capture of Santa Anna himself. Bargaining to save his life and purchase his freedom, Santa Anna declared Texas a free nation. Ecstatic Texans drew up a constitution, made Sam Houston their first president, and called for annexation to the United States.

With the nation in economic crisis and his own party already bickering over who was responsible, the last thing Van Buren wanted as president was a bitter battle over Texas and slavery. He doubted that the Constitution permitted annexation, and he feared that annexation would be construed as meddling in Mexico's internal affairs. Anticipating Texas's application for admission, abolitionists had made opposition to annexation a central issue in their massive petition campaign of 1837–1838, giving the controversy a wide popular foundation in the North. John Quincy Adams had delivered a stirring speech against annexation in the House, and some senators were publicly denouncing slavery in general and especially in Texas. Southerners had responded with their own states' rights petitions. In the end, Van Buren did not submit Texas's request for statehood to Congress.

Pacific Bound

For most white Americans, however, Texas was not the fulfillment of America's manifest destiny. That goal lay in the rich lands beyond the plains. By the time Van Buren left office, the Mississippi River had become the staging ground for a massive migration west.

The migration began modestly enough, as a trickle of missionaries in the 1830s. In 1831 rumors reached the East Coast of four young Indians who had appeared in St. Louis, exhausted and sick, imploring the white clergy there to send religious teachers to their people. Two years later, in 1833, the Methodist *Christian Advocate and Herald* published a letter from a Wyandot Indian who claimed that the Western tribes hungered for instruction in Christianity. Whether true or not, such stories enabled missionaries to claim that they had been invited into Indian communities. In 1834 the Methodist Missionary Society sent the Reverend Jason Lee west to found a mission in the Willamette Valley of Oregon Territory. Two years later, in January 1836, the American Board of Commissioners for Foreign Missions voted to send six people (including two women) to settle permanent missions in Oregon.

For their first mission, the board selected Marcus and Narcissa Prentiss Whitman, a doctor and a Sunday school teacher. In September 1836, after a three-month-long trip west, the Whitmans established their mission among the Cayuse Indians near Fort Walla Walla on the Columbia River. Their fellow missionaries Henry and Eliza Hart Spalding founded a mission 125 miles away among the Nez Percés.

At first, the Whitmans seemed to thrive. Marcus Whitman preached and doctored among the Cayuse and taught the men agriculture, and Narcissa taught school and oversaw the domestic operation of the large mission. Over the following decade, however, as white immigration into the region swelled, the Cayuse came to view the missionaries as the cause of the constant influx of white people and new diseases. In 1847, in response to a deadly measles epidemic, a Cayuse band attacked the mission, killing Marcus and Narcissa Prentiss Whitman and a number of other white people.

By then, overland migrants to the West Coast were so numerous that the roads of Iowa "were literally lined with long blue wagons . . . slowly wending their way over the broad prairies," leaving deep, rutted tracks. In the years of heaviest migration, watering holes were so overused and sanitary conditions so poor that the road west became a breeding ground for typhoid, malaria, dysentery, and cholera.

Most of the migrants were farming families of moderate means, pushed out of the Midwest by the hard times of 1837. Men often made the initial decision to leave, sometimes with little warning to their families. Sarah Cummins later remembered returning home from school one day in Illinois to discover that her father had sold the farm and that "as soon as school closes we are to move." Preparations for the trip took up to half a year and families could expect to spend another half a year on the trail.

Not everyone cherished the prospect of the trip with equal pleasure. Women seem to have felt the wrenching separation from family, church, and community, and the hardship of the trail, more keenly than men. Or, what may have been the case, they seem to have recorded those feelings more often than men. But the excitement of moving west was not limited to men. Narcissa Whitman pronounced herself healthier and in better spirits than ever before in her life as she faced the Overland Trail. Migrants kept their spirits up by singing, telling stories, playing games, and picking wildflowers.

Travelers funneled through St. Louis (where they bought supplies), crossed Missouri to rendezvous with wagon trains near St. Joseph or Independence, Missouri, and then followed one of two main routes west. The northern route, known as the Oregon Trail, zigzagged northwest at roughly the 42nd parallel to the Rocky Mountains. Another line of settlers journeyed southwest out of Independence on the Santa Fe Trail, which led along the Arkansas River through the future state of Kansas before heading into Mexican lands. At Santa Fe, the trail divided, feeding im-

Map 13–2 Major Overland Trails The overland trails to the west started at the Missouri River. The Santa Fe Trail was a conduit for traders and goods to Mexico. The Oregon Trail passed through Wyoming and branched off to California and Oregon.

migrants west along the Old Spanish Trail (mapped by Franciscan missionaries) or south to Chihuahua, Mexico.

Most overland migrants traveled in families, in groups of families from the same neighborhood, and occasionally in entire communities. If they did not have team animals, families pulled their possessions in two-wheeled handcarts. But just having wagons did not ensure an easy trip. For the most part, wagons carried supplies, not people. Most migrants walked west. Moreover, wagons broke down, got stuck, turned over, were washed away in river crossings, or had to be emptied to ease the burden on the animals.

After they left the plains, wagon trains sometimes went days without finding water or game. Women as well as men drove the wagons and herded the cattle, collected firewood, and caught small animals for food. When broken equipment or sickness

Westward Migration The overland journey across the plains was slow and difficult at best, but it quickly entered into American legend and became the subject of romanticized images such as this one.

slowed individual families, the trains were often forced to leave them behind, lest the others not clear the Rocky Mountains before winter. The harrowing dangers of that possibility were immortalized in the story of the ill-fated Donner Party, caught in the Sierra Nevada by an early winter. For four months the group was trapped by snow, without sufficient fuel, blankets, or food, slowly starving. When relief finally arrived in mid-February 1847, "the dead were lying about on the snow, some even unburied, since the living had not strength to bury their dead," according to one survivor. Of the 87 persons snowed in, 42 died. It was not a risk worth taking, even if it meant leaving party members behind on the plains.

For migrants who survived the journey west, the rewards were not always immediately apparent. "My most vivid recollection of that first winter in Oregon," one woman recalled, "is of the weeping skies and of Mother and me also weeping." As soon as their homes were built and their fields plowed, though, many of the newcomers were ready to declare Oregon "this best country in the world." The climate was hospitable to crops of wheat, flax, and corn and to apple and pear orchards. Lumber was plentiful, and the streams ran full of fish. Farther south was the "mild and delightful climate of California," an even greater attraction after 1848, when rumors of "inexhaustible" gold strikes began to filter north and east.

Nations of the Trans-Mississippi West

American settlers considered themselves journeying through national territories. Indigenous communities, like Mah-i-ti-wo-nee-ni's friends and family, viewed the settlers as trespassers in Indian country.

Most wagon trains departed from Missouri, which meant that settlers first crossed Indian Territory, where Native Americans had been guaranteed refuge from white intrusion. Between Independence, Missouri, and the Rocky Mountains lay the Indian nations of the prairies and Great Plains: the Blackfoot and Crow to the northwest; the Sioux, Pawnee, Arapaho, and the two great nations from which Mah-i-ti-wo-nee-ni claimed heritage, the Shoshone and the Cheyenne, through the northern and central Plains; and the Kiowa, Apache, Comanche, and Navajo in the Southwest. Along the Pacific were the Yakima, Chinook, Cayuse, and Nez Percé Indians, and to the south, in California, Pomo, Chumash, Yuma, and many other tribes.

Since most of this vast territory was part of Mexico, and since Great Britain laid claim to Oregon, crossing to utopia meant transgressing the boundaries of those nations, as well.

American penny novelists would depict this contact of peoples as a violent confrontation, in which cunning and bellicose Indians swooped down to massacre naive and well-meaning migrants. In fact, of the more than 250,000 settlers who crossed the plains between 1840 and 1860, fewer than 400 were killed by Native Americans. It was about the same number of deaths as those inflicted by white migrants on the Indians.

Prior to the massive migration of the 1840s, official U.S. policy toward the Indians had been one of removal, by force or by pressured sale of lands and physical relocation. Even in the 1830s observers saw no evidence that Americans recognized a boundary short of the Pacific Ocean. Alexis de Tocqueville noted that "when it promises these unlucky people a permanent asylum in the West," the U.S. government "is well aware of its inability to guarantee this." The trans-Mississippi migrations of the middle of the nineteenth century proved the wisdom of Tocqueville's observation.

By the late 1830s, as the last of the eastern "removals" were completed, federal policy toward Indians began to shift. Removal and resettlement continued to be the primary stated goal, and many western tribes were confined to reservations or moved to Indian Territory. But later removals aimed more overtly at relocation culminating in individual ownership of reservation lands rather than tribal ownership. Such interference with the land customs of Indians was, of course, what many Americans had sought for decades, believing that Native Americans should be brought into the "civilized" political economy of the United States through individual ownership of property. Allotment became the official U.S. policy toward all Indians by the end of the century.

By the mid-1830s, when white Americans started crossing the Mississippi River in huge numbers, most of these nations had already tasted the effects of expansionism. The Comanches (the largest of the southwestern nations) and the Apaches had been at war with Euro-Americans for several centuries. They had fought the Spanish, then the Mexicans, and since the 1820s both the Mexicans and the U.S. settlers in Texas. All of the Plains Indians, especially the Sioux, the Kiowas, and the Comanches, had felt the impact of eastern Indians who had been displaced or officially relocated west. The Sioux, for example, had been at war for decades with the Indians of the old Northwest Territory, who were being pushed across the Mississippi River by white settlers, the militias, and the U.S. Army.

For the western Indians, the effects of the migration of the 1840s were social, cultural, and economic. Although the number of deaths from warfare was low, deaths from disease were far higher. Epidemics took especially high tolls on the children and the old, wiping out both the elders who carried a community's history and collective wisdom and the young people who represented its future. Under demographic stress, native communities confronted missionaries, new forms of medicine, new codes of behavior, new forms of knowledge, and new goods such as guns and alcohol.

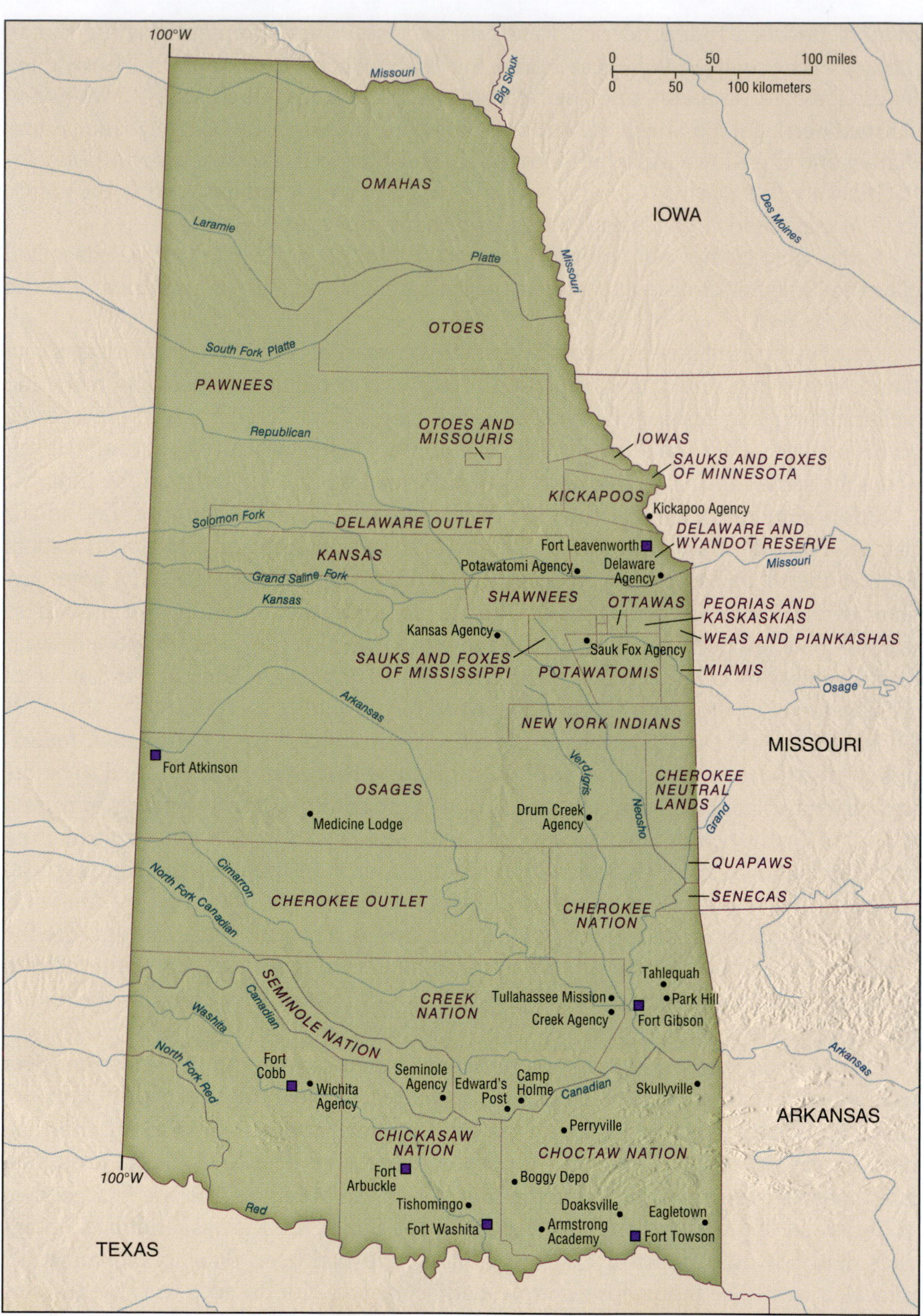

Map 13–3 Major Trans-Mississippi Indian Communities, ca. 1850 Most of the Indians living in the Indian Territories in the 1830s and 1840s had been "removed" from areas east of the Mississippi River. The territories were located west of Arkansas, Missouri, and Iowa. The section to the south (now Oklahoma) was home to Cherokees, Choctaws, Creeks, and Seminoles from the Old Southwest. The northern part (now Kansas and Nebraska) was inhabited by Indians from the Old Northwest.

Contact gradually altered the Indians' social organization and gender division of labor. As it became harder to claim and protect planting grounds, tribes shifted from semiagricultural to more nomadic ways of life. The relative importance of women's foraging and planting diminished, and the relative importance of men's skills as hunters and warriors increased.

By 1840, the northern grasslands and southern plains supported a complex economy of hunting and foraging. The Indians consumed corn, melons, berries, wild sweet potatoes, turnips, and fowl and small game, harvested in a seminomadic way of life, and traded through networks that ran north to south. At the center of this economy stood the bison, supplying not only food but also material for clothing, shelter, and trade.

This way of life was threatened as the bison declined in number. Settlers' need for food had only a minor impact on the buffalo. More deadly was their fascination with hunting and killing such a huge creature, regardless of whether they needed its meat and hides. Recreational hunting parties, as well as bands of hunters intent on wiping out the Indian communities' means of support, took their toll. By 1848, Thomas A. Harvey, western superintendent of Indian affairs, was warning of the inevitable effects of "the immense traveling of emigrant companies over the prairies, and the consequent increased destruction of buffalo."

As early as 1842 and 1843 the Teton Sioux had complained to federal Indian agents that the heavy migrations were harming their hunting grounds. By 1846 the Sioux were demanding that the U.S. government stem the migrations and prevent the migrants from killing animals indiscriminately. When the government ignored the complaints, the Sioux prevented wagon trains from passing until migrants had paid a

Comanche Village In 1834–1835, western artist George Catlin observed the importance of the buffalo to Plains Indians. Here he depicted Comanche women dressing buffalo robes and drying buffalo meat. Notice the presence of horses in the village, a sign of European influence on western Indian life.

toll in money, tobacco, or supplies. Indignant overland travelers criticized the federal government for coddling the Indians and demanded that the trails be reopened.

In the mid-1840s the energies of the federal government were primarily engaged in Texas, where American nationalists were demanding action against Mexico. In the northern plains, the government constructed a chain of forts across the West. These forts were intended as quarters for armed rifle units called dragoons, who would, theoretically, drive the Indians back from intimidating the overland migrants. The strategy was not very effective. During the late 1840s, the Indians continued to exert control over white migration through northern Indian Country.

Slavery and the Political Economy of Expansion

Even as individual Americans poured west, expansion became a source of controversy within the collective politics of the nation. The problem was not the principle of manifest destiny, a principle that few politicians questioned. By the late 1830s, expansion was linked in the public debate with the extension of slavery. That subject, controversial in itself, raised other problems. Southerners viewed northerners as unfaithful to a 50-year-old compromise ratified in the Constitution. Northerners looked with envy on the wealth of the new Southwest (Louisiana, Mississippi, Alabama, and Arkansas) and worried about the political leverage of a new slave state the size of Texas.

> What then ought we to do? Ought we not to move immediately for the admission of Texas into the Union as a slave holding State? Should not the South **demand** it, as indispensable to their security: In my opinion, we have no alternative. To admit Texas as a non-slaveholding State, or to permit her to remain an independent and sovereign non-slave holding state, will be fatal to the Union, and ruinous to the whole country. . . . To the South, it is a question of **safety**; to the North it is one of interest . . . . Would it not be well to break the subject to the people of the South through the public prints? Both parties may unite in that, for it is a **Southern** question, and not one of whiggism and democracy.
>
> ABEL UPSHUR TO JOHN C. CALHOUN, August 14, 1843

Log Cabins and Hard Cider: The Election of 1840

As they approached the election of 1840, the major parties were engaged in a balancing act. Both hoped to exploit certain aspects of regional difference, but without raising the divisive issues associated with slavery. Whigs considered Van Buren vulnerable, both because the nation still languished under the effects of the Depression of 1837 and because he was a northerner who seemed to be blocking the annexation of Texas. Henry Clay, leader of the Whigs, opposed the annexation of Texas, but he calculated that southern Democrats would choose a Kentuckian over a New Yorker. Aware of Van Buren's liabilities in the South, Democrats were eager to keep slavery out of the debates, although Van Buren was willing to have northerners see him as the alternative to a southern president. A number of northern Whigs were suspicious of Clay's ties to the South.

In fact, slavery haunted the election. In June 1839 the USS *Washington* had intercepted the ship *Amistad* in American coastal waters. Although the ship was Spanish owned, it was under the control of its cargo of kidnapped Africans, who were attempting to sail it home to Sierra Leone. Tricked by the ship's pilot, they had sailed instead into Long Island Sound. Almost immediately the case became the center of heated controversy, as pro- and antislavery forces argued over whether the Africans should be returned to slavery. Ultimately the case reached the U.S. Supreme Court, where John Quincy Adams agreed to argue the case for the captives. He would insist that because the international slave trade was illegal in the United States, the Africans must be returned to their homes.

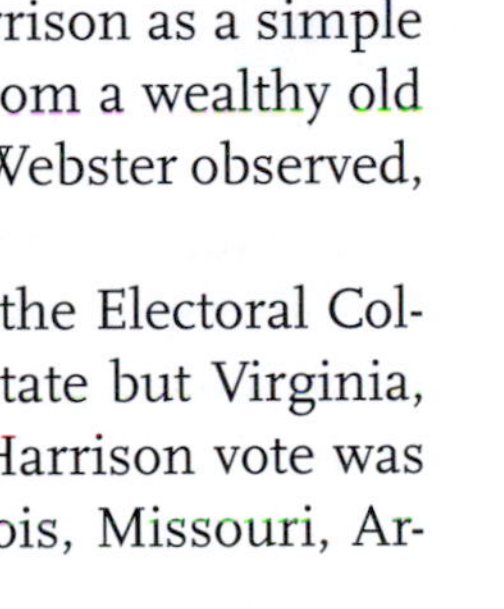

Meanwhile, the election went forward. As anticipated, Van Buren received the Democratic nomination, but in an effort to skirt the explosive sectional issues, the Whigs turned to William Henry Harrison, an outspoken advocate of cheap western land and the hero of the battle of Tippecanoe. Harrison was the candidate, out of the crowded 1836 Whig field, who had run strongest against Van Buren. To bolster the broad appeal of their slate, for their vice presidential candidate the Whigs chose a former Democrat, John Tyler of Virginia, a strong advocate of states' rights, and (at the time) a Clay supporter.

Harrison was a "sentimental" candidate. Through him, the Whigs hoped to evoke feelings of military glory and westward expansion. Studiously avoiding tough issues, they threw their energy instead into crafting a Jackson-like campaign for "Tippecanoe and Tyler, too." When a newspaper editor derided Harrison as a country bumpkin whose highest aspiration in life consisted of sitting on his porch drinking cider, the Whigs took up the image with gusto. In what came to be known as the "Log Cabin and Hard Cider Campaign," the Whigs celebrated Harrison as a simple man of the people (like Jackson). In point of fact, Harrison was from a wealthy old Virginia family. But he could be linked to the West, and, as Daniel Webster observed, Harrison's main appeal was the vague "hope of a better time."

The turnout was large and the popular results were close, but the Electoral College was a different story. Harrison, who had taken every large state but Virginia, triumphed with 234 electoral votes to Van Buren's 60. The anti-Harrison vote was suggestive, however. The Democrats held New Hampshire, Illinois, Missouri, Arkansas, Alabama, Virginia, and South Carolina.

On March 9, 1841, just five days after Harrison took the oath of office, the Supreme Court announced its decision in the *Amistad* case. Speaking for the court, Justice Joseph Story—a longtime opponent of slavery—declared that those on board

Table 13–1 The Liberty Party Swings an Election

Candidate	Party	Actual Vote in New York	National Electoral Vote	If Liberty Voters Had Voted Whig	Projected Electoral Vote
Polk	Democratic	237,588	170	237,588	134
Clay	Whig	232,482	105	248,294	141
Birney	Liberty	15,812	0	—	—

the *Amistad* were "kidnapped Africans, who by the laws of Spain itself were entitled to their freedom." The *Amistad* quickly became a cause celebre among abolitionists, but the impact of the case went beyond activist circles. Heavy newspaper coverage aroused the sympathy even of moderate opponents of slavery, again broadening the antislavery debate and increasing interest in the new Liberty Party.

And Tyler, Too

Whig jubilation at their presidential victory was short lived. Harrison became ill shortly after his inauguration and died on April 4, 1841, the first president to die in office. Harrison was followed in office by his vice president, John Tyler. Most observers assumed that Tyler would function as a caretaker president until the next general election. He soon proved them wrong, setting the precedent for vice presidents to succeed to the full stature and authority of the presidency.

Tyler's ascendancy threw the Whig Party into chaos, for once in office he reverted to his Democratic roots. There was much about Tyler that was reminiscent of Jackson. Not only did he oppose the American System and favor slavery and the annexation of Texas, but, also like Jackson, Tyler was willing to use the full power of the executive to enforce those views. Unlike Jackson in office, Tyler was an enthusiastic advocate of extreme southern states' rights positions.

Tyler's attention was first drawn to diplomatic troubles with Britain. In 1841 the slave crew of the U.S. ship *Creole,* en route from Virginia to New Orleans, had seized control of the vessel and forced it into the port of Nassau, where, by British law, the crew was freed. To no avail, white southerners demanded the return of the crew. Meanwhile, northern anti-British feeling flared over the question of the Oregon Territory, a vaguely defined expanse between northern California and Alaska that Britain and the United States had agreed in 1818 to occupy jointly. By 1842, reports of the North American Pacific Coast as a veritable "storehouse of wealth in all its forests, furs, and fisheries" had stimulated immigration and stirred American desire to claim the Oregon Territory.

In 1842 U.S. Secretary of State Webster and British emissary Ashburton concluded negotiations on the Webster-Ashburton Treaty, which drew a northern boundary between the United States and Canada from Maine to the Rocky Mountains (Oregon was left undivided), established terms of extradition between the two nations, and created a joint effort to restrict the international slave trade. Great Britain also agreed not to interfere with foreign vessels.

Tyler's success in foreign relations was overshadowed by his 1841 break with his own party. Led by Henry Clay, Whigs in Congress succeeded in passing legislation that embodied the Whig platform, including various tariff bills, a national bank bill, and a bill to distribute federal surpluses to states. Tyler vetoed almost every initiative. He denounced federal distribution as inappropriate when the federal government was in deficit. At last, in 1842, Congressional Whigs offered lower tariff increases than Clay wished and detached the tariff from the question of distribution. Citing the need for federal funds, Tyler signed the bill. Tyler supported the repeal of the independent treasury, a Whig goal, but this, too, proved a bitter victory for Clay and the Whig Party, because Tyler vetoed the national bank with which the Whigs wanted to replace the independent treasury.

Tyler soon found himself a president without a party. As early as January 1843, there were calls in the House of Representatives for his impeachment. That year, when Tyler vetoed the bill rechartering the national bank, his entire cabinet resigned, except Webster.

"His Accidency," as opponents dubbed Tyler, proved more resilient than Clay anticipated. Tyler interpreted Democratic gains in the 1842 elections as support for his positions, particularly on the national bank. Urged on by extreme states' rights advocates in Virginia and South Carolina, Tyler took up the cause of the annexation of Texas. After Daniel Webster resigned from the cabinet in the spring of 1843, Tyler fell almost entirely under the influence of southerners who were committed to Texas.

Texas did everything in its power to make annexation an urgent issue. It allowed Great Britain to serve as an intermediary in Texas's efforts to win official recognition from Mexico and hinted that, as an independent republic, Texas might abolish slavery. The idea of an alliance between Texas and Great Britain reawakened old anti-British sentiments in the United States. In addition, the prospect of a non–slave republic so close to their borders filled southerners with dread.

Seeking to capitalize on these anxieties, in 1843 President Tyler secretly opened negotiations with Texas for admission to the Union, expecting to justify the completed treaty as necessary to protect the United States against British influence. In 1844, Tyler submitted a treaty of annexation to Congress. He hoped that the potential for controversy would be buried in American expansionist interests. He was wrong. Even before the treaty was submitted, John Quincy Adams and 12 other Whigs denounced it as constitutionally unauthorized and warned that it would bring the nation to "dissolution." Abolitionists labeled the move a naked power grab by slave owners. Even moderate northerners worried that annexing Texas would cause war with Mexico, consuming taxes and killing soldiers without yielding the North any tangible gains. Some southerners worried that Texas would compete with the depleted lands of the South, harming cotton and sugar profits.

By then, other election-year dramas were afoot. John Calhoun still longed for the presidency. He believed that he had a reasonable chance against Tyler, another southerner, if he could deny Van Buren the Democratic nomination. To that end, Calhoun wrote a note to the British minister that the U.S. goal in Texas was to protect slavery against British abolitionists. As Calhoun hoped, the note became public. The explicit association of Texas and slavery drove Van Buren away from endorsing the treaty, an act that might have made him a stronger candidate in the South. An overwhelmingly sectional vote defeated the treaty in Congress, but Calhoun believed a Democratic victory in 1844 would revive it.

Occupy Oregon, Annex Texas

By the fall of 1844 the American political party system was in disarray. Harrison's impressive victory in 1840 had not signaled a broad endorsement of Clay or the American System, any more than Van Buren's victory in 1836 had signaled a strong hard-money, antibank sentiment. To the contrary, between 1836 and 1844 the party system seemed most successful at polarizing American interests.

Nowhere was that state of affairs more evident than in the 1844 Democratic convention in Baltimore. Van Buren's supporters believed that the party owed him the nomination, yet his liabilities were legion. In the South, proslavery, proannexation Democrats led by Calhoun were vowing to have "a slaveholder for President next time regardless of the man." Andrew Jackson was disappointed with Van Buren's refusal to endorse annexation and encouraged former Tennessee governor James K. Polk to run. In the North, workers and entrepreneurs who had been hard hit by years of deflation were disenchanted with the "Little Magician." Van Burenites were unable to block a convention rule requiring a candidate to receive a two-thirds vote to secure the nomination. Van Buren could not marshal that level of support, but neither could Tyler, Calhoun, or Lewis Cass, a compromise candidate. Finally, on the eighth ballot the convention fell back on Jackson's choice, James Polk. Tyler accepted renomination by a renegade group of supporters, also meeting in Baltimore, who styled themselves Democratic Republicans.

The 1844 Democratic Party ran on the platform of manifest destiny, calling (in language reminiscent of the Missouri Compromise) for "the reoccupation of Oregon and the reannexation of Texas." It was an odd formulation, given that the United States had several times officially denied possession of Texas and had yet to occupy Oregon fully. The platform went even further on Oregon. Although the U.S. claim to Oregon had never extended beyond the 49th parallel, the Democrats now declared their willingness to go to war to gain the entire region ("Fifty-four forty or fight!"). Their bellicose strategy incorporated war fears over Texas into a broader assertion of national destiny.

Meanwhile, in 1844 Henry Clay at long last secured the Whig nomination. Clay was certain that opposition to the extension of slavery was too strong to tolerate a Texas-Oregon compromise and that Americans would not support a war with Mexico. Clay ran primarily as a supporter of the American System as the necessary means for stabilizing economic growth.

The election results suggested a nation teetering on the edge of political division. Polk, annexation, and manifest destiny won, but by only 38,000 of more than 2.5 million votes cast. More striking, James G. Birney of Ohio, the candidate of the new, explicitly antislavery Liberty Party, drew 62,000 votes, most of them from Clay. Had Birney not run, the election might have been a dead heat.

Nevertheless, both Tyler and Congress read the election as a referendum on the Democratic platform and specifically on Texas. Early in 1845, with Tyler still in office, a bill approving annexation passed the House. To move it through the Whig-dominated Senate, Senator Robert Walker of Mississippi suggested the Senate version include the option of negotiating a whole new treaty. Only days away from the presidency, Polk was said to favor this approach, and Whigs thought a revised treaty might better address their objections and get them out of a politically costly position. With the appended option, the Senate approved the treaty. The Whigs expected Tyler to concede the decision to the incoming president, but in the last hours of his presidency he sent notice to Texas that (contingent on its own agreement) the republic was annexed to the United States of America. Mexico immediately severed relations with the United States.

Table 13–2 Personal Income Per Capita by Region: Percentages of United States Average

	1840	1860	1880
United States	100	100	100
Northeast	135	139	141
North Central	68	68	98
South	76	72	51
West	—	—	190

Note: Source: Richard A. Easterlin, "Regional Income Trends, 1840–1950," in Seymour E. Harris (ed.), *American Economic History* (New York; McGraw-Hill, 1961), p. 528.

War with Mexico

The annexation of Texas was the ostensible cause of the outbreak of war with Mexico in April 1846, but

Texas was only a partial explanation for the war. In Polk's eyes, the annexation of Texas was a piece of a larger acquisition: not only Oregon but also present-day New Mexico, Arizona, and California. Certainly, Polk would have been happy to make these acquisitions peacefully, but he was willing to go to war.

Polk's two-track approach to foreign relations soon became evident. In December 1845 he announced his decision to withdraw from negotiations over Oregon, and he called on Congress to terminate the United States–Great Britain Convention of Joint Occupancy. Compromise would constitute an abandonment of American "territorial rights . . . and the national honour," he insisted, and could never be entertained. Polk's rhetoric was more threatening than his intentions: he simultaneously informed his advisors that he was prepared to hear a compromise offer from England. When one came, proposing a boundary at the 49th parallel, Polk submitted it to Congress. By June 1846 the deal had been struck.

In Oregon, Polk threatened war but quickly accepted peace. Thomas Hart Benton later suggested that appearance and intent were reversed in the Mexican borderlands. What Polk really wanted there, Benton claimed, was "a little war," big enough to justify grabbing the Southwest but not so big as to break the budget. Texas provided the excuse.

As a condition of his surrender and release, the Mexican General Santa Anna had agreed to the Rio Grande as the boundary between Texas and Mexico, a boundary that would have run northward to include present-day New Mexico as well as western Texas. The Mexican government had instead drawn the border at the Nueces River, recognizing only about half the territory claimed by Texans. Polk intended to set the boundary at the Rio Grande, and he may have intended to secure not only the disputed Texas territory but also large portions of northern Mexico.

To achieve these aims, he once again played a double game. As late as September, Polk appealed for a peaceful resolution. That month, he dispatched former Louisiana congressman John Slidell to Mexico to offer to purchase New Mexico and Texas for $30 million. The Mexican government refused to receive Slidell.

Meanwhile, Polk prepared for war. In the spring of 1845 he had sent 1,500 soldiers, under the command of General Zachary Taylor, allegedly to protect Texas against a possible invasion by Mexico. When Texas approved union with the United States, Polk reinforced Taylor's troops and ordered them to approach the Rio Grande, while also sending an army under Stephen Kearny into the northern part of the disputed territory. In August 1846, Kearny occupied Santa Fe. At the same time, Polk ordered the U.S. squadron in the Pacific closer to the California coast and directed the U.S. consul in California, Thomas Larkin, to encourage local disaffection with the Mexican government. When American settlers in the Sonoma Valley staged a rebellion in June and July, the representatives of the United States claimed California. Kearny later crossed into California to solidify the claim.

By that time, Polk's brinkmanship on the Rio Grande had produced results. Mexican troops had crossed the river to drive out Taylor's force, and American soldiers had been killed and wounded. In May 1846, Congress declared that "by the act of the Republic of Mexico, a state of war exists" between the two nations.

The United States entered the war unprepared. Although 100,000 volunteers signed up, at the outbreak of hostilities the United States Army had only 7,500 troops. Perhaps Polk shared the widely held expansionist view that Mexico was a "miserable, inefficient" nation. Mexico (and New Spain before it) had always been less interested in its northern provinces than in other parts of the nation. Moreover,

AMERICA AND THE WORLD

>> Lt. Rankin Dilworth in the War with Mexico

Rankin Dilworth was only 18 years old when he entered the United States Military Academy at West Point. Dilworth's father had died some time earlier. Although his mother had remarried, she was apparently a widow again by the time her son applied to the academy. Dilworth described himself as having to "depend upon my own resources," and he may well have seen the army as his one opportunity to get ahead in life. Dilworth was apparently an average cadet, graduating in the middle of his class in 1844, one year behind Ulysses S. Grant, future general of the Union army and president of the United States. But in 1844 neither Grant nor Dilworth was contemplating duty in a civil war. If young Dilworth had his sights fixed on any particular arena of service, it was surely the West, where American territorial ambitions were suddenly creating opportunities for military advancement.

By the spring of 1846, those opportunities were near at hand. Barracked outside of St. Louis, Dilworth's company was ordered in April to southern Texas, where hostilities had already broken out between United States troops and the Mexican army. During the coming weeks they traveled by boat down the Mississippi and by steamer across the Gulf of Mexico to Matamoros, Mexico. From there, they marched up the Rio Grande to Carmargo, Texas, where Dilworth's unit joined with the American expeditionary force under General Zachary Taylor. From Carmargo, the combined force proceeded to Monterrey. From April 28 to September 19, 1846, Dilworth kept an almost daily record of that journey.

The diary suggests that, officer or not, Dilworth was shadowed by nostalgia for home. Viewing the beautiful church in Reynosa made him wonder "if I will ever go to church again where I hear the English language spoken." That night, he dreamed he was in church at home "without a thought of camps or bivouacs, with smiling happy faces around me." Suddenly awakened by the call to guard duty, "in an instant," he wrote, "I found myself on the hot sandy plaza of Reynosa, many, many miles from those I love."

Still, 24 years old and as interested in adventure as in military exploits, Dilworth found much to occupy his attention in the journey south. Especially early in the trip, there were cotillions and elaborate officers' messes. Dilworth also took a keen interest in Mexico. Often waxing romantic, he compared Mexico to "a magnificent flower garden" dotted with plots of "limes, oranges, lemons, [and] pomegranates." He admired young Mexican women, one of whom he declared "the handsomest female that I have seen since I parted with E. M. M." (his sweetheart back East). Dilworth's descriptions of Mexico were not all flattering, however, and he sometimes betrayed the flippant cultural superiority that was so much a part of American expansionism of the 1840s. "The inhabitants present all shades from pure Indian to the white person," he wrote on one occasion. "Their intelligence is in the same scale."

Although Rankin Dilworth enjoyed aspects of the journey south, his diary also recorded the daily, and sometimes needless, hardships that plagued the campaign and would eventually make it infamous in army annals. Swollen with untrained volunteers and newly trained officers (like Dilworth himself), the Mexican campaign was a tutorial in bad luck and bad judgment. Dilworth wrote about tents that collapsed in violent rainstorms, marches through mud so thick that it added 10 pounds to the weight of each boot, and temperatures so hot that soldiers died of heat prostration. He wrote of arrogant and inept officers who could not even march their troops in the right direction. "Some persons occasionally make blunders," he noted, "but others are constantly making them."

On September 19, as his company approached Monterrey, Dilworth encountered an old friend in a different unit. The friend asked Dilworth if he had "heard the 'Elephant' groan," an expression that had by that time become common among the troops to express their bitterness and disappointment. Dilworth did not record his reply. Nor did he add any further entries in the diary. On September 21, General Taylor ordered a dangerous assault on Monterrey, dividing his small band of volunteers and inexperienced professionals into two groups to attack the city from opposite sides. The western troops gained their goals with relative ease, but the eastern forces lost their way in thick cane fields, arriving at the city on heavily fortressed roads where they were caught in deadly Mexican crossfire. Once in the city's narrow streets, they were easy targets for sharpshooters stationed in houses and along rooftops. Remarkably, inch by inch, house by house (often blasting their way through common walls by cannon rather than exposing themselves to sure death on the streets), Taylor's troops carried the day. On September 24, 1846, Mexican general Ampudia offered surrender.

None of this mattered to Rankin Dilworth. During the first day's assault a "twelve-pounder cannon ball" had torn off one of his legs. On September 27, at 24 years of age, he died. His family was unable to pay the costs of having his body returned to Ohio. Lieutenant Rankin Dilworth was buried in Monterrey, Mexico.

the Mexican government had recently undergone a coup and remained unstable. With California guarded by John C. Frémont and the naval squadron, the United States could bring its military power to bear on Mexico City.

Finding the right leader for such a campaign proved tricky. Taylor, the obvious choice, was a Whig of growing popularity. Polk finally settled on Winfield Scott, who also harbored Whig political ambitions. In the late winter of 1847, a naval squadron of 200 ships conveyed Scott's army through the Gulf of Mexico to Veracruz, where his army of 10,000 soldiers forced that city to surrender in April. Scott's troops

Chapultepec Carl Nebel's depiction of the American attack on the Chapultepec fort, near Mexico City, during the Mexican-American War, September 13, 1847.

fought their way to the outskirts of Mexico City. Scott began his final assault on September 8, and on September 14 Mexico City fell.

For all the military brilliance of the American campaign, support for the war steadily eroded. From the beginning, the war raised the question of slavery. Northern Democrats saw the war with Mexico as a transparent ploy to extend slavery. Northern antislavery activists spoke out against the war, and opposition grew as stories of U.S. military atrocities filtered back east.

In spite of the unpopularity of the war, the end of hostilities found Mexico so weak that Polk and his advisors thought of extracting greater concessions. His minister in Mexico, Nicholas P. Trist, opposed this proposal, however. In 1848 Trist negotiated the Treaty of Guadalupe Hidalgo, recognizing the Rio Grande as the border of Texas and granting the United States the territory encompassed in the present states of New Mexico, Arizona, Colorado, Utah, and Wyoming, as well as California. In return, the United States paid Mexico $15 million and assumed war claims of American citizens against Mexico. The Senate approved the treaty on March 10, 1848. The following May 25, Mexico concurred.

Map 13–4 Mexican War General Zachary Taylor's victories in northern Mexico established the Rio Grande as the boundary between Texas and Mexico. Stephen Kearny's expedition secured control of New Mexico. General Winfield Scott's invasion by sea at Veracruz and his occupation of Mexico ended the war.

Although Polk's presidency was dominated by the war with Mexico, the tariff and the independent treasury continued to haunt domestic politics. In each case, Polk was victorious. Like Jackson, Polk opposed protective tariffs, which he saw as benefiting industrialists at the expense of farmers and republican values. Although Whigs in Congress pushed for higher tariffs to support domestic manufacturing, the 1846 tariff eliminated flat duties and revised overall levels downward. Also like Jackson, Polk opposed the national bank. In 1846 he persuaded Congress to reinstate Van Buren's independent treasury to handle the federal government's financial transactions. Meanwhile, he vetoed Whig attempts to enact legislation supporting internal improvements.

The similarities between Jackson and Polk extended to their broader understanding of politics and to the way in which they used the political machinery. Like Jackson, Polk framed policy battles as battles between good and evil, between individual opportunity and elite finance and capital. At the same time, also like Jackson, Polk exercised executive power as the tool of the people's will. He was convinced that the president, not the legislature (Whig controlled by his final years in office) represented the people's will. Before he left office, virtually every important item on his political agenda had been accomplished. Lost for the moment in that flush of victory was the steady erosion of popular support for the Democratic Party.

Conclusion

In 1820, Fanny Wright noted that many observers worried about the differences between the American North and South, but Wright was buoyantly optimistic. If all else failed, she declared, the western states, settled by migrants from both North and South, would always be "powerful cementers of the Union."

By the end of the 1840s, it was clear that Wright's confidence had been misplaced. The war with Mexico revealed just how far apart the North and South had grown. By 1848, the northern tier of states was deeply implicated in a political economy of free labor. The southern states, meanwhile, had grown ever more committed to the political economy of slavery. The Mexican War signaled the beginning of an era in which differences between the North and South would seem undeniable and intractable—and symbolized in the West.

In 1848, Henry David Thoreau mounted a lecture platform in Concord, Massachusetts, to explain his refusal to pay poll taxes, which he considered money paid to support the institution of slavery and its expansion in the war with Mexico. Thoreau declared himself ready to separate from his government—indeed, to see the Union itself destroyed—rather than support the United States in the West. Thoreau's words were fateful: "How does it become a man to behave toward this American government today?" he asked. "I answer, that he cannot without disgrace be associated with it. I cannot for an instant recognize that political organization as my government which is the slave's government also."

Further Readings

John Mack Faragher, *Women and Men on the Overland Trail* (1979). Faragher describes the migration of white Americans into Oregon Territory in the 1840s through the 1860s, including discussions of motivations that prompted families to undertake the trek, the preparations required for the journey, the routes taken, the obstacles faced, and the ways in which the experience of westering differed for women and men.

Jonathan Earle, *Jacksonian Antislavery and the Politics of Free Soil* (2004). Earle's book is an innovative blend of social and political history that traces one of the roots of antislavery politics back to the Jacksonian critique of the "money power."

Reginald Horsman, *Race and Manifest Destiny: The Origins of American Racial Anglo-Saxonism* (1981). Horsman traces the ascendancy of ideas of racial superiority throughout the antebellum years, examining both the presence of racial thinking in broad currents of American culture and the ways in which those intellectual perspectives shaped the politics of westward expansion.

James M. McCaffrey, *Army of Manifest Destiny: The American Soldier in the Mexican War, 1846–1848* (1992). This brief study of the largely volunteer American army of the Mexican War furnishes useful insights into the high politics, the broad military strategies, and the daily experience of common soldiers in Polk's war of expansion against Mexico in 1846.

Sean Wilentz, *The Rise of American Democracy: Jefferson to Lincoln* (2005; College Edition, 2008). No other study goes as far as Wilentz's to put the politics of slavery at the center of the political history of the period.

>> Timeline >>

▼ 1834

First missionaries arrive in Oregon Territory

▼ 1836

Martin Van Buren elected president

Equal Rights Party formed

Whig Party runs candidates for president

Texas declares independence

▼ 1838

"Aroostook" War

Anti-Slavery Petition campaign at height

▼ 1839

Amistad mutiny

▼ 1840

Independent Treasury Bill

Anti-Slavery Society splits

Liberty Party nominates James Birney for the presidency

Large-scale overland migration to West Coast begins

Whig candidate William Henry Harrison elected president

Who, What

Mah-i-ti-wo-nee-ni 433
Henry Clay 435
Tejanos 443
John Tyler 454
Panic of 1837 437
Manifest Destiny 439
The Republic of Texas 445

Review Questions

1. What was the depression of 1837 and what were its origins?
2. Why were Whigs cautious about westward migration?
3. Why was the annexation of Texas so controversial?
4. Did the territorial additions of the 1840s represent a departure (in method or intent) from earlier acquisitions?

For further review materials and resource information, please visit www.oup.com/us/ofthepeople

▼ 1841
John Tyler succeeds Harrison in office
Creole Mutiny

▼ 1842
Webster-Ashburton Treaty

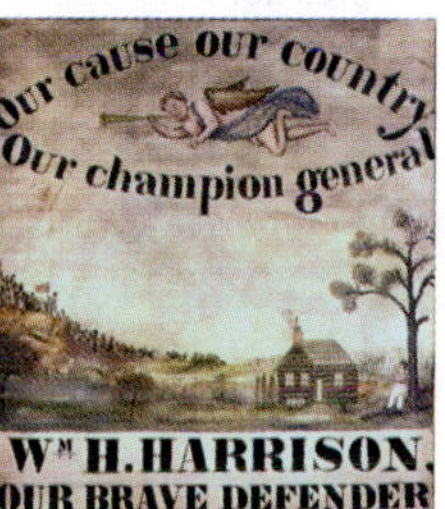

▼ 1844
James Polk is elected president

▼ 1845
The United States annexes Texas

▼ 1846
The United States declares war on Mexico

▼ 1848
Independent women's rights movement begins at Seneca Falls, New York
Treaty of Guadalupe Hidalgo
Teton Sioux tax white settlers passing through their lands

CHAPTER 14

Common Threads

>> In previous chapters you read about the development of the American economy and the expansion of slavery. Notice the ways in which these developments became sources of tension between the North and South during the 1850s.

>> The conflict between Whigs and Democrats during the 1830s and 1840s is sometimes called "the first party system." How did this change in the 1850s?

>> Do you think that by 1860 the Civil War was "irrepressible?"

The Politics of Slavery

1848–1860

AMERICAN PORTRAIT

>> Frederick Douglass

Frederick Douglass denounced the war with Mexico as "disgraceful, cruel, and iniquitous." Northern support for what he saw as a slaveholders' war reinforced Douglass's conviction that the U.S. Constitution had created an unholy union of liberty and slavery. The only solution was for New England to secede. "The Union must be dissolved," Douglass wrote, "or New England is lost and swallowed up by the slave-power of the country."

Douglass had been urging disunion for several years, ever since he became the most compelling antislavery voice in America. His authority derived from his extraordinary intelligence, his exceptional skill as a public speaker, and above all from his personal experience. Frederick Douglass was not simply an abolitionist, he was also the most famous runaway slave in America.

He was born Frederick Augustus Washington Bailey, in Talbot County, Maryland, in 1818. At the age of seven he was sent to Baltimore, where he became a skilled caulker working in the shipyards. There he hired out his labor, paying his master three dollars each week and keeping the rest himself. And there, in Baltimore, he grew to resent the arrangement. For the rest of his life he would associate freedom with the right to earn a living. When Frederick's master revoked their arrangement and demanded that the slave hand over all his earnings, Frederick planned his escape.

On May 3, 1838, Frederick Bailey dressed up as a sailor and boarded a northbound train using a friend's borrowed papers. By September he was calling himself Frederick Douglass and was living and working in New Bedford, Massachusetts, where he began attending antislavery meetings. He subscribed to William Lloyd Garrison's fiery abolitionist newspaper, *The Liberator*. In 1841 he was invited to speak during an abolitionist convention and stunned his listeners with an eloquent recital of his experience as a slave. Garrison himself was in the audience, and he invited Douglass to speak for the American Anti-Slavery Society. For the next several years Douglass was a leading spokesman for the Garrisonian wing of the abolitionist movement.

The Garrisonians concluded that the Constitution was hopelessly corrupted by its compromises with slavery. They saw no point in pursuing political reforms; instead, they advocated the separation of the North from the South. The Garrisonians rejected all violent efforts to overthrow slavery, including slave rebellion. Their preferred solution was moral persuasion of their opponents. Frederick Douglass initially believed all of these things.

The Mexican War was a turning point in Douglass's thinking. By the late 1840s, he saw growing numbers of northerners join the Free-Soil Party, dedicated to halting the expansion of slavery, and he wondered why this could not become a political coalition against slavery itself. During the 1850s Douglass moved further from the Garrisonians: he openly supported slave rebellion, realized that political action was necessary to eliminate slavery, and came to doubt the wisdom of dismissing the Constitution as a proslavery document.

Douglass moved closer to the mainstream of northern politics because antislavery sentiment had reentered the mainstream. Ever since the 1820s, the major parties had studiously avoided the topic of slavery. All attempts to break the silence were met with a hail of racist invective. But the annexation of Texas in the 1830s spurred some abolitionists to push slavery back into national politics, first by flooding the South with antislavery literature, then by inundating Congress with antislavery petitions, and finally by organizing a Liberty Party dedicated to halting slavery's expansion—

continued

>> AMERICAN PORTRAIT *continued*

a position known as "free soil." By 1848 a Free Soil Party was attracting hundreds of thousands of votes.

Even as Garrison and his followers were urging withdrawal from politics, other abolitionists were successfully shoving antislavery back into the political mainstream. By the middle of the 1850s the Whig Party collapsed in the North and in its place emerged the new Republican Party, openly hostile to slavery and sworn to restricting its expansion. Shortly thereafter the Democratic Party split into northern and southern wings. For the first time in American history the political mainstream could accommodate a radical abolitionist like Frederick Douglass, so Douglass moved to the mainstream. By 1861 he was urging the president to uphold the Constitution by suppressing the South's attempt to secede.

OUTLINE 

The Political Economy of Freedom and Slavery

The politics of slavery reemerged at a moment of tremendous economic growth. As the depression of the 1840s lifted, the American zeal for internal improvements revived. The canals that had been constructed between 1800 and 1830 were systematically widened during the 1840s and 1850s to accommodate the new steamboats. Railroad construction, which had collapsed during the depressed 1840s, came back stronger than ever in the 1850s. On the eve of the Civil War, the United States boasted more miles of railroad track than the rest of the world combined. No less spectacular was the rapid adoption of the telegraph. Invented by Samuel F. B. Morse in 1844, the telegraph made it possible for two human beings separated by oceans and continents to sustain virtually instantaneous communication. By 1860, there were 50,000 miles of telegraph wire in America. The first transcontinental line was completed in 1861.

These developments tied all Americans together and so might have inhibited the growth of sectionalism. An efficient transportation and communication network helped integrate the United States into a single national market. But market integration only tied together two different societies based on two very different systems of labor. By the 1850s the differences between North and South overwhelmed the connections that bound them together.

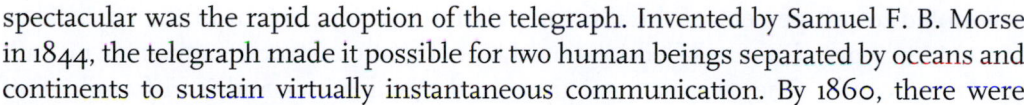

> **Without firing a gun, without drawing a sword, when they [Northerners] make war upon us [Southerners] we can bring the whole world to our feet . . . What would happen if no cotton was furnished for three years? . . . England would topple headlong and carry the whole civilized world with her. No, sir, you dare not make war on cotton. No power on earth dares make war upon it. Cotton is king.**
>
> SENATOR JAMES HENRY HAMMOND,
> South Carolina, 1858

A Changing Economy in the North

The 1850s were booming years for northern farmers. Few rural communities in the North were untouched by the national market. It took less than a week to transport meat and grains from midwestern cities to the East Coast. Because of the dramatic reduction in the cost of transporting commodities, northern farmers could devote more time and effort to producing crops for sale rather than for subsistence at home. Inventions like the steel plow, seed drills, and the McCormick reaper allowed northern farmers to increase their production of goods for market. Between 1820 and 1860 northern farmers quadrupled their productivity.

Farmers could grow more crops for sale because more Americans were living in cities and working for wages. Wage earners produced little of their own food, clothing, or shelter. Yet so productive was American agriculture that the proportion of farmers declined. In 1820, 75 percent of the labor force was devoted to agriculture. By 1860 the figure had dropped to 57 percent. The growth of wage labor in the North was so rapid that native-born workers could not fill the demand for labor in the cities and factories. In the mid-1840s the number of Europeans coming to the United States jumped sharply, and 3 million arrived in the single decade between 1845 and 1854. More than two-thirds were Irish or German, a substantial proportion of whom were Roman Catholic. By 1855 a larger proportion of Americans was foreign born than at any other time in the nation's history.

Many immigrants, especially the Irish, came to America impoverished. Arriving penniless at East Coast ports, they congregated in the growing cities and factory towns of the North. By 1860 immigrants made up more than one-third of the residents in northern cities with populations of at least 10,000.

Impoverished immigrants became wage laborers in numbers that far outstripped their proportions in the population. In New York City, for example, immigrants accounted for 48 percent of the 1860 population but 69 percent of the city's labor force. Men worked in unskilled jobs on the docks, at construction sites, or on railroads and canals. They were conspicuous in the coal mines and iron foundries of Pennsylvania. Women worked as seamstresses, laundresses, or domestic servants. In the textile mills and shoe factories of New England, Irish families worked together, husbands and wives alongside sons and daughters.

Industrialization was not the only reason for the growth of wage labor. By the 1850s a growing middle class of white-collar employees also lived off their wages. These people worked with the increasingly complex accounting records, maintained the expanding files, and kept track of the growing volume of sales. As the scale of industrial production increased, individual businesses opened large downtown stores to sell their goods. Between 1859 and 1862, for example, A. T. Stewart built a huge dry goods store covering a full square block in lower Manhattan. The financial needs of these large-scale enterprises were met by an expanding number of banks, insurance companies, and accounting firms that employed armies of white-collar workers.

Contemplating Emigration to America In this 1854 caricature, an impoverished Irishman on the Dublin docks contemplates booking passage to America, in hopes of economic prosperity.

Thus, economic growth in the North during the 1850s rested on important social changes. A rural society became more urban. Industry was replacing agriculture as the driving economic force. Wage laborers were replacing small farmers and craftsmen. A Protestant nation encountered the first great wave of Catholic immigrants. Machines made it possible for one person to cultivate more acres than ever before. All of this signaled the birth of a political economy based on new sources of wealth and new forms of work.

The Slave Economy

It made sense for a wealthy South Carolina planter like James Henry Hammond to declare in 1858 that "Cotton is king." It had been a prosperous decade for southern slaveholders. Recovering from the economic doldrums of the 1840s, the price of cotton remained steady and the price of slaves rose to new heights. Southern states threw themselves into the business of railroad construction with unprecedented vigor. By 1860 the South had a fairly large railroad network, smaller than the North's but impressive by world standards. Steamboats plied the South's rivers. Telegraph wires sped news of cotton prices from New York to New Orleans and deep into the plantation belt. Southerners boasted of their region's commitment to progress and prosperity. Slavery was thriving. So why shouldn't Senator Hammond confidently defy slavery's critics?

The South had changed in many ways during the previous century. It had expanded across half the continent. Cotton had become the region's most profitable crop. The Atlantic slave trade was closed off, and a native-born, largely Christian slave population had grown up. There were important signs of social change, especially in the upper South. The immigrant workers Frederick Douglass met on the Baltimore docks were caught up in the same process of economic development as the dock workers of New England. The steady sale of slaves from the upper to the lower South reduced the political influence of slaveholders in states like Maryland, Kentucky, and Delaware. Indeed, among whites across the entire South the proportion of slaveholders had been declining for decades. In 1830 one-third of southern white families held slaves. By 1860 the proportion had dropped to one in four.

As slavery expanded it brought commerce but not economic development along with it. The slave economy had always been intensely commercial, more so than northern capitalism. But the slave economy concentrated its profits among slaveholders who were, by 1860, among the richest group of Americans. That wealth enabled the slaveholders to monopolize the best lands wherever they went, to the detriment of small farmers. Moreover the slaveholders reinvested their profits not in machinery that increased productivity but in more slaves. As a result, slaveless farmers in the South were much poorer than their northern counterparts, and the southern economy far less developed than the northern.

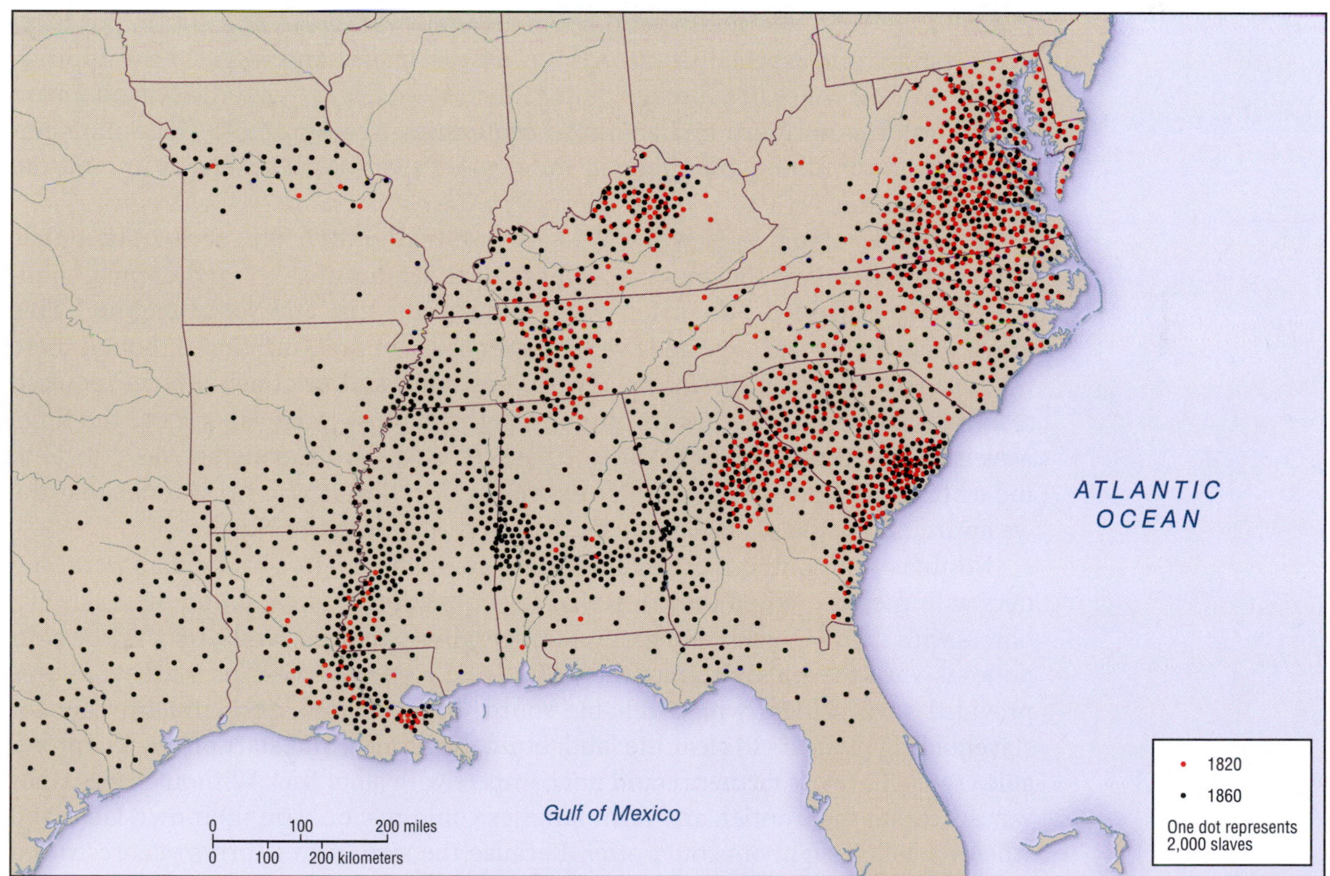

Map 14–1 Slavery's Expansion The westward expansion of the slave economy created political turmoil from 1820 until the Civil War. Sustained by an extensive internal slave trade that sold thousands of humans each year, slavery's expansion required one of the greatest forced migrations in history.

The Importance of the West

Both the North and the South coveted western lands. By 1850 many northerners believed that slavery, if allowed to expand into the West, would deprive free laborers of an important source of prosperity and independence. But slaveholders had come to believe that their prosperity depended on the diffusion, or extension, of the slave economy into the West. The disposition of the land acquired in the war with Mexico therefore forced Americans into a sustained public debate over the future of slavery.

Slavery had expanded more than halfway across the continent of North America in about half a century, from the eastern seaboard to the mines of New Mexico and the plains of Kansas, and white southerners grew accustomed to viewing territorial expansion as a sign of progress. The westward movement of the southern frontier demonstrated the continued strength of the slave economy. To call a halt to that movement was to dam up the wellsprings of southern prosperity. It was an insult to the moral decency of white southerners, an obstacle to their economic vitality. But above all else it was an infringement on the slaveholders' inalienable rights of property, which included the constitutional right to carry their property with them wherever they saw fit. So argued slavery's defenders with increasing vehemence in the 1850s.

But the economic growth of the North created equally strong ties between the East and the West. Mountains and rivers generally ran north and south, but turnpikes, canals, and especially railroads tended to run east and west. Of the approximately 20,000 miles of railroads built in the 1850s, few crossed the Mason-Dixon line to link the northern and southern economies (see Map 14–2). The transportation revolution thus strengthened the ties between northeastern cities and the western frontier.

Northerners came to view the West as essential to their prosperity. The public lands of the West "are the great regulator of the relations of Labor and Capital," Horace Greeley explained, "the safety valve of our industrial and social engine." This safety valve theory was repeated over and over again in the North, even though there was not much truth in it. To move west, buy land, and establish a farm required resources far beyond the means of many, perhaps most, wage laborers at the time. Nevertheless, in the eyes of many northerners, westward expansion was critical to the stability and prosperity of their entire social order. It was no wonder that the westward expansion of slavery caused so much anxiety in the North.

Northern and southern expansion were incompatible. The slaveholders were "settlers with means." When they migrated they bought their wealth and their slave laborers with them. Quickly and easily, they bought up the best lands, usually the river bottoms with the most productive soil and the readiest access to markets. Slaves provided such settlers with a reliable source of labor, making it much easier for slaveholding pioneers to clear the land, build the homes, and start producing profitable crops. Slaveless farmers could not compete with all of this. Without slaves labor was scarce on the frontier, and farm families could rely only on their own labor and whatever help neighbors could offer. Because the size of free farms was restricted by the amount of labor a family could perform, the best lands were more widely dispersed among settlers wherever slavery was excluded. So free farmers quickly came to view the expansion of slavery as a threat to their own prospects in the West.

Map 14–2 Railroad Expansion This map shows that there were two distinct patterns of railroad development in the United States. In the North, rail lines connected the western states to the eastern seaboard. In the South, railroads tied the inland plantation districts to the coastal ports. Few lines connected the North to the South.

Slavery Becomes a Political Issue

Westward expansion forced the issue of slavery back into the political mainstream in the late 1840s. During the heyday of the "second party system," Whigs and Democrats had tacitly agreed to suppress open debates over slavery, but the Mexican War and its consequences made it hard to maintain that silence. For nearly 15 years, national politics would focus on one crucial question: Should Congress restrict the movement of slavery into the West? But behind that question lay a larger moral issue, the wrong and the right of "property in man."

Wilmot Introduces His Proviso

On August 8, 1846, David Wilmot, a Democratic congressman from Pennsylvania, attached to an appropriations bill an amendment banning slavery from all the territories acquired in the war with Mexico. The aim of the famous Wilmot Proviso was to preserve western lands for white settlement. "I plead the cause and rights of the free white man," Wilmot insisted.

> **The Fugitive Slave Law. . . . is a degradation and a scandalous outrage on religious liberty. . . . This vile, infernal law does not interfere with singing of psalms, or anything of that kind, but with the weightier matters of the law, judgment, mercy, and faith. It makes it criminal for you, sir, to carry out the principles of Christianity. It forbids you the right to do right—forbids you to show mercy—forbids you to follow the example of the good Samaritan.**
>
> FREDERICK DOUGLASS,
> August 11, 1852

Initially, northern Whigs and Democrats joined in support of the proviso, while their southern counterparts opposed it. When it was reintroduced in the next session of Congress, however, the proviso went down to defeat. Nevertheless, it paralyzed Congress for several years in the late 1840s, a time when conditions in the West demanded federal legislation. Mormon settlers had been pouring into the basin of the Great Salt Lake, and they required some form of government. The discovery of gold in California brought a rush of settlers and a good deal of disorder to the mining camps of the Sierra foothills and the boomtown of San Francisco. Territorial governments required congressional action, but Congress was frozen by sectional differences.

By 1850, four positions had hardened into place. At one extreme were antislavery northerners who favored a Wilmot-like solution that would ban slavery in all the territories. At the other extreme were the southern followers of John C. Calhoun, who argued that Congress had no right to interfere with the property rights of slaveholders in the territories. In between, there were two compromise positions. Some wanted to extend the Missouri Compromise line, which would have pushed the North-South division all the way to the Pacific Ocean. Finally, there was popular sovereignty, the position later supported by Stephen A. Douglas of Illinois. Popular sovereignty gave settlers the right to decide for themselves whether they would have slavery in their territory.

Prospectors Following the discovery of gold in California, prospectors from around the world headed for the mining camps that sprang up along the foothills of the Sierra Nevada mountains.

The four conflicting positions disrupted the major parties. In the presidential election of 1848 antislavery men bolted both the Democrats and the Whigs and threw their support to the Free-Soil Party. With the Wilmot Proviso as their platform, the Free-Soilers won 14 percent of the northern vote. Meanwhile, proslavery fire-eaters threatened to walk out of the Democratic convention. The Whigs survived this turmoil to elect President Zachary Taylor, a hero of the war with Mexico. The Whig triumph was short lived, however. In 1849 President Taylor urged New Mexico and California to apply directly for admission to the Union without going through the usual territorial stage. California's application for statehood arrived with a constitution that prohibited slavery, provoking a fight over whether new slave states should be admitted to the Union. The House of Representatives, with a strong northern majority, reaffirmed the Wilmot Proviso, condemned the slave trade in Washington, DC, and almost abolished slavery in the District of Columbia. The Senate, which had a strong southern wing, blocked all such measures.

This was no ordinary congressional stalemate. Fistfights broke out in the halls of Congress. Elected representatives challenged each other to duels. Threatening secession, proslavery partisans called for a southern-rights convention to meet at Nashville in June 1850. The stage was set for one of the most dramatic debates in congressional history.

A Compromise Without Compromises

Into this stalemate marched the "great triumvirate" of distinguished old senators, Henry Clay of Kentucky, Daniel Webster of Massachusetts, and John C. Calhoun of South Carolina. Clay, who had been instrumental in securing the Missouri Compromise of 1820, tried one last time to save the Union. He devised a series of eight resolutions designed to balance the conflicting interests of North and South. Under the first pair of measures, California would be admitted as a free state, but the rest of the Mexican territories would have no conditions regarding slavery attached to their applications for statehood. The second pair limited the number of slave states that could be carved out of Texas Territory, but in return required the federal government to assume Texas's debt. The third pair abolished the slave trade in Washington, DC, but protected slavery itself from federal interference. The compromise package included two more provisions that were partial to the South: a formal promise not to interfere in the interstate slave trade and a new fugitive slave law.

Clay gathered all eight provisions of his compromise into a single package, derided by critics as the Omnibus Bill. The senator's goal was simple: to gain enough support from centrists in each party to override both southern fire-eaters and northern Free-Soilers.

Senator Stephen A. Douglas The "Little Giant" from Illinois became the leading advocate of "popular sovereignty" as a solution to the crisis over slavery in the 1850s.

The congressional debate over Clay's package in the spring and summer of 1850 included a series of extraordinary speeches. Daniel Webster eloquently supported the compromise measures. Appealing for sectional harmony, Webster claimed to speak "not as a Massachusetts man, nor as a Northern man, but as an American." Calhoun, by contrast, spoke very much as a southern man. He warned that the bonds tying the sections together had been snapped by the North's continued agitation of the slavery question. If the right of property in slaves was not enforced, the Union would be severed. In response, New York's William H. Seward argued that the Constitution gave Congress every right to restrict slavery in the territories.

The sectional hostilities exposed in the debate suggest why Clay's Omnibus Bill was doomed. Antislavery senators voted against the bill for its various provisions protecting slavery. Proslavery senators opposed it for its restrictions on slavery. On July 31, after months of wrangling, the Senate killed the package. Exhausted and angry, Clay gave up and left Washington. The old generation had failed to resolve the crisis.

From that moment on national politics would be dominated by a new generation of congressional leaders. Seward of New York was one of them. Another was Senator Stephen A. Douglas, the "Little

Giant" from Illinois who used his adroit parliamentary skills to rescue the compromise. He broke the omnibus package up into five separate bills, each designed to win different majorities. Antislavery and moderate congressmen joined to secure the admission of California as a free state. Proslavery congressmen voted with moderates to pass a fugitive slave law. By similar means, Congress settled the Texas border, determined that New Mexico and Utah would apply for statehood under the principle of popular sovereignty, and abolished the slave trade in the District of Columbia. Although proslavery and antislavery forces never compromised on a single issue, the five bills that Douglas and his allies steered through Congress came to be known as the Compromise of 1850.

Anthony Burns Burns was a fugitive slave whose owners were attempting to return him to the South. His 1854 trial created an uproar across the North, but especially in Boston, where the trial was held.

Douglas's efforts were aided by the untimely death of the president. Zachary Taylor's replacement, Millard Fillmore, was more sympathetic to sectional reconciliation. Fillmore pronounced the Compromise of 1850 the "final settlement" of the slavery question. For the next few years moderate politicians across the country avoided all discussion of slavery. In the short run, the compromise apparently worked. A southern-rights convention at Nashville fizzled, and the radical edge of the southern-rights movement was blunted. But fire-eaters in the South and Free-Soilers in the North insisted that the day of reckoning had only been postponed. And in the North, opposition to one feature of the compromise, the fugitive slave law, came with unanticipated intensity.

The Fugitive Slave Act Provokes a Crisis

The Fugitive Slave Act was one of the least-debated features of the 1850 compromise. The Constitution had a fugitive slave clause, and a law enforcing the clause had been in place since 1793. Why, then, did the new Fugitive Slave Act provoke such an uproar? Many northern states had passed laws to restrain fugitive slave catchers by guaranteeing the rights of due process to accused runaways. The 1850 statute took jurisdiction over fugitive slave cases away from northern courts and gave it to federal commissioners who were paid $10 if they ruled that a black captive should be returned to slavery but only $5 if they ruled that the captive was legitimately free. Abolitionists naturally charged that this amounted to a bribe to send captives into slavery.

The Fugitive Slave Act sent waves of terror through northern African American communities. Slaves who had run away decades earlier now faced the prospect

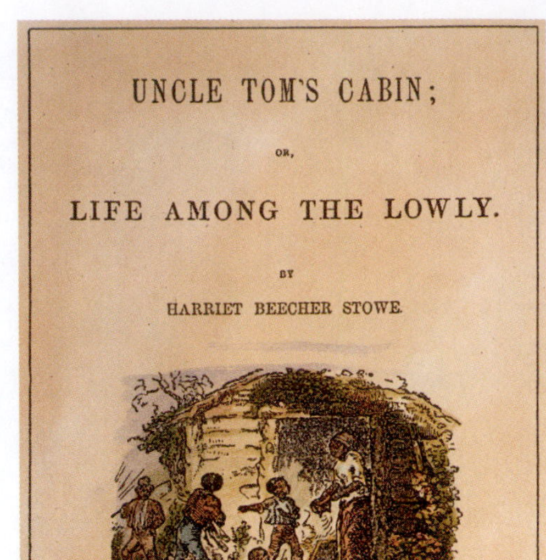
UNCLE TOM'S CABIN;
OR,
LIFE AMONG THE LOWLY.
BY
HARRIET BEECHER STOWE.
VOL. I.
ONE HUNDREDTH THOUSAND.
BOSTON:
JOHN P. JEWETT & COMPANY
CLEVELAND, OHIO:
JEWETT, PROCTOR & WORTHINGTON.
1852.

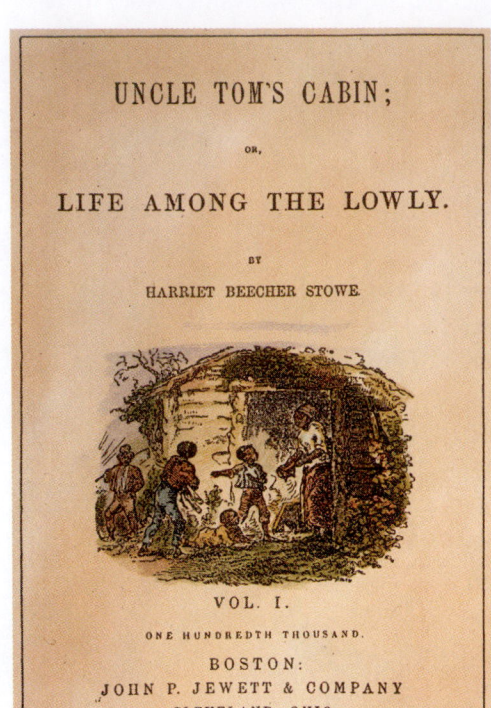

Uncle Tom's Cabin The tremendous popularity of Stowe's book reflected the surprisingly intense northern concern about the Fugitive Slave Act of 1850.

of being captured and sent back to the South. Even free-born blacks feared being kidnapped into slavery, unable to prove their freedom in a court of law. Across the North, vulnerable African Americans moved to the far West, the upper North, or Canada. A convention of blacks denounced the Fugitive Slave Act as "the most cruel, unconstitutional, and scandalous outrage of modern times."

White abolitionists were no less vehement. The Reverend Charles Beecher denounced the Fugitive Slave Act as "the vilest monument of infamy of the nineteenth century." Even white northerners who cared little about the fate of blacks were upset. The South seemed to be imposing its laws and institutions on the North. Appalled by the act, Harriet Beecher Stowe published the great antislavery novel, *Uncle Tom's Cabin,* in 1852. The astonishing success of Stowe's novel was one measure of northern anxiety about the Fugitive Slave Act. In vivid, melodramatic prose, Stowe drew a sentimental portrait of a slave mother and her infant child as they fled from a master who had contracted to sell them apart. Few readers missed the point. Anyone who helped Eliza save her child stood in violation of the Fugitive Slave Act of 1850.

A surprising number of northerners tolerated violations of the Fugitive Slave Act. President Fillmore vowed to enforce the law with federal marshals if necessary, but Frederick Douglass, revealing how far he had moved from his earlier pacifism, advocated violent resistance. "A half dozen or more dead kidnappers carried down South," he suggested, "would cool the ardor of Southern gentlemen, and keep their rapacity in check."

The Election of 1852 and the Decline of the Whig Party

White southerners were outraged by the North's unwillingness to obey the Fugitive Slave Act. The Democratic Party made enforcement of the Compromise of 1850 its rallying cry in 1852. The Democrats, torn by sectional divisions, nominated Franklin Pierce, a northerner thought to be sympathetic to southern interests. Pierce and the Democrats ran on a platform pledged to silencing discussion of slavery by strict federal enforcement of the Compromise of 1850, "the act for reclaiming fugitives included."

The Whigs found no such unifying principle. White southerners abandoned the party because it harbored antislavery advocates, and northern voters punished the

Whigs for their association with the Compromise of 1850. Henry Clay wrote the Fugitive Slave Act. Daniel Webster supported it. Millard Fillmore signed and aggressively enforced it as well. All were Whigs. The Whig Party convention met in Baltimore a month after the Democrats, but it produced no comparable show of unity. After 52 ballots, the convention nominated Winfield Scott of Virginia, despite nearly unanimous southern opposition. The southern delegates secured a platform that reaffirmed the party's commitment to the Compromise of 1850, but this only meant that the Whigs would run a candidate who was objectionable in the South on a platform that was objectionable in the North.

Southern defections all but assured a major Whig defeat in the November election. Pierce won 254 electoral votes and Scott won only 42. The Democratic candidate won 27 out of 31 states. Severely weakened by the 1852 election results, the Whigs found themselves unable to meet another challenge that burst into American politics in the early 1850s: hostility to immigrants, otherwise known as nativism.

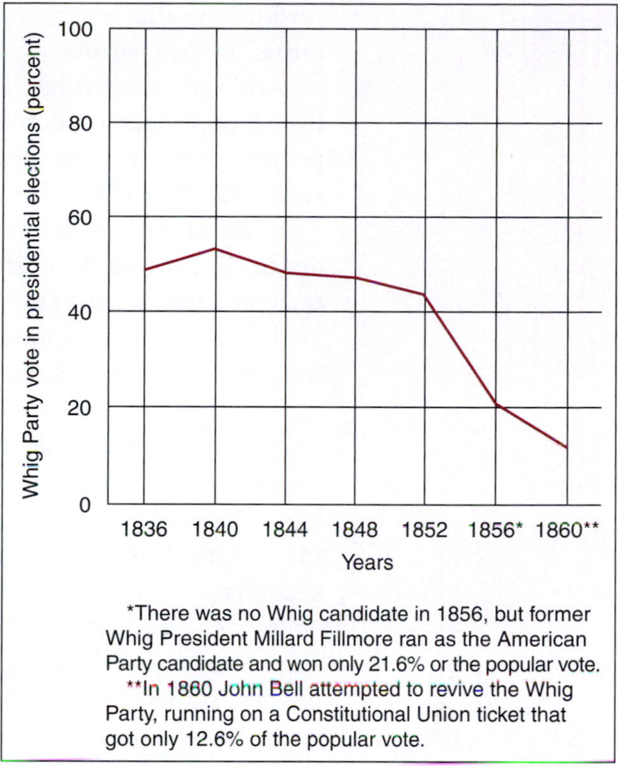
Whig Party vote in presidential elections (percent)
100
80
60
40
20
0
1836 1840 1844 1848 1852 1856* 1860**
Years
*There was no Whig candidate in 1856, but former Whig President Millard Fillmore ran as the American Party candidate and won only 21.6% or the popular vote.
**In 1860 John Bell attempted to revive the Whig Party, running on a Constitutional Union ticket that got only 12.6% of the popular vote.

Figure 14–1 The Decline of the Whig Party

Nativism and the Origins of the Republican Party

The politics of nativism destroyed a Whig Party already weakened by sectionalism. From 1852 through 1854 the nativist American Party gained surprising strength. Hostility to immigrants, however, was not enough to rally northerners concerned about slavery. What, then, would replace the Whig Party in the North? A new and powerful political force, the Republican Party, was dedicated to halting slavery's westward expansion.

The Nativist Attack on Immigration

For a while the arrival of large numbers of Catholic immigrants stirred nearly as much animosity among Yankee Protestants as did slavery. In the early 1850s the Catholic Church was widely known for its conservatism. The pope expressed an abiding contempt for "progress," and the Vatican condemned the liberal

> **Near eighty years ago we began by declaring that all men are created equal; but now from that beginning we have run down to the other declaration, that for some men to enslave others is a "sacred right of self-government." These principles can not stand together. They are as opposite as God and mammon.**
>
> ABRAHAM LINCOLN,
> Peoria, Illinois, October 16, 1854

revolutions that swept across Europe in 1848, revolutions that were widely supported by Americans.

Anti-Catholicism had about it a strong odor of middle-class condescension. Nativism appealed to shopkeepers, independent craftsmen, and white-collar clerks, people for whom the Protestant ethic of steadiness and sobriety amounted to a scriptural injunction. They looked with disdain on a working class of Irish and German immigrants who drank heavily, lived in squalor, and lacked economic independence. But it was immigrant voting, particularly among Irish Catholics, that most unsettled the nativist soul: the Irish voted Democratic.

The Democrats' appeal to Irish Catholics was double-edged. On the one hand, the party's populist rhetoric attracted working-class immigrants who were stung by the snobbery of Yankee Whigs. At the same time, as Democrats stepped up their racist invective, Irish Americans heaped contempt on African Americans with whom they competed for jobs and housing. Democrats cultivated this sentiment, using racism to assimilate Irish working-class voters into American politics at a time when many Americans were organizing to keep immigrants out. The consequences for sectional politics were significant. The Democrats argued that abolition would force white workers into economic competition with an inferior race. With the critical support of the Irish voting bloc, the Democratic Party sponsored new restrictions on the civil rights of free African Americans in many northern states.

In the elections of 1854, voters who believed that immigration was the greatest threat to the American way of life cast their ballots for the American Party. (They were often called "Know-Nothings" because of their origins in a secret organization whose members insisted, when questioned, that they "knew nothing" about it.) Voters who cared more about the threat of slavery voted for the Free-Soil Party. American Party candidates won 25 percent of the vote in New York and 40 percent in Pennsylvania; in Massachusetts, they took control of the state legislature.

In 1854 it seemed as though nativism would eclipse slavery as the great issue of American politics. But slavery and nativism were never entirely separate issues. Middle-class Yankees often viewed the struggle against Catholicism as inseparable from the struggle against slavery. Both were said to represent authoritarianism, ignorance, and a rejection of the "modern" values of individualism and progress. Given the close ties between nativism and antislavery sentiment, it was unclear which issue would eventually prevail. The question was decided on the sparsely settled plains of Kansas and Nebraska (see Map 14–3).

The Kansas-Nebraska Act Revives the Slavery Issue

In 1853, the House of Representatives passed a bill banning slavery in Nebraska Territory on the grounds that it fell north of the Missouri Compromise line. Southerners killed the Nebraska Bill in the Senate. The following year Stephen Douglas reintroduced it, this time organizing the territory on the principle of popular sovereignty.

No one was satisfied with Douglas's proposal. Northerners were outraged that the 1850 agreement to extend the Missouri Compromise line was so quickly scuttled. Militant southerners, suspicious of congressional attempts to regulate slavery in the territories, demanded that the Missouri Compromise be repealed. Douglas withdrew the bill and reintroduced it in January 1854, but with a new twist. He split Nebraska Territory in two, Kansas to the west of the slave state of Missouri and Nebraska to the north of Kansas. Both were to be organized on the principle of

AMERICA AND THE WORLD

>> Slavery as a Foreign Policy

The Pierce administration's disastrous support for the Kansas-Nebraska Act undermined its ability to pursue the expansionist policies of its Democratic predecessors. To be sure, Pierce packed his presidential addresses with bluster about America's right to more Mexican territory and to various parts of the Caribbean, particularly Cuba. But all of Pierce's expansionist efforts were southward, and that meant they all promised the expansion of slavery. This was hardly an accident. Southerners dominated Pierce's cabinet and he appointed slaveholders to crucial diplomatic posts.

Pierce sent a South Carolinian, James Gadsden, to Mexico with instructions to spend up to $50 million to acquire a substantial portion of northern Mexico. Mexico's leader resisted Gadsden's extravagant offer. The American returned to Washington, DC, with a treaty giving the United States just enough territory to build a transcontinental railroad across the southern tier of the nation. But even this was too much for most northern senators. For the first time in American history, Congress rejected land ceded to the United States. The Gadsden Purchase ended up securing only a small piece of land for $10 million to even out the southern border of the United States.

Pierce's expansionist designs fared even worse in Cuba. The president appointed Pierre Soulé, a Louisianan, as minister to Spain. Soulé was instructed to negotiate the purchase of Cuba, with the understanding that if Spain refused to sell he should encourage the Cubans to rise in rebellion. To Soulé's presumptuous behavior the Spanish government offered an extraordinary response. It proposed to free millions of Cuban slaves and arm them for the defense of the island against a possible American invasion.

The United States responded with the Ostend Manifesto, which declared that Cuba was "naturally" a part of the United States and urged Spain to accept an offer of $120 million for the island. If Spain refused, the United States would use all of its power to "wrest" the island of Cuba by force.

The Ostend Manifesto was issued in 1854 at the height of northern reaction against the Kansas-Nebraska Act and was immediately denounced as yet another example of slavery's insatiable hunger for expansion. Expansionism was now hopelessly tainted by its association with slavery. As Pierce's secretary of state, William L. Marcy, admitted, "the Nebraska question" had shattered the Democratic Party in the North "and deprived it of that strength which was needed and could have been more profitably used for the acquisition of Cuba."

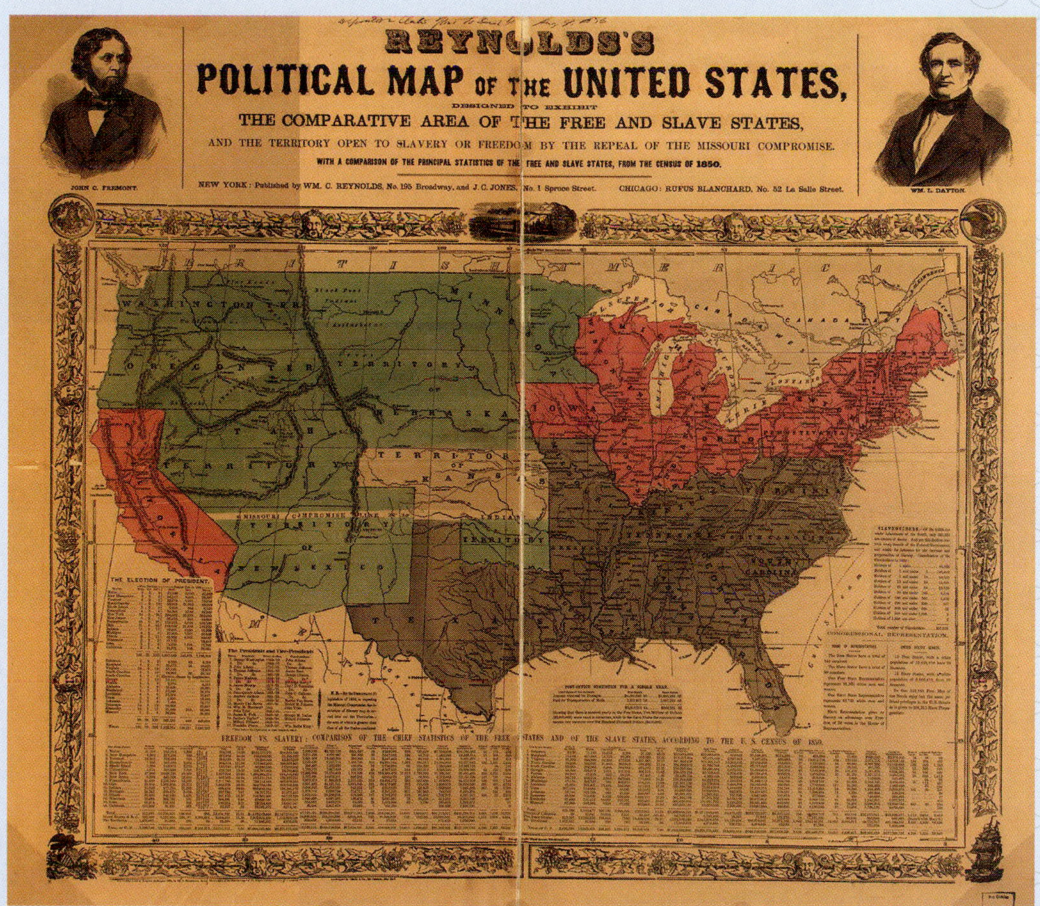

popular sovereignty, but everyone expected that Kansas would become a slave state and Nebraska a free state. To win the support of southern congressmen, the final version of Douglas's bill explicitly repealed the Missouri Compromise of 1820.

Debate over the bill was ferocious: Southerners denied that Congress had the right to regulate slavery in the territories, through popular sovereignty or any other means. Northerners pointed out that the federal government had been regulating slavery in the territories since the 1780s.

In the end, Douglas succeeded in winning passage of the Kansas-Nebraska Act. Yet, as with other southern victories, the act increased support for antislavery politicians in the North. It persuaded many northerners that popular sovereignty was a proslavery swindle, even though Douglas believed that it would produce mostly free states. Yet for that very reason southerners came to mistrust popular sovereignty as well. Douglas had paid a heavy price for his victory. In the 1854 elections the number of northern Democrats in Congress fell from 91 to 25. Over the next several years the fallout from the Kansas-Nebraska Act would split the Democratic Party in two, destroy the credibility of popular sovereignty, and damage expansionism as a political program.

One of the most important consequences of the struggle over the Kansas-Nebraska Act was the emergence of Abraham Lincoln. Stephen Douglas was widely

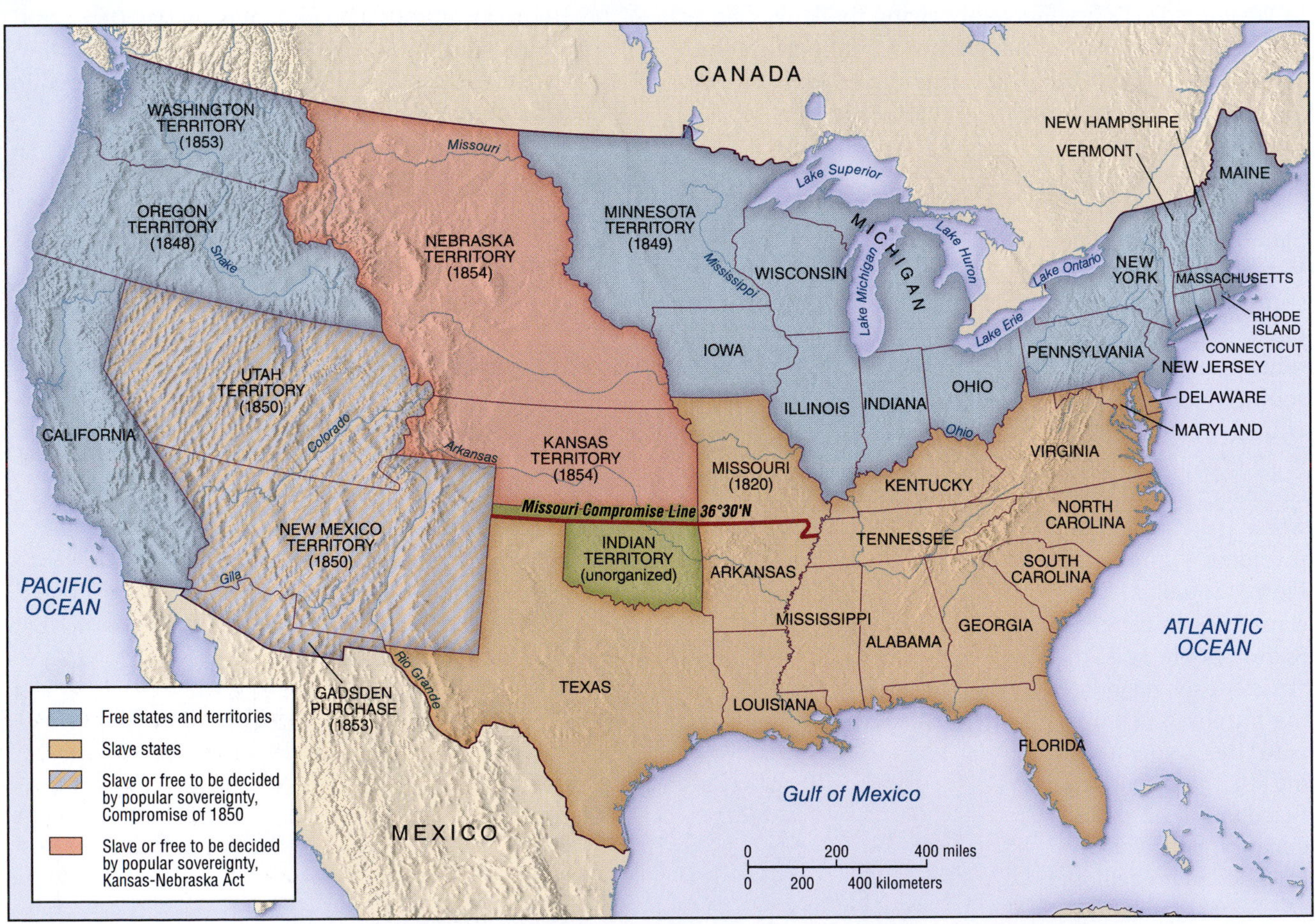

Map 14–3 The Kansas-Nebraska Act of 1854 Stephen Douglas's Kansas-Nebraska Act carved the Kansas Territory out of the larger Nebraska Territory. Because Missouri was already a slave state, the map indicates that slaveholders could move west and settle in Kansas. But because Kansas lay north of the 1820 Missouri Compromise line, many northerners wanted slavery restricted from the territory.

denounced in his home state of Illinois for having helped open Kansas to slavery. When he returned to Illinois, Douglas found himself facing not only hostile voters but the sharp criticism of Lincoln, his longtime political rival. Lincoln had largely abandoned his public life some years before, but the Kansas-Nebraska Act brought him out of semiretirement. He followed Douglas around the state, demanding the restoration of the Missouri Compromise. In Peoria, on October 16, 1854, Lincoln gave a speech summing up his arguments against slavery and had it published. He pronounced slavery "a great moral wrong," insisted on the humanity of blacks, and denounced the dehumanization of slaves. He said that slavery was founded on greed, selfishness, and unrestrained self-interest. It was a remarkable speech, and with it Lincoln reintroduced himself to Illinois voters as one of the state's leading antislavery politicians.

Kansas Begins to Bleed

Under the terms of the Kansas-Nebraska Act, the people in Kansas would determine whether their territory would enter the Union as a slave state or a free state. Elections for the territorial legislature were set for March 1855. Hoping to secure victory for the antislavery forces, the New England Emigrant Aid Company sent settlers opposed to slavery. By election day, however, proslavery settlers probably would have won a fair fight. But on the day the polls opened, proslavery partisans from neighboring Missouri crossed the border and cast thousands of phony ballots. This undermined the legitimacy of the newly elected proslavery legislature. To make matters worse, the new legislature made it a crime to question slavery in Kansas, made it a capital crime to protect fugitive slaves, and expelled the few antislavery members who had been elected.

Free-state settlers responded by repudiating the proslavery government. In January 1856, free-staters elected a governor and legislature of their own. By the spring of 1856, Kansas found itself with two competing governments, a proslavery one in Lecompton and an antislavery one in Topeka. By then, free-state settlers were in the majority. Nevertheless, local sheriffs and federal marshals, backed up by more "border ruffians" from Missouri, tried several times to enter the town of Lawrence to arrest free-staters. They tried again May 21, 1856, only to discover that most of the free-staters had fled. The frustrated Missourians promptly destroyed two printing presses and burned the Free State Hotel to the ground. Although little blood was shed, the eastern press blasted the "sack of Lawrence" as the latest example of proslavery violence. Kansas, they said, was bleeding.

Three days after the sack of Lawrence, Kansas really did begin to bleed, when John Brown launched his famous raid on proslavery settlers at Pottawatomie Creek. Brown was an awesome and in many ways a frightening man, a religious zealot convinced that it was his personal mission to cleanse the nation of the sin of slavery. The wrath of God, not moral persuasion or political organization, was Brown's preferred solution to the problem of slavery.

The day after he learned of the sack of Lawrence, Brown organized a small band of men to take revenge. Among his seven-man legion were four of his own sons and a son-in-law. Armed with finely honed swords and even sharper zeal, Brown's troops went into battle late in the evening on May 24. At their first stop they shot James Doyle in the head, split open the skulls of two of his sons, and then hacked up the bodies. They committed similar atrocities at two other settlers' cabins. Then they went back to their camp, having stolen several horses along the way.

AMERICAN LANDSCAPE

>> Lawrence, Kansas

Eli Thayer was more interested in making money than in spreading freedom when he secured a charter for the Massachusetts Emigrant Aid Society in April of 1854. But one month later, Congress passed the Kansas-Nebraska Act, and Thayer's organization became the focus of a concerted effort to fill Kansas with northern settlers who opposed the spread of slavery. Within a year Thayer's organization had a new name, the New England Emigrant Aid Company, and a treasurer with deep pockets and an even deeper commitment to halting the spread of slavery. His name was Amos Lawrence, and when the settlers reached the western prairie they named their settlement after him. Within a year everybody in America was talking about what was going on in Lawrence, Kansas.

Lawrence quickly became the center of the "free-state" movement in Kansas. The settlers established two antislavery newspapers in the town, the *Kansas Free State* and the *Herald of Freedom*. But they clearly expected more than angry letters to the editor in response. The biggest building in town, the Free State Hotel, was built like a fortress, constructed of thick stone walls to fend off attacks.

If the goal of the New England Emigrant Aid Company was to overwhelm Kansas with free-state settlers who could outvote the proslavery forces, then their campaign failed. When elections for the territorial legislature were held on March 30, 1855, a flood of "border ruffians" crossed into Kansas from Missouri, casting thousands of ballots for candidates who favored slavery. "There are eleven hundred coming over from Platte County to vote," boasted Senator David Rice Atchison, the unofficial leader of the proslavery forces, "and if that ain't enough we can send five thousand—enough to kill every God-damned abolitionist in the territory."

Needless to say, the free-state settlers and their supporters pronounced the elections a fraud, dismissed the new legislature as "bogus," and set up a "government" of their own. Charles Robinson, the "governor" of the free state and the Emigrant Aid Society's agent in Lawrence, wrote stormy letters of protest. "Can such outrageous conduct from Missourians be longer tolerated?" he asked. "Our people are forming military companies." But they needed arms and ammunition. "We want 200 of Sharp's rifles & two cannon for Lawrence people," Robinson wrote. From back east the pastor of Brooklyn's Plymouth Church, the Reverend Henry Ward Beecher, obliged by organizing a campaign to send the rifles out to the frontier. "Beecher's Bibles," the guns were called.

Over the next year the free-state settlers armed themselves in preparation for battle. Meanwhile the proslavery state government grew increasingly impatient with the growing abolitionist stronghold at Lawrence. In April 1856, Sheriff Jones was shot in the back while in Lawrence and the proslavery forces sprang into action. Several free-state leaders were indicted for "treason." Robinson was arrested. A grand jury recommended that the Free State Hotel be demolished and the antislavery newspapers be shut down. The U.S. marshal for Kansas urged all "law abiding" settlers to converge on the town of Lawrence so that he could serve warrants on the free-state leaders.

A posse entered the town where Sheriff Jones, bent on destroying the "hotbed of abolitionism," led 750 men under a flag emblazoned with

the words "Southern Rights." They invaded the offices of both newspapers and tossed the presses into the river. They ransacked the Free State Hotel, fired their cannon at it, then set it on fire. The mob then pillaged several houses and burned down Robinson's house. Only one person was killed, but the town was largely demolished. Newspapers around the country dubbed the attack the "sack of Lawrence."

At stake in the battle over Lawrence were competing conceptions of democracy in America. Over the years southerners had built an aggressive slaveholders' democracy where white men were as proud of their freedom as they were jealous of their property rights in slaves. For the free-state settlers, slavery and democracy were fundamentally incompatible. Thus the war on the Kansas prairie was a prelude to the civil war that would erupt nationwide a few years later.

Whatever it meant to national politics, the sack of Lawrence did not discourage the free-state settlers who lived there. They rebuilt their town, attracted ever more settlers to their cause, and within a few years they were clearly in the majority. For proslavery partisans Lawrence thus survived as a symbol of the abolitionism they so despised. During the Civil War they attacked Lawrence yet again, and yet again the town survived. ●

As blood flowed in the western territories, another battle erupted on the floor of Congress. Prompted by the sack of Lawrence, abolitionist senator Charles Sumner of Massachusetts delivered a two-day harangue exposing the "Crime Against Kansas." Deliberately provocative, the speech was filled with overheated sexual metaphors. Proslavery forces, Sumner declared, had set out to "rape" the virgin territory of Kansas. He accused Senator Andrew Butler of South Carolina of consorting with a "polluted . . . harlot, Slavery." Two days later, Congressman Preston S. Brooks, a nephew of Butler's, walked into a nearly empty Senate chamber and brutally attacked Sumner with his cane.

Across the South, Brooks was hailed as a hero. Southern congressmen prevented his expulsion from the House. Northerners, shocked by the South's reaction to the Sumner-Brooks affair, responded by casting their ballots for a new Republican Party dedicated to halting the expansion of the "slave power."

A New Political Party Takes Shape

The election of 1856 presented Americans with a clear choice. A candidate's position on the Kansas-Nebraska Act betrayed a widening circle of convictions—about slavery's expansion, about the relative value of wage labor and slave labor, and about the morality of human property itself. What was at stake, in other words, was the fundamental conflict between slave and free societies. In the past the Whigs and Democrats had avoided sectional issues by running candidates who appealed to both the North and the South. In 1856 a new major party, the Republicans, appealed exclusively to northern voters.

The First Sectional Election

In 1856 antislavery became the umbrella under which the Democratic Party's opponents in the North could gather. That new umbrella was the Republican Party, and its first presidential candidate was John C. Frémont.

The Republican Party platform called for a prohibition on the expansion of slavery into any western territories, and on this nearly all Republicans were agreed. But a party formed out of former Whigs and Democrats had trouble unifying on

> **Slave labor, in each individual case, and for each small measure of time, is more slow and inefficient than the labor of a free man. . . . Suppose it is admitted that the labor of slaves, for each hour or day, will amount to but two-thirds of what hired free laborers would perform in the same time. But the slave labor is continuous, and every day at least it returns to the employers and to the community, this two-thirds of full labor. . . . [T]he subjection of people of the same race with their masters—of equals to equals . . . would be slavery of the most objectionable kind. It would involve most injustice and hardship to the enslaved—would render it more difficult for the masters to command and enforce obedience—and would make the bonds of servitude more galling to the slaves, because of their being equal to their masters (and, in many individual cases, greatly superior) in natural endowments of mind.**
>
> EDMUND RUFFIN,
> *The Political Economy of Slavery* (1853)

anything else, and decades of partisan rivalry injected a lingering mistrust into the new Republican coalition. Former Whigs wanted the federal government to sponsor the construction of a transcontinental railroad and to set high tariffs to protect industries. They proposed a homestead act to encourage small farmers to settle the West, and supported the creation of land grant colleges to encourage technological innovation in agriculture. But Republicans who had previously been Democrats were often suspicious of such "whiggish" plans for big government. They had become Republicans because they believed that the "money power" they had long opposed as Jacksonian Democrats had become transformed into a "slave power" that now threatened the freedom of northern whites. Opposition to slavery's expansion in the western territories was the overriding issue that held this unwieldy Republican coalition together.

If anything, the Democrats faced an even more daunting challenge. They had to find a candidate acceptable to both the northern and southern wings of the party. They turned to James Buchanan of Pennsylvania, "a northern man with southern principles." Where the Republicans promised to interfere with slavery in the territories, the Democrats pledged "non-interference by Congress with slavery." This wording kept the principle of popular sovereignty alive without actually endorsing it. Northern and southern Democrats could thus unite around a candidate committed, above all else, to ending public discussion of slavery. For decades Democrats shifted the national discussion away from slavery by emphasizing white supremacy. In the 1850s their resort to racist appeals became desperate. Antislavery politics was back in the mainstream, and the Democrats themselves were splitting apart along sectional lines. A newly intensified racism was the only thing that held the Democratic Party together.

Nevertheless, by 1856 the Democrats could claim to be the only national party and that their candidate, Buchanan, was the only one who could prevent the breakup of the Union. Southern leaders repeatedly warned that if Frémont and the Republicans won the presidency, the South would secede. The Democrats played on widespread fears of disunion. The "grand and appalling issue" of the campaign, Buchanan wrote, is "Union or Disunion."

For the first time in their history, Americans were asked to decide in a presidential election whether the Union was worth preserving. That decision had become terribly complicated. The worth of the Union now depended on the kind of society that Union would embrace in the future. Would it be a society whose wealth was based on the labor of slaves or one that staked its prosperity on the progress of free labor?

The Labor Problem and the Politics of Slavery

Northern Democrats warned that a Republican victory would flood the North with emancipated slaves, placing them "side by side in competition with white men." The interest of northern workers therefore required the preservation of southern slavery within the Union. The most articulate spokesman for this view was Stephen Douglas. Douglas did not repudiate the promise of equality in the Declaration of Independence. Instead he argued that the promise was never meant to extend to an "inferior race" of blacks.

Republicans insisted that slavery degraded all labor, black and white, and that the expansion of slavery threatened the economic well-being of free labor in the North. Every precept of classical economics taught them that slavery destroyed the work ethic by withholding from slaves any incentive to diligence and industry. Among the masters, slavery allegedly bred a haughty disdain for hard work and self-discipline. And by stifling the economic progress of the South, slavery was charged with depriving poor whites of the opportunity to get ahead in life. Hobbled by an inefficient workforce and an aristocratic ruling class, the South was said to be doomed to economic backwardness. In contrast, Republicans depicted the North as a society in which labor was free and hard work was rewarded. The Protestant virtues of thrift, sobriety, and diligence were cultivated, opportunities for upward mobility were abundant, and progress was manifest.

Southern spokesmen did not deny that in theory slave labor was less efficient than free labor. They, too, accepted the basic economic principles spelled out by Adam Smith a century earlier. But they made a racial exception to this general rule. Blacks, they argued, did not respond to the incentives of free labor the way whites did. And whites, in turn, could not work efficiently in hot climates such as the South. Slavery solved this dual problem. It was the only way to get blacks to work productively in an otherwise unproductive climate. The proof, the slaveholders argued, was the booming, expanding slave economy. White men who worked hard could get ahead by accumulating land and slaves. The southern labor system provided a poor white man with the opportunity to rise up the social ladder by acquiring slaves "as soon as his savings will admit." Southern Democrats hailed slavery for preserving the economic independence of free whites in terms reminiscent of the Republican defense of wage labor as a stepping stone to self-employment. Slave property was, in this view, a reward for the very same virtues of thrift and industry that Yankees liked to believe they alone embraced.

But for many northerners the only possible explanation for the South's apparent prosperity was the existence of a "slave power" that kept slavery artificially alive by opening the door to its continual expansion. There were many Republicans who believed that "property in man" was simply immoral, that it violated the founding principle of fundamental human equality. But there were other Republicans attracted to the "slave power" theory because it allowed whites to feel threatened by slavery without having to sympathize with the plight of the slaves. The greater evil

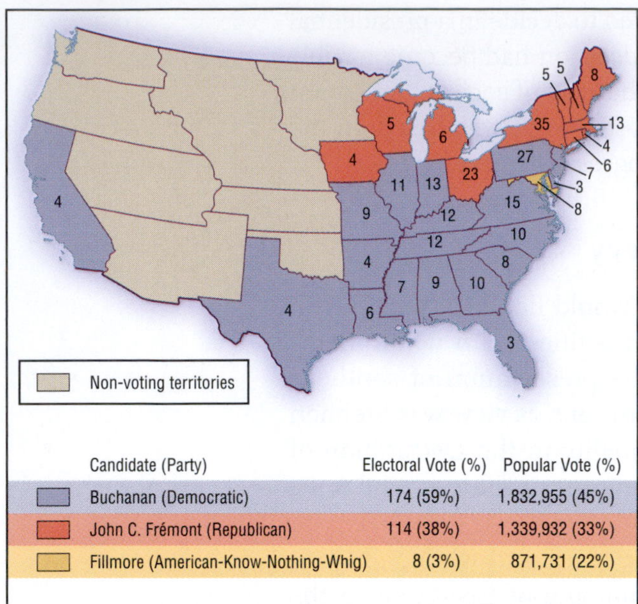

Map 14–4 The Election of 1856 The presidential electoral map of 1856 reveals the growing sectional division. Although he lost the election, the Republican Frémont won a string of victories across the upper North and lost narrowly in Pennsylvania, Indiana, and Illinois. By winning those states four years later, the openly antislavery Abraham Lincoln could be elected president simply by winning the North.

was not the oppression of the slave but the power of the slaveholder. "With the negroes I have nothing to do," one Massachusetts Republican explained, "but with their masters I propose to try conclusions as to our respective political rights."

The Republicans did not succeed in the short run. In 1852 Buchanan won five northern states and all but one of the slave states, winning 45 percent of the popular vote and 174 electoral votes. Frémont swept the upper North and Ohio, winning 114 electoral votes. No one was surprised that Frémont lost; what startled observers was that he did so well. All the Republicans needed to win four years later was Pennsylvania and either Illinois or Indiana. Never before had a clearly sectional party made so strong a showing in a presidential election. The slavery issue would not disappear until slavery itself did.

The Dred Scott Decision

In 1857 Democrat James Buchanan was inaugurated as president. His efforts to silence the slavery issue proved a disastrous failure. By the end of 1858 the most prominent Republican politician in America, William Seward, had declared that the sectional conflict between North and South was "irrepressible." When Buchanan left office in 1861 his party was in disarray, a Republican had been elected his successor, and the Union had collapsed.

Within days of Buchanan's inauguration, the Supreme Court, dominated by southern Democrats, issued one of the most controversial decisions in American history. The case stretched all the way back to 1833, when John Emerson, an army surgeon from Missouri, was assigned to duty at Fort Armstrong, Illinois, and took a slave named Dred Scott with him. Emerson spent two years in Illinois and two more years at Fort Snelling in Wisconsin Territory (now Minnesota). Slavery was illegal in Illinois and Wisconsin Territory. In 1846, after Scott had been brought back to Missouri, he sued his owners, claiming that several years of residence on free soil made him legally free. Having lost his suit in 1854, Scott appealed to the U.S. Supreme Court. By then two questions stood out: First, was Dred Scott a citizen, such that his suit had standing in a court of law? Second, did the laws of the free state of Illinois or the free territory of Wisconsin prevail over the master's property right?

The justices could have issued a narrow ruling that merely upheld the lower court's decision against Scott. But instead the majority decided, with some inappropriate coaxing from President-elect Buchanan, to render a sweeping decision covering some of the most explosive issues of the day.

It was not the majority decision against Scott that created the uproar. The problem was Chief Justice Roger Taney's provocative and highly partisan opinion. Taney argued, first, that Dred Scott was not a citizen because he was black. Since before the republic had been founded, the chief justice reasoned, African Americans had "been regarded as beings of an inferior order . . . so far inferior that they had no rights which the white man was bound to respect." Because their ancestors had been slaves in 1776, Taney reasoned, blacks could not be citizens in 1857. The problem is that it was clearly not true in 1857 or in 1776: free blacks were discriminated against throughout America, but nowhere were they denied all the rights of citizenship. They held property, entered into contracts, brought suits in court, and exercised the rights of speech, press, and assembly.

Second, Taney ruled that slaves were property, just like any other property, and the Constitution "expressly affirms" the right of property in slaves. Dred Scott's residence in Wisconsin Territory could not make him a free man, because the Missouri Compromise, by which Congress excluded slavery from the territory, was an unconstitutional infringement on the right of property. Nor could his residence in Illinois make Scott free, because the right of property includes the right of "sojourn."

Taney's decision made the southern defense of slavery into the law of the land. Neither Congress nor western settlers could legally exclude slavery from the territories, because any such exclusion would trample on the slaveholders' sacred rights of property. And the only human beings who fell into the category of "property" were black slaves. This was a thoroughly political ruling. Taney had declared unconstitutional both the northern Democrats' policy of popular sovereignty and the northern Republican policy of free soil. The one political position left standing by the Court was that of the southern slaveholders. Owning slaves was a right of property, and only blacks could be slaves.

The Lecompton Constitution Splits the Democratic Party

When the Court undermined popular sovereignty as a viable political position, it contributed to the sectional division of the Democratic Party. But the cause of the final Democratic rupture was once again Kansas. In 1858 Congress had to choose between two different constitutions accompanying the territory's petition for admission to the Union. The so-called Lecompton Constitution was drawn up by proslavery partisans, who represented a minority of Kansas residents. Free-staters, knowing they were in the majority, submitted their own constitution to a popular referendum, whereas supporters of the Lecompton Constitution sent their document directly to Congress. President Buchanan supported the proslavery minority. But the leading northern Democrat in the Senate, Stephen Douglas of Illinois, had no choice but to reject the Lecompton Constitution, because it clearly violated his principle of popular sovereignty.

Douglas was in a difficult position. Southern Democrats assailed popular sovereignty as an affront to their rights of property in slaves. Northern critics pointed out that the Dred Scott decision had rendered popular sovereignty meaningless. In their famous 1858 debates, Lincoln shrewdly forced Douglas to confront the issue at Freeport. Given the Dred Scott decision, Lincoln asked, can the people of a territory legally exclude slavery? Although Douglas had answered the question before, he stood his ground. In what became known as the Freeport Doctrine, Douglas argued that the people of a territory could effectively exclude slavery simply by refusing to pass the laws necessary to protect slavery. That way no master would dare go there with his human property. Douglas's logic infuriated southern Democrats and led to the division of the party into northern and southern wings in 1860.

The Irrepressible Conflict

By the late 1850s the conflict between the North and the South began to seem irrepressible, and more and more Americans were saying so. Northern Democrats, led by Stephen Douglas, tried desperately to preserve a middle ground that would prevent the Union from breaking apart. Similarly, the last remaining Whigs in the Border States struggled to devise yet another compromise that would save the Union. But the middle ground was giving way to the irreconcilable positions represented by the Republican Party in the North and the Democratic Party in the South.

More than ever, the Democratic Party in the South was the voice of the slaveholding class, and by the late 1850s it's sole purpose was the defense of the inalienable right of property in slaves. On most matters southern Democrats were staunch advocates of states' rights, fearing the power a strong central government might use to interfere with southern slavery. They opposed protective tariffs, federal support for internal improvements (railroads, canals, turnpikes), and they were suspicious of any effort to reestablish a national bank. But when it came to the protection of slave property, southern Democrats became ardent supporters of strong central government. In response to Stephen Douglas's "Freeport Doctrine," Mississippi Senator Jefferson Davis proposed a federal slave code that would be imposed on any western territory that refused to protect slave property. A federal slave code would provide essential "protection for our slave property in the territories," a Virginia newspaper explained in 1860, adding that property in slaves was a "sacred constitutional right."

Meanwhile northern Republicans were moving in the opposite direction, questioning not only the existence of a constitutional right of property in slaves but the sanctity of property rights themselves. Once upon a time Whigs nurtured a reverence for the rule of law and the authority of the courts. But their Republican descendants, disgusted by the proslavery bias of the Supreme Court, began denouncing the "superstitious reverence" for judges. Judges, Republican Senator Charles Sumner declared, "are but men, and in all ages have shown a full share of human frailty." Republicans also questioned the primacy of property rights. The most powerful Republican in the 1850s, New York Senator William Seward, declared that "property . . . has always a bias toward oppression." And in 1859 Abraham Lincoln praised Thomas Jefferson for elevating human rights over property rights. He repeatedly denounced the Dred Scott decision and argued that there was no such thing as a constitutional right of property in slaves.

As the 1860 elections approached, the business of Congress was once again brought to a standstill by the depth of division over slavery. The number of fistfights, duels, and shouting matches had exploded over the course of the decade—nearly all of them caused by dissension over slavery. So deep were the divisions that the House of Representatives was unable to elect a speaker. After several northern congressmen endorsed an inflammatory antislavery book published by Hinton Rowan Helper, infuriated southern legislators tied Congress up in knots.

For years abolitionists and proslavery writers had been saying that the conflict between the North and the South over slavery was "irreconcilable." Frederick Douglass often said that Liberty and Slavery were at war with one another and that there could be no peace until one or the other was vanquished, until either slavery or freedom was the law everywhere in the land. George Fitzhugh, the most extreme of all proslavery theorists, had long argued the same thing, that the conflict between the slave and free society was irreconcilable. By the late 1850s, such talk had drifted from the margins into the mainstream. Southern politicians began to declare that the slave states were no longer safe within the Union. In Illinois, Abraham Lincoln opened his 1858 race for the U.S. Senate with a speech declaring that "a house divided against itself cannot stand," that a "crisis" was coming and would not end until either slavery had vanquished freedom or freedom had destroyed slavery throughout the Union. The most famous expression of this sentiment came in a speech William Seward gave in Rochester on October 25, 1858. The division over slavery between the North and the South, he said, "is an irrepressible conflict between opposing and enduring forces, and it means that the United States must and will, sooner or later, become either entirely a slaveholding nation, or entirely a free-labor nation."

By the time Seward gave his speech emotions were running so high, North and South, that it was easy to miss the substance of the disagreement behind the hysteria of the rhetoric. In truth, the slaveholders had little choice but to take the position they did. Their economy, their society, and their political power rested on their property rights in slaves. When northerners began to question those rights, the slaveholders had to defend themselves. And despite the overheated rhetoric, the terms on which the slaveholders launched their defense were in their own way reasonable and logical. Slaves *were* property, and property rights were supposed to be sacred. At the same time, it made perfect sense for northerners to defend the superiority of free labor. Their own way of life, not to mention the prosperity of their economy, rested on the basic principle of free labor—that no human being could rightfully own another. The aggressive expansion of slavery, and the disproportionate power of the slaveholders in national

Lincoln-Douglas Debate Poster In 1858 a little-known Illinois Republican, Abraham Lincoln, ran against Stephen A. Douglas for the U.S. Senate. Their seven campaign debates, one of them pictured above, brilliantly spelled out the differences between Democrats and Republicans over slavery. Though Lincoln lost the election, he did so well in the debates that his party nominated him for the presidency two years later.

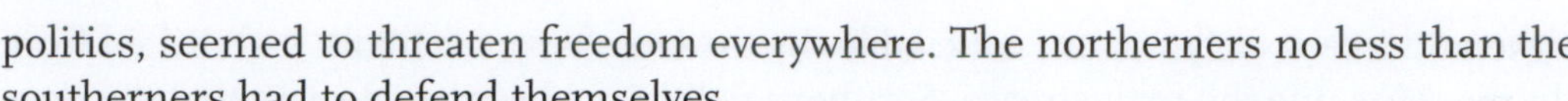

politics, seemed to threaten freedom everywhere. The northerners no less than the southerners had to defend themselves.

But if the conflict between the North and South was irrepressible, that did not mean Civil War was inevitable. The slide from dissension to armed conflict began in late 1859.

The Retreat from Union

Between 1859 and 1860 both the North and the South rejected the sanctity of the Union. In the South the retreat from unionism was a reaction to John Brown's raid on Harpers Ferry. Brown's death was greeted as a martyr's execution throughout much of the North, leading many southerners to conclude that a union of the North and the South was no longer viable. In 1860, with the election of Abraham Lincoln, the North abandoned a long-standing pattern of compromising with slavery for the sake of maintaining the Union.

John Brown's War Against Slavery

In the fall of 1858 the mysterious John Brown reemerged to launch another battle in his private war against slavery. Since the massacre at Pottawatomie Creek, Brown's movements had been obscure. He traveled between Canada and Kansas, New England and Ohio. By the late 1850s he had concocted a plan to invade Virginia and free the slaves. Friends told Brown his plan was unworkable. Frederick Douglass advised him to give it up. But Brown found support from a group of well-connected Bostonians who were dazzled by his appeal to action rather than words. Although they promised more money than they delivered, they delivered enough.

Brown rented a farm in Maryland, about five miles from the town of Harpers Ferry in western Virginia, where a small federal arsenal was located. He apparently planned to capture the arsenal and distribute the guns to slaves from the surrounding area, inciting a slave rebellion. On the evening of October 16, 1859, Brown and 18 followers crossed the Potomac River with a wagonload of guns, cut the telegraph wires leading into Harpers Ferry, overwhelmed a guard, and seized the armory. Brown ordered his men to scour the surrounding countryside to liberate slaves and take slaveholders prisoner. They found Colonel Lewis Washington, a member of the first president's family, and carried him back to Harpers Ferry as a hostage. Brown's mission was accomplished. He sat back and waited for the slaves to rise.

> I John Brown am now quite **certain** that the crimes of this **guilty, land: will** never be purged **away**; but with Blood. I had **as now I think: vainly** flattered myself that without **verry much** bloodshed; it might be done.
>
> JOHN BROWN'S LAST WORDS,
> December 2, 1859

The slaves did not rise, but the armed forces did. Marines were sent from Washington, DC, led by Lieutenant Colonel Robert E. Lee and his assistant, Lieutenant J. E. B. Stuart, both of whom would become leading Confederate generals. On the morning after Brown took control of Harpers Ferry, the militia surrounded the arsenal. The next day Stuart ordered Brown to surrender, and when Brown refused, 12 marines charged the room with bayonets. Two of Brown's men and one marine were killed, and Brown himself was wounded. The rebellion was over in less than two days.

The entire raid was "absurd," Abraham Lincoln later said. "It was not a slave insurrection," he added. "It was an attempt by white men to get up a revolt among slaves, in which the slaves refused to participate." The condemnation of Brown by responsible northerners and the embarrassment of Brown's supporters initially calmed southern outrage over the invasion. Over the next several weeks, however, northern opinion changed from contempt to admiration for Brown. It was not the raid itself that caused this shift of opinion. It was Brown's calm and dignified behavior in prison, at his trial, and at his own hanging. Brown's eloquent statements to the court and on the gallows moved northerners in vast numbers to extraordinary demonstrations of sympathy. On December 2, the day Brown was hanged, northern churches tolled their bells. Militia companies fired salutes. Public buildings across the North were draped in black. Although mainstream politicians disavowed Brown and his raid, white southerners saw that John Brown had become a hero to many northerners.

Northern sympathy for John Brown shocked the white South even more than the actual raid. Across the region, newspapers and politicians responded to Harpers Ferry by questioning the value of the Union itself. The Baltimore *Sun* announced that the South could not "live under a government, the majority of whose subjects or citizens regard John Brown as a martyr and a Christian hero, rather than a murderer and robber." In the end, however, it was not John Brown's raid that led the South to secede from the Union. It was the election of Abraham Lincoln.

Northerners Elect a President

In February 1860, as the nation's focus shifted from John Brown to the coming presidential election, Abraham Lincoln traveled to New York to speak to a large audience of influential eastern Republicans. They were sizing up possible candidates for the coming campaign. Speaking in the great hall of the newly opened Cooper Institute—later known as Cooper Union—Lincoln extended the argument he had made during his debates with Stephen Douglas. When southerners defended their right of property in slaves, Lincoln argued, they were presuming a constitutional right that did not exist. Instead, the Constitution protected slavery in narrow ways and only in the states where it already existed. Moreover, if the slave states seceded from the Union, they would forfeit whatever constitutional protection slavery did have.

John Brown Artist John Curry's painting of John Brown brilliantly captures Brown's larger-than-life personality. The biblical imagery is reminiscent of Moses and suggests Brown's sense of himself as an agent of the Lord sent by God to lead his nation out of bondage.

By making a radical claim—that there was no constitutional right of property in slaves—and by tying it to a threat to interfere with slavery if the South seceded, Lincoln established his antislavery credentials among leaders of the Republican Party. The Cooper Union Address helped Lincoln win his party's nomination, but it also proved to southern Democrats that his election would be a direct threat to slavery.

Lincoln could not hope to win any votes in the South, and for that he was attacked as a "sectional" candidate. But the truth was that by 1860 no major-party candidate could appeal to both the North and the South. For all practical purposes there were two different presidential elections that year. In the slave states a southern Democrat ran against a Constitutional Unionist. In the free states a northern Democrat ran against a Republican. On the surface, slavery in the territories remained the dominant issue. Below the surface, the future of the Union was about to be determined.

The Democratic Party met in April in Charleston, South Carolina, the center of extreme secessionist sentiment. Southern fire-eaters demanded federal recognition of slavery in all the territories as part of the Democratic Party platform. But Stephen Douglas, the leading candidate for the party's nomination, insisted on a reaffirmation of popular sovereignty. Douglas had a bare majority of the delegates supporting him, enough to push his platform through but not enough to win the party's nomination. When Douglas's plank was passed, 49 delegates from eight southern states walked out. The convention was deadlocked. After 57 ballots, the Democrats adjourned, agreeing to reconvene in Baltimore a month and a half later.

But the delay only made matters worse. In Baltimore, 110 southerners nominated their own candidate. Thus the Democrats put up two presidential aspirants in 1860. Stephen Douglas ran in the North advocating popular sovereignty and insisting that the Union itself hung in the balance of the election. John Breckinridge, the southern Democratic candidate, ran on a platform calling for federal recognition of slavery in all the territories. Another candidate, John Bell of Tennessee, tried unsuccessfully to revive the Whig Party by running on a Constitutional Unionist ticket. Neither Douglas, Breckinridge, nor Bell had much chance of winning.

The Republicans were far more united. With the scent of victory in their nostrils, tens of thousands of Republicans poured into Chicago. The leading candidate for the Republican nomination was William H. Seward of New York. But Seward's strength was limited to the uppermost states in the North. In the border states such as Pennsylvania, Indiana, and Illinois, Seward's antislavery politics were seen as too radical, and there was important opposition to him even in his home state of New York. What the party needed was a candidate whose antislavery credentials were unquestioned, but whose moderation could carry the critical states of the lower North. That candidate was Abraham Lincoln. Not only was Lincoln from Illinois, he tempered his radical critique of slavery with a constitutional restraint that made him acceptable to moderates and conservatives in the party. Unlike conservative Republicans, Lincoln did not race-bait very much and he opposed nativist restrictions on immigration. Unlike the party's radicals, Lincoln had supported the enforcement of the Fugitive Slave Act, denounced John Brown's raid on Harpers Ferry, and insisted that the federal government could not interfere in states where slavery already existed. Still, Lincoln made clear his view that slavery was immoral, that owning slaves was not a constitutionally protected property right, that Congress had the right to restrict slavery's expansion into the territories, and that the entire slave system should be placed "in the course of ultimate extinction." No major party had ever run a candidate dedicated to such a proposition.

Throughout the campaign, Lincoln and the Republicans scoffed at secessionist threats coming from the South. Breckinridge the Democrat and Bell the Constitutional Unionist also played down the possibility of disunion. But Stephen Douglas was so convinced that the election of Lincoln would result in secession and war that he actively campaigned as the only candidate who could hold the Union together. When it became clear that Lincoln was going to win, Douglas rearranged his campaign schedule to make a series of speeches in the slave states. He went South "not to ask for your votes for the Presidency," he told his audiences, "but to make an appeal to you on behalf of the Union."

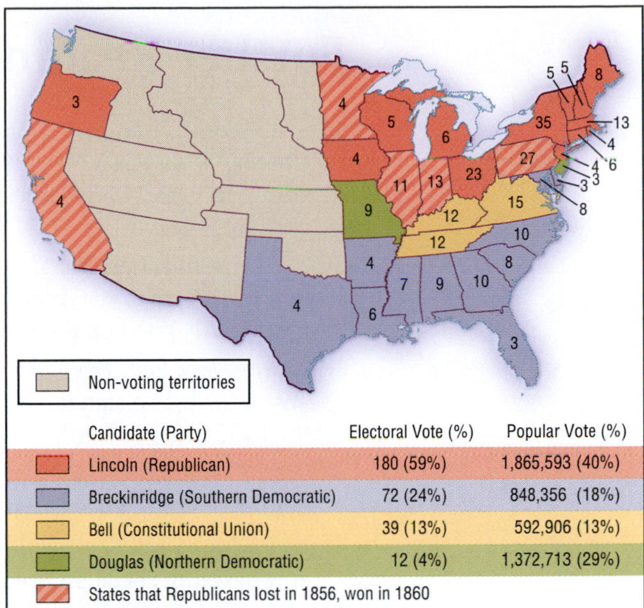

Map 14–5 The Election of 1860 By 1860, no presidential candidate could appeal to voters in both the North and the South. By then, the northern population had grown so rapidly that a united North could elect Lincoln to the presidency without any southern support.

Lincoln won every free state except New Jersey. Douglas got the second largest number of votes but took only one state, Missouri. Breckinridge, the southern Democrat, took 11 slave states, although his support within those states was concentrated in the districts with the lowest proportions of slaves. The slaveholders continued to vote their traditional Whig sympathies, supporting John Bell's Constitutional Unionist candidacy.

Lincoln did not campaign in the South. His name was not even on the ballot in most of the slave states. Nevertheless, he was able to win by appealing exclusively to voters in the North (see Map 14–5). This in turn allowed Lincoln to run on a platform dedicated to slavery's "ultimate extinction." Here was a double vindication for antislavery forces in the North: not only did the Republican victory show wide appeal for an antislavery platform, it also suggested that a dynamic economy based on free labor was bound to grow faster than a slave society. In their own way, white southerners agreed. They concluded that no matter what assurances Lincoln gave them, the future of slavery in the Union was doomed.

Conclusion

Frederick Douglass had misgivings about Lincoln but he sincerely hoped that the Republicans would win the 1860 elections. "Slavery is the issue—the single bone of contention between all parties and sections," he insisted. Slavery and freedom had guided the nation along two diverging historical pathways. The North was developing an urban, industrial economy based on the productive energy of wage labor. In the South, a prosperous slave economy fastened in place a system of intensely commercialized agriculture in which the laborers were commodities as much as the cash crops they produced. The political tensions that arose from these differences finally pushed the nation into civil war. And as the war progressed, the same differences in political economy would shape the destiny of the Union and Confederate forces.

Further Readings

John Ashworth, *Slavery, Capitalism, and Politics in the Antebellum Republic, Volume 2: The Coming of the Civil War, 1850–1861* (2007). A daunting but comprehensive account of competing party ideologies, emphasizing the irreconcilable conflict between the North and the South.

Don E. Fehrenbacher, *The Slaveholding Republic* (2001). A masterful summation of the problem of slavery in national politics from the Revolution to the Civil War. Fehrenbacher is particularly good on the territorial issue.

Eric Foner, *Free Soil, Free Labor, Free Men: The Ideology of the Republican Party Before the Civil War* (1970). The standard interpretation emphasizing the centrality of the labor issue and the fundamental conflict over slavery.

William E. Gienapp, *The Origins of the Republican Party, 1852–1856* (1987). This book is the definitive study, encompassing local as well as national issues.

Bruce Levine, *Half Slave, Half Free: The Roots of the Civil War* (1992). A good brief overview emphasizing social differences between the North and the South.

James Oakes, *The Radical and the Republican: Frederick Douglass, Abraham Lincoln, and the Triumph of Antislavery Politics* (2007). Traces the rise of antislavery politics through the careers of two of its greatest practitioners.

David Potter, *The Impending Crisis, 1848–1861* (1976). An insightful examination of the political crisis of the 1850s.

James A. Rawley, *Race and Politics: "Bleeding Kansas" and the Coming of the Civil War* (1969). The best account of events in Kansas.

Douglas Wilson and Rodney O. Davis, eds., *The Lincoln-Douglas Debates* (2008). The best-edited and most readable edition of the famous debates.

>> Timeline >>

▼ 1838
Frederick Douglass escapes from slavery

▼ 1844
Samuel F. B. Morse invents the telegraph

▼ 1846
David Wilmot introduces his "proviso"

▼ 1847
Treaty of Guadalupe Hidalgo

▼ 1848
Zachary Taylor elected president

▼ 1850
Taylor dies; Millard Fillmore becomes president
Compromise of 1850

▼ 1852
Uncle Tom's Cabin published in book form
Franklin Pierce elected president

▼ 1854
Gadsden Purchase ratified
Kansas-Nebraska Act
Ostend Manifesto

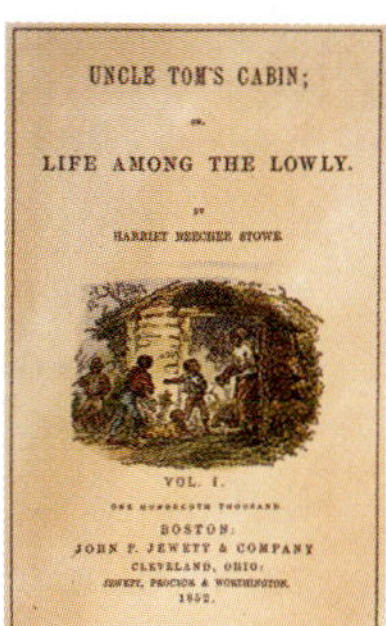

Who, What

Frederick Douglass 465
Stephen Douglas 474
Abraham Lincoln 481
Charles Sumner 482
John C. Frémont 483
Roger Taney 486
John Brown 490
Popular sovereignty 472
Wilmot Proviso 472
Compromise of 1850 474
Fugitive Slave Act 475
Know-Nothings 478
Ostend Manifesto 479
"Bleeding Kansas" 481
The Dred Scott decision 486
Harpers Ferry 490

Review Questions

1. What were the major differences between the northern and southern economies by the 1850s?
2. How did the war with Mexico provoke a conflict over slavery?
3. What did the Republican Party stand for?
4. What was the Kansas-Nebraska Act and why was it so important?
5. What were the major issues in the Lincoln-Douglas debates?

For further review materials and resource information, please visit www.oup.com/us/ofthepeople

▼ 1856
"Bleeding Kansas"
Sumner-Brooks affair
James Buchanan elected president

▼ 1857
Dred Scott decision

▼ 1858
Lincoln-Douglas debates

▼ 1859
John Brown's raid on Harpers Ferry

▼ 1860
Abraham Lincoln elected first Republican president

▼ 1861
South secedes from Union, Civil War begins

CHAPTER 15

Common Threads

>> What made the South secede from the Union?

>> In what ways did the military strategies of the North and South reflect the differences between the two regions?

>> What was the relationship between emancipation and war?

>> Why did the South lose the Civil War? Why did the North win?

>> What happened to the slaves who were freed by the war?

A War for Union and Emancipation 1861–1865

AMERICAN PORTRAIT

>> Edmund Ruffin

Edmund Ruffin was born in 1794 into one of the wealthiest planter families in eastern Virginia. By the age of 20 he was the master of a substantial plantation on the James River. Yet from his youth Edmund Ruffin was discontented and angry. He coveted a political career but his contempt for democracy thwarted him. In 1823 he won election to a four-year term in the Virginia state senate, but he was unwilling to forge the alliances and make the compromises that would bring him political influence. Before his term expired, Ruffin resigned his seat, "tired and disgusted with being a servant of the people." He never held public office again.

During the 1830s and 1840s Ruffin retreated to his plantations, publishing the results of his experiments in crop rotation, drainage techniques, and various new fertilizers. His work paid off in improved productivity, higher profits, and growing public esteem. But Ruffin, more interested in politics than farming, used his fame as an agricultural reformer to spread his proslavery message. By 1850 Ruffin was urging his fellow Virginians to secede from the Union to preserve slavery.

Ruffin made his leap from agricultural reformer to secessionist through the logic of political economy. A more productive slave economy, he reasoned, would protect the South from the growing power of the industrializing North. Inspired by other proslavery authors, Ruffin ended up placing all the world's peoples on a sliding scale that rose from the most savage to the most civilized. Savages, Ruffin asserted, were concerned only with meeting their bare physical needs. By contrast, civilized peoples sought to raise the standard of living by cultivating the mind as well as the body. The only way for barbaric peoples to rise above savagery, Ruffin claimed, was for the powerful and industrious to force shiftless and lazy people to work, usually by enslaving them. Slavery thus spurred both civilization and prosperity.

But Ruffin's general defense of slavery left several important questions unanswered: Who, for example, should be enslaved? Equals could not enslave equals, for that was both morally objectionable and socially disruptive. Southern slavery escaped this problem, Ruffin believed, because whites only enslaved racially inferior blacks. And what of the abolitionist claim that slavery was less efficient than wage labor? Ruffin agreed that in principle slaves lacked the motive of self-interest that made wage laborers more efficient, but he pointed to the exceptional conditions that tipped the balance in the United States. As long as western lands were available to absorb the surplus labor of the North, free laborers would work on their own farms at their own pace. But slaves were compelled to labor on precious cash crops that could be produced in climates where, Ruffin believed, only African Americans could work. As long as these exceptional conditions prevailed, slavery would be as efficient as free labor.

Over time the West was sure to fill up, and when that happened, Ruffin argued, free men and women would have no choice but to sell their labor at miserably low wages. Eventually the cost of free labor would sink so low that it could outperform slavery, but at that point, the misery of free laborers would give rise to socialism and anarchy. Thus northerners would pay the price of perpetual social unrest for their wealth and prosperity. Southern whites, by contrast, had struck the perfect balance between material well-being and social peace. By enslaving an "inferior" race, they could raise the general level of civilization without the disruptions associated with wage labor.

Edmund Ruffin had always believed that slavery was the issue dividing the North from the South. Ironically,

continued

>> **AMERICAN PORTRAIT** *continued*

as the two sections approached war, it was the northerners who clung to the belief that the Union could be held together with slavery intact. Most northerners started out thinking that the war could be fought only to restore the Union. Over time, they came to see it as a struggle to rid the nation of slavery as well. Edmund Ruffin was not surprised that the northern crusade to preserve the Union eventually became a crusade for the abolition of slavery.

OUTLINE 

From Union to Emancipation

Southerners made it clear that they were going to war to preserve their rights of property in slaves. In 1861 Confederate president Jefferson Davis justified secession on the grounds that northern Republican rule would make "property in slaves so insecure as to be comparatively worthless." Southerners talked in general about defending "states' rights" or "property rights," but they were referring specifically to the right of the states to maintain slavery and the right of individuals to hold property in slaves. These were among the cherished principles white southerners believed they had inherited from the Founding Fathers of the nation. Slavery had been legal in

every one of the thirteen colonies represented on the Declaration of Independence. In declaring their own independence, white southerners believed they were affirming rather than rejecting the legacy of the American Revolution. Their rights and prosperity were no longer safe in the Union the Founders had created. So they made a confederacy of their own where slavery could survive unharmed, forever.

But the Union was a sacred thing for most Northerners, a beacon of liberty in a world of tyrannical kings and arrogant aristocracies. To break the Union apart would be treason, but it would also prove to the world that democratic republics could not hold themselves together. If the Union collapsed, "the last best hope" of the oppressed peoples of the world would go down with it. Northerners understood that slavery was the *cause* of the war, but at the outset most supported war to restore the Union, not to destroy slavery. Some did not care enough about the plight of African Americans to support a war to secure their freedom. Those who did care usually agreed with Lincoln and the Republicans that the federal government had no authority to interfere with slavery where it already existed. In his inaugural address of March 1861, Abraham Lincoln reasserted his intention to leave slavery alone in the South. But he also denied there was any such thing as a constitutional right to property in slaves, and he warned that, by seceding, the South risked losing whatever federal protection slavery did enjoy. Like most northerners, Lincoln would fight for the restoration of the Union. Soon after the war began, however, more and more Yankees began asking themselves a question: What would be the point of restoring the Union without also destroying slavery, the very thing that had torn the Union apart?

The South Secedes

As the news of Lincoln's election flashed across the telegraph wires, the South Carolina state legislature called a secession convention. On December 20, 1860, the state withdrew from the Union on the grounds that northerners had elected a president who denied the existence of a right of property in slaves. "They have encouraged and assisted thousands of slaves to leave their homes," South Carolina declared, "and those who remain have been incited . . . to servile insurrection." Within weeks, Mississippi, Florida, Alabama, Georgia, Louisiana, and Texas followed

> **We affirm that these ends for which this Government was instituted have been defeated, and the Government itself has been destructive of them by the action of the non-slaveholding States. Those States have assumed the right of deciding upon the propriety of our domestic institutions; and have denied the rights of property established in fifteen of the States and recognized by the Constitution; they have denounced as sinful the institution of Slavery; they have permitted the open establishment among them of a society, whose avowed object is to disturb the peace and eloin the property of the citizens of other States. They have encouraged and assisted thousands of our slaves to leave their homes; and those who remain, have been incited, by emissaries, books and pictures, to servile insurrection.**
>
> "DECLARATION OF THE CAUSES WHICH INDUCED THE SECESSION OF SOUTH CAROLINA,"
> December, 1860

suit (see Map 15–1). Then, as quickly as it had begun, the secession movement came to a halt. The slave states of the upper South refused to leave the Union simply because Lincoln was elected. Ardent secessionists began to suspect that the South was not unified in its opposition to the North.

The upper South was dominated by cooperationists rather than secessionists. Cooperationists were committed to remaining in the Union, provided the Lincoln administration "cooperated" with the South. Thus even after Lincoln's inauguration Virginia, Arkansas, and Missouri would not secede. The state legislatures of Kentucky and Delaware refused to authorize secession conventions, and in Tennessee and North Carolina the voters refused. Lincoln and many Republicans hoped that if they moved cautiously they could keep the upper South in the Union and thereby derail the secession movement. But cooperationism in the upper South turned out to be a weak foundation on which to rebuild the Union. Cooperationists pledged their loyalty to the Union only if the federal government met certain demands for the protection of slavery.

Cooperationist demands formed the basis of several last-minute attempts at sectional compromise. The most famous was a series of constitutional amendments

Map 15–1 The Secession of the Southern States The South seceded in two stages. During the "secession winter" of 1860/1861, the lower South states seceded in reaction to the election of Abraham Lincoln. The following spring, the upper South seceded in response to Lincoln's attempt to resupply Fort Sumter. The border slave states of Maryland, Delaware, Kentucky, and Missouri never left the Union.

proposed by Senator John J. Crittenden of Kentucky. The Crittenden Compromise would have restored the Missouri Compromise line and guaranteed federal protection of slavery south of that line in all territories currently held or thereafter acquired by the United States. It would have virtually prohibited Congress from abolishing slavery in Washington, DC, and from regulating the interstate slave trade. Finally, it required the federal government to compensate masters who were unable to recover fugitive slaves from the North.

Each of these concessions was unacceptable to the Republicans, especially the one protecting slavery in territories acquired in the future. This struck Republicans as an open invitation for southerners to expand the slave power into Central America, South America, and the Caribbean. In any case, once the lower South seceded, the Republicans concluded that *any* compromise amounted to northern surrender to southern blackmail. They began making nationalist appeals hoping to rally all northerners around the preservation of the Union. By early 1861 northern Democrats who cared little about slavery were nevertheless unwilling to compromise with southern states that had left the Union. For these reasons the Crittenden proposals—like every other compromise scheme—fell on deaf ears throughout the North.

In truth the conflict over slavery had become irreconcilable. By the spring of 1861 most southerners agreed with Edmund Ruffin that there should be no more compromise with the North. Even "cooperationists" insisted that the southern states had every right to secede and should do so if Lincoln committed any act of overt "coercion." It was also clear that the confrontation would come at one of the two forts still held by the Union army in the seceded states—Fort Pickens in Pensacola, Florida, or Fort Sumter in Charleston Harbor. Realizing that Pickens was indefensible, Jefferson Davis sent the flamboyant P. G. T. Beauregard to Charleston Harbor to prepare the defenses against the impending Union invasion. Beauregard captivated Charleston, but more importantly he surrounded Charleston Harbor with more than enough military hardware to capture Sumter.

Out of respect for his long years of service to the cause, southern fire-eaters invited Ruffin to South Carolina, where he was given the privilege of firing one of the first shots of the Civil War. At 4:30 in the morning on April 12, 1861, Ruffin aimed a rifle at Fort Sumter and began shooting. For 33 hours Confederates bombarded the fort, located on an island in Charleston Harbor, to prevent the U.S. government from fortifying its troops with nonmilitary supplies. With no alternative, the Union commander raised the white flag of surrender. Fort Sumter fell to the Confederates, and the Civil War began.

Though he undoubtedly hoped for peace, Lincoln had long since concluded that a war was inevitable. He probably understood that his attempt to resupply Fort Sumter would provoke an armed assault. But by sending only provisions and by announcing in advance that there were no weapons in the cargo headed to Fort Sumter, Lincoln had skillfully maneuvered the South into firing the first shot. For southerners who had declared their independence months earlier, any federal attempt to supply Sumter, whether with food or with weapons, amounted to a declaration of war. And so the war came. The day Fort Sumter surrendered, President Lincoln issued a call to the states for 75,000 militiamen to report for duty within 90 days. The governors of Tennessee, Virginia, North Carolina, Arkansas, Kentucky, and Missouri refused to comply with Lincoln's request. Two days later

Virginia seceded, and within a month Arkansas, Tennessee, and North Carolina did the same. Northern hopes of holding on to the upper South had vanished.

But the South remained divided. Four slave states (Kentucky, Maryland, Delaware, and Missouri) never joined the Confederacy. In the mountains of western North Carolina and eastern Tennessee, unionist sentiment remained strong throughout the war years. Virginia was literally torn apart. The western third of the state voted overwhelmingly against secession, and when the eastern slaveholders decided to leave the Union, western counties formed their own state government. (In 1863 the state of West Virginia was admitted to the Union.) These were among the earliest indications that southern whites were not united. Where slavery was weak, support for secession was weak also. Where slavery thrived, so did the sentiment for secession. Yet despite these internal divisions, support for secession was remarkably widespread in the South, and over the next four years white southerners would put up a long, hard fight to sustain the independence of the Confederacy.

Civilians Demand a Total War

Most Americans expected the war to last only a few months. Lincoln's first call for troops asked volunteers to enlist for 90 days, although he hedged his bets by calling for three-year enlistments as well. Confederate soldiers initially signed up for 12 months. A year later they were required to serve "for the duration" of the war. Although both sides began with relatively limited military and political goals, the conflict steadily descended into a "hard" war that produced shocking numbers of military casualties, horrifying massacres of black prisoners, and a deliberate campaign to undermine civilian morale through the widespread destruction of the homes and farms of southern whites. In the end, hard war would also mean the unconditional surrender of Confederate armies and the destruction of southern slavery.

In the weeks following the Fort Sumter crisis, enthusiasm for war overflowed in both the Union and the Confederacy. Mere military victory was not enough. In the spring of 1861, one southern woman prayed that "God may be with us to give us strength to conquer them, to exterminate them, to lay waste to every Northern city, town and village, to destroy them utterly." The following year southern troops burned the town of Chambersburg, Pennsylvania, to the ground, and in 1864 Jefferson Davis sent Confederate agents to New York City, where they set fire to 10 hotels, hoping to send the city up in flames.

Northerners felt no differently toward southerners. Even before the fighting began, in December 1860, Ohio senator Benjamin Wade talked of "making the south a desert." In the wake of Fort Sumter, one northern judge argued that if the war persisted, the North should "restore New Orleans to its native marshes, then march across the country, burn Montgomery to ashes, and serve Charleston in the same way. . . . We must starve, drown, burn, shoot the traitors." The war had barely begun and the civilians in the North and the South were already pressuring their political leaders to get on with the destruction of the enemy.

The military was more hesitant. For several months both the Union and Confederate commanders concentrated on building up their armies. Neither side was prepared for battle and neither sought it. The entire U.S. Army had only 16,000 troops scattered across the continent. Under the direction of aged war hero General Winfield Scott, Union military strategy was initially designed to take advantage of the North's naval superiority by blockading the entire South, but there was almost no navy, either. Nevertheless, as spring became summer, civilians in both the North and the South demanded something more dramatic. "Forward to Richmond!" cried Horace Greeley, echoing northern sentiment for a swift capture of the new Confederate capital.

Slaves Take Advantage of the War

In the South the enthusiasm for battle was compounded by fantasies of a race war between African Americans and whites. The lower South seceded while still in the grip of the insurrection panics that followed John Brown's raid on Harpers Ferry. Few slaves actually joined with Brown, but that did little to calm the fears of southern whites. Such fears were usually exaggerated. In 1861 this was no longer the case.

As soon as the war began, slaves made strenuous efforts to collect war news. House servants listened in on conversations at the masters' residences and reported the news to field hands in the slave quarters. Every neighborhood had one or two literate slaves who got hold of a newspaper. News of the war's progress spread along what the slaves called the "grapevine telegraph."

Shortly after Lincoln was inaugurated, several slaves in Florida escaped to Fort Pickens, claiming their freedom. In Virginia, scarcely a month after Fort Sumter, Union commander Benjamin F. Butler refused to return three runaway slaves on the grounds that they would have been put to work on Confederate military fortifications. Butler called the runaways "contrabands" of war, and the label stuck. As the number of contrabands mounted, Butler demanded that his superiors clarify Union policy. "As a military question it would seem to be a measure of necessity to deprive

Escaping Slaves Designated "contrabands" of war, these Virginia slaves are escaping to Union lines in August 1862. The Lincoln administration took office with a promise not to interfere with southern slavery, but runaways like those pictured here helped push the Union toward a policy of emancipation.

their masters of their services," he wrote on May 27, 1861. Immediately realizing that Butler's proposal raised fundamental questions, Lincoln called his cabinet together to discuss the matter on May 30. As soon as the meeting adjourned, Secretary of War Simon Cameron telegraphed Butler that his proposal to retain "contraband" slaves "is approved." The Fugitive Slave Act was effectively nullified.

But emancipation was still a long way off. For every runaway who made it to Union lines there were hundreds still trapped in slavery on farms and plantations across the South, and most would remain trapped until the war was over. War disrupted the routines of slave life, but if slavery survived the war, the plantations would recover from the disruption. It had happened many times before in the long history of human slavery; it had even happened in America. Southern slave society had weathered the tremendous upheaval of the American Revolution, and if the slaveholders had anything to say about it, slavery would outlast the Civil War as well. The slaves were determined to win their freedom, but their masters had the guns. For the balance of power to tip in their favor, the slaves would need allies. Specifically, they would need the U. S. government, and the Union army. But that would take time.

Military Strategy and the Shift in War Aims

No single military strategy defined either the Confederate or Union war efforts, if only because there was disagreement on both sides among generals and between the military and civilian authorities about the best way to win the war. But in general the South pursued a defensive strategy. If the Confederate armies could hold off Union attacks, taking advantage of interior lines to move men efficiently to different theaters of war, they might be able to wear down the North until it gave up the fight. Throughout the war Confederate commanders moved their armies like chess pieces across the interior lines of the southern playing field to engage larger Union armies: from the Shenandoah Valley to Manassas, from New Orleans to Shiloh, from northern Virginia to Tennessee. It was, for the most part, a successful strategy. But at various times the Confederates pursued a more aggressive if less successful strategy. Robert E. Lee invaded the North twice, for example, once in September of 1862 and again in July of 1863, and both times his armies were defeated and he was sent scrambling back into Virginia.

The Union forces needed a more aggressive strategy, but it took some time to develop. At the outset General Winfield Scott proposed a gigantic siege of the entire South, choking the Confederacy off from access to the outside world by an increasingly successful blockade. Critics derided this as "the anaconda plan." But long after Scott had retired, the naval squeeze of the South remained a key element of northern military strategy, and some of the most consistently successful northern commanders of the war were admirals, such as David Farragut and Andrew Foote. Lincoln had much more trouble with his generals than with his admirals, particularly in the crucial Army of the Potomac that fought most of the major battles in the East. The problems began with George McClellan, who replaced Scott as general in chief, and who developed a strategy aimed at capturing the Confederate capital of Richmond, Virginia. Eventually Lincoln concluded that capturing territory was no replacement for defeating armies, and until the last year of the war the president struggled with a succession of eastern generals who did not agree that their goal had to be the destruction of the Confederate armies. It was not enough to drive Robert E.

Lee's army out of Maryland or Pennsylvania, Lincoln insisted; the army itself had to be destroyed. For the same reason, the capture of Richmond was a strategic fantasy so long as Lee's armies were parked in waiting somewhere nearby. It was not until 1863, with Grant's successful capture of the Confederate armies trapped in Vicksburg, that Lincoln felt he had a general who shared his strategic commitment to the unconditional surrender of the Confederate armed forces. By then, Lincoln had also embraced a final component of northern strategy, "hard war," aimed at undermining the morale of southern civilians. The most revolutionary piece of the hard-war strategy was emancipation.

The first test of Union and Confederate military strength came on July 21, 1861, when inadequately trained Union and Confederate forces fought by a creek called Bull Run at the town of Manassas Junction, Virginia, 25 miles from Washington. Everyone knew the battle was coming. Spectators with picnic baskets followed the Union army out of Washington to watch from the surrounding hillsides. Among the southerners who came to watch was Edmund Ruffin.

The Confederates took up a defensive line stretching eight miles along Bull Run and waited for the enemy to attack. Taking advantage of their interior lines, the Confederates made the first strategic use of the railroad to rapidly shift reinforcements from the Shenandoah Valley to the battlefield at Manassas. The battle itself, fought by inadequately trained and untested troops, resembled a brutal struggle between two armed mobs more than a well-executed set of maneuvers. Nevertheless, the arrival of Confederate reinforcements proved crucial. And the first battle of Bull Run did establish at least one new military reputation. A southern officer named Thomas J. Jackson, perched on his horse "like a stone wall," inspired his men to drive back the Union advance. (It would not be the last time "Stonewall" Jackson would give the Union army grief.) The green Union troops, unaccustomed to the confusion of the battlefield, turned back in retreat. As they headed east toward Washington, frightened spectators clogged the road in panic and the retreat turned into a rout.

Most southerners were ecstatic, and perhaps somewhat overconfident, as a result of their victory. By contrast, the chaos in the Union ranks shocked the North into the realization that this would be no 90-day war. To discipline the Union troops, Lincoln put George B. McClellan in command of the Army of the Potomac.

The defeat also prompted northerners to start thinking about emancipation. When the war began, the Republicans were pledged to leave slavery undisturbed. Butler's contraband policy was the first crack in that policy, and the Union defeat at Bull Run drove the first wedge into it. Only weeks before Bull Run, the Congress had passed a resolution reaffirming that the war was aimed at nothing more

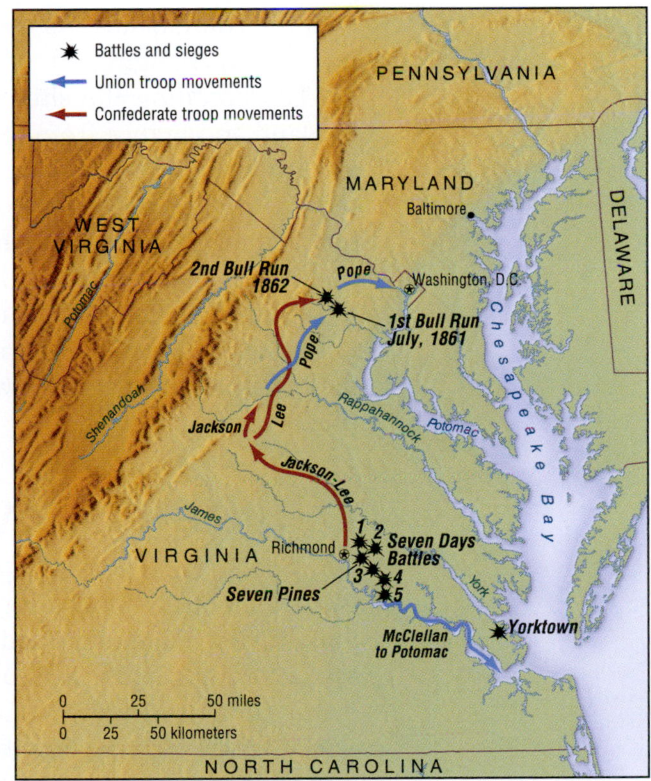

Map 15-2 The Virginia Campaigns of 1861–1862 Between the first and second battles of Bull Run, the Confederate armies in Virginia consistently frustrated northern attempts to capture Richmond, the capital of the Confederate States of America. Superior southern generalship was largely responsible for the northern defeats.

than the restoration of the Union. Even radical Republicans held their tongues. But the humiliating Union defeat suddenly changed all of that. Churches and civic associations across the North began sending petitions declaring that the war could not be won without destroying the slave system that had caused the war. Union soldiers began saying such things in their letters and diaries. The radicals broke their silence and began arguing that emancipation was a "military necessity."

Signaling this shift, the Republican-dominated Congress passed a Confiscation Act within weeks of the battle of Bull Run. For the first time, the federal government committed itself to confiscating any property, including slaves, used to prosecute the war against the United States. Strictly speaking, neither confiscated nor contraband slaves were emancipated. Most Republicans, the radicals included, worried that the Constitution prohibited the government from permanently confiscating property, slaves included. Technically, confiscated slaves would have to be returned to their owners once the war ended. Nevertheless, Senator Crittenden denounced the Confiscation Act as "revolutionary." But Lincoln signed it anyway and more than a few northern military commanders began enforcing the law somewhat liberally.

By the fall of 1861 the Union army was relying on the labor of fugitive slaves to support the northern military effort, thus stretching the definition of "military necessity." In his first annual message in December, President Lincoln urged Congress to pass legislation encouraging the four border states still in the Union to sell their slaves to the federal government, which would then "liberate" them, along with the contrabands. As the new year of 1862 began, the nature of the Civil War was already changing.

Also prodding the shift in war aims was the North's determination to keep England and France from recognizing the Confederate government. The Confederacy hoped to keep Europeans from respecting the Union blockade of southern ports. A diplomatic crisis loomed in late 1861 when an unruly Union navy captain intercepted a British ship, the *Trent,* in Havana. He forced two Confederate commissioners to disembark before allowing the *Trent* to sail on. The commissioners had slipped through the Union blockade and were headed for Europe, hoping to secure diplomatic recognition of the Confederacy. When the British protested, the Lincoln administration wisely backed down and released them. "One war at a time," Lincoln said.

Mobilizing for War

By the end of the first summer, both sides realized that the conflict would last for more than a few months and would demand all the resources the North and South could command. But in 1860 neither side had many military resources to command. By the end of the war approximately 2.1 million men had served in the Union armed forces. Another 900,000 served the Confederacy. To raise and sustain such numbers was an immense political and social problem. To feed, clothe, and arm such numbers of fighters was an equally immense technological problem. To pay for such armed forces was an immense economic problem. As the Civil War progressed, it therefore became a test of the competing economies of the North and the South (see Figure 15–1).

Thomas Nast's *Seventh Regiment Departing for the War from New York City, April 1861* The enthusiasm on display was typical of popular sentiment in both the North and the South at the very beginning of the war. Neither side was prepared for the long and bloody war that followed.

The Confederate States of America

By the spring of 1861 the secessionists had persuaded 11 states to leave the Union. They had convened a constitutional convention in Montgomery, Alabama, and drafted a basic charter for their new government, the Confederate States of America. They had proclaimed Richmond, Virginia, their nation's capital, and they had selected as president an experienced politician and Mississippi planter, Jefferson Davis.

The Confederate constitution varied in a few interesting ways from the U.S. Constitution. The Confederate chief executive served a single, six-year term and had a line-item veto, for example. But the most important constitutional differences had to do with slavery. The slaveholders preferred their markets the same way they preferred their power over the slaves—without restraints. The free market in slaves captured this dual preference perfectly. So it made sense that the Confederate constitution defined slaves as property and protected slavery as an inviolable right of property. It also made sense that the Confederacy's constitution outlawed protective tariffs and severely restricted the government's power to build railroads, canals, and turnpikes. This was the fundamental charter of a highly commercialized slave society.

In addition to these constitutional differences there were several political differences between the U.S.A. and the C.S.A. The most striking was the absence of

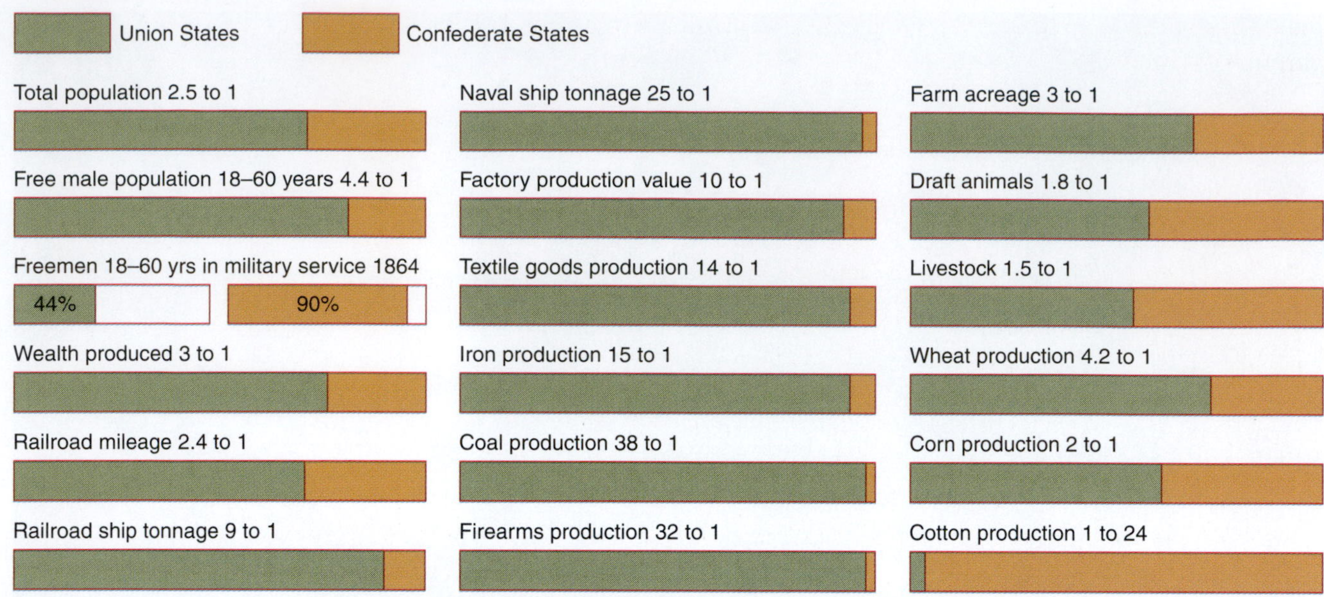

Figure 15-1 The Productive Capacities of the Union and Confederacy Not only did the northern economy dwarf the South's industrial capacity, it also outpaced southern agricultural production in everything but cotton.

a two-party system in the South. The Whig Party had collapsed in the North during the early 1850s, and the Republican Party took its place. Throughout the war, the northern Democrats represented a strong but loyal opposition to the Lincoln administration. In the South, by contrast, the Democratic Party ruled without opposition after the Whigs collapsed. As a result, internal dissent within the Confederacy took the form of factional squabbling within the Democratic Party.

One of the most consistent sources of tension was the South's commitment to states' rights, which often conflicted with the Confederacy's need to mount a concerted defense of the new nation. This led to a series of conflicts between Jefferson Davis and several state governors, in particular Joseph E. Brown of Georgia and Zebulon Vance of North Carolina. Brown and Vance were both loyal Confederates, but in their determination to protect their states they frequently locked horns with the Confederate president. Personalities compounded the problem. Where the governors were arrogant and abrasive, Jefferson Davis was prickly and intemperate.

It is not clear whether any of these political and constitutional differences made much difference to the outcome of the war. Southerners realized soon enough that their devotion to the free market would lose them the war. In the end the Confederacy would sustain itself with a command economy the likes of which the United States has never seen, before or since. Abraham Lincoln was certainly more personable than his Confederate counterpart and better able than Davis to slough off his critics, often with a laugh. But Lincoln's critics were, if anything, more threatening than Davis's. Northern opponents of the war were sometimes violent, though more often they expressed their opposition through the Democratic Party. Like Davis, Lincoln was forced to deal with obstreperous states, and at least a few northern governors seemed determined to undermine the Union war effort. Both presidents suspended habeas corpus and jailed dissidents to counteract the threat of internal subversion. And whatever its internal weaknesses, the Confederate government managed to sustain itself for four years against a massive Union invasion. In the final analysis the Confederacy failed because its armies, not its politics, were weaker than the Union's.

Union Naval Supremacy

The conviction that commerce ruled the world came naturally to the leaders of southern slave society. At the beginning of the war Confederate strategists believed they could bring their enemies to heel by starving them of cotton. By withholding their most valuable cash crop from the market, they would cripple northern industry and force England to recognize Confederate independence.

The Yankees knew better. From the outset northern strategists hoped to use their superior naval forces to prevent the Confederacy from selling its cotton abroad. By the closing months of 1861, the Union navy controlled vast stretches of the Atlantic and Gulf coasts. By early 1862, Union forces were in a position to enforce their blockade, except for a magnificent new weapon designed to thwart Union naval supremacy.

The South refitted an old Union ship, the *Merrimac,* with thick iron plates that rendered it all but impervious to conventional weapons. Rechristened the *Virginia,* the ironclad ship sailed into Union-controlled waters at Hampton Roads, Virginia, on March 8, 1862, and proceeded to wreak havoc on helpless northern ships. But that night the Union's own ironclad, the *Monitor,* arrived from New York. For most of the following day the "battle of the ironclads" raged on, with neither vessel dominating. But a standoff was as good as a defeat for the Confederates because it left the Union navy in control of the coast and better able to enforce its blockade. After the battle the *Virginia* slipped up the James River to assist in the defense of Richmond, but in May the Confederates destroyed their own ironclad rather than allow it to be captured by Union forces.

Beyond the blockade, the greatest achievements of the Union navy came in those rare but crucial occasions when it launched joint operations with the army. This was not easy, because during the Civil War there was no Pentagon and no Joint Chiefs of Staff to coordinate the two branches of the military. Any joint army-navy ventures would depend on the personalities of the commanders involved, or on the direct participation of President Lincoln—the only person who could issue orders to both branches of the armed services. There was a string of successful joint operations early in the war—at Port Royal in November 1861, the capture of New Orleans in early 1862, and most

> **The prevailing ideas entertained by [Thomas Jefferson] and most of the leading statesmen at the time of the formation of the old Constitution were, that the enslavement of the African was in violation of the laws of nature; that it was wrong in principle, socially, morally and politically. . . . Our new Government is founded upon exactly the opposite ideas; its foundations are laid, its cornerstone rests, upon the great truth that the negro is not equal to the white man; that slavery, subordination to the superior race, is his natural and moral condition.**
>
> ALEXANDER STEPHENS,
> Vice President of the Confederate States of America

impressively the collaboration between U. S. Grant and Andrew Foote in the capture of Forts Henry and Donelson a few months later. But just as often, communication between the army and the navy broke down and the results—in the unsuccessful effort to capture Charleston and in the Red River campaign of 1864—were disastrous. Still, by the end of the war the Union had built one of the largest and most modern navies in the world, not to be matched in American history until World War II.

Southern Military Advantages

The Union dominated the naval war, but on land the southern military had several advantages. More southerners had gone to military academies than had northerners. In the early years of the war these graduates brought skill and discipline to the Confederate army that the Union could not match. The South's greatest advantage, however, was that it was defending its own territory. It did not have to invade the North, destroy the Union army, or wipe out the North's industrial capacity. Closer to their sources of supply, the southern armies operated in the midst of a friendly civilian population, except for the slaves.

By contrast, the North had to fight an offensive war. It had to invade the South, destroy the Confederate armies, capture and retain a huge Confederate territory, and wipe out the South's capacity to fight. Northern soldiers fought on unfamiliar ground surrounded by a hostile civilian population, not counting the slaves.

The Union required longer lines of supply and much larger supply provisions. An invading northern army of 100,000 men had to carry with it 2,500 wagons and 35,000 animals. It consumed 600 tons of supplies a day. The farther it penetrated into southern territory, the more its ranks were thinned by the need to maintain increasingly tenuous supply lines. The more territory the Union troops conquered, the more they were shifted from battle duty to occupation forces. As a result, many major battles were fought by roughly even numbers of Union and Confederate troops.

Even in battle the defensive posture of the Confederate army was an advantage. Forts and cities on high ground (like Vicksburg and Fredericksburg) could maintain themselves against large numbers of invading troops. In the Union invasion of northern Virginia in 1864, Confederate general Robert E. Lee repeatedly held off much larger Union forces.

Besides his commitment to destroying enemy armies rather than capturing territory, Lincoln developed a second basic strategy for Union military victory—designed to overcome the advantage the South had in operating from interior lines. To take advantage of the North's superior numbers, Lincoln wanted his generals to launch coordinated attacks on different southern armies at different times. This strategy had worked, for example, in New Orleans. Once Farragut's naval forces had successfully barged past Confederate defenses on the lower Mississippi River, the army was able to capture New Orleans without a fight because the southern troops had been pulled from the city to meet Grant's army at Shiloh. But as with his strategy of engaging armies rather than fighting for territory, Lincoln found that launching coordinated attacks was easier on paper than it was in practice. Until the end of the war the commander in chief was frustrated by Union generals who made excuses for not pressing their armies forward in time, giving the Confederates the ability to continue shifting their own forces about to meet Union assaults that came one after another rather than all at once.

The Battle of Fredericksburg, Virginia, December 13, 1862 This disastrous defeat for the Union Army raised speculation that Lincoln might not issue the Emancipation Proclamation, which he did less than three weeks later.

The Slave Economy in Wartime

Secessionists argued that slavery gave the South several clear military assets. Because they were agricultural workers, the slaves could be shifted easily from cash crops to foodstuffs. With this single stroke, the Confederacy could feed its civilians, supply its armies, and meanwhile cripple the enemy by starving the industrial world's textile mills of desperately needed cotton. With slaves at home doing the work, a very high proportion of white men were able to serve in the southern military. And within the Confederate armies slaves and free blacks were impressed into nonmilitary service as construction workers, teamsters, nurses, and cooks, freeing up more white soldiers to do battle with the enemy. In all of these ways slavery reduced the North's advantage in the number of military-age men.

In certain ways, the relative backwardness of the slave economy had military advantages. Because of slavery the South had remained a largely rural society. Southern country boys knew how to shoot guns and how to ride and treat horses better than shopkeepers and factory workers in the Yankee armies. In the first years of the war the southern cavalry was far superior to its northern counterpart. When the war started, many white southerners assumed that the average Confederate could easily whip two Yankees.

But the southerners assumed incorrectly. They overestimated England's dependence on American cotton and underestimated the strength of Britain's economic ties to the North. The English refused to break the Union blockade of the South or grant diplomatic recognition to the Confederacy. King Cotton diplomacy failed, and so did the slave economy. If slavery freed 60 percent of southern men for military service, it eliminated from military service the 40 percent of the population that was enslaved. When masters and their sons went off to war, the productivity of their farms collapsed and in the end the rural South had trouble feeding itself. With the men gone it was harder to control the slaves left behind and, when Union armies approached, harder still to keep slaves from running off. Even the superiority of the southern cavalry gave way as the Union cavalry improved and the growing use of rifles made traditional cavalry charges deadly.

Above all, slavery diminished the South's industrial strength. Ninety percent of the nation's factories were in the North. Furthermore, the bulk of the Confederacy's industrial capacity was located in the upper South, which was overrun by Union forces early in the war. The South's ability to arm and supply its military was therefore severely restricted. Nevertheless, the South did manage to find enough rifles. The Confederacy also did a remarkable job of producing gunpowder and ammunition. As a result, the Confederate soldier was generally well armed. But he was not well fed or well clothed. The South simply could not provide its army with food enough to keep its soldiers adequately nourished. Confederates often fought in rags and barefoot.

Slavery also crippled the South's ability to finance its war. The cotton crop was systematically embargoed. Because slaves earned no money, they could not be tapped for income taxes as northern workers were. In any case, white southerners remained true to the Jacksonian tradition of resistance to taxation. To finance its military campaign, the South began to print money in huge quantities. By 1865 a Confederate dollar had the purchasing power that one Confederate cent had in 1861.

In the North, prospering farms and growing factories generated substantial taxable income. In addition to the $600 million raised from taxes on incomes and personal property, the Union government eventually sold $1.5 billion worth of government bonds. The North also supplemented its tax revenues by printing money, the famous "greenbacks," which became legally acceptable as currency everywhere in the country. The Union government also floated war bonds. To ease the flow of so many dollars, the Republicans passed the National Bank Act in 1863. This law rationalized the monetary system, making the federal government what it remains today, the only printer of money and the arbiter of the rules governing the nation's banking structure.

On balance the southern slave economy did remarkably well. The Confederacy staggered through the war with ragged soldiers, starving civilians, makeshift factories, and inflated currency. But as long as it could sustain its armies in the field, the Confederacy survived. Johnny Reb and Billy Yank had the ammunition they needed to fight. The question was, did they have the will to fight on and the commanders they needed to win the war?

What Were Soldiers Fighting For?

Political, military, and economic differences are the tangible reasons that armies win or lose wars, but there are also important psychological reasons. Southern soldiers fought from a variety of motives. Many were simply caught up in the initial outburst of enthusiasm. Above all, they fought to protect their homes and their families from Yankee invasion. Most Confederate soldiers took for granted that they were fighting to preserve slavery, and they saw the threat to slavery in personal terms, even when they themselves owned no slaves. In the southern economy slavery was the only real avenue of advancement. To own a slave was an abstract symbol of mastery, but more than that it was the source of southern prosperity.

The defense of homes and slaves gave southern patriotism a concrete and individualistic flavor. The "spirit of 1776" loomed large in the letters and diaries of Confederate soldiers. They saw themselves struggling to preserve the rights and liberties that their forefathers had won from Great Britain. But the right they fought for was the right to own slaves, and the liberty they defended was freedom from government interference with slavery.

Nevertheless, class distinctions affected the levels of patriotism in the Confederate armed forces. Slaveholders and their sons were far more likely to express patriotic sentiments than were soldiers from yeoman families. Troops from states where slavery was relatively unimportant, such as North Carolina, were markedly less enthusiastic about the war than were troops from states like South Carolina, where slavery was strong.

Class divisions were less severe in the Union army. Impoverished immigrants sometimes joined the military to secure a steady source of income and, in later years, a substantial bounty. But Catholic immigrants were less likely to fight than native-born Protestants. As with their southern counterparts, the most common motivation among northern soldiers was patriotism. They, too, thought of themselves as the proud protectors of America's revolutionary heritage, but their patriotism was more abstract. Unlike the Confederates, Yankee troops were not fighting to protect their homes and families from the very real threat of destruction. Rather, they were fighting in defense of northern society in general, and for an idealized notion of what America meant. The Union as a "beacon of liberty" throughout the world was a common theme in the letters and diaries of northern soldiers.

Most northern soldiers believed that slavery had caused the war, but only a few were motivated by antislavery principles, and many would have rejected any idea that they were risking their lives to free slaves. But this was a civilian army, and as northern public opinion turned against slavery so did opinions among northern soldiers. Antislavery views became more common beginning in late 1861, and over the next several years, soldiers' views shifted with the tides of war. There were racist backlashes among Yankee troops, but there was also a steady trend toward support for the abolition of slavery. By the end of the conflict most northern soldiers believed that to restore the Union and destroy the Confederacy they would have to abolish slavery as well.

The Civil War Becomes a Social Revolution

By 1862 the North and the South had built up powerful military machines. At the same time, the North's war aims were shifting to include the abolition of slavery, which meant the destruction of the southern social system. In the spring and summer of 1862, Republicans in Congress and the Lincoln administration adopted the view that emancipation was a military necessity. Within a year they would point to the abolition of slavery to justify the increasingly bloody war. Throughout the South a civil war erupted within the Civil War. As the Union army swept through the South gathering up thousands of slaves fleeing for freedom, the South unleashed a campaign of violence and intimidation aimed at thwarting the unfolding process of emancipation.

> **If we hadn't become sojers, all might have gone back as it was before; our freedom might have slipped through de two houses of Congress and President Linkums' four years might have passed by and notin' been done for us. But now tings can neber go back, because we have showed our energy and our courage and our naturally manhood.**
>
> THOMAS LONG,
> former slave, 1st South Carolina Volunteers

The outcome of this civil war on the ground depended on the fate of the Union and Confederate armies on the field of battle.

Union Victories in the West

In early February 1862, the Union army and navy joined in an aggressive strike deep into Confederate Tennessee. Assisted by the naval bombardment under the direction of Andrew Foote, Ulysses S. Grant's Union forces captured Fort Henry on the Tennessee River and, shortly thereafter, Fort Donelson on the Cumberland River (see Map 15–3). To the shock of Confederate officers at Fort Donelson, Grant insisted on "unconditional and immediate surrender." The Tennessee campaign also persuaded some Union commanders that they could free up their armies by feeding them not from their own extended and vulnerable supply lines but from the goods owned by local civilians.

The war's growing ferocity became clear eight weeks later, at the battle of Shiloh. Southern general P. G. T. Beauregard, the hero of Fort Sumter and Manassas, caught Grant's troops off guard at a peach orchard at Shiloh Church in southern Tennessee. The Confederate's surprise attack on April 6 forced the Union lines steadily backward, although the line did not break. By the end of the day Beauregard was telegraphing Richmond with news of his victory. But on the morning of April 7, Confederate troops were stunned by a counterattack from Union forces. Grant's troops pushed Beauregard's army back over the ground it had taken the day before. When the Confederates finally retreated from Shiloh, the two armies had suffered an astounding 23,741 casualties, dwarfing all previous losses but foreshadowing things to come. The Civil War was quickly becoming a fight for the total destruction of the enemy's forces.

With Confederate forces busy at Shiloh, New Orleans had few defenses beyond two forts on the Mississippi River 75 miles south of the city. But they were impressive forts. It took six days of Yankee bombardment before Union commander David Farragut attempted to break through. In the middle of the night of April 24, Farragut forced his Union fleet upriver through a blaze of burning rafts and Confederate gunfire that lit up the sky. Within a few days the Confederates evacuated both forts and New Orleans fell to Union forces.

Union victories in the West gave rise to northern optimism that war would be over by summer. Republicans took advantage of the mood to enact a bold legislative agenda. During the first half of 1862 Congress and President Lincoln virtually reorganized the structure of national government in the North. Early in the year Lincoln appointed Edwin M. Stanton as secretary of war, and in July he named Henry Wager Halleck as general in chief of the Union forces. Stanton was not much of a military strategist, and Halleck, who was supposed to be, was paralyzed when it came to giving orders to commanders in the field. But both were effective bureaucrats, and, with invaluable help of the Quartermaster General Montgomery Meigs and a brilliant railroad engineer named Henry Haupt, they built a powerful war-making machine that kept the huge, far-flung Union armies well supplied. A similarly effective working relationship developed between Navy Secretary Gideon Welles, his assistant secretary Gustavus Fox, and John Dahlgren, the man in charge of weapons development at the Washington Navy Yard.

Congress was also active. For years Democratic majorities had blocked passage of laws that Republicans considered essential. Now the Republicans had the votes and the popular support to push their agenda through Congress. They began with a critical financial reform. To sustain the integrity of the currency, the Republicans passed a Legal Tender Act protecting northern greenbacks from inflationary pressure. To maintain the manpower of the armed forces, the Republicans instituted the first military draft in United States history. In addition, in 1862 they established a system of land-grant colleges designed to promote the scientific development of American agriculture and passed a Homestead Act that offered land at low prices to settlers in the West. Finally, the Republicans financed the construction of the nation's first transcontinental railroad. Together these laws reflected the Republican Party's commitment to the active use of the central government to preserve the Union and promote capitalist development.

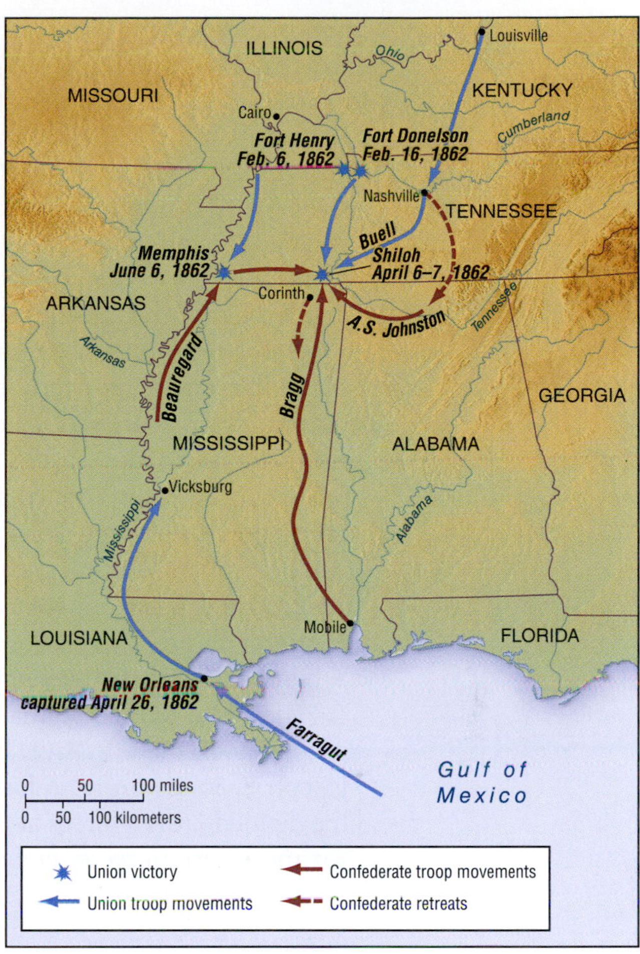

Map 15–3 The War in the West in 1862 As Union armies floundered in the East, northern troops in the West won a decisive series of battles. Here the nature of the war changed. First, General Ulysses S. Grant demanded "unconditional surrender" of the southern troops at Forts Henry and Donelson. Then a bloody battle at Shiloh foreshadowed the increasing brutality of the war. Finally, the western theater produced two of the Union's most effective generals, Grant and William Tecumseh Sherman, and its greatest naval victory, David Farragut's stunning capture of New Orleans.

The Confederate government also reformed its bureaucracy to sustain its military struggle. Southern leaders realized that it was a mistake to withhold the region's cotton from the world market. A year into the war the Confederate economy was showing signs of the weakness that would lead it to the brink of complete financial collapse. To remedy the situation, the Confederate Congress passed a comprehensive tax code, which produced only disappointing revenues. In April 1862 the Confederacy established a national military draft. By centralizing taxation and conscription, however, Jefferson Davis's government at Richmond faced powerful resistance from advocates of states' rights. Thus while military victories in the West allowed northern Republicans to enact an expansive legislative agenda, the Confederate government had trouble winning popular support for its own centralizing measures, despite the success of its troops turned against a massive northern offensive in Virginia.

Southern Military Strength in the East

The Peninsula campaign of 1862 crushed the North's earlier optimism. The goal of the Union army had been to capture the Confederate capital, Richmond, and that was what Lincoln expected George B. McClellan to do as commander of the Army of the Potomac. McClellan's great strength was his ability to administer and train a huge army. He instituted systematic drills and careful discipline and, after their defeat at Bull Run, successfully restored his soldiers' morale. Unfortunately, McClellan was reluctant to fight. He was forever exaggerating the size of his opponents' forces and demanding more troops before he would take the offensive. Throughout the fall and winter of 1861 and 1862, McClellan stubbornly resisted Lincoln's suggestions to attack. McClellan held all politicians in contempt, and none more than the president. He sent insulting dispatches to his superiors and wrote pompous letters to his wife declaring himself the savior of the republic.

Only under intense pressure, and not until his own reputation was at stake, did McClellan devise an overly elaborate strategy to capture Richmond. He very slowly moved his huge army of 112,000 men up the peninsula between the York and James rivers. Instead of directly attacking Richmond, however, McClellan dug in at Yorktown, thinking that he faced a more formidable enemy than he actually did. The Confederates quickly became skilled at manipulating McClellan's weaknesses. They moved small numbers of soldiers back and forth to make him think there were more enemy troops than there really were and planted fake cannons along their lines. Then, during the night of May 4, 1862, the outnumbered Confederates withdrew toward Richmond. When McClellan discovered their escape, he declared it a Union victory.

The Army of the Potomac inched its way up the peninsula toward Richmond, but it never took the offensive. Instead, it was the Confederates, initially led by General Joseph E. Johnston, who forced Union troops into battle. The southerners attacked the divided Union forces at Seven Pines on May 31, and both sides took heavy losses. Far more serious were the brutal battles of the Seven Days beginning in late June. It

Tredegar Iron Works in Richmond, Virginia, 1865 This was the South's largest industrial plant. Because the South lagged so far behind the North in industrial capacity, protecting the Tredegar works was essential to the Confederate war effort.

was during this campaign that Johnston was wounded, and replaced by Robert E. Lee. He repulsed but could not destroy McClellan's larger army. Still, Lee had saved Richmond and sent the Union army lumbering back to new fortifications at Harrison's Landing, where McClellan sat until he was finally ordered to bring his big army back to Washington, DC. There McClellan did what he did best. He revived his soldiers' sagging morale and whipped the Army of the Potomac back into fighting shape. But he still would not do the fighting. Defying the desperate orders of Lincoln and Halleck, McClellan let Union general John Pope take the offensive alone. Hampered by generals loyal to McClellan, Pope led his troops to a disastrous defeat at the second battle of Bull Run (August 29–30), while McClellan's huge army stood by.

By the fall of 1862, the Union and Confederate forces had reached a military stalemate. The North had scored tremendous victories in the West. In the East, however, Robert E. Lee turned out to be one of the most skillful and daring commanders of the war. Stonewall Jackson, Lee's "right arm," had likewise proven himself brilliantly aggressive.

Having turned back the Union invasion on the peninsula and, later that summer, defeated the Union army in a second battle at Bull Run, Lee decided to invade the North. He hoped the Confederacy could win the war in the East before losing it in the West. Lee therefore marched his confident troops across the Potomac into Maryland. McClellan at last met Lee's army at Sharpsburg, Maryland, beside Antietam Creek, on September 17.

McClellan nearly lost Antietam. He had Lee's plans ahead of time, but he took his time and squandered the advantage. Once engaged, McClellan launched his troops in consecutive assaults rather than a single simultaneous maneuver, allowing the Confederates to shift their men around the battlefield whenever the fighting moved to a different location. He held back his own reinforcements, missing a chance to break the center of the Confederate line when it was most vulnerable. By delaying, McClellan gave Confederate reinforcements time to arrive on the scene and turn back an attack on Lee's right. But the Union troops fought with astonishing determination and Lee's men suffered staggering casualties. Unable to maintain the invasion of the North, Lee quickly retreated back into Virginia. It might have been even worse for the South, but despite intense pressure from Washington, McClellan refused to use his fresh reserves to pursue the disoriented southern army as it fell back across the Potomac. When McClellan boasted that his army had forced the Confederates off "our soil," he revealed how far his own vision of Union strategy was from Lincoln's. Its *all* "our soil," Lincoln fumed, and the point was not to send Lee's army back to Virginia

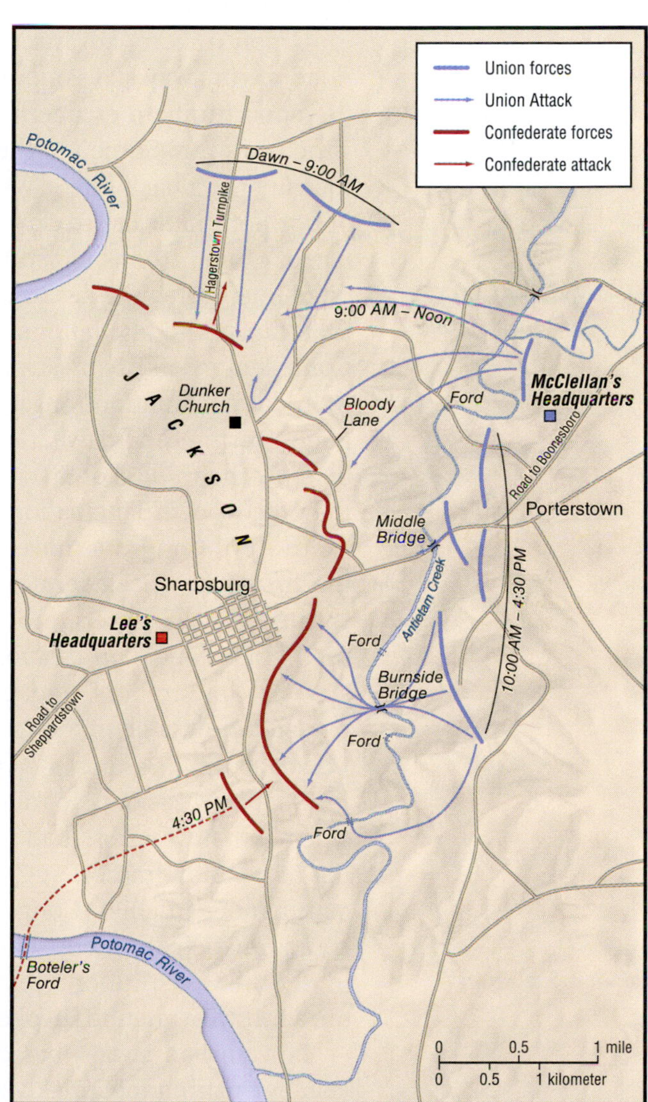

Map 15-4 The Battle of Antietam In September 1862, southern general Robert E. Lee led the Confederacy's first invasion of the North. He was stopped at Sharpsburg, Maryland, by Union troops under the command of George B. McClellan. Antietam was the bloodiest single day of the war, but it was an important turning point for the North. It gave Lincoln the victory he was waiting for to announce the preliminary Emancipation Proclamation.

but to engage and defeat it. The president had run out of patience. He bided his time until the fall elections were over and then fired McClellan. A total of 4,800 soldiers died and 18,000 more were wounded at Antietam, the single bloodiest day of the war. Nevertheless, Antietam was a Union victory, and Lincoln took advantage of it to announce an important shift in northern war aims.

Emancipation as a Military Necessity

By the summer of 1862, northern public opinion was shifting in favor of emancipation. Slave laborers were sustaining the Confederacy, producing the food to feed southern troops, building the fortifications to protect southern armies, working as cooks and mule drivers for rebel regiments. Emancipation took on a double character for many northerners. It was both a military necessity and a moral good.

Union military advances in the plantation South in early 1862 had produced a flood of runaway slaves pouring across northern lines. As slaves took advantage of the opportunity to escape from their masters, Union commanders responded in a variety of ways. Some put the contrabands to work behind Union lines. Others sent the runaways back into slavery, to the horror of African Americans and the dismay of northern radicals. To clarify the situation, in March 1862 Congress prohibited the use of Union troops to return fugitives to the South. Union commanders and soldiers interpreted the law as an invitation to sweep even larger numbers of slaves off their farms and plantations. Edmund Ruffin frequently left his plantation to aid the Confederate defense of Virginia. He returned from one such expedition in July 1862 to find his plantation ransacked, his fields destroyed, and all of his "faithful" slaves gone. During the first year of the war, slaves drifted into Union lines in small numbers. By the middle of 1862 they were coming in by the thousands. A new phase in the process of emancipation had begun.

In April Congress moved further by abolishing slavery in Washington, DC. For the first time, the federal government exercised the power to emancipate slaves. In June 1862 Congress prohibited slavery in the western territories. The following month a second Confiscation Act was passed, this one declaring "forever free" the slaves of any "traitors" engaged in rebellion against the United States. Congress also passed a militia act making it possible for "persons of African descent" to join the Union army.

But there was only so much Congress could do. Many Republicans, even radicals, worried that Congress had no constitutional right to liberate any of the slaves coming into Union lines. If such an authority existed, it resided in the war powers of the commander in chief. Congress could confiscate slaves, but only President Lincoln could emancipate them. Lincoln believed that because slaves were not "property" under the Constitution, he could free slaves by virtue of his war powers. The only question was when to invoke those powers.

Lincoln had always hated slavery, but he did not want to risk an antiwar backlash by pushing too quickly ahead of public opinion. But public opinion was clearly changing. He was searching for a dramatic gesture that would break the military stalemate and convince European powers to side with the Union, and an Emancipation Proclamation would certainly be dramatic. Then, too, something had to be done to clarify the status of the thousands of slave refugees who were now pouring into Union lines.

AMERICA AND THE WORLD

>> The Diplomacy of Emancipation

"The Emancipation Proclamation," Henry Adams wrote from London, "has done more for us here than all our former victories and all our diplomacy. It is creating an almost convulsive reaction in our favor." Adams was attached to the American legation that had been struggling since the war began to prevent England, along with other European nations, from formally recognizing the Confederate States of America. It was unlikely that England would in fact grant diplomatic recognition to the South, and unlikely that France would do it if England did not. But there were powerful elements in Britain, both in and out of Parliament, who openly hoped for Union defeat and called for diplomatic recognition of the Confederacy. With every northern military reversal the South's supporters grew more vocal. And so from the earliest days of the war both Union and Confederate diplomats worked feverishly to forestall or to gain England's formal recognition of the southern nation.

The Emancipation Proclamation tilted the diplomatic balance irreversibly in favor of the North. Huge pro-Union rallies across England declared their support for Union and freedom. At Exeter Hall in London one of the largest such rallies "has had a powerful effect on our newspapers and politicians," Richard Cobden declared. "It has closed the mouths of those who have been advocating the side of the South. Recognition of the South, by England, whilst it bases itself on slavery, is an impossibility."

There was a similar reaction across Europe. As soon as Lincoln publicly proclaimed the emancipation of the slaves as one of the war aims of the Union, nearly all remaining whispers of diplomatic support for the Confederacy were silenced. "The anti-slavery position of the government is at length giving us a substantial foothold in European circles," explained a Union diplomat in the Netherlands. "Everyone can understand the significance of a war where emancipation is written on one banner and slavery on the other."

After January 1, 1863, only the complete military victory of the South over the North could have won substantial diplomatic recognition for the Confederacy. Whatever the Emancipation Proclamation meant for the slavery in the South, it signaled the diplomatic triumph of the North.

Sketch of Queen from *Punch*

On July 22, 1862, Lincoln told his cabinet that he had decided to issue an Emancipation Proclamation. But Secretary of State William Seward warned the president that recent military reverses in Virginia would make such a proclamation seem like an act of desperation to the rest of the world. Lincoln agreed. He would wait for a battlefield victory to make his proclamation public. Antietam provided Lincoln with that victory. On September 22, five days after Lee was turned back, Lincoln issued a preliminary proclamation threatening to free the slaves in areas still in rebellion one hundred days later. One month later he proposed a plan of gradual emancipation in all areas under Union control. Nobody expected any of the seceded states to return to the Union, and on January 1, 1863, Lincoln issued his Emancipation Proclamation.

Company E, 4th United States Colored Infantry, at Fort Lincoln, Washington, DC, 1865 African Americans serving in the Union army symbolized the revolutionary turn the Civil War took once emancipation became the policy of the North. Despite overwhelming loss of life by the African American troops, their bravery impressed many northerners and helped change white attitudes about the goals of the Civil War.

Reactions were swift, and predictable. Jefferson Davis, the president of the Confederate States of America, denounced Lincoln's proclamation as the most despicable act "in the history of guilty man." Abolitionists and free blacks rejoiced and celebrated proclamation day at gatherings all across the North. Other northerners, particularly Democrats, were enraged by the idea that the war was being fought to free the slaves, and some northern soldiers were embittered by the Emancipation Proclamation. "I came out to fight for the restoration of the Union . . . ," one northern soldier wrote, "not to free the niggers." But most Union troops had already reached the conclusion that for the war to end the South had to be destroyed, and that meant the destruction of slavery.

The proclamation itself was both a reaction and a spur to emancipation. Thousands of slaves had been escaping to Union lines throughout 1862, but it took Lincoln's proclamation to clarify their status as free. But the proclamation also increased the pace of emancipation in the South. In low-country South Carolina and New Orleans, slaves celebrated their freedom on January 1, 1863, even though those areas were under Union occupation and were therefore technically unaffected by the proclamation. As Union forces advanced across the South they provided more openings for the slaves to flee, especially from plantations where the master and his sons were away in the army. It made no difference whether a master had been kind or cruel, the slaves left anyway. "We were all laboring under a delusion," one South Carolina planter confessed. "I believed that these people were content, happy, and attached to their masters."

The Proclamation and African Americans On January 1, 1863, African Americans celebrated their freedom all across the country, even in those parts of the South that were technically unaffected by the proclamation. By assuming their freedom in this way, the former slaves gave a far broader meaning to the proclamation than it technically allowed.

Emancipation in Practice: Contraband Camps and Black Troops

The shift in Union policy solved the biggest obstacle to emancipation: it gave the slaves somewhere to go when they left their farms and plantations. There had always been runaway slaves, but the vast majority of them had nowhere to go and ended up returning to their masters. The war gave slaves more opportunities to escape, but it took the U.S. government to give them options. In areas occupied by Union troops early in the war, such as the Sea Islands off low-country South Carolina, the masters had abandoned their plantations and their slaves were, in Lincoln's words, "thus liberated." In occupied regions where the masters remained, such as West Virginia and southern Louisiana, Lincoln required those states to emancipate their slaves as a precondition for admission or readmission to the Union. But for slaves who left their farms and plantations, the Union provided two options, contraband camps and the Union army.

As the number of slave refugees climbed still higher, Union commanders began constructing massive contraband camps all across the South, wherever their armies had swept through an area. Yet the Union was clearly unprepared for the huge numbers pouring into the makeshift camps. Diseases, especially smallpox, raged through the camps. Food and shelter were in short supply. For some slaves the filth and disorder of the camps were so terrible that they left and went back to their farms and plantations. Over time, however, the army and northern volunteers learned how to organize the contraband camps more efficiently. Just across the Potomac River from Washington, DC, on the Arlington estate that had been owned by Robert E. Lee's family, the government built a model contraband camp known as "Freedman's Village." It had a school, a hospital, and a cemetery that was the nucleus for what would later become Arlington National Cemetery.

But most contraband camps were temporary, set up quickly as Union troops moved through an area and just as quickly taken down once the Union army moved on. Such camps were little more than transfer points—the first place slaves went before the army shipped them off to permanent camps or to cities outside the war zones. General Ulysses Grant evacuated thousands of slaves from Vicksburg, for example, and shipped them off to places like Columbus, Ohio. The camps were a major development in the history of emancipation. For the first time the slaves, particularly women, children, and the elderly, had somewhere to go once they escaped from their masters.

AMERICAN LANDSCAPE

>> Freedman's Village, Arlington, Virginia

When Mary Lee's father died in 1857, her husband, Robert E. Lee, became executor of the family's plantation at Arlington, Virginia, across the Potomac River from Washington, DC. The will stipulated that the slaves at Arlington were to be freed, but because the estate was burdened with debts, Lee had the will revoked and took charge of the plantation himself. He began selling off slaves, and within a few years he had broken up all but one of the slave families on the plantation. Expecting to be freed, the slaves were instead worked harder than ever. Lee, they complained, was a "hard taskmaster" and "the worst man I ever saw." They began running away.

When the Civil War broke out, the areas surrounding Washington, DC—including Arlington—came under the control of the Union army almost immediately. Not much happened on the estate until Congress abolished slavery in the nation's capital on April 12, 1862, and large numbers of contraband slaves began escaping into the city from nearby Virginia and Maryland. After Lincoln issued his Emancipation Proclamation on January 1, 1863, the contraband camps in Washington were soon overcrowded and overwhelmed. In May Union officials decided to move the contrabands to a new location, Freedman's Village, to be constructed on the Lee estate at Arlington. Freedman's Village would serve two distinct purposes. First, it would remove the freed people from the crowded, unhealthy camps in the city, where diseases spread rapidly among the refugees. Lieutenant Colonel Elias Greene, the quartermaster for Washington, explained that the "salutary effects of good pure country air" would "prove beneficial" to the contrabands and "will tend to prevent the increase of disease now present among them." Beyond that, Freedman's Village was designed as a model for the dozens of contraband camps that were springing up across the South as more and more slaves came into Union lines and were freed.

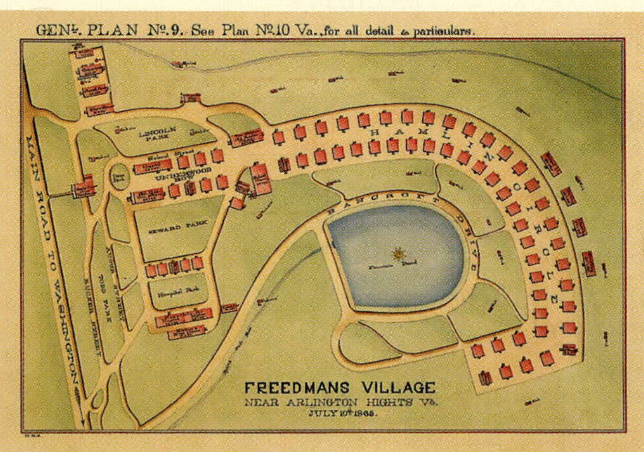

By 1864 Freedman's Village had 50 homes and as many as 2,000 residents. There was a hospital, a laundry, a kitchen, a home for elderly slaves, and a schoolhouse. The buildings were neatly arranged around the pond, and the Village became a destination for visiting dignitaries and a subject for journalists covering the war. But although the facility was a vast improvement over the conditions at most contraband camps, there were complaints from the freed people about the rigid rules they were expected to follow. To pay for the camp the residents were expected to work in the fields adjoining Freedman's Village. They earned a wage of $10 per month, but they had to pay back half of their earnings for the upkeep of the camp. That was hardly enough, they complained, to set them on the road to economic independence. For years the collection of "rents" was a source of tension between the Union army, which ran the camp, and the former slaves who lived there. Yet despite numerous attempts by the government to close Freedman's Village down, the freed people resisted and the camp remained in operation until the end of the century.

By then, however, Arlington had been transformed yet again. On June 15, 1864, the quartermaster general of the Union armies, Montgomery Meigs, wrote to the secretary of war, Edwin M. Stanton, suggesting that "the land surrounding the Arlington Mansion, now understood to be the property of the United States, be appropriated as a National Military Cemetery." Stanton approved the proposal and within weeks the bodies of Union soldiers were being laid to rest at Arlington. Meigs saw to it that the graves were laid out "encircling" the mansion house, and, in the garden once cultivated by Lee's mother-in-law, Meigs placed a mass grave of unknown soldiers who had died at Manassas. By June of 1864 there were 2,600 Union soldiers buried at Arlington National Cemetery.

No one missed the symbolism. By 1863 Robert E. Lee was already recognized as the Confederacy's most daunting military commander. For northerners, that made him a symbol of treason as well. What could be more appropriate than to turn his family's plantation at Arlington first into a model village for former slaves and then into a national grave for fallen Union soldiers? The cemetery would survive as a constant reminder of the past, but Freedman's Village would disappear and with it the hope for the future it once represented.

The second place for slaves to go, at least for young men, was the Union army. Although they had fought in the American Revolution and the War of 1812, blacks had never been allowed in the regular army. The Militia Act of 1862 finally allowed black troops. Lincoln was at first reluctant, but by the end of the year he became an active supporter of black enlistment. Lincoln's final Emancipation Proclamation not only declared all rebel slaves free, it also sanctioned the enlistment of African Americans in the Union army. "The bare sight of 50,000 armed and drilled black soldiers upon the banks of the Mississippi," he said in March 1863, "would end the rebellion at once." Before the war was over, 186,000 blacks had joined, 134,111 of them recruited in the South.

For African Americans themselves, especially for former slaves, the experience of fighting a war for emancipation was exhilarating. In a society that drew increasingly sharp distinctions between men and women, slaves who became soldiers often felt as though they were, in the process, becoming men. "Now we sogers are men," one black sergeant explained, "men the first time in our lives."

Black Union troops were an astonishing spectacle for those still enslaved, but to white southerners, this was the "world turned upside down." As African American troops marched through the streets of southern cities, whites shrieked in horror. They shook their fists at them, spat at them from behind windows, and found it all but impossible to control their rage and indignation. But southern whites were not alone in their opposition to the revolutionary turn the Civil War had taken.

Although they made up nearly 10 percent of the Union army, black soldiers were never treated as the equals of white soldiers. Few African American officers were commissioned, and black soldiers were paid less than whites. They were often held back from combat for fear that Confederates would kill such men if captured. But when they went into combat, blacks performed respectably, and in so doing they changed the minds of many northern whites. Black soldiers were among the most aggressive in spreading emancipation still farther across the Confederacy. Moreover, their numbers tipped the balance of northern and southern forces decisively in favor of the Union army, thereby contributing critically to the defeat of the Confederacy.

The War at Home

African American troops could not end the rebellion "at once," as Lincoln hoped. Instead, the war persisted for two more years. As body counts rose and the economic hardships mounted, civilians in both the North and the South began to register their discontent.

The Care of Casualties

At Shiloh, 24,000 men had fallen in two days of fighting. Almost as many fell during a single day of fighting at Antietam. The following year 50,000 men would die or suffer wounds at Gettysburg. At the battles of Chickamauga and Franklin, Tennessee, Confederate troops would suffer appalling losses. And in Grant's struggle against Lee in the spring of 1864, both sides would lose 100,000 men in seven weeks. Casualties, partly the consequence of inept leadership and inadequately prepared troops, were mostly caused by the fact that military technology had outpaced battlefield tactics. Generals continued to order traditional assaults on enemy lines

> I went unrestrained, into all the largest hospitals. In the first of these an amputation was being performed, and at the door lay a little heap of human fingers, feet, legs, and arms. . . . Soldiers sat by the severely wounded, laving their sores with water. In many wounds the balls still remained and the discolored flesh was swollen unnaturally. There were some who had been shot in the bowels, and now and then they were frightfully convulsed, breaking into shrieks and shouts. Some of them iterated a single word, as, "doctor," or "help," or "God," or "oh!" commencing with a loud spasmodic cry, and continuing the same word until it died away in cadence. The act of calling seemed to lull the pain.
>
> GEORGE TOWNSEND,
> journalist, visiting a field hospital during the Peninsula campaign

even though newly developed rifles and repeating carbines made such assaults almost suicidal.

If advances in military technology multiplied the casualties, primitive medical practices did even more damage. Of the 620,000 soldiers who died, two out of three were felled by disease. Thousands of soldiers were killed by contaminated water, spoiled food, inadequate clothing and shelter, mosquitoes, and vermin. Crowded military camps were breeding grounds for dysentery, diarrhea, malaria, and typhoid fever. Nobody knew what "germs" were and doctors had no idea that sterilization made any difference. No one knew what caused typhoid fever or malaria. There were no antibiotics, and liquor was often the only anesthesia available. There was no cure for gangrene other than amputation, so field hospitals were littered with piles of sawed-off arms and legs.

In one area, nursing, the Civil War advanced the practice of medicine. The Civil War overturned long-standing prejudices against the presence of women in military hospitals. The Confederacy lagged behind in institutional developments, but hundreds of southern women volunteered their services to the southern forces. Even in the North the thousands of women who volunteered their services to the Union army had to overcome institutional barriers against them. In mid-1861, however, northern reformers persuaded Lincoln to recognize the services of the United States Sanitary Commission. A private organization led by men but staffed by thousands of women, the "Sanitary" became a potent force for reform of the Army Medical Bureau. It established the first ambulance corps for the swift removal of wounded soldiers from the battlefield, pioneered the use of ships and railroad cars as mobile hospital units, and made nursing a respectable profession for women after the war ended.

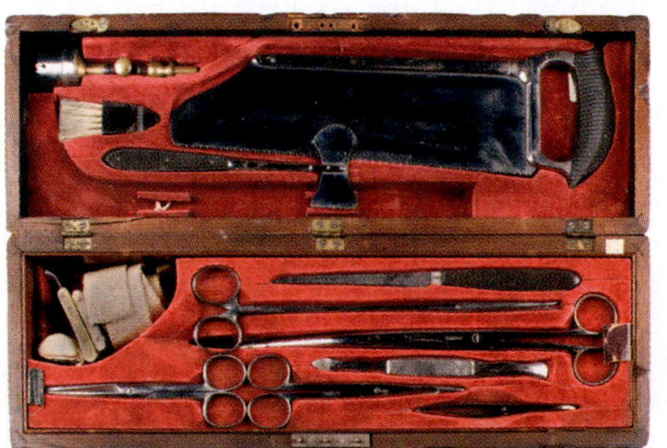

But the heroic efforts of the Sanitary Commission could not undo the fact that the Civil War had caused unprecedented bloodshed. As the war dragged on, and as the aims of the war shifted, Americans raised their voices in opposition to the policies of the Lincoln and Davis administrations.

Northern Reverses and Antiwar Sentiment

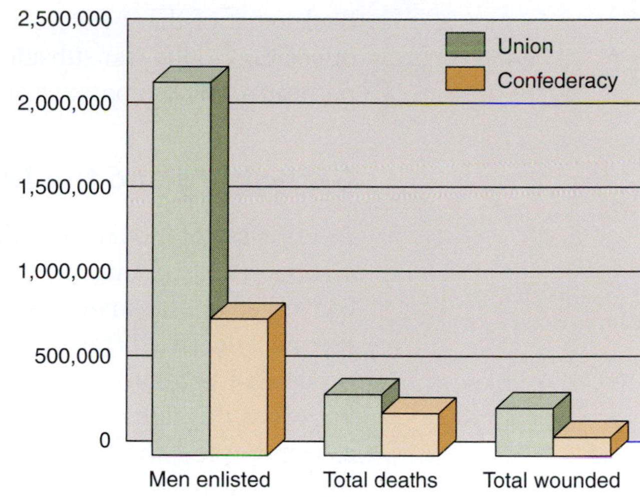

Figure 15-2 Casualties of War

Lincoln struggled for years to find a commander who could stand up to great southern generals like Robert E. Lee and Stonewall Jackson. For failing to crush Lee's army after Antietam, Lincoln at last fired McClellan and gave command of the Army of the Potomac to a reluctant Ambrose Burnside. But Burnside could not hope to match Lee's brilliant, unorthodox strategy. At Fredericksburg, Virginia, on December 13, 1862, Lee's army subjected Burnside's men to a calamitous slaughter. Lincoln quickly replaced Burnside with "Fighting Joe" Hooker, a swaggering braggart who was scarcely better at fighting than Burnside had been. At Chancellorsville, Virginia, in May 1863, Lee overwhelmed Hooker's forces. It was one of the bloodiest Union defeats of the war. Every commander Lincoln had put in charge in Virginia proved more disastrous than the last.

Northern military reverses sustained a wave of political opposition to emancipation. Northern Democrats had always favored compromise with the South on slavery and continued to argue that the only legitimate aim of the war was the restoration of the Union. In the elections of 1862, Peace Democrats (known as Copperheads) took control of the legislatures in Illinois and Indiana and threatened to withhold troops from the war effort. Troops from southern Illinois deserted in droves in early 1863, after the Emancipation Proclamation was issued. Democrats were scandalized when the War Department authorized the formation of African American regiments in early 1863.

With the beginning of military conscription in March 1863, northern Democrats added the draft to their list of Republican outrages. Because northern draftees could escape conscription by paying a $300 commutation fee, many working-class men, especially Irish immigrants, complained that the rich could buy their way out of combat. In fact, the Irish were underrepresented in the Union army, and there were means by which workingmen could pay the commutation fee. But the taint of inequity remained so strong that Congress later abolished commutation.

Drafting white men to fight for black emancipation provoked anger. Dissent became so widespread that Lincoln claimed the constitutional authority to suspend habeas corpus. The Peace Democrats' leading spokesman, Clement L. Vallandigham, repeatedly attacked the president's "despotic" measures. If forced to choose between loss of freedom for whites and continued enslavement of African Americans, he said, "I shall not hesitate one moment to choose the latter alternative."

In 1862 whites protesting the drift toward emancipation rioted in several northern cities. In New York City, Irish Democrats responded to the opening of a draft office by rioting in the streets. Working-class immigrants had suffered most from wartime inflation and were most susceptible to economic competition from African Americans. Their frustration exploded into the great New York City draft riots, which began on July 13, 1863, and continued for several days.

Rioters attacked the homes of leading Republicans and assaulted well-dressed men on the streets, but they mostly attacked blacks. White mobs lynched a dozen African Americans and set fire to the Colored Orphan Asylum. More than 100 people died, most of them rioters killed by police and soldiers. Thereafter violent northern opposition to the war subsided, partly because the draft riots had discredited the Copperheads, but also because of the improving military fortunes of the Union army.

Gettysburg and the Justification of the War

As criticism of the Lincoln administration swelled in the summer of 1863, Lee sensed an opportunity to launch a second invasion of the North. On July 1 the opposing armies converged on the small town of Gettysburg, Pennsylvania. For three days they fought the most decisive battle of the war. On the first day it looked as though the South was on its way to another victory. Confederate troops pushed the Union enemy steadily backward through the streets of Gettysburg and onto the hills south of the town. But as evening fell, the Union army commanded the heights. Through the night Union general George Gordon Meade secured a two-mile line of high ground. On the second day Lee ordered two flanking attacks and a third assault on the Union center, but the Union line held. On the third day, against the strong advice of his trusted general James Longstreet, Lee ordered a direct attack by George Pickett's troops on the strongly fortified Union center. Pickett's charge was a devastating loss for the southern troops. On July 4 the Confederates began their retreat back toward the Potomac River, where rising waters trapped the southerners for more than a week. As he had with McClellan after Antietam, Lincoln furiously urged Meade to go after Lee's trapped army and finish the job. But Meade dithered and by the time he got around to launching an attack the river had subsided and Lee's army escaped. Once again Lincoln was mortified by the insufficiently aggressive instincts of his own generals.

As northerners were celebrating Lee's defeat, news came of another Union victory in the West. For months the Mississippi River town of Vicksburg, Mississippi, had proved invincible, to the endless frustration of General Grant. After a succession of failed maneuvers Grant laid siege to the town. He cut Vicksburg off from all supplies and waited until the soldiers and civilians in the town were starved into submission. For six weeks the people of Vicksburg lived in caves, bombarded by sharpshooters during the day and by cannon fire at night. They subsisted on mules and rats. On June 28, the Confederate soldiers inside the city threatened mutiny, and less than a week later, Vicksburg surrendered. His experience with McClellan had led Lincoln to distrust sieges, and he was at first dubious about Grant's plans. But it wasn't only Vicksburg that surrendered, but a large Confederate army holed up inside it. Lincoln joyfully conceded the error of his doubts and pronounced Grant's Vicksburg campaign "brilliant." The Confederate commander at Port Hudson surrendered shortly thereafter. The Mississippi River was now opened to Union navigation, and the Confederacy was split in two. Vicksburg and Gettysburg, together, were the greatest Union victories of the war.

Gettysburg—The Aftermath The bodies of dead soldiers litter the battlefield at Gettysburg. Shortly thereafter workers rushed to bury the corpses in time for the dedication of the battlefield as a military cemetery. Lincoln's powerful address promised "a new birth of freedom—and that government of the people, by the people, for the people, shall not perish from the earth."

Despite his disappointment with Meade, Lincoln came to realize the significance of the Union victory at Gettysburg. In November, the president went to Gettysburg to speak at the dedication of a military cemetery at the battlefield. There he articulated a profound justification of the Union war effort. The Civil War, Lincoln said, had become a great test of democracy and of the principle of human equality. The soldiers who died at Gettysburg had dedicated their lives to those principles, the president noted. It remained only "for us the living" to similarly "resolve that these dead shall not have died in vain—that this nation, under God, shall have a new birth of freedom—and that government of the people, by the people, for the people, shall not perish from the earth."

With the Gettysburg Address, Lincoln took brilliant advantage of the North's improving military fortunes to elevate the meaning of the war beyond the simple restoration of the Union. After 1863, antiwar sentiment in the North diminished substantially. In the South it exploded.

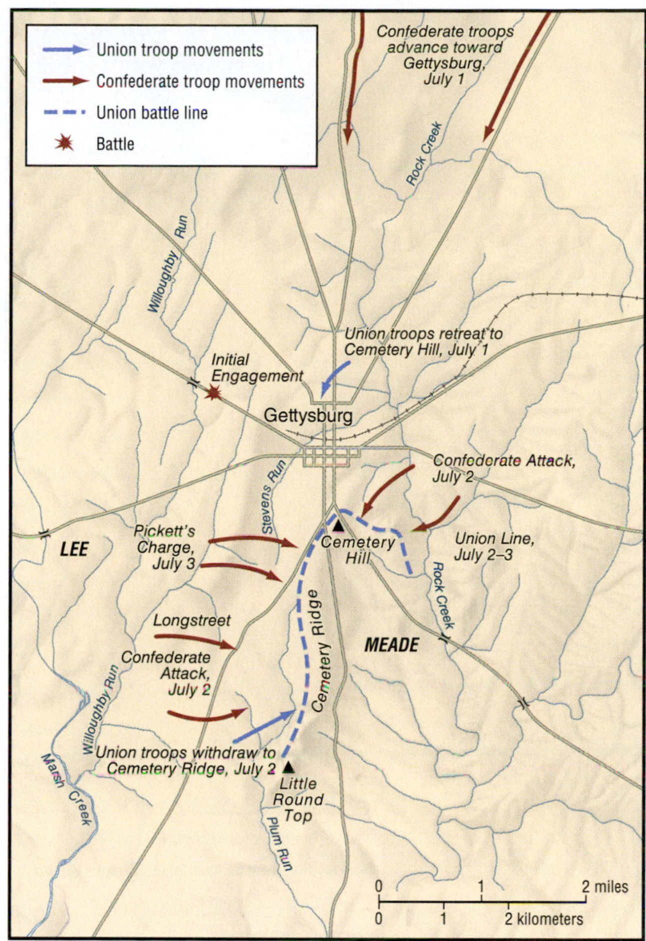

Map 15-5 The Battle of Gettysburg, July 1–3, 1863 In three extraordinary days in Gettysburg, Pennsylvania, the Union army turned back Lee's second invasion of the North. The Union victory, combined with equally important successes in the West at the same time, turned the tide of the war in the North's favor. At the dedication of a military cemetery at Gettysburg a few months later, Lincoln articulated his most profound justification for waging war against the South.

Discontent in the Confederacy

The South was divided over secession from the very beginning. Four slave states—Maryland, Delaware, Kentucky, and Missouri—never even joined the Confederacy. The entire western portion of Virginia "seceded" from the state and rejoined the Union as the new state of West Virginia. As the war became more relentless the divisions grew more disruptive. Brutal guerilla warfare broke out in the mountains of eastern Tennessee and western North Carolina, where hostility to the Confederacy was widespread.

Although most whites in the seceded states remained loyal to the Confederacy, many attacked the government of Jefferson Davis. After Lee's defeat at Gettysburg, Edmund Ruffin littered his diary with vituperative assaults on the Confederate president. Although formed in the name of states' rights, the Confederate government became a huge centralized bureaucracy that taxed white southerners far beyond anything in their prewar experience. The Confederate government burned private stores of cotton and impressed slaves into service, provoking the wrath of the slaveholders for whom the war was being fought in the first place.

The government in Richmond was forever wrestling with the states for control of military enlistments. The South imposed conscription earlier and relied much more heavily on draftees than did the North. A "planter's exemption" designed to thwart emancipation allowed the sons of wealthy slaveholders to purchase replacements, which generated tremendous hostility. Ordinary southerners complained of a "rich man's war but a poor man's fight." The most important resistance came from Georgia, where a trio of powerful politicians (Governor Joseph Brown, Vice President Alexander Stephens, and Senator Robert Toombs) launched a vitriolic

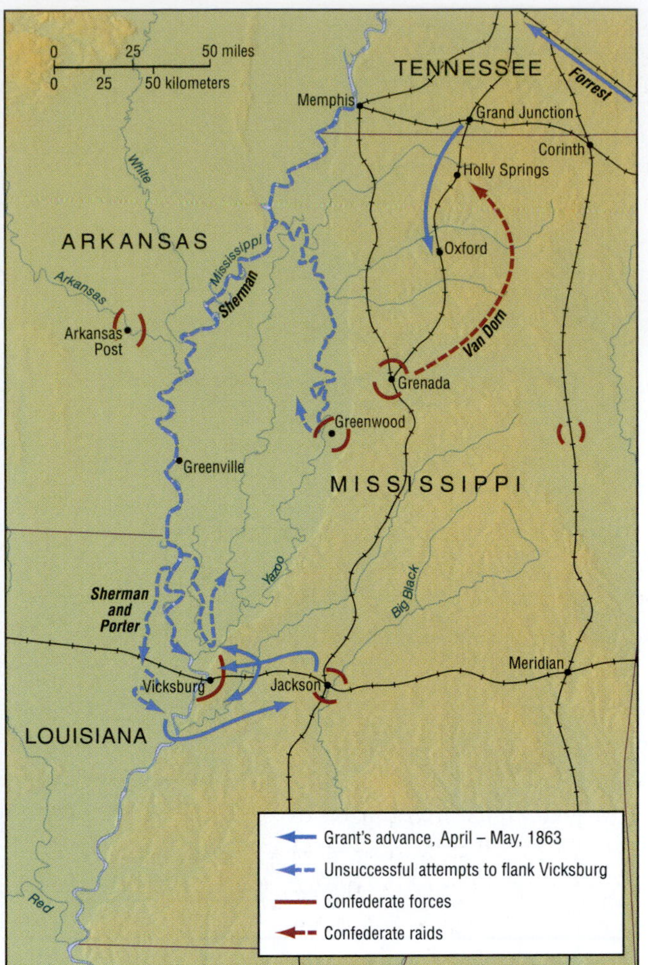

Map 15-6 The Siege of Vicksburg, 1862–1863 After a series of unsuccessful efforts to capture Vicksburg, Mississippi, from the Confederates, Grant settled down for a long siege. After the southern troops surrendered, in July 1863, the Union quickly gained complete control of the Mississippi River and, in so doing, split the Confederacy in two. With the fall of Vicksburg, the Confederacy all but lost the war in the West.

assault on the Confederate government. Faced with swelling internal opposition, Davis followed Lincoln's course and suspended habeas corpus in many parts of the Confederacy.

Southerners, both military and civilian, suffered proportionally far more casualties than did northerners. Day-to-day deprivation and physical destruction were common experiences in the Civil War South. Confederate money was becoming worthless, and the army swallowed up much of the precious food supply. Bread riots erupted in a dozen southern cities in 1863. On April 2, about 1,000 hungry citizens, mostly women, rampaged through the streets of Richmond, Virginia, looting stores for food and clothing. By 1864 life for millions of southerners had become miserable and desperate. Women wrote desperate letters to their husbands and sons in the Confederate armies, begging them to come home and rescue their families from the threat of starvation.

The devastation of the southern economy and the wholesale destruction of southern property sent Edmund Ruffin into a profound depression. All of his money was invested in worthless Confederate war bonds. He could not understand why northerners had not risen in rebellion. Yet Ruffin was also shocked by the disloyalty of ordinary southern whites, and he called for a dictator to take control of the Confederacy. In May 1864 Ruffin's son was killed in battle and his plantation was occupied by Union troops, yet neither Ruffin nor his fellow Confederates abandoned their commitment to a separate nation.

The War Comes to a Bloody End

In the face of civilian bread riots, war weariness, and disloyal slaves, a crippled Confederacy nonetheless sought desperately to maintain itself. At the same time, northern society seemed stronger than ever. Amidst the most ferocious fighting ever witnessed on North American soil, the commander in chief ran for reelection to the presidency and won.

Grant Takes Command

During the summer of 1863, Union forces under the command of William S. Rosecrans succeeded in pushing Braxton Bragg's Confederate troops out of central Tennessee. Bragg retreated all the way to Chattanooga, a critical rail terminal. After some prodding from Washington, Rosecrans began moving his army toward Chattanooga in mid-August; by early September he was joined by Ambrose Burnside. Outnumbered and almost surrounded, Bragg abandoned Chattanooga and retreated into Georgia. Jefferson Davis sent reinforcements and ordered Bragg to return to the offensive. At the same time, Union general George Thomas reinforced Rosecrans and Burnside. On September 19 the two armies discovered each other at Chickamauga Creek in eastern Tennessee. The bloodiest battle of the western theater was about to begin. It lasted two days and ended in the Union troops' retreat and almost total rout.

> [T]he conduct of the Negro in the late crisis of our affairs has convinced me that we were all laboring under a delusion. . . . Born and raised amid the institution, like a greate many others, I believed it was necessary to our welfare, if not to our very existence. I believed that these people were content, happy, and attached to their masters. But events and reflection have caused me to change these opinions. . . . If they were content, happy, and attached to their masters why did they desert him in the moment of his need and flock to the enemy whom they did not know; and thus left their, perhaps, really good masters whom they had known from infancy?
>
> LOUIS MANIGAULT,
> South Carolina planter, June 10, 1865

Weeks after their defeat at Chickamauga, Union armies were still stuck in Chattanooga unable to feed themselves. A frustrated President Lincoln swiftly reorganized the military structure of the western theater, putting General Grant in charge of all Union armies west of the Appalachians. In November 1863 Grant and William Tecumseh Sherman rescued the Union troops trapped at Chattanooga. Together with General Thomas, they dislodged the Confederates from the railroad terminal in eastern Tennessee. Two days later, Union forces routed the enemy at Lookout Mountain, driving Confederate troops into Georgia. The war in the West was nearly over.

Lincoln at last had a general who would fight. In March 1864 he put Grant in charge of the entire Union army. Grant decided on a simple two-pronged strategy: he would take control of the Army of the Potomac and confront Lee's Army of Northern Virginia while Sherman would hunt down and destroy Joseph E. Johnston's troops in Georgia. In these two engagements the Civil War reached its destructive heights. "From the summer of 1862, the war became a war of wholesale devastation," John Esten Cooke explained. "From the spring of 1864, it seems to have become nearly a war of extermination."

The Theory and Practice of Hard War

McClellan, Burnside, and Hooker had all withered under Lee's assaults. When Grant got to Virginia in early 1864 to do battle with Lee, he did not wither. The two generals hurled their men at one another, often directly into the lines of enemy fire. Rebuffed at one spot, they turned and tried again somewhere else. The immediate result was a monthlong series of unspeakably bloody encounters beginning in the spring of 1864. The first battle took place on May 5 and 6, in a largely uninhabited stretch of woods, thick with underbrush and crisscrossed with streams. Appropriately called the Wilderness, the terrain made it difficult to see for any distance and impossible for armies to maintain strict lines. Soldiers and commanders alike were confused by the woods and smoke, by the deafening roar of gunfire, and by the wailing of thousands of wounded. Entire brigades got lost. In two days of fighting, the Union army suffered 17,000 casualties, the Confederates 11,000, and there was more to come.

Grant's goal was to break through Lee's defensive line and capture Richmond. Despite Grant's aggressive maneuvering, though, Lee always managed to take the defensive position. With the smoke still billowing in the Wilderness, Grant marched his army south hoping to outflank Lee at Spotsylvania Court House. As usual, Lee kept one step ahead, and from May 10 to May 12 the bloodbath was repeated. There were another 18,000 Union casualties; another 12,000 Confederates were lost. Still Grant pushed his men farther south. Determined to break through Lee's defenses, Grant waged a series of deadly skirmishes culminating in a frightful assault at Cold Harbor on June 3. Bodies piled on top of bodies until finally Grant realized the hopelessness of the exercise and called a halt. Seven thousand Union men were killed or wounded at Cold Harbor, most of them in the first 60 minutes of fighting. The armies moved south yet again, but when Lee secured the rail link at Petersburg (a link that was critical to the defense of Richmond), Grant settled in for a prolonged siege. The brutal Virginia campaign had not ended the war. More than 50,000 Union men were killed or wounded, but Grant had not destroyed Lee's army or taken Richmond. The war was at a standoff, and Lincoln was up for reelection in November.

Three other military achievements saved the election of 1864 for the Republicans. The first, in late August, was the Union capture of Mobile Bay, the last major southern port still controlled by the Confederates. The entire southern coastline was now virtually sealed. Next came General Philip Sheridan's Union cavalry raid through the Shenandoah Valley in September and his defeat of the Confederate cavalry's raid into Maryland. Ordered by Grant to wipe out the source of supplies for Lee's army, Sheridan's men swept through the Shenandoah Valley, burning barns and killing animals. Sheridan's valley campaign demonstrated that the Union army now had a cavalry that could match and defeat the Confederacy's. Meanwhile, General Sherman took Atlanta, providing Lincoln and the Republicans with a third piece of good news. On September 1, as the election campaign was heating up in the North, Sherman telegraphed Lincoln: "Atlanta is ours, and fairly won."

Map 15-7 The Virginia Theater, 1864–1865 In May and June of 1864, Grant and Lee confronted each other directly in a bloody series of battles in Virginia. The indecisive outcome was a Vicksburg-like siege by Grant, this time of the city of Petersburg, where Lee dug in with his fortified troops. The shockingly high number of casualties, with no clear winner, nearly cost Lincoln his reelection to the presidency in November.

After Atlanta, Sherman came to believe that southern civilians had to be subdued along with the South's armies. He would not attack civilians directly, but he would systematically destroy the homes and farms—indeed, the towns and cities—on which southern civilians depended. The white South had sustained the rebellion, Sherman concluded, and it would remain rebellious until forced to taste the bitter reality of civil war. "War is cruelty," he told the citizens of Atlanta who petitioned him for mercy. The "terrible hardships of war" are inevitable, "and

Atlanta in Ruins Much of Atlanta lay in ruins after General Sherman captured and burned the city. The northern general had made a conscious decision to make war "hell" by destroying the property of the southern civilians who supported the war.

the only way the people of Atlanta can hope once more to live in peace and quiet at home, is to stop the war."

But Sherman was merely the theorist of this type of warfare. Lincoln was its administrator. It was Lincoln who demanded unconditional surrender. It was he who determined to destroy the southern social order by emancipating all the slaves. He stepped back and allowed Grant to pursue his relentless military campaigns. And now he was sanctioning the systematic destruction of the homes, the property, and even the food supplies, of southern civilians. If this was not "total" war, it was something very close to it.

Northern Democrats were horrified by the destructive turn the war had taken. In 1864 they nominated George McClellan, the general Lincoln had fired, for president on a platform advocating compromise, a swift end to the war, and a negotiated settlement with the South. Inevitably, Lincoln's policy of hard war became the major issue of the campaign. The fact that McClellan won 45 percent of the votes suggested that a substantial portion of the northern electorate disapproved of the administration's aggressive policy. But by election day Mobile was in Union hands, Sheridan had laid waste to the Shenandoah Valley, and Sherman had taken Atlanta. The majority of northern voters could smell a Union victory and Lincoln won convincingly. All Confederate

Map 15-8 The Atlanta Campaign and Sherman's March, 1863–1865 Lincoln's reelection was saved in part by Sherman's capture of Atlanta. It was here that Sherman spelled out his theory that war must be made unbearable to southern civilians if the North was to win. From Atlanta he went on to capture Savannah after his famed "march to the sea." Sherman then turned his troops northward to cut an even greater path of destruction through South Carolina.

attempts to offer anything less than unconditional surrender were rejected. Lee's hopes were dashed, and the siege of Petersburg continued.

Sherman Marches and Lee Surrenders

A week after Lincoln's reelection, Sherman's men burned half of Atlanta to the ground, turned east, and marched toward the sea. Confederate general John Bell Hood tried to distract Sherman by moving west toward Alabama and then up into Tennessee, but half of Sherman's army outnumbered Hood's entire force, and half is what Sherman sent to chase Hood down. In two devastating battles, at Franklin and Nashville, Tennessee, Union troops led by George Thomas destroyed Hood's forces. There was almost nothing left of the Confederate army between the Mississippi River and the Appalachian mountains.

Meanwhile Sherman's troops were unleashing their destructive energies through hundreds of miles of Georgia countryside. In late December, Sherman telegraphed Lincoln and presented him with Savannah as a Christmas gift. From Savannah, Sherman's men marched northward. As they crossed into South Carolina, the birthplace of secession, Union soldiers brought the practice of hard war to its ferocious climax. They torched homes and barns, destroyed crops, and slaughtered livestock. With Charleston in Union hands and the state capital of Columbia up in flames,

Sherman continued his movement northward. Once they left South Carolina, however, Union soldiers were better behaved.

By then events in Virginia were bringing the war to a conclusion. Lee's army was fatally weakened when Union forces closed off Petersburg's last line of supply. On April 2, 1865, the Army of the Potomac broke through the Confederate defenses and forced Lee to abandon Petersburg. The next day Confederate leaders abandoned Richmond. Lee moved his tired and hungry troops westward in one last attempt to elude Grant's force, but when he reached Appomattox Court House, Lee surrendered and the war was over.

The Meaning of the Civil War

Despite the draft riots, Copperheads, wartime inflation, and terrible loss of life, the Civil War years had been good for the North's economy. Mechanization allowed northern farmers to increase wheat production, despite the fact that the army drained off one-third of the farm labor force. Huge orders for military rations propelled the growth of the canned-food industry. The railroad boom of the 1850s persisted through the war. By contrast, the slave economy was convincingly defeated. Much of the South lay in ruins. Thousands of miles of railroad track had been destroyed. One-third of the livestock had been killed; one-fourth of the young white men were dead. In 1860 the North and the South had identical per capita incomes and nearly identical per capita wealth. By 1870 the North was 50 percent wealthier than the South.

With Lee's surrender to Grant at Appomattox, the Civil War came to an end.

The redistribution of political power was equally dramatic. Until 1860, slaveholders and their allies had controlled the Supreme Court, dominated the presidency, and exercised disproportionate influence in Congress. The Civil War destroyed the slaveholding class and with it the slaveholders' political power.

Union victory strengthened the advocates of a stronger, more centralized national government. The growth of this "nationalist" sentiment can be traced in the speeches of Abraham Lincoln. When the Civil War began he emphasized the restoration of the "Union." By the end of the war Lincoln was more likely to talk of saving the "nation." An influential new magazine entitled, significantly, *The Nation* was founded in 1865 on the principle that the Civil War had established the supremacy and indivisibility of the nation-state.

But all of this paled beside the destruction of slavery. Emancipation was not what the North intended in 1861, but it clearly was by the end. For in truth, the war had not been enough to destroy slavery. When Lincoln was reelected in November 1864, perhaps half a million slaves had been freed. That meant there were 4 million slaves still in place. Emancipation had been justified as a military necessity, and once the war ended it was not clear that emancipation would continue. Some things had to be done to make sure that it would.

A thirteenth amendment would have to be added to the Constitution, outlawing slavery forever. Lincoln supported such an amendment; it was the only thing he asked to be included in the 1864 Republican Party platform. Once reelected he and the Republicans scrambled to get it through Congress before the war ended and support for emancipation evaporated. Congress finally passed the amendment and sent it to the states, in January of 1865. But it was not ratified until December, and in the intervening months most of the slaves were in fact emancipated. How?

Three of the four border states finally saw the light and emancipated their slaves on their own. Kentucky was the stubborn holdout. When Lee surrendered, many slaves and slaveholders spontaneously concluded that slavery itself was finished, and they began making new arrangements. Officers of the Freedmen's Bureau, an agency of the U.S. Army, stayed on when the war ended and enforced emancipation on farms and plantations across the South. Most importantly, the southern states themselves were required to enact emancipation as a requirement for readmission to the Union. As they did so, in the fall of 1865, millions of slaves across the South were finally liberated. The Thirteenth Amendment sealed the process when it was ratified in December of 1865, liberating the slaves in Kentucky in the process.

Emancipation had not been easy. It took runaway slaves forcing the Union's hands. It took Union troops determined to use slave liberation to put down the southern rebellion. It took tens of thousands of former slaves who put on blue uniforms and pointed their guns at their former owners. It took determined antislavery politicians, in Congress and the White House. It took a gradual but dramatic shift in northern public opinion. It had to overcome sustained and violent resistance by the Confederates. And it took nearly five years. But when it was over, the domestic slave trade was gone, the slave auction houses were closed down, and nobody claimed the fruits of a slave's labor as a right of property.

Six hundred thousand men died during the Civil War. If anything justified the slaughter, emancipation did. Yet even Lincoln was stunned by the price the nation had paid for emancipation. He wondered whether the bloodshed was a form of divine retribution for the unpardonable sin of slavery. In his second inaugural ad-

Lincoln's Second Inaugural Address In his second inaugural address, March 4, 1865, Lincoln suggested that four years of terrible war was the price the nation had to pay for the "offense" of slavery.

dress, in March 1865, he prayed that the "mighty scourge of war may speedily pass away." But, Lincoln added, "if God wills that it continue, until all the wealth piled up by the bond-man's two hundred and fifty years of unrequited toil shall be sunk, and until every drop of blood drawn with the lash, shall be paid by another drawn with the sword, as was said three thousand years ago, so still it must be said, 'the judgments of the Lord, are true and righteous altogether.'"

The bloody war had ended, but there was more blood to be shed. On the evening of April 14, 1865, a disgruntled southern actor named John Wilkes Booth assassinated Abraham Lincoln at Ford's Theater in Washington, DC.

Conclusion

The president who had led the nation through the Civil War would not oversee the nation's reconstruction. Lincoln had given some thought to the question of how to incorporate the defeated southern states into the Union, but when he died neither he nor his fellow Republicans in Congress had agreed on any particular plan. Would the Union simply be restored as swiftly as possible? Or would the South be reconstructed, continuing the revolution begun during the Civil War? At the moment Lincoln died, nobody was sure of the answer to these questions. They would emerge over the next several months and years, as the freed people in the South pressed to expand the meaning of their freedom.

Further Readings

Ira Berlin, et al., *Slaves No More: Three Essays on Emancipation and the Civil War* (1992). This collection gives a well-researched account of the process of emancipation.

Michael Burlingame, *Abraham Lincoln: A Life* (2009). The definitive modern treatment.

William C. Davis, *Look Away: A History of the Confederate States of America* (2002). A lively survey with good coverage of the collapse of slavery.

William W. Freehling, *The South Vs. The South: How Anti-Confederate Southerners Shaped the Course of the Civil War* (2001). Insightful study of the regional divisions within the South.

Gary W. Gallagher, *The Confederate War* (1997). A pugnacious study arguing that southern whites were overwhelmingly loyal to the Confederacy.

Bruce Levine, *Confederate Emancipation: Southern Plans to Free and Arm Slaves During the Civil War* (2006).

Chandra Manning, *What This Cruel War Was Over: Soldiers, Slavery, and the Civil War* (2008). An exceptionally well-researched study proving that soldiers North and South understood that slavery caused the Civil War.

James McPherson, *The Battle Cry of Freedom: The Civil War Era* (1988). A superb one-volume history of the war.

James McPherson, *Trial By War: Abraham Lincoln as Commander in Chief* (2008). This book skillfully demonstrates interconnections between military, political, and social history.

Who, What

>> Timeline >>

▼ 1860
South Carolina secedes

▼ 1861
Lower South secedes
Abraham Lincoln inaugurated
First shots fired at Fort Sumter
Upper South secedes

North declares runaway slaves "contraband"
First battle of Bull Run
McClellan takes command of Army of the Potomac
First Confiscation Act
Trent affair

▼ 1862
Battles of Fort Henry and Fort Donelson
"Battle of the ironclads"
Battle of Shiloh
Union capture of New Orleans
Slavery abolished in Washington, DC
Homestead Act
Confederacy establishes military draft
Peninsula campaign
Slavery prohibited in western territories
Second Confiscation Act, Militia Act, and Internal Revenue Act all passed by northern Congress
Second battle of Bull Run
Battle of Antietam

Review Questions

1. What reasons did southerners give for seceding?
2. What were the relative military advantages of the North and South at the beginning of the war?
3. What made emancipation a "military necessity"?
4. How much antiwar sentiment was there in the Union and the Confederacy?

Websites

Civilwar.com. Contains a massive amount of information on all aspects of the war.

Images of Battle. This site contains a fascinating collection of Civil War letters: http://www.lib.unc.edu/mss/exhibits/civilwar/index.html.

For further review materials and resource information, please visit www.oup.com/us/ofthepeople

Preliminary Emancipation Proclamation
Battle of Fredericksburg

▼ 1863
Emancipation Proclamation
Union establishes military draft
Battle of Chancellorsville
Battle of Gettysburg
Vicksburg surrenders
New York City draft riots
Battle of Chickamauga
Gettysburg Address
Battle of Lookout Mountain

▼ 1864
Wilderness campaign
Battle of Cold Harbor
Siege of Petersburg begins
Sherman captures Atlanta
Philip Sheridan raids Shenandoah Valley
Lincoln reelected
Sherman burns Atlanta and marches to the sea

Battles of Franklin and Nashville

▼ 1864–1865
Sherman's march through the Carolinas

▼ 1865
House of Representatives approves Thirteenth Amendment
Lincoln's second inauguration
Lee surrenders to Grant at Appomattox
Lincoln assassinated

CHAPTER 16

Common Threads 

>> In what ways did emancipation and wartime Reconstruction overlap?

>> When did Reconstruction begin?

>> Did Reconstruction change the South? If so, how? If not, why not?

>> What brought Reconstruction to an end?

Reconstructing a Nation

1865–1877

AMERICAN PORTRAIT

>> John Dennett Visits a Freedmen's Bureau Court

John Richard Dennett arrived in Liberty, Virginia, on August 17, 1865, on a tour of the South during which he sent back weekly reports for publication in *The Nation*. The editors wanted accurate accounts of conditions in the recently defeated Confederate states, and Dennett was the kind of man they could trust. He graduated from Harvard, was a firm believer in the sanctity of the Union, and belonged to the class of elite Yankees who thought of themselves as the "best men" the country had to offer.

At Liberty, Dennett was accompanied by a Freedmen's Bureau agent. The Freedmen's Bureau was a branch of the U.S. Army established by Congress to assist the freed people. Dennett and the agent went to the courthouse because one of the Freedmen's Bureau's functions was to adjudicate disputes between the freed people and southern whites.

The first case was that of an old white farmer who complained that two blacks who worked on his farm were "roamin' about and refusin' to work." He wanted the agent to help find the men and bring them back. Both men had wives and children living on his farm and eating his corn, the old man complained. "Have you been paying any wages?" the Freedmen's Bureau agent asked. "Well, they get what the other niggers get," the farmer answered. "I a'n't payin' great wages this year." There was not much the agent could do. He had no horses and few men, but one of his soldiers volunteered to go back to the farm and tell the blacks that "they ought to be at home supporting their wives and children."

A well-to-do planter came in to see if he could fire the blacks who had been working on his plantation since the beginning of the year. The planter complained that his workers were unmanageable now that he could no longer punish them. The sergeant warned the planter that he could not beat his workers as if they were still slaves. In that case, the planter responded, "Will the Government take them off our hands?" The Freedmen's Bureau agent suspected that the planter was looking for an excuse to discharge his laborers at the end of the growing season, after they had finished the work but before they had been paid. "If they've worked on your crops all the year so far," the agent told the planter, "I guess they've got a claim on you to keep them a while longer."

Next came a "good-looking mulatto man" representing a number of African Americans. They were worried by rumors that they would be forced to sign five-year contracts with their employers. "No, it a'n't true," the agent said. They also wanted to know if they could rent or buy land so that they could work for themselves. "Yes, rent or buy," the agent said. But the former slaves had no horses, mules, or ploughs to work the land. So they wanted to know "if the Government would help us out after we get the land." But the agent had no help to offer. "The Government hasn't any ploughs or mules to give you," he said. In the end the blacks settled for a piece of paper from the Freedmen's Bureau authorizing them to rent or buy their own farms.

The last case involved a field hand who came to the agent to complain that his master was beating him with a stick. The agent told the field hand to go back to work. "Don't be sassy, don't be lazy when you've got work to do; and I guess he won't trouble you." The field hand left "very reluctantly," but came back a minute later and asked for a letter to his master "enjoining him to keep the peace, as he feared the man would shoot him, he having on two or three occasions threatened to do so."

Most of the cases Dennett witnessed centered on labor relations, but labor questions often spilled over into other matters including the family lives of the freed people, their civil rights, and their ability to buy land. The freed people preferred to work their own land, but they lacked the resources to rent or buy farms. Black workers and white owners who negotiated wage contracts had trouble figuring out the limits of each other's rights and responsibilities. The former masters wanted to retain as much of their old authority as possible. Freedmen wanted as much autonomy as possible, while freedwomen were forced to seek the patriarchal protection of their husbands.

continued

>> AMERICAN PORTRAIT *continued*

The Freedmen's Bureau was placed in the middle of these conflicts. Most agents tried to ensure that the freed people were paid for their labor and that they were not brutalized as they had been as slaves. Southern whites resented this intrusion, and their resentment filtered up to sympathetic politicians in Washington, DC. As a result, the Freedmen's Bureau became a lightning rod for the political conflicts of the Reconstruction period.

Conditions in the South raised several questions for lawmakers in Washington. How far should the federal government go to protect the economic well-being and civil rights of the freed people? What requirements should the federal government impose on the southern states before they could be readmitted to the Union? Politicians in Washington disagreed violently on these questions. At one extreme was Andrew Johnson, who, as president, believed in small government and a speedy readmission of the southern states and looked on the Freedmen's Bureau with suspicion. At the other extreme were radical Republicans, who believed that the federal government should redistribute confiscated land to the former slaves, guarantee their civil rights, and give African American men the vote. They viewed the Freedmen's Bureau as too small and weak to do the necessary job. Between the radicals and the president's supporters were moderate Republicans who at first tried to work with the president. But as reports of violence and the abusive treatment of the freed people made their way back to the nation's capital, Republicans shifted toward the radical position.

It went back and forth this way: policy makers in Washington responded to what went on in the South, and events in the South were shaped in turn by the policies emanating from Washington. What John Dennett saw in Liberty, Virginia, was a good example of this. The Freedmen's Bureau agent listened to the urgent requests of former masters and slaves, his responses shaped by the policies established in Washington. But those policies were, in turn, shaped by reports on conditions in the South sent back by Freedmen's Bureau agents like him and by journalists like John Dennett. From this interaction the politics of Reconstruction, and with it a "New South," slowly emerged.

OUTLINE 

Wartime Reconstruction

For several years emancipation overlapped with Reconstruction. Emancipation began early in the war and was not completed until the very end of 1865. Experiments with Reconstruction began during the war, long before emancipation was complete. Indeed, what is known as "Presidential Reconstruction" was also the crucial phase in the completion of emancipation. Congress and the president often had very different ideas about how to reconstruct the defeated Confederacy, but on one thing they agreed from the very beginning. Until the Thirteenth Amendment was ratified in December of 1865, state emancipation was the most legally secure means of abolishing slavery. Congress and the president therefore agreed that before any southern state could be readmitted to the Union, it had to emancipate its own slaves.

After that, however, came several more contentious questions. What system of free labor would replace slavery? What civil and political rights should the freed people receive? During the war Congress and the Lincoln administration responded piecemeal to developments in regions of the South under Union control. A variety of approaches to Reconstruction emerged.

Experiments with Free Labor in the Lower Mississippi Valley

In November 1861, several of the Sea Islands off coastal South Carolina were occupied by Union troops. The slaveholders fled from the advancing Union army, leaving

Slaves Planting Sweet Potatoes Slaves in parts of coastal South Carolina were freed early in the Civil War. Here the freed people on Edisto Island in 1862 are shown planting sweet potatoes rather than cotton. In other parts of the South the former slaves returned to the cultivation of cash crops.

behind between 5,000 and 10,000 slaves. Were they free? Or merely contrabands of war? In December, responding to concerns about the status of contrabands, President Lincoln declared them "liberated." So began the first notable "rehearsal for Reconstruction." By the end of the war the abandoned plantations of the Sea Islands had been reorganized. Slave families were given small plots of their own to cultivate, and in return for their labor they would receive a "share" of the year's crop. When the masters returned after the war to reclaim their lands, the labor system evolved swiftly into what would become known as "sharecropping."

> **A few days ago, a gentleman below the city hired a new overseer, one who was. . . . in the habit of wielding the whip pretty freely, and of using abusive language to the negro women . . . [A] delegation from the field-hands waited upon the proprietor, and very respectfully stated their objections against the newcomer. . . . He dismissed them with an oath. . . . The delegation at once went to their cabins, packed up their little bundles, and started on the road to Fort Jackson. They knew, that, once there, they could get employment. They had not gone far, however, before the master came to his senses. He was no longer the owner of mere chattels. . . . He called them all back; told them they should have any overseer they wanted: upon which they unpacked their bundles, and went quietly to the field, as if nothing had happened.**
>
> GEORGE HEPWORTH,
> surveying the effect of the Banks Plan in Louisiana, 1863

Southern Louisiana also came under Union control early in the war. The sugar and cotton plantations around New Orleans therefore provided another major experiment in the transition from slave to free labor. Unlike the Sea Islands, however, Louisiana's planters did not abandon their plantations, and there were tens of thousands of slaves involved. This created a dilemma for Union commanders. The plantation workers were no longer slaves, but their masters were still in place, so the plantations could not be broken up. And in any case sugar plantations could not be effectively organized into small sharecropping units. The labor system that emerged was unusual in the post-emancipation South, but it played an important role in the politics of Reconstruction.

Union general Nathaniel Banks, hoping to stem the flow of blacks running to Union lines and prevent the shocking number of deaths among blacks in the refugee camps, issued stringent labor regulations designed to put the freed people back to work quickly. The Banks Plan required freed people to sign yearlong contracts to work on their former plantations, often for their former owners. Workers would be paid either 5 percent of the proceeds of the crop or three dollars per month. The former masters would provide food and shelter. African American workers were forbidden to leave the plantations without permission. So harsh were these regulations that to many critics Banks had simply replaced one form of slavery with another. But as harsh as it was, the Banks Plan was not slavery, and most of the freed people returned to work fully aware of the difference. The Banks Plan was implemented throughout the lower Mississippi Valley, especially after the fall of Vicksburg in 1863.

The Banks Plan touched off a political controversy. Established planters had the most to gain from the plan, which allowed them to preserve much of the prewar labor system. Louisiana Unionists, who had remained loyal to the government in Washington, formed a Free State Association to press for more substantial changes. Lincoln publicly supported the Free State movement and issued a Proclamation of Amnesty and Reconstruction to undermine the Confederacy by cultivating the support of southern Unionists. The Proclamation contained, in outline, the first plan for reconstructing the South.

The most important thing Lincoln's plan did was to require Louisiana to abolish slavery, as the price for readmission to the Union. The precedent for such a precondition had been established earlier the same year, when West Virginia was required to emancipate its slaves as a condition for admission to statehood. Lincoln quickly applied that precedent to the seceded states, beginning with Florida and Louisiana. But the attempt to establish a loyal government in Florida foundered, so Louisiana became the first great experiment in wartime Reconstruction.

Charlotte Forten Born to a prominent African American family in Philadelphia, Charlotte Forten was one of many northern women who went to the South to become a teacher of the freed slaves. Forten helped found the Penn School on St. Helena's Island in South Carolina.

Lincoln's Ten Percent Plan Versus the Wade-Davis Bill

Beyond requiring the abolition of slavery, Lincoln's Ten Percent Plan promised full pardons and the restoration of civil rights to all those who swore loyalty to the Union, excluding only a few high-ranking Confederate military and political leaders. When the number of loyal whites in a former Confederate state reached 10 percent of the 1860 voting population, they could organize a new state constitution and government. Abiding by these conditions, Free State whites met in Louisiana in 1864 and produced a new state constitution. It provided for free public education, a minimum wage, a nine-hour day on public works projects, and a graduated income tax. However, although it abolished slavery, it also denied blacks the right to vote.

By the spring of 1864 such denials were no longer acceptable to radical Republicans, a small but vocal wing of the Republican Party. Unionists were active in many parts of the South immediately after the war, and they developed strong ties to leading radicals in Congress, such as Thaddeus Stevens of Pennsylvania and Charles Sumner of Massachusetts. Despite their differences, most radicals favored federal guarantees of the civil rights of former slaves, including the right to vote. Radicals were prepared to use the full force of the federal government to enforce congressional policy in the South. Although the radicals never formed a majority in Congress, they gradually won over the moderates to many of their positions. As a result, when Congress took control of Reconstruction after the elections in 1866, the process became known as radical Reconstruction.

The radicals were particularly strong in New Orleans, thanks to the city's large and articulate community of free blacks. In the spring of 1864 they sent a delegation to Washington to meet with President Lincoln and press the case for voting rights.

MARRIAGE OF A COLORED SOLDIER AT VICKSBURG BY CHAPLAIN WARREN OF THE FREEDMEN'S BUREAU.

Freedman Wedding Because slave marriages had no legal standing, many freed people got married as soon as they could. Pictured here is one such wedding, performed at the Freedmen's Bureau.

The next day Lincoln wrote to the acting governor of Louisiana suggesting a limited suffrage for the most intelligent blacks and for those who had served in the Union army. The delegates to Louisiana's constitutional convention ignored Lincoln's suggestion. Shortly thereafter free blacks in New Orleans and former slaves together demanded civil and political rights and the abolition of the Banks labor regulations. Radicals complained that Lincoln's Ten Percent Plan was too kind to former Confederates and that the Banks Plan was too harsh on former slaves.

Moved largely by events in Louisiana, congressional radicals rejected Lincoln's plan. In July 1864 Congressmen Benjamin F. Wade and Henry Winter Davis proposed a different Reconstruction plan. Under the Wade-Davis Bill, Reconstruction could not begin until a majority, rather than merely 10 percent, of a state's white men swore an oath of allegiance to the Union. In addition, the Wade-Davis Bill guaranteed full legal and civil rights to African Americans, but not the right to vote. Lincoln pocket vetoed the bill because it required Louisiana to emancipate its slaves as a condition for readmission to the Union. Lincoln believed that only he, as commander in chief, could emancipate slaves, as a necessity of war. He included an emancipation provision in his own plan for Louisiana Reconstruction.

The Louisiana experience made several things clear. The radical Republicans were determined to press for more civil and political rights for blacks than moderates initially supported; however, the moderates showed a willingness to move in a radical direction. Equally important, any Reconstruction policy would have to consider the wishes of southern blacks.

The Freed People's Dream of Owning Land

Freedom meant many things to the former slaves. It meant they could move about their neighborhoods without passes, that they did not have to step aside to let whites pass them on the street. Following emancipation, southern blacks withdrew from white churches and established their own congregations, and during Reconstruction the church emerged as a central institution in the southern black community. Freedom also meant literacy. Even before the war ended northern teachers poured into the South to set up schools. The American Missionary Association organized hundreds of such northern teachers. When the fighting stopped, the U.S. Army helped recruit and organize thousands more northern women as teachers. The graduates of the missionary schools sometimes became teachers themselves. As a result, hundreds of thousands of southern blacks became literate within a few years.

More importantly, the former slaves went out of their way to have their marriages secured by the law. There was more to this than sentiment, or even the privacy of the home. In 1865 marriage became an urgent necessity for many recently freed slaves, particularly women. Under slavery black women were valued in part for their labor and in part for their ability to reproduce more slaves. With emancipation black women and their offspring were no longer valuable as property to be accumulated. Hoping to avoid the expense of caring for such workers, planters in some parts of the South began expelling women and children from their plantations in late 1865. Desperate women quickly realized that their best hope for avoiding starvation was to rely on the patriarchal protection of their husbands. Once married, their husbands would demand sharecropping contracts that allowed their families to live with them on the plantations. For the first time in their lives black women across the South became what the law called "domestic dependents." Emancipation moved black women—no longer human property—out of slavery and into patriarchy.

The freed people also wanted land. Without it the former slaves saw no choice but to work for their old masters on their farms and plantations. As the war ended, many African Americans had reason to believe that the government would assist them in their quest for independent land ownership. Marching through the Carolinas in early 1865, Union general William Tecumseh Sherman discovered how important land was to the freed people on the Sea Islands. "The way we can best take care of ourselves is to have land," they declared, "and turn it out and till it by our own labor." Persuaded by their arguments, Sherman issued Special Field Order No. 15 granting captured land to the freed people. By June 1865, 400,000 acres had been distributed to 40,000 former slaves.

Congress seemed to be moving in a similar direction. In March 1865, the Republicans established the Bureau of Refugees, Freedmen and Abandoned Lands, commonly known as the Freedmen's Bureau, which quickly became involved in the politics of land redistribution. The Freedmen's Bureau controlled the disposition of 850,000 acres of confiscated and abandoned Confederate lands. In July 1865, General Oliver Otis Howard, the head of the bureau, issued Circular 13, directing his agents to rent the land to the freed people in 40-acre plots that they could eventually purchase. Many bureau agents believed that to reeducate them in the values of thrift and hard work, the freed people should be encouraged to save money and buy land for themselves. From the bureau's perspective, redistributing land was like giving it away to people who had not paid for it.

From the perspective of the former slaves, however, black workers had more than earned a right to the land. "The labor of these people had for two hundred years cleared away the forests and produced crops that brought millions of dollars annually," H. C. Bruce explained. "It does seem to me that a Christian Nation would, at least, have given them one year's support, 40 acres of land and a mule each." Even Abraham Lincoln seemed to agree. But in April 1865 Lincoln was dead and Andrew Johnson became president of the United States.

Presidential Reconstruction, 1865–1867

When Andrew Johnson took office in April 1865, it was still unclear whether Congress or the president would control Reconstruction policy, and whether that policy would be lenient or harsh. As with so many Democrats, Johnson's sympathy for the common man did not extend to African Americans. Determined to reconstruct the South in his own way and blind to the interests of the freed people, Johnson grew increasingly bitter and resentful of the Republicans who controlled Congress.

The Political Economy of Contract Labor

In the mid-nineteenth century, Congress was normally out of session from March until December. Having assumed the presidency in April 1865, Johnson hoped to take advantage of the recess to complete the Reconstruction process and present the finished product to lawmakers in December. At the end of May the president offered amnesty and the restoration of property to white southerners who swore an oath of loyalty to the Union, excluding only high-ranking Confederate military and political leaders and very rich planters. He named provisional governors to the seceded states and instructed them to organize constitutional conventions. To earn readmission to the Union, the first thing the seceded states were required to do was abolish slavery, preferably by ratifying the Thirteenth Amendment. In addition, Johnson required the states to nullify their secession ordinances and repudiate their Confederate war debts. These terms were far more lenient than those Lincoln and the congressional Republicans had contemplated. They did nothing to protect the civil rights of the former slaves.

> New Orleans, La., August 2, 1866
>
> U. S. Grant, General, Washington, D.C.
>
> The more information I obtain about the affair of the 30th, in this city, the more revolting it becomes. It was no riot; it was an absolute massacre by the police. . . . It was a murder which the Mayor and the police of the city perpetrated without the shadow of a necessity; furthermore, I believe it was premeditated, and every indication points to this. I recommend removing this bad man. I believe it would be hailed with the sincerest gratification by two-thirds of the population of the city. There has been a feeling of insecurity on the part of the people here on account of this man, which is now so much increased that the safety of life and property does not rest with the civil authorities, but with the military.
>
> P. H. Sheridan
> Major-General Commanding

Johnson's leniency encouraged defiance among white southerners. Secessionists had been barred from participating in the states' constitutional conventions, but they participated openly in the first elections held late in the year because Johnson issued thousands of pardons. Leading Confederates thus assumed public office in the southern states. Complying with Johnson's requirements, the former Confederate states began abolishing slavery, and in the fall of 1865 the last great wave of emancipation spread across the South. Right up to the end of the war most slaveholders hoped that they could retain their slaves, even if they were forced to rejoin the Union. When the last holdouts—and there were many thousands of them—were finally forced to accept emancipation they were furious and resentful. Consequently, as Johnson's new state governments were coming into existence a wave of violence spread across the South.

Blacks who had been freed earlier were not immune to the reaction. Restored to power, white southerners demanded the restoration of all properties confiscated or abandoned during the war. In September 1865 Johnson ordered the Freedmen's Bureau to return all confiscated and abandoned lands to their former owners. In late 1865 former slaves were being forcibly evicted from the 40-acre plots they had been given by the Union army or the Freedmen's Bureau. On Edisto Island off South Carolina, for example, the freed people had carved farms out of the former plantations. But in January 1866 General Rufus Saxton restored the farms to their previous owners and encouraged the freed people to sign wage contracts with their old masters. The blacks unanimously rejected his offer, whereupon the general ordered them to evacuate their farms within two weeks.

Alongside their emancipation ordinances the Johnsonian state governments enacted a series of "Black Codes" severely restricting the civil rights of freed people. In many states the Black Codes *were* the emancipation statutes. Vagrancy statutes, for example, allowed local police to arrest and fine virtually any black man. If he could not pay the fine, the "vagrant" was put to work on a farm, often the one owned and operated by his former master. Even more disturbing to the former slaves were apprenticeship clauses that allowed white officials to remove children from their parents' homes and put them to work as "apprentices" on nearby farms.

Presidential Reconstruction left the freed people with no choice but to sign labor contracts with white landlords. The contracts restricted the personal as well as the working lives of the freed people. In one case, a South Carolina planter contractually obliged his black workers to "go by his direction the same as in slavery time." Contracts required blacks to work for wages as low as one-tenth of the crop, and cotton prices were steadily falling. It is no wonder that contract labor struck the freed people as little different from slavery.

Resistance to Presidential Reconstruction

In September 1865, blacks in Virginia issued a public appeal for assistance. They declared that they lacked the means to make and enforce legal contracts, because the Black Codes denied African Americans the right to testify in court in any case involving a white person. In many areas planters blocked the development of a free labor market by agreeing among themselves to hire only their former slaves and by fixing wages at a low level. Finally, there were numerous incidents in which black workers who had faithfully obeyed the terms of their contracts were "met by a contemptuous refusal of the stipulated compensation."

Across the South whites reported a growing number of freed people who would not abide by the humiliating conditions of the contract labor system. Some blacks refused to perform specific tasks, while others were accused of being "disrespectful" to their employers or to whites in general. Most important, thousands of freedmen declined to sign new contracts at the end of the year.

As the white backlash and black defiance spread, reports of violence flooded into Washington. A former slave named Henry Adams claimed that "over two thousand colored people" were murdered around Shreveport, Louisiana, in 1865. Near Pine Bluff, Arkansas, in 1866 a visitor arrived at a black community the morning after whites had burned it to the ground. Blacks were assaulted for not speaking to whites with the proper tone of submission, for disputing the terms of labor contracts, or for failing to work up to the standards white employers expected. Through relentless intimidation, whites prevented blacks from buying their own land or attending political meetings to press for civil rights.

Northerners read these reports as evidence that whites were resisting emancipation and that "rebel" sentiment was reviving in the South. When Congress came back into session in December 1865, moderate Republicans were already suspicious

The Congress owes it to its own character to set the seal of reprobation upon a doctrine which is becoming too fashionable, and unless rebuked will be the recognized principle of our Government. Governor Perry and other provisional governors and orators proclaim that "this is the white man's Government." The whole copperhead party, pandering to the lowest prejudices of the ignorant, repeat the cuckoo cry, "This is the white man's Government." Demagogues of all parties, even some high in authority, gravely shout, "This is the white man's Government." What is implied by this? That one race of men are to have the exclusive right forever to rule this nation, and to exercise all acts of sovereignty, while all other races and nations and colors are to be their subjects, and have no voice in making the laws and choosing the rulers by whom they are to be governed. Wherein does this differ from slavery except in degree? Does not this contradict all the distinctive principles of the Declaration of Independence?

CONGRESSMAN THADDEUS STEVENS,
speech on Reconstruction, December 18, 1865

of presidential Reconstruction. Radicals argued that the contract system made a mockery of their party's commitment to free labor and insisted that the only way to protect the interests of the freed people was to grant them the right to vote.

Congress Clashes with the President

Increasingly distressed by events in the South, Republican moderates in Congress were radicalized. They accepted the need for a more active government in the South and they endorsed voting rights for black men. President Johnson, meanwhile, became obsessed with fears of "negro rule" in the South. When he insisted on the swift readmission of southern states that were clearly controlled by unrepentant Confederates, Congress refused. Instead, the Republicans formed a Joint Committee on Reconstruction to propose the terms for readmission. Established in December 1865, the joint committee reflected Congress's determination to follow its own course on Reconstruction.

In February 1866 Congress voted to extend the life of the Freedmen's Bureau and empowered the bureau to set up its own courts, which would supercede local jurisdictions. The bureau's record during its first year had been mixed. In the crucial area of labor relations, the bureau too often sided with the landowners and against the interests of the freed people. It emancipated thousands of slaves still being held by their owners. It provided immediate relief to thousands of individual freed people, and it assisted in the creation of schools. The bureau's effectiveness varied with the commitments of its agents. Indifferent or even hostile to the needs of the freed people, some agents sided instinctively with the former masters. The more idealistic agents often acted under difficult circumstances to protect the freed people from racist violence, unfair employers, and biased law enforcement officials. For this reason, thousands of freedmen and freedwomen looked to the bureau as their only hope for justice. For the same reason, thousands of southern whites resented the bureau, and they let Andrew Johnson know it.

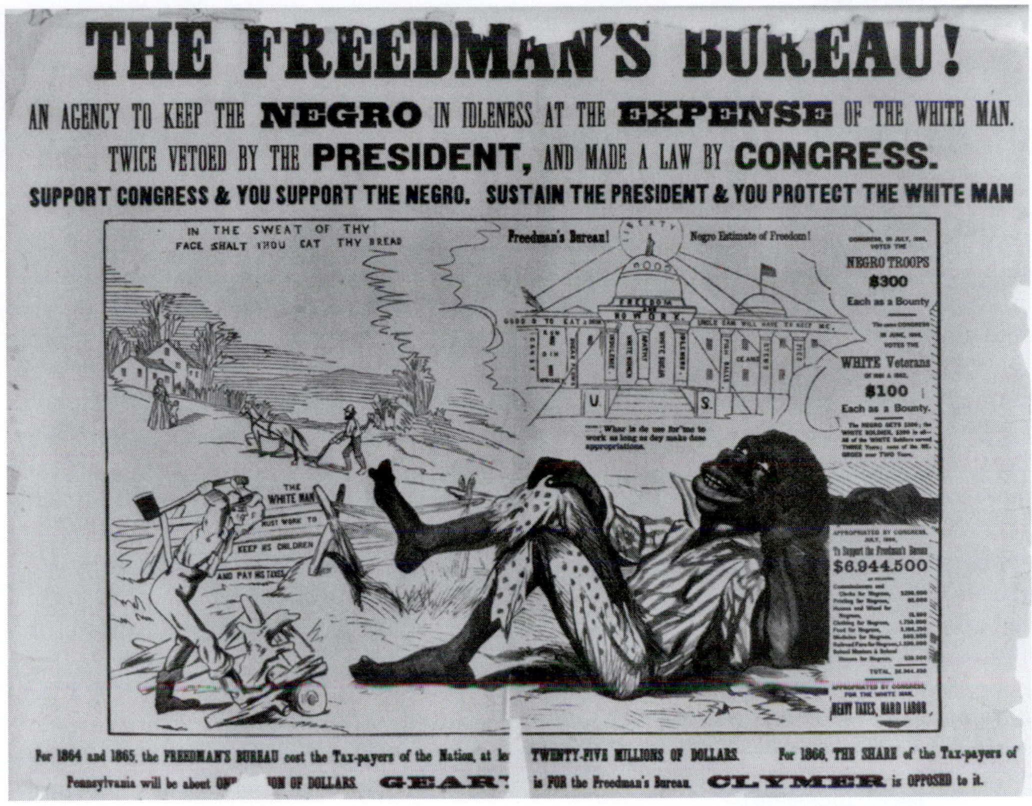

The Freedmen's Bureau Led by President Andrew Johnson, attacks on the Freedmen's Bureau became more and more openly racist in late 1865 and 1866. This Democratic Party broadside was circulated during the 1866 election.

To the amazement of moderate Republicans, Johnson vetoed the bill to extend the life of the Freedmen's Bureau. The president complained that the legislation would increase the power of the central government at the expense of the states. He invoked the Jacksonian ideal of the free market, insisting that the "laws that regulate supply and demand" were the best way to resolve the labor problem in the South. Republicans fell just short of the two-thirds vote they needed to override the veto. Johnson reacted to his narrow victory with a speech attacking the Republicans in Congress and questioning the legitimacy of the Joint Committee on Reconstruction.

Origins of the Fourteenth Amendment

In March 1866 Congress passed a landmark Civil Rights Act. It overturned the Dred Scott decision by granting United States citizenship to Americans regardless of race. This marked the first time that the federal government intervened in the states to guarantee due process and basic civil rights. But President Johnson vetoed the Civil Rights Act of 1866. In addition to the usual Jacksonian rhetoric about limited government, Johnson made an overtly racist argument to justify his veto. He doubted that blacks "possess the requisite qualifications to entitle them to all the privileges and immunities of citizens of the United States."

Johnson's actions and rhetoric forced the moderate Republicans to confront the president. The Republican Congress overrode Johnson's veto of the Civil Rights Act

AMERICAN LANDSCAPE

>> Race Riots in Memphis and New Orleans

A few weeks after Congress passed the Civil Rights Act, white mobs in Memphis rioted for three days. In the year since the war had ended, the city's black population had multiplied four times over as former slaves fled from the countryside in hopes of better opportunities in the city. But whites in Memphis grew increasingly hostile to the presence of so many blacks. "Would to God they were back in Africa, or some other seaport town," the Memphis *Argus* complained, "anywhere but here." Under President Johnson's terms for a newly reconstructed government the old Tennessee elite had been displaced in the city by Irish politicians who proved at least as hostile to freed people as the old guard. Not surprisingly, there were numerous reports of conflict breaking out between whites and blacks on the streets of Memphis.

HARPER'S WEEKLY.
A JOURNAL OF CIVILIZATION.

VOL. X.—No. 491.] NEW YORK, SATURDAY, MAY 26, 1866.

THE MEMPHIS RIOTS.

SCENES IN MEMPHIS, TENNESSEE, DURING THE RIOT—BURNING A FREEDMEN'S SCHOOL-HOUSE.
[SKETCHED BY A. R. W.]

SCENES IN MEMPHIS, TENNESSEE, DURING THE RIOT—SHOOTING DOWN NEGROES ON THE MORNING OF MAY 2, 1866.—[SKETCHED BY A. R. W.]

In this atmosphere of heightened racial tension one incident sparked a riot. On May 1, 1866, two hack drivers—one black, one white—had a traffic accident, and when the police arrived they arrested the black man. Matters soon escalated. A group of black veterans tried to prevent the arrest. A white crowd gathered and began rioting in the streets. Over the next three days white mobs burned hundreds of homes, destroyed churches, and attacked black schools. Five black women were raped and nearly fifty people, all but two of them black, were killed.

Three months later, white mobs in New Orleans rioted as well. Once again both the state and municipal governments were quickly falling into the hands of former Confederates. But the New Orleans massacre had a more explicitly political dimension. The city had a well-established community of free blacks who, by the middle of 1866, had grown disillusioned with the direction Reconstruction was taking in Louisiana and New Orleans. A group of radicals issued a call to bring the state's 1864 constitutional convention back into session. They proposed giving blacks the vote, stripping "rebels" of the franchise, and establishing an entirely new state government. The convention was scheduled to meet on July 30.

But as the delegates met, white mobs set out to stop them. Led by the city's police and firemen, many of them Confederate veterans, whites first attacked a parade of about 200 blacks who were marching to the Mechanics' Institute to support the delegates. When the mob reached the convention hall, deadly violence ensued. They attacked the hall, shooting and killing the delegates as they tried to escape through the windows, even after the victims raised the white flag of surrender. As one Union veteran who witnessed the massacre reported, "the wholesale slaughter and the little regard paid to human life" were worse than anything he had seen in battle. When the mob finally dispersed, 34 blacks and 3 white supporters had been killed, and another 100 had been injured.

The Memphis and New Orleans massacres quickly became political issues in the North, thanks in large part to Andrew Johnson's reaction to them. In late August the president undertook an unprecedented campaign tour designed to stir up voters' hostility to Congress, but his trip backfired. The president blasted congressional Republicans, blaming them for the riots. At one point he suggested that radical congressman Thaddeus Stevens should be hanged. Republicans charged in turn that

Johnson's own policies had revived the rebellious sentiments in the South that led to the massacres.

The elections of 1866 became a referendum on competing visions of what American democracy should mean at that point. For President Johnson "democracy" meant government by local majorities, which often meant white supremacy. For African Americans and a growing number of Republicans in Congress, genuine democracy could only be constructed on a firm foundation of equal civil and political rights. The results were "overwhelmingly against the President," the *New York Times* noted, "clearly, unmistakably, decisively in favor of Congress and its policy." The Republicans gained a veto-proof hold on Congress, and Republican moderates were further radicalized. Congressional Reconstruction was about to begin. ●

and passed another Freedmen's Bureau Bill. Once again Johnson vetoed it, but this time Congress overrode his veto.

To ensure the civil rights of the freed people, the Joint Committee on Reconstruction proposed a Fourteenth Amendment to the Constitution. The most powerful and controversial of all the Constitution's amendments, it guaranteed citizenship to all males born in the United States, regardless of color (see Table 16–1). Although the amendment did not guarantee blacks the right to vote, it based representation in Congress on a state's voting population. This punished southern states by reducing their representation if they did not allow blacks to vote.

By mid-1866, Congress had refused to recognize the state governments established under Johnson's plan, and it had authorized the Freedmen's Bureau to create a military justice system to override the local courts. Congress thereby guaranteed the former slaves basic rights of due process. Finally, it made ratification of the Fourteenth Amendment by the former Confederate states a requirement for their readmission to the Union. Congress and the president were now at war, and Andrew Johnson went on a rampage.

 **Table 16–1** Reconstruction Amendments, 1865–1870

Amendment	Main Provisions	Congressional Passage (2/3 majority in each house required)	Ratification Process (3/4 of all states including ex-Confederate states required)
13	Slavery prohibited in United States	January 1865	December 1865 (27 states, including 8 southern states)
14	1. National citizenship for all men and women born in the U.S.	June 1866	Rejected by 12 southern and border states, February 1867
	2. State representation in Congress reduced proportionally to number of voters disfranchised		Radicals make readmission of southern states hinge on ratification
	3. Former high ranking Confederates denied right to hold office		Ratified July 1868
	4. Confederate debt repudiated		
15	Denial of franchise because of race, color, or past servitude explicitly prohibited	February 1869	Ratification required for readmission of Virginia, Texas, Mississippi, Georgia. Ratified March 1870.

Congressional Reconstruction

Johnson's outrageous behavior during the 1866 campaign, capped by a Republican sweep of the elections, ended presidential Reconstruction. Congressional Reconstruction would be far different. It was an extraordinary series of events, second only to emancipation in its impact on the history of the United States.

Origins of the Black Vote

The Congress that convened in December 1866 was far more radical than the previous one. Nothing demonstrated this as clearly as the emerging consensus among moderate Republicans that southern blacks should be allowed to vote. Radical Republicans and black leaders had been calling for such a policy for two years, but moderate Republicans initially resisted the idea. At most, moderates contemplated granting the vote to veterans and to educated blacks who had been free before the war. Not until early 1867 did the majority of Republicans conclude that the only way to avoid a lengthy military occupation of the South was to put political power into the hands of all male freedmen.

Andrew Johnson finally pushed the moderate Republicans over the line. Ignoring the results of the 1866 elections, Johnson urged the southern states to reject the Fourteenth Amendment. Frustrated Republicans finally repudiated presidential Reconstruction from top to bottom. On March 2, 1867, Congress assumed control of the process by passing the First Reconstruction Act. It reduced the southern states to the status of territories and divided the South into five military districts directly controlled by the army (see Map 16–1). Before the southern states could be readmitted to the Union they had to draw up new "republican" constitutions, ratify the Fourteenth Amendment, and allow black men to vote. The Second Reconstruction Act, passed a few weeks later, established the procedures to enforce black suffrage by placing the military in charge of voter registration. Johnson vetoed both acts, and in both cases Congress immediately overrode the president. This was congressional Reconstruction at its most radical, and for this reason it is often referred to as "radical Reconstruction."

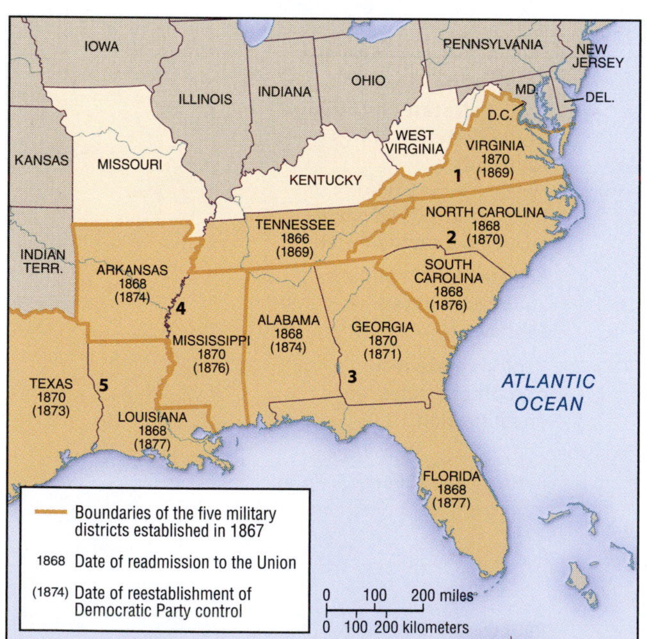

Map 16–1 Reconstruction and Redemption By 1870 Congress readmitted every southern state to the Union. In most cases the Republican Party retained control of the "reconstructed" state governments for only a few years.

Radical Reconstruction in the South

Beginning in 1867 the constitutions of the southern states were rewritten, thousands of African Americans began to vote, and hundreds of them assumed public office. Within six months 735,000 blacks and 635,000 whites had registered to vote across the South. Blacks formed electoral majorities in South Carolina, Florida, Mississippi, Alabama, and Louisiana. In the fall these new voters elected delegates to conventions that drew up progressive state constitutions that guaranteed suffrage for all men, mandated public education systems, and established progressive tax structures.

The governments elected under congressional authority were based on an unstable political coalition. Northern whites occupied a prominent place in the southern Republican Party. Stereotyped as greedy carpetbaggers, they included Union veterans who stayed in the South when the war ended, idealistic reformers, well-meaning capitalists, and opportunistic Americans on the make. More important to the Republican coalition were southern whites, or scalawags. Some of them lived in up-country regions where resistance to secession and the Confederacy had been strongest. Others had been Whigs before the war and hoped to regain some of their former influence. But new black voters were the backbone of the Republican Party in the South. Like the carpetbaggers and scalawags, black voters were a varied lot. Elite black artisans and professionals did not always share the interests of poor black farmers and farm laborers. Nevertheless, most African Americans were drawn together by a shared interest in securing civil rights.

In the long run the class and race divisions within the southern Republican coalition weakened the party, but in the late 1860s and early 1870s the southern Republicans launched an impressive experiment in interracial democracy in the South. Racist legend paints these years as a dark period of "negro rule" and military domination, but military rule rarely lasted more than a year or two, and in only one state, South Carolina, did blacks ever control a majority of seats in the legislature. Blacks who held office came largely from the ranks of the prewar free African American elite. Teachers, ministers, and small businessmen were far more common among black elected officials than were sharecroppers or farm workers. Nevertheless, these Reconstruction legislatures were more representative of their constituents than most legislatures in nineteenth-century America (see Figure 16–1).

Achievements and Failures of Radical Government

Once in office, southern Republicans had to cultivate a white constituency and at the same time serve the interests of the blacks who elected them. To strengthen this biracial coalition, Republican politicians emphasized active government support for economic development. Republican legislatures granted tax abatements for corporations and spent vast sums to encourage the construction of railroads. They preached a "gospel of prosperity" that promised to bring the benefits of economic development to ordinary white southerners.

In the long run, the gospel of prosperity did not hold the Republican coalition together. Outside investors were unwilling to risk their capital on a region marked by political instability. By the early 1870s, black politicians questioned the diversion of scarce revenues to railroads and tax breaks for corporations. Instead, they demanded public services, especially universal education. But more government services meant higher property taxes at a time of severe economic hardship. White small farmers had been devastated by the Civil War. Unaccustomed to paying

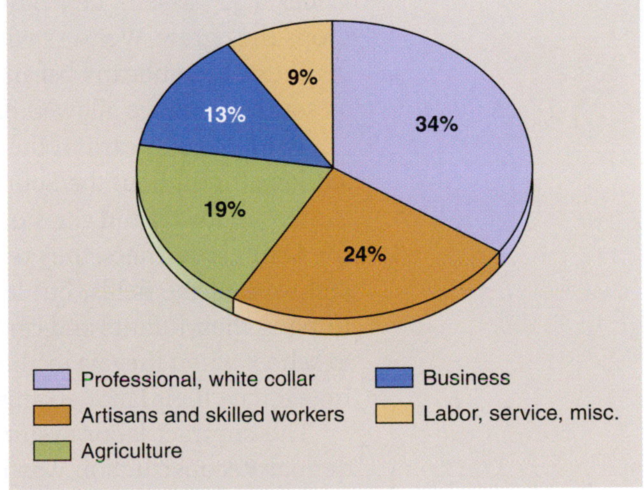

Figure 16–1 Occupations of African American Officeholders During Reconstruction Although former slaves were under-represented among black officeholders, the Reconstruction governments were among the most broadly representative legislatures in U.S. history.

"Radical Members" One of the greatest achievements of congressional Reconstruction was the election of a significant number of African Americans to public office. Only in South Carolina, however, did African Americans ever form a legislative majority.

high taxes, and believing strongly in limited government, they grew increasingly receptive to Democratic appeals for restoration of "white man's government." Thus southern Republicans were unable to develop a program that could unite the diverse interests of their party's constituents.

Despite powerful opposition at home and lukewarm support from Washington, DC, radical governments in the South boasted several important achievements. They funded the construction of hospitals, insane asylums, prisons, and roads. They introduced homestead exemptions that protected the property of poor farmers. One of their top priorities was the establishment of universal public education. Republican legislatures established public school systems that were a major improvement over their antebellum counterparts. The literacy rate among southern blacks rose steadily.

Nevertheless, public schools for southern blacks remained inadequately funded and sharply segregated. In Savannah, Georgia, for example, the school board allocated less than 5 percent of its 1873 budget to black schools, although white children were in the minority in the district. In South Carolina, fewer than one in three school-age children was being educated in 1872.

The Political Economy of Sharecropping

Congressional Reconstruction made it easier for the former slaves to negotiate the terms of their labor contracts. Republican state legislatures abolished the Black Codes and passed "lien" laws, statutes giving black workers more control over the crops they grew. Workers with grievances had a better chance of securing justice, as southern Republicans became sheriffs, justices of the peace, and county clerks, and as southern courts allowed blacks to serve as witnesses and sit on juries.

The strongest card in the hands of the freed people was a shortage of agricultural workers throughout the South. After emancipation thousands of blacks sought opportunities in towns and cities or in the North. And even though most blacks remained in the South as farmers, they reduced their working hours in several ways. Black women still worked the fields, but less often than they had as slaves. They spent more time nursing their infants and caring for their children. And the children themselves went to school when they were able. The resulting labor shortage forced white landlords to renegotiate their labor arrangements with the freed people.

The contract labor system that had developed during the war and under presidential Reconstruction was replaced with a variety of arrangements in different regions. On the sugar plantations of southern Louisiana, the freed people became wage laborers. But in tobacco and cotton regions, where the vast majority of freed people lived, a new system of labor called *sharecropping* developed. Under the sharecropping system, an agricultural worker and his family typically agreed to work for one year on a particular plot of land, the landowner providing the tools, seed, and work animals. At the end of the year the sharecropper and the landlord split the crop, perhaps one-third going to the sharecropper and two-thirds to the owner.

Sharecropping shaped the economy of the postwar South by transforming the way cash crops were produced and marketed. Most dramatically, it required landowners to break up their plantations into family-sized plots, where sharecroppers worked in family units with no direct supervision. Each sharecropping family established its own relationship with local merchants to sell crops and buy supplies. Merchants became crucial to the southern credit system because during the Civil War Congress had established nationwide banking standards that most southern banks could not meet. Therefore storekeepers were usually the only people who could extend credit to sharecroppers. They provided sharecroppers with food, fertilizer, animal feed, and other provisions over the course of the year, until the crop was harvested.

These developments had important consequences for white small farmers. As the number of merchants grew, they fanned out into up-country areas inhabited mostly by ordinary whites. Reconstruction legislatures meanwhile sponsored the construction of railroads in those districts. The combination of merchants offering credit and

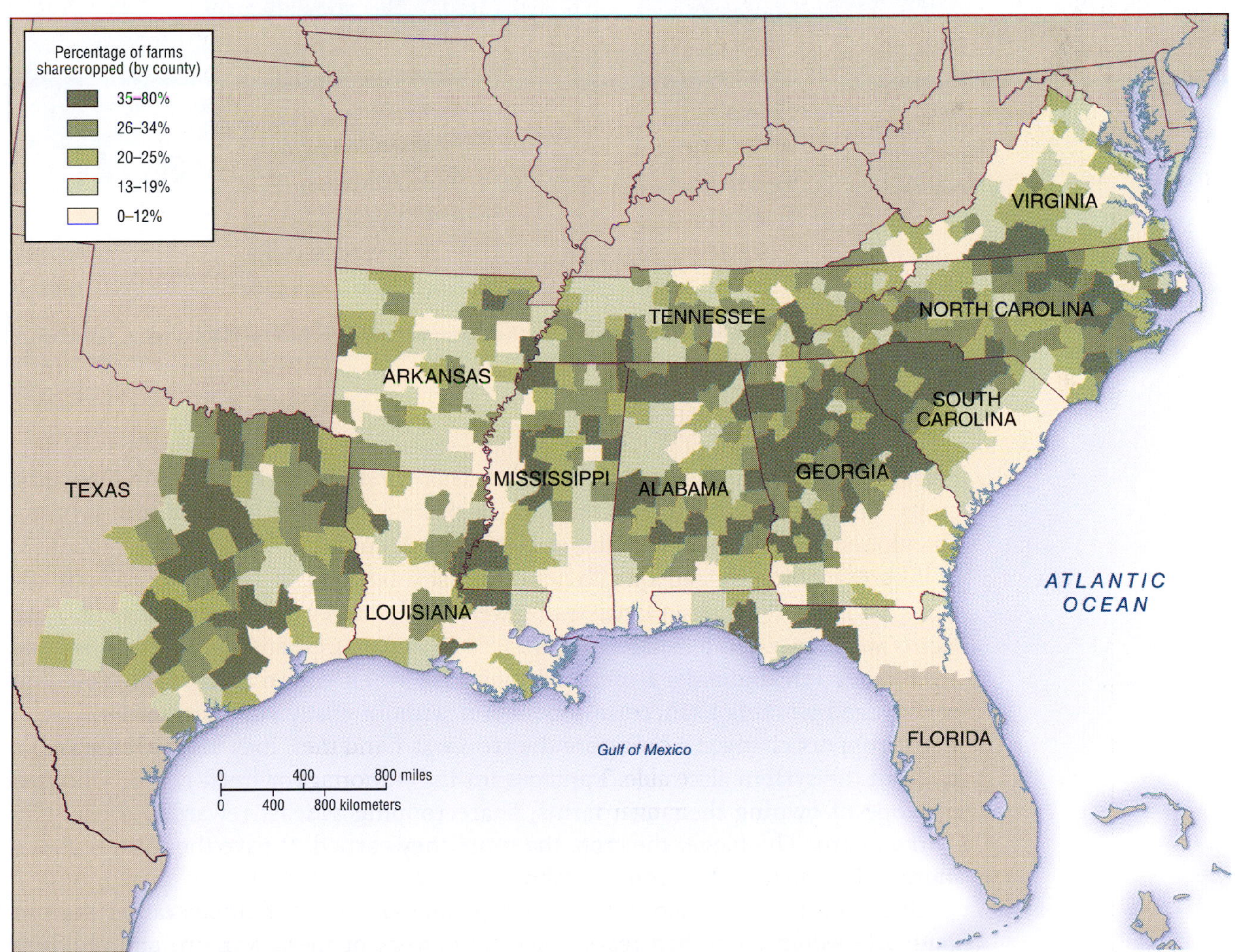

Map 16-2 Sharecropping By 1880 the sharecropping system had spread across the South. It was most common in the inland areas, where primarily cotton and tobacco plantations existed before the Civil War.

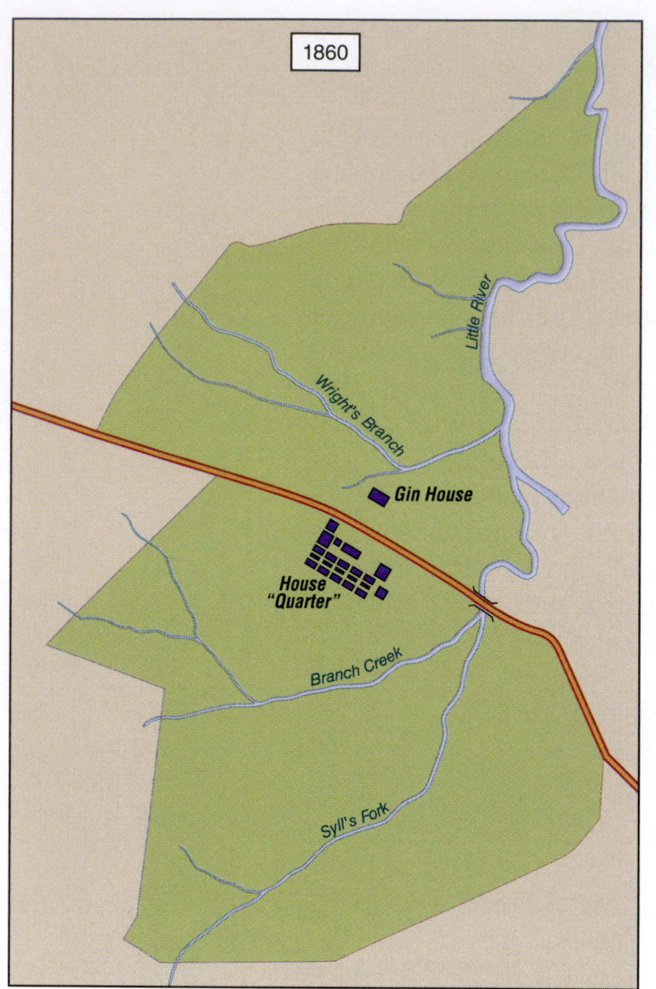

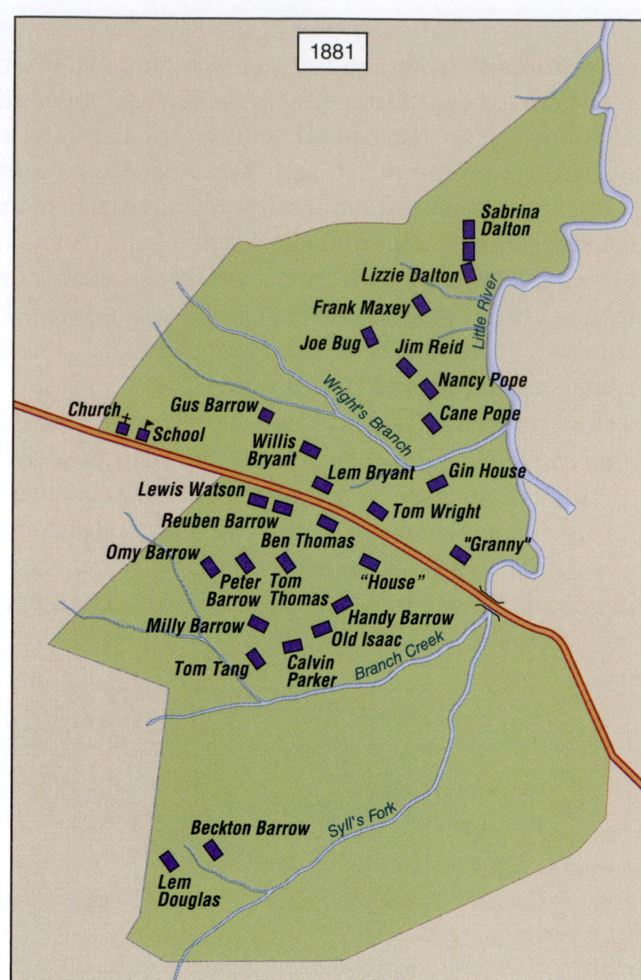

Map 16-3 The Effect of Sharecropping on Southern Plantations: The Barrow Plantation in Oglethorpe County, Georgia Sharecropping cut large estates into small landholdings worked by sharecroppers and tenants, changing the landscape of the South.

railroads offering transportation made it easier for small farmers to produce cash crops. Thus Reconstruction accelerated the process by which the southern yeomen abandoned self-sufficient farming in favor of cash crops.

Sharecropping spread quickly among black farmers in the cotton South. By 1880, 80 percent of cotton farms had fewer than 50 acres and the majority of those farms were operated by sharecroppers (see Map 16–2). Sharecropping had several advantages for landlords. It reduced their risk when cotton prices were low and encouraged workers to increase production without costly supervision. Further, if sharecroppers changed jobs before the crop was harvested, they lost a whole year's pay. But the system also had advantages for the workers. For freed people who had no hope of owning their own farms, sharecropping at least rewarded those who worked hard. The bigger the crop, the more they earned. It gave the former slaves more independence than contract labor.

Sharecropping also allowed the freed people to work in families rather than in gangs. Freedom alone had rearranged the powers of men, women, and children within the families of former slaves. Parents gained newfound control over the lives of their children. They could send sons and daughters to school; they could put them to work. Successful parents could give their children an important head start in life. Similarly, African American husbands gained new powers.

The laws of marriage in the mid-nineteenth century defined the husband as the head of the household. These laws had been irrelevant to slaves, since their marriages had no legal standing. With emancipation the patriarchal assumptions of American family law shaped the lives of freedmen and freedwomen in ways they never had before. Once married, women often found that their property belonged to their husbands. The sharecropping system further assumed that the husband was the head of the household and that he made the economic decisions for the entire family. Men signed most labor contracts, and most contracts assumed that the husband would take his family to work with him.

Sharecropping thereby shaped the social system of the postwar South: It influenced the balance of power between men and women. It established the balance of power between landowners and sharecroppers. It tied the southern economy to agriculture, in particular to cotton production, seriously impeding the region's overall economic development. Yet even as this new way of life was taking shape, the Republican Party was retreating from its commitment to the freed people.

> **Question:** Where did you come from?
> **Answer:** I came from Winston County.
> **Question:** What occasioned your coming here?
> **Answer:** I got run by the Ku-Klux. . . .
> **Question:** What did they do to you?
> **Answer:** . . . They surrounded me in the floor and tore my shirt off. They got me out on the floor; some had me by the legs and some by the arms and the neck and anywhere, just like dogs string out a coon, and they took me out to the big road before my gate and whipped me until I couldn't move or holler or do nothing, but just lay there like a log, and every lick they hit me I grunted just like a mule when he is stalled fast and whipped. . . .
> **Question:** Did they tell you they whipped you because you were a radical?
> **Answer:** They told me, "God damn you, when you meet a white man in the road lift your hat; I'll learn you, God damn you, that you are a nigger, and not to be going about like you thought yourself a white man."
>
> CONGRESSIONAL TESTIMONY OF WILLIAM COLEMAN,
> Macon, Mississippi, November 6, 1871

The Retreat from Republican Radicalism

By the late 1860s the Republican coalition was splintering in ways that weakened the party's continued commitment to radical Reconstruction. By 1868 the Republicans were presenting themselves to voters as the party of moderation. The success of this appeal brought in its wake the last major achievements of Reconstruction.

The Impeachment and Trial of Andrew Johnson

Throughout 1866 and much of 1867, President Johnson waged a relentless campaign against Congress and the radicals. Inevitably, this conflict led to a struggle over control of the military in the South. The First Reconstruction Act placed the entire South under direct military power. The Freedmen's Bureau itself was a branch of the U.S. Army. Judicial authority was vested in the provost marshals. The military also oversaw voter registration. But the president was the commander in chief of the military, and, exercising his authority over the military, Andrew Johnson removed dozens of Freedmen's Bureau officials who enforced the Civil Rights Act of 1866. He replaced Republican provost marshals with men who were hostile to Congress and contemptuous of the former slaves. In short, Johnson went out of his way to undermine the will of Congress.

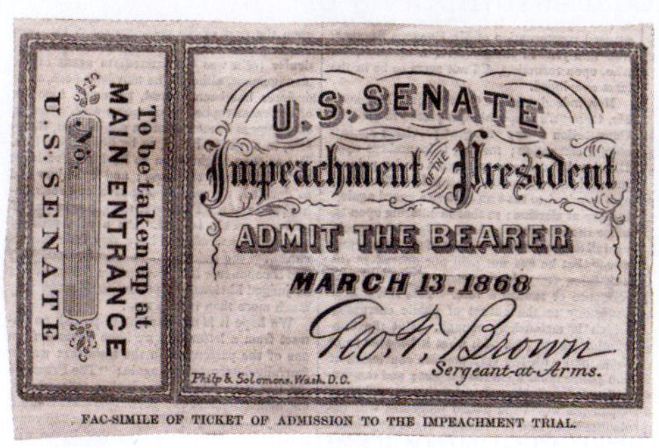

Impeachment Ticket Congressmen were besieged with requests for these tickets to the Senate gallery by constituents who wanted to observe the impeachment proceedings.

Radicals called for Johnson's impeachment, but moderates and conservatives resisted. Instead, Congress hoped to restrain the president by refining the Reconstruction Acts and by using the Tenure of Office Act of March 2, 1867. This act prohibited the president from removing officials whose appointments required Congressional approval. One purpose of the law was to prevent Johnson from firing Secretary of War Edwin M. Stanton, who was sympathetic to the Republicans. A related statute required that all presidential orders to the military pass through General Ulysses S. Grant. Republicans hoped that this would prevent the president from removing military officials who enforced the Reconstruction Acts.

Congress's actions only provoked the president. In his veto messages and public pronouncements Johnson indulged in blatant racist pandering. He played on fears of "amalgamation," "miscegenation," and racial "degeneration." He expressed fear for the safety of white women, when all the evidence suggested that it was black women who were most in danger. In the off-year elections of 1867, northern Democrats played the race card relentlessly and successfully. Democratic victories erased many of the huge Republican gains of 1866 and inspired the president to defy congressional restraints. As a deliberate provocation, Johnson asked Secretary of War Stanton to resign on August 5, 1867. Stanton refused, and the president appointed General Grant as interim secretary of war. Still Stanton would not budge, so in February 1868 Johnson fired him. For this the House of Representatives voted to impeach the president and put him on trial in the Senate.

The New-York Times.

VOL. XVII....NO. 5203 — NEW-YORK, WEDNESDAY, MAY 27, 1868.

IMPEACHMENT.

The Final Vote Taken on the Second and Third Articles.

For all the congressional animosity that Johnson had aroused by his obnoxious behavior, the senators trying him took their job seriously. Many were concerned that the Tenure of Office Act, which Johnson was accused of violating, was in fact unconstitutional. Others wondered whether his technical breach of the law was serious enough to warrant his removal from office. These and other doubts, along with Johnson's promise of good behavior in the future, led the Senate to acquit the president by a single vote.

Republicans Become the Party of Moderation

While Andrew Johnson was on trial in the Senate, voters in Michigan went to the polls and overwhelmingly rejected a new state constitution that granted blacks the right to vote. Coming on the heels of Democratic victories in 1867, the Michigan results were read by Republicans as a rejection of radical Reconstruction.

AMERICA AND THE WORLD

>> Reconstructing America's Foreign Policy

Before the Civil War, Republicans associated expansionism with the slave power and the Democratic Party. But with the triumph of nationalism, the Republicans equated American overseas expansion with the spread of liberty. They went on the offensive. In 1867 Secretary of State William Seward successfully negotiated the purchase of Alaska from Russia. The successful acquisition of Alaska ignited expansionist dreams of eventual U.S. control of all of North America, including Canada and Mexico, and "all the West Indian Islands."

The administration was equally adroit in its negotiations with Great Britain over the settlement of the so-called *Alabama* claims. In 1872 the English accepted responsibility for having helped equip the Confederate navy during the Civil War and agreed to pay over $15 million for damage to American shipping by the *Alabama* and other southern warships built in England.

Two years earlier, in 1870, a coalition of supporters with varying interests came together in support of the annexation of the island nation of Santo Domingo. The Grant administration strongly supported the treaty. Republicans who had once objected to such schemes as tainted by their association with slavery now switched sides and endorsed annexation. It would, they claimed, allow "our neighbors to join with us in the blessings of our free institutions." Thus the abolition of slavery in the United States was said to have purified the motives for American expansion. Even Frederick Douglass endorsed the annexation of Santo Domingo. It would help the island's inhabitants rise out of their truly grinding poverty, Douglass said, by transplanting "within her tropical borders" America's "glorious institutions."

But Grant's aggressive foreign policy did not go uncontested. Grant tried to bulldoze the treaty through Congress, but he was thwarted by Senator Charles Sumner of Massachusetts, the powerful chairman of the Foreign Relations Committee. Sumner took a principled stance against imperial ventures in general, but he was particularly concerned to protect the independence of the black republic of Haiti, which shared the island with Santo Domingo. A handful of Republicans, including Carl Schurz and Oliver P. Morton, likewise opposed the treaty, but most of the party sided with the president. Yet Sumner succeeded in having the treaty rejected, by a 28–28 tie vote, thanks to the opposition of Senate Democrats. They opposed annexation for racist reasons: they objected to incorporating into the United States an island populated by dark-skinned peoples of an inferior race. Thus the prewar alignments on expansionism were largely reversed by the Civil War. The Republican Party became the spearhead of American imperialism, while Democrats largely opposed it.

During the 1868 elections Republicans repudiated the radicals' demand for nationwide black suffrage, arguing that the black vote was a uniquely southern solution to a uniquely southern problem. The northern states should be free to decide for themselves whether to grant African American men the vote. Congress readmitted six southern states to the Union, thereby demonstrating that Republican policies had successfully restored law and order to the South. By nominating General Ulysses Grant as their presidential candidate, the Republicans confirmed their retreat from radicalism. "Let Us Have Peace" was Grant's campaign slogan.

In sharp contrast, the Democrats nominated Horatio Seymour, who ran a vicious campaign of race-baiting. The Democratic platform denounced the Reconstruction Acts and promised to restore white rule to the South. Seymour suggested that a Democratic president might nullify the governments organized under congressional Reconstruction. Where the Republicans promised order and stability, the Democrats seemed to promise continued disruption. Northern fears were confirmed by the violence that swept the South during the election, incited by southern Democrats to keep black voters from the polls.

The Ku Klux Klan, which systematically intimidated potential black voters, was one of several secretive organizations dedicated to the violent overthrow of radical Reconstruction and the restoration of white supremacy. They included the Knights of the White Camelia, the Red Shirts, and the Night Riders. Some tried to force blacks to go back to work for white landlords. Some attacked African Americans who refused to abide by traditional codes of racial etiquette. But in the main, such organizations worked to restore the political power of the Democratic Party in the South. They intimidated white Republicans, burned homes of black families, and lynched African Americans who showed signs of political activism. It is fair to say that in 1868 the Ku Klux Klan served as the paramilitary arm of the southern Democratic Party.

The Ku Klux Klan The Klan was one of a number of racist vigilante groups trying to restore the Democratic Party to power in the postwar South.

As a means of restoring white supremacy, the Klan's strategy of violence backfired. A wave of disgust swept across the North, and the Republicans regained control of the White House, along with 25 of the 33 state legislatures. The victorious Republicans quickly seized the opportunity to preserve the achievements of the Reconstruction.

The Republicans reinforced their moderate image by attempting to restore law and order in the South. Congressional hearings produced vivid evidence of the Klan's violent efforts to suppress the black vote. Congress responded with a series of Enforcement Acts, designed to "enforce" the recently enacted Fifteenth Amendment (see the following section). After some initial hesitation, the Grant administration used the new laws to initiate anti-Klan prosecutions that effectively diminished political violence throughout the South. As a result the 1872 presidential elections were relatively free of disruption.

Reconstructing the North

Although Reconstruction was aimed primarily at the South, the North was affected as well. The struggle over the black vote spilled beyond the borders of the defeated Confederacy. Although not as dramatic as developments in the South, the transformation of the North was still an important chapter in the history of Reconstruction.

The Fifteenth Amendment and Nationwide African American Suffrage

Before the Civil War, blacks in the North were segregated in theaters, restaurants, cemeteries, hotels, streetcars, ferries, and schools. Most northern blacks could not vote, either because they were expressly denied the privilege or because of discriminatory property requirements that blacks alone were required to meet. The Civil War galvanized the northern black community to launch an assault on racial discrimination, with some success. In 1863 California removed the ban on black testimony in criminal courts. Two years later Illinois did the same. During the war, many northern cities abolished streetcar segregation. But when they considered black voting, northern whites retained their traditional racial prejudices. In 1865 voters in three northern states (Connecticut, Wisconsin, and Minnesota) rejected constitutional amendments to enfranchise African American men. In 1867, even as the Republican Congress was imposing the black vote on the South, black suffrage was defeated by voters in Ohio, Minnesota, and Kansas.

The shocking electoral violence of 1868 persuaded many northerners that, given the chance, southern whites would quickly strip blacks of the right to vote. In Iowa and Minnesota, voters finally approved black suffrage. Emboldened by their victory in the 1868 elections, the following year Republicans passed the Fifteenth Amendment to the Constitution. It prohibited the use of "race, color, or previous condition of servitude" to disqualify voters anywhere in the United States. By outlawing voter discrimination on the basis of race, the Fifteenth Amendment protected the most radical achievement of congressional Reconstruction.

The Fifteenth Amendment brought Reconstruction directly into the North by overturning the state laws that discriminated against black voters. In addition, Congress required ratification of the amendment in those southern states still to be readmitted to the Union. Virginia, Mississippi, and Texas did so and were restored to the Union in early 1870. On March 30, 1870, the Fifteenth Amendment became part of the Constitution. For the first time, racial criteria for voting were banned everywhere in the United States, North as well as South.

Women and Suffrage

The issue of black voting divided northern radicals, especially feminists and abolitionists, who had long been allies in the struggle for emancipation. Signs of trouble appeared as early as May 1863 when a dispute broke out at the convention of the Woman's National Loyal League in New York City. One of the convention's resolutions declared that "there never can be a true peace in this Republic until the civil and political rights of all citizens of African descent and all women are practically established." For some of the delegates, this went too far. The Loyal League had been organized to assist in defeating the slave South. Some delegates argued that it was inappropriate to inject the issue of women's rights into the struggle to restore the Union.

By the end of the war, radicals were pressing for black suffrage in addition to emancipation. This precipitated an increasingly rancorous debate among reformers. Abolitionists argued that, while they supported women's suffrage, the critical issue was the protection of the freed people of the South. This, abolitionist Wendell Phillips argued, was "the Negro's Hour." Phillips's position sparked a sense of betrayal among some women's rights activists. For 20 years they had pressed their claims for the right to vote. They were loyal allies of the Republican Party, and now the Republicans abandoned them. It would be better, Elizabeth Cady Stanton argued, to press for "a vote based on intelligence and education for black and white, man and woman." Voting rights based on "intelligence and education" would have excluded virtually all the freed slaves as well as the working-class Irish, Germans, and Chinese. Thus, Stanton's remarks revealed a strain of elitism that further alienated abolitionists.

Not all feminists agreed with Stanton, and as racist violence erupted in the South, abolitionists argued that black suffrage was more urgent than women's suffrage. The black vote "is with us a matter of life and death," Frederick Douglass argued. "I have always championed women's right to vote; but it will be seen that the present claim for the negro is one of the most urgent necessity."

Stanton was unmoved by such arguments. For her the Fifteenth Amendment barring racial qualifications for voting was the last straw. Supporters of women's suffrage opposed the Fifteenth Amendment on the ground that it subjected elite, educated women to the rule of base and illiterate males, especially immigrants and blacks. Abolitionists were shocked by such opinions. They favored universal suffrage, not the "educated" suffrage that Stanton was calling for. The breach between reformers weakened the coalition of radicals pushing to maintain a vigorous Reconstruction policy in the South.

Elizabeth Cady Stanton A leading advocate of women's rights, Stanton was angered when Congress gave African American men the vote without also giving it to women.

The Rise and Fall of the National Labor Union

Inspired by the radicalism of the Civil War and Reconstruction, industrial workers across the North organized dozens of craft unions, Eight-Hour Leagues, and workingmen's associations. The general goal of these associations was to protect northern workers who were overworked and underpaid. They called strikes, initiated consumer boycotts, and formed consumer cooperatives. In 1867 and 1868 workers in New York and Massachusetts launched campaigns to enact laws restricting the workday to eight hours. Shortly thereafter workers began electing their own candidates to state legislatures.

Founded in 1866, the National Labor Union (NLU) was the first significant postwar effort to organize all "working people" into a national union. William Sylvis, an iron molder, founded the NLU and became its president in 1868. He denied that there was any "harmony of interests" between workers and capitalists. On the contrary, every wage earner in America was at war with every capitalist, whose "profits" robbed working people of the fruits of their labor.

Under Sylvis's direction the NLU advocated a wide range of political reforms, not just bread-and-butter issues. Sylvis believed that through successful organization American workers could take the "first step toward competence and independence." He argued for a doubling of the average worker's wages. He supported voting rights for blacks and women. Nevertheless, after a miserable showing in the elections of 1872, the NLU fell apart. By then Reconstruction in the South was also ending.

The End of Reconstruction

National events had as much to do with the end of Reconstruction as did events in the South. A nationwide outbreak of political corruption in the late 1860s and 1870s provoked a sharp reaction. Influential northern Liberals, previously known for their support for Reconstruction, abandoned the Republican Party in disgust in 1872. The end of Reconstruction finally came after electoral violence corrupted the 1876 elections. Republican politicians in Washington, DC, responded with a sordid political bargain that came to symbolize the end of an era.

> Within the last seven years we have passed through the most gigantic war the world ever saw. A rebellion such as no other government could have successfully combated. . . . No man in America rejoiced more than I at the downfall of negro slavery. But when the shackles fell from the limbs of those four millions of blacks, it did not make them **free** men; it simply transferred them from one condition of slavery to another; it placed them upon the platform of the white workingmen, and made all slaves together. I do not mean that freeing the negro enslaved the white; I mean that we were slaves before, always have been, and that that abolition of the right of property in man added four millions of black slaves to the white slaves of the country. We are now all one family of slaves together; and the labor reform movement is a second emancipation proclamation.
>
> SPEECH BY WILLIAM SYLVIS,
> September 16, 1868

Corruption as a National Problem

Postwar Americans witnessed an extraordinary display of public dishonesty. Democrats were as prone to thievery as Republicans. Northern swindlers looted the public treasuries from Boston to San Francisco. In the South, both black and white legislators took bribes. Corruption, it seemed, was endemic to postwar American politics.

If corruption was everywhere in the late 1860s and 1870s, it was largely because there were more opportunities for it than ever before. The Civil War and Reconstruction had swollen government budgets. Never before was government so active in collecting taxes and disbursing vast sums for the public good. Under the circumstances, many government officials traded bribes for votes, embezzled public funds, or used insider knowledge to defraud taxpayers.

The federal government set the tone. In the most notorious case, the directors of the Union Pacific Railroad set up a dummy corporation called the Credit Mobilier, awarded it phony contracts, and protected it from inquiry by bribing influential congressmen. The Grant administration was eventually smeared with scandal as well. Although personally honest, the president surrounded himself with rich nobodies and army buddies rather than respected statesmen. Grant's own private secretary was exposed as a member of the "Whiskey Ring," a cabal of distillers and revenue agents who cheated the government out of millions of tax dollars every year.

State and city governments in the North were no less corrupt. Wealthy businessmen curried favor with politicians whose votes would determine where a railroad would be built, which land would be allocated for rights of way, and how many government bonds had to be floated to pay for such projects. State officials regularly accepted gifts, received salaries, and sat on the boards of corporations directly affected by their votes. Municipalities awarded lucrative contracts for the construction of schools, parks, libraries, water and sewer systems, and mass-transportation networks, creating temptations for corruption. The Tweed Ring alone bilked New York City out of tens of millions of dollars. By these standards the corruption of the southern Reconstruction legislatures was relatively small.

William Marcy Tweed The boss of New York's notoriously corrupt "Tweed Ring" was parodied by the great cartoonist Thomas Nast. His portrayal of the bloated public official became an enduring symbol of governmental corruption.

But corruption in the South was real enough, and it had particular significance for Reconstruction. Southern Republicans of modest means depended heavily on the money they earned as public officials. These same men found themselves responsible for the collection of unusually high taxes and for economic development projects. As elsewhere in industrializing America, the lure of corruption proved overwhelming. The Republican governor of Louisiana grew rich while in office by "exacting tribute" from railroads seeking state favors. Corruption on a vast scale implied petty corruption as well. Individual legislators sold their votes for as little as $200.

In many cases opponents of Reconstruction used attacks on corruption to mask their contempt for Republican policies. Their strategy helped galvanize opposition, destroying Republican hopes of attracting white voters. Finally, corruption in the South helped provoke a backlash against active government nationwide, weakening northern support for

Reconstruction. The intellectual substance of this backlash was provided by influential liberal Republicans, many of whom had once been ardent supporters of radical Reconstruction.

Liberal Republicans Revolt

The label "liberal Republicans" embraced a loosely knit group of intellectuals, politicians, publishers, and businessmen from the northern elite who were discouraged by the failure of radical Reconstruction to bring peace to the southern states and disgusted by the corruption of postwar politics. Although small in number, liberals exercised important influence in northern politics.

At the heart of liberal philosophy was a deep suspicion of democracy. Liberals argued that any government beholden to the interests of the ignorant masses was doomed to corruption. They believed that public servants should be chosen on the basis of intelligence, as measured by civil-service examinations, rather than by patronage appointments that sustained corrupt party machines. Indeed, to liberals, party politics was the enemy of good government.

Liberals therefore grew increasingly alienated from the Republican Party and from President Grant. Above all, they resented the fact that the Republican Party had changed as its idealistic commitment to free labor waned and its radical vanguard disappeared. To the rising generation of Republican leaders, getting and holding office had become an end in itself.

As Republicans lost their identity as moral crusaders, liberal reformers proposed a new vision of their own. In 1872 they supported Horace Greeley as the Democratic presidential candidate. The liberal plank in the Democratic platform proclaimed the party's commitment to universal equality before the law, the integrity of the Union, and support for the Thirteenth, Fourteenth, and Fifteenth Amendments. At the same time, liberals demanded "the immediate and absolute removal of all disabilities" imposed on the South, as well as a "universal amnesty" for ex-Confederates. Finally, the liberals declared their belief that "local self-government" would "guard the rights of all citizens more securely than any centralized power." In effect, the liberals were demanding the end of federal efforts to protect the former slaves.

In the long run, the liberal view would prevail, but in 1872 it did not go over well with the voters. The liberals' biggest liability was their presidential candidate. Horace Greeley's erratic reputation and Republican background were too much, and Democrats refused to vote for him. Grant was easily reelected, but he and his fellow Republicans saw the returns as evidence that Reconstruction was becoming a political liability.

The 1874 elections confirmed the lesson. Democrats made sweeping gains all across the North, and an ideological stalemate developed. For a generation, neither party would clearly dominate American politics. The Republicans would take no more risks in support of Reconstruction.

During his second term, therefore, Grant did little to protect black voters from violence in the South. Not even the Civil Rights Act of 1875 undid the impression of waning Republican zeal. Ostensibly designed to prohibit racial discrimination in public places, the Civil Rights Act lacked enforcement provisions. The bill's most important clause, prohibiting segregated schools, was eliminated from the final version. Southern states ignored even this watered-down statute, and in 1883 the Supreme Court declared it unconstitutional. Thus the last significant piece of

Reconstruction legislation was an ironic testament to the Republican Party's declining commitment to equal rights.

A Depression and a Deal "Redeem" the South

Angered by corruption and high taxes, white voters across the South succumbed to the Democratic Party's appeal for restoration of white supremacy. As the number of white Republicans fell, the number of black Republicans holding office in the South increased, even as the Grant administration backed away from civil rights. But the persistence of black officeholders only reinforced the Democrats' determination to "redeem" their states from Republican rule. Democrats had taken control of Virginia in 1869. North Carolina was redeemed in 1870, Georgia in 1871, and Texas in 1873. Then panic struck.

In September 1873 America's premier financial institution, Jay Cooke, went bankrupt after overextending itself on investments in the Northern Pacific Railroad. Within weeks hundreds of banks and thousands of businesses went bankrupt as well. The country sank into a depression that lasted five years. Unemployment rose to 14 percent as corporations slashed wages. To protect their incomes, railroad workers tried to organize a nationwide union and attempted to strike several times. Their employers, however, repeatedly thwarted such efforts, and the strikes failed.

As the nation turned its attention to labor unrest and economic depression, the Republican Party's commitment to Reconstruction all but disappeared. Democrats regained control of the governments of Alabama and Arkansas in 1874. In the few southern states where black Republicans clung to political power, white "redeemers" used violence to overthrow the last remnants of Reconstruction.

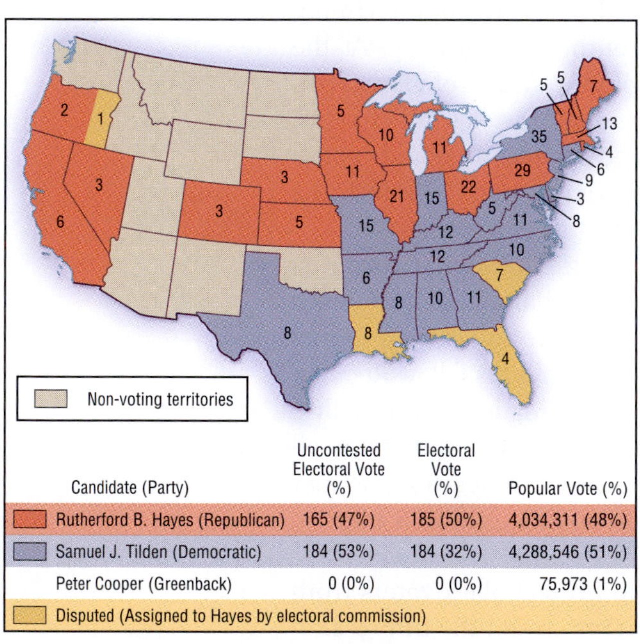

Candidate (Party)	Uncontested Electoral Vote (%)	Electoral Vote (%)	Popular Vote (%)
Rutherford B. Hayes (Republican)	165 (47%)	185 (50%)	4,034,311 (48%)
Samuel J. Tilden (Democratic)	184 (53%)	184 (32%)	4,288,546 (51%)
Peter Cooper (Greenback)	0 (0%)	0 (0%)	75,973 (1%)
Disputed (Assigned to Hayes by electoral commission)			

Map 16–4 The Presidential Election, 1876 In 1876 the Democratic presidential candidate, Samuel Tilden, won the popular vote but was denied the presidency because the Republicans who controlled Congress chose to interpret voting irregularities in Louisiana, South Carolina, Oregon, and Florida in a way that gave their candidate, Rutherford B. Hayes, all of the disputed electoral votes.

Mississippi established the model in 1875, so much so that it became known as "the Mississippi Plan." Confident that authorities in Washington, DC, would no longer interfere in the South, Democrats launched an all-out campaign to regain control of the state government. The Democratic campaign was double edged. Crude appeals to white supremacy further reduced the dwindling number of scalawags. To defeat black Republicans, White Leagues organized a campaign of violence and intimidation to keep blacks away from the polls. Republicans were beaten, forced to flee the state, and in several cases murdered. Washington turned a deaf ear to African American pleas for protection. In the end enough blacks were kept from the polls and enough scalawags voted their racial prejudices to put the Democrats in power. Mississippi was "redeemed."

The tactics used in Mississippi were repeated elsewhere the following year, with dramatic consequences for the presidential election of 1876. Amidst a serious economic depression, and with an electorate tired of Reconstruction, the Democrats stood a good chance of winning the presidency. In fact, the

Democratic candidate, Samuel J. Tilden, won 250,000 more votes than the Republican, Rutherford B. Hayes (see Map 16–4). But electoral fraud in South Carolina, Louisiana, Florida, and Oregon threw the results into doubt.

If all of the electoral votes from those states went to Hayes, he would win, but if even a single electoral vote went to Tilden, he would win, the first Democrat to win the presidency in 20 years. The outcome was determined by an electoral commission with a Republican majority, and the commission awarded every disputed electoral vote to the Republican candidate. When Hayes was inaugurated on March 4, 1877, the legitimacy of his presidency was already in doubt. But what he did shortly after taking office made it appear as though he had won thanks to a sordid "compromise" with the Democrats to end Reconstruction in the South. There is no solid evidence that such a deal was ever actually made. Nevertheless, Hayes ordered the federal troops guarding the Republican statehouses in South Carolina and Louisiana to leave. This order marked the formal end of military occupation of the South and the symbolic end of Reconstruction. By late 1877, every southern state had been redeemed by the Democrats.

The following year the Supreme Court began to issue rulings that further undermined the achievements of Reconstruction. In *Hall v. DeCuir* (1878) the Supreme Court invalidated a Louisiana law that prohibited racial segregation on public transportation. In 1882, the justices declared unconstitutional a federal law that protected southern African Americans against racially motivated murders and assaults. More important, in the Civil Rights Cases of 1883, the Supreme Court declared that the Fourteenth Amendment did not pertain to discriminatory practices by private persons. The Supreme Court thus put the finishing touches on the national retreat from Reconstruction.

Conclusion

Inspired by an idealized vision of a society based on equal rights and free labor, Republicans expected emancipation to bring about a dramatic transformation of the South. Freed from the shackles of the slave power, the entire region would soon become a shining example of democracy and prosperity. If the results were less than Republicans expected, the achievements of Reconstruction were nonetheless impressive. Across the South, African American men and women carved out a space in which their families could live more freely than before. Black men by the tens of thousands elected to office some of the most democratic state legislatures of the nineteenth century. Thousands more black workers repudiated an objectionable contract-labor system in favor of an innovative compromise known as sharecropping. Furthermore, Reconstruction added three important amendments to the Constitution that transformed civil rights and electoral laws throughout the nation.

Nevertheless, the Republicans washed their hands of Reconstruction with unseemly haste. The Republicans left southern blacks unprotected in a hostile world. Sharecropping offered them a degree of personal autonomy but little hope of real economic independence. Democratic redeemers excluded blacks from the substance of power. Tired of Reconstruction, Americans turned their attention to the new and difficult problems of urban and industrial America.

Further Readings

Dan T. Carter, *When the War Was Over: The Failure of Self-Reconstruction in the West* (1985). Particularly good on the crucial year of 1865.

W. E. B. DuBois, *Black Reconstruction in America, 1860–1880* (1935). A work of passion and scholarship, with a devastating critique of the way historians of his day discussed Reconstruction.

Carol Faulkner, *Women's Radical Reconstruction* (2004). One of a number of important recent studies of women and Reconstruction.

Eric Foner, *Reconstruction: America's Unfinished Revolution, 1863–1877* (1988). A modern classic, the best one-volume treatment of the period.

Susan Eva O'Donovan, *Becoming Free in the Cotton South* (2007). A finely grained case study, especially insightful on gender.

Roger Ransom and Richard Sutch, *One Kind of Freedom* (2001, revised edition). The authors provide a clear picture of the breakup of the plantation system and the emergence of sharecropping.

John C. Rodrigue, *Reconstruction in the Cane Fields* (2001). An important study of an important part of the story.

Mark W. Summers, *The Era of Good Stealings* (1993). A lively treatment of the corruption issue.

Who, What

John Dennett 539
Nathaniel Banks 542
Oliver Otis Howard 545
Andrew Johnson 545
U. S. Grant 560
Elizabeth Cady Stanton 562
William Sylvis 563
Horace Greeley 565
Ten Percent Plan 543
Freedmen's Bureau 545
Black Codes 547
Fourteenth Amendment 549
Sharecropping 554
Tenure of Office Act 558
Fifteenth Amendment 561
National Labor Union 562
"Liberal" Republicans 565
Redemption 566

>> Timeline >>

▼ 1863
Lincoln's Proclamation of Amnesty and Reconstruction

▼ 1864
Wade-Davis Bill

▼ 1865
General Sherman's Special Field Order No. 15
Freedmen's Bureau established
Lincoln's second inaugural
Lincoln assassinated; Andrew Johnson becomes president
General Howard's Circular 13
President Johnson orders the Freedmen's Bureau to return confiscated lands to former owners
Joint Committee on Reconstruction established by Congress

▼ 1866
Congress renews Freedmen's Bureau; Johnson vetoes renewal bill
Civil Rights Act vetoed by Johnson
Congress overrides presidential veto of Civil Rights Act
Congress passes Fourteenth Amendment
Congress passes another Freedmen's Bureau Bill over Johnson's veto
Republicans sweep midterm elections

Review Questions

1. What were the three major phases of Reconstruction?
2. What made congressional Reconstruction "radical?"
3. How did Reconstruction change the South?
4. How did Reconstruction change the North?
5. What were the major factors that brought Reconstruction to an end?

Websites

Freedmen's Bureau Online. http://www.freedmensbureau.com/
Reconstruction: The Second Civil War. http://www.pbs.org/wgbh/amex/reconstruction/

For further review materials and resource information, please visit www.oup.com/us/ofthepeople

▼ 1867
First and Second Reconstruction Acts
Tenure of Office Act

▼ 1868
Johnson fires Secretary of War Stanton
House of Representatives impeaches Johnson
Senate trial of Johnson begins
Acquittal of Johnson

Fourteenth Amendment ratified
Ulysses S. Grant wins presidential election

▼ 1869
Congress passes Fifteenth Amendment

▼ 1870
Fifteenth Amendment ratified

▼ 1872
"Liberal Republicans" leave their party
Grant reelected

▼ 1873
Financial "panic" sets off depression

▼ 1875
"Mississippi Plan" succeeds
Civil Rights Act of 1875 enacted

▼ 1876
Disputed presidential election

▼ 1877
Electoral commission awards presidency to Rutherford B. Hayes

CHAPTER 17

Common Threads 

>> In what ways were the problems of Reconstruction and the problems of industrialization similar?

>> What made "big business" different from earlier enterprises?

>> Does the new social order of the late nineteenth century look more like what came before it, or more like what came later on?

The Triumph of Industrial Capitalism 1850–1890

AMERICAN PORTRAIT

>> Rosa Cassettari

In 1884 Rosa Cassettari left the Italian village of Cuggiono, near Milan, to meet her husband Santino, a miner in Union, Missouri. Theirs had been an arranged marriage, and Rosa was reluctant to go, especially because she had to leave behind her infant son. "It is wonderful to go to America even if you don't want to go to Santino," Rosa's friends told her at the train station in Milan. "You will get smart in America. And in America you will not be so poor." Along with millions of others, Rosa entered a stream of migrants coming from the far corners of Europe. At Le Havre, France, she embarked on a ship for America. "All us poor people had to go down through a hole to the bottom of the ship," she remembered. But she was going to "America! The country where everyone would find work! Where wages were so high that no one had to go hungry! Where all men were free and equal and where even the poor could own land!"

Rosa's first taste of America did not live up to such dreams. In New York she was cheated and forced to make the long trip to Missouri with nothing to eat. When she arrived at the town of Union she found a shabby collection of tents and shacks. Life in the mining camp lived up to her fears rather than her hopes. With no doctors or midwives available, Rosa gave birth to a premature child alone on the floor of her cabin. Santino was an abusive husband and a cruel father. Rosa had to supplement his earnings by cooking for 12 additional miners.

Yet Rosa was impressed by many things about America. Poor people did not behave humbly in the presence of the rich, for example, and even in the difficult circumstances of the mining camp Rosa became accustomed to wearing decent clothing and eating meat every day, things she could never do back in Europe.

When Rosa discovered that her husband planned to spend all their savings to open a house of prostitution, she separated from Santino. With the help of her immigrant friends from Missouri, Rosa moved to Chicago with her two children. She took a job at a place called Hull House where the social workers were so impressed by her life story that they wrote it down and published it as *Rosa Cassettari's Autobiography*.

Rosa was one of millions of men and women who were moving around the world in the late nineteenth century. They moved from the countryside to the city or from town to town. They moved from less developed regions to places where industrialization was well under way. The nerve center for all of the movement was a powerful core of industrial capitalist societies, and at the center of the core was the United States. Migrants were on a worldwide trek, but more of them came to the United States than any other nation.

Perpetual human migration, global in its extent, had become a hallmark of the political economy of industrial capitalism. Common laborers moved from place to place because jobs were unsteady. Railroads hired construction workers who moved as the track was laid and had to find other work when the line was finished. African American sharecroppers in the South moved at year's end. Over time they moved into cotton-growing districts, into towns and cities, or out of the South. White tenant farmers moved into mill towns. Native Americans were pushed off their lands throughout the trans-Mississippi West, making room for a flood of white settlers. And all across America the children of farmers abandoned the rural life: they went to mill villages and to huge cities like New York, Chicago, and Philadelphia.

They went looking for work, and for most migrants that meant working in a bureaucracy under professional managers who controlled the work process. It meant working with new and complicated machines. It meant working with polluted air, dirty rivers, or spoiled land. Most of all, industrial capitalism meant wage labor. Working people had been freed from the

continued

>> AMERICAN PORTRAIT *continued*

things that tied them to the land in other places and earlier times, such as feudal dues, slavery, and even independent farming. But wage labor released men and women to move about from community to community, from country to country, and finally from continent to continent. To watch Rosa Cassettari as she traveled from Cuggiono to Missouri and Chicago is to witness one small part of a global process set in motion by the triumph of wage labor.

OUTLINE

The Political Economy of Global Capitalism

The economic history of the late nineteenth century was sandwiched between two great financial panics in 1873 and 1893. Both were followed by prolonged periods of high unemployment and led directly to tremendous labor unrest. The years between the two panics were marked by a general decline in prices that placed a terrible burden on producers. Farmers found that their crops were worth less at harvest time than they had been during planting season. Manufacturers increased production to maintain profits, but the more they produced, the lower prices for their products fell. In search of an inexpensive workforce that could produce more for less, industrialists turned to an international labor market. Amidst financial panics and nationwide strikes, depressions and deflation, Americans experienced a dramatic economic transformation. When it was over, the United States had become the leading capitalist nation on earth.

The "Great Depression" of the Late Nineteenth Century

On July 16, 1877, workers for the Baltimore and Ohio Railroad struck at Martinsburg, West Virginia. Within days the strike spread to the Pennsylvania Railroad, the New York Central, the Great Western, and the Texas Pacific. Governors issued orders for the strikers to disperse and asked for federal assistance. Federal troops were sent to major cities, but confrontations between workers and armed forces only fanned the flames of insurrection. "Other workingmen followed the example of the railroad employees," explained Henry Demarest Lloyd, a prominent social critic. "At Zanesville, Ohio, fifty manufactories stopped work. Baltimore ceased to export petroleum. The rolling mills, foundries, and refineries of Cleveland were closed. . . . Merchants could not sell, manufacturers could not work, banks could not lend. The country went to the verge of a panic." A strike in one key industry now threatened the entire nation.

The railroad strike of 1877 was fueled by an economic depression that began with the Panic of 1873 (see Chapter 16, "Reconstructing A Nation") and spread throughout the developed world. The number of immigrants who had arrived in New York—200,000 every year between 1865 and 1873—fell to less than 65,000 in 1877. Although employment recovered in the 1880s, prices and wages continued to fall. Then in 1893 another panic struck. Once again several major railroads went bankrupt and more than 500 banks and 15,000 businesses shut down. From 1873 to 1896 a "great depression" blighted much of the globe.

The world was shrinking, and most Americans knew it. In 1866 a telegraph cable was laid across the Atlantic Ocean. From that moment, Americans could read about events in Europe in the next morning's newspaper. Railroads slashed the distances that separated eastern from western Europe and the East Coast from the West Coast of the United States. Steamships brought distant ports into regular contact. Midwestern farmers sold their wheat in Russia. Chinese workers laid the tracks of the Union Pacific Railroad. Eastern Europeans worked the steel mills of Pittsburgh. The political economy of capitalism was tying the world's nations together.

The clearest sign of this linkage was the emergence of an international labor market. As economic change swept through the less developed parts of the world, men and women were freed from their traditional ties to the land

---

Chicago, Sunday Oct. 15, 1871

My dear Brother,

I snatch the first moment I have had since one week ago to-night. Our beautiful city is in ruins. The greatest calamity that ever befell a city is upon us. . . .

The fire broke out about eleven o'clock on Sunday night. The wind was blowing heavily from the south-west. The portion of the city where it broke out was thickly settled by the laboring people, on narrow streets and alleys—buildings all of wood—one and two stories high with barns and sheds in alleys. The wind soon increased to almost a gale and it soon became apparent to me that all efforts to stay it were fruitless. . . .

The flames were rushing most frantically, leaping from block to block—whole squares vanishing as though they were gossamer. Men, women and children rushing frantically in all directions to save their lives—some away—but others into traps and places where they were soon surrounded and no retreat left. Hundreds rushed upon the shore of the lake where they had to hug the beach and waters until the flames subsided, giving them a chance to escape. The most heart rending scenes that could be imagined were transpiring in all directions and the tales that are told are most appalling. . . .

Chicago is burned down but not despairing—she has the energy and push and will rise phoenix like from the ashes. . . .

Your affectionate brother,
William.

WILLIAM H. CARTER,
president, Chicago Board of Public Works

AMERICA AND THE WORLD

>> The Global Migration of Labor

Nineteenth-century migrants tended to leave areas already in the grip of social and economic change. Rosa Cassettari, for example, had worked in a silk-weaving factory in Italy. At first, the largest numbers emigrated from the most developed nations, such as Great Britain and Germany. Later in the century, as industrial or agricultural revolution spread, growing numbers of immigrants came from Scandinavia, Russia, Italy, and Hungary (see Map 17–1). As capitalism developed in these areas, small farmers were forced to produce for a highly competitive international market. The resulting upheaval sent millions of rural folk into the worldwide migratory stream.

Improvements in transportation and communication were a sign that capitalism was spreading; they also made migration easier. In 1856, more than 95 percent of immigrants came to America aboard sailing vessels. By the end of the century, more than 95 percent came in steamships. The Atlantic crossing took one to three months on a sailing ship, but only 10 days on a steamship. Beginning in the 1880s, fierce competition among steamship lines dramatically lowered the cost of a transatlantic ticket, making two-way movement easier. Many immigrants went back and forth across the Atlantic, particularly workers in seasonal trades like construction.

But the great migrations of the late nineteenth century were also related to political upheaval. In China, for example, the Taiping Rebellion of 1848 was accompanied by an economic disaster rivaling the Irish potato famine of the same decade. This combination of economic and political disruption sent some 300,000 Chinese to the Pacific Coast of North America between 1850 and 1882. They labored in mines and panned for gold, and large numbers of Chinese workers helped build the transcontinental railroad. Desperate for employment and willing to work for low wages, the Chinese soon confronted racist hostility from American and European workers. Union organizers in San Francisco argued that the Chinese threatened the "labor interests" of white workers. In 1882 Congress responded by passing the Chinese Exclusion Act, banning further immigration from China.

A similar combination of economic and political forces lay beneath European immigration. The revival of employment in the 1880s brought with it a revival of movement. After 1890, immigration from northern and western Europe fell off sharply, as capitalist development made labor scarce in those areas. But by then agrarian crisis and political disruption had set off a wave of emigration from eastern and southern Europe. In Austria-Hungary, for example, the revolution of 1848 brought with it economic and political changes that resulted, by the 1880s, in a profound agrarian crisis. In southern Italy, citrus fruits from Florida and California arrived on the market, and protective tariffs thwarted the sale of Italian wines abroad. Desperate farmers from southern Italy started coming to the United States.

Jewish immigration was propelled by a different combination of politics and economics. The assassination of Czar Alexander II in 1881 was followed by a surge of Russian nationalism. Anti-Jewish riots (called pogroms) erupted in 1881–1882, 1891, and 1905–1906, during which countless Jews were massacred. Anti-Semitic laws forced Russian Jews to live within the so-called Pale of Settlement along Russia's western and southern borders, and the May Laws of 1882 severely restricted Russian Jews' religious and economic life. In the 1880s, Russian Jews began moving to America in significant numbers.

Most immigrants came to America looking for work. Some came with education and skills; some were illiterate. Most came with little more than their ability to work, and they usually found their jobs through families, friends, and fellow immigrants. Letters from America told of high wages and steady employment. Communities of immigrant workers provided the information and the connections that newcomers needed. Large Scandinavian communities settled the upper Midwest; the Chinese were concentrated on the West Coast. Some immigrants settled directly on farms, but the overwhelming number lived in cities.

and hurled into a global stream of wage laborers. Irish women went to work as domestic servants. African Americans took jobs as railroad porters. Wage laborers built and maintained the transportation network, the steel mills, and the petroleum refineries; slaughtered beef in Chicago; sewed ready-made clothing in factories; and staffed department store sales counters.

America Moves to the City

Between 1850 and 1900 the map of the United States was redrawn thanks to the appearance of dozens of new cities (see Figure 17–1). Of the 150 largest cities in the United

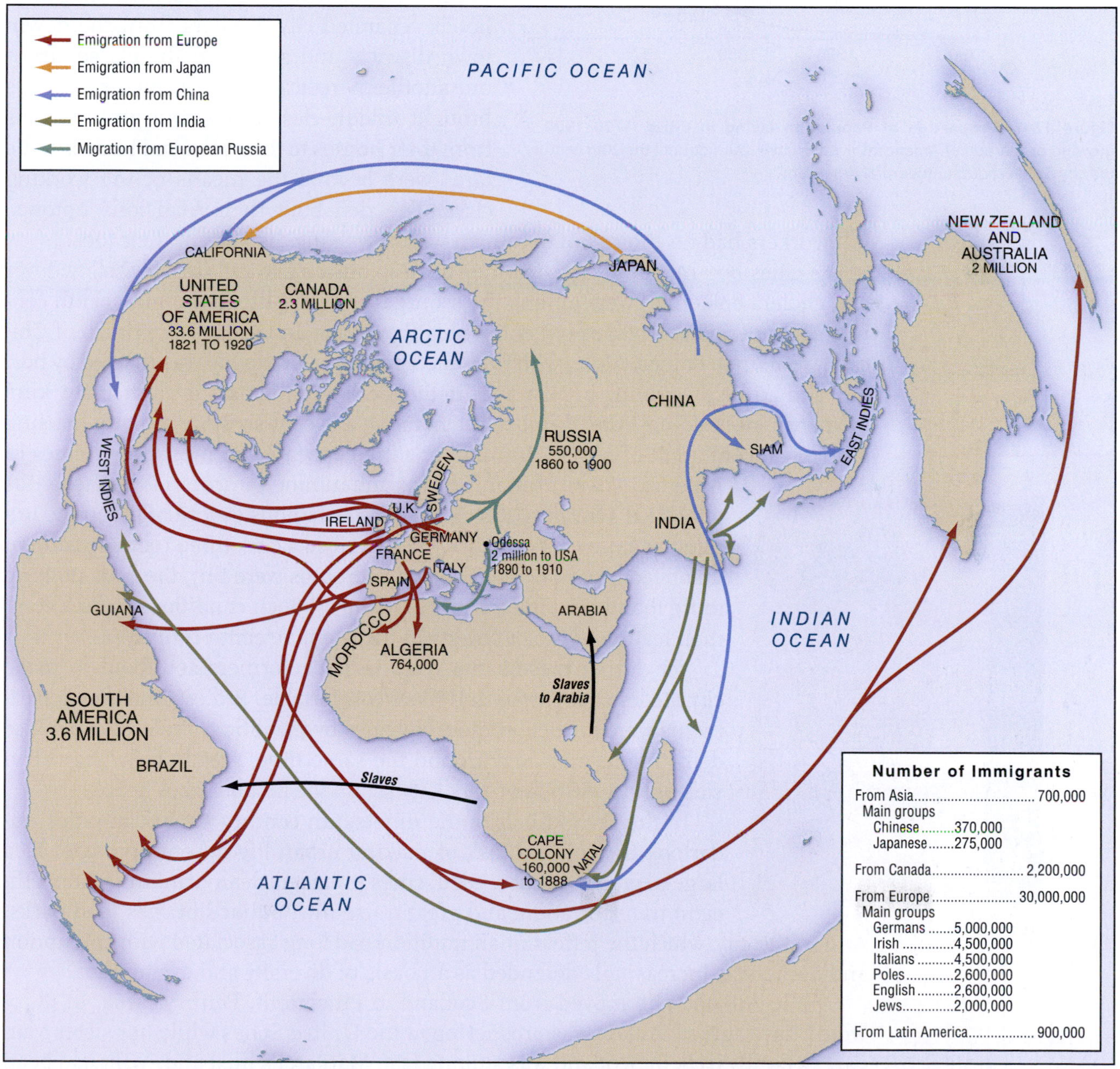

Number of Immigrants

From Asia	700,000
Main groups	
Chinese	370,000
Japanese	275,000
From Canada	2,200,000
From Europe	30,000,000
Main groups	
Germans	5,000,000
Irish	4,500,000
Italians	4,500,000
Poles	2,600,000
English	2,600,000
Jews	2,000,000
From Latin America	900,000

Map 17–1 Patterns of Global Migration, 1840–1900 Emigration was a global process by the late 19th century. But more immigrants went to the United States than to all other nations combined. *London Times Atlas*

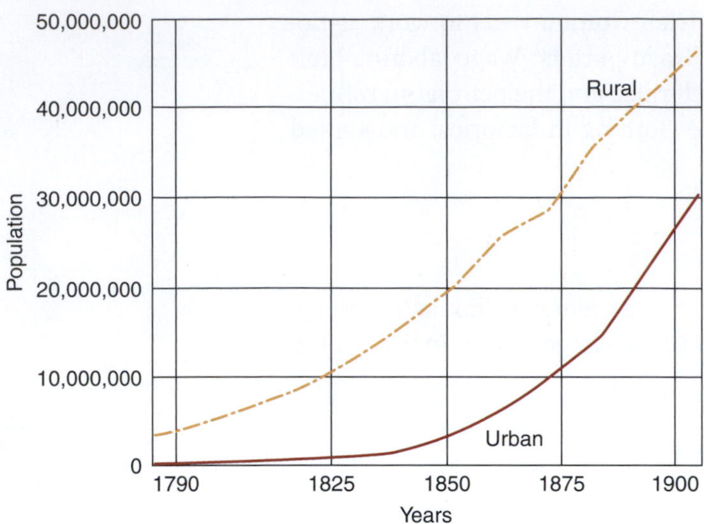

Figure 17–1 Proportion of Population Living in Cities, 1790–1900 A growing proportion of Americans lived in cities, but not until the 20th century did city dwellers outnumber rural Americans.

States in the late twentieth century, 85 were founded in the second half of the nineteenth century. In 1850 the largest city in the United States was New York, with a population of just over half a million. By 1900 New York, Philadelphia, and Chicago each had more than a million residents.

The industrial city was different from its predecessors. By the middle of the nineteenth century the modern "downtown" was born, a place where people shopped and worked but did not necessarily live. Residential neighborhoods separated city dwellers from the downtown districts and separated the classes from one another. Streetcars and commuter railroads brought middle-class clerks and professionals from their homes to their jobs and back, but the fares were beyond the means of the working class. The rich built their mansions uptown, but workers had no choice but to remain within walking distance of their jobs.

As cities became more crowded they became unsanitary and unsafe. Yellow fever and cholera epidemics were among the scourges of urban life in the nineteenth century. Fires periodically wiped out entire neighborhoods. In October 1871 much of Chicago went up in flames. Along with fires and epidemics, urban life was marred by poverty and crime. Beginning in New York in the 1880s, immigrants lived in a new kind of apartment building—the "dumbbell" tenement, a five- or six-story walk-up housing a huge concentration of people. Immigrant slums appeared in most major cities of America, as well as in mill towns and mining camps. In 1890 Jacob Riis published *How the Other Half Lives,* his famous exposé of life in the immigrant slums of New York. He described a dark three-room apartment inhabited by six people. The two bedrooms were tiny, the beds nothing more than boxes filled with "foul straw." Such conditions were a common feature of urban poverty in the late nineteenth century.

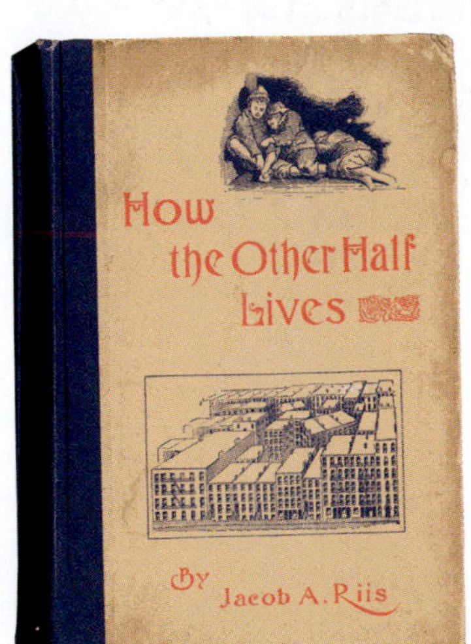

Yet during these same years urban reformers set about to make city life less dangerous and more comfortable. Professional fire departments were formed in most big cities by the 1860s. Professional police departments appeared around the same time, greatly reducing urban violence. In 1866 New York City set up the first board of health.

In the second half of the nineteenth century American cities undertook the colossal task of making urban life decent and safe. To a large degree they succeeded: cities provided clean drinking water, efficient transportation, and great museums, public libraries, and parks. And so the city, which the Jeffersonian tradition had long associated with corruption and decay, was increasingly defended as an oasis of diversity and excitement.

Annie Aitken, who moved from Scotland to Pittsburgh, Pennsylvania, in 1840, would have agreed. Aitken was prospering in the United States while her sister Margaret's family back in Scotland was sinking fast. Margaret's husband, Will, had been a traditional handloom weaver whose livelihood was destroyed by the rise of textile mills. With Aitken's encouragement, in 1848 Will and Margaret Carnegie and their two sons, Tom and Andrew, left Scotland and moved to Pittsburgh. Annie Aitken let her sister's family live rent free in a small house she owned. Her nephew, Andrew, took a job in a textile mill for $1.20 a week. Fifty years later, Andrew Carnegie sold his steel mills to J. Pierpont Morgan for $480 million.

The Lower East Side of Manhattan This busy street scene is from an area swollen with largely Jewish immigrants.

The Rise of Big Business

Before the Civil War the only enterprises in the United States that could be called "big businesses" were the railroads. Indeed, railroads became the model for a new kind of business—big business—that emerged during the 1880s. Big businesses had massive bureaucracies that were managed by professionals rather than owners and were financed through a national banking system centered on Wall Street. They marketed their goods and services across the nation and around the world and generated wealth in staggering concentrations, giving rise to a class of men whose names—Carnegie, Rockefeller, Morgan, and Vanderbilt—became synonymous with American capitalism.

The Rise of Andrew Carnegie

Andrew Carnegie was an immigrant, whereas most businessmen were native born. His childhood in Scotland was marked by poverty, whereas most of America's leading men of business were raised in relative prosperity. Certainly few working families in the late nineteenth century could hope to match Carnegie's spectacular climb from rags to riches. Nevertheless, Andrew Carnegie was the perfect reflection of the rise of big business. In the course of his career, Carnegie mastered the telegraph, railroad, petroleum, iron, and steel industries and introduced modern management techniques and strict accounting procedures to American manufacturing. Other great industrialists and financiers made their mark in the last half of the nineteenth century—Henry Clay Frick, Collis P. Huntington, George M. Pullman, John D. Rockefeller, and Cornelius Vanderbilt—but none of their lives took on the mythic proportions of the Scottish lad who came to America at the age of 12 and ended up the richest man in the world.

"I have made millions since," Carnegie once wrote, "but none of these gave me so much happiness as my first week's earnings." Young Andrew might have been happy to earn a wage, but he was not content with his job in a mill. He enrolled in a night course to study accounting, and a year later got a job as a messenger boy in a telegraph

> **Liberty produces wealth, and wealth destroys liberty. . . . Our bignesses—cities, factories, monopolies, fortunes, which are our empires, are the obesities of an age gluttonous beyond its powers of digestion. . . . The vision of the railroad stockholder is not far-sighted enough to see into the office of the General Manager; the people cannot reach across even a ward of a city to rule their rulers; Captains of Industry "do not know" whether the men in the ranks are dying from lack of food and shelter; we cannot clean our cities nor our politics; the locomotive has more man-power than all the ballot-boxes. . . . This era is but a passing phase in the evolution of industrial Caesars, and these Caesars will be of a new type—corporate Caesars.**
>
> HENRY DEMAREST LLOYD,
> *Wealth Against Commonwealth*, 1894

office. So astute and hardworking was Andrew that by 1851 he was promoted to telegraph operator. In his dealings with the other operators, Carnegie soon displayed the leadership ability that served him throughout his career. He recruited talented, hardworking men and organized them with stunning efficiency.

The most successful businessmen in Pittsburgh, such as Tom Scott, a superintendent for the Pennsylvania Railroad, noticed Carnegie's talents. In 1853, Scott offered Carnegie a job as his secretary and personal telegrapher. Carnegie stayed with the Pennsylvania Railroad for 12 years during a time when railroad construction soared. Railroads stood at the center of the booming industrial economy. They would become the steel industry's biggest customer. Petroleum refiners shipped their kerosene by rail. Mining corporations needed railroads to ship their coal and iron. Ranchers shipped their cattle by rail to the slaughterhouses of Chicago, and meat packers distributed butchered carcasses in refrigerated railroad cars. Thus his position at the Pennsylvania Railroad gave Carnegie an unrivaled familiarity with the workings of big business.

By the mid-1850s, the largest factory in the country, the Pepperell Mills in Biddeford, Maine, employed 800 workers, while the Pennsylvania Railroad had more than 4,000 employees. If the men who maintained the track fell down on the job, if an engineer arrived late, or if a fireman came to work drunk, trains were wrecked, lives were lost, and business failed. The railroads thus borrowed the disciplinary methods and bureaucratic structure of the military to ensure that the trains ran safely and on time.

The man who introduced this organizational discipline to the Pennsylvania Railroad was Tom Scott, the man who hired Andrew Carnegie. J. Edgar Thomson, the Pennsylvania's president, was a pioneer of a different sort. He established an elaborate bookkeeping system that provided detailed knowledge of every aspect of the Pennsylvania's operations. Scott used the statistics Thomson collected to reward managers who improved the company's profits and eliminate those who failed.

Carnegie succeeded. After Scott was promoted to vice president in 1859, Carnegie took Scott's place as superintendent of the western division, where he helped make the Pennsylvania Railroad into a model of industrial efficiency. By 1865 the Pennsylvania had 30,000 employees and had expanded its line east into New York City and west to Chicago. It was the largest private company in the world.

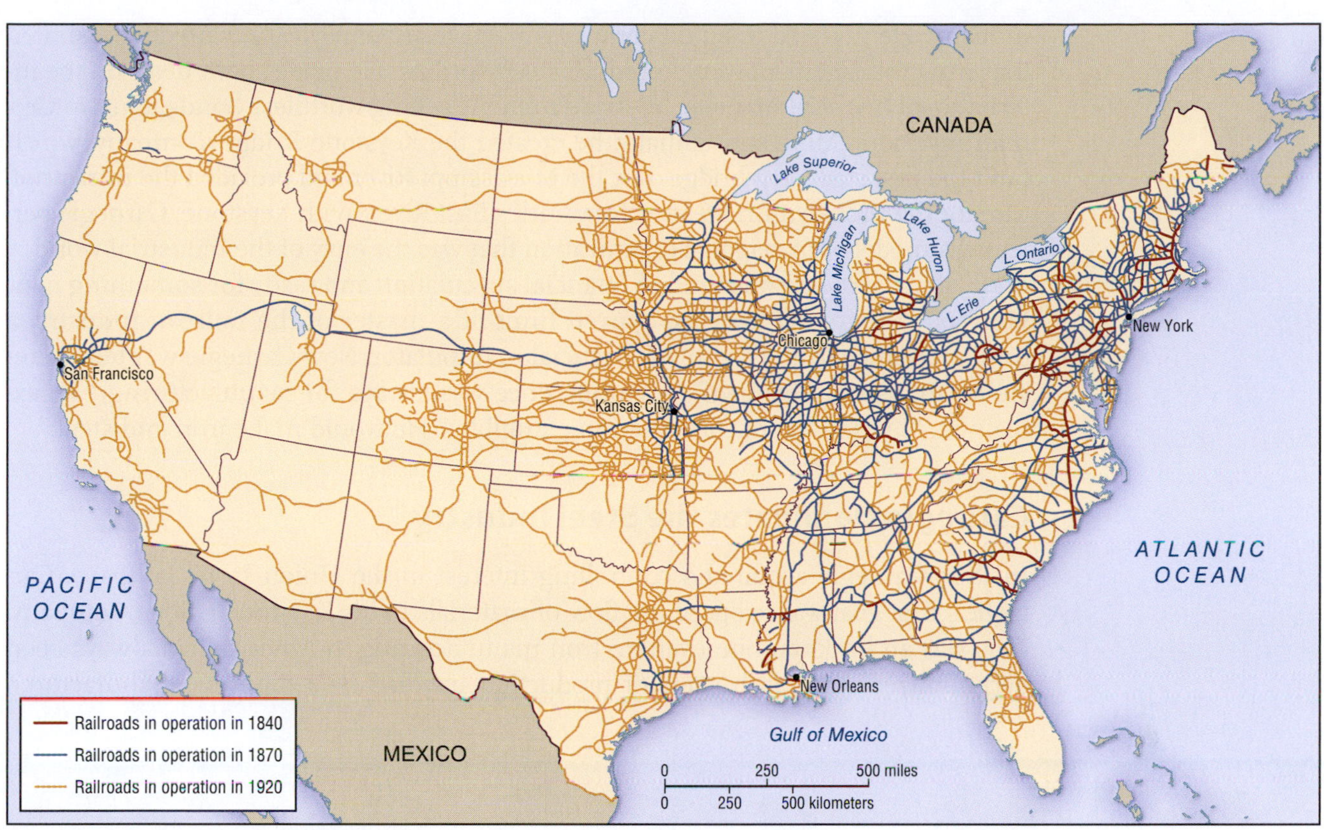

Map 17-2 The Growth of Railroads, 1850–1890 Railroads were more than a means of transportation; they were also America's first "big business." Railroad management established the model for running huge industrial corporations, and the growth of railroads sustained the initial growth of the iron and steel industries.

Carnegie's experience at the Pennsylvania Railroad gave him a keen understanding of the modern financial system. Railroads dwarfed all previous business enterprises in the amount of investment capital they required and in the complexity of their financial arrangements. Railroads were the first corporations to issue stocks through sophisticated trading mechanisms that attracted investors from around the world. To organize the market in such vast numbers of securities, the modern investment house was developed. J. Pierpont Morgan grew rich selling railroad stocks. The House of Morgan prospered greatly from its association with Andrew Carnegie, for there was no shrewder investor in all of America.

Carnegie Becomes a Financier

Carnegie began making money from money in 1856. On Tom Scott's advice Carnegie borrowed $600 and invested it in Adams Express Company stock, which soon began paying handsome dividends. Carnegie had become a successful capitalist, and for the next 15 years he made a series of financial moves that earned him several more fortunes.

Carnegie invested in the Woodruff Sleeping Car Company in the late 1850s and, a decade later, used his shares and influence to help George Pullman win near-monopoly control of the industry—and make millions in the bargain. Carnegie brokered a similar deal that created the Western Union monopoly of the telegraph industry. He invested in an oil company in western Pennsylvania and demonstrated that strict management would produce steady profits. He made shady deals on the international financial markets; he made millions selling worthless bonds to naive German investors. More substantially, he created the Keystone Bridge Company, which built the first steel arch bridge over the Mississippi River and provided the infrastructure for the Brooklyn Bridge over New York's East River. With Keystone, Carnegie perfected a model of managerial organization that was the envy of the industrial world.

By 1872 Carnegie was tired of financial speculation and ready for something new. He was 37 years old and had proven himself a master of the railroad industry, a brilliant manager, and a shrewd financial manipulator. Now Carnegie wanted to create an industry of his own. "My preference was always for manufacturing," he explained. "I wished to make something tangible." He would make iron and steel.

Carnegie Dominates the Steel Industry

In 1865 Carnegie acquired a controlling interest in the Union Iron Company. Carnegie's first goal was to speed the flow of materials to his Keystone Bridge Company. This was an important innovation. Iron manufacturing in America had always been decentralized, with each stage of production handled by a different manufacturer.

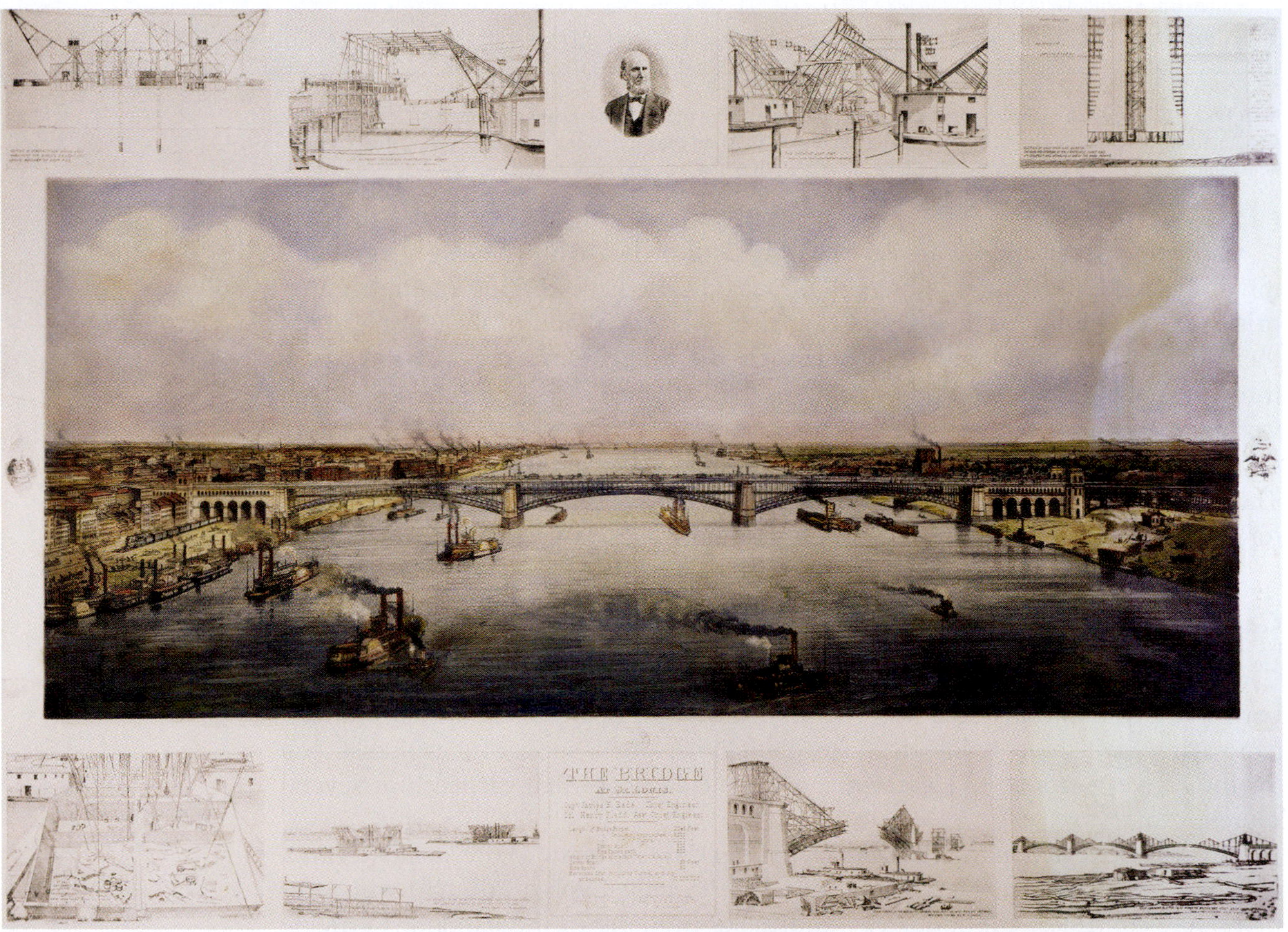

The Eads Bridge The steel arches of the Eads Bridge across the Mississippi River at St. Louis were both an engineering marvel and a triumph of Andrew Carnegie's managerial skills.

But Carnegie forced Union Iron and Keystone Bridge to coordinate their operations, thereby eliminating middlemen and making production more efficient. Carnegie also forced Union Iron to adopt the managerial techniques and accounting practices he had learned at the Pennsylvania Railroad. By keeping a strict account of all costs, Carnegie could locate the most wasteful points in the production process and reward the most efficient workers. Because he knew exactly what his costs were, Carnegie figured out that his iron mill would be more profitable if he invested in expensive new equipment. He ran his furnaces at full blast, wearing them out after only a few years and replacing them with still more modern machines. Carnegie's great achievement was his introduction of modern management techniques to American industry, but it was in steel rather than iron that Carnegie would prove the worth of those techniques.

As with so many industries, the development of steel was driven by the development of railroads. Traditional iron rails deteriorated rapidly, and as trains grew larger and heavier, iron withered under the load. J. Edgar Thomson, head of the Pennsylvania Railroad, began experimenting with steel rails in 1862. Steel was also a better material for locomotives, boilers, and railroad cars themselves. In the 1860s two developments cleared the path for the transition from iron to steel. First, Henry Bessemer's patented process for turning iron into steel became available to American manufacturers. Second, iron ore began flowing freely onto the American market from deposits in northern Michigan.

Andrew Carnegie was uniquely situated to take advantage of these developments. His experience with Union Iron taught him how to run a mill efficiently, and he

Chinese Laborers Building Railroad This 1877 picture of a Southern Pacific Railroad trestle shows the construction methods used in building the first railroad across the Sierra Nevada.

had access to investment capital. In 1872 Carnegie built a steel mill, the Thomson Works. Despite a worldwide depression, the steel mill was profitable from the start.

Big Business Consolidates

In the late nineteenth century the names of a handful of wealthy capitalists became closely associated with different industries: Gustavus Swift in meat packing, John D. Rockefeller in oil refining, Collis P. Huntington in railroads, J. P. Morgan in financing, and Andrew Carnegie in steel (see Map 17–3). These powerful individuals, sometimes called "robber barons," represented a passing phase in the history of American enterprise. Most big businesses were so big that no single individual or family could own them. They were run by professionally trained managers, and the highest profits went to companies with the most efficient bureaucracies. Because the businesses were so big and their equipment was so expensive, they had to be kept in operation continuously. An average factory could respond to an economic slowdown by closing its doors for a while, but big businesses could not afford to do that.

Beginning in the 1880s big businesses developed strategies designed to shield them from the effects of ruinous competition. The most common strategy was vertical integration, the attempt to control as many aspects of a business as possible, from the production of raw materials to the sale of the finished product. Carnegie integrated the steel industry from the point of production forward to the distribution of steel but also backward to the extraction of iron ore. He bought iron mines to produce his own ore, and railroads to ship the ore to his mills and the finished product to market. His Keystone Bridge Company then purchased the steel.

In 1882 John D. Rockefeller devised a new solution to the problem of ruinous competition by forming the Standard Oil Trust. Rockefeller had founded Standard Oil in 1867 in Cleveland, Ohio. Like Carnegie, Rockefeller surrounded himself with the best managers and financiers to build and run the most efficient modern refineries, but he was more willing than Carnegie to use ruthless tactics to wipe out his competitors. Rockefeller extracted preferential shipping rates from the railroads, giving him a critical advantage in the savagely competitive oil business. In 1872 Rockefeller began imposing on the national oil refining industry the same control that he had already achieved in Ohio. As president of the National Refiners' Association he formed cartels with the major operators in other states. But the cartels were too weak to eliminate independent refiners.

Rockefeller therefore set out to control the entire oil industry by merging all of the major companies together under Standard Oil. By 1879 the Standard Oil monopoly was largely in place, but not until 1882 was it formalized as a "trust," an elaborate legal device by which different producers came together under the umbrella of a single company that could police competition internally. In 1889 the New Jersey legislature passed a law that allowed corporations based in that state to form "holding companies" that controlled companies in other states. Thus the trust gave way to the holding company, with Standard Oil of New Jersey as its most prominent example. Within a decade many of the largest industries in America were dominated by massive holding companies.

Rockefeller's Standard Oil monopoly was a notorious example of how big business had changed the American economy. Rockefeller himself came to represent a powerful new class of extraordinarily wealthy businessmen. Their names—Carnegie, Rockefeller, Morgan, Harriman, and others—soon became associated with the upper class of the new social order of industrial America.

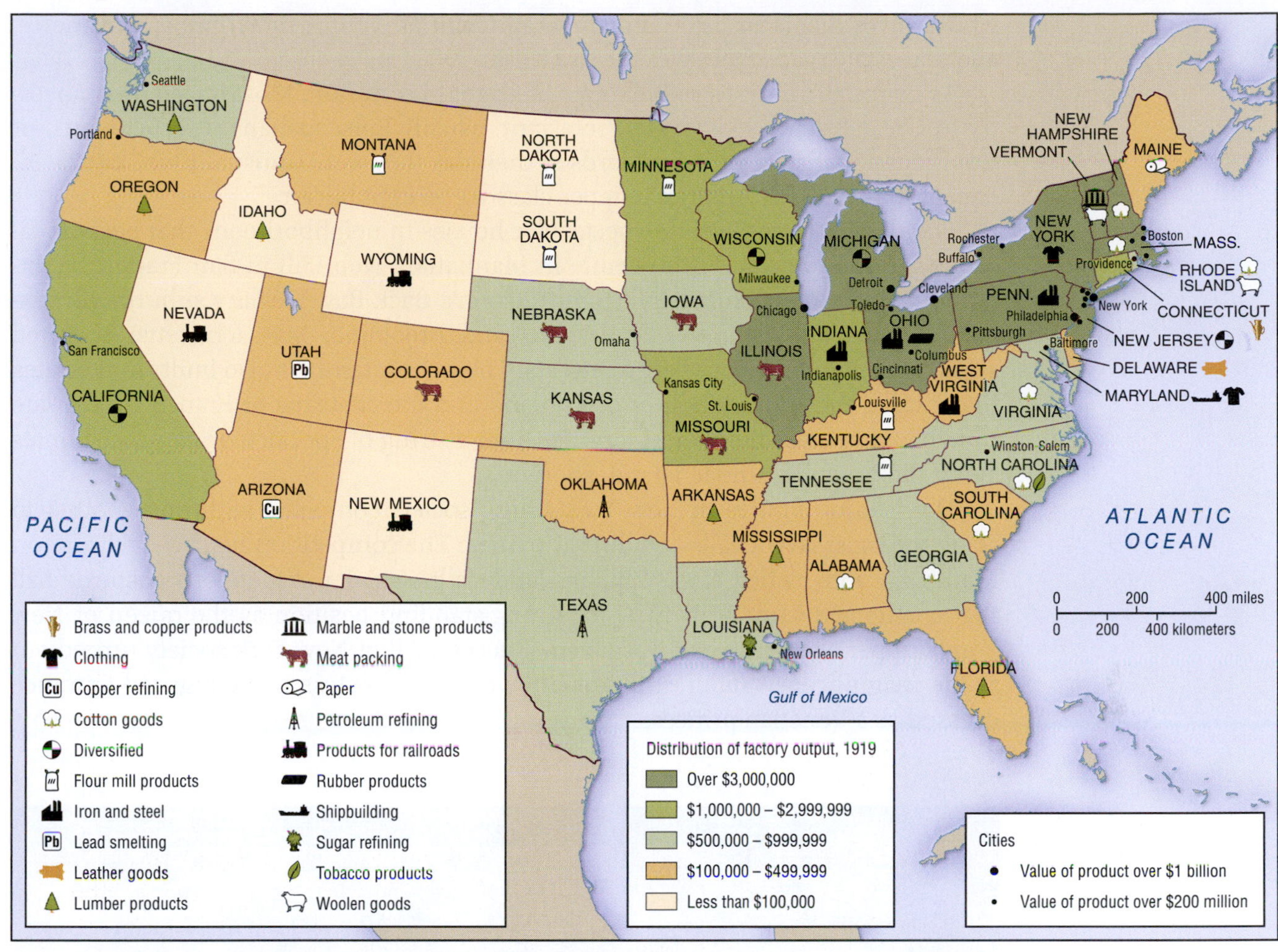

Map 17–3 Major American Industries, ca. 1890 An industrial map of late 19th-century America shows regions increasingly defined not by their crops but by their major industries.

A New Social Order

Classes were not supposed to exist in the United States the way they existed in Europe, as many Americans continued to believe in the late nineteenth century. Yet the reality of class divisions was so obvious that it had become part of public discussion. It was hard not to notice the conspicuous gap between the astonishing wealth of Andrew Carnegie and the daily struggles of Rosa Cassettari.

> The most valuable class in any community is the middle class, the men of moderate means, living at the rate of a thousand dollars a year or thereabouts.
>
> WALT WHITMAN, 1858

Lifestyles of the Very Rich

Between 1850 and 1890 the proportion of the nation's wealth owned by the 4,000 richest families nearly tripled. At the top of the social pyramid rested some 200 families worth more than $20 million each. Concentrated in the Northeast, especially in New York, these families were known throughout the world for their astonishing wealth. Spread more evenly across America were the several thousand millionaires whose investments in cattle ranching, agricultural equipment, mining, commerce, and real estate made them wealthy capitalists.

As a group America's millionaires had a lot in common. Most traced their ancestry to Great Britain. Most were Protestant, usually Episcopalians, Presbyterians, or Congregationalists. By the standards of their day they were unusually well educated. Except in the South, America's upper class voted Republican.

The upper classes lived in spectacular houses in neighborhoods that became famous for their wealth: Fifth Avenue in Manhattan, Nob Hill in San Francisco, Rittenhouse Square in Philadelphia, and Boston's Back Bay. Wealthy suburbs (Brooklyn Heights, Philadelphia's Main Line, and Brookline, Massachusetts) acquired similar reputations as privileged retreats. The richest families also built rural estates that rivaled the country homes of England and the chateaus of France. In the late nineteenth century the richest families built a string of spectacular summer homes along the Newport, Rhode Island, shoreline.

The leading figures in New York's high society competed with one another to stage the most lavish balls and dinner parties. The competition reached a climax on March 26, 1883, when Mrs. William Vanderbilt staged a stupendous costume ball that challenged Mrs. William Astor's long-standing position as the queen of New York's upper class. The ball was a great success. All of New York society turned out at the magnificent Vanderbilt mansion, where the hostess made a grand entrance dressed as a Venetian princess.

Biltmore Estate The homes of the industrial rich were huge by comparison with those of their antebellum predecessors. Pictured here is the immense Biltmore Estate outside Asheville, North Carolina. Built by George Vanderbilt in the late 1800s, Biltmore had 255 rooms and required a railroad of its own to bring the construction materials to the building site.

It was left to the new middle class to preserve the traditional virtues of thrift and self-denial.

The Consolidation of the New Middle Class

In 1889 *The Century Dictionary* introduced the phrase "middle class" in the United States. The new term reflected a novel awareness that American society had become permanently divided in a way that earlier generations had stoutly denied.

Professionals were the backbone of the new middle class that emerged in the nineteenth century. All professions defined what it meant to be a member of their tribe, organized themselves into professional associations, and set educational standards for admission. By these means professionals could command high salaries and enjoy both prestige and a comfortable standard of living. Between 1870 and 1890 some 200 societies were formed to establish the educational requirements and maintain the credentials of their members. Even the management of corporations became a professional occupation, as business schools were created to train professionals in the science of accounting and the art of management. Some professionals succeeded in having their standards written into law. In most states, by 1900, doctors and lawyers could practice legally only when licensed under the auspices of professional associations.

Behind the new professional managers marched an expanding white-collar army of cashiers, clerks, and government employees. They were overwhelmingly men, and they earned annual incomes far beyond those of independent craftsmen and factory workers. They also enjoyed much better opportunities for upward mobility. A beginning clerk might make only $100 a year, but within five years his salary could be closer to $1,000. At a time when the average annual income of a skilled factory worker in Philadelphia was less than $600, over 80 percent of the male clerks in the Treasury Department earned over $1,200 a year.

As it developed, the middle class withdrew from the messy uncertainties of the central city. Improved roads and mass-transit systems allowed middle-class families to escape the urban extremes of great wealth and miserable poverty. Middle-class residents idealized the physical advantages of trees, lawns, and gardens, as well as the comfortable domestic life that suburbs afforded.

Only the most successful craftsmen matched the incomes and suburban lifestyles of white-collar clerks. Butchers might earn more than $1,600 annually, for example, but shoemakers averaged little more than $500. A shoemaker who owned his own tools and ran a small shop maintained the kind of independence that was long cherished among middle-class Americans, yet his income scarcely distinguished him from skilled factory workers. The manual crafts were therefore a bridge between the remnants of the independent middle class and the growing industrial working class made up of men and women like Rosa Cassettari.

The Industrial Working Class Comes of Age

"When I first went to learn the trade," John Morrison told a congressional committee in 1883, "a machinist considered himself more than the average workingman; in fact he did not like to be called a workingman. He liked to be called a mechanic." Morrison put his finger on one of the great changes in the political economy of nineteenth-century America. Before the Civil War, urban workingmen were skilled laborers who were referred to as artisans and mechanics. "Today," Morrison explained, the mechanic "is simply a laborer." Big businesses replaced mechanics with semiskilled or unskilled factory laborers. For traditional mechanics, this felt like downward mobility.

But most factory operatives and common laborers were migrants (or children of migrants) from small towns and farms. Few, therefore, experienced factory work as a degradation of their traditional skills, as John Morrison did. But most migrants did experience industrial labor as a harsh existence. Factory operatives worked long hours in difficult conditions performing repetitious tasks with little job security.

The clothing industry is a good example of the lives of urban workers. The introduction of the sewing machine in the 1850s gave rise to sweatshops where work was subdivided into simple, repetitive tasks. One group produced collars for men's shirts, another produced cuffs, and another stitched the parts together. Jobs were defined to ensure that workers could be easily replaced. Factory operatives learned this lesson quickly. They were young; often they were women or children who moved into and out of different factory jobs with astonishing frequency. But even among men, factory work was at best unsteady. The business cycle swung hard and often, leaving few factory operatives with secure, long-term employment.

At the bottom of the hierarchy of wage earners were the common laborers, whose trademark was physical exertion. Their numbers grew throughout the century until by 1900 common laborers accounted for a third of the industrial workforce. Hundreds of thousands of common laborers worked for railroads and steel companies. Before Andrew Carnegie and his competitors revolutionized their industry, for example, no more than 20 percent of iron and steel workers were common laborers. By the 1890s, 40 percent of steel workers were common laborers.

Common laborers were difficult to organize into effective unions. A large proportion were immigrants and African Americans, and ethnic differences and language barriers often frustrated the development of workers' alliances. Even the kind of work common laborers performed inhibited the growth of effective unions. It was rarely steady work. Men who laid railroad tracks or dug canals and subway tunnels generally moved on when they finished. Common labor was often seasonal; as a result, unskilled workers changed jobs frequently. Common laborers were unusually mobile and easily replaceable, and they increasingly came from parts of the world where the idea of organized labor was unknown. Even when they did organize, common laborers faced the biggest, most powerful, most effectively organized corporations in the country.

A great deal of the wage work done by women fell into the category of common labor. In 1900 women accounted for nearly one of every five gainfully employed Americans. They stood behind the counters of department stores, and young Irish women worked as domestics in northern middle-class homes. In the South, African American women worked as domestics. A smaller proportion of women held white-collar jobs, as teachers, nurses, or low-paid clerical workers and sales clerks.

The same hierarchy that favored men in the white-collar and professional labor force existed in the factories and sweatshops. In the clothing industry, for

Women Workers in a New York City Hat Factory, ca. 1900 In the hierarchy of wage laborers, women were the lowest paid and the least skilled.

example, units dominated by male workers were higher up the chain of command than those dominated by women. Indeed, as the textile industry became a big business, the proportion of women working in textile mills steadily declined. The reverse trend appeared among white-collar workers. As department stores expanded in the 1870s and 1880s, they hired low-paid women, often Irish immigrants, with none of the prospects for promotion still available to men. White-collar work was not a signal of middle-class status for women as it was for most men in the late nineteenth century.

The story was somewhat different for married women and their children. As few as 1 in 50 working-class wives and mothers took jobs outside the home. Women supplemented the family income by taking in boarders or doing laundry. Most often, however, working-class families survived by sending their children to work. Even in the families of the highest-paid industrial workers, 50 percent of the children worked. Among the poorest working-class families, three out of four children worked. Child labor was a clear sign of class distinction. The rich sent their daughters to finishing schools and their sons to elite boarding schools, middle-class parents sent their children to public schools, and working-class families sent their children to work. This was especially true in the South, where sharecropping was becoming a form of wage labor.

Sharecropping Becomes Wage Labor

As the southern economy recovered from the devastation of the Civil War, many observers predicted a bright future for the region. Optimists saw a wealth of untapped natural and human resources, a South freed from the constraints of an inefficient slave labor system ripe for investment, brimming with opportunities, and ready to go.

African American Exodus from the South "Remarkable Exodus of Negroes from Louisiana and Mississippi—Incidents of the Arrival, Support and Departure of the Refugees at St. Louis." Notice the four scenes: 1) "Procession of refugees from the steamboat landing," 2) "Embarkation for Kansas," 3) "Feeding the refugees at one of the colored churches," and 4) "St. Louis colored citizens welcoming the immigrants upon arrival."

In an age when Americans were building railroads at an exuberant clip, southerners built them faster. By 1890 nine out of ten southerners lived in a county with a railroad. By then impressive steel mills were coming to life in Birmingham, Alabama. The Piedmont Plateau (running along the eastern foothills of the Appalachian Mountains from Virginia to Georgia) was dotted with textile mills bigger and more efficient than those in New England. Southerners were migrating from the countryside to the towns, expanding the production of cotton into new areas, bringing the rich soil of the Mississippi Delta under cultivation. For ordinary southerners, however, especially African Americans, there was no great prosperity in the New South.

After the war most blacks returned to work on land they did not own (see Chapter 16). In place of the master-slave relationship emerged a new labor relationship between landlords and sharecroppers. Between the landlords and croppers, supplying the credit that kept the system alive, arose a powerful class of merchants. At the beginning it was unclear how much power the landlords, the merchants, and the sharecroppers each had. The most important question was who owned the cotton crop at the end of the year: the sharecropper who produced it, the landlord who owned the farm, or the merchant who loaned the supplies needed until the crop came in. The answer would be decided in the state legislatures and courts where the credit laws were written and interpreted.

The resolution was legally complete by the middle of the 1880s. First the courts defined a sharecropper as a wage laborer. The landlord owned the crop and paid his workers a wage in the form of a share of what was produced. Landlords also won a stronger claim on the crop than the merchant creditors. The struggle among landlords, sharecroppers, and merchants was therefore settled in favor of the landlord.

Under the circumstances, merchants were reluctant to loan money to sharecroppers. Many left the plantation districts and moved to the up-country, where they established commercial relations with white yeomen farmers. Trapped in a cycle of debt, white farmers in the 1880s began losing their land and falling into tenancy. Meanwhile, in the "black belt" (where most African Americans lived and most of the cotton was produced), successful landlords became merchants while successful merchants purchased land and hired sharecroppers of their own. By the mid-1880s, black sharecroppers worked as wage laborers for the landlord-merchant class across much of the South.

Sharecropping differed in two critical ways from the wage work of industrial America. First, sharecropping was family labor, depending on a husband and father who signed the contract and delivered the labor of his wife and children to the landlord. Second, because sharecropping contracts were yearlong, the labor market was restricted to a few weeks at the end of each year. If croppers left before the end of the year, they risked losing everything.

The political economy of sharecropping impoverished the South by binding the region to a single crop—cotton—that steadily depleted the soil even as prices fell. Yet for most southern blacks there were few alternatives. Over time a small percentage of black farmers purchased their own land, but their farms were generally tiny and the soil poor. The skilled black artisans who had worked on plantations before the Civil War moved to southern cities where they took unskilled, low-paying jobs. Industrialization was not much help for African Americans. Northern factories were segregated, as were the steel mills of Birmingham, Alabama, and the Piedmont textile mills. Black women worked as domestic servants to supplement their husbands' meager incomes. Wage labor transformed the lives of southern blacks, but it did not bring prosperity.

Hoping to escape the poverty and discrimination of southern life, a number of former slaves moved west. One group, the Exodusters, began moving to the Kansas prairie during the mid-1870s. By 1880 more than 6,000 blacks had joined them, searching for cheap land on which to build independent farms. The Exodusters became locked in the same battles with cattlemen that troubled white farmers, and blacks who settled in cow towns like Dodge City and Topeka found the same pattern of discrimination they had known in the South. Nevertheless, some of the Exodusters did manage to buy land and build farms. In this respect, the black exodus was similar to the movement of Americans headed west for relief from the constraints of urban and industrial America.

Clearing the West for Capitalism

The Homestead Act, passed by Congress during the Civil War, was designed to ensure that the West would be settled by hardworking, independent small farmers. And millions of farmers actually did settle in the West during the second half of the nineteenth century. Their movement has become the stuff of legend.

AMERICAN LANDSCAPE

>> Mining Camps in the West

Rosa Cassettari's experience in the mining camps of Missouri was not unique. But it is overshadowed by the more famous mining camps of California and the Far West. Mining fever began in 1848 when James Marshall discovered gold close to John Sutter's mill on the American River near what is now Sacramento, California. Thousands of prospectors poured into California during the 1850s, panning for gold wherever rumors of a vein hit, pulling up stakes and generating boomtowns and ghost towns with dizzying speed. "Every few days news would come of the discovery of a brand-new mining region," Mark Twain wrote from California. "Immediately the papers would teem with accounts of its richness, and away the surplus population would scamper to take possession." Eventually word of new discoveries pulled prospectors eastward from California. Tens of thousands of miners flooded into Colorado in 1859. Meanwhile prospectors in Nevada discovered the largest single vein in American history, the Comstock Lode, which would yield 350 million dollars worth of gold and silver during the 1860s and 1870s alone. Similar rushes transformed parts of Idaho in 1862 and Montana in 1864.

Western mining camps were extraordinary places. They were peopled by settlers from a variety of backgrounds. In the gold-country camps on the western slope of the Sierra Nevada, native-born Yankees lived among British subjects, Chinese immigrants, Mexicans, Spaniards, and African Americans. This was a male-dominated world of violence, vigilantism, and multicultural interaction. Alone or in small groups they would pan for gold in the beds of the rivers and streams that poured out of the Sierra Nevada mountains. This was known as placer mining. Once the surface gold had been captured, miners would shovel dirt into boxes or sluices to capture gold and silver by running water over it. Only a few miners struck it rich this way, although their stories captured the imaginations of thousands.

Marcus Daly, for example, came to America as a penniless Irish immigrant and struck it rich in the gold fields of California. But his biography says less about the prospects for success among individual miners than it does about the larger transformation in the mining frontier. With the wealth he accumulated on his own, Daly persuaded a group of San Francisco investors to back his plans to dig a silver mine deep into the ground at Butte, Montana. They did not find silver, but they did strike one of the largest veins of copper in the world. The Anaconda mine made Daly and his partners rich, but it also symbolized the changes that had taken place in western mining. Daly became the supervisor of a large group of engineers and wage laborers. Anaconda extracted and smelted its own ore, then shipped its high-grade copper around the world to cities and industries anxious to harness the power of electricity that was transmitted across copper wires. By 1883 the United States was the largest producer of copper on earth.

The world of the placer miners disappeared almost as quickly as it arose. As the years passed, the miners moved from west to east, into and then across the Sierra Nevada, following the news of new strikes in Idaho, Montana, Nevada, and Colorado. But as the surface riches were quickly snapped up, the remaining veins of gold and silver proved too deep for any one prospector to reach. It took heavy machines to get at the ore buried deep underground, and machinery required capital investments beyond the means of ordinary miners. Most of the wealth taken from the Comstock mines, for example, was extracted by corporations using powerful tools to dig deep into the earth. So mining corporations steadily bought up the settlers' claims and created a more permanent industrial presence in the western states. Mark Twain's experience was typical: having gone out to prospect for gold on his own, he ended up selling his labor for wages. "I went to work as a common laborer in a quartz mill," he explained, "at ten dollars a week and board."

Yet the mining camps, however brief their existence, represented a temporary alternative to the permanent inequalities of the industrial economy. As rough and violent as they were, the camps were also experiments in spontaneous democracy in which men came together, governed themselves, and agreed on the rules by which they would live. ●

But these hardy individuals did not settle an empty prairie. Waiting for them in the West were native peoples, some helpful and many hostile. And far from escaping the hierarchy of industrial capitalism, the settlers brought it with them. By the time the director of the U.S. Census declared the frontier "closed" in 1890, the political economy of the American West was composed of railroad tycoons and immigrant workers, commercial farmers and impoverished Native Americans.

The Overland Trail

"Left home this morning," Jane Gould wrote in her diary on April 27, 1862. Along with her husband, Albert, and their two sons, Jane loaded a covered wagon in Mitchell, Iowa, and joined a group of migrants on the Overland Trail to California (see Map 17–3). It would be a long and difficult journey. Albert got sick shortly after they left, and Jane had to nurse him, drive the wagon, and care for the children. The farther they traveled, the more distressed Jane became. The Overland Trail was littered with the remnants of wagon trains that had gone before, including discarded furniture, dried bones, and lonely graves. In early October the Goulds reached their new home in the San Joaquin Valley. Five months later, Jane's husband died.

A popular image pictures the West as a haven for rugged men who struck out on their own, but most migrants went in family groups, and the families were mostly middle class. Few poor people could afford the expense of the journey and still hope to buy land and set up a farm in the West.

The journey across the Overland Trail became safer over the years. In the late 1840s the U.S. government began building forts along the overland routes. Besides protecting migrants from Indians, the forts became resting points for wagon trains. By the 1850s Mormon settlers in Utah had built Salt Lake City into a major stopping point. Migrants came to rely on the facilities there to ease the journey. Also during the 1850s, the government began to pursue a long-term solution to the growing problem of Native American–white relations in the West.

The Origins of Indian Reservations

In 1851 more than 10,000 Native Americans from across the Great Plains converged on Fort Laramie in Wyoming Territory. All the major Indian peoples were

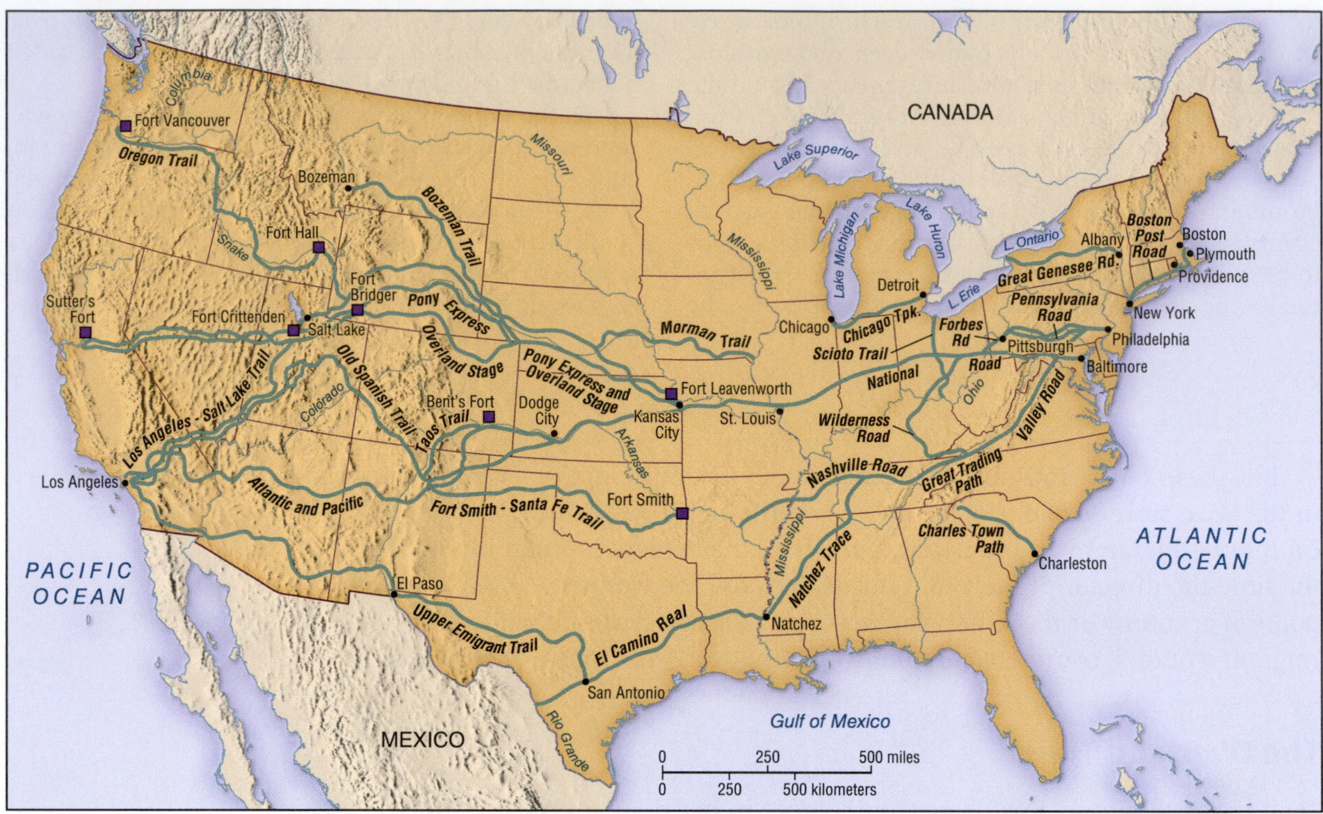

Map 17–4 The Overland Trail There was no transcontinental railroad until the late 1860s. Before then, and even thereafter, most settlers moved west on a series of well-developed overland trails.

represented: Sioux, Cheyenne, Arapaho, Crow, and many others. They came to meet with government officials who hoped to develop a lasting means of avoiding Indian–white conflict. Since the discovery of gold a few years earlier, white migrants had been crossing through Indian territory on their way to California, most of them already prejudiced against the Indians. U.S. officials wanted to prevent hostility between whites and Indians from breaking out into violence and to restrain the conflicts among Indians themselves. They proposed the creation of a separate territory for each Indian tribe, with government subsidies to entice the Indians to stay within their territories. This was the beginning of the reservation system, and for the rest of the century the U.S. government struggled to force the Indians to accept it.

From the start, the reservation system was corrupt and difficult to enforce. Agents for the Bureau of Indian Affairs cheated Indians and the government alike, sometimes reaping huge profits. But primarily, the reservations failed because not all Indians agreed to restrict themselves to their designated territories, leading to armed confrontations and reprisals.

By the late 1860s the tensions between Indians and whites were at a fever pitch, as Senator James R. Doolittle of Wisconsin discovered on a fact-finding mission through the West. In Denver he asked an audience of whites whether they preferred outright extermination of the Indians to a policy of restricting Indians to reservations. The crowd roared its approval for extermination. Army officers agreed. The government "must act with vindictive earnestness against the Sioux," General William Tecumseh Sherman declared.

Senator Doolittle and his colleagues resisted the calls for extermination, opting instead for a more comprehensive reservation policy. The government pursued this approach by means of two important treaties that divided the Great Plains into two huge Indian territories. The Medicine Lodge Treaty, signed in Kansas in October 1867, organized thousands of Indians across the Southern Plains. In return for government supplies, most of the Southern Plains peoples agreed to restrict themselves to the reservation. The Northern Plains Indians did not sign onto the reservation so readily. A treaty was drafted, but a band of holdouts demanded further government concessions. Inspired by their leader Red Cloud, the Indians insisted that U.S. forces abandon their forts along the Bozeman Trail. When the government agreed, Red Cloud signed the Fort Laramie Treaty in November 1868.

Red Cloud respected the treaties for the rest of his life, but they nevertheless failed. Most white settlers still preferred extermination to reservations, and not all the Plains Indians approved of the treaties. Nor did the U.S. Army abide by the reservation policy. Within weeks of Red Cloud's signature on the Fort Laramie Treaty, for example, the Seventh Cavalry led by Colonel George Armstrong Custer massacred Cheyennes at Washita, Oklahoma, on November 27, 1868. As long as the U.S. Army sustained the settlers' hunger for extermination, Indian "policy" was made on the battlefield rather than in government offices.

By 1870 it was clear that western Indians would not voluntarily retire to reservations and that the military could not force them into surrender. If any further

Indian Village Routed, Geronimo Fleeing from Camp Oil on canvas by Frederic Remington, 1896.

Map 17-5 Conflicts in the West In the late 19th century, battles between whites and Native Americans erupted all across the western half of the continent.

evidence of the Indian resistance was needed, it came in South Dakota, where, after discovery of gold in the Black Hills, thousands of whites poured onto Indian territory. When the Lakota Sioux rejected demands that they cede their lands to the miners, the government sent in the army, led by General Custer. Custer was an arrogant man, and he made two critical mistakes. First he divided his army in two, and then he failed to keep them in communication with each other. Custer and hundreds of his men were slaughtered at Little Bighorn, Montana, in 1876 by 2,000 Indian warriors led by Sitting Bull and Crazy Horse.

The Destruction of Indian Subsistence

Custer's Last Stand did not signal any change of fortunes for the Plains Indians. By the 1870s whites had learned that they could undermine Native American society most effectively by depriving Indians of their sources of subsistence, especially the bison. "Kill every buffalo you can," a U.S. Army colonel urged one hunter. "Every buffalo dead is an Indian gone." Federal authorities did not actually sponsor the mass killing of the bison; they merely turned a blind eye. Railroads joined the pro-

Ghost Dance, Wood Engraving, ca. 1890 The Ghost Dance swept across the Plains among Native Americans threatened with destruction by white settlement.

cess, sponsoring mass kills from slow-moving trains as they crossed the prairies. Some 13 million bison in 1850 were reduced, by 1880, to only a few hundred.

With their subsistence destroyed, Chief Sitting Bull and his starving men finally gave up in 1881. The Sioux war ended in 1890 with a shocking massacre of 200 Native American men, women, and children at Wounded Knee, South Dakota.

In the Northwest in 1877 the Nez Percés, fleeing from Union troops, set out on a dramatic trek across the mountains into Yellowstone in an attempt to reach Canada. The Nez Percés eluded government troops and nearly made it over the Canadian border. However, hunger and the elements did what the Union army had failed to do. Chief Joseph and his exhausted people agreed to go to their reservations.

Reformers who advocated reservations over extermination always believed that the Indians should be absorbed into the political economy of capitalism. By "confining the Indians to reservations," explained William P. Dole, Lincoln's Commissioner of Indian Affairs, "they are gradually taught and become accustomed to the idea of individual property." Most white settlers considered Native Americans an inferior race

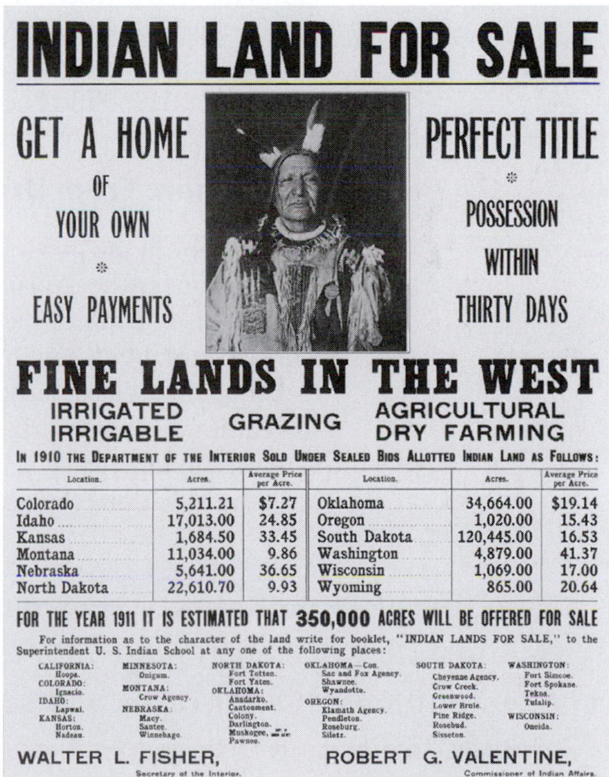

Indian Land For Sale Within a couple of decades of the passage of the Dawes Act, most Native American lands were sold to white settlers.

worthy of destruction. By contrast, Dole believed that "Indians are capable of attaining a high degree of civilization." But reformers like Dole equated civilization with the cultivation of "individual property." Accordingly, reformers set out to destroy Native American society. They introduced government schools on Indian reservations to teach children the virtues of private property, individual achievement, and social mobility.

The reformers' influence peaked in 1887 when Congress passed the Dawes Severalty Act, the most important piece of Indian legislation of the century. Under the terms of the Dawes Act, land within the reservations was broken up into separate plots and distributed among individual families. The goal was to force Indians to live like stereotypical white farmers. But the lands allotted were generally so poor, and the plots so small, that their owners sold them as soon as they were allowed. By the early twentieth century there were virtually no reservations left, except for a few parcels in the desert Southwest. With the Indians subdued, the path was cleared for the capitalist transformation of the West.

The Economic Transformation of the West

A few hundred civilians died in Indian attacks during the late nineteenth century. More than 5,000 died building the railroads. Lawless violence and wild speculation were very much a part of the western experience, as were struggling families, temperance reformers, and hardworking immigrants. By 1900 the West provided Americans with the meat and bread for their dinner tables, the wood that built their homes, and the gold and silver that backed up their currency. The West was being drawn into the political economy of global capitalism.

Cattlemen: From Drovers to Ranchers

The cowboy is the great mythic figure of the American West: a rugged individual, a silent loner who scorned society for the independence of the trail. Like many myths, this one has elements of truth. Cowboys were usually unattached men. They worked hard, but when their work was over they played just as hard, spending their earnings on a shave, a new suit of clothes, and a few good nights in town. Driving cattle was hard work, often dangerous, and even more often boring. Civil War veterans, emancipated slaves, displaced Indians, and Mexican vaqueros all became cowboys at various times. Cowboys were poorly paid, their work was unsteady, and their chances of reaching real independence were slim.

> **The Great Pacific Railway is commenced. . . . Immigration will soon pour into these valleys. Ten millions of emigrants will settle in this golden land in twenty years. . . . This is the grandest enterprise under God!**
>
> GEORGE FRANCIS TRAIN

Longhorn cattle were as much a part of western legend as the cowboys who drove them. With the destruction of the bison and the westward spread of the railroads, it became possible to drive huge herds of Texas longhorns north onto the Great Plains. With relatively little capital, cattle herders could make substantial profits. Cowboys drove gigantic herds, sometimes numbering half a million, to a town with a railroad connection from which the cattle could be shipped, such as Abilene, Wichita, or Dodge City, Kansas. Cattlemen sold half of their stock to eastern markets and the other half in the West, to Californians, or to the government, which purchased beef to feed soldiers and Indians on reservations.

But the Texas longhorn had several drawbacks that eventually led to its replacement. Most seriously, it carried a tick that devastated many of the grazing animals that came into contact with it. In addition, the longhorn took a long time to fatten up and never produced good beef. Wealthy investors began to experiment with hybrid cattle that did not carry the deadly tick, fattened up quickly, and produced higher quality meat. By the early 1880s investors were pouring capital into mammoth cattle-herding companies. At the same time it was becoming clear that the Great Plains were seriously overstocked. The grazing lands were depleted, leaving the cattle weak from malnutrition. In the late 1880s several severe winters devastated the sickly herds.

Open-range herding became so environmentally destructive that it was no longer economically feasible. In addition, long drives became increasingly difficult as farmers settled the plains and fenced in their lands. By the 1890s huge cattle companies were giving way to smaller ranches that raised hybrid cattle. The western railroad network was by then so extensive that it was no longer necessary to drive herds hundreds of miles to reach a railhead. Cowboys became ranch hands who worked for regular wages, like miners and factory workers.

In the mid-1880s, more than 7 million head of cattle roamed the Great Plains, but their numbers declined rapidly, and in their place came sheep. Sheep fed on the growths that cattle would not eat. In fact, the sheep ate so many grasses that they proved even more ecologically destructive than cattle. Nevertheless, by 1900 sheepherding had largely replaced the cattle industry in Wyoming and Montana and was spreading to Nevada. Sheepherding had one other crucial advantage: it did not interfere with small farmers as much as cattle driving did.

Commercial Farmers Subdue the Plains

Between 1860 and 1900, the number of farms in America nearly tripled, thanks largely to the economic development of the West. On the Great Plains and in the desert Southwest, farmers took up former Indian lands. From San Francisco to Los Angeles, white settlers poached on the estates of Spanish-speaking landlords, stripping them of their natural resources and undermining their profitability. Over time Hispanic ranchers gave way to Euro-American farmers. The Hispanic population of Los Angeles fell from 82 percent in 1850 to 19 percent in 1880. A similar pattern displaced the Mexican American landowners in New Mexico and Texas.

This ethnic shift signaled profound changes in the ecology and political economy of the West, driven by the exploding global demand for western products. Cattle ranchers were feeding eastern cities. Lumber from the Pacific Northwest found its way to Asia and South America. By 1890 western farmers produced half of the wheat grown in the United States, and they shipped it across the globe.

But farming in the arid West was different from farming in the East. To begin with, the 160-acre homesteads envisioned by eastern lawmakers were unrealistic:

farms of that size were too small for the economic and ecological conditions of western agriculture. From the beginning, western farmers were businessmen. To produce wheat and corn for the international market they needed steel plows, costly mechanical equipment, and extensive irrigation. To make these capital investments, western farmers mortgaged their lands. For mechanized, commercial agriculture to succeed on mortgaged land, western farms had to be much bigger than 160 acres.

Most western agricultural settlement took place not on government-sponsored homesteads but through the private land market. By some estimates land speculators bought up nearly 350 million acres of western lands from state or federal governments or from Indian reservations. Railroads were granted another 200 million acres by the federal government. The more farmers who settled in the West, the more agricultural produce they could regularly ship back East. Therefore, railroads set up immigration bureaus and advertised for settlers, offering cheap transportation, credit, and agricultural assistance, filling up the Great Plains with settlers from the East Coast and from Ireland, Germany, and Scandinavia. In 1890 the director of the Bureau of the Census reported that the frontier had at last been filled.

Changes in the Land

The trans-Mississippi West was no Garden of Eden waiting for lucky farmers to move in and reap the land's abundant riches. The climate, particularly in the Great Plains and the desert Southwest, was too dry for most kinds of farming. The sod on the plains was so thick and hard that traditional plows ripped like paper; only steel would do the job. With little wood or stone to build houses, farmers lived first in dugouts or sod houses. Fierce winter blizzards gave way to blistering summers, each rocked by harsh winds. Yet settlers seemed determined to overcome, and to overwhelm, nature itself. To build fences where wood was scarce, manufacturers invented barbed wire. Windmills dotted the prairie to pump water from hundreds of feet below ground. Powerful agricultural machinery tore through the earth, and new strains of wheat from Europe and China were cultivated to withstand the brutal climate.

The western environment was transformed. Wolves, elk, and bear were exterminated as farmers brought in pigs, cattle, and sheep. Tulare Lake, covering hundreds of square miles of California's Central Valley, was sucked dry by 1900. Hydraulic mining sent tons of earth and rock cascading down the rivers flowing out of the Sierra Nevada, raising water levels to the point where entire cities became vulnerable to flooding. The skies above Butte, Montana, turned grey from the pollutants released by the copper-smelting plants. Sheepherding destroyed the vegetation on the eastern slopes of the Rocky Mountains and the Sierra Nevada.

By the turn of the century, the bison had all but disappeared, and the Indians had been confined to reservations. Industrial mining corporations, profitable cattle ranches, and mechanized farms now dominated the West. The frontier was gone, and in its place were commercial farmers whose lives were shaped by European weather, eastern mortgage companies, commodity brokers, and railroad conglomerates. Cowboys sold their labor to cattle companies owned by investors in Boston and Glasgow. Mining and lumber corporations employed tens of thousands of wage laborers. Big cities sprang up almost overnight. San Francisco had 5,000 inhabitants in 1850, but by the time the Gold Rush was over, in 1870, there were 150,000 people living there. Denver was incorporated in 1861 but its population hovered at just below 5,000 until the railroad came in 1870. Twenty years later Denver had more than 100,000 inhabitants. Whatever it was in American mythology, the West was well on its way to becoming a part of an urban, industrial nation.

Conclusion

Rosa Cassettari and Andrew Carnegie never met, but together their lives suggest the spectrum of possibilities in industrializing America. Both were immigrants who, caught up in the political economy of industrial capitalism, made their way to the United States. Yet the same grand forces touched the two immigrants in different ways. Cassettari moved to a mining camp west of the Mississippi River before making her way to Chicago—the city that opened the West to the dynamism of industrial capitalism. Carnegie migrated, almost overnight, from the preindustrial world of Scotland to the heart of the Industrial Revolution in America—Pittsburgh, with its railroads, oil refineries, and steel mills. Cassettari struggled all her life and achieved a modest level of comfort for herself and her children. She did as well as most immigrants could hope for, and in that sense her biography reflects the realities of working-class life in industrial America. Cassettari's experience with failure—the harsh life of the mining camp and a bad marriage—impelled her to move on in search of something better. It was success, however, that made Carnegie itch for something different. By 1890, having made his millions, he remade himself by becoming a patron of culture. He moved to New York and traveled the world, befriending the leading intellectuals of his day. He built libraries and endowed universities. He had helped create an industrial nation. Now he set out to re-create American culture.

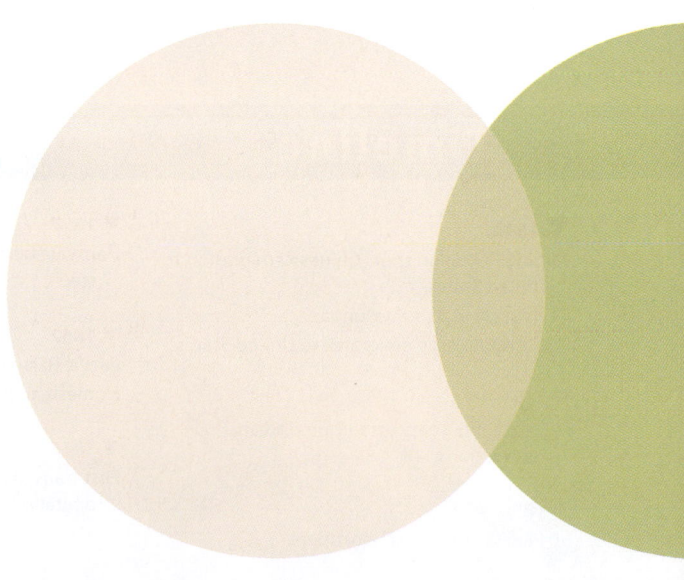

Further Readings

Alfred D. Chandler, *The Visible Hand: The Managerial Revolution in American Business* (1977). The standard account of the rise of corporate bureaucracy.

William Cronon, *Nature's Metropolis: Chicago and the Great West* (1991). Meticulously charts the way Chicago's influence stretched across much of the West.

Eric Hobsbawm, *The Age of Empire: 1875–1914* (1987). Establishes the global context for the industrial transformation of the United States.

Maldwyn Jones, *American Immigration*, 2nd ed. (1992). Unusually sensitive to the political and economic background to global migration.

David Montgomery, *The Fall of the House of Labor: The Workplace, the State and American Labor Activism, 1865–1925* (1987). Shows how the rise of big business changed the daily labor of the American working class.

David Nasaw, *Andrew Carnegie* (2006). Does an especially good job of putting Carnegie's life into the larger historical context.

Gregory Nobles, *American Frontiers: Cultural Encounters and Continental Conquest* (1997). A brief survey reflecting the latest scholarship in western history.

Heather Cox Richardson, *West From Appomattox: The Reconstruction of America After the Civil War* (2007). An intelligent and highly readable survey of American history in the late nineteenth century.

Richard White, *'It's Your Misfortune and None of My Own': A History of the American West* (1991) is a comprehensive survey by a leading historian of the West.

C. Vann Woodward, *Origins of the New South, 1877–1913* (1951) is one of the great works of American historical literature.

>> Timeline >>

▼ 1848
Taiping Rebellion spurs Chinese emigration to United States
Revolution in Austria-Hungary
Andrew Carnegie emigrates to United States

▼ 1851
Fort Laramie Treaty establishes Indian reservations

▼ 1856
St. Paul's boarding school opens

▼ 1857
Henry Bessemer develops process for making steel

▼ 1862
Pacific Railroad Act
Homestead Act

▼ 1865
First transatlantic telegraph cable begins operation

▼ 1867
Medicine Lodge Treaty

▼ 1868
Second Fort Laramie Treaty
Washita Massacre

▼ 1871
October: Great Chicago fire

Who, What

Rosa Cassettari 571
Jacob Riis 576
Andrew Carnegie 577
Tom Scott 578
James Doolittle 592
Red Cloud 593
Sitting Bull 595
Tenement 576
Bessemer Process 581
Monopoly 582
Trusts 582
Fort Laramie 591
Overland Trail 591
Reservations 592
Longhorn cattle 596

Review Questions

1. What were the major features of "global" capitalism in the late nineteenth century?
2. Describe the new social order of industrial America.
3. How did western Indians respond to westward expansion?
4. How was the West absorbed into the national and international market?

Websites

A Coal Miner's Work. http://people.cohums.ohio-state.edu/kerr6/courses/History563/A%20Coal%20Miner's%20Work.htm

The Chinese in California. http://memory.loc.gov/ammem/award99/cubhtml/cichome.html

The Northern Great Plains, 1880–1920. http://memory.loc.gov/ammem/award97/ndfahtml/ngphome.html

For further review materials and resource information, please visit www.oup.com/us/ofthepeople

▼ 1872
Edgar Thomson Steel Works open near Pittsburgh

▼ 1873
Financial panic, followed by depression

▼ 1876
Custer's Last Stand at Little Bighorn

▼ 1878
American Bar Association founded

▼ 1881
Czar Alexander II of Russia assassinated

▼ 1882
Chinese Exclusion Act
John D. Rockefeller forms Standard Oil trust
Edison Electric Company lights up New York buildings

▼ 1887
Dawes Severalty Act

▼ 1890
Jacob Riis publishes *How the Other Half Lives*
Massacre at Wounded Knee, South Dakota
Director of U.S. Census declares frontier "closed"

▼ 1893
Financial panic, followed by depression

CHAPTER 18

Common Threads 

>> How did American culture in the late nineteenth century reflect the rise of big cities and big business?

>> What, if anything, is the difference between popular culture and high culture?

>> What was new about artistic realism?

>> Was culture a political issue in the late nineteenth century?

Cultural Struggles of Industrial America 1850–1895

AMERICAN PORTRAIT

>> Anthony Comstock's Crusade Against Vice

Anthony Comstock devoted most of his adult life to putting the owners of brothels, gambling dens, abortion clinics, and dance halls out of business. "You must hunt these men as you hunt rats," Comstock declared, "without mercy." There was little in his background to foreshadow such zeal. While still a young man Comstock moved from rural Connecticut to New York City, where he worked as a clerk in a dry goods store. White-collar careers of this sort were a familiar path for native-born Protestant men in the middle of the nineteenth century. Fame came to him in 1873 when the United States Congress enacted a statute that bore his name. The Comstock Law banned the production, distribution, and public display of obscenity. Thereafter, Comstock spent much of his life chasing down and prosecuting pornographers, prostitutes, and strippers.

Comstock and many like-minded citizens were genuinely disturbed by the municipal corruption that kept police departments from enforcing obscenity laws. To overcome this obstacle, reformers established private organizations with quasi-official authority. Among the most influential was Anthony Comstock's New York Society for the Suppression of Vice, commonly known as the SSV. Founded in 1873, the SSV was dedicated to "the enforcement of laws for the suppression of the trade in, and circulation of, obscene literature and illustrations, advertisements, and articles of indecent or immoral use." As head of the society, Comstock was appointed a special agent of the U.S. Post Office. Along with other SSV leaders, Comstock disregarded the rights of due process by entrapping his victims. But Comstock and others defended their actions by pointing out that the established legal procedures of the police and the judiciary were ineffective in preventing the sale of smut.

Comstock's chief concern was the protection of children. In his most famous book, *Traps for the Young* (1883), he warned that obscenity was enticing American youngsters into deviant ways by artificially nourishing youthful appetites and passions until they exerted "a well-nigh irresistible mastery over their victim." The evils that trapped America's children were concentrated in the cities that, in the late nineteenth century, attracted millions of young people. Urban life was relatively anonymous and it was also driven by vast amounts of cash. In the last third of the nineteenth century the income of nonfarm employees in America rose steadily, while prices declined. Except for the very poorest workers, urban Americans had more money to spend and more time to spend it than ever before. And if industrial workers enjoyed more leisure time, white-collar employees enjoyed even more. The big city offered Americans bawdy new entertainments that violated long-established standards of respectability. Pornography was not a new thing in the late nineteenth century, but it was more widespread than ever before.

For Comstock, cities were cesspools of vice and corruption, the breeding ground for immigrant slums thought to be devoid of "culture." At the time, many educated Americans thought that "culture" referred only to the great works of Western art, literature, and music. High culture, in this sense, was a healthy alternative to the sordid realities of urban and industrial America. Ironically, the best artists and writers of the late nineteenth century were "realists" who wanted art to reflect the gritty realities of everyday life. While Anthony Comstock tried to suppress the vices of the city, realists embraced them, translating them into compelling fiction and dramatic canvases.

In the second half of the nineteenth century, cultural clashes were as much a part of industrial capitalism as

continued

>> **AMERICAN PORTRAIT** *continued*

were class conflict and political upheaval. Rural Americans were often ambivalent about urban culture, attracted by its freedom but repelled by its licentiousness. Native-born Protestants, often genuinely concerned to help immigrants, were at the same time condescending and suspicious of immigrant folkways. Defenders of high culture resisted the lure of popular culture. Amateur sportsmen sniffed at the emergence of spectator sports. Victorian moralists assailed the collapse of traditional gender distinctions. Yet these struggles reflected the efforts of Americans to absorb the dramatic social transformations that accompanied the rise of industrial capitalism.

OUTLINE 

The Varieties of Urban Culture

Americans both loved and hated the cities they lived in, and their mixed feelings were reflected in the variety of entertainments they embraced during the second half of the nineteenth century. They swooned over romanticized re-creations of the Plains wars on the western frontier, and they paid good money to watch nostalgic minstrel shows about plantation life in the Old South. But as the economy developed, the nation's love affair with the countryside gave way to popular entertainments that idealized the city as never before. These new entertainments rested more than ever on the technological marvels of American industry. Beginning in the 1880s, electricity lit up the big city after dark, making it possible to create new forms of urban "night life." By 1900 electricity was powering the trolleys and subways that brought tens of thousands of Americans into new "downtown" districts (see Figure 18-1). Stores, businesses, and factories were the hallmarks of the older downtowns. But leisure activities attracted tens of thousands to the new city centers. In growing numbers Americans went to theaters, music halls, concert saloons, baseball stadiums, and sports arenas. City life, long associated with poverty and crime, now came to mean fun and excitement as well.

Minstrel Shows as Cultural Nostalgia

In the late nineteenth century the western frontier became one of the most popular themes in American show business. As rugged pioneers gave way to wage earners, commercial farmers, and industrialists, the mythology of the West grew. The most spectacular example of this was Buffalo Bill Cody's hugely successful Wild West Show, which toured the country parading live Indians before delighted urban spectators. Audiences watched displays of horsemanship and highly stylized reenactments of the Plains wars. America's fascination with a romanticized frontier was one example of a popular nostalgia for ways of life that were thought to have been simpler than the life of the city. Nowhere was this nostalgia more obvious than in the minstrel shows.

Minstrel shows were the most significant form of public entertainment for most of the nineteenth century. During the 1830s and 1840s minstrel shows were dominated by white performers in blackface. Although the minstrels stereotyped plantation slaves as happy and carefree, the earliest performances were not as viciously racist as they became later. In the mid-1850s, however, the tone of blackface minstrel shows changed. As the slavery controversy forced white northerners to take sides on a divisive issue, popular troupes like New York's Christy Minstrels took the side of the slaveholders. During the Civil War and Reconstruction, minstrel shows attacked white reformers in the North who supported emancipation and black rights. They portrayed blacks with gross racial stereotypes and subjected

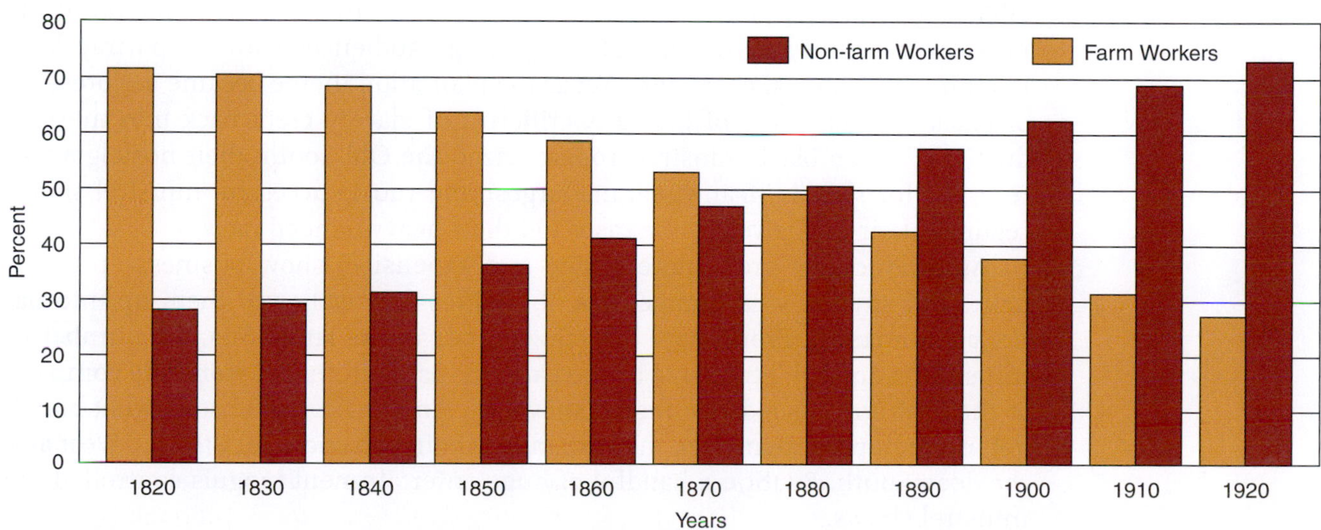

Figure 18–1 Growth of the Nonfarm Sector Underpinning the rise of urban culture was the emergence of a wage-earning labor force. Concentrated in cities, wage earners had cash at their disposal to spend on the amusements cities had to offer.

> **Amusement is not only a great fact and a great business interest, it is also a great factor in the development of the national character. If a wise philanthropist could choose between making the laws of any people and furnishing their amusements, it would not take him long to decide. The robust virtues are nurtured under the discipline of work; if the diversions can be kept healthful, a sound national life will be developed. The ideals of the people are shaped, and their sentiments formed, to a large extent, by popular amusements.**
>
> REVEREND WASHINGTON GLADDEN, *Applied Christianity*, 1886

abolitionists to ridicule. Minstrel troupes staged corrupted versions of *Uncle Tom's Cabin*, stripped the novel of its abolitionist theme, and reduced the plot to a simplistic story of beleaguered southern whites. Yet throughout the period, minstrel shows continued to poke fun at the aristocratic pretensions of cultural elites. Indeed, minstrel shows commonly combined racism with populism, lampooning elites by playing them in blackface wearing fancy clothes and putting on airs.

In the 1870s minstrel shows grew larger and more elaborate. J. H. Haverly led the way. He hired the most players, dressed them in the gaudiest costumes, placed them in the most spectacular sets, and had them perform the widest variety of numbers. He toned down the emphasis on blackface singers and plantation themes and added scantily clad women and off-color routines. Haverly expanded his audiences with extensive advertising. By 1881 he had theaters in New York, Brooklyn, Chicago, and San Francisco; three national minstrel troupes; and four touring comedy theaters. Of Haverly's three companies, two were white and one was black. There were other black companies as well. As national minstrel shows abandoned their commitment to authentic representations of southern life, blacks often took to the stage and kept the plantation theme alive, operating within the racial stereotypes established by prewar whites in blackface. The most famous black minstrel of the nineteenth century, Billy Kersands, drew huge audiences with his portrayals of ignorant and comical characters. Yet as the plantation theme became the preserve of black players, some of the early criticism of slavery crept back into the productions. When black minstrels romanticized the Old South, their nostalgia was reserved for slaves. Meanwhile, the largest and most successful minstrel shows retained their exclusively white casts and their heavy-handed racism.

As productions grew more ornate and expensive, show business entrepreneurs put smaller local troupes out of business or swallowed them up into national companies. From more than 60 troupes in the late 1860s, the number of minstrel troupes fell to just 13 by the early 1880s. Differences from one company to the next diminished as minstrel shows became uniform and somewhat bland. Yet, more popular than ever, they expanded their audiences into the far West and the deep South. By 1890 a handful of huge entertainment moguls controlled the minstrel shows.

Minstrel shows never lost their nostalgic appeal to rural America. However, by the late nineteenth century they looked more and more like vaudeville, an art form that was born and bred in the big city.

The Origins of Vaudeville

Unlike the minstrels, vaudeville shows did not rely on nostalgia. Rather, vaudeville and its cheaper cousins (concert saloons and dollar theaters) flourished in American cities after elites succeeded in distinguishing serious theater from variety shows. As the cost of a ticket to a Shakespeare production rose beyond the means of most working people, urban audiences turned to inexpensive houses that offered music, singing, sketches, and variety acts. At first the audiences in such theaters were rowdy and exclusively male. Yet these concert saloons and variety theaters attracted patrons from up and down the social scale. In 1883 a Chicago guidebook claimed that the city's variety theaters were patronized not only by "the lower class of society, but [by] journalists, professional men, bankers, railroad officials, politicians, and men of rank in society." Even so, there were no blacks.

Increasingly, however, there were women. Beginning in the 1880s, a handful of show business entrepreneurs tried to develop variety theaters that appealed to audiences with both men and women. The respectability of a mixed audience was one of the distinguishing signs of vaudeville. Vaudeville producers booked a variety of acts to appeal to a broad audience. They also developed continuous performances, which allowed patrons to come to a vaudeville show any time of the day or evening. Continuous performances kept the prices down, thereby increasing the size of the potential audience. Locating downtown in the heart of the city had the same effect. Theater owners also regulated smoking and, over time, banned alcohol consumption, thus promoting the image of family entertainment. Finally, they booked great opera singers or distinguished musicians for brief appearances, in a conscious effort to enhance vaudeville's reputation for respectability.

BILLY KERSANDS.
CALLENDER'S (GEORGIA) MINSTRELS.

Billy Kersands African American minstrels such as Billy Kersands moderated the racism characteristic of the extremely popular white minstrels.

Growing audiences made it possible for vaudeville producers to construct huge and ornate theatrical "palaces" that housed ever more elaborate productions. The high cost of such theaters kept the number of competitors down. As a result, a handful of companies came to dominate the vaudeville theater industry, much as minstrel companies had become concentrated in the hands of a few owners. By the turn of the century, vaudeville was one of the most popular forms of public entertainment in American cities. But minstrel shows and vaudeville theaters were not the only places Americans went during their leisure time.

Sports Become Professional

As growing numbers of Americans went to the theater to be entertained, still more went to the baseball park or sports arena. For a significant segment of the urban population, sports became something to watch rather than something to do.

AMERICA AND THE WORLD

>> World's Fairs

To celebrate the accomplishments of urban and industrial society, the city of London hosted a spectacular world's fair at the Crystal Palace in 1851. Over the next 50 years the cities of the Western world became showcases for the technological and cultural achievements of industrial capitalism. By 1900 there had been expositions in Paris, Vienna, Brussels, Antwerp, Florence, Amsterdam, Dublin, and even Sydney, Australia. Most celebrated the achievements of the host countries and the civic pride of their sponsoring cities, as well as the triumph of technology and the progress of humanity. American fairs were no exception. Several major American cities—including St. Louis, San Francisco, and Chicago—sponsored world expositions in the late nineteenth and early twentieth centuries.

The first major world's fair in the United States took place in Philadelphia in 1876, timed to commemorate the centennial of American independence. In keeping with the theme of global interaction, the fair's sponsors asked the nations of the world to build pavilions of their own. The pavilions were arranged to reflect not the harmony of nations, but the differences among the world's "races." Americans were only beginning to develop such ideas in 1876, but the broad outlines of the racial categories were already evident. France and its colonies, "representing the Latin races," were grouped together, as were England and its colonies, "representing the Anglo-Saxon races," and "the Teutonic races," represented by Germany, Austria, and Hungary. Within 20 years, these racial categories would harden into an elaborate hierarchy that embraced all the peoples of the world.

Nowhere was this hierarchy more visible than at the greatest fair of the century, the World's Columbian Exposition in Chicago in 1893. Built on Lake Michigan several miles south of downtown, the Chicago fair had twice as many foreign buildings as its Philadelphia predecessor, covered 686 acres, and attracted 25 million visitors. The exposition was divided between the White City and the Midway Plaisance. The White City showcased American industrial might with immense steam engines and the latest consumer goods. But the Midway Plaisance boasted carnivals, the first Ferris wheel, games, and sideshows. It also featured an ethnographic exhibit providing a popular rendition of principles of scientific racism. The exhibit portrayed the "races" of the world in a hierarchy from the most civilized (Europeans) to the least civilized (Asians and Africans).

Where earlier forms of popular entertainment had romanticized preindustrial society and the rural life, the world's fairs celebrated the global economy, industrial enterprise, and urban life. The White City, the heart of the World's Columbian Exposition in Chicago, was an idealized vision of urban life. Rural simplicity had given way to the majestic city as the model for civilization.

The Cover of *The Youth's Companion,* World's Columbian Exposition at Chicago Issue, 1893 The World Columbian Exposition in Chicago was the largest of the world's fairs that became popular in the late 19th century. Among other things, they were celebrations of the technology and city life that were becoming the characteristics of modern, industrial civilization.

As the number of spectators increased, baseball and prizefighting became professionalized. Prizefighting had long been a disreputable amusement of shady bars and lower-class streets, but during the 1880s it became an organized sport attracting a huge national audience. Richard Kyle Fox, owner of the *National Police Gazette,* used his popular magazine and his considerable financial resources to transform boxing. Because Fox put up the prize money, he had the power to reform the sport. He made it both more profitable and more respectable, and he introduced standardized rules.

As prizefighting grew in popularity, entrepreneurs sponsored matches at indoor rings where they could control unruly audiences with police and security guards. Thereafter, as prizefighter John L. Sullivan explained in 1892, "the price of admission is put purposely high so as to exclude the rowdy element, and a gentleman can see the contest, feeling sure that he will not be robbed . . . or in any way be interfered with." Although prizefighting never completely lost its aura of disrepute, by the 1890s it was one of the most popular spectator sports in America, second only to baseball.

Like prizefighters, baseball players became professionals in the last half of the nineteenth century. By the 1860s baseball had become tremendously popular among city dwellers, particularly immigrants and their children. They formed leagues in urban neighborhoods all across the country. But not until 1869, when the Cincinnati Red Stockings went on tour and charged admission, did baseball become a professional spectator sport. Soon thereafter standardized rules appeared for the first time.

Within a decade the owners of eight baseball clubs had formed a National League that had all the earmarks of a corporate cartel. It restrained the power of players, restricted the number of teams to one per city, prohibited Sunday games, banned the sale of alcohol at ballparks, hired umpires, and set schedules and admission prices. Chafing under these restrictions, many players jumped to a new American Association that formed in 1882. The owners regrouped, however, and within a year the two leagues merged and quickly reinstated the restrictions on players. In reaction the players formed a league of their own but were unable to match the wealth and power of the owners. By the mid-1890s the National League controlled professional baseball.

Baseball idealized the principle of success based purely on merit. Objective statistics identified the best players without respect to their personal background. A model of ordered competition, the baseball meritocracy provided a useful lesson in the way capitalist society was supposed to work. Professional players became working-class heroes, many of them having risen from factories and slums. But professional baseball reflected the realities as well as the ideals of American capitalism. The owners' cartel prevented professional athletes from taking advantage of the market. In addition, baseball's meritocracy had no place for the merits of black players. Even the seating arrangements in ballparks reflected America's social divisions. Working-class fans sat in the bleachers, the middle class occupied the stands, and elites took the box seats.

The popularity of sports was reflected in the growing numbers of participants as well as spectators. As daily work became more sedentary, especially for white-collar workers, Americans spent more time in physical recreation. During the late nineteenth century, "the sporting life" became an American pastime. The

Women and Men on Bicycles in New York City, on Riverside Drive Prosperity and shorter working hours gave many middle-class Americans more leisure time than ever before. Bicycling was only one of the many physical activities that became wildly popular in the late 19th century.

popularity of bicycling exploded, for example, particularly after the invention of the modern "safety bike" in 1888. Within a decade there were 10 million bicycles in the United States. Men joined the YMCA or organized local baseball teams. At Harvard, Yale, and Princeton young men took up football, basketball, and rowing. At Smith, Vassar, and Berkeley young women played baseball, basketball, and tennis. In urban neighborhoods ethnic groups organized Irish, Italian, and German baseball teams. Women began riding bicycles, swimming, and playing golf and croquet.

But appearances were deceptive. The sports craze mirrored the inequalities and anxieties of industrial America. Men who believed that independence was a sign of masculinity became concerned that wage labor would make them soft and "feminine." A vocal segment of the American elite turned to athletic activities as an antidote to the supposedly feminizing tendencies of industrial capitalism. Theodore Roosevelt, the product of an old and wealthy New York family, and who became president of the United States, believed that "commercial civilization" placed too little stress on "the more virile virtues." There was, Roosevelt argued, "no better way of counteracting this tendency than by encouraging bodily exercise and especially the sports which develop such qualities as courage, resolution and endurance."

As baseball and prizefighting became popular and professional, elites reacted by glorifying the amateur ideal, embracing vigorous athletic activity for its own sake rather than for monetary reward. In the late nineteenth century wealthy Americans pursued the sporting life at elite colleges, exclusive racetracks, and private athletic clubs, country clubs, and yacht clubs. By the turn of the century, the most exclusive

colleges in the Northeast had formed football's Ivy League, a designation that became synonymous with elite private universities.

The rigors of sport taught elite men how to face the rigors of business competition, weeded out the weak, and prepared society's leaders for the contest of daily life. Thus the elite's attraction to rugged sports reinforced a self-serving view of American society: in an increasingly global and competitive capitalism the best nations, like the best men, would rise to the top.

The most significant attempt to spread such values was the founding of the Young Men's Christian Association (YMCA) in 1851. By 1894 there were 261 YMCAs across the nation. A strong reform impulse sustained the YMCA movement. Its founders hoped that organized recreational activity would distract workers from labor radicalism. Classroom instruction and organized games would assimilate immigrants to the laws, customs, and language of the United States. Take away Anthony Comstock's fanatic tinge, and the YMCA can be seen as an extension of the movement to suppress vice: it hoped to provide wholesome amusements to young men who might otherwise succumb to the temptations of city life.

The Elusive Boundaries of Male and Female

Anthony Comstock saw the city as a place where traditional morality broke down, particularly standards of sexual propriety. In fact, the political economy of industrial capitalism and the triumph of wage labor compelled men and women to rethink traditional conceptions of masculinity and femininity. As they did so, spectacular new cities and newfound leisure time offered Americans unprecedented opportunities to test the conventional boundaries of sexual identity.

The Victorian Construction of Male and Female

Until the mid-1700s most European doctors believed that there was only one sex: females were simply inferior, insufficiently developed males. Sometime after 1750, however, scientists and intellectuals began to argue that males and females were fundamentally different, that they were "opposite" sexes. For the first time it was possible to argue that women were naturally less interested in sex than men or that men were "active" while women were "passive." Nature itself seemed to justify the infamous double standard that condoned sexual activity by men but punished women for the same thing.

In the nineteenth century, Victorians drew even more extreme differences between men and women. Taking its name from the long reign of Britain's Queen Victoria, the "Victorian" era is often stereotyped as an age of sexual repression and cultural conservatism. Like many stereotypes, the image of the puritanical Victorian is simplistic but not without a grain of truth. Victorian boys were reared on moralistic stories of heroes who overcame their fears. In this way boys were prepared for the competitive worlds of business and politics, worlds from which women were largely excluded. To be a "man" in industrial America was to work in the rough-and-tumble world of the capitalist market. Men proved themselves by their success at making a living and therefore at taking care of a wife and children.

Victorian men defined themselves as rational creatures whose reason was threatened by their overwhelming sexual drives. Physical exertion was an important device for controlling a man's powerful sexual urges. A growing number of physicians warned that masturbation was an unacceptable outlet for these drives. Medical experts urged men to channel their sexual energies into strenuous activities such as sports and, conveniently enough, wage labor. Masculinity was defined as the ability to leave the confines of the home and compete successfully in the capitalist labor market.

Where masculinity became a more rigid concept, femininity became less certain. Women's schools established their own sports programs. Thousands of women took up bicycling, tennis, and other physical activities. Yet at the same time the stereotype persisted that women were too frail to engage in the hurly-burly of business and enterprise. Lacking the competitive instinct of the male, the female was destined to become a wife and mother within the protective confines of the home. Just as men congregated in social clubs and sports teams, a "female world of love and ritual" developed. Middle-class women often displayed among themselves a passionate affection that was often expressed in nearly erotic terms. But genuinely passionate female sexuality was deeply disturbing to the Victorians. Evidence of sexual passion among women was increasingly diagnosed, mostly by male doctors, as a symptom of a new disorder called "neurasthenia."

Over time the differences between men and women were defined in increasingly medical terms. Victorian doctors redefined homosexuality as a medical abnormality, a perversion, and urged the passage of laws outlawing homosexual relations. The new science of gynecology powerfully reinforced popular assumptions about the differences between men and women. Distinguished male physicians argued that the energy women expended in reproduction left them unable to withstand the rigors of higher education. In extreme cases physicians would excise a woman's clitoris to thwart masturbation or remove her ovaries to cure neurasthenia.

On the assumption that motherhood was a female's natural destiny, doctors pressed to restrict women's access to contraception and to prohibit abortion. Before the Civil War many Americans tolerated abortion in the first three months of pregnancy, though they did not necessarily approve of it. This began to change as the medical profession seized control over the regulation of female reproduction. The American Medical Association (AMA, founded in 1847) campaigned to restrict the activities not only of quacks and incompetents but also of female midwives and abortionists. Doctors, most of whom were males, accepted prevailing assumptions about the maternal destiny of women. Hence doctors opposed attempts by women to interfere with pregnancy. The AMA supported passage of the Comstock Law, which outlawed the sale of contraception. Doctors also pushed successfully to criminalize abortion.

Victorians Who Questioned Traditional Sexual Boundaries

In a new economy based on wage labor large numbers of Americans, especially young men, now found themselves with cash and leisure time. The anonymity of huge cities gave them the opportunity to defy established standards of sexual behavior. Freed from the constraints of parents and the scrutiny of small-town life, wage earners frequented prostitutes in unprecedented numbers, attended shows that featured sexually provocative entertainers, read erotic novels, and purchased pornographic prints. Many Americans began to explore unconventional sexual practices.

The major venues of popular amusement flouted Victorian standards of propriety by using sexual titillation to attract and entertain audiences. Can-can girls, off-color jokes, and comedy skits focusing on the war of the sexes were increasingly popular. Even the styles of clothing that consumers purchased in mass quantities were a rejection of the stifling conventions of the Victorian middle class. Trousers got looser, starched collars disappeared, and women's dresses were simplified and became considerably more comfortable. The sensuous human body became an

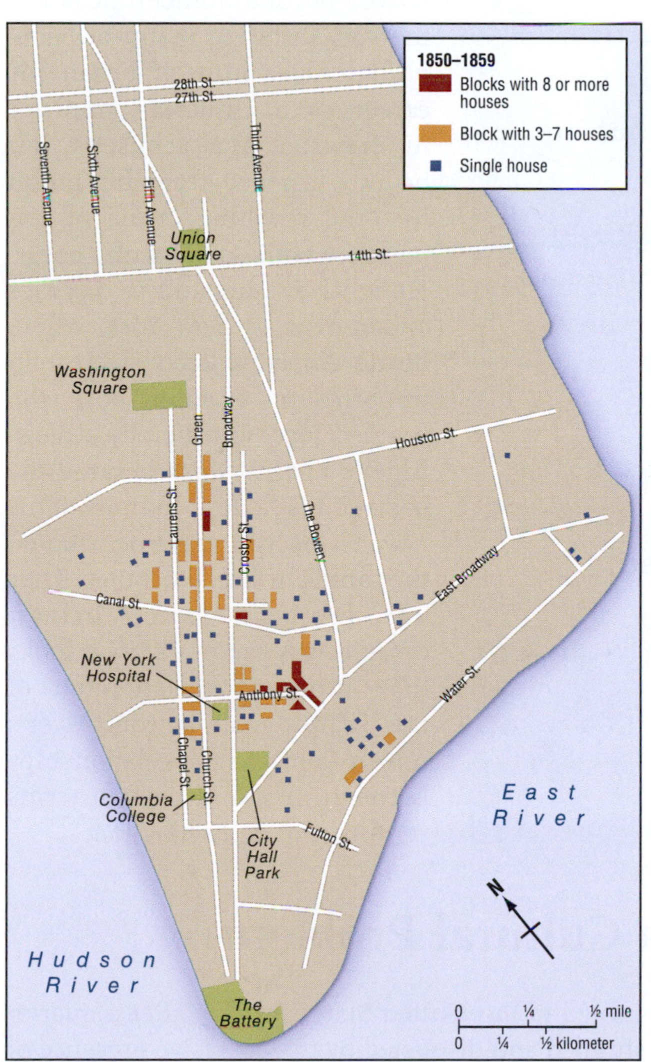

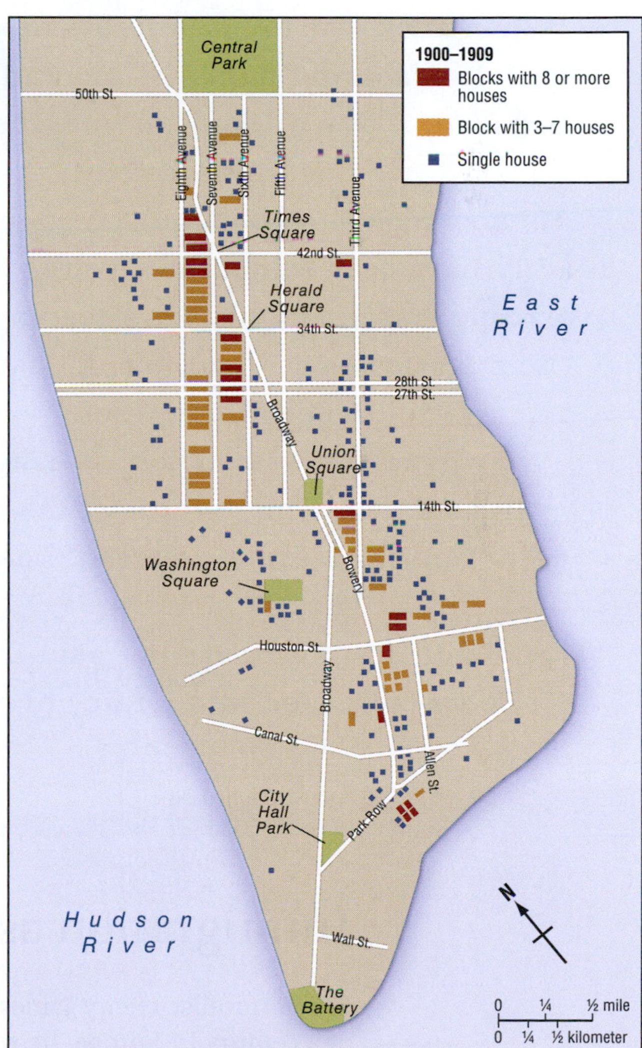

Map 18-1 Houses of Prostitution, 1850–1859 and 1900–1909 One measure of the sexual freedom characteristic of city life was the explosive increase in prostitution. As the demand for prostitution rose, so did attempts to suppress it. *Timothy J. Gilfoyle,* City of Eros *(New York: W. W. Norton, 1992), p. 33.*

object of fascination in much of the popular culture. Minstrels, musical variety shows, and the vaudeville theater all glorified female sexuality. For the first time male sports heroes were openly admired for their physiques.

There were homoerotic themes running through Horatio Alger's popular novels. Once rescued from rags and gainfully employed, Alger's hero typically set up house with a roommate. These households were fastidiously neat, and their inhabitants were thrifty and sober. The only difference from an ideal middle-class household was that both inhabitants were male. In one case, two male roommates, having both been saved and made respectable, actually "adopted" a little boy, a street urchin named "Mark the Matchboy." But the novels often moved beyond homoeroticism to the very different realm of pedophilia. Alger himself began his career as a Unitarian minister in Brewster, Massachusetts, but he was expelled from his pulpit for "the revolting crime of unnatural familiarity with boys." He left New England in disgrace and moved to New York, where he developed a keen interest in the problems of young boys who roamed loose on the city streets. Alger's charity work became the basis of his fiction. In most of his novels, the young heroes shared the same physical attributes. They were dirty but handsome. In most cases it was the boy's good looks that attracted the attention of the wealthy male patron. Alger's novels depicted the relationships between men and boys in terms reminiscent of a seduction.

> **[I]n spite of his dirt and rags there was something about Dick that was attractive. It was easy to see that if he had been clean and well dressed he would have been decidedly good-looking. . . .**
>
> **When Dick was dressed in his new attire, with his face and hands clean, and his hair brushed, it was difficult to imagine that he was the same boy.**
>
> **He now looked quite handsome, and might readily have been taken for a young gentleman, except that his hands were red and grimy.**
>
> **"Look at yourself," said Frank, leading him before the mirror.**
>
> **"By gracious!" said Dick, staring back in astonishment, "that isn't me, is it?"**
>
> **"Don't you know yourself?" asked Frank, smiling.**
>
> **"It reminds me of Cinderella," said Dick, "when she was changed into a fairy princess."**
>
> HORATIO ALGER, *Ragged Dick*

Immigration as a Cultural Problem

When novelist Henry James returned to the United States in 1907 after a quarter of a century in Europe, he was stunned and disgusted by the pervasive presence of immigrants in New York City. On the streetcars, he confronted "a row of faces, up and down, testifying, without exception, to alienism unmistakable, alienism undisguised and unashamed." James was one of the many native-born Americans who assumed that their culture was Protestant, democratic, and English speaking. They

were deeply disturbed, therefore, by the arrival of vast numbers of immigrants who were none of those things, and by the way ethnic subcultures seemed to flourish in United States cities. Yet among immigrants and their children, an ethnic identity was often a sign of assimilation into a broader American culture.

Josiah Strong Attacks Immigration

"Every race which has deeply impressed itself on the human family has been the representative of some great idea," Josiah Strong wrote in *Our Country*. Greek civilization was famed for its beauty, he explained, the Romans for their law, and the Hebrews for their purity. The Anglo-Saxon race had two great ideas to its credit, Strong argued. The first was the love of liberty, and the second was "pure spiritual Christianity." Published in 1885, Strong's best-selling book was revised and reprinted in 1891 and serialized in newspapers across America. Strong spoke to the concerns of vast numbers of native-born Americans who saw themselves as the defenders of Anglo-Saxon culture. Strong was optimistic that as representatives of "the largest liberty, the purest Christianity, the highest civilization," the powerful Anglo-Saxon race would "spread itself over the earth."

> **Go and see in our public schools the children of German, Irish, Bohemian, and Italian parents, waving the Stars and Stripes on the glorious Fourth, and you will fully appreciate the meaning of my statement, that education is solving the problem.**
>
> RICHARD BARTHOLDT, 1896

But there was a problem. Strong and his followers believed that the Anglo-Saxon in America was threatened by the arrival of millions of immigrants. By 1900 more than 10 million Americans were foreign born. The typical immigrant, he warned, was not a freedom-loving Anglo-Saxon Protestant but a "European peasant." Narrow-minded men and women "whose moral and religious training has been meager or false," immigrants brought crime to America's cities and undermined the nation's politics. Immigrants voted in blocks, and their influence was enhanced by the fact that they were concentrated in big cities. "[T]here is no more serious menace to our civilization," Strong warned, "than our rabble-ruled cities."

At the core of the problem was the fact that immigrants could not be assimilated into the American way of life. "Our safety demands the assimilation of these strange populations," Strong wrote. But they were coming in such huge numbers that assimilation was becoming impossible (see Map 18–2). Worst of all—in Strong's view—the Catholic Church held millions of immigrants in its grip, filling their heads with superstition rather than "pure Christianity." It did not help that immigrants had large numbers of children. Through its elaborate network of parochial schools, the Catholic Church was training new generations to love tyranny rather than liberty.

Strong and his readers need not have worried. The millions of immigrants who came to the United States adapted quickly to American society. Indeed, Strong misread much of his own evidence. By cultivating the German vote or the Irish vote, for example, political machines went far toward assimilating immigrants into American political culture. Nor were immigrants as slavishly subservient to the Catholic

Immigrants Immigrants often crowded into "tenements," a new form of apartment building that actually improved living conditions for many of America's poor city dwellers.

Church as Strong thought. In the end, the church played an ambiguous role in the cultural history of American immigrants.

From Immigrants to Ethnic Americans

Critics like Strong scarcely noticed the regional and class differences that immigrants brought with them. In the middle of the nineteenth century, most immigrants came with loyalties to their regions and villages, but not to their nationality. In New York City German-speaking immigrants thought of themselves primarily as Bavarian or Prussian rather than as German. Irish immigrants identified with their home counties more than their native country. Immigrant churches across America were torn by such regional conflicts.

After immigrants arrived in the United States, however, regional differences began to decline. One reason was the growth of secular fraternal organizations. Fraternal organizations often began as mutual aid societies designed to help newcomers find jobs and housing. In 1893 mineworkers formed the Pennsylvania Slovak Catholic Union to help cover burial expenses for those killed in the mines. Most often, however, middle-class immigrants took the lead in forming fraternal organizations; in other cases local priests played prominent roles. Regardless of their leadership, about half of all immigrants eventually joined ethnic fraternal societies.

As they grew, fraternal organizations became national in their scope, as immigrants constructed a new "ethnic" identity that united all members under a single

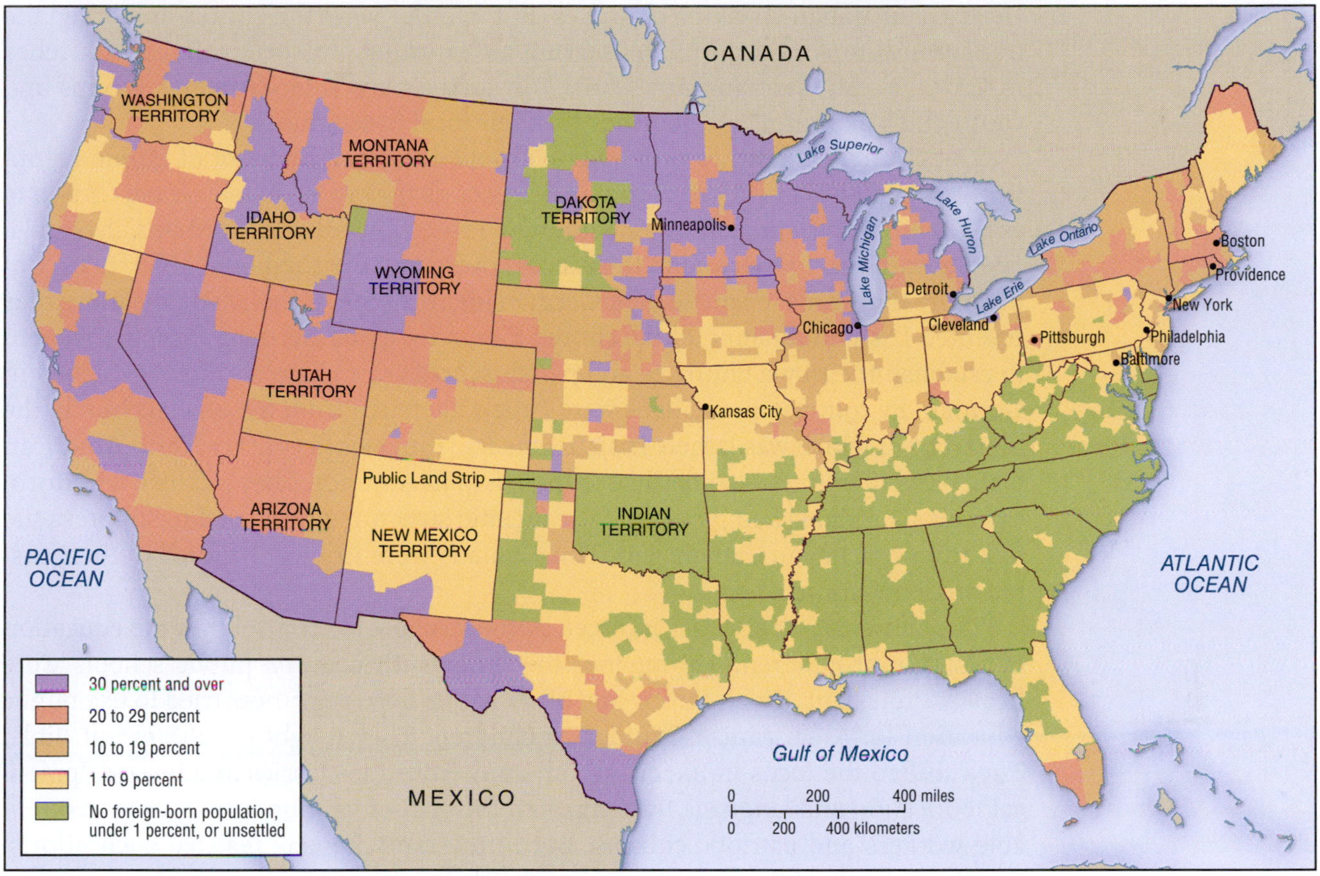

Map 18–2 Population of Foreign Birth by Region, 1880 *Clifford L. Lord and Elizabeth H. Lord,* Lord & Lord Historical Atlas of the United States *(New York: Holt, 1953).*

national rubric. In some cases immigrant businessmen led the drive toward the development of a unified ethnic identity. Marco Fontana, who ran the Del Monte company in California, encouraged the growth of an "Italian" identity among his workers. He found that regional loyalties hindered the efficient operation of his enterprises. Eventually, immigrants began to think of themselves as members of ethnic groups that shared the same national ancestry.

It was not merely coincidental that immigrants developed "national" identities in the United States. Nationalism was spreading throughout the Western world during the nineteenth century. While immigrants in America were coming to see themselves as Irish or Italian, the same thing was happening back home in Ireland and Italy. In the United States the Civil War had unleashed a wave of nationalistic fervor, and a series of liberal revolutions did the same thing in Europe. As the decades passed, immigrants brought to America an increasingly powerful sense of their ethnic identities.

The Catholic Church and Its Limits in Immigrant Culture

The Roman Catholic Church played a complicated role in the development of ethnic cultures among immigrants. In some cases churches were established to preserve Old World traditions. Local priests sometimes collected donations to build

German- or Italian-speaking churches. But in other ways the church smoothed the transition into American life by serving as a mutual aid society. Polish churches in Chicago and German parishes in Milwaukee used their women's groups and youth clubs as mutual aid societies for their local immigrants.

The church sometimes unintentionally sped the development of ethnic identities. The Irish became more devout in America as they came to rely on the church to assist them in resisting an overwhelmingly Protestant culture. Germans also gravitated toward the church and in the process overcame their regional differences. But the more they came to equate their German identity with Catholicism, the more they resented Irish domination of the church hierarchy. Thus German Catholics worked to establish their own churches and parish schools or to have sermons preached in German. By contrast, the Italians were largely alienated from the official church, the hierarchy of which was largely Irish. By the late nineteenth century North American bishops were trying to standardize Catholicism in America. They published uniform catechisms, established powerful bureaucratic structures, and tried to suppress the folk rituals of Italian Catholicism. Thus Italians were ironically united in their suspicion of the church.

The church's power was reinforced by the struggle for control over the education of immigrant children. Throughout the nineteenth century, public schools were heavily Protestant. Josiah Strong and other native-born reformers tried to use public education to "Americanize" immigrant children. They taught the Protestant Bible. They shifted the focus in the classroom away from the classics and toward "practical" education and language training, with the goal of turning immigrants into reliable workers and patriotic citizens. But immigrants fiercely resisted such efforts, and the bulwark of their resistance was the church.

During the second half of the nineteenth century both the Catholic and Lutheran churches established parochial school systems to protect immigrant children from the biases of public education. So comprehensive was the Catholic Church's effort that by 1883 all but two parishes in the city of Chicago had their own parochial schools. Ironically, parochial education contributed to assimilation among immigrants. Catholic or Lutheran schools in Irish or German parishes reinforced the growth of distinctively American ethnic identities and bound ethnicity to an increasingly standardized and Americanized Catholicism or Lutheranism.

Immigrant Cultures

Despite assimilation, the ethnic identities that immigrants developed in America remained distinctive. Irish Americans, for example, fused together songs from various parts of Ireland and added piano accompaniment. Similarly, Polish immigrant bands expanded beyond the traditional violin of their homelands by adding accordions, clarinets, and trumpets. But the results were still distinctively Polish American or Irish American music. Hundreds of immigrant theaters sprang up offering productions that adjusted traditional plot lines to the New World. Jewish plays told of humble peddlers who outwitted their prosperous patrons. Italian folktales emphasized the importance of the family. In these ways distinctive ethnic identities, adapted to urban and industrial America, developed.

One of the most distinctive features of immigrant culture was family size. At a time when middle-class families had only two or three children, immigrant families remained large. There were sound economic reasons for this. There were no child-labor laws restricting the employment of minors and few compulsory-education laws requiring children to attend school. Working-class families relied heavily on the incomes of their children, particularly teenagers. Children in the immigrant working class were expected to contribute to the economic well-being of their families.

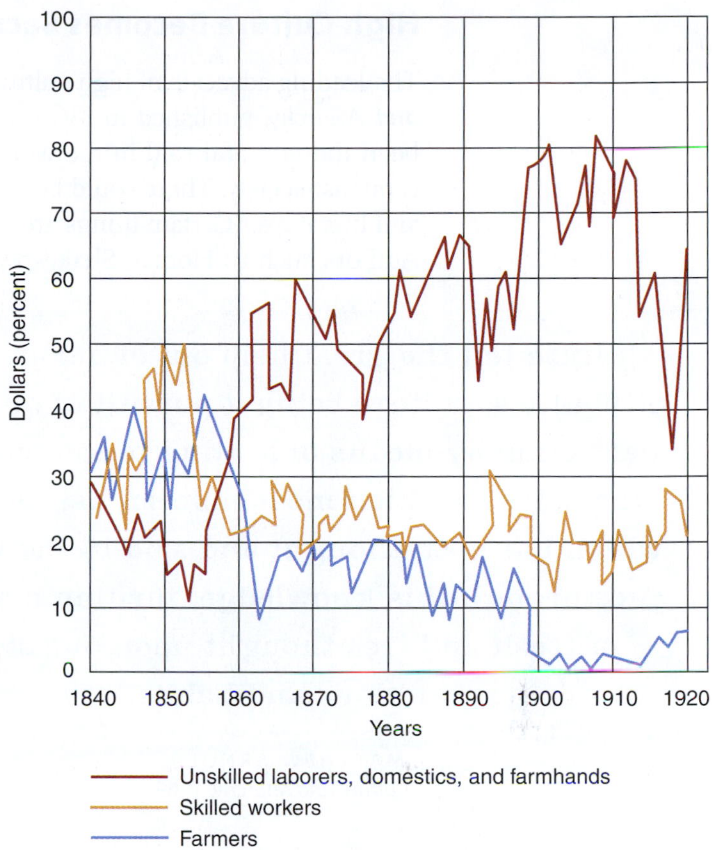

Figure 18-2 Working-Class Immigration, 1840–1920 *U.S. Bureau of the Census.*

At the turn of the century, Italian mothers in Buffalo, New York, had an average of 11 children. Among Polish wives the average was closer to eight. In Pennsylvania's coal-mining district, working-class immigrant women had 45 percent more children than native-born women. But the death rate among immigrant children was also high. In 1900, one out of three Polish and Italian mothers had seen one of their children die before his or her first birthday.

As ethnicity developed in the late nineteenth century, class divisions were increasingly difficult to isolate from cultural distinctions. The middle class, for example, was overwhelmingly native born, white, Anglo-Saxon, and Protestant. The working class was, by contrast, African American, foreign born, Catholic, or Jewish. By 1900, 75 percent of the manufacturing workers in the United States were immigrants or the children of immigrants. In large cities, five out of six new manufacturing jobs were filled by immigrants and their children. In the South, wage laborers were overwhelmingly black sharecroppers. It was in this context that educated elites constructed a definition of high culture that would distinguish the middle classes from the allegedly uncultivated and uncultured working classes.

The Creation of High Culture

During the second half of the nineteenth century many leading intellectuals sought to isolate and define a tradition, *high culture,* that stretched through Western history from ancient Greece and Rome to the present. By the 1890s high culture embodied principles of social, cultural, and political hierarchy that were firmly installed in museums, libraries, and universities across the United States. A "Western tradition" had been created as an antidote to the new forms of popular culture that had emerged in the same decades.

High Culture Becomes Sacred

The leading advocate of high culture was an Englishman, Matthew Arnold. In *Culture and Anarchy*, published in 1869, Arnold promoted the study of "the best which has been thought and said in the world" as a source of stability amidst the "anarchy" of capitalist society. There could be no question as to which were "the best" works of art and literature. "Certain things are not disputable," *Harper's Magazine* declared in 1867. Authors such as Homer, Shakespeare, and Dante "are towering facts like the Alps or the Himalayas. . . . It is not conceivable that the judgment of mankind upon those names will ever be reversed." American elites looking for firm moral guidelines were establishing a canon of great cultural achievements and turning to it the way earlier generations had looked to holy scripture. Secular culture took on the qualities of the sacred.

> **Culture [is] the great help out of our present difficulties; culture being a pursuit of our total perfection by means of getting to know, on all the matters which most concern us, the best which has been thought and said in the world; and through this knowledge, turning a stream of fresh and free thought upon our stock notions and habits.**
>
> MATTHEW ARNOLD,
> *Culture and Anarchy*, 1869

Lurking beneath the sacred view of culture was the fear that the modern world had undermined traditional values, especially religious values. "Organizations are splitting asunder, institutions are falling into decay, customs are becoming uncustomary," one observer complained in 1865. Particularly troubling was the apparent decline in religious fervor. Middle-class men and women often confessed to a loss of their own faith.

The middle class never lost its faith entirely. On the contrary, Victorians retained their overwhelmingly Protestant orientation and their deep suspicion of Roman Catholicism. What they lost was a strong theology and missionary zeal. Victorians moved restlessly from one denomination to another, but few found the spiritual satisfaction or moral guidance they sought. As religious fervor waned, the Victorian middle class looked for comfort in more secular pursuits.

Thomas Wentworth Higginson typified this shift. Nurtured in the reform movements of antebellum New England, Higginson had been an abolitionist and supporter of women's rights. During the Civil War he commanded a famed regiment of African American troops. Fully engaged in the politics of his day, Higginson was equally at home in the literary culture of his native New England, turning to culture for relief from the sordid realities of urban life and industrial capitalism.

In 1871, two years after Matthew Arnold published *Culture and Anarchy*, Higginson made a strikingly similar case. Culture, he explained, "pursues" art and science for their intrinsic worth. It "places the fine arts above the useful arts." It sacrifices "material comforts" for the sake of a "nobler" life. At its best, Higginson believed, culture "supplies that counterpoise to mere wealth which Europe vainly seeks to secure by aristocracies of birth." Like Matthew Arnold, Higginson saw culture as a defense against materialism.

Higginson shared the Victorian conviction that culture was an attribute of the middle classes. At the top of the social order stood an increasingly dissolute and un-

restrained capitalist class. At the bottom, poor working men and women lived lives utterly devoid of gentility and cultural refinement. Yet these very classes, the greedy capitalists at the top and the ignorant masses below, seemed to grow in influence as capitalism developed. To counteract this threat, American elites worked to transform American cities into centers of high art and cultural distinction.

The Emergence of a Cultural Establishment

Advertisement for *Hamlet* Shakespeare was the most popular playwright in mid-19th-century America. This 1863 playbill advertised the appearance of one of the most popular Shakespearean actors of the time.

In the early nineteenth century Shakespeare was the most popular playwright in America. Traveling through the country in the 1830s, Alexis de Tocqueville encountered Shakespeare even in "the recesses of the forests of the New World. There is hardly a pioneer's cabin but that does not contain a few odd volumes of Shakespeare." In established theaters, Shakespearean plays were performed more than any others, and the repertoire was not limited to a few classics. American audiences were familiar with a substantial body of Shakespeare's work.

A Shakespearean play was usually performed as the centerpiece of an entire evening's entertainment that included music, dancing, acrobats, magicians, and comedians. The show generally ended with a short humorous skit, or farce. Audiences attending these shows came from all walks of life, and they often made a noisy crowd. They generally preferred highly melodramatic renditions of Shakespeare in which the moral ambiguities were smoothed out and the lessons made sharp and clear. Ideally the ending was always satisfying. Good always triumphed over evil. Instead of committing suicide, Romeo and Juliet lived happily ever after. By 1850 Americans were so familiar with Shakespeare that politicians could safely make allusions to his plays without fear of losing an audience.

All of this changed in the second half of the nineteenth century. Shakespeare was redefined as high culture, and performances of his plays were separated from popular entertainment. This shift was evident as early as the 1850s, when a San Francisco theater announced that its production of *A Midsummer Night's Dream* would be performed by itself, with "NO FARCE." The entertainments that had once accompanied Shakespearean performances became the basis of the vaudeville theater, and theater audiences became segregated by class. The respectable classes retreated from the boisterous houses into quieter theaters, where the prices rose beyond the means of ordinary working people.

The same thing happened to opera and to orchestral music. Opera changed from an eclectic and highly popular art form to an elite entertainment. Italian immigrants who began arriving in the United States in the late nineteenth century noticed the difference. Back home opera was widely popular, and certain composers, Verdi in particular, were heroic figures whose work addressed the national aspirations of millions of Italians. But in America opera had become associated with high fashion and elite culture, and the opening of the opera season became synonymous with the opening of the "social season" among the very rich.

AMERICAN LANDSCAPE

>> The Modern University

At the same time that American elites were endowing museums and libraries, they stepped up their commitment to the establishment of distinguished private universities. Cornell, Johns Hopkins, Vanderbilt, Stanford, and the University of Chicago all appeared between the late 1860s and the 1890s. Wealthy businessmen had good reason to endow great universities. The political economy of industrial capitalism rested on technological developments, which in turn depended on up-to-date scientific learning. Research universities played a central role in such developments and provided the training for the new business and engineering elite. And finally, corporate philanthropists agreed with many Americans that a great Western nation required great universities.

The new colleges reflected a new conception of how universities should be organized. Daniel Coit Gilman, the first president of the Johns Hopkins University in Baltimore, created specialized departments of history, English, and the various sciences that were responsible for recommending appointments and promotions and for developing courses. He encouraged the publication of academic journals and established the first university press in 1878. Gilman had created the modern university with a faculty of specialists dedicated to research and the training of other scholars. His innovations spread quickly and led to the undergraduate major; the system of numbered courses, unit requirements, and electives; and PhD programs with research seminars and dissertations based on original research.

In this new setting, the study of modern literature entered the college curriculum for the first time. Some professors, influenced by German scholarship, emphasized sentence structures, word roots, and forms of publication. This approach appealed to those who sought to make the study of literature into a science. But beneath the surface was a set of assumptions about the intrinsic superiority of western European languages. A leading Oxford scholar, Friedrich Max Müller, saw "an unbroken chain between us and Cicero and Aristotle." Müller and his American followers created a canon of great works that they believed defined culture of the "West." They also defined the study of literature as the preserve of specialists.

Leading scholars in the new "social sciences" of sociology, anthropology, and political science also divided the world into great and inferior nations. At the top stood the so-called Teutonic nations of western Europe and North America. This hierarchy, far from reflecting the biases of its creators, was grounded in the objective methods of pure science—or so anthropologists, sociologists, and professional economists claimed. Science was becoming the model for the production of all human knowledge.

As the modern university emerged it reflected the inequalities of the age. Only a tiny fraction of Americans attended college, most of them were men, most of the men were native born, and very few of those rose out of the working class. State universities and land-grant colleges were more open to a wider range of students, but in the late nineteenth century colleges and universities hardened rather than softened the barriers of caste and class. In the late twentieth century Americans would come to view widespread access to a college education as one of the great promises of democracy. But a century earlier the greatest seats of learning produced some of the most sustained attacks on democracy itself. ●

The Vanderbilt University Campus, ca. 1900 Founded in 1873, Vanderbilt was one of a large number of private and public universities established in the late 19th century.

Something similar was happening to orchestral music. In the first half of the nineteenth century local bands sprang up in thousands of communities across America (3,000 of them by 1860) with a repertoire that included popular and classical pieces. Beginning in the 1840s, classical music became the preserve of elite symphony orchestras in large cities.

Orchestra Hall in Chicago This is one of many stately auditoriums built to house America's major symphony orchestras in the second half of the 19th century. Pictured here are the Chicago Symphony Orchestra and Theodore Thomas, Auditorium Theater, 1897.

Symphonies and opera companies cost a lot of money. Orchestras like the New York Philharmonic and the Chicago Symphony needed expensive new halls. Opera companies needed endowments. Serious theater needed generous patrons. Thus great infusions of private wealth were necessary to support lavish arts programs. In the late nineteenth century, the rich formed an alliance with leading performers and intellectuals to create a cultural establishment that endures to this day. Opera houses and symphony halls were built with and sustained by the patronage of the wealthy. They were the architectural embodiment of high culture.

Great cities required great museums as well. Americans built a stunning array of secular temples devoted to the world's great art. Major museums were founded in New York, Boston, Philadelphia, and Chicago in the 1870s. Spectacular new public libraries appeared at the same time. By 1900 many Americans had come to associate "culture" with impressive institutions lodged in major cities. By this reasoning, for example, the cultural life of Chicago was embodied not in the immigrant neighborhoods or the popular theaters, but in the Art Institute, Symphony Hall, and the Chicago Public Library.

Social Darwinism and the Growth of Scientific Racism

In 1859 Charles Darwin published his masterpiece of evolutionary theory, *On the Origin of Species.* Several scientists had already suggested that life had evolved over a long period of time, but Darwin offered the first persuasive explanation of how this might have taken place. He argued that a process of "natural selection" favored those biological changes that were most suited to the surrounding environment. In Darwinian theory, natural selection was the single most important explanation for the vast array of life forms on earth. American scientists were remarkably receptive to Darwinism. Asa Gray at Harvard and Joseph Le Conte at the University of California spread the evolutionary word in their influential textbooks on botany and geology. By 1900 virtually all the science textbooks used in American high schools embraced evolution.

Darwin's remarkable influence did not stop with the natural sciences. Social scientists applied the theory of natural selection to social evolution. This combination of social theory with evolutionary science was known as social Darwinism. Social Darwinists argued that human inequality was the outcome of a struggle for survival in which the fittest rose to the top of the social ladder. This theory made the rich seem more fit than the poor; it made blacks seem less fit than whites. To social Darwinists, inequality was the natural order of things. In this way Darwin's theory—one of the greatest scientific discoveries of all time—was twisted into a pseudoscientific defense of the new social order of industrial capitalism.

From the moment Darwin published his findings, the theory of natural selection was invoked to sustain a theory of African racial inferiority. Racists had argued that emancipation would force blacks to compete with their white superiors and that this competition would end in the disappearance of the African race. When the 1890 census seemed to show that the African American population was declining, racial theorists rushed into print with a series of influential studies claiming to show that blacks were withering under the strain of competition with whites. In 1892 biologist Joseph Le Conte weighed in with an article on "The Race Problem in the South." In conditions of free competition with whites, Le Conte argued, blacks faced either "extinction" or permanent subordination. Only the protection of whites could shield blacks from their natural fate.

Far more influential than the Le Conte article was Frederick L. Hoffman's full-length treatise, *Race Traits and Tendencies of the American Negro,* published in 1896. Hoffman's book quickly established itself as one of the most important studies of race relations written in the nineteenth century. Hoffman himself was a statistician, and the tables and figures scattered throughout his book gave it the authoritative air of the new social sciences. All of those numbers, Hoffman claimed, led to one inescapable conclusion: ever since they had left the protective cover of slavery, blacks had shown clear signs of moral degeneration and were doomed to poverty and social inferiority.

Social scientists like Hoffman prided themselves on their commitment to the truth as it was revealed in facts and statistics. Like advocates of high culture, sociologists and anthropologists claimed to have isolated the definitive truths of human society. But not all "realists" sought solace in the past or justified the inequalities of the present. The best American artists of the late nineteenth century openly embraced the realities of urban and industrial America.

Artistic Realism Embraces Urban and Industrial America

In the second half of the nineteenth century, artists and writers embraced the world that Anthony Comstock wanted to suppress, that Matthew Arnold wanted to escape, and that Thomas Wentworth Higginson wanted to fix. "This is the age of cities," writer Hamlin Garland declared. "We are now predominantly urban and the problem of our artistic life is practically one of city life." Artists like Garland called themselves "realists" and saw themselves as part of the first major artistic movement that was grounded in urban and industrial America. As writer Fanny Bates put it, the people of the cities "live more in realities than imagination."

The Triumph of Literary Realism

In April 1861 the *Atlantic Monthly* published a powerful story called "Life in the Iron Mills" by a writer named Rebecca Harding. Her story created a sensation. Rarely had the dreary lives of ordinary workers been presented in such relentless detail. In the decades to come, the best writers in America joined in the crusade to make fiction realistic. The leading spokesperson for realistic fiction was William Dean Howells, the author of one of the best-known realist novels, *The Rise of Silas Lapham,* and editor of the *Atlantic Monthly,* one of a handful of influential magazines that championed literary realism.

Realists tried to bridge the gap between "high" and "popular" culture by making great literature out of the details of everyday life. To "enjoy the every-day life," Sarah Orne Jewett explained in *Deephaven,* one must "find pleasure in thought and observation of simple things, and have an instinctive, delicious interest in what to other eyes is unflavored dullness." By writing about failed businessmen or runaway slaves, writers like Howells and Mark Twain hoped to reveal both courage and cowardice in the lives of ordinary men and women. This was the great achievement of Twain's *Huckleberry Finn.*

The characters in realistic novels were flawed men and women who struggled with the moral dilemmas they encountered in their daily lives. In Howells's best novel, Silas Lapham had to decide whether to mislead the men who wanted to buy his failing paint company. Huck Finn had to decide whether to turn in a runaway slave. Yet neither Lapham nor Finn was "heroic" in the way that earlier heroes were. Lapham was an ill-educated social climber who drank and talked too much. Huck Finn was a barely literate seeker of adventure who played hooky, spoke improper English, and spun absurd fantasies. In the end both Silas Lapham and Huck Finn made the right moral decisions, but neither found his decision easy to make, and Lapham suffered for having done so. Thus realism meant not merely the evocation of the themes of ordinary life, but the creation of characters who were psychologically complex and therefore more "realistic." For Henry James, psychological realism was the whole point and his characters—Isabel Archer in *Portrait of a Lady* is a good example—are among the most vivid and compelling in all American literature.

The realist movement was greeted with shock by the defenders of the genteel tradition of American letters. In March 1885 the public library committee of Concord, Massachusetts, banned *Huckleberry Finn* from its shelves, denouncing it as "the veriest trash." Members of the committee characterized Twain's masterpiece as "rough, coarse and inelegant, dealing with a series of experiences not elevating, the whole book being more suited to the slums than to intelligent, respectable people."

Realists dismissed such criticism as evidence of the "feminine" taste that prevailed in American letters, and they saw realism as a "masculine" alternative to sentimental writing that appealed to women novel readers. In their commitment to the unvarnished truth, realists thought of themselves as "virile and strong." But female realists also rejected the assumption, common to sentimental fiction, that women's lives should be bounded exclusively by the needs of their husbands and children. "The public demands realism and they will have it," the novelist Willa Cather declared. Louisa May Alcott wanted her female characters to be "strong-minded, strong-hearted, strong-souled, and strong-bodied." Realistic writers thus challenged the sentimental depiction of women as nervous, frail, and destined only for the domestic life.

Other authors, most notably Walt Whitman, pushed the radical possibilities of realism even further. Like most realists, Whitman aspired to "manly" writing. Through his poems he hoped "to exalt the present and the real, to teach the average man the glory of his daily walk and trade." He was the poet of the city who filled his verse with vivid details of urban life. For Whitman that meant he would embrace the "goodness" as well as the "wickedness" of modern America. Just as vaudeville flirted more and more openly with sexual titillation, Whitman wrote more and more openly about eroticism, as in this passage from *Leaves of Grass:*

> Have you ever loved the body of a woman?
> Have you ever loved the body of a man?
> Do you not see that they are exactly the same to all in all nations and
> times all over the earth?
>
> If anything is sacred the human body is sacred,
> And the glory and sweet of a man is the token of manhood untainted,
> And in man or woman a clean, strong, firm-fibred body, is more beau-
> tiful than the most beautiful face.

Thus Whitman, like so many realists, fused the themes of popular culture with the forms of "high" art.

Walt Whitman One of America's greatest poets, Whitman was a champion of the diversity and excitement of city life.

Painting Reality

In 1878 New York artist John Ferguson Weir declared that "art, in common with literature, is now seeking to get nearer the reality, to 'see the thing as it really is.'" Like the best writers of the post–Civil War era, the finest painters rejected romanticism. Winslow Homer and Thomas Eakins shifted the emphasis of American painting from sentiment to realism, from unspoiled nature to the facts of social life in urban and industrial America. Realists did not always paint the city, but even when they depicted rural life, or in Winslow Homer's case the life of the seafarer, realists generally avoided the romanticized scenes of nature that had been so popular in the early nineteenth century.

Winslow Homer was, in the words of one critic, a "flaming realist—a burning devotee of the actual." He left several important bodies of work, all realistic in different ways. A series of Civil War studies, notably *Prisoners From the Front* (1866), presented ordinary soldiers with ragged uniforms and worn, tired expressions. This was a sharp departure from a tradition of painting military men in heroic poses. As an illustrator for *Harper's Weekly,* the first successful mass-circulation magazine in America, Homer also drew realistic scenes of factories, railroad workers, and other aspects of industrial life.

Two of Homer's most enduring contributions were his sensitive depictions of African Americans and his remarkable portrayals of seafaring men struggling against nature. At a time when intellectuals were perfecting theories of black racial inferiority and minstrel shows presented blacks in the grossest stereotypes, Winslow Homer represented blacks as varied men and women who worked hard and struggled with dignity against the difficulties of everyday life. In the process, Homer produced some of his finest paintings.

Thomas Eakins was an even more thoroughgoing realist, determined to drain his paintings of all romantic sentiment. He wielded his paintbrush with the precision of a scientist in a laboratory. Indeed, in his effort to represent the human body with perfect accuracy, Eakins attended medical school. After studying for several years in Europe, Eakins returned to his native Philadelphia in 1870 and was soon shocking viewers with warts-and-all portraits of his own sisters. Eakins, one critic sniffed, "cares little for what the world of taste considers beautiful."

Eakins established his reputation with a series of lifelike paintings of rowers. Even at the beginning of his career, Eakins could render scenes with startlingly three-dimensional effects. In 1875, he shocked the art world once again with *The Gross Clinic,* a large canvas depicting the gruesome details of a surgical procedure. The selection committee for the 1876 Philadelphia Centennial Exposition rejected *The Gross Clinic* on the grounds that "the sense of actuality about it was . . . oppressive."

Eakins was fascinated by the human form. He photographed dozens of naked men and women and used some of them as the basis for full-scale paintings. *The Swimming Hole* (ca. 1884) was based on a photograph Eakins had taken. By 1886 the

The Swimming Hole Thomas Eakins was a pioneer in the artistic use of photography. By using photography as the basis for painting, and by using scenes from ordinary life as the basis of high art, Eakins demonstrated his commitment to artistic realism.

directors of the Academy had had enough. Eakins was fired after he pulled the loincloth from a male model posing before a group of female students.

Critics complained that Eakins was obsessed with nudity, but for Eakins himself the exact details of the human body were merely the entryway into a deeper exploration of the characters and personalities of his subjects. In the late 1880s and 1890s Eakins produced a number of portraits that were stunning both for their physiological accuracy and their psychological penetration. Like Winslow Homer's portrayals of blacks, Eakins's women were thoughtful and dignified. *Miss Amelia C. Van Buren* (1891) conveys its subject's intelligence and complexity with no sacrifice of accuracy. Eakins thereby did for painting what Henry James did for literature. Both demonstrated that distinguished works of art could be impressively realistic and at the same time deeply insightful.

Is Photography Art?

As city life became the subject matter of painters and writers, a major technological development—photography—created a new medium of artistic expression. The camera had been invented scarcely a generation earlier, in 1839, by a Frenchman named Louis Daguerre. By the early 1860s photographic technology had improved dramatically. For one thing, cameras had become more portable. Mathew Brady knew how to take advantage of it. In the fall of 1862 Brady mounted an exhibit of Civil War photographs in his New York gallery. This was the first time a large viewing public was able to see realistic pictures of the most gruesome facts of war. His exhibition had electrifying effects. By the 1880s journalists used photographs to heighten the reality, the sense of "truth," conveyed by their stories. The effect of Jacob Riis's *How the Other Half Lives,* published in 1890, was enhanced by the fact that he included a series of dramatic photographs documenting the misery of the urban poor. Photography had become part of the body of factual evidence.

The camera's eye inevitably fascinated realistic writers and artists. In the second half of the nineteenth century photography set the standard for accurate representation to which many artists aspired. Thomas Eakins, for example, used the camera to freeze images that he intended to paint on canvas. He photographed horses in motion to guide him as he painted. Eakins soon became a skilled photographer, producing hundreds of portraits of his subjects. He took numerous photos of the naked human form, and not always as a basis for later paintings. Eakins was one of the first artists to recognize the artistic element of photography itself. His work thereby raised questions that remain unanswered: Is a painting based on a photograph a work of art? Is photography art?

Some writers applauded the camera's capacity to capture the "truth." Writers as varied as Walt Whitman and Harriet Beecher Stowe used photographic metaphors to describe the effects they hoped to achieve with their words. But others were not persuaded that the photograph could ever be a genuine work of art. The camera captures only "the external facts," *The Galaxy* magazine declared, it "does not tell the whole truth."

Anthony Comstock worried a great deal about the difference between art and photography. Millions of copies of great and not-very-great works of art flooded the market in the late nineteenth century. Photographs of naked men and women suddenly became a new form of readily accessible pornography. "Is a photograph of an obscene figure or picture a work of art?" Comstock asked. "My answer is emphatically, No."

Civil War Photography Pioneered by Mathew Brady's New York studio, Civil War photography was part of a larger artistic movement toward realism. The photos were not simply graphic; the best of them were works of art.

Artists who paint nude portraits use lines, shadings, and colors in ways that "seem to clothe the figures"; their artistry diverts the viewers' attention from the nudity. Photographers have no such artistic devices at their disposal, Comstock explained. "A photograph of a nude woman in a lewd posture, with a lascivious look on her face," was to Comstock no work of art, for it lacked "the skill and talent of the artist."

Conclusion

When Comstock questioned whether photography could be art, he was participating in a larger debate about what counted as culture in the new world created by industrial capitalism. Did it include the popular culture of the city, or was American culture restricted to the nation's great libraries, universities, museums, and opera houses? And what was culture supposed to do for people? Americans argued over whether culture should maintain traditional values or boldly face up to the realities of the new political economy.

These cultural struggles easily spilled over into politics. Urban reformers proposed public policies to elevate the cultural level of slum dwellers. Elites convinced politicians to subsidize the construction of huge public libraries. Nevertheless, American politics in the late nineteenth century had not yet become cultural politics. The issues that brought Americans into the streets and into the voting booths remained, for the most part, economic issues. Just as American culture was transformed by the rise of cities and industry, the problems of industrial capitalism became the focus of American politics in the late nineteenth century.

Further Readings

John D'Emilio and Estelle Freedman, *Intimate Matters: A History of Sexuality in America* (1988). An innovative overview with important chapters on the late nineteenth century.

Elliot J. Gorn and Warren Goldstein, *A Brief History of American Sports* (1993). An intelligent introduction to the subject.

John Higham, *Strangers in the Land: Patterns of American Nativism, 1860–1925* (1955). The classic study of the response of native-born Americans to immigrants.

Lawrence Levine, *Highbrow/Lowbrow: The Emergence of Cultural Hierarchy in America* (1988). Traces the origins of the distinction between "high" and "low" culture in the nineteenth century.

John Matteson, *Louisa May Alcott and Her Father* (2007). A beautiful study of an important realist author.

Roy Rosenzweig, *Eight Hours for What We Will: Workers and Leisure in an Industrial City, 1870–1920* (1983). A pioneering work demonstrating the importance of leisure time to industrial workers.

David Shi, *Facing Facts: Realism in American Thought and Culture, 1850–1920* (1995). A broad, insightful overview.

Robert Toll, *Blacking Up: The Minstrel Show in Nineteenth-Century America* (1974). The first and still the best survey of the subject, especially good at tracing changes over time.

Alan Trachtenberg, *The Incorporation of America: Culture and Society in the Gilded Age* (1982). Shows the connections between culture and industrial society.

Who, What

>> Timeline >>

▼ 1851
YMCA is founded
First world's fair is held at Crystal Palace in London

▼ 1859
Charles Darwin publishes *On the Origin of Species*

▼ 1861
Rebecca Harding publishes "Life in the Iron Mills"

▼ 1862
Mathew Brady exhibits Civil War photos at his New York studio

▼ 1866
New York Athletic Club opens
Horatio Alger expelled from his pulpit in Brewster, Massachusetts

▼ 1869
Cincinnati Red Stockings charge admission to watch baseball games
Matthew Arnold publishes *Culture and Anarchy*

▼ 1870
Metropolitan Museum of Art and Boston Museum of Fine Arts are founded

▼ 1870s
National League is formed; baseball becomes professional

▼ 1871
Walt Whitman publishes *Democratic Vistas*

▼ 1873
New York Society for the Suppression of Vice (SSV) founded
Congress enacts the Comstock Law

▼ 1875
First Harvard-Yale football game is played
Thomas Eakins paints *The Gross Clinic*

▼ 1876
World's fair held in Philadelphia
Philadelphia Museum of Art founded
Daniel Coit Gilman becomes first president of Johns Hopkins University

Review Questions

1. In what ways was American culture "urbanized" in the late nineteenth century?
2. How did immigration affect American culture?
3. What were the major features of the high cultural establishment that developed in this period?
4. What was "artistic realism?"
5. Did American culture become more repressed or more eroticized in the second half of the nineteenth century?
6. In what ways did American culture reflect the patterns of race relations in the late nineteenth century?

Websites

On the Lower East Side. http://tenant.net/Community/LES/contents.html
The World's Columbian Exposition. http://xroads.virginia.edu/~MA96/WCE/title.html

For further review materials and resource information, please visit www.oup.com/us/ofthepeople

▼ 1878
Johns Hopkins establishes the first university press

▼ 1879
Art Institute of Chicago founded

▼ 1880s
Richard Kyle Fox professionalizes prizefighting

▼ 1881
Henry James publishes *Portrait of a Lady*

▼ 1883
Anthony Comstock publishes *Traps for the Young*

▼ 1884
Mark Twain publishes *The Adventures of Huckleberry Finn*
Thomas Eakins paints *The Swimming Hole*

▼ 1885
William Dean Howells publishes *The Rise of Silas Lapham*
Josiah Strong publishes *Our Country*

▼ 1888
Modern "safety" bike invented

▼ 1890
Jacob Riis publishes *How the Other Half Lives*

▼ 1891
Thomas Eakins paints *Miss Amelia C. Van Buren*

▼ 1893
World's Columbian Exposition held in Chicago

▼ 1894
Vaudeville producer B. F. Keith opens the New Theatre in Boston

▼ 1896
Frederick L. Hoffman publishes *Race Traits and Tendencies of the American Negro*

CHAPTER 19

Common Threads

>> How did both culture and politics reflect sharp distinctions between men and women? How did culture and politics break those distinctions down?

>> What was the overriding issue of American politics in the late nineteenth century?

>> Was American politics headed for a crisis in the 1890s?

The Politics of Industrial America 1870–1892

AMERICAN PORTRAIT

>> Luna Kellie and the Farmers' Alliance

Luna Kellie was the daughter of a railroad worker, but as a young girl she dreamed of one day raising a family on a farm of her own. Born in 1857, Luna grew up in towns along the Northern Pacific Railroad line. At one point her father did try to make a go of farming in Minnesota, but when the farm failed he moved the family to St. Louis, Missouri. There Luna met and married James T. Kellie. But she still hoped for a large family and a big house, so at the age of 18 Luna moved with her husband and their infant to a homestead in Hastings, Kansas.

Life on the prairie was a far cry from the dreams of Luna Kellie's youth. She gave birth to twelve children, two of whom died. They lived in an eight-by-twelve-foot sod house dug into the side of a hill. Overworked and exhausted, physically weakened by the strain of childbirth and constant work, Luna kept dreaming of a better future. She read an article in *Harper's* about the great geysers of Yellowstone and imagined a family trip. "Our trip never materialized," she recalled years later, "but we put in some happiest hours of life planning it."

What Luna Kellie imagined as a life of sturdy independence turned out to be an impoverished and isolated existence. It was an experience common to many American farmers, men and women alike. She tried to find connections with friends and neighbors wherever she could, but there was not much choice. Her family joined a Methodist church, but when an arrangement to care for a neighbor's cows in return for milk failed, Luna's husband became estranged from the church's pastor. Schools were even scarcer than churches, but Luna went out of her way to become active in the school district, where she took part in discussions over whether women should have the right to vote.

Luna and her husband were not able to make a go of their farm. Like many rural women, Luna shared the responsibility for managing the farm with her husband. She kept a garden, which helped feed the family and brought in extra income from the sale of chickens and eggs. As Luna taught herself how to maintain the livestock and grow fruit trees, her husband learned how to grow spring wheat on the forbidding Kansas plains. But no matter how hard they worked, a lethal combination of declining prices and high interest rates clamped the farm down in perpetual debt. After seven years Luna and her husband lost the farm. They struggled to keep themselves afloat by raising chickens, sheep, and livestock.

The more Luna Kellie came to understand the burdens on farmers in the late nineteenth century, the more attracted she was to organized efforts to relieve their plight. She became active in the Farmers' Alliance, the largest and most powerful of all such efforts. Nor was Luna Kellie alone. On the contrary, she was but one of the 250,000 women who joined the Farmers' Alliance, making it the largest women's organization in the United States at the time.

Luna Kellie was one of a large number of rural women who became active in the Populist movement.

For Kellie, the Alliance held out the hope of realizing the dreams of her youth. It advocated education for the young, scientific farming, business methods, and organized cooperation among producers. The reforms the Alliance advocated would bring progress and prosperity to rural America. They would break down the stifling isolation of rural life, bringing farmers together in cooperative enterprises and at the same time linking rural Americans to the progressive world of cities and industry. For Kellie, and for thousands of other farmers, the mere existence of the Alliance already established many of those connections. In 1892, when the Nebraska

continued

>> AMERICAN PORTRAIT *continued*

Farmers' Alliance affiliated with the National Farmers' Alliance and Industrial Union, she was elected state secretary. Kellie worked as tirelessly on Alliance business as she had on her own farm. She wrote countless letters. She edited and set the type for articles for the Alliance newspaper.

Without ever setting foot outside her home, Luna Kellie found herself at the center of a vast network of farmers who learned from each other by discussing the issues of greatest concern to men and women like themselves. Those issues started from a basic concern for improving the lives of rural Americans, but the discussions quickly expanded into broader questions of political reform. For by 1892 the Farmers' Alliance had become the backbone for the most important political insurgency of the late nineteenth century, the Populist Party.

OUTLINE

Two Political Styles

There were two distinct political styles in late nineteenth-century America: one was partisan, the other was voluntary. Partisan politics included all the eligible voters who counted themselves as Democrats or Republicans, attended party parades and electioneering spectacles, and cast their ballots in record numbers. This was largely a world of men. The second political style, voluntarism, embraced a vast network of organizations, including women's assemblies, reform clubs, labor unions, and farmers' groups.

The Triumph of Party Politics

In the late nineteenth century American men voted along very strict party lines. Political parties printed and distributed their own ballots, and loyal Republicans and

Democrats simply dropped a party ballot in the appropriate box. Party allegiances and discipline were strict, and campaigns were carefully organized. At no other time in American history did voters ally themselves so tightly to the two major parties.

And never again would so large a proportion of American men participate in presidential elections. From the 1840s through the 1860s an average of 69 percent of those eligible voted in presidential elections. During the final quarter of the century, the average rose to 77 percent. The figures were less impressive in the South, although they followed the same general pattern. Between 1876 and 1892, nearly two out of three southern men cast ballots in presidential elections. In the North, 82 percent of men went to the polls every four years between 1876 and 1892. In the presidential elections of 1896 and 1900, northern voter turnout peaked at 84 percent.

Newspapers played a critical role in maintaining this level of political participation. Most editors were strong party advocates. Papers survived with the help of official advertisements and contracts to print ballots and campaign documents. Strong-willed editors such as Horace Greeley of the *New York Tribune* and William Cullen Bryant of the *New York Evening Post* became influential party leaders. Papers editorialized relentlessly in favor of their candidates and their party and slanted stories to show their party in the most favorable light. Some papers printed logos boasting of their partisan affiliation. "Republican in everything, independent in nothing," the *Chicago Inter Ocean* declared. Newspapers thus presented to their readers a starkly partisan world in which the difference between parties was the same as the difference between good and evil.

> **A New England Village of olden time—that is to say, of some forty years ago—would have been safely and well governed by the votes of every man in it; but, now that the village has grown into a populous city, with its factories and workshops, its acres of tenements-houses, and thousands and ten thousands of restless workmen, foreigners for the most part, to whom liberty means license and politics means plunder . . ., the case is completely changed, and universal suffrage becomes a questionable blessing. Still we are told it is an inalienable right. Suppose for an instant that it were so, wild as the supposition is. The community has rights as well as the individual, and it has also duties. It is both its right and its duty to provide good government for itself, and, the moment the vote of any person or class of persons becomes an obstacle in doing so, this person or class forfeits the right to vote. . . .**
>
> FRANCIS PARKMAN,
> "The Failure of Universal Suffrage," 1878

Spectacular political campaigns reinforced the partisan attachments promoted by newspapers. The parties organized political clubs to drum up enthusiasm for elections. Military marching companies organized the party foot soldiers as well. The clubs and marching groups in turn organized an endless series of competing party parades. Marchers rang bells, set off cannons, raised banners, and unfurled flags. Millions of American men, perhaps a fifth of all registered voters, participated in these huge spectacles.

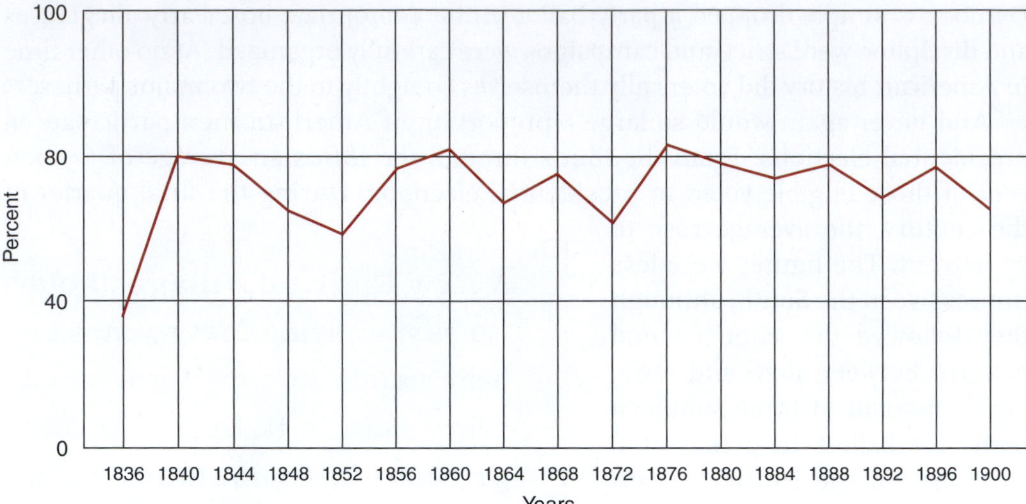

Figure 19–1 Percent of Eligible Voters Casting Ballots Between 1840 and 1896 a huge proportion—often 80 percent—of those eligible to vote did so in presidential elections. In the 20th century turnout dropped substantially.

Conspicuously absent from these events were the candidates themselves, particularly in presidential contests. Throughout the nineteenth century it was considered unseemly for presidential candidates to stump for votes. Those who did campaign—for example, Stephen Douglas in 1860, Horace Greeley in 1872, or James G. Blaine in 1884—were notoriously prone to losing the election. As the *Philadelphia Inquirer* explained in 1884, "It is better that the country should make its choice between the two candidates from what they know of their public records rather than from what they may learn of their personal appearance."

Masculine Partisanship and Feminine Voluntarism

Party politics was a largely masculine activity in the late nineteenth century. Both major parties functioned like fraternal organizations, and voting was increasingly referred to as a "manly" or a "manhood" right. Denying a man his right to vote was like denying his masculinity. If the electoral sphere of campaigns and voting was a man's world, the private sphere of home and family was widely understood as a woman's world. In practice, women always participated in the background of popular politics. They sewed the banners, decorated the meeting halls, prepared the food for rallies and picnics, and joined the parades dressed as symbolic representations of the Goddess of Liberty or some similarly feminine icon. Nevertheless, politically active women opted for a different style of politics.

The stereotypes of the public man and the private woman rested on the assumption that women were destined to remain at home as protectors of the family's virtue. By the middle of the century, increasing numbers of women used that female stereotype to develop their own form of political activism. Female virtue justified women's support for moral reform movements such as abolitionism and temperance. Thus many women entered the public sphere to protect the private sphere. By defining "the family" in broad terms, women expanded the horizons of political activity beyond the confines of the two-party system. In this way, a stereotype that initially restricted feminine political activity became a justification for women's increasing participation in public crusades.

Women pursued politics as representatives of voluntary associations that were dedicated to specific reforms, such as Sabbatarian laws that would prohibit working and drinking alcohol on the Sabbath, or the struggles against slavery, prostitution, and poverty. Because it grew out of voluntary associations rather than political parties, this style of political activity is known as voluntarism. Most of those who joined voluntary associations came from the educated middle class, and voluntary associations inevitably reflected the class biases of their members. By upholding the home as the special preserve of feminine authority, for example, reformers ignored the fact that working-class families depended heavily on the labor of children.

Sometimes women's associations copied the style of partisan politics, staging mass marches and rallies. But because many politically active women were critical of the emotional style of mass politics, voluntary associations concentrated less on rousing voters than on educating them and lobbying elected officials. Although men also joined voluntary associations, they were dismissed by mainstream politicians as "namby-pamby, goody-goody gentlemen." In the late nineteenth century, voluntarism was associated with feminine politics and party politics was associated with masculinity.

The Critics of Popular Politics

The combination of partisanship and voluntarism made American politics more "popular" than ever before. Women and men, blacks and whites, immigrants and the native born, working class and middle class all found places in the popular politics of

"Women on Top" A satirical cartoon from 1869 belittled the campaign for women's suffrage. Entitled "Women on Top," the image reflected the common assumption that electoral politics was strictly a masculine activity.

the late nineteenth century. But not all Americans appreciated popular politics. After the Civil War a small but influential group of conservatives reacted with disgust to the American rage for politics. Contemptuous of partisanship, they advocated a new style of nonpartisan politics and questioned the principle of universal suffrage. Because they laid the groundwork for a new style of politics that would prevail in the twentieth century, the critics were ahead of their time.

"Universal suffrage can only mean in plain English the government of ignorance and vice," Charles Francis Adams complained in 1869. Adams spoke for a traditional American elite that saw popular politics as a degradation of public life. To such men, economic independence was the precondition for political virtue, among voters and public officials alike. The fact that the American working class was made up largely of blacks, Asians, and Catholic immigrants only made matters worse.

But blatantly antidemocratic rhetoric was a losing proposition in the late nineteenth century. Elites who hoped to maintain political influence learned to avoid direct assaults on the principle of universal suffrage. Instead they became advocates of good government: government run by professionals rather than party bosses, and staffed by civil servants rather than party favorites. They became, in short, advocates of *nonpartisan* politics.

Nonpartisan politics was a reaction against the upheavals of urban and industrial development. Many elites were haunted by what they saw as the twin evils of radicalism and immigration. In the wake of the nationwide strikes of 1877, *The Nation* magazine, a reliable barometer of elite opinion, asked whether an "alien" proletariat had transformed universal suffrage from a democratic blessing into a nightmare for the "well-to-do and intelligent" classes. In 1881, supporters of good government organized the National Civil Service Reform League to prevent political parties from filling government positions with their supporters. Victory came two years later with the establishment of a Civil Service Commission that would assign federal jobs on the basis of merit rather than patronage.

But civil service reform would not stop the phenomenal growth of a working-class electorate made up largely of recent immigrants. Political opposition to immigration, known as nativism, had enjoyed some success in the 1850s, and in 1882 nativists had secured a congressional ban on the further immigration of Chinese. Anti-Catholicism spread across the country, especially in the Midwest in the late 1880s. Immigrants were Catholic and working class, so Yankee Protestants often saw working-class radicalism as a double threat. One nativist pointed to the "two lines" of foreign influence that were threatening the American republic. One line led to the radical politics of "agrarianism" and "anarchy." The second line tended toward Catholic "superstition." Both led "by different roads to one ultimate end, despotism!"

By the mid-1890s, as the number of immigrants from eastern and southern Europe increased, nativist rhetoric grew more racist. It was no longer merely radicals and Catholics who were swarming into the United States, but darker-skinned peoples from Italy, Russia, and eastern Europe. Social scientists wrote treatises on the inherent intellectual inferiority of such peoples, giving the imprimatur of science to the most vicious stereotypes. Italians were said to be genetically predisposed to organized violence, Jews to thievery and manipulation. Anti-immigrant parties and nativist societies appeared across America.

Throughout most of the nineteenth century, however, the critics of popular politics remained a vocal minority. Most Americans entered the political arena with

As the Number of Immigrants to America Swelled, So Did Opposition to Them This 1891 cartoon blames immigration for causing a host of social and political evils.

deep concerns over the problems of a society that was rapidly becoming more urban and industrial. Industrial capitalism generated the issues that dominated American public life in the late nineteenth century.

Economic Issues Dominate National Politics

By the late nineteenth century, Americans were accustomed to the idea that government should oversee the distribution of the nation's natural resources. After the Civil War, federal officials distributed public lands to homesteaders and railroads and granted rights to mining, ranching, and timber companies. During these same decades, the rise of big business led growing numbers of Americans to believe that the government should regulate the currency and also protect American commerce and workers from ruinous foreign competition. Given the even balance of the two major parties, it is not surprising that the outcome was a policy that split the difference. High protective tariffs protected workers, while the gold standard remained largely intact. Meanwhile the Supreme Court restricted the government's ability to regulate the domestic market. But this was never a stable compromise. On the contrary, struggles over economic policy were at the center of national politics throughout the late nineteenth century.

Weak Presidents Oversee a Stronger Federal Government

Starting in the mid-1870s, the Democrats and Republicans had nearly equal electoral strength, and from 1876 through 1896 not a single president enjoyed a full term during which his own party controlled both houses of Congress, nor did any

> **In Grover Cleveland the greatness lies in typical rather than unusual qualities. He had no endowments that thousands of men do not have. He possessed honesty, courage, firmness, independence, and common sense. But he possessed them to a degree other men do not.**
>
> ALLAN NEVINS

president during these years take office with an overwhelming electoral mandate. After Grant's reelection in 1872, no president was elected to two consecutive terms until 1900.

In some cases, a president took office already tainted by the process that put him there, as was certainly true of Rutherford B. Hayes's election in 1876. Hayes's fellow Republicans were annoyed by his efforts to conciliate the southern Democrats, who were conducting congressional investigations of his election, and frustrated by the president's contradictory position on civil service reform. Hayes forbade his party from raising money by assessing Republican officeholders, and he wrestled with the mighty Roscoe Conkling, Republican boss of New York City, for control of the New York Customs House—the most lucrative source of patronage in America. But although Hayes spoke for civil service reform, he acted the role of the party patron by lavishly rewarding his own supporters. Civil service reformers soon turned away from Hayes.

In 1877 Hayes took one important step toward strengthening the presidency. When railroad workers went on strike, Hayes dispatched federal troops to suppress them. This was an important precedent. Later presidents would often exercise their authority to intervene directly in disputes between workers and employers. But except for calling out the troops, Hayes's policy was to do nothing whatsoever to relieve the distress caused by the depression of the 1870s. Millions of Americans were suffering from the sharp fall in wages and prices, yet Hayes vetoed a bill that would have modestly inflated the currency. By 1880 the president was so unpopular that his fellow Republicans happily took him up on his offer not to run for reelection.

The results of the 1880 election were typical of the era. Republican James A. Garfield won the presidency by a tiny margin. He received 48.5 percent of the votes, and Democrat Winfield Hancock received 48.1 percent. As usual, the Republicans did best in New England, the upper Midwest, and the West. The Democrats swept the South but also took New Jersey, Nevada, and California. As a general rule, the Republicans appealed to southern blacks and to a northern middle class that was native born and overwhelmingly Protestant. The Democrats could count on strong support from working-class immigrants and southern whites.

As usual, economic issues dominated the 1880 campaign. But this did not mean that the Democrats and Republicans differed on economic policy. Both parties were addicted to the patronage system, so neither pressed for civil service reform. In theory the Democrats favored lower tariffs than the Republicans. In practice neither party advocated free trade and both parties had strong "protectionist" blocs (those who supported high tariffs to protect American business) as well as significant numbers who favored lower tariff rates. Neither party wanted to reverse the prevailing deflationary policies. Finally, while Republicans made periodic gestures in support of southern blacks, they had abandoned the freed people of the South. Thus Garfield's victory for the Republicans in 1880 did not foreshadow any major shifts in government policy.

On July 2, 1881, the president was shot by a lunatic who claimed to be a disappointed office seeker. Garfield died two months later, and Chester A. Arthur, the product of a powerful patronage machine, became president. The assassination that put him in office made it dangerous for the president to resist the swell of popular support for civil service reform. The Republicans in control of Congress did resist, however, and Democrats swept into office on a tide of resentment against Republican corruption and patronage. The following year Congress passed, and President Arthur signed, the landmark Pendleton Civil Service Act.

The Pendleton Act prohibited patronage officeholders from contributing to the party machine that gave them their jobs. More important, the law authorized the president to establish a Civil Service Commission to administer competitive examinations for federal jobs. Before the century ended, the majority of federal jobs were removed from the reach of the patronage machines. The Pendleton Act was a major turning point in the creation of a stable and professional civil service.

Although Arthur signed the Pendleton Act, he squandered his chance of gaining popular credit as a reformer by distributing lavish patronage to his supporters in a shameless bid for reelection in 1884. He likewise threw away an opportunity to lead the way on tariff reform. With the return of prosperity in the late 1870s and early 1880s, government coffers bulged with surplus revenues from import taxes. Cries for lower tariffs grew louder, but the president succumbed to the political manipulations of the high-tariff forces in Congress. The so-called Mongrel Tariff he signed in 1883 did nothing. Arthur was no more successful in his attempts to strengthen the navy or carry out an aggressive foreign policy. To make matters worse, the economy began to slow down again. Arthur approached the 1884 elections a tainted president. His fellow Republicans would not even renominate him.

The Democrats nominated Grover Cleveland. In his brief career as mayor of Buffalo and governor of New York, Cleveland had developed a reputation as an honest man and a moderate. Cleveland, the first Democrat elected to the presidency in nearly 30 years, made reconciliation between the North and the South a theme of his administration.

Letter from Charles Guiteau The original letter written by Charles J. Guiteau, in which he concludes "*I had no ill will to the president*," after he shot President James Garfield to death in a Washington, DC, train station.

Cleveland's conviction that the federal government should defer to southern whites derived in part from his commitment to local government. Accordingly, Cleveland was not an activist president. During his first two years in office he initiated no new programs, but neither did he thwart congressional moves to strengthen the authority of the central government. Cleveland approved legislation that raised the Agriculture Department to the status of a cabinet office and signed the Dawes Severalty Act of 1887, which placed the federal government in direct control over most Native Americans (see Chapter 17, "The Triumph of Industrial Capitalism"). In the same year, Cleveland signed the Interstate Commerce Act, the first federal legislation designed to regulate big business. It empowered a five-member Interstate Commerce Commission to curb monopolistic and discriminatory practices by railroads.

I WANT MY PA!
Another voice for Cleveland.

Republican Campaign Poster from the 1888 Presidential Election This poster assails the Democratic candidate, Grover Cleveland, on both personal and ideological grounds. Cleveland supported lower tariffs, and is therefore derided as an advocate of free trade. He had also fathered a child out of wedlock, hence the image of the infant.

Cleveland earned few points for merely signing laws passed by Congress, so when his fellow Democrats lost control of the House of Representatives in 1886, he decided to take the lead on some important issue. The issue he chose was the tariff. In December 1887, shortly before his reelection campaign was to begin, Cleveland devoted his annual message to Congress almost entirely to sharp reductions in the tariff. He insisted that he was not an advocate of free trade; he simply thought that the tariff was too high.

Having staked so much on tariff reduction, the president merely watched passively as Congress produced a doomed bill that was biased in favor of southern interests. When his own party included only a weak endorsement of tariff reform in the 1888 platform, Cleveland did nothing. Throughout his campaign for reelection, he spoke not one word on the subject. Cleveland went before the voters with no tariff reform, and little else, to show for his four years in office.

Running a skillful campaign on an overtly protectionist platform, the Republicans won back the White House in 1888. A Republican president, Benjamin Harrison, at last presided over a Republican majority in Congress. Making good on their campaign promises, Republicans enacted high tariff rates. The Harrison-McKinley Tariff of 1890 also gave the president the authority to raise or lower tariffs with nations that opened their markets to American businesses. Thus the legislation gave the president important new authority in the conduct of foreign affairs. Also in 1890 the Republicans passed the Sherman Anti-Trust Act, declaring it illegal for "combinations" to enter into arrangements that would restrain competition. By failing to define precisely what constituted a "restraint of trade," the Sherman Act left it to the probusiness courts to decide.

The Republicans received little credit for their efforts, and part of the problem was the president himself. Nicknamed "the human iceberg," Harrison was too stiff and pompous to rally the people. But the larger problem was the rising discontent among voters. In 1890 they put the Democrats back in control of the House of Representatives, and in 1892 they reelected Grover Cleveland president. Once again, however, a president took office without a popular majority. Cleveland was the last of a string of relatively weak presidents (see Table 19–1).

But the weakness of the executive did not indicate an inactive central government. In

Table 19–1 Razor-thin Electoral Margins in the Gilded Age

Year	Popular Vote	% of Popular Vote	Electoral Vote
1876	4,036,572	48.0	185
	4,284,020	51.0	184
1880	4,453,295	48.5	214
	4,414,082	48.1	155
	308,578	3.4	—
1884	4,879,507	48.5	219
	4,850,293	48.2	182
1888	5,477,129	47.9	233
	5,537,857	48.6	168

addition to the Pendleton Act, the Interstate Commerce Act, and the Sherman Anti-Trust Act, the government tried to inflate the currency by modestly increasing the amount of silver in circulation. By maintaining high tariffs, politicians effectively protected the wage rates of workers and the economic security of businesses. Nevertheless, the weakness of the federal government left growing numbers of Americans with the impression that the political system could not solve the problems associated with the political economy of industrial capitalism.

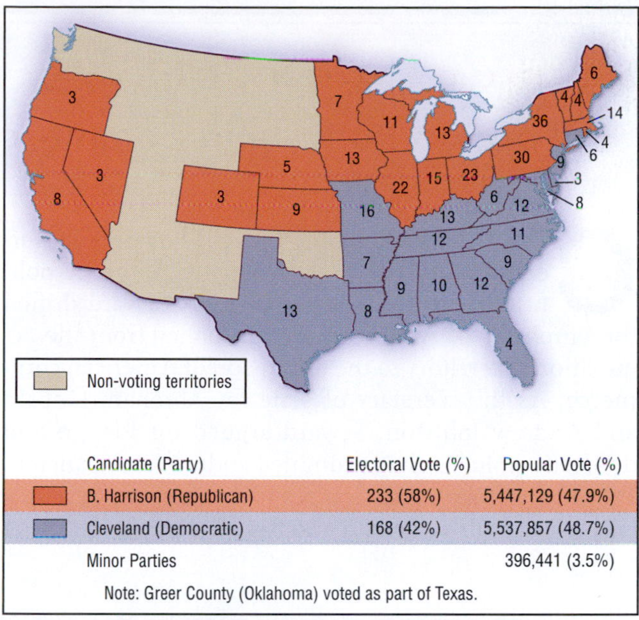

Candidate (Party)	Electoral Vote (%)	Popular Vote (%)
B. Harrison (Republican)	233 (58%)	5,447,129 (47.9%)
Cleveland (Democratic)	168 (42%)	5,537,857 (48.7%)
Minor Parties		396,441 (3.5%)

Note: Greer County (Oklahoma) voted as part of Texas.

Map 19–1 The Election of 1888

Government Activism and Its Limits

There are two standard themes in the political history of the late nineteenth century. The first theme stresses that government in this era was replete with corruption and bribery. The second theme emphasizes that the late nineteenth century was the great age of limited government and unregulated markets. After the retreat from Reconstruction, the government stepped back and allowed the new industrial economy to grow at its own rapid pace. There is a kernel of truth in each of these themes. Corruption was a real problem in late nineteenth-century politics, and the government's regulatory powers were trivial compared to what would come later. Nevertheless, government in the late nineteenth century did become somewhat more involved in the regulation of the economy. The conflicting impulses toward limited and active government can be seen most clearly in one of the most disruptive issues of late nineteenth-century American politics, the regulation of the currency.

Greenbacks and Greenbackers

People have always disagreed over how much money governments should produce and how they should produce it. During the eighteenth century, American colonists complained that there was not enough money in circulation to sustain their economic needs. In the first half of the nineteenth century, Americans fought over how much power the government should give to banks to regulate the amount of money in circulation. After the Civil War, capitalist development sparked another political debate over the role of government in the organization of the economy.

During the Civil War, the U.S. government printed $450 million worth of "greenbacks" to support the Union effort. Greenbacks were paper bills that were backed by the government's word, but not by the traditional reserves of gold or silver. When the war ended, most Americans agreed that the greenbacks should be withdrawn from circulation. But after the depression of the 1870s a growing number of Americans demanded that the government keep the greenbacks in circulation. Those who wanted to return to the gold standard by making greenbacks convertible for "specie"—gold or silver—were called *resumptionists,* that is, they

AMERICA AND THE WORLD

>> Foreign Policy and Commercial Expansion

Capitalist development reshaped American foreign policy just as it dominated domestic politics. In the 1860s William Henry Seward shifted the emphasis of American foreign policy from the acquisition of territory to the expansion of American commerce. As the secretary of state for Abraham Lincoln and Andrew Johnson, Seward argued for foreign and domestic policies that promoted industrial expansion. Prewar southern expansionism had dampened Seward's enthusiasm for the acquisition of more land: he came to believe that "political supremacy follows commercial supremacy," and so he shifted his attention to the opening of American markets in Latin America, Canada, and the Pacific region, including Asia. Territorial expansion did not come to an end, but it took a back seat to commercial expansion.

In the late 1860s, as congressional Republicans struggled with President Johnson over Reconstruction, many of Seward's plans got caught in the crossfire. His biggest success came on April 9, 1867, when the Senate

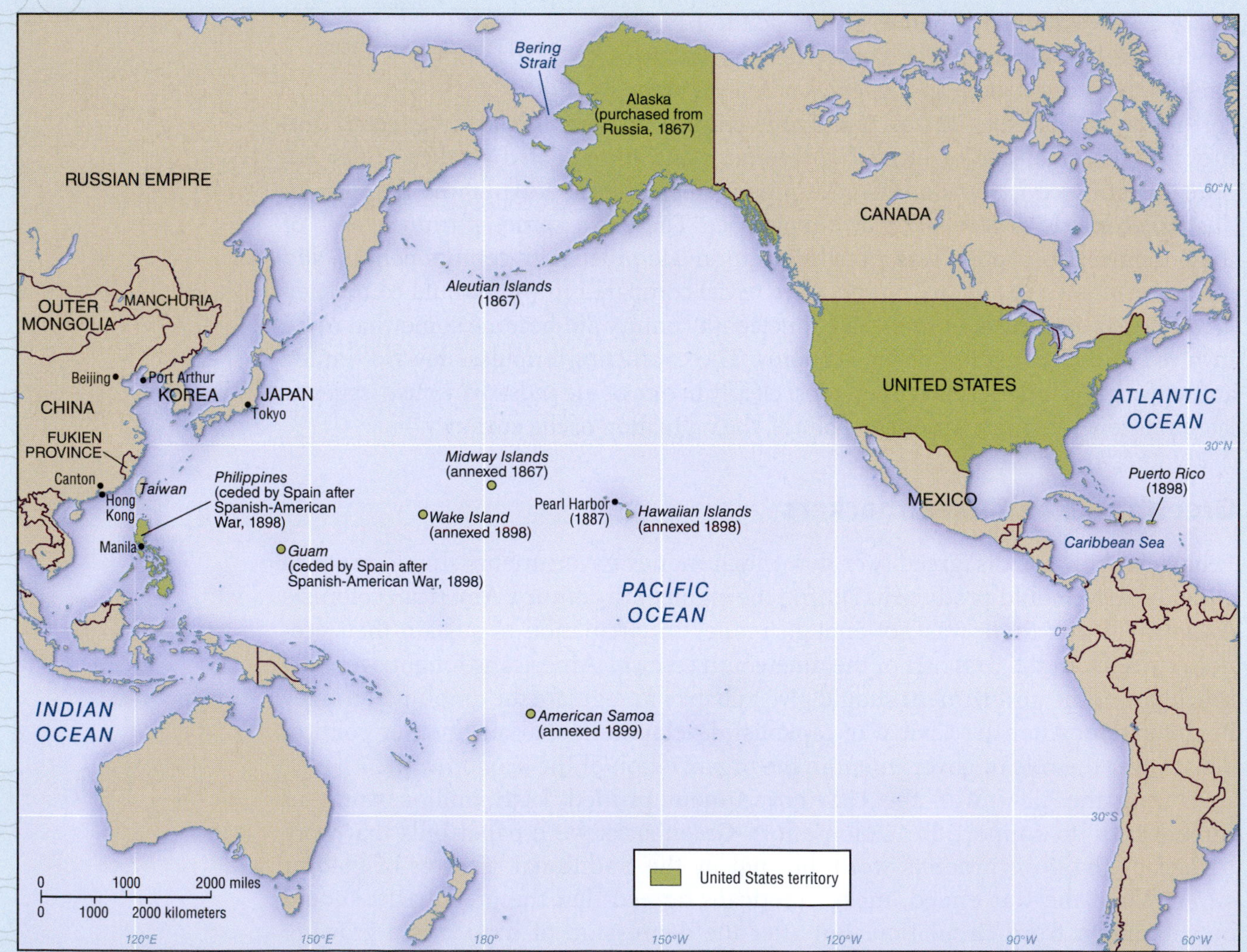

Map 19–2 American Expansion, 1857–1898 By the 1860s, Secretary of State William Henry Seward established the principle that American foreign policy would be driven by commercial interests.

ratified the treaty purchasing Alaska for $7.2 million. A few months later, however, the Senate blocked a treaty with Denmark for the purchase of the Virgin Islands. Seward likewise failed to win approval for a naval base in Santo Domingo and a treaty with Colombia giving the United States exclusive rights to build a canal across the isthmus of Panama. President Grant and Senator Charles Sumner revived long-standing American hopes of annexing Canada, but the Canadians seemed intent on cementing their ties to Great Britain.

European powers thwarted U.S. territorial ambitions in Latin America, but so did racist concerns about bringing large numbers of nonwhites into the United States. A rebellion in Cuba in 1868 heightened American interest in annexing the island. But Secretary of State Hamilton Fish had long resisted the idea of absorbing half a million Cubans of "every shade and mixture of color." Similar inhibitions led the Senate to reject President Grant's 1869 treaty with Santo Domingo.

Despite America's continued expansionist efforts, however, Seward believed that commercial rather than territorial expansion would drive American foreign policy in the future. Those commercial interests were increasingly global. Between 1860 and 1897 American exports tripled, surpassing $1 billion per year. After 300 years of trade deficits, in 1874 America's exports began to surpass its imports. Nearly 85 percent of those exports were agricultural commodities, but the growth of industrial exports was even more spectacular. Iron and steel exports jumped by 230 percent between 1888 and 1898. John D. Rockefeller's Standard Oil corporation shipped three-quarters of its kerosene overseas between the 1860s and the 1880s. In the 1880s, U.S. multinational corporations became a fixture of international commerce.

Aggressive secretaries of state reaffirmed Seward's commitment to commercial expansion. In 1886, for example, James G. Blaine worried openly that rapidly industrializing European nations were diverting Latin American commerce away from the United States. Concern for access to foreign markets pushed successive administrations to assert America's exclusive right to build a canal across Central America. The canal, President Harrison argued in 1891, "is the most important subject now connected with the commercial growth and progress of the United States." Hoping to thwart European commercial expansion by forging ties of friendship with Latin America, the United States convened the first Pan-American Conference in 1889.

Mexico provided the most vivid demonstration of U.S. commercial expansion. Although Americans had been buying up property in Mexico since before the Civil War, political instability limited Mexico's attractiveness as an investment. In 1876, however, Porfirio Díaz seized power in Mexico and began a reign of 35 years that proved a boon to American commercial interests. American investors quickly swarmed into Mexico, building railroads, selling life insurance, and digging oil wells. By 1910 Americans owned 43 percent of all the property in Mexico, more than Mexicans themselves owned.

United States attention also turned toward Asia and the South Pacific. In the 1880s the United States nearly went to war with England and Germany over disputed claims to Samoa. An 1876 reciprocity treaty gave Hawaiian sugar favored treatment on the American market, prompting a huge influx of Hawaiian sugar into the U.S. market (along with a backlash against the treaty by sugar producers on the mainland). By 1886, however, two-thirds of Hawaiian sugar was produced on American-owned plantations. Consequently, President Cleveland supported the treaty's renewal by referring to "our close and manifest interest in the commerce of the Pacific Ocean." By the 1890s American power in Hawaii had grown so great that it provoked among native Hawaiians a backlash that culminated in Queen Liliuokalani's ascension to the throne in January 1891. Two years later, Hawaiians favorable to the United States dethroned the queen. The Senate rejected the annexation treaty submitted by President Harrison, but eventually, under President William McKinley, Hawaii was annexed to the United States.

The United States treaded somewhat more cautiously in East Asia, where European powers had long-established ties. The United States negotiated treaties with Japan and Korea that substantially increased American access to Asian markets.

From 1865 to 1890 the Senate repeatedly rejected treaties negotiated by presidential emissaries, but a succession of powerful secretaries of state compensated for a succession of weak presidents. By the late 1880s America's extensive global interests began to shape the nation's military policy. In 1890 Congress approved the construction of the first modern warships, and the Supreme Court extended the president's control over "our international relations." The growing links between commercial and diplomatic interests were reviving the powers of the American presidency.

wanted the government to resume specie payments. Those who wanted the government to keep greenbacks in circulation to help inflate the currency were called greenbackers.

The supporters of the gold standard associated sound money with sound religion. In 1878, for example, the *Christian Advocate* compared greenbackers to atheists. And in fact, greenbackers were often radical critics of industrial society. They formed a Greenback-Labor Party, which garnered more than 1 million votes in the 1878 congressional elections and elected 14 members of Congress. But the sound-money forces won out, and in 1879 the $300 million in greenbacks that were still in circulation were made convertible into gold.

> **I do not believe that the power and duty of the General Government ought to be extended to the relief of individual suffering which is in no manner properly related to the public service or benefit. A prevalent tendency to disregard the limited mission of this [government] power and duty should, I think, be steadfastly resisted, to the end that the lesson should constantly be enforced that though the people support the Government the Government should not support the people.**
>
> GROVER CLEVELAND

Supporters of inflation next took up the issue of "free silver." To counteract the deflationary trend, they argued, the government should add to the amount of money in circulation by allowing the unlimited coinage of silver. In 1878 the inflationists and sound-money forces in Congress passed the Bland-Allison Act authorizing the Treasury to purchase silver and mint it in amounts tied to the amount of gold being minted. With the return of prosperity in the 1880s the currency question died down, to be revived with the arrival of another severe depression in the 1890s.

Growth of the Central Government

Despite the inevitable retrenchment that followed the Civil War, the size of the central government grew as new bureaucracies were created in the late nineteenth century. Congress consolidated the United States Geological Survey in 1879, established the Interstate Commerce Commission in 1887, and created the Department of Justice in 1870 and the Department of Agriculture in 1889.

The number of civilian federal employees rose from 53,000 in 1871 to 256,000 in 1901. These numbers reflected the emergence of a professional civil service. In 1883, when Congress passed the first civil service law, 13,780 federal jobs were "classified," meaning that applicants had to pass an exam to qualify. Fifteen years later, 89,306 federal positions were classified, amounting to nearly half of the jobs in the national government. This expansion of the number of civil service jobs substantially weakened the power of the Democratic and Republican parties. As the proportion of "classified" federal jobs swelled, the patronage well dried up.

By the turn of the century, however, only the rudiments of a modern federal government were in place. The Interstate Commerce Commission lacked the power to enforce its own rulings, so it was forced to rely on the courts, which were dominated by supporters of big business. The Sherman Anti-Trust Act was even weaker.

Few monopolies were threatened, much less broken up, by it. Finally, only about 15 percent of the wage-labor force was actually protected by the high tariffs. By 1900 the federal government had developed in important ways, yet it remained small and weak by later standards. Indeed, it was not the federal but rather the state and municipal governments that responded most aggressively to the problems of urban and industrial society.

States Regulate; Municipalities Reform

Even as Americans called on their government to do more and more, politicians proclaimed their opposition to the taxes and bureaucracies that active government required. The result was a jarring contradiction. At the state level, politicians enacted policies of retrenchment. In contrast to the steady expansion of the federal government, for example, late-nineteenth-century state legislatures passed fewer laws and lowered taxes.

But state politicians also established new regulatory bodies to govern the exploding municipalities of urban and industrial America. During the late nineteenth century, state officials often transferred municipal power from elected officials and party politicians to experts and specialists on unelected boards. Mayors, city council members, and aldermen lost much of their authority over budgets, schools, police, and parks. For example, reformers handed control of the police to commissions staffed by middle-class citizens rather than by working-class immigrants. Parks commissions, sanitation commissions, public health commissions, and transportation commissions were generally staffed by middle-class professionals who were appointed to their posts and who prided themselves on their "nonpartisan" approach to government. The quality and professionalism of police and fire services increased dramatically over the course of the nineteenth century.

As states retrenched, cities increased their property taxes to pay for streets, sewers, reservoirs, and public transportation. In the late nineteenth century city governments produced some of the great urban achievements of American history. Huge public parks, such as Central Park in New York and Golden Gate Park in San Francisco, sprang up across the country. At the same time, cities sponsored spectacular feats of engineering and architecture. New Yorkers built the Brooklyn Bridge; Chicagoans literally reversed the flow of the

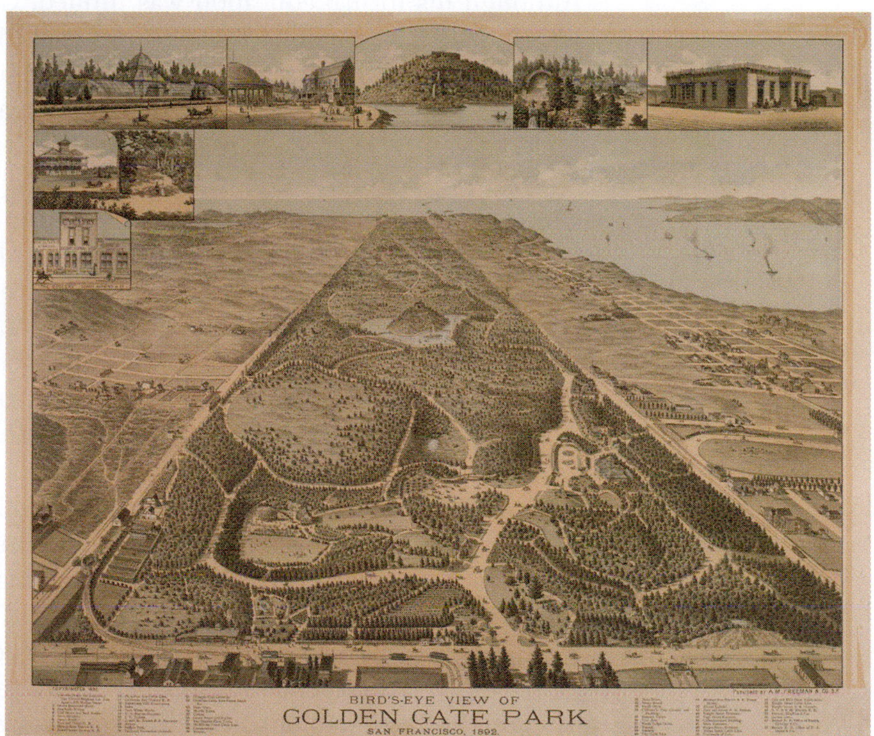

Bird's-Eye View of Golden Gate Park San Francisco's Golden Gate Park, designed by Frederick Law Olmsted, was one of the most impressive of the great municipal parks built in cities across America in the late 19th century.

Chicago River. Municipal governments went a long way toward enhancing the civility and decency of urban life in America.

Yet Americans grew dissatisfied with their governments. Some were disgusted by corruption and inefficiency; others were offended by the hoopla of popular politics. To a significant number, government policies seemed inadequate to the demands of urban and industrial America. The powers of government grew slowly, but they were dwarfed by the private power of huge new corporations. Frustrated by piecemeal reforms, middle-class Americans turned to radical campaigns for social and economic transformation.

Middle-Class Radicalism

In the late nineteenth century a number of middle-class radicals argued that economic development had undermined individual liberty and equality. Yet while their attacks on capitalism were severe, their assumptions were surprisingly traditional. They were usually frightened, not motivated, by socialism. They often worried that if substantial reforms were not undertaken, a discontented working class would overthrow the reign of private property. Their radical critiques of industrial society exposed deep wells of discontent among Americans.

Henry George and the Limits of Producers' Ideology

Henry George was born in Philadelphia in 1839, the son of middle-class parents. Although his formal education was limited, George traveled extensively and read widely. Like many middle-class Americans of his generation, he was shocked by the fact that as the United States grew richer the number of poor people grew as well. He studied the problem for many years and in 1879 published his conclusions in a best-selling book called *Progress and Poverty.*

George's explanation rested on what historians have called producers' ideology. It started from the assumption that only human labor could create legitimate wealth. Anything of value, such as food, clothing, or steel rails, came from the world's producing classes. By contrast, stockbrokers, bankers, and speculators made money from money rather than from the goods they produced. Producers' ideology therefore deemed their wealth illegitimate. Starting from these premises, Henry George divided the world into two classes: producers and predators.

The harmony of capital and labor was a central theme of producers' ideology. Henry George dreamed of a world in which working people owned their own farms and shops, making them both capitalists and laborers. His critique of industrial capitalism thus harkened back to Thomas Jefferson's vision of a society of small farmers and independent shopkeepers. America used to be that way, George believed, but as society "progressed," the land was monopolized by a wealthy few. Producers were forced to go to work for wealthy landholders. Employers then invested in technology that increased the productivity of their workers, but they kept the added wealth for

> **The tramp comes with the locomotive, and almshouses and prisons are as surely the marks of material progress as are costly dwellings, rich warehouses, and magnificent churches.**
>
> HENRY GEORGE, *Progress and Poverty*, 1879

John F. Weir's 1877 Painting *Forging the Shaft: A Welding Heat* This painting graphically depicts the forms of industrial wage labor that Henry George feared. He advocated tax policies that would restore a Jeffersonian economy of small, independent producers.

themselves. Technology thus multiplied the wealth of the predators at the expense of the producers.

George's solution for the inequities of industrial society was a so-called Single Tax on rents. Because all wealth derived from labor applied to land, he reasoned, rents amounted to an unnatural transfer of wealth from the producers to the landlords. To thwart that transfer, George suggested taxing rents and improvements on land at prohibitive levels. This would discourage the accumulation of land by the landowning class. All other taxes would be abolished, including the tariffs that protected big business.

George presented his Single Tax as an alternative to the dangerous socialist doctrines that he thought were spreading among the working class. George attacked as "faulty" the socialist idea that there was an inherent conflict between labor and capital. He opposed government regulation of the economy, and he was a fiscal conservative, suspicious of proposals to counteract deflation by putting more money in circulation. Despite his apparent radicalism, George's popularity testified to the strength of middle-class concerns about the political power of the working class.

Edward Bellamy and the Nationalist Clubs

In 1888 Edward Bellamy, a 38-year-old Massachusetts editor, published a best seller with a critique of capitalism even more powerful than Henry George's. Bellamy's *Looking Backward* was a utopian novel set in the future. The plot revolves around Julian West, who goes to sleep in Boston in 1887 and wakes up in the year 2000.

AMERICAN LANDSCAPE

>> The "Crusade" Against Alcohol

A few days before Christmas in 1873, Dr. Diocletian Lewis arrived in Hillsboro, Ohio, to speak on the evils of alcohol. He had given the speech many times before, but on this occasion the women who came proved unusually responsive. Lewis told them how, when he was a boy, his mother saved his father from drink by persuading a local saloonkeeper to stop selling liquor. The next morning a group of Hillsboro women met for prayer and then marched through the town urging local merchants to stop selling liquor. Inspired by their success, the women kept up the pressure through the winter of 1873/1874.

The Crusade, as it came to be called, quickly spread to more than 900 towns and cities in 31 states and territories. The women closed down thousands of liquor stores and saloons and secured written pledges from hundreds of druggists and hotel keepers not to sell alcohol. With the dramatic success of the Crusade of 1873/1874, temperance was reborn as a movement dominated by women.

From these humble, almost accidental, beginnings, there grew one of the late nineteenth century's largest outlets for women's political activism. Under the auspices of the Woman's Christian Temperance Union, women took up causes that stretched well beyond the suppression of alcohol. Voting and office holding were restricted to men, but the WCTU expanded democratic participation to include tens of thousands of women. ●

His host, Doctor Leete, introduces West to the miraculous changes that have taken place. Technological marvels have raised everyone's standard of living. Boston has become a clean and orderly city. The great problems of industrial civilization have been solved. This was possible, Doctor Leete explains, because Americans had overcome the "excessive individualism" of the late nineteenth century, which "was inconsistent with much public spirit."

What about "the labor question?" Julian West asks. It had been "threatening to devour society" in 1887 when West fell asleep. Bellamy's critique of capitalism is contained in Doctor Leete's answer to West's question. In the early years of the American republic, the doctor explains, workers and employers lived in harmony. Upward mobility was common. This changed when "great aggregations of capital" arose. Like Henry George's, Bellamy's criticism of capitalism was grounded in traditional Jeffersonian ideals. For both authors the triumph of wage labor led to concentrations of wealth that undermined the harmony of capital and labor.

But where *Progress and Poverty* proposed the restoration of the simple virtues of Jeffersonian society, *Looking Backward* imagined a high-tech future in which consumer goods were provided in abundance. What got produced and what got consumed would no longer be left to the chaotic whims of the market. Instead, in Bellamy's ideal world production and consumption would be harmonized by an obscure process of centralized planning. The result would be a consumer's utopia of widespread abundance.

Where Henry George reasserted the values of hard work and self-restraint, Edward Bellamy embraced the modern cult of leisure. For Henry George, technology led to misery and inequality, but for Edward Bellamy, machines would free mankind from the burdens and inequities of the modern world.

In spite of these differences, Bellamy and George were both motivated by a profound fear of militant workers. *Looking Backward* catered to a middle-class craving for order amidst the chaos of industrial society. Decisions about what to produce were made collectively, and society as a whole owned the means of production. Yet Bellamy was contemptuous of socialism and called his vision "nationalism." Under nationalism, the restoration of social peace was so complete that there was little or no need for government. This vision inspired thousands of middle-class Americans to form "Bellamy Clubs" or "Nationalist Clubs," particularly in New England.

The Woman's Christian Temperance Union

"Edward Bellamy's wonderful book" likewise inspired Frances Willard, president of the Woman's Christian Temperance Union (WCTU). She called nationalism "the fulfillment of man's highest earthly dream." Fifteen years earlier such support would have been impossible. At first "conservatives" who wanted to restrict the WCTU's activity to the suppression of liquor dominated the organization. But Willard had grander visions, and so, apparently, did the WCTU's members. In 1879 they elected Willard their national president, a position she held until her death in 1898.

The temperance movement broadened its interests and grew steadily more radical and more popular. It embraced women's suffrage, workers' rights, and finally "Christian socialism." Nevertheless, the WCTU's appeal and its radicalism were restricted by its predominantly prosperous membership. The middle-class Protestant bias of the WCTU was consistent with its disdain for most forms of party politics.

To be sure, the WCTU convened huge rallies, but Willard contrasted them to party conventions. WCTU gatherings were depicted as clean, well-disciplined affairs with oratory that was substantive rather than bombastic. Unlike the major parties, the WCTU combined education with interest-group pressure. Willard and her associates gave speeches, wrote articles, published books and newspaper columns on the evils of drink, organized petition campaigns, and lobbied officeholders. The crusade against alcohol grew into a broad-ranging political campaign to alleviate the problems of a new industrial society. In this sense the WCTU was typical of American politics in the late nineteenth century.

Under Willard's direction the WCTU endorsed women's suffrage and formed an alliance with the country's largest labor union. Willard supported laws restricting the workday to eight hours and prohibiting child labor. Even the WCTU's attitude toward alcohol changed. By the 1890s Willard viewed drunkenness as a public health problem rather than a personal sin, a problem of political economy rather than individual failure. Accordingly, temperance advocates supported reforms designed to relieve poverty, improve public health, raise literacy, alleviate the conditions of workers, reform prisons, suppress public immorality, and preserve peace. In the end, Willard attributed the evils of liquor to the inequities of corporate capitalism.

Three factors explain the WCTU's success. The first was Frances Willard's paradoxically conservative approach to radical reform. Her justification for female political activism always came back to women's distinctive calling as protectors of the home. The second reason for the WCTU's success was its decentralized structure. Willard left the local chapters of the union free to adjust their activities to suit their particular needs. In the southern unions there was little talk of women's suffrage. Willard called this the "Do Everything" policy. Finally, the WCTU appealed to middle-class women who felt isolated by a culture that restricted them to the home. Women found in the WCTU a source of camaraderie as well as political activism. The WCTU dwarfed most other women's political organizations in the late nineteenth century. By the early 1890s, for example, the National American Woman Suffrage Association had 13,000 members; the less-radical General Federation of Women's Clubs had 20,000. The WCTU had 150,000 adult members and 50,000 in its young women's auxiliary. The only reform organization to attract more women was the Farmers' Alliance.

For all its success, however, temperance remained a middle-class reform movement. The organization rested on a constituency that was concentrated in cities, especially in the North. The WCTU did not attract many immigrants, for example. The official policy of religious toleration was undermined by the prejudices of middle-class members. For many temperance advocates immigrants were the Union's targets rather than its constituents, and the strong Protestant identity of the WCTU limited its appeal among working-class Catholics. One of its first major campaigns in the 1870s was aimed at replacing altar wine with grape juice in Christian services, a switch that Irish Catholics and German Lutherans were unwilling to make. As radical as it was, the WCTU would never reflect the interests of black sharecroppers, white tenant farmers, or immigrant workers. Nevertheless, like the Single-Taxers and the Bellamy Clubs, WCTU reformers reflected a growing sense that the American political system was unable to solve the problems of an industrial political economy.

Discontent Among Workers

Radicalized workers shared the conviction that mainstream politics could not confront the problems of industrial capitalism. Labor radicals began to question one of the premises of producers' ideology—that American democracy was secured by a unique harmony between capital and labor. Labor agitation often became violent, and employers demanded that government use its police powers to put down strikes. But if the harmony of capital and labor had been destroyed, advocates of the producers' ideology continued to search for a political solution to the labor problem.

The Knights of Labor and the Haymarket Disaster

Between 1860 and 1890 wages overall grew by 50 percent, but the bulk of the growth was confined to elite skilled and semiskilled workers in a handful of industries, such as printing and metalworking. The vast majority of workers suffered directly from the deflation and economic instability of the late nineteenth century. By 1880, 40 percent of industrial workers lived at or below the poverty line, and the average worker was unemployed for 15 to 20 percent of the year. To relieve their plight, American workers sought political solutions to economic problems.

The most important labor organization to emerge from the crisis of the 1870s was the Noble and Holy Order of the Knights of Labor. Founded in 1869, the Knights of Labor was inspired by the producers' ideology and admitted everyone from self-employed farmers to unskilled factory workers. It appealed to a nostalgic vision of a world dominated by ordinary working people. Nevertheless the Knights of Labor advocated a host of progressive reforms, including the eight-hour day, equal pay for men and women, the abolition of child and prison labor, inflation of the currency to counteract the deflationary spiral, and a national income tax.

By the late 1870s leaders realized that the union needed a strong national organization to hold various locals together. A new constitution, drawn up in 1878, required all members to pay dues and allowed the national organization to support local boycotts and thereby boost its credibility among workers. Thereafter the Knights grew rapidly, from 19,000 members in 1881 to 111,000 in 1885. True to the producers' tradition, leader Terence Powderly favored the consumer boycott over the strike. His approach proved most successful during the sharp recession of 1884, when trade union strikes were being broken. By 1886 membership in the Knights skyrocketed to more than 700,000.

Liberty *versus* Anarchy. In this image published in *Harper's Weekly* (September 4, 1886), cartoonist Thomas Nast depicted a massive female Liberty crushing the Haymarket defendants in her hands, presumably rescuing the republic in the process.

But the more the Knights of Labor grew, the more the strains among its members showed. The interests of shopkeepers and small-factory owners were very different from those of wage laborers. The critical issue dividing self-employed producers from wage-earning producers was the use of the strike as a weapon of organized labor. Self-employed producers preferred the consumer boycott, and so did the leadership of the Knights of Labor. By contrast, wage laborers saw the strike as their most powerful weapon.

With the return of prosperity, trade unions called for a nationwide strike for the eight-hour day. On May 1, 1886, workers across the country walked off their jobs in one of the largest and most successful labor walkouts in American history. In Chicago 80,000 workers went out on strike. The Chicago job action was largely peaceful until May 4, when, at an anarchist rally at Haymarket Square near downtown, someone from the crowd tossed a bomb into a line of police. One policeman was killed instantly, and seven more died within days. The number of civilian casualties was never determined. Although the bomb thrower was never identified, eight anarchists were tried for inciting violence, and four were put to death.

Anarchists—who questioned the legitimacy of all government power—had been active in Chicago for several years. Although they had little influence on the labor movement, their fiery rhetoric advocating the use of violence made them conspicuous. At the Haymarket rally on the evening of May 4, anarchist speakers used the same violent rhetoric. Samuel Fielden, for example, urged his listeners to "throttle" and "kill" the legal system or else, he warned, "it will kill you." This remark provoked detective James Bonfield to rush 170 policemen to the dwindling rally, and into this crowd of policemen someone threw a bomb.

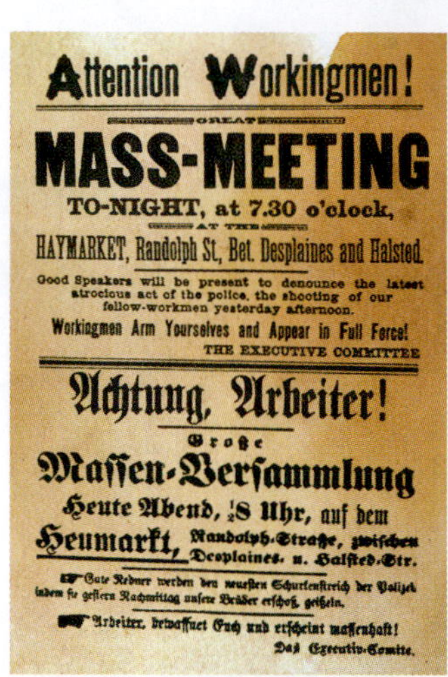

Haymarket was a turning point in American labor politics. With the support of its president, Terence Powderly, the Knights of Labor had tried to prevent its locals from supporting the May Day walkouts. Powderly had put himself into a bind. Members resented his failure to support the strikes, while outside the union a wave of revulsion against labor agitation swept the country. The Knights of Labor never recovered from the Haymarket disaster. Thereafter worker agitation split dramatically into two competing wings. Small farmers formed their own organizations, and wage laborers organized separately into industrial trade unions.

Agrarian Revolt

The late nineteenth century was a desperate time for American farmers, especially in the West and South. To compete they had to buy expensive agricultural equipment, often from manufacturers who benefited from tariff protections. Then they had to ship their goods to market on railroads that charged higher rates to small farmers than to big industrialists. When their goods reached a market, they faced steadily declining prices.

As the economy became global, southern cotton had to compete against cotton from India and the Near East. Western wheat competed with Russian and eastern European wheat. To keep up, farmers increasingly went into debt, and in a deflationary spiral the money they borrowed to plant their crops was worth more when it came time to pay it back, while their crops were worth less. Farmers mortgaged their homes and land. The proportion of owner-occupied farms declined while the number of tenants rose.

Farmers were traditionally opposed to active government, but they began to press for government action. But farmers were notoriously hard to organize. They were scattered over large sections of the country, they were committed to an ideology of economic independence, and they were traditionally hostile to government intervention. If American farmers were to pursue their political agenda effectively, they needed to overcome these and many other obstacles.

One of the first attempts to organize farmers was the Patrons of Husbandry, generally called the Grange. The Grange began to attract large numbers of farmers during the depression of the 1870s and claimed 1.5 million members by 1874. Consistent with producers' ideology, the Grange organized cooperatives designed to eliminate the role of merchants and creditors. By storing grain collectively, farmers held their products back from the market in the hope of gaining control over commodity prices. But inexperience made the Grange cooperatives difficult to organize and sustain. After 1875 their membership dwindled.

> **[W]e meet in the midst of a nation brought to the verge of moral, political, and material ruin. Corruption dominates the ballot-box, the Legislatures, the Congress, and touches even the ermine of the bench. The people are demoralized; most of the States have been compelled to isolate the voters at the polling places to prevent universal intimidation and bribery. The newspapers are largely subsidized or muzzled, public opinion silenced, business prostrated, homes covered with mortgages, labor impoverished, and the land concentrating in the hands of the capitalists. The urban workmen are denied the right to organize for self-protection, imported pauperized labor beats down their wages, a hireling standing army, unrecognized by our laws, is established to shoot them down, and they are rapidly degenerating into European conditions. The fruits of the toil of millions are boldly stolen to build up the fortunes for a few, unprecedented in the history of mankind; and the possessors of these, in turn, despise the Republic and endanger liberty. From the same prolific womb of governmental injustice we breed the two great classes—tramps and millionaires.**
>
> THE OMAHA PLATFORM,
> July 4, 1892

The National Farmers' Alliance and Industrial Union, known simply as the Farmers' Alliance, was much more effective than the Grange. Founded in Texas in 1877, the Farmers' Alliance spread rapidly across the South, the West, and the upper Plains states. The goal of the Alliance was not to restore rural America to Jeffersonian simplicity, but to bring American farmers into the modern world of industry and prosperity. The Alliance focused above all on education, broadly conceived. That meant public schools for their children and the spread of scientific agriculture and sound business practices among themselves. To spread the word, the Alliance built a remarkable network of newspapers and lecturers to help liberate individual farmers from their rural isolation. Yet the appeal of the Farmers' Alliance transcended politics and economic reform. For men and women alike the Farmers' Alliance offered a chance to escape the stifling isolation of rural life. It appealed to the desire among tens of thousands of farmers to claim a share in the progress and prosperity of American life.

Nevertheless, at its core the Alliance was a reform organization calling for a specific set of economic policies. Above all, the farmers wanted to inflate the currency, sometimes by the circulation of more silver currency, sometimes by the circulation of more paper currency, or "greenbacks," and sometimes by a combination of the two. Inspired by the successful example of highly organized corporations, especially railroads, the Farmers' Alliance also supported a system of cooperative "subtreasuries" that would allow farmers to pool their products and store them in warehouses until the best prices were available. In the meantime the Alliance cooperative would sustain its members through low-interest loans.

By the late 1880s the Farmers' Alliance had attracted millions of members, concentrated in the southern, western, and Plains states. Its potency was demonstrated at a huge meeting at Ocala, Florida, in 1890. The Ocala Platform supported a host of reforms that joined economic progress to democratic reform. In addition to planks calling

Kansas Farmers Organizing to Attend a Populist Party Gathering

for the free coinage of silver, lower tariffs, and a government system of subtreasuries, the platform also called for a constitutional amendment providing for direct election of senators. Finally, the Alliance called for strict government regulation, and if necessary direct government ownership, of the nation's railroad and telegraph industries.

The Farmers' Alliance steered clear of politics and instead judged political candidates by the degree to which they supported the reforms advocated in the Ocala Platform. But very little such support was forthcoming from either of the major parties. Farmers' Alliance members therefore formed their own third parties, with some success on the Great Plains in the election of 1890. Out of these initial forays into politics came the most significant third party of the late nineteenth century, the People's Party, otherwise known as the Populists.

The Rise of the Populists

On February 22, 1892, a huge coalition of reform organizations met in St. Louis, including Single Tax advocates inspired by Henry George, greenbackers who wanted an inflationary currency policy, representatives of the Knights of Labor, and members of the Farmers' Alliance. Together they founded the People's Party and called for a presidential nominating convention to meet in Omaha, Nebraska, on July 4. There they nominated General James B. Weaver of Iowa for president and drew up the famous Omaha Platform, a vigorous restatement of the proposals laid out two years earlier by the Farmers' Alliance. Like the Ocala Platform, the Omaha Platform demanded an inflationary currency policy and subtreasuries. The Populists also called for a graduated income tax, direct government ownership of the railroad and telegraph industries, and the redistribution of lands owned by the railroads.

In the 1892 elections the Populist presidential candidate won about 1 million votes, and the Populists elected several senators, representatives, governors, and state legislators. But there was no support among wage earners in the industrial centers of the North and East. The Populist platform, for all its talk of the unity of working people, was frankly incompatible with the interests of industrial workers, who favored the protective tariffs that shielded the industrial economy. Inflation would only undermine the value of their wages and raise the price of commodities, and income taxes would shift the tax burden from landowners and importers to wage laborers. Conversely, farmers who hired workers had every reason to oppose the eight-hour day and laws restricting child labor.

Southern Populists faced a particularly daunting challenge. They could not hope to win without the support of the largest class of impoverished farmers, black sharecroppers. But any attempt to build a multiracial alliance of white and black Populists was met with an avalanche of racial demagoguery from Democratic politicians. White Populists had a hard enough time overcoming their own racial prejudices. The Farmers' Alliance had always been strictly segregated, with the Colored Farmers' Alliance kept at arm's length from the central organization. And in truth the economic interests of the two groups were not always compatible. But for political purposes they did need one another, and this made some amount of cross-racial cooperation desirable. Leading black Populists were fully aware of the limits of any alliance they might enter into with white reformers. But the *need* for a coalition of whites and blacks had a tendency to contradict the entrenched racial prejudices of white farmers. It also made the extremist racial demagoguery of the Democratic Party all but inevitable. Third parties are hard to sustain in the best of circumstances, but in the face of such attacks Populism in the South could not survive.

Conclusion

After the Civil War the problems of industrial capitalism placed increasing strain on the political system. The two major parties were so closely matched in electoral strength that neither could risk bold new programs to meet the needs of a new political economy. So restless workers, desperate farmers, and an anxious middle class turned in increasing numbers to voluntary organizations, labor unions, and farmers' alliances.

The politics of industrial society reached a dramatic turning point in the 1890s. During that decade American voters went to the polls in record numbers. Organized farmers made their most radical demands; labor agitation reached a violent climax. And as night follows day, a conservative reaction set in. Movements to restrict the number of voters emerged, particularly in the South. Opponents of immigration made significant strides. The Supreme Court declared constitutional one of history's greatest social experiments, systematic racial segregation. In short, radicalism and reaction reached their peak in the 1890s. During the closing decade of the nineteenth century, a recognizably modern America was born.

Further Readings

Richard Franklin Bensel, *The Political Economy of American Industrialization, 1877–1900.* Argues that the Republican Party was the "agent" of industrialization.

Ruth Bordin, *Woman and Temperance: The Quest for Power and Liberty, 1873–1900* (1981). *Woman and Temperance* is the best single volume available on the subject.

Leon Fink, *Workingmen's Democracy: The Knights of Labor and American Politics* (1983). A case study, with broad implications, showing the connections between political mobilization and labor organization.

Walter LaFeber, *The New Empire: An Interpretation of American Expansion, 1860–1898* (1963). Links American foreign policy to commercial expansion.

Michael McGerr, *The Decline of Popular Politics: The American North, 1865–1928* (1986). Particularly strong on the culture of popular politics in the late nineteenth century.

Charles Postel, *The Populist Vision* (2007). Outstanding. The best book on populism.

John L. Thomas, *Alternative America: Henry George, Edward Bellamy, Henry Demarest Lloyd, and the Adversary Tradition* (1983). A sensitive examination of middle-class radicalism and its limits.

>> Timeline >>

▼ **1867**
United States purchases Alaska from Russia
Patrons of Husbandry (the Grange) founded

▼ **1869**
Noble and Holy Order of the Knights of Labor founded
Suez Canal opened

▼ **1870**
Department of Justice created

▼ **1872**
Grant reelected

▼ **1873**
"Crusade" against alcohol begins in Hillsboro, Ohio

▼ **1874**
WCTU is formed

▼ **1876**
Rutherford B. Hayes elected president
Porfirio Díaz seizes power in Mexico

▼ **1877**
Farmers' Alliance founded

▼ **1878**
Bland-Allison Act

▼ **1879**
Frances Willard becomes president of the WCTU
Henry George publishes *Progress and Poverty*

▼ **1880**
James Garfield elected president

▼ **1881**
Garfield assassinated; Chester Arthur becomes president
WCTU endorses women's suffrage

▼ **1883**
Pendleton Civil Service Act
"Mongrel Tariff"

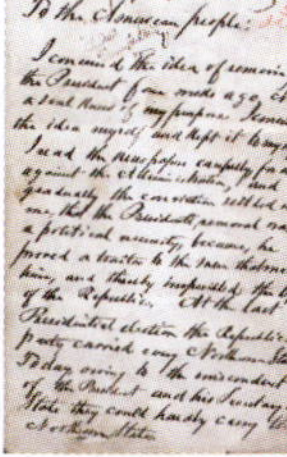

Who, What?

Luna Kellie 633
Charles Francis Adams 638
Henry George 648
Frances Willard 651
Terence Powderly 653
James B. Weaver 656
The Nation 638
Pendleton Act 641
Sherman Act 642
Greenbackers 643
Nationalist Clubs 649
The WCTU 651
Knights of Labor 652
Farmers' Alliance 655
Populism 656

Review Questions

1. Describe the two major "styles" of politics in the late nineteenth century.
2. What were the major issues in national politics in this period?
3. What did Henry George, Edward Bellamy, and Frances Willard have in common?
4. What did the Farmers' Alliance stand for?

For further review materials and resource information, please visit www.oup.com/us/ofthepeople

▼ 1884
Grover Cleveland elected president

▼ 1886
Nationwide strike for eight-hour day
Riot at Haymarket Square in Chicago

▼ 1887
Interstate Commerce Act
Four Haymarket anarchists executed
Dawes Severalty Act

▼ 1888
Benjamin Harrison elected president

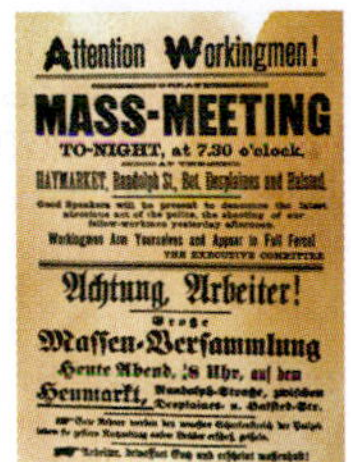

Edward Bellamy publishes *Looking Backward*

▼ 1889
United States convenes first Pan-American Conference
Department of Agriculture created

▼ 1890
Harrison-McKinley Tariff
Sherman Anti-Trust Act
Ocala Platform

▼ 1891
Queen Liliuokalani assumes the Hawaiian throne

▼ 1892
Omaha Platform of the People's Party
Grover Cleveland reelected

▼ 1893
Queen Liliuokalani overthrown

▼ 1898
Frances Willard dies

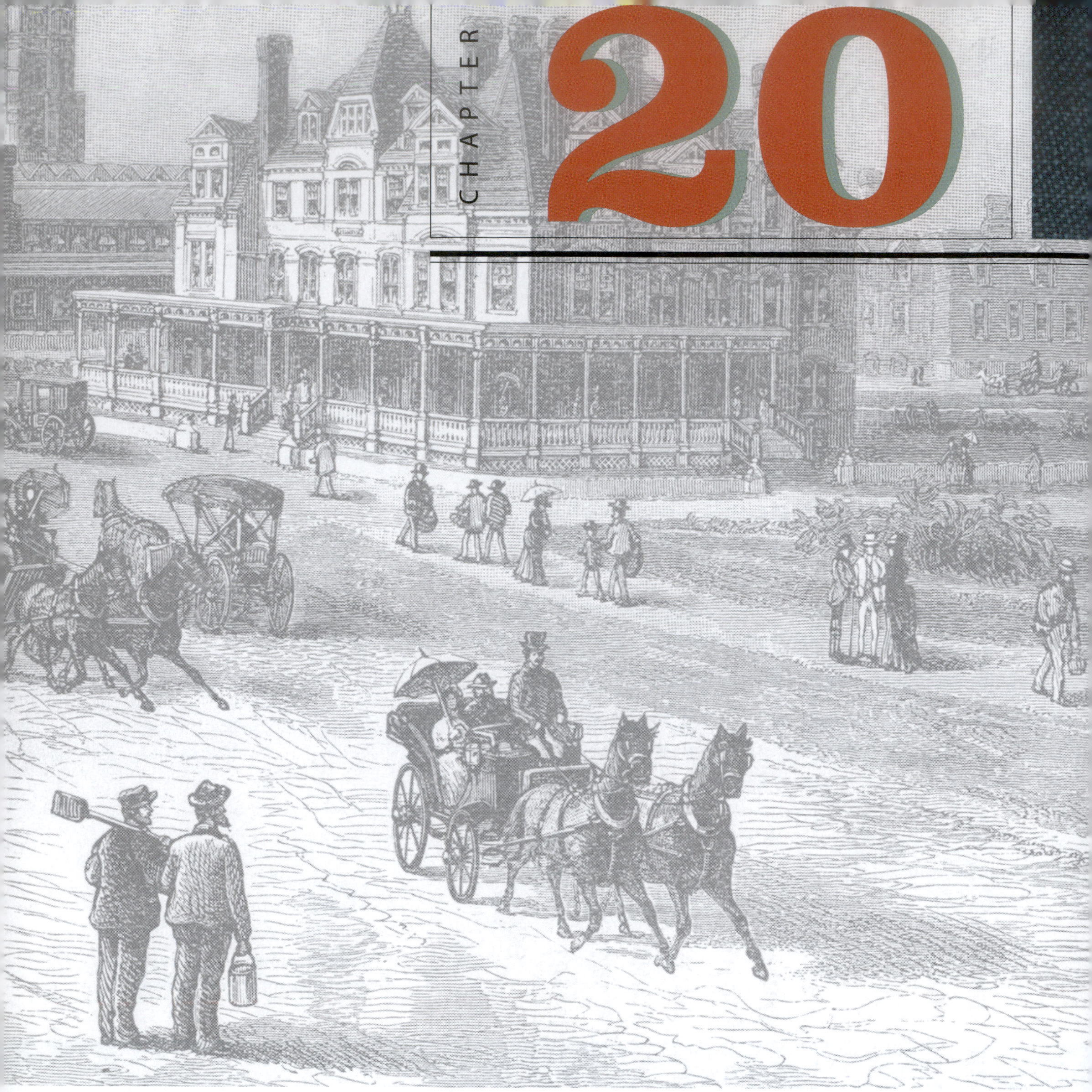

CHAPTER 20

Common Threads

>> How did industrial ideals of efficiency and organization change democratic practice in America during the early 1900s?

>> Did the choices Americans made about how to run their economy set the United States on a course for overseas conflict?

>> What did it mean to be modern? How did the pace of technological change affect Americans' outlook?

Industry and Empire

1890–1900

AMERICAN PORTRAIT

>> J. P. Morgan

It was a short distance from the Arlington Hotel to the White House, and although it was icy and dark, J. Pierpont Morgan chose to walk. He pulled his scarf up around a scowling face known to millions of newspaper readers. He had not wanted to come to Washington. There were "large interests" that depended on keeping the currency of the United States sound, he told a Treasury official, and those interests were now in jeopardy. The commander in chief of the nation's bankers was going to meet the president to keep the United States from going bankrupt.

The events leading up to this urgent meeting stretched back five years to 1890, when business failures in Argentina toppled London's venerable Baring Brothers investment house and triggered a collapse in European stock prices. Depression spread through Britain, Germany, and France. Anxious European investors began selling off their substantial American holdings. For two years, good harvests staved off the inevitable, but in early 1893 the panic reached the United States. The Philadelphia and Reading Railroad folded in February. Fourteen thousand businesses soon followed, along with more than 600 banks.

Summer brought more bad news from abroad. The government of India stopped minting silver, causing U.S. silver dollars to lose one-sixth of their value. Wall Street went into another tailspin. In New York 55,000 men, women, and girls in the clothing industry were thrown out of work. Banks refused to cash checks, and coins of all kinds vanished from circulation. The governor of Nebraska instructed the police to deal leniently with the thousands of homeless poor people on the roads. Breadlines formed. "For thorough chaos I have seen nothing since the war to compare with it," the historian Henry Adams observed. "The world surely cannot remain as mad as it is."

For Grover Cleveland the madness was only starting. The anger of workers and farmers, simmering for decades, was boiling over. The president called Congress into special session and pledged to keep the dollar on the gold standard, but it was not enough. A wave of strikes swept the country. Unemployed workers battled police on the Capitol grounds. By January 1895 so many panicky investors were cashing government bonds that the Treasury's gold reserve was half gone, and it looked as if the remainder might last only two weeks. Reluctantly, Cleveland asked his aides to open negotiations with Morgan.

Admired and reviled, Morgan was known as the preeminent financial manipulator of the late nineteenth century. Born to wealth in Hartford, Connecticut, he had been a Wall Street fixture since before the Civil War. Like his contemporaries, steelmaker Andrew Carnegie and oil magnate John D. Rockefeller, Morgan's skill lay in organization. He restructured railroads, rooting out corruption, waste, and competition and driving down wages. Instead of taking risks, he eliminated them. His style was to gather the leaders of warring firms for a meeting aboard his mammoth yacht, the *Corsair*, and strike a bargain that allowed everyone to profit. Cleveland was about to place the Treasury in this man's hands.

The president opened the meeting by suggesting that things might not be so bad; perhaps a new bond issue would stabilize the Treasury. No, Morgan replied flatly, the run on gold would continue until European investors regained confidence. As things stood, they had more faith in the House of Morgan than in the government. If the president agreed, Morgan would arrange a private loan and personally guarantee the solvency of the U.S. Treasury. After a stunned silence, the two men shook hands. News of the deal instantly calmed the bond markets. The crisis was over. The *New York Sun* reported that the deal struck between the country's political and economic

continued

>> AMERICAN PORTRAIT *continued*

chief executives "revived a confidence in the wealth and resources of this country," but Populist newspapers denounced it as a conspiracy and a "great bunco game."

Culminating two decades of economic turbulence, the Panic of 1893 permanently transformed the American political economy. Businessmen like Morgan created even larger corporate combinations and placed them under the control of professional managers. They used technology and "scientific management" to take control of the workplace and push laborers to work faster and harder. Workers resisted, and the 1890s witnessed brutal clashes between capital and labor. Looking for jobs and schools, country people moved to the city and found both promise and danger. Social mobility among African Americans aroused fears in whites, and southerners created a system of formal segregation, enforced by law and terror. Amid growing violence, industrial workers, Native Americans, and African Americans debated how best to deal with the overwhelming forces ranged against them.

The 1890s were also a turning point in American political history. After the 1896 election, many Americans voluntarily withdrew from the electoral process. Others were systematically removed from the voter rolls through a process known as "disfranchisement." African American leaders and union organizers urged their followers to turn away from politics in favor of "bread and butter" economic issues. Torchlight parades and flag raisings became scarce, and the masculine, public spectacle of nineteenth-century politics died out. Patriotism, once synonymous with partisanship, now became identified with the United States' global military and economic ambitions. Civic events featured army bands and cannon salutes. Newspapers conjured up foreign threats. As Americans became more conscious of their military power, they watched the horizon, fearing that well-being at home could hinge on events as far away as China.

Americans began to feel that their economy's links to the world—and the changes manufacturing and rapid communications brought to politics and daily life—separated the events of their times from everything that had happened before. Morgan's rescue required transactions on two continents, instantaneously coordinated by telegraph. The speed of industry, trade, and information, the ability of machines and technology to span distance and time created a sense that the environment and the future could be controlled. Many felt that the peoples who possessed this newfound control—the modern countries—stood apart from those living in other lands whose thought and action were not guided by science and the streams of information issuing from transoceanic cables.

Between 1890 and 1900 Americans made their country recognizably modern. Those with the means to do so enlarged, accelerated, and rationalized the settings of work and daily life. Financiers and giant corporations assumed control of the American economy. Huge cities grew. The significance of voting declined, and a decade that opened with a global economic catastrophe ended with a dramatic display of the global reach of U.S. power.

OUTLINE

The Crisis of the 1890s

Financial convulsions, strikes, and the powerlessness of government against wealth rudely reminded Americans of how much their country had changed since the Civil War. When Illinois sent Abraham Lincoln to Congress, Chicago's population was less than 5,000; in 1890 it exceeded 1 million. Gone was the America of myth and memory, where class tensions were slight, and upward (or at least westward) mobility seemed easy. Many Americans, a British diplomat noted, foresaw the imminent collapse of civilization: "They all begin with the Roman Empire and point out resemblances." Others, however, felt that the United States was passing into a new phase of history that would lead to still greater trials and achievements.

> **Chicago is the product of modern capitalism, and, like other great commercial centers, is unfit for human habitation.**
>
> EUGENE V. DEBS

Hard Times

Chicago in 1893 captured the hopes and fears of the new age. To celebrate the 400th anniversary of Columbus's discovery of America, the city staged the World's Columbian Exposition, transforming a lakefront bog into a gleaming vision of the past and the future, but just outside the exposition's gates lay the city of the present. In December 1893 Chicago had 75,000 unemployed, and the head of a local relief committee declared that "famine is in our midst." In the nation's second-largest metropolis, thousands lived in shacks or high-rise tenements in which each densely packed floor had only a single bathroom. Jobs were hard to find, and when groups of men gathered at the exposition's gates to beg for work, the police drove them away.

As the depression deepened, the Cleveland administration ordered troops to guard Treasury branches in New York and Chicago. Jobless people banded together into "industrial armies," many with decidedly revolutionary aims. Hundreds heeded the call of Jacob Coxey, a prosperous Ohio landowner and Populist. Coxey appealed in 1894 to the unemployed to march on Washington and demand free silver and a public road-building program that would hire a half-million workers. When Coxey set out with 100 followers, reporters predicted the ragged band would disintegrate as soon as the food ran out, but well-wishers turned out by the thousands to greet the Coxeyites and offer supplies for the trip.

Industrial armies set out from Boston, St. Louis, Chicago, Portland, Seattle, and Los Angeles. When Coxey arrived in Washington on May 1 with 500 marchers, Cleveland put the U.S. Army on alert. The march ended ignominiously. In front of the Capitol, police wrestled Coxey into a paddy wagon, and his disillusioned army dispersed. Still, after the march no one could deny that something was seriously wrong. Ray Stannard Baker, a reporter for the *Chicago Record*, acknowledged that "the public would not be cheering the army and feeding it voluntarily without a recognition, however vague, that the conditions in the country warranted some such explosion."

The Overseas Frontier

At noon on September 16, 1893, thousands of settlers massed along the borders of the Cherokee Strip, a 6-million-acre tract in northwestern Oklahoma. In the next six hours the population of Wharton, Oklahoma, grew from zero to 10,000 and the

AMERICA AND THE WORLD

>> Singer Sewing Machine Company

Before the Russian Revolution, St. Petersburg's grandest boulevard, the Nevskii Prospekt, was known according to one tourist for its "cathedrals, the grocery of Elisieff Brothers, and the Singer Sewing Machine Company's establishment." The headquarters of Kompaniya Singer was Russia's tallest building. Completed in 1904, the six-story tower was topped by an illuminated globe bearing the name Singer in gilded letters. It symbolized the global reach of one of America's preeminent manufacturers.

Isaac Merritt Singer did not invent the sewing machine; he invented a way to market it. Elias Howe, who applied for the first U.S. patent in 1845, invented a device with an oscillating eye-pointed needle that made a locking stitch fed continuously from spools mounted on an overhanging arm. It seemed a practical, labor-saving device, but Howe soon found that tailors and shoemakers who made a living by hand sewing had no use for it. His principal customers viewed the gadget with hostility.

Singer, a machinist from Rochester, New York, made Howe's device smaller, added a decorative cabinet, and sold it as an article for the home. He employed young women to demonstrate the machine in shop-front "sewing centers." Salesmen went door to door, and in the 1880s, Singer introduced buying on the "installment" plan, whereby customers could purchase a new machine by putting down a dollar a week. It was a "psychological fact, which has come to light in this sewing machine business," he asserted, that "a woman would rather pay $100" in installments "than $50 outright." By 1867, Singer was the largest manufacturer of sewing machines in the world, producing 43,000 a year.

The federal government aided this growth in two ways. The need for military uniforms during the Civil War outstripped the capacities of hand tailors, and Singer promoted machine sewing as a patriotic duty women could perform for the country. "We Clothe the Union Army," the company proclaimed. Secondly, the government imposed a 35 percent tariff on imported sewing machines, preventing European makers from challenging Singer in its home market.

With its domestic base secure, Singer expanded. By 1890, it had an international merchandising network that sold three-quarters of the world's sewing machines. A German consul general in Istanbul reported that Singer's "ingeniously organized selling apparatus, extending to the smallest places" gave it "an almost unassailable position."

The sales formula did not work everywhere. In India, agents complained that they were not allowed to speak to women. Chinese merchants were suspicious of the "iron tailor." The company had trouble collecting installments from Kyrgyz nomads, who never stayed put long enough to make payments. A Singer representative in Charkoff, Russia, was ordered to leave on the grounds that he was "a foreign Jew." In Japan, however, the adoption of Western-style military uniforms during the Sino-Japanese War (1894–1895) provided a ready market, and Japanese outfitters adopted the faster-moving treadle models. Europe, the Philippines, Mexico, and Russia all became significant markets.

Alarmed by Singer's success, European governments began protecting their colonial and home markets. In 1893, French courts ordered Singer to reveal information about its earnings and stock dividends. Other governments raised import taxes or set quotas to exclude American machines. Singer responded by forming separate national subsidiaries that could claim local, rather than American, origin. When the Spanish-American War broke out in 1898, the Singer offices in Madrid flew the Spanish flag and donated to the war fund. The locals were not fooled. The newspaper *El País* called Singer "an immense octopus whose tentacles encircle Spain and crushes it, snatching from it the savings of its workers in order to aggrandize the miserable, iniquitous, cowardly disgusting North American nation."

The company prided itself on bringing democracy and fair dealing to the world. In the Middle East, Singer machines carried the brand *Hurriya*, Arabic for "freedom." By the turn of the century, the company had over 4,000 branch offices, located on every inhabited continent. It opened a string of factories overseas, in Montreal (1882),

Floridsdorf, Austria (1882), Kilbowie, Scotland (1883), Podolsk, Russia (1902), and Wittenberg, Prussia (1904).

Growth slowed in the more tumultuous twentieth century. The agent in Teheran had to flee a revolution in 1907, and ten years later Red Guards stormed the St. Petersburg office with guns drawn. The mass armies deployed in World War I wore factory-made uniforms, and the postwar market for ready-to-wear clothing undercut demand. German bombers pounded the Scotland plant to rubble in 1941, and four years later the Soviet army smashed the Wittenberg factory.

Singer was a forerunner of a global commerce in consumer goods that the United States would dominate in the late twentieth century. Portable and practical, the machine itself had universal appeal, and its marketing was infinitely adaptable. In 1891, Singer's advertising department issued trading cards showing the peoples of the world in native costume. The images were strikingly different from racialized depictions common in that period. Although the fabrics and colors varied, the peoples of other cultures looked very much alike, each with their sewing machine, a global community of consumers.

last great land rush came to an end. The line of settlement that had been marked on census maps throughout the nineteenth century had ceased to exist.

Frederick Jackson Turner, a historian at the University of Wisconsin, explained the implications of this event. Steady westward movement had placed Americans in "touch with the simplicity of primitive life," he explained, and allowed the nation to renew the process of social development continuously. The frontier furnished "the forces dominating the American character," and without its rejuvenating influence, democracy itself might be in danger. Turner's thesis resonated with Americans' fears that modernity had robbed their country of its unique strengths. For the previous 10 years, Populists and financiers had worried that the end of free land would signal trials for free institutions. "There is no unexplored part of the world left suitable for men to inhabit," Populist writer William "Coin" Harvey claimed, "and now justice stands at bay."

That assertion turned out to be premature. More homesteaders claimed more western lands after 1890 than before, and well into the twentieth century new "resource frontiers"—oil fields, timber ranges, Alaskan ore strikes—were explored. Irrigation technology and markets for new crops created a bonanza for dry-land farmers. Nonetheless, the economic and social upheavals of the 1890s seemed to confirm Turner's contention that new frontiers would have to be found overseas.

While farmers had always needed to sell a large portion of their output abroad, until the 1890s manufactured goods had sold almost exclusively through domestic distribution networks. As the total volume of manufactured goods increased, the composition of exports changed. Oil, steel, textiles, typewriters, and sewing machines made up a larger portion of overseas trade. American consumers still bought nine-tenths of the output of domestic factories, but by 1898 the extra tenth was worth more than $1 billion (see Figure 20–1).

As American firms entered foreign markets, they discovered that other nations and empires guarded their markets with restrictive tariffs just as the United States did, to promote domestic manufacturing. Government and business leaders acknowledged that to gain a larger share of world trade, the United States might have to use political or military leverage to pry open foreign markets. Their social Darwinist view of the world—as a jungle in which only the fittest nations would survive—justified engaging in global competition for trade and economic survival.

Recognizing that a strong navy could extend America's economic reach, Congress authorized the construction of three large battleships in 1890. Four years later,

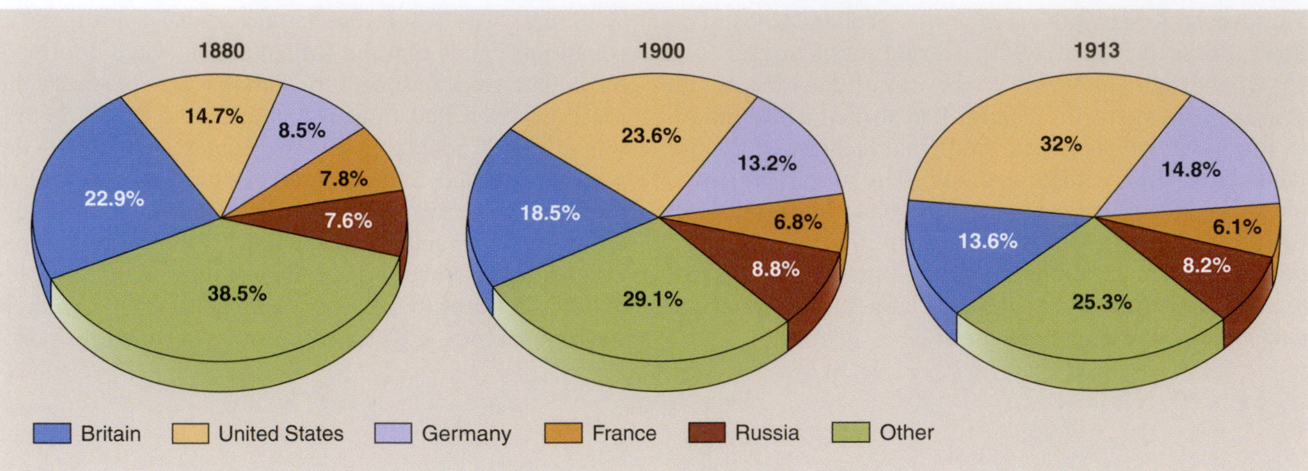

Figure 20–1 Relative Shares of World Manufacturing The United States was a significant industrial power by 1880, and by the turn of the century it moved into a position of dominance.

an official commission investigated the feasibility of a canal across Central America. A newly organized National Association of Manufacturers urged the government to open foreign markets. The administration created a Bureau of Foreign Commerce and urged U.S. consuls to seize opportunities to extend sales of American industrial products abroad.

Congress also knew that tariff rates could influence the expansion of trade. Before 1890, taxes on imports had been set high to raise revenue and to help domestic manufacturers by making foreign goods unaffordable. The Harrison-McKinley Tariff of 1890 did something different. It allowed the president to use the tariff to punish countries that closed their markets to U.S. goods or reward them for lifting customs barriers. This "bargaining tariff" put the full weight of the U.S. economy behind the drive to open markets around the world.

The United States began to reorganize itself to compete in a global marketplace. The struggle required the executive branch to enlarge the military and take on additional authority. It also meant that domestic industries had to produce higher-quality goods at less cost to match those being turned out in Germany or Japan. Employers and workers had to gear up for the global contest for profits.

The Drive for Efficiency

In mines, factories, and mills, production relied on the knowledge of skilled workers. Laborers used their knowledge to set work routines, assure their own safety, and bargain with managers who wanted to change the pace or conditions of work. As profits stagnated and competition intensified, managers tried to prevent labor from sharing control over production. In the struggle for control in the workplace, employers relied on three allies: technology, scientific management, and federal power. Workers resisted, organizing themselves and enlisting the support of their communities.

Advances in management techniques enabled employers to break routines favored by laborers and to dictate new methods. Frederick Winslow Taylor, the first "efficiency expert," reduced each occupation to a series of simple, precise move-

AMERICAN LANDSCAPE

>> Pullman, Illinois

When economist Richard T. Ely first saw the industrial town of Pullman in 1885, he thought he was looking at the future. A planned suburb entirely owned by one company and inhabited by its employees, Pullman seemed "a forerunner of better things for the laboring classes." On broad streets named for famous inventors—Watt, Fulton, Morse, and, of course, Pullman—mechanics, shopkeepers, and company officials lived side by side in tidy homes with gas heat and indoor plumbing. Pullmanites shopped under the glass roof of the Arcade, the first indoor shopping mall, and benefited from a library, a theater, and a school provided by their employer. Surrounded by culture and natural beauty, Pullman workers were, by company estimate, 40 percent more refined, thrifty, and wholesome than other workers.

George Mortimer Pullman's name was synonymous with luxury. With the help of Andrew Carnegie, he had become the preeminent maker of passenger railroad cars. By the 1880s every railroad in the country used Pullman sleeping cars, dining cars, and observation cars.

In 1880 he decided to centralize his scattered factories into a single site on Lake Calumet, south of Chicago. He asked Solomon S. Beman, a young architect, and Nathan Barrett, a landscape designer, to build a model town around the plant. By the following year, there were 1400 dwellings, public parks, gardens, a hotel, a school, and a church, all designed in a gracious "secular gothic" style. By 1893 it was home to 12,000 residents.

Pullman was not designed as art or charity, but for business. Happy, healthy workers were expected to produce more, and in Pullman's estimate, they did. Modern sewers and plumbing made the air and water safe. The death rate in Pullman was less than half that in nearby neighborhoods. There were no saloons. Drinkers had to walk miles to one of the 30 taverns at the edge of the company property on Kensington Avenue.

The theater's management screened out "immoral" shows. An exhibit at the Columbian Exposition claimed Pullman was making a new kind of worker, "distinct in appearance, in tidiness of dress, in fact in all the external indications of self-respect."

Other companies rushed to copy Pullman's success. Chocolate makers built Hershey, Pennsylvania, and near Cincinnati the producers of floating soap colonized the model town of Ivoryville. But the residents of Pullman were less enthusiastic. Despite low rents and spacious homes, most Pullmanites moved out within a year or two. Even those who stayed saw the arrangement as temporary. "We call it camping out," one woman told Ely. The town was nicer than any they had lived in before, but "the general complaint seems to be that they were too much under Mr. Pullman's thumb."

Pullman had no newspaper, no clubs, no elected officials. The school board was manned by company executives. When a group of women organized a charity, the company ordered it stopped. Political activity, especially on behalf of Democratic candidates, was discouraged. When shopkeeper John P. Hopkins put up a sign for Grover Cleveland, his lease was revoked. The town's one church was for "artistic effect" only. No congregation met there.

After staying several weeks, Ely concluded that "the idea of Pullman is un-American." It was impossible

continued

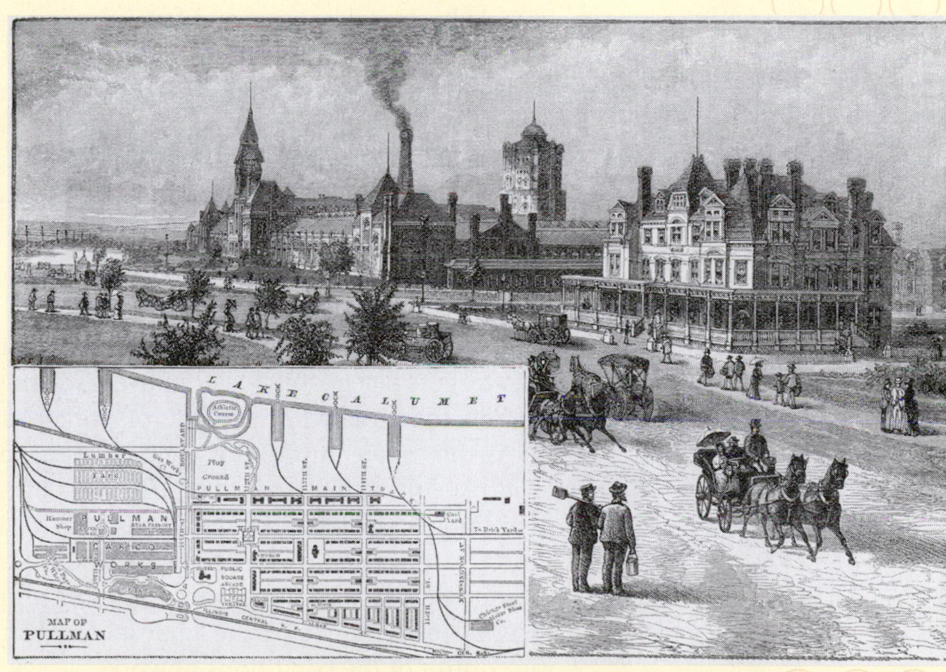

>> **AMERICAN LANDSCAPE** *continued*

for the residents to escape the overshadowing power of the company, which owned the houses, the shops, even the streets. There was not a single piece of property that was privately owned, and leases could be terminated in 10 days. In the factories, workers assembled sumptuous railroad cars that only reminded them of the wealth they could not attain.

When the Panic of 1893 hit, Pullman laid off 2,000 of his 5,000 employees and cut wages to the others by 25 percent. Rents dropped in Chicago, but not in Pullman. Many residents could not afford rent or food, but there were no charities or municipal agencies to help. There was only the company.

Desperate workers organized in the spring of 1894 and joined Eugene V. Debs's American Railway Union (ARU). On May 11, they struck. George Pullman cut off credit for workers at the stores in the Arcade and then went on vacation. In June, Pullman workers asked the entire ARU to join the strike. "We struck because we were without hope," one worker told the convention. The ARU voted to make the strike national; ARU switchmen would refuse to switch Pullman cars onto trains.

The strike shut down 20 railroads in the West and Midwest. Almost no traffic moved through Chicago, the nation's hub. The U.S. attorney general vowed to meet the strike with force, and President Cleveland sent 2,000 troops to Chicago. Fighting between workers and soldiers broke out at the stockyards and in the Illinois Central switchyard. Troops fired into crowds of workers, killing 20 and wounding 60 others. Debs was jailed for "interfering with the mails." The union was broken. The town of Pullman remained peaceful, but residents saw, over the tops of their houses, a column of smoke rising from the Columbian Exposition. The White City was on fire.

Three years later, George Pullman died of a heart attack. His obituaries mixed praise for his achievements with criticism of his stubborn refusal to head off one of the bloodiest labor conflicts in U.S. history. The next year, the city of Chicago absorbed Pullman and the company town became a neighborhood where voters could choose their own aldermen. Efficient, paternal corporate rule gave way to the messy but democratic politics of a big city. A writer for *The Nation* noted that what working people wanted most was a chance to own a place of their own. "Mr. Pullman in his scheme for a model community for American workmen overlooked this peculiar American characteristic. Hence, in my humble opinion, these tears." ●

ments that could be easily taught and endlessly repeated. To manage time and motion scientifically, Taylor explained, employers should collect "all of the traditional knowledge which in the past has been possessed by workingmen" and reduce "this knowledge to rules, laws, and formulae."

Taylor's stopwatch studies determined the optimal load of a hand shovel (21.5 pounds), how much pig iron a man could load into a boxcar in a day (75 tons), how much the man should be paid (3.75 cents per ton), and how much he should eat (3500 calories). Even office work could be separated into simple, unvaried tasks. Taylorism created a new layer of college-educated "middle managers" who supervised production in offices and factories.

Although Taylorism accelerated production, it also increased absenteeism and worker dissatisfaction. Telephone operators had a 100 percent yearly turnover rate. Another new technique, "personnel management," promised to solve this problem with tests to select suitable employees, team sports to ward off boredom, and social workers to regulate the activities of workers at home.

As the nineteenth century ended, management was establishing a monopoly on expertise and using it to set the rhythms of work and play, but workers did not easily relinquish control. In the 1890s, the labor struggle entered a new phase. New unions confronted corporations in bloody struggles that forced the federal government to decide whether communities or property had more rights. Skilled workers asserted leadership over the labor movement, and they rallied to the cause of retaining control of the conditions of work.

Taylorism Corporations used stopwatches and social workers to stretch each machine and worker to full capacity. The method was called "Taylorism."

Progress and Force

To accelerate production, employers aimed to seize full control over the workplace. They had private detective agencies at their disposal, the courts on their side, and federal troops ready to act. In Pennsylvania and Chicago this antagonism led to bloody confrontations.

In 1892 Andrew Carnegie's mill at Homestead, Pennsylvania, the most modern steelworks in the world, turned out armor plating for American warships and steel rails for shipment abroad. In June Carnegie's partner, Henry Clay Frick, broke off talks with the plant's American Federation of Labor–affiliated union and announced that the plant would close on July 2 and reopen a week later with a nonunion workforce. The union contended that Frick's actions constituted an assault on the community, and the town agreed. On the morning of July 6, as 300 armed guards tried to land from barges, they were raked by gunfire. Townspeople placed the company guards under arrest.

The victory was short-lived. A week later the governor of Pennsylvania sent in the state militia, and under martial law strikebreakers reignited the furnaces. Homestead became one of labor's most celebrated battles, but it broke the union and showed that corporations, backed by government, would defend their prerogatives at any cost.

The Pullman strike, centered in Chicago, paralyzed the nation's railroads for two weeks in the summer of 1894. It pitted the American Railway Union (ARU) against 24 railroads and the powerful Pullman Company over the company's decision to cut pay by 30 percent. The calm at the center of the strike was Eugene V. Debs, charismatic president of the ARU, who urged strikers to obey the law, avoid violence, and respect strikebreakers. When Cleveland sent in the army over the governor's protests, enraged crowds blocked tracks and burned railroad cars. Police arrested hundreds of strikers. Debs went to jail for six months and came out a Socialist. Pullman and Homestead showed that the law was now on the side of the proprietors.

Newspapers, magazines, and novels portrayed Pullman and Homestead as two more battles in an unending war against the savage opponents of progress. Frederic Remington, famous for his reporting on wars against the Navajo and Apache Indians, covered the Pullman strike for *Harper's Weekly*. In his account, rough-hewn cavalrymen, having defeated the Sioux, now came to rescue civilization from the unions.

The business elite's influence over cultural expression allowed it to define the terms of this contest, to label its enemies as enemies of progress. Workers did not object to efficiency or modernization, but they wanted a share of its benefits and some control over the process of change. With state and corporate power stacked against them, the workers' goals appeared beyond reach.

Just as the massacre at Wounded Knee in 1890 had ended the armed resistance of Native Americans, the violence at Homestead and Chicago signified that the struggle of industrial workers had entered a new phase.

Corporate Consolidation

In a wave of mergers between 1897 and 1904, investment bankers consolidated leading industries under the control of a few corporate giants. J. P. Morgan led the movement. His goal was to take industry away from the industrialists and give it to the bankers. Bankers, he felt, had better information about the true worth of an industry, and they could make better decisions about its future. Financiers could create the larger and leaner firms needed to take on foreign competitors.

Morgan's greatest triumph was the merger of eight huge steel companies, their ore ranges, rolling mills, railroads, and shipping lines into the colossal U.S. Steel. Announced in March 1901, the merger created the world's largest corporation. Its capital amounted to 7 percent of the total wealth of the United States (by comparison, Wal-Mart's total assets in 2008 amounted to one and one half percent of the gross national product). U.S. Steel's investors (Morgan especially) earned profits "greatly in excess of reasonable compensation," according to one government report.

Bankers outnumbered steelmakers on U.S. Steel's board, and they controlled the company. *McClure's* magazine reported that the new company was "planning the first really systematic effort ever made by Americans to capture the foreign steel trade." Morgan's son wrote to his stepmother that "Father is in the same category with Queen Victoria." He did not say what category his father's employees and customers fell into.

A Modern Economy

Grover Cleveland's bargain with Morgan revived the industrial economy, but farm prices, wages, and the president's popularity remained flat. Cash-strapped farmers in the West and South grumbled against the president's hard-money policies and cozy relationships with plutocrats like Morgan. Calling out troops to crush the Pullman strike cost Cleveland the support of northern workers. The escalating cycle of economic and political crises, farmer and labor insurgencies, middle-class radicalism, and upper-class conservatism fractured political parties. Democrats, Republicans, and Populists all called for stronger government action, but each party split over what action to take. In 1896 the "currency question" dominated a watershed election that transformed the two major parties and destroyed the third.

The year 1896 was the last time presidential candidates openly debated great economic questions in terms that had been familiar to voters since Thomas Jefferson ran for president in 1800; 1896 was also the first recognizably modern presidential election. It was the first time a successful candidate fully employed the advertising and fund-raising techniques of twentieth-century campaigns.

> **Whatever questions may at one time or another disturb the minds of the mass of men who hold the franchise in England, France, Germany, or other European countries, the plain people have never for a moment believed it possible that they were competent to settle currency and banking questions.**
>
> DR. ALBERT SHAW,
> political scientist, October 1896

Currency and the Tariff

The soundness of the dollar, which Morgan and Cleveland worked so hard to preserve, was a mixed blessing for Americans. Based on gold, the dollar helped sell American goods in foreign markets, especially in Europe, where currencies were also based on gold. The United States traded on a much smaller scale with countries—like Mexico or China—that used silver. "Without exception," Cleveland's secretary of commerce explained, "prices are fixed in the markets of countries having a gold standard." Gold, however, was valuable because it was scarce, and many Americans suffered from that scarcity. The low prices and high interest rates Populists complained of were a result of the gold standard.

Increasing the money supply would reduce interest rates and make credit more available. There were two ways to put more money in circulation: the government could print paper "greenbacks," or it could coin silver. "Free silver" advocates generally favored coining a ratio of 16 ounces of silver for each ounce of gold. Populists initially wanted greenbacks but later found silver an agreeable compromise. Western mining interests pushed silver as well. The Republican and Democratic parties officially endorsed the gold standard, but by 1896 each party had a renegade faction of silverites. To Americans in the 1890s, the crucial political issues—jobs, foreign trade, the survival of small farms, and the prosperity of big corporations—boiled down to one question: Would the dollar be backed by gold or silver? The election of 1896 was "the battle of the standards."

The Cross of Gold

A dark mood hung over Chicago as delegates arrived at the Democratic convention in July 1896. They had come to bury Cleveland and the party's commitment to the gold standard along with him. The draft platform denounced Cleveland for imposing "government by injunction" during the Pullman strike. When the platform

Victor Debreuil, *The Cross of Gold* (ca. 1896) Debreuil was known for his realistic still lifes of coins, greenbacks, and photographs. Artists and citizens in the 1890s used the "'money question" to ask what was valuable, true, and real in the modern age.

came before the full convention, delegates had to decide whether the party would stand for silver or gold and who would replace Cleveland as the candidate for president.

Both questions were decided when a former congressman from Nebraska, William Jennings Bryan, mounted the stage. Handsome and only 36 years old, he was an electrifying speaker. "You come and tell us that the great cities are in favor of the gold standard," he said. "Destroy our farms, and the grass will grow in the streets of every city in the country!" Bryan delivered his lines in the rhythmic cadence of a camp preacher. "We will answer their demand for a gold standard by saying to them"—he paused stretching out his arms in an attitude of crucifixion—"You shall not press down upon the brow of labor this crown of thorns. You shall not crucify mankind upon a cross of gold!" The hall exploded with cheers. Bryan won the nomination handily.

Two weeks later the Populists, meeting in St. Louis, also nominated Bryan. The Ocala and Omaha platforms, which imagined comprehensive changes in the money system and American institutions, had been reduced to a single panacea: silver. Republicans overwhelmingly adopted a pro-gold plank, drafted with the approval of J. P. Morgan, and nominated William McKinley, the governor of Ohio and a supporter of industry. The parties could hardly have offered two more different candidates or two more different visions of the future.

The Battle of the Standards

In one of the most exciting electoral contests since the Civil War, the candidates employed new techniques in radically different ways. McKinley ran like an incumbent: he never left his home. Instead, delegations came to him. Some 750,000 people from 30 states trampled McKinley's grass and listened to speeches affirming the candidate's commitment to high tariffs and sound money. The speeches were set in type and distributed as newspaper columns, fliers, and pamphlets throughout the country. The campaign used public relations techniques to educate the electorate on the virtues of the gold standard. Posters reduced the campaign's themes to pithy slogans like "Prosperity or Poverty," or "Vote for Free Silver and Be Prosperous Like Guatemala."

The genius behind the campaign was a Cleveland coal-and-oil millionaire named Marcus Hanna who bankrolled his publicity blitz with between $3 million and $7 million raised from industrialists. He assessed a share of the campaign's expenses from corporations and banks based on calculations of the profitability and net worth of each. The combination of big money and advertising revolutionized presidential politics.

With only $300,000 to spend, Bryan ran like a challenger even though his party occupied the White House. He logged 29,000 miles by rail and buggy and made more than 500 speeches in 29 states. Oratorical ability had won Bryan the nomination, but audiences were unaccustomed to hearing a candidate speak for himself, and many considered it undignified. "The Boy Orator has one speech," wrote an unsympathetic Republican, John Hay. "He simply reiterates the unquestioned truths that . . . gold is vile, that silver is lovely and holy."

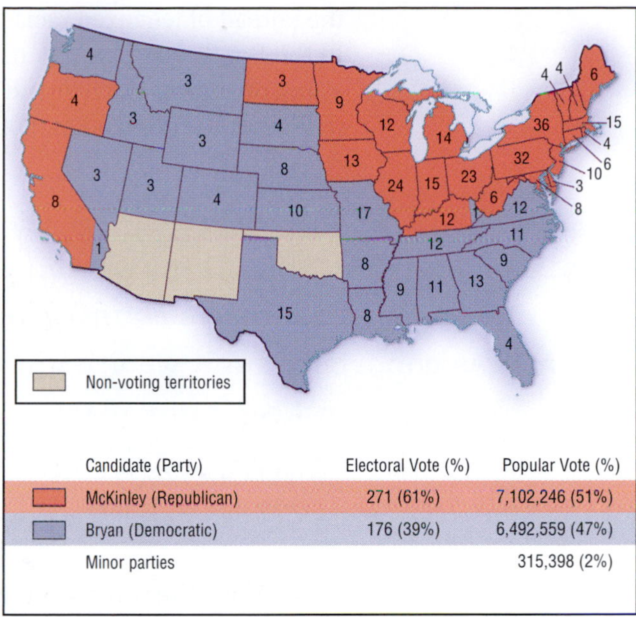

Non-voting territories
Candidate (Party) | Electoral Vote (%) | Popular Vote (%)
McKinley (Republican) | 271 (61%) | 7,102,246 (51%)
Bryan (Democratic) | 176 (39%) | 6,492,559 (47%)
Minor parties | | 315,398 (2%)

Map 20–1 The Election of 1896 William McKinley's "front-porch campaign" carried the northern industrial states, along with the key farm states of Iowa and Minnesota, securing a narrow victory over Bryan.

Despite the scorn of eastern newspapers, industrialists genuinely feared the prospect of a Bryan presidency. "He has succeeded in scaring the gold bugs out of their five wits," Hay remarked. Factory owners threatened to close shop if Bryan won. Just before election day, the global markets that McKinley praised returned the favor. Crop failures abroad doubled the price of wheat in the Midwest, raising farm incomes and alleviating the anxieties that made farmers flock to Bryan. In the final tally, Bryan won the South and West decisively, but McKinley won the populous states of the industrial Northeast, as well as several farm states in the upper Midwest, capturing the Electoral College by a majority of 271 to 176.

The election of 1896 changed the style of campaigns and shifted the political positions of both major parties. By pushing currency policies to improve the lives of workers and farmers, Bryan's Democrats abandoned their traditional commitment to minimal government that stretched back to Andrew Jackson. The Republicans recognized that the electorate would judge the president on his ability to bring prosperity to the country. Electoral democracy now had a distinctly economic cast. As president, McKinley asserted his leadership over economic policy, calling Congress into special session to pass the Dingley Tariff Act, which levied the highest taxes on imports in American history. He extended the reach of presidential power even more dramatically through an expansionist foreign and military policy.

In the election of 1896 fundamental economic questions—who is the economy supposed to serve? what is the nature of money?—were at stake in a closely matched campaign. No wonder voter turnout hit an all-time high. Administrative agencies took over those issues after the turn of the century, but Americans long remembered that raucous campaign when the nation's economic future was up for grabs. As late as the 1960s, schoolchildren still recited the Cross of Gold speech.

The Retreat from Politics

The economy improved steadily after 1895, but this latest business panic and its aftermath left lasting marks on corporate and political culture. Industrial workers made a tactical retreat in the face of a new political and legal climate. In the South, depression, urbanization, and the modernizing influence of railroads accelerated the spread of legalized racial segregation and disfranchisement. What was happening in the South was part of a nationwide decline of participatory politics. With the slackening of agrarian unrest and the exhaustion of resistance to corporate capitalism, politics lost some of its value. Voter participation declined, and Americans felt less of a personal stake in election campaigns. Disaffected groups—such as labor and African Americans—had to devise new ways to build community and express resistance.

> I want to give you niggers a few words of plain talk and advice. You might as well understand that this is a white man's country, as far as the South is concerned, and we are going to make you keep your place.
>
> WILLIAM C. OATES, Alabama governor, 1895

The Lure of the Cities

In the South as in the North, people left the countryside and moved to towns and cities. By 1900 one out of six southerners lived in town. With the lone exception of Birmingham, Alabama, southern cities were not devoted to manufacturing but to commerce and services. Doctors' offices, haberdasheries, dry goods stores, and groceries could be found near warehouses where cotton was stored, ginned, and pressed and near the railway station where it was shipped to textile mills.

The growth of villages and towns in the South was the product of rural decay. Crop liens, which gave bankers ownership of a crop before it was planted, and debt drove people from the countryside. The young and the ambitious left first, while older and poorer residents stayed behind.

While white newcomers settled on the outskirts of towns, African Americans moved into industrial districts along the railroad tracks. Cities became more segregated as they grew. By 1890 most blocks in the larger cities were either all black or all white. Still, towns offered things that were missing in the country, such as schools. A Little Rock, Arkansas, resident noted that newly arrived African American parents were "very anxious to send their children to school." Jobs were often available, too, although more frequently for women than for men. Men looked for seasonal labor at farms or lumber camps some distance from town. This meant families faced a tough choice between poverty and separation.

Despite setbacks, the newcomers gained a place for themselves in urban life. By 1890 every southern city had an African American business district with churches, insurance companies, lawyers, doctors, undertakers, and usually a weekly newspaper. Benevolent and reform organizations, sewing circles, and book clubs enriched community life. There were limits to how high educated African Americans could ascend. Professionals like lawyers, doctors, and nurses had to work within their community. Jobs on the bottom rung of the corporate ladder—clerk, salesman, telephone operator, stenographer, railroad conductor—were reserved for whites.

Inventing Jim Crow

In June 1892 Homer Plessy boarded the East Louisiana Railway in New Orleans for a trip to Covington, Louisiana. Having purchased a first-class ticket, he attempted to board the whites-only car and was arrested under a Louisiana law that required

African Americans and whites to ride in "equal but separate accommodations." Before Judge John H. Ferguson could try the case, Plessy's lawyer appealed on the grounds that the separate-car law violated the Constitution's Fourteenth Amendment.

When *Plessy v. Ferguson* came before the Supreme Court in April 1896, lawyers for the state of Louisiana argued that the law was necessary to avoid the "danger of friction from too intimate contact" between the races. In separate cars, all citizens enjoyed equal privileges. Plessy's lawyer, Albion Tourgée, replied that the question was not "the equality of the privileges enjoyed, but the right of the state to label one citizen as white and another as colored." In doing so, the government gave unearned advantages to some citizens and not to others. The issue for Tourgée was not racial conflict or even prejudice, but whether the government should be allowed to divide people arbitrarily. The court upheld the "separate but equal" doctrine. The Plessy decision provided legal justification for the system of official inequality that expanded in the twentieth century. Informal segregation had existed since the Civil War. People associated with members of their own race when they could, and when they could not—at work, in business, or when traveling—unwritten local customs usually governed their interaction. By the 1890s those informal customs were being codified in law. Railroads, as symbols of progress, were a chief point of contention.

Mary Church Terrell (1863–1954) Activist, suffragist, and educator, Terrell tried to unite the struggles for women's rights and civil rights. "A white woman has but one handicap to overcome," she wrote. "I have two—both sex and race."

The political and economic tensions created by the depression helped turn racist customs into a rigid caste division. Competition for jobs fed racial antagonisms, as did the migration into cities and towns of a new generation of African Americans, born since the war, who showed less deference to whites. New notions of "scientific" racism led intellectuals and churchmen to regard racial hostility as natural. Angry voters in many southern states deposed the coalitions of landowners and New South industrialists that had governed since Reconstruction and replaced them with Populist "demagogues."

Between 1887 and 1891 nine states in the South passed railroad segregation laws. Trains began pulling separate cars for African Americans, called "Jim Crow" cars after the name of a character in a minstrel show. Soon Jim Crow laws were extended to waiting rooms, drinking fountains, and other places where African Americans and whites might meet.

Segregation was also enforced by terror. The threat of lynching poisoned all relations between the races, and African Americans learned that they could be tortured and killed for committing a crime, talking back, or simply looking the wrong way at a white woman. Lynchings occurred most frequently in areas thinly populated by whites, but killings and mob violence also occurred in the largest cities. Between

Lynchings Were Public Spectacles When 17-year-old Jesse Washington was killed in Waco, Texas, in 1916, a crowd of several thousand, including the mayor, police chief, and students from Waco High, attended the event on the lawn of city hall. Afterwards, the murderers posed for a photograph and sold their victim's teeth for $5 apiece.

1882 and 1903, nearly 2,000 African American southerners were killed by mobs. Victims were routinely tortured, flayed, castrated, gouged, and burned alive, and members of the mob often took home grisly souvenirs like a piece of bone or a severed thumb.

Many African American southerners fought segregation with boycotts, lawsuits, and disobedience. Ida Wells-Barnett, a Nashville journalist, organized an international antilynching campaign (see Chapter 21, "A United Body of Action"). Segregation was constantly negotiated and challenged, but after 1896 it was backed by the U.S. Supreme Court.

The Atlanta Compromise

When Atlanta invited African American educator Booker T. Washington to address the Cotton States Exposition in 1895, northern newspapers concluded that a new era of racial progress had begun. The speech made Washington the most recognized African American in the United States. Starting with 40 students and an abandoned shack, Washington had built Tuskegee Institute into a nationally known institution, the preeminent technical school for African Americans. Washington was a guest in the stately homes of Newport and at Andrew Carnegie's castle in Scotland. When Atlanta staged an exposition to showcase the region's industrial and social progress, the organizers asked Washington to speak.

Washington's address stressed racial accommodation. It had been a mistake, he argued, to try to attain equality by asserting civil and political rights. "The wisest among my race understand that agitation of questions of social equality is the extremest folly," he said, "and that progress in the enjoyment of all the privileges that will come to us must be the result of severe and constant struggle rather than artificial forcing." He urged white businessmen to employ African American southerners "who have, without strikes and labor wars, tilled your fields, cleared your forests, builded your railroads and cities." Raising his hand above his head, stretching out his fingers and then closing them into a fist, he summarized his approach to race relations: "In all things that are purely social, we can be as separate as the fingers, yet one as the hand in all things essential to mutual progress." The largely white audience erupted into applause.

Booker T. Washington With voting rights denied to African Americans, Booker T. Washington urged vocational education as the surest route to economic advancement.

Washington's "Atlanta Compromise" stressed the mutual obligations of African Americans and whites. African Americans would give up the vote and stop insisting on social equality if

white leaders would keep violence in check and allow African Americans to succeed in agriculture and business. White industrialists welcomed this arrangement, and African American leaders felt that for the moment it might be the best that could be achieved.

Disfranchisement and the Decline of Popular Politics

After the feverish campaign of 1896, elections began to lose some of their appeal. Attendance fell off at the polls. Some 79 percent of voters cast ballots in the battle of the standards; eight years later the figure was down to 65 percent. More visibly, the public events surrounding campaigns drew thinner crowds. Organizers fretted about apathy, which seemed to have become a national epidemic.

In the South, the disappearance of voters was easy to explain. As Jim Crow laws multiplied, southern states disfranchised African Americans (and one out of four whites) by requiring voters to demonstrate literacy, property ownership, or knowledge of the Constitution before they could register. Louisiana added the notorious grandfather clause, which denied the vote to men whose grandfathers were prohibited from voting.

Whites saw disfranchisement and segregation as modern, managed race relations. Demonizing African Americans enforced solidarity among white voters, who might otherwise have voted on local or class interests.

No new legal restrictions hampered voting in the North and West, but participation fell there, too. This withdrawal from politics reflected the decline of political pageantry as an element of cultural and social life, but it also reflected the disappearance of intense partisanship. For American men, the cliffhanger contests of the late nineteenth century provided a sense of identity that matched and strengthened ethnic, religious, and neighborhood identities.

A developing economy with new patterns of recreation, class relations, and community participation undermined the habits of partisanship, but so did the new style of campaigns. The emphasis on advertising, education, and fund-raising reduced the personal stakes for voters. Educated middle- and upper-class voters liked the new style, feeling that raucous campaigns were no way to decide important issues. They sought to influence policy more directly, through interest groups rather

 **Table 20–1** The Spread of Disfranchisement

	State	Strategies
1889	Florida	Poll tax
	Tennessee	Poll tax
1890	Mississippi	Poll tax, literacy test, understanding clause
1891	Arkansas	Poll tax
1893, 1901	Alabama	Poll tax, literacy test, grandfather clause
1894, 1895	South Carolina	Poll tax, literacy test, understanding clause
1894, 1902	Virginia	Poll tax, literacy test, understanding clause
1897, 1898	Louisiana	Poll tax, literacy test, grandfather clause
1899, 1900	North Carolina	Poll tax, literacy test, grandfather clause
1902	Texas	Poll tax
1908	Georgia	Poll tax, literacy test, understanding clause, grandfather clause

than parties. Unintentionally, they discarded traditions that unified communities and made voters feel connected to their country and its leaders.

Organized Labor Retreats from Politics

Workers also withdrew from politics as organized labor turned away from political means and goals and redefined objectives in economic terms. As traditional crafts came under attack, skilled workers created new organizations that addressed immediate issues: wages, hours, and the conditions of work. The American Federation of Labor (AFL), founded in 1886, built a base around skilled trades, and grew from 150,000 members to more than 2 million by 1904. The AFL focused on immediate goals that would improve the working lives of its members. Its founder, Samuel Gompers, was born in London's East End and apprenticed as a cigar maker at the age of ten. Three years later his family moved to New York, where Gompers joined the Cigar Makers' International Union.

Although affiliated with the Knights of Labor, the cigar makers were more interested in getting higher wages than in remaking the economy. They concentrated on shortening work hours and increasing pay. High dues and centralized control allowed the union to offer insurance and death benefits to members while maintaining a strike fund. Gompers applied the same practices to the AFL. His "pure and simple unionism" made modest demands, but it still encountered fierce resistance from corporations, which were backed by the courts.

In the 1895 case of *In re Debs,* the Supreme Court allowed the use of injunctions to criminalize strikes. The court then disarmed one of the few weapons left in labor's arsenal, the boycott. In the 1908 case of *Loewe v. Lawlor,* popularly known as the Danbury Hatters case, the court ruled that advertising a consumer boycott was illegal under the Sherman Anti-Trust Act.

Gompers believed that *industrial unions,* associations that drew members from all occupations within an industry, lacked the discipline and shared values needed to face down corporations and government, and that unions organized around a single trade or craft would break less easily. However, because the AFL was organized by skill, it often ignored unskilled workers, who were often women or recent immigrants. Because employers used unskilled newcomers to break strikes or to run machinery that replaced expert hands, Gompers excluded a large part of the labor force. Organizers recruited Irish and German workers through their fraternal lodges and saloons while ignoring Italian, African American, Jewish, and Slavic workers. The union attacked female workers for stealing jobs that rightfully belonged to men.

Even leaders who rejected Gompers's philosophy and strategy built unions that represented the immediate interests of their members. Under the leadership of Eugene V. Debs, railroad workers merged the old railroad brotherhoods into the ARU in 1893. The United Mine Workers (UMW), founded in 1890, unionized coal mines in Pennsylvania, Ohio, Indiana, and Michigan. The ARU and the UMW were industrial unions that tried to organize all of the workers in an industry. These new unions faced determined opposition from business and its allies in government. "Our government cannot stand, nor its free institutions endure," the National Association of Manufacturers declared, "if the Gompers-Debs ideals of liberty and freedom of speech and press are allowed to dominate."

American Diplomacy Enters the Modern World

The Republican victory in 1896 gave heart to proponents of prosperity through foreign trade. Before the turn of the century, the new president announced, the United States would control the markets of the globe. "We will establish trading posts throughout the world as distributing points for American products," Senator Albert Beveridge forecast. "Great colonies, governing themselves, flying our flag and trading with us, will grow about our posts of trade." McKinley sought neither war nor colonies, but many in his party wanted both. Called "jingoes," they included Assistant Secretary of the Navy Theodore Roosevelt, John Hay, the ambassador to London, and Senators Beveridge and Henry Cabot Lodge. Britain, France, and Germany were seizing territory around the world, and jingoes believed the United States needed to do the same for strategic, religious, and economic reasons. Spain was the most likely target. Madrid clung feebly to the remnants of its once-vast empire, now reduced to Cuba, the Philippines, Guam, and Puerto Rico. Under Cleveland, the United States had moved away from confrontation with Spain, but McKinley, at first reluctantly but later enthusiastically, pushed for the creation of an American empire that stretched to the far shores of the Pacific.

> **Nobody wants to arouse America's anger. The United States is a rich country.**
>
> OSWALD FREIHERR VON RICHTHOFEN, German foreign minister, 1898

Sea Power and the Imperial Urge

Few men better exemplified the jingoes' combination of religiosity, martial spirit, and fascination with the laws of history than Alfred Thayer Mahan. A naval officer and strategist, he told students at the Naval War College that since the Roman Empire, world leadership had belonged to the nation that controlled the sea. Published in 1890, his book *The Influence of Sea Power upon History, 1660–1783* became an instant classic.

In his first paragraph, Mahan connected naval expansion and empire to the problem of overproduction that the United States faced. A great industrial country needed trade; trade required a merchant fleet; and merchant shipping needed naval protection and overseas bases. Colonies could provide markets for goods and congregations for Christian missionaries, but more importantly they offered a springboard for naval forces that could protect sea lanes and project power into the great land masses of Asia, Latin America, and Africa.

Mahan urged the United States to build a canal across Central America, allowing manufacturers on the Atlantic coast to "compete with Europe, on equal terms as to distance, for the markets of eastern Asia." He felt that naval bases should be established along routes connecting the United States with markets in Latin America and the Far East. Congress and the Navy Department began implementing these recommendations even before McKinley took office.

Mahan was not the only prophet who saw resemblances to the Roman Empire. Brooks Adams's *The Law of Civilization and Decay* (1895) spelled out the implications of the closing of the frontier: greater concentration of wealth, social inequality, and eventually collapse. To repeal this "law" the United States needed to seek a new frontier in Asia where it could regenerate itself through combat. Sharing the social

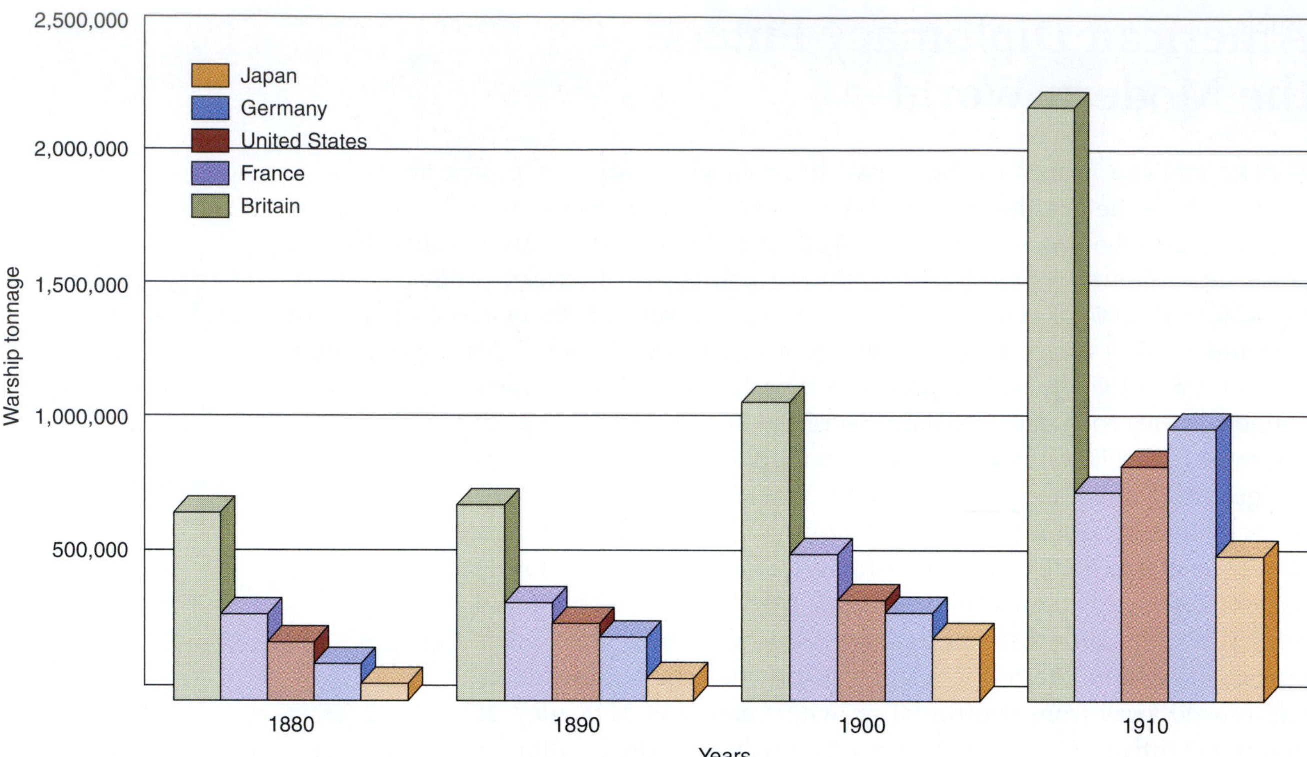

Figure 20–2 Warship Tonnage of the World's Navies Naval strength was the primary index of power before World War I. The United States held onto third place in the naval arms race, while Germany and Japan made significant gains. *Paul Kennedy,* Rise and Fall of the Great Powers *(New York: Random House, 1987), p. 203.*

Darwinist belief (see Chapter 18) that nations and races were locked in a savage struggle for survival, Mahan and Adams expected the United States to prevail and benefit from the approaching conflict.

If subduing continents with cross, Constitution, and Gatling gun appealed to anyone, it was Theodore Roosevelt. As a politician and strategist, Roosevelt paid keen attention to new ideas and forces that were magnifying the power of some nations and diminishing others. Imperialism seemed to him the essential characteristic of modernizing countries. He was the image of the modern frontiersman, a writer, soldier, and politician. Between stints in the state assembly and as New York City police commissioner, he raised cattle in the Dakota Territory, reading books by the campfire at night to the amusement of his fellow cowpunchers. Roosevelt was acutely conscious of how modern forces—globalized trade, instant communications, the reach of modern navies, and imperialism—had altered the rules of domestic and international politics. He sought to position the United States at the center of these modernizing currents, a place that would have to be earned, he felt, both on foreign battlefields and at home, where the material and technological gains of the nineteenth century had not yet been translated into the social and moral advancement that marked a true civilization.

The Scramble for Empire

For jingoes, China was the ultimate prize to be won in the global contest for trade and mastery. It had more people than any other country, hence more customers and more souls to be brought to Christ. The number of American missionaries in China doubled in the 1890s. Many of them came from the Student Volunteer Movement, which promised "the evangelization of the world in this generation" and had chapters on nearly every college campus. Even though no more than 1 or 2 percent of U.S. exports had ever gone to Chinese ports, manufacturers believed that if any country could absorb the output of America's overproductive factories, it was China. James B. Duke founded the British-American Tobacco Company based on "China's population of 450 million people, and assuming that in the future they might average a cigarette a day." In 1890 Standard Oil began selling kerosene in Shanghai. Fifteen years later, China was the largest overseas market for American oil. Mahan had predicted that China would be the arena for the coming struggle for industrial and military supremacy, and by 1897 he appeared to be right.

Missionaries in China Thanks to the work of missionaries in China, Mark Twain observed, "the people who sit in darkness . . . have become suspicious of the blessings of civilization."

In 1894 Japan declared war on China, and within months it occupied Korea, Manchuria, and China's coastal cities. When the fighting was over, Western powers seized slices of Chinese territory. In November 1897, German troops captured the port of Qingdao on the Shandong Peninsula. An industrial area on the northeast coast, Shandong was the center of American missionary activity, investment, and trade. To Americans, the invasion of Shandong presaged the beginning of an imperial grab for territory and influence. In the 1880s European powers had carved up Africa. Now it appeared that the same thing was about to happen in China. "It is felt," the *Journal of Commerce* declared, "that we stand at the dividing of the ways, between gaining or losing the greatest market which awaits exploitation." The McKinley administration watched the events unfolding in China carefully, but in the winter of 1897/1898 the Departments of State and War had more pressing concerns closer to home.

War with Spain

While other European powers were expanding their empires, Spain was barely hanging on to the one it had. Since the 1860s its two largest colonies, Cuba and the Philippines, had been torn by revolution. Between 1868 and 1878 Cuban nationalists fought a prolonged war of independence. Spain ended the war by promising autonomy but not independence. U.S. officials wanted an end to Spanish rule, but their disappointment at this peaceful outcome did not last long. The McKinley Tariff and the Panic of 1893 ruined the island's chief export industry, sugar. Groaning under a crushing debt, Spain reneged on its promise, and in 1895 the rebellion resumed, quickly overrunning two-thirds of the island. The rebels practiced a "scorched earth" policy, dynamiting trains and burning plantations in an attempt to force Spain out.

Spain retaliated with a brutal campaign of pacification, killing nearly 100,000 civilians, but it was no use. The Spanish army was disintegrating. Cuban rebels, in full control of the countryside, prepared a final assault on the cities. U.S. officials, many of whom wanted to annex the island, now worried Cuba would gain full independence. McKinley explored the options of either purchasing it from Spain or intervening on the pretext of ending the "strife." William Randolph Hearst's *New York Journal* and other newspapers favored the latter, inciting readers with lurid stories of Spanish atrocities and Cuban rioting. Cuba sold newspapers. "Is there no nation," one editorialist asked, "wise enough, brave enough, and strong enough to restore peace?"

McKinley moved quickly toward confrontation. When riots erupted in the Cuban capital he asked the navy to send a warship to Havana. Theodore Roosevelt selected one of the newest battleships, the *Maine*. The arrival of the *Maine* reduced tensions for a while, but on February 15 an explosion ripped through the ship. Almost the entire crew of 266 perished. Navy investigators later concluded that the explosion had been internal, probably in the new oil-fired boilers, but the newspapers alternately blamed Spanish and Cuban treachery. Hearst printed a full-page diagram showing the ship being destroyed by a "sunken torpedo."

McKinley hesitated, mindful of the budget and the unfolding events in China, but Roosevelt ordered Commodore George Dewey's Asiatic Squadron to prepare for an attack on the Philippines. Congress appropriated $50 million for arms. Spanish emissaries tried to gain support from other European countries, but they were rebuffed.

In March the economic picture took a turn for the better, and McKinley sent Spain an ultimatum demanding independence for Cuba. On April 11 he asked Congress for authorization to use force, and Congress responded by passing a declaration of war. Expansionists such as Roosevelt, Mahan, and Adams would not have had their way if war had been less popular. Corporate interests favored it, immigrants and southerners saw it as a way to assert their patriotism, and newspapers found it made good copy. "We are all jingoes now," declared the *New York Sun*.

Neither side had many illusions about how the fighting would turn out. Going to war with Spain, novelist Sherwood Anderson wrote, was "like robbing an old gypsy woman in a vacant lot at night after the fair," but the war opened with a cliffhanger that even Hearst could not have invented. On May 1 news arrived that Dewey's Asiatic Squadron was in battle against the Spanish fleet in Manila Bay in the Philippines. The war had begun not in Cuba, but instead half a world away on the far edge of the Pacific Ocean. There the information stopped. The telegraph cable connecting Manila to the outside world had been cut. Official Spanish reports were vague, but they alleged that the Americans had suffered a "considerable loss of life." Dewey's squadron contained only two modern cruisers, but all of its ships were steel hulled in contrast with Spain's wooden vessels. For six anxious days the American public awaited word from the Far East.

It arrived in the early morning hours of May 7, interrupting a poker game in the newsroom at the *New York Herald*. The paper's Hong Kong correspondent had been at the battle. Dewey destroyed Spain's entire fleet of 12 warships without suffering a single serious casualty. The country went wild with relief and triumph. New York staged a parade on Fifth Avenue. A Dewey-for-president movement began. In Washington, McKinley consulted a map to see where the Philippines were. Roosevelt quit his job and ordered Brooks Brothers to make him a uniform.

The war in Cuba unfolded less spectacularly. The navy bottled up Spain's Atlantic fleet in the Bay of Santiago de Cuba. When the ships attempted to escape, American warships cut them to pieces. "Don't cheer, men," an officer ordered the gun crews. "Those poor devils are dying." A bit of drama was provided by the voyage of the USS *Oregon*, which left its West Coast base and traveled at top speed around the southern tip of South America in 68 days to join the Atlantic fleet too late for the fighting. Its journey, tracked by newspapers around the country, dramatized the need for a canal connecting the Atlantic and the Pacific.

In the years before the war, Congress had poured money into the navy but not the army, and it took some time before soldiers could be trained and equipped. Recruits were herded into camps in Florida without tents, proper clothing, or latrines. There were few medical supplies or doctors. In unsanitary camps, soldiers in woolen uniforms died of dysentery and malaria. Of the 5,462 U.S. soldiers who died in the war with Spain, 5,083 succumbed to disease, a scandal that forced the government to elevate the status of the surgeon general and to regard sanitation and disease prevention as important to national defense.

The army landed on the Cuban coast and marched inland to engage Spanish defenders. A cavalry general, Joseph Wheeler, an ex-Confederate from Alabama, urged his men on, yelling, "The Yankees are running! Damn it, I mean the Spaniards!" Roosevelt came ashore with the First Volunteer Cavalry, known as the "Rough Riders." He recruited, trained, and publicized the regiment, and afterwards he wrote its history, all with an eye to symbolism. An assortment of outlaws, cowboys, Ivy League athletes, New York City policemen, a novelist, and a Harvard Medical School graduate, its membership combined frontier heroism with eastern elite leadership. The regiment traveled with its own film crew and a correspondent from the *New York Herald*.

Spanish forces stubbornly resisted around the city of Santiago. Their Mauser rifles had a longer range and a faster rate of fire than American weapons. At San Juan Hill, 500 defenders forced a regiment of the New York National Guard to retreat. The all–African American 9th and 10th Cavalry took their place along with the Rough Riders, with Roosevelt cautiously waiting until Gatling guns could be brought up from the rear. "The negroes saved that fight," a white soldier reported. The capture of Santiago effectively ended Spanish resistance. When fighting ended in August, U.S. troops occupied Cuba, Guam, Puerto Rico, and the city of Manila. The war had lasted only four months.

As American and Spanish diplomats met in Paris to conclude a peace treaty, McKinley had to decide which occupied territories to keep as colonies. Congress, not wanting to inherit the island's $400 million in debt, had already resolved not to annex Cuba. McKinley decided that Guam and Puerto Rico would make ideal naval bases.

The president also seized the opportunity to annex the island nation of Hawaii. In 1893 American sugar planters, led by Sanford Dole, overthrew the islands' last queen, Liliuokalani, and petitioned for annexation (see Chapter 19). They were motivated by the Harrison-McKinley Tariff, which would ruin the planters financially unless they could somehow reconnect Hawaii's trade to the United States. Annexation was their best chance, and they had a powerful ally in the U.S. Navy. Mahan had identified the deep-water anchorage at Pearl Harbor, on Oahu, as a vital base. McKinley now decided to take up Dole's annexation offer.

The Philippines presented more of a problem. Its 7,000 islands were far from the United States and had a population of several million. What the United States needed was a naval base and a coaling station close to the China coast, but holding just one island would be impossible if another power controlled the others. Shortly after Dewey's victory, British and German warships anchored in Manila Bay, clearly intending to divide up whatever territory the United States did not claim. McKinley felt trapped.

"The United States, whatever it might prefer as to the Philippines, is in a situation where it cannot let go," he advised his negotiators.

One consideration McKinley did not take into account was that the Philippines had already declared independence. With Dewey's encouragement, rebels under the command of Emilio Aguinaldo had liberated the countryside surrounding Manila and laid siege to the city. At Malolos, 25 miles north of Manila, a national assembly, including lawyers, doctors, professors, and landowners from across the archipelago, issued a constitution. By the time the U.S. Army finally arrived in 1899, Filipinos throughout the country had overthrown the Spanish and rallied to their new government.

Spanish negotiators recognized Cuban independence and surrendered most of Spain's empire to the United States for free, but they gave up the Philippines only after the United States agreed to pay $20 million, or as an American satirist calculated, $1.25 for every Filipino. The treaty was signed December 10, 1898.

The Anti-Imperialists

Many prominent Americans opposed both the annexation of new colonies and the approaching war with the Philippines. During the treaty fight in Congress in January 1899, they tried to mobilize opinion against the treaty. The movement included ex-presidents Grover Cleveland and Benjamin Harrison, William Jennings Bryan, labor unionists including Samuel Gompers and Eugene Debs, writers such as Mark Twain and Ambrose Bierce, and industrialists including Andrew Carnegie. The anti-imperialists advanced an array of moral, economic, and strategic arguments. Filipinos and Hawaiians, they said, had sought American help in good faith and were capable of governing themselves. The islands could not be defended. Instead of using the Pacific Ocean as a barrier, U.S. forces would be exposed to attack at Pearl Harbor or Manila. Carnegie argued that imperialism distracted attention from domestic problems and took tax money that could be spent at home. White supremacists asked whether Filipinos would become citizens or be allowed to vote and emigrate to the mainland.

The most moving objections came from those who believed imperialism betrayed America's fundamental principles. "Could there be a more damning indictment of the whole bloated ideal termed 'modern civilization' than this amounts to?" William James asked. To Mark Twain imperialism was only the newest form of greed. "There is more money in it, more territory, more sovereignty, and other kinds of emolument, than there is in any other game that is played." Opponents of annexation organized an Anti-Imperialist League and lobbied for the rejection of the Paris Treaty.

Congress whittled away at anti-imperialist objections, banning Philippine immigration, placing the colonies outside the tariff walls, and promising eventual self-government. Jingoes had the momentum of military victory on their side. Anti-imperialists could not offer a vision comparable with naval supremacy, the evangelization of the world, or the fabled China market. On February 6, 1899, the U.S. Senate ratified the Paris Treaty and annexed the Philippines. A day earlier, on the other side of the world, the Philippine-American War began.

The Philippine-American War

McKinley believed he had annexed islands full of near savages "unfit for self-rule," but the Philippines by 1899 had an old civilization with a long tradition of resistance to colonialism. When Magellan discovered the islands in 1521, he found a literate

Map 20–2 **Spanish-American War, Caribbean**

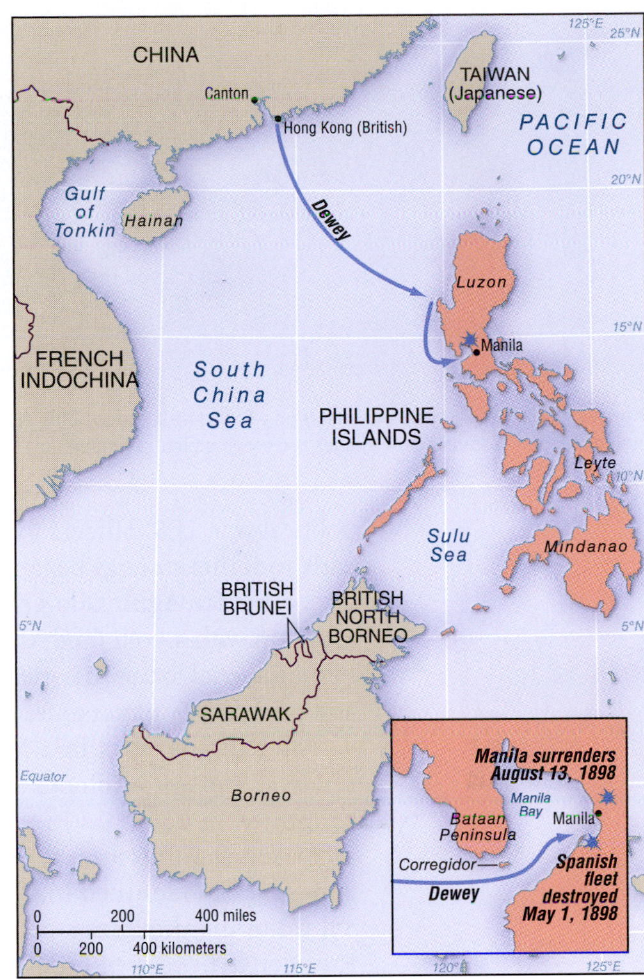

Spanish-American War, Pacific

population linked by trade ties to India, Japan, and China. The Spanish converted most Filipinos to Catholicism and established schools and a centralized government. Manila's oldest university was older than Harvard. By 1898 much of the upper class, the *illustrados,* had been educated in Europe.

Dewey gave Aguinaldo his word that America desired no colonies. Aguinaldo continued to trust the Americans long after the arrival of fresh troops made it clear that the United States intended to stay. On February 4 an argument between American and Filipino sentries ended in gunfire. Aguinaldo was despondent: "No one can deplore more than I this rupture. I have a clear conscience that I endeavored to avoid it at all costs."

Kansas volunteers drove the Filipino armies into the mountains. Aguinaldo abandoned conventional warfare for a guerilla strategy, which proved effective. Some 4,000 Americans were killed during the war and another 3,000 wounded out of a total force of 70,000. Frustrated by guerilla conflict, American soldiers customarily executed prisoners, looted villages, and raped Filipino women. An American general on the island of Samar ordered his soldiers to kill everyone over the age of 10. One soldier wrote home, "No cruelty is too severe for these brainless monkeys, who can appreciate no sense of honor, kindness, or justice. I am in my glory when I can sight some dark skin and pull the trigger."

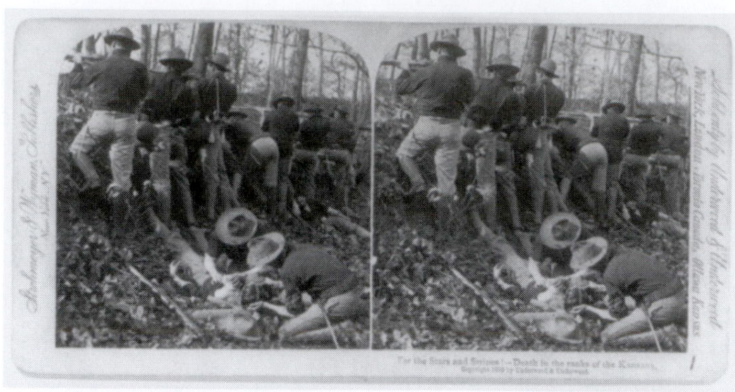

Kansas Volunteers Kansas volunteers on a firing line in Luzon, 1899. New technologies, such as stereoscope images and moving pictures, made the Philippine War vivid for Americans.

The army's preferred mode of torture was "the water cure," in which water was forced down a prisoner's throat until the abdomen swelled, and then forced out again by kicking. When Congress investigated these practices, military officials argued that in a savage war such measures were necessary. Filipinos were "half-civilized," they explained, and force was the best language for dealing with them.

Newspaper accounts of torture and massacres fueled opposition in the United States to the war, but just as the anti-imperialist movement gained steam, U.S. forces scored some victories. Recognizing that they were fighting a political war, U.S. officers took pains to win over dissidents and ethnic minorities. In early 1901 this strategy began to pay off. When American troops intercepted a messenger bound for Aguinaldo's secret headquarters, Brigadier General Frederick Funston came up with a bold (and, under the rules of war, illegal) plan. He dressed a group of Filipinos loyal to the American side in the uniforms of captured Filipinos, and, posing as a prisoner, Funston entered Aguinaldo's camp and kidnapped the president.

After three weeks in a Manila prison, Aguinaldo issued a proclamation of surrender. "Enough of blood, enough of tears and desolation," he pleaded. Resistance continued in Batangas Province, south of Manila, for another year. The U.S. Army increased the pressure by imposing the same reconcentration policies the United States had condemned in Cuba, and produced the same result. Perhaps as much as a third of the province's population died of disease and starvation. On July 4, 1902, President Theodore Roosevelt declared the war over.

The American flag flew over the Philippines until 1942, but the colony never lived up to its imperial promise. Instead of defending American trade interests, U.S. troops were pinned down in Philippine garrisons, guarding against sporadic uprisings and the threat of Japanese invasion. The costs of occupation far exceeded the profits generated by Philippine trade. The colony chiefly served as an outlet for American reformers and missionaries, who built schools, churches, and agricultural colleges. A small group of colonists sought statehood, but as the Philippines became more closely tied to the United States, Americans liked their colonial experiment less and less. Labor unions feared a flood of immigration from the islands, and farmers resented competition from Philippine producers; in 1933 Congress voted to phase out American rule.

The Open Door

As Americans celebrated their victories, European powers continued to divide China into quasi-colonial "concessions." An alarmed imperial court in Beijing began a crash program of modernization, but reactionaries within the government overthrew the emperor and installed the conservative "dowager empress" Ci Xi. In the countryside, Western missionaries and traders came under attack from local residents led by street-corner martial artists known as Boxers. In 1899, a British author, Charles Beresford, lectured across the United States promoting his book *The Breakup of China*. Large audiences turned out to hear what they already feared, that the approaching disintegration of China would mean the exclusion of U.S. trade. Just as the United States arrived at the gateway to the Orient, the gates were swinging closed.

Secretary of State John Hay watched events in China with growing apprehension. "The inherent weakness of our position is this," he wrote McKinley. "We do not want to rob China ourselves, and our public opinion will not allow us to interfere, with an army, to prevent others from robbing her. Besides, we have no army." Casting about for some means to keep China's markets open, McKinley turned to William Rockhill, a legendary career foreign service officer who had lived in China and had been the first westerner to visit Tibet. He, in turn, consulted his friend Alfred Hippisley, an Englishman returning from service with the British-run Chinese imperial customs.

Together, Rockhill, Hippisley, and Hay drafted an official letter known as the Open Door Note. Sent to each of the imperial powers, it acknowledged the partitioning of China into spheres, and it observed that so far none of the powers had closed its areas to the trade of other countries. The note urged each of the powers to continue this policy and to declare publicly their intention to keep their concessions open to the trade of the other powers.

The Open Door was mostly bluff. The United States had no authority to ask for such a pledge and no military power to enforce one. The foreign ministers of Germany, Japan, Russia, Britain, and France replied cautiously at first, agreeing to issue a declaration when the others had done so, but Hay adroitly played one power off another, starting with Britain and Japan, whose trade interests gave them a stake in the Open Door. Once the two strongest powers in China had agreed, France reluctantly acquiesced. Russia and Germany, rather than challenge the other powers, did likewise. Hay proclaimed the Open Door a diplomatic watershed on the order of the Monroe Doctrine. The United States had secured access to China without war or partition, but the limits of Hay's success soon became apparent.

In early 1900, the antiforeign Boxer movement swept through Shandong province. Armed Chinese attacked missions and foreign businesses, destroyed railroads, and massacred Chinese Christians. Empress Ci Xi recruited 30,000 Boxers into her army and declared war on all foreign countries. The Western powers rushed troops to China, but before they could arrive Chinese armies laid siege to Western embassies in Beijing. An international force of British, Russian, Japanese, and French troops gathered at Tianjin to march to the rescue. European powers appeared all too eager to capture the Chinese capital.

Without consulting Congress, McKinley ordered American troops into battle on the Asian mainland. Five thousand soldiers rushed from Manila to Tianjin. John Hay issued a second Open Door Note, asking the allied countries to pledge to protect China's independence. Again, the imperial powers reluctantly agreed rather than admit their secret plans to carve up China. On August 15, 1900, U.S. cavalry units under General Adna Chaffee reached Beijing along with Russian Cossacks, French Zouaves, British-Indian sepoys, German hussars, and Japanese dragoons. After freeing the captive diplomats, the armies of the civilized world looted the city. The United States was unable to maintain the Open Door in China for long. Russia and Japan established separate military zones in northeast China in defiance of the Beijing government and American protests, but the principle of the Open Door, of encouraging free trade and open markets, guided American foreign policy throughout the twentieth century. It rested on the assumption that, in an equal contest, American firms would prevail, spreading manufactured goods around the world, and American influence with them. Under the

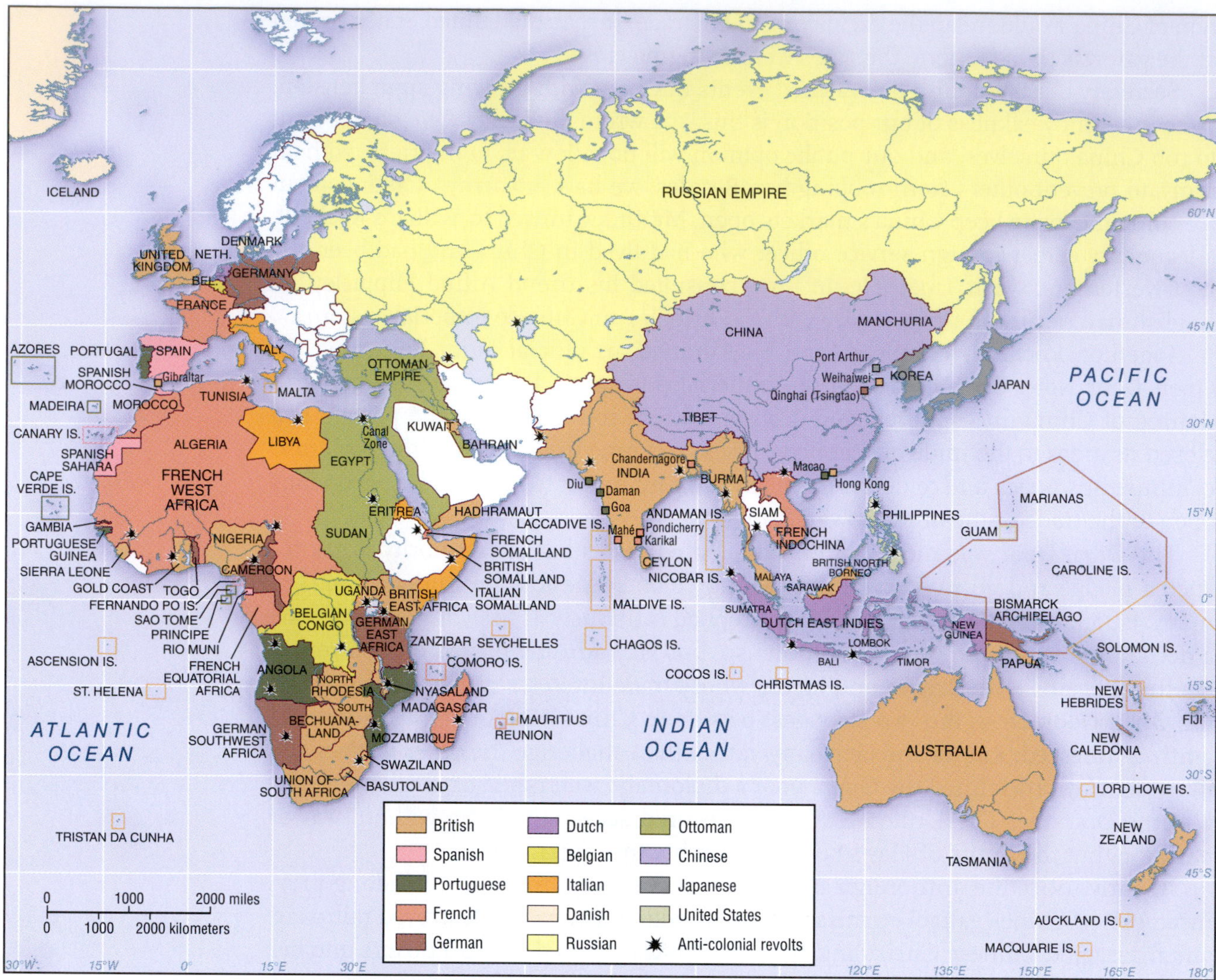

Map 20–3 The Imperial World Modern imperialism reached its apex between 1880 and 1945. Most of Africa, the Middle East, and Asia, a third of the world's population, was absorbed into global empires linked by telegraph and steamship to centers of government and commerce in London, Paris, Tokyo, and Washington, DC.

Open Door, the United States was better off in a world without empires, a world where consumers in independent nations could buy what they wanted. Just one year after the Spanish-American War, Hay's notes rejected imperial expansion in favor of trade expansion. This bold new strategy promised greater gains, but it placed the United States on a collision course with the great empires of the world.

Conclusion

In the turbulent 1890s the social and economic divisions among Americans widened. The hope that a solution to these divisions could be found outside the United States was short-lived. Imperialism promised new markets and an end to the wrenching cycle of depression and labor strife. The United States conquered an overseas empire and challenged other empires to open their ports to free trade, but the goal of prosperity and peace at home proved elusive.

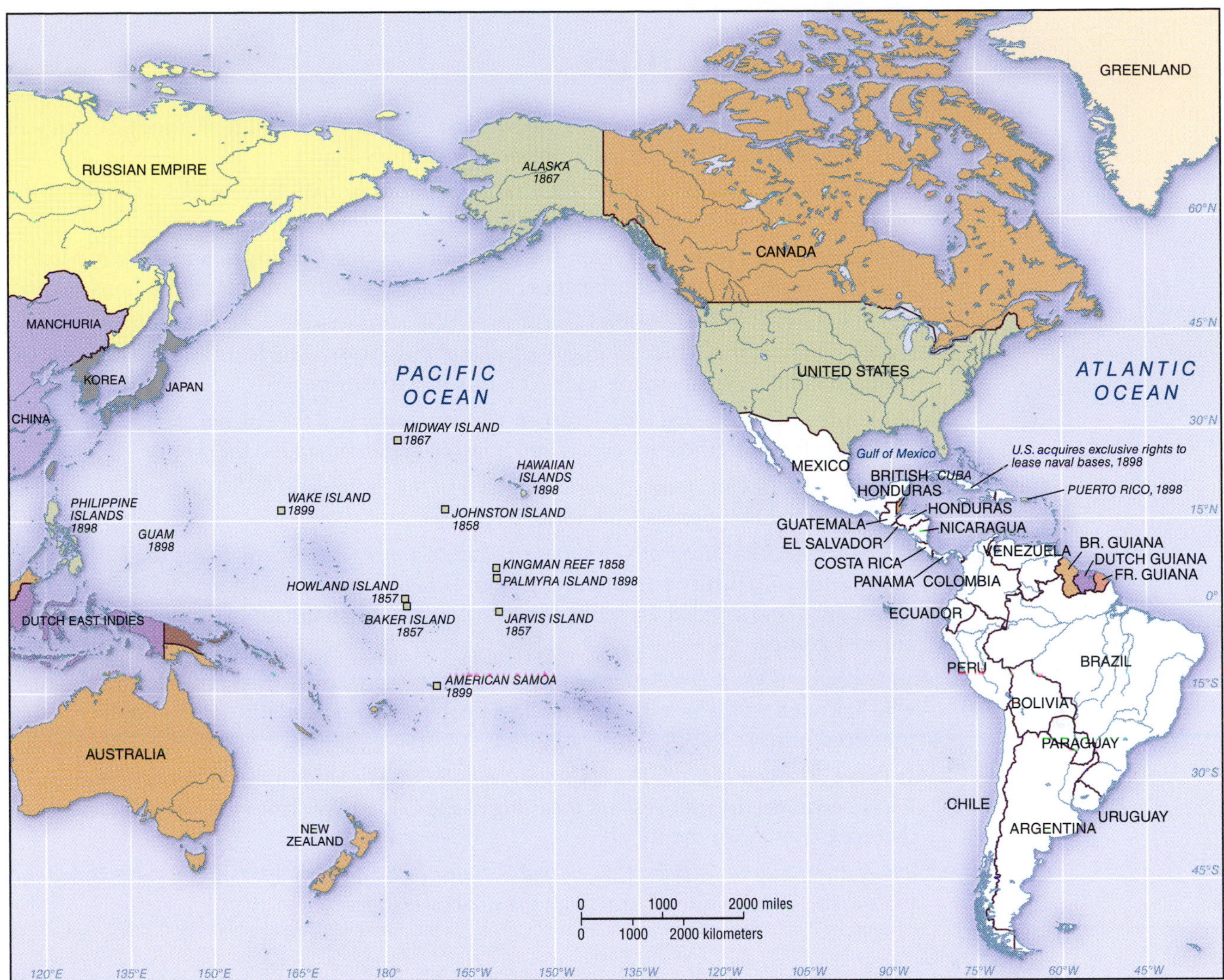

In many ways social Darwinism became a self-fulfilling prophecy, as competition rather than compromise prevailed. Workers and businessmen, farmers and bankers, middle-class radicals and conservatives, whites and African Americans saw each other as enemies. Racial segregation showed that middle ground, where whites and African Americans could meet on equal terms, had disappeared. Workers, farmers, African Americans, radicals, and reformers had to decide what was politically possible and devise new bargaining strategies.

Economic recovery and victory in global conflict closed the decade on an optimistic note. Prosperity, power, and technology seemed to have rewritten the rules of human affairs to America's advantage. Henry Adams, standing in the American exhibit at the Paris Exposition of 1900, contemplated a 40-foot dynamo—a "huge wheel, revolving within arm's length at some vertiginous speed, and barely murmuring"—and felt as if he had crossed a "historical chasm." The machine's silent force, scarcely understood or controlled and emanating from "a dirty engine house carefully kept out of sight," seemed a metaphor for the modern age.

Further Readings

Edward L. Ayers, *The Promise of the New South: Life After Reconstruction* (1992). A study of daily life, work, and politics in the turn-of-the-century South.

H. W. Brands, *The Reckless Decade: America in the 1890s* (1995). A lively look at some of the decade's noteworthy events and characters.

Ron Chernow, *The House of Morgan: An American Banking Dynasty and the Rise of Modern Finance* (1990). The life and business of J. P. Morgan and his heirs, the lions of Wall Street for more than a century.

James B. Gilbert, *Perfect Cities: Chicago's Utopias of 1893* (1991). The fears and dreams that led Chicago's elite to create the World's Columbian Exposition.

Robert Kanigel, *The One Best Way: Frederick Winslow Taylor and the Enigma of Efficiency* (1997). The most famous efficiency expert and how his system changed the world.

Stanley Karnow, *In Our Image: America's Empire in the Philippines* (1989). America's colonial venture in the Philippines from 1898 to 1986.

Paul A. Kramer, *The Blood of Government: Race, Empire, the United States, and the Philippines* (2006). To justify war and occupation, U.S. officials invented new theories of racial dominance and divided Filipinos into "civilized" Christians and "savage" Muslim and animist groups.

David L. Lewis, *W. E. B. Du Bois: Biography of a Race, 1868–1919* (1993). The story of the man who "pleaded with a headstrong, careless people to despise not Justice," and the era that produced him.

Louis Pérez, *The War of 1898: The United States and Cuba in History and Historiography* (1998). Pérez separates the motives and meaning of the Cuban War from the nationalist legends that have grown around it.

Nick Salvatore, *Eugene V. Debs: Citizen and Socialist* (1982). From the railroad yards to federal prison, the story of one of America's great labor leaders.

>> Timeline >>

▼ 1890

Global depression begins

United Mine Workers founded

Battle of Wounded Knee ends Indian wars

Harrison-McKinley Tariff passed

Alfred T. Mahan publishes *The Influence of Sea Power Upon History, 1660–1783*

Standard Oil markets kerosene in China

▼ 1892

Homestead strike

▼ 1893

Financial crisis leads to business failures and mass unemployment

World's Columbian Exposition, Chicago

Cherokee Strip land rush

American sugar planters overthrow Queen Liliuokalani of Hawaii

▼ 1894

Coxey's Army marches on Washington

Pullman strike

U.S. commission charts canal route across Nicaragua

▼ 1895

Morgan agrees to Treasury bailout

National Association of Manufacturers founded

Brooks Adams publishes *The Law of Civilization and Decay*

Booker T. Washington gives "Atlanta Compromise" address

Revolution begins in Cuba

Japan annexes Korea and Taiwan

▼ 1896

Plessy v. Ferguson declares "separate but equal" facilities constitutional

Mary Church Terrell founds National Association of Colored Women

William McKinley elected president

Who, What?

Review Questions

1. What new techniques and practices made U.S. industries more efficient?
2. What motivated Americans to seek an empire?
3. Why did some observers find the Pullman experiment "un-American"?
4. Which cities were the main centers of industry and culture in the 1890s?
5. How did the concept of individual rights evolve in reaction to new economic conditions? Name key figures who articulated a concept of democratic rights, and describe their ideas.
6. Contrast the arguments for empire with the rhetoric of the anti-imperialists. Which dangers to the nation and democracy did each side stress?
7. Why was the issue of currency so important to Americans in 1896? What was at stake?

For further review materials and resource information, please visit www.oup.com/us/ofthepeople

▼ 1897
Germany captures Qingdao, on China's Shandong Peninsula
McKinley issues formal protest to Spain

▼ 1898
Maine explodes in Havana's harbor
United States declares war on Spain
Dewey defeats Spanish fleet at Manila Bay
In the Treaty of Paris, Spain grants Cuba independence, cedes Guam, Puerto Rico, and the Philippines to the United States
Aguinaldo proclaims Philippine independence

▼ 1899
Senate votes to annex Puerto Rico, Hawaii, and the Philippines
Philippine-American War begins
Hay issues first Open Door Note

▼ 1900
Hay issues second Open Door Note
U.S. Army joins British, French, Russian, German, and Japanese forces in capture of Beijing
Great Exposition of Paris showcases American technology
William McKinley reelected

▼ 1901
Aguinaldo captured
McKinley assassinated; Theodore Roosevelt becomes president

▼ 1902
Roosevelt declares Philippine-American war over

CHAPTER 21

Common Threads 

>> What political problems arose from the transition to an urban, industrial, and national society?

>> How did women's activism on social issues change the style and content of politics?

>> Why did party politics decline at the same time that national interest groups emerged?

>> How did the new interventionism transform the administration of cities and states?

>> In what ways did Progressivism enlarge the president's powers over foreign policy and the economy?

A United Body of Action

1900–1916

AMERICAN PORTRAIT

>> Alice Hamilton

On an October morning in 1902, three distinguished friends, Maude Gernon of the Chicago Board of Charities, Gertrude Howe, kindergarten director at Hull-House, and Dr. Alice Hamilton, a professor of pathology at Northwestern University, stood over sewer drains catching flies. The prey was abundant, and the women methodically trapped dozens in test tubes. Hamilton organized the expedition in the midst of a typhoid epidemic. The disease ravaged Chicago's 19th Ward, a working-class neighborhood where Hull-House stood. To find out why, Hamilton investigated the surrounding tenement houses, which often had illegal outdoor privies rather than indoor plumbing. It was then that she noticed the flies. Army doctors in the Spanish-American War found a link between flies and poor sanitation and the spread of typhoid. Hamilton incubated her test tubes for several days, examined them under a microscope, and confirmed that Chicago's flies carried the typhoid bacillus.

When her findings appeared in the *Journal of the American Medical Association* a few months later, they touched off a furor. Hull-House attacked the Board of Health for failing to enforce the sanitary codes, and an inquiry discovered that landlords bribed sanitation inspectors to overlook the outhouses. Further investigations found that drinking water was pumped straight from Lake Michigan, without any purification, and that broken pumping equipment channeled raw sewage into the water mains. Through a chain of bribery and neglect, Chicago's city government was responsible for an epidemic that killed hundreds of people.

Hamilton, who grew up in affluent surroundings in Fort Wayne, Indiana, attended medical school at the University of Michigan, later going on to do advanced work in bacteriology and pathology at Leipzig and Munich. Despite her training, it was difficult for her to find work, but in Chicago she found support at Hull-House, a "settlement house" founded by women who wanted to live among the poor. Hamilton lived there for 22 years. Her work concerned occupational disease, which she began studying in Germany. In the United States she noticed a "strange silence on the subject" of job-related disease. Her early research linked the working conditions of Jewish garment workers to the tuberculosis that frequently claimed their lives.

After the typhoid scandal, Hamilton began looking into stories of poisoning among workers at the National Lead Company. Clouds of metallic dust filled the plant, and employees came home from work glistening with lead. The company refused to admit its high absenteeism had anything to do with the work. Hamilton interviewed workers' wives and priests in the neighborhood. One foreman told her that lead workers "don't last long at it. Four years at the most, I should say, then they quit and go home to the old country." "To die?" she asked. "Well," he replied, "I suppose that is about the size of it." Searching hospital records, she documented a pattern of chronic lead poisoning. Confronted with these findings, the company agreed to install ventilators and create a medical department. Hamilton pushed for state laws on occupational disease, and in 1911 Illinois became the first state to pass legislation giving workers compensation for job-related disability.

Hamilton's activism was noteworthy but not unique. She was one of millions of people in the early twentieth century who reshaped democracy by participating in a new type of politics. Responding to the challenges of immigration, industrialization, and urbanization, Americans agitated for change. They worked from outside the two-party system, forming their own organizations.

continued

>> AMERICAN PORTRAIT *continued*

Women, who did not have the vote, took the lead and created a new style of activism.

Some activists feared the uncontrolled power of corporations, while others feared the uncontrolled passions of the poor. Both called themselves progressives, and they shared certain understandings about democracy. They optimistically believed in people's ability to improve society, but they were pessimistic about the ability of people, particularly nonwhite people, to improve themselves. Science and religion, as Progressives understood them, supported these beliefs and justified the supervision of human affairs by qualified experts.

Although reformers accepted industry as a modern necessity, they were outraged by the worst consequences of industrialism: the trail of disease, waste, and corruption the factory system left behind. They sought a middle ground between revolutionary socialism and uncontrolled corporate capitalism. Finally, they belonged to a movement that had national reach. Progressivism, as it came to be called, was the first and perhaps the only reform movement experienced by all Americans. Wide-circulation magazines carried the agitation into every town and county.

OUTLINE 

Toward a New Politics

Progressivism displaced the intensely partisan politics of the late nineteenth century. The political and economic crises of the 1890s left Americans disillusioned with traditional parties. A growing Socialist movement threatened to lead Americans in a more radical direction if moderate reform failed. Protestant churches became outspokenly critical of capitalism's abuses, and new interpretations of Christian ethics lent a moral urgency to reform. The mounting dangers of urban life, some of which

Alice Hamilton encountered, gave educated, affluent Americans a sense that civic problems needed to be dealt with immediately. Women took leading roles, using pressure groups to extend their influence while also seeking the vote.

Egged on by a national press, progressives organized at the local, state, and national levels to solve the problems of the new industrial world. Although they sometimes pined for the (probably imaginary) security of smaller towns and bygone eras, progressives recognized that large-scale industrial capitalism was here to stay. They worked as troubleshooters, laboring to make an erratic and brutal system more predictable, efficient, and humane. In pushing for reform, however, they were willing to enlarge the authority of the state and to use state power to tell people what was good for them. As reform gained momentum, mayors, governors, and presidential candidates identified themselves and their agendas as progressive.

> A city is in many respects a great business corporation, but in other respects it is enlarged housekeeping. . . . May we not say that city housekeeping has failed partly because women, the traditional housekeepers, have not been consulted?
>
> JANE ADDAMS, 1907

The Insecurity of Modern Life

Most people who lived in cities at the turn of the century had grown up in the country. They remembered living in communities where people knew each other, where many of the foods they ate and clothes they wore were made locally. These communities were less dependent on outsiders or big corporations. For many Americans, living in a modern metropolis meant depending on strangers. Meat and bread came not from a familiar butcher or baker, but from packinghouses hundreds or thousands of miles away. Tap water, fuel, and transportation to work were all supplied by

A Tale of Two Kitchens The house where Woodrow Wilson was born in 1856 (left) used food, fuel, water, and lighting supplied locally or even just outside the door. The kitchen in the house where he died in 1924 (right), used gas and electricity from hundreds of miles away, as well as food and appliances that came from national suppliers.

large, anonymous corporations. Unknown executives made decisions that affected the livelihoods, savings, and safety of thousands of people. City dwellers felt more sophisticated than their parents but also less secure.

City living carried risks. Inspecting a Chicago market, journalist Upton Sinclair found milk laced with formaldehyde, peas colored green with copper salts, and smoked sausage doctored with toxic chemicals. Druggists sold fraudulent cures for imaginary diseases. Dozens of patent medicines—including aspirin, cocaine, and heroin—advertised themselves as the remedies for everything from hay fever to cancer.

Even staying indoors involved hazards. Tenement blocks housing hundreds of people often had no fire escapes or plumbing. Tragedy reminded New Yorkers of these dangers on March 25, 1911, when fire engulfed the Triangle Shirtwaist Company on the top three floors of a ten-story building. Five hundred Jewish and Italian seamstresses were trapped; many jumped from ledges in groups, holding hands. In all, 146 died. Such episodes demonstrated that an unregulated economy could be both productive and deadly.

Government often added to the problem. Regulation supplied a pretext for kickbacks and bribery. In 1904 and 1905, journalist Lincoln Steffens uncovered corruption in state after state. In New York, insurance companies paid off state representatives and even a U.S. senator in return for favorable legislation. Trials in San Francisco disclosed that boss Abraham Ruef ruled the city with a slush fund donated by public utilities. The Minneapolis police, with the connivance of the mayor's office, protected brothels and gambling dens in return for bribes. Elections made the system less accountable, not more. By creating a demand for campaign funds and jobs, elections became invitations to graft.

The rising middle class found public and corporate irresponsibility particularly infuriating. In the stately Victorian "streetcar suburbs," business managers, accountants, engineers, lawyers, and doctors became conscious of themselves as a class, but they felt trapped between the two dominant social groups, the rich and the masses of wage laborers. "We do not like to acknowledge that Americans are divided into two nations," Jane Addams observed, but the tiny middle class could see itself as imperiled by both groups or, alternatively, as the only possible mediator between them. By virtue of their education and experience, members of the middle class had their own ideas on how organizations, such as utility companies, cities, and states, should run. Modern corporations had to have clear lines of authority, an emphasis on efficiency, and reliable sources of information. Yet these virtues were frustratingly absent from civic life.

The Decline of Partisan Politics

Participation in elections declined by choice and coercion. Nationally, 79 percent of the electorate voted in 1896, but four years later only 73 percent voted, and by 1904 the total fell to 65 percent. Literacy tests accounted for much of the decline in the South, but in all regions the old spectacular style of electioneering, with torchlit parades, mass rallies, and flagpole raisings, gave way to campaigns that were more educational and less participatory. "Listless" was how one observer described the 1904 turnout. "There is much apathy on the part of the public as regards the campaign—more than I have ever seen before." Worse from the parties' point of view, the voters who did turn out split their tickets. The ethnic and sectional loyalties that

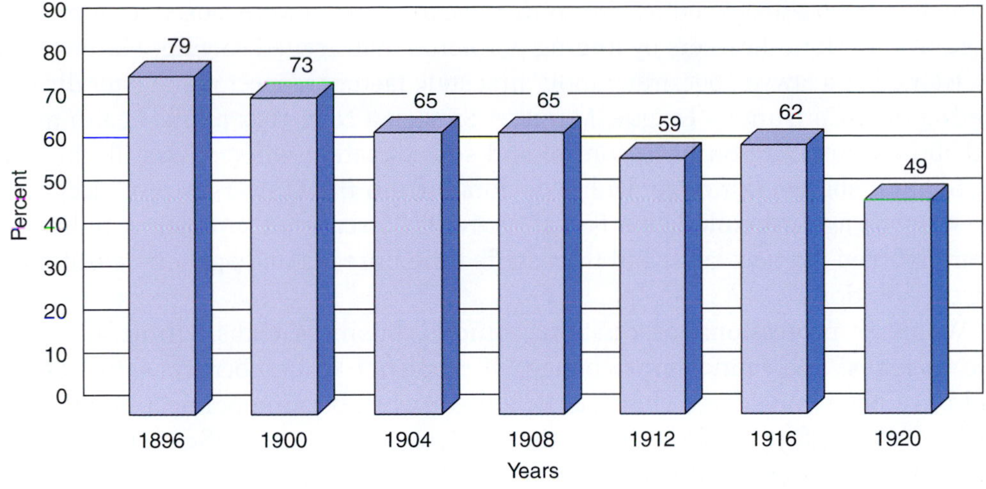

Figure 21–1 Voter Participation, 1896–1920 After the intense partisanship and high-stakes elections of the 1890s, campaigns became more "educational" and voters lost interest.

led people to vote a straight party ballot in the late nineteenth century seemed to be weakening.

Increasingly, Americans participated in politics through associations. Voluntary and professional societies took over functions that once belonged to the parties: educating and socializing voters and even making policy. These "interest groups" worked outside the system to gather support for a particular cause or proposal. Many were patterned after corporations, with a board of directors and state and local chapters. Built on the idea that reform was a continuous process, they strove for permanence. Some, like the National Association for the Advancement of Colored People (NAACP), the Salvation Army, and the Sierra Club, remain prominent after a century.

Social Housekeeping

The mounting clamor for social change aroused latent political strength in unexpected places. Women's social clubs had been nonpolitical before the turn of the century. Dedicated to developing public talents like art, speaking, reading, and conversation, they were typically highly organized, with local, state, and national chapters. A General Federation of Women's Clubs was formed in 1890. Within 10 years the urgency of social problems led many clubs to launch campaigns on behalf of free kindergartens, civil service reform, and public health. "Ladies," Sarah P. Decker announced at her inauguration as head of the federation in 1904, "Dante is dead. He has been dead for several centuries, and I think that it is time that we dropped the study of his inferno and turned attention to our own." Following her advice, clubwomen turned from developing public skills to exercising them.

A growing cohort of professional women also energized reform. The first generation of graduates from the new women's colleges had reached adulthood, and some, like Alice Hamilton, had attained advanced degrees at a time when few men went to college. These "new women," as historians have called them, had ambitions and values that set them apart from women of their mothers' generation. About half of the female graduates did not marry. Since career paths were closed to them, educated women found careers by finding problems that needed solving. Florence Kelley, trained as a lawyer, became Illinois' first state factory inspector and later directed the National Consumers League. Margaret Sanger, a New York public health nurse, distributed literature on birth control and sex education when it was illegal to do so. Sophonisba Breckinridge, with a doctorate from the University of Chicago, led the struggle against child labor. Female activists "discovered" problems, publicized them, lobbied for new laws, and then staffed the bureaus and agencies administering the solutions.

Women's professional associations, unions, business clubs, ethnic and patriotic societies, and foundations changed the practice of democracy. Activities that had once been considered charity or volunteer work became political. Some, such as the YWCA (1894) and the International Council of Nurses (1899), had a global reach. The experiences of women's clubs and associations taught activists the importance of cooperation, organization, and expertise. When women's clubs built a playground and donated it to the city or urged lawmakers to address an issue, they increased their own stake in the political system. They gave themselves new reasons to demand full citizenship.

The women's suffrage movement quietly built momentum in the early years of the century. Women had gained the vote in four states—Colorado, Wyoming, Utah, and Idaho—early on, but between 1896 and 1910 no other states adopted a women's suffrage amendment. The movement encountered stubborn opposition from the Catholic Church, machine politicians, and business interests.

Competing suffrage organizations joined forces under the National American Woman Suffrage Association (NAWSA). Led by Carrie Chapman Catt and Anna Howard Shaw, NAWSA developed a strategy based on professional lobbying and publicity. Suffragists appealed to clubwomen and middle-class reformers by cultivating an image of Victorian respectability and linking suffrage to moderate social causes, such as temperance and education. NAWSA eventually narrowed its constituency and became less democratic, but initially its strategy paid off. After 1910, five states adopted suffrage amendments in rapid succession, but the opposition rallied and defeated referendums in three eastern states.

Frustrated with the glacial pace of progress, Alice Paul's National Woman's Party adopted more radical tactics, picketing the White House and staging hunger strikes. Despite setbacks, women led the transformation of politics through voluntary organizations and interest groups and were on the threshold of even greater gains.

Evolution or Revolution?

The Socialist Party's swelling membership seemed to confirm its claims that the future would be revolutionary rather than progressive. At its founding meeting in Indianapolis in 1901, the party declared confidence in the inevitability of capitalism's downfall. By 1912, Eugene V. Debs, the party's candidate for president, garnered almost a million votes, some 6 percent of the total. "Gas and water" Socialists, who demanded public ownership of utilities, captured municipal offices in smaller cities across the country. In the Plains states, socialism drew strength from primitive Baptist and Holiness churches and held revival-style tent meetings. The party's stronghold was Oklahoma, where almost one-quarter of the electorate voted Socialist in 1914.

Although tinged with religion, Socialists' analysis of modern problems was economic. They maintained that the profit motive distorted human behavior, forcing people to compete for survival as individuals instead of joining to promote the common good. Driven by profits, corporations could not be trusted to look after the welfare of consumers or workers. Socialists demanded the collective ownership of industries, starting with ones that most directly affected the livelihoods and safety of people: the railroads and city utilities. Although their ambitions collided with corporate values, they had faith that America could make the transition without violence. Above all, they were sure socialism was coming, "coming like a prairie fire," a Socialist newspaperman told his readers. "You can see it in the papers. You can taste it in the price of beef."

"Social Gospel" clergymen preached this coming millennium. Washington Gladden, a congregational pastor from Columbus, Ohio; Walter Rauschenbusch, a Baptist minister from New York; William Dwight Porter Bliss, who founded the Society for Christian Socialists; and George Herron, an Iowa Congregationalist, were among the prominent ministers who interpreted the Bible as a call to social action. Their visions of the Christian commonwealth ranged from reform to revolution, but they all believed that corporate capitalism was organized sin, and that the church had an obligation to stand against it.

When the Industrial Workers of the World (IWW) talked about revolution they meant class war, not elections. Founded in 1905, the IWW unionized some of the most rugged individuals in the West: miners, loggers, and even rodeo cowboys (under the Bronco Busters and Range Riders Union). Gathering unskilled workers into "one big union," the Wobblies challenged both the AFL's elite unionism and the Socialists' gradualism. Membership remained small, fewer than 100,000, but the union and its leader, William "Big Bill" Haywood, had a reputation for radicalism. At IWW strikes in Lawrence, Massachusetts, and Paterson, New Jersey, strikers clashed with police and staged parades in which thousands of marchers carried red flags. To sensationalist newspapermen and anxious middle-class readers, these activities looked like signs of approaching class warfare.

Conservatives and reformers alike felt the hot breath of revolution on their necks, and socialism's greatest influence may have been the push it gave conservatives to support moderate reform. Theodore Roosevelt warned that unless something was done the United States would divide into two parties, one representing workers, the other capital.

The failure of the two parties to deal with urgent problems created a chance to redefine democracy. As the new century began, Americans were testing their political ideals, scrapping the old rules, and getting ready to fashion new institutions and laws to deal with the challenges of modern society.

The Progressives

Historians have found it difficult to define the progressives. They addressed a wide variety of social problems with many different tactics, but for people of the time the connectedness was apparent. A rally to end child labor, for instance, might draw out young lawyers, teachers, labor unionists, woman suffragists, professors, and politicians. "Scores of young leaders in American politics and public affairs were seeing what I saw, feeling what I felt," journalist William Allen White remembered. A series of overlapping movements, campaigns, and crusades defined the era from 1890 to 1920.

Progressivism was a political style, a way of approaching problems. Progressives had no illusions that wage labor or industrialism could be eliminated or that it was possible to re-create a rural commonwealth. Big cities and big corporations, they believed, were permanent features of modern life, but progressives shared an optimistic conviction that modern institutions could be made humane, responsive, and moral.

In choosing solutions, progressives relied on scientific expertise as a way to avoid the clash of interests. The generation raised during the Civil War knew democracy was no guarantee against mass violence. Rival points of view could be reconciled more easily by impartial authority. Like the salaried managers many of them were, progressives valued efficiency and organization. No problem could be solved in a single stroke. Instead, true remedies could be enforced only by persistent action.

Convinced that science and God were on their side, progressives did not balk at imposing their views on other people, even if democracy got in the way. Such measures as naming "born criminals" to be put on probation *before* committing a crime were called "progressive." To southern progressives "scientific" principles justified racial segregation. Popular opposition posed a strategic rather than a philosophical problem. Progressives demanded more democracy when it led to "good government," but if the majority was wrong, in their view, progressives handed power to unelected managers. The basic structure of American government and economy, they felt, should not be open to political debate.

> **I've come here to write the Uncle Tom's Cabin of the labor movement.**
>
> UPTON SINCLAIR,
> Chicago, 1904

More than anything else, progressives shared an urgency. "There are two kinds of people," Alice Hamilton learned from her mother, "the ones who say, 'Someone ought to do something about it but why should it be I?' and the ones who say, 'Somebody must do something about it, then why not I?' "Hamilton and other progressives never doubted that they were the second kind.

Social Workers and Muckrakers

Among the first to hear the call to service were the young women and men who volunteered to live among the urban poor in "settlement houses." Stanton Coit established the first on New York's Lower East Side in 1886, but the most famous was Hull-House, which opened in Chicago three years later. Its founders, Jane Addams and Ellen Starr, bought a run-down mansion at the center of an inner-city ward thick with sweatshops, factories, and overcrowded tenements. The women of Hull-House opened a kindergarten and a clinic, took sweatshop bosses to court, investigated corrupt landlords, criticized the ward's powerful alderman, and built the first public playground in Chicago.

Addams drew together at Hull-House a remarkable group of women with similar backgrounds. Florence Kelley organized a movement for occupational safety laws. Julia Lathrop headed the state's Children's Bureau. All three women were raised in affluent Quaker homes during or shortly after the Civil War, and their parents were all abolitionists. Like Alice Hamilton, all three attended college and afterward traveled or studied in Europe.

The Hull-House Choir in Recital, 1910 Chicago, according to Lincoln Steffens, was "loud, lawless, unlovely, ill-smelling, new; an overgrown gawk of a village." Addams and other settlement workers sought to tame this urban wilderness through culture and activism.

As the fame of Hull-House spread, women (and some men) organized settlement houses in cities across the country. By the turn of the century there were more than 100, and by 1910 more than 400. Reformers often began by using social science techniques to survey the surrounding neighborhoods, gathering information on the national origins, income, housing conditions, and occupations of the local people. Addams released *Hull-House Maps and Papers*, a survey of the 19th Ward, in 1895. One of the Progressive Era's most ambitious research projects was the Pittsburgh Survey, a massive investigation of living and working conditions in the steel city published in six volumes between 1909 and 1914. Survey data confirmed that the causes of poverty were social, not personal, contradicting a common belief that the poor had only themselves to blame. Settlements did "social work" rather than charity.

Surveys re-created a social world with statistics accompanied by maps, photographs, and in some cases three-dimensional models. In 1900, housing reformers in New York exhibited a scale cutaway model of a tenement block, allowing visitors to see from a bird's-eye perspective how overcrowding, the arrangement of rooms, and the size of air shafts contributed to disease and crime. Shelby Harrison, director of surveys for the Russell Sage Foundation, explained that the survey itself was reform. It relied "upon the correcting power of facts . . . plus such a telling of facts that will make them common knowledge. It is believed to be the American experience that people will act upon facts when they have them."

This statistical outlook motivated settlement workers to attack urban problems across a broad front. "If parks were wanted, if schools needed bettering," Jacob Riis wrote, "there were at the College Settlement, the University Settlement, the Nurses' Settlement, and at a score of other such places, young enthusiasts to collect the facts and urge them, with the prestige of their non-political organization to back them." Social workers labored to make food safe, repair housing, and sponsor festivals and pageants. Working conditions, especially for women and children, drew special attention, but employers, landlords, and city bosses were not the only targets. The "young enthusiasts" attacked working-class vices—gambling, saloons, and brothels. Supporters participated vicariously by reading *The House on Henry Street, The City Wilderness, Twenty Years at Hull-House,* and other popular books written by settlement workers.

The loudest voice of progressivism came from a new type of journalism introduced in 1902. In successive issues, *McClure's* magazine published Lincoln Steffens's investigation of graft in St. Louis, and Ida Tarbell's "History of the Standard Oil Company," sensational exposés that disclosed crimes of the nation's political and economic elite. As periodicals competed for a mass readership, the old partisan style of journalism gave way to crusades, celebrity correspondents, and "sob sister" features. The new ten-cent magazines, like *Everybody's, Cosmopolitan,* and *McClure's,* had national audiences and budgets big enough to pay for careful, in-depth investigations. The result was a type of reporting Theodore Roosevelt disdainfully called "muckraking." Readers loved it, and an article exposing some new corporate or public villainy could easily sell half a million copies.

Muckrakers named names. Upton Sinclair described the grisly business of canning beef. Ray Stannard Baker investigated railroads and segregation. Samuel Hopkins Adams catalogued the damage done by narcotics in popular medicines. Tarbell exposed Standard Oil's methods: camouflaged companies, espionage, sweetheart deals, and predatory pricing. The series ran in 24 straight issues and shattered the notion that industrial giants competed in a free market. Amid a national outcry, the Justice Department sued Standard Oil in 1906 for conspiracy to restrain trade.

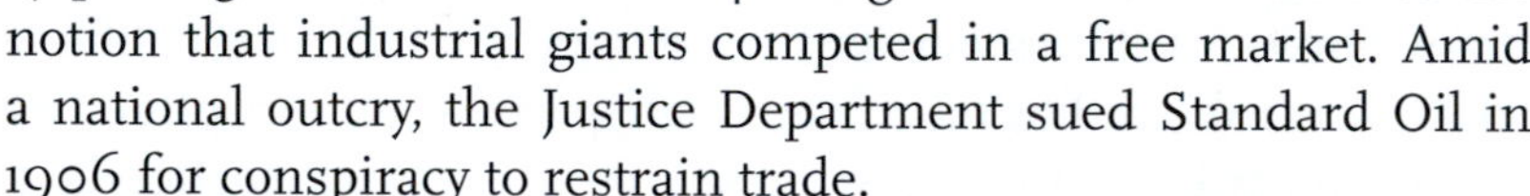

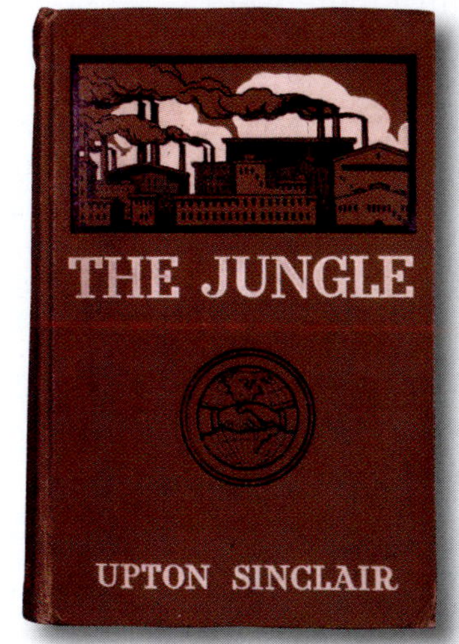

The ten-cent magazines projected local problems onto a national canvas. Newspapers had covered municipal corruption before, but Steffens's series in *McClure's* revealed that bribery, influence peddling, and protection rackets operated in nearly every major city, and for the same reason: an insidious alliance between city officials and local monopolies. Magazines also carried news of progressive victories, allowing solutions adopted in Toledo or Milwaukee to spread quickly. Muckraking declined after 1912, the victim of corporate advertising boycotts and declining readership, but while it lasted, "public opinion" became a force that could shake politicians and powerful corporations.

Dictatorship of the Experts

For doctors, lawyers, and engineers, reform offered a chance to apply their skills to urgent problems. Not accidentally, the Progressive Era coincided with the rise in influence of the social sciences and the professions. Experts could mediate potentially violent conflicts between rival interests and eliminate the uncertainties of democracy. Scientific advances seemed to justify this faith. In just a generation, antiseptic

AMERICA AND THE WORLD

>> The Calorie

Just after breakfast on March 23, 1896, Professor Wilbur Atwater sealed a student in an airtight chamber in the basement of Wesleyan University's Judd Hall. The apparatus was described by the press as resembling a meat locker, a single room lined with copper and zinc. Atwater carefully recorded the change in temperature inside the cell while the student, A. W. Smith, rested, lifted weights, and ate measured portions of bread, baked beans, hamburger, milk, and potatoes. The device was a calorimeter, a tool previously used to measure the efficiency of engines and explosives.

The national press was riveted by the story of the "prisoner of science," but the results were even more startling. Atwater proved a theory European scientists had advanced 50 years earlier, that the human body had the thermodynamic properties of a machine. Both its intake—food—and its output—physical or mental exertion—could be measured in uniform units called calories. The discovery had immense military and industrial implications, allowing rations and wages to be calculated for maximum energy-producing efficiency. Congress voted funds to build a calorimeter in Washington, and government scientists compiled charts that proved another fact scientists had thought highly unlikely: all people, regardless of climate or race, need exactly the same number of calories to thrive. When it came to food, all men were created equal, after all.

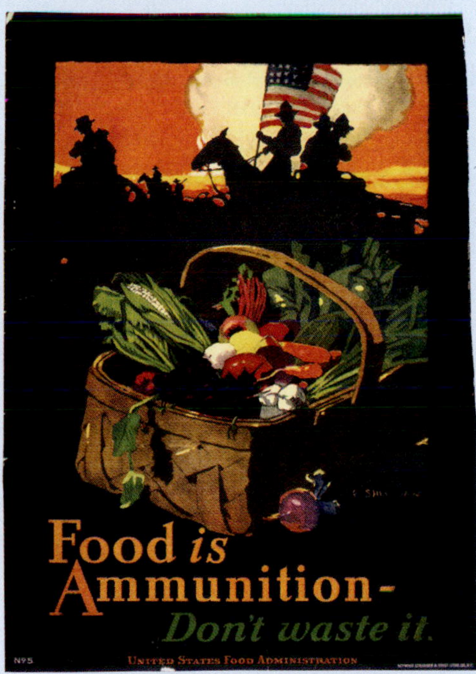

Food is
Ammunition-
Don't waste it.
United States Food Administration

Before the calorie, it was no more possible to measure appetite than to measure beauty or intelligence. Eating habits varied widely among cultures and individuals, and dietary knowledge was closer to a religion than a science. The calorie opened the way for the systematic study of nutrition. The discovery of vitamins in 1914 brought the machine theory of the body into question, but the calorie remained the only universal gauge of food consumption.

World War I provided the first practical applications. After Germany's invasion of Belgium in 1914 devastated the neutral country, a wealthy mining engineer, Herbert Hoover, organized American charities to prevent famine. The Belgium Relief used the calorie to ration food supplies, and soon Europeans learned to count what they ate by American numbers. When the United States entered the war, Hoover mobilized the country's food supply to feed the Allied armies. He particularly prized wheat, "the largest supply of calories available" for the war effort. American families were told how to count calories and save wheat by cleaning their plates and avoiding "overeating." Restaurants helpfully listed calorie counts on the menu.

In the wake of victory in 1918, Europe's ports opened to American relief shipments, and Hoover's organization commanded the food supply from central Europe as far east as Moscow. The calorie briefly even became a unit of currency. Immigrants could send a check from New York to their relatives in Poland or Lithuania to be cashed at food banks for a fixed number of calories. The newly formed League of Nations discussed using the calorie to rationalize the world's food supply, perhaps eliminating famines permanently.

Calorie consciousness revolutionized global cuisine in the interwar years. The discovery that Japanese sailors could eat just as much as their British counterparts prompted the Imperial Navy to provision its ships with high-calorie pork and chicken dipped in batter (tempura). These new recipes, popularized as the national cuisine, became what we know today as Japanese food. Greek and Mexican cookbook writers added flour to increase calorie counts. But while nationalists used calories to assert entitlement to a full plate, newspapers around the world urged women to count calories to stay thin. The calorie measured the food needs of whole populations, rather than individuals, but despite doctors' warnings, "dieting" became a global fad.

To many people, quantification took all the pleasure out of eating. Dutch historian Johan Huizinga saw the calorie as a peculiarly American "Taylorism of the mind."

continued

>> **AMERICA AND THE WORLD** *continued*

Indian nationalist leader Mahatma Gandhi rejected the calorie as yet another imperial ploy to control the world's hungry masses, this time through science. Insisting that each body had its own needs and each food its own spiritual value, he made hunger and self-denial into weapons in the independence struggle.

Nutrition came to be seen as a solution to economic and political problems. A 1936 League of Nations report proposed that the global agricultural depression could be solved if surplus calories in the industrial countries could be exported to countries, such as China, with caloric deficits. The proposal led in 1942 to the creation of the Food and Agriculture Organization, the first component of the United Nations system. The United States fought World War II, President Franklin D. Roosevelt proclaimed, to guarantee "freedom from want."

Since ancient times, communities and nations have always kept a close eye on food supplies, but the calorie made food and nutrition an international concern. It implied that humanity had a single appetite, and that those who had food had obligations to those who did not, even if they were on opposite sides of the world. Back in the twentieth century, many a child who refused to eat his asparagus got a stern reminder of that duty.

techniques, X-rays, and new drugs generated a whole new understanding of disease. Electric light, recorded sound, motion pictures, radio, and flight confirmed science's ability to shape the future.

Social workers copied doctors, diagnosing each case with clinical impartiality and relying on tests and individual histories. Newly professionalized police forces applied the techniques of fingerprinting, handwriting analysis, and psychology to law enforcement. Dietitians descended on school cafeterias, banishing pierogies and souvlaki and replacing them with bland but nutritionally balanced meals. Reformers tried (but failed) to simplify spelling and bring "efficiency" to the English language.

Trust in science sometimes led to extreme measures. One was the practice of eugenics, an attempt to rid society of alcoholism, poverty, and crime through selective breeding. "We know enough about eugenics so that if the knowledge were applied, the defective classes would disappear within a generation," the president of the University of Wisconsin predicted. Persuaded that genetics could save the state money in the long run, the Indiana legislature passed a law in 1907 authorizing the forced sterilization of "criminals, idiots, rapists, and imbeciles." Patients with epilepsy, psychiatric disorders, or mental handicaps who sought help at state hospitals were surgically sterilized. Criminals received the same treatment. Seven other states also adopted the "Indiana Plan."

Behind the emphasis on expertise lay a thinly veiled distrust of democracy. Education was one example. Professional educators took control of the schools away from local boards and gave it to expert administrators and superintendents. They certified teachers and classified students based on "scientific" intelligence tests. To reformers, education was far too important to be left to amateurs, like teachers, parents, or voters.

Progressivism created new social sciences and made universities into centers of advocacy. Sociology was a product of the progressive impulse. The study of government became political science, and "scientific" historians searched the past for answers to modern problems. John R. Commons, Richard Ely, and Thorstein Veblen escaped from the old debates over classical theory and used economics to study how modern institutions developed and functioned. Legal scholars like Louis Brandeis and Roscoe Pound called for revising the law to reflect social realities.

This stress on expertise made Progressive-Era reforms different from those of the Gilded Age and earlier. Instead of trying to gain success at a single stroke—by passing a law or trouncing a corrupt politician—progressives believed in process. When they could, progressives set up permanent organizations and procedures that would keep the pressure on and make progress a habit.

Progressives on the Color Line

In her international crusade against lynching, Ida B. Wells-Barnett pioneered some of the progressive tactics of research, exposure, and organization. A schoolteacher in Memphis, Wells-Barnett documented mob violence against African Americans and mobilized opinion in the United States and Britain. Cities that condoned extralegal executions soon faced a barrage of condemnation from church groups and women's clubs. As her Afro-American Council took on national and then international scope, she joined forces with white suffragists, social workers, and journalists, but her cause fell outside of the progressive mainstream. Many reform groups sympathized with white southerners or wanted to avoid dividing their membership over race.

Reformers debated as to how much progress non-Anglo-Saxons were capable of, but they were inclined to be pessimistic. Eugenics gave white supremacy the endorsement of science. A new technology, the motion picture, showed its power to rewrite history from a racial viewpoint in D. W. Griffith's classic *Birth of a Nation* (1915), which romanticized the Klan's campaign of terror during Reconstruction. Policy was often based on assumptions about the capabilities of various races. Trade schools, not universities, were deemed appropriate for educating Filipinos and Hawaiians. Progressives took Native American children from their families and placed them in boarding schools. Electoral reform in Texas meant disfranchising Spanish-speaking voters.

Ida B. Wells-Barnett with Her Children Ida Wells-Barnett, journalist and activist, made lynching an international issue through her writing and speaking tours.

Wells-Barnett was not alone in finding doors through this wall of racial ideology. William Edward Burghardt DuBois documented the costs of racism in *The Philadelphia Negro* (1898). The survey spoke the progressives' language, insisting that discrimination was not just morally wrong but inefficient, since it took away work and encouraged alcoholism and crime. DuBois transformed the politics of race as profoundly as Addams transformed the politics of cities.

Raised in Massachusetts, DuBois learned Latin and Greek in public schools. At 17, he went to Fisk University in Tennessee, where he "came in contact for the first time with a sort of violence that I had never realized in New England." He also had his first encounter with African American religion and gospel music. The songs he heard in church were "full of the voices of the past." DuBois later studied at Harvard and Berlin.

DuBois and Booker T. Washington came to espouse opposing visions of African Americans' place in the United States. Both emphasized the importance of thrift and hard work. DuBois, however, rejected Washington's willingness to accept legal inequality. Gradually, DuBois came to believe that the Atlanta Compromise (see Chapter 20) led only to disfranchisement and segregation. He disliked the way Washington's influence with white philanthropists silenced other voices. Five years after the Atlanta speech he opened a sustained attack on Washington's "Tuskegee Machine."

In *The Souls of Black Folk* (1903), DuBois argued that the strategy of accommodation contained a "triple paradox": Washington had urged African Americans to seek industrial training, build self-respect, and become successful in business, while asking them to stop striving for higher education, civil rights, or political power. How could a people train themselves without higher education or gain self-respect without having any of the rights other Americans enjoyed? How could African Americans succeed in business without having the political power to protect themselves or their property? Economic, political, and educational progress had to move together. Like other progressives, DuBois insisted on the importance of process and organization. African Americans could not stop demanding the vote, equality, or education.

In July 1905, DuBois and 28 prominent African American leaders met on the Canadian side of Niagara Falls (no hotel on the U.S. side would admit them) to organize a campaign against racial violence, segregation, and disfranchisement. The Niagara Movement was one of several such organizations. In 1909, Wells-Barnett, Addams, and other reformers created the National Association for the Advancement of Colored People to carry on the fight in the courts. In 1915 the NAACP won a Supreme Court decision outlawing the grandfather clause, which denied the vote to descendants of slaves, but another 40 years passed before it succeeded in overturning *Plessy v. Ferguson*.

Progressives in State and Local Politics

Progressives were of two minds about the public. Walter Lippmann, a journalist and reformer, could write fondly of "the voiceless multitudes," and contemptuously of the "great dull mass of people who just don't care." Progressives' tactics betrayed this split vision. To bring the cities under control, they made city government less democratic and more "businesslike." Reforms at the state level, however, expanded voters' power to initiate legislation and remove corrupt officeholders. In both cases, the changes enlarged the influence of the small-town and urban-middle-class reform constituency while reducing that of immigrants and the working class.

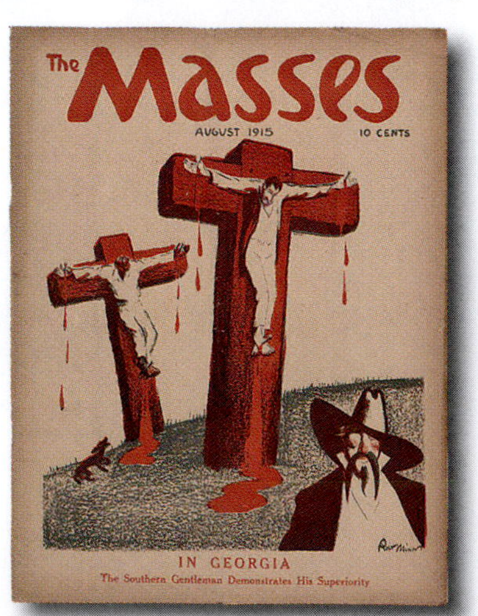

Redesigning the City

The machine politicians who ran American cities proved remarkably adaptable to changing conditions. To immigrants and factory workers, the local boss was one of the few people looking out for the average person. He rushed to fire scenes to aid homeless victims. He distributed turkeys in poor neighborhoods at Christmas. When a family member was jailed or thrown out of work, the machine politician stood ready to post bail or find a job. Jane Addams acknowledged that for popularity, she could not compete with Johnny Powers, the local ward boss, this "big manifestation of human friendliness, this stalking survival of village kindness."

> **Four years ago, the city of Galveston was almost wiped from the face of the earth. . . . Today, Galveston is practically a new city, with more advantages than were enjoyed in the days before the storm, a more economical administration, and a better financial showing than has ever been known in the history of the city.**
>
> *WASHINGTON POST,*
> June 10, 1904

Powers and other aldermen sheltered the brothels, saloons, and gambling dens that, in Addams's view, exploited honest workers. Hull-House organized to beat Powers in 1895, and in reacting to defeat the reformers revealed their frustrations with democracy. The reformers nominated an Irish bricklayer, William Gleeson, on the assumption that the 19th Ward's working-class voters would prefer a candidate of their own status. But voters said they wanted someone grander to represent them, and Powers, with his big house and diamond buttons, seemed just the type. Gleeson was thoroughly trounced. Addams was "puzzled, then astounded and indignant" at the outcome.

With officials like Powers in charge, corporations could do what they liked, so long as they padded the right wallets. "If you want to get anything out of the council," the

"Annual Parade of the Cable-Trolley Cripple Club," from *The Verdict,* March 20, 1899 Injuries caused by privately run utilities led to demands for public supervision of essential services.

head of the Chicago Chamber of Commerce advised, "the quickest way is to pay for it—not to the city, but to the aldermen." City machines lost their appeal not by providing too few services, but too many. As tax burdens grew, wealthier voters clamored for reform. Progressives set out to replace paternalism with efficient, scientific administration.

After the depression of 1893, scores of associations sprang up to criticize municipal government. The structure of many cities resembled the federal system in miniature. A mayor, elected by the whole city, presided over a council of representatives from each neighborhood, or ward. This system diluted the influence of the "better classes" and allowed a few powerful wards to rule the city. In 1899 Louisville's Conference for Good City Government proposed a new model, later known as the "strong mayor" system. It gave more power to the mayor and required each council member to represent the whole city. Two years later, after a hurricane and tidal wave destroyed Galveston, Texas, the devastated city experimented with an even bolder plan. The recovery would be managed by a commission of five elected officials, each of whom managed a city department. Des Moines, Iowa, copied and improved on Galveston's design, and by 1911 some 160 cities had commission governments.

The commission resembled a corporate board of directors. Professionalism and accountability, the skills that made for business success, could make a city run, too. This philosophy led Detroit voters to elect Ford Motor Company's chief efficiency expert, James Couzens, as mayor. Other cities, led by Dayton, Ohio, tried to improve on the city-commission plan by placing local government in the hands of an unelected "city manager."

Middle- and upper-class professionals led this revolution in city government, and they gained the most from it. The new city officials could explain where tax money was spent, and they responded to criticisms from leading citizens and newspapers, but there were no turkeys at Christmas. Getting a job or help from the city meant filling out the proper forms. Reform administrations targeted urban "vice," which included the whole range of working-class recreations. Voters also learned that businesslike efficiency did not lower taxes. Budgets continued to grow along with the public's demand for services.

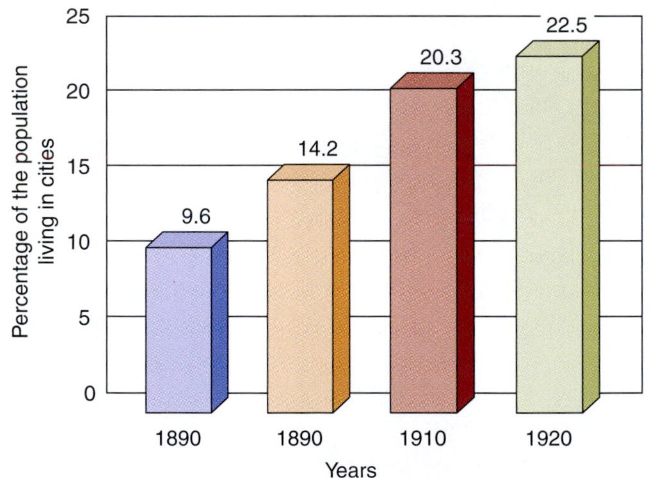

Figure 21–2 Percentage of the Population Living in Cities, 1890–1920 Cities and towns underwent dramatic growth around the turn of the century. Offices, department stores, and new forms of mass entertainment—from vaudeville to professional sports—drew people to the city center. Railroads and trolleys allowed cities to spread outward, segregating residents by class. *Kennedy,* Rise and Fall of the Great Powers, *p. 200.*

Reform Mayors and City Services

While commissioners rewrote the rules, a new breed of reform mayors cleaned up their cities. Samuel "Golden Rule" Jones, a Welsh immigrant who earned a fortune in the Pennsylvania oilfields, won election three times as independent mayor of Toledo. He enacted the eight-hour day for city employees, pushed for public ownership of city utilities, and staged free concerts in the parks. Like Tom Johnson in Cleveland and Hazen Pingree in Detroit, Jones worried less about inefficiency and saloons and more about utilities. Milwaukee, Schenectady, and other cities bought or regulated the private monopolies that supplied lighting, garbage removal, water, and streetcars.

The reform mayor's efforts to humanize the urban environment were supported by architects and engineers who endeavored to improve urban life through the arrangement of public space. A City Beautiful movement sought to soften the urban landscape with vistas, open spaces, and greenery. The District of Columbia, with its commission government, broad avenues, and parks adjacent to federal buildings, furnished a model of city planning, and Congress sought to make it a model of municipal reform as well by introducing a model child-labor law, slum-clearance plan, and school system, but representatives from the industrial North and the segregated South found it easier to agree on parks and monuments than on social legislation. Spatial arrangement performed social and educational functions indirectly. Well-ordered scenes were designed to Americanize and uplift immigrant city dwellers. New York enacted zoning laws in 1916, and "city planners" joined the ranks of specialists by organizing themselves as a profession.

Progressivism and the States

Reform at the state level varied by region. The East mimicked the tactics and agenda of urban reform. New York's progressive governor, Charles Evans Hughes, passed laws prohibiting gambling and creating a state commission to regulate utilities. In southern states, progressivism often meant refining the techniques of segregation and disfranchisement, freeing white voters to disagree among themselves about schools or crime. Lynching and mob assaults on African Americans were weekly occurrences in the Progressive Era. White leaders justified segregation and violence in terms used to justify urban reform in the North: the "better classes" had an obligation to rein in the excesses of democracy.

States in the West and Midwest produced the boldest experiments. Oregon introduced the secret ballot, voter registration, and three measures originally proposed by the Populists: the initiative, recall, and referendum. The initiative allowed voters to place legislation on the ballot by petition; the referendum let the legislature put proposals on the ballot; and the recall gave voters the chance to remove officials from office before the end of their terms. In his inaugural address as governor of New Jersey, Woodrow Wilson observed that Oregon had brought "government back to the people and protect[ed] it from the control of the representatives of selfish and special interests." Other states soon adopted all or part of the "Oregon system."

The best known of the progressive governors was Robert M. "Fighting Bob" La Follette, whose model of state government came to be known as the "Wisconsin Idea." Elected governor in 1900, La Follette pushed through a comprehensive program of social legislation. Railway and public-utility commissions placed the state's largest corporations under public control. A tax commission designed a "scientific" distribution of the tax burden, including an income tax. Other commissions regulated hours and working conditions and protected the environment. Wisconsin also implemented the direct primary, which allowed party nominees to be chosen directly by the voters rather than by party caucuses.

Few machine politicians had as much personal power as the reform governors did. Wisconsin papers reserved the term "demagogue" for La Follette, but the demagogic reform governors dispelled much of the public's cynicism and brought policy making out of the "smoke-filled rooms." By shaking up city halls and statehouses, progressives made government more responsive to demands for reform, but they

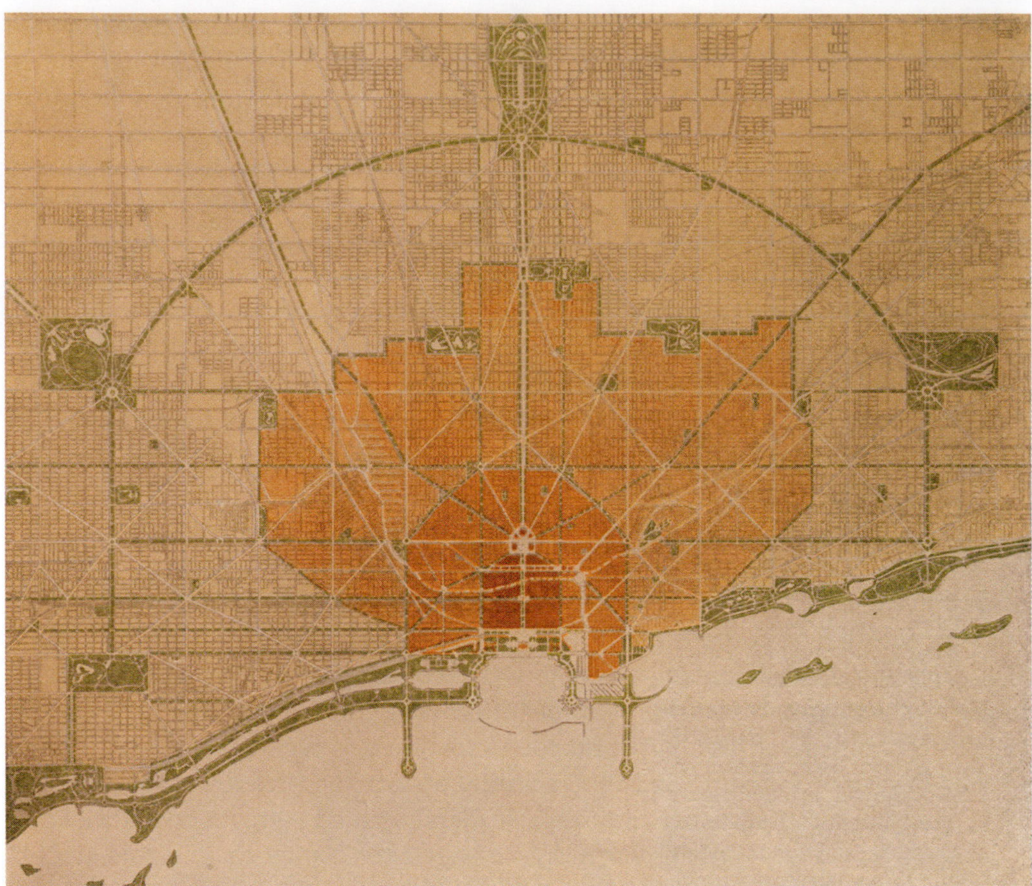

Daniel Burnham's City Plan for Chicago, 1909 Through comprehensive planning, Burnham sought to save cities from "the chaos incident to rapid growth." He drafted designs for Washington, Cleveland, San Francisco, and Manila.

knew that social problems did not respect city and state boundaries. National corporations and nationwide problems had to be attacked at the federal level, and that meant capturing the White House.

The President Becomes "The Administration"

If Theodore Roosevelt stood at the center of the two great movements of his age, imperialism and progressivism, it was because he prepared himself for the part. The Roosevelt family was one of the oldest in New York and wealthy enough to afford comfort, but Theodore embarked instead on a series of pursuits that were unusual for a man of his class. After graduating from Harvard in 1880, he married, started law school, wrote a history of the War of 1812 (he would write four other works, including the four-volume *Winning of the West*), bought a cattle ranch in the Dakota Territory, and, most surprisingly, ran for the state legislature.

Roosevelt's political bid stunned his family and friends, who believed government was no place for gentlemen. Roosevelt himself described his colleagues as "a stupid, sodden, vicious lot, most of them being equally deficient in brains and virtue." Avoiding the "rough and tumble," he argued, only conceded high offices to those less fit to lead. Albany's politicos hardly knew what to make of the young swell who appeared at the capitol wearing a monocle and carrying "a gold-headed cane in one hand and a silk hat in the other." Roosevelt's flair for publicity got him noticed, and in 1886 the Republican Party nominated him for mayor of New York. He finished a poor third, behind the Tammany nominee and the Socialist candidate.

A turn as head of New York's board of police commissioners from 1895 to 1897 deepened Roosevelt's commitment to reform. The commission supervised an army of 38,000 policemen. Muckraking journalists Lincoln Steffens and Jacob Riis showed Roosevelt the dismal tenement neighborhoods that housed Irish and Italian immigrants. Roosevelt's crackdown on saloons and corruption in the police department earned him a reputation as a man who would not be intimidated, even by his own party's bosses, and when McKinley captured the presidency he named Roosevelt assistant secretary of the navy. The Spanish-American War catapulted him to national fame, and in quick succession he became governor of New York, vice president, and then president of the United States.

> **Theodore Roosevelt began the work of turning the American mind in the direction which it had to go in the Twentieth Century.**
>
> WALTER LIPPMANN

Roosevelt believed that to restore democracy—"genuine democracy"—America needed a mission. "We must have a genuine and permanent moral awakening without which no wisdom of legislation or administration really means anything." He spoke more often about the responsibilities, duties, and character of citizens than about their choices. In the White House, he set out to find great tasks—principles to be upheld, isthmuses to be cut, and lands to be conserved—that inspired a spirit of common purpose and tested the national will. In the process, he rewrote the president's job description, seizing new powers for the executive branch and turning the presidency into "the administration."

The Executive Branch Against the Trusts

Roosevelt approached politics the way Addams approached poverty, studying it, living in its midst, and carefully choosing his battles. His fear of radicalism was borne out in September 1901. President William McKinley was shaking hands at the Pan American Exposition in Buffalo, New York, when a man thrust a pistol into his chest and fired twice. The assassin, Leon Czolgosz, came from the Cleveland slums and claimed to seek vengeance for the poor.

Roosevelt entered the White House at the age of 42, the youngest man to attain the presidency. He was the first president to call himself a progressive, and the first, according to Lippmann, "who realized clearly that national stability and social justice had to be sought deliberately and had consciously to be maintained," and that "the promise of American life could be realized only by a national effort."

Unsatisfied to be merely the standard-bearer of his party, he set out to remake the executive as the preeminent branch of government, the initiator of legislation, molder of public opinion, and guardian of the national interest at home and abroad. "I believe in a strong executive," he explained, "I believe in power." Instead of asking Congress for legislation, he drafted bills and lobbied for them personally. He believed federal administrators should intervene in the economy to protect citizens or to save business from its own short-sightedness. McKinley had already decided action against the trusts was necessary, but his plans were not as bold as his successor's.

Challenging the corporations would be no easy task. Roosevelt took office less than a decade after J. P. Morgan rescued the federal Treasury. In an 1895 decision, the Supreme Court gutted the Sherman Act, one of the few laws that allowed federal action against monopolies. The underfunded Interstate Commerce Commission possessed only theoretical powers. Roosevelt admitted to Congress that "publicity is the only sure remedy which we can now invoke." He used it to the limit. Wall Street took notice when in his first inaugural he asserted that trusts "are creatures of the State, and the State not only has the right to control them, but it is duty bound to control them." In 1903 Roosevelt established a Department of Commerce and Labor that required annual reports, making corporate activities transparent.

The Justice Department revitalized the Sherman Act with vigorous prosecutions of the worst offenders. To send a message to Wall Street, Roosevelt selected cases for maximum publicity value. Attorney General Philander Knox filed suit against J. P. Morgan's holding company, Northern Securities. Morgan expected that the matter could be settled in the usual way, and his attorney asked how they might "fix it up." "We don't want to fix it up," Knox replied. "We want to stop it." When the Court handed Roosevelt a victory in 1904, Americans cheered.

With this case, Roosevelt gained an undeserved reputation as a "trust buster." Although he opposed serious abuses, he distinguished between good and bad trusts, and believed government should encourage responsible corporations to grow. His thinking mirrored that of progressive writers like Herbert Croly, editor of *The New Republic,* who imagined a professionalized, central government staffed by nonpartisan experts who would monitor the activities of big corporations to assure efficiency and head off destructive actions.

Not all progressives agreed. Louis Brandeis and Woodrow Wilson envisioned a political economy of small, highly competitive firms kept in line by regular applications of the Sherman Act. To Roosevelt, there was no going back to an economy of small businesses. Only large combinations could compete on a world scale. It was government's obligation not to break them up but to regulate them. He secured passage of the Hepburn Act (1906), which allowed the commission to set freight rates and banned "sweetheart" deals (of the kind Standard Oil enjoyed) between carriers and favored clients. The Elkins Act (1910) regulated telephone, telegraph, and cable communications. The Pure Food and Drug Act (1906) responded to Upton Sinclair's stomach-turning exposé of the meatpacking industry by making it a crime to ship or sell contaminated or fraudulently labeled food and drugs. Under Roosevelt, the federal government gained the tools to counterbalance the power of business. It grew to match its responsibilities. The number of federal employees almost doubled between 1900 and 1916.

The Square Deal

Roosevelt's exasperation with big business reached a peak during the coal strike of 1902. The United Mine Workers represented 150,000 miners in the coalfields of eastern Pennsylvania. The miners, mostly Polish, Hungarian, and Italian immigrants, earned less than $6 a week, and over 400 died yearly to supply the coal to run railroads and heat homes. Seventy percent of the mines were owned by six railroads, which in turn fell under the control of the usual financiers—Morgan and Rockefeller, among others. The owners refused to deal with the union, declaring it a band of outlaws. When the miners struck in May 1902, they had the public's sympathy. Editorials, even in Republican newspapers, urged the president to take the mines away from the owners.

The "gross blindness of the operators" infuriated Roosevelt. Coal was the only fuel for heating, and a strike might cause hundreds to freeze. After failing to get the sides to negotiate, he invited union officials and the operators to Washington so that he could personally arbitrate. John Mitchell, head of the mine workers, eagerly accepted the president's offer, but the owners flatly refused.

For Roosevelt this was the final straw. He drew up plans for the army to move into the coalfields and place the mines under government control. The owners capitulated, agreeing to submit the dispute to a federal commission. The result was a compromise: miners received a 10 percent increase in pay and a nine-hour workday, but owners did not have to recognize the union.

Roosevelt's direct action made the federal government a third force in labor disputes. For the first time a strike was settled by federal arbitration, and for the first time a union had struck against a strategic industry without being denounced as a revolutionary conspiracy. The government would no longer automatically side with the corporations. Instead, Roosevelt offered an understanding: "We demand that big business give the people a square deal; in return, we must insist that when anyone engaged in big business honestly endeavors to do right, he shall be given a square deal."

Theodore Roosevelt Theodore Roosevelt ran in 1912 at the head of a new Progressive Party ticket. His candidacy split the Republicans, allowing Wilson to gain a plurality.

Conserving Water, Land, and Forests

When Roosevelt felt important issues were at stake, he seldom accepted the limits of his office. He enraged Congress by stretching the definitions of presidential power, nowhere more so than in the area of conservation. When Congress sent him a bill to halt the creation of new national forests in the West, Roosevelt first created or enlarged 32 national forests then signed the bill. To stop private companies from damming rivers, he reserved 2,500 of the best hydropower sites by declaring them "ranger stations." The energy behind his program came from Gifford Pinchot, the chief forester of the United States, who saw conservation as a new frontier. Unsettled, undeveloped lands were growing scarce, and Pinchot convinced the president that hope for the future lay in using the available resources more efficiently. Forests, deserts, and ore ranges were to be used, but wisely, scientifically, and in the national interest.

One of the first victories for the new policy of resource management was the Newlands Reclamation Act (1902), which gave the Agriculture Department authority to build reservoirs and irrigation systems in the West. In the next four years, 3 million acres were "reclaimed" from the desert and turned into farms. To prevent waste, Roosevelt put tighter controls on prospecting, grazing, and logging. Big lumber and mining companies had few complaints about rationalized resource administration, but small-scale prospectors and ranchers found themselves shut out of federal lands. Naturalists, like John Muir (see feature), also resisted, pointing out that nature was to be appreciated, not used.

By 1909, conservation had become a national issue. Hikers, sightseers, and tourism entrepreneurs drawn to the new parks and forest reserves were forming a powerful constituency. By quadrupling the acreage in federal reserves, professionalizing the forest service, and using his "bully pulpit" to build support for conservation, Roosevelt helped create the modern environmental movement.

TR and Big Stick Diplomacy

Imperial and commercial expansion put new strains on foreign and military policy after the turn of the century. U.S. investors wanted Washington to use its leverage to protect their overseas factories and railroads against civil wars and hostile governments. Diplomatic and military budgets grew to meet these demands. The diplomatic corps replaced political cronies with trained professionals. Commercial attachés issued reports on foreign business conditions. Conducting foreign relations was no longer a matter of weathering "incidents" but of making policy.

Roosevelt's view of world affairs flowed from his understanding of the past and the future. Global trade and communications, he believed, united "civilized" nations. His foreign policy aimed to keep the United States in the mainstream of historical processes such as commerce, imperialism, and military (particularly naval) modernization. He felt a duty to interfere with "barbarian" governments in Asia, Latin America, or Africa that blocked progress. The United States had an obligation, he felt, to overthrow governments and even seize territory when it was acting in the interests of the world as a whole.

Building an interoceanic canal topped Roosevelt's list of foreign-policy priorities. A canal would be a hub of world trade and naval power in the Atlantic and

AN AMERICAN LANDSCAPE

>> The Hetch Hetchy Valley

When landscape painter Albert Bierstadt visited in 1875, he saw a panorama of waterfalls. The canyon walls towered 2,500 feet above a wide, forested meadow populated by herds of elk. Twenty-five years later, San Francisco's mayor James Phelan beheld the perpendicular cliffs and the pure glacier water tumbling into the Tuolumne River and saw his city's answer to the problems of "monopoly and microbes."

The Hetch Hetchy Valley hypnotized naturalists and hydraulic engineers equally because of its magnificence and its location. It was only 152 miles from San Francisco, close enough to lure visitors or, alternatively, to channel its waters to the city. A village of less than a thousand in 1848, the City by the Bay was by 1900 the nation's ninth largest, with 340,000 people. Only water kept it from growing larger.

Hemmed in by ocean on three sides, San Francisco faced a chronic scarcity of water. As the Gold Rush swelled the population, farsighted entrepreneurs bought up all available water supplies and formed the Spring Valley Water Company, which held a monopoly on the city's water for 60 years. Water tycoons supported the city's political machine, led by "Boss" Abe Ruef. The company's water was neither cheap nor safe, a liability demonstrated by occasional outbreaks of cholera and typhus.

When voters elected Phelan at the head of a reform ticket in 1897, they expected him to do something about water. What the Republican mayor wanted to do was to dam the Hetch Hetchy and build an aqueduct across the Central Valley, thus breaking the monopoly and making water an abundant, safe public utility.

Local and national obstacles stood in the way. The city's board of superintendents, controlled by Ruef, sided with Spring Valley and thwarted efforts to build a city reservoir. But it was even harder to get permission from the federal government. Hetch Hetchy was located in Yosemite National Park, one of the first nature preserves, created in 1890 to save its peaks and waterfalls from wanton destruction. The parks system itself was new, and the philosophy of conservation—how to preserve natural resources, and for what purposes—was evolving rapidly. Phelan found an ally in Gifford Pinchot, who filled the newly created office of chief forester.

continued

Albert Bierstadt, *Hetch Hetchy Canyon* (1875)

>> **AMERICAN LANDSCAPE** *continued*

Pinchot's father had made millions in the lumber trade, and Gifford studied scientific forestry in France, where timber was seen as a crucial strategic and economic resource. The job of forestry was "to grow trees as a crop," he argued, and the two principal threats to any resource were inefficient use and monopoly control. On this point he and Phelan saw eye to eye. The few hikers who might enjoy Hetch Hetchy's magnificence were clearly less important than the need "to supply pure water to a great center of population."

Natural and political disasters worked to Phelan's advantage. After the great 1906 earthquake and fire destroyed San Francisco's downtown and vividly demonstrated the need for a water supply, Congress passed a waiver allowing the city to apply to use part of Yosemite's land. The following year, a lurid scandal led to a bribery conviction for Ruef and disgrace for his followers. But just as the way seemed clear, an outpouring of petitions and letters urged the secretary of the interior to save the Hetch Hetchy.

The campaign was orchestrated by the 1,000-member Sierra Club and its ascetic founder, John Muir. A wilderness explorer and naturalist, Muir gained a national following through his writings on the transcendent, spiritual aspects of the natural world. "Dam Hetch Hetchy!" he remonstrated. "As well dam for water tanks the people's cathedrals and churches." Historians have characterized the debate between Muir and Pinchot as a contest between rival concepts of environmentalism—conservation for use versus preservation for nature's sake—but the two men also represented opposing interpretations of democracy and the dangers it faced in the modern world.

"Conservation is the most democratic movement this country has known for generations," Pinchot believed. The Hetch Hetchy project would replace unbridled corporate power with management of natural resources for the public good.

Democratic values were scientific values: efficiency, expertise, and "the greatest good, for the greatest number, for the longest time." For Muir, nature was a refuge where democratic values could survive amid the "gobble gobble" culture of self-interest and scientific progress. The valley had to be preserved not just to save the trees, but to "save humans for the wilderness." Only there could people share the nonmaterial values in which democracy took root.

Because people were essential to their vision of the valley, the Sierra Club did not advocate leaving the area pristine. They imagined roads and hotels, managed by the park service, that would make Hetch Hetchy a weekend retreat for harried city dwellers. The public outcry threw dam advocates off balance, but eventually they were able to cast the "nature lovers" as unwitting tools of the water and power monopolies.

The Roosevelt administration wavered, but in 1913, Phelan got his dam. Muir died a year later. Today the Hetch Hetchy aqueduct delivers 300 million gallons of water a day to San Francisco. But the battle for the valley gave birth to a modern environmental movement. When municipal and mining interests encroached on the Yosemite and Yellowstone preserves in the following decades, they were opposed by a national constituency that saw both activism and wilderness as national legacies. ●

Pacific, and Roosevelt aimed to prevent French or British engineers from building it. He negotiated a deal to buy out a failed French venture in the Colombian province of Panama.

A civil war in Colombia complicated his plans. In 1902 American diplomats brokered a peace between modernizers led by José Marroquín and traditionalists who wanted to isolate the country from outside influences. The fundamentalists fiercely opposed the canal, which would thrust Colombia into the crossroads of world trade. Marroquín favored it, but he knew war would erupt again unless the Americans gave Bogotá full control over the canal. For Roosevelt, control was not negotiable.

In the spring of 1903 Panamanian senators, upset by the rejection of the U.S. offer, began conspiring to secede. Panama had had revolutions before, but the United States had always stepped in to preserve Colombia's sovereignty. Together with Philippe

Map 21–1 Growth of Public Lands Responding to a national conservation movement, Roosevelt set aside public lands for use as parks and managed-yield forests. The National Park Service was founded in 1916.

Bunau-Varilla, who represented shareholders in the French company, the Panamanians lobbied U.S. officials to support their plot. Bunau-Varilla predicted a revolution for November 3, thereby assuring that the rebels, the Colombian army (which had been bribed into surrendering), and U.S. warships would all be on hand.

The revolution went off without a hitch, and Roosevelt presented the new Panamanian government a treaty that gave less and took more than the one offered to Colombia. The president was defensive about his behavior, claiming that he had acted "with the highest, finest, and nicest standards of public and governmental ethics." Congress launched an investigation. "I took the canal and let Congress debate," Roosevelt said, "and while the debate goes on the canal does also." Engineers, led by George W. Goethals, removed a mountain to let water into the isthmus and built another to shore up an artificial lake. Colonel William C. Gorgas defeated malaria and yellow fever, reducing the death rate in Panama to below that of an average American city. The canal, a 50-mile cut built at a cost of $352 million and more than 5,600 lives, opened in 1914.

Once construction was under way, Roosevelt acted to protect the canal from other powers. Poverty in the Caribbean states created opportunities for imperial governments to establish bases on Panama's doorstep. In 1902 Germany came close to invading Venezuela over an unpaid loan, but Roosevelt stepped in to mediate. When the Dominican Republic reneged on its loans two years later, four European nations laid plans for a debt-collecting expedition.

Roosevelt went before Congress in December 1904 and announced a policy later known as the Roosevelt Corollary. It stipulated that when chronic "wrongdoing or impotence" in a Latin American country required "intervention by some civilized nation," the United States would do the intervening. Its language captured the president's worldview. White "civilized" nations acted; nonwhite "impotent" nations were acted upon. The following month the United States took over the Dominican Republic's customs offices and began repaying creditors. The economic intervention turned military in 1916, when the United States landed marines to protect the customs from Dominican rebels. U.S. troops stayed until the early 1920s.

By enforcing order and administrative efficiency in the Caribbean, Roosevelt extended progressivism beyond the borders of the United States; the movement gained footholds in the Far East, too. In 1906 the U.S. federal courts took the unusual step of creating a court outside the United States, in Shanghai, China, to control prostitution in the American community there.

Taft and Dollar Diplomacy

Enormously popular at the end of his second term, Roosevelt chose his friend, William H. Taft, to succeed him. Taft gained national attention as a circuit judge with decisions that enlarged federal power to regulate trusts. As governor general of the Philippines he brought municipal reform to Manila. Taft easily defeated William Jennings Bryan in the 1908 election, and as president he began consolidating Roosevelt's gains. He sent to the states constitutional amendments for the direct election of senators and the income tax. His administration increased antitrust enforcement and levied the first tax on corporations. Satisfied that his legacy would continue, Roosevelt left for a tour of Africa.

In the Caribbean, Taft put the Roosevelt Corollary into action. The United States bought up the debts of Honduras and Nicaragua. Taft persuaded four New York banks to refinance Haiti's debt to prevent German intervention there. Taft intended "dollar diplomacy" to replace force as an instrument of policy, "substituting dollars for bullets," but in most cases, dollars preceded bullets. For Caribbean nations, American protection meant high import taxes. A revolt usually followed. Marines went into Honduras and Nicaragua in 1912. They stayed in Central America until 1933.

Dollar diplomacy also aimed to harness economic power for diplomatic purposes. Shortly after his inauguration, Taft mobilized a consortium to finance China's Chinchow-Aigun railway. Railroads were instruments of power in North China, and Taft felt he could drive a wedge between the imperial powers—Britain, Russia, and Japan—and compel them to resume open-door trade. Instead, they joined forces against the United States and the Open Door. Despite the setback, Taft still believed military force was outmoded and economic power was what mattered.

Taft disappointed both conservatives and progressives in his party. He first urged Congress to reduce the tariff, but then signed the Payne-Aldrich Tariff in 1909,

Map 21–2 United States in the Caribbean U.S. troops intervened repeatedly in the Caribbean and Central America to protect investments and guard against perceived threats to order. Panama, Nicaragua, Haiti, and the Dominican Republic were under nearly constant U.S. occupation until the mid-1920s. *Thomas Paterson et al.,* American Foreign Relations *(D.C. Heath, 1995), vol. 2, pp. 55, 40.*

which raised rates on steel, cotton, silk, and other important imports. Taft's secretary of the interior, Richard Ballinger, sided with ranchers and miners who opposed Roosevelt's resource-management policies. When Pinchot fought back, Taft fired him. When the Ballinger-Pinchot affair brought the party's divisions into the open, Roosevelt began to believe his country needed him back.

Rival Visions of the Industrial Future

After Roosevelt returned in 1910, Pinchot, La Follette, Croly, and others trooped to his home at Sagamore Hill to complain about Taft. The former president denied his interest in the Republican nomination, but a friend acknowledged that "no thirsty sinner ever took a pledge that was harder for him to keep." Roosevelt reentered politics because his views had evolved, and because politics was what he knew best. Just 54 years old, his energy was undiminished. He took more radical positions on corporations, public welfare, and labor than he had during his presidency. The election of 1912 became a race that would define the future of industrial America.

The New Nationalism

At a sunbaked junction in Osawatomie, Kansas, in August 1910, Roosevelt declared that "the essence of any struggle for liberty . . . is to destroy privilege and give the life of every individual the highest possible value." He laid out a program he called the New Nationalism. It included the elimination of corporate campaign contributions, regulation of industrial combinations, an expert commission to set tariffs, a graduated income tax, banking reorganization, and a national workers' compensation program. "This New Nationalism regards the executive power as the steward of the public welfare." The message drew cheers.

From the beginning, Roosevelt had the newspapers while Taft had the delegates. The nomination fight tested the new system of direct primaries. Taft's control of the party machinery gave him an advantage in states that chose delegates by convention, but in key states Roosevelt could take his campaign to the voters. When the convention met in Chicago in June 1912, Taft's slim but decisive majority allowed him to control the platform and win over undecided delegates. Grumbling that he had been robbed, Roosevelt walked out.

Roosevelt returned to Chicago in August to accept the nomination of the newly formed Progressive Party. The delegates were a mixed group. They included Hiram Johnson, the reforming governor of California; muckraking publisher Frank Munsey; imperialist senator Albert Beveridge; and J. P. Morgan's business partner George W. Perkins. The party platform endorsed the New Nationalism, along with popular election of senators, popular review of judicial decisions (which would allow the voters to second-guess the courts), and women's suffrage. Women served as delegates, and Jane Addams gave the speech seconding Roosevelt's nomination. The gathering had an evangelical spirit. Roosevelt spoke apocalyptically. "Our cause is based on the eternal principles of righteousness," he said. "We stand at Armageddon and we battle for the Lord."

The 1912 Election

Meanwhile in Baltimore the Democratic convention nominated a former college professor and governor of New Jersey. Like Roosevelt, the young Woodrow Wilson defied his family's expectations by pursuing a political career. He took an unusual route. Obtaining a doctorate in government from Johns Hopkins University in 1886, he published his first book, *Congressional Government,* at the age of 28. It advocated reforming the federal structure by enlarging the power of the executive branch. As a professor and later president of Princeton University, he became a well-known lecturer and commentator for the new national political magazines like *Harper's* and *The Atlantic.* In 1910 he won election as governor of New Jersey and enacted a sweeping program of progressive reforms. For Democrats, smarting from a string of defeats under Bryan's leadership, Wilson offered a new image and the ability to unite the South and the East under a progressive program.

With Roosevelt in the race, Wilson had to stake his own claim to the progressive constituency. With the help of Louis Brandeis, Wilson devised a program called the New Freedom. It challenged Roosevelt on his fundamental approaches to the economy and politics. Simply regulating the trusts, Wilson argued, would not make the economy friendly to consumers, workers, or small entrepreneurs. Instead, it would create a paternalistic bureaucracy. Wilson wanted antitrust laws that would allow a lean but powerful government to return competition and economic mobility to the marketplace. Both men agreed on the importance of a strong executive, but they had different economic formulas. Roosevelt appealed to a collective, national interest, while Wilson stressed the needs of individual consumers and investors. The political philosophy and style of New Nationalism was evangelical, aiming to inspire people to work for the common good. Wilson appealed to reason and self-interest.

On election day, Wilson won fewer votes than Bryan had in any of his races, but the split in the Republican Party gave him a plurality. He won 42 percent of the popular vote, compared to 27 for Roosevelt, 23 for Taft, and 6 for Debs. Although his margin was thin, Wilson could interpret Taft's repudiation and the large combined vote for the progressive candidates as a mandate for change. "What the Democratic Party proposes to do," he told his followers, "is to go into power and do the things the Republican Party has been talking about doing for sixteen years."

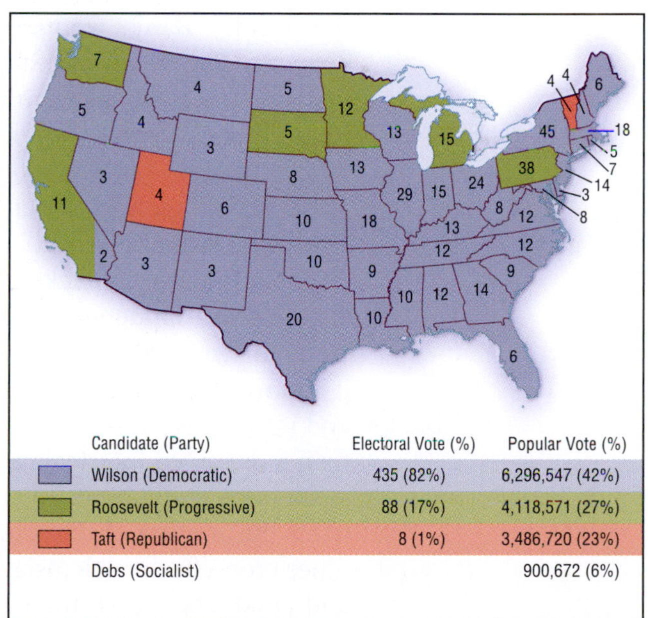

Candidate (Party) Electoral Vote (%) Popular Vote (%)
Wilson (Democratic) 435 (82%) 6,296,547 (42%)
Roosevelt (Progressive) 88 (17%) 4,118,571 (27%)
Taft (Republican) 8 (1%) 3,486,720 (23%)
Debs (Socialist) 900,672 (6%)

Map 21–3 The Election of 1912 The election pitted rival visions of progressivism against each other. The decentralized regulation of Wilson's "New Freedom" had more appeal than Roosevelt's far-reaching "New Nationalism."

The New Freedom

Within a year and a half of his inauguration, Wilson produced one of the most coherent and far-reaching legislative programs ever devised by a president.

Drawing on his long study of congressional politics, he seized the advantage of his party's majority and exercised an unprecedented degree of personal control through the majority leaders in both houses. The New Freedom advocated lower tariffs, increased competition, and vigorous antitrust enforcement. Three monumental bills passed through Congress in rapid succession.

The first bill was the Underwood-Simmons Tariff (1913), which made the first deep cuts in tariff rates since before the Civil War. The bill overturned one of the cornerstones of Republican economic policy, the protectionist tariff, and it helped farmers and consumers by lowering prices and increasing competition, but Wilson argued that its real beneficiaries would be manufacturers. Lower tariffs would help persuade other countries to reduce taxes on imports from the United States, he reasoned, opening new markets for American-made goods. Wilson created an expert Tariff Commission in 1916 to carry tariff bargaining to a new level. The most-favored-nation policies it implemented (and which remain standard practice) induced European powers to open their empires to American goods. The Singer, Ford, and Camel brand names began appearing in bazaars, souks, and godowns from Caracas to Mandalay. The Underwood-Simmons Tariff also permanently shifted the revenue base of the federal government from taxes on imports to taxes on income.

Wilson's next target was the banking system. When Steffens and Lippmann investigated banking for *Everybody's* magazine in 1908, they found its structure was "strikingly like that of Tammany Hall: the same pyramiding influence, the same tendency of power to center on individuals who did not necessarily sit in the official seats, the same effort of human organization to grow independently of legal arrangements." Money poured into investment houses but scarcely trickled to western farmers. The Federal Reserve Act of 1913 set up a national board to supervise the system and created 12 regional reserve banks in different parts of the country. Banks were now watched to assure that their reserves matched their deposits. The system's real advantage was the flexibility it gave the currency. The Federal Reserve Board could put more dollars into circulation when demand was high and retire them when it subsided. Regional banks could adjust the money supply to meet the needs of different parts of the country. The system broke Wall Street's stranglehold on credit and opened new opportunities for entrepreneurship and competition.

Finally, Wilson attacked the trusts. He established the Federal Trade Commission (FTC), an independent regulatory commission assigned to enforce free and fair competition. It absorbed the functions of Roosevelt's Bureau of Corporations, but it had more far-reaching powers, including the right to subpoena corporate records and issue cease-and-desist orders. The Clayton Antitrust Act (1914) prohibited price fixing, outlawed interlocking directorates, and made it illegal for a company to own stock in its competitor. To enforce these provisions citizens were entitled to sue for triple the amount of the actual damages they suffered. In 1916 Wilson produced another crop of reform legislation, including the first national workers' compensation and child-labor laws, the eight-hour day for railroad workers, and the Warehouse Act, which extended credit to cash-strapped farmers.

These programs furthered Wilson's goal of "releasing the energies" of consumers and entrepreneurs, but they also helped business. Businessmen headed many of the regulatory boards, and the FTC and Federal Reserve Board brought predictability and civility to unruly markets. The New Freedom implemented reform without resorting to the elaborate state machinery that the New Nationalism envisioned or that European industrial nations were assembling. The New Freedom linked liberal reform to individual initiative and the free play of markets.

Conclusion

By 1900 America's political economy had outgrown the social relationships and laws that served the rural republic for most of the nineteenth century. Squeezed between the indifference of corporate elites and the large, transient immigrant communities that controlled urban politics, middle-class reformers created a new style of political participation. They experimented with the structure of decision making at the municipal and state levels and vested the state with responsibility for the quality of life of its citizens. Progressives challenged but never upset the system. Above all, they wanted managed, orderly change. Science and the pressure of informed opinion, they believed, could overcome resistance without open conflict.

The progressive presidents continued this movement on the national stage. Roosevelt and Wilson touted their programs as attacks on privilege, but both presidents helped position the federal government as a broker among business, consumer, and labor interests. "Democracy is now setting out on its real mission," William Allen White observed, "to define the rights of the owner and the user of private property according to the dictates of an enlightened public conscience." In less than two decades, the federal government overcame its reputation for corruption and impotence and adapted to a new role at the center of economic and social life. The concept of a "national interest" that superceded individual and property rights and needed to be protected through continuous action was now firmly ingrained. The president's leadership now extended beyond the administration to Congress and public opinion. These achievements created a modern central government just at the time when military, diplomatic, and economic victories made the United States a global power. War and its aftermath would curtail the progressive movement, as the consensus favoring a strong central government would be tested by events unfolding in Europe.

Further Readings

Jane Addams, *Twenty Years at Hull-House* (1910). In her autobiography, Addams urges respect for the traditions of immigrants and action against the causes of crime and poverty.

Harry Bruinius, *Better for All the World: The Secret History of Forced Sterilization and America's Quest for Racial Purity* (2006). In 1927, the Supreme Court upheld state laws that sterilized women against their will. Eugenic policies, which had their origins in the Progressive Era, remained in force for much of the twentieth century.

John Milton Cooper Jr., *The Warrior and the Priest: Theodore Roosevelt and Woodrow Wilson in American Politics* (1983). A dual biography of the progressive presidents compares their backgrounds, philosophies, and political styles.

Maureen A. Flanaghan, *Seeing with Their Hearts: Chicago Women and the Vision of a Good City, 1871–1933* (2002). Beginning with the Great Fire in 1871, women organized to rebuild a safer, cleaner, and more orderly Chicago.

Louise W. Knight, *Citizen: Jane Addams and the Struggle for Democracy* (2005). Knight analyzes Addams's complex attitude toward democracy and her search for a politics of justice and equity.

J. Anthony Lukas, *Big Trouble: A Murder in a Small Western Town Sets Off a Struggle for the Soul of America* (1997). The anxiety and tension of the Progressive Era West comes to the surface in the trial of three labor leaders for the murder of a former governor of Idaho.

Michael E. McGerr, *A Fierce Discontent: The Rise and Fall of the Progressive Movement in America, 1870–1920* (2005). Traces the rise and fall of a middle-class movement that veered between desperation and utopianism.

Kevin Starr, *Inventing the Dream: California Through the Progressive Era* (1985). The century's first decade in a state that was defining a distinct local identity through planning, art, and reform.

Robert H. Wiebe, *The Search for Order, 1877–1920* (1967). This classic study of progressivism traces the movement's origins to the middle class's yearning for a lost Eden of small towns and personal relationships.

Who, What?

Eugene V. Debs 698
W. E. B. DuBois 705
Theodore Roosevelt 710
Woodrow Wilson 722
Interest groups 697
Eugenics 704
Commission plan 708
Initiative, recall, and referendum 709

>> Timeline >>

▼ 1889
Hull-House founded

▼ 1890
General Federation of Women's Clubs founded

▼ 1893
Illinois passes eight-hour day for women

▼ 1895
National Association of Manufacturers organized

▼ 1900
Robert La Follette elected governor of Wisconsin

▼ 1901
Socialist Party of America founded

Galveston introduces commission government

McKinley assassinated; Theodore Roosevelt inaugurated president

▼ 1902
Newlands Reclamation Act funds construction of dams and irrigation systems

Alice Hamilton investigates Chicago's typhoid epidemic

McClure's publishes first episodes of Ida Tarbell's "History of the Standard Oil Company" and Lincoln Steffens's "The Shame of the Cities"

Roosevelt settles anthracite strike

▼ 1903
Roosevelt establishes Department of Commerce and Labor

Panama declares independence from Colombia

W. E. B. DuBois publishes *The Souls of Black Folk*

▼ 1904
Justice Department sues Standard Oil under the Sherman Anti-Trust Act

U.S. Supreme Court orders Northern Securities Company dissolved as an illegal combination

Roosevelt elected president

The Roosevelt Corollary announced

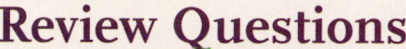

Review Questions

1. Were the progressives' goals conservative or radical? How about their strategies?
2. Why did reformers feel that privately owned utilities caused corruption?
3. What were the Oregon system and the Wisconsin Idea?
4. Theodore Roosevelt has been called the first modern president. In what ways did he change the presidency?
5. Did the progressives' emphasis on research and documentation indicate their respect for public opinion, or not?
6. Choose one level of government—local, state, or federal—and describe three key progressive reforms.

Websites

San Francisco Public Utilities Commission, "Hetch Hetchy Virtual Tour," http://www.creatf.com/hetchy/watershedtour.html

Sierra Club, "Hetch Hetchy: Time to Redeem a Historic Mistake," http://www.sierraclub.org/ca/hetchhetchy/

Ida B. Wells, "Lynch Law in Georgia," 1899, http://www.loc.gov/exhibits/odyssey/educate/barnett.html. Read the exposé of racial violence that inspired a worldwide antilynching movement.

For further review materials and resource information, please visit www.oup.com/us/ofthepeople

▼ 1905
U.S. takes over Dominican customs
Industrial Workers of the World founded
Roosevelt mediates end to Russo-Japanese War

▼ 1906
Hepburn Act passed, allowing the Interstate Commerce Commission to set freight rates
Pure Food and Drug Act requires accurate labeling

▼ 1907
Indiana passes forcible sterilization law

▼ 1908
William H. Taft elected president

Supreme Court upholds maximum-hours laws for women in *Muller v. Oregon*

▼ 1909
Payne-Aldrich Tariff goes into effect
NAACP founded

▼ 1910
Taft fires chief forester Gifford Pinchot
Elkins Act authorizes Interstate Commerce Commission to regulate electronic communications
Roosevelt announces the New Nationalism

▼ 1911
Triangle Shirtwaist Company fire

▼ 1912
U.S. troops occupy Nicaragua
Woodrow Wilson elected president

▼ 1913
Federal Reserve Act reorganizes banking system
Underwood-Simmons Tariff

▼ 1914
Panama Canal completed
Clayton Act strengthens antitrust enforcement

▼ 1916
New York City enacts zoning laws
Federal workers' compensation, child-labor, and eight-hour-day laws passed

CHAPTER 22

Common Threads 

>> As a progressive, Wilson was committed to order, efficiency, and gradual reform. How did his policies toward Mexico and Europe reflect this commitment?

>> Both the Philippine-American War of 1899 and U.S. involvement in World War I in 1917 provoked dissent at home. Why did the government tolerate opposition in the first case but suppress it in the second?

>> How did the repression of the war years set the stage for the Red Scare and the Ku Klux Klan?

A Global Power

1914–1919

AMERICAN PORTRAIT

>> Walter Lippmann

Walter Lippmann had just arrived in Brussels in July 1914 when the trains suddenly stopped running. At the station, "crowds of angry, jostling people, carrying every conceivable kind of package" were trying to leave the city. This looked, he confided in his diary, like the beginning of a war. Four weeks earlier, Austria-Hungary's crown prince, Archduke Ferdinand, had been shot as he drove through the Serbian city of Sarajevo. Austria threatened to attack unless Serbia found and punished the terrorists. Russia mobilized to come to Serbia's defense. As stock markets tumbled and banks collapsed, Lippmann found himself caught up in a conflict between the world's most powerful states: Austria and Germany on one side, Russia, France, and Britain on the other. As land borders closed, he escaped across the channel to England.

In the twilight of August 4, he stood with an anxious crowd on the terrace outside the House of Commons, as Britain's foreign minister, Sir Edward Grey, asked Parliament for a war resolution. In Berlin, the Reichstag declared war on France. "We sit and stare at each other and make idiotically cheerful remarks," Lippmann wrote, "and in the meantime, so far as anyone can see, nothing can stop the awful disintegration now. Nor is there any way of looking beyond it: ideas, books, seem too utterly trivial, and all the public opinion, democratic hope, and what not, where is it today?"

Twenty-four years old, Lippmann had come of age in the Progressive Era. As a student at Harvard, he came to believe that reason and science would allow his generation to "treat life not as something given but as something to be shaped." After graduation, he set out to become a journalist, studying under Lincoln Steffens and helping to start a magazine called the *New Republic*. "It was a happy time, those last few years before the First World War," he later remembered; "the air was soft, and it was easy for a young man to believe in the inevitability of progress, in the perfectibility of man and of society, and in the sublimation of evil."

The European war crushed those hopes. Just days after Lippmann left Belgium, German armies sliced through the neutral nation in a great wheeling maneuver that aimed to encircle the French army, but before the ring could be closed, reserve troops from Paris, many of them rushed to the front in taxicabs, struck the German flank and stopped the advance at the Marne River in northeastern France. By November, the Western Front had stabilized into the bloody stalemate that would prevail for the next four years, absorbing between 5,000 and 50,000 lives a day. The machine gun defeated all attempts to break through the enemy's trench lines. Colossal artillery, poison gas, submarine warfare, aerial bombardment, and suicide charges would each be used in desperate bids to break the deadlock, and all would fail.

The carnage horrified Americans. German soldiers terrorized Belgian civilians in retaliation for guerilla attacks, killing over 5,000 hostages and burning the postcard medieval city of Louvain. The gruesome tragedy of war in the heart of the modern world made Americans feel simultaneously fortunate and guilty to be so uninvolved. "We Americans have been witnessing supreme drama, clenching our fists, talking, yet unable to fasten any reaction to realities," Lippmann told his readers. "We are choked by feelings unexpressed and movements arrested in mid-air." For three years, Americans watched as a civilization they had admired sank into barbarism. They recoiled from the war's violence and the motives behind it, and they debated what, if anything, they could do to stop it.

When the United States entered the fight in 1917, it mobilized its economy and society to send an army of a million to Europe. The war disrupted and culminated

continued

>> **AMERICAN PORTRAIT** *continued*

the progressive movement. In the name of efficiency, the state stepped in to manage the economy as never before, placing corporations under federal supervision but allowing them profits and a measure of autonomy. The war transformed many of the most controversial items on the progressive social agenda—women's suffrage, prohibition of alcohol, restrictions on prostitution—into matters of national urgency. The federal government used its control of the mails to punish political dissenters. On the battlefield, American forces brought swift triumph, but victory failed to impose a new stability. Defeated powers collapsed into revolution and anarchy. New ideologies threatened American ideals. The experience of war brought home the dangers of a modern, interdependent world, but it also revealed the United States' power to shape the global future.

OUTLINE

The Challenge of Revolution

Like other progressives, Wilson saw threats arising from rapid change in the industrial world. Revolution, militarism, and imperial rivalries threatened global stability just as surely as labor wars, reckless corporations, and corrupt officials threatened the republic internally. Wilson opposed radicalism at home and abroad, and he tried to fashion institutions and processes to foster orderly change. Stability, like reform, was not a goal but a process, but Wilson also believed it had to be forced on those who resisted. Opponents "who will not be convinced," he wrote, deserved to be "crushed."

Imposing order, the president believed, was both a duty and an opportunity for the United States. An expanding commercial power like the United States had talent, technology, and capital to share. "Prosperity in one part of the world ministers to prosperity everywhere," he declared, but it could only do so in safe markets. Imperialism and revolution endangered the trade necessary for peace in the world and growth at home. It was the government's duty to assure the safety of goods and investments in order to secure American prosperity and its benefits for the world.

This combination of idealism and self-interest, humanitarianism and force, produced a seemingly contradictory foreign policy. Wilson renounced "dollar diplomacy," only to use Taft's tactics himself in China. He atoned for the imperialism of prior administrations, but he intervened repeatedly in Central America. Secretary of State William Jennings Bryan negotiated a series of conciliation, or "cooling-off," treaties that required arbitration before resorting to war, but Wilson was seldom willing to submit his own policies to arbitration. He believed the United States had a mission to promote democracy, yet he considered many peoples—including Filipinos—unready to govern themselves.

These contradictions are explained by Wilson's view of history. As he saw it, modern commerce and communications were creating a global society with new rules of international conduct. Meanwhile, relics of the past—militarism and revolution—threatened to "throw the world back three or four centuries." Resolving the struggle between the past and the future would require "a new international psychology," new norms and institutions to regulate conflict. Wilson's sympathies lay with Britain and France, but with Europe aflame, the United States, the sole voice of reason, had to remain aloof. "Somebody must keep the great economic processes of the world of business alive," he protested. He was also preoccupied with matters closer at hand. In April 1914, American troops invaded Mexico in an attempt to overthrow its revolutionary government.

> **We intend to teach the Mexicans to elect good men.**
>
> WOODROW WILSON

The Mexican Revolution

In May 1911, rebels took control of Mexico City, ending over three decades of enforced order and rapid industrialization under the dictatorship of Porfirio Díaz. Díaz and a clique of intellectuals and planners known as the *científicos* had spanned the country with railroads and made Mexico one of the world's leading oil exporters. They confiscated communal lands, forcing Indians to farm as tenants on commercial *haciendas*. Foreign investment poured in, and by 1911 Americans owned 40 percent of the property in the country. Mexicans grew to resent foreign businessmen and the regime's taxes. When Francisco Madero's revolt broke out, the army folded, Díaz fled to Spain, and power changed hands in a nearly bloodless coup.

The fall of Díaz gave the United States little cause for concern: Madero held an election to confirm his presidency. But in February 1913, just two weeks before Wilson's inauguration, General Victoriano Huerta seized power and had Madero shot. Mexican states raised armies and revolted against Huerta's regime, beginning one of the twentieth century's longest and bloodiest civil wars. In the mountains south of Mexico City, Emiliano Zapata led a guerilla resistance. Meanwhile along Mexico's northern border, Venustiano Carranza organized a constitutionalist army.

Wilson denounced Huerta, gave arms to Carranza's soldiers, and sent 7,000 marines to occupy Mexico's largest port city, Veracruz, in April 1914. The invasion radicalized the revolution, unifying all sides against the United States. When Carranza deposed Huerta a few months later, he promised to nationalize U.S. oil fields. Still determined to "put Mexico on a moral basis," Wilson pressured Carranza to resign while providing arms to his enemy, Francisco "Pancho" Villa. Villa briefly seized the capital at the end of 1914, but Carranza counterattacked, driving Villa's army north toward the border. Reluctantly, Wilson recognized the Carranza government and cut ties to Villa. Stung by Wilson's betrayal, Villa crossed the border and attacked the 13th Cavalry outpost at Columbus, New Mexico, killing 17 Americans and stealing horses and guns.

Furious, Wilson sent 10,000 troops under General John J. Pershing into Mexico. Pershing never found Villa, but the invasion once again unified Mexicans against the United States. Wilson now faced a choice between declaring war or giving up the hunt. He ordered Pershing home. After three years of trying to bring democracy and stability to Mexico, Wilson had nothing to show for his efforts. Carranza was seeking German arms, the civil war still raged, and American property was more in danger than ever. Wilson's failure to tame revolution and nationalism in Mexico foreshadowed disappointments he would experience in trying to bring order to the rest of the world.

Bringing Order to the Caribbean

In principle, Wilson opposed imperialism, but his desire to bring order to neighboring countries led him to use force again and again. He sent the marines into more countries in Latin America than any other president. Marines quashed a revolution

Map 22–1 Mexican Invasion Routes to Veracruz General John Pershing led 10,000 troops together with observation aircraft and a convoy of trucks 419 miles into Mexico on a fruitless hunt for Francisco Villa's band. Federal forces loyal to Carranza confronted Pershing near Parral, bringing the U.S. advance to a halt.

in Haiti in 1915, then occupied the country. They landed in the Dominican Republic the following year to supervise an election, and stayed to fight a guerilla war until 1924. Wilson kept marines in Honduras, Panama, and Nicaragua, and briefly sent troops into Cuba.

Progressive senators wondered why Wilson busted trusts and reorganized banks at home but put the marines at their service abroad. Senators Robert La Follette and George Norris argued that revolutions might be necessary in some countries to protect the rights of the many against the power of the few. On August 29, 1914, some 1,500 women, dressed in black, marched down Fifth Avenue in New York City to oppose wars in the Caribbean and Europe. Peace advocates, like Jane Addams, saw signs that the United States was being drawn toward war.

A One-Sided Neutrality

As German armies crossed Belgium in August 1914, Woodrow Wilson declared a policy of strict neutrality and called on Americans to "be impartial in thought as well as in action." The war took him by surprise, and like Addams he found it "incredible" that civilized nations could display such savagery. His first worry was that America's immigrant communities would take sides. Shortly after the crisis began, 450 steelworkers from Gary, Indiana, enlisted in the Serbian army. Irish Americans, who wanted independence for their homeland, sided with Germany against England. The Allies (Britain, France, Italy, and Russia) and the Central powers (Germany, Austria-Hungary, and Turkey) each used propaganda to manipulate U.S. opinion.

Wilson dispatched his closest aide, Colonel Edward House, to Europe with offers to broker a peace agreement. Privately the president believed that a German victory would be a catastrophe. Protected by Britain's control of the seas, the United States had expanded its influence during the previous century. If the Allies were defeated, he told his brother-in-law, "the United States, itself, will have to become a military nation, for Germany will push her conquests into South America." With Europe and possibly Asia controlled by a single power, the United States would be vulnerable and alone.

Modern warfare and commerce made true neutrality difficult, and in the implementation a bias became clear. The belligerent powers desperately needed everything the United States had to export. As purchasing agent for France and Britain, J. P. Morgan's firm soon became the world's largest customer, buying more than $3 billion worth of armaments, food, textiles, steel, chemicals, and fuel. Factories hired extra shifts, and farm prices rose to an all-time high. U.S. loans to the Allies grew to $2.5 billion by 1917, but the Central powers received only $127 million in credit. Trade with the Central powers meanwhile sank from $170 million to less than $1 million by 1916. An Allied victory would make the United States the world's leading creditor, while defeat might mean financial collapse. Although the United States had not formally taken sides, the American economy was already in the war on the side of the Allies.

Wilson's response to the British and German naval blockades reinforced the tilt toward the Allies. Both sides violated the "freedom of the seas" by imposing blockades, Britain with mines and warships, Germany with submarines. Wilson considered Britain's violation justifiable, but he reacted differently toward Germany. Britain's surface fleet was able to capture civilian ships as required by international law, but a German *Unterseeboot* or U-boat—a small, fragile submarine with a crew of only 32 men—could not do that without giving up the stealth and surprise that were its only weapons.

The *Lusitania's* Last Voyage

Germany posted advertisements in American newspapers warning passengers not to travel on ships bound for the war zone; Americans were horrified by the targeting of ships carrying civilians. The State Department was divided. Robert Lansing, the department's counselor, condemned submarine attacks as an offense against law and morality, but Bryan wanted to bar Americans from traveling on belligerent ships. Wilson sided with Lansing and declared that Germany would be held to "strict accountability" for American lives or property.

On the afternoon of May 7, 1915, submarine U-20 sighted the luxury liner *Lusitania* off the coast of Ireland. A torpedo detonated against the starboard side behind the bridge. In 18 minutes the massive ship broke apart and sank. Of almost 2,000 passengers aboard, 1,198 drowned, including 94 children. Among the drowned were 124 Americans. The newspapers reacted with rage and horror, but Wilson's advisers again disagreed on how to respond. Bryan wanted to balance a protest with a denunciation of Britain's violation of neutral rights. Wilson ignored him and demanded that submarine warfare stop altogether. He hinted that unless his demands were met, the United States would break relations.

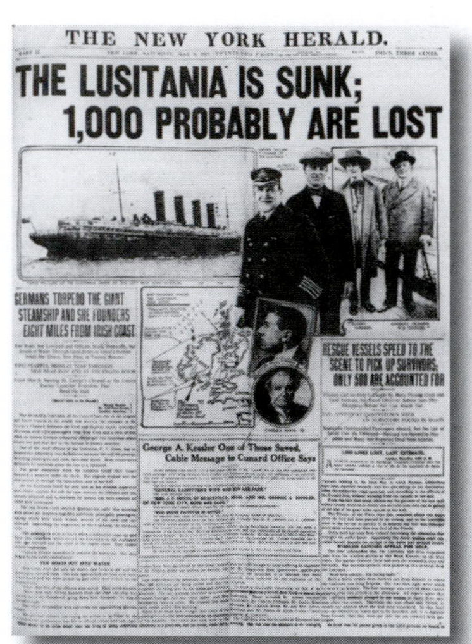

THE NEW YORK HERALD.

THE LUSITANIA IS SUNK; 1,000 PROBABLY ARE LOST

GERMANS TORPEDO THE GIANT STEAMSHIP AND SHE FOUNDERS EIGHT MILES FROM IRISH COAST

RESCUE VESSELS SPEED TO THE SCENE TO PICK UP SURVIVORS; ONLY 500 ARE ACCOUNTED FOR

George A. Kessler One of Those Saved, Cable Message to Cunard Office Says

Public opinion was equally divided. Lippmann told a friend in England that "the feeling against war in this country is a great deal deeper than you would imagine by reading editorials." When Germany promised not to attack passenger liners without warning, Wilson accepted this pledge as a diplomatic triumph. It momentarily restored calm, but official and public opinion had turned against Germany. The *Lusitania* crisis, Lippmann predicted, "united Englishmen and Americans in a common grief and a common indignation" and might "unite them in a common war."

The Drift to War

The *Lusitania* disaster opened a gap between progressives on the issue of the war. Peace advocates such as Addams, Bryan, and La Follette urged a stricter neutrality. Others believed war, or preparations for war, were justified. Theodore Roosevelt clamored for it. He endorsed the preparedness campaign mounted by organizations like the National Security League and the American Defense Society. Thousands of preparedness supporters marched down New York's Fifth Avenue under an electric sign declaring "Absolute and Unqualified Loyalty to our Country."

Preparedness leagues, headed by businessmen and conservative political figures, called attention to the state of the armed forces, equipped only for tropical wars, and lacking trucks, planes, and modern arms. The preparedness campaign appropriated patriotic rituals once reserved for elections. Wilson himself led the parade in

AMERICAN LANDSCAPE

>> Plattsburg Training Camp

Dawn rose over Lake Champlain as a special train pulled onto a siding near the old army barracks at Plattsburg, on the lake's New York side. The passengers, young men in their 20s and early 30s, some in civilian clothes, others already in uniform, filed from the cars and stood at attention on the platform. These were no ordinary recruits. They included diplomat and Morgan partner Willard Straight, Thomas Miller, a 29-year old congressman, Raynal C. Bolling, a top executive at United States Steel, southern plantation owners, Ivy League professors, the editor of *Vanity Fair*, and the mayor of New York.

They were there for four weeks of push-ups, forced marches, and intensive military training, although none had actually enlisted in the army. Drill sergeants called them "tourists," but the recruits saw themselves as the bearers of a new martial spirit. "This was young America," one observed, "a very decent sort of thing, a thing even thrilling to touch shoulders with for a little time."

The camp was conceived in New York's Harvard Club by an alliance of generals, businessmen, and professors. Leonard Wood, commander of the army's eastern division, wanted to create an army reserve that could be used in a foreign war. University presidents suggested that he organize a summer military camp for college students. Students needed the discipline and exercise, and the army needed educated commanders. The president of Harvard explained that the camps would train "a class of men" that would supply "a large proportion of the commissioned officers" in the next war. Private businessmen provided funds, and the first college camps bivouacked at Gettysburg, Pennsylvania, and Monterey, California, in the summer of 1913.

When war erupted in Europe the following summer, young business leaders clamored for a camp of their own. Over a thousand people jammed the Harvard Club on June 14, 1915, five weeks after the *Lusitania* disaster, to hear Wood announce the Businessmen's Military Training Camp at Plattsburg. Word spread through alumni societies and professional associations, and 1,300 of "the best and most desirable men" signed up. Plattsburg emptied "the whole table at Delmonico's," one organizer beamed. Young men from the wealthiest and most prestigious families shelled out $30 for a khaki uniform and mess kit.

ARE YOU TRAINED TO
DEFEND YOUR COUNTRY?
PLATTSBURG

The press sniped at this new fashion for militarism, but Willard Straight replied that the camp's organizers "do not propose to militarize the American nation. They seek rather to civilize the American military." Harvard was out to show West Point how to run an army, but two weeks of close-formation drill was enough to give the "tourists" a new respect for professional soldiers. The recruits answered reveille at 5:55 A.M. After breakfast and inspection, calisthenics and drill began at 7:25 and went until supper. Top college athletes found it gruelling. Regular infantry marched 30 miles in a day, but at the end of four weeks the recruits could barely manage 10.

At evening campfires, recruits discussed politics, war, and what the Plattsburg experience meant. Theodore Roosevelt, who had three sons and a nephew at the camp, came one evening to denounce "the professional pacifist, the poltroon, and the college sissy" who were

continued

>> **AMERICAN LANDSCAPE** *continued*

trying to keep the United States out of the war. Some recruits agreed with Roosevelt that the United States must be prepared for war, but others saw preparedness as a way to avoid war. They agreed that young Americans, and particularly the rich, could benefit from military drill.

Over the previous decades, the upper class had detached itself from American society, retreating into exclusive schools, neighborhoods, and recreational enclaves, a process known as "social closure." Aloofness undermined its claim to leadership in a democratic society, and nowhere more than in the military. The officers and men of the regular army came from the rural South and West, from farming and working-class families. Few in the corporate elite sent their children to West Point and almost none to the enlistment depots. The heroes of the coming war would become the elected leaders of the future, and Plattsburg was Wall Street's chance to claim a share of military glory.

Recruits talked about the wholesome, democratic influence of military training. It instilled "discipline, manliness, and that comradeship in a high common purpose which grows so slack . . . in a society governed by purely economic conditions," one observed. A millionaire looked like anyone else in uniform, and a journalist remarked that "each reservist left his worldly goods, his 'pull,' his record of past performances at home." Just as in sports, the only standard was how well one performed now. The camp included a large number of college athletes, including Yale fullback Frank Butterworth; Hamilton Fish Jr., the captain of Harvard's football team; and his coach, Percy Haughton. Not surprisingly, recruits saw what one described as the "obvious parallel between a football team and an army, and between the training of a fullback and a first-rate squad leader." War, he wrote, was the "real game."

In articles written afterwards, and memoirs many years later, the recruits remembered the emotions stirred by watching the flag lowered at sunset to the solemn strains of a bugle sounding retreat. "There is a fine restraint in military ceremony," Harvard philosophy professor Ralph Barton Perry noted, "that enables the purest product of New England self-repression to *feel*." "I do not believe that anyone in the camp," John J. McCloy, an Amherst college student who would become an adviser to five presidents, told a friend, "no matter how tired or blue he felt, ever 'stood retreat' without having a tiny thrill run up his spine." Like McCloy, many of the young men at Plattsburg fought in World War I, served the federal government in World War II, and ran law firms, industries, embassies, and government agencies during the cold war. For them, Plattsburg was the beginning of America's adventure in world leadership. "Plattsburg was not just a military training camp," historian Kai Bird later wrote, "it was, in a way, a secular retreat for a whole generation. There, amid simple, material surroundings, the upper class elite underwent a conversion experience of patriotism." ●

Washington in 1916, wearing a red tie, white trousers, and a blue blazer. "What a picture," Mrs. Wilson remembered, "as the breeze caught and carried out the Stars and Stripes!"

Hundreds of young Americans, positive that a German victory would mean the defeat of civilization, went to Paris to enlist. The French army soon had an American Volunteer Corps and a squadron of American fliers, the Lafayette Escadrille, whose exploits filled American newspapers. Magazines reprinted the romantic poems of Alan Seeger, a Harvard graduate who volunteered for the foreign legion. While Americans slept "pillowed in silk and scented down," Seeger wrote, "I've a rendezvous with death/At midnight in some flaming town." Wilson increasingly felt that to shape the world order to come after the war, Americans would have to meet that rendezvous.

The Election of 1916

Although Wilson increasingly felt the United States would need to enter the fight, he campaigned for reelection under the slogan "He kept us out of war." The preparedness issue reunited Theodore Roosevelt and the Republicans behind Supreme Court

Justice Charles Evans Hughes, who attacked Wilson for failing to defend American honor in Mexico and Europe. Woman suffragists campaigned against Wilson. They whistle-stopped across the country in a train called the *Golden Special* and picketed the White House with signs asking, "Mr. President? How long must women wait for liberty?" Although the Republicans remained dominant, Hughes proved an inept campaigner. He won pivotal states in the North and East—New York, Pennsylvania, and Illinois—but lost in the South and West. Wilson won narrowly; a shift of a few thousand votes in California would have cost him the election. Republicans controlled the House and the Senate. Still, reelection freed Wilson to pursue a more vigorous foreign policy. As Lippmann realized, "What we're electing is a war president—not the man who kept us out of war."

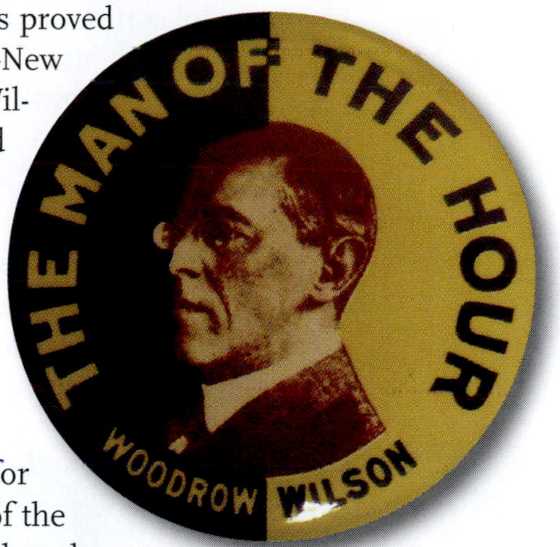

The Last Attempts at Peace

After the election, Wilson launched a new peace initiative. Looking for an opening for compromise after years of stalemate, he asked each of the belligerent powers to state its war aims. Each insisted on punishing the other and enlarging its own territories. Going before Congress in January 1917, the president called for a "peace without victory," based on self-determination of all nations and the creation of an international organization to enforce peace.

Germany toyed with accepting Wilson's proposals but decided to wait. With the defeat of Russia in 1917, it could begin shifting armies from the eastern front to France. U-boats once again torpedoed British passenger liners and American merchant ships. In late February, British naval intelligence officers showed the U.S. ambassador in London a telegram from the German foreign minister, Arthur Zimmermann, plotting an alliance with Mexico. The Zimmermann Telegram provoked alarm in the West, where antiwar feeling had been strongest. If Wilson did not declare war now, Roosevelt declared, he would "skin him alive."

Americans disagreed then, as historians do today, on why the United States went to war. Critics pointed to the corporate interests that stood to gain. Publicly and in private, Wilson stressed two considerations: the attacks on American ships and the peace settlement. The treaty conference afterward would settle scores of issues in which American interests would be involved. Unless it took part in the conflict, Wilson told Jane Addams, the United States would have to shout "through a crack in the door."

War Aims

Rain was falling on the evening of April 2, 1917, as Wilson went to ask Congress for war. Some onlookers on Pennsylvania Avenue cheered and waved paper flags while others stared silently at the president's limousine. The war, Wilson told the assembly, was in its last stages. American armies could bring it to a merciful end. The United States had tried to stand apart, but it had failed. Neutrality had provided no safety for travelers or trade. The only hope for avoiding future wars that might pose even graver dangers to the nation was to place the United States in a position to dictate the peace, to establish a "concert of free peoples." This would be a war to end all wars, to make the world safe for democracy.

In urging Congress to vote for war, the president explicitly rejected the aims of the Allies. "We have no quarrel with the German people," he said of the nation that would soon be at the receiving end of U.S. artillery. His argument was with the kaiser and all other emperors and autocrats who stood in the way of his plan for a new world order. Wilson realized, however, that imperial France and Britain did not stand for democracy or self-determination either. "We have no allies," he claimed, but the United States would fight with Britain and France as an "associated power."

Edward House assembled a secret committee, known as the Inquiry, to draft a peace proposal that would be both generous enough to show "sympathy and friendship" to the German people and harsh enough to punish their leaders. Made up of economists, historians, geographers, and legal experts, it met in the cramped offices of the American Geographical Society in New York. House named Lippmann as the group's secretary. Working day and night, the Inquiry produced a set of 14 recommendations that redrew the boundaries of Europe, created a league of nations, and based peace on the principles of freedom of the seas, open-door trade, and ethnic self-determination.

Wilson and the Draft Lottery The AEF was the first U.S. army chosen primarily by conscription. The selective service registered 24 million men and chose 3 million of them—some through a draft lottery—to enlist.

The Fight in Congress

During the ovation after Wilson's speech to Congress, one senator stood silently, his arms folded across his chest. La Follette told his colleagues that if this was a war for democracy, it should be declared democratically. The country had voted only five months earlier for the peace candidate for president, and there were strong reasons to suspect a declaration would fail a national vote. Representatives who polled their districts found that voters opposed American entry, in many places by two to one. Midwestern farmers, William Allen White reported from Iowa, "don't seem to get the war."

Prowar representatives blocked La Follette's move for a referendum and brought the declaration to a vote on April 6, when it passed by a margin of 82 to 6 in the Senate and 373 to 50 in the House. As debate turned to questions of how to pay for the war and who would fight in it, divisions resurfaced. Wilson wanted universal conscription, the first draft since the Civil War. The 1917 draft law deputized 4,000 local boards to induct men between 18 and 45. Both supporters and opponents believed the draft would mold citizens. It would "break down distinctions of race and class," said one representative, turning immigrants into "new Americans." La Follette countered that the new Americans would be like the new Germans, militarist "automatons" indoctrinated by the army.

Newspapers and politicians denounced the antiwar progressives as traitors who belonged either in jail or in Germany. They had too few votes to stop conscription, but they managed to make an exemption for conscientious objectors and to reduce some taxes on sugar, bread, and coffee used to pay for the war. The voices of opposition were soon silenced by patriotic calls for unity at all costs. There was little room in wartime America for dissent or divided loyalties. "I pray God," Wilson avowed, "that some day historians will remember these momentous years as the years which made a single people of the great body of those who call themselves Americans."

Mobilizing the Nation and the Economy

News of the war declaration, carried in banner headlines on Easter Sunday, 1917, set the nation abuzz with activity. William Percy, a college student from Mississippi, rushed home to Greenville and found women "knitting and beginning to take one lump of sugar instead of two, men within draft age were discussing which branch of the service they had best to enter, men above draft age were heading innumerable patriotic committees and making speeches." Wilson recognized that he was asking for an unprecedented effort. Raising an army of over 3 million, supplying it with modern equipment, and transporting it across submarine-infested waters to France were herculean feats. By midsummer, there were more men at work building barracks than had been in both armies at Gettysburg. Americans would spare from their dinner plates and send to Europe 1.8 million tons of meat, 8.8 million tons of grain, and 1.5 million tons of sugar. Factories that produced sewing machines, automobiles, and textiles would retool to make howitzers and tanks.

> We need more business not less. . . . Now is the time to open the throttle.
>
> HOWARD E. COFFIN, War Industries Board member and founder of Hudson Motors, April 1917

Accomplishing these tasks placed tremendous strains on the American people and economy. Wilson and others feared that it could widen political divisions and destroy the achievements progressives had made in the previous 15 years, but others felt that sharing the sacrifices of war would consolidate the gains. "We shall exchange our material thinking for something quite different," the General Federation of Women's Clubs predicted. "We shall all be enfranchised, prohibition will prevail, many wrongs will be righted." Lippmann hoped war would bring a new American revolution. "We are living and shall live all our lives now," he predicted, "in a revolutionary world."

Enforcing Patriotism

Authorities dealt severely with dissent. Suspicions about the loyalties of ethnic communities and rumors of German saboteurs fed the hysteria. There had already been mysterious explosions. On July 30, 1916, across the river from New York City, the largest arms storage facility in the country blew up, perforating the Statue of Liberty with shrapnel. Thousands of pounds of shells and guns bound for Russia were lost. Four days after Wilson declared war, saboteurs struck again, blowing up a munitions factory outside of Philadelphia and killing 112 workers, mostly women and girls. Federal agents rounded up large numbers of aliens, but the fear of internal enemies persisted.

Congress gave the president sweeping powers to suppress dissent. The Espionage Act (1917) and the Sedition Act (1918) effectively outlawed opposition to the war and used the postal service to catch offenders. Although there was no link between the labor movement and sabotage, unions were the prime target. The Justice Department raided the Chicago offices of the Industrial Workers of the World and sent 96 leaders to prison on charges of sedition. William D. "Big Bill" Haywood was sentenced to 20 years. Eugene V. Debs, leader of the Socialist Party, received 10 years for telling Ohioans they were "fit for something better than slavery and cannon fodder."

States also passed laws criminalizing activity deemed unpatriotic. Indiana's Council for Defense licensed citizens to raid German homes, prevent church services in German, and make sure German Americans conserved meat and wheat and bought war bonds. Towns, schools, and clubs with German-sounding names changed them. East Germantown, Indiana, became Pershing. Hamburgers became "liberty sandwiches." School systems in the Midwest that for decades had taught math and science in German stopped teaching the language altogether. Americans who had once proudly displayed their ethnicity now took pains to disguise it.

Pacifist faiths encountered their own ordeals. Some sects had come to America to avoid conscription in Germany or Russia. Many could not comply even with the conscientious objector statute, which required submission to military control. Fifteen hundred Mennonites fled to Canada to avoid being placed in camps. Thirty-four Russian Pentecostals were arrested in Phoenix, Arizona, turned over to the army, court-martialed, and sent to Leavenworth.

The government's propaganda effort was managed by the Committee on Public Information (CPI) under former muckraker George Creel. It made films, staged pageants, and churned out display ads, billboards, posters, leaflets, and press releases. The CPI sold the war by telling Americans they were fighting to save their own homes. One poster showed a fleet of German bombers passing over a shattered, headless Statue of Liberty. Like Wilson, however, propaganda distinguished between Germany and the German people. The CPI distributed leaflets in German offering "Friendly Words to the Foreign Born." It cast immigrants as potential patriots, and women as symbols of progress and sacrifice. Creel drafted Charles Dana Gibson, whose "Gibson Girl" ads personified glamour, to depict women as mothers, nurses, and patriotic consumers. Advertising mobilized American thought on behalf of the war effort and, in the process, advanced progressive agendas.

Regimenting the Economy

The first prolonged conflict between industrial nations, World War I introduced the public to the term "total war." By 1917 all of the resources, manpower, and productive capacities of the combatants had been mobilized. It soon became clear that the economy of the United States would have to be planned and centralized in new ways.

The navy planned a vast shipyard on Hog Island, near Philadelphia, with 250 buildings, 80 miles of railroad track, and 34,000 workers. When finished it would be larger than Britain's seven largest shipyards combined, but in April 1917, Hog Island was 847 acres of swamp. Steelmaker Charles M. Schwab, in charge of the project, signed contracts for machinery, cement, steel, and timber. Manufacturers loaded materials on trains headed east. The result was the Great Pile Up, the biggest traffic jam in railroad history. Without enough workers to unload, stationmasters began to back cars up on sidings in Philadelphia. Within weeks cars could get no closer than Pittsburgh or Buffalo, and loads were being dumped on the outskirts of cities. Schwab begged the railroads to cooperate, to no avail. The voluntary system had failed, and on January 1, 1918, Wilson nationalized the railroads.

The Hog Island fiasco demonstrated the need for supervision of the economy. Wilson created a War Industries Board (WIB) to regulate prices, manufacturing, and transport. The job was enormous. After the first WIB administrator had a nervous breakdown, Wilson found the overseer he needed in Bernard Baruch, a Wall Street financier, who believed in regulation by "socially responsible" businessmen. He recruited corporate executives to fill top positions and paid them a dollar a year. The president of the Aluminum Company of America became chairman of the WIB's

Hog Island Shipyard Building the massive shipyard at Hog Island was a major feat. The railroad network broke down under the strain, leading Wilson to nationalize the railroads.

aluminum committee, and a former top executive of John Deere was named to head the agricultural implements section.

The dollar-a-year men regimented the economy and put business at the service of government, but they also guaranteed profits and looked after their own long-term interests. One of their innovations, the "cost-plus" contract, assured contractors the recovery of costs plus a percentage for profit. Under these arrangements, the Black and Decker Company used its factories to make gun sights, Akron Tire made army cots, and the Evinrude Company stopped making outboard motors and turned out grenades. Each company built up revenues to launch new product lines after the war. Standardization also helped industry. The WIB set standard designs and sizes for everything from shirts to lug nuts, ridding the economy of wasteful diversity. One steel executive observed, "We are all making more money out of this war than the average human being ought to."

Not all businesses submitted willingly to "war socialism." The Ford Motor Company had just set up a national dealer network, and it refused to stop making cars. When other automakers followed suit, the board threatened to cut off the industry's supply of coal and steel, amounting to "confiscation of the industry," one carmaker sputtered. After months of negotiations, the auto manufacturers agreed to cut production by three-fourths. The delay hurt. When American troops went into battle they had a grand total of two tanks.

The war economy was a culmination of two movements: Wall Street's drive for corporate consolidation and the progressives' push for federal regulation. Businessmen recognized that the WIB could rationalize the economy. These "New Capitalists" wanted to end cutthroat competition and make business predictable. They encouraged workers to identify with the company through stock sharing and bonus plans. The WIB's example of government-industry cooperation would serve as a model in crises that would face the nation in future decades.

The Great Migration

The war economy gave Americans new choices and opportunities. As factories geared up, corporate managers faced a shortage of labor. The draft took eligible employees from the cities, and the usual source of new workers—Europe—was sealed off by a screen of U-boats. Elbert Gary, head of U.S. Steel, wanted to import laborers from China, but other employers found a ready supply in the South. In small towns and rural junctions, labor recruiters arrived offering free rides to the North and well-paid employment on arrival. Large manufacturers came to rely on the labor of former sharecroppers. Westinghouse employed 25 African Americans in 1916; by 1918 it employed 1,500. The Pennsylvania Railroad recruited 10,000 workers from Florida and Georgia. In some northern cities, a thousand migrants were arriving each week. This massive movement from the rural South to the urban North and West came to be called the Great Migration.

Lynchings, intimidation, and a declining southern economy encouraged migration. Almost half a million people came north during the war years—so many that some counties emptied out, creating panic among whites left behind. Mississippi lost 75,000 workers, leaving farms without tenants and delivery wagons without drivers. "We must have the Negro in the South," the Macon, Georgia, *Telegraph* pined. "It is the only labor we have. . . . If we lose it, we go bankrupt." Southern states banned recruiters. In some places, migrants encountered violence, provoking still more migration. "Every time a lynching takes place in a community down south," one observer noted, "you can depend on it that colored people will arrive in Chicago within two weeks."

Archibald Motley, Jr., *Nightlife* (1943) In his paintings, Archibald Motley captured the vibrancy and freedom of Chicago at the height of the Great Migration. Motley grew up in the "Back of the Yards" neighborhood during World War I and began sketching in poolrooms, churches, and gambling halls before attending the Art Institute.

African American workers moved into jobs at the bottom of the pay scale: janitors, domestics, and factory hands. Rent, groceries, and other necessities were substantially more expensive in the cities. Still, African American workers could earn wages 70 percent higher than what they were used to at home. Almost no one went back. The new arrivals adapted to the rhythms of city life. "South State Street was in its glory then, a teeming Negro street with crowded theaters, restaurants, and cabarets," Langston Hughes wrote of Chicago in 1918. "Midnight was like day. The street was full of workers and gamblers, prostitutes and pimps, church folks and sinners." To Carl Sandburg this vibrant community was "spilling over, or rather being irresistibly squeezed out into other residence districts."

Housing was scarce, and African American renters found their options limited to overcrowded districts wedged between industrial zones and unfriendly white neighborhoods. W. E. B. DuBois noted that residential patterns in Philadelphia changed dramatically. At the turn of the century African Americans had lived in many neighborhoods, but by the end of the war they were concentrated in one area, the Seventh Ward. Ghetto neighborhoods were both expensive and decrepit. On Chicago's South Side, rents were 15 to 20 percent higher than in white neighborhoods, and the death rate was comparable to that of Bombay, India. White property owners and real estate agents worked to create the ghettos and enforce their boundaries. On Chicago's South Side, the Hyde Park Property Association organized to "Make Hyde Park White." A real estate agent explained that African American homeowners "hurt our values." When discrimination failed to deter "undesirables," they used dynamite. From 1917 to 1919 there were 26 bombings of African American residences in Chicago. On July 2, 1917, in East St. Louis, an arms manufacturing center in southern Illinois, competition for housing and political offices led a mob of white workers to attack "Black Valley," an African American neighborhood along the Southern Railroad track. Forty-seven people were killed and six thousand left homeless.

After East St. Louis, white mobs found African American neighborhoods less easy to attack. When a mob invaded a Washington, DC, ghetto three years later, residents fought back with guns. "New Negroes are determined to make their dying a costly investment for all concerned," an African American newspaper explained drily. "This new spirit is but a reflex of the Great War." The New Negro, urban, defiant, demanding rather than asking for rights, became the subject of admiring and apprehensive reports. Police kept files on suspected militants, but northern cities offered a mobility and anonymity that translated into freedom.

Reforms Become "War Measures"

On August 3, 1917, thousands of protestors marched in New York under signs demanding "Why not make America safe for democracy?" In the wake of the East St. Louis outrage, the NAACP urged Congress to outlaw lynching as a "war measure." African Americans were not alone in using the president's language to justify reform. Carrie Chapman Catt told Wilson that he could enact women's suffrage "as a 'war measure' and enable our women to throw, more fully and wholeheartedly, their entire energy into work for their country." Advocates of progessive change demanded that the United States practice at home the ideals it fought for abroad.

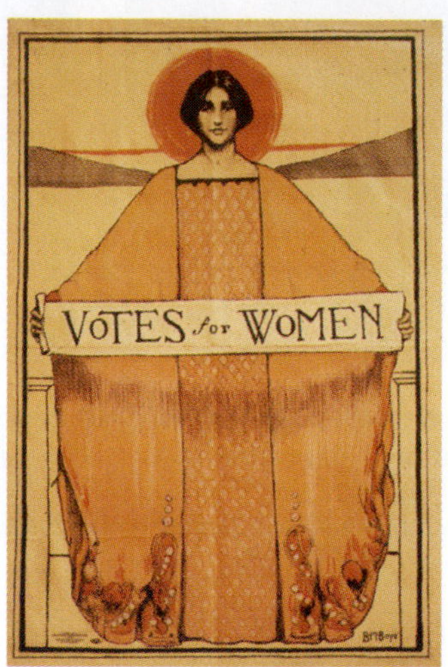

Suffragists hitched their cause to the national struggle. Catt's National American Woman Suffrage Association (NAWSA) abandoned its strategy of lobbying state by state and worked to identify women with the national cause. Members sold liberty bonds and knitted socks for the Red Cross, making clear that they expected to be rewarded with a constitutional amendment. Alice Paul's National Woman's Party (NWP) picketed the White House gate with signs quoting Wilson's demand for all peoples to "have a voice in their own governments." When Wilson announced his support in 1918, he cited women's war service as the reason. The Nineteenth Amendment was finally ratified in 1920, "so soon after the war," according to Jane Addams, "that it must be accounted as the direct result of war psychology."

As it had for African Americans, the shortage of labor increased opportunities for women. Although fewer than 1 in 20 women workers were new to the labor force, many took jobs previously considered "inappropriate" for their sex. Women replaced men as bank tellers, streetcar operators, mail carriers, and in heavy-manufacturing firms. Many of these opportunities vanished as soon as the war was over, but in rapidly expanding sectors like finance, communications, and office work women made permanent gains. By 1920, more than 25 percent labored in offices or as telephone operators, and 13 percent were in the professions. The new opportunities made work a source of prestige and enjoyment for women. Alice Hamilton remarked on the "strange spirit of exaltation among the men and women who thronged to Washington, engaged in all sorts of 'war work' and loving it." Army General Order 13 set standards for women's work, including an eight-hour day, prohibitions on working at night or in dangerous conditions, and provisions for rest periods, lunchrooms, and bathrooms. The government also empowered women consumers, encouraging them to report on shopkeepers who charged above the official price.

Wilson authorized a National War Labor Board to intervene in industries "necessary for the effective conduct of the war." The board set an unofficial minimum wage. For the first time the federal government recognized workers' rights to organize, bargain collectively, and join unions. Unskilled workers earned higher real wages than ever before. When the Smith and Wesson Company refused to acknowledge its workers' right to bargain collectively, the army seized the factory and recog-

nized the union. There were limits, however, to how far the administration would go to keep workers happy. When skilled machinists at the Remington Arms plant in Bridgeport, Connecticut, made demands the board considered excessive, Baruch threatened to have them drafted and sent to France.

Prohibition did not please workers either, but beer, wine, and spirits were early casualties of war. The Anti-Saloon League and the Woman's Christian Temperance Union had assembled a powerful antiliquor coalition by 1916. Congress would have passed Prohibition without war, but in the rush to mobilize, temperance became a patriotic crusade. Military regulations prohibited liquor first in the vicinity of army camps. Finally, in 1919 the states ratified the Eighteenth Amendment, banning the "manufacture, sale, or transportation of intoxicating liquors." At midnight on January 28, 1920, the Anti-Saloon League celebrated the dawn of "an era of clear thinking and clean living." America was "so dry it couldn't spit," according to Billy Sunday. He overstated the case. By some estimates, after the ban illegal speakeasies in New York outnumbered the saloons they replaced. Bootleggers and smugglers slaked American thirsts, but liquor prices rose and consumption declined. Americans never again drank anything like the average two and a half gallons of pure alcohol per person annually imbibed before Prohibition.

The war also lent patriotic zeal to antivice crusaders. During the Progressive Era, muckrakers exposed the police-protection rackets that allowed gambling dens and brothels to thrive. Within days of the declaration of war, reformers identified prostitutes as enemies of the health of American troops. Gonorrhea afflicted a quarter of the Allied forces in France, and middle-class Americans were appalled. When French premier Georges Clemenceau offered brothels for the American army, the secretary of war told his aide, "Don't show this to the president or he'll stop the war." Before 1917, reformers targeted commercial vice as a source of political and social corruption, but afterward they directed their efforts at women as carriers of disease.

The army acted against liquor and prostitution to protect the welfare of soldiers, but it shrank from challenging racial injustice even when lives were at stake. At training camps in the South, it was often unclear who had more authority, uniformed African American soldiers or white local officials. Clashes could easily turn violent. A riot in Houston in August 1917 began when soldiers from nearby Camp Logan rushed to the aid of an African American woman being beaten by police. Before it was over, 20 policemen and soldiers were dead and 54 soldiers received life sentences in the largest court-martial in U.S. history.

After the Houston riot, African American units were dispersed across the country. They were not allowed to assemble in full companies or join their officers until they were in France. Training was continually interrupted by menial assignments like road building or freight handling. The army remained segregated. Worse, many southern communities used military discipline to strengthen their own Jim Crow laws. Encouraged by the army's "work or fight" order, which required draft-age men to either enlist or get a job, states and localities passed compulsory work laws that applied to women and older men. The laws were intended to keep laborers in the fields and servants in the kitchens at prewar wages.

In the "war welfare state" created by full mobilization, the government served as a mediator among labor, industry, and other organized interests. Social activism became a matter of lobbying federal agencies who could either dictate sweeping changes from Washington or use wartime powers to maintain the status quo. Success required organization and an ability to tie one's goals to the government's national and international ambitions.

Over There

When the U.S. Senate took up the enormous war budget the president submitted in April 1917, the finance committee questioned Major Palmer E. Pierce about what would be done with all of that money. "Clothing, cots, camps, food, pay," he replied, "and we may have to have an army in France." "Good Lord!" exclaimed Senator Thomas Martin of Virginia. "You're not going to send soldiers over there, are you?" After the horrors of the Somme and Verdun, where men were fed to the Spandau guns by the tens of thousands, it hardly seemed reasonable to send Americans to such a place. "One would think that, after almost four years of war, after the most detailed and realistic accounts of murderous fighting, . . . it would have been all but impossible to get anyone to serve," one veteran later recalled. "But it was not so, we and many thousands of others volunteered."

Americans went to France optimistically believing they could change the war and the peace. Trench warfare was not for them. They planned to fight a war of movement, sweeping in formations across open fields, as Americans had at Antietam and Gettysburg. The Europe they expected to see would confirm their opinion that their immigrant ancestors had made the right choice. To a remarkable degree, they got the war they wanted. Europeans watched their civilization destroy itself in the Great War, but Americans saw theirs rising. Soldiers, "doughboys," said so in their letters, echoing the words of their leaders, their newspapers, and the volumes of poetry they carried with them into battle.

> **This western-front business couldn't be done again, not for a long time. . . . This took religion and years of plenty and tremendous sureties and the exact relation that existed between the classes.**
>
> F. SCOTT FITZGERALD, *Tender Is the Night*

Citizens into Soldiers

Enlisting, training, and transporting soldiers began in a rush. Camps housing 400,000 recruits went up in the first 30 days. A Wisconsin man saw Fort Sheridan "alive with enthusiastic recruits, with an atmosphere somewhat like that of a college campus on the eve of a big game." To Secretary of War Newton D. Baker's surprise, conscription went smoothly, and soon 32 camps were in operation, housing 1.3 million men. Commander John J. Pershing arrived in France in June along with 40,000 men and the first of some 16,000 women who would serve in the American Expeditionary Force (AEF).

Neither the Wilson administration nor the Allies initially anticipated that soldiers would be the United States' main contribution to the war effort. Britain urgently needed financial support, and Wilson advanced $200 million immediately, the first of an eventual $10 billion in loans to the Allies. Funds, food, and ammunition were needed more urgently than men, but that changed in October 1917, when German and Austrian forces smashed through the Italian lines at Caporetto, capturing 275,000 men and finishing the war on that front. When the Bolshevik Revolution curtailed Russian resistance in the east in November, Britain and France saw that by the next spring Germany would be able to mass its armies on the line between Ostend and Switzerland and break through to Paris. The war became a race between the United States and Germany to see who could place the most men on the Western Front in 1918.

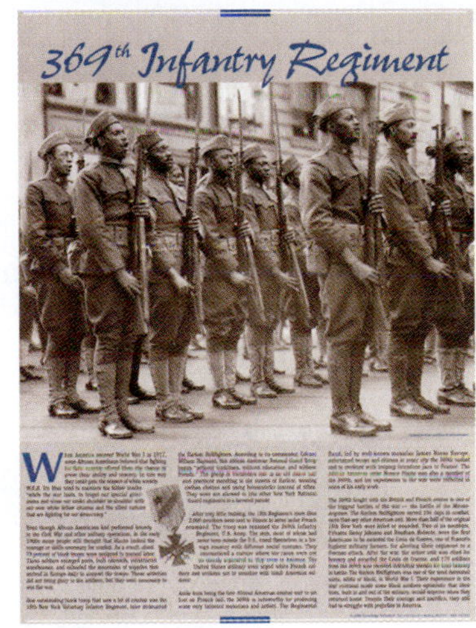

To get troops to the war the United States needed ships, but the American merchant fleet was smaller in 1917 than it was during the Civil War. For a time the United States had to cut back draft calls because it lacked ships to transport soldiers. Men shared berths, sleeping in shifts. The navy, meanwhile, cured the U-boat problem. The addition of the American destroyer fleet allowed the Allies to convoy effectively for the first time, cutting losses dramatically and banishing submarines from the sea lanes. When a torpedo was sighted, destroyers would sprint to the far end of the wake and deploy depth charges in a circle around the U-boat. By July 18, some 10,000 troops a day boarded the "Atlantic Ferry" for the ride to France.

The Fourteen Points

In December 1917, the Inquiry sent the president a memorandum titled "The War Aims and the Peace Terms It Suggests." Wilson redrafted it and presented it to Congress on January 8, 1918. The Fourteen Points outlined U.S. objectives, but more fundamentally they offered a different basis for peace than any that had been proposed up to that point. Unlike nineteenth-century wars waged for limited territorial or political objectives, the Great War was a total war, fought for unlimited aims. The principal belligerents—Britain, France, Russia, Germany, and Austria-Hungary—were global empires whose trade and law spanned continents and oceans. Germany hoped not only to defeat Britain but also to take its empire. France wanted to destroy Germany's future as a great power, economically and militarily. Wilson replaced these imperial visions of total victory with a peace based on limited gains for nations, instead of empires.

The Fourteen Points were grouped around four themes: national self-determination; freedom of the seas; enforcement of peace by a league of nations; and open diplomacy. The Inquiry's memorandum included a thick sheaf of maps marked with new European boundaries based on national, ethnic identities. The new state of Poland, for instance, should govern only territories with "indisputably Polish populations." Point three restated the Open Door, urging international free trade. Wilson thus hoped to eliminate what he saw as the two leading causes of war, imperial and commercial rivalry. By calling for an end to secret diplomacy, he aimed to appeal directly to the people of Europe, over the heads of their governments. The expectation was that the hope of a just peace would weaken the enemy nations' will and inspire the Allies to fight harder. Creel printed 60 million copies and had them distributed around the world. Planes dropped copies over Germany and Austria.

Wilson hoped the Fourteen Points would dispel not only the old dream of empire but also the new one of socialist revolution. On November 7, two months before Wilson presented the points to Congress, Russian workers overthrew the Provisional Government of Alexander Kerensky. The one-party regime of the Bolsheviks, led by Vladimir Lenin, summoned workers everywhere to rise against their governments and to make peace without indemnities or annexations. "The crimes of the ruling, exploiting classes in this war have been countless. These crimes cry out for revolutionary revenge." In December, Lenin revealed the contents of the secret treaties, unmasking the imperial ambitions of the Allies. He sued for peace based on the principle of self-determination. The Council of People's Commissars allocated 2 million rubles to encourage revolutions around the world and called "upon the working classes of all countries to revolt."

Two world leaders—Lenin and Wilson—now offered radically different visions of the new world order, and Lenin was putting his into effect. The Bolsheviks' contempt for democracy angered Wilson, but he continued to hope that the revolution would move in a more liberal direction and that Russia would stay in the war. Those hopes ended with the Treaty of Brest-Litovsk, signed by Russia and Germany in March 1918. The treaty showed the fearful price of defeat in modern war. Russia lost the Ukraine, Poland, and Finland, three-quarters of its iron and steel, one-quarter of its population, and most of its best farmland. Those assets went to the Germans, who began integrating them into their war machine. With its eastern front secure, Germany began transferring 10 divisions a month to the west.

Wilson was the first, but not the last, American president to be haunted by the specter of a German-Russian alliance, uniting the immense war-making resources of Europe and Asia. Wilson's strategic vision replaced Alfred Thayer Mahan's. Sea power threatened U.S. security less, in Wilson's view, than the great land powers of Eurasia. He refused to recognize the Bolshevik government, and he sent 7,000 American troops to Russia to support anti-Bolshevik forces on the eastern front. U.S. and Japanese forces invaded Siberia from the east. The Bolshevik government now counted the United States among its enemies. Meanwhile, the battle for the control of Europe was about to begin.

The Final Offensive

The German high command knew the spring offensive would be the last. Their exhausted economy no longer could supply food or ammunition for a sustained effort. Breadlines, strikes, and industrial breakdowns foreshadowed the chaos that would follow defeat. Risking everything, the German commander Erich Ludendorff launched his offensive on March 21, 1918. Specially trained shock troops hurled the British Fifth Army back to Amiens. In May they penetrated French lines as far as Soissons, 37 miles from Paris. As gaps opened in the lines, French general Ferdinand Foch and General

Douglas Haig of Britain appealed urgently to Pershing to put American troops under British and French command. Pershing opposed the idea. Born in Missouri six months before the Civil War began, the AEF's commander had attended West Point at a time when cadets learned tactics by studying Shiloh and Chickamauga. He wanted the American army to play its own part in the war.

Pershing criticized European commanders for remaining on the defensive when the war could be won only by "driving the enemy out into the open and engaging him in a war of movement." Imagining himself a General Grant replacing European McClellans, he saw trenches not as protection against modern weaponry but as symbols of inertia. Pershing favored massed assaults on the main German force in which the sheer numbers of American troops would overwhelm the enemy. Infantry commanders, he decided, "must oppose machine guns by fire from rifles." In envisioning Europe's war as a replay of the U.S. Civil War, Pershing revealed a habit of mind that would typify American geopolitical thinking for the next century: the belief that Americans could understand the world through the prism of their own experience. He was not alone in wanting a clean, decisive alternative to trench warfare. Billy Mitchell, head of the army's aviation section, noted that while the Allies had been "locked in the struggle, immovable, powerless to advance for three years . . . we could cross the lines of these contending armies in a few minutes in our aeroplanes."

The German onslaught interfered with Pershing's plans. On May 27, German divisions pierced French lines at Château-Thierry and began advancing on Paris at a rate of 10 miles a day. The French government considered whether to abandon the capital or surrender. Bowing to urgent requests, Pershing threw the AEF into the breach. It was springtime in France as column upon column of fresh American troops filled the roads from Paris to the front. Photographs show doughboys marching to meet the enemy across fields of wildflowers. "We are real soldiers now and not afread [sic] of Germans," John F. Dixon, an African American infantryman from New York, wrote home. "Give my love to Claypool, Mary, June, and Grace. Tell them I say war is more than a notion. Our boys went on the battlefield last night singing." Ahead of them lay five German divisions, poison gas, minefields, rolling artillery barrages, and machine guns emplaced in interlocking fields of fire. The Americans stopped the Germans, but at a fearful cost. The marine brigade that took Belleau Wood suffered 4,600 casualties, half the force. Without artillery or tanks, they assaulted machine gun nests head-on, with rifles. The Americans stopped the German drive.

By mid-July, the initiative passed to the Allies. On September 12, Foch allowed Pershing to try his tactics against the St. Mihiel salient, a bulge in the French lines which, unknown to the Allies, the Germans had already begun to evacuate. The doughboys raced behind the retreating enemy past their planned objectives, even outdistancing their own supply wagons. Pershing was delighted. St. Mihiel had vindicated his strategy, and he yearned for another chance. It came two weeks later, at the battle of the Meuse-Argonne.

Ten miles northwest of Verdun, the Argonne Forest contained some of the most formidable natural and man-made defenses on the Western Front. Atop parallel ridges lay three fortified trench lines, *Stellungen*—barriers of concrete pillboxes, barbed wire, artillery, and observation posts—named for Wagnerian witches, Giselher, Kriemhilde, and Freya. Half a million German troops had defended these fortifications for four

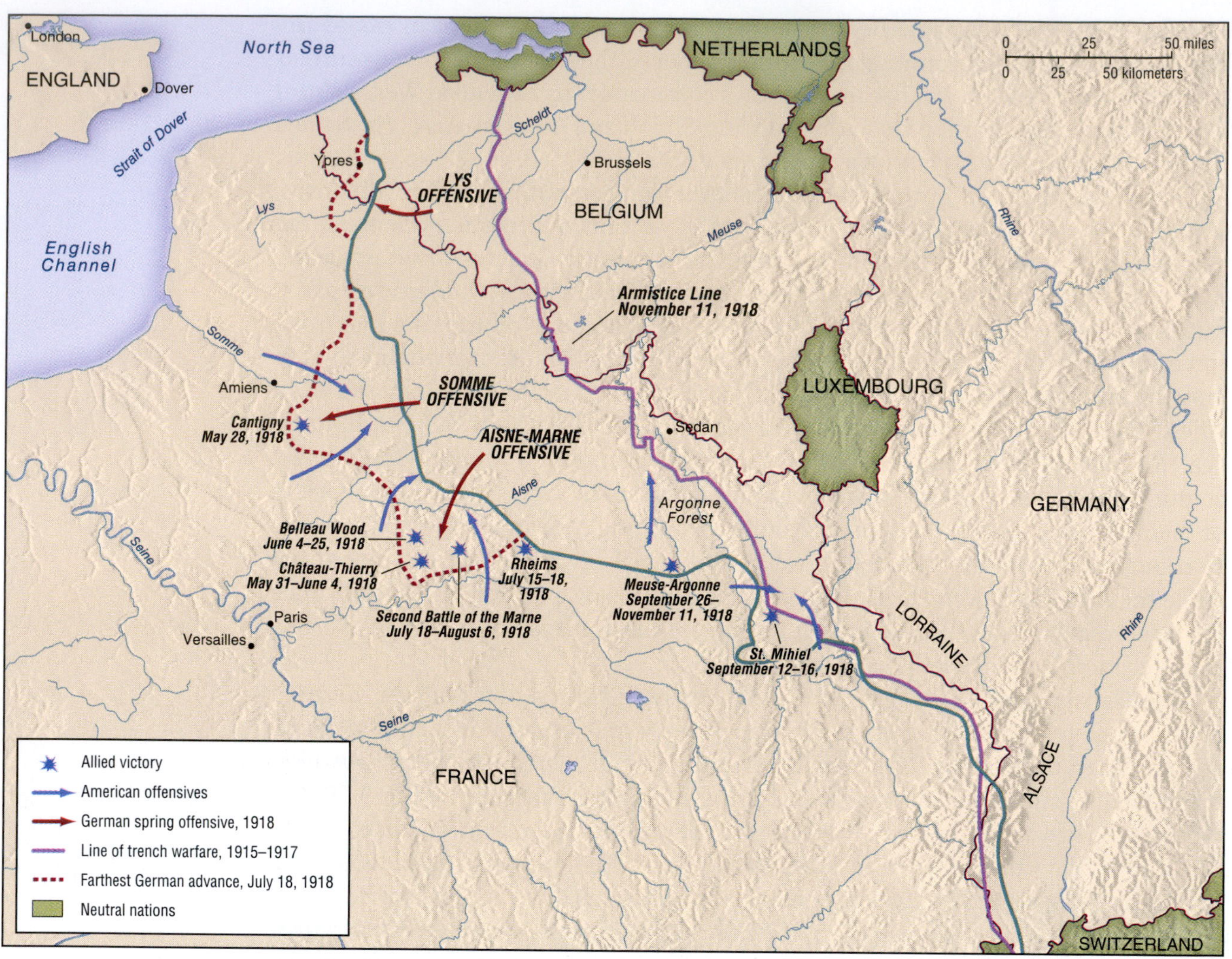

Map 22–2 Western Front, 1918 On the western front, the opposing armies fought from trenches fortified with earthworks and barbed wire. The parallel trench lines stretched thousands of miles from the North Sea to Switzerland.

years. Against this force, Pershing arrayed the American First Army, 1,031,000 men. The average doughboy at the Meuse-Argonne had a total of four months of training, and some had as little as 10 days. Pershing's battle plan called for overwhelming the German defenses with speed and numbers, breaching the Giselher Stellung, and reaching the second trench line, 10 miles inside the German front, the first day.

"Moving slowly forward, never heeding the bursting shells, nor gas, we followed a road forking to the left . . . into no man's land. It was soon noticed that we were in the bracket of a German barrage," a soldier wrote from the battlefield. Breaking through the first line of German trenches after a day and a half, the battle turned into a deadly crawl up the Romagne Heights into the teeth of the Kriemhilde Stellung. "We came to the spot where the fellow was hit during the night—he had one boot and leg blown off," Lt. Robert Sawyer of Texas wrote in his diary. "The dead seemed to be in hundreds, though I am quite sure it was my imagination." In two weeks of fighting, 26,277 Americans died. French soldiers reported seeing the American dead lying in rows, cut down by machine guns as they marched in formation. American divisions "suffer wastage out of all proportion to results achieved," a British observer noted. Finally, on November 10, American troops reached their objective and dynamited the rail line connecting the cities of Metz and Sedan. Meanwhile, Germany announced that it would accept the Fourteen Points as the basis for an armistice and negotiations. At 11:00 A.M. on November 11, 1918, the guns fell silent.

American intervention had been decisive. The American economy, two and a half times the size of Germany's, lent its immense industrial and agricultural productivity to the Allies at a crucial moment. American naval strength and manpower also tipped the balance. Pershing failed to transform strategy—it remained a mechanized war of attrition until the end—but by striking the final blow, Americans had the illusion that their way of war had been triumphant. American losses, 116,516 dead, were smaller than the British (908,371), the French (1.4 million), or the Germans (1.8 million), but they still show the colossal destructiveness of the kind of industrial war fought on the Western Front. In just six months, the United States suffered twice as many combat deaths as in the Vietnam War and almost a third as many as in World War II.

The Western Front From 1914 to 1918, the western front was the largest metropolis on earth, in Robert Cowley's phrase, an "unreal city" whose inhabitants—8,000 of whom died each day—worked in an industry of destruction.

While they fought on the same battlefields, Americans and Europeans fought two vastly different wars. The Americans' war, swift and victorious, bore almost no resemblance to the European experience, a prolonged catastrophe that consumed an entire generation. For Europeans, the mental world of the prewar era, with its optimistic faith in modernity, in the ability of science and democracy to create a better future, vanished forever. Confidence in the inevitability of progress became a distinctive feature of U.S. culture in the postwar era. In much of the world "American" became almost synonymous with "modern," but not everywhere. In the East another political and economic system shouted its claim to the future.

Revolutionary Anxieties

Americans celebrated the armistice with bonfires, automobile horns, church bells, and uplifted voices. New York's Metropolitan Opera interrupted a performance to sing the anthems of the Allied nations. Wilson told Congress that "everything for which America fought has been accomplished," but he observed that the situation in Russia cast doubt on the durability of peace. Even before the armistice, German revolutionaries took power in Bavaria. Over the next months, revolutions broke out throughout eastern Europe. From the trenches of Flanders to the Sea of Japan, not a single government remained intact, and in Moscow the new Soviet state towered above the ruins of the old regimes.

> **The Department of Justice has undertaken to tear out the radical seeds that have entangled American ideas in their poisonous theories.**
>
> ATTORNEY GENERAL A. MITCHELL PALMER, 1920

Wilson in Paris

For Wilson, the moment he had planned for in 1917 had arrived—the United States could help set the terms of peace—but war had exhausted the president. Confident that the public would view the nation's victory as his victory, he committed mistakes. Had he remained in Washington, some historians have argued, he could have taken credit for the achievements of his negotiators while keeping a close eye on his critics. Instead, he went to Paris, staking the treaty's success on his own popularity. He passed up a chance to include in the delegation a prominent Republican, like Lodge, who could guide the treaty through Congress afterwards. A member of the British cabinet, Winston Churchill, observed that "if Mr. Wilson had been either simply an idealist or a caucus politician, he might have succeeded. His attempt to run the two in double harness was the cause of his undoing."

In December 1918, Walter Lippmann, now an army captain, watched Wilson's triumphal entry into Paris. Crowds lined the streets, and as the procession crossed the Pont du Concorde into the center of the city, a great cheer went up, echoing off the walls of the Chamber of Deputies. "Never has a king, never has an emperor received such a welcome," *L'Europe Nouvelle* declared. For the next month, Wilson toured France, Italy, and Britain with cries of "Viva Veelson" ringing in his ears. An Italian mayor compared his visit to the second coming of Christ. "They say he thinks of us, the poor people," a workingman remarked, "that he wants us all to have a fair chance; that he is going to do something when he gets here that will make it impossible for our government to send us to war again. If he had only come sooner!"

By the time he arrived for the treaty talks at the Palace of Versailles, two of the Fourteen Points had already been compromised. Britain refused to accept the point on freedom of the seas, which would thwart the use of the Royal Navy in a future conflict. Wilson's own actions also undercut his position on point six, respect for Russia's sovereignty, since American troops were occupying Russian Siberia. Wilson was unable to prevent Britain, France, and Japan from dividing Germany's colonies among themselves and imposing harsh peace terms. Germany had to sign a humiliating "war guilt" clause and pay $33 billion in reparations, enough to cripple its economy for decades. "God gave us the Ten Commandments and we broke them," Clemenceau quipped. "Wilson gave us the Fourteen Points—we shall see."

Council of Four Peace Conference Ending WWI The Big Four. From left to right, David Lloyd George of Great Britain, Vittorio Orlando of Italy, Georges Clemenceau of France, and Woodrow Wilson of the United States gather outside Hotel Crillon before the Paris Peace Conference in 1919.

Wilson concentrated on the League of Nations, which might make up for the treaty's other weaknesses and provide some safety against the rising tide of revolution. He took the lead in drafting the League Covenant, which committed each member to submit disputes to arbitration and pledged them to take action against "any war or threat of war."

The Senate Rejects the League

To many observers in the United States the Treaty of Versailles betrayed the goals Americans had fought to attain. "This is Not Peace," declared the *New Republic*. Congress saw the League of Nations less as a way to prevent wars than as a guarantee that the United States would be involved. Americans were "far more afraid of Lenin than they ever were of the Kaiser," Lippmann wrote. "We seem to be the most frightened lot of victors the world ever saw." To Republican leaders, like Henry Cabot Lodge, the United States' best bet was to look to its own security, keep its options open, and work out its international relations independently rather than as part of an alliance or league.

In early March 1919, before the treaty was concluded, Lodge and 38 other senators—more than enough to defeat the treaty—signed a petition opposing the League of Nations. James A. Reed of Missouri said the covenant would turn American foreign policy over to foreigners. Editorials described scenarios in which American troops would be automatically summoned to settle blood feuds in the Balkans. Wilson knew he would have to fight, but he believed that in the end the Senate would not reject the treaty.

AMERICA AND THE WORLD

>> The Influenza Pandemic of 1918

The 57th Vermont Pioneer Infantry marched for hours through the rain on the night of September 29, 1918, from Camp Merritt, New Jersey, to open ferries that carried them down the Hudson to Hoboken, where they boarded the U.S.S. *Leviathan* for the trip to France. The 9,000 tired and wet soldiers and 200 nurses aboard the country's largest and fastest troop transport were nervous about U-boats they might encounter in the Atlantic, but they had a deadlier enemy, one that came on board with the men of the 57th.

Within hours of embarkation, every bed in the ship's infirmary was full, and every patient had symptoms that were all too familiar to military doctors: aches in the legs and back, nosebleed, and, in extreme cases, the blue lips and ears, the thin, gasping breaths that indicated advanced pneumonia. But though doctors recognized the signs, they knew nothing about how to treat or prevent Spanish influenza. They could only comfort patients and try, futilely, to separate the sick from the well on the overloaded ship. By the time it arrived in France, 1,700 passengers were down with "the flu." Ninety had died during the passage and 200 more would perish within days of landing.

The 1918 pandemic affected nearly every spot on the globe, killing over 30 million people, far more than died in the world war. Called Spanish because the king of Spain was the first well-known figure to die, the flu was first observed at Fort Riley, Kansas, where the virus may have jumped from pigs to humans. War and commerce accelerated its spread. Men from all of Europe and colonial nations in Asia and Africa came together in the trenches and then carried the disease by steamship and locomotive to every continent. In August the flu mutated into an exceptionally lethal strain. Patients showed signs of massive pneumonia and usually died within three days.

It spread westward across North America, following the path of the railroads, and within weeks encircled the world in a fatal embrace, killing 6 million in India, 200,000 in Japan, and 675,000 in the United States. In Cincinnati, Ohio, and Harbin, China, farmers noticed that the disease killed hogs in the same proportion that it killed humans, roughly one in ten. A steamer from San Francisco put in at Tahiti on November 16, and within the next three weeks 10 percent of the population died. Isolated habitations newly tied to global conduits of trade and communications were hit hardest. The virus arrived in Eskimo villages on postal dogsleds and by camel caravan to Arabian towns. Australia closed its ports in a vain effort to shut out the disease.

At the Paris Peace Conference, delegate and Plattsburg veteran Willard Straight died, and President Wilson, Walter Lippmann, Edward House, and the entire American delegation were sick. When Wilson spoke of war and revolution as contagions spreading across the world, it was a terror his audience knew well. At the height of the pandemic in Philadelphia, churches, schools, saloons, and theaters were shut; San Francisco required everyone to wear surgical masks in public. Trolley cars were used as hearses, and the dead were interred in mass graves. Katherine Anne Porter, who nearly died, described the "noiseless houses with the shades drawn, empty streets, the dead cold light of tomorrow."

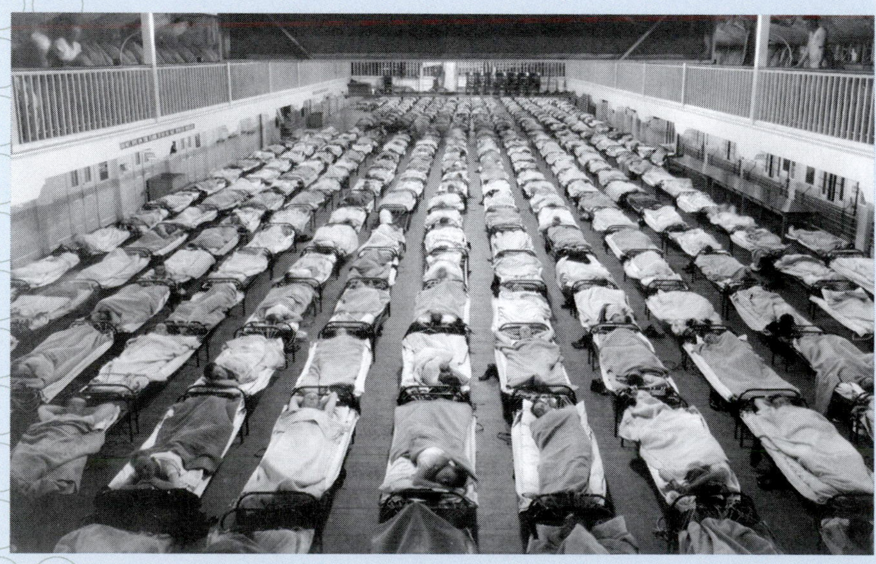

World war aroused a fervid nationalism, but the pandemic revealed that parliaments and autocrats were equally powerless in the face of catastrophe on this scale. Citizens accused their governments of apathy. The British Raj was in "a state of coma," the Bombay *Chronicle* complained. At Cartwright, on Canada's Labrador Coast, a minister wrote bit-

terly of his "resentment at the callousness of the authorities, who sent us the disease by mail-boat, and then left us to sink or swim." American soldiers in Brest took up red flags and mutinied, demanding to be released from flu-infested Camp Pontanezen.

One of the first acts of the new League of Nations in 1920 was to establish an international health organization to track the movement of epidemics. Agents at port cities collected reports of influenza, typhus, smallpox, cholera, and other plagues and sent them by telegraph to centers at Geneva and Singapore, allowing quarantines to be established or lifted when danger had passed. Quarantines disrupted trade, and League members wanted to control panic as much as disease. In 1948, the service became the World Health Organization (WHO), an affiliate of the United Nations.

Nearly a century later, air transport and global food-supply chains have made every epidemic into a potential pandemic. Outbreaks of communicable disease—or livestock infections, such as mad cow disease—touch off a global response. In March 2003, a strange pneumonia appeared in China, Canada, Viet Nam, and Singapore, reviving memories of the 1918 flu. A WHO doctor, an Italian tending an American patient in a Hanoi hospital, identified it as a new virus: Severe Acute Respiratory Syndrome (SARS). The WHO issued travel alerts, established quarantine procedures at airports, and dispatched epidemiological teams to trace the outbreak to its source. National governments resisted, attempting to conceal the extent and danger of the disease from the media, but the WHO prevailed and the outbreak was contained. Still, experts counted us lucky. No cure has yet been found for viral diseases, and had SARS spread at the rate of the Spanish flu, the toll would have numbered in the millions. In April 2009, a lethal flu virus—transferred, like the 1918 strain, from pigs—emerged in Mexico and spread through New York and Toronto to the rest of the world. Once again, the WHO mobilized a global response. For disease trackers, 1918 remains the benchmark, the standard for how destructive a modern plague can be—and might be again.

In September, Wilson went "over the heads" of Congress and stumped for the treaty on a nationwide tour. He assured listeners in Sioux Falls that "the peace of the world cannot be established without America." He promised the citizens of Salt Lake City that China's independence would be respected. Traveling more than 8,000 miles and speaking before large audiences without loudspeakers took a toll on the president's health. After a speech in Pueblo, Colorado, he became so ill that he was rushed back to Washington, where he suffered a stroke that left him paralyzed on his left side and unable to concentrate for more than a few minutes a day. Mrs. Wilson and the president's physician kept his condition a secret and refused to allow anyone to see him.

It was at this moment, with Wilson secluded in the White House, that the Senate voted against ratification. Down to the end, Wilson refused to allow Senate Democrats to accept any modifications. Even Lippmann's *New Republic,* which had been a mouthpiece for the Wilson administration throughout the war, called the treaty's demise "desirable and wholesome." Lodge and the Republicans were not ready to retreat into isolation, but they preferred diplomatic strategies that employed the United States' economic strength rather than its relatively weak military. They also saw Latin America as more critical than Europe to U.S. security. Lodge even toyed briefly with the idea of two leagues, one for each hemisphere.

Meanwhile, European governments organized the League of Nations without delegations from the United States or the Soviet Union. Over the next decade, U.S. influence abroad grew enormously. American automobiles, radios, and movies could be seen in far corners of the globe. However, the United States was cautious in its diplomatic dealings in Europe and Asia, in order to avoid being drawn into what the *New York Tribune* called the "vast seething mass of anarchy extending from the Rhine to the Siberian wastes."

Red Scare

On May 1, 1919, a dozen or more mail bombs were sent to prominent Americans: J. P. Morgan, John D. Rockefeller, senators, cabinet officials, and Supreme Court Justice Oliver Wendell Holmes. None of the explosive packages reached its intended target, but one injured a maid in the home of Senator Thomas Hardwick and another exploded at the residence of Attorney General A. Mitchell Palmer in Washington, nearly injuring Franklin and Eleanor Roosevelt, who lived next door. Investigations later showed that the bombings were the work of lone lunatics, but many people quickly concluded that the United States was under attack. Since the Russian Revolution, newspapers, evangelists, and government officials had fed fears of Bolshevism. "The blaze of revolution was sweeping over every American institution," Palmer alleged, "licking at the altars of the churches, leaping into the belfry of the school bell, crawling into the sacred corners of American homes."

Revolutions in Europe terrified conservatives in the United States and led them to look for Soviet terrorists, particularly among immigrants and unionized workers. They drew no distinctions among Socialists, anarchists, Communists, and labor unionists; they were all "red." Seattle's mayor called in the army to break a dockworkers strike. When steelworkers in Gary, Indiana, struck for higher wages and shorter hours in September 1919, Judge Elbert Gary, president of U.S. Steel, denounced them as followers of "anarchy and Bolshevism" and other doctrines "brought directly from Russia." During the war they had worked 12 hours a day, 7 days a week, for an average wage of $28 a week. Enlisting the help of local loyalty leagues, Judge Gary broke the strike.

Using the patriotic rhetoric of the war, industry leaders labeled strikers as dangerous aliens. They persuaded allies in the courts to take action, and a series of Supreme Court decisions made union activity virtually illegal. In 1919 the Court allowed antitrust suits to be filed against unions, and it later outlawed boycotts and picketing. Then, in January 1920, a series of crackdowns known as the Palmer raids rounded up and deported 250 members of the Union of Russian Workers. In one night, 4,000 suspected Communists were arrested in raids across the country; some said this was not enough. "If I had my way with these ornery, wild-eyed Socialists and IWWs," evangelist Billy Sunday allowed, "I would stand them up before a firing squad and save space on our ships."

The Sacco and Vanzetti Trial The trial of Sacco and Vanzetti, depicted here by Ben Shahn, came to symbolize the arbitrary injustices of the Red Scare. Their trial became an international cause celebre.

The most notorious case associated with the "Red Scare" began in May 1920 when Nicola Sacco and Bartolomeo Vanzetti, a shoemaker and a fish peddler, were arrested for robbing a shoe company in South Braintree, Massachusetts. Two men died of gunshot wounds during the robbery, and ballistics experts claimed that the bullets came from Sacco's gun. The trial, however, focused less on the evidence than on the fact that the defendants were Italian and anarchists. The state doctored evidence and witnesses changed testimony, but the judge favored the prosecution. The appeals lasted six years, during which protests for their release mounted. As the day of the execution approached, labor parties organized worldwide boycotts of American products. Riots in Paris took 20 lives. Uruguayan workers called a general strike. Governments called on the president to intervene, but on August 23, 1927, Sacco and Vanzetti died in the electric chair.

Americans who had talked in 1917 about making the world safe for democracy now seemed ready to restrict their own freedoms out of fear. Lippmann found it "incredible that an administration announcing the most spacious ideals in our history should have done more to endanger fundamental American liberties than any group of men for a hundred years." By the end of 1920, the original terror subsided, but labor unions and social radicals would have to fend off the charge of communism for decades to come.

Conclusion

Wilson tried to lead America toward what he called a new world order, a world where nations and international law would count more than empires and where the United States could light the way toward progress, stability, and peace. What he failed to recognize was that for many Americans this future was filled with terrors as well as promise. The strains of war had introduced new divisions in American society. Progressivism, which had given coherence and direction to social change, was a spent force. The growth of federal administration, the new powers of big business, internal migrations, and new social movements and values added up to what Lippmann called a "revolutionary world." Many of the changes that began during the war had not fully played out, nor were their consequences apparent, but Americans entered the 1920s with a sense of uneasiness. They were aware that their nation was now the world's strongest, but they were unsure about what that might mean for their lives.

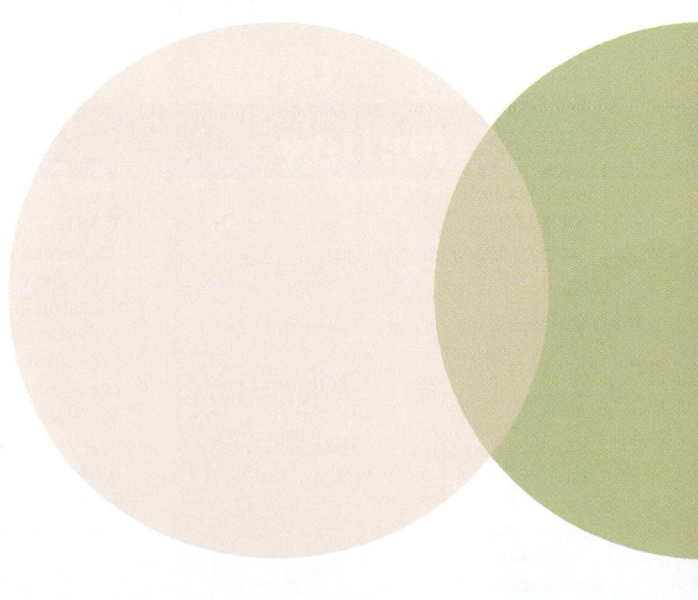

Further Readings

Nancy K. Bristow, *Making Men Moral: Social Engineering During the Great War* (1996). Reformers and women's groups used military training to mold men into model citizens.

John Eisenhower, *Intervention! The United States and the Mexican Revolution, 1913–1917* (1993). The story of the U.S. occupation of Veracruz and Pershing's search for Pancho Villa.

Meirion Harries, *The Last Days of Innocence: America at War, 1917–1918* (1997). Lively anecdotal history of the war years.

David M. Kennedy, *Over Here: The First World War and American Society* (1980). An examination of the home front during World War I.

Edward G. Lengel, *To Conquer Hell: The Meuse-Argonne, 1918* (2008). The experience of combat in the American sector of the Western Front.

N. Gordon Levin Jr., *Woodrow Wilson and World Politics* (1968). Levin analyzes progressive president's response to the disorder of world politics.

Erez Manela, *The Wilsonian Moment: Self-Determination and the International Origins of Anticolonial Nationalism* (2007). The global reaction to Wilson's revolutionary doctrine of self-determination.

H. C. Peterson and Gilbert C. Fite, *Opponents of War, 1917–1918* (1957). On wartime peace movements and the Wilson administration's attempts to suppress dissent.

Linda R. Robertson, *The Dream of Civilized Warfare: World War I Flying Aces and the American Imagination* (2003). While infantrymen died by the thousands for a few yards of mud, Americans dreamed of soaring above the Western Front and winning the war in the skies.

Ronald Steel, *Walter Lippmann and the American Century* (1980). More than any other journalist, Lippmann shaped American foreign policy in the twentieth century.

Who, What?

Porifirio Díaz 729
George Creel 738
Bernard Baruch 739
Langston Hughes 741
Carrie Chapman Catt 742
John J. Pershing 747
Neutrality 731
Propaganda 737
Cost-plus contract 740
Suffrage 742
Red Scare 754

>> Timeline >>

▼ 1911
Mexican Revolution begins

▼ 1912
Woodrow Wilson elected president

▼ 1914
U.S. troops occupy Veracruz, Mexico
World War I begins

▼ 1915
U.S. troops occupy Haiti (until 1934)
Lusitania sunk

THE NEW YORK HERALD.
THE LUSITANIA IS SUNK; 1,000 PROBABLY ARE LOST

▼ 1916
U.S. forces invade Mexico in search of Pancho Villa
U.S. forces enter the Dominican Republic
Woodrow Wilson reelected.

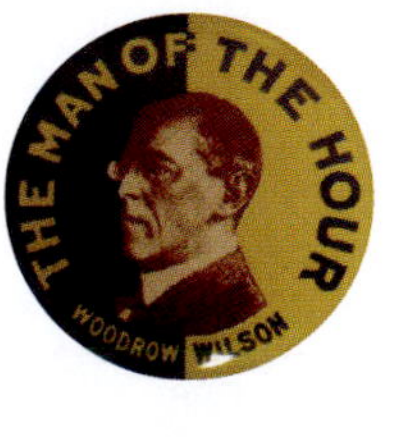

▼ 1917
Russian czar abdicates; parliamentary regime takes power
U.S. declares war on Germany
East St. Louis riot
Houston riot
October Revolution overthrows Russian government; Lenin takes power

▼ 1918
Wilson announces U.S. war aims: the Fourteen Points
Wilson nationalizes railroads

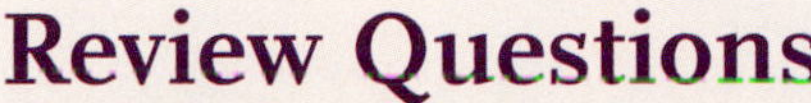

Review Questions

1. Did the war help or hurt the progressive movement?
2. Allied commanders wanted to use American troops as a reserve, but Pershing wanted his soldiers to enter the battle as an army. Why was that so important to him?
3. Did Senate Republicans reject the League of Nations because they wanted the United States to withdraw from the world, or because they wanted to deal with the world in a different way?
4. Managing the pace of change posed a tricky problem for leaders in the early twentieth century. How did Wilson try to control the dynamic of social and political change? What methods of change was he unwilling to accept?
5. Why were American leaders so much more concerned about sedition and dissent during World War I than they were during the Civil War or World War II?
6. How did mobilization for war advance the progressive agenda? In what ways did it set progressives back?

Websites

Carrie Chapman Catt. From American National Biography Online. A powerful advocate for peace and women's suffrage, she and Alice Paul orchestrated the state-by-state campaign for the nineteenth amendment.

From the Home Front and the Front Lines. Library of Congress online exhibit. The Veterans History Project draws together diaries, oral histories, photographs and other artifacts from America's twentieth century wars. http://www.loc.gov/exhibits/treasures/homefront-home.html

For further review materials and resource information, please visit www.oup.com/us/ofthepeople

Sedition Act outlaws criticism of the U.S. government

U.S. troops stop German advance

Wilson sends troops to Siberia

Armistice ends fighting on the Western Front

Influenza pandemic peaks in September

▼ 1919

Eighteenth Amendment outlaws manufacture, sale, and transport of alcoholic beverages

Versailles Treaty signed in Paris

Mail bombs target prominent government and business figures

Gary, Indiana, steel strike

U.S. Senate rejects Versailles Treaty

▼ 1920

Nineteenth Amendment secures the vote for women

Palmer raids arrest thousands of suspected Communists

Sacco and Vanzetti arrested on charges of robbery and murder

CHAPTER 23

Common Threads 

>> How did the Industrial Revolution continue to affect culture and politics, as well as the economy?

>> What differentiated the modern culture of the 1920s from the popular culture of the Gilded Age and the Progressive Era?

>> Why did individualism continue to be such an important force in American life?

>> How did the Republican New Era of the 1920s mark a break from the progressive politics of the 1900s–1910s?

>> What were the long-term implications of a political and cultural order so dependent on material prosperity?

The Modern Nation

1920–1928

AMERICAN PORTRAIT

>> "The Queen of the Waves"

On August 6, 1926, Gertrude Ederle walked across the beach at Cape Gris-Nez on the French coastline. Her body and her bright red swimsuit were heavily greased. At 7:00 A.M., the 19-year-old from New York City plunged into the water and began to swim toward the coast of England.

"Trudy," the daughter of a German immigrant butcher, was a champion distance swimmer who had won medals at the 1924 Olympics, but no woman had ever completed the long, hazardous swim across the English Channel. In fact, only five men had accomplished the feat. Ederle herself had tried and failed the year before. Exhausted, she had been pulled from the water by her coach, who rebuked her for playing the ukulele instead of practicing hard in the preceding weeks.

This time was different. Despite the tides, the chill water, and the threat of sharks, Ederle persevered, spurred on by her competitive instincts, her eagerness to please her mother, and her father's promise to buy her a new car, a roadster, if she succeeded.

Inspired by thoughts of that roadster, Ederle fought the choppy waves and hunted for a favorable tide. Finally, after 14 hours and 31 minutes in the water, she came ashore at Kingsdown, England, at 9:40 P.M. Ederle had become the first woman to swim the channel and had made the crossing faster than any of the men before her. "I am a proud woman," Trudy announced as she walked up the English beach.

Back in the United States, newspapers trumpeted Ederle's stunning achievement in page-one headlines and analyzed it in editorials. Ederle came home to a tumultuous ticker tape parade in New York. "No President or king, soldier or statesman," reported the *New York Times,* "has ever enjoyed such an enthusiastic and affectionate outburst of acclaim by the metropolis as was offered to the butcher's daughter . . . hailed as the 'Queen of the Waves.'" President Calvin Coolidge sent his congratulations. Trudy was overwhelmed with offers to endorse products and to appear on stage and in the movies.

Gertrude Ederle's enormous reception said a great deal about the United States in the 1920s. Once again at peace, America could afford to indulge an interest in the exploits of a long-distance swimmer. The nation's dynamic industrial economy seemed effortlessly to produce plenty of roadsters, movies, and prosperity.

Ederle herself exemplified a new national culture, rooted in the needs of the booming consumer economy, that broke sharply with the forms and conventions of the past. Emphasizing the importance of pleasure, this modern culture celebrated leisure activities such as dancing, channel swimming, ukulele playing, and other diversions. The ukulele-playing Ederle loved "all normal pleasures, including a jazzy dance now and then." The new culture glorified the purchase and consumption of material goods such as the roadster Ederle wanted and the merchandise she advertised. The teenage swimmer embodied still other aspects of the new culture—its fascination with youth, its endorsement of a more indulgent, child-centered family life, and its infatuation with pleasure-seeking, independent, nontraditional women.

Ederle—the solitary swimmer and enthusiastic consumer—also exemplified the resurgent individualism that shaped the politics of the 1920s. It was no wonder that President Coolidge, a staunch Republican, congratulated Ederle. She seemed to prove that individuals could still achieve great things and find happiness in an increasingly organized, centralized, bureaucratized society.

In the euphoria of the ticker tape parade, it was easy to conclude that Americans welcomed the emerging cultural and political order as much as they welcomed Trudy Ederle. In fact, many people were troubled by the changes of the 1920s. The modern order did not reflect the values of millions of Americans. Neither did it speak to the social and economic inequalities that plagued national life. As a result the new cultural and political order faced a powerful backlash, just as Ederle faced a hostile tide in the English Channel. Nevertheless, like the swimmer, the new culture and politics seemed to overcome all opposition as the decade moved to a close.

OUTLINE

A Dynamic Economy

By and large, the 1920s were a prosperous time for America. After a recession during 1920 and 1921, the economy continued to grow. Consumer prices remained steady throughout the decade, and jobs were plentiful; the unemployment rate went as low as 1.8 percent in 1926. Wages jumped: the nation's net income—the value of its earnings from labor and property—leapt from $64.0 billion in 1921 to $86.8 billion in 1929. This prosperity was driven by the dynamism of the evolving industrial economy. New technologies, increased efficiency, a maturing automobile industry, and new businesses all contributed to the economic gains.

> The man who builds a factory, builds a temple. The man who works there, worships there.
>
> PRESIDENT CALVIN COOLIDGE, January 1925

Despite the general prosperity, the transformation of the economy involved defeats for organized labor and decline for many farmers. The relative weakness of agriculture and the strength of industry helped to turn the United States into a predominantly urban nation. In the prosperous 1920s, as always, industrial capitalism was a transforming force.

The Development of Industry

Several long-term factors shaped the development of American industry in the 1920s. In their continuing quest for more efficient production, businessmen made use of a flood of new technologies and other innovations. The federal government issued more patents for new inventions—421,000 of them—than in any preceding decade. The industrial economy also made greater use of technical expertise. During the 1920s, the number of engineers in the country nearly doubled.

The switch from coal to electricity, under way since the 1910s, was an important innovation in factories. By the end of the 1920s, electricity powered more than two-thirds of American manufacturing plants. Henry Ford's car company pioneered another critical innovation, the system that became known as Fordism or mass production. By the 1910s, Ford, like other American manufacturers, used interchangeable parts, simple and accurate machine tools, and electric power to speed output at its Highland Park factory complex in Detroit, Michigan. However, auto production was slowed by traditional manufacturing practice. Frames, transmissions, and other key subassemblies remained in place on stands while teams of workers moved from one stand to another to work. Eager to meet the rising demand for the popular Model T car, Ford's managers reversed the process by "moving the work to the men." Beginning in 1913, the Ford plant added conveyor belts and chains to send subassemblies past groups of stationary workers. Instead of making an entire engine or subassembly, a worker might tighten a few bolts or install a single part. The results were astonishing: in 1914, Ford produced 300,000 Model Ts; in 1923, the company produced more than 2 million. Other manufacturers raced to copy Fordism, the company's techniques.

Ford Assembly Line Mass production at work: the assembly line at the Ford Motor Company plant in Dearborn, Michigan, 1928.

Mass production, electrification, and other innovations spurred an extraordinary increase in productivity for American industry. Output per worker skyrocketed 72 percent from 1919 to 1929.

Along with increased productivity, the rise of several industries drove the economy. Auto production now dominated as textiles, railroads, iron, and steel had earlier. In 1921, there were 9.3 million cars on American roads. By 1929, the figure had reached 23 million. By producing all those cars, auto manufacturers stimulated demand for plate glass, oil, gasoline, and rubber.

Other sectors of the industrial economy also grew rapidly. The demand for processed foods, household appliances, office machinery, and chemicals increased dramatically. Emerging industries such as aircraft demonstrated their potential economic importance.

Arguably the first powered, fixed-wing flight had occurred in December 1903, when Wilbur and Orville Wright brought their "Flyer" to the beach at Kitty Hawk, North Carolina. With Orville lying at the controls, the fragile plane flew 120 feet in 12 seconds. But the civilian airplane industry did not take off until the 1920s. Aircraft production rose from less than 300 in 1922 to more than 6,000 in 1929. By then, fledgling airlines were flying passengers on scheduled flights.

The Trend Toward Large-Scale Organization

The development of industry reinforced the trend toward large-scale organization that was basic to U.S. capitalism (see Chapter 17). Only giant corporations, with thousands of employees and hundreds of millions of dollars in capitalization, had the financial resources to pay for mass production. A wave of mergers meant that these big businesses controlled more factories and assets than ever. By 1929, corporations produced 92 percent of the nation's manufactured goods.

The largest firms also benefited from more efficient organizational structures. When the recession of 1920 and 1921 left big corporations with too many unsold goods, companies reorganized. Now top managers, aided by financial, legal, and other experts, oversaw the work of semiautonomous divisions that supplied different markets. At General Motors, for example, the Chevrolet division produced huge numbers of relatively inexpensive cars, while the Cadillac division turned out a smaller number of expensive cars. The new organizational system made corporations more flexible, efficient, and responsive to changes in consumer demand.

Corporate growth was not confined to industry. Chains such as A. & P. grocers and F. W. Woolworth's variety stores increased their share of the nation's retail sales from 4 percent to 20 percent. Just 1 percent of the nation's banks managed nearly half of the country's financial assets. By 1929, just 200 corporations held about one-fifth of national wealth.

Giant firms and their leaders had often been the targets of suspicion, hostility, and reform during the Progressive Era, but the decade's prosperity led many Americans to soften their attitude toward business. There were fewer calls to break up or regulate giant corporations. Big businessmen had seemed to be selfless, patriotic supporters of the U.S. effort in World War I. Now their companies were apparently leading the nation into a new period of economic well-being. To ensure a better image, businessmen paid for extensive public relations campaigns that stressed their commitment to ethical behavior and social service. Basking in the glow of public approval, big business confidently forecast a central role for itself in the nation's destiny. "The modern business system, despised and derided by innumerable reformers, will," a businessman predicted, "be both the inspiration and the instrument of the social progress of the future."

The Transformation of Work and the Workforce

Businessmen's quest for productivity had sweeping consequences for American workers. Industrial efficiency was not just a matter of electricity and machines. To speed up production, the managers at Ford and other factories had to change the nature of work.

Accordingly, the spirit of scientific management continued to sweep through American industry. Laboring under ever-tighter supervision, workers were pushed to work faster and harder. In textile mills, for instance, workers faced the "stretch-out," the requirement that they tend more looms than before. Ford's system of mass production shared Frederick Winslow Taylor's determination to simplify and regiment labor. The result of that determination was less-satisfying work. Instead of making a whole engine, a Ford assembly line worker might spend his day turning a few nuts on one engine after another. In 1913, the company's labor turnover rate soared to 380 percent as unhappy workers quit their jobs.

As production became more efficient, the nation experienced a net loss of about a million jobs in manufacturing, coal mining, and railroading. The growth of other kinds of employment more than compensated for this decrease, however. The ranks of white-collar workers increased 80 percent from 1910 to 1930, when nearly one worker in three did white-collar work rather than manual labor. The nation had already begun a long evolution from an industrial economy based on manual labor to a postindustrial economy based on white-collar work in sales and service.

Economic development also encouraged the continuing, gradual movement of women into the paid workforce. By the end of the 1920s, women made up a majority of clerical workers. In 1900, 22.1 percent of women had worked for pay; by the 1940s, the percentage would reach 27.1 As in the past, most women workers were unmarried.

Despite these changes, women still faced discrimination in the workplace. Overwhelmingly concentrated in low-wage occupations such as domestic service, factory work, and agriculture, they were paid less than men who did comparable work. Female sales workers, for example, earned between 42 and 63 percent of the wages paid to their male counterparts. Hardly any women held high-level managerial jobs. Moreover, there was still resistance to the idea that women should work outside the home. Most people continued to believe that a woman's place was in the home, especially if she had children. Many men feared that paid labor would make women too independent. Only economic necessities—families' need for income and employers' need for workers—reconciled American society to women's employment in the 1920s.

The Defeat of Organized Labor

The American labor movement did not respond effectively to the transformation of work and the workforce. In an age of increasing economic organization, workers became less organized. In 1920 nearly one nonagricultural worker in five belonged to a union. By 1929, little more than one in ten was a union member. The labor movement was especially weak in the developing mass-production industries such as automobiles and steel and barely addressed the growing ranks of clerks and other white-collar workers.

The weak state of organized labor partly resulted from prosperity. Earning relatively good wages, many workers were less interested in joining unions. To show that unions were unnecessary, corporations promoted welfare capitalism, a set of highly publicized programs ranging from lunch-hour movies to sports teams to profit-sharing plans supposedly beneficial to workers. Many firms created company unions purported to represent the interests of workers. But as it became clear that these groups did not give employees a real voice in management, their membership dwindled.

While some firms tried to win over their workers with baseball teams and company unions, many employers used tougher tactics to battle the labor movement. Management crusaded for the "open shop"—a workplace free of labor organization—and found an ally in the judicial system. Rulings by the U.S. Supreme Court such as *Duplex Printing Press Co. v. Deering* (1921) and *Bedford Cut Stone Co. v. Journeymen Stone Cutters' Assn.* (1927) made it easier for lower courts to grant injunctions against union activities. State and federal courts issued injunctions to stop unions from striking and exercising their rights and allowed businesses to sue unions for damages. Businesses used old antiunion tactics such as the demand that workers sign "yellow-dog contracts" promising not to join a union.

The labor movement also hurt its own cause. The leadership of the major national organization, the AFL, was increasingly conservative and timid. The heads of the AFL, mostly white males of western European extraction who represented skilled crafts, had little interest in organizing women workers and wanted nothing to do with socialists, radical unionists, or African American workers. The AFL was slow to admit or even pay attention to the Brotherhood of Sleeping Car Porters, the assertive union of African American workers organized in 1925 under socialist A. Philip Randolph. Despite pleas from Randolph and others, the AFL failed to organize unskilled workers, many of whom were African Americans or white immigrants from eastern and southern Europe.

Weakened by internal divisions, welfare capitalism, the open-shop crusade, and the courts, the labor movement did not challenge the ongoing transformation of industrial labor. Nationwide, the number of strikes and lockouts dropped from 3,411 in 1920 to 604 in 1928. All too often, these labor actions ended in defeat for workers.

The Decline of Agriculture

Against the backdrop of national prosperity, American agriculture continued its long decline. Prices for basic crops such as cotton and wheat fell, and the number of farms dropped.

The larger story of decline obscured important signs of growth and health. Some agricultural sectors were as dynamic as industry, and for the same reasons—increased efficiency promoted by new technologies and large-scale organization. Mechanization, including the introduction of such tractors as the huge Fordson built by the Ford Motor Company, made farm labor more efficient. So did the increasing development of irrigation systems since the turn of the century. By the 1920s, the irrigated farms of the Southwest were producing bumper crops of cotton, fruits, and vegetables. The Southwest also witnessed the rise of huge farms with hundreds and even thousands of acres, whose owners could afford mechanization and irrigation. These innovative "factories in the fields" depended on the old-fashioned exploitation of farm labor, as well as on size and technology. In California's Imperial Valley and elsewhere, migrant workers labored in harsh conditions for low pay in order to create modern, large-scale agriculture.

Ironically, the dynamism of the agricultural economy created a problem for many American farmers. Midsize farms, too big to be run by their owners alone and too small to make mechanization practical, could not compete with the vast "factories in the fields." Increased efficiency, meanwhile, led to bumper crops that did not always find a market at a good price. Farmers were hurt by changes in Americans' diet, such as declining consumption of bread and potatoes, and by the rise of competitors overseas. Producing too much, American farmers could not export enough of their surplus crops to foreign countries. The resulting glut reduced the price of farm products. As their incomes lagged behind those of urban workers, farmers yearned for the return of high pre–World War I agricultural prices that would restore parity between city and country.

Farmers' purchasing power did improve toward the end of the decade, but the basic reality did not change. As a Georgia farmer observed, "The hand that is feeding the world is being spit upon."

The Urban Nation

The woes of agriculture contributed to a long-term shift in the geographical distribution of the American population. For the first time, according to the federal census of 1920, a majority of Americans—54 million out of 105 million—lived in urban territory. This did not mean the United States had become a nation of big cities. The census defined "urban territory" as places with as few as 2,500 people. Many "urban" areas were really small towns little removed from rural life. Nevertheless, the population of the United States was no longer predominantly rural.

***Arrangement—New York*, ca. 1925** The city—modernistic and smoky—loomed over the new culture of the 1920s: Czech-American artist Jan Matulka's vision of New York City.

The decline of farming spurred this transformation. As agricultural prices fell, millions of Americans fled the nation's farms. While the total U.S. population increased by 17 million during the 1920s, the farm population actually declined by more than 1.5 million.

At the same time, the dynamic growth of the industrial economy swelled the population of towns and cities. In the 1920s, factory production was still centered in urban areas. Manufacturing gave many cities their identity. Detroit was becoming the "motor city." Akron, Ohio, was the home of the nation's rubber production. Pittsburgh, Pennsylvania, and Birmingham, Alabama, symbolized the steel industry. Most of the new white-collar jobs were located in cities. Corporations also put their headquarters in cities, especially the two largest, Chicago and New York.

The rise of the automobile contributed to the emergence of the urban nation as well. The car made it practical for Americans to live in suburbs and drive into the city to work and to shop. In the 1920s, the suburban lifestyle was still reserved mostly for the well-to-do. Elite suburbs, such as Grosse Pointe and Ferndale outside Detroit, and Beverly Hills, Glendale, and Inglewood outside Los Angeles, grew explosively. The transformation of the countryside into suburbs was a powerful symbol of the new urban nation.

A Modern Culture

The 1920s saw the full emergence of a modern culture that had been gradually taking shape for decades. But Americans now felt themselves surrounded by something fundamentally new—a term they used over and over to describe their world. So perfectly symbolized by Gertrude Ederle, the new culture extolled the virtues of modernity and pleasure. Rooted in the nation's economic development, the new culture reflected both the needs of businessmen who had to sell the goods rolling off assembly lines and the desires of Americans with more money and free time than ever. Supported by advertising and installment buying, the culture of leisure and consumption offered spectator sports, movies, popular music, radio, and sex. The new culture entailed new views of gender, family life, and youth and placed renewed emphasis on the old values of individualism in an increasingly organized society.

The Spread of Consumerism

Encouraged by big business, many Americans increasingly defined life as the pursuit of pleasure. They were invited to find happiness in leisure and consumption rather than in work. This philosophy of consumerism saturated American society by the end of the decade.

The increased efficiency and profitability of the economy enabled American employers to allow their workers higher wages and more leisure hours. Some employers, most notably Ford, also raised wages in order to hold on to workers alienated by the drudgery of mass production. And Ford himself intentionally increased workers' pay to enable them to buy the products of modern factories. As a result, the incomes of workers and other employees reached a new high in the 1920s. Factory workers' real wages rose 19 percent from 1914 to 1923.

> **Every morning, Every evening,**
> **Ain't we got fun/**
> **Not much money, Oh but honey,**
> **Ain't we got fun**
>
> RICHARD A. WHITING, RAYMOND B. EGAN, AND GUS KAHN, 1921

Many workers had more time to enjoy their wages. For salaried, middle-class workers, the annual vacation had become a tradition by the 1910s. Although blue-collar workers seldom enjoyed a vacation, they spent less time on the job. Some employers, including Henry Ford, instituted a five-day workweek during the 1920s. More commonly, businesses shortened their workday. As a result, the average workweek fell from 47.4 hours in 1920 to 44.2 in 1929. "The shorter work day brought me my first idea of there being such a thing as pleasure," said one young female worker. "Before this time it was just sleep and eat and hurry off to work."

A change in attitude accompanied these changes in wages and workdays. The work ethic seemed less necessary in a prospering economy. Thanks to Fordism and Taylorism, work was less satisfying, too. In these circumstances, people justified pleasure as an essential antidote to labor. As early as 1908, a magazine announced that "Fun Is a Necessity." Many Americans now agreed.

"Would your husband marry you again?" Like this advertisement for Palmolive Soap, advertising in the 1920s often sold products by making consumers feel insecure and inadequate.

The advertising industry encouraged the new attitude toward pleasure. Although advertising agencies had first appeared in the 1850s and 1860s, the business did not reach maturity until the 1920s. During the 1920s, ads appeared everywhere—in newspapers and magazines, on billboards and big electric signs. Major advertising agencies such as J. Walter Thompson and Batten, Barton, Durstine, and Osborn became concentrated in New York City, home to so many corporations. Impressed by successful ad campaigns for Listerine antiseptic and mouthwash and Fleischmann's yeast, big business increasingly turned to advertising agencies to sell goods and services. Expenditures for advertising leaped from $682 million in 1914 to nearly $3 billion by 1929.

Advertising, like the new culture, optimistically embraced change and trumpeted the new. Ad men believed they were bringing the benefits of modernity to Americans. According to advertisements, purchasing the right products would solve people's problems, make up for the drudgery of work, and bring fulfillment. To enthusiastic ad men, advertising became as important as the products it sold. In his best-selling book, *The Man Nobody Knows* (1925), ad executive Bruce Barton portrayed Jesus Christ as a great advertiser, who had turned his disciples into a sales force "that conquered the world" with the new product, Christianity.

Along with advertising, business used installment loans to encourage Americans to buy goods and services "on time." Credit buying spread so rapidly that the nation's total consumer debt more than doubled from 1922 to 1929. As a result, the sales of such consumer goods as pianos, washing machines, and automobiles boomed. Americans had bought just 181,000 automobiles in 1910; they bought 4,455,000 in 1929. Thanks to the availability of another kind of loan, the mortgage, more Americans were able to invest in a home of their own. Spending on new private housing jumped from $1.2 billion in 1915 to $2.0 billion in 1920 and then to a staggering $5.0 billion by 1924. All this loan-driven spending helped power the economic prosperity of the 1920s.

New Pleasures

The culture of the 1920s offered many pleasures, especially sports, movies, popular music, and radio. Gertrude Ederle was part of a golden age for spectator sports. Although people still avidly played games themselves, they also passively observed other people's games more than ever before. Tennis, boxing, and auto racing flourished during the decade. The American Professional Football Association, which became the National Football League, played its first season in 1920. Although crowds packed stadiums for college football games, baseball remained the most popular American sport. A huge network of minor-league baseball teams covered the nation. Meanwhile, the popularity of major-league baseball surged, thanks in part to the exploits of the New York Yankees' home run–hitting outfielder, Babe Ruth.

While spectator sports enthralled millions, another passive pleasure, the movies, was undeniably the most popular consumer attraction of the 1920s (see Table 23–1). Little more than a novelty when first shown in the mid-1890s, silent films had rapidly matured into a big business commanding the loyalty of millions of Americans. In city neighborhoods in the 1900s, crowds packed into stuffy "nickelodeons"—converted storefront theaters that showed short, silent one-reel films for the low price of a nickel. The movies quickly became longer and more sophisticated. Spreading through the cities and into the suburbs, theaters became larger and more elegant. By the 1920s, lavish movie "palaces," such as the Roxy in New York and the Tivoli in Chicago, evoked the Orient and other exotic faraway places. Nationwide, attendance doubled from 40 million a week in 1922 to 80 million a week in 1929.

Booming attendance fueled the growth of a handful of corporations, including Warner Brothers and RKO, that dominated the film industry. By the 1920s, the center of movie production had shifted from New York to Hollywood, California. As the film industry began to be called "Hollywood," the business grew still bigger toward the end of the decade, when film studios learned how to synchronize sound and moving images in such films as *The Jazz Singer* of 1927.

 **Table 23–1** Spending for Recreational Services, 1909–1929

Year	Total (millions of dollars)	Motion Picture Theaters (millions of dollars)	Spectator Sports (millions of dollars)
1909	377	###	###
1914	434	###	###
1919	806	###	###
1921	911	301	30
1923	1082	336	46
1927	1405	526	48
1929	1670	720	66

Historical Statistics of the United States, Millennial Online Edition (Cambridge: Cambridge University Press, 2008), Table Dh309–318.

= No Data

It was fitting that one of the first "talking pictures" was about the impact of jazz. Popular music in general and jazz in particular played an important role in the new consumer culture. Created by African Americans in the 1910s, jazz was a rhythmically and harmonically innovative music that featured improvised solos and a hot beat. The new music emerged in various places around the country, but its first great center was the streets, brothels, and dives of New Orleans. The Louisiana city was home to the first major jazz composer, Jelly Roll Morton, and to the first jazz superstar, trumpeter and singer Louis Armstrong. As jazz became nationally popular, Morton, Armstrong, and the focus of jazz moved on, as did so many African Americans, to Chicago and New York City (see Chapter 22).

***The Jazz Singer* Premiere** The dazzling allure of a new pleasure—the "talking picture"—draws a big opening-night crowd to Warners' Theatre, New York City, October 6, 1927.

The new music quickly attracted white Americans, especially the young, who yearned for something more daring than the relatively sedate popular music of the day. Even the name—a reference perhaps to speed or sexual intercourse—conjured up pleasure and liberation. Soon white musicians were contributing to the evolution of the music. For many whites, jazz summed up a period seemingly dominated by the pursuit of liberating pleasures. The 1920s became known as the "Jazz Age," after the title of a 1922 book of short stories by F. Scott Fitzgerald.

The great popularity of jazz and other musical genres was made possible by the phonograph, originated by Thomas Edison in the 1870s and modified by other inventors. In the 1920s, the electrical recording microphone dramatically improved the sound quality of records and made the new music accessible to millions of Americans.

A newer technological innovation, the radio, also allowed Americans to hear popular music. After Italian inventor Guglielmo Marconi transmitted the first radio waves through the air in 1895, a series of innovations made possible the inauguration of commercial radio broadcasting in the United States by 1920. The federal government began licensing radio stations the next year.

Like the movies, radio quickly became corporatized big business. By 1923, there were more than 500 stations. In 1926, the first permanent network of stations, the National Broadcasting Company (NBC), took to the airwaves. Americans tuned in to hear broadcasts of live music, news, sports, and soap operas. To meet the demand for radios, manufacturers turned out more than 2 million sets a year by 1925. Radio, like the movies, played a key role in disseminating the values of consumerism, as corporations rushed to advertise their products by sponsoring radio programs.

A Sexual Revolution

Along with such new pleasures as radio and movies, the modern culture offered a new attitude toward an old pleasure, sex. By the 1920s, Americans' sexual attitudes and behavior were clearly changing. People openly discussed sex and placed a new emphasis on the importance of sexual satisfaction, primarily in marriage. And there were signs of greater sexual exploration among unmarried young people.

In the nineteenth century, Americans, especially middle-class Victorians, had tended to maintain a discreet silence about sex. But that silence gave way in the twentieth century. During the Progressive Era, reformers forced the public discussion of such sexual issues as prostitution and venereal disease. The reformers, anxious to limit and control extramarital sexual behavior, hardly wanted to glorify sexual pleasure. But they helped pave the way for a more open and approving depiction of sexuality.

The popular amusements of the 1910s and 1920s inundated Americans with sexual images. From the beginning, the movies explored sexual topics in such films as *The Anatomy of a Kiss* and *A Bedroom Blunder*. Some popular music featured suggestive songs about sex such as "It's Tight Like That" and "I Need a Little Sugar in My Bowl." Popular dances such as the grizzly bear, the shimmy, and the turkey trot promoted close physical contact or sexually suggestive steps. The contrast with the culture of the late nineteenth century was startling. As early as 1913, a magazine concluded that "Sex O'Clock" had struck in the United States.

The increased openness about sex reflected the growing belief that sexual pleasure was necessary and desirable, particularly within marriage. Married couples increasingly considered intercourse as an opportunity for pleasure as well as procreation. Experts insisted that healthy marriages required sexual satisfaction for both partners.

The new view of marital sexuality helped to change attitudes toward contraception. By the 1910s, an emerging grassroots movement, led by socialists and other radicals, promoted sex education and contraceptives, which were largely illegal. The crusade's best-known figure was the fiery former nurse and socialist organizer, Margaret Sanger, who coined the term "birth control." Although Sanger once had to flee the country to avoid prosecution, birth control gradually became respectable—and widely practiced—in the 1920s.

Despite the growing belief in the importance of sexual satisfaction, most adult Americans still condemned premarital sex. Nevertheless, premarital intercourse apparently became more common. Many couples believed that intercourse was acceptable if they were "in love" and intended to marry. There was also an apparent increase in "petting"—sexual contact short of intercourse.

While changing some of their attitudes about sexual behavior, most heterosexual Americans still condemned homosexuality. Nevertheless, a sexual revolution was under way.

Changing Gender Ideals

Shifting sexual attitudes were closely tied to new gender ideals. By the 1920s, Americans' sense of what it meant to be female was changing. Since the late nineteenth century, Americans had been talking about the independent, assertive "New

Woman" who claimed the right to attend school, vote, and have a career. The "New Woman" of the 1920s was now a sexual being, too. An object of male desire, she was also a fun-loving individual with desires of her own.

The sexual nature of women was central to a new movement, known as feminism, that had emerged in the 1910s. The feminists, like earlier female reformers, were generally white, well-educated, Protestant, urban women. Concentrated in New York's Greenwich Village, the feminists broke with the older reformers by insisting on sharing the sexual opportunities and satisfactions that men had presumably long enjoyed. Unlike the older generation of activist women, the feminists were unwilling to give up marriage and children in order to have careers outside the home. Feminism insisted on women's right to pleasure and satisfaction in all phases of life, from the most public to the most intimate.

Small in number, the feminists commanded a great deal of attention. Several of their ideas and practices were too radical for many American men and women. Much of the nation rejected altogether some feminists' decision to retain their maiden names in married life or to explore sexual relationships outside of marriage. Most fundamentally, many Americans were unwilling to accept the feminist insistence on full equality with men.

Nevertheless American culture proved rather open to the more liberated view of female sexuality that emerged from feminism, experts, and the movies. The most popular image of the American woman of the 1920s was the vivacious young "flapper," with her short skirt, bound breasts, and bobbed hair. The flapper was likely to wear cosmetics and to smoke cigarettes—practices once associated only with prostitutes.

Notions of masculinity were also changing. With the growing emphasis on female needs and desires, men were urged to be attentive and responsive and to focus on the home. As the world of work became less satisfying, experts told men to look for fulfillment in family life. The family man of the 1920s, unlike the stereotypical Victorian man, was not supposed to be a distant, stern patriarch. Instead, he was a companion to his wife and a doting friend to his children.

In practice, many men still defined themselves in terms of their work rather than their domestic life. Moreover, American society still regarded women as the primary caretakers of children. Despite the clear change in domestic values, many men were still relative outsiders in the home.

The Family and Youth

Changing gender ideals were directly related to a reconsideration of family life and youth. Although whole families still labored together in California fields and North Carolina textile mills, most Americans no longer regarded the family as a group of productive workers. Child-labor laws increasingly made sure that boys and girls spent their time in school rather than in the workplace. The family became primarily a unit of leisure and consumption. The home was the place where men, women, and children found pleasure and fulfillment, where they used their Fleischmann's yeast and Listerine mouthwash and congregated around the radio.

Reflecting the values of the modern culture, parents became more likely to indulge their children, who enjoyed more toys, possessions, spending money, and pleasures than had earlier generations. The automobile gave young people more

AMERICAN LANDSCAPE

>> "Flaming Youth" on Campus

College and university campuses were the laboratories for "flaming youth." During the 1920s, male and female college students created a distinctive youth culture within the larger modern culture. Campus life reflected central features of twentieth century society: the desire for individual freedom and the need to cope with organization. The culture of the "advance guard of the younger generation" also reflected the uneven development of American democracy in the Jazz Age.

On one level, higher education was anything but democratic. Traditionally, colleges and universities were for the elite. In 1899, only 238,000 students—little more than 2 percent of Americans aged 18 to 24—enrolled in institutions of higher learning. Only 85,000 of those students were women. But as the dynamic economy demanded educated white-collar workers, more middle-class families found the means to send their sons and daughters to college. By 1929, 1.1 million students—7.2 percent of 18- to 24-year-olds—were enrolled. Thanks to changing attitudes toward women, 480,000 female students were on campus.

The development of public-supported colleges and universities made this growth possible. In just three years from 1919 to 1922, enrollments doubled from 3,000 to 6,000 at the University of Illinois and from 4,000 to 8,000 at Ohio State University. Less elitist than leading private institutions, the public schools were at the forefront of a more democratic student culture.

That culture celebrated independence. "To me the Jazz Age signifies an age of freedom in thought and action," explained a coed at the University of Denver. "The average young person of today is not bound by the strict conventions which governed the actions of previous generations." Liberated from the constraints of home and workplace, college students had the space to pursue their desires. "We were big-eyed with wanting," said Hoagy Carmichael, a student at Indiana University, "with making fun."

On campuses across the country, students held "petting parties." They forced college officials to tolerate racy new dances such as the toddle, the shimmy, the Charleston, and the black bottom. By the end of the decade, about two out of three students defied Prohibition (see Chapter 22) by drinking on and off campus. Public drunkenness was no longer a scandal. Women students engaged in the "unladylike," sexually suggestive practice of smoking. "College," sniffed a dean at Princeton, "has unfortunately become a kind of glorified playground . . . a paradise of the young."

Students' quest for pleasure shaped their politics. While Carmichael and his friends paid little attention to most public issues, they believed strongly in individual rights. Students regarded sex and other satisfactions as a private matter. College newspapers criticized Prohibitionists and other moral reformers who wanted to regulate individual behavior.

Even as they reflected the individualist values of the modern culture, college students adapted to the growing power of organization. Collegiate life became more bureaucratic as administrators coped with rising enrollments. Students themselves turned to organizations in the 1920s. Nationwide, the number of fraternities and sororities shot up during the decade. By 1930 about one student in three belonged to a fraternity or sorority; Hoagy Carmichael joined Kappa Sigma. On many campuses, Greek houses included most student leaders and set the tone of campus fashion for the "barbs," the barbarians who made up the rest of the student body.

Fraternities and sororities were places where college students could try out smoking and other freedoms. But the Greek system also forced its members to come to terms with organization. As the campus newspaper at Cornell University explained, the fraternity "crushes individuality." Initiation rites and hazing taught new members that they were expected to conform to the norms of the group. The distinctive culture of "flaming youth," like the new national culture, embraced organization as well as freedom, conformity as well as individualism.

mobility, too. With their new freedom, they could begin to create their own separate culture. One sign was the dramatic spread of petting among high-school youth, newly free from parental control.

Most adults accepted this situation partly because they admired and envied youthfulness. The modern culture, unhappy with work and anxious for fun, glorified youth. In 1923 the writer Samuel Hopkins Adams, writing under a pseudonym, published the novel *Flaming Youth,* about sexually adventurous, fast-living young people; the title became a catchphrase for the youth culture of the 1920s.

The Celebration of the Individual

The emphasis on the individual, so evident in changing views of sex, gender, family, and youth, was a fundamental aspect of the modern culture. In addition to Gertrude Ederle and Babe Ruth, Americans admired a host of sports heroes and heroines, including tennis player Helen Wills Moody, boxer Jack Dempsey, golfer Bobby Jones, and football running back Red Grange. In the 1920s, the movie industry increasingly focused public attention on the distinctive personalities of stars. Individualism was basic to the "New Woman," too.

The resurgence of individualism was not surprising. The belief in the importance of the individual was deeply engrained in the American culture. Paradoxically, the development of industrial capitalism intensified the importance of both individuals and organizations. As corporations grew larger and produced more, these giant firms needed to stimulate consumerism, the gratification of individual needs and desires.

First Nonstop Solo Transatlantic Flight Charles A. Lindbergh pictured in front of the *Spirit of St. Louis* just before taking off from Roosevelt Field, New York, for Paris, on May 20, 1927.

There were serious obstacles to true individualism in the 1920s. Powerful organizations, including corporations, controlled individual life. Even the most famous individual exploit of the decade depended on organization. On May 20–21, 1927, Charles A. Lindbergh flew his monoplane, the *Spirit of St. Louis,* from New York City to Paris. This first nonstop solo crossing of the Atlantic made Lindbergh an international symbol of what an individual could accomplish, but Lindbergh's feat relied on a group of businessmen who put up the money and a corporation that built the plane. Organization and individualism, the new and the old, were interdependent in the 1920s.

The Limits of the Modern Culture

The modern culture had clear limits in the 1920s. For millions of Americans, much of the consumer lifestyle was out of reach. The spread of the new values was as limited as the spread of prosperity. Many Americans, among them artists and intellectuals, were unwilling to define their lives by the pursuit of pleasure, leisure, and consumption. For them modern society, with its emphasis on all things new, including the "New Negro," the "New Woman," and the "New Era," represented an unwelcome abandonment of old values. In different ways, fundamentalist Christians, immigration restrictionists, and the Ku Klux Klan demanded a return to an earlier United States. Mexican Americans, African Americans, and others found that the new culture, like the old, treated them like second-class citizens.

> I feel most colored when I am thrown against a sharp white background. . . . Among the thousand white persons, I am a dark rock surged upon, and overswept, but through it all, I remain myself. When covered by the waters, I am; and the ebb but reveals me again.
>
> ZORA NEALE HURSTON, 1928

The Limits of Prosperity

Despite the general aura of prosperity, low incomes and poverty persisted in the 1920s. As late as 1928, six out of ten American families made less than the $2,000 a year required for the "basic needs of life." Despite the housing boom, most American household heads—52 percent in 1930—still did not own their own home.

These statistics were not simply a reflection of the difficult lives of rural Americans. In the towns and cities of the increasingly urban nation, there was still a stark divide between middle- and upper-class existence on one hand, and working-class reality on the other. In their pioneering anthropological study of a small midwestern city in the 1920s, Helen and Staughton Lynd discovered that the "division into the working class and business class . . . constitutes the outstanding cleavage in Middletown." The working class of "Middletown"—it was in fact Muncie, Indiana—had less money and leisure to enjoy the new culture. As the Lynds reported in *Middletown* (1929), about a third of the city still did not own automobiles.

The "Lost Generation" of Intellectuals

Many artists and intellectuals felt alienated from the United States of the 1920s. For white, mostly male writers and artists who came of age during World War I, the conflict represented a failure of Western civilization, a brutal and pointless exercise in destruction. Its aftermath left these Americans angry at what the poet Ezra Pound called "an old bitch gone in the teeth . . . a botched civilization." It also left them alienated and rootless. In a nation supposedly devoted to individualism, they did not feel free. They were, as the writer Gertrude Stein described them, a "Lost Generation." Some of them, such as Stein and her fellow writer Ernest Hemingway, left the United States for Paris and other places in Europe.

However prosperous and peaceful, the postwar years did not reassure the Lost Generation about the course of American life. Artists and intellectuals argued that the nation had not changed much at all. In such works as *Winesburg, Ohio* (1919), novelist Sherwood Anderson portrayed a still-repressive society that denied people real freedom and individuality. The acid-tongued critic H. L. Mencken, editor of the magazine the *American Mercury,* condemned a provincial and parochial culture still dominated by the "booboisie" and its rural values.

At the same time, other American artists and intellectuals feared that their country had changed too much. Although excited by the potential of the machine, they criticized the routinized work and superficial pleasures of modern life. In his 1922 novel *Babbitt,* Sinclair Lewis satirized a midwestern Republican businessman whose consumerism made him a conformist, not an individualist. F. Scott Fitzgerald, in such fiction as *This Side of Paradise* (1920) and *The Great Gatsby* (1925), conveyed the sense of loss and emptiness in the lives of fashionable "flaming youth" in the "Jazz Age."

From a different angle, 12 southern intellectuals, including Allen Tate, Robert Penn Warren, Donald Davidson, and John Crowe Ransom, attacked the modern culture in *I'll Take My Stand: The South and the Agrarian Tradition* (1930). Their essays offered a spirited defense of the rural, traditional culture and lamented an industrial consumer society that demeaned work and exalted individualism.

The artists and intellectuals did not set off a mass rebellion against modern culture, but they did express the ambivalence and uneasiness many people felt. In different and contradictory ways, artists and intellectuals laid out an agenda for Americans as they came to terms with modern, consumer society in the decades to come.

Fundamentalist Christians and "Old-Time Religion"

For many Americans of faith, the rapid growth of the modern culture promoted a sense of profound and unsettling change. "The world has been convulsed," declared *Presbyterian Magazine.* "The most settled principles and laws of society have been attacked." The new culture was troubling because it was so secular. American society seemed to define life in terms of material satisfaction rather than spiritual commitment. Many Protestants, feeling that their own churches had betrayed them, resented the influence of liberal Protestants who had tried to accommodate their faith to the methods and discoveries of science and scholarship.

Fundamentalists, or opponents of liberalism, took their name from *The Fundamentals,* a series of essays by conservative Protestant theologians that appeared beginning in 1909. Fundamentalists emerged all around the country, but they were strongest in rural areas and in the South and West. By the end of World War I, fundamentalists dominated the Southern Baptist Convention and were fighting liberals for control of the northern churches.

Fundamentalists rejected liberalism above all for its willingness to question the historical truth of the Bible. The fundamentalist movement urged people to return to biblical, patriarchal, and denominational authority, to what came to be called "old-time religion."

The high point in the fundamentalist-liberal battle came in a courtroom in Tennessee in 1925. That year, a high-school biology teacher, John Scopes, defied a new state law banning the teaching of "any theory that denies the story of the divine creation of man as taught in the Bible, and that teaches instead that man has descended from a lower order of animals." Scopes's trial became a national media event. The chief lawyer for the prosecution was William Jennings Bryan, the former Democratic presidential candidate and secretary of state who had become a leading crusader for fundamentalism. While Bryan was a longtime champion of rural America, Scopes's attorneys—Clarence Darrow and Dudley Field Malone—represented the city and modern culture. (Malone had helped to finance Gertrude Ederle's swim across the English Channel.) In a dramatic confrontation, Darrow called Bryan to the stand and forced him to concede that the Bible might not be literally accurate. Although Scopes was convicted and fined, the fundamentalists lost some credibility and Bryan died soon after. In the next several years, other southern and western states passed antievolution laws, but similar measures failed in the more urbanized Northeast.

The Scopes trial did not end the war between fundamentalism and liberalism. Fundamentalists were numerous. Their hostility to liberal Protestantism and modern culture would affect American life for decades to come.

Nativists and Immigration Restriction

While fundamentalist Christianity sought a return to old-time religion, a resurgent nativist movement wanted to go back to an earlier, supposedly more homogenous America. As mass migration from Europe to the United States resumed after World War I, nativist feeling revived among Americans from western European backgrounds. Thanks to the Russian Revolution and the domestic Red Scare, they associated immigrants with anarchism and radicalism and derided southern and eastern Europeans as inferior races that would weaken the nation.

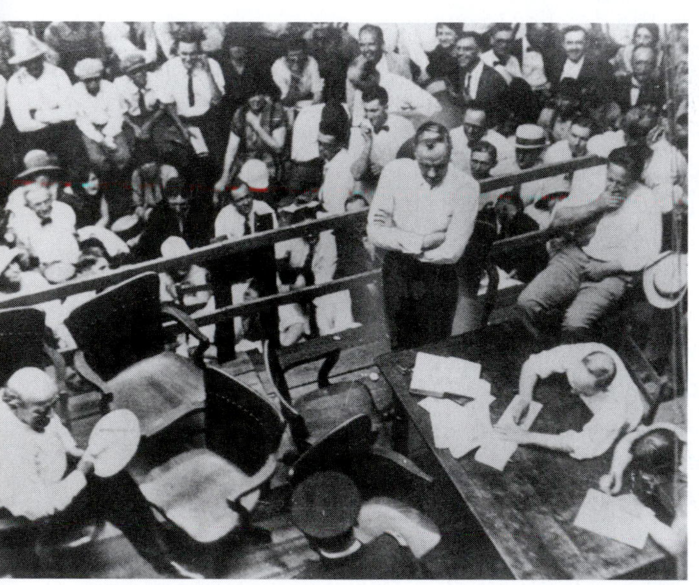

Scopes Trial The battle between liberalism and fundamentalism: Clarence Darrow, lawyer for John Scopes in his 1925 trial for teaching evolution, confronts chief prosecutor William Jennings Bryan on the witness stand.

Responding in 1921, Congress overwhelmingly passed a law temporarily limiting the annual immigration from any European country to 3 percent of the number of its immigrants who had been living in the United States in 1910. This quota sharply reduced the number of new immigrants from southern and eastern Europe, but nativists wanted even tougher action. Congress responded with the National Origins Act of 1924. This limited the annual intake from a European country to 2 percent of the number of its immigrants living in the United States in 1890—a time when there were few southern and eastern Europeans in America. The act also excluded Japanese immigrants altogether. The legislation had the desired effect: immigration fell from 805,000 arrivals in 1921 to 280,000 in 1929 (see Table 23–2).

The Rebirth of the Ku Klux Klan

Table 23–2 The Impact of Nativism: Immigration, 1921–1929

	Arrivals (in thousands)		
Origin	**1921**	**1925**	**1929**
Eastern Europe and Poland	138	10	14
Southern Europe	299	8	22
Asia	25	4	4
Mexico	31	33	40
Total	805	294	280

Historical Statistics of the United States, (Cambridge: Cambridge University Press), I, 401. Itemized groups do not add up to totals.

Nativism and fundamentalism helped spur another challenge to the new cultural order of the 1920s. In 1915, the Ku Klux Klan, the vigilante group that had terrorized African Americans in the South during Reconstruction, was reborn in a ceremony on Stone Mountain, Georgia, and it enjoyed explosive growth after World War I. The "Invisible Empire" borrowed the rituals of the nineteenth-century Klan, including its costume of white robes and hoods and its symbol of a burning cross. Like the old Klan, the twentieth-century version was driven by a racist hatred of African Americans, but the new Klan took on new targets, including Jews, Roman Catholics, immigrants, religious liberalism, and change in general.

The Invisible Empire condemned modern culture, charging that the nation now valued "money above manhood." Klan rallies rang with denunciations of big business. Above all, the Klan condemned pleasure, "the god of the young people of America." The Klan was hostile to the new gender ideals, to birth control and freer sexuality, and to the independence of youth. Klansmen and Klanswomen yearned for an earlier America in which white Protestant males had power over women, youth, and other groups and had nothing to fear from big business.

The Klan's tactics were a blend of old and new. Seeing themselves as an army of secret vigilantes, some Klan members supported the age-old tactics of moral regulation—intimidation, flogging, and sometimes lynching—in order to scare people into good behavior. At the same time, much of the Invisible Empire repudiated violence and used the latest advertising techniques to boost its membership.

For several years, the Klan proved extraordinarily successful. Despite its extremist views, the Invisible Empire had a mainstream membership, flourishing in every region, in cities as well as the countryside. At its peak, the organization enrolled perhaps 3 to 5 million secret members. Because so many politicians sympathized with the Klan or feared its power, the organization had considerable political influence. Working with both major parties, the order helped to elect governors, senators, and other officials.

KKK Parade, August 19, 1925 Members of the Ku Klux Klan marching down Pennsylvania Avenue in Washington, DC, to celebrate the organization and its defense of "traditional" values.

At the height of its power, however, the Invisible Empire collapsed under the weight of scandal. The Klan seemed lawless and hypocritical when its leaders were revealed to be caught up in financial scandal, alcohol, pornography, adultery, kidnapping, and murder. Most people realized they had nothing to fear from such Klan targets as Communists, unions, and Jews. Millions of Americans, however uneasy about the new culture, had no desire to support prejudice, lawbreaking, and violence in a futile attempt to go back to the past. The Klan's membership dropped precipitously in the late 1920s.

Mexican Americans

Despite the activities of immigration restrictionists and the Klan, the United States became in some ways more diverse than ever. Perhaps a million to a million and a half Mexicans entered the United States legally or surreptitiously between 1890 and 1929. Many left to avoid the upheaval of the Mexican Revolution of 1910 (see Chapter 22) and to escape the agricultural transformation that made it difficult for the rural poor to earn a living off the land. Meanwhile, the dynamic U.S. economy created opportunities for impoverished Mexican immigrants. Ironically, the restrictionist immigration legislation of the 1920s helped ensure that Mexicans would find work in the United States. Unable to get enough European or Asian workers, employers turned eagerly to Mexico as a source of cheap seasonal labor. In particular the Southwest's rapidly developing economy needed Mexican workers for mines, railroads, construction gangs, and, above all, farms.

Mexican American Workmen Laborers pause for the camera while making adobe bricks at the Casa Verdugo, Glendale, California, ca. 1920.

Like a large number of immigrants from Europe, many Mexican migrants did not plan to stay in the United States. They traveled back and forth to their homeland, or returned permanently. Gradually, however, many chose to stay as they developed economic and family ties in the United States. The National Origins Act, which made it costly, time consuming, and often humiliating for Mexicans to cross the border, also encouraged migrants to remain in the United States. As a result, the official Mexican population of the United States rose from 103,000 in 1900 to 478,000 by 1920. At the turn of the century, the majority of immigrants lived in Texas and Arizona, but California, with its booming agricultural economy, rapidly became the center of the Mexican population. The city of Los Angeles, growing phenomenally in the early twentieth century, attracted perhaps 190,000 Mexicans by 1930.

Mexican immigrants, like so many other ethnic groups in the United States, wrestled with complex questions about their national identity. Were they still Mexicans or had they become Americans or some unique combination of the two nationalities? In varying degrees, the migrants clung to their old national identities and adapted to their new home.

Mexican Americans, eager to hold onto the advantages they had won by birth and longtime residence in the United States, feared that the newcomers would compete for jobs and cause native-born whites to denigrate all Mexicans alike. The immigrants, in turn, often derided Mexican Americans as *pochos*—bleached or faded people—who had lost their true Mexican identity.

Nevertheless, ethnic Mexicans created a distinctive culture in the United States. For all their differences, they shared a sense of common cultural origins and common challenges. In a white-dominated society, they saw themselves as *La Raza*—The Race—set apart by heritage and skin color.

Poverty and discrimination also contributed to a sense of common Mexican American identity. In many towns and cities, ethnic Mexicans were effectively segregated in certain neighborhoods—*barrios*—in poor conditions. Largely ignored by corporations marketing goods nationwide, Mexican Americans supported their own businesses, listened to their own Spanish-language radio programs, and bought records made by their own musicians. Anglo-American prejudice also tended to drive Mexicans together. Many whites stereotyped them as a lazy and shiftless race who would take jobs from native-born workers and who could not be assimilated into American life and culture. Still other white Americans, drawing on the reform techniques of the Progressive Era, wanted to "Americanize" ethnic Mexicans by teaching them English and middle-class values and homemaking practices.

Their sense of common identity encouraged Mexican Americans to struggle for economic progress and equal rights. In 1928, farm workers in California created La Unión de Trabajadores del Valle Imperial (Imperial Valley Workers Union) in a successful fight for higher wages. A year later, Mexican American businessmen and professionals in Texas formed the League of United Latin American Citizens (LULAC) in Texas.

African Americans and the "New Negro"

Like Mexican Americans, African Americans found the new cultural terrain of the United States appealing but unsatisfying. They enjoyed and helped to create the new culture, but it did little to alter discrimination against blacks. In both South and North, African Americans still lived with economic and political inequality.

While discrimination had not changed, many African Americans insisted that they had. The decade that talked about the "New Woman" also talked about the "New Negro." The term went back to the late nineteenth century; in 1900, Booker T. Washington titled one of his books *A New Negro for a New Century*. By the 1920s, the increased use of "New Negro" reflected a fresh sense of freedom as African Americans left the southern countryside for cities. It was also the product of frustration as African Americans encountered inequality along with opportunity in urban areas. The "New Negro" was militant and assertive in the face of mistreatment by whites. "The time for cringing is over," said an African American newspaper.

The "New Negro" was also defined by a profound sense of racial difference. Applauding the distinctiveness of their life and culture, African Americans spurred the Harlem Renaissance. Harlem, the section of upper Manhattan in New York where many African Americans had moved since the turn of the century, became a center of artistic and intellectual creativity. Novelists such as Zora Neale Hurston, Jessie Fauset,

Claude McKay, Jean Toomer, and Dorothy West; poets such as Langston Hughes, Sterling Brown, and Countee Cullen; and artists such as Aaron Douglas and Augusta Savage produced a new birth of African American creativity. In different ways, these women and men explored and celebrated the nature of American blackness in 1920s America and its origins in Africa.

The militance of the "New Negro" was reflected in the development of the NAACP, which turned increasingly to African American leadership. The organization's key figure, W. E. B. DuBois, became more critical of whites and more determined that white-dominated nations should return Africa to African control. The NAACP also pushed the cause of African American civil rights more aggressively and attacked the white primary system that denied African Americans any say in the dominant Democratic Party organizations of the South. The NAACP continued a longtime antilynching campaign, which bore fruit in the 1920s, as southern whites were increasingly embarrassed by vigilante justice.

For a time, the NAACP's efforts were overshadowed by the crusades of Marcus Garvey. A Jamaican immigrant to New York City, Garvey founded the Universal Negro Improvement Association (UNIA), which became the largest African American activist organization of the 1920s. Less interested in political rights and integration, Garvey focused on African American pride and self-help and on Africa. He exalted "a new Negro who stands erect, conscious of his manhood rights and fully determined to preserve them at all times." So Garvey urged African Americans to develop their own businesses and thus become economically self-sufficient. Like DuBois, he insisted that the imperial powers give up their colonial control of the African continent. Sure that blacks could never find equality in a white-dominated nation, Garvey believed African Americans should return to Africa.

While the NAACP attracted mostly middle-class members, UNIA developed a vast following among the African American working class. In 1919, Garvey launched an economic self-help project, the Black Star Line, which, he promised, would buy ships and transport passengers and cargo from the United States to the West Indies, Central America, and Africa. Many of his followers invested in the Black Star Line, but it collapsed due to mismanagement. Garvey himself was indicted for mail fraud in connection with the project. By the end of the decade, federal authorities had deported him to Jamaica, and the UNIA had lost its mass following.

African American Activism Marcus Garvey presides at the 1922 UNIA convention, Liberty Hall, New York City.

As the fate of the UNIA suggested, militance could be costly for African Americans. The NAACP also saw its membership drop dramatically during the decade. Nevertheless, African Americans' struggles laid the groundwork for more successful struggles in the future.

A "New Era" in Politics and Government

The economic and cultural transformations of the 1920s shaped American democracy in profound but contradictory ways. Modern culture helped empower ordinary people and transform the style of politics. But organized groups—big business above all—affected public life more decisively. Reflecting this balance of power, a succession of conservative Republican presidents monopolized the White House during the decade. In a decade so fascinated by all things "new," the Republicans inevitably claimed to represent a "New Era" in American politics and government. But in fact, the Republican ascendancy of the 1920s mostly meant the return of an older vision centered on minimalist government, individualism, and a less internationalist foreign policy. The mix of old ideology and new political styles failed to galvanize the democratic system in a prosperous time: the 1920s became an age of apathy and low voter turnout.

> **Men do not live by bread alone. Nor is individualism merely a stimulus to production and the road to liberty; it alone admits the universal divine inspiration of every human soul.**
>
> HERBERT HOOVER, *American Individualism*, 1922

The Modern Political System

In some ways, the cultural changes of the 1920s stimulated equality. The celebration of feats such as Ederle's Channel crossing reinforced the idea that the individual could make a difference in politics, too. The emphasis on female freedom and empowerment encouraged women to exercise their newly won right to vote.

The modern culture also hastened the emergence of a political style taking shape since the late nineteenth century. Copying big business, politicians used advertising to appeal to the electorate. In the Gilded Age, voters had been active participants, joining clubs and marching in parades during campaigns. Now, citizens were political consumers choosing candidates just as they chose mouthwash or automobiles.

The shift to advertising was necessary, too, because the major parties' control over the media had dramatically decreased. Traditionally partisan, many newspapers now took a more independent stand. The new radio stations and movie theaters had no political affiliations at all. With the decline of intense partisanship, political ad campaigns focused more on the personality and activities of individual candidates than on the parties themselves.

Economic and cultural change also benefited big business and other organized groups. In Washington, Congress was besieged by lobbyists from corporations, business groups, professional organizations, and single-issue pressure groups such as the Anti-Saloon League. Organizations employed a political style that emphasized the use of supposedly objective, nonpartisan facts to educate legislators and voters. Unorganized Americans had less chance of influencing the political process.

The new, less partisan politics did a poor job of mobilizing voters on election day. Nationwide, voter turnout fell from 79 percent for the presidential election of 1896 to just 49 percent in 1920 and 1924. A number of factors accounted for this drop-off: African Americans in the South had been effectively disfranchised, and newly enfranchised women were less likely to vote than men, but white male turnout dropped dramatically, too.

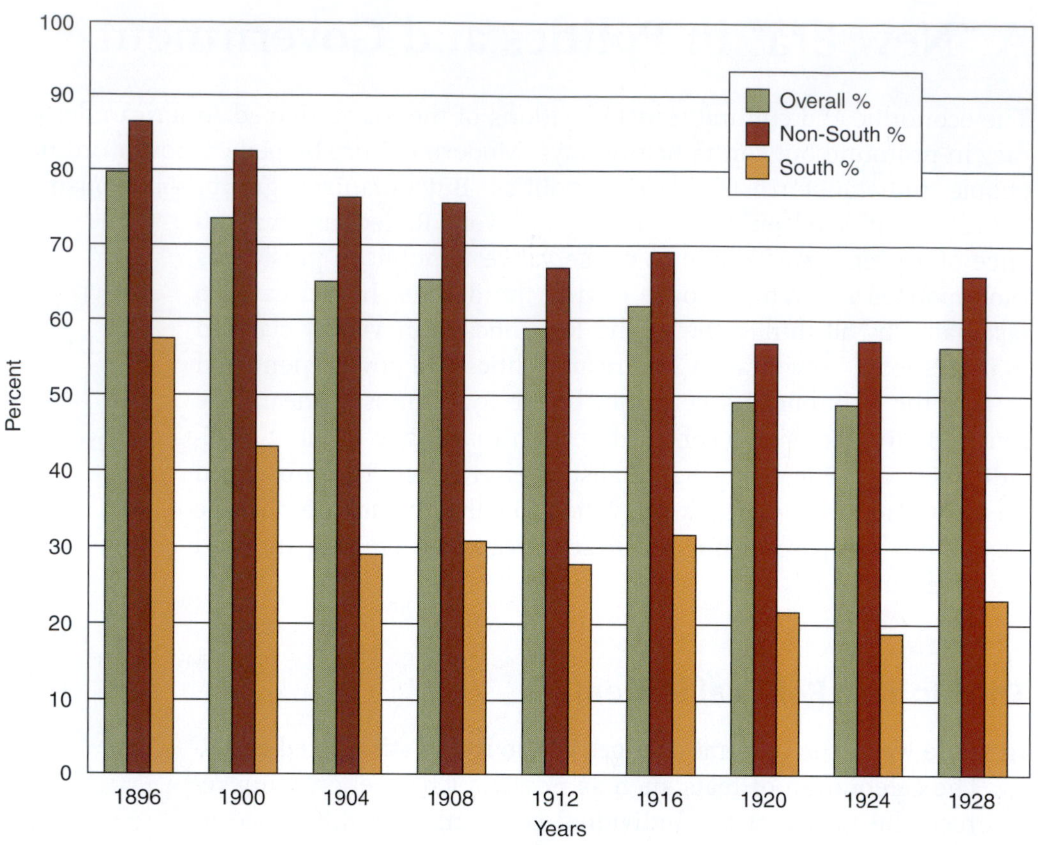

Figure 23–1 Declining Voter Turnout, 1896 to 1928 Why was turnout so much lower in the South?

The Republican Ascendancy

The chief beneficiaries of the new politics were the Republicans. Determined to win back the White House in 1920, the Republican Party chose an uncontroversial, conservative ticket. Handsome and charismatic, presidential nominee Warren G. Harding of Ohio had accomplished little during a term in the Senate. His running mate, Governor Calvin Coolidge of Massachusetts, was best known for his firm stance against a strike by the Boston police the year before.

The Republican ticket was not imposing, but neither was the opposition. The Democratic presidential nominee, Governor James M. Cox of Ohio, was saddled with the unpopularity of the Woodrow Wilson administration. His running mate, Franklin Roosevelt of New York, was a little-known cousin of former president Theodore Roosevelt who had served as assistant secretary of the navy.

While the Democrats ran an ineffective campaign, the Republicans made excellent use of advertising. And Harding neatly appealed to the reaction against Wilson's activist government, offering a return to "normalcy" after the progressive innovations that had disrupted American society during and after the war.

Harding won a huge victory with 60.3 percent of the popular vote, a new record; he won 37 states for a total of 404 electoral votes. The Republican Party substantially increased its majorities in the House and the Senate.

The Harding administration was plagued by revelations of fraud and corruption, some involving the so-called Ohio Gang, political cronies from Harding's home state. The director of the Veterans' Bureau, caught making fraudulent deals with federal property, went to prison. One of the Ohio Gang, fearing exposure of the group's influence-peddling schemes, committed suicide in 1923. The revelations shook the president, who complained about "my damn friends, my God-damn friends."

Harding died suddenly of a misdiagnosed heart attack in August 1923, but the scandals continued. Congressional hearings revealed that former secretary of the interior Albert B. Fall had apparently accepted bribes in return for leasing U.S. Navy oil reserves at Teapot Dome, Wyoming, and Elk Hills, California. Teapot Dome, as the scandal came to be called, eventually earned Fall a fine and a jail term. In 1924, another member of Harding's cabinet, Attorney General Harry Daugherty, resigned because of his role in the Ohio Gang.

The Teapot Dome Scandal The revelations of governmental corruption threatened to roll over politicians of both parties in 1923 and 1924.

The parade of scandals damaged the reputation of the dead president, but they did not seriously harm his party or his successor, Calvin Coolidge. The former vice president—so reserved in public that he was called "Silent Cal"—proved well suited to the political moment. The picture of rectitude, Coolidge restored public confidence in the presidency after the Harding scandals.

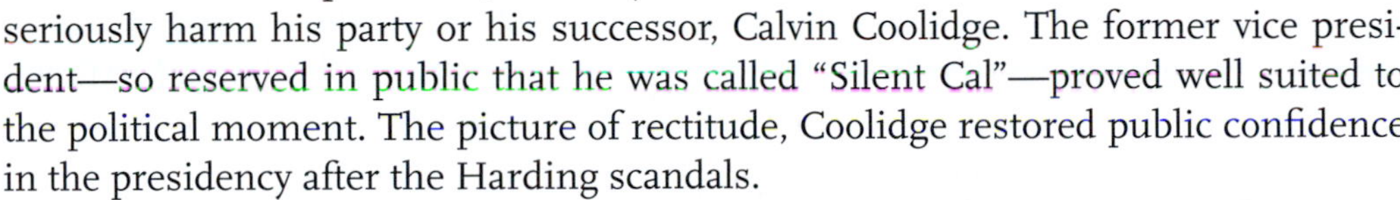

In 1924, Coolidge easily won the presidency in his own right against the Democrat John W. Davis, a colorless, conservative corporate lawyer from West Virginia, and the standard-bearer of the new Progressive Party, Senator Robert M. La Follette of Wisconsin. The choice, insisted Republicans, was either "Coolidge or Chaos." Holding onto the White House and to their majorities in Congress, the Republicans continued their ascendancy.

The Politics of Individualism

In office, the Republicans practiced the politics of individualism. Eager to serve big business, they denounced the activist, progressive state and called instead for less government and more individual freedom. Coolidge declared that "the chief business of the American people is business." Harding bluntly summed up the Republican prescription for America: "Less Government in Business and More Business in Government."

Despite such slogans, Republicans sometimes used government power to spur economic development. The Federal Highway Act of 1921 provided federal matching grants to improve the nation's roads, and the Fordney-McCumber Tariff of 1922 restored high taxes on imports to shelter American producers from foreign competition.

These measures were exceptions, however. Above all, the Harding and Coolidge administrations called for "economy"—reduced government spending and lower taxes. The Republicans also condemned budget deficits and pledged to reduce the national debt; they succeeded on all counts. Federal expenditures dropped from $6.4 billion in 1920 to $3.1 billion in 1929. Congress repeatedly cut income and other taxes, but the federal government still produced annual budget surpluses and reduced its debt.

Republicans' commitment to minimal government was obvious in their lax enforcement of Progressive Era legislation. During the Harding and Coolidge administrations, the federal government made only weak attempts to carry out Prohibition. Harding himself kept a private stock of liquor in the White House. The Republicans also allowed the regulatory commissions of the Gilded Age and the Progressive Era to atrophy. The Interstate Commerce Commission (ICC) and the Federal Trade Commission (FTC) were effectively controlled by the businesses they were supposed to regulate.

Herbert Hoover, the secretary of commerce in both the Harding and Coolidge administrations, had a more activist view of the government's role in the economy than either of his bosses. Trained as an engineer, Hoover had become a national hero by supervising the government's effort to relieve famine in Europe during and after World War I. Sensitive to business interests, Hoover used the Commerce Department to promote "associationalism"—organized cooperation among business trade groups. However, businessmen did not trust one another enough to make voluntary cooperation effective, and Hoover did not advocate federal action to force them to cooperate. Afraid of too much government, Hoover believed above all in what he called "American individualism."

Republican Foreign Policy

After America's intense involvement in international affairs during World War I, the 1920s were a period of relative withdrawal. No crisis thrust foreign policy to the center of American life. Nevertheless, the United States, the world's greatest economic power, played an active role around the globe.

The aftermath of World War I, like other postwar periods, found Americans eager to reduce the size of the military and to avoid new conflict. Horrified by the "Great War," women's groups and religious organizations joined a surging international peace movement. Activists' calls for disarmament helped push the Harding administration to organize the Washington Naval Conference of 1921–1922. In the first international arms-reduction accord, the United States, Great Britain, and Japan agreed to scrap some of their largest ships and, along with France and Italy, promised to limit the tonnage of their existing large ships, abandon gas warfare, and restrict submarine warfare.

The peace movement was less successful in its second goal, outlawing war. In 1928, the United States and 14 other countries signed the Kellogg-Briand Pact foreswearing war as an instrument of national policy. Enthusiastically received in the United States and elsewhere, the measure nevertheless contained no effective mechanism to stop a nation from going to war. U.S. membership in a world court, the third major goal of the peace movement, was not achieved in the 1920s. Too many Americans believed that the court, like the League of Nations, would undermine U.S. sovereignty.

While Americans debated membership in the court, the U.S. economy became increasingly bound up in the world economy. American investment grew substantially overseas during the 1920s, American bankers made major loans around the world, and Ford and other American companies exported their products around the world. More U.S. corporations became multinational firms by building plants overseas.

The growth of American economic activity abroad complicated the foreign policy priorities of the Harding and Coolidge administrations. In the 1920s, the United States had more interests than ever to protect overseas, but the American people were wary of government action that might lead to war. Many Americans were also

AMERICA AND THE WORLD

>> "Jazz-band partout!"

Even as political leaders pulled back from an activist foreign policy, American culture spread across the world in new ways. The rapid diffusion of jazz music epitomized the powerful global impact of the new, modern culture emerging in the United States. As early as 1920, a popular French song proclaimed *"Jazz-band partout!"*—"Jazz band everywhere!": "They're jazz bands by day, by night/ They're jazz bands everywhere/ It's all the rage in Paris, it makes men crazy."

Jazz itself was the product of globalization: the new music resulted from the long-term encounter between the musical cultures that Europeans and Africans had brought to the Americas. As World War I ended, jazz became, in turn, an agent of U.S. musical globalization. African American musicians had been part of the American army sent to France in 1917. The pioneering "Hell Fighters" band of the 369th Infantry Regiment, led by the orchestra leader Lt. James Reese Europe, helped introduce the French to the new music. After the war, some of his musicians returned to Europe. Meanwhile, American jazz groups began to tour overseas. Both the white musicians of the Original Dixieland Jazz Band and the African American musicians of Will Marion Cook's Southern Syncopated Orchestra visited England in 1919. Sam Wooding's band for the Chocolate Kiddies revue began an extended tour in 1925 that took African American jazz to Germany, Scandinavia, Spain, the USSR, and South America. Meanwhile, phonograph records conveyed the excitement of this swinging, hot music throughout the world.

The new sounds from America had a profound but complicated impact on listeners overseas. Noble Sissle, one of James Reese Europe's musicians, reported the dramatic effect of a jazz "spasm" at a Hell Fighters concert in France: "The audience could stand it no longer; the 'jazz germ' hit them and it seemed to find the vital spot, loosening all muscles and causing what is known in America as an 'eagle rocking fit. . . .'" Jazz seemed at once primitive and modern to the French. On one hand, it conjured up fantasies about African American sensuality and the mysteriousness of the African jungle. On the other, jazz conveyed the excitement of modern life in the industrial age. "The jazz band is the panting of the machine, the trepidation of the automobile. . . ." said a French critic. Above all, jazz seemed quintessentially American to its French audience. The music, a French writer observed, "has helped us finally to discover and to understand the United States." And so French audiences responded enthusiastically. "All through France, the same thing happened," Noble Sissle happily observed. "Then I was . . . satisfied that American music would one day be the world's music."

That was a worrisome prospect for some French musicians and writers. "[D]oes the whole world," one complained, "have to be American?" A number of French creative artists feared that jazz would simply sweep French music away: the French song, the *chanson,* would no longer be heard in the cafes and concert halls of France. "The violins have left and jazz is king!" lamented a French poet. "The French *chanson* is truly very sick . . . could it die?" But the *chanson* did not die: jazz did not simply Americanize France. Just as white and black Americans had heard and absorbed each other's music for generations, so French musicians accommodated, modified, and reinterpreted American jazz. By the mid-1930s, the greatest jazz-guitar player in the world was a French Gypsy, Django Reinhardt, whose many records incorporated French popular music as well as the distinctive, traditional sounds of the Gypsies.

Jazz was indeed *partout*. The music was one sign of the internationalization of the new American culture in the 1920s. It was a reminder, too, that the United States could not simply remake the world in its own image, musical and otherwise.

American Pianist Eubie Blake (1883–1983) and singer Noble Sissle (1889–1975), who helped bring jazz, the new American music, to Europe.

"NO MORE WAR" A meeting of the Washington State branch of the Women's International League for Peace and Freedom, 1922.

uneasy about imperialism, the nation's continuing military role in its own possessions and in supposedly sovereign nations.

In these circumstances, the Harding and Coolidge administrations tried to pull back from some of the imperial commitments made by presidents Taft and Wilson in the 1910s. The U.S. Marines withdrew from the Dominican Republic in 1924. They also withdrew from Nicaragua in 1925 but returned the next year when the country became politically unstable.

The Harding and Coolidge administrations also attempted to promote a stable world in which American business would thrive. During the 1920s, the United States was involved in negotiations to increase Chinese sovereignty and thereby reduce the chances of conflict in Asia. The United States also tried to stabilize Europe in the years after World War I. With the quiet approval of Republican presidents, American businessmen intervened twice to help resolve the controversial issue of how much Germany should be expected to pay in reparation to the Allies.

The "New Era" in Politics Meets the New Culture of Pleasure President Warren G. Harding and New York Yankees slugger Babe Ruth at a ball game in Yankee Stadium, 1923

Extending the "New Era"

The Republicans' cautious foreign and domestic policies proved popular. There was no serious challenge to the Republican ascendancy as the decade came to a close. In fact, the backlash against modern culture hurt the Democrats more than the Republicans. The Democratic Party depended on support not only from nativists, fundamentalists, and Klansmen, but also from their frequent targets—urban Catholics and Jews. The antagonism among these constituencies helped doom the Democrats' chances in the 1924 and 1928 elections.

In 1928, the Democrats nominated Al Smith, the governor of New York, for president. The first Irish Catholic presidential nominee of a major party, Smith displeased fundamentalists and nativists. Moreover, his brassy, urban style—his campaign theme song was "The Sidewalks of New York"—alienated many rural Americans. Smith represented a new generation of urban, ethnic Democrats who were ready to use activist government to deal with social and economic problems. Their brand of urban liberalism would be influential in later years, but Smith's politics and background could not galvanize a majority of voters in 1928.

Meanwhile, Herbert Hoover, the Republican nominee, polled 58.2 percent of the popular vote and carried 40 states for a total of 444 electoral votes—the Republicans' largest electoral triumph of the decade. Moreover, the Republicans increased their majorities in both the House and the Senate. "The New Era" would continue.

Candidate (Party)	Electoral Vote (%)	Popular Vote (%)
Hoover (Republican)	444 (82%)	21,391,993 (58%)
Smith (Democratic)	87 (17%)	15,016,169 (41%)
Thomas (Socialist)		267,835 (1%)
Minor parties		62,890 (-)

Map 23–1 The Election of 1928 Herbert Hoover's landslide victory extends the Republican "New Era."

Conclusion

The Republicans' victory in 1928 underscored the triumph of modern culture. Just as Gertrude Ederle overcame the tides in the English Channel, the "New Era" swept past the challenges of nativists, fundamentalists, and Klansmen . As Hoover prepared to take over the White House, the appeal of the modern culture, rooted in the needs of the industrial economy, appeared undeniable. It offered a renewed sense of individual worth and possibility. It promised new freedom to women and youth. It held out an alluring vision of material pleasures—a life devoted to leisure and consumption—to all Americans.

Nevertheless, the modern culture and its Republican defenders were vulnerable. The political "New Era" of the 1920s was especially dependent on the state of the economy. Perhaps more than ever before in American history, the nation's dominant value system equated human happiness with the capacity to pay for pleasures. What would happen if Americans lost their jobs and their purchasing power? The new culture and the "New Era" had survived the dissent of alienated and excluded Americans in the 1920s. It would not survive the sudden end of prosperity.

Further Readings

Susan Currell, *American Culture in the 1920s* (2009). A concise introduction to the emerging modern culture of the 1920s.

David Greenberg, *Calvin Coolidge* (2006). A brief, positive assessment of this Republican president.

Thomas Hine, *The Rise and Fall of the American Teenager* (2000). A useful, wide-ranging account.

Edward J. Larson, *Summer for the Gods: The Scopes Trial and America's Continuing Debate over Science and Religion* (1997). A vivid narrative account of the battle over evolution in Tennessee.

Jackson Lears, *Fables of Abundance: A Cultural History of Advertising in America* (1994). Puts the developments of the 1920s in broader context.

Robert S. Lynd and Helen Merrell Lynd, *Middletown: A Study in Contemporary American Culture* (1929). This pioneering sociological study of Muncie, Indiana, charts the spread of modern culture in an American community.

Nancy MacLean, *Ku Klux Klan: The Making of the Second Ku Klux Klan* (1994). Portrays the Klansmen's hostility to the modern culture.

David Nasaw, *Going Out: The Rise and Fall of Public Amusements* (1993). The evolution of movies, sports, and other amusements that helped to constitute the consumer culture of the 1920s.

George Sánchez, *Becoming Mexican American: Ethnicity, Culture, and Identity in Chicano Los Angeles, 1900–1945* (1993). A sensitive exploration of the Mexican encounter with life in the United States.

Who, What?

Henry Ford 761
Bruce Barton 767
Margaret Sanger 770
John Scopes 776
Marcus Garvey 780
Calvin Coolidge 782
Warren G. Harding 782
Herbert Hoover 784
Fordism 761
New Woman 770-71
Fundamentalism 775
New Negro 779
New Era 781

Review Questions

1. What caused the transformation of the industrial economy in the 1910s and 1920s? How did that transformation benefit or harm different economic groups such as big business, workers, and farmers?
2. Why did the modern culture emerge in the 1920s and not before?
3. How did views of sexuality, gender, family, and youth change in the 1920s? Why was individualism so important to the modern culture?

>> Timeline >>

▼ 1913
Introduction of assembly line at Ford Motor Company

▼ 1918
End of World War I

▼ 1919
Black Star Line founded by Marcus Garvey
Original Dixieland Jazz Band and Will Marion Cook's Southern Syncopated Orchestra bring jazz to England

▼ 1920
Commercial radio broadcasting
Warren G. Harding elected president

▼ 1922
Fordney-McCumber Tariff
Sinclair Lewis, *Babbitt*

▼ 1923
Teapot Dome scandal
Calvin Coolidge succeeds Harding as president

▼ 1924
National Origins Act

4. Why was there such a widespread backlash against the modern culture of the 1920s? Why did the backlash fail?
5. Why did the Republican Party dominate the emerging political system of the 1920s? How did Republican policies reflect the economic and cultural changes of the decade?
6. Did the United States become more or less democratic a nation in the 1920s?
7. How would the emergence of consumer culture shape the United States beyond the 1920s?

Websites

Emergence of Advertising in America, 1850–1920 (http://library.duke.edu/digitalcollections/eaa/) is a huge searchable database of advertisements and pamphlets.

A Guide to Harlem Renaissance Materials, from the Library of Congress (http://www.loc.gov/rr/program/bib/harlem/harlem.html), provides a jumping-off point to a variety of collections about African American life and culture.

The Margaret Sanger Papers Project of New York University (http://www.nyu.edu/projects/sanger/) offers a selection of the birth control advocate's writings and speeches.

Prosperity and Thrift: The Coolidge Era and the Consumer Economy, an American Memory project of the Library of Congress (http://memory.loc.gov/ammem/coolhtml/coolhome.html), is an outstanding multimedia collection on politics and society in the 1920s.

The Red Hot Jazz Archive (http://www.redhotjazz.com/) offers a history and plenty of examples of the new music of the 1920s.

Women Working, 1800–1930, a project of the Harvard University Library Open Collections program (http://ocp.hul.harvard.edu/ww/), includes many items from the 1920s among its digitized books, pamphlets, photographs, and other materials.

For further review materials and resource information, please visit www.oup.com/us/ofthepeople

▼ **1925**
Founding of the Brotherhood of Sleeping Car Porters
Bruce Barton, *The Man Nobody Knows*
Scopes trial

▼ **1926**
Gertrude Ederle's swim across the English Channel

▼ **1927**
Charles Lindbergh's solo transatlantic flight

▼ **1928**
Kellogg-Briand Pact
Herbert Hoover elected president

▼ **1929**
Stock market crash

▼ **1932**
Franklin Roosevelt elected president

CHAPTER 24

Common Threads 

>> Contrast government's response to the Depression against its actions in earlier "panics" in 1893 and 1877.

>> How did Franklin D. Roosevelt's Democratic Party differ from the one that nominated William Jennings Bryan or Woodrow Wilson?

>> How did the New Deal redefine what it meant to be "liberal" or "conservative"?

A Great Depression and a New Deal 1929–1940

AMERICAN PORTRAIT

>> Margaret Mitchell

Margaret Mitchell wrote her first and only book, *Gone with the Wind,* to earn extra money, and she was more than a little surprised when it became a runaway best seller as soon as it was published in June 1936. Stores sold out before the first shipments arrived. At a bookstore appearance fans tore buttons from Mitchell's coat to keep as souvenirs, and crowds gathered outside her Atlanta apartment. In four days, almost 1,200 letters from admiring readers arrived.

Most wrote to tell Mitchell how her story had renewed their faith in themselves. For an urban, industrial society in the depths of the century's worst economic crisis, *Gone with the Wind* conjured up a rural past in which Americans struggled and triumphed. Mitchell's fiercely determined heroine, Scarlett O'Hara, survived the collapse of her world in the Civil War through sheer force of will. "I'm going to live through this," Scarlett resolved at her lowest point, "and when it's over, I'm never going to be hungry again." Her eventual triumph reaffirmed the values of self-reliance and individualism at a time when many Americans wondered if those values still mattered.

In 1936 the Great Depression—the worst economic collapse in United States history—was nearly seven years old. The stock market crash in October 1929 preceded an uninterrupted four-year decline in nearly every sector of the economy. On farms across America hard work was rewarded with failure and poverty. In cities and towns there was little work to be found. Since the time of Andrew Jackson, Americans had grown to feel that democracy rested on shared values of individualism, private property, and a capitalist market economy. Now, with millions unemployed, these principles, and the relationship between them, were openly questioned. Politicians had few answers, and Americans felt alone and vulnerable.

The popularity of *Gone with the Wind* suggests that even in the depths of the Depression Americans still clung to the promise of individual opportunity. "We Americans have all been taught, from childhood, that it is a sort of moral obligation for each of us to rise, to get up in the world," the writer Sherwood Anderson explained. Steeped in the precepts of individualism, impoverished Americans blamed themselves for the economy's failure. "It's my own fault," explained a wheat farmer who worked hard his whole life only to lose his farm and move in with relatives. "I wasn't smart enough." Everywhere the theme of individual responsibility was reinforced. *Gone with the Wind* echoed advice books, newspapers and magazines, radio shows and movies that encouraged Americans to confront the Great Depression by working harder than ever. "In the final analysis," one advertisement from 1932 declared, "we are responsible for our own defeats and our own victories."

While millions of Americans were heartened by Scarlett's old-fashioned individualism, other readers turned to updated versions of American values. Atop the nonfiction bestseller list of 1937 sat Dale Carnegie's *How to Win Friends and Influence People,* a book that told readers how to become rich and famous. Carnegie, born poor on a Missouri farm, reinvented himself by moving to New York and adopting the last name of a steel tycoon. He sprinkled his writings with the names of celebrities ("Martin Johnson, the African explorer" and "Arnold Reubens . . . originator of the four-decker sandwich") who overcame their own setbacks by following a few simple steps. Where Scarlett O'Hara represented the lone heroine overcoming adversity as an individual, Carnegie's hero was a team player, an "organization man" who knew how to manipulate others for his personal advantage.

One figure, especially, captured the tension between old and new versions of American individualism in his viselike

continued

>> AMERICAN PORTRAIT *continued*

grip. In 1938 Action Comics introduced Superman, who in his first year thwarted two European wars, foiled evil businessmen and insane scientists, and rescued helpless politicians by the planeload. He was the creation of two Cleveland teenagers, Jerry Siegel and Joe Shuster, who sold the rights to the comic for a quick $130. Superman's dual identity reflected the split personality of Dale Carnegie's mild-mannered manipulator. Clark Kent, reared in rural Kansas, was a big-city organization man, a reporter for a large daily paper. But beneath his grey flannel suit he was Superman, who could right society's wrongs in a single bound. In an early issue, he turned his super strength against the Depression, tearing Metropolis's slums apart with his bare hands and forcing city officials to rebuild. The "man of the future" revived the fantasy of the rugged individual able to remake society on his own terms.

Society's emphasis on individual responsibility had important implications for the way voters and politicians responded to the economic disaster. For the first four years of the Depression, the federal government offered solutions that relied on individuals' willingness to help each other and themselves. But the persistence of the Depression strained the public's faith, and in 1933 the administration undertook a dramatic series of experiments to relieve the plight of individuals. These experiments, known collectively as the "New Deal," permanently changed the relationship between Americans and their government. Voters relied on elected officials not just to represent their interests, but to protect their livelihoods. Yet by the late 1930s the ingrained suspicion of big government began to revive, and the New Deal ground to a halt. Margaret Mitchell and her character Scarlett ended the decade in triumph. In 1939 she was immortalized on screen in the Technicolor film version of *Gone with the Wind*, which swept the 1940 Academy Awards.

OUTLINE

The Great Depression

In the fall of 1929 declining confidence in the stock market sent tremors throughout the economy. By Thursday, October 24, panic had set in as brokers rushed to unload their stocks. Prices rallied briefly, but on October 29, "Black Tuesday," stock values lost over $14 billion, and within the month the market stood at only half its precrash worth. Hundreds of corporations and thousands of individuals were wiped out. On Wall Street, the symbol of prosperity in the 1920s, mounted police had to hold angry mobs back from the doors of the stock exchange. Although the crash did not cause the ensuing depression, it did expose underlying weaknesses and shatter the confidence President Herbert Hoover relied on for recovery. His optimistic speeches would echo hollowly over the ensuing years of widespread unemployment, hunger, and homelessness.

Causes

No single factor explains the onset or persistence of the Great Depression. No one among the politicians, bureaucrats, business leaders, and others responsible for addressing the problem had a clear idea of why things had gone so wrong. Economists and historians still debate the issue today. Yet, even if no definitive account can be given, it is clear that structural flaws in the national and international economies along with ill-conceived government policies were at fault.

> **Now everyone will get back to work instead of cherishing the idea that it is possible to get rich overnight.**
>
> ALFRED P. SLOAN, Chairman, General Motors, October 27, 1929

In the 1920s the base of the economy had begun to shift. No longer was it driven by steel, coal, textiles, railroads, and other heavy industries. Now, new industries that sold complex consumer goods like automobiles became the driving force. In addition to cars, sales of radios, clothing, processed foods, and a whole range of consumer products grew dramatically. This shift toward a vibrant new consumer-oriented economy was fueled by favorable business conditions, job growth, and plentiful credit that allowed consumers, mainly those in the relatively small middle class, to purchase more and more goods and services. The limits of this market had, however, been reached even before the Great Crash. When the stock market fell, the collapse of purchasing power caused by mass unemployment and the loss of savings slowed the transition to the new economy.

A rickety credit and financial system added to the problems of the late 1920s. Even in good times banks failed by the hundreds. For banks in rural areas these failures could be traced to persistently low farm prices, but all over America financial institutions suffered from inept and even criminal management. Banks were virtually unregulated, and in the boom atmosphere of the 1920s many bet depositors' money on stocks or large, risky loans. Bank failures magnified the impact of the crash; many thousands lost money they thought was safely saved.

Like banks, corporate finance was free from regulation and given to misrepresentation, manipulation of stock prices, and corrupt insider deals. Few could be sure whether investments were going into sound companies or worthless paper.

Government missteps and poor policies also had a role. The Republican administrations of the 1920s were committed to reducing government interference in the economy, lowering taxes on the wealthy, and reducing spending. As a result, little was done to address the banking mess, the problems of farmers, or the growing reliance on credit. The Federal Reserve could have dampened speculation in stocks or, after the Depression began, expanded the currency to promote growth. Concerned more about keeping the dollar strong than maintaining employment, the Harding and Coolidge administrations throttled back spending and the money supply, worsening the eventual collapse.

The Depression was magnified by an international economy still reeling from the effects of World War I. Under the peace terms, Germany owed $33 billion in reparations to Britain and France, who in turn owed billions in war debts to the United States. Only U.S. bank loans to Germany made these huge payments possible, so throughout the 1920s funds that could have created jobs and industries went instead into this financial merry-go-round. The cycle was broken at the onset of depression in the United States. European nations attempted to protect themselves by devaluing their currencies and raising trade barriers. The result was a steady decline in their economies that made payments on reparations or loans impossible. The whole cycle reached a breaking point in 1931, and the international financial system came crashing down, bringing with it many more American banks and helping to further deepen the economic crisis.

Descending into Depression

The Great Depression was a year old when an unemployed worker in Pottstown, Pennsylvania, sat down and wrote a harsh letter to President Hoover. "I am one of the men out of work," he explained, "but the rich don't care so long as they have full and plenty." With winter coming on he pleaded with Hoover to speed up aid to "the struggling starving working class [of] under nourished men, women, and children." Such misery, he added, "really is alarming [in] this so called prosperous nation."

The statistics alone were alarming. Between 1929 and 1933 every index of economic activity showed a steadily worsening slide. The gross national product shrank from $104.4 billion in 1929 to $74.2 billion in 1933. The combined incomes of American workers fell by more than 40 percent. Bank failures increased, from 640 in 1928 to 2,294 in 1931. A *New York Times* index of business activity dropped from 114.8 in June of 1929 to 63.7 in March of 1933. Both exports and imports fell by more than two-thirds.

Table 24–1 Labor Force and Unemployment, 1929–1941 (Numbers in Millions)

		Unemployment	
Year	**Labor Force**	**Number**	**% of Labor Force**
1929	49.2	1.6	3.2
1930	49.8	4.3	8.7
1931	50.4	8.0	15.9
1932	51.0	12.1	23.6
1933	51.6	12.8	24.9
1934	52.2	11.3	21.7
1935	52.9	10.6	20.1
1936	53.4	9.0	16.9
1937	54.0	7.7	14.3
1938	54.6	10.4	19.0
1939	55.2	9.5	17.2
1940	55.6	8.1	14.6
1941	55.9	5.6	9.9

Source: *United States Department of Commerce,* Historical Statistics of the United States (1960), p. 70.

As business activity collapsed, joblessness skyrocketed. Periodic bouts of unemployment had always been a feature of capitalist economies, even in good times. What distinguished the Great Depression was the extent and duration of unemployment. At the lowest point of the slump in the early 1930s, between 20 and 30 percent of wage earners were out of work. In some cities the jobless percentage was much higher, with Chicago and Detroit approaching 50 percent, Akron 60 percent, and Toledo a crushing 80 percent. In 1933, the Bureau of Labor Statistics estimated that as many as one in three workers, more than 12,600,000 Americans, were unemployed.

Behind the grim statistics lay terrible human costs. In the spring of 1930, as the first Depression winter came to an end, breadlines appeared in major cities. Apple peddlers crowded street corners hoping to earn a few nickels to replace some of their lost wages. The unemployed could be seen in the thousands, Sherwood Anderson wrote, "men who are heads of families creeping through the streets of American cities, eating from garbage cans; men turned out of houses and sleeping week after week on park benches, on the ground in parks, in the mud under bridges." Unemployed men and women stood in lines at factory gates desperately seeking work, at soup kitchens hoping for a meal, and at homeless shelters that were already overflowing.

The basic necessities—food, clothing, and shelter—were suddenly hard to get. "I have always been able to give my family a decent living," a struggling father in Seattle explained, "until economic conditions got so bad I was unable to make it go any longer." Schoolteachers reported growing numbers of students were listless from hunger. Big-city hospitals began receiving patients suffering from nutritional disorders, including children with rickets, a disease caused by a deficiency of vitamin D. Deficient diets caused another disease, pellagra, to reappear in many parts of the South. *Fortune* magazine ran an article on Americans who had actually starved to death. Embarrassed mothers sent children to school in rags. Men wrapped newspapers beneath their shirts as protection from the cold or put cardboard in their shoes to cover the holes. Desperate families, their savings gone, unable to pay the rent, "doubled up" by moving in with relatives. More and more tenants were evicted; more and more banks foreclosed on mortgages. Apartments stood vacant and homes went unsold, yet by 1932 more than a million homeless men, women, and children occupied shantytowns on the outskirts of towns and cities or slept in doorways and alleys. Hoboes appeared everywhere, traveling railroads and highways in a constant search for something to eat, somewhere to live, someplace to work.

Effects of the Dust Bowl Drought and modern agriculture churned the Great Plains into silica powder that was carried by windstorms. Over half the patients in Kansas hospitals in 1935 suffered from dust pneumonia.

Farmers faced a double catastrophe of economic and environmental disaster. Farmers in the Plains states and the West aggressively increased production in the 1920s and then watched helplessly as the markets for corn, wheat, beef, and pork collapsed in the wake of the crash. Between 1929 and 1932, the income of American farmers dropped by two-thirds. Then the drought struck. Between 1930 and 1936, the rains all but stopped in large parts of the South, the Southwest, and the Great Plains. Exposed by decades of wasteful farming practices, the earth dried up and blew away. Spectacular dust storms carried topsoil hundreds of miles through the air, giving a new name—the Dust Bowl—to a large swath of the Southern Plains. Dust and depression ripped thousands of farm families from the land in Texas, Kansas, Oklahoma, and Arkansas, sending these "Okies," "Arkies," and "Texies" off to California in search of work.

The Great Depression affected nearly everyone in America, but it was most severe for those already disadvantaged. While the environmental shock of the Dust

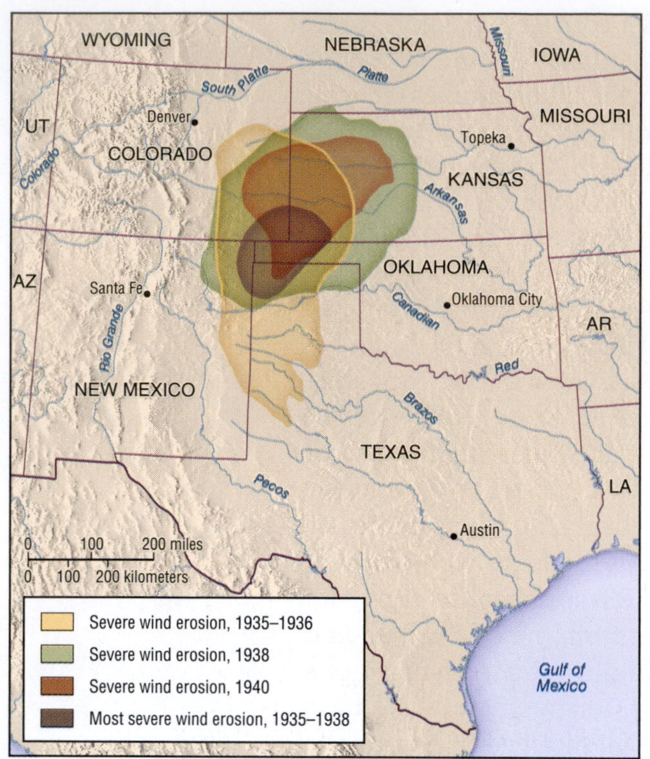

Map 24–1 Extent of the Dust Bowl The Dust Bowl of the 1930s eventually spread across thousands of square miles of the Southern Plains.

Bowl affected many poor white farmers, the larger agricultural depression was even more devastating for sharecroppers on the southern cotton lands, workers in the wheatfields of the Midwest, and the vast migrant labor pools that traveled up and down the East and West coasts picking fruits and vegetables. In cities, African Americans, who held the least secure jobs, found themselves pushed from menial service tasks and unskilled work by desperate white workers.

By 1932 private charities, the major social safety net before the Depression, failed to meet the needs of desperate citizens. Ethnic organizations such as the Bohemian Charitable Association or Jewish Charities in Chicago had been a bulwark against adversity for members of their own groups. Now they found themselves overwhelmed. Summing up the state of charities, Arthur T. Burns, the president of the Association of Community Chests and Councils, flatly declared that "the funds we have are altogether inadequate to meet the situation."

Public monies were just as scarce. Only eight states provided any form of unemployment insurance; most of it was meager. Such state welfare agencies as existed tended to be poorly funded in the best of times and were now stretched beyond their limits. Entire cities slid toward insolvency as their tax bases dwindled. Many states were expressly forbidden by their constitutions to borrow for social welfare expenditures. Frustrated politicians and citizens looked to the federal government for a solution, but beyond pensions for veterans, little existed in the way of a social welfare state. There was no social security for the elderly and disabled, no federal unemployment insurance for those who lost their jobs, and no food stamps to relieve hunger.

The federal government thus found itself under unprecedented pressure to do something, anything, to relieve the Depression. Even bankers and businessmen abandoned their resistance to a strong central government. The president of Columbia University suggested a dictatorship might provide more effective leadership. Others warned of social revolution if the government did not act. Most of the pleas for federal action were aimed at the administration, and Herbert Hoover himself came to symbolize the failures of the federal government. The newspapers that jobless men wrapped themselves in were called "Hoover shirts"; shantytowns were "Hoovervilles." In the popular imagination, Hoover and the Great Depression became inseparable.

Hoover Responds

In many ways, Hoover was ideally qualified to handle this emergency. He had experience with natural and human catastrophes. Orphaned at a young age, Hoover grew up in small-town America and worked hard to educate himself. He was trained

A Hooverville in Seattle, Washington As the Depression deepened, the homeless settled in "Hoovervilles" on the edge of city centers.

as an engineer at Stanford University, then roamed the world building and managing mining operations. He became a millionaire by his mid-20s. Like many other young progressives, Hoover sought to apply skills from the business world to solve social problems. He won fame as an administrator of emergency relief, saving Belgium from starvation during World War I and overseeing rescue efforts during the Great Mississippi Flood of 1927.

He came into the presidency with a well-developed theory on the role of government in a modern economy. His vision centered on the belief that complex societies required accurate economic information, careful planning, and large-scale coordination. At the same time, Hoover rejected the idea that a large and overbearing government could provide these services without crushing the creativity and flexibility essential to a capitalist economy. His political philosophy, associationalism, envisioned a federal government empowered to gather information and encourage voluntary cooperation among businesses but forbidden to intervene further. This voluntarist dream fit well with the dominant ideology of America, and it was no surprise that Hoover easily won the presidency in 1928.

Once in office Hoover lost no time in implementing his ideas. One of his first achievements was the Agricultural Marketing Act of 1929, designed to raise farm incomes and rationalize production. Since the turn of the century, farmers had been plagued by a "paradox of plenty." Modern techniques produced more food and fiber than Americans could consume, so the more farmers grew, the less they earned. The bill established a Federal Farm Board to establish cooperatives for purchasing and distributing surplus crops. It issued $500 million in loans to stabilize prices, but it did not limit production or dictate prices.

When the market crashed, Hoover's initial response was consistent with his overall vision. His goal was to get business to promise to cooperate to maintain wages and investment. In 1931, as banks were failing at a rate of 25 a week, he encouraged the formation of the National Credit Corporation, in which banks were urged to pool resources to stave off collapse. Rather than distribute unemployment insurance or poor relief, he tried to persuade companies not to lay off workers and to contribute to charities for the homeless and unemployed. But the breadth and depth of the Depression overwhelmed all of Hoover's schemes. Crop prices fell so low that farmers began to blockade cities and demand adequate compensation for their crops.

Hoover had never failed before in his life, and he worked tirelessly to fight the Depression. By 1932, he reluctantly conceded the need for more aggressive government programs, even at the risk of deficit spending. He proposed a Reconstruction Finance Corporation (RFC) authorized to loan $2 billion to revive large corporations. Plans to increase government revenues and allow the Federal Farm Board to distribute surpluses to the needy were also enacted. But it was too little too late. The Depression was three years old and showed no signs of lifting.

The Republican administration's policies did not simply fail to relieve the Depression but, rather, increased its severity. Unable to control members of his own party, Hoover watched helplessly as Congress passed the Hawley-Smoot Tariff in 1930. The tariff raised import duties to their highest level in history, stifling hopes that international trade might help the economy and wreaking untold damage on the weak nations of Europe. Despite the president's misgivings about the tariff, he signed the bill into law. At the same time, Hoover opposed other measures that might have relieved poverty or stimulated recovery. He vetoed massive public works bills sponsored by congressional Democrats. Finally, Hoover's stubborn commitment to the gold standard and a balanced budget choked off hopes of a turnaround.

Hoover, whose popularity had plummeted as the Depression deepened, reinforced his reputation as a cold and aloof protector of the privileged classes by his response to the Bonus Marchers in 1932. In 1924 Congress had issued the veterans of World War I a "bonus" to be paid in 1945. But as the Depression threw millions out of work, veterans asked to have their bonuses paid early. In the summer of 1932, veterans formed a "Bonus Expeditionary Force" to march on Washington. Arriving on freight cars and buses, over 20,000 Bonus Marchers encamped on the Capitol grounds. "Families were there galore, just couples and families with strings of kids," one marcher remembered. Hoover ordered the army to remove the march-

The Bonus Army Expeditionary Force, or Bonus Marchers The Bonus Marchers arrived in Washington, DC, in the summer of 1932 to ask Congress to pay World War I veterans' payments early.

ers. General Douglas MacArthur exceeded his orders and attacked the marchers with tanks and mounted cavalry. Major George S. Patton, sabre drawn, galloped through the encampment, setting fire to the miserable tents and shacks of the veterans. Among those he attacked was Joseph T. Angelino, who won the Distinguished Service Cross in 1918 for saving Patton's life. Americans were shocked by photographs of MacArthur calmly sipping coffee and standing in a pool of blood. Hoover's silent support solidified his reputation for callousness.

As Congress struggled to devise policies to relieve unemployment and suffering, Hoover flatly dismissed the "futile attempt to cure poverty by the enactment of law." Arrogant and aloof, the president questioned the integrity and suspected the motives of everyone who disagreed with his policies. By the end of his presidency the "Great Humanitarian" had become sullen and withdrawn. It was a dispirited Republican Convention that met in Chicago to nominate Hoover for reelection in 1932.

The First New Deal

When the Democratic Convention chose a presidential candidate in 1932, Franklin Delano Roosevelt flew from Albany, New York, to Chicago to accept the nomination in person, a dramatic gesture in an age new to air travel and personal politics. "I pledge myself," he told the enthusiastic crowd, "to a new deal for the American people." The phrase stuck, and, ever since, the assortment of reforms enacted between 1933 and 1938 has come to be known as the New Deal. The programs came in two great waves commonly referred to as the "first" and "second" New Deals. The first commenced with the Hundred Days, a three-month burst of executive and legislative activity following FDR's inauguration. The first New Deal continued through 1934.

> **TVA is more an example of democracy in retreat than democracy on the march.**
>
> REXFORD TUGWELL, New Deal economist

The Election of 1932

The Depression reached its lowest depths as the 1932 election approached, and the Republicans seemed headed for disaster. Their inability to develop a legislative program to attack the Depression had already cost them control of the House. But the Democrats had to overcome serious internal divisions if they were to take advantage of the situation.

Throughout the 1920s the Democratic Party had been split along cultural lines between the ethnically diverse, wet (i.e., anti-Prohibition), urban wing concentrated in the North and the East, and the Anglo-Saxon Protestant, rural southern and western wings. Ideological divisions on a whole range of issues separated northeastern business Democrats from western populists, and urban progressives from southern conservatives.

The leading candidate for the Democratic nomination, New York's Governor Franklin D. Roosevelt, had the background to overcome many of these divisions. He came from an upstate rural district and his interest in conservation endeared him to many westerners. He had built ties to the southern Democrats while serving as Woodrow Wilson's assistant secretary of the navy and, during the 1920s, as a sometime resident of Warm Springs, Georgia. As governor of New York he built a strong record of support for progressive social reforms that appealed to urban liberals.

Roosevelt turned out to be the ideal candidate. As a distant cousin of Theodore Roosevelt, he had a recognizable name. FDR also had immense personal charm. Despite having been crippled by polio since 1921, he proved a tireless campaigner and would go on to become one of the most visible of modern presidents. He was a born patrician, a blue-blooded member of the American aristocracy, raised in wealth and educated at Groton and Harvard. Yet he spoke in clear, direct language that ordinary Americans found persuasive and reassuring.

During the campaign, Roosevelt simultaneously embraced old orthodoxies and enticed reformers with hints of more radical changes. He promised to cut government spending and provide government relief for the poor. How he would do both, FDR declined to say, but it hardly mattered. In November 1932, the Republicans were swept out of office in a tide of popular repudiation. FDR and the Democrats

took control of the national government with the promise of "a new deal" for the American people.

Behind the scenes during the campaign, Roosevelt worked hard to develop a program to fight the Depression. While governor of New York, FDR had recruited intellectuals who provided him with an influential diagnosis of the Great Depression. Known as the "Brains Trust," they attempted to convince Roosevelt that the Depression was caused by the economy's fundamental defects. The core of the problem, they told FDR, was the maldistribution of wealth within the United States. Because the rich held onto too large a share of the profits of American industry, the economy was producing much more than Americans could consume.

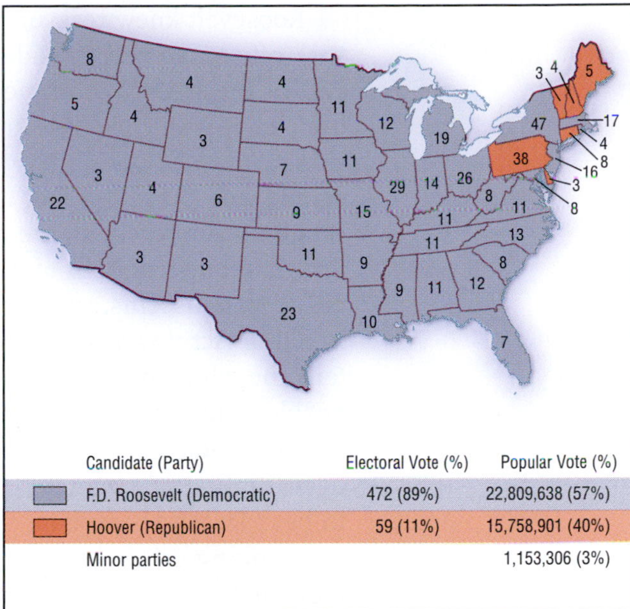

Candidate (Party)
Electoral Vote (%)
Popular Vote (%)
F.D. Roosevelt (Democratic) 472 (89%) 22,809,638 (57%)
Hoover (Republican) 59 (11%) 15,758,901 (40%)
Minor parties 1,153,306 (3%)

Map 24–2 The Presidential Election of 1932 By November 1932 most American voters blamed the Depression on Hoover and the Republicans. The Democrats, led by FDR, swept into office by huge electoral margins.

Despite the influence of the Brains Trust, Roosevelt never fully bought their ideas or allowed any one group to dominate his thinking. It was FDR's comfort with experimentation and chaos that would hold his administration together and make it capable of confronting the confusing persistence of the Depression. Where Hoover had retreated into dogmatism, FDR endorsed "bold, persistent experimentation." Above all, he ordered his officials, "try something." And rather than trying to unite his followers behind a single idea or policy, Roosevelt seemed to enjoy watching his advisers feud. He acted as a dealmaker, arranging the final bargains and compromises for the exhausted combatants. The president, one adviser said, was "the boss, the dynamo, the works."

FDR Takes Command

As the president-elect and his advisers discussed their approach to the Depression in the weeks before the inauguration, the ailing American banking system took a sharp turn for the worse. In mid-February the governor of Michigan declared an eight-day bank holiday. In one of the nation's most important manufacturing states, nearly a million depositors could not get their money. Stock prices dropped on the news, and the anxious rich began shipping their gold to safer countries. Panic struck and banks saw their funds fly out of the tellers' windows at an alarming rate. On the morning of the inauguration New York and Illinois, the two great centers of American finance, joined most of the other states in calling a bank holiday. The New York Stock Exchange and Illinois Board of Trade also closed. To many, it seemed like the end of the American economy that had so recently been the envy of the world.

With commerce at a standstill the nation turned expectantly to the new president: Roosevelt did not disappoint. "First of all," he declared, "let me assert my firm belief that the only thing we have to fear is—fear itself, nameless, unreasoning, unjustified terror." In another time and place such words might have sounded empty, but in the midst of a frightening financial collapse FDR's speech revitalized the nation almost overnight.

Roosevelt knew reassuring words alone would not end the crisis. On the day he took office, the new president declared a national bank holiday to last through the end of the week. He immediately instructed his new secretary of the Treasury to draft emergency legislation and called Congress into special session. When Congress convened on March 9, the drafting team had finished a bill, barely, and presented one pencil-marked copy for its consideration. Congress was ready to act. Breaking all precedent, the House unanimously shouted its approval of the bill after less than one half hour of debate; that evening the Senate voted to do the same with only seven dissents, and the president signed it into law that night. The Emergency Banking Act was a modest reform. It gave the Treasury secretary the power to determine which banks could safely reopen and which had to be reorganized. It also enabled the RFC to strengthen sound banks by buying their stocks.

On Sunday night, a week after taking office, FDR went on national radio to deliver the first of his many "fireside chats." Sixty million people tuned their radios to hear Roosevelt explain, in his resonant, fatherly voice, his measures to address the banking crisis. He assured Americans that their money would be "safer in a reopened bank than under the mattress." This was a tremendous gamble because the government was not completely sure how solid most banks truly were, but it worked. The next day, 12,756 banks reopened, some in style. Five thousand customers of the Consolidated National Bank of Tucson, Arizona, were welcomed into a lobby decked with flowers and a band playing "Happy Days Are Here Again." The run stopped and deposits began flowing back into the system. The immediate crisis was over.

Once the banking crisis had been resolved in March 1933, Roosevelt wanted to ensure that the financial system would remain sound for the long run. He moved to restrict banks' speculations while guaranteeing their profitability. The Glass-Steagall Banking Act of 1933 imposed conservative banking practices nationwide. Chancy loans, stock investments, and shady business practices by banks were outlawed, and close federal oversight guaranteed the stability of the U.S. banking system until Glass-Steagall was repealed in 1999. In addition, the newly created Federal Deposit Insurance Corporation protected deposits. Two years later, the Banking Act of 1935 reorganized the Federal Reserve, bringing the entire system under more centralized and democratic control. Together, these laws established the credibility of the U. S. banking sys-

FDR Photographed During One of His Fireside Chats Hoover broadcast his speeches on radio, but Roosevelt's "fireside chats" took advantage of the intimacy of the new medium.

tem. One reason the banking system had become so vulnerable was its ties to the unregulated securities markets. So in 1933 the administration sponsored a Truth in Securities Act that required all companies issuing stock to disclose accurate information to all prospective buyers. The following year Congress passed the Securities and Exchange Act. Where the 1933 law regulated companies, the 1934 legislation regulated the markets that sold stocks. It prohibited inside trading and other forms of manipulation. It gave the Federal Reserve Board the power to control how much credit was available and it established the Securities and Exchange Commission, which quickly became one of the largest and most effective regulatory agencies in the country.

Federal Relief

Roosevelt's unemployment programs departed sharply from Hoover's relief strategies. In May, Congress passed a bill providing a half billion dollars for relief and creating the Federal Emergency Relief Administration (FERA) to oversee it. Lacking the organization to dispense money across the nation, the federal government passed on funds to existing local and state agencies. Headed by Harry Hopkins, a shrewd social worker and Roosevelt confidant from New York, FERA distributed money at a terrific rate. As winter came on, however, Hopkins convinced Roosevelt that only a massive new federal program could avert disaster. At FDR's request, Congress created the Civil Works Administration (CWA), which employed 4 million men and women. During the winter, the CWA built or renovated over half a million miles of road and tens of thousands of schools and other public buildings. When spring came the CWA was eliminated—Roosevelt did not want the nation to get used to a federal welfare program—but FERA continued to run programs on a smaller scale.

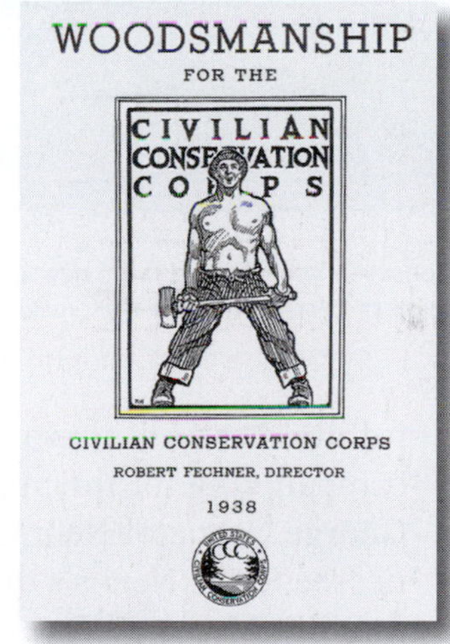

WOODSMANSHIP
FOR THE
CIVILIAN CONSERVATION CORPS
CIVILIAN CONSERVATION CORPS
ROBERT FECHNER, DIRECTOR
1938

Roosevelt generally came to relief only out of necessity, but he was enthusiastic about one program, the Civilian Conservation Corps (CCC). FDR believed that life in the countryside and service to the nation would have a positive moral impact on the young men of the cities and those "wild boys" whom the Depression had compelled to roam the nation. The CCC employed these young men building roads and trails in the national parks. By the time the program was discontinued in 1942, it had dramatically transformed America's public lands and employed over 3 million teenagers and young adults.

The Farm Crisis

"I don't want on the relief if I can help it," a Louisiana farm woman wrote to the first lady, Eleanor Roosevelt, in the fall of 1935. "I want to work for my livin.'" But she was desperate. She asked Mrs. Roosevelt to send money to save the family cow "for my little children to have milk." One child was sick and the doctor was no longer

Eleanor Roosevelt Eleanor Roosevelt wrote a syndicated newspaper column, personally inspected government projects, and acted as a presidential adviser, all new roles for a first lady.

able to give her the medicine "unless we pay him some for he is in debt for it." The landlord was threatening to evict them unless they got a mill plow, which they could not afford. She had turned to the first lady because of Mrs. Roosevelt's reputation for caring about the poor, but political realities would limit what the first lady, or her husband, could do to help this woman and thousands like her.

By the spring of 1933, farmers in many parts of the country were desperate. Prices of basic commodities like corn, cotton, wheat, and tobacco had fallen so low that it was not even worth the cost of harvesting. The banking crisis left farmers without access to the necessary credit to continue, and millions faced the stark prospect of foreclosure, homelessness, or dust storms.

FDR saw a stark "imbalance" between city and country as a root cause of the Depression. While the land remained the only real source of wealth, modern cities absorbed all of the countryside's water, produce, talent, and population. The Dust Bowl was a consequence of this ecological distortion. His aim was to restore a more even pattern of development across the landscape, with small manufacturing towns, suburbs, and farms linked to centers of culture and commerce. The New Deal program that came closest to fulfilling each of these goals was the Tennessee Valley Authority, or TVA. While campaigning for the presidency, Roosevelt had endorsed the proposal by Senator George Norris of Nebraska to develop the Muscle Shoals property along the Tennessee River. Norris's dream was realized when Congress created the TVA within the first Hundred Days. The TVA was a "corporation clothed with the power of government but possessed of the flexibility and initiative of a private enterprise." According to its administrator, it aimed to change the environment, the economy, the way of life, and the "habits, social, economic, and personal" of a region that spanned nine states.

One of the most ambitious projects of the entire New Deal, the TVA was also astonishingly successful. The dams eventually built by the TVA served many purposes. They controlled flooding in the Tennessee Valley, created reservoirs for irrigation, and provided cheap hydroelectric power. Electricity not only made life more comfortable for millions of farm families, it also made it possible for industry to move into new areas, thus bringing jobs to some of the poorest parts of the country. Jesus "is the greatest thing that can happen to any man," a Tennessee preacher testified, "but the next greatest thing is electricity."

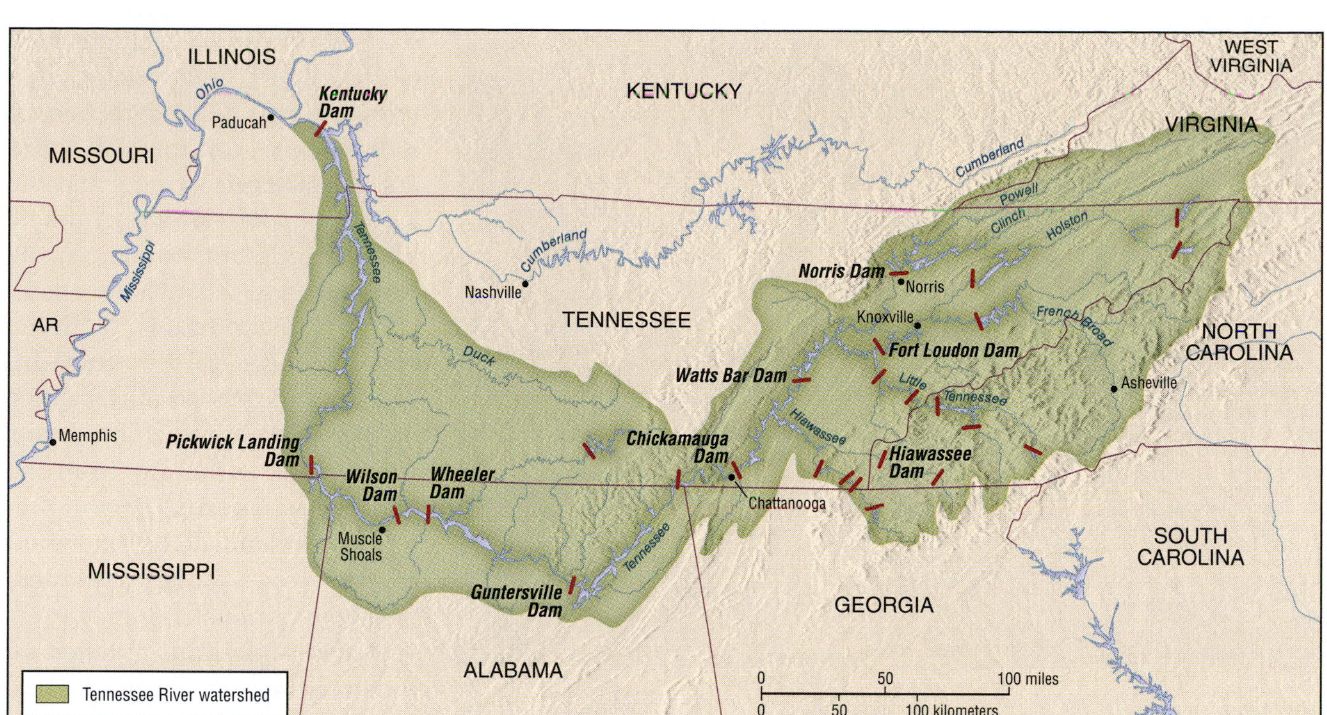

Map 24–3 TVA Projects The Tennessee Valley Authority (TVA) was one of the most ambitious of all New Deal projects. A network of dams provided electricity, irrigation, and flood control to many of the poorest regions of the South.

The TVA took responsibility for soil conservation, reforestation, improved navigation, and the manufacture of fertilizer and aluminum. During the course of the Roosevelt administration, the poor, mountainous region along the Tennessee–North Carolina border went from growing cotton to manufacturing aircraft and components for nuclear weapons. The average income of the area's residents increased tenfold. As a comprehensive, centrally planned development scheme, the TVA came closest to the Brains Trusters' vision of how a modern "democracy on the march" should work. But it was an exception among New Deal programs, which tended to be more fragmented and improvisational.

Headed by Henry Wallace, founder of the Pioneer Hi-Bred Corn Company, the Agriculture Department was an idea factory in the first Hundred Days. An emergency farm bill gave Wallace broad powers to control production, buy up surpluses, regulate marketing, and levy taxes. Conservation and reclamation projects drained swamps, irrigated deserts, and altered the weather, planting a "shelterbelt" of forest across the Great Plains to break the force of windstorms. The Agricultural Adjustment Act established a system of subsidies, price controls, and production limits that turned agriculture into a regulated industry. After 1933, farmers, once fiercely independent, essentially worked for the federal government. The New Deal farm system permanently altered the American diet by making processed grains, grain-fed meat, sugar, and dairy products cheap and plentiful relative to unsubsidized fresh vegetables, fruits, and fish.

In many respects, however, the New Deal did little for the rural poor. Price supports and production controls helped farmers who owned their own land. Similarly,

The Norris Dam New Dealers idolized civil engineering projects such as the Norris Dam, which they saw as symbols of a new national consensus. "A river has no politics," David Lilienthal explained. "Development anywhere helps everyone everywhere."

soil conservation, irrigation, rural electrification, and various long-term reforms tended to benefit independent commercial farmers. Subsistence farmers and the landless poor—overwhelmingly Mexican migrant workers in the Far West, and tenants and sharecroppers, black and white, in the cotton South—gained little. Indeed, an unintended consequence of New Deal production limits was to take work away from the poorest Americans. These programs accelerated the migration of poor, often barely educated, people into industrial cities.

Native Americans suffered an especially severe form of rural poverty. Shunted onto reservations in the late nineteenth century, by 1930 the majority of American Indians were landless, miserably poor, and subjected to the corrupt paternalism of the Bureau of Indian Affairs. Alcoholism, crime, and infant mortality were all more common on reservations than they were even among the poorest whites. John Collier, FDR's commissioner of Indian affairs, was determined to correct the situation, and the Indian Reorganization Act of 1934 gave him the power to try. Collier reversed decades of federal attempts to assimilate Native Americans into the cultural mainstream. Under the New Deal, forced land sales ended, and reservations were actually enlarged. Tribal democracy replaced bureaucratic authority. But Congressional opponents, even western liberals, resented Collier's attempts to preserve traditional culture. Even on its own terms Collier's plan could be only partially successful. What worked for Pueblo communities might not work for the Navajo, for example. And Indians themselves were divided over policies and goals. As a result, while the New Deal relieved some poverty among Native Americans, it did not develop a satisfactory long-term solution.

The Blue Eagle

FDR had no fixed plan for industrial recovery and preferred to wait until business interests could agree on one before acting. Congress, however, moved independently to pass a bill aimed at spreading employment by limiting the workweek to 30 hours. Heading off what he thought an ill-conceived plan, Roosevelt put forward his last proposal to become law in the first Hundred Days: the National Industrial Recovery Act. It mandated that business, labor, and government officials negotiate a "code" restructuring each industry into a national cartel. The code would set trade practices, wages, hours, and production quotas. The hope was to raise prices by limiting production while simultaneously protecting the purchas-

ing power of workers. The NIRA reversed decades of antitrust law. Organized labor received protections from Section 7(a) of the act, which guaranteed unions the right of collective bargaining. Finally, $3.3 billion was earmarked for jobs creation through a Public Works Administration.

The NIRA was a bold idea, but it suffered from many of the same problems as Hoover's earlier schemes. It quickly brought together representatives from hundreds of industries to draw up their respective codes, but the process tended to be dominated by business. Few strong unions existed, and the government lacked expertise in industrial management. Smaller businesses were shut out, leaving America's largest corporations to write the codes in their interest. For a time in 1933 and 1934 the NRA's Blue Eagle, the symbol of compliance with the codes, flew proudly in the windows of shops and factories. Soon, however, dissatisfaction with the program dampened enthusiasm, and by 1935 the eagle had come to roost atop a shaky and unpopular agency.

The Second New Deal

The first Hundred Days had been extraordinary by any standard. Congress had given the president unprecedented power to regulate the economy. The financial system had been saved from collapse. Federal relief had been extended to the unemployed. The agricultural economy was given direct federal support. A "yardstick" for the nation's public utilities had been created by the TVA. And a bold experiment in industrial planning had been attempted. Almost everyone was dazzled by what had happened, but not everyone was pleased. Critics pointed out that much of this legislation was poorly drafted, overly conservative, or downright self-contradictory. If Hoover had been too rigid, FDR struck even his admirers as hopelessly flexible. By 1935 the New Deal was besieged by critics from all directions. But rather than becoming demoralized, Roosevelt responded to political criticism and judicial setbacks by keeping Congress in session throughout the hot summer of 1935. The result was another dramatic wave of reforms known as the second New Deal.

> Those taxes were never a problem of economics. They are politics all the way through. . . . With those taxes in there, no damn politician can ever scrap my social security program.
>
> FRANKLIN DELANO ROOSEVELT

Critics Attack from All Sides

In May 1935 one of William Randolph Hearst's emissaries traveled to Washington to warn Roosevelt that the New Deal was becoming too radical. Hearst had long been one of the most powerful newspaper publishers in America, and like many businessmen he had "no confidence" in Roosevelt's advisers. But by 1935 Roosevelt was losing patience with the business community. Saving capitalism had

AMERICAN LANDSCAPE

>> Angola, Louisiana

"Angola was a pleasant place to live back then," Patsy Spillman remembers of her childhood in the 1930s. "You could get inmates as cooks, yard boys, house boys; you could have two or three of them if you wanted." "It was wonderful," her sister JoAn agrees. "I was the princess, and my daddy and mother were the king and queen, and we had servants, and we didn't want for anything." There were occasional problems. Once, a convict put rat poison in the girls' milk. Another time, the Himel family down the road had their throats slit by a prisoner attempting to escape. JoAn and Patsy were the daughters of John Spillman, a guard "captain" at the Louisiana State Penitentiary at Angola. Their home was a plantation house inside the prison.

Apart from the striped uniforms, Angola in the 1930s resembled a pre–Civil War plantation, 18,000 treeless acres of cotton and sugarcane bounded on one side by the Tunica Hills and on the other three by the earthen levees holding back the Mississippi River. Inmates, organized into work gangs, slept in military-style "camps" and rose before dawn to chop cotton and cane and refine sugar in the prison's own mill, the Pelican State Factory. Guards, all of whom were white, flogged prisoners, most of whom were black, with a leather strap, an average of three beatings a day between 1928 and 1940. "Angola was probably the closest thing to a feudal system in America at the time," one warden observed, "the guard captains being the lordly aristocrats and the inmates as the downtrodden serfs."

To the warden and the state, the prison's main purpose was to turn a profit, not to reform prisoners or even to keep them alive. With the economy in crisis, the voters and legislators wanted to lower property taxes while increasing state spending on roads, education, and jobs. To save money, Governor Huey Long demanded that that prison system be self-supporting, or even return revenue to the state. Democratic pressures created the system of convict slavery at Angola.

Blues legend Huddie Ledbetter, known as Leadbelly, served time in Angola, where he was discovered by music producers.

Before 1928, many southern states had a "convict lease" system that allowed planters and private businesses to rent chain gangs of prisoners. In the 1930s that system disappeared, as Long and other governors realized that the state could as easily reap the proceeds for itself. While two-thirds of American workers were unemployed, convict laborers nationwide produced $75 million a year in shirts, shoes, cement, license plates, and other goods and services. Inmates at Angola were treated as state property and taken from the prison to repair roads, tend gardens at the governor's mansion, and even to perform minstrel shows. To maximize gains, prisoners at Angola worked 60 hours a week and were paid two cents a day. They grew their own food, slept in unheated barracks, used the same bucket for a toilet and to hold drinking water, and had no medical care. Epidemics regularly swept through the camps. In the 1930s, an average of 41 prisoners died each year.

No walls stood between the prisoners and the outside. The prisoners guarded themselves. Fewer than 20 free captains, along with 600 "trusty" convicts with rifles, guarded over 4,000 prisoners. Trusties were rewarded for shooting prisoners who stepped over the "deadlines" that surrounded work areas. Chase teams of mounted men hunted down escapees with dogs. Survivors were "hotboxed" in tiny airless cells at the notorious Red Hat camp, where they received only bread and water. Desperation drove prisoners to keep trying. On September 10, 1933, 12 prisoners took advantage of a Sunday baseball game to shoot a captain and two trusties and steal a car. They were rounded up in hours. The following year, 15 Red Hats working an okra field brandished wooden pistols and disarmed two trusties, but other guards shot them down.

The system established in the 1930s has proven surprisingly resilient. Voters continue to demand that prisons turn a profit. When the population topped 4,000 inmates in the 1950s, the prison was deemed overcrowded. Today it has 5,100; over half are lifers and 87 are awaiting execution. Prisoners still work five days a week, raising soybeans and cattle instead of sugar. Pay has risen to two cents an hour. The prison's revenue streams are now adapted to the region's tourist economy. Vacationers can explore a museum on the site of the old Red Hat camp and attend an annual rodeo, where convicts ride bulls to the delight of a paying audience. In 1976, inmates began publishing a newspaper, *The Angolite*, which won a Pulitzer Prize for reporting on prison life. Its editor likes to quote the essayist William Hazlitt, who wrote that "We are all, more or less, slaves of opinion." ●

always been one of Roosevelt's goals, but shortsighted businessmen and financiers never appreciated his efforts. They had their own reasons for detesting the New Deal, and in the long run they proved more potent critics than all of Roosevelt's radical opponents combined.

The fate of the Communist Party illustrates the difficulties radicals faced during the New Deal. On the one hand, the 1930s were "the heyday of American Communism," as perhaps a quarter of a million Americans, disillusioned with capitalism, joined the Communist Party (CPUSA). The Communists organized labor unions and took the lead in defending the Scottsboro Boys, a group of nine young African American men falsely accused of raping two white women in Alabama. Yet the party's appeal was greatest after 1935, when, on orders from the Soviet Union, it adopted a "popular front" strategy in support of the New Deal. Thus, the Communists were most popular when they surrendered their revolutionary aims. Most of those who joined had left the party by the end of the decade.

Populist radicals gave Roosevelt more trouble. Father Charles Coughlin was a Catholic priest in Detroit who attracted listeners to his weekly radio show by blaming the Depression on international bankers and Wall Street. His solution was to nationalize the banking system and inflate the currency. FDR was careful not to anger Coughlin, and at first the radio priest defended Roosevelt and blamed the New Deal on Communist and Jewish influence in Washington. But by 1935 Coughlin turned on the president. He formed his own organization, the National Union for Social Justice, which pressured Congress to enact further reforms.

A California physician, Dr. Francis Townsend, offered an agenda especially popular among older Americans devastated by the Depression. Through a transaction tax of 2 percent, the government would fund retirement pensions of $200 per month. By requiring the elderly retirees to spend all of their pensions each month, the program was supposed to pump money into the economy and thereby stimulate a recovery. "Townsend clubs" advocating this scheme sprang up across the country and a *Townsend National Weekly* spread the word. Huey Long's "Share Our Wealth" program was more comprehensive than Townsend's and more popular than Father Coughlin's. As governor of Louisiana, Long slapped steep taxes on the oil industry which he used to build or renovate roads, schools, hospitals, and Louisiana State University. In the process, he amassed nearly dictatorial powers, controlling the legislature and the state police. Long was a loyal but critical supporter of FDR during the first Hundred Days. But by 1934 he was proposing his own alternative to the New Deal.

Long believed that the Depression was caused by the maldistribution of income. Consequently, his program for recovery called for the radical redistribution of wealth through confiscatory taxes on the rich and a guaranteed minimum income of $2,500 per year. Townsend's, Coughlin's, and Long's plans all rested on a crucial kernel of truth about the condition of the American economy. The currency did need to be inflated. Elderly Americans were indeed desperate, and wealth was unequally distributed. Roosevelt eventually defused these movements by adopting parts of their programs.

The business community's rising hostility concerned FDR as he prepared for his 1936 campaign. It would be several years before bankers would even admit the New Deal had saved the financial system. Wall Street never admitted it. And after some initial gestures of cooperation, most industrialists became vocal critics of the NIRA. As criticism of the New Deal grew, a conservative U.S. Supreme Court moved to strike down many of the key laws of the first Hundred Days. On May 27, 1935, in *Schechter Poultry Corporation v. United States,* the Court invalidated the NIRA. The case had been brought by a small New York poultry company, but it was financed by larger companies interested in killing the Blue Eagle. The justices ruled the NIRA unconstitutional and did so in a way that made it difficult for Congress to regulate the national economy to any significant degree. Roosevelt feared the setback portended the elimination of most of his achievements, and his fears were borne out in January 1936, when the Court overturned the Agricultural Adjustment Act.

The Second Hundred Days

FDR loved a good fight. No longer concerned about attracting the support from business, the president welcomed criticism and shot right back. After 1935 the rhetoric became noticeably more radical. When the Supreme Court invalidated the NIRA, Roosevelt kept Congress in session through the sweltering Washington summer and forced through a raft of legislation in a "second Hundred Days," which marked the beginning of the second New Deal.

A few of the new proposals were designed to salvage pieces of the NIRA and AAA or to silence radical critics. Hoping to undermine the "crackpot ideas" of Huey Long, Roosevelt proposed a Revenue Act that would encourage a "wider distribution of the wealth." The Revenue Act raised estate and corporate taxes and pushed personal income taxes in the top bracket all the way up to 79 percent. Despite the political motives behind the bill, it made certain economic sense. Before the 1935 Revenue Act, most New Deal programs had been financed by regressive sales and excise taxes. Thereafter, programs were funded with progressive income taxes that fell most heavily on those best able to pay.

The first New Deal had been preoccupied with the dire emergency of 1933. The second New Deal left a more enduring legacy. The administration put the finishing touches on its program to ensure the long-term security of the nation's financial system and extend the relief programs that had helped so many to survive. It put in place a social security system that became the centerpiece of the American welfare state for the remainder of the century, and it allied itself with organized labor, thereby creating a new and powerful Democratic Party coalition. By the time Congress adjourned in late August 1935, the most important achievements of the New Deal were in place.

Social Security for Some

Bolstered by big Democratic gains in the 1934 elections, FDR pursued a massive effort to fund work relief by sponsoring the Emergency Relief Appropriations

Bill. Providing nearly $5 billion, more than the entire 1932 federal budget, it was called by some members of his administration the "Big Bill." This appropriation breathed new life into the relief programs of the first New Deal and created a new Works Progress Administration (WPA), headed by Harry Hopkins. The WPA lasted for eight years, employing as many as 3.3 million Americans. WPA workers built infrastructure: bridges, schools, libraries, and sewer systems, the Blue Ridge Parkway across Virginia and the Carolinas, and over 800 airports. The WPA commissioned artists to decorate post offices, and historians to collect the stories of mill workers and former slaves. At Indiana University, the WPA paid undergraduates to build a student union. WPA lexicographers wrote a Hebrew-English dictionary. "There are rabbis who are broke," Hopkins explained. The program was hugely popular.

Critics complained with some justice that the WPA put people to work on meaningless "make-work" jobs or that many of the workers were incompetent to perform the jobs they were given. Political corruption was a more serious problem. WPA officials, especially at the local level, often used the agency as a patronage machine. Party regulars were sometimes favored with public works projects, and individual jobs were awarded on the basis of party loyalty. Corruption was not rampant, but there was enough of it to provide ammunition to the WPA's opponents. In many states, particularly in the South, local officials openly discriminated against African Americans. The WPA was never able to employ all those who needed work, but for millions of Americans it provided a critical source of immediate relief from the very real prospect of hunger and misery.

In addition to short-term relief, the New Deal created a permanent system of long-term economic security. In 1932 there were no national programs of unemployment insurance, workers' compensation, old-age pensions, or aid to needy children. The states were only slightly more able to care for citizens. As a result, most Americans had little or no protection from economic calamity.

The Social Security Act of 1935 took a critical first step toward providing such protection. It established matching grants to states that set up their own systems of workers' compensation, unemployment insurance, and aid to families with dependent children. Even more importantly, the federal government itself created a huge new Social Security system that guaranteed pensions to millions of elderly Americans. FDR insisted that it be funded as an insurance plan with payroll taxes paid by employees and employers. He hoped that this would protect the system from the political attacks that welfare programs commonly encountered.

Most New Dealers hoped to go much further. Secretary of Labor Frances Perkins wanted to include agricultural laborers and domestic servants, mostly women and African Americans, in the new Social Security system. But that would have provoked enough opposition from southern conservatives to kill the entire program. The administration also preferred federal rather than state programs of workers' compensation and unemployment insurance. There was, however, no federal bureaucracy in place that could have run such programs, and in any case there was fierce opposition to the idea of taking such programs away from the states.

Local and factional opposition thus limited the New Deal's plans for nationalized social welfare and economic security. Welfare and insurance programs were weaker in the South than in the North and weaker for women and African Americans than for white men. Despite such strong opposition, the New Deal actually accomplished a great deal. By 1939 every state had established a program of unemployment insurance and assistance to the elderly. Welfare bureaucracies across the country were professionalized to meet the demands of the federal system. Almost overnight the Social Security system became the federal government's first huge social welfare bureaucracy. More Americans than ever before were thereby protected from the ravages of unemployment, disability, poverty, and old age.

Labor and the New Deal

The 1930s saw unions take a new role in America's political economy. During that decade the number of Americans organized in unions leaped by the millions, and by 1940 nearly one in four nonfarm workers was unionized. Labor organizations overcame resistance from employers to enroll workers in the economy's core industries, including steel, rubber, electronics, and automobiles. Unions also became key players in the Democratic Party. None of the leading New Dealers, Roosevelt included, had anticipated this in 1932. Nevertheless, in critical ways the New Deal fostered the growth of organized labor and its inclusion in the Democratic electoral coalition.

The Roosevelt administration had never adopted the past government attitude of outright hostility toward unions. Rather, over the course of the 1930s FDR moved from grudging acceptance to open support for organized labor. Across the country, workers responded to the change. Section 7(a) allowed unions to launch huge organizing drives, and labor began to flex its muscle with a spontaneous wave of strikes. Mill workers in the South launched brave, but doomed, strikes against textile manufacturers. Dockworkers in San Francisco organized a tremendously successful general strike throughout the city. At the same time, the NIRA inspired a talented group of national leaders, in particular John L. Lewis of the United Mine Workers, Sidney Hillman of the Amalgamated Clothing Workers, and David Dubinsky of the International Ladies' Garment Workers.

Employers fought back against this new worker militancy. They used all the methods to intimidate workers—espionage, blacklisting, and armed assault—that had worked so well in earlier decades. But when it became clear that the federal government would now protect workers seeking to organize and bargain collectively, employers formed company unions to thwart independent action by workers themselves. By 1935 the employers seemed to be winning, particularly in May when the Supreme Court declared the NIRA, including Section 7(a), unconstitutional. In 1935 militancy among workers declined and the unionization drive seemed to be stalled. But the hopes of organized labor were kept alive by an influential and imaginative liberal senator from New York named Robert Wagner.

Wagner took the lead in expanding the limited protections of Section 7(a) into the National Labor Relations Act, also known as the Wagner Act. Although he had few ties to organized labor, Wagner believed workers had a basic right to join unions. He also hoped that effective unions would stimulate the economy by raising wages, thereby building consumer purchasing power. Like Section 7(a), the Wagner Act guaranteed workers the right to bargain collectively with their employers, but it also outlawed company unions, prohibited employers from firing workers after a strike, and restricted many of the other tactics traditionally used by companies to inhibit the formation of unions. Most importantly, the Wagner Act created the National Labor Relations Board (NLRB) to enforce these provisions. In the summer of 1935 FDR, perhaps convinced that businessmen could not be counted on to support industrial planning, declared the Wagner Act "must" legislation, and the bill became law.

While Wagner and his colleagues moved in Congress, John L. Lewis and Sidney Hillman took another course. In 1935 they pressed the conservative leadership of the American Federation of Labor to accept the principle of industrial unions, which would organize workers in an entire sector of the economy such as steel. The traditionalists of the AFL rejected the idea and held fast to the notion that workers should be organized by their crafts rather than by whole industries. Thwarted by the AFL leadership, Lewis, Hillman, and their allies formed a rival organization that eventually became the Congress of Industrial Organizations (CIO).

The CIO proceeded to organize some of the most powerful and prosperous industries in the country. Although none of these efforts depended on the Wagner Act for their initial success, the government's new attitude toward organized labor played an important role. For example, when the United Automobile Workers initiated a series of "sit-down strikes" against General Motors, neither FDR nor the Democratic governor of Michigan sent in troops to remove workers from the factories that they were occupying. This sent a powerful message to the leaders of industry and helped to win the strike against the most powerful corporation in America. In addition, the NLRB protected the new unions from an employer counterattack during the recession that hit the economy in 1937.

Thus by the late 1930s a crucial political alliance had been formed. A newly vigorous labor movement had become closely associated with a reinvigorated national Democratic Party. Thanks to this alliance, American industrial workers entered a new era. Having won the ability to organize with the help of the government, industrial workers used their power to increase wages, enhance job security, improve working conditions, and secure their retirements. Organized labor now had a stake in preserving the system from economic collapse. As much as the banking and financial reforms of the first New Deal, the successful unionization of industrial workers helped stabilize American capitalism.

The New Deal Coalition

Franklin Roosevelt believed that to overcome his varied opposition and win his bid for reelection he needed to create a coalition far broader than that of 1932. By 1936, the Democratic Party was transformed in fundamental ways. For the first time since the Civil War, a majority of voters identified themselves as Democrats, and the Democrats remained the majority party for decades to come. FDR achieved this feat by forging a powerful coalition between the competing wings of the party. In the end, however, the same coalition that made the New Deal possible also limited its progressivism.

The rural South had been overwhelmingly Democratic for a century, but urban voters in the North became the party's new base. This shift was well under way during the 1920s, when Al Smith's two presidential bids attracted ethnic blue-collar voters. Symbolism and substance attracted the urban working class to the New Deal. FDR offered prominent ethnic Americans an unprecedented number of federal appointments. Jews and Catholics (Italian as well as Irish) served Roosevelt as advisers, judges, and cabinet officers. More importantly, thousands of working-class city dwellers found relief from the Depression through jobs with the CWA, the WPA, or the CCC. Those same New Deal programs generated a flood of patronage appointments that endeared Roosevelt to local Democratic machines. Finally, FDR's support for labor was reciprocated by the unions. The CIO alone poured $600,000 into Roosevelt's campaign, replacing the money no longer forthcoming from wealthy donors, and its members formed an army of volunteers to help get out the vote. Thus the Democratic Party became, by 1940, the party of the urban working class.

The New Deal's programs also help to explain a dramatic shift of allegiance among African American voters. Since Reconstruction, southern blacks had supported the party of Lincoln, but as they migrated to the urban North they gained voting strength and abandoned the Republican Party. By 1936 northern blacks voted overwhelmingly for FDR, even though the Democrats were weak on the issue of civil rights. The New Deal included no legislation against discrimination, and FDR silently allowed Congress to reject antilynching laws. New Deal agencies did, however, offer more assistance to poor, unemployed African Americans than previous federal programs. And some New Dealers such as Harold Ickes, Harry Hopkins, and Will Alexander committed themselves to equal rights. Mary McLeod Bethune, a prominent African American educator and close friend of Eleanor Roosevelt, served the New Deal as director of the National Youth Administration's Office of Negro Affairs, which gave jobs and training to some 300,000 young African Americans. Besides controlling her own Special Negro Fund, Bethune successfully pressured other New Deal administrators to open their programs to blacks. With perhaps a million African American families depending on the WPA by 1939, black voters had solid economic reasons for joining the New Deal coalition.

A similar logic explains why women reformers threw their support to the Democrats in the 1930s. Once again, FDR had no feminist agenda, and New Deal programs discriminated against women by offering lower pay and restricting jobs by sex. But as with African Americans, women benefited in unprecedented numbers from New Deal welfare and jobs programs. For the first time in American history, a woman, Frances Perkins, was appointed to the cabinet. "At last," said Molly Dewson, director of the Women's Division of the Democratic National Committee, "women had their foot inside the door."

The most prominent female reformer associated with the New Deal was Eleanor Roosevelt. She was in many ways the last great representative of a woman's reform tradition that flourished in the Progressive Era. She had worked in a settlement house and campaigned for suffrage and progressive causes. Eleanor and Franklin made a remarkable political couple. Millions of Americans read Eleanor's opinions in her weekly newspaper column, "My Day." She became for many Americans the conscience of the New Deal, the person closest to the president who spoke most forcefully for the downtrodden. Her well-deserved reputation for compassion protected her husband in at least two ways. Liberals who might have been more critical of the New Deal instead relied on Eleanor Roosevelt to push the president in the direction of more progressive reform. At the same time, conservatives who were charmed by FDR's personality blamed all the faults of the New Deal on his wife. "It was very simple," one southern journalist explained. "Credit Franklin, better known as He, for all the things you like, and blame Eleanor, better known as She, or 'that woman,' for all the things you don't like." This way, southern conservatives reasoned, "He was cleared, She was castigated, and We were happy."

Although four years of the New Deal had not lifted the Depression, the economy was making headway. Jobs programs had put millions of Americans to work; the banking crisis was over; the rural economy had been stabilized. Based on this record and the backing of his powerful coalition of southern whites, northern urban voters, the labor movement, and many other Americans, FDR won reelection by a landslide in 1936. He captured over 60 percent of the popular vote and, in the Electoral College, defeated his Republican opponent Alf Landon in every state but Maine and Vermont. Landon, the governor of Kansas, even lost his home state. The new Democratic coalition also won sweeping command of the Congress. Seventy-six Democratic senators faced a mere 16 Republicans. In the House, the Democratic majority was even stronger, 333 to 89. Roosevelt now stood at the peak of his power.

Crisis of the New Deal

When the members of the new Congress took their seats in 1937 it seemed as if Roosevelt was unbeatable, but within a year the New Deal was all but paralyzed. A politically costly fight to "pack" the Supreme Court at last gave Roosevelt's conservative opponents a winning issue. A sharp recession further encouraged the New Deal's enemies and provoked an intellectual crisis within the administration itself. In 1938, when the Republicans regained much of their congressional strength, the reform energies of the New Deal were largely spent. Within a year the nation turned its attention to rising threats from overseas.

> **Last Spring I thought you really intended to do something. Now I have given it all up. Henceforward I am swearing eternal vengeance on the financial barons and I will do every single thing I can to bring about communism.**
>
> INDIANA FARMER TO FDR,
> October 16, 1933

Conservatives Counterattack

With conservative opponents vanquished, it seemed as if New Dealers could finish the job begun in 1933. Administration progressives like Frances Perkins hoped that legislation already passed could now be strengthened.

FDR himself appeared to be poised to launch the next great wave of New Deal reforms, but one apparently immovable barrier stood in the way: the U.S. Supreme Court. The Court had already struck down the NIRA and the AAA, and recent rulings made it seem that neither Social Security nor the Wagner Act were safe from the Court's nine "old men." Before he went on, Roosevelt wanted to change the Court. He had not yet had the opportunity to appoint any new justices, and pundits joked that the elderly judges refused to die. Sure that a constitutional amendment supporting his program would take too long or fail, FDR launched a reckless and unpopular effort to "reform" the Court. He proposed legislation that would allow the president to appoint a new justice for every sitting member of the Court over 70 years of age. This "court packing" plan, as Roosevelt's opponents labeled it, would have given the president as many as six new appointments.

Conservatives had long complained of FDR's "dictatorial" powers, and the court plan seemed to confirm their warnings. They formed the National Committee to Uphold Constitutional Government and skillfully cultivated congressional allies, allowing Democrats to take the lead in opposing the court reform. Even the New Deal's allies refused to campaign for the president's bill, and it took all of his political power and prestige to keep it before a hostile Congress. By the end of the summer of 1937, it was over and the bill defeated.

Ironically, Roosevelt eventually won his point. Several of the justices soon retired, giving FDR the critical appointments he needed to swing the Court in the administration's favor. The Supreme Court backed away from its narrow conception of the role of the federal government; nevertheless, FDR's court plan proved a costly mistake. The defeat of court reform emboldened the president's opponents. In November 1937 the administration's critics issued a Conservative Manifesto calling for balanced budgets, states' rights, lower taxes, and the defense of private property and the capitalist system. It heralded the themes around which conservatives would rally for the remainder of the century. In some cases, opposition was purely a matter of interest group pressure, but behind the manifesto lay some hard political realities that drove the conservatives into opposition.

Southern congressmen, for example, were motivated by a desire to preserve white privilege. Federal programs that offered alternatives to subsistence wages disturbed entrenched systems of political and economic dominance. Southern conservatives blamed the New Deal. "You ask any nigger in the street who's the greatest president in the world. Nine out of ten will tell you Franklin Roosevelt," one white southerner declared. "That's why I think he's so dangerous."

In the rural South and West there were growing fears that the New Deal was becoming too closely tied to the urban working class in the Northeast. To counteract this trend, conservatives appealed to the deeply rooted American suspicions of central government. Still, conservatives were not strong enough to block all New Deal legislation. Farm-state representatives needed Roosevelt's support. In late 1937 the administration succeeded in passing housing and farm tenancy reforms. In 1938 Congress passed the Fair Labor Standards Act, requiring the payment of overtime after 40 hours of work in a week, establishing a minimum wage, and eliminating child labor. Even with flagging support, FDR could enact proposals blocked during the Progressive Era.

However, the 1938 congressional elections gave the conservatives the strength they needed to bring New Deal reform to an end. The president tried to purge leading conservatives by campaigning against them, but the attempt failed. Republicans gained 75 seats in the House and were now strong enough in the Senate to organize an effective anti–New Deal coalition with southern Democrats. By then, a jolting recession had created a crisis of confidence within the New Deal itself.

AMERICA AND THE WORLD

>> The Global Depression

In 1930, mulberry trees covered the hills of the Japanese islands of Hokkaido and Honshu. In parts of Japan, two-thirds of the cultivated land was fodder for the silkworms that produced Japan's leading export. Over 2 million families depended on silk, which went chiefly to the United States, where it was made into the fashionable stockings worn by American women.

The silk market was the one bright spot in Japan's economy after World War I. Chinese consumers had boycotted Japan to protest land grabs during the war. In 1923, an earthquake followed by fires and a tidal wave leveled Tokyo and Yokohama. Japan was not alone: in much of the world, economies stagnated in the 1920s under the burden of war reparations and war loans. One of the worst-hit was Italy, where lingering unemployment contributed to the rise of Benito Mussolini's fascist government in 1922. But the New York Stock Exchange crash triggered a global depression. As the world's leading creditor, producer, and consumer, the United States exported its financial disaster to the world.

Countries tied to a single commodity or to the American market suffered most. After the crash, American women stopped buying stockings, and the price of silk dropped by three-quarters. By the end of 1931, Japanese silk farmers were broke; by the next year, they were starving. Similar catastrophes unfolded in the rubber-growing regions of Malaya and the coffee farms of Guatemala. International prices for Australian wool, Cuban sugar, Canadian wheat, and Egyptian cotton plummeted. Brazil, unable to export coffee, used it to fuel locomotives. Everywhere, it seemed, the environment and the economy joined forces to destroy farmers. In Rwanda a famine aggravated by the loss of tin exports killed 40,000. In China, 25 million people fled when the Yangtze River broke its banks in 1935.

The disruption of trade intensified conflict in India, Africa, and other areas under imperial rule. Unable to collect taxes at the ports, colonial governments imposed head taxes or government monopolies that shifted burdens onto the rural poor. The distress of the peasantry intensified demands for independence in India, and Mohandas Gandhi's satyagraha, civil resistance, reached a peak in 1932, when 32,500 nonviolent protestors filled the jails. The French government of Indochina (Vietnam) forced rice farmers to pay taxes in gold. Uprisings against French rule grew in frequency and violence as the Depression wore on, as did insurgencies against the U.S. colony in the Philippines. In the industrial countries, jobless people stood in breadlines and built shanties near the centers of civilization and culture. More than 2 million workers were unemployed in Britain. American loans to Germany dried up in 1930, and by the end of the year two out of every five Germans were out of work. This catastrophe, together with a hyperinflation that wiped out the savings of most of central Europe's middle class, silenced the voices of political moderates. This was the worst economic crisis in memory, and voters demanded extreme action. Each country now looked out for itself, marshaling scarce resources and forming self-contained economies known as autarkies. Under nationalist leaders Getulio Vargas and José Félix Uriburu, Brazil and Argentina restricted trade and steered investment into industry. The Soviet Union, already cut off from the capitalist world, built "socialism in one country." Japan merged its colonies in Taiwan, Korea, and Manchuria into a "Greater East Asia Co-Prosperity Sphere." The 1932 Ottawa Accords merged Britain, its empire, Canada, and Australia into

continued

No Fireside Chat José Uriburu broadcasting shortly after taking power in a military coup in 1930. Uriburu's dictatorship began a period of Argentina's history known as "the infamous decade."

>> **AMERICA AND THE WORLD** *continued*

a self-contained economic bloc. In Germany, this policy was called *Grossraumwirtschaft*, the economics of large areas. It was the policy of the National Socialist (Nazi) Party led by Adolf Hitler.

Autarky exacted heavy demands on citizens, requiring them to sacrifice prosperity, liberty, and lives for the nation. Efficiency was more important than democracy, and regimes around the world became more ruthless and less free. Even to Americans, dictatorships had a high-tech, modern sheen. "If this country ever needed a Mussolini," Senator David A. Reed remarked, "it needs one now." In 1927, an Indiana automaker unveiled a new streamlined model, the Studebaker Dictator. FDR and other American leaders drew the connections between global trade, autarky, repression, and war. "If goods don't cross borders," Secretary of State Cordell Hull observed, "armies will." As another global war loomed, they recognized it as a contest between dictatorship and democracy, but also as a conflict between economic systems. The outcome would mean either autarky or a New Deal for the world. ●

The Liberal Crisis of Confidence

During the 1936 campaign Roosevelt was stung by the conservative criticism of his failure to balance the budget. He had leveled the same charge against Hoover four years earlier, but the demands of the Depression made it difficult and dangerous to reduce government spending. Furthermore, deficit spending seemed to be helping resuscitate the economy.

Hoping to silence his conservative critics after his reelection, Roosevelt ordered a sharp cutback in relief expenditures in 1937. On top of an ill-timed contraction of the money supply ordered by the Federal Reserve and the removal of $2 billion from the economy by the new Social Security taxes, Roosevelt's economy measure had a disastrous effect. Once again, the stock market crashed and industrial production plummeted. Even the relatively healthy automobile, rubber, and electrical industries were seriously hurt. Instead of being silenced, opponents carped about the "Roosevelt Recession" and accused the administration of destroying business confidence.

Among the president's advisers, the competition between the budget balancers and the deficit spenders intensified. This was an important turning point in the intellectual history of the New Deal, as well as of twentieth-century American politics. Until 1938, the orthodoxy that associated economic health with balanced budgets was firmly entrenched in government and the business community. Experience with the recession of 1937–1938 converted young New Dealers to the newer economic theories associated with John Maynard Keynes, the great English economist. During periods of economic stagnation, Keynes argued, the government needs to stimulate recovery through deficit spending. The goal of fiscal policy was no longer to encourage production, but rather to increase purchasing power among ordinary consumers. Roosevelt himself never fully embraced these theories, but more and more members of his administration found them attractive. Moreover, the massive inflow of government funds during World War II brought breathtaking economic revival and seemed to confirm the wisdom of Keynesian economics. Until the 1980s, presidents of both parties subscribed to

Keynesian theory, although they differed on what kind of government programs federal spending should buy.

Conclusion

The New Deal did not bring an end to the Depression, and this was undoubtedly its greatest failure. Nevertheless, FDR achieved other important goals. "I want to save our system," he told a White House visitor in 1935, "the capitalistic system." By this standard, the New Deal was a smashing success. By allowing Americans to survive the worst collapse in the history of capitalism while preserving core freedoms, the New Deal reaffirmed democracy at a time when most of the industrialized world chose dictatorship. The New Deal also created a system of security for the vast majority of American people. National systems of unemployment compensation, old-age pensions, and welfare programs grew from the stout sapling planted during the 1930s. Farm owners received new protections, as did the very soil of the nation. Workers were granted the right to organize, hours of labor were limited, child labor ended, and wages held above the bare minimum. Moreover, the financial system was stabilized and made more secure, to the benefit of investors, depositors, and the economy as a whole.

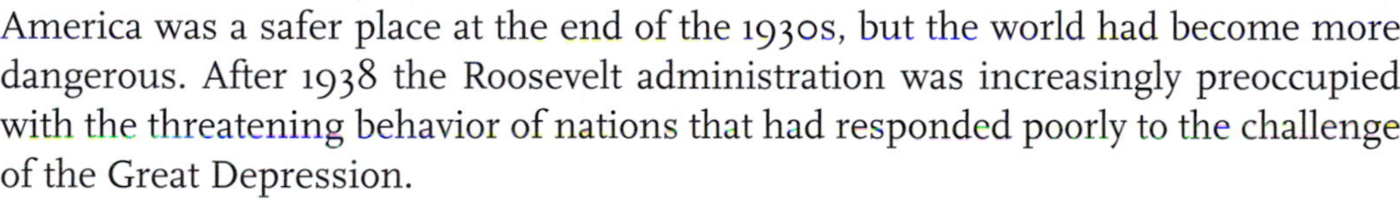

America was a safer place at the end of the 1930s, but the world had become more dangerous. After 1938 the Roosevelt administration was increasingly preoccupied with the threatening behavior of nations that had responded poorly to the challenge of the Great Depression.

Further Readings

Ben S. Bernanke, *Essays on the Great Depression* (2000). A distinguished economist compares the strategies different nations used to attack the economic crisis and finds that those who abandoned the gold standard first recovered faster.

Alan Brinkley, *The End of Reform* (1995). An intellectual history of the "internal crisis" of the New Deal.

Lizabeth Cohen, *Making a New Deal: Industrial Workers in Chicago, 1919–1939* (1990). This work successfully combines labor history with the history of popular culture.

James Goodman, *Stories of Scottsboro* (1994). A highly readable retelling of one of the most notorious trials of the 1930s through the eyes of various participants.

David E. Hamilton, *From New Day to New Deal: American Farm Policy from Hoover to Roosevelt, 1928–1933* (1991). How economists in Washington dealt with a farm crisis that had no explanation in economic theory.

Ellis W. Hawley, *The New Deal and the Problem of Monopoly: A Study in Economic Ambivalence* (1966). One of the first and most authoritative economic histories of the New Deal.

Richard Hofstadter, *The American Political Tradition* (1948). The critical chapter on FDR is a classic that anticipated later treatments of the broker state.

David M. Kennedy, *Freedom from Fear: The American People in Depression and War* (1999). A strong recent synthesis of the period from 1933 to 1945.

William E. Leuchtenberg, *Franklin D. Roosevelt and the New Deal* (1963). Still the best short survey of the New Deal and the president who made it.

Arthur Schlesinger Jr., *The Age of Roosevelt,* 3 vols. (1957–1960). A literary and scholarly masterpiece of heroic history.

Amity Shlaes, *The Forgotten Man: A New History of the Great Depression* (2008). This revisionist account criticizes FDR for the New Deal's excesses and defends Hoover's noninterventionist approach.

Who, What?

Herbert Hoover 797
FDR 801
Huey Long 809
Eleanor Roosevelt 814
The New Deal 800
CCC 803
TVA 804
Social Security 811
Wagner Act 812
Autarkies 817

>> Timeline >>

▼ 1928
Herbert Hoover elected president

▼ 1929
Stock market crash

▼ 1930
Hawley-Smoot Tariff enacted

▼ 1931
National Credit Corporation authorized

▼ 1932
Franklin Roosevelt elected president

▼ 1933
FDR declares a bank holiday
First Hundred Days
Emergency Banking Act passed
Economy Act passed
Civilian Conservation Corps (CCC)
United States goes off the gold standard
Agricultural Adjustment Act (AAA)
Emergency Farm Mortgage Act
Tennessee Valley Authority (TVA)
Truth in Securities Act

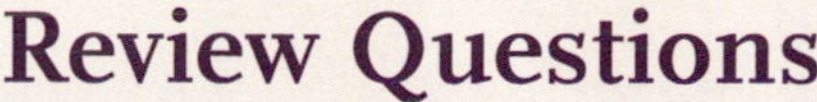

Review Questions

1. Did the stock market crash cause the Great Depression?
2. How did Roosevelt's philosophy of government differ from Hoover's?
3. What setbacks caused FDR to launch a second New Deal?
4. Compare the American response to the Depression to that of Britain, Germany, and Japan. Why did other industrial countries choose different paths?
5. What were Franklin Roosevelt's attributes as a leader? What aspects of his style inspired confidence or animosity?
6. Histories of the Depression focus on national statistics and large-scale programs. How could you retell the story of the 1930s from a local, personal perspective?

Websites

PBS, "Jim Crow Stories." The 1930s were years of struggle for African Americans in the segregated South. Hear of these experiences firsthand, from those who lived through them. http://www.pbs.org/wnet/jimcrow/stories.html

WBUR Radio, "Haunting the Quabbin." What happens when a federal dam project comes to an area? The Quabbin Reservoir brought water and power to Boston and created jobs for some, but whole towns lay at the bottom of the valley flooded by the new dam. http://www.insideout.org/documentaries/hauntingquabbin/

For further review materials and resource information, please visit www.oup.com/us/ofthepeople

National Industrial Recovery Act (NIRA)
Glass-Steagall Banking Act
Farm Credit Act

▼ 1935
Second Hundred Days
NIRA declared unconstitutional
National Labor Relations Act
Social Security Act

▼ 1936
AAA overturned
Gone with the Wind published
FDR reelected

▼ 1937
FDR announces "court packing" plan
Economy goes into recession

▼ 1938
Second Agricultural Adjustment Act
Fair Labor Standards Act
New Deal opponents win big in Congress

▼ 1939
Administrative Reorganization Act
British actress Vivien Leigh stars in *Gone with the Wind*
Britain and France declare war on Germany

CHAPTER 25

Common Threads 

>> What strategic and domestic issues were at stake in the debate over American entry into the war?

>> Did the war consolidate, or overturn, New Deal reforms?

>> In what ways did the war generate economic opportunities and highlight issues of civil rights?

The Second World War

1941–1945

AMERICAN PORTRAIT

>> A. Philip Randolph

"Who is this guy Randolph," Joseph Rauh wondered, and "what the hell has he got on the President of the U.S.?" It was June 1941 and Rauh, a government attorney, had just been instructed to draft a presidential order prohibiting discrimination on grounds of "race, color, creed, or national origin" in defense industries. It was a radical departure from decades of official support for legalized racism. It would use the economic muscle of the federal government to overturn job segregation nationwide, and in the process make enemies for President Franklin Roosevelt. Rauh was enthusiastic, but he couldn't understand why FDR, with his reliance on southern votes, would even consider it. The president was bending to pressure, Rauh learned, from African Americans led by a charismatic organizer named A. Philip Randolph.

Raised in Florida and educated at New York's City College, Randolph had founded the largest African American labor union, the Brotherhood of Sleeping Car Porters, in 1925. Porters traveled the railroads as baggage handlers and valets, and during the Depression years Randolph's influence extended into every downtown station and rural depot reached by the Brotherhood's magazine, the *Messenger.*

In 1941, it looked to Randolph like only a matter of months before the United States entered the war raging in Europe and Asia. He believed, according to FBI informants, "that Negroes make most fundamental gains in periods of great social upheaval." War would create an opportunity to achieve equality, but only if African Americans demanded it. "The Negro sat by idly during the first world war thinking conditions would get better," he told an audience in Oklahoma City. "That won't be the procedure during the duration of this conflict."

In January 1941, Randolph called for African Americans to march to Washington to demand an end to job discrimination. Only 3 percent of workers in war industries were people of color. "The administration leaders in Washington will never give the Negro justice," he declared, "until they see masses, ten, twenty, fifty thousand Negroes on the White House lawn." The March on Washington Movement (MOWM) was largely bluff. No buses were chartered, and there were no plans for where the thousands would sleep and eat, but Roosevelt and the FBI believed it enough to try to head it off.

A protest march would embarrass the government, and Roosevelt had the power to accede to Randolph's demands. Using the leverage of federal defense contracts, the president could desegregate a large portion of the economy without even asking Congress. He opened negotiations with Randolph through Eleanor Roosevelt. The organizers agreed to cancel the march in return for a presidential directive—Executive Order 8802—establishing a Fair Employment Practices Committee to assure fairness in hiring.

It was a victory for civil rights and for Randolph personally. If the Emancipation Proclamation had ended physical slavery, the New York *Amsterdam News* declared, E.O. 8802 ended "economic slavery." Within a year, thousands of African Americans would be working at high-tech jobs in aircraft factories and arms plants. Randolph had recognized that war created an opening for changing the economic and political rules of the game. The social upheaval of war touched all Americans. The armed forces sent millions, to serve and fight, everywhere from the Arctic to the tropics. Millions of others left home to work in plants producing war materiel. Government stepped in to run the economy, and corporations, labor, the states, and universities fashioned new relationships to the federal government. The war stimulated revolutionary advances

continued

>> **AMERICAN PORTRAIT** *continued*

in science, industry, and agriculture. The United States itself became the foremost military and economic power in a world destroyed by war.

These changes enlarged the discretionary powers of the federal government and particularly the presidency. Americans willingly, even eagerly, accepted personal sacrifices and greater federal authority as part of the price of victory. As the March on Washington Movement proved, the president's enhanced powers could enlarge the freedoms and opportunities enjoyed by Americans, but they could also restrict individual liberties. Many Japanese Americans spent the war imprisoned in "relocation centers," and just six months after Roosevelt signed Executive Order 8802, the FBI placed Randolph's name on a list of persons to be placed in "custodial detention" in the event of a national emergency. The war unsettled the economy and society, enlisting all Americans in a global crusade and arousing both idealism and fear.

OUTLINE

Island in a Totalitarian Sea

Randolph's movement capitalized on a world crisis that reached back to the treaty that ended World War I. The Depression heightened international tensions, turning regional conflicts in Africa, Europe, and Asia into tests of ideology and power. In 1937 Japan attacked China. Two years later when Germany invaded Poland, France and Britain declared war, beginning World War II in Europe. As with the last war, Americans had time to reflect on the origins of the world crisis before it affected them directly. Most blamed the conflict on the failures of the Versailles Treaty and the desperation caused by the global Depression. Nations and empires were solving economic problems with military force.

Americans were divided, however, on how their country ought to respond. Isolationists believed the United States should stay out of war and secure the Western Hemisphere against attack. But Roosevelt and other internationalists believed the United States had to support the nations fighting Germany and Japan. The alternatives reflected different visions of America's role in the world and responsibilities at home. Internationalists saw a free-trading open-door world economy as a solution to international conflict. Isolationists worried about growing federal power and the ambitions of Britain and the Soviet Union. The threat of fascism forced Americans to ask whether their own economy and government could measure up in the competition between nations.

Internationalists and isolationists both knew war would change American society. The future of world politics and the world economy would be shaped by America's choice of allies and war aims. In 1940, most Americans opposed aid to the enemies of fascism, fearing that giving such aid would lead the United States to become involved. When France's defeat left Britain to fight alone, the polls shifted as more Americans saw aid to Britain as an alternative to U.S. involvement. Japan's attack on Pearl Harbor in December 1941 ended a debate that divided the nation.

> **If Hitler destroys freedom everywhere else, it will perish here. Ringed around by a world hostile to our way of life, we should be forced to become a great military power.**
>
> *FORTUNE* MAGAZINE, June 1941

A World of Hostile Blocs

The Depression destroyed the liberal international order based on free trade. For a century, governments around the world had favored policies that increased the movement of goods, people, and investment across borders. The steamship and telegraph accelerated that trend. In many respects, the world economy was more "globalized" before World War I than it is today. Movement toward an open-door world slowed during World War I and the 1920s, and then stopped completely with the Depression. World trade shrank from almost $3 billion a year in 1929 to less than $1 billion in 1933. Empires and nations began to restrict the movement of goods, capital, and people, and to regiment their societies in the pursuit of national self-sufficiency. Everywhere, it seemed, governments became more ruthless and less free.

Dictators enticed their followers with visions of imperial conquests and racial supremacy. Mussolini promised to build a new Roman Empire in Africa and the Mediterranean. Japanese schoolchildren learned that they belonged to a "Yamato race," purer and more virtuous than the inferior peoples they would one day rule. In Germany, Hitler built a state based on racism and brutality. Urging Germans to defend themselves against the *Untermenschen,* subhumans, in their midst—Jews, Gypsies, homosexuals—he suspended civil rights, purged non-Aryans from government and the professions, and compelled art, literature, and science to reflect the Nazi Party's racial conception of the world. A secret police, the Gestapo, hunted down enemies of the regime, and a Nazi army, the SS, enforced party rule.

Jews were the main target of Nazi terror. In 1935, the Nuremberg Laws stripped Jews of citizenship and outlawed intermarriage with members of the "Aryan race." On the night of November 9, 1938, Nazi stormtroopers and ordinary citizens rampaged throughout Germany, burning synagogues and destroying Jewish shops, homes, and hospitals, killing 100 Jews and arresting 30,000 more. *Kristallnacht,* the "night of the broken glass," alerted Americans to the scale of the terror. Until then FDR thought international opinion would restrain Hitler. Now he was no longer sure.

The American president grew apprehensive as Germany, Italy, and Japan, together known as the Axis powers, sought to solve their economic problems through military conquest. Italy invaded Ethiopia in 1935. In July 1937, Japan attacked China. The following year, Hitler's troops marched into Austria. Roosevelt worried the Axis would soon control most of Europe and Asia, but American leaders had an even darker fear, one they scarcely breathed: that in a world of rival economic blocs, totalitarianism would outcompete democracy. Free markets and free labor might be no match for the ruthless, modern efficiency of the fascist states. The United States would be, Assistant Secretary of State Adolf Berle worried, "an old-fashioned general store in a town full of chain stores." It would have to regiment its own citizens just to keep up. The United States would be forced to enlist industry, labor, and agriculture into a "state system," *Fortune* magazine predicted, "which, in its own defense, would have to take on the character of Hitler's system."

The Good Neighbor

Some believed the United States ought to retreat into its own self-contained sphere, and in the early 1930s policy briefly took that direction. The Hawley-Smoot Tariff of 1930 blocked most imports, but within a year, FDR reversed course and began pushing trade as the answer to America's economic problems. He reacted mainly to the vision of his single-minded secretary of state, Cordell Hull. A conservative former senator from Tennessee, Hull believed the Open Door was the cure for dictatorship and depression. The best way to ensure peace, he argued, was to give all countries equal access to the world's markets. In a world of empires and blocs, Hull's formulation turned an old foreign policy tradition, the Open Door, into a bold plan for building international peace and prosperity.

Using loans and the lure of the vast American market, Roosevelt and Hull slowly began to reopen markets in Latin America. The "Good Neighbor" policy—encouraging trade and renouncing the use of force—actually began with Herbert Hoover. FDR expanded the policy and made it his own. A new Export-Import Bank financed transactions, and a Reciprocal Trade Act lowered tariffs. Hull surprised the Pan American Conference at Montevideo, Uruguay, in 1933 by approving a declaration that no nation had the right to intervene in the affairs of another. Good Neighbor policies undermined German and Japanese economic ventures, and Latin American governments invited the FBI to track down Axis agents on their soil.

In 1938, after absorbing Austria, Hitler demanded part of Czechoslovakia's territory. Czechoslovakia's allies, Britain and France, agreed to negotiations, and in a meeting at Munich in September they yielded to Hitler's demands. FDR cabled Hitler a last-minute appeal for restraint, but he accepted the final decision. The victors of World War I feared that a small war over Czechoslovakia would escalate into a larger one. After World War II, the term "Munich" came to symbolize the failure of attempts to appease aggressors, but in 1938 Americans were unsure how best to guard their freedoms in a hostile world.

America First?

As the Axis threat grew, Roosevelt pushed for a buildup of U.S. forces, but Congress and the public disagreed. Disillusioned by the results of the last war, the public earnestly wanted to stay out of the conflicts in Europe and Asia. Polls indicated that more than 70 percent believed the United States had been tricked into World War I. Half a million students pledged that if another war came, they would refuse to serve. Senator Gerald P. Nye charged that the munitions industry was lobbying for war. Pacifists, economic nationalists, and veterans groups, backed by the *Chicago Tribune* and the Hearst newspapers, comprised a powerful isolationist constituency that aimed to prevent the United States from being drawn into hostilities.

From 1935 to 1937, Congress passed annual Neutrality Acts prohibiting loans and credits to nations engaged in war. The action took place against the backdrop of the Spanish Civil War in which Fascist forces, aided by Germany and Italy, fought against democratic, Loyalist forces aided by the Soviet Union. The war aroused passions in the United States, and some 3,000 Americans volunteered to fight with the Loyalists. Precisely for that reason, Congress decided to stay out of the conflict. The Neutrality Acts restricted the president's ability to aid the enemies of fascism just as Munich made the danger clear.

Charles Lindbergh and the America First Committee campaigned against involvement in Europe's war. With Britain's defeat likely, they urged neutrality and defense of the Western Hemisphere as the only chance to keep America safe.

After the fall of 1939, Roosevelt watched his worst nightmare come true, as the United States became an island in a world dominated by force. The Soviet Union signed a nonaggression treaty with Germany. The full terms of the Nazi-Soviet pact were secret, leading diplomats to fear the worst, a totalitarian alliance stretching from the Rhine to the Pacific. In September, German armies struck Poland, using tanks and dive-bombers to slice deep into the interior. Reporters used the new term *Blitzkrieg,* "lightning war," to describe the German tactics. Hitler and Soviet leader Josef Stalin split Poland between them. Britain and France declared war on Germany.

The following April, Nazi armies invaded Denmark and Norway. On May 10, 1940, Hitler launched an all-out offensive in the West. Tank columns pierced French lines in the Ardennes Forest and turned right toward the English Channel. France folded along with Belgium and the Netherlands. Britain stood alone against the German onslaught. Roosevelt now had to reckon with the possibility that Britain might surrender, placing the British fleet, control of the Atlantic, and possibly even Canada in Hitler's hands. Already the German air force, the *Luftwaffe,* was dueling for control of the skies over southern England.

Determined to shore up this last line of defense, Roosevelt used his powers as commander in chief to bypass the Neutrality Acts. In June 1940, he submitted a bill to create the first peacetime draft in American history. He declared army weapons and supplies "surplus" so they could be donated to Britain. In September 1940, he traded Britain fifty old destroyers for leases to eight naval bases in Newfoundland, Bermuda, and the Caribbean.

The isolationists now found themselves isolated. Sympathy for Britain grew as radio audiences heard the sounds of air attacks on London. Two-thirds of the public favored the draft, but isolationists were not ready to give up. In September 1940, the America First Committee launched a new campaign that urged Americans to distance themselves from Europe and prepare for their own defense. Charles A. Lindbergh and Senator Burton Wheeler headlined America First rallies. The only reason for the United States to become involved, Lindbergh argued, "is because there are powerful elements in America who desire us to take part. They represent a small minority . . . but they control much of the machinery of influence and propaganda."

Roosevelt worried the 1940 election would become a referendum on intervention. Isolationist senator Robert Taft was a leading contender for the nomination, but the Republicans chose Wendell L. Willkie, an anti–New Deal internationalist. In his acceptance speech, Willkie endorsed the draft and expressed sympathy for Britain. With defense and foreign policy issues off the table, the only thing Willkie had to offer was a younger, fresher face. FDR won an unprecedented third term by a 5-million-vote margin.

Means Short of War

British prime minister Winston Churchill waited until after election day to broach the delicate but urgent issue of war finances. Britain had been buying arms on a "cash and carry" basis, but it was now out of funds. The Neutrality Act prohibited new loans, but without arms Britain would have to surrender. FDR gave his cabinet a weekend to come up with a plan, and the following Monday he produced the answer himself. Instead of loaning money, the United States would lend arms and equipment. Roosevelt compared the idea to lending a garden hose to a neighbor whose house is on fire. "There would be a gentleman's obligation to repay," but since there would be no loans, it would not violate the Neutrality Act. Lend-Lease, as the program came to be called, put the U.S. "arsenal of democracy" on Britain's side and granted FDR unprecedented powers to arm allies. The Lend-Lease bill, H.R. 1776, passed the Senate by a two-to-one margin in 1941.

Repayment took the form of economic concessions. Hull saw Lend-Lease as a chance to crack one of the largest autarkic blocs, the British Empire. He insisted that in return for aid, Britain had to discard the Ottawa Accords and open its empire to American trade. Churchill's economic adviser, John Maynard Keynes, reluctantly agreed. Britain was now, at least formally, committed to the Open Door. Later that year Churchill and Roosevelt met aboard the cruisers *Augusta* and *Prince of Wales* off the Newfoundland coast to issue a declaration of war aims, the Atlantic Charter. It assured all nations "victor and vanquished" equal access to the trade and raw materials of the world.

In June 1941, Hitler stunned the world again by launching a lightning invasion of the Soviet Union. Three million men backed by 3,000 tanks slashed through the Soviet defenses and rolled toward Moscow and Leningrad. Secretary of War Henry Stimson predicted that in three months the Axis would control Europe and Asia, but George C. Marshall, the army's chief of staff, reckoned that this might be a turning point. If the Soviet army could hold the area between Moscow and the Black Sea, the Germans would have a long winter. Roosevelt shared his optimism. The eastern front took pressure off Britain and gave the Allies a real chance to defeat Hitler. Roosevelt extended Lend-Lease aid to Moscow. The German columns advanced without interruption, but to the dismay of Hitler's officers, Russian soldiers did not respond to *Blitzkrieg* as French and Polish soldiers had. "Even when encircled, the Russians stood their ground and fought," a Nazi general reported.

German U-boats concentrated on severing Britain's lifelines, sinking half a million tons of shipping a month. To ease the burden on the British navy, Roosevelt fought an undeclared naval war against Germany in the western Atlantic. The U.S. Navy convoyed merchant ships as far as Iceland, where British destroyers took over. FDR said he was offering "all aid short of war," but it was not far short. In September a U-boat fired torpedoes at the USS *Greer,* and the destroyer threw back depth charges. Roosevelt ordered aggressive patrols to expel German and Italian vessels from the western Atlantic. In the Battle of the Atlantic he had crossed the line from neutrality to belligerency, and he appeared to be seeking an incident that would make it official.

Japan, meanwhile, probed into Southeast Asia. In 1939, Japanese militarists had adopted a "go south" strategy, planning to capture oil fields in the Dutch East Indies and encircle China. Because the Philippines, a U.S. territory, lay across the invasion route, the question for the Japanese was not whether to declare war on the United States, but when. In July 1941, Japanese troops established bases in French Indochina. Roosevelt saw this as a threat, but, preoccupied with war in Europe, he wanted to forestall war in the Pacific. U.S. diplomats opened talks with Japan while Marshall dispatched a fleet of B-17s in an attempt to deter an attack. When Japanese troop convoys moved into the South China Sea, Hull broke off negotiations and cut off U.S. oil exports, Japan's only source of fuel. On November 27, Marshall warned army and navy commands in Hawaii and the Philippines to expect "an aggressive move by Japan" in the next few days. The Philippines, Thailand, and Malaya were the likely targets.

On Sunday afternoon, December 7, Americans listening to the radio heard that aircraft "believed to be from Japan" had attacked U.S. bases at Pearl Harbor in Hawaii. At 7:40 A.M. Hawaii time, 181 planes had bombed and strafed the airfields on Oahu, destroying or damaging more than 200 planes on the ground. Bombers then made a run at the 96 ships of the U.S. Pacific Fleet anchored next to each other. Three torpedoes struck the battleship *Oklahoma,* capsizing it with 400 crew members aboard. Alongside her the *Maryland* went down, spreading flaming oil over the shallow waters. A bomb exploded in the *Arizona*'s forward magazine, breaking the ship in half and killing over a thousand men. Hours later, more bad news came from the Philippines, where Japanese bombers also caught American planes on the ground. The following day, President Roosevelt appeared before Congress to ask for a declaration of war against Japan. Only one representative, Montana's Jeannette Rankin, voted no. On December 11, Germany honored its alliance with Japan and declared war on the United States.

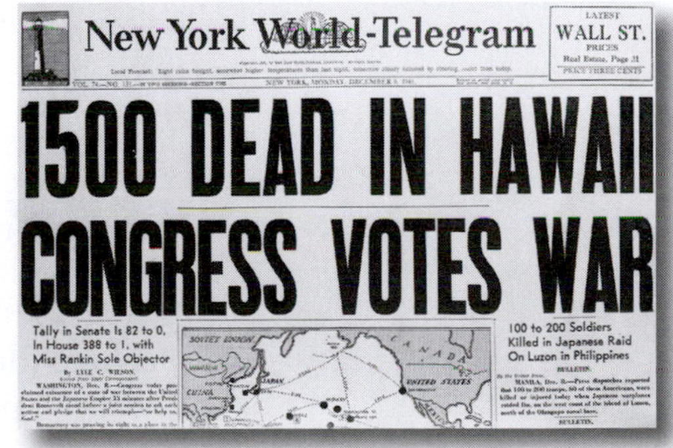
New York World-Telegram

LATEST WALL ST. PRICES

Real Estate, Page 31

1500 DEAD IN HAWAII

CONGRESS VOTES WAR

Tally in Senate Is 82 to 0, In House 388 to 1, with Miss Rankin Sole Objector

100 to 200 Soldiers Killed in Japanese Raid On Luzon in Philippines

Some historians have argued that Roosevelt knew of the approaching attack but withheld warnings, in order to draw the United States into war. In fact, naval authorities at Pearl Harbor anticipated an attack but expected it to come in a different form. They doubted that Japan had the ability or audacity to

Pearl Harbor Japan's attack on the U.S. Navy's principal Pacific base at Pearl Harbor brought the United States into World War II. For Japan, it was the opening phase of a campaign to capture European and American colonies in Asia.

project air and sea power across the Pacific in secrecy. When Japanese planes destroyed American aircraft on the ground in the Philippines nine hours after the Pearl Harbor attack, Douglas MacArthur observed that the bombers must have been flown by Germans. Such preconceptions blinded commanders to the warning signs.

Turning the Tide

For the Allies there was only bad news in the first half of 1942. Japanese invaders walked over the numerically superior British and Dutch armies in Southeast Asia and captured the American islands of Guam and Wake. In February, the "impregnable" fortress of Singapore surrendered, with most of the Australian and Indian armies still inside. Japan's Combined Fleet commanded the waters between Hawaii and India, striking at will. MacArthur declared Manila an open city and staged an Alamo-style defense of the Bataan Peninsula and the fortress island of Corregidor.

Few could see it, but the tide was beginning to turn. The Soviets stopped the German advance in front of Moscow. On April 18, U.S. Colonel James Doolittle's B-25 bombers raided Tokyo. Roosevelt wanted to hold the line in the Pacific while coming to the aid of Britain and the Soviet Union as soon as possible. This meant stopping Japan, creating an American army, and putting it into action on the other side of the Atlantic. None of those jobs would be easy.

Midway and Coral Sea

"We can run wild for six months or a year," Admiral Isoroku Yamamoto prophesied before designing the victorious attack on Pearl Harbor, "but after that I have utterly no confidence." Panic-stricken Americans imagined enemy landings in California,

Map 25-1 World War II in the Pacific, 1942–1945 Japan established a barrier of fortified islands across the western Pacific. U.S. forces penetrated it westward from Hawaii and from Australia northward through the Solomon Islands to the Philippines.

> Through the haze I saw Marines stumble and pitch forward as they got hit. I then looked neither right nor left but just straight to my front. The farther we went, the worse it got.
>
> EUGENE B. SLEDGE, Battle of Peleliu, September 1944

but Japan's strategy was never so ambitious. It called for fortifying a defensive screen of islands in the western Pacific and holding the Allies at bay until they sued for peace. "The fact that the Japanese did not return to Pearl Harbor and complete the job was the greatest help for us," Chester W. Nimitz, the U.S. Pacific commander, later remembered, "for they left their principal enemy with time to catch his breath, restore his morale, and rebuild his forces."

After the Doolittle raid, the Japanese realized their error and laid plans to lure the U.S. Pacific Fleet into battle. The increase in radio traffic helped Commander Joseph Rochefort, who had already partly succeeded in breaking the Japanese codes. In late April, he was confident enough to tell Nimitz that Japan was planning an attack on Port Moresby on the island of New Guinea. Nimitz dispatched two carriers, *Lexington* and *Yorktown,* to intercept the invasion convoy and its carrier escorts. The Battle of Coral Sea was the first between carrier task forces, an entirely new type of sea battle. Sailors never saw the enemy's ships, only their aircraft, which struck with devastating speed. Planes from *Yorktown* turned back the Japanese transports while *Lexington*'s dive bombers dispatched the carrier *Shoho*. The Japanese retaliated, fatally crippling the *Lexington* and ripping a hole in *Yorktown*'s deck. The two sides withdrew after fighting to a draw.

Yamamoto next chose to attack the U.S. fleet directly. Sending a diversionary attack toward the Aleutians, he aimed his main attack at Midway, the westernmost outpost of the Hawaiian chain. Yamamoto gambled that Nimitz would divide his forces, allowing the Combined Fleet to crush the remnant guarding Hawaii. But trusting Rochefort's code breakers, Nimitz knew the real target was Midway. He also learned from Coral Sea that aircraft, not battleships, were the winning weapons. He hastily assembled task forces around the carriers *Hornet* and *Enterprise* and reinforced airfields on Midway and Oahu. Crews worked night and day to repair the *Yorktown* in time for the battle. The American fleet was still outnumbered, but this time surprise was on its side.

When Japanese aircraft encountered stiff resistance from Midway's flak gunners on the morning of June 4, they returned to their carriers and prepared for an unplanned second attack. With bombers, bombs, and aviation fuel littering their decks, Japan's four carriers were vulnerable. Defending Zeros had been drawn down to the water by a U.S. torpedo bomber attack. At that moment dive bombers from *Yorktown* and *Enterprise* burst out of the clouds. They destroyed three carriers in a matter of minutes. The mighty Combined Fleet ceased to exist. Midway put Japan on the defensive and allowed the United States to concentrate on building an army and winning the war in Europe.

Gone with the Draft

The German army that overran France in May 1940 consisted of 136 mechanized divisions of 17,000 men each. The United States had only five divisions and was still using horse cavalry. "Against Europe's total war," *Time* observed, "the U.S. Army looked like a few nice boys with BB guns." Realizing the danger, military officials drew up plans for a 10-million-man force. As in World War I, the United States had to find ways to house, equip, and transport the army, but this time it would be five times larger. By December 1941, 2 million men and 80,000 women had enlisted. A year later the total exceeded 5 million.

The 99th Pursuit Squadron, Known as the Black Eagles The Black Eagles trained at the Tuskegee Institute and engaged the Luftwaffe in the skies over North Africa.

Buses rolled into the new camps and unloaded recruits in front of drill instructors. Boot camp aimed to erase the civilian personality and replace it with an instinct for obedience and action. Selectees, as they were called, learned that there were three ways of doing things: the right way, the wrong way, and the army way. Eugene Sledge left college to join the marines and found himself standing in line at a camp in San Diego. "Your soul may belong to Jesus," his drill instructor bellowed, "but your ass belongs to the Marines." After 13 weeks of calisthenics, close-order drill, road marches, and rifle practice, he was assigned to the infantry.

Recruits hungered for a weekend pass, but in base towns in the South and West, where many bases were located, there was little for them to do except loiter on street corners and look for trouble. The War Department joined several charities in creating the United Services Organization (USO), to provide a "home away from home" with meals, dances, movies, and wholesome entertainment. Still, wherever there were large numbers of men on leave, soldiers fought with each other and with the locals. Distinctions of apparel and race could stimulate violence. Southerners lynched African American soldiers for wearing their uniforms. In 1943, riots erupted in Harlem after police arrested an African American soldier in uniform. The same year, sailors in Los Angeles attacked Mexican American shipyard workers who wore distinctive "zoot suits." In both cases the clothes signified a disruption of the established social order, a process accelerated by the war.

The army leadership struggled to preserve its racial traditions amid wartime changes. Like the multiethnic imperial armies of Britain and France, the U.S. Army consisted of segregated units, some with special functions. The Japanese American 442nd Regimental Combat Team and the marines' Navajo "code talkers" became well known. African Americans served in the army in segregated units, and until 1942 they were excluded from the navy altogether. Roosevelt ordered the services to admit African Americans and appointed an African American brigadier general, Benjamin O. Davis, but injustices remained. Even blood plasma was segregated in military hospitals.

Two issues aroused the most anger among African Americans: exclusion from combat and the treatment of soldiers at southern bases. Many GIs in uniform experienced the indignity of being refused service at restaurants where German prisoners of war were allowed to eat. Mutinies and race riots erupted at bases in Florida, Alabama, and Louisiana where African American soldiers were housed separately and denied furlough privileges. The army responded by sending African American GIs to the war theaters.

Though desperately short of infantrymen, the army kept African Americans out of frontline units and assigned them to menial chores. Combat symbolized full citizenship, and the NAACP pressed Roosevelt to create African American fighting units. An African American infantry division, the 92nd, went into battle in Italy; three air units—among them the 99th Pursuit Squadron, known as the Tuskegee Airmen—flew against the *Luftwaffe;* and one mechanized battalion, the 761st Tanks, received a commendation for action in the Ardennes. However, most African Americans went into the line individually as replacements, as during the Battle of the Bulge in late 1944. Racially mixed units aroused few complaints in the field, the NAACP noted; resistance to desegregation came mainly from Washington.

With manpower in short supply, the armed forces reluctantly enlisted women. Congress passed legislation creating the Women's Army Corps (the WACs) in 1942. The navy signaled its reluctance in the title of its auxiliary, the Women Accepted for Volunteer Emergency Service (WAVES). Eventually more than 100,000 women served as mechanics, typists, pilots, cooks, and nurses, but the unusual feature of the U.S. forces was not how many women served, but how few. Nearly every other warring country mobilized women for industry and combat, leaving the state to perform traditionally female jobs: caring for children, the sick, and the elderly, functions that continued after the war. Publics in Europe, Canada, and Australia came to accept this government role, but in the United States "welfare" continued to be associated with poor relief.

The Winning Weapons

During World War II weapons technology advanced with blinding speed. The quality of a nation's weapons often depended on how recently they had moved from the drafting table to mass production. Entering the war late, the United States gained a technological edge. American factories tooled up to produce models using the latest innovations, but many of these would not reach the fighting fronts until 1943 or later.

Until then, troops had to make do with weapons that were outclassed by their Axis counterparts. Marines went into action on Guadalcanal wearing World War I–era helmets and carrying the 1903 Springfield rifle. Japan's Zero was substantially faster and lighter than any American fighter. After 1943, the advantage began to pass to the Americans. The M1 rifle was the finest infantry weapon in the war. Artillery was precise and lethal, and American crews were skilled practitioners of the devastating "time-on-target" technique, which delivered shells from several directions simultaneously, leaving no place to hide. In the air, the elegant P-51 Mustang, a high-speed ultra-long-range fighter, could escort bomber groups from Britain as far as Berlin.

It dominated the French skies after D-Day. American four-engine bombers—the B-17 Flying Fortress and the B-24 Liberator—were superior in range and capacity to German or Japanese air weapons. In 1944, the B-29 Superfortress, with its 141-foot wingspan, 10-ton bomb load, and awesome 4,200-mile range, took to the skies over the Pacific. Uniquely adapted to city-busting raids, the Superforts incinerated one Japanese city after another. American tanks, however, remained inferior to their German counterparts throughout the war, owing to the army's failure to recognize the importance of this weapon.

Lawrence Beall-Smith, *Task Force Hornets* (1943) Carrier warfare was unique to the Pacific theater, where opposing fleets used aircraft to strike each other across vast expanses of ocean.

Quantity was often a substitute for quality, however, and American designers sometimes cut corners to make a product that could be mass produced. The results were impressive. When Allied troops landed in France in 1944, they enjoyed a superiority of 20 to 1 in tanks and 25 to 1 in aircraft. When Roosevelt set a production target of 50,000 aircraft in 1940, the Germans considered it a bluff, but American factories turned out almost 300,000 planes during the war. Often, abundance resulted in attrition tactics that pitted American numbers against Axis skill. An American soldier in Salerno asked a captured German lieutenant why he had surrendered. "The Americans kept sending tanks down the road," the German replied. "Every time they sent a tank, we knocked it out. Finally, we ran out of ammunition, and the Americans didn't run out of tanks."

Americans also developed a number of secret weapons. The War Department funded defense laboratories at Johns Hopkins, MIT, Harvard, and other universities, forging a permanent link between government, science, and the military. American and British scientists invented one of the first "smart" bombs, the proximity fuse, which set its own range by bouncing a radio signal off its target. To keep it from falling into Axis hands, Allies used it only for the air defense of London, on ships in the Pacific, and in the worst moments of the battles of Iwo Jima and the Bulge. Collaboration between American and British scientists produced improvements in sonar and radar, penicillin, and the atomic bomb.

The Manhattan Project that produced the atomic bomb was the war's largest military-scientific-industrial enterprise. In 1939, Albert Einstein warned Roosevelt that the Germans might invent a nuclear weapon. The National Academy of Sciences concluded that a weapon of "superlatively destructive power" could be built, and General Leslie R. Groves was put in charge of the project, which eventually employed 600,000 people and cost $2 billion. World War II's marriage of technology and war changed warfare, and it also changed science. Researchers and inventors had once worked alone on problems of their own choosing. Now they worked in teams at government-funded laboratories on problems assigned by Washington.

The Second Front

To reassure Britain and the Soviet Union, FDR adopted a "Europe First" strategy, holding the line against Japan while directing the main effort at Nazi Germany. The Allies had little in common except that Hitler had chosen them as enemies. Britain was struggling to preserve its empire. The Soviet Union had once been allied with Germany and had a nonaggression pact with Japan. Roosevelt needed to keep this shaky coalition together long enough to defeat Hitler. His greatest fear was that one or both of the Allies would make a separate peace or be knocked out of the war before the American economy could be mobilized. Stalin and Churchill each had their own opinions about how to use American power, and their conflicting aims produced bitter disputes over strategy.

As the Nazis closed in on the Soviet oil fields during 1942, Stalin pleaded with Britain and the United States to launch an invasion of France. Roosevelt and Marshall also wanted a second front. Since the Civil War, U.S. military doctrine had favored attacking the main body of the enemy's army, which could be done only in northern Europe. But to the British, the idea of a western front evoked the horrors of the trench warfare of World War I. Britain could not sustain those losses a second time in a century. Instead, Churchill wanted to encircle the Nazi empire and attack the "soft underbelly" of the Axis from the Mediterranean.

Concerned about U-boats and the inexperience of American troops, FDR reluctantly accepted Churchill's plan. A month after Pearl Harbor he had promised Stalin a second front "this year." In late 1942, he postponed it to the spring of 1943. Finally, in June 1943, he told Stalin it would not take place until 1944. The delays reinforced Stalin's suspicions that the capitalist powers were waiting for the USSR's defeat.

Instead of invading Europe, the Americans chose a softer target, North Africa, and troops commanded by Lt. Gen. Dwight Eisenhower landed in Algeria and Morocco on the morning of November 8, 1942. As they advanced east to link up with British forces attacking into Tunisia, German tank divisions under General Erwin Rommel burst through the Kasserine Pass and trapped American columns in high, rocky terrain. Panicky troops fled, blowing up their ammunition stores. One GI described the Panzers as "huge monsters, with a yellow tiger painted on their sides." Once through the pass, Rommel briefly had a chance to encircle and defeat the Allied forces, but his Italian commanders ordered him to advance in another direction. The Americans and British regrouped for a counterattack.

Ernie Pyle, the popular war correspondent, reassured American readers that "though they didn't do too well in the beginning, there was never at any time any question about American bravery." Eisenhower was not so sure. He sacked the commander responsible for defending the Kasserine and replaced him with Maj. Gen. George S. Patton. The army increased basic training from 13 to 17 weeks and reviewed its doctrine and weapons. For Patton, the Kasserine debacle showed that firepower delivered by air, tanks, and artillery was more reliable than infantry. His preference for technology over bravery became ingrained in American strategy.

Map 25–2 World War II in Europe, 1942–1945 While the Soviets reduced the main German force along the eastern front, the British and American Allies advanced through Italy and France.

Allied forces captured Tunis and Bizerte on May 7, bagging 238,000 German and Italian prisoners. Rommel escaped to fight the Americans again in France a year later. At that time he would encounter a different American army, larger, more experienced, and equipped with the newest weapons. As it mobilized to fight the Axis, the United States was changing too. Industry and people were shifting around. Government took on new functions, and industry shifted into high gear.

Organizing for Production

To defeat regimented, totalitarian enemies, Americans had to gear their economy for war. Big government and corporations made possible the "miracle of production" that was winning the war and raising living standards. During the height of the Depression, FDR had never been bold enough to use deficit spending to stoke up the economy (a technique economists call a "Keynesian stimulus"), but during the war, half the money the federal government spent was borrowed, and nobody complained. The economy boomed. War contracts created 17 million new jobs. Industrial production doubled. The employment dial reached "full" in 1942 and stayed there until Japan surrendered.

> When Hitler put his war on wheels, he rolled it right down our alley.
>
> GEN. BREHON B. SOMERVELL

War industries worked by a new set of rules. Contractors depended on the government for financing, materials, and labor. New war plants, built at taxpayer expense, went up in towns that had seen little industry before. As industry moved, workers moved with it, changing jobs, migrating to the new boomtowns, and organizing themselves into a powerful political and economic force.

A Mixed Economy

The Roosevelt administration added new war agencies to control prices, assign labor, and gear up industry. It dusted off the tried-and-true methods from World War I—dollar-a-year men and "cost plus" contracts—and added new incentives, such as tax breaks for retooling and federal loans and subsidies. "You have to let business make money out of the process," Secretary of War Henry Stimson explained, "or business won't work." Sometimes it still wouldn't, and the government seized at various times the steel industry, the railroads, the coal mines, and even a department store chain.

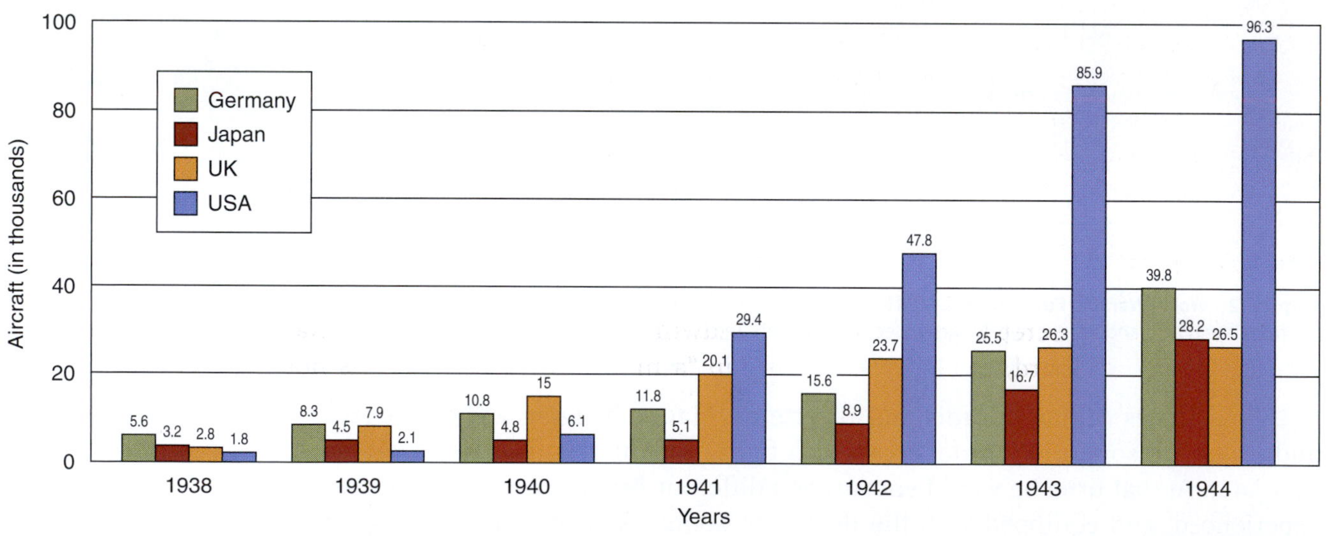

Figure 25-1 Number of Military Aircraft Produced U.S. production of military equipment lagged at first, but once in high gear it dwarfed that of the rest of the world. *I. C. B. Dear,* The Oxford Companion to World War II *(Oxford University Press, 1995), p. 22.*

A View of a Military Aircraft Facility in Long Island, New York, October 1942 Mass produced weapons allowed U.S. forces to win by attrition, wearing down the enemy with sheer weight and numbers.

Output soared. A Ford plant at Willow Run, Michigan, turned out a fleet of B-24s larger than the whole *Luftwaffe*. Cargo ships, which took longer than a year to build in 1941, were coming out of the Kaiser Shipyards in an average of 56 days. Entirely new industries such as synthetic rubber and Lucite (a clear, hard plastic used for aircraft windshields) appeared overnight. Industrial techniques applied to agriculture—mechanization and chemical herbicides and pesticides—raised output by one-third with 17 percent fewer farmers. Enterprising corporations patriotically increased their market share. Coca-Cola's mobile bottling plants followed the front lines, creating a global thirst for their product. Wrigley added a stick of gum to each K ration and made chewing gum a national habit.

Business leaders regained the prestige they had lost during the Depression. Major corporations like General Electric, Allis-Chalmers, and Westinghouse ran parts of the super-secret Manhattan Project. Edwin Witte, a member of the National War Labor Board, called this partnership "a mixed economy, which is not accurately described as either capitalism or socialism." Witte was sure that "individual initiative, work, and thrift count as much as ever" in the new economy, but he could not say how.

Most business was still small; 97 percent of manufacturing, for example, came from firms with just a few hundred employees. During the war, however, Congress and the administration drew a line between large high-tech firms, its partners in the business of national defense, and "small business" that had to be mollified with tax breaks and loans. "Small business" acquired its own federal agency and lobbying groups, while major corporations such as Boeing and General Electric negotiated long-term contractual relationships with the federal government. World War II permanently divided the economy into separate "government" and "market" sectors, each with its own rules and ways of dealing with Washington.

Industry Moves South and West

Although Detroit got its share, the bulk of war contracts went to states in the South and Southwest and on the Pacific Coast, shifting industry's center of gravity. Airplanes flown in World War I came from Dayton, Ohio, and Buffalo, New York, but the B-29 Superfortress, the most advanced plane at the end of World War II, was made in Seattle, Washington, Omaha, Nebraska, Wichita, Kansas, and Marietta, Georgia. The Manhattan Project's largest facilities at Oak Ridge, Tennessee, Hanford, Washington, and Los Alamos, New Mexico, likewise broke the historic pattern that had concentrated industry in the Northeast and Midwest.

There were several reasons for this shift. Industries that needed power gravitated to the huge hydroelectric grids created by the New Deal. Aluminum plants went up along the Tennessee and Columbia rivers to take advantage of abundant power from federal dams. The federal government also encouraged construction in the middle of the country to lessen the danger from enemy bombers. Corporations

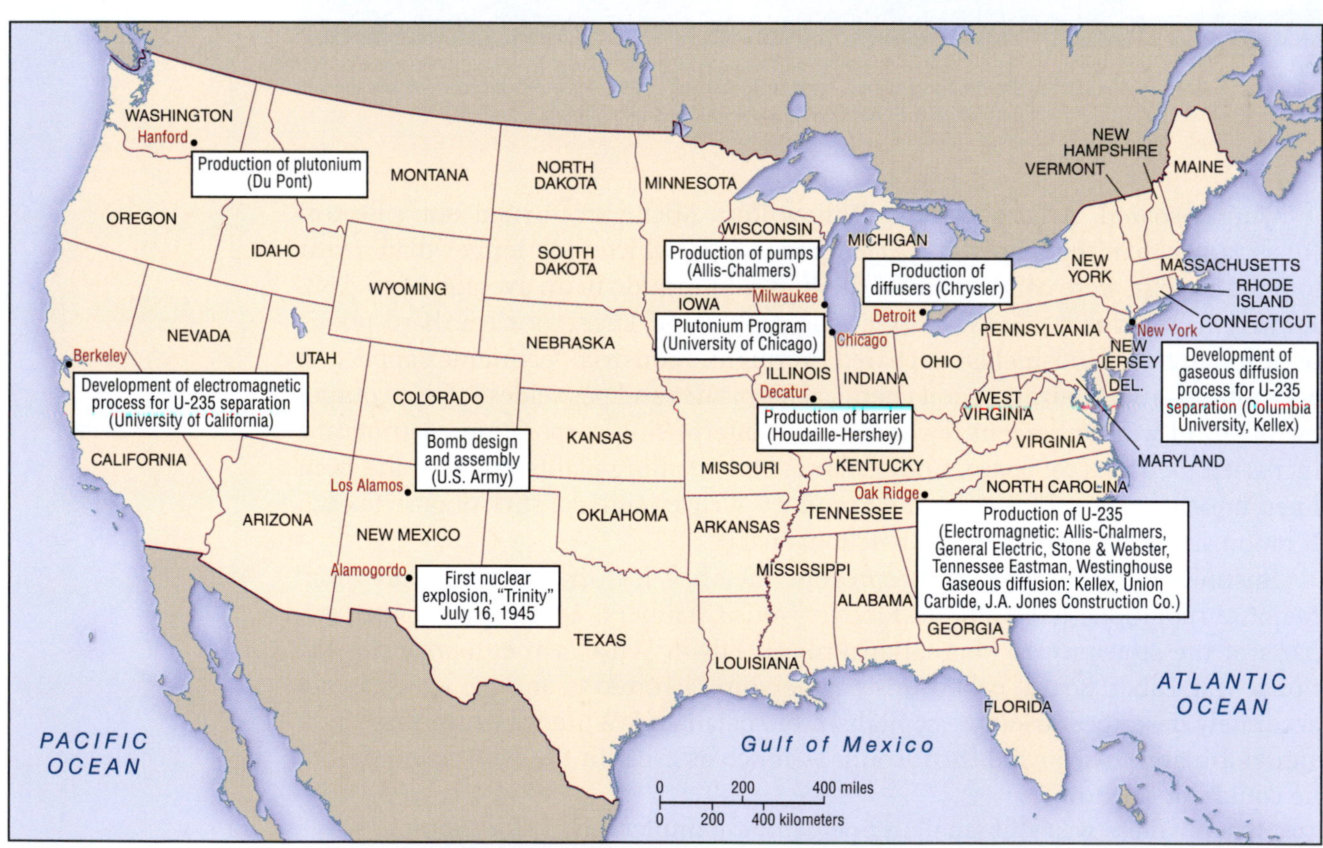

Map 25–3 The Manhattan Project The Manhattan Project created a new kind of collaboration between industry, government, and science. In a pattern of federal spending that would continue after the war, much of the new infrastructure was located in the South and West.

moved south and west to find low-wage nonunion workers. Powerful southern and western senators, who controlled military appropriations, also steered new factory development into their states.

The results were visible. The population of the West increased by 40 percent. Towns became cities overnight. The population of San Diego doubled in 1942. Los Angeles, Houston, Denver, Portland, Seattle, and Washington, DC, became wartime boomtowns. While "old" industries such as automobiles and steel remained the mainstay of the economy above the Mason-Dixon Line, the Sunbelt states of the South and West became the home of the gleaming industries of the future: plastics, aluminum, aircraft, and nuclear power.

Few people objected to government direction of the economy when it meant new jobs and industry in regions that had been poor. A 1942 Gallup poll showed that two-thirds of Americans wanted the federal government to register all adults and assign them to war work as needed. The Office of Price Administration enlisted women consumers to enforce price ceilings, and thousands wrote in to inform on their local grocers. Citizens volunteered for scrap drives, bond drives, and blood drives, and they dug victory gardens. The war effort was so popular that the administration did not worry much about propaganda. Roosevelt and other war managers—many of them former progressives—had learned a lesson from World War I: in gaining public support, inducements worked better than coercion.

New Jobs in New Places

As it had during World War I, the need for workers pushed up wages, brought new employees into the workforce, and set people on the move in search of better opportunities. It also swelled the ranks of organized labor from 10 million to almost 15 million between 1941 and 1945. The federal government enlisted labor as a partner in the war effort. Unions grew because of a federally mandated "maintenance of membership" policy, by which new employees automatically joined the union. Through the National Defense Mediation Board, the Roosevelt administration encouraged cooperation, furthering a process begun by the New Deal. When wildcat locals of the United Auto Workers struck North American Aviation plants in Los Angeles in 1941, Stimson sent the army to break the strike, but the NDMB then forced management to accept the union's wage demands. Through a combination of carrots and sticks, federal administrators encouraged a more collaborative, managerial style of union leadership. Unions did not have to struggle for membership or recognition; in return, they curbed militant locals and accepted federal oversight. Decision making moved from the one-story brick "locals" that dotted factory districts around the country to the marble headquarters of national unions in Washington, DC.

People moved to jobs, rather than the other way around, and some 4 million workers, taking with them another 5 million family members, migrated to the new sites of war production. "Scarcely a section of the country or a community of any size escaped the impact of this great migration," according to an official report. Some 200,000 Mexican *braceros* crossed the border to harvest crops. San Francisco's African American population doubled in a single year. At the peak of the migration, African Americans were arriving in Los Angeles at a rate of 300 to 400 a day. By leaving Mississippi to take a factory job in Los Angeles, a sharecropper could increase his salary six- or sevenfold. Migrants moved into cities crowded

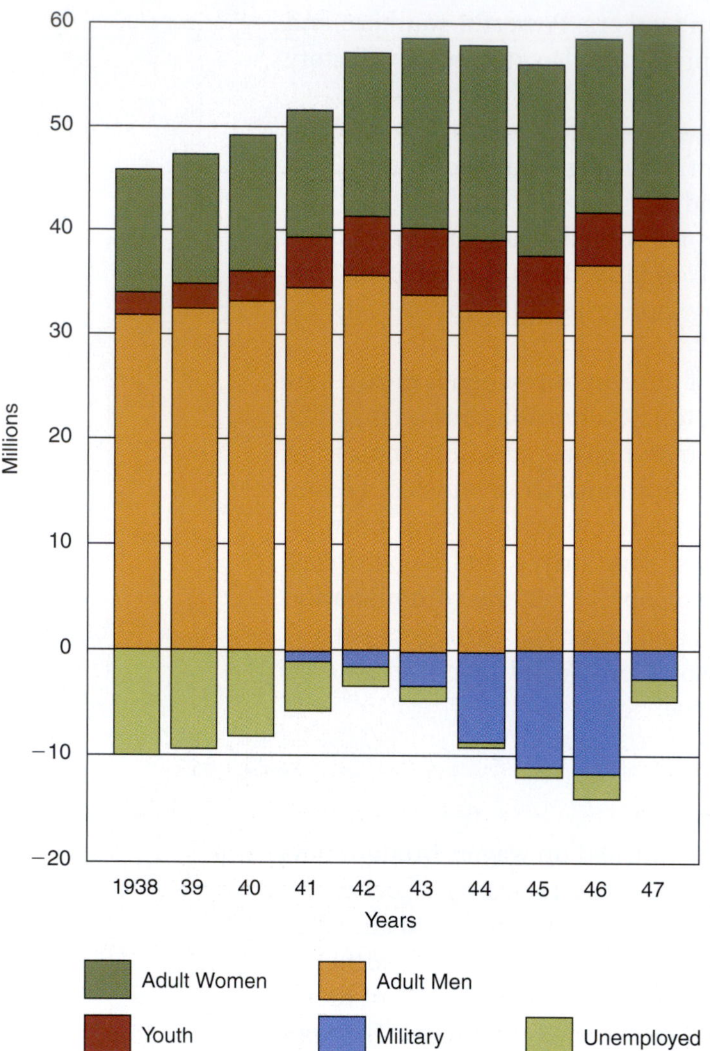

Figure 25-2 Makeup of U.S. Labor Force, 1938–1947 *Dear,* Oxford Companion to World War II, *p. 1182.*

with newcomers, families of overseas military personnel, ex-farmers seeking industrial jobs, and refugees from Europe.

Workers were generally happy with higher wages, but many would have been glad to have a decent place to live. New York, which had plenty of housing, suffered from unemployment while new factories were located in places with no housing. There were no rooms to rent within miles of Willow Run. In southern and western towns, workers "hot bedded"—slept in shifts in boardinghouses—or lived in cars. Frustrations over the housing shortage sometimes boiled over into racial conflict. In 1943, when the federal government constructed 1,000 units in Detroit, mob violence erupted over who would take possession of the dwellings. After two days of rioting, federal troops occupied the city. Housing remained a chronic problem throughout the war and for several years afterward.

Women in Industry

"Rosie the Riveter," the image of the glamorous machinist laboring to bring her man home sooner, was largely a creation of the Office of War Information. Industry needed workers, and the OWI promised women that running heavy machinery was no more difficult than using kitchen appliances. Some 36 percent of the wartime labor force was female, but that was only marginally higher than the peacetime figure. Few women left housework to take a job in an aircraft factory solely for patriotic reasons. Instead, the war economy shifted women workers into new roles, allowing some to move from service jobs into industry and those with factory jobs to take better-paid positions.

The number of manufacturing jobs for women grew from 12 million to 16.5 million, with many women moving into heavy industry as metalworkers, shipwrights, and assemblers of tanks and aircraft, jobs that had been off-limits before. Employers had once refused to hire women for such heavy labor, but under the pressures of wartime they found that machinery could take away some of the physical strain and actually improve efficiency. Women worked coke ovens in the hottest parts of steel plants; they operated blast furnaces and rolling mills. For many women, the war offered the first real chance for mobility.

Even so, employers did not offer equal pay. Unions either refused women membership or expelled them when the war ended. Employers gave little help to women trying to juggle job and family. The Lanham Act provided the first federal support for day care, but the 2,800 government centers were not nearly enough. "Latchkey children," left home alone while their mothers worked, were said to be a major problem. Experts saw female labor as necessary for the war effort but dangerous in the long run. "Many of them are rejecting their feminine roles," a social worker complained. "They wish to control their own fertility in marriage, and say they never wanted the children which had been thrust upon them." After the war, women were expected to yield their jobs to returning servicemen. They were blamed for neglecting their duties and encouraging juvenile delinquency, a backlash that had begun to build even before the war ended.

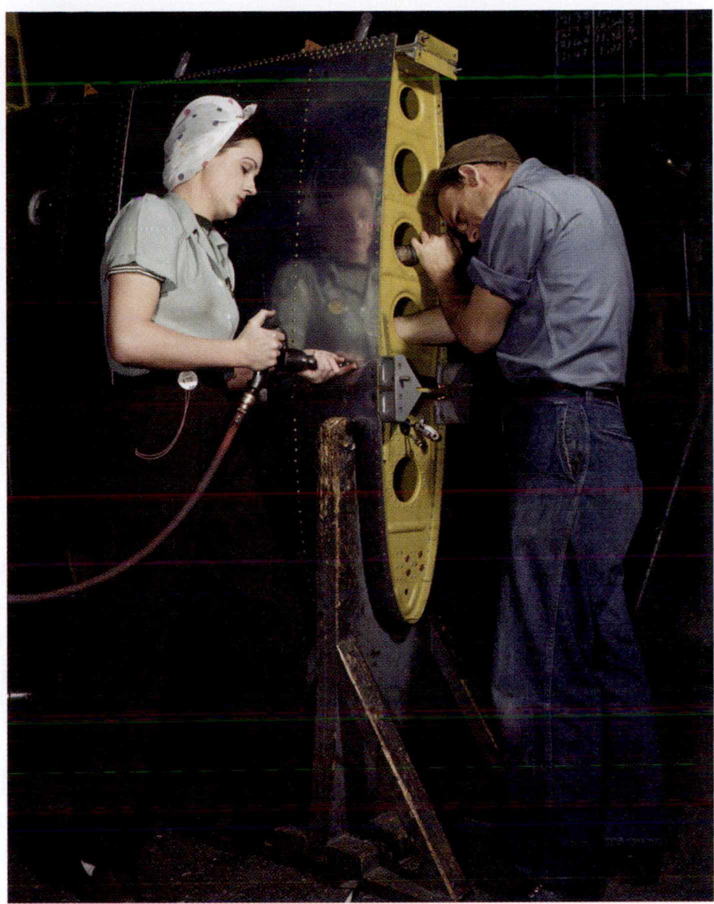

Flush riveting of aluminum wing panels required a steady hand. War industries employed thousands of women.

Between Idealism and Fear

In the movies Americans marched to war (and war plants) singing patriotic tunes by George M. Cohan, but in real life this war was noticeably free of high-minded idealism. Americans had already fought once to end all wars and keep the world safe for democracy. They were not ready to buy that bill of goods again. Journalist John Hersey asked marines on Guadalcanal what they were fighting for. "Scotch whiskey. Dames. A piece of blueberry pie. Music," they replied. Things were no clearer on the home front, where to writer Dwight Macdonald the war seemed to represent "the maximum of physical devastation accompanied by the minimum of human meaning." In one wartime advertisement, Goodyear Rubber Company asked, "What can you say to those whose hearts bear the aching burden of this conflict? That their sons have died in a noble cause? That the nation mourns with them?" Obviously not.

If Americans weren't sure what they were fighting for, they knew what they were fighting against: totalitarianism, gestapos, and master races. Throughout the war and after, totalitarianism provided a powerful symbol of what America and Americans ought to oppose. The president of the U.S. Chamber of Commerce denounced the New Deal as "fascist" and "totalitarian." Labor unions and civil rights groups used the same words to brand their enemies, but wartime rhetoric also held Americans to a higher standard of tolerance. "Religion makes no difference, except to a Nazi or somebody as stupid," Frank Sinatra explained in *The House I Live In* (1945), before bursting into song: "All races and religions; that's America to me."

> **If Hitler wins, down with the blacks! If the democracies win, the blacks are already down.**
>
> W. E. B. DUBOIS, 1941

Wartime leaders struggled to fill the inspirational vacuum, crafting some of the twentieth century's most stirring restatements of the democratic creed. Winston Churchill spoke of the destiny of the "English-speaking peoples," a global community with an inheritance of liberty and culture to protect. In his State of the Union address in January 1941, Franklin Roosevelt aspired to a world based on the "Four Freedoms": freedom of speech, freedom of worship, freedom from want, and freedom from fear. A month later, *Life* magazine published an essay by its founder, Henry Luce, entitled "The American Century." Coming before the United States had entered the war, at a moment when the Allies were falling back, it confronted defeatism with a powerfully optimistic vision. It foresaw a globalization of democracy, "a sharing with all people of our Bill of Rights, our Declaration of Independence, our Constitution, our magnificent industrial products, our technical skills." Luce put science and material abundance on a par with democracy among the gifts America had to offer the world. The administration responded with a bold plan for applying the Four Freedoms in practice. Vice President Henry Wallace proclaimed that in the "Century of the Common Man," nations would "measure freedom by standards of nutrition, education and self-government." He equated democracy—as American leaders would do in the postwar period—with schools, jobs, food, and a New Deal for the world.

African Americans sought to attain the four freedoms in an atmosphere of increasing racial hostility. Detroit was just one of many cities in which rapid economic growth touched off racial conflict. In Maryland, Michigan, New York, and Ohio white workers engaged in "hate strikes" to prevent the hiring of African American workers. Over 3,000 white employees of a naval shipyard burned African American neighborhoods in Beaumont, Texas, in June 1943. Curfews, rumors of riots, and white citizens' committees kept many other cities on edge.

African Americans responded by linking their struggle for rights in the United States to the global war against fascism. Thurgood Marshall, chief counsel for the NAACP, compared the Detroit rioters to "the Nazi Gestapo." In 1942, the *Pittsburgh Courier* launched the "Double V" campaign explicitly to join the struggles against racism and fascism in a fight for "victory at home as well as abroad." "Defeat Hitler, Mussolini, and Hirohito," it urged, "by Enforcing the Constitution and Abolishing Jim Crow." Membership in the NAACP grew tenfold during the war. In Chicago, students and activists inspired by the nonviolent tactics of Indian nationalist Mohandas Gandhi organized the Congress of Racial Equality (CORE), which desegregated restaurants and public facilities in the North. The NAACP won a legal victory in the Supreme Court case of *Smith v. Allwright* (1944), which invalidated all-white primary elections.

The experience of war may have been the greatest catalyst to change. Many African American veterans returned from the war determined not to accept discrimination any longer. Amzie Moore came back to Cleveland, Mississippi, after serving in the army and was elected head of the local NAACP chapter. "Here I am being shipped overseas," he said of his service in the Pacific, "and I been segregated from this man who I might have to save or he save my life. I didn't fail to tell it." The war prepared Moore and a generation of African Americans for the struggle ahead.

Japanese Internment

Idealism was no match for fear, and in the days after Pearl Harbor, panicky journalists, politicians, and military authorities perpetrated an injustice on American citizens of Japanese descent. Ominous signs reading "Civilian Exclusion Order" went up in California and the Pacific Northwest in February 1942. They instructed "Japanese aliens and non-aliens" to report to relocation centers for removal from the Pacific Coast "war zone." The Western Defense Command of Lt. Gen. John L. DeWitt and the *Los Angeles Times,* believing the Japanese planned to invade the West Coast, aroused the public against the Japanese "menace." FBI investigators found no suspicious plots and told the president so, but the press continued to print rumors. "The Pacific Coast is officially a combat zone," columnist Walter Lippmann observed. "There is plenty of room elsewhere for [the Japanese] to exercise his rights." Responding to the press, DeWitt, and the California congressional delegation, FDR ordered the relocation.

Internees and civil-liberties lawyers challenged the legality of confining American citizens without charge or trial. Fred Korematsu, a welder from San Leandro, California, took a new name and had his face surgically altered in a futile attempt to stay out of the camps. When he was arrested, the American Civil Liberties Union used his case to challenge the exclusion order. Supreme Court Justice Hugo Black upheld the evacuation policy as justified by "military necessity." In January 1947, the army's Western Defense Command applauded the record of the evacuation program and suggested that it could be used as a model for the treatment of suspect populations during the next national emergency.

No Shelter from the Holocaust

The United States might have saved more of the victims of Hitler's "final solution" had it chosen to do so. A combination of fear and anti-Semitism and a desire to avoid unwanted burdens led American leaders to dismiss the Holocaust as someone else's problem. The State Department, worried that spies and saboteurs would sneak in among the refugees, erected a paper wall of bureaucratic restrictions that kept the flow of immigrants to a trickle. Refugees found it easier to get a visa from China than from the United States. In 1939, the *St. Louis* steamed from Hamburg with 930 Jewish refugees aboard. American immigration officials refused to let the refugees ashore because they lacked proper papers—papers that would have had to be furnished by their Nazi persecutors. The ship and its passengers returned to Germany.

Once it began, Nazi Germany's systematic extermination of the Jews made news in the United States. Stories in the *New York Times* as early as 1942 described the deportations and concluded that "the greatest mass slaughter in history" was under way. At Auschwitz, Poland, in the most efficient, high-tech death camp, 2,000 people an hour could be killed with Zyklon-B gas. Jewish leaders begged War Department officials to bomb the camp or the rail lines leading to it. The city of Auschwitz was bombed twice in 1944, but John J. McCloy, the assistant secretary of war, refused to target the camp, dismissing it as a humanitarian matter of no concern to the army. Roosevelt, who also knew of the Holocaust, might have rallied public support for Hitler's victims. His inaction, according to historian David Wyman, was "the worst failure of his presidency."

AMERICAN LANDSCAPE

>> Manzanar

Jeanne Wakatsuki's exile into internment began with a Greyhound bus ride from Los Angeles across the Mojave Desert. When the shades came up a mile from her destination, she saw "a yellow swirl across a blurred, reddish setting sun. The bus was being pelted by what sounded like splattering rain. It wasn't rain. This was my first look at something I would soon know very well, a billowing flurry of dust and sand churned up by the wind through Owens Valley." Its lakes and rivers emptied by the Los Angeles aqueduct, Owens Valley was a man-made desert.

Temperatures ranged from 115 degrees in summer to well below freezing in winter. On an alkali flat beneath the towering Inyo Range, workmen were building the Manzanar Relocation Camp, 600 wood and tar paper barracks that would soon house more than 10,000 people. Each family received 20 square feet of floor space and an iron cot and army blanket for each member. Prisoners made the other furnishings themselves, filling burlap bags with straw for mattresses, making privacy screens from newspaper, crafting chairs and tables from spare lumber.

The prisoners fed themselves. They tilled the dry soil and planted tomatoes, turnips, radishes, watermelons, and corn. They also raised cattle, pigs, and poultry, making the camp self-sufficient in both meat and vegetables. "People who lived in Owens Valley during the war still remember the flowers and lush greenery they could see from the highway as they drove past the main gate," Wakatsuki later wrote. Prisoners opened repair shops, laundries, a newspaper, a clinic, and a cemetery. They practiced medicine and law. The Manzanar Co-Op, which sold retail and mail-order goods, did $1 million in business in 1944.

Manzanar was like a small city, except that it was surrounded by wire and armed guards. The camp administrators created a network of informants to spy on inmates. In December 1942, four prisoners beat up a man suspected of being an informant. When one was arrested, a group of prisoners demonstrated in front of the administration building to demand his release. Nervous guards fired into the crowd, killing two young men and wounding eight others. "You can't imagine how close we came to machine-gunning the whole bunch of them," a camp official explained. "The only thing that stopped us, I guess, were the effects such a shooting would have had on the Japs holding our boys in Manila and China."

It was the last "uprising" at the camp. Administrators censored the newspaper, prohibited expressions of Japanese culture, and required all meetings to be conducted in English. The community within the camp remained forever divided. Young men denounced their elders for respecting the law even when it was unjust. Administrators, with their persistent questionnaires, separated the angry from the docile and drew up blacklists.

Defiance was severely punished. Over 8,000 internees who would not renounce the emperor were separated from their families and sent to a camp at Tule Lake, California, and 263 young men who refused military service went to federal prison. Still, the majority of draft-eligible men in the camps served in the armed forces, many in intelligence and combat roles. The separation of the loyal from the disloyal, and the placement of so many in positions of trust, removed all justification for continuing to hold loyal Japanese Americans, apart from the political embarrassment their sudden release would cause.

Those who could—college students who gained admission to eastern universities, workers with contracts elsewhere, those who joined the armed forces—left, leaving only the very old and the very young. "What had to be endured was the climate, the confinement, the steady crumbling of family life," Wakatsuki wrote in her memoir, *Farewell to Manzanar.* "In such a narrowed world, in order to survive, you learn to contain your rage and your despair, and you try to re-create, as well as you can, your normality, some sense of things continuing." ●

When American soldiers penetrated Germany in 1945, they gained a new understanding of what they were fighting for and against. On April 15, Patton's Third Army liberated the Buchenwald death camp. Radio commentator Edward R. Murrow described the scene for listeners in the United States: the emaciated, skeleton-like survivors, the fetid piles of the dead, the ovens. "I pray you to believe what I have said about Buchenwald," he said. "I have reported what I saw." Eisenhower ordered photographs and films to be taken, and he brought German civilians from the surrounding communities to witness the mass burial, by bulldozer, of the corpses. Many GIs doubted that the things they had witnessed would be believed. "We got to talk about it, see?" one told reporter Martha Gellhorn. "We got to talk about it if anyone believes us or not."

Americans went into the First World War flushed with idealism and became disillusioned in victory's aftermath. The Second World War followed the reverse trajectory. Americans slowly came to see that their shopworn ideals offered what little protection there was against the hatred and bigotry that afflicted all nations, including their own. Rose Mclain of Washington State wrote her husband in the Pacific to promise "that our children will learn kindness, patience, and the depth of love . . . that they shall never know hate, selfishness and death from such [a war] as this has been."

Closing with the Enemy

"The Americans are so helpless," Joseph Goebbels, Hitler's propaganda minister, exclaimed in 1942, "that they must fall back again and again upon boasting about their matériel." After the North Africa campaign, the United States made good on its boasts. The American army was small—only 5 million compared to Germany's 9 million—but it was amply supplied and agile. Tactics emphasized speed and firepower, a combination suited to a nation so fond of the automobile. In 1944 and 1945 the United States carried the war to Japan and into the heart of Europe with a destructiveness never before witnessed. As the war drew to a close, Americans began to anticipate the difficulties of reconstructing the postwar world and to create institutions to structure a global economy at peace.

Taking the War to Europe

Using North Africa as a base, the Anglo-American Allies next attacked northward into Italy, knocking one of the Axis powers out of the war. In Sicily, where the Allies landed in July 1943, Patton applied the mobile, aggressive tactics he had advocated since 1940. Slicing the island in half with a thrust from Licata to Palermo and trapping a large part of the Italian army, he swung east to Messina but arrived too late to block the Germans' escape. The defeat shook Italy. Parliament deposed Mussolini and ordered his arrest. German troops took control and fiercely resisted the Allied landings at Salerno in September. Winter rains stopped the Anglo-American offensive south of Rome. "Vehicles were bogged above the axles," General Mark Clark grumbled, "the lowlands became seas of mud, and the German rearguard was cleverly entrenched in the hills." American troops finally broke through to Rome on June 5, 1944.

> **At the suggestion of Dr. Conant, the Secretary agreed that the most desirable target would be a vital war plant employing a large number of workers and closely surrounded by workers' houses.**
>
> MINUTES,
> Interim Committee of Scientific Advisers to the Secretary of War, May 31, 1945

The assault on France's Normandy coast the next day, D-Day, finally created the second front the Soviets had asked for in 1942. Early on the morning of June 6, 1944, the Allied invasion armada, thousands of supply and troopships and hundreds of warships, assembled off England's Channel coast and began the run into beaches designated Juno, Gold, Sword, Utah, and Omaha. Hitler had fortified the beaches with an "Atlantic Wall" of mines, underwater obstacles, heavy guns, and cement forts. Americans waded ashore on the lightly held Utah Beach without much difficulty, but on Omaha the small boats headed straight into concentrated fire from shore batteries. The boats unloaded too soon, and men with full packs plunged into deep water. Floating tanks equipped with rubber skirts overturned and sank with crews inside. Commanders briefly considered calling off the attack, but soldiers in small groups began moving inland to outflank German firing positions. By the end of the day, they held the beach.

Eisenhower's greatest fear was another Italy. The hedgerow country behind the beaches contained the most defensible terrain between the Channel and Germany. Each field and pasture was protected by earthen mounds topped with shrubs, natural walls that isolated troops. When a column of GIs crossed a hedgerow, "the Germans could knock off the first one or two, cause the others to duck down behind the bank and then call for his own mortar support," according to one infantryman. "The German mortars were very, very efficient." However, just as had happened on Omaha Beach, the defects of the generals' strategy were compensated by the initiative of men at the lowest ranks of the army. On their own, tankers experimented with devices to gouge holes through the hedgerows. Sergeant Curtis G. Culin crafted a set of tusks out of steel girders from a German roadblock. Thus equipped, "rhino" tanks could burst into an enemy-held enclosure and cover infantry following through the gap. By the end of the month the U.S. advance broke through the German defenses and captured the critical port city of Cherbourg.

Once in the open country, highly mobile American infantry chased the retreating enemy across France to the fortifications along the German border. There, in the Ardennes Forest, where panzers had pierced French lines in 1940, Hitler's armies rallied for a final desperate counterattack. Thirty divisions, supported by 1,000 aircraft, hit a lightly held sector of the American lines, broke through, and opened a "bulge" 40 miles wide and 60 miles deep in the Allied front. Two whole regiments were surrounded and forced to surrender, but the 101st Airborne, encircled and besieged at Bastogne, held on to a critical road junction, slowing the German advance

and allowing the Allies to bring in reinforcements. The Battle of the Bulge lasted a month and resulted in more than 10,000 American dead and 47,000 wounded, but the German army had lost the ability to resist.

Mitchell Jamieson's *Burial Grounds* (1944) Wartime censors carefully spared the American audience images of the anonymous, mass death of modern war, but scenes such as this one in Normandy always followed major battles.

Island Hopping in the Pacific

To get close enough to aim a knockout blow at Japan, the United States had to pierce the barrier of fortified islands stretching across the western Pacific. The army and the navy each had a strategy, and the two services bickered over supplies and the shortest route to Tokyo. Gen. Douglas MacArthur favored a thrust northward from Australia through the Solomon Islands and New Guinea to retake the Philippines. Nimitz preferred a thrust across the central Pacific to seize islands that could be staging areas for an air and land assault on Japan.

By November 1943, MacArthur's American and Australian forces had advanced to Bougainville, the largest of the Solomon Islands and the nearest to the Japanese air and naval complex at Rabaul. Jungle fighting on these islands was especially vicious. Atrocity stories became self-fulfilling, as each side treated the other without mercy, killing prisoners and mutilating the dead. Both sides fought with "a brutish, primitive hatred," according to Eugene Sledge, whose marine comrades kept gold teeth and skulls as trophies. Air attacks pulverized Rabaul's airfields and harbor in early 1944, opening the way for an advance into the southern Philippines.

Meanwhile, Nimitz launched a naval attack on Japan's island bases. With 11 new aircraft carriers, each holding 50 to 100 planes, the Fifth Fleet attacked Tarawa, a tiny atoll that contained 4,500 Japanese troops protected by log bunkers and hidden naval guns. Coral reefs snagged landing craft, forcing troops to wade ashore under heavy fire. Americans were shocked by the scale of the losses, more than 3,000 dead and wounded, for such a small piece of territory, but it was only one of many island battles. "Island hopping" from Tarawa to the Marshall Islands and then to the Marianas, American forces bypassed strongly held enemy islands and moved the battle lines closer to Japan.

The Allied capture of Saipan, Tinian, and Guam in July 1944 brought Japan within range of B-29 bombers. General Curtis LeMay brought his 21st Bomber Command to Saipan in January 1945 and began launching a new kind of air offensive against Japanese cities. LeMay experimented with low-level attacks using a mix of high explosives (to shatter houses) and incendiaries (to set fire to the debris). The proper mix could create a "firestorm," an inferno in which small fires coalesced into a flaming tornado hundreds of feet high. On the night of March 9, 1945, LeMay sent

334 bombers to Tokyo to light a fire that destroyed 267,000 buildings. The heat was so intense that the canals boiled, oxygen was burned from the air, and 83,000 people died from flames and suffocation. In the following months LeMay burned more than 60 percent of Japan's urban areas. Americans felt city busting was justified, but, as historian Ronald Spector has written, bomber crews "realized that this was something new, something more terrible than even the normal awfulness of war."

Building a New World

As the war progressed across Europe and the Pacific, Allied leaders met to discuss their visions of the world after victory. Meeting in Casablanca in 1943, Roosevelt and Churchill agreed to demand the unconditional surrender of the Axis powers, to give the Allies a free hand to set the terms of peace. No country planned for peace as carefully or extensively as the United States. The State, War, and Navy departments undertook a comprehensive survey of the world, examining each country and territory to determine its importance to the United States. The planners had only sketchy ideas about where future threats would come from, but based on experience they believed that American security would depend on having a functioning international organization, a global system of free trade, and a worldwide network of American military bases.

The loosely organized League of Nations stood little chance of maintaining the peace in the 1930s. Roosevelt envisioned a stronger organization led by regional powers who would act as "policemen" within designated spheres of influence. The new organization would disband empires, placing "trusteeships" over colonial territories preparing for self-government. The world after victory would be a world of nations, not empires or blocs. In September 1944, delegates from 39 nations met at the Dumbarton Oaks estate in Washington, DC, and sketched out a plan for a United Nations (UN) organization comprising a general assembly, in which all nations would be represented, and an executive council made up of the United States, China, the Soviet Union, Britain, and France.

To American leaders, the lesson of the 1930s had been that without prosperity there could be no peace. They wanted to remove the economic conditions that caused desperate people to follow dictators into war. A true victory, they imagined, would create an open-door world, in which goods and money could move freely, eliminating the need or justification for conquest. In 1943, before the UN existed as an organization, the United States created the United Nations Relief and Rehabilitation Administration (UNRRA) to provide food and medicine to areas retaken by the Allies. The Bretton Woods Conference (see feature) set conditions for a postwar expansion of trade. The army established schools at major universities where officers studied languages and discussed strategies for instilling a democratic culture in enemy nations. The invasion of Italy provided a first test of these techniques, and the United States drew on its resources as an immigrant nation to staff civil-affairs units with Italian-speaking officers.

Military planners were not ready to stake America's future security entirely on trade or international organizations. Pearl Harbor had shown that the Atlantic and Pacific oceans offered no protection against aggression. Military leaders could imagine aircraft and rockets striking deep into the American heartland without warning. Beginning in 1943, they laid plans for a global system of military bases from

AMERICA AND THE WORLD

>> Bretton Woods

As Allied armies struggled for control of Normandy in late June 1944, 300 economists, diplomats, and translators from 44 nations converged on the Mount Washington Hotel in Bretton Woods, New Hampshire. Army MPs were still tacking carpet and painting the lobby as they arrived. The hotel had gone out of business during the Depression, but a new owner, David Stoneman, reopened it in early 1944 in the hope that skiing would become popular once the war was over. With most big hotels already converted into barracks, this remote, run-down hotel was one of the few places where the United States could host a global conference.

Roosevelt and Churchill convened the conference to deal with the staggering economic problems that would follow the war. International trade had collapsed; several major world currencies—the franc, the mark, and the yen—were or soon would be valueless; Britain and the Soviet Union were approaching bankruptcy; and two-thirds of the world's gold reserves were held by one country, the United States. Allied leaders also recognized that peace in the postwar world would require a global system in which every nation could control its economic future.

Preventing a renewed Depression required each nation to combat unemployment, applying all its monetary and trade resources for self-recovery. Reporter I. F. Stone noted that the new international economy would have to accommodate this "positive governmental interference" in ways that the gold standard had never allowed. Every nation would need a welfare state, and no nation could be allowed to fail. "Prosperity is indivisible," Treasury Secretary Henry Morgenthau warned at the conference's opening session.

The use of gold as an international currency had expanded trade in the nineteenth century, but in the twentieth century it amplified economic crises and political instability by radically reducing consumption and employment in debtor countries. By the 1930s, the world economy had broken into rival blocs, each settling accounts using a different metal or currency (sterling, gold, the yen, etc.). To knit together an indivisible prosperity, the conferees at Bretton Woods needed to find substitutes for gold and empire: a new way to settle international debts, encourage trade expansion, and still allow national governments to pursue full employment.

Two strong personalities vied to be the architect of the postwar order. John Maynard Keynes, the brilliant British economist, wanted to create a global currency unit, the "bancor," that would allow a centralized world bank to expand or shrink the money supply as needed. The chief of the American delegation, Harry D. White, held that a world currency would be unnecessary if every lira, zloty, and balboa could be converted into U.S. dollars. Convertibility was the economic equivalent of a military alliance, and the United States should "attract other currencies into its orbit of influence."

The conference debated these proposals for a month. The United States' massive gold reserves gave its delegation a strong hand. White's assistant, Dean Acheson, settled a controversy over the location of the new world financial institutions—in Washington—by explaining simply "you fellows will have to give way in this matter, you know, if the fund is

continued

>> **AMERICA AND THE WORLD** *continued*

to go through." The conference's final resolutions were nearer to White's vision than to Keynes's.

The International Monetary Fund would manage international accounts. It fixed the relationship between gold and the dollar at $35 an ounce and pegged all other currencies to the dollar at fixed rates of exchange. The system brought an unprecedented predictability to international trade: the profits of Mexican wheat farmers no longer depended on the value of the peso but only on the value of wheat. The International Bank for Reconstruction and Development (later known as the World Bank) would promote growth and trade, Keynes explained, and "raise the standard of life and condition of labor everywhere."

Between them, the "Bretton Woods institutions" possessed broad powers to manage the global movement of capital. The IMF held to the system of fixed exchange rates until 1973, after which it managed the float of currencies against one another. IMF and World Bank loans have financed an expanding repertoire of development projects and reforms. By the 1990s, an international antiglobalization movement criticized the Bretton Woods institutions for enforcing international trade rules at the expense of local business, cultural diversity, and the environment. In 1944, however, critics of the new system objected that the plan gave national governments far too much leeway. The plan, columnist Walter Lippmann complained, provided "almost unlimited domestic freedom and diversity at the expense of international conformity and stability." After the straitjacket of the gold standard, the new rules seemed slack.

Contention between global and local interests began right there in the lobby at the Mount Washington. When deliberations went into overtime, delegates told the reservations clerk they needed three more days to straighten out the planet's finances. Stoneman went to Morganthau and explained that he had a hotel to run, other guests had booked rooms, and the conferees would have to leave. Morgenthau replied that the army could seize the hotel, if necessary. The hotel keeper caved. Score one for the forces of globalization. ●

the Azores to Algiers, Dhahran, Calcutta, Saigon, and Manila, encircling the vast Eurasian land mass. Planners could not say who the next enemy would be. Germany, Japan, the Soviet Union, and even Britain might present future threats. With such an extensive base network, the United States could act against any challenger before it could strike. If the United States attacked "*before and not after* a series of Munich conferences," one admiral explained, "the personal following of any future Hitler would be limited to a few would-be suicides." Britain and the Soviet Union looked upon this base system warily, suspecting they might be its targets, but American leaders were willing to take diplomatic risks to attain the security they felt they required.

The Fruits of Victory

Despite rumors of the president's failing health, Americans elected Franklin Roosevelt to a fourth term in 1944 by a margin of 53.5 percent to 46 percent for the challenger Thomas E. Dewey. On April 12, 1945, less than three months after his inauguration, Roosevelt died suddenly of a cerebral hemorrhage at Warm Springs, Georgia. "Mr. Roosevelt's body was brought back to Washington today for the last time," reporter I. F. Stone wrote on April 21, 1945. "Motorcycle police heralded the procession's approach. The marching men, the solemn bands, the armored cars, the regiment of Negro soldiers, the uniformed women's detachments . . . the coffin covered with a flag. . . . In that one quick look thousands of us said goodbye to a great and good man, and to an era." In Paris, French men and women offered condolences to American GIs. Flags flew at half staff on Guadalcanal, Kwajalein, and

Map 25–4 A Global War Polar-projection maps such as this one became popular during the war and afterwards became the symbol of the United Nations. This perspective shows the war's geopolitical logic, the struggle on two fronts for control of the large central land mass of Eurasia.

Tarawa. The president died just days before Allied troops in Europe achieved the great victory for which Roosevelt had struggled and planned. On April 25, American and Soviet troops shook hands at Torgau in eastern Germany. On April 30, with Soviet soldiers just a few hundred yards away, Hitler committed suicide in his Berlin bunker. On May 8, all German forces surrendered unconditionally.

Harry S. Truman, the new vice president and former senator from Missouri, was now commander in chief. Shortly after he took office, aides informed him that the Manhattan Project would soon test a weapon that might end the war in Asia. The first atomic explosion took place in the desert near Alamogordo, New Mexico, on July 16, 1945. Truman, meeting with Churchill and Stalin at Potsdam, Germany, was elated by the news. He informed Stalin while Churchill looked on, watching the expression of the Soviet leader. The bomb had been developed to be used against the Axis enemy, but by the time Truman learned about it, American leaders already saw it as a powerful instrument of postwar diplomacy.

As American forces neared the Japanese home islands, defenders fought with suicidal ferocity. On Okinawa, soldiers and civilians retreated into caves and battled to the death. GIs feared the invasion of Japan's home islands, where resistance could only be worse. Then on August 6, a B-29 dropped an atomic bomb on Hiroshima. Two days later the Soviet Union declared war on Japan, and Soviet armies attacked deep into Manchuria, heartland of the Co-Prosperity Sphere. On August 9, the United States dropped a second atomic bomb, this time on Nagasaki. It detonated 1,900 feet above Shima Hospital. In a fraction of a second, the hospital and nearly a square mile of the city center ignited. Bricks and granite melted in the nuclear fire. People were vaporized, some leaving shadows on the pavement. A few days later a French Red Cross worker saw the ruins of Hiroshima. "Not a bird or an animal to be seen anywhere. . . . On what remained of the station facade the hands of the clock had been stopped by the fire at 8:15. It was perhaps the first

V-J Day Jubilant crowds greeted V-J Day in New York. Many soldiers newly returned from Europe were on their way to the Pacific.

time in the history of humanity that the birth of a new era was recorded on the face of a clock."

Conclusion

Emperor Hirohito announced Japan's unconditional surrender on August 14. In New York, crowds celebrated, but in most of the world there was silence and reflection. Thirty million people had been killed; great cities lay in ruins. At the end of the war, the United States' economic, scientific, and military mastery reached a pinnacle never attained by any of the great empires of history. Two-thirds of the world's gold was in American treasuries; half of the world's manufactured goods were made in the United States. At its height, imperial Britain controlled 25 percent of the world's wealth. In 1945, the United States controlled 40 percent. America's air armada, almost 80,000 planes, 10 times the size of the *Luftwaffe,* dominated the skies; its naval fleet had more ships than the navies of all its enemies and allies combined. Senator Claude Pepper asked Navy Secretary James Forrestal where he intended to put all of the 1,200 warships at his disposal. "Wherever there's a sea," Forrestal replied. Then there was the atomic bomb. The rest of the world looked for signs of how the United States would use its formidable wealth and power.

The war's sudden end meant Americans had to reconvert to a "peacetime" economy, preferably one more stable and prosperous than the depression economy of the 1930s. A. Philip Randolph predicted government would have to take a larger role in raising wages and stimulating key industries, such as housing, if soldiers returning home were to find jobs and goods to buy. The future looked tenuous. America could either succumb to "a native variety of fascism" in the postwar period, or open an era of expanding rights, democracy, and material abundance.

Further Readings

Thomas Childers, *Wings of Morning* (1995). A historian reconstructs the lives and war experiences of the last B-24 crew shot down over Germany.

I. C. B. Dear, *The Oxford Companion to World War II* (1995). Easily the best single-volume reference work on the war. Contains full descriptions of battles and campaigns, biographies of leading figures, chronologies, maps, and as many statistics as you could want.

Michael D. Doubler, *Closing with the Enemy: How GIs Fought the War in Europe, 1944–1945* (1994). World War II has been seen as a "general's war," but Doubler explains how the tactics that beat the Nazis came from the bottom up. The U.S. Army's ability to listen to the lowliest GIs was its best asset.

Doris Kearns Goodwin, *No Ordinary Time: Franklin and Eleanor Roosevelt: The Home Front in World War II* (1994). The story of the nation at war through the eyes of the family that led it.

E. B. Sledge, *With the Old Breed at Peleliu and Okinawa* (1990). A classic memoir, the story of a marine infantryman's war in the Pacific told with candor and feeling.

Ronald H. Spector, *Eagle Against the Sun: The American War with Japan* (1985). A comprehensive history of the Pacific War from a leading military historian.

Who, What?

Charles Lindbergh 828
Chester W. Nimitz 832
Benjamin O. Davis 833
George S. Patton 836
Braceros 841
Rosie the Riveter 842
Atomic bomb 835
Internment 845
City busting 849

>> Timeline >>

▼ 1930
Hawley-Smoot Tariff constricts trade
Depression becomes global

▼ 1933
Hitler becomes chancellor of Germany
President Roosevelt devalues the dollar
The United States recognizes the Soviet Union

▼ 1934
Reciprocal Trade Act passed
Export-Import Bank created

▼ 1935
Congress passes first Neutrality Act

▼ 1937
War begins in Asia

▼ 1938
Mexico nationalizes oil fields
Munich agreement gives Hitler Sudetenland

▼ 1939
War begins in Europe

▼ 1940
Germany defeats France, Netherlands, Belgium
Destroyers-for-bases deal between the United States and Britain

▼ 1941
Lend-Lease passed
Executive Order 8802 ends discrimination in defense industries
Roosevelt and Churchill sign Atlantic Charter
Germany invades the Soviet Union
Japan attacks the United States at Pearl Harbor
United States declares war on Axis powers

New York World-Telegram
WALL ST.
1500 DEAD IN HAWAII
CONGRESS VOTES WAR

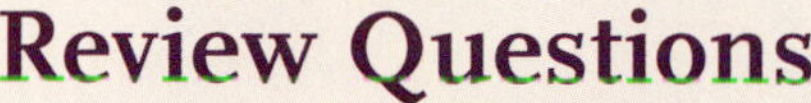

Review Questions

1. Which was more important to victory at Midway, planning or luck?
2. Why did the population of the West grow so rapidly during the war?
3. Contrast isolationist and internationalist viewpoints. Did they imagine different futures for the United States?
4. Thurgood Marshall worried about the emergence of "gestapos" in America. What did he mean?
5. According to American leaders, what caused World War II? How did their answers to that question affect their plans for the postwar world?
6. The government used propaganda and repressive laws to control domestic opinion during World War I. Why was there no repeat of those policies in World War II?
7. Some historians blame Roosevelt for luring the United States into war. How might that historical view be rooted in the isolationist/internationalist debate?

Websites

American Radioworks, Public Radio International, "Radio Fights Jim Crow," http://americanradioworks.publicradio.org/features/jim_crow/. During the war years, civil rights activists and the federal government producd a radio series that tried to mend racial divisions and unite the nation to win the war.

Franklin Roosevelt, "State of the Union Address: The Four Freedoms," January 6, 1941, http://millercenter.org/scripps/archive/speeches/detail/3320. Hear and read Franklin Roosevelt's statement of war aims.

Smithsonian Air and Space Museum, "Black Wings: African American Pioneer Aviators," http://www.nasm.si.edu/interact/blackwings/.

For further review materials and resource information, please visit www.oup.com/us/ofthepeople

▼ 1942

Philippines fall to Japan

Internment of Japanese Americans begins

Battles of Coral Sea and Midway turn the tide in the Pacific

Allies land in North Africa

▼ 1943

Allies land in Sicily

Churchill and Roosevelt meet at Casablanca

U.S. troops advance to Bougainville

Marines capture Tarawa

▼ 1944

U.S. troops capture Rome

Allied landings in Normandy

U.S. troops capture Saipan

Bretton Woods Conference

Roosevelt reelected for fourth term

▼ 1945

Roosevelt dies

Harry S. Truman becomes president

Germany surrenders

Truman meets Churchill and Stalin at Potsdam

Atomic bombs dropped on Hiroshima and Nagasaki

Japan surrenders

CHAPTER 26

A WARNER BROS. Picture

MISSION TO MOSCOW

Common Threads 

>> Why did friction over Germany, Poland, and the Mediterranean turn into a cold war affecting the entire world?

>> How did the need for constant vigilance interfere with democratic values?

>> The specter of the Depression hung over postwar economic planners. How did they try to avoid another decline as they reconverted the war economy?

The Cold War

1945–1952

AMERICAN PORTRAIT

>> Esther and Stephen Brunauer

Esther Caukin and Stephen Brunauer were an American success story. Born in California in 1901, Esther benefited from the increasing opportunities for women in the twentieth century. She graduated from Mills College, earned a doctoral degree from Stanford, and became an administrator for the American Association of University Women. In 1931, she married Stephen Brunauer, a successful chemist who had come to the United States from Hungary in Eastern Europe.

The Brunauers were patriots who hated fascism. In the 1930s, Esther tried to educate Americans about the threat from Adolf Hitler's Germany. When World War II came, she went to work in the U.S. State Department. Stephen also worked for the government as an explosives expert in the navy. After the war, he traveled to Hungary to gather scientific intelligence for the government and to help Hungarian scientists emigrate to the United States. With fascism defeated and their careers well launched, the Brunauers had succeeded. Like most Americans, they could have looked forward to a happy, prosperous future. But then it all went wrong.

In 1947 a congressman accused Esther of being one of the "pro-Communist fellow travelers and muddle heads" in the State Department. One of her speeches, he said, was "echoing Soviet propaganda." That year, a federal agency refused to let Stephen attend a meeting about atomic energy because he had once, as a student in the 1920s, belonged to the Young Workers' League, a group with Communist ties. Somehow, even though they hated Communism as much as they hated fascism, the Brunauers found their patriotism questioned.

Then things got worse. On March 13, 1950, Senator Joseph McCarthy of Wisconsin charged Esther and Stephen with espionage and links to known Communists. Esther, McCarthy testified, had engaged in "Communist-front activities"; Stephen had access "to some of the topmost secrets" of the U.S. military and constituted "a grave security risk of the highest order." McCarthy demanded that the subcommittee subpoena federal records in order to find out whether the Brunauers were Communists who had betrayed their country. Stephen immediately denied he had ever been a Communist. "I am a loyal American," Esther insisted.

Two weeks later Esther took the witness stand to defend herself and her husband before the subcommittee. Rejecting McCarthy's charges, she accused the senator himself of betraying American values. His sudden and unfounded attack was, she said, "in violation of the traditions of fairness which are among our oldest heritages." Esther revealed how much McCarthy's accusations had already hurt her family. Since the 13th, they had received "anonymous telephone calls at all hours of the day and night, accompanied by threats and profanity." "Get out of this neighborhood, you Communists," one caller warned, "or you will be carried out in a box." "We are all upset and bewildered," Esther reported. "All of you who have families . . . how would you feel if it were happening in your home." Esther finished her testimony by offering letters of support from a senator, a former senator, and a college president. Dismissing McCarthy's charges, the college president, who was a brother of General Dwight D. Eisenhower, maintained that it was "un-American" to call Esther a "Communist sympathizer."

A majority of the subcommittee agreed. In July, the subcommittee's report concluded that McCarthy's charges against the Brunauers were "contemptible," "a fraud and a hoax." But the damage had been done. Despite the subcommittee report, there was enough doubt about the Brunauers that the State Department and the navy were no longer willing to risk keeping such controversial people on the job. In 1951 the navy suspended Stephen from his position, and the State Department suspended Esther from hers. Esther fought her suspension but found herself charged with "close and habitual association" with

continued

>> AMERICAN PORTRAIT *continued*

her husband. In 1952, the State Department fired her as a "security risk." The real reason for her dismissal, Esther told the press, was "political expediency." Their careers destroyed, the Brunauers left Washington to try to rebuild their lives out of the spotlight in Illinois.

How had it happened? How had the optimism of 1945 degenerated into suspicion? Those were questions that most Americans could have asked in one way or another. Like the Brunauers, Americans lived in a country and a world that had been saved from ruin. At home, the economic boom of World War II had swept away the Great Depression. Abroad, the United States had helped to destroy the threat of fascism. Understandably, Americans could have expected the postwar world to be stable and safe.

Before two years had passed, however, a tense peacetime confrontation with the Soviet Union disrupted American life. Convinced that the Soviets intended to expand their power and spread Communism across Europe, U.S. leaders challenged their former allies. While this "cold war" developed, Americans also faced the task of maintaining prosperity in peacetime. Organized labor, women, and African Americans struggled to preserve and extend their rights and opportunities. President Harry Truman and the Democratic Party struggled as well to preserve their power and implement a liberal agenda.

However unsettling, the cold war was not an aberration. The confrontation with Communism was deeply rooted in the core values of American democracy at the close of World War II. Truman and other leaders saw the Soviet system as inimical to free institutions, civil rights, and the capitalist system revived by the New Deal. Moreover, they worried that if a Communist coalition became too strong, the United States would have to defend itself by regimenting the economy and restricting individual rights—effectively turning America into a "garrison state." To contain Soviet expansion, the U.S. government took unprecedented peacetime actions—massive foreign aid, new alliances, a military buildup—that helped to transform the political economy in the 1940s and beyond.

Dramatic though they were, the new American policies did not prevent the cold war from widening and intensifying. By 1950, the nation was fighting a hot war on the other side of the world in Korea. By then, too, Americans knew that the Soviet Union had nuclear weapons that could conceivably devastate the United States. In turn, the Truman administration stepped up military spending and developed more powerful nuclear weapons. As the cold war seemed to spiral out of control, fear gripped American society. A frenzied search for Communist subversives at home threatened civil liberties and destroyed the careers of Esther and Stephen Brunauer. They suffered more than most people, but in one way or another, the cold war unsettled the lives of all Americans for years to come. ●

OUTLINE

Origins of the Cold War

In a span of two years, the United States and the Soviet Union went from a wartime alliance to the protracted rivalry known as the cold war. The sweeping, long-term consequences of the cold war made it particularly important for Americans to understand the origins of the conflict. From the outset, the United States and the Soviet Union tried to pin the blame for the cold war on each other. For a long time, Americans wanted to believe that the Soviet Union, authoritarian and expansionist, was solely responsible. However, historians have gradually offered a more critical perspective, and they generally agree that actions by both countries caused the cold war.

> **One way of life is based upon the will of the majority, and is distinguished by free institutions, representative government, free elections, guarantees of individual liberty, . . . The second way of life is based upon the will of a minority forcibly imposed upon the majority. It relies upon terror and oppression.**
>
> HARRY S. TRUMAN,
> March 1947

Ideological Competition

There is less agreement about the precise sources of the conflict. Ideological, political, military, and economic factors all clearly played a role. Ever since the founding of the Soviet Union toward the end of World War I, Soviets and Americans were ideological adversaries. They had essentially different political systems. The Soviet Union (the USSR) was committed to Communism and socialism, the United States to democracy and capitalism. Despite their differences, the two countries fought as allies in World War II. Wartime decisions, especially about the arrangement of the postwar world, laid the groundwork for animosity after 1945. In peacetime, the Soviet Union and the United States were the only countries strong enough to threaten each other, and the recent experience of both countries showed that with modern arms enemies could strike with devastating suddenness. Moreover, they had quite different political, military, and economic ambitions. By 1947 those different goals produced open antagonism. With the United States' vow to combat the spread of Communism, the cold war was under way. The Union of Soviet Socialist Republics (USSR) emerged from the Russian Revolution of 1917 and the civil war that followed. Vladimir Lenin's Bolshevik Party introduced a socialist economy in which the state—the government—owned factories and farms. At home, the Soviet Union practiced forms of economic and social regimentation Americans recognized from Nazi Germany and imperial Japan, limiting individual rights, including freedom of speech and religion, and achieving a self-contained autarkic economy. Abroad, the new nation endorsed the revolutionary overthrow of capitalism.

The Soviets' Marxist ideology obviously set them at odds with American ideals. The vast majority of Americans favored a capitalist economy, in which private citizens owned property. They celebrated individualism, freedom of speech, freedom of religion, and democratic government based on free elections. Communists believed all modern societies would eventually eliminate religion and private property and value the collective good over the rights of the individual.

Nevertheless, open conflict between the two countries was not inevitable. While American leaders hated Communism, the USSR was weak and hemmed in by powerful neighbors, Germany in the west and Japan in the east. It posed no military threat to the United States in the 1920s and 1930s. The Soviets could even be helpful to American interests. President Franklin Roosevelt, eager to promote trade and restrain Japanese expansion, officially recognized the Soviet Union in 1933.

Uneasy Allies

World War II demonstrated that, despite their differences, the United States and the Soviet Union could become allies. After the German invasion of the USSR and the Japanese attack on Pearl Harbor, the United States and the Soviets were thrown together in the war against fascism in 1941. Still, they were uneasy allies at best. For many Americans, the lesson of the war was that the United States could not tolerate aggression. No new dictator should ever be able to take over other European countries unopposed, as Hitler did, nor should any single power be allowed to dominate Eurasia. By 1945 some Americans already equated the Soviets with the Nazis by denouncing totalitarianism or "Red Fascism."

Each country had experiences that underlay its determination to protect itself from future disasters. American leaders believed autarkic trade blocs had caused both the Great Depression and the war that followed, and they resolved to rebuild the world economy as a single system, with reduced trade barriers and uniform rules. Soviet leaders feared a repeat of the last two wars, in which Poland and Eastern Europe had been staging areas for invasions that claimed millions of Russian lives. But the lessons they drew from war led them to opposite solutions: American leaders favored an interdependent system, with open borders allowing goods, information, and people to move freely; Soviet leaders felt only a closed system and tight controls on its periphery would give it real protection.

Wartime decisions also aggravated tensions between the United States and the Soviet Union. In 1943 the American government created ill feeling by excluding the Soviets from the surrender of Italy to the Allies. The delay of the Allied invasion of France until 1944 embittered the Soviets, who were desperately resisting the Germans at the cost of millions of lives. The American government further strained relations by sharing news of its secret atomic bomb project with the British but not with the Soviets.

Decisions about the postwar world led to trouble as well. At a conference in Yalta in the Soviet Union in February 1945, Franklin Roosevelt, Josef Stalin, and British prime minister Winston Churchill proposed a self-contradictory vision of the postwar world. The "Big Three" supported national self-determination, the idea that countries should decide their own future. They also agreed that countries should act collectively to deal with world problems. They laid plans for the United Nations, an organization that would encourage states to cooperate in keeping the world secure. But they also believed powerful nations should dominate other nations within a "sphere of influence." In these areas—Latin America and the Pacific for the United States; Africa and the Middle East for Britain; and Eastern Europe for the Soviet

Union—each power could act independently and limit the self-determination of smaller states. Clearly, spheres of influence and unilateral action conflicted with democracy, self-determination, and collective action.

The conflict was made apparent when the three leaders dealt with the critical issue of the future of Poland, the Soviets' neighbor to the west. Despite talk of self-determination and democracy, Stalin wanted to install a loyal Polish government. He could not risk an independent Poland that might become a gateway for another

Map 26–1 Cold War in Europe, 1950 Five years after World War II, the cold war had divided Europe into hostile camps, with NATO members allied with the United States and Warsaw Pact signers tied to the Soviet Union.

invasion. Churchill and Roosevelt, however, favored a self-governing Poland under its prewar leaders. Stalin agreed to elections but came away feeling that Roosevelt had given him a free hand in Poland. This lack of clarity set the stage for future misunderstandings.

From Allies to Enemies

The United States' ambitions for global military and economic security appeared threatening to the Soviet Union. To prevent a future Pearl Harbor, the Pentagon erected a chain of air and naval bases that encircled Europe and Asia. The Bretton Woods agreement placed the United States at the center of a global economy with rules that worked to the disadvantage of controlled, socialist economies. The Roosevelt administration did not see these steps as antagonistic, but Stalin recognized that their effect was to cage his ambitions within a ring of bombers and dollars.

Disagreements over Germany sharpened these suspicions. The United States wanted defeated Germany to rejoin the world economy. Having been attacked by Germany twice in the last 50 years, the Soviets wanted the country divided and weakened forever. In the end, the Big Three agreed to split it into four zones of occupation. The United States, the USSR, Great Britain, and France would each administer a zone. Although Berlin lay within the Soviet zone, the four conquering powers would each control a section of the capital. The Big Three also agreed that eventually Germany would be reunified, but they did not indicate when or how.

The uncertainties and contradictions of Yalta led to disagreements even before the war ended. When Vice President Harry Truman succeeded Roosevelt in April 1945, he objected to the Soviets' attempt to take tight control of Poland. Promising to "stand up to the Russians," the new president held a tense meeting in Washington with the Soviet Foreign Minister, V. M. Molotov. With "words of one syllable," the president "gave it to him straight 'one-two to the jaw.'" "I have never been talked to like that in my life," Molotov answered. "Carry out your agreements," snapped Truman, "and you won't get talked to like that."

When Truman met with Stalin and the British prime minister in Potsdam in July, relations were more cordial. Because Soviet troops occupied most of Eastern Europe and much of Germany, there was little Truman could do about Stalin's actions there. There was no progress on planning the future reunification of Germany. But Truman learned during the meeting that the test of the atomic bomb in Nevada had been a success. The new weapon would increase U.S. influence everywhere in the world. Sailing home to the United States, he called Stalin "an S.O.B.," but admitted that "I guess he thinks I'm one too."

National Security

After the war, relations between the United States and the Soviet Union deteriorated. Although Stalin was still committed to overthrowing capitalism, his immediate concerns were in Eastern Europe and along the southern border with Turkey and Iran. The Soviet leader also wanted to keep Germany and Japan from menacing his country again. As an added measure of security the USSR built a completely self-reliant economy. The United States, by contrast, did not have to worry about securing its borders or supplies. Equipped with nuclear weapons, the United States was stronger than any rival. But American leaders feared that impoverished and vulnerable states around the world would voluntarily align themselves with Soviet power. Every election in Europe, coup in the Middle East, or uprising in Asia had the potential to add a piece to a future Communist war machine. Recalling the collapse of empires and alliances in the late 1930s, they could imagine chains of events that could leave the United States suddenly alone and vulnerable.

> We may be likened to two scorpions in a bottle, each capable of killing the other, but only at the risk of his own life.
>
> J. ROBERT OPPENHEIMER, 1953

The Truman Doctrine

To avoid this dismaying scenario, American leaders favored the quick reconstruction of nations, including Germany and Japan, within a world economy based on free trade. They also needed military bases to keep future aggressors far from American shores. The opposing needs and interests of the Soviet and U.S. systems soon translated into combative rhetoric. In February 1946 Stalin declared capitalism and Communism incompatible. A month later, Winston Churchill, the former British prime minister, spoke at Fulton, Missouri. Introduced by Truman, Churchill ominously declared that "an Iron Curtain has descended across the Continent" of Europe. Central and Eastern Europe, the former prime minister warned, "lie in the Soviet sphere." Churchill called for an alliance against this menace.

In February 1946, George Kennan, an American consul in Moscow, sent the State Department a long telegram reflecting a new attitude. The Soviet leadership, he explained, believed "there can be no permanent peaceful coexistence" between capitalism and socialism. Stalin and his regime were sure that capitalist nations, beset by internal problems, would attack socialist nations. Acting on this fear, the USSR would, Kennan insisted, try to penetrate and destabilize other nations and align them with the Communist bloc. The Communist system needed to expand to survive.

More concerned than ever, Truman took aggressive steps to counter apparent Soviet expansion in the Mediterranean. The USSR had been pressing Turkey for control of the Dardanelles, a key waterway. Meanwhile in Greece, a civil war pitted Communist guerillas against a monarchist government backed by Britain. By 1947 the British could no longer afford the war and wanted to pass the burden to the Americans. Truman told Congress on March 12, 1947, that the world faced a choice between freedom and totalitarianism. "The free peoples of the world look to us," he insisted. "If we falter in our leadership, we may endanger the peace of

***George Kennan* by Ned Seidler** George Frost Kennan emerged as the principal strategist, author of the containment doctrine.

Iron Curtain In Winston Churchill's image, an "iron curtain" divided Europe, but soon similar barriers would mark the frontiers of containment in Asia and the Middle East.

the world—and we shall surely endanger the welfare of this Nation." The president announced what became known as the "Truman Doctrine." The United States must "support free peoples who are resisting attempted subjugation by armed minorities or by outside pressures." The speech, observed *Life* magazine, was "a bolt of lightning." Congress voted overwhelmingly to send aid to Greece and Turkey.

The crisis marked a turning point. In 1947, Walter Lippmann coined the term "cold war" to describe the American-Soviet confrontation. There was no formal declaration of war, but with the announcement of the Truman Doctrine, confrontation had certainly begun. Dividing the world into good and evil, the United States was ready to support "free peoples" and oppose Communism. Former allies were now bitter antagonists.

Was the confrontation inevitable? There is no way for historians to prove other outcomes were not possible, but it is difficult to see how the United States and the Soviet Union could have avoided friction. They had a history of hostility, and they both possessed great military power. It is harder to be sure that the form confrontation took—the cold war—was inevitable. It was the product of choices, such as Truman's decision to give aid to Greece, and perceptions, such as Kennan's conclusion that the Soviets were bent on expansion. Those choices and perceptions were not the only ones that could have been made. With good reason, Americans would wonder for decades whether the cold war could have been different.

Containment

As the United States implemented strategies for containing Soviet expansion through a combination of diplomatic, economic, and military moves, the scope of the confrontation widened to include the entire world. In 1949 China's civil war ended in a Communist victory. In 1950, just five years after the end of World War II, the United States went to war again, this time to save a non-Communist regime in South Korea. As the cold war spread, it became more dangerous. When the Soviets exploded their own atomic bomb, the United States also dramatically stepped up military spending and built a hydrogen bomb. As the arms race spiraled, the cold war seemed frighteningly out of control.

Committed to opposing Soviet and Communist expansion, the Truman administration had to figure out just how to fight the cold war. Once again, the diplomat George Kennan helped give expression to American thinking about the confrontation with the Soviets. Writing under the pen name "X," he argued that "the main element of any United States policy toward the Soviet Union must be that of a long-term, patient but firm and vigilant containment of Russian expansive tendencies."

The term "containment" aptly described American policy for the cold war. The United States worked to hold back the Soviets for the next 40 years, but "containment,"

AMERICAN LANDSCAPE

>> Dhahran

In the years after World War II an American city grew in the Arabian Desert. Starting with just 92 pioneers in 1942, Dhahran grew into a city of over 5,000 Americans, working and living in air-conditioned offices, clubhouses, movie theaters, and homes that looked, according to the *New York Times,* as if they had been lifted from Florida by magic carpet.

The clean, modern facilities inside the American zone contrasted sharply with the ragged tents and desert heat outside. Although larger than most, Dhahran was like thousands of compounds built all over the world during the cold war to house the expatriates who staffed the corporate headquarters, military bases, and embassies that looked after the United States' global interests.

America's interest in Arabia was oil. In the 1930s, U.S. companies struck a bargain with Ibn Saud, patriarch of a nomadic clan, securing rights until 2005 to any petroleum found in an area twice the size of Texas. When a huge reserve was found near Dhahran in 1938, pipelines, refineries, and machine shops sprang up overnight, making the oil consortium, known as ARAMCO, into the largest U.S. private overseas investment. And as the company grew, so did the power of its partner, Ibn Saud. By the late 1940s, Americans began to refer to the company's territory as "Saudi Arabia."

Before World War II, the Saud family was one of several Bedouin clans vying for control over the Arabian Peninsula. With oil wealth, Saud transformed his chieftaincy into a monarchical state, centralizing authority, raising taxes, and using radio to spread Wahabism, a puritanical faith that rejected liberal, pluralist Islamic practices in favor of Koranic literalism and a strict code of Sharia justice. Punishments for minor offenses included stoning and amputation. Saud's decrees allowed no labor unions, prohibited music and the education of women, and forced nomadic Arabs into settlements.

Oil money financed these policies, but ARAMCO officials refrained from criticizing Saudi rule. The king's relationship with the company was, the crown prince explained, "founded on mutual profit, with both parties respecting the rights of the other."

In the atmosphere of the cold war, security for the company and the Saudi regime became vital U.S. interests. The U.S. Pacific Fleet consumed nearly three-quarters of ARAMCO's oil, and the remainder fuelled European construction under the Marshall Plan. If rebels or the Soviets cut off Saudi oil, Defense Secretary James Forrestal warned, Americans would be reduced to driving four-cylinder cars. The residents of Dhahran were supplying an essential ingredient of the American way of life, and making a million dollars a day for the company in the process.

With its tennis courts and ranch homes, Dhahran looked like a suburb of Houston or Miami. It had its own

continued

Dhahran, 1952 The "American Camp" at Dhahran was a complete American suburb, with a golf course, Little League, tract homes, and segregated schools.

>> **AMERICAN LANDSCAPE** *continued*

PTA and scout troop, a country club, libraries, and television station. It resembled American cities in another way, too. It was racially segregated. Outside the gates of the American colony, ARAMCO built an "intermediate camp" to house 2,000 Italian and Palestinian skilled workers. Further out lay the "coolie camp," a squalid settlement of wood and grass huts housing the 14,000 Arabs who drilled the oil, laid the pipe, and paved the roads.

Each settlement had its own separate electrical and water systems, schools, and clinics, except for the Arab camp, which had none of those things. The American colony had the country's only swimming pools and hospitals. No Arabs allowed. The clearest distinction between the nationalities was in climate. Americans could live, work, and shop entirely in air-cooled surroundings, but Arabs dug ditches and hauled loads in temperatures averaging 120 degrees in the shade for a starting wage of 90¢ a day. "For most Americans," one observer noted, differences of language and religion "and fear of local diseases made friendship with the Arabs hard to establish."

Arabs resented being third-class citizens in their own country, but complaints were not tolerated in Saud's kingdom. Americans drank liquor and appeared in public unveiled, flouting Sharia laws that Saud's religious police sternly enforced in the Arab community. Bedouin shepherds complained that pipelines fenced them in. Literate Arabs resented United States support for Israel. By the early 1950s, occasional flashes of violence in the workplace unsettled the community. In the autumn of 1953, Dhahran erupted in a general strike as 13,000 Arabs walked off the job to protest the arrest of workers attempting to organize a union. The U.S. community met the challenge, manning the pumps to keep the oil flowing. Together with Saud's U.S.-trained police they broke the strike.

ARAMCO and the king recognized the strike as a wake-up call and responded with a combination of paternalism and force. The company raised wages to over a dollar a day and built a hospital and concrete dormitories for Arab workers. Saud built a modern military equipped with U.S. jets and tanks. More Saudis took white-collar positions in the company, but the number of Americans living in the country continued to grow. Executives continued to hope that the American example would make Saudi society more tolerant, progressive, and democratic, but the company adapted readily to the kingdom's autocratic customs. ARAMCO refused to hire Jews, for fear of offending their hosts. The company helped the king seize lands from rival tribes, and from neighboring Yemen.

An opportunistic partnership between an American industry and an antidemocratic monarchy had become a permanent alliance. The cold war created many such relationships, and U.S. officials worried that so many of America's allies were dictators and kings rather than elected leaders. But the Soviet threat, they believed, did not allow the United States to choose its friends. That time would come when the danger had passed. ●

as Kennan described it in 1947, was still a vague concept. Truman and his successors had to decide just where and when to contain the Soviet Union, and they also had to decide what combination of diplomatic, economic, and military programs to use.

One thing became clear quickly. Containment would not rely primarily on the United Nations. Like the United States, the Soviet Union had a veto over actions by the United Nations Security Council. From the beginning, they used the veto to frustrate American efforts. The United Nations would become another arena for rivalry, not an instrument of American policy.

Truman and his advisors revolutionized American policies on foreign aid, overseas alliances, and national defense. Soon after the decision to help Greece and Turkey, the United States confronted a ruined Europe which Winston Churchill described as "a rubble-heap, a charnel house, a breeding ground of pestilence and hate." Fearing an impoverished Europe would embrace Communism, Truman and his advisors were determined to help rebuild. In a speech at Harvard University in June 1947, Truman's new secretary of state, General George C. Marshall, proposed a "European Recovery Plan" to combat "hunger, poverty, desperation and chaos" and to promote "political and social conditions in which free institutions can exist." The

Soviets declined to join and refused to allow Eastern European countries to participate, but 16 nations eagerly supported what became known as the "Marshall Plan."

"The Marshall Plan saved Europe," Truman boasted. From 1948 to 1952, $13 billion from the United States went to boost agricultural and industrial output, increase exports, and promote economic cooperation. Whole cities were rebuilt. By 1950, participating countries had already exceeded prewar production by 25 percent. Politically, prosperity helped stabilize Western European governments and weaken the region's Communist parties. In the process, Western European nations were bound more tightly to the United States.

Whatever the weather
We only reach welfare
together

Containment required more than aid. It also demanded the kind of military alliances that the United States historically avoided. Such entanglements, Americans had long believed, might drag the nation into unnecessary wars. But facing the challenge of the cold war, leaders now saw alliances as a way of preventing, rather than provoking, armed conflict. In 1949, the United States joined 10 Western European nations and Canada to form the North Atlantic Treaty Organization (NATO). Under the NATO agreement, an attack on any member nation would be treated as an attack on all. To strengthen the American commitment to Western Europe, Congress appropriated $1.3 billion in military aid for NATO countries, and Truman ordered American troops to the Continent. General Dwight D. Eisenhower, the commander of the Allied invasion of France in World War II, agreed to become the supreme commander of NATO forces.

Containment also required a government organized for vigilance. In 1947 Congress passed the National Security Act, creating a Central Intelligence Agency (CIA) to gather and assess information for the president and a National Security Council (NSC) to advise him on military and political threats. The act placed the army, navy, and air force under a single command, the Joint Chiefs of Staff, and a single cabinet secretary, the secretary of defense. The term "national security" was itself a novelty; it provided a blanket justification for responses to all kinds of threats, actions including election rigging, proxy wars, and other "covert operations" by the CIA. Congress briefly considered requiring all young men to undergo military training. Instead it passed a new Selective Service Act the draft for men between 19 and 25.

Taking Risks

Containment entailed risks. There was always the chance that the simmering conflict could boil over into a world war. One particularly dangerous hot spot was Berlin. In 1948, the Americans, British, and French began to unify their zones of occupation in Germany into a single unit under a new currency, the deutschmark. Faced with a revived anti-Communist western Germany, Stalin sealed off his own German zone of occupation. On June 24, the Soviets cut road and rail transport into Berlin, the jointly occupied German capital. Truman figured Stalin was bluffing, and as the sole nuclear power, the United States could call the bluff. "We stay in Berlin, period," Truman snapped. But the 2.5 million citizens of the American, British, and French sectors were at risk of running out of food and coal. Sending an armed supply convoy through the Soviet blockade could provoke a shooting war.

Instead, the Truman administration supplied Berlin by air. American transport planes carried 2,500 tons of food and fuel a day. Along with this massive airlift, the

Truman administration sent to Britain two squadrons of B-29 bombers: significantly, the kind of planes that dropped the atomic bombs on Japan. In May 1949 the Soviets ended the blockade. Put to the test, the strategy of containment had worked. U.S. countermeasures had seemingly deterred Soviet expansion. But the risks were plain.

The dangers became even greater for the United States later that year. In early September, American planes found radioactivity in the air over the Pacific, evidence that the Soviet Union had exploded an atomic bomb. The U.S. monopoly of nuclear weapons, which had boosted Truman's confidence, was over. Suddenly, the confrontation with the Soviets had potentially lethal consequences for the American people. It was now, a Republican senator somberly observed, "a different world."

Global Revolutions

The cold war soon spread from Europe to shape the politics of the whole world. Civil and postcolonial strife in Asia, Africa, the Middle East, and Latin America came to be seen as part of the conflict between the nuclear superpowers.

In China, the nationalist government of Jiang Jieshi had waged a civil war against Mao Zedong's Communist rebels since the 1920s. Both sides joined forces to fight the Japanese during World War II, but while combat experience strengthened the Communists, it weakened Jiang's corrupt and unpopular regime. When Japan surrendered, U.S. forces helped Jiang regain control of Chinese cities and Truman urged the two sides to reach a permanent settlement, but the civil war resumed. Congressional Republicans saw China as a key cold war battleground, but Truman doubted the United States could influence the outcome in this vast, populous, rural country. He sent the nationalists $2 billion in aid but refused to send troops. In December 1949 the defeated nationalists fled the Chinese mainland for the island of Taiwan, and Republicans angrily blamed the administration for the "loss" of China.

With most of Asia now in Communist hands, American strategists began to rethink containment. Before 1949, the danger zones were in the world's industrial heartlands, Europe and Japan. Now it seemed that brushfire wars could spread nearly anywhere. Resentful peasants manned Mao's armies, and the rural "third world" seemed especially vulnerable. To implement containment in Latin America, Truman organized a coordinated defense, known as the Rio Pact, through which the United States would provide training, weapons, and advisers for Latin American militaries. The Organization of American States (OAS), created in 1948, promoted stability and economic development from its headquarters in Washington.

Territories formerly of little interest to American strategists, such as Southeast Asia and Africa, became vital to national security. Although the Truman administration favored self-determination, it tolerated Latin American dictatorships, European colonial dominion, and South Africa's white supremacist state because these undemocratic regimes opposed Communism.

Korea

With the United States working to hold off Communism at so many points, it was probably not surprising that the nation was eventually drawn into war. Nevertheless, the news that U.S. troops were in battle in Korea startled Americans in 1950,

AMERICA AND THE WORLD

>> Underdevelopment

As the opening acts of the cold war unfolded, a second global drama, in some ways more consequential, played out in Asia, the Middle East, and Africa. Subjugated peoples struggled for and claimed independence, and European colonial systems crumbled. By the end of the 1940s, for the first time in history, a majority of the world's people lived in nations, instead of empires.

Decolonization ripped apart systems of authority and trade. After years of conflict, new nations often gained little but freedom. They inherited economies without industry or markets, governments with no schools, roads, or tax collectors, and restless populations living in deep poverty. The Truman administration recognized that, although the movement toward nationalism could not be stopped, with luck, it might be managed.

In the fourth point of his 1949 inaugural address, Truman announced a "bold new program for making the benefits of our scientific advances and industrial progress available for the improvement and growth of underdeveloped areas." The "Point Four" program was the United States' first global foreign aid program, but Truman's real innovation was in redefining terms. By calling the new nations underdeveloped, Truman asserted that nations were entitled to growth, that all nations would one day be fully developed.

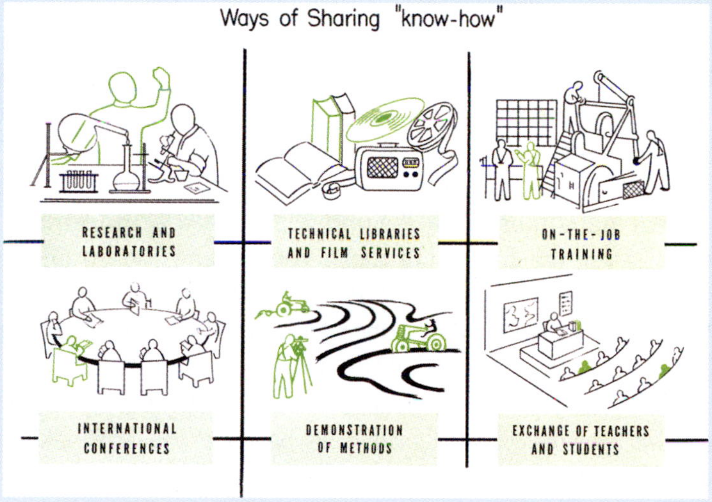

National leaders eagerly accepted the new terms. Truman "hit the jackpot of the world's political emotions," *Fortune* magazine reported. Delegations from Ecuador, Pakistan, and Egypt lined up to ask for technical assistance. "America's attitude is our salvation," an Afghan prince declared. "We are free of the threat of great powers using our mountain passes as pathways to empire. Now we can concentrate our talents and resources on bettering the living conditions of our people."

While nationalists struggled for freedom from outside interference, development made it the obligation of every responsible government to open the door to foreign experts. Countries that had expelled foreign advisers a few years earlier welcomed teams of economists from the World Bank and the Ford Foundation. UN commissions on food, health, and education measured each nation's progress toward universal goals that would mark its arrival as a fully modern state. Development directed the nationalist energies into economic channels and away from political actions that might endanger U.S. interests. It was Point Four's purpose, Secretary of State Dean Acheson noted, to "use material means to a non-material end."

Nationalist leaders also remarked on how material changes altered the spiritual and cultural outlook of people. Hydroelectric dams were the temples of modern India, declared Prime Minister Jawaharlal Nehru at the dedication of an enormous water project modeled on the TVA. "When we undertake a big work, our minds open out a little." Some contended that development might replace the cold war with a peaceful competition to modernize the world under rival economic theories.

Others argued that poverty went beyond aid, technical knowledge, or even states of mind. A Brazilian delegate at the first Point Four conference explained that poverty was caused by the terms of trade: Latin American agricultural exports steadily declined in value, while manufactured imports from the United States steadily increased in price. Economies became wealthy and technically advanced, in other words, by pushing others into backwardness. Development created underdevelopment.

But the success of the Marshall Plan and Japan's reconstruction gave Americans tremendous confidence in

continued

>> **AMERICA AND THE WORLD** *continued*

their ability to make over whole societies. In the 1950s, social scientists devised theories of "nation building." For their own convenience, academic specialists divided the world into three parts, each with a distinct set of problems: a democratic, developed "first world," a Communist "second world," and the underdeveloped "third world," which contained most of the nations and two-thirds of the people on earth.

If the United States could ease the third world's ascent, MIT economist Walt W. Rostow predicted, it could create "an environment in which societies which directly or indirectly menace ours will not evolve." Military strategies against guerilla insurgencies increasingly employed development techniques to stabilize governments and win (in Mao Zedong's phrase) the "hearts and minds" of the people.

Aid officials often said that development and democracy went together. As peasants became consumers and workers, they would demand more choice in how they lived their lives and who their leaders were. By giving freely of its resources and know-how, America could "export democracy." But in practice, development programs seldom asked ordinary people what kind of progress they wanted. Aid reinforced a centralized state, channeling funds to unelected planning commissions and economic experts who made decisions that affected millions of people.

By the 1960s, "nation building" by planners and social scientists had become central to U.S. containment strategy. The long U.S. struggle in Vietnam, which began with military aid in 1950 and ended with defeat in 1975, would test the theory that stimulating development would increase democracy and security. That idea, Henry Kissinger later concluded, was "clearly wrong."

But by then, a system of national and international institutions to guide the development of nations was already in place. Leaders and electorates around the world judged national success by the statistical yardstick of economic growth. While few people fully accepted Truman's hunch that prosperity would guarantee peace, even fewer were ready to reject it entirely. Underdevelopment had taken a permanent place on the agenda of global problems. ●

because the conflict was so far from areas considered strategically important. But the Korean War was firmly rooted in the logic of the cold war.

Korea, a peninsula bordering China and the Soviet Union, had been liberated from the Japanese in 1945. American and Soviet troops jointly occupied the territory, splitting it into two zones at the 38th parallel. American policy makers opposed the popular nationalist Kim Il Sung, who was a Communist, and acted unilaterally to install a regime in the southern zone under Syngman Rhee, an anti-Communist. By 1948, Korea effectively had two governments, each claiming jurisdiction over the whole. In June 1950, after incidents along the 38th parallel, Kim's army, led by Soviet-made tanks, invaded the South.

Truman responded boldly. By itself, South Korea was not strategically important, but the president and his advisors believed the Soviet Union was behind the North Korean attack. After the "loss" of China, the Truman administration could not afford another Communist victory in Asia. "By God," the president swore, "I am going to let them have it!" His administration secured approval from the United Nations for international action in Korea. Troops from 15 countries eventually fought under the UN flag, but nine-tenths of the UN force in Korea came from the United States. America was at war then—or was it? Claiming that the conflict was only a "police action," Truman never asked Congress for a declaration of war. For the first time, but not the last, a president committed troops to battle in the cold war without regard for the Constitution.

At first, the fighting did not go well. U.S. troops, unprepared and understrength, fell back toward the coast. But in the summer, General Douglas MacArthur used the U.S. Navy's control of the seas to put troops ashore at Inchon on the west coast of South Korea, deep behind enemy lines. North Korea's main armies were cut off and destroyed. Within weeks, the South had been reclaimed.

Then Truman and his advisers made a fateful decision. Rather than just contain Communism, they wanted to roll it back. Truman gave the order to invade North Korea and reunify the peninsula. MacArthur, who privately thirsted for war with the Chinese Communists, pushed northward, ever closer to China. Fearing an American invasion, the Chinese issued warnings, sent their forces into North Korea, and then, on November 25, unleashed a massive attack on UN troops. MacArthur's shattered army fled to South Korea and regrouped to defend it.

The Korean "police action" settled into a troubling stalemate. A frustrated MacArthur wanted to expand the war effort and fight back aggressively, but the chastened Truman administration, giving up on reunification, was prepared to accept the old division at the 38th parallel. That was too much for MacArthur, who broke the U.S. military's unwritten rule against public criticism of civilian leaders. "There is no substitute for victory," MacArthur lectured in 1951. Truman, fed up, fired his popular general in April. Meanwhile, the war dragged on.

The Korean stalemate underscored difficult realities of the cold war. Containment had the potential to sacrifice American lives in minor, nondecisive wars. Since each conflict had to be stopped short of nuclear disaster, U.S. troops also had to be prepared, as the saying went, to "die for a tie"—to fight for something less than victory. In this kind of conflict, leaders had to sustain the confidence of allies, undecided nations, and citizens at home that, despite setbacks, the West would eventually win. Psychology was more important than territory.

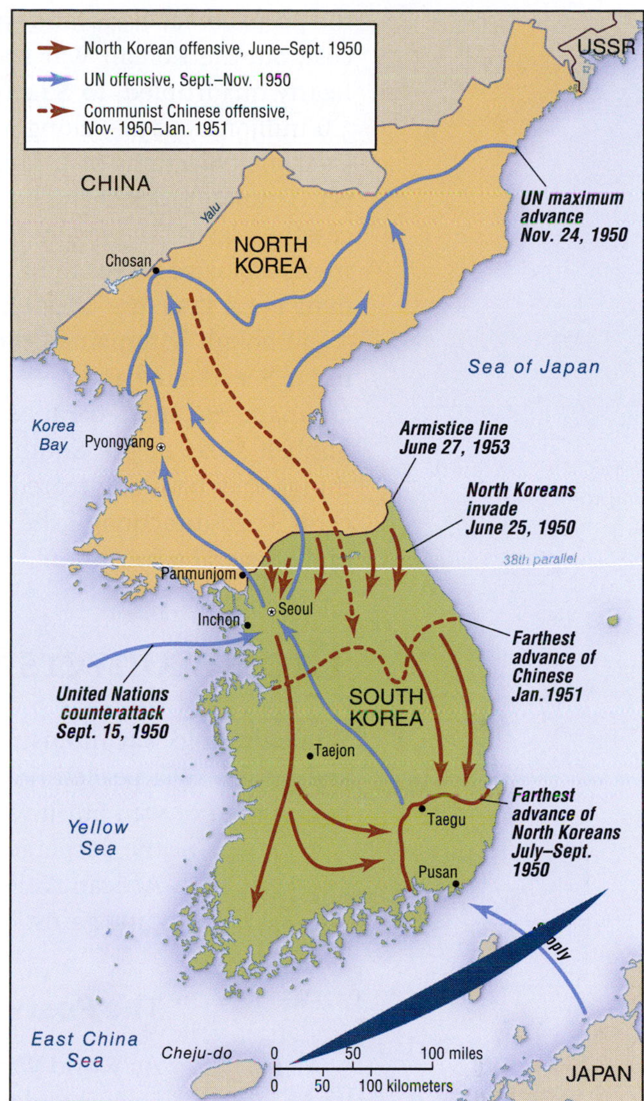

Map 26–2 The Korean War, 1950–1953 The shifting lines of advance mark the back-and-forth struggle that would end with stalemate and the division of Korea.

NSC-68

Before Korea, the Truman administration tried to balance its international and domestic agendas—limiting spending on the military, for instance, to boost economic recovery. By the 1950s, containment became the first priority. Escalating the U.S. effort, the administration challenged revolutionary movements even in peripheral areas, such as Southeast Asia. Colonial struggles, such as the Vietnamese rebellion against their French overlords, came to be seen as critical challenges to the non-Communist West.

In April 1950, the National Security Council approved a secret guideline known as NSC-68. Citing a growing list of threats and the "possibility of annihilation," it stipulated that the United States should triple defense spending, impose order in the postcolonial areas, and seek more powerful weapons. Truman worried about the cost, but the Korean War soon convinced him. By 1952, defense expenditures had nearly quadrupled, to $44 billion. Meanwhile, the armed forces grew—reaching 3.6 million by 1952—along with the list of combat theaters, now including Vietnam. Over the objections of J. Robert Oppenheimer, the director of the Manhattan Project, Truman ordered the building of "the so-called hydrogen or superbomb." Successfully tested in November 1952, the atom-fusing, thermonuclear bomb had far more explosive power than the atomic bomb, but it did not stop the arms race. Less than a year later, the USSR had its own "H-bomb."

Although it remained top secret until the 1970s, NSC-68 profoundly changed the U.S. economy and political system. The military buildup was paid for with deficit financing, and federal borrowing generated jobs and growth, particularly in the Sunbelt areas of the South and West. To fight the cold war, Americans accepted things they had long feared: secrecy, debt, alliances, a massive standing army, and centralized direction of the economy. Each of these innovations magnified the role of the federal government.

The Reconversion of American Society

While the cold war intensified, domestic policy focused on restoring the economy and society to a peacetime footing. "Reconversion" was a welcome process for a nation tired of war, but it was also a cause for worry. Americans feared a return to the desperate economic conditions of the 1930s. Labor, women, and African Americans, especially, wanted to hold on to and extend wartime gains.

> We are living in a period in which there are going to be witch-hunts, hysteria, and red-baiting by the most vicious group of congressmen that have gathered under the dome of the Capitol.
>
> WALTER REUTHER, labor union president, 1947

The Postwar Economy

As World War II ended, it seemed likely that the economy would slide back into depression. Millions of unemployed servicemen returned home at a time when government was cutting spending. The disaster never came. Unemployment rose to almost 4 percent the year after the war but never approached the double-digit rates of the 1930s. Despite brief downturns, the economy remained vibrant. This resilience reflected several factors, including veterans' choices, the federal role, the gradual transformation of industry, and U.S. economic dominance. Returning veterans did not strain the economy, partly because half of them went to school rather than work. Under the GI Bill of 1944 the federal government paid for up to three years of education for veterans. Spending by the federal government also helped to prevent a return to the economic conditions of the 1930s. With the end of World War II, federal expenditures decreased dramatically, but the government was still spending far more than it did during the 1930s. The GI Bill illustrated how that spending stimulated the economy. Pumping nearly $14.5 billion into the educational system, the bill encouraged colleges and universities to expand. As veterans swelled enrollments, institutions hired new faculty. Entire new educational systems, such as the State University of New York, were created.

Reconversion accelerated economic transformations that World War II started. In the late 1940s, industrial production was still concentrated in the Northeast and Midwest but there were already signs of change. Military spending helped shift factories and population toward the South and West. In the 1940s, the population of the western states grew by 50 percent while the population of the East grew by only 10 percent. The nature of the economy was changing, too. Oil and natural gas replaced coal as the principal source of power. New industries, such as plastics, electronics, and aviation, were growing rapidly.

Finally, the dominance of the United States in the world economy facilitated reconversion. At the end of World War II, the U.S. economy was roughly the size of the European and Soviet economies combined. As late as 1950, America, with only 6 percent of the world's population, accounted for a staggering 40 percent of the value of all the goods and services produced around the globe. Demand for American exports provided jobs but also stoked inflation. Ultimately production caught up, and by the late 1940s, the economy was beginning a prolonged peacetime boom.

The Challenge of Organized Labor

Organized labor had never been more powerful than at the end of World War II. One-third of nonagricultural civilian workers belonged to unions. The Democratic Party paid attention to the interests of influential unions such as the Congress of Industrial Organizations (CIO), and after pledging not to strike during World War II, organized labor was eager to test its clout. Workers wanted wage increases to cope with inflation and reward workers for their contribution to wartime profits. In Europe and Japan, unions were gaining control over the way corporations did business, and some American unionists wanted a similar role in management. Not surprisingly, corporations were reluctant to give up any of their power or profits. Along with conservatives in Congress, they branded the unions as agents of Communism.

The result was a huge wave of strikes as soon as the war ended in August 1945. At the start of 1946, 2 million workers were on strike. Machinists in San Francisco, longshoremen in New York City, and other workers across the country called a record 4,985 strikes that year. "[L]abor has gone crazy," an anxious Truman told his mother.

Significant work stoppages took place in automobile factories, coal mines, and railroad yards. Late in 1945, the United Auto Workers (UAW) struck General Motors (GM) for a 30 percent raise in hourly wages, access to the company's account books, and more say in company decisions. UAW vice president Walter Reuther insisted that higher wages would stimulate consumption without forcing the company to raise prices. GM rejected union interference in management decisions. When the strike finally ended after 113 days, the UAW won only some of its wage demands. It marked a turning point for labor. Unions never again made such bold demands to participate in management, and instead focused on pay and benefits.

The coal and railroad strikes were even more contentious than the GM work stoppage. Members of the United Mine Workers (UMW) and the railway unions refused to accept arbitration by the federal government. As the coal supply dwindled, power systems suffered "brownouts," and railroad passengers were stranded. The situation tested the strong relationship, forged in the New Deal, between the Democratic Party and organized labor. Truman ordered federal takeovers of both the mines and the railroads. "Let Truman dig coal with his bayonets," snarled John L. Lewis, leader of the

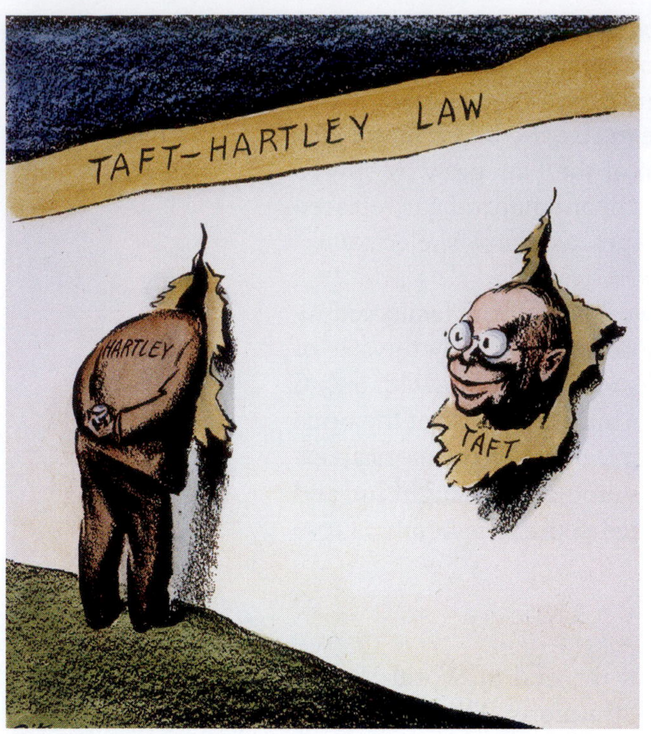

Containment on the Home Front. Although Congress passed the Taft-Hartley Act in 1947 to forestall an impending coal strike, United Mineworkers leader John L. Lewis ignored the act and struck anyway.

UMW. But the strikes came to an end in May. Much of the public applauded the president's action. Many Americans believed that Lewis, Reuther, and the other union leaders had become too powerful, arrogant, and demanding for the good of the country.

Counting on the public's unhappiness with unions, probusiness Republicans in Congress soon moved to limit the power of organized labor, which had been boosted by the Democratic New Deal. In 1947, a coalition of Republicans and conservative, mostly southern, Democrats passed the Taft-Hartley Act, a sweeping modification of federal labor law. The measure made it easier for employers to hire nonunion workers and to oppose the formation of unions. The bill also limited unions' right to organize and engage in political activity. Most humiliating of all, it compelled union leaders to swear that they did not belong to the Communist Party.

Despite these setbacks, workers and unions still prospered. Landmark contract negotiations between the UAW and GM offered a peaceful and lucrative model of labor relations. In 1948 the UAW won guaranteed cost-of-living adjustments, known as COLAs, and an annual wage increase tied to rises in worker productivity. In the so-called Treaty of Detroit, signed in 1950, the UAW obtained other increases and a pension plan in an unusually long-term contract lasting five years. The UAW contracts replaced confrontation with cooperation and strikes with security. In return for pensions and protection against inflation, the autoworkers gave management stable, predictable labor relations over the long term.

The Treaty of Detroit ended a difficult period for organized labor. Thanks to such lucrative contracts as the Treaty of Detroit, many workers were more secure than ever before, but reconversion also limited the power of organized labor. Aggressive strikes produced mixed results, public hostility, and government interference. Reconversion revealed the limits of the Democratic Party's support for labor as well. With the end of the strike wave, unions effectively abandoned their demand to participate in management in postwar America.

Opportunities for Women

Reconversion also posed special challenges to the status of American women. During World War II, the shortage of male labor had expanded women's opportunities for employment. Working women prized the income and the sense of satisfaction they gained from performing jobs traditionally monopolized by men. But there was a widespread belief, encouraged by employers and government officials, that women should surrender jobs to returning veterans. The number of women in the labor force dropped 13 percent from 1945 to 1946, but reconversion did not send displaced female workers home for good. Three-quarters of the women who wanted to stay at work after the war managed to find jobs.

Women's role in the postwar workplace was the product both of their desire and of financial necessity. Most, of course, needed to earn a living for themselves or their families. By 1953 the number of women in the workforce matched the level of 1945. A higher percentage of women were employed than before World War II. The number in nontraditional jobs increased, too. More women than ever before were skilled craftspersons, forepersons, physicians, and surgeons.

The number of married women in the postwar labor force was especially notable. The cultural prejudice against women's employment had always applied most strongly to married women and mothers, but economic realities overcame cultural prejudices. Increasingly, employers needed women workers. By 1947 there were already more married women than single women in the wage labor force.

The armed forces, like civilian employers, initially cut back the number of women in the ranks when the war ended, but reconversion did not cause a return to the prewar days when women had almost no place in the military. Congress granted women permanent status in the armed forces and merged the separate women's military organizations, such as the Women's Army Corps, into the regular armed services.

Despite these gains, women continued to face discrimination. The majority had to settle for traditionally female, traditionally low-paying jobs in offices, stores, and factories. Women's hourly pay rose only half as much as men's pay in the first years after the war. In the military, women were largely confined to noncombatant roles such as nursing. There were no women generals.

Secretarial Pool Despite official discouragement, large numbers of women worked in offices and other settings after World War II.

Women faced discrimination in the larger society as well. There was little interest in women's rights. After a meeting with female activists, Truman dismissed a constitutional amendment guaranteeing equal rights for women as a "lot of hooey." Despite the lack of support for women's rights, women's opportunities were gradually expanding in the years after World War II; the combination of women's desires and the economy's needs was slowly promoting the feminization of the labor force.

Civil Rights for African Americans

Like women, African Americans had made significant gains during World War II. They had filled new roles in the military and higher-paying jobs in the civilian economy, and aggressively pushed their demand for civil rights. Like women, African Americans sought to preserve and extend these rights and opportunities in the face of substantial resistance.

Several factors, including economic change, legal rulings, and wartime experiences, stimulated the drive for equal rights and opportunities after World War II. By the end of the war, the transformation of the southern economy was undermining the system that segregated African Americans and denied them the right to vote. As the mechanization reduced the need for field hands, African Americans continued to leave farms for the region's growing cities and for the North and West. One of the fundamental rationales for segregation—the need for an inexpensive and submissive labor force to work the fields—was disappearing. The developing southern economy also attracted white migrants from other regions, people less committed to segregation and disfranchisement. Meanwhile, the African American migrants to northern and western cities increased African American votes and political influence in the nation.

In fighting the Nazis during the war and the Communists afterwards, the United States dedicated itself to universal freedoms. The United Nations Declaration on Human Rights committed member states to guarantee rights to education, free movement, assembly, and personal safety. Truman often stated that disregard for human rights was "the beginning of tyranny, and too often, the beginning of war." But Kennan noted that, since the United States did not respect the rights of its own citizens, such statements only "invite charges of hypocrisy against us." African Americans appealed to the UN, the courts, and the press to recognize these commitments.

During the 1940s, a series of decisions by the U.S. Supreme Court struck at racial discrimination and encouraged African Americans to challenge inequality. In *Smith v. Allwright* in 1944, the court had banned whites-only primary elections. In *Morgan v. Virginia* in 1946, the court ruled that interstate bus companies could not segregate passengers. In *Shelley v. Kraemer* in 1948, the court banned restrictive covenants, the private agreements between property owners not to sell houses to African Americans and other minorities. These and other court decisions made discriminatory practices vulnerable and raised the possibility that African Americans might have a judicial ally in their struggle for justice.

African Americans' war experiences also encouraged them to demand more from the United States. Veterans, having fought for their country, now expected it to give them justice. Reconversion could not mean a return to the old days of discrimination. "Our people are not coming back with the idea of just taking up where they left off," an African American private wrote. "We are going to have the things that are rightfully due us or else."

That kind of determination spurred civil rights activism after World War II. In the South, African Americans increasingly demanded the right to vote after *Smith v. Allwright*. The National Association for the Advancement of Colored People (NAACP), the oldest civil rights organization, set up citizenship schools in southern communities to show African American voters how to register. The campaign was driven, too, by individual and spontaneous actions. In July 1946 Medgar Evers, a combat veteran who had just reached his 21st birthday, decided to try to vote in the Democratic Party's primary election in Decatur, Mississippi.

Slain American Civil Rights Activist Medgar Evers (1925–1963) Medgar Evers fought for democracy in France and Germany, and then returned to fight for it again in Mississippi.

Such activism met resistance from whites deeply committed to disfranchisement and segregation. A white mob kept Evers from voting in 1946. In Georgia, whites killed an African American voter. More often, they manipulated registration laws to disqualify voters. A voter who wanted to register might have to answer such questions as "How many bubbles are there in a bar of soap?" Nevertheless, African American voter registration in the South, only 2 percent in 1940, rose to 12 percent by 1947. With that widening margin came the election of a few African American officials and improved service from local government.

While the campaign for voting rights went forward, civil rights activists fought segregation in all parts of the country. The interracial Congress of Racial Equality (CORE) took the lead in protesting public discrimination. To test the Supreme Court's decision in *Morgan,* CORE sent an integrated team of 16 activists on a two-week bus trip through the upper South, where they met with violence and arrests. Activists hardly dented segregation in the South in the 1940s, but they had more success promoting antidiscrimination laws in the North. By 1953, fair-employment laws had been adopted in 30 cities and 12 states.

Activists also pressured Truman to support civil rights. In the spring and summer of 1946, picketers marched outside the White House with signs that read, "SPEAK, SPEAK, MR. PRESIDENT." Racial discrimination was an embarrassment for a nation claiming to represent freedom and democracy around the world, but support for civil rights was a political risk for a politician dependent on white support. Nevertheless, Truman took significant steps.

In the fall of 1946, a presidential committee report, *To Secure These Rights,* called for strong federal action against lynching, vote suppression, job discrimination, and civil rights violations, including segregation in the armed forces. Admitting that "there is a serious gap between our ideals and some of our practices," Truman insisted "this gap must be closed." Furious white southern politicians and newspapers said Truman was "stabbing the South in the back."

African Americans, meanwhile, kept the heat on Truman. To protest discrimination in the military, A. Philip Randolph, the head of the Brotherhood of Sleeping Car Porters, proposed a boycott of the draft. Warned that he would be accused of treason, he replied that "if that is the only way we can get democracy, we will have to face it." In July 1948 Truman responded with Executive Order 9981, creating a committee to phase out discrimination in the military. At the same time, Truman established the Fair Employment Board, which moved more slowly against discrimination in federal hiring.

During the Truman years, the most publicized blow to racial inequality came not from the White House but the baseball diamond. When the Brooklyn Dodgers called up infielder Jackie Robinson from the minor leagues in 1947, he became the first African American man in decades to play in the majors. A strong, self-disciplined former soldier, Robinson took taunts and beanballs on the field and death threats in the mail. Fast, powerful, and exciting, he finished the season as the National League's Rookie of the Year. Robinson's success paved the way for increasing numbers of African American players in the majors over the next several years.

Robinson's success also spelled the end of the Negro Leagues, the organizations created when African Americans were banned from the major leagues. As would sometimes be the case, integration undermined distinctly African American institutions. Nonetheless, the achievements of Robinson, Larry Doby, and other pioneering African American major leaguers sent a powerful message for civil rights and underscored the limits of reconversion. On the whole, African Americans preserved and sometimes managed to expand their wartime gains while still encountering injustice and inequality in almost every aspect of daily life. In one respect, at least, African Americans, women, and organized labor shared a common experience in the first years after World War II. For each of these groups, reconversion turned out to be better than feared and worse than hoped. African Americans, women, and workers all struggled to preserve and expand their rights and opportunities in the political economy of the late 1940s. They all confronted the limits of their power to change the society around them.

The Frustrations of Liberalism

During the Great Depression, liberalism, in the form of Franklin Roosevelt's New Deal, had reshaped American democracy, thrusting the federal government more deeply than ever into economic and social life. But the liberal Democratic agenda, with its calls for further federal activism, had stalled during World War II. In the first years after the war, it met with more frustration. Liberals and the Democratic Party strained to show that they had answers for a nation no longer facing an economic or military emergency. Harry Truman struggled to prove that he was a worthy successor to Roosevelt.

The Democrats' Troubles

An accidental president, Harry Truman faced skepticism from many Americans. Liberals wondered whether he shared their ideals. They were incensed when he fired FDR's trusted aide Henry Wallace after Wallace criticized Truman's policy toward the USSR. Conservatives and moderates also had doubts about his agenda. During the Depression, Americans had been willing to endorse government interventions in the economy, but in a fairly prosperous peacetime, people felt less need for government and more need for individual freedom.

The president embraced more of liberalism than the liberals expected. Shortly after he took office in 1945, he presented a legislative program that included proposals on education, employment, insurance, social security, and civil rights. Yet a full-employment bill, reflecting the liberal belief that the federal government should take responsibility for securing jobs and prosperity, met overwhelming conservative and moderate opposition. Watered down by Congress, the resulting Employment Act of 1946 created a Council of Economic Advisors for the president but did nothing to increase the economic role of the federal government.

> **I'm "not familiar with the term 'cold war.'"**
>
> 46 PERCENT OF AMERICANS, Gallup poll, December 1948

Truman and the liberals suffered an even sharper defeat over the president's sweeping proposal for a national health insurance system that would guarantee medical care to all Americans. The plan gave the federal government powers to manage the insurance system and set doctors' and hospitals' fees. Conservatives and the medical profession promptly condemned Truman's proposal as "the kind of regimentation that led to totalitarianism in Germany." The bill failed, and so did most of Truman's domestic proposals.

Nevertheless, the federal role in national life continued to grow in cold war America. Medical care offered a notable example. The Veterans Administration established a vast network of federal hospitals to care for returning soldiers. In 1946, the Hill-Burton Act appropriated federal money for the construction of hospitals. That same year, Congress created a research lab, later called the Centers for Disease Control, in Atlanta, Georgia, to monitor infectious diseases. Congress also reorganized the National Institutes of Health in 1948 and established the National Institute of Mental Health in 1949. Even though national health insurance was defeated, the federal role grew.

While Truman struggled with domestic and foreign policy, he became increasingly unpopular. "To err is Truman," went the joke. The president looked weak and ineffective to some Americans, tyrannical and overbearing to others. "Had Enough?" asked Republicans. Many had. In the 1946 congressional elections, the voters gave the Republicans a majority in both the House of Representatives and the Senate for the first time in 16 years.

Truman's Comeback

The 1946 elections seemed to point toward Truman's defeat two years later, but the president managed a stunning comeback. It began with the Republican majority that took control in Congress in 1947. Led by Senator Robert Taft of Ohio, they hoped to beat back New Deal liberalism and substitute a different understanding of American democracy. Refuting "the corrupting idea that we can legislate prosperity, legislate equality, legislate opportunity," Taft wanted "free Americans freely working out their destiny." The Taft-Hartley Act was a blow to liberals and the administration, but Republicans found themselves hamstrung by Americans' ambivalence about liberalism. Few were enthusiastic about bold new programs such as national health insurance, but there was little sentiment to roll back the New Deal. Americans clearly wanted to hold on to the benefits they had. Besides Taft-Hartley, the Eightieth Congress did not accomplish much, and soon Truman was campaigning against a "do-nothing Congress."

Nevertheless, things looked bad for Truman. By March 1948 only 35 percent of the people approved of his performance. Moreover, his party was splitting apart. On the left, his former secretary of commerce Henry Wallace was running for president as a "Progressive." On the right, Democratic governor Strom Thurmond of South Carolina was running as a "Dixiecrat," appealing to white supporters of segregation. Losing Democratic votes to both Wallace and Thurmond, Truman seemed certain to lose in November. Or so his Republican opponent, Governor Thomas E. Dewey of New York, thought. Dewey believed a moderate, uncontroversial campaign would do the trick, but Truman worked to pull the New Deal majority back together. Climbing aboard his railway car, Truman visited more than half the states on a "whistle-stop" campaign. The president reached out to African Americans, labor, farmers, senior citizens, and other beneficiaries of New Deal liberalism. "Give 'em hell, Harry," the crowds shouted, and he did. He hammered home the difference between the Democrats' and Republicans' visions of the political economy. "The Democratic Party puts human rights and human welfare first," he declared. "These Republican gluttons of privilege . . . want a return of the Wall Street economic dictatorship."

On election day, Wallace and Thurmond received only a million votes each. Dewey attracted fewer votes than he had four years before. Holding together Roosevelt's coalition, Truman won the presidency in his own right with only 49.5 percent of the vote (see Map 26–3). Moreover, the Democrats recaptured the House and the Senate. The triumph did not last long. Like Taft two years before, Truman soon discovered that an election victory did not mean a mandate. In his State of the Union address in January 1949, Truman declared that "every individual has a right to expect from our Government a fair deal." But the president's "Fair Deal" legislation made little headway in Congress. Despite Truman's comeback, the liberal vision, so influential in the 1930s, could not dominate the politics of cold war America.

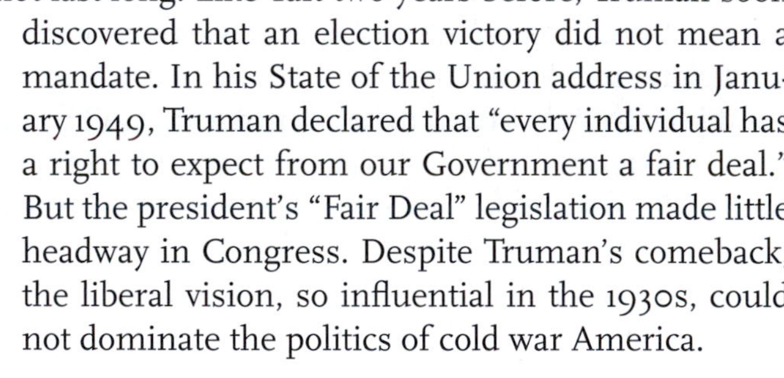

Candidate (Party)	Electoral Vote (%)	Popular Vote (%)
Truman (Democratic)	303 (57%)	24,105,812 (49.5%)
Dewey (Republican)	189 (36%)	21,970,065 (45.1%)
Thurmond (States' Rights Democratic)	39 (7%)	1,169,063 (2.4%)
Wallace (Progressive)		1,157,172 (2.4%)
Minor parties		272,713 (0.6%)

Map 26–3 The 1948 Presidential Election Segregationist and progressive candidacies were expected to undermine the Democratic majority, but the Roosevelt coalition returned Truman to the White House for a second term.

Fighting the Cold War at Home

While conservatives and liberals battled over domestic policy, the cold war increasingly intruded into every aspect of life. As the drafters of NSC-68 had hoped, the billions of dollars in defense expenditures stimulated economic growth, but in the short run, the main by-product was fear. Doubt and insecurity pervaded American culture in the late 1940s. Americans added a new fear of nuclear weapons to their old fear of immigrants. Above all, society succumbed to a largely irrational dread of hidden traitors in Hollywood, Washington, the universities, and the public library. To fight the cold war at home, anti-Communist crusaders such as Joe McCarthy hunted for disloyal Americans. By the 1950s, McCarthyism was a powerful force capable of destroying the lives of thousands of Americans, including Esther and Stephen Brunauer.

Doubts and Fears in the Atomic Age

Despite the U.S. triumph in World War II, American culture was surprisingly dark and pessimistic in the late 1940s. The rise of fascism, the Holocaust, and the bombings of Hiroshima and Nagasaki raised troubling questions about the direction of progress and the innate goodness of humankind. The cold war did nothing to calm those concerns. Even the welcome prosperity of the reconversion period did not soothe Americans' sense of doubt. People felt insignificant and powerless in an age of giant corporations, big unions, big government, and superbombs.

Americans revealed their unease in a variety of ways. Not long after the announcement of the Truman Doctrine in 1947, people suddenly began seeing lights in the sky. There were reports of "flying saucers" over 35 states and Canada. Some Americans even believed the federal government was covering up the truth about these unidentified flying objects. In a nuclear-armed world, columnist Joseph Alsop observed, the saucer scare was a reminder that "man-made horrors are quite real, quite imminent possibilities."

Meanwhile, Hollywood films explored popular fears. In 1946, *The Best Years of Our Lives* traced the difficult, sometimes humiliating readjustment of three returning veterans. The same year, *It's a Wonderful Life* told the story of a small-town banker forced to accept the disappointment of his unfulfilled dreams. Both films expressed reservations about the morality of capitalism and the chances of achieving happiness in the modern world. A new cinematic genre, film noir, offered an even darker view of individuals trapped in a confusing, immoral world. "I feel all dead inside," confessed the detective in *The Dark Corner* (1946). "I'm backed up in a dark corner and I don't know who's hitting me."

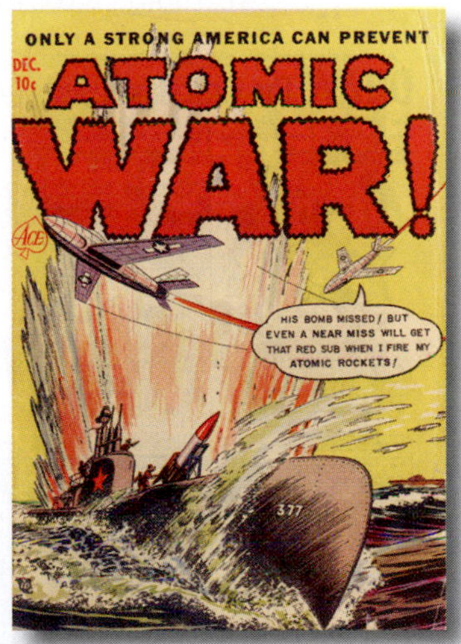

Nuclear weapons were perhaps the greatest source of fear. The unprecedented power of the atomic bomb dominated the popular imagination. For many Americans, this was the Atomic Age. They dealt with their anxiety about the new age in a variety of ways. Some people tried dark attempts at humor. Americans drank "atomic cocktails" and danced to the "Atomic Polka." American women wore the new "bikini," the explosively scanty two-piece bathing suit named for the Pacific atoll where the United States tested the H-bomb. The Soviets' development of the atomic bomb and then the hydrogen bomb was impossible to laugh away.

Americans' fear was also reflected in the hardening of attitudes toward foreigners. In 1945, a welcoming nation eased the immigration process for the foreign wives of American servicemen by passing the War Brides Act, but as the cold war intensified, other potential migrants met a hostile reception. The Immigration and

Nationality Act of 1952 tightly restricted immigration, particularly from Asia. It also kept out Communists and homosexuals and allowed the deportation of American citizens suspected of disloyalty.

The Anti-Communist Crusade

Americans may have feared disloyalty most of all. Many believed the real Communist threat came from within their own country. Historians debate the origins of this second "Red Scare." Some trace the anti-Communist crusade to a conservative reaction against the rising power of labor, African Americans, women, and other disempowered groups. Others blame the Truman administration for stoking fear to justify unprecedented military activity and spending. Although the new Red Scare was not solely a political creation—anti-Communism had deep roots in American culture—politicians in both parties gave domestic anti-Communism its particularly dangerous form.

The crusaders had to search hard for Communists at home. The Communist Party of the United States of America (CPUSA), a legal political party, was tiny and losing followers. Infiltrated by FBI and police informants, it never received more than a microscopic 0.3 percent of the popular vote. Just to be sure, the Truman administration charged 12 party leaders with violations of the Smith Act, which had criminalized membership in "a group advocating . . . the overthrow of the government by force." In 1949, 11 were convicted and sent to jail.

Open Communists posed less of a threat than secret ones, and in fact, self-professed former Communists and spies were seen as the most reliable informants on the hidden network of traitors presumed to be operating throughout the country. The hunt for these "subversives" was led by the House of Representatives' Un-American Activities Committee (HUAC). In 1947 HUAC held hearings on supposed Communist plots in Hollywood. The film industry cooperated, but eight screenwriters, a producer, and a director cited their First Amendment rights and declined to

***The Subway* (1950)** Modernist painter George Tooker captured the claustrophobic anxiety of the McCarthy era in paintings like *The Subway* and *Government Bureau* (1956). In popular fiction and noir films, social conformity only thinly concealed a mounting hysteria.

testify. The "Hollywood Ten" were convicted of contempt of Congress and sent to jail for up to a year. Hollywood got the message. Film studios "blacklisted"—refused to hire—writers, directors, and actors even remotely suspected of Communist ties. Avoiding controversial subjects, the studios put out overwrought anti-Communist movies such as *The Red Menace* and *I Was a Communist for the FBI*.

Afraid of looking "soft" on Communism, the Truman administration encouraged the idea that there was a real problem with domestic Communism. "Communists," declared Truman's attorney general, Tom Clark, "are everywhere—in factories, offices, butcher shops, on street corners, in private businesses—and each carries with him the germs of death for society."

Late in 1946 the president set up a committee to investigate "employee loyalty." The next year he created a permanent loyalty program. Any civil servant could lose his or her job by belonging to any of the "totalitarian, Fascist, Communist or subversive" groups listed by the attorney general. The loyalty program proceeded with little regard for due process. People accused of disloyalty could not challenge evidence or confront their accusers, and they were presumed guilty until they proved their own innocence. Although only about 300 employees were actually discharged, Truman's loyalty program helped create the impression that there must be a serious problem in Washington.

The Hunt for Spies

There was, in fact, spying going on inside the federal government. The Soviet Union, just like the United States, carried out espionage abroad. The Canadian government found evidence of a spy ring that had passed American atomic secrets to the Soviets during World War II. Through its intercepts of Soviet communications, the CIA had a good idea of the scale of the spying and who was involved, but for its own reasons, the agency chose not to share this information with Congress, prosecutors, or even the president.

Thanks to information from the Canadian case, the FBI began to suspect Alger Hiss, an aide to the secretary of state, was a Soviet agent. Hiss was quietly eased out of his job. Then, in 1948, HUAC took testimony from Whittaker Chambers, an editor of *Time* magazine who claimed to have been a Soviet agent in the 1930s. Chambers accused Hiss of passing secret documents. Educated at elite schools before joining the Roosevelt administration, Hiss epitomized New Deal liberalism. He denied the charges and said he had never even met Chambers. He initially appeared more credible than the rumpled Chambers, an admitted perjurer, but Congressman Richard Nixon of California, a Republican member of HUAC, forced him to admit that he had in fact known Chambers under an alias. With help from the FBI, Chambers charged that Hiss had given him secret information in the 1930s. In front of reporters, Chambers pulled rolls of microfilm out of a hollowed-out pumpkin on his Maryland farm. The film contained photographs of secret documents. Hiss could not explain these "Pumpkin Papers." Under the statute of limitations, it was too late to try Hiss for spying, but it was not too late to indict him for lying to Congress. Hiss's perjury trial ended in a hung jury in 1949, but a second jury convicted him in January 1950. While Hiss sat in prison for almost four years, Chambers wrote a best seller and Nixon became a senator. The case was a great triumph for Republicans and conservatives and a blow to Democrats and liberals.

As the Hiss case ended, another scandal stimulated Americans' fears. In early 1950, British authorities arrested Klaus Fuchs, a physicist who had worked at the U.S. nuclear research facility in Los Alamos, New Mexico. The investigation led eventually to David Greenglass, who worked on the atomic bomb project, and his brother-in-law, Julius Rosenberg. Julius, a former member of the CPUSA, and his wife Ethel were convicted of conspiring to steal atomic information, in a trial that was controversial owing to its anti-Semitic overtones and because the act protecting atomic secrets became law after the spying allegedly took place. Though they had two young sons, both Rosenbergs were sentenced to death. Ignoring appeals for clemency from around the world, the federal government finally electrocuted the Rosenbergs in June 1953.

There now seems little disagreement that the USSR obtained American nuclear secrets, but the impact was probably not as great as conservatives feared or as small as liberals insisted. Most likely, espionage sped up the Soviets' work on an atomic bomb that they would have eventually produced anyway.

The Rise of McCarthyism

Two weeks after Hiss's conviction, one week after Truman's announcement of the decision to build the hydrogen bomb, and just days after the arrest of Klaus Fuchs, Senator Joseph McCarthy of Wisconsin suddenly and spectacularly took command of the anti-Communist crusade. Speaking to the Republican Women's Club of Wheeling, West Virginia, the previously obscure senator claimed to have names of 205 Communists working in the State Department. In fact, McCarthy had no new information. Instead, he dredged up a handful of old accusations, including the ones against the Brunauers.

Nevertheless, McCarthy was instantly popular and powerful. Frightened by new geopolitical and technological dangers, many people wanted to believe in a senator bold enough to fight back. Some shared McCarthy's resentment of privileged elites—New Dealers, diplomats, scientists—the powerful figures he derided as "egg-sucking phony liberals" and "bright young men . . . born with silver spoons in their mouths." For some Americans—immigrants, midwesterners, Catholics, and fundamentalists—support for McCarthy was a way to prove that they were more patriotic than educated or wealthy elites. "McCarthyism" was a way to assert local, civic control over national cultural life. Even Democratic legislators voted for the Internal Security Act of 1950, which forced the registration of Communist and Communist-front groups, provided for the deportation of allegedly subversive aliens, and barred Communists from defense jobs. Refusing to "put the Government of the United States in the thought control business," Truman vetoed the bill, but Congress overrode his veto.

Eventually, McCarthy went too far. Angry that one of his aides, David Schine, had not received a draft deferment, the senator launched an investigation of the army. The secretary of the army, Robert T. Stevens, refused to cooperate and claimed that McCarthy had tried to get preferential treatment for Schine. In April 1954, before a television audience of 20 million people, McCarthy failed to come up with evidence of treason in the army. When he tried unjustifiably to smear one of the army's young lawyers as a Communist, the senator was suddenly exposed. "Have you no sense of decency, sir, at long last?" asked the army's chief counsel, Joseph Welch. It was an electric moment. The Senate hearings came to no judgment, but Americans

did. McCarthy's popularity ratings dropped sharply. By the end of the year, the Senate finally had the courage to condemn him for "unbecoming conduct."

The fall of McCarthy did not end McCarthyism. Schools forced teachers to sign loyalty oaths. Faculty members at several universities lost their jobs, and deans passed the names of suspect students to the FBI. Communism had become a useful charge to hurl at anything that anybody might oppose—labor unions, civil rights, even modern art. Politicians and communities attacked nonrepresentational, abstract expressionist artists as "tools of the Kremlin" and "our enemies." To protect themselves, groups policed their own membership. Labor unions, led by Reuther and other liberals, drove out Communist leaders and unions. The Cincinnati Reds renamed their team the "Redlegs" to make sure no one associated the world's oldest professional baseball team with Communism.

Across the country, Americans became more careful about what they said out loud. Many Americans had come to believe, along with McCarthy, that the civility and routines of democracy, the attention to rights and fairness, left America exposed to a ruthless adversary not bound by similar codes of conduct. Even as the Senate was censuring McCarthy, James Doolittle, the heroic World War II aviator, handed the Central Intelligence Agency a report on counterespionage and countersubversion. It explained that America faced "an implacable enemy whose avowed objective is world domination by whatever means and at whatever cost." "There are no rules in such a game," it concluded. "If the United States is to survive, long-standing American concepts of 'fair play' must be reconsidered."

Conclusion

By the time Esther Brunauer lost her job in 1952, the cold war had disrupted American life. To contain Communism, the United States had made unprecedented commitments that transformed the nation's economy. American society sorted through the unfinished business of reconversion, including the role of government and the rights and opportunities of labor, women, and African Americans. Despite these changes, the cold war had widened and intensified. Just seven years after dropping the first atomic bomb on Japan, Americans were again at war in the Far East and were forced to live with the threat of their own nuclear annihilation. They lived, too, with the frenzied search for subversives. American society seemed to be out of control.

As Esther and Stephen Brunauer moved back to Illinois to find peace and rebuild their lives, other Americans needed peace as well. They wanted the fighting in Korea to end. Anxious to avoid a nuclear holocaust, they wanted the confrontation with the Soviets to stabilize. Meanwhile, American society adjusted to a postwar economy, sorting out the role that government, labor, race, and gender would have in the new cold war order.

Further Readings

Kai Bird and Martin J. Sherwin, *American Prometheus: The Triumph and Tragedy of J. Robert Oppenheimer* (2005). Oppenheimer, the genius behind the Manhattan Project and a victim of McCarthyism, personified the contradictions of the early cold war.

Richard M. Fried, *Nightmare in Red: The McCarthy Era in Perspective* (1990). Provides a concise overview of the anti-Communist crusade.

William Graebner, *The Age of Doubt: American Thought and Culture in the 1940s* (1991). Probes the fears and insecurities that shaped American society during the cold war.

Alonzo L. Hamby, *Man of the People: A Life of Harry S. Truman* (1995). A full biography of the first cold war president.

Melvyn P. Leffler, *A Preponderance of Power: National Security, the Truman Administration, and the Cold War* (1992). One of several important conflicting accounts of the origins of the cold war.

Nelson Lichtenstein, *The Most Dangerous Man in Detroit: Walter Reuther and the Fate of American Labor* (1995). Examines the hopes and frustrations of the labor movement after World War II.

David M. Oshinsky, *A Conspiracy So Immense: The World of Joe McCarthy* (1983). An engaging, evenhanded biography of the most famous anti-Communist crusader.

Arnold Rampersad, *Jackie Robinson: A Biography* (1997). Explores the complicated man who integrated major league baseball.

Allen Weinstein, *Perjury: The Hiss-Chambers Case* (1978). Provides a thorough, controversial study of one of the most controversial episodes of the cold war.

Who, What?

Douglas MacArthur 873
Walter Reuther 875
Jackie Robinson 880
Alger Hiss 885
Central Intelligence Agency 869
National independence movements 870
38th parallel 873
NSC-68 874
Taft-Hartley Act 876

>> Timeline >>

▼ 1945

Yalta conference

Harry S. Truman inaugurated

Potsdam Conference

Industrial strikes break out

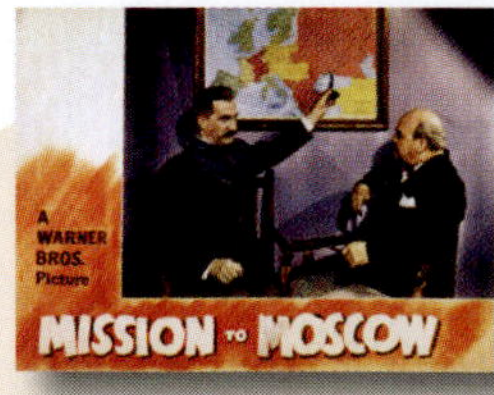
A WARNER BROS. Picture
MISSION TO MOSCOW

▼ 1946

Winston Churchill's "Iron Curtain" speech

George Kennan's "long telegram" on Soviet expansionism

Employment Act of 1946

Morgan v. Virginia

Election of Republican majorities in House and Senate

▼ 1947

Announcement of Truman Doctrine

Beginning of Federal Employee Loyalty Program

CORE's "Journey of Reconciliation"

Integration of major league baseball by Jackie Robinson

HUAC Hollywood hearings

Rio Pact

Taft-Hartley Act

National Security Act

Presidential commission reports on civil rights

▼ 1948

Shelley v. Kraemer

Congressional approval of Marshall Plan

Truman's Executive Order 9981

Beginning of Berlin crisis

Whatever the weather
We only reach welfare
together

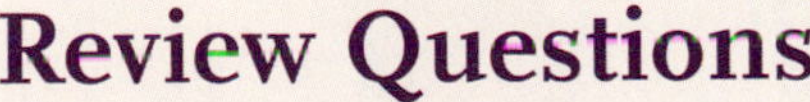

Review Questions

1. How did the National Security Act change the executive branch?
2. Why did Truman see Korea as important enough to defend?
3. Why were struggles in the workplace more intense in the late 1940s than during the Depression or World War II?
4. McCarthyism attacked government, science, education, theater, and Hollywood. Does this pattern reveal anything about the nature of American anxiety in the 1950s?
5. Two-thirds of the world's peoples gained their independence between 1945 and 1961. How did the cold war affect this movement toward nationhood?
6. In the 1950s and 1960s, historians debated the question of who started the cold war. In the 1990s, it became more interesting to ask *when* it started. Why the change, and what questions might historians today ask?

Website

America Abroad Media, "Banking on the Future: Global Development and the World Bank," http://www.americaabroadmedia.org/programs/view/id/52. Since World War II, the World Bank has worked to rebuild countries ravaged by war and colonialism and to create a unified world economy. It carries on the mission Truman launched with his Point Four address.

For further review materials and resource information, please visit www.oup.com/us/ofthepeople

Selective Service Act
Truman elected president

▼ 1949
Formation of North Atlantic Treaty Organization
Communist takeover of mainland China

▼ 1950
NSC-68
Alger Hiss's conviction for perjury
Joe McCarthy's speech in Wheeling, West Virginia
Treaty of Detroit
Beginning of Korean War
Internal Security Act of 1950

▼ 1951
Truman fires General Douglas MacArthur

▼ 1952
Immigration and Nationality Act
Test of hydrogen bomb

▼ 1953
Execution of Ethel and Julius Rosenberg

▼ 1954
Army-McCarthy hearings

CHAPTER 27

Common Threads 

>> Did the character of the cold war change from the 1940s to the 1950s?

>> Why did consumerism change the way Americans lived?

>> Why did diversity and individuality survive in the 1950s?

>> What was the impact of the Eisenhower administration on democracy?

>> How would the emerging discontents of the 1950s affect society and politics in the next decades?

The Consumer Society

1945–1961

AMERICAN PORTRAIT

>> Gene Ferkauf

At the end of World War II, Harry Ferkauf owned two luggage stores in midtown Manhattan in New York City. An immigrant Jewish man from Eastern Europe, he haggled with customers over prices in the old way and made a decent living. He did not want or expect much more. After all, he had barely kept his business alive during the Great Depression.

Harry's son, Eugene, who managed one of the stores, was unwilling to accept the old limits. After the war, Gene began offering discounts on luggage, watches, and other goods. Local storeowners resented this low-priced competition. Father and son argued frequently over Gene's strategy. In 1948, Gene quit the business and put all his savings into his own discount store on East 46th Street that would compete with the full-priced stores of the other merchants.

Gene envisioned a new kind of store, where customers could buy appliances and other goods without haggling, at low, fixed prices. Discounting his merchandise by a quarter and even a third, Gene could not make much money from a single sale. But if he sold enough televisions and refrigerators, he would earn more than his father ever had. On opening day, crowds filled the small shop and spent $3,000. Harry, who usually took in about $50 a day, was impressed.

In a few years, Gene had five successful discount stores in and around New York City. The business was called "E. J. Korvettes"—E for Eugene, J for his partner Joe Zwillenberg, and Korvettes after the small, quick Canadian warships of World War II. Korvettes appealed to a new generation, more optimistic than the older generation that had survived the Depression. Eager to buy televisions and other appliances, these younger people were unafraid to go into debt. Prosperous, they were leaving their parents' neighborhoods in the city for new suburbs. Gene Ferkauf understood these people; he was one of them. He, too, moved from his small $75-a-month urban apartment in Brooklyn to a $75,000 suburban "mansion" in Jamaica, Queens.

Gene had made it big. Closing the stores in New York, Korvettes built suburban stores in several states. In 1955, the partnership became a corporation. Gene had left his father's world behind.

Gene Ferkauf's success reflected one of the central developments that shaped American society after World War II. Along with the cold war, economic prosperity transformed the nation in a host of ways. Just as Gene left his father's world behind, American society left behind the sense of economic limits and constraints that characterized the Great Depression and the war. The 1950s marked the culmination of the nation's long transformation into a full-fledged consumer society. Gene Ferkauf profited because mainstream culture celebrated consumption and pleasure instead of work and self-restraint and because televisions and suburbs defined the consumer lifestyle.

The emergence of the consumer society strongly affected American culture and politics. The prosperous 1950s helped to produce a more homogeneous, seemingly more harmonious society, characterized by decreasing class differences, changing gender relations, and a baby boom. Enjoying the benefits of consumerism, American voters demanded less from government. In later years, American culture would look back nostalgically at the 1950s as a prosperous golden age, but the consumer society had its conflicts, failures, and limits. In different ways, many Americans chafed against the conformity and constraints of the 1950s. The benefits of the consumer society did not reach every group; consumerism did not solve the problem of racial inequality or end the cold war. By the close of the decade, many Americans worried about the inadequacies of the consumer society, even as they enjoyed its benefits. ●

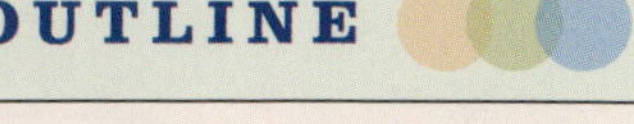

OUTLINE

Living the Good Life

Consumerism was not a new development: much of the consumer lifestyle existed by the 1920s (see Chapter 23). But it was only in the 1950s that consumer values and habits finally dominated the American economy and culture. Never before had so many Americans had the chance to live the good life.

They tended to define that "good life" in economic terms. A dynamic, evolving economy provided more leisure and income. Sure of prosperity, Americans had the confidence to spend more of their time and money in the pursuit of pleasure. Millions of people lived the dream of home ownership in new suburbs, bought flashy automobiles, purchased their first televisions, and enjoyed a new openness about sex.

Economic Prosperity

Consumerism could not have flourished without prosperity. Despite three short recessions, the 1950s were a period of economic boom. The economy grew solidly, and the gross national product—the value of all the country's output of goods and services—grew at an average of 3.2 percent a year.

Several major factors spurred this economic growth. The shortage of consumer goods during and just after World War II had left Americans with money to spend. Because of the cold war, the federal government was also ready to spend money. Washington's expenditures for the defense buildup and foreign aid helped to stimulate the demand for American goods and services. Robust capital spending by the nation's businesses also helped ensure economic growth. At the same time, the industrial economy was evolving. Traditional heavy manufacturing—the production of steel and automobiles—was still crucial to national prosperity, but newer industries such as electronics, chemicals, plastics, aviation, and computers became increasingly important.

> **See the USA in your Chevrolet**
> **America is asking you to call**
> **Drive your Chevrolet through the USA**
> **America's the greatest land of all.**
>
> CHEVROLET COMMERCIAL JINGLE, 1950

The emergence of the computer business was especially significant for the long-term transformation of the economy. In 1946, two engineers at the University of Pennsylvania, J. Presper Eckert Jr. and John William Mauchly, completed the first fully electronic digital computer, loaded with hot bulky vacuum tubes. The Electronic Numerical Integrator and Computer (ENIAC) weighed more than 30 tons and filled a large room. Then Eckert and Mauchly produced the UNIVAC 1 (Universal Automatic Computer), a more advanced machine that was used to count census data in 1951 and presidential election returns in 1952.

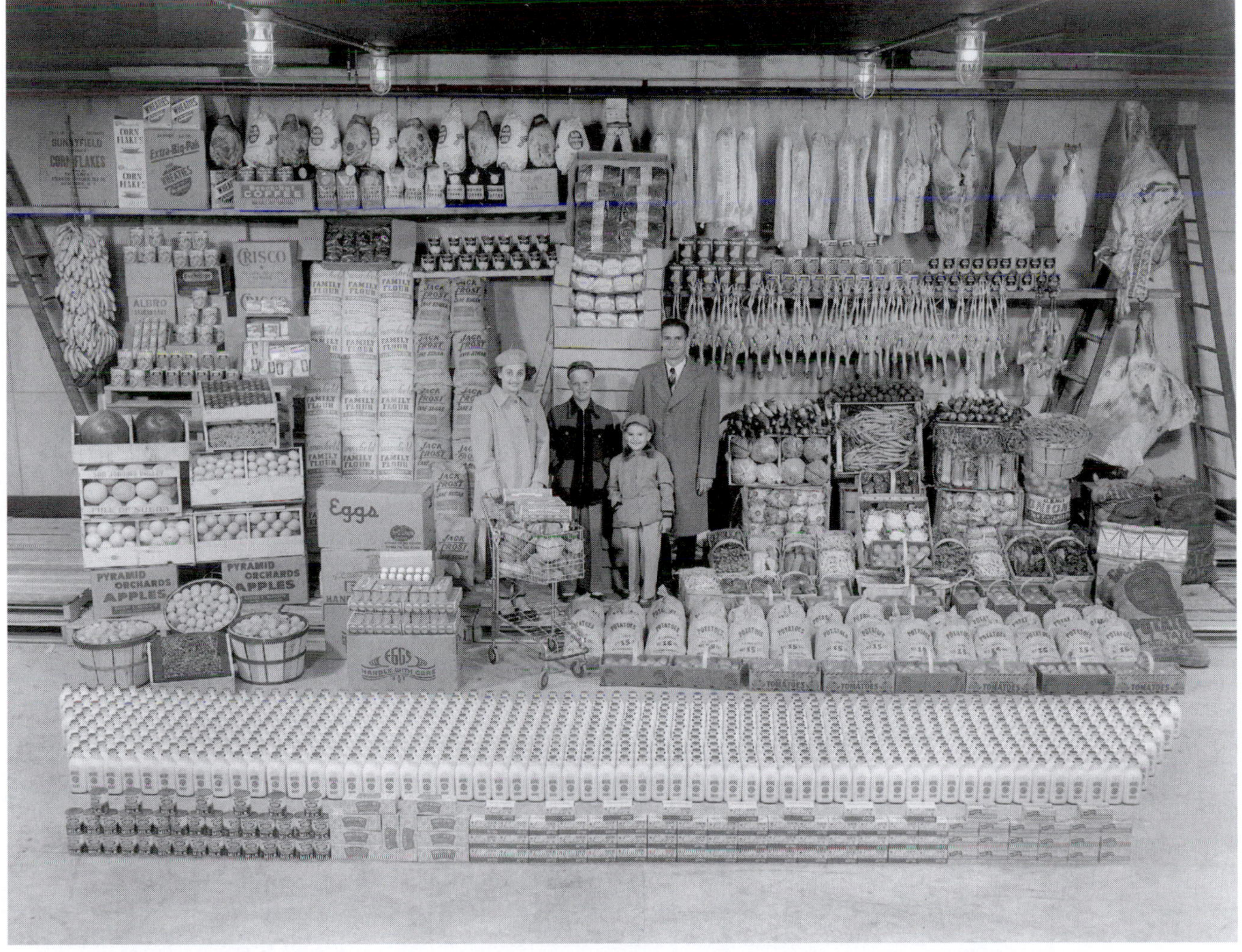

The New Affluence All the groceries consumed by a white-collar DuPont Chemical worker, his wife, and their two children in 1951.

ENIAC The first fully electronic digital computer fills a room in 1946.

As tiny solid-state transistors replaced vacuum tubes, computers became smaller, more powerful, and more common. By 1958, American companies were producing $1 billion worth of computers a year. Because computers were still so large and expensive, they were used mostly by universities, corporations, the Department of Defense, and other federal agencies. By 1961, there were about 10,000 computers in use, and the nation was on the brink of the computer age.

As American industry continued to evolve, the nation's distribution and service sectors played a larger economic role than ever before. While the number of manufacturing jobs barely changed, employment in retail stores like E. J. Korvettes increased 19 percent. Jobs in the service sector, such as restaurants, hotels, repair shops, hospitals, and universities, jumped 32 percent. The United States had begun to develop a postindustrial economy, less dependent on production and more dependent on service and consumption.

Economic prosperity greatly benefited big business. New corporations such as E. J. Korvettes emerged and grew. Thanks to a wave of mergers, established corporations became still larger. By 1960, corporations earned 18 times as much income as the rest of the nation's businesses combined.

Prosperity also boosted corporations' popularity. Even liberals, once critical of corporate power, now celebrated the benefits of large-scale business enterprise. Businessmen exuded confidence. "What is good for the country is good for General Motors, and vice versa," Charles Wilson, the head of GM, supposedly announced.

Benefiting from prosperity, American workers enjoyed high employment, low inflation, and rising incomes. Typically, less than 5 percent of the workforce was out of a job at one time. Wages rose dramatically. Factory workers' average hourly pay more than doubled between 1945 and 1960. Moreover, consumer prices rose less than 2 percent per year. As a result, the percentage of Americans living in poverty fell from as much as 30 in the late 1940s to 18 in 1959.

The economy also gave Americans more leisure time. By the 1950s, the 40-hour workweek was commonplace in American factories. Many workers now looked forward to two- or three-week paid annual vacations. As life expectancy increased and the economy boomed, more and more Americans could expect to retire at age 65 and then live comfortably off their pensions and Social Security.

Workers' well-being produced labor peace, which in turn stimulated prosperity. After the contentious relations of the 1940s, workers and employers were more likely to resolve their differences without strikes and lockouts. When the relatively aggressive Congress of Industrial Organizations (CIO) merged with the American Federation of Labor (AFL) to become the gigantic AFL-CIO in 1955, the union movement seemed to become more bureaucratic and complacent. "American labor never had it so good," crowed a trade union leader. Workers and corporations alike had the means to live the good life.

The Suburban Dream

For growing numbers of people, the good life meant a house in the suburbs. Most Americans had never owned their own homes. Suburbs had been mainly for the well-to-do. But entrepreneurship, efficient construction methods, inexpensive land, and generous federal aid made possible a host of affordable-housing developments outside the nation's cities. Along with Gene Ferkauf and his family, much of America moved to the suburbs in the 1950s.

William J. Levitt's pioneering development, Levittown, illustrated how entrepreneurship, low-priced land, and new construction techniques fueled a suburban housing boom. Levitt came back from military service in World War II with an optimistic vision of the future. He wanted to make houses affordable for middle-class and working-class people. Drawing on his military experience and on the assembly-line techniques of automaker Henry Ford, he intended to build houses so efficiently that they could be sold at remarkably low prices. Levitt bought 1,000 acres of cheap farmland not far from a Korvettes on New York's Long Island. He put up simple houses, with prefabricated parts, no basements, and low price tags. The original Cape Cod–style house cost $7,990, an appealing price for young couples trying to finance their first home.

Like Korvettes, Levittown quickly became a huge success. Buyers signed 1,400 contracts for houses on a single day in 1949. The development grew to 17,500 dwellings housing 82,000 people. Levitt soon built more Levittowns, as did imitators all around the country.

The federal government helped develop the suburbs. To make home ownership more affordable, the government allowed buyers to deduct mortgage interest payments from their federal income taxes. Federal legislation also guaranteed loans to the millions of military veterans. To help make commuting practical, the National System of Defense Highways Act of 1956 encouraged the construction of freeways connecting cities and suburbs.

Under such favorable conditions, the United States quickly became a nation of suburban home owners. As the rate of home ownership increased 20 percent between 1945 and 1960, nearly one-third of Americans lived in places like Levittown. The suburban dream had become an everyday reality.

AMERICAN LANDSCAPE

>> Levittown, New York

For many Americans, the first Levittown epitomized the virtues and defects of suburbia, consumerism, and democracy in post–World War II America. The new community seemed to be a democratic triumph, a visual reminder of upward mobility and equality of condition. The male heads of Levittown households tended to be prosperous blue-collar workers, veterans of World War II reaching for middle-class status for their growing, baby boom families. As an observer noted, Levittown was a "one-class community." Most households had an annual income of about $3,500 to $4,000, just enough to afford a place in the suburb.

From another angle, Levittown seemed less democratic. The suburb was notable for who didn't live there. Amid all the young families, there were few teenagers or senior citizens. There were hardly any African Americans, either.

The homogeneity of Levittown was no accident. The developer, William Levitt, had planned it that way. Levittown's first four-room Cape Cod houses came in only five models that differed very little from each other. To observers, the houses and streets of the new development all appeared to be the same. In fact, William Levitt even admitted that he had once gotten lost in all the look-alike streets of his suburb. The uniform style and cost of the houses ensured that the new development would attract only one class of residents. So-called restrictive covenants—special clauses in housing deeds—ensured that only whites bought property in Levittown.

Levitt also tried to impose uniform behavior on his residents. Community rules forbade putting up fences or hanging out the wash on weekends. Some of the residents themselves promoted conformity in Levittown. They wrote the local newspaper to attack neighbors who broke the rules. A nonconformist could expect to be labeled a "commie" or a "Russkie."

In Levittown, as in the rest of America, there was a heavy emphasis on domesticity. The design of the community and its houses reflected the domestic values of the period. The small Cape Cod homes encouraged family "togetherness." With so little private space, family members congregated around the kitchen table or in front of the TV in the living room. The wives of Levittown were expected to spend weekdays doing domestic tasks at home, rather than working at a paying job. That was how Levitt could assume these women would not need to hang out laundry on the weekends. Because the kitchen was supposed to be the center of women's lives, that room was placed at the front of the Cape Cod houses in Levittown.

The design of Levittown also supported men's domestic role. Former apartment dwellers found they had to spend time at home mowing their new lawns. Moreover, Levittown had few traditionally masculine public places—bars, firehouses, ball fields, and the like. Instead, the community promoted family togetherness away from home with plenty of playgrounds and swimming pools for children and their parents. As the local property owners association concluded, "Levittown is a child-centered community."

Despite the power of conformity, Levittown also revealed the survival of individuality in America. In time, the suburb became less homogeneous. With each succeeding year, the Levitts offered houses with a bit more variety. In 1949, they replaced the Cape Cod model with new ranch-style houses. The following years saw new features, including car-

The Suburban Dream. A young family stands proudly in front of a typical house in 1950s Levittown.

ports. As the 1950s wore on, residents turned houses into expressions of their individual tastes. They built garages and patios. They added rooms, gardens, signposts, and distinctive paint jobs. Despite the rules, they put up fences. "The houses take on the personalities of their owners," wrote a suburban resident.

In this way, as in others, Levittown was a product of 1950s America. This pioneering suburb revealed the power of domesticity and conformity. Levittown also demonstrated both the limits of democracy and the persistence of individuality in the consumer society.

The Pursuit of Pleasure

The consumer society depended on Americans' eagerness to pursue pleasure. Businesses made sure that nothing would prevent Americans from buying goods and services. If their wages and salaries were not enough, consumers could borrow. Along with federally guaranteed mortgage loans, people could now get credit cards. In 1950, the Diners Club introduced the credit card for well-to-do New Yorkers. By the end of the decade, Sears Roebuck credit cards allowed more than 10 million Americans to spend borrowed money. In 1945, Americans owed only $5.7 billion for consumer goods other than houses. By 1960, they owed $56.1 billion.

In the 1950s, discount stores such as Korvettes made shopping seem simpler and more attractive, and so did another new creation, the shopping mall. In 1956, Southdale, the nation's first enclosed suburban shopping mall, opened outside Minneapolis, Minnesota. Consumers bought meals more easily, too. The first McDonald's fast-food restaurant opened in San Bernardino, California, in 1948. Taken over by businessman Ray Kroc, McDonald's began to grow into a national chain in the mid-1950s.

To get to McDonald's, the Southdale Mall, Korvettes, and Levittown, Americans needed cars. In the 1950s, automobiles reflected Americans' new sense of affluence and self-indulgence. Big, high-compression engines burning high-octane gasoline powered ever-bigger cars stuffed with new accessories—power steering, power brakes, power windows, and air-conditioning. Unlike the drab autos of the Great Depression, the new models featured "Passion Pink" and "Horizon Blue" interiors and two-tone and even three-tone exteriors studded with shiny chrome.

Automakers used that chrome to solve one of the main problems of a consumer society—getting people who already had plenty to want to buy even more. How could

Icons of the Consumer Society The first enclosed mall in the United States—Southdale, outside Minneapolis, Minnesota.

Detroit persuade Americans to trade in old cars that were running just fine and purchase new ones? The answer was what General Motors' chief designer called "dynamic obsolescence," the feeling that last year's model was somehow inadequate. So the automakers changed chrome, colors, and tail fins from year to year (see Table 27–1).

More than ever, automakers offered cars as a reflection of a driver's identity. The car of the 1950s clearly announced its owner's affluence. General Motors' line of cars rose up the socioeconomic ladder, from the ordinary Chevrolet, to the more prosperous Pontiac, Oldsmobile, and Buick, all the way up to the sumptuous success symbol, the Cadillac.

Automobiles also spoke to gender identities. Detroit designed the interior of cars to appeal to women. Inside, the autos of the 1950s seemed like living rooms. The exterior offered men power and sexuality. Automakers tried to make them feel like they were flying supersonic jets. While the back of a 1950s car looked like the winking afterburners of a jet, the front spoke to something else. The chrome protrusions on 1950s Cadillacs were known as "Dagmars," after the name of a large-breasted female television star. A car, as a Buick ad promised, "makes you feel like the man you are."

It was not remarkable that the chrome on a Cadillac would make Americans think of a television star. In the 1950s, television became a central part of American life. Technological advances made TV sets less expensive. As sales boomed, there were new opportunities for broadcasters. By 1950, the Federal Communications Commission (FCC) had licensed 104 TV stations, mostly in cities. By 1960, 90 percent of the nation's households had a television (see Table 27–2). In 15 years, TV had become a part of everyday life.

Table 27–1 Automobiles and Highways, 1945–1960

Year	Factory Sales (in 1,000s)	Registrations (in 1,000s)	Miles of Highway Completed (in 1,000s)
1945	69.5	25,796.9	3,035
1946	2,148.6	28,217.0	5,057
1947	3,558.1	30,849.3	15,473
1948	3,909.2	33,355.2	21,725
1949	5,119.4	36,457.9	19,876
1950	6,665.8	40,339.0	19,876
1951	5,338.4	42,688.3	17,060
1952	4,320.7	43,823.0	22,147
1953	6,116.9	46,429.2	21,136
1954	5,558.8	48,468.4	20,548
1955	7,920.1	52,144.7	22,571
1956	5,816.1	54,210.9	23,609
1957	6,113.3	55,917.8	22,424
1958	4,257.8	56,890.5	28,137
1959*	5,591.2	59,453.9	32,633
1960	6,674.7	61,682.3	20,969

*Denotes first year for which figures include Alaska and Hawaii.

Source: *Historical Statistics of the United States, Millennial Online Edition* (Cambridge University Press, 2008), Table Df347–352 and Table Df213–217

From its early days, television reinforced the values of consumer society. Advertisements for consumer products paid for programming that focused mainly on pleasure and diversion. Nightly national news broadcasts lasted only 15 minutes. There were operas, documentaries, and live, original dramas in what some critics consider television's golden age, but most of the broadcast schedule was filled with variety shows, sports, westerns, and situation comedies. As television undermined the popularity of radio and movie theaters, the three major broadcasting companies quickly created TV networks and dominated the new industry.

Table 27–2 Television, 1941–1960

Year	Television Stations	Households with Television Sets (in 1,000s)
1941	2	—
1945	9	—
1950	104	3,875
1955	458	30,700
1960	579	45,750

Source: George Thomas Kurian, *Datapedia* (Lonham, MD: Bernan Press, 1994), pp. 299–300.

American culture also became more open about sexuality. Dr. Alfred C. Kinsey of Indiana University commanded enormous public attention with two pioneering academic studies—*Sexual Behavior in the Human Male* (1948) and *Sexual Behavior in the Human Female* (1953). To his readers' surprise, Kinsey reported that Americans were more sexually active outside of marriage than had been thought. The Supreme Court contributed to sexual openness by overturning a ban on a film version of D. H. Lawrence's often erotic novel, *Lady Chatterley's Lover,* in 1959. The new candor about sexuality was epitomized by *Playboy* magazine, first published by Hugh Hefner in December 1953. Featuring pictures of bare-breasted women, *Playboy* presented sex as one part of a hedonistic consumer lifestyle complete with flashy cars, expensive stereos, and fine liquor.

A Homogeneous Society?

The spread of consumerism reinforced a sense of sameness in America during the 1950s. It seemed as if the United States was becoming a homogeneous society whose members bought the same products, watched the same TV shows, worked for the same corporations, and dreamed the same dreams. Some observers worried that Americans had become conformists willing to sacrifice their individuality in order to be like one another. Declining class differences strengthened the feeling that people were becoming more alike, as did a rush to attend church and have children. Along with the renewed emphasis on religion and family, Americans faced pressure to conform to gender roles.

Nevertheless, the United States remained a heterogeneous society. While class and ethnic differences among whites decreased, race remained a powerful divider. Despite fears of conformity, the nation still encouraged difference and individuality.

The Discovery of Conformity

In the years after World War II, sociologists and other writers noticed a disturbing uniformity across American society. A variety of factors promoted homogeneity. During the frenzied search for domestic Communists, people did not want to risk accusations by appearing different or unusual. Moreover, as corporations merged and small businesses disappeared, Americans worked for the same giant companies. Levittown and the other new suburbs intensified the sense of homogeneity. In 1957, one writer described suburbanites as "people whose age, income, number of children, problems, habits, conversations, dress, possessions, perhaps even blood types are almost precisely like yours."

> **Little boxes on the hillside**
> **Little boxes made of ticky tacky**
> **Little boxes on the hillside, little boxes all the same**
> **There's a green one and a pink one and a blue one and a yellow one**
> **And they're all made out of ticky tacky and they all look just the same.**
>
> MALVINA REYNOLDS'S SONG ABOUT SUBURBIA, "LITTLE BOXES" (1962)

Americans, some observers believed, actually wanted to be like one another. In *The Lonely Crowd* (1950), sociologist David Riesman argued that instead of following their own internalized set of values, Americans adjusted their behavior to meet the expectations of the people around them. In *The Organization Man* (1956), William H. Whyte Jr. suggested that the conformist white-collar workers of big corporations were making the United States more like the totalitarian Soviet Union.

The Decline of Class and Ethnicity

The apparent decline of social class differences reinforced the sense of homogeneity. By the 1950s, the old upper class—the families of the Gilded Age industrialists and financiers—no longer single-handedly controlled and managed America's big businesses. Thanks to the Great Depression and income and inheritance taxes, the largest American fortunes were smaller than at the beginning of the twentieth century. As sociologist C. Wright Mills argued in *The Power Elite* (1956), an interlocking group of military, political, and economic managers ran the nation's institutions. But this rather drab group didn't have the bold swagger or the dynastic ambitions of the Gilded Age robber barons.

Meanwhile, the ranks of American farmers continued to decrease. As agriculture became more efficient and corporatized, the number of farms fell from more than 6 million in 1944 to just 3.7 million in 1959. Although manual and service workers remained the nation's largest occupational group, they seemed to be a less distinctive social class. In this era of labor peace, well-paid blue-collar workers appeared content with American society. Labor leaders endorsed consumerism and anti-Communism. Some observers argued that American workers had become essentially middle class in their buying habits and social values. The middle class itself was burgeoning. By 1960, the white-collar sector made up 40 percent of the workforce.

Even ethnic differences no longer seemed significant. Whites from different national and religious backgrounds mixed together in the new suburbs. The rate of intermarriage between ethnic groups increased. Anxious to prove their loyalty during the cold war, newer Americans were reluctant to emphasize their origins. Ethnicity had apparently disappeared in the national melting pot of the consumer society.

Many Americans, especially powerful ones, had long wanted to believe that the United States was a unified society devoted to middle-class values. In the 1950s, there was probably more basis for this belief than ever before.

The Resurgence of Religion and Family

A renewed emphasis on religion and family contributed to the homogeneity of American society. The nation's political leaders, fighting the cold war, encouraged religiosity. Freedom of religion, they insisted, differentiated the United States from allegedly godless Communist nations. To underscore the national commitment to religion, the federal government put the words "In God We Trust" on all its currency. Meanwhile, denominations adapted religion to the consumer society. Charismatic preachers such as Roman Catholic bishop Fulton J. Sheen and Protestant evangelist Billy Graham used television to bring religion to Americans in a new way.

Partly as a result, Americans became more involved with organized religion. In 1945, 45 percent of the nation belonged to one religious denomination or another; by 1960, that figure had reached 61 percent. Weekly church attendance increased, too, reaching a peak of 49 percent in 1958. By 1960, there were 64 million Protestants, 42 million Roman Catholics, and fewer than 6 million Jews (see Table 27–3).

American culture also celebrated what *McCall's* magazine christened family "togetherness." Manufacturers promoted TV viewing as a way of holding families together. Detroit presented its big automobiles as "family" cars.

"Togetherness" meant the nuclear family, with a mother, a father, and plenty of children. After decades of decline, the birthrate rose unexpectedly in the 1940s. Beginning in 1954, Americans had more than 4 million babies a year. Thanks to new drugs, nearly all these infants survived. Antibiotics reduced the risk of diphtheria, typhoid fever, influenza, and other infections. The Salk and Sabin vaccines virtually wiped out polio. As a result, the average number of children per family went from 2.4 in 1945 up to 3.2 in 1957, and the population grew by a record 29 million people to reach 179 million.

Like the religious revival, the "baby boom" of the 1940s and 1950s is somewhat difficult to explain. For more than 100 years, Americans had reduced the size of their families in order to ease burdens on mothers and family budgets and to provide more attention, education, and material resources to children. The economic prosperity of the cold war era may have persuaded couples that they could afford to have more children. Prosperity alone did not explain why American culture became so much more

Table 27–3 Religious Revival and Baby Boom, 1945–1960

Year	Membership of Religious Bodies (in 1,000s)	Live Births (in 1,000s)
1945	71,700	2,858
1946	73,673	3,411
1947	77,386	3,817
1948	79,436	3,637
1949	81,862	3,649
1950	86,830	3,632
1951	88,673	3,823
1952	92,277	3,913
1953	94,843	3,965
1954	97,483	4,078
1955	100,163	4,104
1956	103,225	4,218
1957	104,190	4,308
1958[1]	109,558	4,255
1959[2]	112,227	4,245
1960	114,449	4,258

[1]Includes Alaska.
[2]Denotes first year for which figures include Alaska and Hawaii.
Source: George Thomas Kurian, *Datapedia* (Lanharn, MD: Bernan Press, 1994), pp. 37, 146.

child centered during these years. In his *Common Sense Book of Baby and Child Care* (1946), pediatrician Benjamin Spock urged parents to raise their children with less severity and more attention, warmth, tenderness, and fun. *Baby and Child Care* outsold every other book in the 1950s except, not surprisingly, the Bible.

Maintaining Gender Roles

As many social differences seemed to disappear, American culture nevertheless reemphasized the distinctions between the sexes. During the baby boom, women were expected to be helpful wives and devoted mothers. Men were encouraged to define themselves primarily as family providers.

The 1950s underscored the differences between genders in a variety of ways. Blue became the color for boys and pink the color for girls. Standards of beauty highlighted the physiological differences between women and men. The image of the slim girlish flapper of the 1920s had long since faded away; now more voluptuous actresses such as Dagmar, Jayne Mansfield, and Marilyn Monroe defined femininity.

Nevertheless, gender roles grew more similar during the 1950s. Society stressed a man's domestic role more than before. Experts urged husbands to do some of the housework and to spend more time nurturing their children, although few men lived up to the new ideal.

Female roles evolved more dramatically. To help pay for the consumer lifestyle, many wives had to leave the domestic sphere and find a job. In 1940, 15.6 percent of married women were in the paid workforce. By 1960, that percentage had nearly doubled to 31.0, and women made up more than one-third of the labor force. Gene Ferkauf's wife, while taking care of their child, helped publicize the first Korvettes store. Most women held clerical and sales positions. Thanks to the spread of labor-saving devices, fewer women took the traditional female job of domestic servant.

To a degree, American culture supported the expanding role of women outside the home. In the cold war competition with the Soviets, Americans celebrated the supposedly greater freedom and opportunity for women in the United States. Television featured situation comedies with feisty women, such as Lucy Ricardo in *I Love Lucy* and Alice Kramden in *The Honeymooners,* who got out of line and stood up to their husbands.

Nevertheless, women had little help coping with jobs and bigger families. Congress voted an income tax deduction for child-care costs in 1954, but little first-class child care was available. At work, women were expected to watch men get ahead of them. Women's income was only 60 percent of men's in 1960.

American culture strongly condemned women and men who strayed outside conventional gender norms. *Modern Woman: The Lost Sex,* a 1947 best seller by Marynia Farnham and Ferdinand Lundberg, censured feminism as the "deep illness" of "neurotically disturbed women" with "penis envy." Psychologists and other experts demonized lesbians and gay men. As police cracked down on gay bars, unmarried men risked accusations of homosexuality. The dominant culture expected males to be heterosexual husbands and fathers. Those roles, in turn, made men more likely to conform to social expectations. "Once a man has a wife and two young children," the writer Gore Vidal observed, "he will do what you tell him to."

Persisting Racial Differences

In spite of the many pressures toward conformity, American society remained heterogeneous. Although suburbanization broke down ethnic differences among whites, it intensified the racial divide between those whites and African Americans. The nation's suburbs were 95 percent white in 1950. As whites moved into Levittown and other suburbs, African Americans took their place in cities. By 1960, more than half of the black population lived in cities, where they were typically kept out of white neighborhoods.

Native Americans, living on their reservations, were also set apart. In 1953, Congress did try to "Americanize" the Indians by approving the termination of Indians' special legal status as sovereign groups. Termination meant the end of the traditional rights and reservations of more than 11,000 Native Americans. The new policy was intended to turn them into members of the consumer society.

It did not turn out that way. As reservations became counties in the 1950s and early 1960s, Indians had to sell valuable mineral rights and lands to pay taxes. Despite short-term profits, tribes faced poverty, unemployment, and social problems. Encouraged by the federal government's new Voluntary Relocation Program, about one in five Native Americans moved to the city. Some tribes, including the Catawba, the Coquille, the Klamath, and the Menominee, began long legal fights to reclaim tribal status. But whether they lived on reservations or on crowded city blocks, the nation's quarter of a million Indians remained largely separate and ignored.

The increasing migration of Puerto Ricans also reinforced the multiracial character of American society. Beginning in the 1940s, a large number of Puerto Ricans, who were U.S. citizens, left their island hoping for more economic opportunity on the mainland. By 1960, the Puerto Rican population in the mainland United States had reached 887,000, two-thirds of it concentrated in the East Harlem section of New York City. These new migrants found opportunities in the United States, but they also found separation and discrimination.

Mexican immigration further contributed to racial diversity. After 1945, increasing numbers of Mexicans left their impoverished homeland for the United States, particularly the booming Southwest. Congress, bowing to the needs of southwestern employers, continued the Bracero Program, the supposedly temporary wartime agreement that had brought hundreds of thousands of laborers, or *braceros,* to the United States. Meanwhile, illegal Mexican migration increased dramatically.

Like other Mexican migrants before them, the newly arrived met a mixed reception. As in the years before World War II, Mexicans already living in the United States worried that the new migrants would compete for jobs, drive down wages, and feed American prejudice. Many white Americans did indeed deride them as *mojados,* or "wetbacks," because so many had supposedly swum the Rio Grande River to get into the United States illegally. Mexican Americans feared that the federal government would use the provisions of the Internal Security Act of 1950 and the Immigration and Nationality Act of 1952 to deport Mexicans and thereby break up families. The government's intention became clear in 1954 with the launching of Operation Wetback, which sent more than 1 million immigrants back to Mexico in that year alone.

About 3.5 million Mexican Americans were living in the United States by 1960. The great majority worked for low wages in the cities and on the farms of the Southwest. Many continued to live in *barrios* apart from whites. Because of Operation Wetback and other instances of prejudice, some Mexican Americans became more vocal about

The Plight of Mexican "Wetbacks" Illegal immigrants taken off freight trains in Los Angeles, after two days without food or water, in 1953. They were probably sent back to Mexico.

their circumstances and their rights. The League of United Latin American Citizens denounced the impact of the Immigration and Nationality Act. More outspoken was the American GI Forum, an organization of Mexican American veterans formed when a funeral parlor would not bury a deceased comrade in Three Rivers, Texas, in 1949. Such assertiveness made it all the harder for white Americans to ignore the presence of Mexican Americans in the consumer society.

The experiences of Hispanics, Mexican Americans, Native Americans, and African Americans underscored the continuing importance of race in the United States. Mostly living apart, whites and nonwhites faced different conditions and different futures. Prosperity and consumerism did not change that reality. As long as race was such a potent factor in national life, the United States would never be a homogeneous society. In the 1960s, white Americans would have to face that fact.

The Survival of Diversity

Along with race, a variety of forces ensured the survival of diversity. Despite the appearance of suburbs and discount stores all over the country, the states continued to differ from each other. As in the past, internal migration and the expansion of national boundaries promoted diversity. During the 1950s, more than 1.6 million people, many of them retired, moved to Florida. As a result, the state increasingly played a distinctive national role as a center for retirement and entertainment.

Meanwhile, other Americans moved westward. During the 1950s, California gained more than 3 million new residents. California earned a reputation as the pioneer state of the consumer society, the home of the first Disneyland amusement park and the first McDonald's.

The admission of two new states highlighted the continuing diversity of the United States. In 1959, Alaska and Hawaii became, respectively, the 49th and 50th states in the Union. Racially and culturally diverse, climatically and topographically distinctive, they helped make certain that America was not simply a land of corporations and Levittowns.

Popular music also exemplified the continuing diversity of the United States. Big swing bands gave way to such popular singers as Frank Sinatra and Patti Page. Jazz split into different camps—traditional, mainstream, and modern. Country music, rooted in white rural culture, included cowboy songs, western swing, honky-tonk, bluegrass, and the smooth "Nashville sound." A range of African American musical forms, including blues, jazz, and vocal groups, became known as "rhythm and

blues" (R & B). Gospel music thrilled white and African American audiences. Mexican Americans made Tejano music in Texas, and Cajuns played Cajun music in Louisiana, and German and Polish Americans danced to polka bands in Illinois and Wisconsin.

R & B collided with country music to create rock and roll. By 1952, white disc jockey Alan Freed was playing R & B on his radio show, "Moondog's Rock 'n' Roll Party," out of Cleveland. In 1954, a white country group, Bill Haley and the Comets, recorded the first rock-and-roll hit, "Rock Around the Clock." Rock and roll produced both African American and white heroes in its first years—Chuck Berry, Fats Domino, Jerry Lee Lewis, and Buddy Holly, among others.

The biggest rock-and-roll sensation of all was a young white singer and guitar player, Elvis Presley. Born in Mississippi and raised in near poverty in Memphis, Tennessee, Presley drew on a variety of musical genres to create a distinctive personal style in an age of supposed conformity. "Who do you sound like?" he was asked. "I don't sound like nobody," he said.

Because of Presley and other musicians, the sound of American popular music was anything but homogeneous. Because of the distinctiveness of Florida, California, Alaska, Hawaii, and other states, the United States was hardly monolithic. In these ways, at least, American society remained diverse after World War II.

The Eisenhower Era at Home and Abroad

Prosperity encouraged Americans to demand less from government in the 1950s. In a period of rapid social change and continuing international tensions, most people wanted reassurance rather than boldness from Washington. The politics of the decade were dominated by President Dwight D. Eisenhower, a moderate leader well suited to the times. His middle-of-the-road domestic program, "Modern Republicanism," appealed to a prosperous electorate wary of government innovation. But Eisenhower's anti-Communist foreign policy did little to diminish popular anxieties about the cold war in the short run and laid the groundwork for trouble in the Middle East and Southeast Asia in the long run.

"Ike" and 1950s America

Eisenhower, a charismatic military hero with a bright, infectious grin, would have been an ideal public figure in almost any era of American history, but the man known affectionately as "Ike" was especially suited to the 1950s. The last president born in the nineteenth century, he had successfully accommodated the major changes of the twentieth. Raised on the individualistic values of the rural Midwest, Eisenhower adopted the bureaucratic style of modern organizations. He succeeded in the military after World War I, not because he was a great fighter or strategist, but because he was a great manager. A believer in teamwork, Eisenhower was the quintessential "organization man." As a commander in

> **Would it not be better to compete in the relative merits of washing machines than in the strength of rockets? Is this the kind of competition you want?**
>
> VICE PRESIDENT RICHARD NIXON TO SOVIET PREMIER NIKITA KHRUSHCHEV,
> "Kitchen Debate," Moscow, July 24, 1959

Mamie and Dwight Eisenhower The first lady and the president were reassuring figures in the turbulent transition to the Cold War and consumerism in the 1950s.

World War II, Eisenhower worked to keep sometimes fractious allies together. After the war, he deepened his organizational experience as president of Columbia University and then as the first commander of the armed forces of NATO.

Just as he accommodated the rise of big organizations, Eisenhower accommodated the extension of the nation's commitment abroad. Ike had grown up among people who often feared American involvement in the world's problems. But his military career rested on his acceptance of an activist role for the United States around the world.

Eisenhower easily fit the dominant culture of the 1950s. He was an involved, loving husband and father. In a society zealously pursuing pleasures, he was famous for his many hours on the golf course. His wife, Mamie, eagerly wore the "New Look" fashions inspired by designer Christian Dior and avidly watched television soap operas.

Nominated for president by the Republicans in 1952, Eisenhower ran against Adlai Stevenson, the liberal Democratic governor of Illinois. Stevenson, witty and eloquent, was no match for Eisenhower. Running a moderate, conciliatory campaign, the former general avoided attacks on the New Deal and promised to work for an end to the Korean War. Meanwhile, his tough-talking running mate, Senator Richard Nixon of California, accused Stevenson of being soft on Communism. The Republican ticket won big with 55 percent of the popular vote and 442 electoral votes. The Republican Party took control of the White House and both houses of Congress for the first time in 20 years.

Modern Republicanism

Eisenhower advocated Modern Republicanism for the American political economy. This philosophy attempted to steer a middle course between traditional Republican conservatism and Democratic liberalism. With a conservative's faith in individual freedom, the president favored limited government and balanced budgets, but Eisenhower the organization man believed that Washington had an important role to play in protecting individuals. Eisenhower also recognized that most Americans did not want to give up such liberal programs as Social Security and farm subsidies.

Accordingly, the Eisenhower administration limited the reach of the government by decreasing regulation of business and cutting taxes for the wealthy. With the Submerged Lands Act of 1953, the federal government turned over offshore oil resources to the states for private exploitation. With the Atomic Energy Act of 1954, Washington allowed private firms to sell power produced by nuclear reactors.

Nevertheless, the Eisenhower administration did little to undermine the legacy of the New Deal and the Fair Deal. Eisenhower went along with increases in Social Security benefits and farm subsidies. Despite his belief in balanced budgets, his administration produced several budget deficits. Federal spending, including the highway program, helped fuel the consumer economy.

Modern Republicanism frustrated liberals as well as conservative "Old Guard" Republicans, but many Americans appreciated the president's moderation. "The public loves Ike," a journalist observed. "The less he does the more they love him."

Eisenhower's popularity was confirmed at the polls in 1956. In a repeat of 1952, Eisenhower and Nixon defeated Adlai Stevenson again. This time Eisenhower won an even bigger victory, with 58 percent of the popular vote and 457 electoral votes.

An Aggressive Cold War Strategy

Like President Harry Truman before him, Eisenhower was committed to opposing Communism at home and around the world. The president helped the crusade against alleged Communist subversives and tolerated its excesses. He refused to criticize the tactics of Senator Joseph R. McCarthy in public and declined to stop the execution of the convicted atomic spies, Julius and Ethel Rosenberg, in 1953. Eisenhower denied the security clearance that J. Robert Oppenheimer, the former director of the Manhattan Project, needed to continue work on the government's nuclear projects. Thousands of other alleged security risks also lost their federal jobs during the Eisenhower era.

While Truman had pledged only to contain further Communist expansion, Eisenhower and his advisers talked aggressively of rolling back Soviet power in Europe and freeing already "captive peoples" from Communism. Secretary of State John Foster Dulles threatened "instant, massive retaliation" with nuclear weapons in response to nuclear and even nonnuclear Soviet aggression. To support this threat, the U.S. military adopted the "New Look" strategy, named after Mamie Eisenhower's favorite fashions, that de-emphasized costly conventional armies and increased the nuclear arsenal with long-range bombers, missiles, and the first nuclear-powered submarines. Not surprisingly, the New Look stirred fears of nuclear war.

The president also used the CIA to counter Communism by stealthier means. At the president's direction, the CIA carried out secret activities once considered unacceptable: as a presidential commission observed, the cold war was "a game" with "no rules." At home, the agency explored the possible uses of lysergic acid diethylamide—the dangerous hallucinogenic drug known as LSD—by using it on hundreds of unwitting Americans. Some of them went mad and at least one killed himself. Abroad, the agency gave secret aid to pro-American regimes and ran secret programs against uncooperative governments.

In August 1953 a covert CIA operation, code-named Ajax, orchestrated a coup that removed Mohammad Mossadeq, the nationalist prime minister of oil-rich Iran. Eisenhower and Dulles feared that this "madman," who had nationalized Iran's oil fields, would shut out U.S. business and open the way for Communism and the Soviet Union. The young Iranian monarch, Shah Mohammad Reza Pahlavi, who had effectively ceded power to Mossadeq, now reclaimed it. The shah gratefully accepted $45 million in U.S. aid, turned his back on the Soviets, and made low-priced oil available to American companies.

The next year, PBSUCCESS, a secret CIA operation modeled on Ajax, overthrew another foreign leader. Eisenhower and Dulles worried that a "Communist infection" in the Central American nation of Guatemala could spread to the United States–controlled Panama Canal and farther north to Mexico. In fact, the Soviet Union had made no effort to help Guatemala's new president, Jacobo Arbenz Guzmán, who supported the redistribution of land and threatened the interests of a powerful

The "New Look" of Defense in the Eisenhower Era A ceremony honors the production of the 1,000th B–47 Stratojet, the long-range bomber capable of delivering nuclear weapons in an attack on the Soviet Union.

American corporation, United Fruit. In June, PBSUCCESS used misleading "disinformation," a small force of Guatemalan exiles, and CIA-piloted bombing raids to persuade Arbenz Guzmán to resign.

More openly, Eisenhower intensified efforts to shape perceptions of American culture and values abroad. In 1953, the administration gathered various information and propaganda efforts together in a new United States Information Agency (USIA), overseen by the State Department. Active in 76 countries by 1960, the agency published pamphlets, promoted the exchange of visitors with other nations, beamed the radio broadcasts of Voice of America around the world, and collaborated with the CIA on propaganda and psychological warfare. The growth of the USIA underscored that the cold war was a global struggle about culture and ideas as well as military power.

Avoiding War with the Communist Powers

Despite its tough talk, the Eisenhower administration tried to avoid direct confrontation with the two major Communist powers, the People's Republic of China and the Soviet Union. Eisenhower knew he had to end the Korean conflict. As he promised in his 1952 campaign, Eisenhower traveled to Korea to observe conditions firsthand and then pushed to end the military stalemate that ultimately killed 33,629 Americans. A cease-fire agreement in July 1953 left the United States without a victory. Although North and South Korea remained divided, the agreement ended a costly, difficult war. It was, Eisenhower declared, "an acceptable solution."

Ending an old war with one Communist power, the Eisenhower administration avoided a new conflict with the other. In October 1956, Hungarians, spurred on by American propaganda broadcasts, rose up against their pro-Soviet government. The Soviet Union sent troops to break the rebellion. Despite talk of "captive peoples" and "massive retaliation," the Eisenhower administration did not intervene to help the Hungarian rebels.

Fundamentally, Eisenhower would not break with Truman's policy of containment. Cautious about military confrontation with the Soviets and the Chinese, Eisenhower declined to unleash nuclear weapons that would "destroy civilization." Although he dispatched CIA agents to conduct covert operations, the president was more reluctant than Truman to send American soldiers into open battle.

At the same time, Eisenhower, like Truman, knew the cold war was an economic and political fight. The Eisenhower administration maintained foreign aid programs and fought a propaganda war with the Soviets. In front of a model American kitchen in Moscow in 1959, Vice President Richard Nixon and Soviet leader Nikita Khrushchev argued the merits of their two systems. Not surprisingly, Nixon turned this "Kitchen Debate" into a celebration of the prosperity and freedom of the consumer society.

AMERICA AND THE WORLD

>> Popular Music as a Cold War Weapon

By the 1950s, music, like other forms of popular entertainment, had long served as a vehicle for spreading American culture around the world. It was only natural, then, for the United States government to make popular music a weapon in the cold war struggle against Communism.

The State Department particularly used jazz, a uniquely American improvised music, to sell a democratic image of the United States. In 1955, Washington's worldwide radio service, the Voice of America, began broadcasting *Music U.S.A.*, hosted by Willis Conover. "Jazz is a cross between total discipline and anarchy," Conover explained. "The musicians agree on tempo, key and chord structure but beyond this everyone is free. . . . It's a musical reflection of America." Conover also believed that jazz, largely created by African Americans such as the trumpeter and singer Louis Armstrong and the composer and bandleader Duke Ellington, sent the true message of racial equality in the United States. "Jazz corrects the fiction that America is racist," Conover insisted.

Music U.S.A. became a remarkable hit. The show soon reached an audience of about 30 million people in 80 countries. "Conover's daily two-hour musical program has won the United States more friends than any other activity," declared an Egyptian weekly in 1959. Conover himself saw the show's popularity as a sign of the spread of American values. "[P]eople in other countries love jazz because they love freedom," he observed. "Jazz also helps them to believe that America is the kind of country that they want to believe it is."

Washington sent well-known jazz musicians on overseas concert tours sponsored by the president's Special International Program for Cultural Relations and overseen by the State Department. The most popular touring jazzman was Louis "Satchel Mouth" Armstrong, who became known as "Ambassador Satch." Beginning in 1956, the African American trumpeter and singer won over white audiences in Europe and black audiences in Africa. "I feel at home in Africa . . .," Armstrong proclaimed. "I'm African-descended down to the bone, and I dig the friendly ways these people go about things." "Through his superb jazz musicianship," a Kenyan newspaper wrote, "Satchmo has given expression to the often inarticulate feelings of his people, once oppressed, but now, although there are blots on the record, moving rapidly towards full and equal citizenship of the great country he represents."

Armstrong's message and music disturbed the Soviet Union. Concerned about the impact of jazz around the world, the Soviet leadership also worried that the music made its own young people rebellious back home. Soviet composers, visiting the United States in 1959, denounced Armstrong's music as "vulgar," "unnatural," and "a long way from good taste." When cheering throngs welcomed "this son of our African race" to the Congo in 1960, the Soviets charged that Ambassador Satch was only there to "distract" the African nation from the reality of white

continued

"Ambassador Satch" Jazz trumpeter Louis "Satchel Mouth" Armstrong represents the United States in Cairo, Egypt, 1961.

>> **AMERICA AND THE WORLD** *continued*

European power. The State Department happily declared Armstrong "the most effective unofficial goodwill ambassador this country had."

Armstrong usually played his propaganda role to perfection. He dodged difficult questions about the identity and the loyalty of black Americans. "Do you feel like an American in Africa or an African in America?" he was asked. "I just feel in place, man." But during the Little Rock crisis in 1957, this African American rebelled against his role. The trumpeter was outraged by white treatment of black students and by President Eisenhower's reluctance to intervene. "The way they are treating my people in the South, the government can go to hell," Armstrong fumed. "It's getting so bad, a colored man hasn't got any country." Armstrong refused to represent the United States on a scheduled trip to Moscow. "The people over there ask me what's wrong with my country," he demanded, "what am I supposed to say?"

As the State Department discovered, jazz, in the person of Louis Armstrong, really was the sound of democratic freedom, and therefore impossible to control completely. "[M]usic," Armstrong concluded, "is stronger than nations."

The Eisenhower administration took some modest steps to improve relations with the Soviets. Responding cautiously to the Soviets' interest in "peaceful coexistence," Eisenhower told the United Nations that he wanted to pursue disarmament and the peaceful use of atomic power. The president proposed an "Atoms for Peace" plan in which an international agency would experiment with nonmilitary uses for nuclear materials. The Soviets, however, dragged their feet.

The president made another attempt at improving relations with the Soviets. In July 1955, Eisenhower joined Khrushchev in Geneva, Switzerland, for the first meeting between an American president and a Soviet leader since World War II. Eisenhower's proposal for "Open Skies"—a plan to allow each side to fly over the other's territory—sparked some optimism about American-Soviet relations. That optimism ended by May 1960, when the Soviets shot down an American U-2 spy plane flying high over the USSR. After the Eisenhower administration denied the entire affair, Khrushchev triumphantly produced the captured pilot, Francis Gary Powers, along with pieces of the plane. The U.S.-Soviet rivalry would continue.

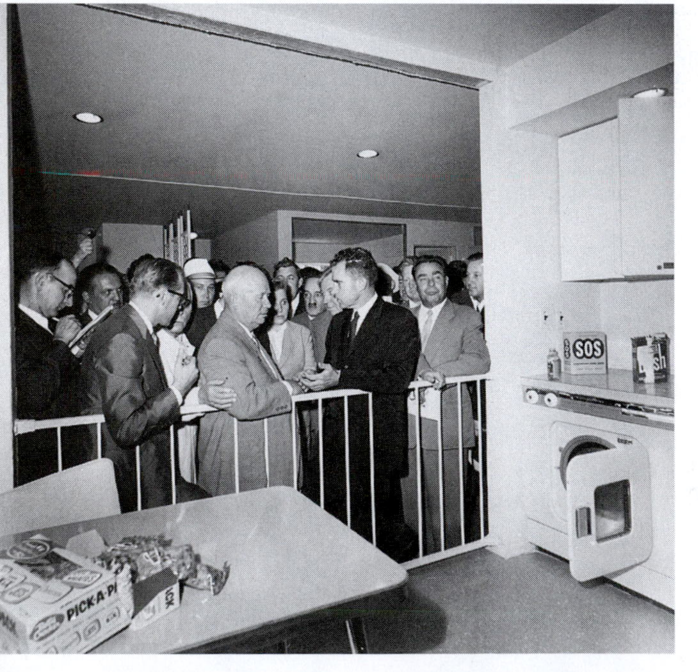

"Kitchen Debate" Vice President Richard Nixon upholds the virtues of the consumer society in an argument with Soviet leader Nikita Khrushchev at an exhibition in Moscow in 1959.

Crises in the Third World

Although Eisenhower worried most about the fate of Western Europe, his administration increasingly focused on the threat of Communist expansion in Africa, Asia, Latin America, and the Middle East. These relatively rural, unindustrialized regions, which made up the so-called third world, were enmeshed in the confrontation between the "first world" of industrialized, non-Communist nations and the "second world" of industrialized, Communist countries. Plagued by poverty, violence, and civil war, many third world societies struggled to break free from imperial domination.

Under Khrushchev, the Soviet Union tried to exploit third world discontent and conflict. Anxious to preserve America's influence and access to natural resources, the Eisenhower administration stood ready to counter Soviet moves with the techniques of containment—aid, trade, and alliances. Eisenhower offered increased foreign aid to third world countries and tried to stimulate trade with them. He also pursued closer military ties, including individual defense pacts with the Philippines, South Korea, and Taiwan.

Eisenhower's approach to the third world was sorely tested in Southeast Asia. When he took office in 1953, the United States continued to support France's war to hold on to Vietnam and its other Southeast Asian colonies. Despite vast American aid, the French could not defeat the nationalist forces of the Viet Minh, led by the Communist Ho Chi Minh and helped by the mainland Chinese. By 1954, the Viet Minh had surrounded French troops at Dien Bien Phu in northern Vietnam. Unwilling to fight another land war in Asia, Eisenhower refused to send American troops and rejected the use of atomic bombs. Without further help from the United States, France surrendered Dien Bien Phu in May.

In 1954, peace talks at Geneva produced an agreement to cut Vietnam, like Korea, in half. Ho Chi Minh's forces would stay north of the 17th parallel; his pro-French Vietnamese enemies would stay to the south of that line. The peace agreement stipulated that a popular election would unite the two halves of Vietnam in 1956. Certain that Ho Chi Minh and the Communists would win the election, the United States refused to sign the agreement. The president feared that a Communist takeover of Vietnam would deprive the West of raw materials and encourage the triumph of Communism elsewhere. Comparing the nations of Asia and the Pacific to "a row of dominoes," Eisenhower explained that the fall of the first domino—Vietnam—would lead to the fall of the rest, including Japan and Australia.

Instead, the Eisenhower administration worked to create an anti-Communist nation south of the 17th parallel. To protect South Vietnam, the United States joined with seven nations to create the Southeast Asia Treaty Organization (SEATO) in 1954 (see Map 27–1). To ensure South Vietnam's loyalty, the Eisenhower administration backed Ngo Dinh Diem, an anti-Communist who established a corrupt, repressive government. The United States sent military advisers and hundreds of millions of dollars to Diem.

By thwarting the Geneva Accords and establishing an unpopular regime in the South, Eisenhower ensured that Vietnam would be torn by civil war in the years to come. In the short run, however, Eisenhower had avoided war and seemingly stopped the Asian dominoes from falling.

Eisenhower soon confronted another crisis in the Middle East. Gamal Abdel Nasser, who had seized power in Egypt in 1954, emerged as a forceful spokesman for Arab nationalism and Middle Eastern unity. Fearing that Nasser would open the way for Soviet power in the Middle East, John Foster Dulles withdrew an offer to aid the Egyptians. Nasser struck back by taking over the British- and French-owned Suez Canal in 1956. In retaliation, Britain and France, with Israel's cooperation, moved against Nasser. As Israeli troops fought their way into Egypt in October, Britain and France stood ready to take back the Suez Canal. Eisenhower, fearing the invasion would give the Soviets an excuse to move into the Middle East, threatened the British, French, and Israelis—U.S. allies—with economic sanctions. They soon withdrew.

Map 27–1 America's Cold War Alliances in Asia Members of SEATO (the Southeast Asia Treaty Organization) and signers of other treaties with the United States. Through these pacts, the Eisenhower administration hoped to hold back the threat posed by Communist mainland China.

The Suez crisis was a pivotal moment. Before a joint session of Congress in January 1957, Eisenhower promised that the U.S. would intervene to protect any Middle Eastern nation threatened by "power-hungry Communists." The president implemented this "Eisenhower Doctrine" by sending troops to Lebanon the next year. In 1959, the United States joined with Turkey and Iran to create a Middle Eastern defense alliance known as the Central Treaty Organization (CENTO) for its geographical position between NATO and SEATO.

Eisenhower had helped to stabilize the Middle East and Southeast Asia temporarily, but he had also drawn the United States more deeply into these crisis-ridden regions and increased the odds of future trouble. In the 1960s and 1970s, the United States would have to deal with Eisenhower's legacy in the third world.

Map 27–2 America's Cold War Alliances in the Middle East Located between the members of NATO and SEATO, the members of CENTO (the Central Treaty Organization) joined with the United States to deter the threat of international Communism sponsored by the Soviet Union to the north.

Challenges to the Consumer Society

While the Eisenhower administration managed crises abroad, American society confronted challenges at home. In different ways, a rebellious youth culture, the alienated beat movement, a nascent environmental movement, and the divisive civil rights struggle upset the stability of the Eisenhower era. They demonstrated that consumerism had not solved all the nation's problems or won over all of its citizens.

Rebellious Youth

"Never in our 180-year history," declared *Collier's* magazine in 1957, "has the United States been so aware of—or confused about—its teenagers." In the 1950s, the emergence of a distinct youth culture, built around rock and roll, customized cars, comic books, and premarital sexual exploration, troubled many adults. The youth culture was the culmination of a trend apparent since the 1920s and 1930s. As more and more teenagers attended high school, they were segregated in their own world. Within that world, they developed their own values and practices. In the 1950s, young people claimed rock and roll as their own music. They wore blue jeans; they read comic

> **America when will you be angelic?**
> **When will you take off your clothes?**
> **When will you look at yourself through the grave?**
>
> ALLEN GINSBERG, "America" (1956)

books and teen magazines. Expressing their individuality, boys modified standard Detroit cars into customized "hot rods." Teens were attracted to alienated and rebellious movie characters such as the troubled son played by James Dean in *Rebel Without a Cause* (1955) and the motorcycle-gang leader played by Marlon Brando in *The Wild One* (1953). Worried adults feared that youth were copying the movies and defying authority. A wave of juvenile delinquency appeared to be sweeping the country.

Many young people were rebellious, but not nearly as much as adults feared. Despite all the publicity, juvenile delinquency did not actually increase after World War II and neither did rates of sexual intercourse among teenagers. Girls, although restless and attracted to such figures as James Dean and Elvis Presley, never played a very visible role in the male-dominated youth culture of the 1950s. Most young people never questioned the political system. On the whole, youth culture exaggerated rather than rejected the values of adult, consumer society.

The early career of Elvis Presley illustrated the boundaries of youthful rebellion. Presley's appeal rested on an unsettling combination of rock-and-roll music and open sexuality. Presley's style—his sensual mouth, disheveled "duck's ass" haircut, and gyrating hips—powerfully amplified the music's sexuality.

Despite his appeal to teenagers, Presley remained relentlessly polite and soft spoken, devoted to his parents and deferential to interviewers. Buying a pink Cadillac and other luxury cars, he was caught up in the consumer culture. Like Gene Ferkauf and millions of other Americans, Presley joined the suburban migration when he bought his house, Graceland, on the outskirts of Memphis, Tennessee. Presley was a new version of the old American dream of upward mobility.

Still, many adults blamed Presley, rock and roll, and mass media for the spread of dishonesty, violence, lust, and degeneration among young Americans. One popular television program showed Presley only from the waist up. To get rid of blue jeans and other teenage fashions, high schools imposed dress codes on their students. There was a crusade against comic books, teen magazines, and movies that were supposedly "brainwashing" teenagers. In well-publicized hearings from 1954 to 1956, the Senate's Subcommittee to Investigate Juvenile Delinquency focused attention on the corrupting power of the mass media.

A Less-than-rebellious Youth Culture As his father Vernon looks on, rock and roll star Elvis Presley kisses his mother, Gladys, on the eve of his induction into the army in 1958..

However, the campaign against youth culture had little impact in a society devoted to free speech and consumerism. Television networks, movie studios, record labels, and comic book companies did not stop catering to teenagers with spending money. Many adults found youth culture appealing.

The Beat Movement

A second group of rebels was smaller in numbers but a bit older and much more critical of American society. The beat movement, which emerged in New York City in the 1940s, expressed a sense of both alienation and hope. The term "beat" itself referred to a feeling of physical and emotional exhaustion and also to a state of transcendence, the "beatific."

Worn down by contemporary culture, the beats searched hopefully for a way to get beyond it.

Uptown at Columbia University and downtown in Greenwich Village, Allen Ginsberg, Jack Kerouac, John Clellon Holmes, William Burroughs, and others wanted, as one of them put it, "to emote, to soak up the world." Beats explored their sexuality, sampled mind-altering drugs, and investigated the spirituality of Eastern religions. In a society captivated by bright colors, "beatniks" declared their alienation from consumerism by wearing black. Kerouac captured the spirit of their odyssey in his novel about a trip across America, *On the Road* (1957). During the decade, San Francisco emerged as a center of beat culture. There, Allen Ginsberg published his long poem, "Howl" (1956), which evoked the beats' sense of alienation: "I saw the best minds of my generation destroyed by madness, starving hysterical naked, . . ."

Few in number, the beats sometimes seemed absurd, but their dark vision of America attracted a great deal of attention. The beat movement was a clear sign of budding dissatisfaction with consumer society, conventional sexual mores, and politics as usual.

The Rebirth of Environmentalism

A rebirth of environmental consciousness was one more indication of worry about consumerism. By the late 1950s, Americans were more concerned about the environment than at any time since the Progressive Era at the beginning of the twentieth century. The environmental threat was obvious in the cities. A well-publicized pall of smog seemed to hang perpetually over Los Angeles, so dependent on cars instead of subways and trains. Americans could no longer ignore the fact that their large, flashy automobiles, the symbol of the consumer society, were polluting the air.

The environmental threat was obvious in the countryside, too. Even as they moved into new suburban developments built on old farms, some Americans lamented the disappearance of undeveloped land. They began to criticize society's cavalier attitude toward the natural world. In the mid-1950s, environmentalists, led by the Sierra Club and the Wilderness Society, successfully blocked the construction of the Echo Park Dam in the upper basin of the Colorado River because the project would have inundated a national park, the Dinosaur National Monument. A new environmental movement, determined to protect wilderness lands from development, emerged from the battle.

The Struggle for Civil Rights

The African American struggle for civil rights also challenged the Eisenhower era. By the 1950s, segregation was under increasingly effective attack in the courts and on the streets. Focusing on public schools, the NAACP assaulted the discriminatory legacy of the Supreme Court's *Plessy v. Ferguson* ruling of 1896 (see Chapter 20). In 1951 the organization's special counsel, Thurgood Marshall, combined five school lawsuits, including African American welder Oliver Brown's challenge to the constitutionality of a Kansas state law that allowed cities to segregate their schools. Because of the law, Brown's eight-year-old daughter, Linda, had to ride a bus 21 blocks to a "colored only" school even though there was a "white only" school just three blocks from home. When the Brown case reached the Supreme Court in December 1952, Marshall attacked the *Plessy* argument that justified "separate but equal" facilities for whites and African Americans. As a result of segregation, Marshall maintained, Linda Brown and other African Americans received both an inferior education and a feeling of inferiority. He concluded that segregation violated the citizenship rights guaranteed by the Fourteenth Amendment.

In May 1954, the Court, led by new Chief Justice Earl Warren, handed down its ruling in *Brown v. Board of Education, Topeka, Kansas*. Overturning the *Plessy* decision, the justices ruled unanimously that public school segregation was unconstitutional under the Fourteenth Amendment. "Separate but equal has no place," Warren announced. African Americans and white liberals were jubilant. The ruling was, an African American newspaper exulted, "a second emancipation proclamation." Marshall himself foresaw the dismantling of school segregation before the end of the decade.

It did not work out that way. When the Supreme Court ruled on the enforcement of its decision in 1955, the justices turned to local school boards, dominated by whites, to carry out the integration of the schools. Federal district courts were to oversee the process of desegregation, which should occur with "all deliberate speed." In other words, school segregation had to end, but not right away.

Taking heart from this ruling, many whites refused to give up Jim Crow. For some white southerners, as one put it, a "reasonable time" for the end of segregation would be "one or two hundred years." In 1956, 101 congressmen signed a "Southern Manifesto" calling on their home states to reject the *Brown* ruling. Amid calls for massive resistance to desegregation, White Citizens' Councils formed in southern states to prevent schools from integrating. Some states passed laws intended to stop school integration. There was violence, too. In October 1955, white Mississippians killed Emmett Till, a 14-year-old black boy from Chicago, who had supposedly whistled at a white woman. Till was shot in the head, bludgeoned, and wired to a factory fan.

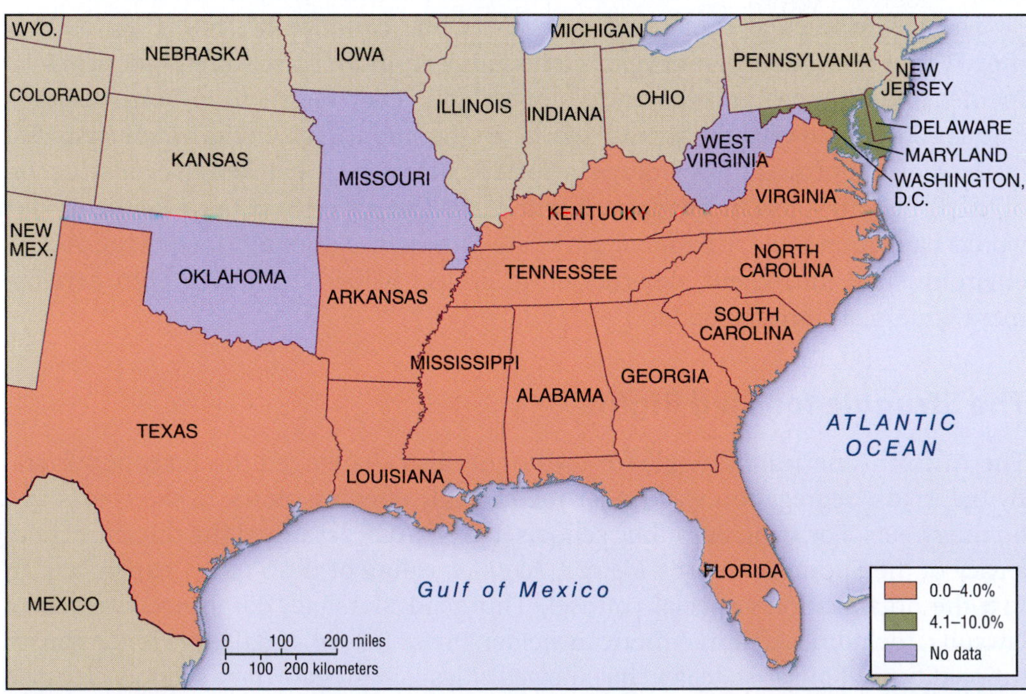

Map 27–3 African Americans Attending Schools with White Students in Southern and Border States, 1954
The small percentages indicate just how successfully segregation had separated the races before the Supreme Court ruled in *Brown v. Board of Education, Topeka, Kansas* in 1954.

African Americans, encouraged by the court's action, were ready to fight even harder against segregation. In Montgomery, Alabama, the NAACP wanted to test the state law dictating segregation on the city's buses. On December 1, 1955, Rosa Parks, a 42-year-old African American tailor's assistant and NAACP official "tired of giving in," boarded a bus to go home from work. Local custom required an African American to give up her seat to a white passenger and move to the back of the bus, but when the bus driver told her to move, Parks would not get up. As she said, "my feet hurt." More than that, she wanted to find out "once and for all what rights I had as a human being and a citizen." The angry driver thought she had none; he had Parks arrested.

Seizing on Parks's arrest, African American men and women began to boycott the city's bus system. Twenty-six-year-old Martin Luther King Jr., pastor of the Dexter Avenue Baptist Church, agreed to lead the boycott. The son of a noted Atlanta preacher, King was already developing a brilliant oratorical style and a philosophy of nonviolent protest against segregation.

The boycott met immediate resistance. The city outlawed carpools and indicted the leaders; African American homes and churches were bombed. In November 1956, however, the U.S. Supreme Court ruled Alabama's bus-segregation law unconstitutional. By then, the boycott had cost the bus company and downtown store owners dearly, and the white community had lost the will to resist. The city settled with the boycotters and agreed to integrate the buses. "We just rejoiced together," one of the boycotters remembered. "We had won self-respect."

Montgomery showed that a combination of local activism and federal intervention could overcome Jim Crow in southern communities. It established a charismatic new leader with a powerful message, and it soon brought forward a new civil rights organization, when King helped found the Southern Christian Leadership Conference. For one journalist, Montgomery "was the beginning of a flame that would go across America."

The flame did not travel easily. In 1957, the school board of Little Rock, Arkansas, accepted a federal court order to integrate the city's Central High School, but in September the state's segregationist governor, Orval Faubus, called out National Guard troops to stop black students from enrolling. Even after meeting with President Eisenhower, Faubus would not order the troops away from the school. When he finally did remove the soldiers, an angry mob of whites made it impossible for the African American students to stay. "Two, four, six, eight," cried the mob, "we ain't going to integrate."

Little Rock created a dilemma for the president. Not a believer in racial equality, Eisenhower wanted to avoid the divisive issue of civil rights. He privately opposed the *Brown* ruling and gave only mild support to the weak Civil Rights Act of 1957, which offered no real protection for African Americans' right to vote.

An Unlikely Criminal Arrested for refusing to give up her bus seat to a white passenger, Rosa Parks poses for her official "mug shot" in December 1955.

Little Rock, Arkansas, September 1957 African American student Elizabeth Eckford braves a hostile crowd of white students to integrate Central High School, September 6, 1957.

The president knew, however, that his government was being defied in Little Rock and humiliated around the world. The Soviets, he complained, were "gloating over this incident and using it everywhere to misrepresent our whole nation." So Eisenhower sent in troops of the crack 101st Airborne of the U.S. Army. With that protection, nine African American students went to Central High.

Like the Montgomery bus boycott, Little Rock demonstrated that a combination of federal action, however reluctant, and African American courage could triumph over "massive resistance." The Central High crisis showed, too, how the cold war helped tip the balance against segregation. Competing with the Soviets for support from the multiracial third world, no president could afford the embarrassment of racial inequality at home. Segregation and discrimination would continue to upset the stability of Eisenhower's America. It was, the president concluded, "troublesome beyond imagination."

An Uneasy Mood

Youth culture, the beat movement, the environmental movement, and the civil rights struggle contributed to an uneasy mood in America by the end of the 1950s. Even people who did not share the beats' values worried that the consumer society was flawed. Some intellectuals believed that "softheaded high living" had left the nation "cultureless." For the critic Lewis Mumford, modern automobiles were "fantastic and insolent chariots" and suburbs were "a low-grade uniform environment from which escape is impossible." Consumerism itself could seem like a trap. In his best seller *The Hidden Persuaders* (1957), Vance Packard played on the fears that advertisers were manipulating American consumers.

Americans were troubled, too, by signs of corruption in the consumer society. In 1958, they learned that record companies had paid Alan Freed and other disc jockeys to play particular records on the radio. The same year, Americans were shocked by revelations that contestants on popular TV quiz shows had secretly been given the answers to questions in advance.

While Americans worried about whether the consumer society was corrupt, they wondered whether it could meet the challenge of the cold war. In October 1957, the Soviet Union sent *Sputnik,* the world's first satellite, into orbit, setting off a wave of fear in the United States. If the Soviets could send up a satellite, they could be ahead in nuclear weapons and economic growth too. Americans felt suddenly more vulnerable.

Sputnik intensified concerns about the quality of American education. A diverse and growing student population, along with rising parental demands, had strained the nation's schools. Now Americans worried that the schools were not preparing children to compete with the Soviets in science and technology. In 1958, Congress, previously reluctant to provide aid to schools, passed the National Defense Education Act. To win what Senator Lyndon Johnson called the "battle of brainpower," this wide-ranging measure promoted instruction in science, math, and foreign languages, supported construction of new schools, and offered loans and fellowships to students.

Sputnik forced Washington to accelerate the space program. The first U.S. satellite launch collapsed in flames—*Flopnik,* the world's press called it. At the end of January 1958 the government successfully launched its first satellite, *Explorer I.* Later that year, Congress created the National Aeronautics and Space Administration (NASA) to coordinate space exploration. These initiatives did not wipe away fears about the fate of a society caught up in consumerism and the cold war, however. "What we are really worried about," one magazine emphasized, "is that the whole kit and caboodle of our American way of life—missiles and toasters, our freedoms, fun, and foolishness—is about to go down the drain."

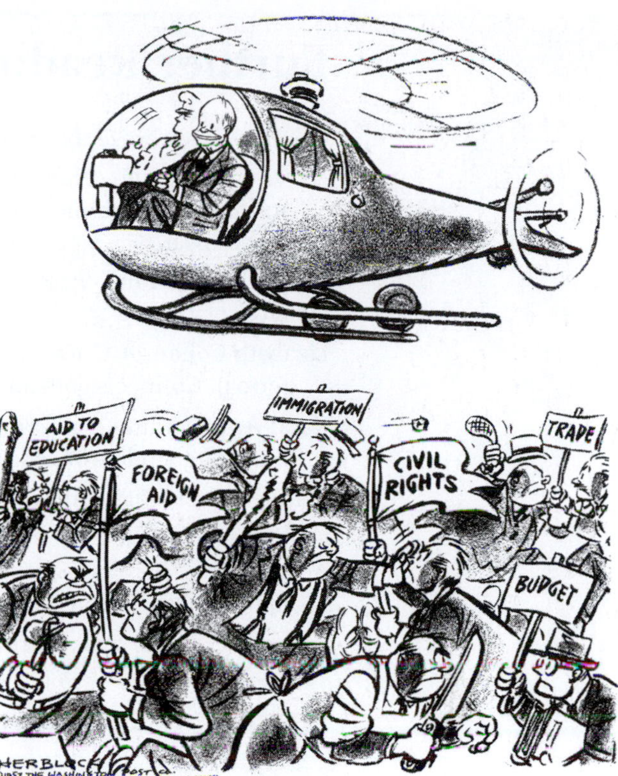

"The Helicopter Era" Cartoonist Herblock lampoons President Dwight Eisenhower's apparent lack of involvement in the nation's problems.

Eisenhower did little to change the national mood. Slowed by poor health, the president now seemed old and out of ideas. In 1960, he even had to create a Commission on National Goals to help figure out what the country should do. A few days before the end of his presidency in January 1961, Eisenhower fed the uncertain mood with a somber warning in his farewell address. Noting that cold war spending had built up the military and the defense industry, he cautioned against allowing this "military-industrial complex" to gain too much power. "We must never let the weight of this combination endanger our liberties or democratic processes," Eisenhower cautioned. It was a stunning admission that the cold war might destroy rather than save democracy in America.

Eisenhower's difficulties were a sign of new stresses on American society. The great majority of Americans were not about to give up the benefits of the prosperous consumer economy, but many people worried whether consumerism and Modern Republicanism were enough to meet the challenges of the cold war world.

Conclusion

Along with the cold war, the triumph of consumerism dramatically affected the United States in the 1950s. The booming consumer economy gave Gene Ferkauf and other Americans a new sense of security and affluence during the unsettling confrontation with Communism. Breaking with the past, they moved to the suburbs, had record numbers of children, bought televisions at E. J. Korvettes, and defined life as the pursuit of material pleasures. Consumerism helped promote homogeneity and conformity in American society and spurred the victory of Dwight Eisenhower and his moderate approach to government. For a moment, perhaps, it seemed as if America had achieved stability and harmony in a dangerous cold war world, but that feeling did not last. At the close of the 1950s, many Americans wanted more for themselves and their country. They questioned whether the consumer society could provide prosperity, democracy, and security for all its citizens. The next decade would give them an unsettling answer.

Further Readings

Stephen E. Ambrose, *Eisenhower: Soldier and President* (2007). Readable biography.

David L. Anderson, *Trapped by Success: The Eisenhower Administration and Vietnam, 1953–1961* (1993). Examines the American decision to support South Vietnam after the French withdrawal.

Michael T. Bertrand, *Race, Rock, and Elvis* (2000). The impact of Elvis Presley on southern race relations.

Lizabeth Cohen, *A Consumers' Republic: The Politics of Mass Consumption in Postwar America* (2003). Connects consumerism to broader political trends.

Karal Ann Marling, *As Seen on TV: The Visual Culture of Everyday Life in the 1950s* (1996). Engaging studies of consumer culture.

Joanne Meyerowitz, ed., *Not June Cleaver: Women and Gender in Postwar America, 1945–1960* (1994). An important set of revisionist essays on women after World War II.

Adam Rome, *The Bulldozer in the Countryside: Suburban Sprawl and the Rise of American Environmentalism* (2001). Revealing study of the emergence of environmental consciousness.

Kathryn C. Statler and Andrew L. Johns, eds., *The Eisenhower Administration, the Third World, and the Globalization of the Cold War* (2006). Useful range of essays on key aspects of foreign policy.

Who, What?

William J. Levitt 895
Alfred Kinsey 899
Dwight Eisenhower 905
Richard Nixon 906
John Foster Dulles 907
Martin Luther King Jr. 917
Rosa Parks 917
Dynamic obsolescence 898
Modern Republicanism 906
Massive retaliation 907
Domino theory 911

Review Questions

1. How did the consumer society of the 1950s differ from the modern culture of the 1920s?

>> Timeline >>

▼ 1947
Levittown suburban development
Announcement of Truman Doctrine

▼ 1948
First McDonald's fast-food restaurant
Alfred Kinsey, *Sexual Behavior in the Human Male*

▼ 1950
Diners Club credit card

▼ 1951
UNIVAC 1 computer

▼ 1952
Dwight D. Eisenhower elected president

▼ 1953
First suburban E. J. Korvettes store
Korean cease-fire

▼ 1954
"Baby boom" birthrate over 4 million per year
Supreme Court school desegregation decision, *Brown v. Board of Education, Topeka, Kansas*
Army-McCarthy hearings
Creation of divided Vietnam in Geneva peace talks

▼ 1955
Formation of AFL-CIO

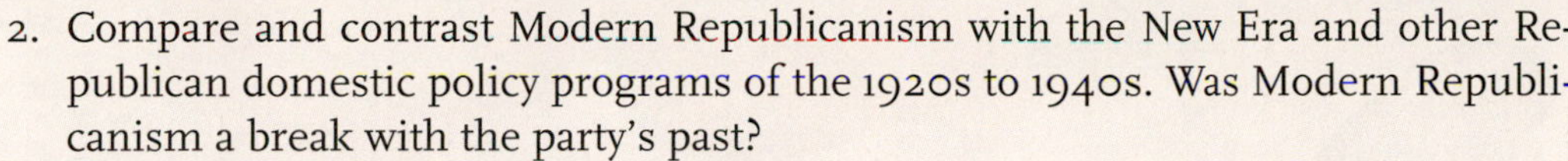

2. Compare and contrast Modern Republicanism with the New Era and other Republican domestic policy programs of the 1920s to 1940s. Was Modern Republicanism a break with the party's past?
3. Why did the civil rights movement make progress in the 1950s?
4. What was Eisenhower and Dulles's strategy for fighting the cold war? Was it successful?
5. Why did social-class differences decrease after World War II? Did class still matter?
6. On balance, did the domestic and international events of the 1950s leave Americans more or less well-off than before? Did the decade make American democracy stronger?

Websites

The Digital Documents and Photographs Project of the Dwight D. Eisenhower Presidential Library & Museum (http://www.eisenhower.archives.gov/index.html) has digitized many documents and photographs dealing with key issues of Eisenhower's administration.

The Digital Library of Georgia (http://dlg.galileo.usg.edu/?Welcome), with plenty of civil rights materials, cartoons, photographs, and other items from the 1950s, is a particularly good example of the digital resources of state libraries and historical societies.

The Literature & Culture of the American 1950s, University of Pennsylvania (http://www.writing.upenn.edu/~afilreis/50s/home.html), has a broad, idiosyncratic collection of texts.

The Prelinger Archives (http://www.archive.org/details/prelinger) is a treasure trove of newsreels, commercials, and other films from the 1950s and other decades.

Television News of the Civil Rights Era, 1950–1970, University of Virginia (http://www.vcdh.virginia.edu/civilrightstv/), offers streaming video footage of speeches, interviews, Klan rallies, desegregation, and other events, mainly in Virginia.

For further review materials and resource information, please visit www.oup.com/us/ofthepeople

▼ 1955–56
Montgomery, Alabama, bus boycott

▼ 1956
National System of Defense Highways Act
William H. Whyte Jr., *The Organization Man*
Suez crisis
Reelection of President Eisenhower

▼ 1957
Eisenhower Doctrine
School desegregation crisis, Little Rock, Arkansas
Jack Kerouac, *On the Road*
Soviet *Sputnik* satellite launch

▼ 1958
National Defense Education Act
TV quiz show scandals

▼ 1959
Alaska and Hawaii statehood
Nixon-Khrushchev "Kitchen Debate" in Moscow

▼ 1960
President Eisenhower's Commission on National Goals
Soviet downing of U.S. U-2 spy plane
John F. Kennedy elected president

▼ 1961
Eisenhower's farewell address on "military-industrial complex"

▼ 1965
U.S. escalation of Vietnam War

CHAPTER 28

Common Threads

>> How did the prosperity of the 1950s shape the politics of the 1960s?

>> What was the impact of the civil rights movement on other groups?

>> How did the new liberalism, the new conservatism, and the New Left define democracy?

>> How did anti-Communism shape U.S. foreign policy?

>> How would desires for rights and worries about limited resources continue to shape American society beyond the 1960s?

The Rise and Fall of the New Liberalism 1960–1968

AMERICAN PORTRAIT

>> Lt. Fred Downs

On the night of January 10, 1968, Second Lieutenant Fred Downs of the U.S. Army looked up at the stars over the coast of South Vietnam. Only 23, he was thousands of miles from the Indiana farm where he had grown up. His job now was to lead a platoon of American soldiers in the war to protect anti-Communist South Vietnam from Viet Cong insurgents and the North Vietnamese army. Downs faced his duty with absolute confidence. "I knew we would never be beaten," he declared.

Still, the months in Vietnam had tested Downs severely. The hot sun "cooked" him by day, the rain drenched him by night, and leeches sucked his blood. He worried about stepping on land mines and booby traps. He worried whether he could trust the South Vietnamese. He worried whether his country was fighting the war the right way. Too often, the Americans' advanced weapons didn't work: frighteningly, his M16 rifle jammed in the middle of a fight. Downs was wounded four times, but he put aside his worries and kept fighting.

Much of the time, Lt. Downs and his men went out hunting for the enemy on "search and destroy" missions. To his frustration, the Viet Cong and the North Vietnamese were hard to find. When he did get close to them, the result was a "deadly game of hide and seek." Downs shot and killed Viet Cong and North Vietnamese soldiers with his rifle. He stabbed a soldier to death in the throat with a bayonet. He killed women. He watched his own men die.

Despite all his experiences, Downs never lost his confidence. "My men thought I was invulnerable," he reported. "I did too." On the night of January 10 he saw "no clouds on my horizon." "Nothing would happen to me," he believed.

Fred Downs's story mirrored the experience of his country in the 1960s. With growing confidence in its wealth, power, and wisdom, the United States cast aside the cautious politics of the 1950s and began bold new projects at home and abroad. Across the political spectrum, Americans offered new solutions for the problems of consumer society, civil rights, and the cold war. Increasingly the nation turned to a vigorous liberalism that pledged to confront Communism abroad and reform life at home. To save South Vietnam, the federal government sent Lt. Downs and hundreds of thousands of other soldiers around the world. To create a "Great Society" in the United States, the government tried to wipe out poverty, heal race relations, protect consumers and the environment, and improve education and health care.

By 1968, these efforts had torn the nation apart. As the 1960s ended, the confidence that sustained Fred Downs and his country would be gone. ●

OUTLINE

New Ideas, New Leaders

The popular discontents at the close of the 1950s created an opportunity for new ideas and new leaders in the 1960s. Buoyed by the nation's power and prosperity, Americans faced the new decade with a sense of both urgency and optimism. From right to left, activists, intellectuals, and politicians offered conflicting solutions for America's domestic and international problems.

> **As a social system we seek the establishment of a democracy of individual participation, governed by two central aims: that the individual share in those social decisions determining the quality and direction of his life; that society be organized to encourage independence in men and provide the media for their common participation.**
>
> THE PORT HURON STATEMENT, 1962

Grassroots Activism for Civil Rights

By 1960, a new generation of African Americans was impatient with the slow, "deliberate speed" of the desegregation ordered by the Supreme Court in *Brown v. Board of Education* (see Chapter 27). Young blacks were ready to go beyond court cases and boycotts and try new tactics. In 1960, grassroots activists, committed to peaceful civil disobedience, spurred a wave of sit-ins and the formation of a new civil rights organization.

The sit-ins began in Greensboro, North Carolina. On February 1, four black male students from North Carolina Agricultural and Technical College politely insisted on being served at the whites-only lunch counter of the local Woolworth store. When the white waitress refused their order, the students, who would become known as the Greensboro Four, stayed all afternoon. Returning the next day with about thirty male and female colleagues, the four were again denied service. Soon hundreds of African American students from North Carolina A & T and other campuses, along with some white students, were besieging lunch counters. Under pressure, Woolworth and other large stores allowed their lunch counters to serve African Americans. "I felt," concluded Franklin McCain, one of the Greensboro Four, "as though I had gained my manhood."

The new tactic spread quickly across the South and North. There were wade-ins at whites-only beaches, kneel-ins at whites-only churches, and even paint-ins at whites-only art galleries. The demonstrations forced reluctant whites to open up lunch counters and other facilities to black patrons. The demonstrations also helped produce a new organization, the Student Nonviolent Coordinating Committee (SNCC). The SNCC (pronounced "Snick") brought together white and black young people, influenced by "Judaic-Christian traditions" and eager to create "a social order permeated by love."

Energizing the civil rights movements, the sit-ins demonstrated that ordinary people could successfully confront the powerful. This example of grassroots activism inspired Americans to confront other problems as well.

The Greensboro Sit-Ins, February 2, 1960 African American college students at the whites-only lunch counter of Woolworth on the second day of protest in Greensboro, North Carolina. The first two students from the left, Joseph McNeill and Franklin McCain, had helped start the sit-ins the day before.

The New Liberalism

Out of power during the 1950s, liberal intellectuals and politicians, mostly Democrats, had been forced to reconsider their ideas and plans. By the 1960s, the liberals were offering a fresh agenda that responded to the civil rights movement, consumerism, and the cold war confrontation with Communism.

A powerful faith in economic growth drove the new liberalism. To meet its domestic and international challenges, the United States, liberals believed, had to expand its economy more rapidly. As one liberal economist observed, growth would provide "the resources needed to achieve great societies at home and grand designs abroad." By manipulating its budget, the federal government could keep the economy growing. The right amount of taxes and expenditures would ensure full employment, strong consumer demand, and a rising gross national product.

Growth alone would not make America great, the liberals cautioned. A society devoted mainly to piling up personal wealth and spending it on consumer goods was fundamentally flawed. Economic growth had to be used to create a better, more satisfying life for all Americans. Because the private sector could not solve pressing national problems, the federal government had to step in to deal actively with poverty, racial inequality, pollution, housing, education, world Communism, and other problems.

Like the liberals of the 1930s and 1940s (see Chapter 24), 1960s liberals believed in employing government to correct problems created or ignored by the private sector. Nevertheless, the new liberalism differed from the old in important ways. New Dealers had worried most of all about restoring prosperity in the Great Depression; the new liberals almost took prosperity for granted. They were sure that the economy could pay for a host of reforms. The old liberals had feared that big business and class conflict posed dangers for the United States. Their successors generally saw racial divisions as the country's greatest domestic problem.

The New Conservatism

Conservatives had been out of power even longer than the liberals. In the 1930s, Herbert Hoover's failure to halt the Great Depression had discredited the conservative faith in minimalist government; then Hitler's aggression had undercut the conservative belief in isolationism. In 1950, critic Lionel Trilling could declare that America had no conservative ideas, only a liberal intellectual tradition.

By then, conservative ideas had already begun a quiet resurgence. In 1951, conservative intellectual William F. Buckley's book *God and Man at Yale* attacked his alma mater for its liberalism and denial of individualism. Two years later, theorist Russell Kirk published *The Conservative Mind* to prove that there was in fact a conservative tradition in America. In 1955, Buckley and Kirk founded the magazine *National Review* to serve as a forum for conservative ideas, including the rejection of isolationism in favor of staunch anti-Communism.

Conservatives soon had a new political hero in outspoken Senator Barry Goldwater of Arizona. With a western belief in individual freedom and fear of federal power, Goldwater was a blunt opponent of New Deal liberalism. A major general in the air force reserve, he was also a staunch advocate of a more aggressive stance toward Communism.

By 1960, the growing conservative movement had its own younger generation of activists. That year, the Young Americans for Freedom gathered at Buckley's estate in Sharon, Connecticut, to adopt a manifesto. The Sharon Statement called for government to protect individual liberty by preserving economic freedom and maintaining a strong national defense.

Conservative Hero Senator Barry Goldwater Campaigns for President, 1964 "Y.A.F." stands for Young Americans for Freedom, the collegiate activists who helped advance the conservative agenda in the 1960s.

The New Left

At the opposite end of the political spectrum, another young group, inspired by civil rights activism and troubled by student life on campus, rejected both conservatism and liberalism. By the early 1960s many students felt confined and oppressed in overcrowded and impersonal colleges and universities. These schools ordered students' lives through parietal rules that governed eating in dining halls, drinking alcohol, keeping cars on campus, and socializing in dorm rooms. Female students were subject to particularly strict rules, including curfews.

Some of these youth created the New Left, a radical movement that attempted to build a more democratic nation. The key organization of the New Left was Students for a Democratic Society (SDS), which emerged in 1960 to produce "radical alternatives to the inadequate society of today." During its national convention at Port Huron, Michigan, in 1962, SDS approved an "Agenda for a New Generation" that laid out its developing vision. An answer to the Sharon Statement, the Port Huron Statement argued that American society denied people real choice and real power in their lives. The answer, SDS claimed, was "participatory democracy." The members of SDS did not believe that liberalism would promote real democracy in America. SDS did not expect much help from the old left of socialists and Communists, with their Marxist faith in the revolutionary power of the working class. Instead, the Port Huron Statement looked to students to lead the way by fighting for control of their schools. The message began to resonate: SDS membership rose from 2,500 to 10,000 in late 1965.

The Presidential Election of 1960

As so often in American history, new ideas didn't immediately transform mainstream politics. Fought out in the political center, the presidential election of 1960 offered a choice between a vaguely liberal Democratic future and a moderate Republican status quo. The Democratic nominee, Senator John F. Kennedy of Massachusetts, was open to the liberals' agenda and shared their optimism. Only 42 when he announced his candidacy, Kennedy was youthful, energetic, and charismatic. Although he had compiled an undistinguished record in Congress, he promoted a sense of expectation. The candidate exuded, said one of his speechwriters, "the promise, almost limitless in dimensions, of enormous possibilities yet to come."

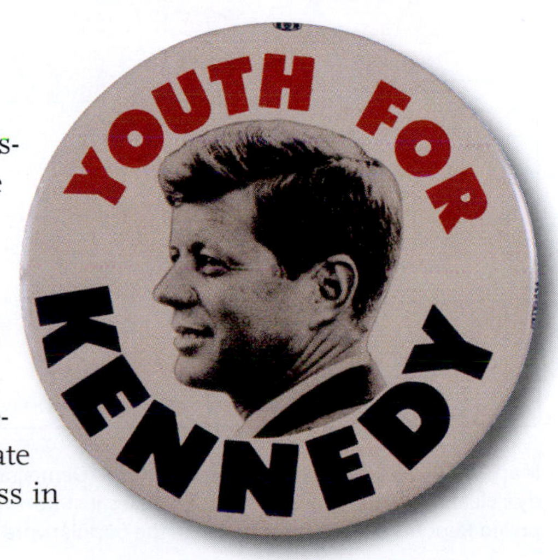

The ideas of the New Left resonated throughout the 1960s. Here a crowd estimated at 3,500 gathers outside an administration building at the University of California, Berkeley for a protest sponsored by the Free Speech Movement, led by Mario Savio (center), January 1965.

Kennedy gave voice to that promise during the campaign. Americans, he explained, stood "on the edge of a New Frontier—the frontier of the 1960s—a frontier of unknown opportunities and paths, a frontier of unfulfilled hopes and threats." The United States needed to foster economic growth, rebuild slums, end poverty, improve education for the young, and enhance retirement for the old.

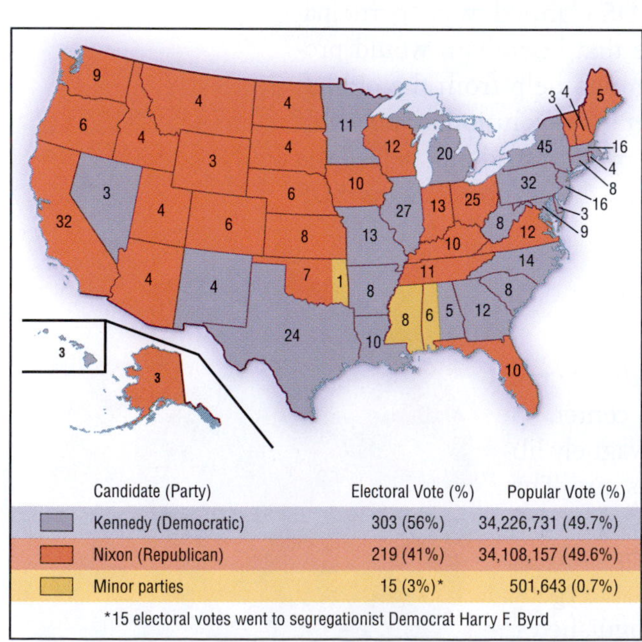

Candidate (Party) Electoral Vote (%) Popular Vote (%)
Kennedy (Democratic) 303 (56%) 34,226,731 (49.7%)
Nixon (Republican) 219 (41%) 34,108,157 (49.6%)
Minor parties 15 (3%)* 501,643 (0.7%)
*15 electoral votes went to segregationist Democrat Harry F. Byrd

Map 28–1 The Presidential Election, 1960 Democrat John F. Kennedy's clear margin in the electoral vote belies just how narrowly he outpolled Republican Richard M. Nixon in the popular vote.

In contrast, Kennedy's Republican opponent, Vice President Richard Nixon of California, represented the cautious Eisenhower administration that favored balanced budgets, limited government, and qualified acceptance of New Deal programs. Nixon embraced neither the bold programs and dynamic economic growth of the new liberalism nor the soaring individualism and strident anti-Communism of the new conservatives.

Despite Kennedy's stirring rhetoric and apparent triumph in televised debates, the election was the closest in history. Kennedy managed to keep much of the Democratic New Deal coalition of liberals, workers, and African Americans together, but he won by less than 120,000 votes (see Map 28–1). However narrowly, the voters had turned to a Democrat, influenced by liberal ideas, who was eager to explore the New Frontier.

The New Frontier

Style and Substance

From the first moments of his presidency, Kennedy voiced the confident liberal faith in America's unlimited power and responsibility. "Let every nation know," he declared in his inaugural address in January 1961, "that we shall pay any price, bear any burden, meet any hardship, support any friend, oppose any foe to assure the survival and the success of liberty. This much we pledge—and more." Kennedy's extravagant promise perfectly captured the optimistic spirit of the early 1960s.

So did the president's space program. The exploration of space, the ultimate frontier, seemed like an ideal occupation for confident Americans in the 1960s. Moreover, the space race allowed Kennedy to reject cautious Eisenhower policies and confront the Soviet challenge. In April 1961 the Soviet Union sent up the first astronaut to orbit Earth. The next month, NASA managed only to launch astronaut Alan Shepard for a brief, suborbital flight. Once again Americans feared "that the wave of the future is Russian."

> **The 1930s taught us a clear lesson: aggressive conduct, if allowed to go unchecked and unchallenged, ultimately leads to war. This nation is opposed to war. . . . We will not prematurely or unnecessarily risk the costs of worldwide nuclear war in which even the fruits of victory would be ashes in our mouth; but neither will we shrink from that risk at any time it must be faced.**
>
> JOHN F. KENNEDY,
> Address on the Cuban Missile Crisis, October 22, 1962

The Kennedy administration responded with dramatic rhetoric and the abundant resources of the growth economy. Insistent on "beating the Soviets," the president boldly pledged to land "a man on the moon before the decade is out." Apollo, the moon project, got under way with 60,000 workers and billions of dollars. Meanwhile, in February 1962 astronaut John Glenn became the first American to orbit Earth. That year the United States launched Telstar, the first sophisticated communications satellite. In all, the space program mixed practical achievements such as Telstar with less practical, more symbolic gestures such as manned space flights.

That mixture of style and substance reflected the Kennedy administration as a whole. The president maintained a dynamic, energetic image, but his administration, hampered by a weak electoral mandate, did not venture too far out onto the liberal New Frontier.

For liberals, the persistence of poverty amid prosperity stood as a chief failure of the consumer society and an embarrassment for the United States around the world. Liberals argued that the poor needed help from the federal government to become productive workers and contribute to economic growth. Increasing the productivity of the poor was not a simple matter, however. Liberals contended that the battle against poverty should include improved housing, education, health, and job opportunities, as well as job training.

Kennedy supported some modest antipoverty measures. In 1961 he signed into law the Area Redevelopment Act to help revive depressed areas. He also signed the

Omnibus Housing Act to clear slum housing and bring urban renewal to inner cities. But these measures were not enough to wipe out poverty.

Civil Rights

Grassroots activism for civil rights posed a critical challenge for the Kennedy administration. In one place after another, attempts to break down segregation and promote African American voting met with resistance.

After the Supreme Court outlawed the segregation of interstate bus terminals, a small group of African American and white "Freedom Riders" traveled south on buses to test the decision in the spring of 1961. The Freedom Riders met with beatings from white citizens and harassment from local authorities. Only then did the Kennedy administration send federal marshals to protect them.

White resistance proved effective, especially if there were no federal marshals around. In 1961, when SNCC started a voter-registration drive in Mississippi, white people struck back. SNCC workers were beaten and shot. When SNCC tried to register black voters in the small city of Albany, Georgia, members of the Albany Movement, as it was called, were beaten and arrested. Martin Luther King Jr., leader of the Southern Christian Leadership Conference (SCLC) and veteran of the Montgomery bus boycott of 1955–1956, came to Albany and got arrested, too, but segregation still ruled in the city.

SNCC activists resented the lack of presidential support. Kennedy found himself caught in a bind. Like earlier cold war presidents, he understood that racial inequal-

Hosing Down Civil Rights Demonstrators, Birmingham, Alabama, May 1963 Shocking pictures such as this one earned international sympathy for the civil rights movement.

ity damaged the United States' image abroad, but the president also knew that the civil rights issue could split the Democratic Party.

The defiance of southern whites gradually pushed Kennedy toward action. In 1962 the governor of Mississippi, Ross Barnett, disregarded a federal court order by preventing a black student from enrolling at the University of Mississippi. When federal marshals escorted the student, James Meredith, to school, white students pelted them with rocks and Molotov cocktails. After the rioting killed two people and wounded more than one hundred marshals, Kennedy called in federal troops to stop the violence and allow Meredith to enroll.

Two confrontations in Alabama forced the president's hand in 1963. In April, Martin Luther King Jr. and the SCLC tried to end segregation in the southern steel-making center Birmingham, perhaps the most segregated city in America. The city's public safety commissioner, Eugene "Bull" Connor, was a stereotypical racist white southern law-enforcement officer. To win a badly needed victory, King and local allies planned to boycott department stores and overwhelm the jails with arrested protestors. In the next days, Connor's officers arrested demonstrators by the hundreds. Ignoring a judge's injunction against further protests, King ended up in solitary confinement. In a powerful statement, "Letter from Birmingham Jail," King rejected further patience: "We must come to see . . . that 'justice too long delayed is justice denied.'" Out on bail, King pushed harder with the SCLC for justice, with demonstrations by thousands of young African American students.

Goaded by the new protests, "Bull" Connor turned fire hoses on young demonstrators, set dogs on them, and hit them with clubs. Shocking pictures of the

"I Have a Dream" Martin Luther King, Jr. at the Lincoln Memorial, Washington, DC, August 28, 1963.

scenes, shown around the world, increased the pressure on the white leadership of Birmingham and on President Kennedy. Mediators from Kennedy's Justice Department arranged for a deal in which the SCLC gave up the demonstrations, and local businesses gave up segregation and promised to hire African Americans. However, soon thereafter the Ku Klux Klan marched outside the city, and bombs went off at the home of King's brother and at SCLC headquarters. In response, African Americans rioted in the streets of Birmingham. Kennedy was forced to send federal troops to keep the peace.

A second confrontation in Alabama drew the president still deeper into the civil rights struggle. The state's segregationist governor, George Wallace, defied federal officials and tried to stop two black students from enrolling at the University of Alabama. In an eloquent televised address, Kennedy finally admitted that there was "a moral crisis" and called for sweeping civil rights legislation.

Two months later, on August 28, a march on Washington brought together a crowd of nearly 200,000 people, including 50,000 whites, at the Lincoln Memorial to commemorate the 100th anniversary of the Emancipation Proclamation and to demand "jobs and freedom." Whites and African Americans, workers and students, singers and preachers joined hands to sing the stirring civil rights anthem, "We Shall Overcome." Martin Luther King Jr. moved the nation with his vision of racial harmony. "I have a dream," he said, "that one day . . . little black boys and black girls will be able to join with little white boys and white girls as sisters and brothers." King looked forward to "that day when . . . black men and white men, Jews and Gentiles, Protestants and Catholics, will be able to join hands and sing . . . 'Free at last! Free at last! Thank God Almighty, we are free at last!'"

Kennedy's address and the March on Washington marked a turning point. The surging grassroots movement for racial equality had created broad-based support for civil rights and finally forced the federal government to act.

Flexible Response and the Third World

More confident about the economy than President Eisenhower had been, Kennedy believed the nation could afford to spend more money on the military. He also abandoned the doctrine of massive retaliation, Eisenhower's threat to use nuclear weapons against any Soviet aggression. Kennedy and his advisers preferred flexible response, a strategy that enabled the president to choose different military options, not just nuclear weapons, in dealing with the Soviets. While spending generously on nuclear weapons, the Kennedy administration built up the country's conventional ground forces and special forces—the highly trained troops, known as Green Berets, who could fight in guerilla wars. Flexible response better prepared the United States for challenges around the world.

Kennedy was more willing than Eisenhower to intervene in the affairs of the third world. This was partly a reflection of Kennedy's characteristic confidence about American power and partly a response to Soviet actions. In January 1961 Nikita Khrushchev announced Soviet support for "wars of national liberation," insurgencies against established governments in Asia, Africa, and Latin America. In reply, Kennedy encouraged democracy and prosperity in developing countries.

To counter the appeal of Communism, his administration supported modernization for Africa, Asia, and Latin America; that is, policy makers wanted these continents to develop capitalist, democratic, independent, and anti-Communist regimes along the lines of the United States. In 1961, the Kennedy administration created the Peace Corps to send thousands of young volunteers to promote literacy, public health, and agriculture around the world. The Peace Corps reflected not only the idealism and anti-Communism of the Kennedy years but also many Americans' arrogant sense of superiority. Not surprisingly, the organization was not always welcomed by the people it was supposed to help. To promote the modernization of Latin America, Kennedy announced the formation of the Alliance for Progress in 1961. Over the next eight years, this venture provided $20 billion for housing, health, education, and economic development for poorer countries in the Western Hemisphere.

The Kennedy administration sometimes helped to thwart third world independence and democracy in the name of anti-Communism. In some cases, the United States intervened in the domestic affairs of supposedly independent countries. In the Republic of the Congo, the CIA engineered the election of an anti-Communist leader. The CIA secretly tried to manipulate elections in Chile as well. The United States also backed antidemocratic, but anti-Communist, regimes in Argentina, Guatemala, Haiti, and Honduras.

Similarly, Kennedy wanted to bring down Fidel Castro, whose successful Cuban Revolution was an example for the rest of Latin America. Taking office, the president inherited a plan from the Eisenhower administration for a CIA-directed invasion of the island by anti-Communist Cuban exiles. To conceal U.S. responsibility, Kennedy canceled U.S. flights that would have protected the invaders. As a result, nearly all 1,500 exiles who landed at the Bay of Pigs in April 1961 were killed or captured by Castro's troops. Embarrassed, Kennedy turned to the CIA, which launched "Operation Mongoose," an unsuccessful secret campaign to kill or depose Castro. The Cuban leader, aware of the American plot, declared himself a Communist and turned to the Soviets for help.

Two Confrontations with the Soviets

Kennedy faced two direct confrontations with the Soviet Union. In 1961, Khrushchev threatened to stop Western traffic into West Berlin, which was surrounded by Soviet-dominated East Germany. In response, Kennedy called up reserve troops, asked Congress to increase defense spending, and hinted at a preemptive nuclear strike against the Soviets. Khrushchev backed down, but the East German government built a barbed-wire-and-concrete fence between East Berlin and West Berlin. By halting the embarrassing flight of East Germans to freedom in West Berlin, the so-called Berlin Wall defused the crisis and became a symbol of cold war Europe, a visible "iron curtain" that separated Communists and non-Communists.

In 1962 Kennedy entered a more dangerous confrontation with the Soviet Union. On October 15 photos from an American spy plane showed that the Soviets were building launch sites in Cuba for nuclear missiles that could strike the United States. In tense secret meetings, Kennedy and his advisers debated how to force the Soviet Union to withdraw the missiles. On October 22, he put ships in place to intercept Soviet vessels bound for Cuba. That night, a somber Kennedy told a television audience about the Russian missiles and demanded their removal. Fearing a nuclear war, Americans waited for the Soviets' response. Khrushchev,

The Tension of the Cuban Missile Crisis Customers in a store watch President John F. Kennedy address the nation, October 22, 1962.

unable to confront the United States in its own hemisphere, backed down. The Soviets withdrew the missiles in exchange for the removal of obsolete American missiles from Turkey.

The Cuban Missile Crisis both eased and intensified the cold war. Faced with a nuclear conflict, neither side found the prospect appealing. To ensure Soviet and American leaders could communicate in a crisis, a teletype "hotline" was installed between the White House and the Kremlin. In 1963 the two powers also approved a Limited Test Ban Treaty halting aboveground tests of nuclear weapons. On the other hand, the Cuban crisis made both the Soviets and the Americans more determined to stand firm against each other.

Kennedy and Vietnam

Kennedy inherited a deteriorating situation in South Vietnam in 1961. Ngo Dinh Diem's anti-Communist government faced increasing attacks from the Viet Cong guerillas determined to overthrow his regime. Diem also faced the Viet Cong's new political organization, the National Liberation Front, which was trying to mobilize his Communist and non-Communist opponents. In addition, he faced the continuing hostility of Ho Chi Minh's Communist government in North Vietnam, which was secretly sending soldiers and supplies into South Vietnam.

Like Eisenhower, Kennedy tried to shore up the Diem government by providing advice and financial aid. Further, Kennedy sent American advisers, including the Special Forces, to teach the South Vietnamese army how to stop the Viet Cong insurgency. Before Kennedy took office, there were 900 American troops filling noncombat roles in South Vietnam. At his death, there were more than 16,000.

Despite all this support, Diem's regime spiraled downward. His army could not stop the Viet Cong. A cold, unpopular ruler, he alienated his own people. In 1963 Americans were shocked by pictures of South Vietnamese Buddhists burning themselves to death with gasoline as a protest against the government. Losing confidence in Diem, the Kennedy administration did nothing to stop a military coup that resulted in the murder of the South Vietnamese leader at the beginning of November.

What Kennedy would have done in Vietnam will never be known. On a trip to Dallas, Texas, on November 22, 1963, the president was shot while riding in an open limousine at 12:33 p.m. Two bullets tore through Kennedy's throat and skull, and doctors pronounced him dead half an hour later. That afternoon, police arrested Lee Harvey Oswald for the shooting. A quiet former marine, Oswald had spent time in the Soviet Union. Two days later, as police transferred him from a jail, he was shot and killed by Jack Ruby, the troubled owner of a local nightclub.

Americans were shocked and numbed by the assassination and its aftermath. Some could only believe the assassination was the product of a dark conspiracy, but there was never proof of such a plot. The presidency of John Kennedy, little more than 1,000 days long, left a sad sense of unfulfilled promise. To many Americans, Kennedy's White House seemed like Camelot, the royal seat of the mythical English King Arthur who led the Knights of the Round Table before his tragic death in battle. The reality of the New Frontier was less magical. Kennedy gave voice to the new liberalism, but he seldom translated liberal ideas into action. In later years, some Americans wanted to believe that Kennedy, if he had lived, would have kept the United States from escalating the Vietnam War. Yet there was no compelling evidence that the president intended to withdraw American troops. Instead, Kennedy's commitment only made it more difficult for his successor to pull the United States out of Vietnam.

The Great Society

After Kennedy's death, Lyndon Johnson and the Democratic-controlled Congress carried out most of the liberal agenda. A flood of new laws addressed poverty, race relations, consumer and environmental protection, education, and health care. At the same time, the liberal majority on the Supreme Court afforded new protections for individual rights. By the mid-1960s, the principles of the new liberalism, turned into law, were transforming American government and society.

Lyndon Johnson's Mandate

In background and personality, the new president, Lyndon Johnson, seemed far different from his slain predecessor. Born to modest circumstances in rural Texas, he had made his own fortune, largely through political connections.

> **The Great Society rests on abundance and liberty for all. It demands an end to poverty and racial injustice, to which we are totally committed in our time. But that is just the beginning. The Great Society is a place where every child can find knowledge to enrich his mind and to enlarge his talents. It is a place where leisure is a welcome chance to build and reflect, not a feared cause of boredom and restlessness. It is a place where the city of man serves not only the needs of the body and the demands of commerce but the desire for beauty and the hunger for community.**
>
> LYNDON JOHNSON,
> Commencement Address, University of Michigan, May 22, 1964

He was never an eloquent public speaker or a charismatic figure. But he was an especially effective legislator who knew how to bully and cajole Senate colleagues into making a deal.

Despite obvious differences in style and background, there were fundamental similarities between Johnson and Kennedy. Both were products of the Democratic Party that had engineered the New Deal, won World War II, and fought the cold war. Both shared the liberals' expansive sense of American might. "Hell, we're the richest country in the world, the most powerful," Johnson declared. "We can do it all."

Taking office, Johnson stressed continuity with his predecessor. Yet the situation had changed. Kennedy's martyrdom left Americans more willing to accept political innovation. Rather than discourage people, his death seemed to inspire them.

The presidential election of 1964 strengthened Johnson's mandate. The contest offered voters an unusually clear choice between competing solutions for America. Influenced by the new liberalism, Johnson stood for activist government, growth economics, and civil rights. His Republican opponent, Barry Goldwater, stood unequivocally for the new conservatism. "We have gotten where we are," he declared, "not because of government, but in spite of government."

It was not much of a contest. Democrats portrayed Goldwater as a dangerous radical who would gut popular programs and perhaps start a war. Johnson, in contrast, was supposed to be a statesman and a man of peace. He won 61.1 percent of the popular vote, 44 states, and 486 electoral votes. Moreover, the Democrats increased their majorities in the House and Senate. It was a greater victory than Johnson's hero, Franklin Roosevelt, had ever enjoyed.

"Success Without Squalor"

With his mandate, Johnson moved to enact a legislative program that would rival Roosevelt's New Deal. At the University of Michigan in May, 1964, he had called for the creation of the "Great Society"—"a society of success without squalor, beauty without barrenness, works of genius without the wretchedness of poverty." To create that society, Johnson turned to the ideas of the new liberalism. His administration pushed through new laws that aimed to wipe out poverty, end segregation, and enhance the quality of life for all Americans.

Johnson, like many Americans, was disturbed by the persistence of poverty in the consumer society: by the standards of the day, nearly one in five Americans was poor. Declaring "unconditional war on poverty," the Johnson administration won congressional approval of the Economic Opportunity Act of 1964, which created an independent federal agency, the Office of Economic Opportunity (OEO), to spend nearly $1 billion on antipoverty programs. The OEO managed Volunteers in Service to America (VISTA), whose workers taught literacy and other skills in impoverished areas. It ran the Job Corps, which taught necessary job skills to poor youth, and implemented Community Action Programs (CAPs), which encouraged the poor to organize themselves in American cities. By supporting the "maximum feasible participation" of the poor, the CAPs, unlike other poverty programs, had the potential to redistribute power away from local officials.

The War on Poverty President Lyndon Johnson, hat in hand, talks with a family of poor sharecroppers in Nash County, North Carolina, May 1964.

In 1965 and 1966 Congress continued the war on several fronts. It established an expanded food stamp program and created Head Start, which provided early schooling, meals, and medical exams for impoverished preschool-aged children. To protect the rights of the poor, the Legal Services Program brought lawyers into slums. To improve urban life, the Model Cities Program targeted 63 cities for slum clearance and redevelopment. Congress also created the Department of Housing and Urban Development in 1965 and the Transportation Department in 1966 partly to help manage antipoverty programs.

To improve the quality of life, Congress used the fruits of economic growth to furnish security, opportunity, and cultural enrichment. The Great Society took a major step toward national health insurance when Congress created Medicare in 1965. This program provided the elderly with insurance coverage for doctors' bills, surgery, and hospitalization. At the same time, Congress created Medicaid, a program that helped the states provide medical care to the nonworking poor.

The Johnson administration confronted the growing issue of consumer protection. In 1965, Ralph Nader, an intense young lawyer, published a disturbing book, *Unsafe at Any Speed,* charging that car manufacturers cared more about style and sales than about safety. American cars lacked safety features, such as seat belts, that could save lives. Moreover, Nader reported, executives at General Motors had ignored safety defects in the Chevrolet Corvair. Faced with these revelations, General Motors seemed to confirm its arrogance by trying to discredit Nader rather than promising immediately to improve the Corvair. In response, Congress passed the National Traffic and Motor Vehicle Safety Act of 1966, which set the first federal safety standards for automobiles, and the Highway Safety Act, which required states to establish highway safety programs.

The president and Congress adopted the new liberals' belief in using the federal government to support education at all levels. The Elementary and Secondary School Act of 1965 channeled $1.3 billion into school districts around the country.

The Higher Education Act of 1965 encouraged youth to attend college by offering federally insured educational loans.

The Great Society included programs for cultural enrichment. In 1965 Congress established the National Endowment for the Arts to fund the visual and performing arts, and the National Endowment for the Humanities to support scholarly research. The Public Broadcasting Act of 1967 established a nonprofit corporation to support educational and cultural programming. Before long, the Corporation for Public Broadcasting would be giving money for such commercial-free television shows as *Sesame Street.*

Protection of the environment was a natural issue for liberals to address. In the 1960s Americans had become further sensitized to the ecological threat that the consumer economy posed to the countryside because of the best-selling book *Silent Spring* (1962), which emphasized the dangerous power that human beings held over the natural world. The author, marine biologist Rachel Carson, warned that environmental contamination from pesticides, like nuclear weapons, threatened human survival. Here was a problem, created by the booming consumer economy, that government could solve.

During Johnson's presidency, more than 300 pieces of legislation led to the expenditure of more than $12 billion on environmental programs. In 1963 the Clean Air Act encouraged state and local governments to set up pollution-control programs. Two years later, amendments established the first pollution-emission standards for automobiles. The Air Quality Act of 1967 further strengthened federal authority to deal with air pollution. Meanwhile, the Water Quality Act of 1965 and the Clean Waters Restoration Act of 1966 enabled states and the federal government to fight water pollution. The Wilderness Act of 1964 responded to environmentalists' calls for a system of wilderness lands protected from development. Johnson's wife, Lady Bird, campaigned to limit outdoor advertising and contribute to the beautification of the nation's highways.

Preserving Personal Freedom

The new liberalism contained a paradox: liberals wanted both to enhance the power of the federal government and to expand individual rights. Their concern for individual rights was apparent in their support for civil rights for African Americans and in a series of decisions by the Supreme Court, led by Chief Justice Earl Warren.

Several rulings by the Court protected the freedom to speak out and to live free from undue governmental interference. In *New York Times v. Sullivan* in 1964, the justices encouraged free speech by making it more difficult for public figures to sue news media for libel. In addition, two decisions protected the rights of people accused of crimes. In 1963 the Court ruled in *Gideon v. Wainwright* that governments had to provide lawyers to poor felony defendants. Three years later, *Miranda v. Arizona* required police to inform individuals of their rights when they were arrested, including the right to remain silent and the right to an attorney.

The Warren Court also protected sexual and religious freedom. In 1965 in *Griswold v. Connecticut* the Court threw out a state law that banned the use of contraceptives. Affirming individuals' right to privacy, the justices in effect kept government out of the nation's bedrooms. In 1963 the Court acted to prohibit mandatory prayer in the nation's public schools. *School District of Abington Township v. Schempp* prohibited state and local governments from requiring public school students to say the Lord's Prayer or read the Bible.

The Supreme Court's rulings were controversial. Some people charged that the Court was "driving God out" of the classroom. Others believed that the Court had gone too far to protect the rights of alleged criminals. Some conservatives demanded the impeachment of Chief Justice Warren. Through its rulings, the liberal majority on the Court substantially increased individual freedom, but few people had yet thought much about the tension between expanding both individual rights and government power.

Much of the liberal agenda had been accomplished by 1967. The Great Society's programs added up to a major change in American democracy. Government claimed more authority than ever to manage many Americans' daily lives. The Great Society brought a massive expansion of the size, cost, and power of the federal government (see Table 28–1).

That expansion would be controversial for years to come. Some Great Society measures—Medicare in particular—proved to be enormously expensive. Conservatives did not welcome an enlarged federal government, and some corporations resented the government's regulation of business in the name of consumer protection. Despite these concerns, the various attempts to improve the quality of life represented some of the major accomplishments of the new liberalism. The War on Poverty was at least a partial success. Mainly because of the ongoing economic boom, the percentage of people living in poverty decreased to 13 percent by 1970. But that meant that 25 million Americans were still poor. Moreover, poverty was unevenly distributed. About a third of African Americans and a quarter of Americans of Spanish origin were impoverished as the 1970s began. Still, the liberal War on Poverty made a significant, enduring difference in American life.

The Death of Jim Crow

As Johnson became president, the battle for civil rights became still more intense. In the 10 weeks after the Birmingham confrontation, 758 demonstrations led to 14,733 arrests across the United States. When a bomb killed four African American girls in a Baptist church in Birmingham in September, African American rioters burned stores and destroyed cars, and the police killed two more children.

The violence continued the following year: CORE, SNCC, SCLC, and the NAACP had created the Council of Federated Organizations (COFO) to press for African American voting rights in Mississippi. Robert Moses, an African American schoolteacher, led the COFO crusade uniting young African American and

 **Table 28–1** Expanding the Federal Government, 1955–1970

Year	Civilian Employees (thous.)	Total Spending (millions)	Defense (millions)	Space (millions)	Health (millions)	Education and Manpower (millions)
1955	2,397	$68,509	$40,245	$74	$271	$573
1960	2,399	$92,223	$45,908	$401	$756	$1,060
1965	2,528	$118,430	$49,578	$5,091	$1,704	$1,284
1970	2,982	$196,588	$80,295	$3,749	$12,907	$1,289

Source: *Historical Statistics of the United States* (1976), II, 1102, 1116.

AMERICAN LANDSCAPE

>> "The Long Cool Summer" of Greenville, Mississippi

The dramatic pictures of brave marchers, menacing dogs, ominous police, and murdered activists can make the civil rights movement seem like a continuously violent confrontation. But civil rights, like much social change, was also a more quiet process, a slow dance in which blacks and whites gradually, haltingly created and accepted a new, more democratic order. That was the case in Greenville, Mississippi, in the "Freedom Summer" of 1964, when civil rights workers fanned out across the state to ensure the voting rights of African Americans. While there was turbulence and violence in much of the state, Greenville witnessed what the local newspaper, the *Delta Democrat-Times*, described as "The Long Cool Summer."

Like the rest of Mississippi, Greenville, a city of 41,000 in the state's rich cotton-growing delta, was segregated. Although African Americans made up half the city's population, they faced second-class social and economic status. "I don't like it," a young black man declared, "when the white man works an easy job for $25 a day and I work a mean one for $3." African Americans lived with second-class political status, too: thanks to state-imposed literacy requirements and poll taxes, black voters had long been effectively disfranchised. Few African Americans were registered to vote in Greenville; the city had no black elected officials.

The Council of Federated Organizations (COFO), a coalition of leading civil rights groups, intended to change that with the voting-rights drive known as Freedom Summer. In the fall of 1963, COFO organizers visited the city to plan their campaign. In the spring of 1964, white and black activists moved into Greenville. The arrival of these outsiders, mostly in their 20s, touched off a wave of speculation and anxiety among the city's whites. The enactment of the federal Civil Rights Act of 1964, banning segregation, intensified fears of demonstrations, confrontations, and bloodshed. "There are many of us . . . who are today dismayed by the attitude, actions and statements of some of the young men and women who are temporarily within the state," declared the *Democrat-Times*. "At times it would appear that nothing less than a calculated attempt to provoke wholesale violence is their aim."

Despite these fears, local officials urged "patience and self-control." In fact, COFO's strategy focused, not on demonstrations, but on voter registration. "If you can't vote you have no power." COFO presented voting as an "alternative to violence," Fred Anderson, an African American official of the Student Nonviolent Coordinating Committee, told local blacks. "If you get the vote you don't have to shoot a gun," a COFO leader insisted. "You can pull a trigger with a vote and kill off a politician." To help encourage black activism, COFO set up two summer "freedom schools" in Greenville. "Mississippi schools are poisoning your kids' minds," Anderson explained.

In July, COFO began to bring African Americans to the county courthouse to register to vote. The first day, 100 took the preliminary registration test; the turnout was so large that 35 would-be voters were still outside when the office closed for the day. The next day, another 45 began the registration process. And so the COFO drive went on. "There was no sustained violence, no bombings, no riots, no murders and no unruly mass demonstrations," the *Democrat-Times* reported. "[R]owdies of both races never felt free to follow the course tolerated in other state communities."

Why were the African Americans of Greenville able to begin reclaiming their democratic rights with so little upheaval? Certainly, the nonconfrontational tactics of COFO made a difference. The city's growth and relative prosperity probably made whites more secure about sharing power. At least some whites accepted that American democracy demanded the registration of African Americans. "This is their undeniable right," the *Democrat-Times* conceded, "and what they seek is entirely within the American political pattern." The paper also pointed out that southern whites faced "inevitable changes" because of the federal government and the national civil rights movement; for many whites, it probably seemed pointless to disrupt the quiet lines of would-be black voters.

There was one final, ironic explanation for The Long Cool Summer of Greenville. As the editor of the *Democrat-Times* noted, most of the city's whites didn't care enough to exercise their right to vote. The paper suggested that Greenville also needed a voting drive for whites, "to make our democratic republic more truly democratic." Paradoxically, blacks won the vote in Greenville because whites cared so little about their own rights. ●

white activists to register black voters and start "Freedom Schools" for African American children. The effort, known as Freedom Summer, met hostility from whites. Two white activists, Michael Schwerner and Andrew Goodman, and one African American activist, James Chaney, were found, shot to death, near Philadelphia, Mississippi. Eventually a white deputy sheriff, a local Klan leader, and five other whites were convicted of "violating the rights" of Chaney, Goodman, and Schwerner. The violence continued in Mississippi throughout Freedom Summer. Homes and churches were burned, and three more COFO workers were killed.

Lyndon Johnson could not escape the events in Mississippi. In the summer of 1964, the Mississippi Freedom Democratic Party (MFDP) sent a full delegation to the Democratic National Convention in Atlantic City, New Jersey. The MFDP delegates, including the eloquent Fannie Lou Hamer, hoped at least to share Mississippi's convention seats with the whites-only Democratic Party delegation. Hamer, the daughter of sharecroppers, told the Credentials Committee how she had been jailed and beaten for trying to register African American voters. Afraid of alienating white southerners, Johnson tried to stop the publicity and offered the delegates two seats in the convention. "We didn't come all this way for no two seats," Hamer retorted. The MFDP delegation went away empty-handed.

Johnson and the Democratic Party were clearly not ready to share power with African American activists, but they were ready to end legalized segregation. In July, Congress adopted the Civil Rights Act, which outlawed racial discrimination in public places. The measure also set up an Equal Employment Opportunity Commission (EEOC) to stop discrimination in hiring and promotion. Even the schools gradually became integrated. In 1964 hardly any African American students attended integrated schools; by 1972 nearly half of African American children attended integrated schools.

"VOTE" Marching for African-American voting rights, Alabama, 1965.

However, across the South, most African Americans still could not vote. In January 1965 the SCLC and SNCC tried to force the voting-rights issue with protests in Selma, Alabama. Predictably, the demonstrations produced violent opposition and helpful publicity. The sight of state troopers using tear gas, cattle prods, and clubs on peaceful marchers built support for voting rights.

Seizing the moment, Johnson called for the end of disfranchisement, and Congress passed the Voting Rights Act of 1965. This powerful measure forced southern states to give up literacy tests used to disfranchise black voters and empowered federal officials to make sure that African Americans could register to vote. In three years, Mississippi saw African American registration increase from 6 percent to 44 percent of eligible voters.

Together with the Civil Rights Act of 1964, the Voting Rights Act transformed the South. These twin achievements of the civil rights movement and the Great Society effectively doomed Jim Crow and laid a foundation for African American political power. However, the struggle for racial equality was far from over

The American War in Vietnam

The war in Vietnam was the decisive event for the new liberalism and the nation in the 1960s. American participation in the conflict reflected the liberals' determined anti-Communism and their boundless sense of power and responsibility. Driven by these beliefs, Johnson made the fateful decision to send American troops into battle in 1965. When the war did not go according to plan, Americans divided passionately over the conflict, and the economy faltered. By the end of 1967 the war was destroying the Great Society.

Johnson's Decision for War

Kennedy's assassination made little difference for American defense and foreign policies. Johnson, too, was a committed cold warrior with an optimistic view of American power. He kept flexible response in place and was equally willing to undermine the independence of third world countries. In 1965, Johnson sent 22,000 American troops to the Dominican Republic to stop an increasingly violent struggle for political power. The president violated the sovereignty of this Caribbean nation without obtaining evidence of a Communist threat and without consulting Latin American countries as required by treaty.

At first, Johnson followed Kennedy's policy in Vietnam. The new president believed in the domino theory, the idea that the fall of one country to Communism would lead to the fall of others. Like many Americans who had witnessed the rise of Adolf Hitler in the 1930s, Johnson thought it was a mistake to tolerate any aggression. The president also felt he could not turn his back on commitments made by Kennedy, Eisenhower, and Truman. As one weak government followed another, Johnson sent more aid and advisers to South Vietnam and stepped up covert action against the North.

This secret activity helped Johnson get congressional approval to act more aggressively. On August 2, 1964, a U.S. destroyer, the *Maddox,* was cruising a few miles off the coast of North Vietnam in the Gulf of Tonkin, in order to monitor communications. When three North Vietnamese torpedo boats unsuccessfully attacked the *Maddox,* the American ship sank two of the boats and damaged a third. Two days later the *Maddox,* along with a second U.S. destroyer, fired at a nonexistent North Vietnamese attack. Johnson ordered retaliatory strikes from U.S. aircraft carriers and asked Congress for the power to protect American military personnel. With only two dissenting votes, Congress approved what became known as the Tonkin Gulf Resolution, which gave the president the authority, without a declaration of war, to use military force to safeguard South Vietnam. Even though Johnson knew there had been no real threat to the United States, he had misled Congress to obtain a "blank check" to fight in Southeast Asia.

He soon cashed it. After American soldiers were killed in a Viet Cong attack on a U.S. base in February 1965, Johnson authorized air strikes against North Vietnam itself. In March the United States began Operation Rolling Thunder, a series of bombing raids on military targets in North Vietnam.

When the raids failed to deter the North Vietnamese and Viet Cong, Johnson had a disagreeable but clear choice. If he wanted to save both South Vietnam and his reputation, he had to commit American ground troops to battle; otherwise, he would be blamed for the loss of South Vietnam to Communism. In July 1965, Johnson gave the order to send 180,000 soldiers to fight in South Vietnam without a declaration of war.

Johnson's decision was the ultimate expression of the new liberalism. The president went to war not only because he opposed Communism, but also because he had faith in American wealth and wisdom. Johnson believed that the United States could transform a weak, divided South Vietnam into a strong, united, modern nation. Even though he was cautious about going to war, Johnson could not accept that the United States might lose. Moreover, he believed that the United States could afford to fight a war abroad and still build the Great Society at home. It was a fateful choice.

Fighting a Limited War

Johnson and his advisers believed the United States did not need all its power to save South Vietnam (see Map 28–2). Unlike World War II, America would not attack civilian targets, use nuclear weapons, and demand "unconditional surrender." Instead of another total war, Vietnam was to be a limited war in which the U.S. forces, led by General William Westmoreland, would use conventional weapons against military targets. The goal was not to take over territory but rather to kill enough enemy soldiers to persuade the North Vietnamese and the Viet Cong to give up. Relying on America's superior technology, Westmoreland expected the United States to prevail by the end of 1967.

Westmoreland's strategy turned out to be poorly suited to the realities of Vietnam. As Fred Downs discovered, the North Vietnamese and the Viet Cong usually escaped by hiding in tunnels, fleeing through the jungle, fighting mainly at night, or retreating into Cambodia, Laos, and North Vietnam. Their strategy was to live long enough for a frustrated U.S. military to leave South Vietnam.

American troops fought well. Yet at the close of 1967, too many North Vietnamese and Viet Cong were still alive and committed to the overthrow of South Vietnam. Meanwhile, the United States had lost many troops: 9,000 died in 1967 alone. Even though there were now half a million troops in Westmoreland's command, he had not won the war on schedule. He had not lost the war, either. But the United States was running out of time to win (see Table 28–2).

The War at Home

The war in Vietnam had a divisive impact back home. An impassioned antiwar movement, led by SDS and other student radicals, emerged to condemn American policy. For the New Left, the war confirmed their analysis of America's ills. Communism in Southeast Asia, they believed, did not pose a real threat to the United States. But the misguided cold war had led liberals to support an antidemocratic regime. The war

Map 28–2 America's War in Vietnam, 1965–1968 The many military bases suggest how much power the United States had to commit to South Vietnam; the many major battles show how hard American troops had to fight to protect the South Vietnamese regime from the Viet Cong and from the North Vietnamese soldiers who traveled the Ho Chi Minh Trail.

Table 28–2 The Escalating War in Vietnam, 1960–1968

Year	U.S. Troops	U.S. Battle Deaths	S. Vietnamese Battle Deaths	N. Vietnamese and Viet Cong Battle Deaths (estimated)
1961	3,164	11	(three-year	12,000
1962	11,326	31	total =	21,000
1963	16,263	78	13,985	21,000
1964	23,310	147	7,457	17,000
1965	184,000	1,369	11,403	35,382
1966	385,000	5,008	11,953	55,524
1967	486,000	9,378	12,716	88,104
1968	536,000	14,589	27,915	181,149

Sources: Michael Clodfelter, *Vietnam in Military Statistics*, 46, 57, 209 and 258; Fox Butterfield, ed., *Vietnam War Almanac*, 50, 54, 57, 64, 102, 132, 158, 192; Shelby Stanton, ed., *Vietnam Order of Battle*, 333.

also revealed how undemocratic America had become. Johnson, the New Left pointed out, had ignored the Constitution by sending troops into battle without a declaration of war. In addition, the selective service law was forcing a repugnant choice on young men: they could either fight this illegal war or obtain student deferments to stay in school and prepare for empty lives as corporate employees in the consumer society.

A growing number of liberals and Democrats shared at least some of the radicals' analysis. These "doves" acknowledged that the United States was backing an antidemocratic government in a brutal and apparently unnecessary war. The conflict appeared to be a civil war among Vietnamese rather than some plot to expand Soviet or Chinese influence at the cost of the United States. Meanwhile, the war had

The Toll of War A South Vietnamese refugee, displaced by American bombing.

shattered many liberals' and Democrats' overconfident view of the Great Society. The United States, confessed Senator J. William Fulbright of Arkansas in 1966, was a "sick society" suffering from an "arrogance of power." The nation apparently could not solve major problems as readily as the liberals had believed a few years earlier.

Some African Americans viewed the conflict as a painful illustration of American racism. A disproportionate number of poor African Americans, unable to go to college and avoid the draft, were being sent to kill nonwhites abroad on behalf of a racist United States. First SNCC and then Martin Luther King Jr. condemned the war. Refusing to be drafted, boxer Muhammad Ali was sentenced to jail and stripped of his championship in 1967.

The growing opposition to the war produced large and angry demonstrations. In 1965 students and faculty staged "teach-ins" at college campuses to explore and question American policy in Vietnam. In April, 20,000 people gathered at the Washington Monument to protest the war. Some young men risked jail by returning or burning their draft cards. On campuses, students protested the presence of recruiters trying to hire workers for defense contractors. In October 1967 the National Mobilization Committee, known as the "Mobe," staged Stop the Draft Week. As part of the protest, radicals in Oakland, California, tried to shut down an army draft induction center, fought with police, and briefly took over a 25-square-

Stop the Draft Week Protestors and police in front of an induction center, Oakland, California, October 1967.

block area of the city. Meanwhile, nearly 100,000 people rallied in Washington, DC, to protest the war.

Despite the protests, most Americans supported the war. To many people, the demonstrators were unpatriotic. "America—Love It or Leave It," read a popular bumper sticker. "Hawks," mostly conservative Republicans and Democrats, wanted Johnson to fight harder. Nevertheless, by October 1967 support for the war had fallen to 58 percent, in one public opinion poll, and only 28 percent of the people approved of Johnson's conduct of the war.

Bad economic news contributed to the public mood. Massive government spending for the war and the Great Society had overstimulated the economy. With jobs plentiful, strong consumer demand drove up prices, which in turn put upward pressure on wages. Anxious about inflation, the Federal Reserve contracted the money supply, making it harder for businesses to get loans. When interest rates reached their highest levels since the 1920s, there were fears of a financial panic. Despite liberal economic policies, the United States had not created perpetual prosperity after all.

By the end of 1967 the war had put enormous stress on the Great Society. It undermined liberals' commitment to anti-Communism and their confidence in American power and wisdom. By dividing the nation, the conflict also undermined support for the Great Society. By weakening the economy, furthermore, the Vietnam War made it harder to pay for the Great Society. The United States could not, as Johnson believed, "do it all." The new liberalism had reached its crisis.

The Great Society Comes Apart

Liberals attained power in the early 1960s because their agenda responded to popular discontent with the consumer society, but even as Congress enacted that agenda, many Americans were expressing new dissatisfactions that liberalism could not accommodate. The Black Power movement, the youth rebellion, and a reborn women's movement exposed the limits of the liberal vision. In 1968 the strain of new demands, the Vietnam War, and economic realities tore apart the Great Society and destroyed the fortunes of Lyndon Johnson, the Democratic Party, and the new liberalism.

> [T]he world is all messed up. The nation is sick. Trouble is in the land. Confusion all around. . . . But I know, somehow, that only when it is dark enough, can you see the stars. And I see God working in this period of the twentieth century in a way that men, in some strange way, are responding—something is happening in our world. The masses of people are rising up. And wherever they are assembled today . . . the cry is always the same—"We want to be free."
>
> MARTIN LUTHER KING JR.,
> last speech, Memphis, Tennessee, April 3, 1968

The Emergence of Black Power

For many African Americans, the Great Society's response to racial inequality was too slow and too weak. Even as the civil rights movement reached its climax, a wave of more than 300 race riots from 1964 to

1969 dramatized the gap between the promise of the Great Society and the reality of life in black America. When a white policeman shot a 15-year-old African American in the Harlem district of New York in July 1964, angry African Americans burned and looted buildings. In August 1965 friction between white police and African American citizens touched off a riot in the Watts section of Los Angeles, where 40 percent of the mostly African American population lived in poverty. In five days more than 1,000 fires burned, and 34 people died. The wave of riots peaked in Detroit, in July 1967, when 43 people died before U.S. Army paratroopers stopped the violence (see Map 28–3).

To many onlookers, the riots were, in the words of an official report on Watts, "senseless," but the disturbances flowed from the real frustrations of African Americans. Despite the civil rights movement's successful challenge to legalized segregation in the South, African Americans still lived with poverty and discrimination all across the country. Northern cities, the center of the riots, had been largely ignored by Martin Luther King Jr. and other civil rights leaders. The riots signaled that the civil rights movement and the new liberalism, for all their accomplishments, had not addressed some of the most difficult problems of racial inequality.

For years King and other activists had relied on nonviolent demonstrations and ties to white liberals to achieve integration, but that approach proved ineffective in the North. In 1965, King confronted "the Negro's repellent slum life" in Chicago by joining marches protesting the de facto segregation of the city's educational sys-

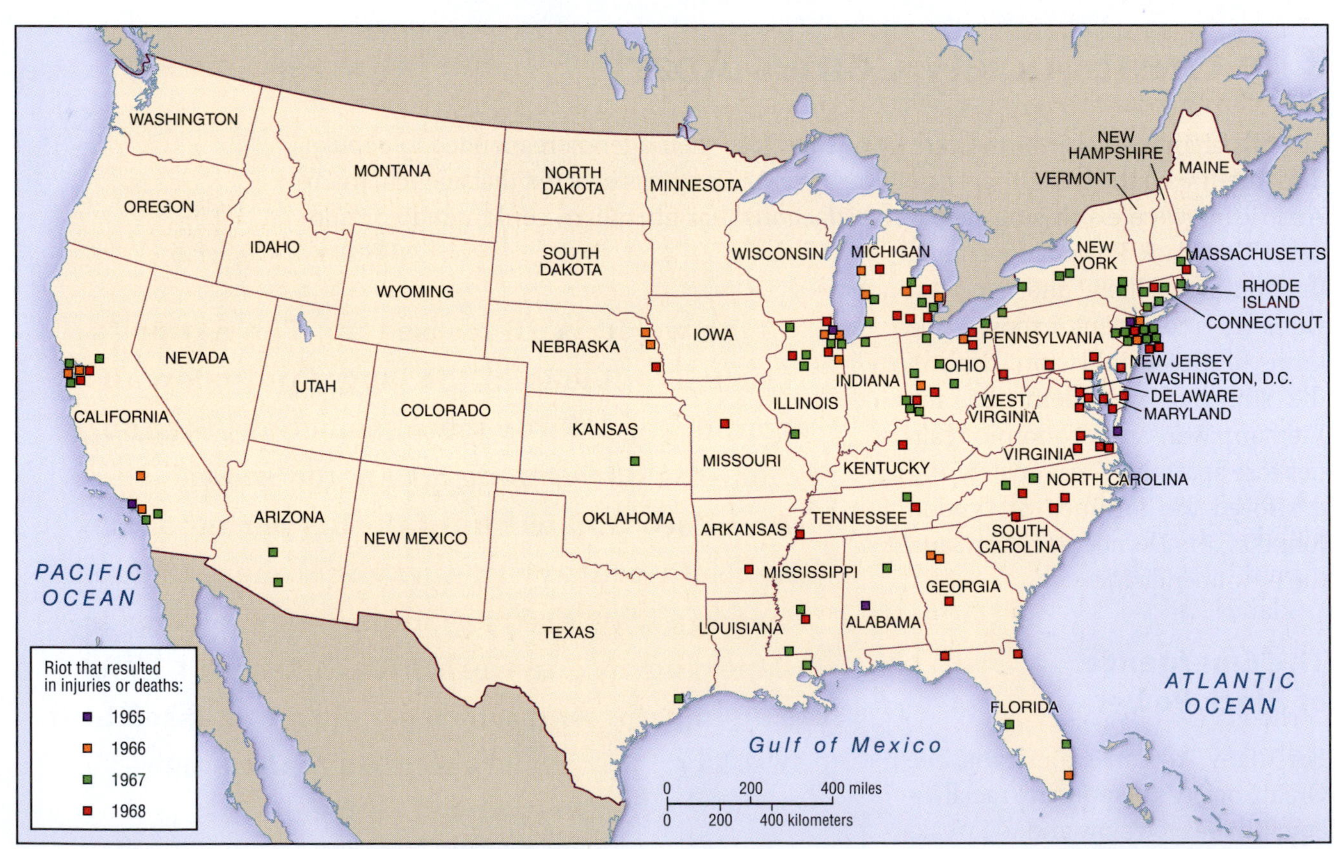

Map 28–3 Race Riots, 1965–1968 The clusters of riots in the Northeast, Midwest, and California emphasize that race was not just a southern issue in the 1960s. *Mark C. Carnes et al.,* Mapping America's Past *(New York: Henry Holt and Co., 1996), p. 217.*

tem. King faced the determined opposition of the city's Democratic political boss, Mayor Richard Daley. Reluctant to challenge the powerful mayor, the Johnson administration would not give King real support. In 1966, King returned to lead the "Chicago Movement" to wipe out slums and win access to better housing in white neighborhoods. "Go back to Africa," white demonstrators chanted. Daley accepted a compromise on fair housing but repudiated it as soon as King left town. Under the leadership of 24-year-old Jesse Jackson, Operation Breadbasket threatened demonstrations and boycotts against businesses that refused to hire African Americans. The project produced few results; King's nonviolent tactics had failed.

African Americans already had the example of a different approach to the problem of black-white relations. The Nation of Islam believed that whites were devils and African Americans were God's chosen people. The Black Muslims, as they were known, preached separation of the races and the self-reliance of African Americans. One of the Muslims' most powerful preachers was Malcolm X, a former pimp, drug pusher, and convict who angrily rejected integration and nonviolence. "If someone puts a hand on you," he said, "send him to the cemetery." Malcolm X moderated his view of whites before being gunned down, apparently by Muslims, in 1965. But he was best known for his militant call "for the freedom of the 22 million Afro-Americans by any means necessary."

By the mid-1960s, many African Americans were willing to follow at least some of Malcolm X's example. Rejecting the longtime goal of integration, they now emphasized maintaining and celebrating a separate African American identity. Now, many African Americans declared that "Black is beautiful." In asserting their distinctive identity, some African Americans accentuated their African heritage. They wore African robes and dashikis, explored African language and art, and observed the seven-day holiday Kwanzaa, based on an African harvest festival. Instead of working with white liberals and depending on the federal government, some African American activists insisted blacks needed to create their own institutions. In 1966, SNCC ousted its white members.

In rejecting nonviolence and integration, a number of African American activists adopted a more militant stance. "What we gonna start saying now is Black Power!" Stokely Carmichael told a rally in Mississippi. The new slogan had different meanings for different people. The most radical interpretation came from the Black Panthers, who were first organized in Oakland, California, by Huey P. Newton and Bobby Seale. Dressed in black clothes and black berets, the Panthers armed themselves to protect their neighborhoods from white police. Newton, admiringly described by an associate as "the baddest motherfucker ever to step foot inside of history," went to jail after a shootout with police. The Panthers also founded schools and promoted peaceful community activism, but they were best known in the media for their aura of violent militance.

Black Panther Organizers Huey Newton and Bobby Seale

Particularly because of the violent image of the Panthers, many people, African American and white, were hostile to the new slogan. For King and his allies, Black Power all too obviously meant repudiation of nonviolent integration. For many whites, Black Power stirred fears of violence. For white leaders like Richard Daley, Black Power meant giving up political authority to African Americans. For Lyndon Johnson, Black Power obviously meant a rejection of his Great Society.

The Youth Rebellion

The anti–Vietnam War movement was part of a broader rebellion against adult authority and expectations. The battle began at the University of California at Berkeley in 1964. That fall, the university's administration banned political speaking and organizing at the one street corner where it had been allowed. When a civil rights activist was arrested for defying the ban in October, hundreds of students sat down around the police cars, trapping the officers for 32 hours. After the standoff, students created the Free Speech Movement (FSM) to pursue greater student involvement in the educational process. When the university refused to accept that demand, students took over the main administration building. Speaking that day, the student leader Mario Savio reflected the ideas of the New Left. "We have an autocracy which runs this university," he exclaimed. "[W]e're a bunch of raw material[s] that . . . don't mean to end up being bought by some clients of the University, be they the government, be they industry, be they organized labor, be they anyone! We're human beings!" The administration eventually succumbed to faculty protests and a student boycott of classes and agreed to new rules on free speech.

Americans had never seen anything quite like the Berkeley protests. Here were privileged students, on their way to comfortable middle-class lives, condemning society, storming a building, and being dragged off by the police. Many people were infuriated; some younger Americans were inspired.

As campus activism flourished, young people were also creating the rebellious lifestyle that became known as the counterculture. Less politically oriented than the New Left, the counterculture challenged conventional social values. By the mid-1960s, many younger Americans were condemning conformity, careerism, materialism, and sexual repression as they groped toward an alternative lifestyle.

The counterculture rested on the enjoyment of rock music, drugs, and sexual freedom. Beginning in 1964, the sudden popularity of the Beatles, the Rolling Stones, and other British rock groups brought back a rebellious note to rock and roll. The Beatles' irreverent attitude toward authority, symbolized by their long hair, helped create "Beatlemania" in the United States. Young Americans loved the Beatles' first movie, *A Hard Day's Night,* in 1964, because, a student wrote, "all the dreary old adults are mocked and brushed aside."

Rock also became more socially and politically conscious in the 1960s. Bob Dylan, Simon and Garfunkel, and other musicians rooted in folk music sang about racism, nuclear weapons, and other issues.

Rock music often sang of the virtues of drugs and sex, two more elements of the counterculture. The use of marijuana, the hallucinogen LSD, and other drugs increased during the 1960s. The counterculture saw drugs, most of them illegal, as a way of flouting adult convention and escaping everyday reality for a more liberated consciousness.

Sex offered a similar mix of pleasure and defiance. On campuses across the country, students demanded greater freedom, including the repeal of the parietal rules that restricted the mixing of male and female students in dorms. By the end of the decade, students were living together before marriage, to the consternation of college authorities and other adults.

Many young people hoped that the counterculture would weave sex, drugs, and rock into a new lifestyle. Novelist Ken Kesey joined with his followers, the Merry Pranksters, to set up a commune, complete with "Screw Shack," outside San Francisco. The Merry Pranksters used drugs to synchronize with the cosmos and attain a state of ecstasy. By 1965 Kesey had created the "acid test," which fused drugs, rock, and light shows into a multimedia experience. The acid test helped establish the popularity of "acid rock," the "San Francisco sound" of Jefferson Airplane and the Grateful Dead.

The purest form of the countercultural lifestyle was created by the hippies, who appeared in the mid-1960s. Hippie culture centered in the Haight-Ashbury section of San Francisco. Rejecting materialism and consumerism, hippies celebrated free expression and free love. They wanted to replace capitalism, competition, and aggression with cooperation and community. One group of hippies, the Diggers, gave away clothes and food and staged the first "Human Be-In" at Golden Gate Park "to shower the country with waves of ecstasy and purification."

The youth rebellion was easy to exaggerate. There were not many full-time hippies. The countercultural lifestyle quickly became conformist consumerism, as young Americans flocked to buy the right clothes and records.

The counterculture also had roots in the orthodox culture it attacked. By the close of the 1950s, adults themselves had become ambivalent about consumerism, conventional morality, and institutional authority. Sexual freedom for youth was encouraged partly by the greater sexual openness of mainstream culture, the Supreme Court's *Griswold* decision, and the introduction of the oral contraceptive ("the pill") in 1960. Americans chafed at the authority of religious denominations. The pop art paintings of Andy Warhol and Roy Lichtenstein, the productions of the Living Theater, the essays of Susan Sontag, and the novels of Thomas Pynchon broke with formal, artistic conventions.

Nevertheless, the counterculture was a disruptive force in 1960s America. Like the Black Panthers, hippies deeply influenced young people and adults. The counterculture encouraged Americans to question conventional values and authority and to seek a freer way of life.

The Rebirth of the Women's Movement

By the 1960s American women were reacting against the difficult social roles enforced on them after World War II. More women than ever went to college, but they were not expected to pursue long-term careers. More women than ever worked outside the home, but they were still expected to devote themselves to home and family. Women also had to put up with the continuing double standard of sexual behavior, which granted men more freedom to seek sexual gratification outside of marriage. By the start of the new decade, educated middle-class women, in particular, questioned their second-class status. In part, they were inspired by the example of the civil rights movement.

Two best-selling books reflected these women's complaints. In *The Feminine Mystique* (1963), journalist Betty Friedan described "the problem that has no name," the growing frustration of educated, middle-class wives and mothers who had subordinated their own aspirations to the needs of men. Meanwhile, journalist Helen Gurley Brown rejected unequal sexual opportunities in her book, *Sex and the Single Girl* (1962). Brown did not challenge male sexual ethics, just as Friedan did not challenge male careerism. Instead, like Friedan, Brown wanted equal opportunity for women, both in and out of marriage. She explained, coyly, that "nice, single girls do."

The complaints of Friedan, Brown, and other women received attention but little action from men. In 1961 Kennedy appointed the Presidential Commission on the Status of Women, chaired by Eleanor Roosevelt. The commission's cautious report, *American Women,* documented gender discrimination but reaffirmed women's domestic role. In 1963 Congress passed the Equal Pay Act, which mandated the same pay for men and women who did the same work, but the measure, full of loopholes, had little impact on women's comparatively low earnings. A year later, Title VII, a provision slipped into the Civil Rights Act of 1964, prohibited employers from discriminating on the basis of sex in hiring and compensating workers. Yet the Equal Employment Opportunity Commission (EEOC) did little to enforce the law.

Male inaction pushed women to organize. In 1966 Betty Friedan and a handful of other women, angry at the EEOC, formed the National Organization for Women (NOW). Although frustrated with the Great Society, Friedan and the founders of NOW expressed essentially liberal values. They saw NOW as "a civil rights organization," and wrote a "Bill of Rights" for women that focused on government action to provide rights and opportunities. NOW also demanded access to contraception and abortion.

NOW's platform was too radical for many women and not radical enough for others. Some younger women, particularly activists in the civil rights movement and the New Left, wanted more than liberal solutions to their problems. By the fall of 1967, activists were forming new groups dedicated to "women's liberation." Influenced by the New Left, radical feminists blamed the capitalist system for the oppression of women, but a growing number of radicals saw men as the problem. Like African Americans in the Black Power movement, radical women talked less about rights and more about power. Their slogan was "Sisterhood Is Powerful!" Like the Black Power movement and the New Left, radical feminists rejected collaboration with male liberal politicians.

Few in number, radical feminists nevertheless commanded public attention. In September 1968, New York Radical Women organized a protest against the annual Miss America pageant in Atlantic City, New Jersey. The pageant, they said, was an act of "thought control" intended "to make women oppressed and men oppressors; to enslave us all the more in high-heeled, low-status roles." The protestors threw bras, girdles, makeup, and other "women-garbage" into a "Freedom Trash Can." Then they crowned a sheep "Miss America."

Not surprisingly, men and many women were generally uncomfortable with radical feminism. Onlookers at the Miss America protest called the women "lesbians" and "screwy, frustrated women."

Conservative Backlash

The rebellions against the Great Society strengthened the conservative movement. Just two years after humiliating defeat in the presidential election of 1964, conservative figures won new national prominence. Two politicians in particular became focal points for many Americans' resentment against feminism, civil rights and black power, the counterculture and the antiwar movement, and the new liberalism.

George Wallace, former governor of Alabama, increasingly combined his hostility to civil rights and federal power with a populist appeal to working-class and middle-class whites. In 1964, he ran for the Democratic presidential nomination calling for "law and order." Encouraged by his success in northern primaries that year, Wallace prepared to mount an independent campaign aimed at the "average man—your taxi driver, your steel and textile worker" in 1968. Now he played on anger over the youth rebellion and the antiwar movement, as well as the civil rights movement. "If I ever get to be President and any of these demonstrators lay down in front of my car," Wallace vowed, "it'll be the last car they ever lay down in front of." Wallace's independent campaign loomed as a threat to the two major parties.

Meanwhile, former actor Ronald Reagan became a major conservative force in the Republican Party. A lifelong liberal Democrat, the amiable Reagan had moved to the right and supported Barry Goldwater in 1964. Two years later, Reagan ran for governor of California vowing to "clean up the mess at Berkeley," with all its "Beatniks, radicals and filthy speech advocates" and its "sexual orgies so vile I cannot describe them." He opposed high taxes, Medicaid, and other liberal activism. Condemning the antiwar movement, Reagan also favored escalation of the U.S. war effort in Vietnam.

1968: A Tumultuous Year

In 1968 the stresses and strains of the Great Society came together to produce the most tumultuous year in the United States since World War II. In January, the Viet Cong and North Vietnamese launched bold, sometimes suicidal attacks all over South Vietnam on the first day of Tet, the Vietnamese New Year. Although U.S. and South Vietnamese forces inflicted punishing losses on the attackers, the Tet Offensive shocked Americans. If the United States was winning the war, how could the North Vietnamese and the Viet Cong have struck so daringly? Many Americans who had supported the decision to send troops into South Vietnam now began to believe the war was unwinnable.

The Tet Offensive doomed Johnson's increasingly troubled administration. The president needed to send reinforcements to Vietnam, but he knew public opinion would oppose the move. As it was, he could not even pay for more troops. The economy would not support both the war and the Great Society any longer. The political situation was bad, too. On March 12 Senator Eugene McCarthy of Minnesota, an antiwar candidate with little money and seemingly no chance of success, nearly beat Johnson in New Hampshire's Democratic primary. Four days later, Senator Robert Kennedy of New York, the younger brother of John Kennedy, announced his own candidacy for the Democratic nomination. The charismatic Kennedy, opposed to

AMERICA AND THE WORLD

>> International Student Protest, 1968

The unrest had built on campus almost from the moment it opened in 1964. Many students hated the sterile, modern buildings, erected in the midst of a big-city slum. The students also chafed at the many rules: no cooking in the dorms; no changes to the furniture; no males in females' rooms. The campus represented, one student critic complained, "an assembly-line conception of educational organization." As the student body grew from 2,000 to more than 12,000 by the fall of 1967, the Vietnam War escalated half a world away. When six local leaders of the antiwar movement were arrested, radical students rushed into the university administration building and occupied the dean's office. "Professors," they wrote on the walls, "you are past it and so is your culture!"

The protest took place, not in the United States, but on the Nanterre campus of the University of Paris. The student movement of the 1960s was, in fact, a global phenomenon. In Europe, Asia, and Latin America as well as the United States, mostly middle-class students criticized the authority of universities and governments, demanded more freedom, and condemned the Vietnam War. The wave of protest surged and reached its crest in the spring of 1968. In Western Europe, there were vast student demonstrations, strikes, and confrontations with police. Even in authoritarian, pro-Soviet Eastern Europe, students protested against universities and police. In Japan, students protested the Vietnam War. In Brazil, students confronted their universities' rigid governance and the nation's repressive military regime.

There were significant differences among these protest movements. In the United States, the New Left rejected the Old Left and did not see organized labor as an ally. In Western Europe, students were influenced by socialism and eager to make common cause with workers and unions. In France, the result was a general strike of students and workers unlike anything seen in the United States. While American protestors seldom criticized the Soviet Union, East European students condemned their own Communist governments and the USSR.

Nevertheless, important commonalities united the international student movements of the 1960s. They generally had common origins in youthful uneasiness about the cold war and the repressiveness of modern, bureaucratized society dominated by big organizations. The movements reflected a powerful yearning for free-

dom and free expression. The simultaneity of these largely separate national protests was a product of rapid communication in this age of satellites and television: students learned quickly what was going on elsewhere around the globe. The rise of student movements was a reminder, too, of the global influence of the United States: America's war in Vietnam angered students abroad; America's student movement set the example for protest around the world.

Finally, the international student protests produced a common reaction—a frightened backlash from educators, police and military, and politicians. Tear gas, water hoses, and clubs were common sights in 1968. As in the United States, the result of protest was often the triumph of conservatism and the status quo. In France, the movement that began with Nanterre ended in the reelection of President Charles de Gaulle. The harshest backlash came in Czechoslovakia: the Soviets invaded, killed and wounded more than 700, and ended any loosening of authority. But in the long run, the international student movements also signaled a persisting, even growing, demand for freedom and democracy in the face of great organizations and worldwide superpower competition.

the war, would be a formidable opponent for the president. Besieged by the war, the economy, and the presidential campaign, Johnson went on television the night of March 31. He announced that he had ordered a halt to the bombing of much of North Vietnam and indicated his willingness to talk peace with the North Vietnamese. Then Johnson, drained by events, announced that he would not run again for president.

Johnson painfully accepted new limits to the Great Society. Congressional leaders forced him to agree to spending cuts for Great Society programs. Despite liberal pressure, Johnson did not have the money or the clout for new welfare programs, new initiatives to improve race relations, or even the space program, that symbol of great liberal dreams. The president continued the Apollo program but abandoned other space projects. The Great Society was coming back down to earth.

Meanwhile, the United States was torn by upheaval and violence. In the first six months of 1968, students carried out demonstrations at 101 colleges and universities. On April 4, a white man assassinated Martin Luther King Jr. in Memphis, Tennessee, where he had gone to support striking African American and white sanitation workers. King's assassination set off riots in more than 100 cities. Forty-one African Americans and five whites died. African Americans "have had all they can stand," two black psychologists wrote.

The violence soon spread to the presidential campaign. After winning the California Democratic primary on the evening of June 5, Robert Kennedy was shot in a Los Angeles hotel by Sirhan Sirhan, a troubled Palestinian. Kennedy's death the next

The Anguish of Vietnam President Lyndon Johnson listens to a tape-recorded report on the state of the American effort in South Vietnam, 1968.

The Funeral Procession of Martin Luther King, Jr., Atlanta, Georgia, April 9, 1968 The widowed Coretta Scott King, center, walks with her family.

morning left Eugene McCarthy to contest the Democratic presidential nomination with Vice President Hubert Humphrey of Minnesota, who still supported the American war effort in Vietnam. Humphrey won the nomination at the Democratic convention in Chicago in August, but the party was deeply divided. Outside the convention hall, Mayor Daley's police battled in the streets with antiwar demonstrators.

The Republican Party nominated Richard Nixon, the man who lost to John Kennedy in 1960. A critic of the Great Society, Nixon promised to end the Vietnam War and unify the country. Like the more conservative Reagan and Wallace, Nixon tried to exploit the nation's social divisions with promises to speak for "the forgotten Americans, the nonshouters, the nondemonstrators." Wallace, meanwhile, appealed even more bluntly to frustrated middle- and working-class whites.

Unlike 1960, Nixon won this time. Although Humphrey made it close by repudiating Johnson's Vietnam policy, the vice president could not overcome the troubles of the Great Society. Nixon attracted 43.4 percent of the popular vote to Humphrey's 42.7 percent and Wallace's 13.5 percent. Running strongly in every region of the country, Nixon piled up 301 electoral votes. Although the Democrats retained control of the House and Senate, the party's eight-year hold on the White House had been broken.

Conclusion

The upheavals of 1968 marked the end of illusions about limitless American power. John Kennedy's confident nation—able to "pay any price, bear any burden, meet any hardship, support any friend, oppose any foe"—had vanished. By 1968 the

American economy could no longer "pay any price." The United States could not successfully support its friends in South Vietnam. The government could not create the Great Society. Instead, the nation was deeply divided by generation, race, and gender. The assassinations of Robert Kennedy and Martin Luther King Jr. dramatized the breakdown of democracy.

The year 1968 was tumultuous for Lt. Fred Downs, too. On the morning of January 11, he walked through a gate and stepped on a mine. The explosion threw him into the air, ripped through his eardrums, tore away pieces of his legs and hips, mutilated his right hand, laid bare the bones of his right arm, and blew off his left arm at the elbow. Horrified, Downs looked at his wounds. "I felt," he recalled, "the total defeat of my life."

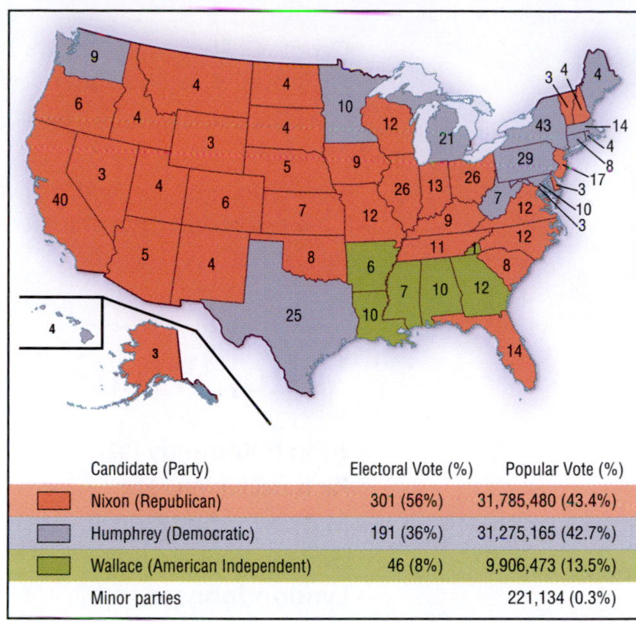

Candidate (Party)	Electoral Vote (%)	Popular Vote (%)
Nixon (Republican)	301 (56%)	31,785,480 (43.4%)
Humphrey (Democratic)	191 (36%)	31,275,165 (42.7%)
Wallace (American Independent)	46 (8%)	9,906,473 (13.5%)
Minor parties		221,134 (0.3%)

Map 28–4 The Presidential Election, 1968 Like the 1960 election, this was another close contest with widespread consequences. But this time, former vice president Richard M. Nixon was the winner.

Back in the United States, Downs had to deal with the loss of his arm, his confidence, and his plans. At a military hospital, he had to learn how to use a prosthetic arm and to accept the breakup of his marriage. He also had to learn how to deal with a divided, angry America. On the street, a man pointed to the hook sticking out of Downs's left sleeve. "Get that in Vietnam?" the man asked. Downs said he had. "Serves you right," the man snapped, and walked away. The United States, like that man, would have a difficult time coming to terms with the events of the 1960s.

Further Readings

Terry H. Anderson, *The Movement and the Sixties* (1995), offers a sweeping chronicle of the varieties of protest in the 1960s. Robert Cohen and Reginald E. Zelnik, eds. *The Free Speech Movement: Reflections on Berkeley in the 1960s* (2002). Perspectives on this key moment of emerging student radicalism.

Robert Dallek, *An Unfinished Life: John F. Kennedy, 1917–1963* (2003). Carefully researched, balanced treatment.

Gareth Davies, *From Opportunity to Entitlement: The Transformation and Decline of Great Society Liberalism* (1999). How Lyndon Johnson's program went wrong.

Betty Friedan, *The Feminine Mystique* (1963). Pioneering liberal-feminist exploration of the plight of middle-class women.

George C. Herring, *America's Longest War: The United States and Vietnam, 1950–1975*, 4th ed. (2001). A balanced overview of the war.

Mark Kurlansky, *1968: The Year That Rocked the World* (2003). A readable survey of global unrest.

Howell Raines, *My Soul Is Rested: Movement Days in the Deep South Remembered* (1977). A moving collection of interviews that vividly re-create the struggle against segregation.

Who, What?

John F. Kennedy 927
Richard Nixon 928
Martin Luther King Jr. 930
George Wallace 932
Lyndon Johnson 935
Fannie Lou Hamer 941
Black Panthers 949
Mario Savio 950
Betty Friedan 952
Sit-ins 924
Participatory democracy 927
Flexible response 932
War on Poverty 937
Limited war 943

Review Questions

1. How did the new liberalism differ from the liberalism of the New Deal and the Fair Deal? How did the new conservatism differ from the old?
2. Compare and contrast the New Frontier and the Great Society. Did their goals differ?
3. Why was the civil rights movement able to attain its major goals by the mid-1960s?

>> Timeline >>

▼ 1955–56
Montgomery, Alabama, bus boycott

▼ 1957
Soviet *Sputnik* satellite launch

▼ 1960
Greensboro, North Carolina, lunch-counter sit-ins
Sharon Statement
John F. Kennedy elected president

▼ 1961
First U.S. suborbital space flight, by Alan Shepard
Freedom Rides

▼ 1962
Port Huron Statement
Integration of University of Mississippi
Cuban Missile Crisis

▼ 1963
Birmingham, Alabama, civil rights protests
Civil rights march on Washington, DC
Assassination of John F. Kennedy

▼ 1964
Civil Rights Act of 1964

4. How did the United States fight the cold war in the 1960s? Was America winning by the end of the decade?
5. Compare liberal and radical feminism. Were these movements incompatible with each other?
6. Compare the Black Power movement, the New Left, and the counterculture. Did any of these want radical change for the United States?

Websites

Free Speech Movement Digital Archive, from the Bancroft Library of the University of California (http://bancroft.berkeley.edu/FSM/), offers a wealth of documents and other resources for studying student activism on the Berkeley campus.

The Lyndon Baines Johnson Library and Museum website (http://www.lbjlib.utexas.edu/) includes many primary sources, including speeches, photographs, oral histories, national-security documents, audio, and video.

The National Security Archive of George Washington University (http://www.gwu.edu/~nsarchiv/) features excellent collections on the Cuban Missile and Berlin crises.

The Vietnam Center and Archive website, maintained by Texas Tech University (http://vietnam.ttu.edu/index.php), includes many oral histories of the war.

The online Voices of Civil Rights exhibit of the Library of Congress (http://www.loc.gov/exhibits/civilrights/) includes words and images of the African American, Chicano, and Native American struggles of the 1960s.

For further review materials and resource information, please visit www.oup.com/us/ofthepeople

Lyndon Johnson's "War on Poverty"
Free Speech Movement
Tonkin Gulf incidents
Lyndon Johnson's landslide election as president

▼ 1965
U.S. escalation of Vietnam War
Voting Rights Act of 1965

Water Quality Act
Watts race riot

▼ 1966
National Organization for Women (NOW)

▼ 1967
Air Quality Act
Stop the Draft Week

▼ 1968
Tet Offensive in Vietnam
Assassinations of Martin Luther King Jr. and Robert F. Kennedy
Richard Nixon elected president

▼ 1975
Surrender of South Vietnam to North Vietnam

Common Threads 

>> How did economic problems continue to shape American life from the 1960s to the 1970s?

>> Why did liberalism continue to influence politics in the 1970s?

>> How did a sense of limits drive Richard Nixon's foreign and domestic policies?

>> Did American society become more democratic in the 1970s?

>> What were the ways the Vietnam syndrome would affect the United States after the 1970s?

Living with Less
1968–1980

AMERICAN PORTRAIT

>> "Fighting Shirley Chisholm"

At the end of the 1960s, Shirley Chisholm, an African American congresswoman from Brooklyn, New York, worried about her country. Amid the upheaval of the Great Society, the United States "sometimes seemed to be poised on the brink of racial and class war." Blacks, women, the poor, and the young demanded change, but the political system refused to meet their needs. "Our representative democracy is not working," Chisholm declared. "It is ruled by a small group of old men."

It was not in Chisholm's nature to give in. Born to working-class West Indian parents in Brooklyn, she had pushed her way to a master's degree and a career as an educator. Running as "Fighting Shirley Chisholm," she won election to Congress from her poor, predominantly black and Puerto Rican district in 1968. In January 1972, she became the first black and first female candidate for the Democratic presidential nomination. "You've never had anyone looking like me running for President," Chisholm declared. "Other kinds of people can steer the ship of state besides white men."

Chisholm's campaign continued the 1960s battle for rights. Chisholm wanted to create a coalition of African Americans, women, and the young "to get their share of the American dream and participate in the decision-making process that governs our lives."

Chisholm campaigned hard in several primaries. But with little money and organization, she had little chance. Chisholm had to fight for equal time on television. Black male politicians withheld their support. Black voters wondered whether an African American could really win. Her female and black supporters squabbled. The Chisholm campaign ended in defeat in California.

Chisholm's daring presidential candidacy enhanced her reputation. In November, she won reelection to Congress with a huge majority. But she was worn down. "I am tired," she admitted. "I am tired of fighting, fighting, fighting all the time." Still, Chisholm did not regret her presidential bid. "I ran for the Presidency in order to crack a little more of the ice which has congealed to nearly immobilize our political system and demoralize people," she explained. "I ran for the Presidency, despite hopeless odds, to demonstrate sheer will and refusal to accept the status quo."

Chisholm's failed campaign was part of a collision between Americans' aspirations for equality and new political, economic, and cultural realities. As the struggle for rights and opportunities expanded in the 1970s, the nation's economy and global influence continued to weaken. Without enough oil and industrial jobs, the United States no longer seemed a land of unlimited possibilities. Americans worried whether the nation could afford to meet everyone's needs in an age of dwindling resources. As a magazine concluded, the American people were "Learning to Live with Less."

The result was not the "racial and class war" that Chisholm feared. But neither did the liberal Great Society give way to a stable new order dominated by one party or ideology. Instead, workers, employers, politicians, and families struggled with the consequences of limited resources and power. While Americans puzzled over the relationship between the economy and government and between the nation and the world, the political system broke down in scandal and failure. ●

OUTLINE

A New Crisis: Economic Decline

During the social, political, and military crises of the 1960s, Americans had largely taken the economy for granted. Prosperous and growing, the United States seemed destined to remain the world's preeminent economic power. But the economy had faltered as the Great Society came apart. By the 1970s, it was in crisis. The failings of business, government, and economists, a shortage of oil, intensifying foreign competition, and the multinational strategies of giant corporations combined to weaken the foundations of prosperity. By the end of the 1970s, the United States seemed to be in economic decline.

Weakness at Home

There were signs of economic weakness almost everywhere in the 1970s. Although the economy continued to grow, corporate profits and workers' productivity fell off. Unemployment increased; inflation, which usually dropped when unemployment rose, also increased. At best, the economy seemed stagnant. The unprecedented combination of high unemployment and high inflation led to the coining of a new word—stagflation—to describe the nation's economic predicament (see Table 29–1).

Table 29–1 Stagflation in the 1970s

Year	Inflation % Change	Unemployment % Change	Combined* % Change
1970	5.9	4.9	10.8
1971	4.3	5.9	10.2
1972	3.3	5.6	8.9
1973	6.2	4.9	11.1
1974	11.0	5.6	16.6
1975	9.1	8.5	17.6
1976	5.8	7.7	13.5
1977	6.5	7.1	13.6
1978	7.7	6.1	13.8
1979	11.3	5.8	17.1
1980	13.5	7.1	20.6

*"Combined" means annual percentage changes of inflation and unemployment.

Source: *Statistical Abstract of the United States*, 1984, pp. 375–76, 463; tables 624–25, 760. (1971 inflation data from *Statistical Abstract*, 1973, p. 348, table 569.)

Corporations were partially responsible for the weak state of the economy. Corporate leaders had tended to maximize short-term profits at the cost of the long-term health of their companies. Some companies had not plowed enough of their earnings back into research, development, and new equipment. As a result, some American products seemed less innovative and reliable. Detroit's automobiles, so attractive and advanced in the 1950s, now struck consumers as unglamorous, inefficient, and poorly made. Ford's new Pinto sedan had to be recalled because its fuel tank was prone to explode.

Long an emblem of security and stability, corporations themselves appeared as vulnerable as the Pinto. In 1970, the Penn Central Railroad became the largest corporation in American history to go bankrupt. That year, only massive federal aid saved Lockheed Aircraft from going under as well.

The federal government also played a part in the nation's economic predicament. Massive federal spending had stimulated the economy from the 1940s to the 1960s but did not have the same effect in the 1970s. Some analysts claimed that Washington had diverted too much of the nation's talent and resources from the private sector to military projects during the cold war. In addition, the government's huge expenditures for the Vietnam War promoted inflation.

Economists did not give federal policy makers much help. In the 1960s, liberal economists had been confident that they understood the secret of maintaining prosperity. The novel problem of stagflation left them baffled. "The rules of economics," admitted the chairman of the Federal Reserve, "are not working quite the way they used to."

The Energy Crisis

An emerging energy crisis intensified economic problems. By 1974, the nation had to import over a third of its oil from foreign countries, particularly from the Middle East. The energy needs of the United States and other western countries empowered the Organization of the Petroleum Exporting Countries (OPEC), a group of third world nations that had joined together to get higher prices for their oil. In October 1973, war broke out between Israel and a coalition of Arab nations including Egypt and Syria. Arab members of OPEC refused to send petroleum to the United States and other nations that supported Israel in the conflict. OPEC soon raised oil prices nearly 400 percent.

The effect of the oil shortage spread well beyond gas stations. In some states, truck drivers blockaded highways to protest the high cost of fuel and low speed limits. Lack of fuel grounded some airline flights. Heating oil for homes and businesses was also in short supply. Communities opened shelters for people who could not afford to heat their homes. Although the Arabs ended the oil embargo in March 1974, the underlying energy problem remained.

The Energy Crisis Motorists crowd around an open gas station, New York City, December 1973.

Competition Abroad

Weakened by trouble at home, the United States was all the more vulnerable to increasingly tough competition from abroad. Thanks to American aid after World War II, Japan and Western European countries now had efficient, up-to-date industries. By the 1970s, these nations rivaled the United States, not only abroad, but even in the American market.

The rise of Japan was the most dramatic of these developments. For decades, Americans had derided Japanese goods. Yet by the 1970s, Japan's modern factories turned out high-quality products. Japanese televisions and other electronic goods filled American homes. Japanese cars—small, well made, and fuel efficient—attracted American buyers worried about the high price of gas.

Because of such competition, the United States fell back in the global economic race. In 1950, the nation had accounted for 40 percent of the value of all the goods and services produced around the world. By 1970 that figure was down to 23 percent. By the end of the 1970s, the United States imported more manufactured goods than it exported.

The Multinationals

Multinational corporations—firms with factories and other operations in several nations—played a key role in the economic crisis. Taking advantage of new technologies and lower trade barriers, corporations in the United States and Western Europe had moved aggressively into global markets after World War II. All told, multinationals accounted for about 15 percent of the world's annual gross product. The biggest multinationals had annual sales larger than the annual product of some countries.

AMERICA AND THE WORLD

>> Carl Gerstacker's Dream

In February 1972, Carl A. Gerstacker, chairman of the multinational Dow Chemical Company, confessed his secret fantasy to an audience of executives, economists, and policy makers at a White House conference. "I have long dreamed of buying an island owned by no nation," Gerstacker revealed. But this sober executive did not plan to escape to his island and enjoy a life of solitary primitive leisure. Instead, Gerstacker wanted to take Dow Chemical along. "If we were located on such truly neutral ground," he explained, "we could then really operate in the United States as U.S. citizens, in Japan as Japanese citizens and in Brazil as Brazilians rather than being governed in prime by the laws of the United States." The multinational would effectively be on its own, free to do as it pleased without interference from the U.S. government.

Gerstacker's audience probably did not wonder whether he had been working too hard lately. By the 1970s, the leaders of American multinationals felt surprisingly few ties to their home country. "We are not an American company," a U.S. oil executive told a congressional committee. Explaining why most of his company's top executives came from foreign countries, an executive vice president of Bendix responded that "nationality is unimportant." So unattached to the United States or any other country, multinational leaders did not believe their companies should let patriotism interfere with business. "It is not proper for an international corporation to put the welfare of any country in which it does business above that of any other," a spokesman for Dow's competitor, Union Carbide, sanctimoniously observed. As Carl Gerstacker concluded, giant corporations were becoming not so much multinational or international as "anational" and "nationless."

Multinational leaders seemed to prefer a world with no nations at all. Eager to create a unified global economy, these executives felt that governments only got in the way. They imposed tariffs on exports and imports, regulated and limited trade, taxed profits, dictated working conditions, nationalized resources, and started wars. "The world's political structures are completely obsolete," fumed Jacques Maisonrouge, a French-born senior vice president of IBM. "They have not changed in at least a hundred years and are woefully out of tune with technological progress." Nation-states represented the past; multinationals, creating new technologies and serving the planet, represented the future. José Béjarano, vice president of the Latin American division of Xerox, declared, "The multinational corporation today is a force that can serve global needs of mankind far better than the medieval concept of nation states." Of course, the heads of the multinationals conveniently forgot how often their firms had turned to the U.S. government for diplomatic and military support when other nations had threatened their investments over the decades.

Few Americans shared the antinational vision of men like Béjarano. Around the world, the United States and other nation-states, fueled by the intense patriotism of their citizens, were not about to disappear—or leave the multinationals alone. As Gerstacker acknowledged, U.S. tax laws made it impossible for Dow Chemical to move its headquarters to his island paradise. For all their impact on the world around them, the multinational executives were ahead of their time. But they could fantasize. With the fervent certainty of a prophet in a crowd of unbelievers, John J. Powers, president of the drug company Pfizer, insisted a unified global economy "is no idealistic pipe dream but a hard-headed prediction." Time would tell.

U.S. firms made up the majority of the largest multinationals in the 1970s. As Americans struggled, U.S. multinationals still earned large profits because their overseas units were often more profitable than their domestic operations. Not surprisingly, these American firms rapidly expanded abroad. In 1957, just 9 percent of American investments went abroad; by 1972, the figure had reached 25 percent.

The multinationals' most controversial foreign investment was the transfer of manufacturing from the United States to nations with lower wages and less restrictive labor laws. As corporations shifted production to plants just over the Mexican border or to facilities in Asia, American plants closed with stunning job losses. The combination of overseas production and foreign competition was devastating. In 1954, U.S. companies had made 75 percent of the world's televisions. Twenty years later, U.S. companies produced less than 25 percent—and almost all of that production took place in Mexico and overseas.

Responding to critics, multinational executives argued that investment abroad increased jobs and prosperity in the United States. Capital invested in Mexico and Asia came back home, the executives insisted, as dividends to stockholders and tax payments to the government. It was unclear whether the multinationals or their critics were right.

The Impact of Decline

Economic decline began to reshape life in the United States in the 1970s. It seemed as if the Industrial Revolution was being reversed. As factories closed, Americans witnessed the deindustrialization of their country. Huge steel plants, the symbol of American industrial might, stood empty. These developments intensified the trend, first evident in the 1950s, toward a service-centered economy. In the 1970s, most new jobs were in the sales and retail sectors. The United States, a union official lamented, was turning into "a nation of hamburger stands."

For workers, the consequences of deindustrialization were demoralizing. Heavy industry had been the stronghold of the labor movement. Organized labor lost members, power, and influence. By the late 1970s, less than one in four workers belonged to a union.

The shift away from unionized industrial jobs eroded workers' incomes. After rising from the 1950s into the 1960s, workers' spendable income began to drop. To keep up, more and more women took full-time jobs outside the home: the percentage of women in the workforce, 36 percent in 1960, rose to 50 percent in 1980—the highest level in American history to that time. Many Americans could not find work, however. As the huge baby boom generation came of age, the economy did not produce enough jobs. The unemployment rate, which had dipped as low as 2.8 percent in 1969, jumped up to a high of 9 percent only six years later.

Economic decline accelerated the transformation of America's regions. The energy crisis and deindustrialization sped up the shift of people and power from north to south and east to west (see Map 29–1). With its cold, snowy winters, the North was especially vulnerable to the oil embargo and higher energy prices. America's Snowbelt now seemed a less attractive place to live and do business. In the 1970s, the sight of empty, decaying factories made the Northeast and the Midwest America's "Rustbelt."

AMERICAN LANDSCAPE

>> Youngstown, Ohio

For more than 75 years, workers made steel in the open-hearth furnaces at the Campbell Works of the Youngstown Sheet and Tube Company. Opened just after the start of the twentieth century, the huge mill was one of the plants that gave the community of Youngstown, in northeast Ohio, its reputation as a "Steel City." In exchange for hard labor, the Campbell Works also gave generations of Youngstown's workers a chance for prosperity. "Youngstown," a resident observed, "was a place in which the American Dream seemed to have come true for many working-class families."

The dream came to a sudden end in 1977. By then, the mill was an inefficient "antique" that made steel more slowly and expensively than new mills. On September 19 the parent company of Youngstown Sheet and Tube, Lykes Corporation, announced it was closing down the Campbell Works and transferring some production to a new facility in Illinois. As many as 5,000 workers would lose their jobs. Once a symbol of American industrial might, the Campbell Works had instantly become a symbol of deindustrialization and decline on that "Black Monday" in 1977.

The announcement of the shutdown stunned the mill's employees. To many, it was like another Pearl Harbor. Some workers realized right away that their way of life was gone. On the way home, they threw their hard hats and work boots into the Mahoning River.

Although many workers hoped that the Campbell Works could be saved, the Lykes Corporation refused to reopen the mill. The company claimed that the low price of foreign steel, especially from Japan, and the high cost of U.S. environmental regulations made it impossible to operate the mill at a profit. A coalition of workers and churches tried to buy the mill, but their plan fell through. Congress and President Jimmy Carter, believing the Campbell Works was too inefficient to save, refused to help. Carter, an angry worker grumbled, "ought to run for president of Japan."

In the end, there was no way to save the Campbell Works. The workers lost their jobs, and much more. They felt cut off from their past and their future. "Our fathers worked here and our grandfathers worked here," said a union official. "Now I face the prospect of this turning into a ghost town." The optimistic future of the American Dream had disappeared. "They used to tell us: 'Get out of high school, get a job in a mill and you're fixed for life,'" said a steelworker. "Now I know better."

Facing such bleak prospects, a quarter of the labor force at Campbell Works moved away from Youngstown. Many of them went to the booming Sunbelt. About half of the workers stayed on in Youngstown and found new jobs. Many of those jobs did not pay nearly as well as work at Youngstown Sheet and Tube. The remaining quarter of the workforce also stayed on but found no work at all.

Other Youngstown residents also suffered because of the closing of the Campbell Works. Business dropped in the taverns where steelworkers had gone for a drink after the job. Other stores missed the steelworkers' patronage. "It will kill our business," a Youngstown store owner lamented.

The shutdown at Youngstown Sheet and Tube was just the beginning of deindustrialization in Youngstown. By 1980, the "Steel City" was dotted with the decaying hulks of empty mills. Other communities feared they would be next. "There are going to be a few more Youngstowns before it's over," an economist predicted.

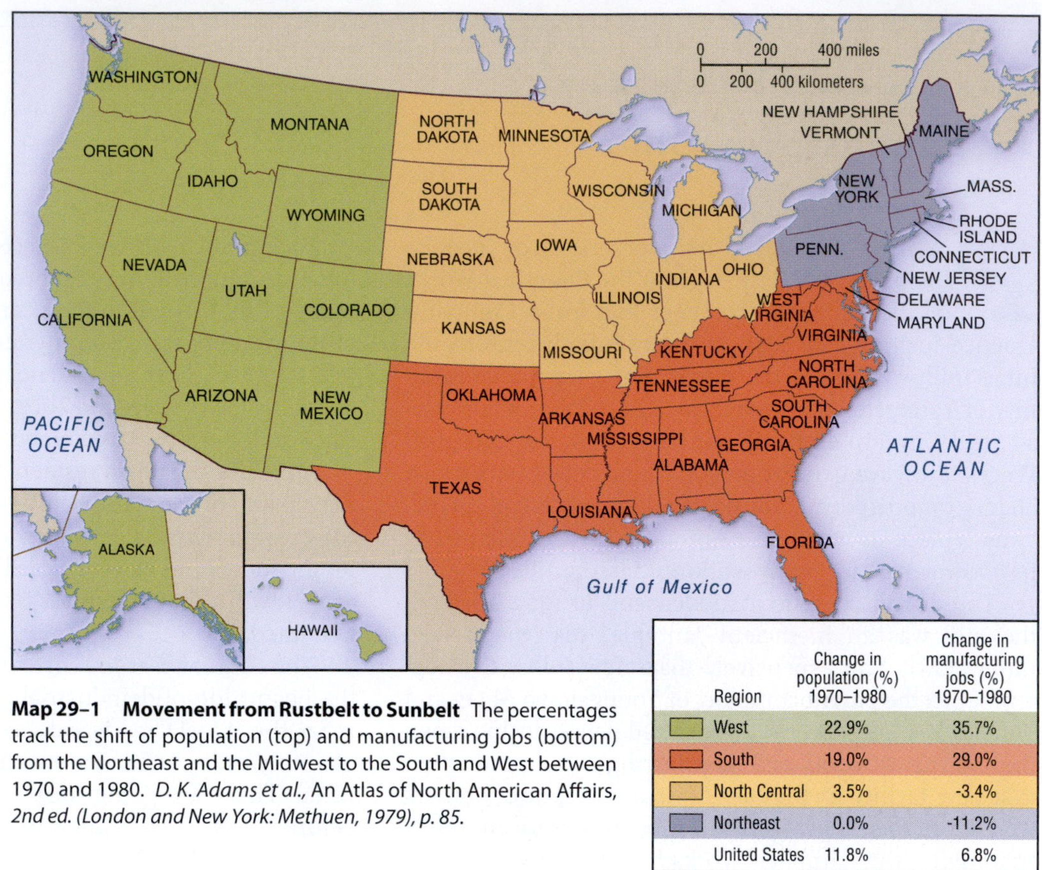

Region	Change in population (%) 1970–1980	Change in manufacturing jobs (%) 1970–1980
West	22.9%	35.7%
South	19.0%	29.0%
North Central	3.5%	-3.4%
Northeast	0.0%	-11.2%
United States	11.8%	6.8%

Map 29–1 Movement from Rustbelt to Sunbelt The percentages track the shift of population (top) and manufacturing jobs (bottom) from the Northeast and the Midwest to the South and West between 1970 and 1980. *D. K. Adams et al.,* An Atlas of North American Affairs, *2nd ed. (London and New York: Methuen, 1979), p. 85.*

Fleeing deindustrialization, many northerners migrated south to the band of states ranging from Florida to California. As the Sunbelt boomed, farms turned into suburbs, and cities such as Orlando, Houston, Phoenix, and San Diego exploded in size. If anything, Texas and the southwestern states, rich in oil and natural gas reserves, profited from the energy crisis. The Sunbelt was home to new high-technology businesses: aerospace firms, electronics companies, and defense contractors. The Sunbelt was also at the cutting edge of the service economy, with its emphasis on leisure and consumption. More retirees moved to Florida than to any other state. Tourists flocked to the original Disneyland in California and the new Disney World in Florida. They gambled their money in Las Vegas.

> All I want is my damn job back.
>
> MARY FARMER KINNEY, a laid-off African American autoworker in Hamtramck, Michigan, 1979.

Confronting Decline: Nixon's Strategy

Richard Nixon was the first president to confront the decline of America's prosperity and power. He recognized that the failure of the war in Vietnam marked the end of America's cold war pretensions. He accepted, too, that the American economy had weakened. Despite his long opposition to Communism and the New Deal, Nixon was a pragmatist, open to new realities and approaches as he coped with the nation's problems.

A New Foreign Policy

> . . I think of what happened to Greece and Rome . . . great civilizations of the past, as they have become wealthy, as they lost their will to live, to improve, they then have become subject to the decadence which eventually destroys a civilization. The United States is now reaching that period.
>
> RICHARD NIXON, 1971

The president and his national security advisor, Henry Kissinger, still regarded Communism as a menace and saw the cold war rivalry between the United States and the Soviet Union as the defining reality of the modern world. However, Nixon and Kissinger understood that the relative decline of American power dictated a new approach to the cold war.

The twin pillars of the new foreign policy were the Nixon Doctrine and détente. In July 1969, the president announced that the United States "cannot—and will not—conceive all the plans, design all the programs, execute all the decisions and undertake all the defense of the free nations of the world." America would continue to provide a nuclear umbrella, but its allies would have to defend themselves against insurgencies and invasions. This Nixon Doctrine amounted to a repudiation of the Truman Doctrine, the 1947 promise "to support free peoples who are resisting attempted subjugation by armed minorities or by outside pressures" (see Chapter 26).

The United States also pursued a new relationship with the Soviet Union and the People's Republic of China. Nixon and Kissinger wanted to lessen the cost of America's rivalry with these two Communist nuclear powers. Separate agreements with the Soviet Union and China would, the American leaders hoped, keep those two nations from combining forces against the United States. Nixon and Kissinger therefore worked to establish détente, the relaxation of tensions.

At the start of Nixon's presidency, the United States had not recognized the legitimacy of the People's Republic of China. Instead, America supported the Communists' bitter foes, the Nationalist Chinese regime on Taiwan. In February 1972, Nixon became the first American president to go to mainland China. He gave the Chinese leaders what they most wanted—a promise that the United States would eventually withdraw its troops from Taiwan. The two sides also made clear that they opposed any Soviet attempt to dominate Asia.

Nixon's trip brought American policy in line with the reality of the 1970s and underscored the gradual ending of anti-Communist hysteria back home in America. As Nixon intended, the trip also left the Soviets with the frightening possibility of a Chinese-American alliance.

Architects of Détente President Richard Nixon and his National Security Advisor, Henry Kissinger, 1972.

Détente at the Great Wall of China, 1972 President Nixon, with his wife Pat, became the first American president to visit mainland China.

Nixon did not want a confrontation with the Soviets, the only power that could destroy America with nuclear weapons. The United States no longer had clear military superiority. Instead, the president sought détente. Above all, he wanted the Soviets to agree to limit their long-range or strategic nuclear arsenals. The Soviets also wished to reduce the expense and danger of the cold war and to counter Nixon's overture to the Chinese. Moreover, they badly needed American grain to help feed their own people.

Under these circumstances, the two sides began talks on the Strategic Arms Limitation Treaty (SALT I) in 1969. In May 1972, three months after his trip to China, Nixon became the first American president to travel to Moscow, where he signed the SALT treaty, limiting for five years the number of each nation's nuclear missiles. An Anti–Ballistic Missile (ABM) treaty sharply limited the number of defensive missiles that the two sides could deploy. Although they did not stop the arms race, the ABM and SALT treaties symbolized the American and Soviet agreement that "there is no alternative to . . . peaceful coexistence."

Ending the Vietnam War

The Nixon administration sought better relations with the Soviet Union and the People's Republic of China in part to help end the Vietnam War. Nixon and Kissinger hoped the Soviets and the Chinese would pressure the North Vietnamese to accept a peace agreement. The president needed such an agreement. Nixon knew the United States could not win the Vietnam War. Meanwhile, the ongoing conflict divided the American people and undermined American prestige and power around the world. But Nixon did not want the United States to look weak.

To appease public opinion, Nixon began to bring American soldiers home in 1969. Without those soldiers, he had a hard time persuading North Vietnam to accept the continued existence of South Vietnam. The president attempted to resolve this dilemma with a policy known as "Vietnamization," or encouraging the South Vietnamese to take over their own defense. However, the South Vietnamese military alone could not beat back the Communists.

Accordingly, Nixon turned to U.S. airpower to support South Vietnamese troops and intimidate the North Vietnamese. In March 1969, he authorized B-52 raids on North Vietnamese sanctuaries in Cambodia. Because bombing this neutral country might outrage American and world opinion, the president kept the raids secret. However, the Cambodian operation did not force North Vietnam to make peace. Secret negotiations between Henry Kissinger and North Vietnamese diplomats also went nowhere.

Meanwhile, Nixon's actions angered many Americans. News of the secret bombings leaked out. In October, millions of Americans participated in Moratorium Day, a dramatic break from business as usual, to protest the war. In November, more than 250,000 people staged a "March Against Death" in Washington. That month, Americans learned about one of the most troubling episodes of the war. On March 16, 1968, United States soldiers had shot and killed between 200 and 500 unarmed South Vietnamese women, children, and old men in the hamlet of My Lai. This atrocity led to the 1970 court-martial and eventual conviction of Lieutenant William Calley Jr. for mass murder.

The Vietnam War Comes to Cambodia Cambodian landscape devastated by the 1969 bombings that President Nixon tried to keep secret.

Demonstrations and public opinion did not stop the president from using violence to force a peace agreement. When General Lon Nol, the new pro-American leader of Cambodia, appealed for United States aid to stop a Communist insurgency, a joint United States–South Vietnamese force invaded Cambodia to look for North Vietnamese troops in April 1970. The Cambodian invasion produced turmoil in the United States. Students demonstrated on campuses across the country. On May 4, National Guard troops fired at an unarmed crowd of protestors at Kent State University in Ohio. Four students died. Ten days later, state police killed two African American students at Jackson State College in Mississippi. These deaths intensified the outrage over the invasion of Cambodia. Students went out on strike at about 450 campuses.

Some Americans, angered by the demonstrating college students, mobilized in support of the president and the war. In New York City, construction workers attacked student demonstrators. "The country is virtually on the edge of a spiritual—and perhaps physical—breakdown," New York's mayor lamented. "For the first time in a century, we are not sure there is a future for America."

As American troop withdrawals continued, the war and the peace negotiations dragged on. Meanwhile, the *New York Times* began publishing the so-called Pentagon Papers, a secret government history of the American involvement in Vietnam. The documents, which made clear that the Johnson administration had misled the American people, further undermined support for the war. The Nixon administration tried unsuccessfully to persuade the Supreme Court to block publication of the papers.

Unable to stop the publication of the Pentagon Papers or secure a peace agreement, Nixon stepped up efforts to pressure North Vietnam into a settlement. When the North Vietnamese army swept across the border into South Vietnam in March 1972, the president struck back with Operation Linebacker, an aerial attack against North Vietnam. When negotiations stalled again, the president intensified the air raids in December. On January 27, 1973, negotiators signed a peace agreement in Paris. For the United States, at least, the Vietnam War was over.

Nixon had promised "peace with honor" in Vietnam. But the agreement did not guarantee the survival of our South Vietnamese ally. The cease-fire came at a heavy cost. Twenty thousand Americans and more than six hundred thousand North and South Vietnamese soldiers had died since Nixon took office in 1969. The number of civilian casualties will never be known. Nixon had ended U.S. participation in the Vietnam War, but the president's critics asked whether four more years of fighting had really been necessary when the result was such a flawed peace agreement.

Chile and the Middle East

Détente, a practical accommodation with Soviet power, did not mean that the Nixon administration accepted the rise of potentially hostile regimes around the world. To stop the spread of socialism and Communism, Nixon, like the presidents before him, was willing to subvert a democratically elected government and tolerate an authoritarian substitute. In 1970, he ordered the CIA to block the election of Salvador Allende, a Marxist, as president of Chile. Allende was elected anyway. "I don't see why we need to stand by and watch a country go communist due to the irresponsibility of its own people," Kissinger fumed. "The issues are much too important for the Chilean voters to be left to decide for themselves." The CIA then helped destabilize Allende's regime by aiding right-wing parties, driving up the price of bread, and encouraging demonstrations. When a military coup deposed Allende in 1973, the United States denied responsibility and offered financial assistance to the new military dictator, General Augusto Pinochet.

In the Middle East, the Nixon administration also displayed both its continuing hostility to Communism and its inability to shape events decisively. During the Six-Day War in 1967, Israel had defeated Egyptian and Syrian forces and occupied territory belonging to Egypt, Syria, and Jordan. Seeking revenge, Egypt and Syria attacked Israel in October 1973, on Yom Kippur, the holiest day of the Jewish calendar. When the United States sent critical supplies to Israel, Arab countries responded with the oil embargo. Meanwhile, the Soviets supplied the Arabs and pressed for a role in the region. Determined to keep out the Soviet Union, Nixon put American nuclear forces on alert. Kissinger mediated between the combatants, who agreed to pull back their troops in January 1974. Although the embargo ended, American weakness was obvious. Supporting Israel, the United States still needed the Arabs' oil. Nixon and Kissinger held back the Soviet Union, but they could not bring peace to the Middle East.

Taming Big Government

The problem of decline, imaginatively addressed in Nixon's foreign policy, proved more difficult to handle at home. Nixon took office with the conventional Republican domestic goals of taming big government. He wanted the federal government to balance its budget and shed some of its power.

So, Nixon's administration cut spending for some programs, including defense. The fate of the space program epitomized the new budgetary realities. On July 20, 1969, a lunar landing module touched down on the moon. As astronaut Neil Armstrong set foot on the surface, he proclaimed, "That's one small step for man, one giant leap for mankind." The United States had beaten the Soviets to the moon. This triumph suggested that there was still no limit to what Americans could do.

There were, however, firm limits to what the space program could do. The administration slashed NASA's budget.

In 1969, the president called for a New Federalism, in which Washington would return "a greater share of control to state and local governments and to the people." Three years later, the administration persuaded Congress to pass a revenue-sharing plan that allowed state and local governments to spend funds collected by the federal government.

Despite his commitment to Republican ideology, Nixon took the same pragmatic approach to domestic problems that he did to foreign affairs. Although the president pushed for the New Federalism, he left popular New Deal and Great Society programs largely intact. Despite his budget cuts, the government kept spending vast amounts of money. By 1971, the cost of big government, combined with the unsettled economy, had produced a huge, un-Republican budget deficit.

The president did try to reform the federal welfare system put in place by the New Deal. Like many Republican conservatives, Nixon believed that welfare made the federal bureaucracy too large and the poor too dependent. During the president's first term, his administration tried to replace the largest federal welfare program, Aid to Families with Dependent Children, with a controversial system inspired by presidential aide Daniel Patrick Moynihan, a Harvard sociologist. Moynihan's Family Assistance Plan would have provided poor families with a guaranteed minimum annual income, but it also would have required the heads of poor households to accept any jobs available. Opposed by both liberals and conservatives, the program failed to pass Congress.

Meanwhile, the Nixon administration went along with several liberal initiatives that expanded the government's regulatory powers. By the end of the 1960s, many Americans worried that corporations did not protect workers, consumers, or the environment. A grassroots environmental movement grew rapidly, particularly on college campuses. On April 22, 1970, tens of millions of Americans celebrated the first Earth Day. Echoing anti–Vietnam War activism, they staged teach-ins, demonstrations, and cleanup campaigns. "If you care about this mess," one marcher's sign read, "why not stop it?" After this great initial turnout, Earth Day became an annual event.

Liberals in Congress responded to popular opinion by establishing three new federal regulatory agencies: the Environmental Protection Agency (EPA), the Occupational Safety and Health Administration (OSHA), and the Consumer Product Safety Commission. These agencies considerably enhanced the government's power over corporations, as did a series of measures to safeguard coastlines and endangered species and to limit the use of pesticides, the strip-mining of coal, and the pollution of air and water.

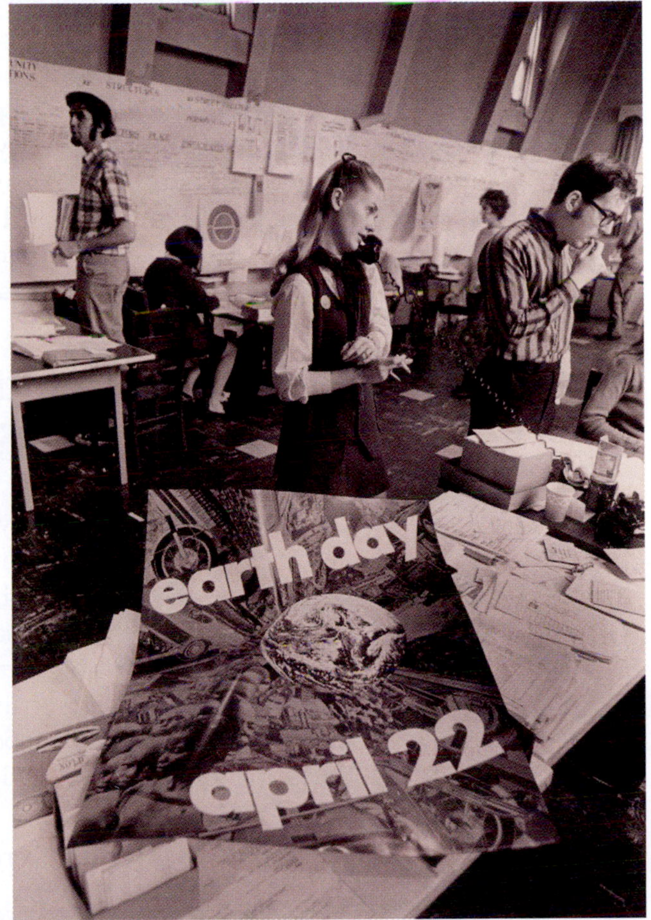

The Grassroots Environmental Movement Organizing the first Earth Day, April 22, 1970.

An Uncertain Economic Policy

Nixon, like most Republicans, believed government should not interfere much in the economy. But high inflation, rising unemployment, and falling corporate profits tested the president's commitment to Republican orthodoxy. He was unable to persuade business to control price increases and organized labor to limit wage demands.

Meanwhile, the U.S. dollar was in crisis. Since the Bretton Woods conference during World War II (see Chapter 25), many other nations had tied the value of their own currencies to the dollar. The value of the dollar, in turn, had been supported by the U.S. commitment to give an ounce of gold in return for 35 dollars. The U.S. commitment to the gold standard had stabilized the international financial system and helped spur worldwide economic development for more than two decades. But by the 1970s, the United States' weakening economy had undermined the dollar: strong European economies had too many dollars and too little confidence in the United States, and the U.S. government didn't have enough gold. If other countries demanded gold for their dollars, Washington would be unable to pay and panic would follow.

Confronting inflation, monetary crisis, and economic weakness, Nixon announced his New Economic Policy in August 1971. To prevent the breakdown of the monetary system, the president took the United States off the gold standard by ending the exchange of gold for dollars. To strengthen U.S. producers against foreign competitors, Nixon lowered the value of the dollar and slapped new tariffs on imports; as a result, American goods would sell more cheaply abroad and foreign goods would cost more in the United States. To slow inflation, the president authorized a freeze on wages and prices.

The New Economic Policy did strengthen the international monetary system and help U.S. producers. But wage and price controls did not solve the underlying economic problems that caused inflation. The ongoing cost of the Vietnam War, along with the Arab oil embargo, continued to drive up prices. Deindustrialization continued, too. Nixon and his advisers had no domestic counterpart to détente.

Refusing to Settle for Less: Struggles for Rights

Despite the troubled economy, many Americans, like Shirley Chisholm, refused to settle for less. In the late 1960s and 1970s, African Americans and women continued their struggles for the rights that they had long been denied. Their example inspired other disadvantaged groups to demand recognition. Mexican Americans, Native Americans, and gays and lesbians organized and demonstrated for their causes. But other Americans, worried about preserving their own advantages in an era of limited resources, were often unwilling to support these new demands for rights and opportunities. At times, the result was almost the "racial and class war" that Chisholm dreaded.

African Americans' Struggle for Racial Justice

As the civil rights struggle continued, attention focused on two relatively new and controversial means of promoting racial equality—affirmative action and mandatory school busing. First ordered by the Johnson administration, affirmative action required businesses, universities, and other institutions receiving federal money to provide opportunities for women and nonwhites. Supporters viewed the policy as a way to make up for past and present discrimination. Opponents argued that affirmative action was itself a form of discrimination reducing opportunities for whites, particularly white men.

Somewhat surprisingly, Nixon, despite his commitment to limited government, generally supported affirmative action. His administration developed the Philadelphia Plan, which encouraged the construction industry to meet targets for hiring minority workers. In 1978, the Supreme Court offered qualified support for affirmative action with its decision in *Regents of the University of California v. Allan Bakke*. The justices ruled that the medical school of the University of California at Davis could not deny admission to Bakke, a white applicant who had better grades and test scores than some minority applicants accepted by the institution. While the court barred schools from using fixed admissions quotas for different racial groups, it did allow educational institutions to use race as an admissions criterion. By the end of the 1970s, affirmative action had become an important means of increasing diversity in schools and other institutions.

School busing was more controversial than affirmative action. By the late 1960s, the Supreme Court had become impatient with delays in integrating the nation's schools. Even in the North, where there had been no de jure or legal segregation, there was still extensive de facto segregation. In *Swann v. Charlotte-Mecklenburg Board of Education* in 1971, the court upheld the mandatory busing of thousands of children to desegregate schools in the Charlotte, North Carolina, area. But many Americans opposed busing, because they did not want integration or did not want children taken out of neighborhood schools.

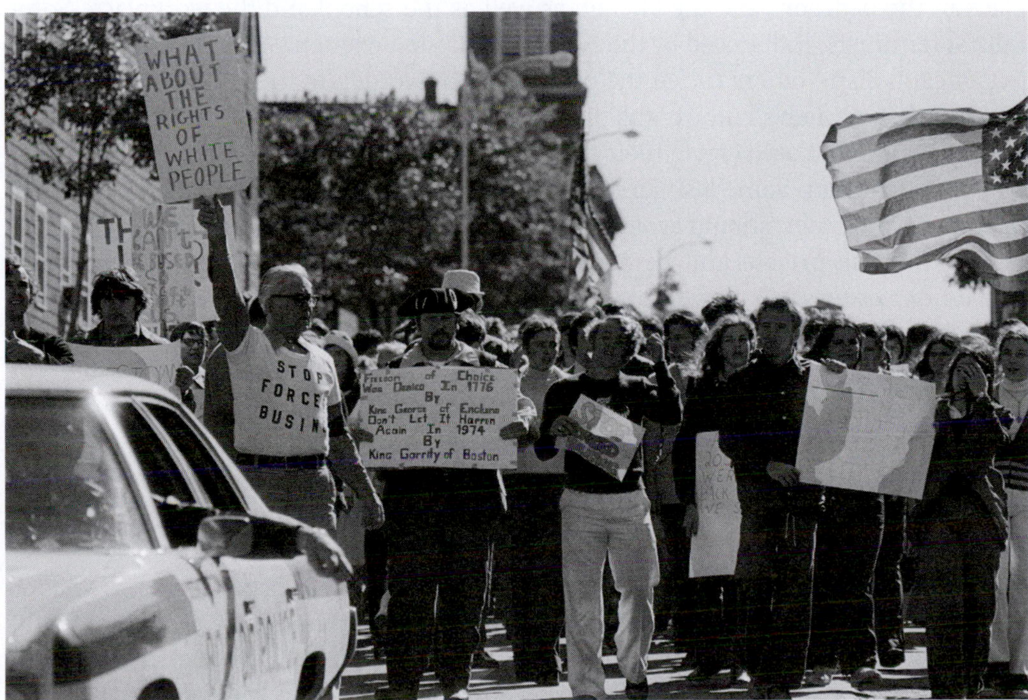

Protesting Mandatory Busing White demonstrators, some dressed in colonial costume, march against court-ordered school busing in Boston in September 1970.

Nixon sided with the opponents of busing. Privately ordering his aides to enforce busing less vigorously, the president publicly called for a "moratorium" on new busing plans. Some communities implemented busing peacefully. Others faced protest and turmoil. In 1974, a federal court ordered busing in Boston. When the white-dominated local school committee refused to comply, a federal judge imposed a busing plan on the community. Working-class and lower-middle-class whites formed Restore Our Alienated Rights (ROAR) and other organizations to protest plans to bus students between the predominantly African American neighborhood of Roxbury and the largely Irish American neighborhood of South Boston. In "Southie," whites taunted and injured black students. Although violence spread and continued through the fall, the busing plan went into effect. With busing and affirmative action, the civil rights movement seemed to have reached its limits: many Americans were unwilling to go any further to ensure racial equality.

Women's Liberation

By the 1970s, the movement for women's liberation was flourishing. Many women were coming together in "consciousness-raising" groups to discuss a broad range of issues in their lives. To commemorate the 50th anniversary of the ratification of the women's suffrage amendment to the Constitution, thousands marched in the Women's Strike for Equality on August 26, 1970.

The women's liberation movement, like the struggle for African American equality, was diverse. Liberal feminist groups, such as the National Organization for Women (NOW), concentrated on equal public opportunities for women. Radical feminists focused on a broader range of private and public issues. Oppression, they insisted, took place in the bedroom and the kitchen as well as the school and the workplace. Some radical feminists, influenced by the New Left, blamed women's plight on the inequalities of capitalism; others traced the oppression of women to men. Cultural feminists insisted that women's culture was different from and superior to male culture. They felt that women should create their own separate institutions rather than seek formal equality with men. Some lesbian feminists took this separatist logic one step further to argue that women should avoid heterosexual relationships.

Linking the private and personal with the public and political, the women's movement necessarily fought on many fronts. More women who married decided to keep their maiden names rather than adopt their husbands' surnames. Rather than identifying themselves by their marital status, many women abandoned the forms of address "Miss" or "Mrs." for "Ms." Women's liberation made its mark on the media. In 1972, Gloria Steinem began to publish the feminist magazine *Ms.* On television, popular sitcoms portrayed independent women. Some feminists condemned the availability of pornography, which, they argued, incited violence against women.

In the 1970s, feminists focused especially on three public issues—access to abortion, equal treatment in schools and workplaces, and passage of the equal rights amendment (ERA) to the Constitution. Long effectively outlawed, abortions were generally unavailable or unsafe. In *Roe v. Wade* in 1973, the Supreme Court ruled a Texas antiabortion law unconstitutional on the grounds that it violated the "right to

privacy" guaranteed by the Ninth and Fourteenth Amendments. With this decision, abortion began to become legal and widely available.

Like the civil rights movement, the women's movement demanded equal treatment in schools and workplaces. Women filed many complaints against discrimination by employers. At first reluctant, the Nixon administration moved to open up government employment to women and to press colleges and businesses to end discriminatory practices. In 1972, Congress approved Title IX of the Higher Education Act, which required schools and universities receiving federal funds to give equal opportunities to women and men in admissions, athletics, and other programs.

The women's movement also continued the longtime struggle to enact the ERA. "Equality of rights under the law," the amendment read, "shall not be denied or abridged by the United States or by any State on account of sex." In 1972 Congress passed the ERA. If 38 states had ratified the amendment within 7 years, it would have become law. But after 28 states had ratified within a year, the ERA met heavy opposition. To male critics, feminists were a "small band of braless bubbleheads" who suffered from "defeminization." Some women feared that equal rights would end their femininity and their protected legal status. Conservative activist Phyllis Schlafly organized an effective campaign against the ERA. Although more states ratified the amendment, some rescinded their votes and the ERA never became law.

The ERA's defeat underscored the challenges that the women's movement faced. Women still did not have full equality in American society. Nevertheless, women had more control over their bodies, more access to education, and more opportunity in the workplace.

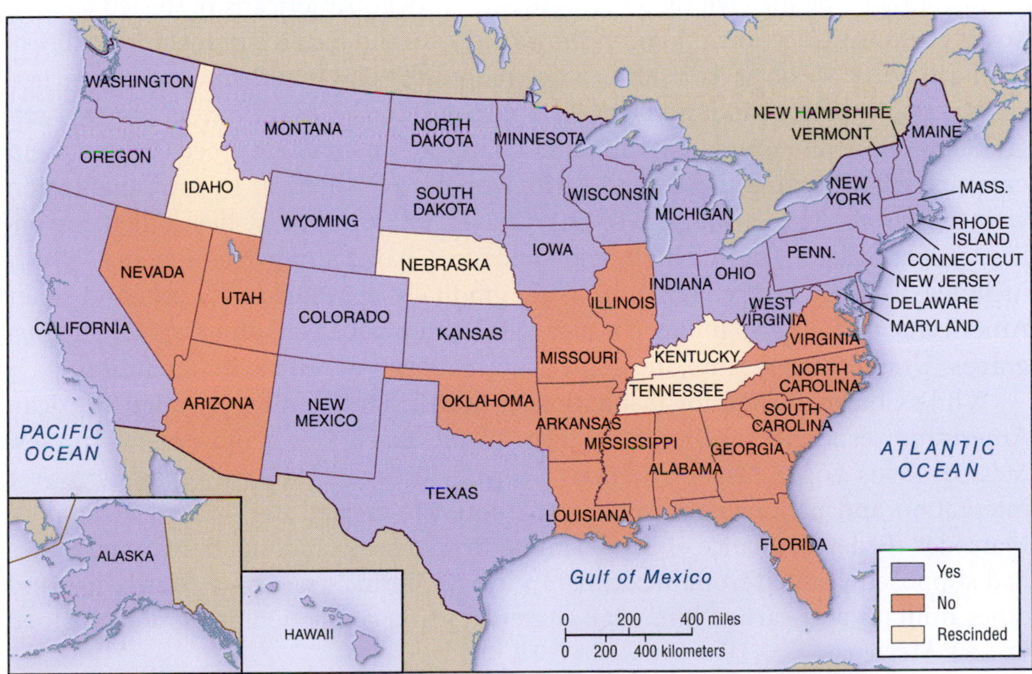

Map 29–2 The Equal Rights Amendment (ERA) Despite substantial support in state legislatures across the country, the ERA faced crippling opposition in the mountain West and the South.

Mexican Americans and "Brown Power"

In the 1960s and 1970s, Mexican Americans, the second-largest racial minority in the United States, developed a new self-consciousness. Proudly identifying themselves as Chicanos, Mexican Americans organized to protest poverty and discrimination.

Despite federal efforts to keep out Mexican immigrants, the Mexican American population grew rapidly. By 1980, at least 7 million Americans claimed Mexican heritage. The great majority lived in Arizona, California, Colorado, New Mexico, and Texas. By the 1970s, most Mexican Americans lived in urban areas. More than 1 million lived in Los Angeles. Holding an increasing percentage of skilled and white-collar jobs, Mexican Americans nevertheless earned substantially less as a group than did Anglos (white Americans of non-Hispanic descent). One in four Mexican American families lived in poverty in the mid-1970s.

Mexican Americans faced racism and discrimination. The media stereotyped them as lazy and shifty. Schools in their neighborhoods were underfunded. In some California schools, Mexican American children could not eat with Anglo children. California and Texas law prohibited teaching in Spanish.

Although Mexican Americans were not legally prevented from voting, gerrymandering diluted their political power. Despite its large Mexican American population, Los Angeles had no Hispanic representative on the city council at the end of the 1960s. The justice system often treated Mexican Americans unfairly.

The combination of poverty and discrimination marked Mexican American life. In cities, many Mexican Americans were crowded into *barrios,* run-down neighborhoods. In the countryside, many lived without hot water or toilets. Infant mortality was high, and life expectancy was low. Nationwide, almost half of the Mexican American population was functionally illiterate.

Encouraged by the civil rights movement, Mexican Americans protested against poverty and injustice for migrant farm workers. In the fertile San Joaquin Valley of California, the Mexican Americans who labored for powerful fruit growers earned as little as 10¢ an hour and lived in miserable conditions. César Chávez, a former migrant worker influenced by Martin Luther King Jr.'s nonviolent creed, helped them organize what became the United Farm Workers of America. In 1965 this union went on strike. The growers, accusing Chávez of Communist ties, called for police, strikebreakers, intimidation, and violence. Chávez's nonviolent tactics, which included a 25-day hunger strike in 1968, gradually appealed to liberals and other Americans. Chávez also initiated a successful nationwide consumer boycott against grapes. Under this pressure, the grape growers began to settle with the union.

While Chávez turned for inspiration to Martin Luther King Jr., other Mexican Americans responded to the nationalism of the Black Power movement. In New Mexico, Reies López "Tiger" Tijerina, a former preacher, favored separatism over integration and nationalism over assimilation. He created the Alianza Federal de Mercedes (Federal Alliance of Land Grants) to take back land that the United States had supposedly stolen from Mexicans. In 1967, Tijerina's raid on a courthouse and other militant acts earned him a jail sentence and a reputation as the Robin Hood of New Mexico.

Mexican American activism flourished in the late 1960s. In East Los Angeles, the Brown Berets, a paramilitary group, showed the influence of the Black Panthers.

In California in 1969, college students began the Movimiento Estudiantil Chicano de Aztlán (Chicano Student Movement of Aztlán). The organization was known by its initials, MEChA, which spelled the word for "match" in the Spanish dialect of Mexican Americans. MEChA was meant to be the match that would kindle social change for Chicanos. In Crystal City, Texas, a boycott of Anglo businesses led to the formation of La Raza Unida ("The Unified Race"), a political party that won control of the local school board in 1970. Thousands of students marked September 16, 1969, Mexican Independence Day, with a boycott of high schools.

All these protests and organizations reflected a strong sense of pride and a powerful desire to preserve the Mexican American heritage. Reflecting a strong, assertive sense of group identity, activists more frequently referred to Mexican Americans as "Chicanos." The term had uncertain origins, but its connection to group pride was obvious. "A Chicano," declared reporter Rubén Salazar, "is a Mexican-American with a non-Anglo image of himself." Chicano activists wanted bilingual education and Mexican American studies in the schools, and equal opportunity and affirmative action in schools and workplaces. Most fundamentally, Mexican American activism reflected the desire for empowerment, for what some called "Brown Power."

On the whole, white Americans paid less attention to Chicano activism than they did to African Americans' struggles. But Mexican American activists made some important gains. On the national level, Congress prohibited state bans on teaching in Spanish.

Asian American Activism

Asian Americans also pressed for rights and recognition as the 1960s ended. Like Mexican Americans, they confronted a history of discrimination in the United States. They, too, had to contend with denigrating stereotypes and hurtful epithets.

The small size of the Asian American population limited organization and protest, but the Immigration Act of 1965 had made possible increased Asian migration to the United States. From the 1960s through the 1970s, the war in Southeast Asia, political conditions in the Philippines, and economic opportunity spurred waves of Asian immigration. By 1980 America was home to more than 3 million Asian immigrants, including 812,000 Chinese, 781,000 Filipinos, and 716,000 Japanese. Overall, there were 3.7 million Americans of Asian descent. The majority lived in the Pacific states and in cities.

Asian American activism followed the pattern of other minority movements. By the late 1960s, Asian Americans were demonstrating a new ethnic self-consciousness and pride. Many Asian Americans saw themselves not only as Chinese or Japanese, inheritors of a particular national and ethnic heritage, but as members of a broader, pan-Asian group.

In 1968, the Asian American Political Alliance (AAPA) emerged on the campus of the University of California at Berkeley to unite Chinese, Japanese, and Filipino students. Asian Americans pushed for Asian-studies programs on college campuses. By the end of the 1970s, a number of colleges and universities had responded to Asian American students' demands for courses and programs.

Asian American activism spread beyond campuses. In 1974 protests forced the hiring of Chinese American workers to help build the Confucius Plaza complex in

New York City's Chinatown. In San Francisco, activists brought suit against the public school system on behalf of 1,800 Chinese pupils. In *Lau v. Nichols* in 1974, the Supreme Court declared that school systems had to provide bilingual instruction for non-English-speaking students.

In the 1970s, Japanese groups demanded compensation for the U.S. government's internment of Japanese Americans during World War II. In 1976 Washington did rescind Executive Order 9066, the 1942 presidential directive that allowed internment to occur. But the federal government did not make a more comprehensive settlement until 1988.

Asian Americans, like Chicanos, made only limited gains by 1980. However, Asian Americans had developed a new consciousness and new organizations; they had also forced real change at the local and national levels.

The Struggle for Native American Rights

After many years of decline and stagnation, the Indian population had grown rapidly since World War II (see Map 29–3). By 1970, there were nearly 800,000 Native Americans, half of whom lived on reservations. Native Americans were divided into about 175 tribes and other groups, but, like Mexican Americans and African Americans, they were united by poor living conditions and persistent discrimination. Native Americans had the lowest average family income of any ethnic group. Reservations had especially high unemployment rates. Many Indian children attended substandard schools.

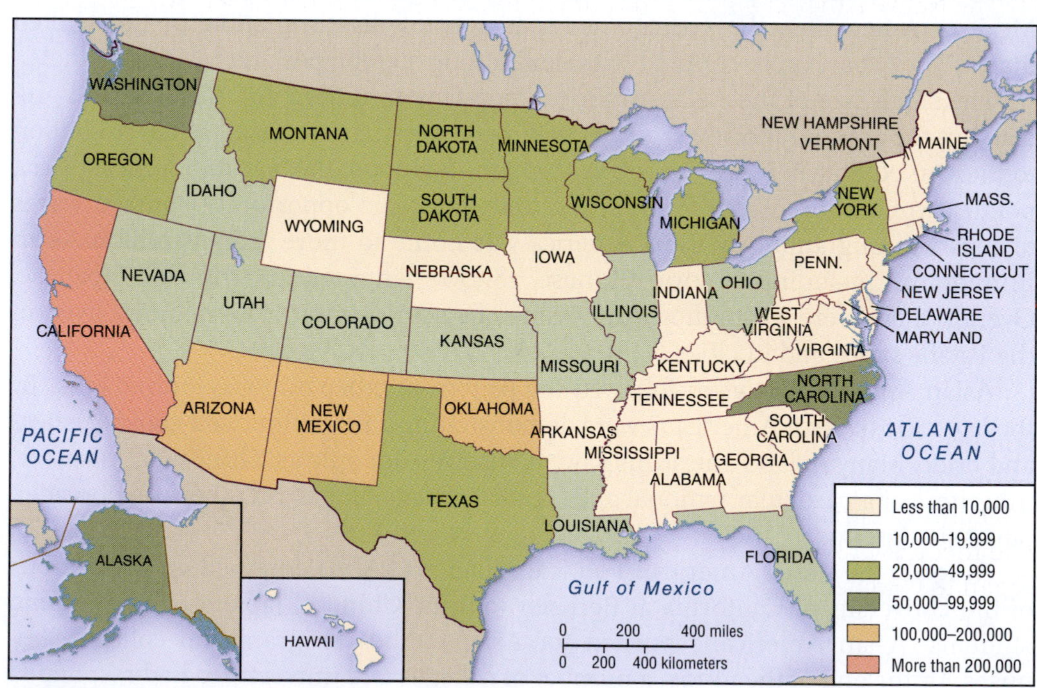

Map 29–3 Native American Population, 1980 After rapid growth in the years following World War II, the Native American population remained largest west of the Mississippi River and, above all, across the Southwest. But there were substantial numbers of Native Americans in every region. *Data from* Statistical Abstract of the United States, 1973 *(Washington: U.S. Bureau of the Census, 1973), p. 348; and* Statistical Abstract of the United States, 1984 *(Washington: U.S. Bureau of the Census, 1984), pp. 375–376, 463, 760.*

Native American life was shaped by the Indians' unique relationship with the federal government. Many resented the Bureau of Indian Affairs (BIA), which had long patronized and exploited tribes. Like African American and Mexican American separatists, some Native Americans began to see themselves as a nation apart. Calling themselves "prisoners of war," these Native Americans struck an aggressive stance, expressed in such slogans as "Custer Had It Coming" and "Red Power."

Beginning in the 1960s, a Native American movement emerged to protest federal policy, combat stereotypes, unite tribes, and perpetuate their cultures. Native Americans called for an end to employment discrimination and to the sale of Indian lands and resources to corporations. Activists staged "hunt-ins" and "fish-ins" to protest lost hunting and fishing rights. Native Americans also condemned the use of Indian symbols by schools and sports teams and demanded Indian-centered school curricula.

Some Indians favored more radical action. Copying the Black Panthers, a group of red-beret-clad Native Americans in Minneapolis, Minnesota, formed an "Indian Patrol" to defend against the police. The patrol evolved into the American Indian Movement (AIM), which spread to other cities. In 1969, AIM activists occupied the abandoned federal prison on Alcatraz Island in San Francisco Bay and told the authorities to leave. The occupiers unsuccessfully offered the government "$24 in glass beads and cloth" for the prison, which they planned to convert into a Native American museum and center. In 1972 and 1973, AIM took over BIA headquarters in Washington and the BIA office in Wounded Knee, South Dakota, where federal troops had massacred Indians in 1890.

The Native American rights movement made few gains in a society worried about limited resources and an uncertain future. Through the Indian Self-Determination Act of 1975, the federal government did allow Native Americans more independence on the reservations. Still, Native Americans themselves were divided about their relationship to the government. Many tribal leaders wanted to continue selling off their lands through the BIA, but AIM assailed Native Americans who accepted the BIA's authority. Despite such divisions, the movement had forced American society to confront the inequitable treatment of Indians more directly than at any time since the Great Depression.

Homosexuals and Gay Power

Singled out for persecution in the McCarthy era, most homosexual men and women had learned to conceal their sexual identity in public. Mainstream American culture mercilessly ridiculed homosexuals as "faggots," "queers," and "dykes." The medical profession treated homosexuality as an illness. In the late 1960s, that began to change.

A catalyst for change was the struggle of women, racial minorities, and students. Another was a police raid on the Stonewall Inn, a gay bar in New York City's Greenwich Village, in June 1969. Such raids were commonplace, but this time, to the surprise of the police, gay men resisted. The next night, the police beat and arrested gay protestors, who yelled, "Gay Power!"

Stonewall became a rallying cry for gay activism. The Gay Liberation Front, the Student Homophile League, and other organizations appeared. Activists picketed companies that discriminated against gays, and homosexuals socialized more openly. On the first anniversary of Stonewall, 10,000 gay men and lesbians paraded down New York's Sixth Avenue. "Two, four, six, eight!" marchers chanted. "Gay is just as good as straight!" The gay movement began to have an effect on mainstream culture. In 1974, the American Psychiatric Association decided that homosexuality was not a "mental disorder" and that homosexuals deserved equal rights.

The emerging movements for gay, Native American, and Chicano rights, along with the ongoing crusades of women and African Americans, made a deep impact on the 1970s. American society could not escape demands for equal rights and opportunities for all people. Women, gays, African Americans, Native Americans, and Chicanos did not win full equality, but these groups made important gains despite the troubled economic climate of the 1970s.

Backlash: From Radical Action to Conservative Reaction

By the close of the 1960s, American society reverberated with demands to end the war in Vietnam and allow equal rights at home. Some activists believed the United States would indeed be torn apart and remade by the "racial and class war" that Shirley Chisholm feared; but the revolution never came. Radical movements squabbled and fell apart. Many Americans abandoned activism for their own private concerns; others angrily rejected protest movements. Encouraging this backlash, President Nixon won reelection in 1972.

"The Movement" and the "Me-Decade"

Many activists believed that the struggles of women and minorities, along with student protests and the antiwar movement, were creating a single coalition, known simply as "the Movement." At the close of the 1960s, it sometimes seemed as if the Movement might truly take shape. In August 1969, an astonishing crowd of nearly half a million mostly young people gathered for a music festival on a dairy farm near Woodstock in upstate New York. For three days, they created a temporary utopia dedicated to love and other countercultural values and vocally opposed to the Vietnam War. What activist Abbie Hoffman called the "Woodstock Nation" briefly symbolized the possibility of a true mass-based coalition for radical change.

Nevertheless, the Movement stalled. "We had the dream and we are losing it," lamented the activist Julius Lester the year of Woodstock. The different protest groups never merged, and they were often hostile to each other. Black activists, for instance, criticized white activists for neglecting poverty and other working-class problems.

> **We are letting the people of America know that we will not sit still for this government to take away our basic parental rights. We will fight, and we will never, never quit. Our enemies can go straight to hell.**
>
> STATE SENATOR WILLIAM BULGER
> addressing an antibusing rally, Boston, 1975

The "Woodstock Nation," August 1969 Perhaps half a million people created a huge temporary community celebrating countercultural values.

In addition, key groups within the Movement fell apart. Plagued by internal divisions, SDS held its last convention in 1969. The violent Weathermen called for "Days of Rage" in the "pig city" of Chicago in October 1969, but only a few hundred protestors showed up. Transient radical groups bombed or burned corporate headquarters and other "establishment" targets but succeeded only in giving the New Left and the Movement a bad name. The FBI secretly penetrated Black Panther chapters and worked to discredit the organization. Panther leaders fled the country, went to jail, or died at the hands of police. Radical feminist groups also declined as women's liberation increasingly focused on liberal demands, such as the ERA.

Some protest movements lost their targets. After the widespread demonstrations of 1970, the antiwar movement declined as the United States pulled out of Vietnam. The student movement declined as young people lost some of their grievances. Around the country, colleges and universities eased parietal rules and other regulations. In 1971, the states completed ratification of the Twenty-sixth Amendment to the Constitution, which lowered the voting age to 18.

The revolution also failed to materialize because many people turned away from activism and political engagement. Some were disillusioned by the failure of the Great Society and the duplicity of the Johnson and Nixon administrations. Others were disappointed by the limited accomplishments of radicalism. Still others found themselves caught up in therapeutic and religious movements, as Americans focused on their inner needs rather than on political change.

The 1970s, announced the writer Tom Wolfe, were the "Me-Decade." Wolfe and other observers believed Americans had become self-absorbed and narcissistic. The cause, explained the historian and social critic Christopher Lasch, was the crisis of capitalism in "an age of diminishing expectations." The fears about the self-absorbed Me-Decade were as exaggerated as the hopes for the revolutionary Movement. People did not stop hoping and working for change, but in a time of economic decline and political disappointment, many Americans felt they could not afford the expansive liberal dreams of the 1960s. They had to look out for themselves.

The Plight of the White Ethnics

The "new American revolution" was a victim of anger as well as apathy. Most lower-middle-class and working-class whites rejected the Movement. They decried radical feminism and resented the students and protestors who had avoided fighting in Vietnam. They also increasingly rejected the new liberalism of the 1960s. Feeling threatened by urban renewal projects, welfare spending, and court-ordered busing, many whites believed the Great Society did too little for them and too much for minorities and young radicals. Most of all, the white working and middle classes feared the consequences of economic decline. In a decade of deindustrialization, they faced the loss of their jobs and their standard of living. "I work my ass off," said an ironworker. "But I can't make it."

The media painted an unflattering portrait of these Americans as frustrated racists and reactionaries. In reality, they were not all so racist and forlorn. They took renewed pride in the ethnic heritage that set them apart from other Americans. "White ethnics" were self-consciously German American or Irish American, like the opponents of busing in Boston. They were "PIGS"—Poles, Italians, Greeks, and Slovaks.

The white ethnics used their heritage to affirm an alternative set of values—their own counterculture. For them, ethnicity meant a commitment to family, neighborhood, and religion in place of the individualistic American dream and the centralizing federal government. In response, some colleges and universities created ethnic-studies programs. In 1972, Congress passed the Ethnic Heritage Studies Act to "legitimatize ethnicity" and promote the study of immigrant cultures. Most important, the white ethnics formed a large potential voting bloc, attractive to politicians.

Television's View of the White Ethnic The popular 1970s comedy *All in the Family* derided its main character, the conservative Archie Bunker, who was upset with his feminist daughter, his liberal son-in-law, and all the social change around him.

The Republican Counterattack

Nixon tried to combine the white ethnics and white southerners in a Republican counterattack against radicalism, liberalism, and the Democratic Party. The president condemned protestors and demonstrations. "Anarchy," the president declared, "this is the way civilizations begin to die." The Nixon administration used more than words against protestors. The president ordered IRS investigations to harass liberal and antiwar figures. He used the FBI to infiltrate and disrupt the Black Power movement, the Brown Berets, and the New Left. He even made illegal domestic use of the CIA to obstruct the antiwar movement.

To oppose the forces of disruption, Nixon called for support from "the great silent majority of my fellow Americans." With his "southern strategy," the president reached out to Sunbelt voters by opposing busing, rapid integration, crime, and radicalism. He also tried to create a more conservative, less activist Supreme Court. In 1969, he named the cautious Warren Burger to succeed Earl Warren as chief justice. To fill another vacancy on the court, Nixon nominated first a conservative South Carolina judge, Clement Haynsworth, who had angered civil rights and union leaders, and then Judge G. Harrold Carswell of Florida, a former avowed white supremacist. Both nominations failed, but the president had sent an unmistakable message to the "silent majority" and to white southerners.

The counterattack paid off in the 1972 presidential election. The Republican ticket of Nixon and Vice President Spiro Agnew benefited from some unforeseen occurrences. More than any other politician, George Wallace, the segregationist governor of Alabama, rivaled Nixon's appeal to the "silent majority." But Wallace's campaign for the Democratic nomination came to an end when a would-be assassin's bullet paralyzed him from the waist down. In addition, the Democratic vice-presidential nominee, Senator Thomas Eagleton of Missouri, had to withdraw over revelations about his treatment for depression.

Nixon did not really need good luck in 1972. The Democrats chose a strongly liberal senator, George McGovern of South Dakota, for president. McGovern's eventual running mate was another unabashed liberal, Sargent Shriver, a brother-in-law of the Kennedys. The Democratic ticket—which endorsed busing and affirmative action and opposed the Vietnam War—alienated white ethnics, white southerners, and organized labor.

Carrying 49 out of 50 states, Nixon easily won reelection in November 1972. With nearly 61 percent of the popular vote, the president scored almost as big a triumph as Lyndon Johnson in 1964, but Nixon's victory was deceptive. The Republican counterattack had not produced a partisan political realignment: the Democrats still controlled both houses of Congress.

Nevertheless, the 1972 election was a sign that the traditional Democratic coalition was breaking up. More broadly, Nixon's triumph, along with the failure of the Movement, the rise of the white ethnics, and the self-absorption of the Me-Decade, showed that the glory days of liberalism and radicalism were over.

Political Crisis: Three Troubled Presidencies

Nixon's triumph turned out to be his undoing. The discovery of illegal activities in the president's campaign led to the revelation of other improprieties and, finally, to his resignation. Nixon's successors, Gerald Ford and Jimmy Carter, could not master the problems of a divided nation discovering the limits of its power. Unable to handle the conflicting issues of rights and economic decline, the three troubled presidencies of the 1970s intensified the sense of national crisis. The decade ended with Americans wondering whether their democracy still worked.

Watergate: The Fall of Richard Nixon

Nixon's fall began when five men were caught breaking into the offices of the Democratic National Committee in the Watergate complex in Washington, DC, just before

2:00 A.M. on June 17, 1972. The five burglars had ties to Nixon's campaign organization, the Committee to Re-Elect the President (CREEP). They were attempting to repair an electronic eavesdropping device that had been previously planted in the Democrats' headquarters.

At first, Watergate had no impact on the president. He won reelection easily, but gradually, a disturbing story emerged. Two reporters for the *Washington Post*, Bob Woodward and Carl Bernstein, revealed payments linking the five burglars to CREEP and to Nixon's White House staff. The burglars went on trial with two former CIA agents, who had directed the break-in for CREEP. Faced with heavy sentences in March 1973, the burglars admitted that "higher-ups" had planned the break-in and orchestrated a cover-up. One of those higher-ups, Nixon's presidential counsel John Dean, revealed his role in the Watergate affair to a grand jury. By the end of April, the president had to accept the resignations of his most trusted aides, H. R. "Bob" Haldeman and John Ehrlichman. To emphasize his commitment to justice, Nixon named a special federal prosecutor, Archibald Cox, to investigate Watergate.

> **America is not over the hill as a people. But tomorrow is not going to get better in the way that people in 1955 would say that tomorrow would be better. That's gone.**
>
> FRANZ HELDNER,
> a college art teacher, New Orleans, 1975

In the end, the president was trapped by his own words. A Senate committee, chaired by Sam Ervin of North Carolina, began hearings on Watergate in May 1973. Testifying before the committee, a White House aide revealed that a secret taping system routinely recorded conversations in the president's Oval Office. Claiming "executive privilege," Nixon refused to turn over tapes of his conversations after the break-in. When Archibald Cox continued to press for the tapes, Nixon ordered him fired on Saturday, October 20, 1973. Attorney General Elliot Richardson and a top aide refused to carry out the order and resigned. A third official finally discharged Cox. Nixon's "Saturday Night Massacre" set off a storm of public anger. Nixon had to name a new special prosecutor, Leon Jaworski. The Democratic-controlled House of Representatives began to explore articles of impeachment against the president. "I am not a crook," Nixon insisted.

By 1974, it became clear that the Nixon administration had engaged in a shocking range of improper and illegal behavior. Infuriated by news leaks in 1969, Henry Kissinger had ordered wiretaps on the phones of newspaper reporters and his own staff. Two years later, the White House had created the "Plumbers," a bumbling group of operatives to combat leaks, including the release of the Pentagon Papers. Anxious to win in 1972, Nixon's men had also engaged in dirty tricks to sabotage Democratic presidential aspirants. Nixon's personal lawyer had collected illegal political contributions, "laundered" the money to hide its source, and then transferred it to CREEP.

Nixon himself had ordered the secret and illegal bombing of Cambodia. He had impounded (i.e., refused to spend) money appropriated by Congress for programs he disliked. He had secretly approved the use of federal agencies to hurt "political enemies."

As a result of the Watergate break-in and other scandals, many of Nixon's associates had to leave office. No fewer than 26, including former attorney general John Mitchell, went to jail. Vice President Spiro Agnew was found to have accepted bribes as the governor of Maryland in the 1960s. In October 1973 Agnew accepted a plea bargain deal and resigned as vice president. He was replaced by Republican Congressman Gerald R. Ford of Michigan.

Under growing pressure to release his tapes, Nixon tried to get away with publishing selected edited transcripts. Revealing a vulgar, rambling, and inarticulate president, the transcripts only fed public disillusionment. In July 1974 the House Judiciary Committee voted to recommend to the full House of Representatives three articles of impeachment—obstruction of justice, abuse of power, and defiance of subpoenas.

Nixon still wanted to fight the charges, but the Supreme Court ruled unanimously that he had to turn over his tapes to the special prosecutor. The tapes showed that Nixon himself had participated in the cover-up of Watergate as early as June 23, 1972. The president had conspired to obstruct justice and had lied repeatedly to the American people. Almost certain to be impeached, the president agreed to resign rather than face a trial in the Senate. On August 9, 1974, Nixon left office in disgrace. "My fellow Americans, our long national nightmare is over," the new president, Gerald Ford, declared. "Our constitution works."

Putting a Brave Face on Scandal Forced to resign from office because of Watergate, Richard Nixon gives a victory sign as he prepares to fly away from the White House, August 1974.

Gerald Ford and a Skeptical Nation

At first, Gerald Ford was a welcome relief for a nation stunned by the misdeeds of Richard Nixon. Modest and good-humored, the new president seemed unlikely to abuse the authority of the White House. But Ford also seemed stumbling and unimaginative in the face of the nation's declining prosperity and power. Moreover, his administration had no popular mandate. Ford was the first unelected vice president to succeed to the presidency. His vice president, former New York governor Nelson Rockefeller, had not been elected either.

Ford had to govern a nation that had grown skeptical about politicians. Johnson's deceitful conduct of the Vietnam War and Nixon's scandals raised fears that the presidency had grown too powerful. To reestablish its authority, Congress passed the War Powers Act of 1973, which allowed the president to send troops to hostile situations overseas for no more than 60 days without obtaining congressional consent. In 1975 Congress conducted hearings on the secret operations of the CIA. Amid revelations about the agency's improper roles in domestic spying and the assassination of foreign leaders, the House and Senate created permanent committees to oversee the agency. Ford had to ban the use of assassination in American foreign policy.

Soon after taking office, Ford himself fed public skepticism about the presidency by offering Nixon a full pardon for all crimes committed as president. Ford's popularity dropped immediately and his presidency never fully recovered.

Ford's handling of economic issues did not make up for the pardon. A moderate Republican, the president did not want the federal government to take too active a role in managing the economy. But like Nixon, he could not stop some liberal initiatives. Congress, reflecting popular concern about corporations and the environment, strengthened the regulatory power of the Federal Trade Commission and extended the 1970 Clean Air Act.

Ford had no solutions for deindustrialization and stagflation. Believing inflation was the most serious problem, Ford did little to stop rising unemployment, which topped 9 percent. His anti-inflation program, known as WIN for "Whip Inflation Now," mainly encouraged Americans to control price increases voluntarily. Ford wore a WIN button on his lapel, but inflation continued.

In foreign affairs, the president had to accept limits on American power. Despite the 1973 cease-fire agreement, the fighting continued in Vietnam. Ford promised to protect South Vietnam, but Congress cut the administration's requests for monetary aid to the Saigon government. Sending American armed forces back to South Vietnam was out of the question. When North Vietnamese troops invaded early in 1975, panicked civilians fled southward and Congress refused to provide any more aid. As Saigon was overrun, the last Americans evacuated in helicopters. Thousands of loyal South Vietnamese fled with them, but many more were left behind. For more than 20 years, the United States had worked to preserve an independent, anti-Communist South Vietnam. Yet, on April 30, 1975, South Vietnam surrendered. There was nothing Ford could do to prevent the final, ignominious failure of America's Vietnam policy.

The president could also do nothing to save the pro-American government of Cambodia from Communist insurgents, the Khmer Rouge, earlier in April 1975. Ford did act the next month when the Khmer Rouge captured an American merchant ship, the *Mayaguez,* off Cambodia. At the cost of 41 deaths, United States marines rescued the 39-man crew. Despite the rescue, the United States no longer wielded much power in Southeast Asia.

The policy of détente with the Soviet Union was supposed to help America cope with its limited power, but détente was clearly in trouble during the Ford administration. The United States and the Soviets failed to agree to a second Strategic Arms Limitation Treaty (SALT II). American critics of détente, including Democratic Senator Henry Jackson of Washington, claimed that the policy sapped American defenses and overlooked human rights violations by the Soviets. In

1974, Jackson added an amendment to a trade bill linking commerce to freedom for Soviet Jews to emigrate. The Jackson-Vanik Amendment helped sour the Soviets on détente. In turn, Ford further alienated American conservatives when he traveled to Helsinki, Finland, in 1975 to sign an agreement accepting the post–World War II boundaries of European nations.

Ford's troubles were reflected at the polls. The Democrats made large gains in the congressional elections in 1974. Two years later, Ford won the Republican nomination for president, replacing Rockefeller with a more conservative vice-presidential nominee, Senator Robert Dole of Kansas. The Democrats' presidential choice was a far cry from the liberal George McGovern. Former Georgia governor Jimmy Carter ran as a moderate who promised efficiency rather than new reforms.

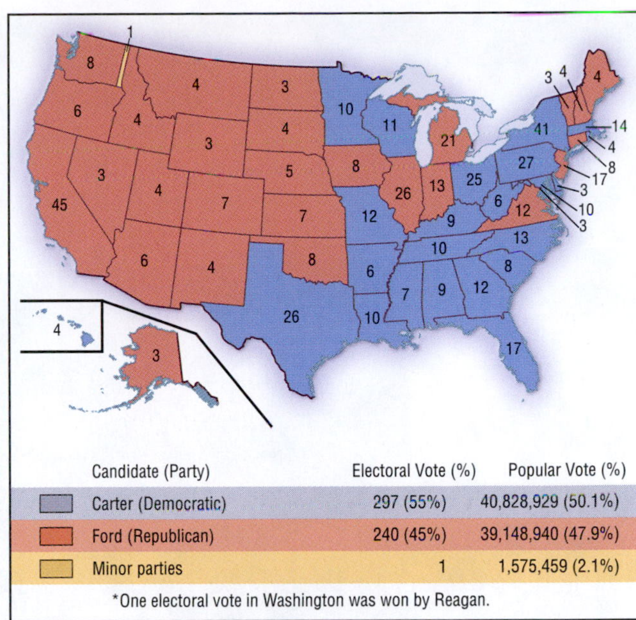

Candidate (Party) Electoral Vote (%) Popular Vote (%)
Carter (Democratic) 297 (55%) 40,828,929 (50.1%)
Ford (Republican) 240 (45%) 39,148,940 (47.9%)
Minor parties 1 1,575,459 (2.1%)
*One electoral vote in Washington was won by Reagan.

Map 29–4 The Presidential Election, 1976 Jimmy Carter managed to reestablish the Democratic Party's appeal to white southerners.

With low turnout at the polls, Carter took 50.1 percent of the vote to Ford's 48 percent. The Democrats won a majority in the Electoral College by carrying much of the industrial Northeast and taking back almost all the South from the Republicans. The outcome was less an endorsement of Carter than a rejection of Ford, who became the first sitting president to lose an election since Herbert Hoover during the Great Depression in 1932.

"Why Not the Best?": Jimmy Carter

As he took office in 1977, Jimmy Carter seemed capable and efficient. A graduate of the Naval Academy, he had served as an engineer in the navy's nuclear submarine program and successfully managed his family's peanut farm before entering politics. Carter's commitment to perfectionism was captured in the title of his autobiography, *Why Not the Best?*

Carter responded more energetically and imaginatively than Ford to the nation's problems. But Carter came to be seen as a weak, uncertain leader. More important, he faced the same intractable problems that had bedeviled Ford.

Like his predecessor, Carter had trouble putting to rest the recent past. The president met angry criticism when he pardoned most American men who had resisted the draft during the Vietnam War, offending many veterans and conservatives

Carter also had to contend with increasing popular resentment of government. Many Americans believed that government regulation and taxation had gotten out of hand. When the Endangered Species Act of 1973 forced a halt to the construction of a Tennessee dam because it threatened the survival of the snail darter, a small local fish, it seemed as if the federal government worried more about fish than about people's need for electricity and recreation.

The West was the stronghold of antigovernment sentiment in the 1970s. Assailing the bureaucrats in Washington, DC, the Sagebrush Rebellion demanded state control over federal lands in the West. Businessmen in the West also wanted Washington to

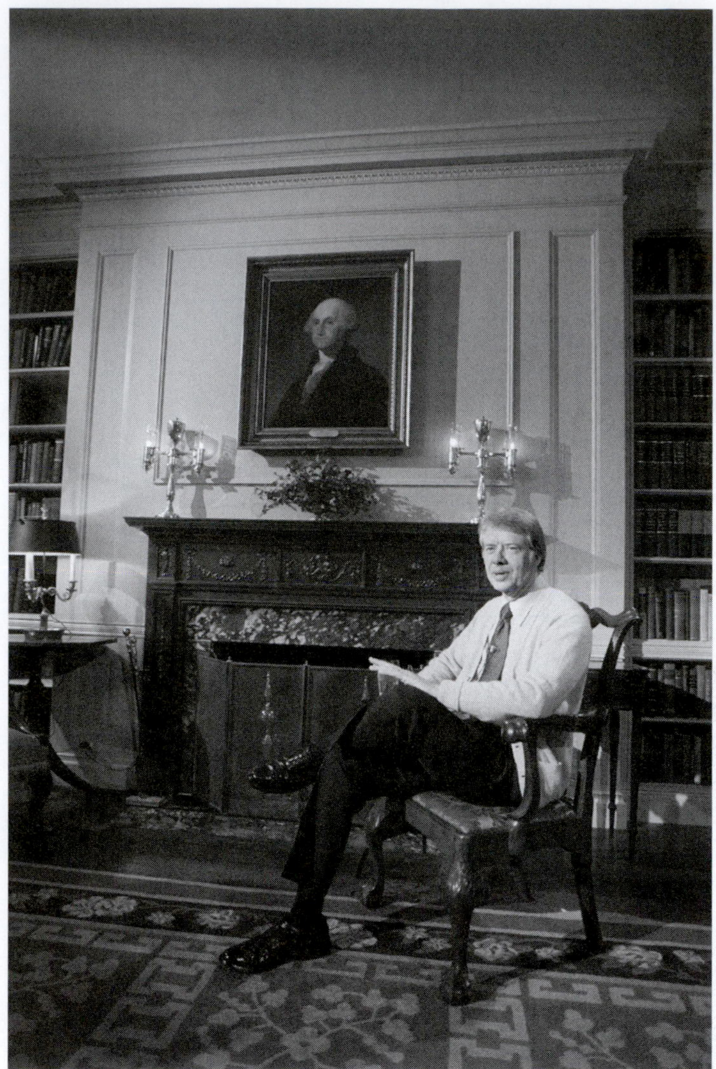

President Jimmy Carter Wearing a beige wool cardigan instead of a suit jacket, the new President asks Americans to conserve energy, February 2, 1977.

allow more exploitation of oil, forests, and other resources on federal lands. Meanwhile, California became the center of an antitax movement in 1978. Angered by high taxes and government spending in their communities, California voters passed Proposition 13, which sharply reduced property taxes.

As always, antigovernment sentiment was inconsistent. Many of the same people who attacked taxes and regulation expected aid and benefits from Washington. When the giant automaker Chrysler faced bankruptcy in 1979, the government had to save the company with a $1.5 billion loan guarantee. When Carter moved to cancel federal water projects in the West in 1977, he encountered a storm of protest from the heart of the Sagebrush Rebellion.

Carter was most successful when he moved to limit government. By the 1970s, some economists were advocating deregulation of businesses as a way to lower costs, increase competition, and improve services. In 1978, the government removed price controls on the airline industry. In the short run the move lowered fares, but in the long run it drove some airlines out of business.

Deregulation was a sign of a changing balance of political power. Big business, under attack since the 1960s, now lobbied effectively against regulation, organized labor, and taxes. Liberals, meanwhile, had lost influence. As a result, Congress never created the Consumer Protection Agency advocated by consumer activists. Legislation to make labor organization easier also failed. In 1978, Congress watered down the Humphrey-Hawkins Bill, which reasserted the government's responsibility to ensure full employment. When Carter tried to raise taxes on business, Congress instead cut taxes on capital gains and added more loopholes to the tax law.

Carter attempted, with mixed results, to adjust the economy to the realities of living with less. His program of voluntary wage and price controls did not stop soaring inflation. After fuel shortages forced some schools and businesses to close in the harsh winter of 1976/1977, Carter addressed the energy crisis. The president told Americans that "the energy shortage is permanent" and urged them to conserve. His energy plan included establishment of the Department of Energy, taxes on gas-guzzling automobiles and large consumers of oil, tax incentives to stimulate production of oil and gas, and development of nuclear power. But conservatives thought the program expanded government authority. Liberals and environmentalists objected to its support for nuclear power and oil-company profits. The final plan, passed in 1978, was considerably weakened, but it did encourage conservation.

Nuclear power, a key part of Carter's energy plan, soon lost much of its appeal. In March 1979 a nuclear reactor at Three Mile Island, Pennsylvania, nearly suffered a catastrophic meltdown. As 100,000 frightened residents fled their homes, the reactor had to be permanently closed. Around the country, utilities scrapped plans for new nuclear power plants.

Three Mile Island fed broader anxieties about the environmental damage caused by industrial capitalism. Americans wondered whether their neighborhoods would suffer the fate of Love Canal, near Niagara Falls, New York. There, hazardous waste buried by a chemical company caused so many cases of cancer, miscarriages, and other health problems that residents had to move away. Despite business concerns about regulation, Washington created a "superfund" of $1.6 billion to clean up hazardous-waste sites. The Carter administration also took control of 100 million acres of Alaska to prevent damage from economic development.

At first, Carter had more success with foreign policy than with domestic affairs. Continuing Nixon's de-escalation of the cold war, Carter announced that "we are now free of the inordinate fear of Communism." The president did not abandon Nixon's emphasis on détente with the Soviet Union, but he focused on supporting human rights and democracy and building harmony around the world. In 1978, Carter won Senate approval of a treaty yielding ownership of the Panama Canal to Panama at the end of the century. The treaty signaled a new and more respectful approach to Central and Latin America.

In 1978, Carter also mediated the first peace agreement between Israel and an Arab nation. Bringing together Israeli and Egyptian leaders at the Camp David presidential retreat, Carter helped forge a framework for peace that led to Israel's withdrawal from the Sinai Peninsula and the signing of an Israeli-Egyptian treaty. The agreement did not settle the fate of the Israeli-occupied Golan Heights and Gaza Strip or the future of the Palestinian people, but it did establish a basis for future negotiations in a region torn by conflict for centuries.

Carter viewed a commitment to human rights and democracy abroad as a way of recapturing the international respect that the United States had lost during the Vietnam War. In practice, however, his administration did not speak out consistently against the violation of rights around the world. Instead, Carter was supportive of authoritarian American allies such as the rulers of Iran and the Philippines who clearly abused human rights in their own countries.

Carter's foreign policy suffered from the eventual collapse of détente. The president did reach agreement with the Soviets on the SALT II treaty, but the Senate was reluctant to ratify the agreement. Then, in December 1979, the Soviet Union invaded its southern neighbor, Afghanistan. In response, Carter withdrew the SALT II treaty, stopped grain shipments to the Soviet Union, forbade American athletes to compete in the 1980 Olympics in Moscow, and increased American military spending. These moves had no effect on the Soviet invasion, but détente was obviously over, and the direction of American foreign policy had become unclear.

By 1979, Carter was a deeply unpopular president. He had not stabilized the economy or set out a coherent foreign policy. After pondering the situation at the Camp David retreat for 11 days in July, the president came back to tell a television audience that the nation was suffering a "crisis of spirit." The president offered a number of proposals to deal with the energy crisis, but he spoke most strongly to the state of the nation. "All the legislation in the world can't fix what's wrong with America," Carter maintained. "What is lacking is confidence and a sense of community." The speech only seemed to alienate more Americans.

Carter became still more embattled when the Shah of Iran was overthrown by the followers of an Islamic leader, the Ayatollah Ruholla Khomeini, early in 1979. The Shah had long received lavish aid from the United States. Now, the Iranian revolutionaries, eager to restore traditional Islamic values, condemned America for imposing the Shah and modern culture on their nation. In the wake of the revolution, oil prices rose. Once again, Americans had to contend with gas lines, and inflation spread through the economy.

The situation worsened when Khomeini condemned the United States for allowing the Shah to receive medical treatment in New York. On November 4, students loyal to Khomeini overran the United States embassy in Teheran, the Iranian capital, and took 60 Americans hostage. Carter froze Iranian assets in the United States, but he could not compel the release of the hostages. As days passed, the United States seemed helpless. In the spring of 1980, the frustrated president ordered a secret military mission to rescue the hostages. On April 24, eight American helicopters headed for a desert rendezvous with six transport planes carrying troops and supplies. When two helicopters broke down and an-

Disaster in the Iranian Desert, April 1980 The wreckage of this Army helicopter, part of the failed attempt to free American hostages in Iran, symbolizes the weakness of the United States at the start of the 1980s.

other became lost, the mission had to be aborted. An accident left eight soldiers dead. The hostages remained in captivity. The limits of American power seemed more obvious than ever.

Conclusion

As the 1970s ended, Shirley Chisholm was still deeply worried about her nation. Noting the many problems of the United States, the congresswoman concluded "there was a real crisis . . . in this country. . . . Government was being conducted by crisis." The mixture of economic decline and aspirations for rights and opportunity had proved too much to handle. To Chisholm, the nation even seemed to be undoing the changes of the liberal 1960s. "Lots happened in the '60s," she noted sadly. "What's happening today? Every gain has been eroded." As always, Chisholm refused to give in to pessimism. "I will continue to do what I'm doing—fighting, fighting, fighting," she vowed, "because I realize that this country is moving to the right." As the 1980s would reveal, Chisholm was correct about the direction of the United States. After the political uncertainty of the 1970s, the nation would finally deal with economic decline and the other challenges of the decade by embracing a new conservatism. The future lay to the right.

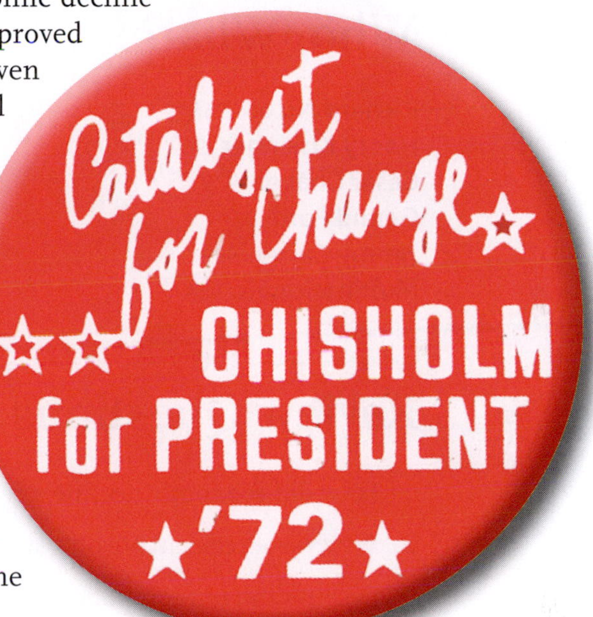

Further Readings

Beth L. Bailey and David Farber, eds., *America in the Seventies* (2004). A collection of scholarly essays.

Jefferson Cowie and Joseph Heathcott, eds., *Beyond the Ruins: The Meanings of Deindustrialization* (2003). Case studies of economic decline.

Robert Dallek, *Nixon and Kissinger: Partners in Power* (2007). A joint study of the architects of détente.

Ronald P. Formisano, *Boston Against Busing: Race, Class, and Ethnicity in the 1960s and 1970s* (1991). Neatly analyzes the white resistance to school desegregation.

Ignacio Garcia, *Chicanismo: The Forging of a Militant Ethos Among Mexican Americans* (2000). Offers a balanced account of the emerging Chicano rights movement.

Eric Marcus, *Making History: The Struggle for Lesbian and Gay Equal Rights* (2002). Moving, candid oral histories that personalize the gay and lesbian liberation movement.

Rick Pearlstein, *Nixonland: The Rise of a President and the Fracturing of America* (2008). An opinionated account of the dominant political figure of the 1970s.

Bruce J. Schulman, *The Seventies: The Great Shift in American Culture, Society and Politics* (2001). Provides an overview of the period.

Who, What?

Richard Nixon 968
Henry Kissinger 969
César Chávez 978
Gerald Ford 987
Jimmy Carter 989
Multinationals 964
Deindustrialization 966
Détente 969
Affirmative action 974
Busing 974
Roe v. Wade 976
Watergate 985

Review Questions

1. How did economic decline affect the lives of Americans?
2. Why was President Nixon's strategy for ending the Vietnam War so controversial?
3. Discuss the foreign policies of the Nixon administration, including détente and the Nixon Doctrine. How did these policies mark a departure from previous American approaches to the cold war?
4. How did the demands of the African American civil rights movement change from the 1960s to the 1970s?

>> Timeline >>

▼ 1965
Decision to send U.S. troops into battle in South Vietnam

▼ 1968
Assassinations of Martin Luther King Jr. and Robert F. Kennedy
Election of Richard Nixon

▼ 1969
Secret bombing of Cambodia
Stonewall Riot in New York's Greenwich Village
Apollo 11 moon landing
Nixon Doctrine

▼ 1970
First Earth Day
Invasion of Cambodia

▼ 1971
United States off gold standard
Ratification of Twenty-sixth Amendment, lowering voting age to 18
Supreme Court busing decision, *Swann v. Charlotte-Mecklenburg Board of Education*

▼ 1972
President Nixon's trips to the People's Republic of China and the Soviet Union
Strategic Arms Limitation Treaty (SALT I) and Anti–Ballistic Missile (ABM) Treaty
Congressional passage of equal rights amendment
Watergate burglary
Reelection of President Nixon

▼ 1973
Peace agreement to end Vietnam War
Supreme Court ruling to legalize abortion, *Roe v. Wade*

5. Discuss the Republican counterattack of the late 1960s and early 1970s. How did Nixon and his party take advantage of discontent?
6. Analyze the troubled presidencies of Nixon, Ford, and Carter. Did these leaders create their own problems, or did they face impossible situations?

Websites

The Jimmy Carter Library and Museum (http://www.jimmycarterlibrary.org/documents/) includes documents, photographs, and the diary of an American hostage in Iran.

The Electronic Reading Room of the Federal Bureau of Investigation (http://foia.fbi.gov/room.htm) features files the FBI maintained on gay activists, the Weathermen, and the Watergate affair.

Nixontapes.org (http://www.nixontapes.org/) offers the most complete collection of the secret Oval Office recordings that brought down a presidency.

Oyez (http://www.oyez.org/) is a growing, comprehensive guide to the history of the Supreme Court, featuring audiotapes of such modern cases as *Roe v. Wade*.

The scanned and transcribed materials of Documents from the Women's Liberation Movement, Duke University Library (http://scriptorium.lib.duke.edu/wlm/), make an excellent guide to the varieties of feminism in the 1960s and 1970s.

The Center for Working-Class Studies at Youngstown State University (http://www.centerforworkingclassstudies.org/) features online resources including documents, photos, and poetry about Youngstown, "Steel City U.S.A."

For further review materials and resource information, please visit www.oup.com/us/ofthepeople

▼ 1973–74
OPEC oil embargo

▼ 1974
Boston busing struggle
Resignation of President Nixon

▼ 1975
Surrender of South Vietnam to North Vietnam
Helsinki Agreement

▼ 1976
Announcement of the "Me-Decade" by Tom Wolfe
Jimmy Carter elected president

▼ 1977
Carter's energy plan

▼ 1978
Camp David peace accords
Supreme Court affirmative action decision, *Regents of the University of California v. Allan Bakke*

▼ 1979
Accident at Three Mile Island nuclear power plant

▼ 1979–81
Iranian hostage crisis

▼ 1980
Ronald Reagan elected president

CHAPTER 30

Common Threads 

>> How did Ronald Reagan's approach to economic decline differ from his predecessor Jimmy Carter's?

>> How did conservatism's emphasis on personal responsibility shape the economic and social policies of the Reagan administration?

>> Why was religion so important to the Reagan Revolution?

>> How would the emergence of microcomputing shape the economy beyond the 1980s?

The Triumph of Conservatism 1980–1991

AMERICAN PORTRAIT

>> Linda Chavez

"On Election Day 1980," Linda Chavez recalled, "I did something I had never imagined I could do: I voted for a Republican for president." A lifelong Democrat, she rejected her party's nominee, incumbent Jimmy Carter, and pulled the lever instead for the conservative GOP candidate, Ronald Reagan.

As Chavez admitted, she made "an unlikely conservative." The daughter of an Anglo mother and a Mexican American father, Chavez had grown up in the Mexican American neighborhoods of Albuquerque, New Mexico, and Denver, Colorado. Her father, like most Mexican Americans, was a Democrat. Chavez herself was drawn to the party and its causes. As a girl in the early 1960s, she joined the civil rights organization CORE and demonstrated against racial discrimination outside a Denver Woolworth store. As a young woman, Chavez had gone to work for the Democratic National Committee, a liberal Democratic congressman, two liberal teachers unions, and the Carter administration.

Despite her partisan commitments, Chavez had been quietly changing. As an undergraduate at the University of Colorado at Boulder in the late 1960s, Chavez discovered that she did not have to settle for her parents' working-class existence. "For the first time," she said, "I realized that I could control my own destiny." Chavez also felt that the university's affirmative action programs shortchanged Mexican Americans by admitting unqualified students, allowing them to flounder academically, teaching them to blame their problems on racism, and then leaving them to drop out.

From those realizations, Chavez gradually developed a new political outlook in the 1970s. She believed that individuals should take responsibility for their lives. "[T]hinking of yourself as a victim and hating those that have oppressed you doesn't get you anywhere," Chavez concluded. She rejected affirmative action programs, race-based hiring quotas, busing, and bilingual education as misguided liberal attempts to create equality in America.

Meanwhile, her stint in the Carter administration left her skeptical about another liberal article of faith. "The federal government was not at all what I expected," Chavez confessed. "Nothing—and almost no one—worked." She was troubled, too, that Carter and the Democrats did not support anti-Communism and a strong defense.

In some ways, Chavez felt that she was not the one who had changed. "Hispanics tend to be fairly traditional," she insisted, "somewhat conservative on social issues, and very patriotic and prodefense." It was her party that had changed by adopting controversial solutions to racial and gender inequality and by abandoning its longtime commitment to the containment of Communism. In 1976, Chavez stayed home rather than vote for Carter. By 1980, she was ready to vote for Reagan, another longtime Democrat who felt that his party had changed.

In one respect, Linda Chavez was an unusual figure: there were hardly any prominent Mexican American conservatives, male or female. But her transformation from liberal Democrat to conservative Republican typified a basic change of the 1980s. Still coming to terms with economic and political decline, a new majority of Americans, including businesspeople, evangelical Christians, and "Reagan Democrats" like Chavez, turned toward a conservative vision of the country. Rejecting the pessimism of the 1970s, these Americans wanted to believe that individual and national success were still possible. The new conservative majority was more open to materialism and to a government that left people free to succeed or fail.

continued

>> AMERICAN PORTRAIT *continued*

The trend toward conservatism had wide-ranging consequences. Eager to restore old social, economic, and political values, Reagan set out to recast the United States by cutting taxes, reducing government regulation, and diminishing union power to restore economic growth. The president also embraced a conservative social agenda including attacks on affirmative action and abortion. Abroad, he carried out a foreign policy dedicated to confronting Communism. Despite scandals, setbacks, and compromises, Reagan and the new conservatism arrested fears of America's decline and altered the nation's politics and culture for a generation.

OUTLINE 

Creating a Conservative Majority

In the 1970s and 1980s, the conservative movement continued its rise to power. The New Right drew strength from the transformation of the economy, the changing reputation of big business, and the growth of evangelical Christianity. The power of the conservative coalition became clear in the 1980 presidential election, when voters sent Ronald Reagan to the White House.

The New Economy

Conservatism benefited from the gradual emergence of a postindustrial, computer-centered economy. As deindustrialization continued, technological change pointed the way to national economic revival. Along with other innovations, semiconductors—transistorized integrated circuits attached to small silicon crystals—allowed manufacturers to shrink the computer. By the late 1970s they could put the power of an old, room-sized mainframe computer into a box that would fit on a desktop. In 1981, the computing giant IBM introduced its first personal computer, or PC. By the end of the 1980s, Americans were buying 7 million PCs a year (see Figure 30–1).

> **We see our lives as boundless. . . . Yes, we read about high interest rates and an economy that may hamper our success. But we don't think of that as meaning us.**
>
> MARK SANDERS, a junior at the University of Texas at Austin, 1984

Computers seemed to promise a way out of national economic decline. The microcomputer bolstered older companies such as IBM and created new firms such as Apple and Dell; it enriched new entrepreneurs such as Steve Jobs, a founder of Apple, and Bill Gates, a founder of the software firm Microsoft. Whereas Asian manufacturers built most consumer-electronics products, American companies dominated computer hardware and software.

The growth of the computer industry inspired utopian dreams of a high-technology society built on the production of knowledge rather than things. Promoting literacy and education, the computer would lift up the poor and disadvantaged. Unlike the old industrial economy, the computerized economy would cut down on pollution and the consumption of raw materials. By enabling people to work at home, the microcomputer would eliminate commuting and relieve urban congestion.

The vitality and promise of the computer-driven economy helped conservatism. The traditional faith of conservatives in capitalist free enterprise, unaided by government, seemed to be confirmed by the appearance of new industries, new companies, and new jobs. Correspondingly, there was seemingly less need for the government intervention in the economy that liberals preferred.

The emergence of the new economy also benefited conservatism by stimulating the continued flow of people, jobs, and political power from the North and East to the South and West. Computing did revive parts of the Rustbelt. In Massachusetts, a string of computer companies sprang up around Boston along Route 128 to replace the textile mills and shoe factories that had long since left the state. But computing more visibly benefited the Sunbelt, the birthplace of the new conservatism in the 1950s and 1960s. Dell's headquarters were in Texas. Apple was one of many computer firms clustered in Silicon Valley outside San Francisco. Rustbelt industrial cities such as Pittsburgh and Detroit lost population, while some Sunbelt counties more than doubled in population. The shifting regional

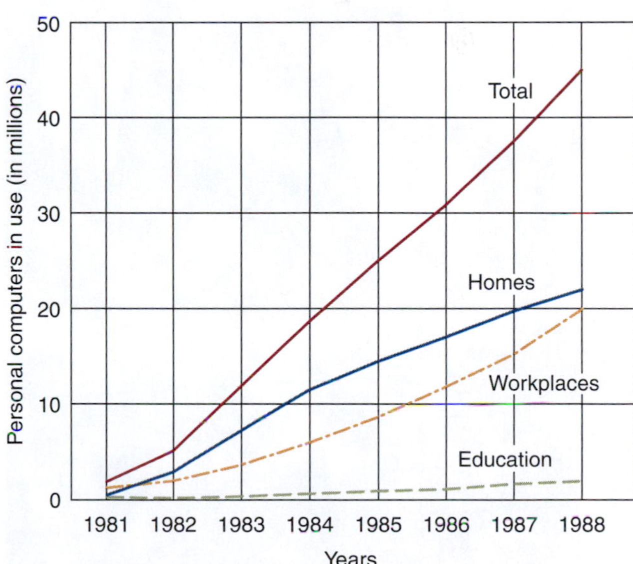

Figure 30–1 The Rise of the Personal Computer The rapid rise in the number of microcomputers in use in homes, workplaces, and schools in the 1980s inspired hopes that the nation's economic decline had ended. Statistical Abstract of the United States, 1989 *(Washington, D.C.: U.S. Bureau of the Census, 1990), p. 743;* Statistical Abstract, 1993 *(Washington, D.C.: U.S. Bureau of the Census, 1994), p. 761.*

balance had direct political consequences. Reapportionment in 1980 gave more congressional seats and electoral votes to the relatively conservative states of the Sunbelt.

A Revolution on a Desktop In 1981, the new IBM PC or personal computer conveniently offered the power of an old room-filling mainframe computer.

The Rehabilitation of Business

While the 1980s pointed to a utopian future, the decade also recalled the cutthroat capitalism of the turn of the twentieth century. A wave of corporate takeovers and mergers swept across the economy. Aggressive investment bankers and entrepreneurs such as Michael Milken and Ivan Boesky used a variety of techniques, such as junk bonds—high-risk, high-paying securities—to finance takeovers. Executives took golden parachutes, huge payments for selling their companies and losing their jobs. Enormous deals merged some of the largest American corporations. In 1985 General Electric bought RCA for $6 billion. In 1986 alone there were more than 4,000 mergers worth a total of $190 billion. The biggest deal of all came in 1988 when RJR Nabisco was sold for $25 billion and the company's President and CEO received a $53 million golden parachute.

Michael Milken One of the aggressive leaders of the corporate takeover movement of the 1980s, his tactics, including the use of junk bonds, soon landed him in jail.

The takeover wave, along with the growth of the computer industry, helped rehabilitate business and its values, which had been assailed in the 1960s and 1970s. Although some observers criticized the concentration of so much economic power, others saw the takeovers as a sign of economic vitality. They argued that the mergers created larger, more efficient companies able to compete more successfully. These observers praised takeover artists as models of entrepreneurial energy and creativity. The media enthusiastically reported the achievements and opinions of Milken, Boesky, Jobs, and Gates. *Dallas, Dynasty,* and other popular television shows wallowed happily in the fictional sagas of wealthy, freewheeling businessmen and their families. Business was more respectable than at any time since the 1950s.

So was materialism. Business figures helped legitimize the pursuit and enjoyment of wealth. "Everybody should be a little greedy," Boesky advised. "You shouldn't feel guilty." There was renewed interest in lavish living. "Thank goodness it's back," gushed the *New York Times,* "that lovely whipped cream of a word—luxury."

The baby boom generation reflected the new appeal of business values. Abandoning social action, former 1960s radicals such as Yippie (Youth Independent Party) leader Jerry Rubin took up business careers. By 1983 the media were talking about the emergence of yuppies, young urban professionals in their 20s and 30s. Uninterested in reform, these optimistic, self-centered baby boomers were supposedly eager to make lots of money and then spend it on BMW cars, Perrier water, and other consumer playthings. Although the transition from idealistic Yippies to radical yuppies was exaggerated, the yuppie stereotype underscored how much Americans aspired to a more conservative, money-centered way of life.

The Rise of the Religious Right

At the same time American culture celebrated materialism, many Americans still turned to spirituality to find meaning in their lives. Their choice of denominations reinforced the trend to conservatism. Such mainline Protestant denominations as the United Methodist Church, the Episcopal Church, and the Presbyterian Church, USA, had attracted a declining share of the nation's church members since at least 1940. Meanwhile, evangelical churches boomed (see Map 30–1). By the 1980s, the Southern Baptist Convention was the largest American Protestant denomination.

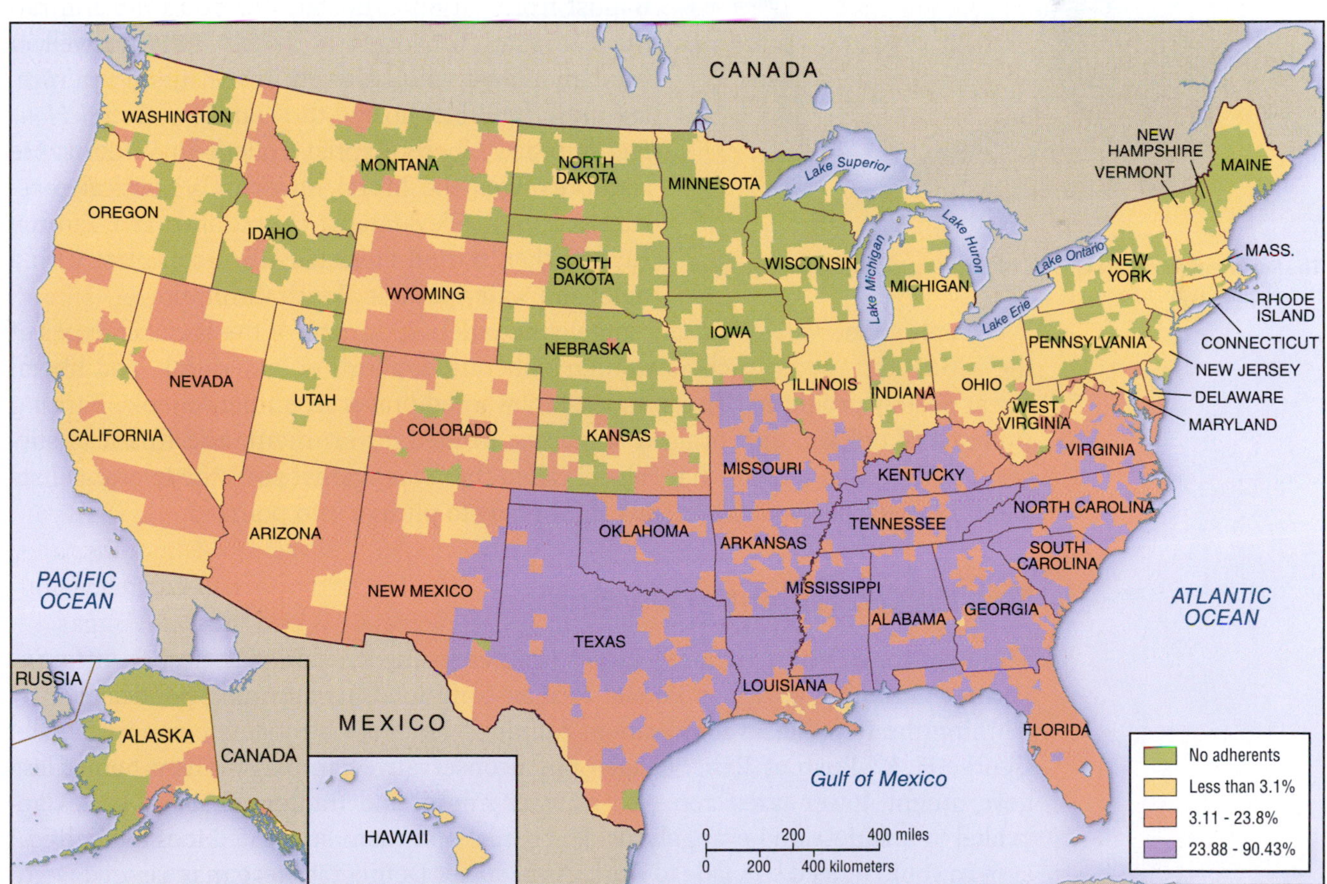

Map 30–1 The Growth of Evangelical Christianity The Southern Baptist Convention's share of the population, by county, reveals its gradual spread beyond its traditional base in the South by 1990. *Peter L Halvorson and William M. Newman,* Atlas of Religious Change in America, 1952–1990 *(Cincinnati, Ohio: Glenmary Research Center, 1994), p. 120.*

Such smaller evangelical bodies as the Assemblies of God and the Church of God more than doubled in size from the 1960s to the 1980s.

The changing balance between mainline and evangelical churches had social and political consequences. The mainline denominations often took moderate or liberal positions on such social issues as civil rights and abortion, but the evangelical churches were much more likely to support conservative positions. Troubled by social change and emboldened by their own growth, evangelicals wanted to spread a conservative message across American culture and politics.

The emergence of "televangelists" was the most obvious result of this impulse. From 1978 to 1989 the number of Christian television ministries grew from 25 to 336. In addition to their own television shows, the most successful televangelists had their own networks, colleges, political groups, and even an amusement park. Pat Robertson, a born-again Baptist from Virginia, hosted *The 700 Club* and ran the Christian Broadcast Network. Jerry Falwell, a fundamentalist who believed in the literal interpretation of the Bible, hosted the *Old Time Gospel Hour* and founded Liberty Baptist College in Virginia. He also organized the Moral Majority, a political pressure group. A televangelist couple, Jim and Tammy Faye Bakker, started Heritage USA, complete with a hotel and water park, in South Carolina.

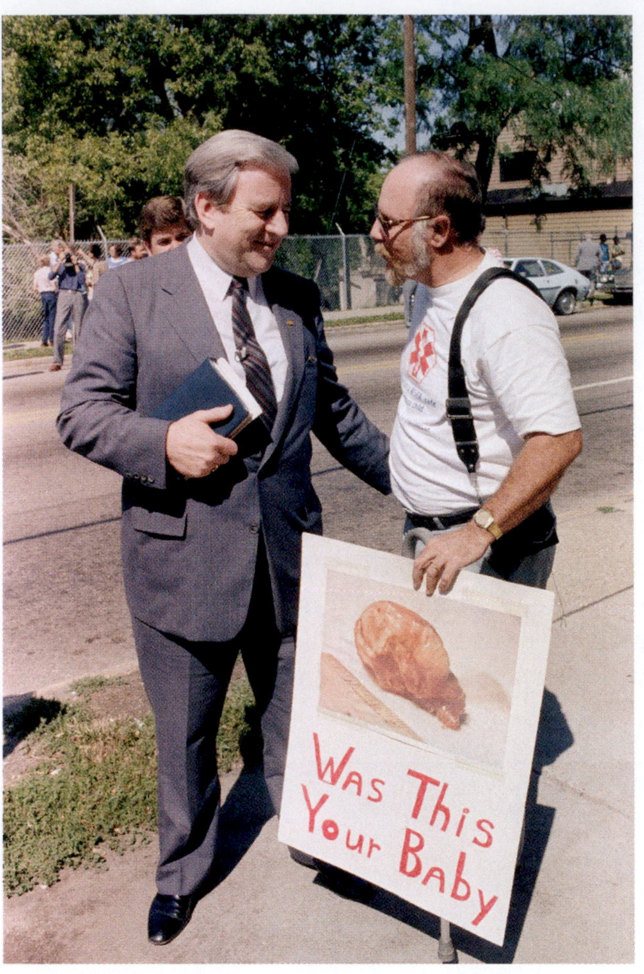

The Reverend Jerry Falwell Falwell (left), fundamentalist and leader of the religious right.

Deeply conservative, the televangelists condemned many of the social changes of the 1960s and 1970s, such as women's liberation, abortion, gay rights, and liberal Great Society programs. The broadcasters wanted prayer in public schools. Earning millions of dollars, they praised low taxes, limited government, and financial success. Determined to win what Falwell called the "war against sin," the televangelists were the spearheads of a religious right ready to plunge into politics.

The 1980 Presidential Election

The new conservative majority came together in the presidential election of 1980. Former California governor Ronald Reagan continued his stunning political rise by winning the Republican nomination. Although he chose a moderate running mate, George H. W. Bush of Texas, Reagan ran a conservative campaign. His vision of less government, lower taxes, renewed military might, and traditional social values appealed to business and evangelicals. His genial optimism suggested that the political system could indeed be made to work. As a former Democrat, Reagan reassured Democrats and independents that they too could find a home in the Republican Party.

Meanwhile, the Democratic nominee, incumbent president Jimmy Carter, struggled with the double burdens of a weak economy and the ongoing hostage crisis in

Iran. His moderate and sometimes conservative policies had alienated liberal Democrats. His poor economic record had alienated the party's white ethnics. Moderate Republican congressman John Anderson of Illinois, who ran as an independent, drew more voters away from Carter than from Reagan. Meanwhile, the Republican nominee focused relentlessly on the continuing decline of American fortunes during Carter's presidency. In the last presidential debate before election day, Reagan told the audience, "I think . . . it might be well if you would ask yourself, are you better off than you were four years ago?"

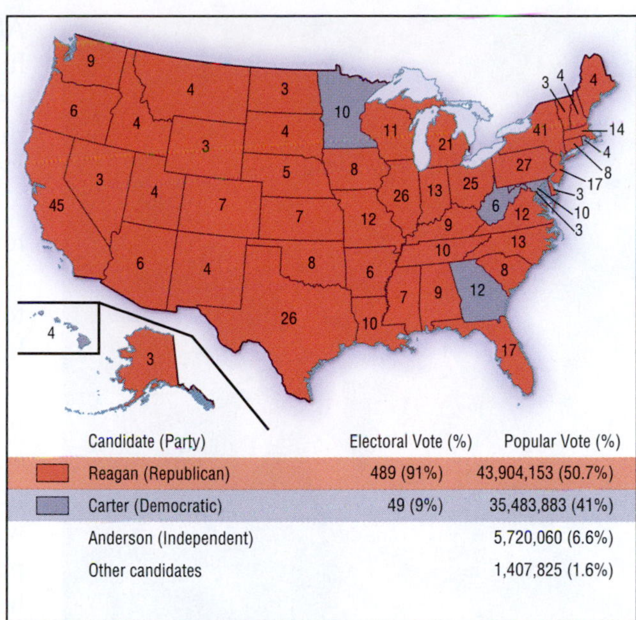

Candidate (Party) Electoral Vote (%) Popular Vote (%)
Reagan (Republican) 489 (91%) 43,904,153 (50.7%)
Carter (Democratic) 49 (9%) 35,483,883 (41%)
Anderson (Independent) 5,720,060 (6.6%)
Other candidates 1,407,825 (1.6%)

Map 30–2 The Presidential Election, 1980 As in other elections, a narrow victory in the popular vote translated into a landslide in the electoral college.

Americans answered that question by giving Reagan the presidency. The Republican nominee carried all but four states and the District of Columbia (see Map 30–2). Reagan managed only 50.7 percent of the popular vote, but his tally, combined with Anderson's 6.6 percent, suggested the extent of popular disaffection with Carter and the Democratic Party. Although the Democrats held on to the House of Representatives, Republicans took control of the Senate for the first time since 1962. Sixteen years after Barry Goldwater's conservative candidacy had ended in a crushing defeat, the nation had turned sharply to the right.

The Reagan Revolution at Home

Ronald Reagan shaped American life more decisively than any president since Franklin Roosevelt. Reagan's style—folksy and optimistic—made him popular, but the Reagan years were more than a triumph of style. With some justice, his supporters believed that the president spurred a "Reagan Revolution," a sweeping conservative transformation of American economic and political life.

The Reagan Style

The Reagan Revolution was partly a matter of style. Despite the frustrations of the 1960s and 1970s, Reagan exuded optimism. Rather than teach Americans how to live with less, he embraced luxury. Reagan's presidency signaled a confident, even opulent, new era. On inauguration day, as if to mark the belated end of the frustrating 1970s, the Iranian government finally released its American hostages. In his inaugural address, Reagan firmly rejected pessimism about the nation's future. "We are not," the new president declared, "doomed to an inevitable decline." That night, he and his wife Nancy danced at a series of lavish balls. The Reagan inaugural cost five times more than Jimmy Carter's had four years earlier.

> **In this present crisis, government is not the solution of our problem.**
>
> RONALD REAGAN, inaugural address, January 1981

Even while the Reagans continued their lavish lifestyle in the White House, the president retained a popular, common touch.

The Return of Confident Luxury Newly-inaugurated President Ronald Reagan dances with his wife Nancy at a ball, January 1981.

After his career in movies and television, he knew how to speak simply and effectively to the American people. Although the president did not always absorb the details of issues, he became known as the "Great Communicator."

Reagan also appeared to enjoy and master his job. After the troubled presidencies of the 1970s, Reagan made the presidency seem manageable again. Even though he took office as America's oldest president at the age of 69, he projected an image of vigor and energy.

The president even managed to survive an assassination attempt. On March 30, 1981, John W. Hinckley, a troubled young loner, shot and wounded Reagan, his press secretary, and a policeman. Reagan's chest wound was more serious than his spokesmen admitted, but the president met the situation with good humor. "Honey," he told his wife, "I forgot to duck." The president's popularity soared.

Shrinking Government

More than just a master of style, Reagan offered a clear conservative alternative to the liberal policies of the New Deal and the Great Society. Above all, he denied that a large, activist federal government could deal with the challenges of American life in the 1980s. Accordingly, Reagan wanted to shrink the government's size and reduce its power.

The president's efforts to shrink the federal government met with mixed success. In his 1982 State of the Union address, Reagan, like the previous Republican president, Richard Nixon, endorsed the New Federalism, a plan to transfer federal programs and tax revenues to the states. Reagan insisted the New Federalism would promote efficiency and economic growth, but governors worried that their states would be saddled with expensive responsibilities. In the end, the federal government transferred only a few programs.

Reagan also created a commission, headed by business executive J. Peter Grace, to explore ways the federal government could save money. The Grace Commission claimed that Washington could save more than $400 billion over three years, partly by making it more difficult for Americans to qualify for welfare, pension, and other benefits. Congress was unwilling to make such reforms. The commission also called for the line-item veto, which would allow a president to reject particular spending programs in Congress's annual budget without having to veto the entire budget bill. Congress was not ready to give Reagan so much new power.

The president had more success when he attacked social welfare programs. Like many other conservatives, Reagan condemned antipoverty programs as a waste of federal resources that sapped the work ethic and the morals of the poor. Reagan and his followers believed that the nation thrived when workers had to succeed or fail on their own. He wanted reductions in food stamps, school meal programs, and aid to cities. In response, Congress cut appropriations for urban public housing and eliminated job training for the unemployed.

Reagan found it nearly impossible to touch Medicare and Social Security, two expensive and popular programs that benefited most Americans. The Social Security system proved especially difficult to cut. By the 1980s there was growing concern that workers' Social Security payments would eventually not be enough to cover the cost of benefits to retirees. After a long struggle, Congress produced the Social Security Reform Act of 1983, which raised the minimum age for full benefits from 65 to 67 and made retirees pay taxes on some benefits. The measure did little to reduce the total cost of the program. By 1984, Reagan was promising not to cut Social Security.

Although expenditures for welfare programs continued to rise, the Reagan administration managed to slow the growth of such spending. Benefits did not expand dramatically; there were no costly new programs. As expenditures for national defense grew, welfare outlays fell from 28 percent of the federal budget in 1980 to 22 percent by 1987. Reagan did not reduce the federal government overall, but he did succeed in shrinking the relative size of some parts of it that he disliked.

Reaganomics

For Reagan and his followers, shrinking the government also meant decreasing Washington's role in the economy. True to conservative ideology, they argued that the nation prospered most when government left Americans free to manage their own businesses and keep their own earnings. The Reagan administration worked to lower taxes, deregulate business, and cut federal support for unions.

"Reaganomics" drew on a new theory known as supply-side economics. Beginning in the 1970s, economist Arthur Laffer had offered an alternative to the liberal, Keynesian economics that had guided federal policy since the New Deal. While Keynesians believed that increased consumer demand would spur economic growth, Laffer contended that an increased supply of goods and services was the key to growth. He rejected the Keynesian prescription for raising government spending to put more money in the hands of consumers. To promote prosperity, he believed government should cut, rather than hike, taxes. By leaving more money in the hands of businesses, government would allow them to invest in more production of goods and services. The increase in supply would stimulate prosperity and increase, rather than decrease, tax revenues.

Supply-side economics was controversial. To liberal critics it seemed to be an excuse to let the rich keep more of their money. Even some Republicans doubted that a tax cut would produce more tax revenues. But the supply-side approach fit neatly with conservative dislike for high taxes and big, active government.

Following supply-side principles, Reagan asked a joint session of Congress in 1981 to cut taxes dramatically. Impressed by Reagan's popularity and the electorate's increasing conservatism, the Democratic-controlled House joined the Republican-dominated Senate to pass the Economic Recovery Act of 1981 (also known as the Kemp-Roth Bill). An important victory for Reagan, this measure cut federal income taxes 5 percent the first year and then 10 percent in each of the next two years. It especially benefited the wealthy by making the tax structure less progressive and by reducing the tax rate on the highest individual incomes and on large gifts and estates.

Like other conservatives, Reagan believed that federal rules and requirements hamstrung American business and prevented economic growth. Accordingly, his administration stepped up the campaign for deregulation begun by Jimmy Carter. The government cut the budgets of such key regulatory agencies as the Environmental Protection Agency and the Occupational Safety and Health Administration. The Reagan administration also made sure that government officials did not strictly enforce regulatory rules and laws. Further, the administration deregulated the telephone industry. In 1982 the government broke up the giant American Telephone and Telegraph Company into smaller regional companies and allowed new firms such as Sprint and MCI to compete for AT&T's long-distance business.

Reagan moved to lift environmental restrictions on American businesses. His administration made it easier for timber and mining companies to exploit wilderness areas and allowed oil companies to drill off the Pacific coast. The administration also opposed environmentalists' demands for laws to protect against acid rain—air pollution, caused by industrial emissions, that harmed lakes, forests, and crops, especially in the Northeast and Canada.

Reaganomics also meant weakening organized labor, already suffering from deindustrialization. Ironically, Reagan, once the head of the Screen Actors Guild, was the first former union official to serve as president. Like most conservatives, Reagan believed that unions obstructed business and limited the freedom of individual workers. He believed as well that the federal government had done too much to encourage organized labor since the New Deal.

Reagan made probusiness appointments to the National Labor Relations Board. More important, he took a strong antiunion stance during a strike by the Professional Air Traffic Controllers Organization (PATCO) in 1981. Despite a law forbidding strikes by federal workers, PATCO walked out to protest unsafe conditions in the air traffic control system. Reagan fired the striking controllers, refused to hire them back, and replaced them with nonunion workers. The president's action encouraged business to take a hard line with employees. By the end of the 1980s, the union movement was weaker than at any time since the Great Depression.

Reaganomics did not quite have the effect that its supporters anticipated. In the short run, Reagan's measures did not prevent a sharp recession, which began in the fall of 1981. As the Federal Reserve Bank fought inflation by raising interest rates, the economy slowed, and unemployment increased. Reaganomics also increased the federal budget deficit. The supply-side theory that tax cuts would boost tax revenues and balance the budget proved incorrect.

By the spring of 1984, the recession had ended. Thanks largely to the Federal Reserve's monetary policy, the high inflation of the 1970s was over. The economy began a long period of growth and higher employment, and Reagan's supporters gave the president credit. His critics charged that the deficit rather than Reaganomics had produced the boom and that the deficit would ultimately hurt the economy. In the mid-1980s, however, Reaganomics appeared to be a success. Certainly "stagflation," the combination of stagnant economic growth and high inflation that plagued the 1970s, was over.

Organized Labor Confronts the Reagan Revolution These and other striking members of the Professional Air Traffic Controllers Organization would soon be fired by President Ronald Reagan in 1981.

The 1984 Presidential Election

The changing impact of Reaganomics shaped national politics. In the depths of the recession, the Republicans lost 26 House seats in the midterm congressional elections of 1982. But with the return of prosperity, the president was easily renominated in 1984. Reagan ran against a liberal Democratic nominee, former vice president Walter Mondale of Minnesota. The Democrat, confronting a popular incumbent, made bold moves. Mondale chose the first female vice-presidential nominee of a major party, Representative Geraldine Ferraro of New York. To prove his honesty and openness, Mondale made the politically foolish announcement that he would raise taxes as president. The Democrat was also saddled with the disappointing record of the Carter administration and the alienation of white working- and middle-class Democrats.

Reagan ran an optimistic campaign emphasizing the renewal of America. "It's morning again in America," a Reagan campaign commercial announced. "Life is better, America is back," another commercial declared. "And people have a sense of pride they never felt they'd feel again." Mondale would jeopardize all that, the Reagan campaign charged, with tax increases and favors to such "special interests" as labor unions, feminists, and civil rights activists.

Election day revealed both the strength and the weakness of the Reagan Revolution. The contest was a personal triumph for the president. With his conservative message, Reagan polled 58.8 percent of the popular vote and lost only the District of Columbia and Mondale's home state of Minnesota. Reagan's big vote did not translate into a sweeping victory for his party. Holding on to the Senate, the Republicans failed to win a majority in the House of Representatives.

The Reagan Revolution Abroad

Reagan's foreign policy, like his domestic policy, rested on old conservative values. The president rejected the main diplomatic approaches of the 1970s—Richard Nixon's détente with the Soviet Union and Jimmy Carter's support for international human rights. Instead, the Reagan Revolution revived the strident anti-Communism of the 1940s and 1950s. The president moved to restore the nation's military and economic power in order to challenge the Soviet Union and stop Communism in the Western Hemisphere. Communism, however, had little to do with such difficult international issues as conflict in the Middle East, terrorism, and economic relations with Japan and developing nations. Nevertheless, the Reagan Revolution abroad plainly refocused American policy on the cold war confrontation with Communism.

Restoring American Power

After losing the Vietnam War, the United States had cut back its armed forces and become reluctant to risk military confrontations abroad. Reagan set out to restore American power in the 1980s—and the will to use it.

Like most conservatives, the president did not believe that cutting government spending should include cutting the armed forces. Under Reagan, the nation's defense spending more than doubled, from $134 billion in 1980 to more than $300 billion by 1989. Reagan's administration built up all branches of the armed services and ordered development of controversial weapons systems. Construction of the B-1 strategic jet bomber, stopped by Jimmy Carter, resumed. Reagan began development of the B-2 Stealth bomber, an innovative plane that could evade detection by enemy radar. He won congressional approval for the MX Peacekeeper, a nuclear missile with multiple warheads. He also persuaded Congress to authorize work on the neutron bomb, a nuclear weapon that could spread lethal radiation over a half-mile radius.

As he pursued his military buildup, Reagan faced a growing mass movement against nuclear weapons. In both Europe and the United States, millions of people, frightened by the horror of nuclear war, called for a halt to the introduction of new nuclear arms. In June 1982, a crowd of 700,000 gathered in New York's Central Park to demand a nuclear freeze. The National Conference of Catholic Bishops supported the freeze and declared nuclear war immoral. But Reagan rejected the movement as naive and Communist-infiltrated. The best way to ensure peace, he believed, was to keep developing weapons.

The military buildup was a matter of changing attitudes as well as increasing weapons and budgets. In the wake of the Vietnam War, many Americans were reluctant to endorse U.S. intervention abroad. They feared that the nation might become entrapped in another costly, losing, possibly immoral battle overseas. This "Vietnam syndrome" threatened the Reagan administration's foreign policy. The president could not afford to let other countries think the United States would not back up its words with action. Accordingly, Reagan used his speeches to stir up patriotic emotion. The president also tried to persuade Americans that the Vietnam War had been "a just cause," well worth supporting.

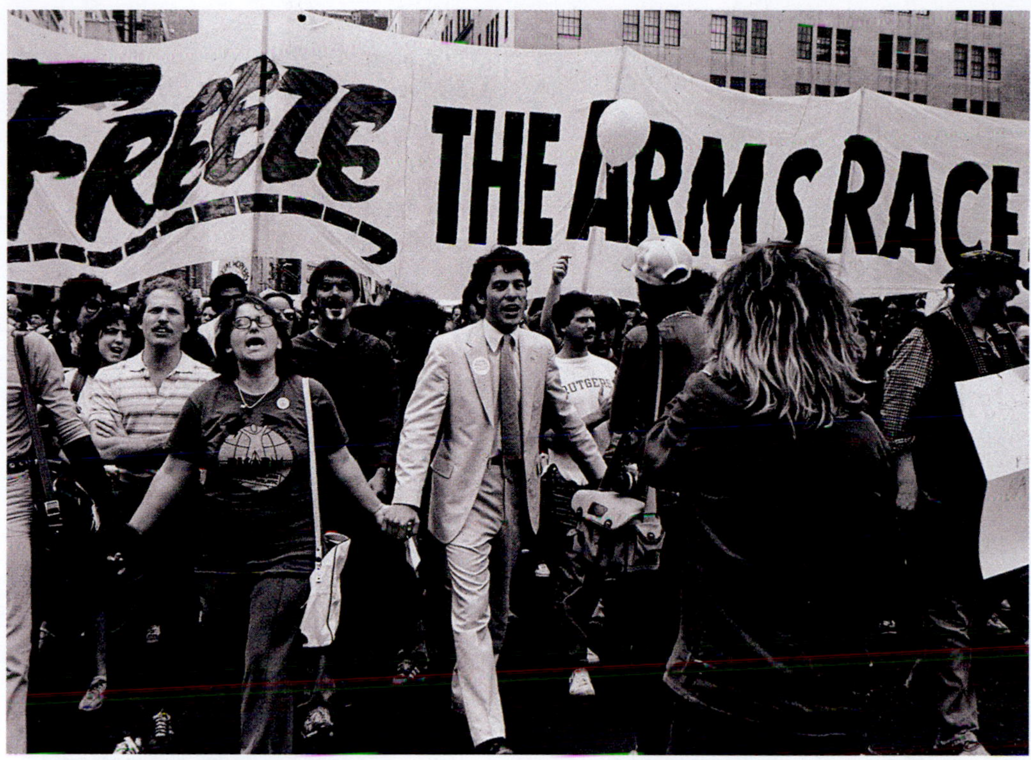

Some of the 700,000 Demonstrators at the Nuclear Freeze Rally in New York City's Central Park, June 1982 For a time, the movement to halt new nuclear weapons challenged President Reagan's plans for an arms buildup.

By the mid-1980s, Reagan had succeeded in restoring much of America's military power. It remained to be seen, however, whether Americans were willing to use that power abroad.

Confronting the "Evil Empire"

The main purpose of the military buildup was to contain the Soviet Union. Suspicion of the Soviets and their Communist ideology was the heart of Reagan's diplomacy. In the early 1980s, Reagan called the USSR the "evil empire" and insisted that the Soviet Union and its Communist allies were doomed by failing economies and unpopular regimes. Communist ideology, Reagan declared, would end up "on the ash heap of history."

Reagan avoided cooperation with the Soviet Union and held no summit meetings during his first term. The Reagan administration openly supported the mujahedeen, the Afghan rebels who were resisting the Soviets. More important, the president avoided arms-control agreements with the Soviets during his first term. Instead, he used the American military buildup to pressure the USSR. Reagan refused to submit the second Strategic Arms Limitation Treaty, signed by Jimmy Carter, to the Senate for ratification. In response to the United States' deployment of new intermediate-range nuclear missiles in Western Europe, the Soviets walked out of arms-control talks in 1983.

That year, Reagan put even more pressure on the USSR when he announced plans for the Strategic Defense Initiative (SDI), a space-based missile-defense

The Dream of President Reagan's "Star Wars" An artist's illustration of how the Reagan administration's Strategic Defense Initiative would knock Communist missiles out of the sky.

system that would use lasers and other advanced technology to shoot down nuclear missiles launched at the United States. Although funded by Congress, SDI was a long way from reality in 1983. Critics, convinced SDI was science fiction, called the plan "Star Wars," after the epic space movie.

The American initiative doubly threatened the Soviets. SDI seemingly made the USSR vulnerable to attack. Since the 1950s, the Americans and the Soviets had relied on the theory of *mutual assured destruction* as a deterrent to war: since a nuclear war would destroy both sides, the theory ran, there was no incentive for either nation to start one. Now SDI raised the possibility that the United States could survive a nuclear attack and therefore might be willing to start a war with the Soviets. To avoid this threat, the Soviets would need to develop their own SDI. There was the second threat: the USSR would have to divert scarce resources and perhaps weaken their economy in order to compete with the United States.

While the United States pressed the Soviets, Reagan clearly wanted to avoid open confrontation with the major Communist powers. In 1983, a Soviet fighter plane shot down an unarmed Korean airliner, killing all 269 passengers and crew. Although a U.S. congressman was one of the victims, Reagan responded with restraint. A year later, Reagan traded visits with the premier of the People's Republic of China and encouraged cultural exchanges, economic cooperation, and a nuclear-weapons agreement.

The Reagan Doctrine in the Third World

The Reagan administration also changed American foreign policy toward the third world. Reagan, along with other conservatives, had been impatient with the Carter administration's attempts to promote human rights abroad. The United States, conservatives believed, needed to back anti-Communist, pro-American governments, whether or not they respected human rights. Jeane J. Kirkpatrick, who became Reagan's ambassador to the United Nations, called for a distinction between totalitarian regimes hostile to the U.S. and authoritarian governments friendly to American interests. Critics claimed that this distinction was meaningless and insisted that the nation should not support antidemocratic governments. The administration adopted Kirkpatrick's view, which became known as the Reagan Doctrine.

During the president's first term, his administration applied the Reagan Doctrine aggressively in Central America and the Caribbean (see Map 30–3). Determined to keep Communism out of the Western Hemisphere, the United States opposed the

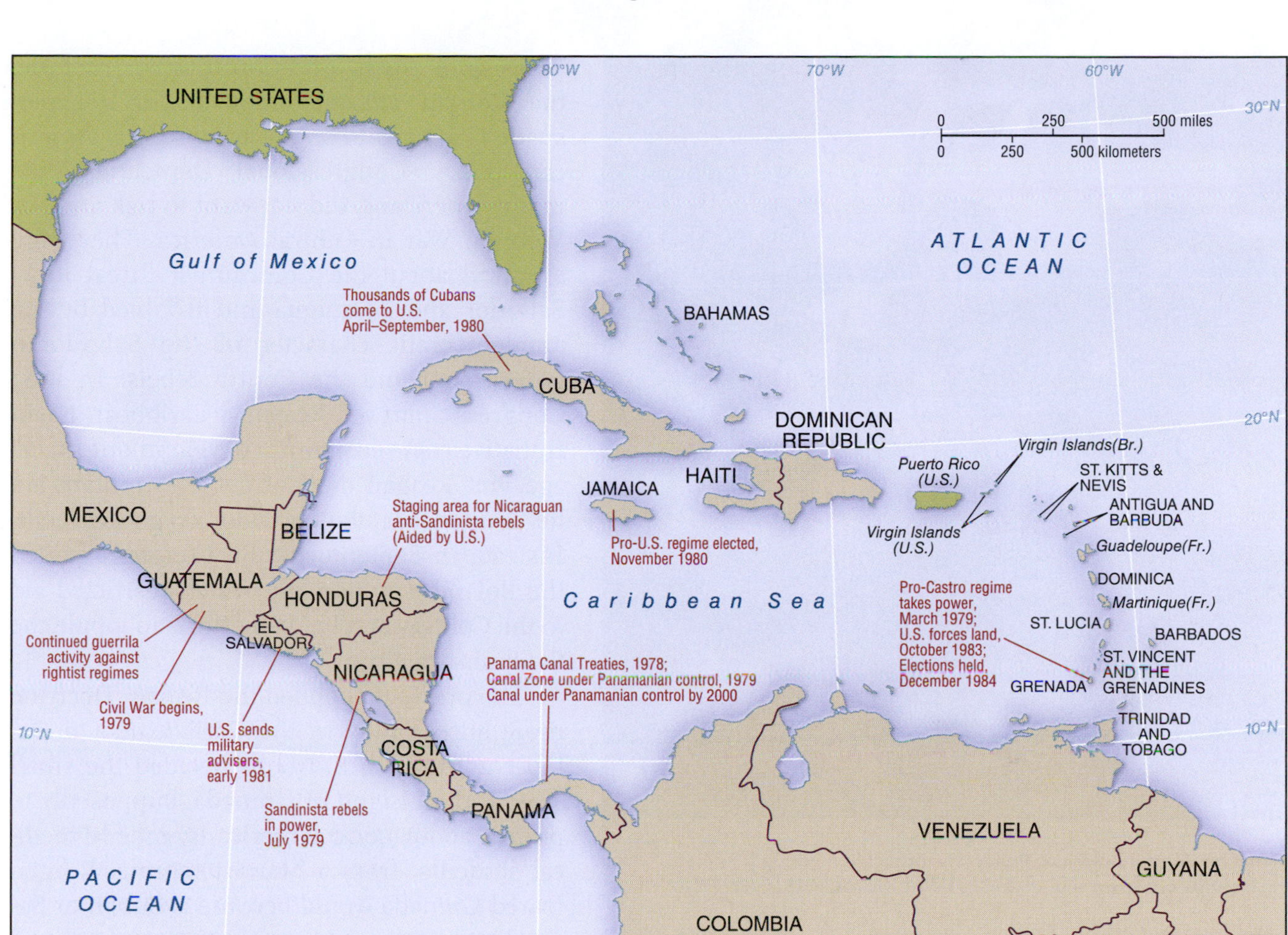

Map 30–3 The Reagan Doctrine in Central America and the Caribbean Events that shaped Reagan's anti-Communist initiative in the Western Hemisphere.

Marxist Sandinista government of Nicaragua and supported the repressive anti-Communist government of neighboring El Salvador.

The Sandinistas had come to power in the late 1970s by overthrowing the dictatorship of Anastasio Somoza with the encouragement of the Carter administration. The Reagan administration believed the Sandinistas were too friendly to the Soviet Union and to leftist rebels in El Salvador. Reagan halted aid to Nicaragua in April 1981 and directed the CIA to train, arm, and supply the Contra rebels, who opposed the Sandinistas. Many of the Contras had ties to the oppressive Somoza government, but Reagan praised them as "freedom fighters" and "the moral equivalent of our Founding Fathers."

Meanwhile, the president strongly backed the right-wing military government of El Salvador, which was locked in a deadly civil war with pro-Sandinista and pro-Cuban rebels. Ultimately, some 75,000 people died in the conflict. Employing infamous "death squads," the military government engaged in kidnapping, torture, and murder. Nevertheless, Reagan did not want this brutal, undemocratic regime to fall. El Salvador, the president explained, was "a textbook case of indirect armed aggression by Communist powers."

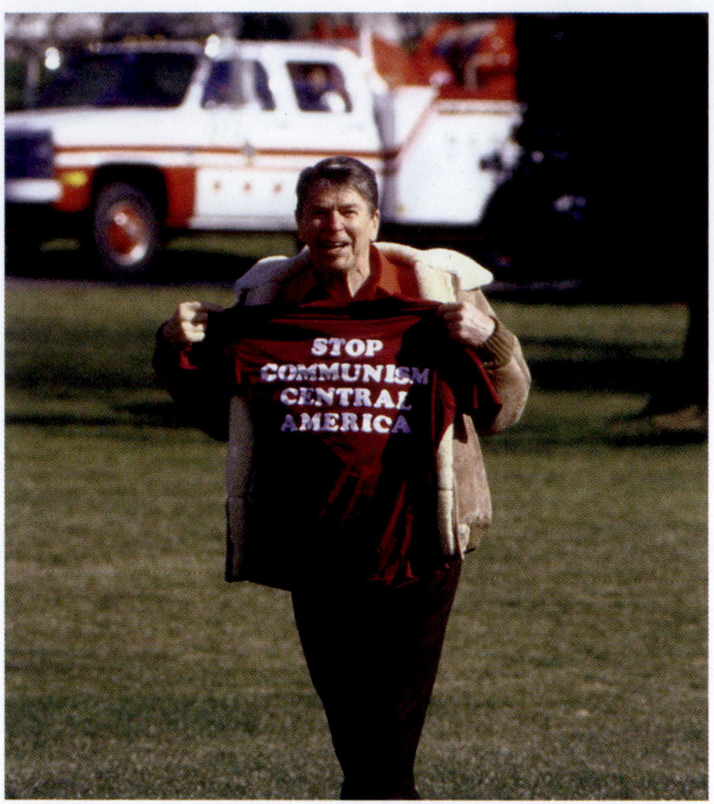

Reagan's Central American Policy The president holds up a T-shirt summing up his approach to the region: "STOP COMMUNISM CENTRAL AMERICA."

Despite such anti-Communist rhetoric, the Reagan administration could not persuade Congress to support its Central American policy. Congressional Democrats, like many Americans, did not want to risk another Vietnam War in Central America. They were skeptical about the Communist threat to El Salvador and Nicaragua and troubled by the antidemocratic character of the Salvadoran government and the Contra rebels. In 1983 Congress approved Reagan's Caribbean Basin Initiative, an economic development package, but Reagan did not get the military aid he wanted for the Salvadoran government. Instead, in September 1982 Congress passed the Boland Amendment, which restricted aid to the Contras and banned efforts to topple the Sandinista regime.

The president applied the Reagan Doctrine more successfully in the Caribbean. On October 25, 1983, U.S. troops invaded the small West Indian island of Grenada, supposedly to protect about 1,000 Americans, mostly medical students, from a Marxist regime. Reagan feared Grenada would become a Cuban or Soviet base close to U.S. shores. The invading force quickly secured the island and replaced the government with a pro-American regime. Critics charged that Reagan had undermined the sovereignty of another state in order to win an easy military victory. For the president's supporters, the invasion was a welcome demonstration of the Reagan Doctrine and an antidote to the Vietnam syndrome.

The president also implemented the Reagan Doctrine in Africa. With its commitment to human rights, the Carter administration had condemned the long-standing policy of *apartheid*—racial separation—pursued by the white government of South Africa. Reagan, despite America's own struggle with racial segregation, would not take a similarly strong stance. Rather than impose economic sanctions on the South African regime, the president endorsed a mild policy of diplomatic discussions known as "constructive engagement" while South Africa suffered violence and near civil war. Reagan held back because his administration viewed the South African regime as a vital ally in the struggle against Communism in southern Africa. During the 1980s, the United States supported South African military intervention in Angola, Mozambique, and Namibia against groups aided by Cuba and the Soviet Union. More than a million people died in these conflicts.

The Middle East and Terrorism

The Reagan Doctrine was not much help in dealing with the Middle East and the growing problem of terrorism. Communism and the Soviet Union, the focus of Reagan's foreign policy, had little impact on Middle Eastern issues in the 1980s.

As before, the United States wanted to ensure its supply of oil and to support its longtime ally, Israel. There was no new Arab oil embargo during the Reagan years, but the administration could not bring peace to the Middle East or end the threat of terrorism.

Reagan found it difficult to build on the Camp David Accords between Israel and Egypt, which were supposed to lead to self-government for the Palestinian Arabs who lived in the Israeli-occupied West Bank and Gaza Strip. However, Israel and the Palestine Liberation Organization (PLO), the official representative of the Palestinians, remained at odds. The PLO continued to threaten Israel from bases in neighboring Lebanon. In the spring of 1982, the Israelis invaded Lebanon, which was already convulsed by a civil war between Muslims and Christians.

To end the Israeli invasion and stabilize Lebanon, the United States sent marines to join an international peacekeeping force. On October 23, 1983, a terrorist killed 241 Americans by driving a truck bomb into marine headquarters at Beirut. The attack shocked Americans and marked a low point of Reagan's administration. The president did not retaliate. He did not want to reward terrorism by removing U.S. troops from Lebanon. Nevertheless, he pulled out the soldiers in 1984, even though there was still no peace in Lebanon and no agreement between the Israelis and the PLO.

The Threat of Terrorism U.S. Marines carry a survivor from the rubble of marine headquarters in Beirut, Lebanon, after a truck bomb explosion in October 1983.

The attack on the marine headquarters illustrated the growing threat of terrorism against the United States and its allies. Reagan vowed to make terrorists "pay for their actions," but terrorism proved hard to stop. Acts of terrorism by Palestinians and Libyans drew quick American reprisals in the 1980s. After Palestinians murdered an American passenger on a cruise ship in the Mediterranean in 1985, U.S. planes forced down the Egyptian airliner carrying the escaping terrorists. The Reagan administration believed that Muammar Qaddafi, leader of the North African nation of Libya, supported terrorism. In 1982 U.S. Navy fighter planes shot down two Libyan fighters off the Libyan coast. After American soldiers died in a terrorist bombing in West Germany in 1986, U.S. jets bombed several targets in Libya, among them the military barracks and headquarters including Qaddafi's personal residence. Among the 40 or so dead was one of the Libyan leader's daughters. Qaddafi, whom Reagan called "the mad dog of the Middle East," seemed to become less critical of the United States, but the threat of terrorism did not go away.

Reagan also acted to safeguard America's oil supply. During a war between Iran and Iraq, the United States sent navy ships to protect oil tankers in the Persian Gulf. As in Lebanon, American intervention was costly. In May 1987 Iraqi missiles struck the U.S. destroyer *Stark,* killing 37 of its crew. The Reagan administration, unwilling to help Iran, accepted Iraq's apology. In July 1988, the U.S.

missile cruiser *Vincennes* accidentally shot down an Iranian airliner, killing 290 passengers. An American apology did little to quell Iranian anger, but the Iran-Iraq war soon ended, and with it the threat to America's oil supply.

The United States and the World Economy

Middle Eastern oil was only one of the economic factors shaping Reagan's foreign policy. The president had to deal with strains on the world economy. Like twentieth-century presidents before him, Reagan believed strongly that free trade would boost national economies around the world. He believed, too, that his conservative formula of tax cuts, lower government spending, and less government regulation would benefit other nations. But after years of relative economic decline, the United States could not always impose its will on other nations.

Reagan did successfully force his views on debt-ridden, relatively weak third world countries. By the end of the 1980s, the developing nations owed foreign banks more than $1.2 trillion in loan payments. Mexico was more than $100 billion in debt. American banks stood to lose heavily if Mexico and other nations defaulted on loans. American producers stood to lose, too, if these countries could not afford to buy U.S. goods. The Reagan administration nevertheless refused to protect American banks from loan defaults, instead forcing debtor countries to adopt freer trade, deregulation of business, and government austerity programs in return for new loans.

The Reagan administration had much less power to dictate trade policy with Japan. As Japanese exports flowed into the United States, Americans increasingly resented Japan's domination of the Japanese home market. Congress, believing the Japanese discriminated against American goods, pushed for retaliation. Japan placed voluntary quotas on its export of steel and automobiles to the United States. Although the Reagan administration devalued the dollar to make American goods cheaper, the trade imbalance continued. In 1988 the president signed the Omnibus Trade and Competitiveness Act, which allowed the government to place high tariffs on Japanese goods if Japan continued to discriminate against American goods. However, as long as Americans wanted to buy Japanese products, retaliation was unlikely. By 1989 a Japanese car, the Honda Accord, had become the biggest-selling model in the United States for the first time.

Many of those Accords had been made in the United States. Even as the Reagan administration struggled to open up Japanese markets for American goods, Japanese firms greatly increased their direct investment in the United States. Honda, for instance, built a new factory in Marysville, Ohio, to produce Accords for the American market. As Japanese companies built or took over other manufacturing facilities, many Americans wondered whether the global expansion of trade was really beneficial to their country after all.

The Battle over Conservative Social Values

For all of Ronald Reagan's success in the early 1980s, the new conservatism met with considerable opposition. The conservatives' social values were especially controversial. Eager to combat the legacies of the 1960s, many conservatives, like Linda Chavez, wanted to restore supposedly traditional values and practices. The conservative agenda collided head-on with one of the chief legacies of the 1960s—disadvantaged groups'

AMERICA AND THE WORLD

>> Japanese Management, American Workers

Until the 1980s, American workers had generally missed one of the quintessential experiences of globalization—management by foreigners. For decades, it was the workers of other countries who found themselves adapting to foreign managerial techniques, often those of U.S. multinational companies and their American executives. But with the weakening of American industry and the rebuilding of the Japanese and West European economies, expansive foreign firms began to set up operations in the United States in the 1970s and 1980s.

Japanese firms rushed to invest. By 1988, more than 300,000 American workers labored for Japanese companies in the United States. The most publicized Japanese ventures came in the auto industry, long dominated by U.S. manufacturers and their pioneering mass production techniques. In the 1980s, leading Japanese auto manufacturers set up factories in such places as Marysville, Ohio, Smyrna, Tennessee, and Fremont, California. In these and other facilities, Japanese companies set about teaching Americans new ways to work.

The Japanese approach emphasized the importance of the group over the individual. Japanese managers urged their American workers to see the company as a harmonious family whose members had the same interests. To foster harmony, the Japanese eliminated reserved parking spaces and dining rooms for management and time clocks for labor. At the Nissan plant in Smyrna, managers and workers wore the same blue uniform. The Japanese also tried to improve communication with workers and draw them into decision making. To empower workers and increase efficiency, Japanese companies often gave workers the means to stop production to eliminate a problem—something U.S. firms seldom did.

Japanese companies tried to make factory life more pleasant. Plants were clean and efficient. At the Nissan factory in Smyrna, workers had basketball hoops and Ping-Pong tables close to their stations for use during breaks. But the Japanese companies also banned smoking and radios. More important, management pushed workers to speed up production. Japanese companies also wanted workers to be flexible enough to do different jobs in a plant.

Some workers enthusiastically accepted the new approach. "I love it," gushed Nancy Nicholson, a laid-off factory worker who found a job in a Japanese plant in Virginia. "They make you feel like a part of a family." Workers appreciated that Japanese managers put in long hours and seemed devoted to efficiency and quality.

Laboring harder than before, many American workers were not quite so enthusiastic. They felt that the Japanese were hostile to unions, African Americans, and women. Some American managers charged that their Japanese employers would not promote them to top jobs. But most employees were glad to have a well-paying job that might last. "This plant is our survival," explained a union representative at the General Motors–Toyota plant in Fremont.

Japanese executives had some criticisms of their own. They felt that American workers needed too many instructions and too much motivation to do a job. Still individualistic, the Americans were not "team players" ready to confess mistakes or perform work outside their job description. "Americans are too sensitive about fairness," complained Kosuke Ikebuchi, after his years in the United States. Japanese veterans of the United States generally concluded their American subordinates were less productive than Japanese workers.

Despite such criticism, the Japanese companies seemed successful in the United States in the 1980s. Typically, Japanese-run units showed gains in productivity and quality. At the General Motors–Toyota plant in Fremont, workers turned out a car in 20 hours compared to 28 hours at another GM plant. Moreover, that car was more likely to satisfy buyers than the typical product of American-run companies.

> I bought feminism, and a lot of other things. It didn't work in any way, in my marriage or in child rearing. I'm talking about anarchy.
>
> NADA JAGERSON, a conservative Christian activist from San Bernardino, California, 1985

demands for equal rights and opportunities. Moreover, many Americans were unwilling to abandon the social changes of the last generation. Faced with such opposition, conservatives failed to achieve much of their vision for American society.

Attacking the Legacy of the 1960s

The new conservatism was driven by a desire to undo the liberal and radical legacies of the 1960s. Conservatives blamed federal courts for much of the social change in the United States over the last generation. In the 1960s and 1970s liberal justices with an activist conception of the courts' role had supported defendants' rights, civil rights, affirmative action, busing, and abortion while rejecting such conservative causes as school prayer.

Determined to take control of the courts, Reagan appointed many staunch, relatively young conservatives to the federal bench and the Supreme Court. In 1981 Sandra Day O'Connor, a fairly conservative judge from Arizona, became the Court's first woman justice. When Chief Justice Warren Burger retired, Reagan replaced him with conservative William Rehnquist. With the appointments of two more conservatives, Antonin Scalia and Anthony Kennedy, the Supreme Court seemed ready to turn away from liberalism.

It did not quite work out that way. In the 1980s the Court followed conservative views in limiting the rights of defendants. Ruling in *United States v. Leon* and *Nix v. Williams* in 1984, the justices made it easier for prosecutors to use evidence improperly obtained by police. However, on a variety of other issues, the court took a moderate stance. In *Wallace v. Jaffree* in 1985, the Court disappointed evangelical Christians and other advocates of school prayer by invalidating an Alabama law that allowed schools to devote a minute each day to voluntary prayer or meditation.

Prayer was just one element of conservatives' broad plan to reform public education. They believed that the federal government had played too large a role in the schools since the 1960s. Parents, meanwhile, had too little say in the education of their children. Conservative educational reformers preferred to use market forces rather than government power to reform the schools. They wanted to dismantle the federal Department of Education. In addition, they wanted the government to enable parents to choose the best schools—public or private—for their children, with federally funded vouchers or tax credits to help pay for the choice.

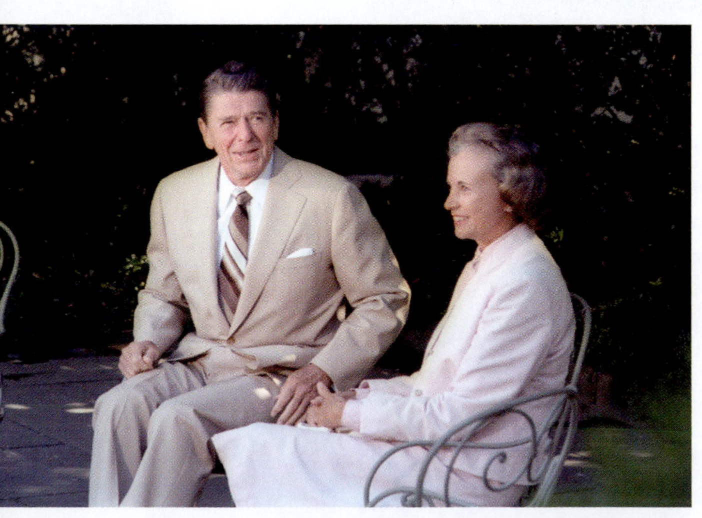

The First Woman Supreme Court Justice Sandra Day O'Connor, with President Reagan, who had nominated her to the court, 1981.

Because many Americans were worried about the quality of the schools, conservatives had a golden opportunity. In 1983 a federal study, *A Nation at Risk,* documented American students' shortcomings, especially in math and science. Despite such revelations, Congress refused to adopt the voucher system or to abolish the Department of Education.

Drug use was another issue that conservatives traced to the 1960s. In the early 1980s, drugs again became a major public concern with the spread of crack, a cheap but addictive form of cocaine. The sale and use of crack, especially in the cities, led to crime and violence. In 1986 the president and his wife, Nancy, announced a "national crusade" for a "drug-free" America. Their campaign encouraged young people to "Just Say No" to drugs, implemented drug testing for federal employees, and imposed mandatory minimum sentences for some drug use. The "war on drugs" was controversial. Critics ridiculed the "Just Say No" slogan as naive and ineffective. They also condemned new federal and state sentencing laws, which put millions in jail, as unfair to African Americans and expensive to taxpayers. Despite the new penalties and expenditures, drug use did not decrease appreciably.

Women's Rights and Abortion

One of the chief legacies of the 1960s was the women's rights movement. The new conservatism condemned feminism and lamented the changing role of women in America. Many conservatives, especially evangelical leaders, blamed feminists and liberal government for encouraging women to abandon their traditional family role for paid jobs. The conservative movement was especially determined to halt federal initiatives, such as affirmative action programs and the equal rights amendment (ERA), that used government power to protect women's rights (see Chapter 29).

The conservative agenda on women's rights met with mixed results. The campaign for the ERA, already lagging in the 1970s, ended unsuccessfully, but affirmative action programs, designed to promote the hiring of women, continued. So did women's push into the workplace and public life as more and more American families needed two incomes. By 1983 women made up half of the paid workforce. As their economic role expanded, American women received more recognition from the political system. Ironically, Reagan himself gave women new public prominence by choosing Jeane J. Kirkpatrick and Sandra Day O'Connor for important offices.

Women still did not enjoy equality in America. They were generally paid less than men doing the same sort of work, and they had less opportunity to break through the glass ceiling and win managerial jobs. Moreover, commentators had begun to note the feminization of poverty. Unmarried or divorced women, many with children, made up an increasing percentage of the poor. This suffering and inequality, liberals and feminists argued, disproved the conservative claim that women did not need special protection.

For many conservatives, the right to abortion, guaranteed by the Supreme Court in *Roe v. Wade* in 1974, was the most troubling sign of the changed status of women. A growing Right to Life movement passionately denounced abortion as the murder of the unborn, practiced by selfish women who rejected motherhood and family.

Conservatives failed to narrow abortion rights significantly in the 1980s. Reagan successfully urged Congress to stop the use of federal funds to pay for abortions, but a constitutional amendment outlawing abortion stalled in the Senate. In 1983 and 1986, the Supreme Court made rulings that upheld *Roe v. Wade*.

Gays and the AIDS Crisis

The gay rights movement was another legacy of the 1960s that troubled many conservatives. Evangelical leaders such as Jerry Falwell condemned homosexuality on

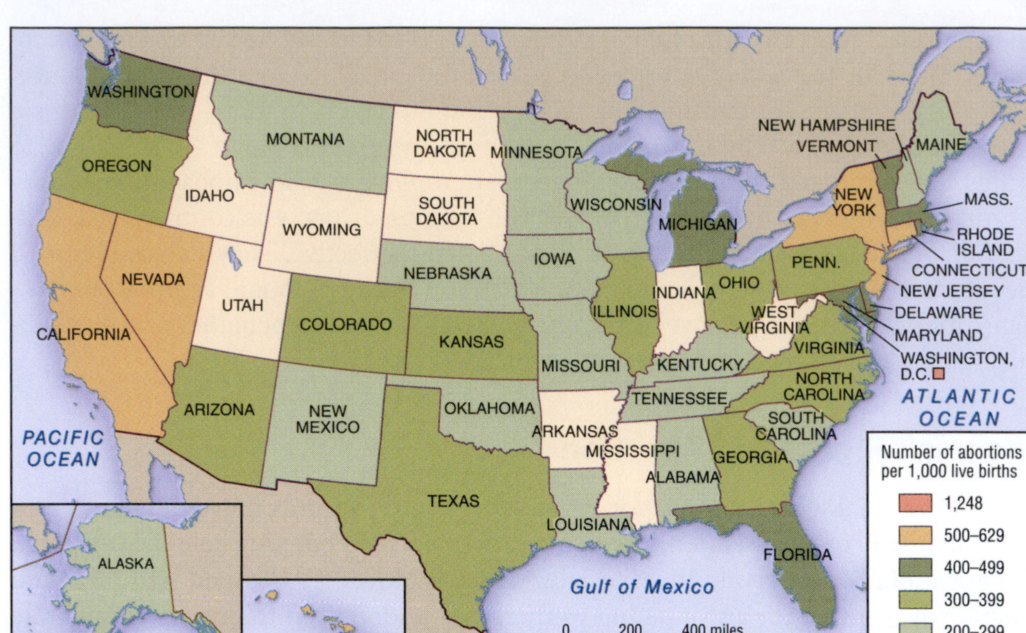

Map 30–4 Abortion in the 1980s The rate of abortions across the United States 14 years after the Supreme Court's decision legalizing abortion in *Roe v. Wade. Timothy H. Fast and Cathy Carroll Fast,* The Women's Atlas of the United States, *rev. ed. (1995), p. 166.*

religious grounds. Some people believed that the public acceptance of equal rights for gay men and women would promote immorality and corrupt children. In 1977 Anita Bryant, a former Miss America, launched a national crusade, Save Our Children, to protest the passage of a gay rights ordinance in Dade County, Florida, where Miami is located. Voters soon repealed the measure. In San Francisco in 1978, Harvey Milk, the first avowedly gay member of the city's board of supervisors, was assassinated, along with the mayor, by a former supervisor. Many gays were shocked when the assassin received only a short jail sentence.

Despite such opposition, the gay rights movement made progress in the 1980s. By the end of the decade, most states had repealed sodomy laws that criminalized gay sex. In 1982 Wisconsin became the first state to pass a law protecting the rights of gay men and women. At the federal level, however, a majority of the U.S. Supreme Court dismissed a gay man's right to sexual privacy as "facetious" in *Bowers v. Hardwick* in 1986.

The battle over gay rights took place against a tragic backdrop. In 1981 the Centers for Disease Control began reporting cases of acquired immune deficiency syndrome (AIDS), a disease that destroyed the body's immune system and left it unable to fight off infections and rare cancers. By the mid-1980s, researchers had traced AIDS to different forms of the human immunodeficiency virus (HIV) that were transmitted in semen and blood. But no cure had been found. By 1990 there were nearly 100,000 recorded deaths from the AIDS epidemic in the United States (see Figure 30–2).

Because 75 percent of the first victims were gay men, Americans initially considered AIDS a homosexual disease. Some people, including evangelical leaders, believed this "gay cancer" was God's punishment for the alleged sin of homosexuality. As soon became clear, however, AIDS could also be transmitted by heterosexual

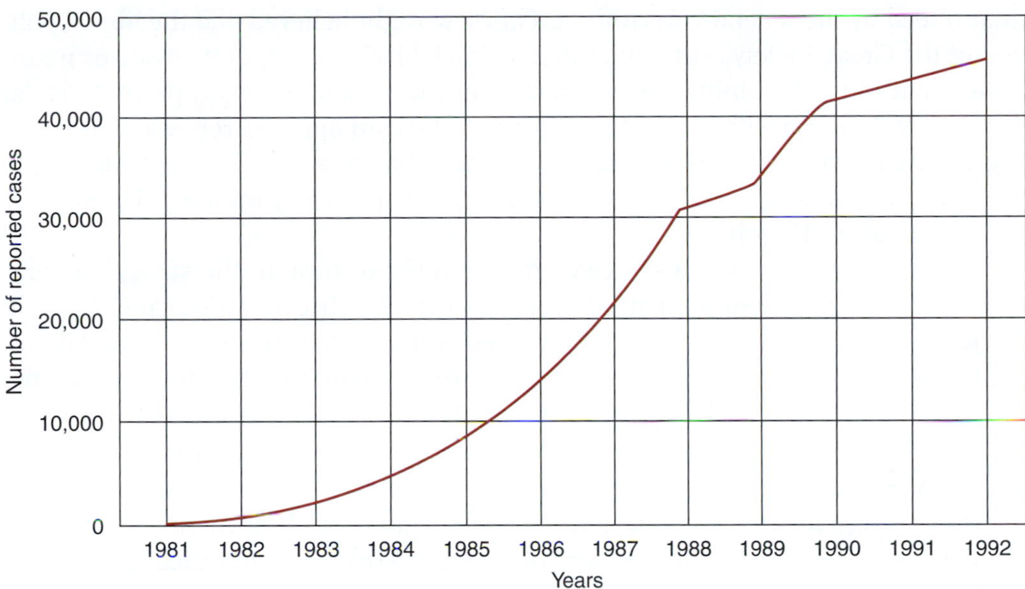

Figure 30–2 The Rapid Rise of AIDS Statistical Abstract of the United States, 1989, *p. 111*; Statistical Abstract, 1993, *p. 203.*

intercourse, by intravenous drug use that involved sharing needles, and by tainted blood transfusions.

Public understanding of AIDS and HIV gradually increased. Nevertheless, the specter of "gay cancer" promoted homophobia and slowed the public response to the disease. Gay activists pushed for government action. The AIDS Coalition to Unleash Power, known as ACT UP, and other organizations staged demonstrations and acts of civil disobedience to focus attention on the crisis. Nevertheless, the Reagan administration did not fund research on AIDS for several years. Meanwhile, the disease continued to spread.

The AIDS epidemic complicated the struggle over gay rights. For some Americans, the disease reinforced the conservative condemnation of homosexuality. For others, the suffering of AIDS victims engendered sympathy and compassion. As the 1980s ended, the conservative backlash against gay rights had not succeeded, but the AIDS epidemic continued.

"How Many More Must Die?" Gay rights advocates protest President Bush's AIDS policies in the Maine town where he was vacationing in September 1991.

African Americans and Racial Inequality

Conservatives were uneasy with still another legacy of the 1960s, the expansion of African American civil rights and benefits guaranteed by the federal government. The New Right believed that the liberal policies of the Great Society hurt, rather than helped, black people. Conservatives maintained that individual initiative, and not government action, would promote racial equality. In keeping with these ideas, President Reagan opposed renewal of the Voting Rights Act and condemned busing and affirmative action. The president, like many Republicans, opposed the creation of a national holiday marking the birthday of Martin Luther King Jr.

The conservatives' tough stance came at a difficult time in the struggle for racial equality. Compared with the 1950s and 1960s, African Americans' crusade for justice and opportunity generally slowed in the 1970s and 1980s. Despite legal equality, African Americans faced persisting racism and discrimination. Disproportionately clustered in manual occupations, African Americans were particularly hurt by the deindustrialization and economic decline of the 1970s and 1980s. After years of improvement, African Americans' economic status relative to whites stagnated or declined during the Reagan era. African Americans still made less money than whites did for comparable work and had much less chance to attain managerial positions.

Economic hardship and persistent discrimination did not affect all African Americans equally. In the 1980s the African American middle class continued to thrive. Among college-educated Americans, the incomes of black men rose faster than those of whites into the mid-1980s. Middle-class African Americans could afford to move to better housing, often in suburbs and integrated areas. Meanwhile, working-class African Americans found their wages stagnating or falling compared with those of white workers. In the 1970s and 1980s, poverty rates rose faster among African Americans than among whites. The feminization of poverty hit black families particularly hard. In 1985, 75 percent of poor African American children lived in families headed by a single female. Observers feared that there was now a permanent African American underclass living segregated in inner-city neighborhoods with poor schools and widespread crime.

As in the past, African American culture, driven by the distinctiveness of the black experience, proved dynamic and controversial. In the poverty and decay of the Bronx in New York City in the 1970s, young African Americans had begun to create a powerful new music, rap. Reflecting the diversity of the city's culture, pioneering rap artists such as Kool Herc, Afrika Bambaataa, and Grandmaster Flash drew on Caribbean musical practices and the popular dance music disco, as well as on African American linguistic and musical traditions. Rap typically featured spoken lyrics over a driving percussive "break" beat, often sampled from recordings of other music. The new sound was part of a loose African American cultural movement known as hip-hop, which included graffiti art and break dancing.

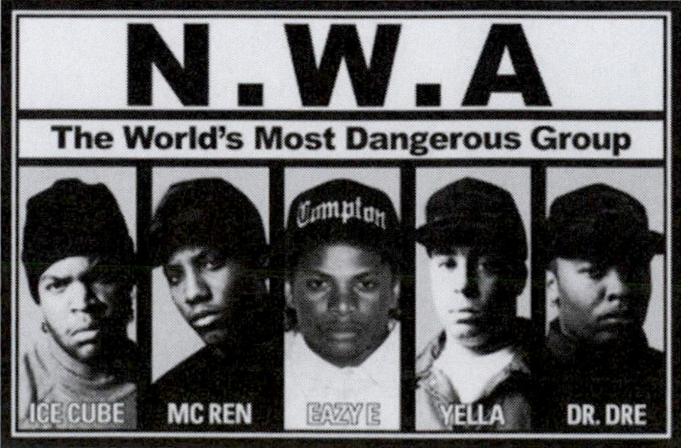

Rap was the first new musical form to rival the impact of jazz in the 1920s and rock and roll in the 1950s. Spreading rapidly around the country, rap crossed boundaries of race, class, and nation to appeal to middle-class, white, and eventually international audiences. Commercially successful, rap was also controversial for its often blunt, unblushing look at ghetto life. The subgenre of gangsta rap, with its first-person celebrations of gang life, violence, and misogyny in such tracks as N.W.A.'s "Fuck tha Police," proved particularly provocative to conservatives and other Americans. In the meantime, rap deeply influenced other genres of music—yet another instance of the powerful impact of African Americans on American culture.

African Americans also mobilized to fight for equality and opportunity. Across the nation, the number of African American elected officials increased markedly. The Reverend Jesse Jackson, a protégé of Martin Luther King Jr., won wide attention. Preaching self-esteem and economic self-help for African Americans, Jackson was the leader of Operation PUSH—People United to Save Humanity. In 1984 Jackson challenged Walter Mondale for the Democratic presidential nomination. His campaign suggested how far American society had come in accepting African American political participation.

African American activism made it difficult for Reagan and other conservatives to undo the civil rights revolution, as did the persistence of discrimination and inequality. Most Americans seemed to accept that some federal action was essential to redress the imbalance between races in America. Despite Reagan's opposition, in 1982 Congress voted to extend the Voting Rights Act for 25 years. In 1983 the Supreme Court ruled overwhelmingly against Bob Jones University, an evangelical institution that attempted to retain its tax-exempt status even though it prohibited interracial dating and engaged in other forms of racial discrimination. The court also rejected the Reagan administration's bid to set aside local affirmative action programs. In other decisions, the justices limited affirmative action somewhat, but this important liberal program survived the Reagan administration.

The battles over the rights of African Americans, gays, and women underscored the limits of conservatism. Many Americans were not ready to undo the social and cultural legacies of the 1960s. New cultural expressions, such as rap, clashed with conservative values. The result was a stalemate. Disadvantaged groups made relatively little political progress in the 1980s, but conservatives also made little progress in their social and cultural agenda.

"The Decade of the Hispanic"

After the upheavals of the 1960s and 1970s, the Hispanic experience in the United States took on a quieter, more confident tone in the 1980s. Hispanics were not a homogeneous group but a diverse population defined by geographical, cultural, and even linguistic differences. In New York City, Puerto Ricans predominated; in South Florida, Cubans; and in the long arc from South Texas to Southern California, Mexican Americans. The census of 1980 revealed that Hispanics were the nation's fastest-growing minority group. The birthrate for Hispanic women was 75 percent higher than the national average. Most immigrants to the United States were Hispanic. Looking ahead, demographers predicted that Hispanics would outnumber African Americans and become the nation's largest minority group within a generation.

These population numbers shaped the outlook of both Hispanics and the rest of American society. There was a new sense in the 1980s that the Hispanics mattered,

AMERICAN LANDSCAPE

>> San Antonio

In the 1980s, tourists still came to San Antonio, Texas, to glimpse the past. Strolling the Paseo del Rio, the sunken, tree-lined River Walk along the San Antonio River, they visited the chain of Roman Catholic missions erected by the colonizing Spanish in the eighteenth century. The tourists usually stopped at the most famous of the old mission buildings, the Alamo, where a Texian and Tejano garrison died fighting the Mexican army in 1836.

Some hundred and fifty years later, San Antonio had also become a place to see the future. By the 1980s, Hispanics, concentrated on the West Side, made up a majority of the city's population. Home to nearly a million people, San Antonio was the largest Hispanic-majority city in the nation. Here was a glimpse, perhaps, of how the United States would develop in the years to come.

In San Antonio, the increase in the Mexican American population translated into political power. For decades, the city's Anglo business elite had controlled the community. But by the 1970s, the emerging Hispanic majority threatened to sweep away Anglo domination. COPS—Citizens Organized for Public Service—practiced a divisive, confrontational politics on behalf of Mexican Americans who lacked quality housing, education, and job opportunities. COPS animated Mexican American voters and shook the Anglo elite. Then, in 1977, the federal government used the federal Voting Rights Act to destroy a critical instrument of elite power, at-large elections for city council. San Antonio had chosen council members in citywide contests that virtually guaranteed victory for white candidates. Now the city had to adopt single-member council districts, which meant that the barrios on the West Side could elect candidates of their own. Five of the eleven positions went that year to Chicanos, who allied with a black councilman to create a majority.

The results were disappointing: confrontational politics brought few gains for Chicanos. Then, the Democrats nominated a young councilman, Henry Cisneros, for mayor in 1981. An urban planner from the West Side, Cisneros argued that Mexican Americans would not flourish unless business also flourished in San Antonio. His campaign appealed successfully both to the barrios of the West Side and to the Anglo neighborhoods of the North Side. On election day, Cisneros became the first Mexican American mayor of San Antonio since 1842. At a victory party, Cisneros embodied the artful culture balance that spurred Chicano power in San Antonio: dressed in a Ralph Lauren business suit, the mayor happily broke a traditional piñata.

Reelected three times, Cisneros aggressively pursued his economic vision for San Antonio. Here, again, the city offered a glimpse of the future for the United States. San Antonio's fragile economy had depended on tourism and U.S. military bases. Now Cisneros wanted to create a "no-smokestack" economy of high-technology firms. As Advanced Micro Devices, Control Data, and other corporations invested in San Antonio, electronics plants sprang up along Interstate Loop 410 on the city's North Side. As Cisneros pushed to expand tourism, Sea World opened and a $200 million shopping plaza came to the River Walk.

With his term coming to an end, Cisneros designated 1988 "The Year of Emergence," when the nation would have to take note of San Antonio's redevelopment. "This is a city that has had to learn to accommodate different points of view," he maintained. Others were not so sure. San Antonio was still a poor city, above the national average in unemployment and below it in income. Proud of Cisneros, Mexican Americans still lived less well than whites. To some, Cisneros's accommodation of business had shortchanged the West Side. The community, warned the president of COPS, wanted "development, not exploitation." Only time would tell who was right. San Antonio gave glimpses of the future, not the whole picture. ●

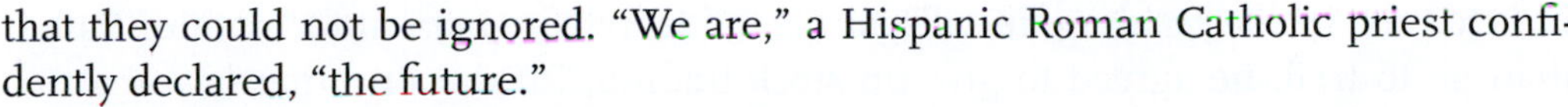

that they could not be ignored. "We are," a Hispanic Roman Catholic priest confidently declared, "the future."

In this consumer society, the growing importance of the Hispanic population could be measured in goods and services. Hispanic culture affected the nation's foodways. From the 1970s into the 1980s, more and more Americans discovered "Tex-Mex," the distinctive cuisine of the Tejanos, the Mexican Americans of South Texas. Consumers flocked to Tex-Mex restaurants to enjoy enchiladas and tamales covered with chili, refried beans, and Spanish rice, all with plenty of cheese and salsa. By the 1990s, salsa had passed catsup as the best-selling condiment in the United States.

Meanwhile, American business, recognizing the size of the Hispanic market, moved to attract Spanish-speaking consumers. The Coors brewery enthusiastically declared the 1980s "The Decade of the Hispanic." By 1983, Coors and other companies could advertise their products in the growing Spanish-language media, including newspapers, magazines, and 67 television stations.

For politicians, the 1980s were also "The Decade of the Hispanic." The Republican Party, long unable to attract a majority of African Americans, hoped that overwhelmingly Roman Catholic Hispanic voters, like Linda Chavez, would respond to the new conservatism's emphasis on values, family, and religion. Thanks to Reagan's anti-Communism, Republicans did attract Cuban Americans, so many of whom were refugees from the regime of Fidel Castro. However, most Hispanics, including Mexican Americans, emphasized economic issues over foreign policy and cultural appeals. Mainly working class, the Hispanic population continued to grapple with poverty and struggle for educational and economic opportunity in the United States. In these circumstances, the majority, unlike Linda Chavez, preferred the more activist economic and educational policies of the Democrats.

The increasing importance of Hispanic voters helped temper the response to another critical number in American political life—the perhaps 3 million illegal immigrants who had slipped across the border from Mexico into the United States. The Immigration Reform and Control Act of 1986, known as the Simpson-Mazzoli Act, imposed harsher penalties on Americans who knowingly brought illegal aliens into the country and hired them. But the measure also reflected the sentiments of Mexican Americans and other Americans by offering amnesty to illegal aliens who had arrived since 1981.

From Scandal to Triumph

The stalemate over social values was not the only sign that there were limits to conservatism in the 1980s. Scandals plagued business and religious figures who had helped create the conservative climate of the decade. Policy setbacks, economic woes, and scandals plagued the Reagan administration. For a time, the conservatives' triumph was in doubt, but then the cold war began to come to an end.

Business and Religious Scandals

By the mid-1980s the new conservatism was suffering a series of business and religious scandals. In 1986 Ivan Boesky, the swaggering Wall Street deal maker, was indicted for insider trading, the illegal use of secret financial information. Rather than go to trial, he agreed to give up stock trading, inform on other lawbreakers, spend two years in jail, and pay a $100 million fine. In 1987 Michael Milken, the junk bond king, was indicted on fraud and racketeering charges. His eventual plea bargain agreement included a 10-year jail sentence and a stunning $600 million fine, the largest judgment against an individual in American history.

Such scandals provoked second thoughts about the celebration of business and materialism. Critics pointed out that Boesky's and Milken's business methods had hurt the economy by saddling corporations with a great deal of debt and little cash to pay for it. Lavish lifestyles no longer seemed quite so attractive.

> **At its best, the Reagan Presidency provided a tonic of self-confidence that helped to restore vigor to the national economy and psyche; at its worst, it fostered greed, chauvinism and intolerance.**
>
> R. W. APPLE, 1989

Scandal touched religion as well as commerce. Leading televangelists were caught in embarrassing predicaments. In 1987 Americans learned that Jim Bakker had defrauded investors in Heritage USA and paid hush money to hide an adulterous liaison with a church secretary. The scandal hurt the reputation of Jerry Falwell, who had taken over Bakker's organization. In 1988 Falwell resigned from his own Moral Majority. That same year, televangelist Jimmy Swaggart admitted that he "had sinned" with prostitutes.

Political Scandals

The Reagan administration had its own scandals. Before the end of the president's first term, more than 20 officials of the EPA resigned or were fired over charges of favoritism toward lobbyists and polluters. In 1985 Secretary of Labor Raymond Donovan resigned after becoming the first cabinet officer ever indicted. In 1988 Reagan's friend and attorney general, Edwin Meese III, resigned amid questions about his role in the corrupt awarding of government contracts to a defense firm. To critics, the administration's "sleaze factor" stemmed from the president's contemptuous conservative attitude toward government and his eagerness to please business.

In his second term, Reagan faced much more damaging accusations. In October 1986, Sandinista soldiers in Nicaragua shot down a transport plane attempting to supply the Contra rebels. It soon became clear that the plane had been part of a secret effort by the Reagan administration to violate the Boland Amendment's ban on aid to the Contras. Then, a Lebanese magazine reported that the United States had traded arms to Iran. Despite denials from the president, the government had sold arms to win the release of American hostages held by terrorists in Lebanon. The Reagan administration had broken the president's pledge not to negotiate with terrorists and had violated a ban on arms sales to Iran. Americans soon learned that the arms deal and the Nicaraguan plane crash were connected. Government officials had illegally used proceeds from the arms sale to pay for supplying the Contras.

The scandal that became known as the Iran-Contra affair had the potential to drive Reagan from office. If the president had ordered or known about the arms deal and the supply effort, he might have faced impeachment. The Reagan administration underwent three separate investigations. These inquiries made clear that the president was probably deeply involved in the Iran-Contra affair, but none turned up enough evidence to impeach him.

Nevertheless, the Iran-Contra affair badly damaged Reagan's reputation. Several of his associates left office and faced jail sentences. Former national security adviser Robert "Bud" McFarlane pleaded guilty to withholding information from Congress. His successor, Rear Admiral John Poindexter, was allowed to resign. Poindexter's charismatic aide, Marine Lieutenant Colonel Oliver North, had to be fired. Meanwhile, the director of the CIA, William Casey, died in 1987, the day after testimony implicated him in the effort to aid the Contras. Much of the public concluded that the president must have known about his associates' dealings; his popularity dropped.

Setbacks for the Conservative Agenda

Against this backdrop of scandal, conservatives faced a series of policy setbacks. The Democratic-controlled House of Representatives was less cooperative during Reagan's second term. Democrats became even more combative after winning majorities in both the House and Senate in the congressional elections of 1986.

Accordingly, Reagan had to compromise more often with Congress. In 1985 the president called for a Second American Revolution, a comprehensive overhaul of the income tax system. But the Tax Reform Act that Congress passed in 1986 did not lower and simplify income taxes nearly as much as the president had wanted.

Reagan also met outright defeat in Congress. In 1988, a coalition of Democrats and Republicans passed a bill compelling large companies to give workers 60 days' notice of plant closings and layoffs. Reagan opposed this liberal, prolabor measure, but he allowed the bill to become law without his signature.

The president faced repeated defeat on environmental policy. During the 1980s there was growing concern about environmental hazards. In December 1984 the subsidiary of a U.S. corporation accidentally allowed toxic gas to escape from a pesticide plant in Bhopal, India. The emission killed more than 2,500 people and injured 200,000. In April 1986 an explosion and fire allowed radioactive material to escape a nuclear power plant at Chernobyl in the Soviet Union. The accident killed more than 30 people, injured more than 200, exposed countless others to radioactivity, and caused extensive environmental damage.

In this alarming context, Reagan's conservative hostility to environmentalism was no longer so appealing. The president had to accept the extension of the federal Superfund program to clean up hazardous waste in the United States in 1986. The next year, Congress overrode his veto of a bill renewing the Water Quality Control Act. In 1988 the Reagan administration signed an international agreement placing limits on emissions linked to acid rain.

A Vulnerable Economy

Even the economy, the centerpiece of the Reagan Revolution, became a problem during the president's second term. During the 1980s the gap between rich and poor widened sharply. While the average family income, after taxes, of the highest-paid tenth of Americans rose 27 percent from 1977 to 1988, the average family

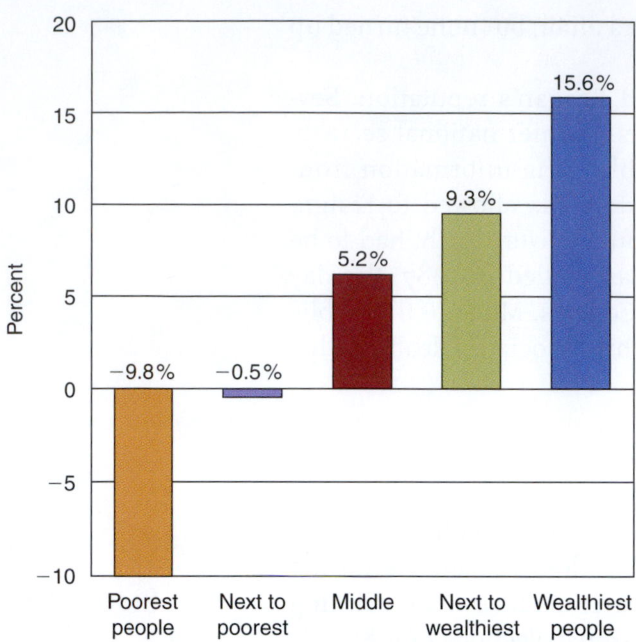

Figure 30–3 Changes in Families' Real Income, 1980–1990 The Reagan Revolution had very different consequences for rich and poor. *Copyright © 1989 by the New York Times Co. Reprinted by Permission.*

income of the poorest tenth fell 11 percent (see Figure 30–3). In the 1980s only the rich earned more and kept more. Other Americans faced economic stagnation or decline.

The falling incomes of the poorest Americans ensured the persistence of poverty. Twenty-nine million Americans lived below the poverty line in 1980. Ten years later, that figure had grown to almost thirty-seven million. Despite Reaganomics, the United States had one of the highest poverty rates among industrialized nations.

One of the most visible consequences of poverty was homelessness. In the 1980s the number of homeless Americans increased markedly. The sight of men and women sleeping on sidewalks, their belongings in shopping carts, was common during the Reagan years.

Homelessness, poverty, and inequality produced a spirited debate in the 1980s. Democrats and liberals blamed these problems on Reaganomics. The president, they charged, had done nothing to stop the erosion of high-paying factory jobs. His welfare, housing, and job-training cuts hurt the poor, while his tax cuts and deregulation helped the rich. In response, conservatives and Republicans maintained that activist, liberal government had hurt manufacturing and weakened the economy. Moreover, welfare programs caused poverty by destroying poor people's work ethic and making them dependent on handouts.

Not surprisingly, neither side persuaded the other. In reality, both liberal and conservative policies had produced flawed economic results. Lyndon Johnson's spending for the Great Society, along with the cost of the Vietnam War, had begun to undermine the economy in the 1960s. His antipoverty programs had been less effective than liberals wanted to admit, but the Reagan Revolution had offered no solution to poverty, either. Reaganomics did not reinvigorate manufacturing or substantially boost middle-class incomes.

There were other signs of economic vulnerability by the mid-1980s. Despite the promises of Reaganomics, the federal budget deficit did not disappear. Instead, between 1981 and 1986, as the government cut taxes and increased defense spending, the deficit soared from $79 billion to $221 billion—a staggering new record.

Like poverty and inequality, the deficit was controversial. Some economists believed the deficit was a sign of great economic weakness; others believed it did not matter. Democrats and liberals blamed Reagan for the budgetary red ink. Reagan's supporters blamed Congress for failing to cut the budget.

In fact both the president and Congress were to blame. Neither Republicans nor Democrats wanted to reduce such popular benefits as Medicare and Social Security. Congress enacted the Balanced Budget and Emergency Deficit Control Act of 1985, known as the Gramm-Rudman Act, which promised automatic cuts to balance the budget by 1990. The next year, a Supreme Court ruling critically weakened the mea-

sure. The deficit remained high during Reagan's last years in office, and the national debt—the total amount owed by the federal government to its creditors—reached $2.6 trillion.

Along with this burgeoning debt, the Reagan years produced a growing international trade deficit. In 1980 the annual value of imports was $25.4 billion greater than the value of the nation's exports. By 1986 that gap had grown to $145.1 billion. American business was still not able to compete with foreign producers in the 1980s. Consumers at home and abroad found foreign goods more attractive than ever. Reaganomics had not solved the problem of America's relative decline in the world economy.

Doubts about Reagan's economic policy increased when the stock market plummeted unexpectedly on Monday, October 19, 1987, losing 508 points, or 23 percent of its value. It was the biggest one-day decline since "Black Tuesday" in October 1929. The market drop reflected underlying economic problems including the federal budget deficit, the trade deficit, and deindustrialization, plus lax regulation of Wall Street by the Reagan administration. The crash seemed to be a mortal blow to the Reagan Revolution. "What crashed was more than just the market," a journalist concluded. "It was the Reagan Illusion: the idea that there could be a defense buildup and tax cuts without a price, that the country could live beyond its means indefinitely."

Reagan's Comeback

Beset by scandals and economic troubles, Reagan began a comeback. He showed a remarkable ability to withstand scandal and defeat. Opponents dubbed him the "Teflon president" because nothing seemed to stick to him. That was a tribute to Reagan's political skills as well as many Americans' real affection for him. After a series of disappointing presidencies, Americans seemed unwilling to let Reagan fail.

The economy also helped the president. Notwithstanding Americans' fears, the stock market crash did not lead to depression or recession. The market soon recovered and the economy continued to grow.

Reagan's comeback was probably helped most of all by the transformation of the Soviet Union. By the mid-1980s the Soviets suffered from a weakening economy, an unpopular war in Afghanistan, and a costly arms race. At this critical juncture, Mikhail Gorbachev became General Secretary of the Communist Party. The dynamic and charismatic Gorbachev signaled a new era with a series of stunning reforms. At home, he called for restructuring the economy (*perestroika*) and tolerating more open discussion (*glasnost*). Abroad, he sought an easing of tensions with the United States and the West.

Gorbachev's reforms gave the U.S. government a politically popular opportunity to thaw cold war tensions. Reagan met with the Soviet leader in a series of positive summits beginning in Geneva, Switzerland, in November 1985. Visiting West Berlin in June 1987, the president challenged Gorbachev to "tear down" the Berlin Wall. Meanwhile, it became apparent that the Soviets were, in fact, changing their foreign policy, as they withdrew their troops from Afghanistan and eased their control over Eastern Europe.

The United States and the Soviets also made striking progress on arms control. In December 1987 Reagan and Gorbachev signed the Intermediate-Range Nuclear Forces Treaty (INF), promising to destroy more than 2,500 intermediate-range nuclear missiles. For the first time, the two powers had agreed to give up a weapon altogether.

The INF treaty signaled a permanent easing of tensions. The cold war, so intense just a few years earlier, suddenly ended. Asked in 1988 about calling the USSR the "evil empire," Reagan replied, "I was talking about another time, another era." Reagan's presidency ended in 1989; a year later, the United States and the Soviet Union agreed to end production of chemical weapons and reduce existing stockpiles. In 1991, the two nations signed the START (Strategic Arms Reduction Talks) Treaty, which called for each side to reduce its arsenals of nuclear weapons as much as 30 percent.

Meanwhile, the Soviet Union weakened. In 1989, Gorbachev could do nothing to stop the collapse of its repressive allies in Eastern Europe. Hard-line Communist regimes toppled in Bulgaria, Czechoslovakia, Hungary, Poland, and Rumania. Most dramatically, a new East German government agreed in November to allow travel through the Berlin Wall, which had symbolized the cold war division of Europe. As jubilant Berliners dismantled the wall, it epitomized the collapse of Communism. Accepting the transition to democracy, the Soviets withdrew their troops from Eastern Europe.

Powerless to stop its allies from abandoning Communism, the Soviet leadership soon could not save itself. Despite Gorbachev's attempts to improve life in the Soviet Union, many people were unhappy with the low standard of living, Communist repression, and the unpopular war in Afghanistan. Estonia, Latvia, Lithuania, and other republics chafed under Russia's domination of the USSR. In 1990 Russia itself chose a charismatic president, Boris Yeltsin, who quit the Communist Party, supported independence for the republics, and challenged Gorbachev. The next year, Gorbachev had to resign as party leader and president of the Soviet Union. The Soviet parliament suspended the Communist Party. As one republic after another declared its independence, the USSR ceased to exist.

With the collapse of the Soviet Union, the United States and its allies had won the cold war. Conservatives insisted that Reagan's defense buildup had pushed the Soviets into a military and economic race they could not win and so had forced them to surrender. Democrats maintained that the buildup and the president's harsh rhetoric had actually slowed the thaw in U.S.-Soviet relations. America won the cold war, they argued, because of its long-term strength and strategy. With typical modesty, Reagan himself seemed to agree with the Democrats in a speech at Fulton, Missouri, where Winston Churchill had decried the iron curtain and the onset of the cold war in 1946. "The road to a free Europe that began there in Fulton led," Reagan observed, "to the Truman Doctrine and the Marshall Plan, to NATO and the Berlin Airlift, through nine American presidencies and more than four decades of military preparedness."

Meanwhile, Americans did not celebrate very much as the Berlin Wall came down and the Soviet Union collapsed. The cold war had cost a great deal in money and lives. Many Americans wondered whether Communism had posed a mortal danger to the United States in the first place.

The Fall of the Berlin Wall On November 11, 1989, a man helps dismantle the barrier that divided East and West Berlin and symbolized the division between communism and the west during the cold war.

Conclusion

Reagan left office with the highest popularity rating of any president since the beginning of modern polling in the 1930s. His comeback culminated the triumph of the new conservatism. Americans would debate the nature of that triumph for years to come. The nation did not embrace much of the conservative social agenda. The Reagan Revolution did not solve such basic economic problems as poverty. It even worsened some problems, such as inequality and the budget deficit.

Nevertheless, the conservative triumph was real. Reagan successfully combated the sense of national decline that had pervaded America in the 1970s. His presidency reinvigorated faith in capitalist innovation, minimal government, and American military power. At the end of the 1980s, business values and evangelical religion claimed a more prominent place in American culture.

The accomplishments of the new conservatism, as Reagan's troubled second term indicated, were fragile. The nation's economic revival was shaky, as was the revival of its spirit. Americans were still worried about the future. "I think," a businessman concluded, "the '90s are going to be much trickier than the 1980s."

Further Readings

Connie Bruck, *The Predators' Ball: The Inside Story of Drexel Burnham and the Rise of the Junk Bond Raiders* (1989). A vivid account of the controversial business practices of the 1980s.

Lou Cannon, *Ronald Reagan: A Life in Politics* (2004). A journalistic two-volume biography offering perhaps the best insight into Reagan and his remarkable career.

Paul Freiberger and Michael Swaine, *Fire in the Valley: The Making of the Personal Computer* (2000). Anecdotal account of a critical development in the creation of a new economy.

William Martin, *With God on Our Side: The Rise of the Religious Right in America* (2005). Places the evangelical movement of the 1980s in long-term context.

Gil Troy, *Morning in America: How Ronald Reagan Invented the 1980s* (2005). A scholarly survey of society during the Reagan Revolution.

Sean Wilentz, *The Age of Reagan: A History, 1974–2008* (2008). A sweeping account of the conservative ascendancy.

Who, What?

Ivan Boesky 1000
Yuppies 1001
Rev. Jerry Falwell 1002
Ronald Reagan 1002
Sandra Day O'Connor 1016
Mikhail Gorbachev 1027
Religious right 1001
Reaganomics 1005
Reagan Doctrine 1010

Review Questions

1. What were the main values and goals of the new conservatism in the 1980s? What role did business and religion play in shaping the conservative movement?
2. What was the Reagan Revolution in domestic policy? How did Reagan's domestic programs reflect conservative values?

>> Timeline >>

▼ 1973–74
OPEC oil embargo

▼ 1979–1981
Iranian hostage crisis

▼ 1980
Ronald Reagan elected president

▼ 1981
IBM personal computer
Air traffic controllers' strike
Economic Recovery Act

▼ 1982
Nuclear freeze rally in New York City
Boland Amendment

▼ 1983
Strategic Defense Initiative
U.S. invasion of Grenada
Terrorist attack on U.S. Marines in Lebanon

▼ 1984
Reelection of Ronald Reagan

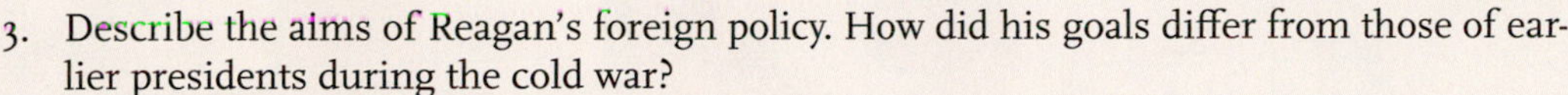

3. Describe the aims of Reagan's foreign policy. How did his goals differ from those of earlier presidents during the cold war?
4. What groups resisted the conservative social agenda in the 1980s? Did the desire for equal rights and opportunities conflict with conservatism?
5. What factors limited the triumph of the new conservatism? Did conservatives really succeed in the 1980s?
6. How did the conservatism of the 1980s differ from earlier forms of conservatism in the twentieth century?

Websites

Hartford Institute for Religion Research (http://hirr.hartsem.edu/) offers many resources for the study of religion in the 1980s, as well as other eras.

The Living Room Candidate (http://www.livingroomcandidate.org/) is a fascinating collection of presidential campaign commercials from 1972 to the present, including Reagan's from 1980 and 1984.

Making the Macintosh: Technology and Culture in Silicon Valley, Stanford University (http://library.stanford.edu/mac/index.html), explores the early history of the path-breaking Apple computer.

The Public Papers of President Ronald W. Reagan, Ronald Reagan Presidential Library (http://www.reagan.utexas.edu/archives/speeches/publicpapers.html), is a searchable collection of all the public statements of the "Great Communicator" as president.

For further review materials and resource information, please visit www.oup.com/us/ofthepeople

▼ 1985
General Electric purchase of RCA
Gramm-Rudman Act

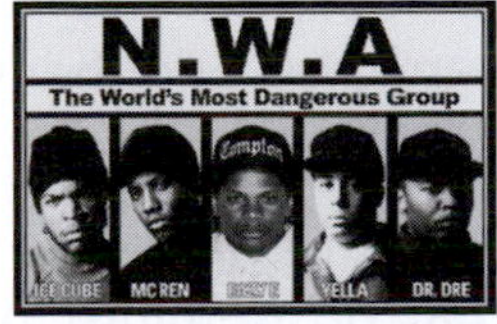

▼ 1986
U.S. bombing of Libya
Tax Reform Act
Revelation of Iran-Contra affair

▼ 1987
Stock market crash
Intermediate-Range Nuclear Forces Treaty

▼ 1988
Omnibus Trade and Competitiveness Act

▼ 1991
Collapse of the Soviet Union

CHAPTER 31

Common Threads 

>> What were some of the most pervasive consequences of technological change in the last decades of the 1900s? Where and when did these changes begin? How did they unfold?

>> How did the new conservatism of the 1980s continue to impact American politics and culture?

>> Did the African American civil rights movement extend its influence beyond the twentieth century?

>> What were the main uncertainties of a post–cold war, postindustrial, postfeminist, post–civil rights society?

"A Nation Transformed"

1989–2008

AMERICAN PORTRAIT

>> Tiger Woods

"Hello world," smiled 20-year-old Stanford undergraduate Tiger Woods as he became a professional golfer in 1996. A talented prodigy ready to take on the world, Woods was a distinctive product of global forces. His father, Earl, was part African American, Native American, and Chinese. A U.S. Army officer, the elder Woods had met Kultida Punsawad in Thailand during the Vietnam War. Kultida, part Thai, Chinese, and Dutch, had become Earl's wife and Tiger's mother.

Tiger quickly succeeded. In 1997, he became the youngest player to win the prestigious Masters tournament at the Augusta National Golf Club. Setting record after record, Woods became the greatest golfer and the best-paid athlete of his generation.

Observers interpreted Woods's success as a triumph for African Americans. Golf was a notoriously segregated sport; blacks had long been denied admission to elite clubs such as Augusta. Woods's Masters victory, the first for a nonwhite, seemed like one more milestone in the struggle for African American civil rights.

Woods himself fed that perception. "[E]ven though I'm mathematically Asian," he said, "if you have one drop of black blood in the United States, you're black." But Woods also defined himself as the sum of all his parents' racial identities. The golfer was, he said in 1997, "Cablinasian"—a mixture of Caucasian, black, Indian, and Asian. "As proud as I am of Tiger Woods, I realize I have to share him," said a veteran African American civil rights activist. "He is part of a new reality. [P]eople are going to have to get comfortable with it."

Many observers welcomed Woods as an emblem of a more diverse nation. "He is more than just one race, he is many races," said a radio talk show host. "And that's what makes us Americans, because we're the melting pot. We're kind of mutts." The African American television personality Oprah Winfrey dubbed Woods "America's son."

Yet sometimes he did not seem American. Representing the nation in the Ryder Cup, Woods, who also had Thai citizenship, felt that he was "playing for the United Nations, not the United States." His parents held up their multiracial son as a transnational man with a globalizing mission. "He can hold everyone together," his mother said. "He is the Universal Child." "[H]e's qualified through his ethnicity to accomplish miracles," Earl Woods agreed. "He's the bridge between the East and the West." Tiger's transnational image became even stronger when he married a Swedish model in 2004.

As the world drew together in new ways, Woods's racial and national identities made him an ideal figure—"a one-man symbol of globalization in the twenty-first century." American, Asian, and European multinational corporations paid him lavishly to reach the expanding global marketplace. Woods's greeting "Hello World" was the slogan of his Nike marketing campaign. Playing a game invented in Scotland, the American traveled the world to promote golf courses, credit cards, computer video games, watches, coffee, automobiles, jet planes, laser eye surgery, and corporate consulting, technology, and international job outsourcing.

Despite his transnational image, Woods's activities sometimes seemed to serve U.S. values and interests. In the Philippines in 1998, he promoted a golf community built on land taken from thousands of peasants. "Tiger Woods should be barred from entering the country and from propagating golf," the peasants' lawyer insisted. "We have globalization, we have privatization, we have land conversion, all of these are just complete manifestations of U.S.-dictated policies."

Distinctive as he was, Tiger Woods epitomized forces changing the United States. As his endorsements reflected, an emerging information economy still manufactured

continued

>> AMERICAN PORTRAIT *continued*

automobiles but leaned towards computing, medical services, and leisure. Like Woods, with his ties to multinationals, jet travel, and outsourcing, the new economy was increasingly globalized. The multiracial golfer, who embraced his mother's Buddhism, also reflected a new social and cultural diversity in America.

While Woods profited handsomely in a changing world, the United States struggled with the consequences of the information economy, globalization, and diversity. Although conservatism continued to shape American democracy, conservatives had less success shaping social and cultural change. America's place in a globalizing world was uncertain, particularly after a devastating terrorist attack in September 2001 and then a stunning stock market collapse in September 2008. Americans lived, as the commission investigating the attack put it, in "a nation transformed." But the exact nature of that transformation still remained unclear as the new president—as transnational as Tiger Woods—prepared to take office amid a national crisis.

OUTLINE

The Age of Globalization

By the end of the twentieth century, Americans increasingly felt enmeshed in global forces. That had always been the case, of course. Throughout its history, the nation had been defined by its relationship to the world; the cold war had been one more phase in this relationship. But Americans' global connection entered a new, more self-conscious phase beginning in the 1980s. During the decade, the term "globalization" first came into use to describe the web of technological, economic, military, political, and cultural developments binding people and nations ever more tightly together. The cold war's end, technological advances, the spread of multinationals and other organizations, the creation of transnational economic alliances, and a new wave of immigration all drew the United States deeper into globalization.

> **Globalization is not just a trend, not just a phenomenon, not just an economic fad. It is the international system that has replaced the cold-war system.**
>
> THOMAS L. FRIEDMAN, 1999

The Cold War and Globalization

For two generations, the cold war had both facilitated and hindered globalization. In some ways, the confrontation between the United States and the Soviet Union linked the world more closely together. Each power had forged a host of ties to other nations. To hold off Communism, the United States had established regional military alliances around the world. To rebuild Western European and Asian economies, America had lowered trade barriers and created the World Bank and the International Monetary Fund.

Still, the cold war inhibited globalization, too. The United States and the Soviet Union had largely avoided trading with each other. Each power had discouraged its allies from ties with the other side.

The collapse of the Soviet Union in 1991 opened the way to further globalization. Key international mechanisms such as the World Bank and the United Nations remained in place. But now nations and companies could forge new ties more freely across the old cold war divide.

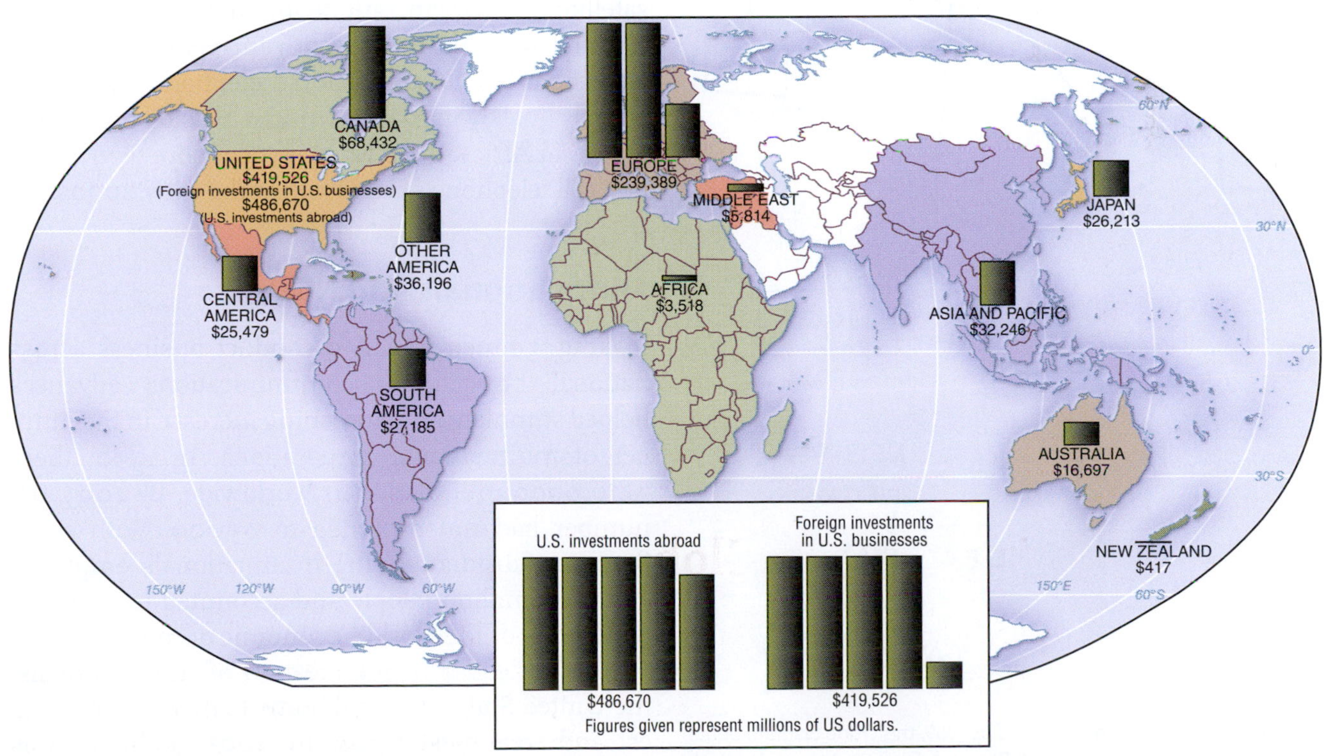

Map 31–1 The Globalization of the U.S. Economy In 1992, the large value of U.S. investment in other regions around the world was nearly equaled by the value of foreign investments in the United States.

New Communications Technologies

New communications technologies were especially important in speeding up the global flow of news, ideas, and money. The Internet, another product of the cold war, emerged from a Department of Defense search in the 1960s for a means of maintaining communications in the event of a nuclear attack on America. Aided by the development of the telephone modem and fiber-optic cable, the Internet spread quickly through universities, across America, and around the world in the 1990s and 2000s. At first, people used the Internet to send and receive electronic messages, but by the middle of the 1990s, computer users also explored the World Wide Web, a rapidly expanding segment of the Internet that blended text, graphics, audio, and video. The new "information superhighway" of the Web and the Internet enabled people to do research, create and exhibit art, listen to music, share photographs and films, and buy and sell online. By 2000, some 304 million people from more than 40 nations were using the global information superhighway.

Communications satellites also played a critical role in globalization. Following the U.S. deployment of Telstar and other satellites in the 1960s, Canada, Japan, and several other nations had launched their own. In the 1990s, the ready availability of global satellite communications revolutionized the news business. Cable News Network (CNN), founded in 1979 by the flamboyant American entrepreneur Ted Turner, used satellite uplinks to provide live televised coverage of news events around the world. Turner wanted CNN to be a "positive force in the world, to tie the world together." The huge success of CNN inspired the creation of satellite news organizations in other countries.

Improvements in telephony further facilitated globalization. Mobile and cellular telephones spread especially quickly in many countries outside the United States. In Africa, there were already more than 15 million cell telephone subscribers in the early 2000s.

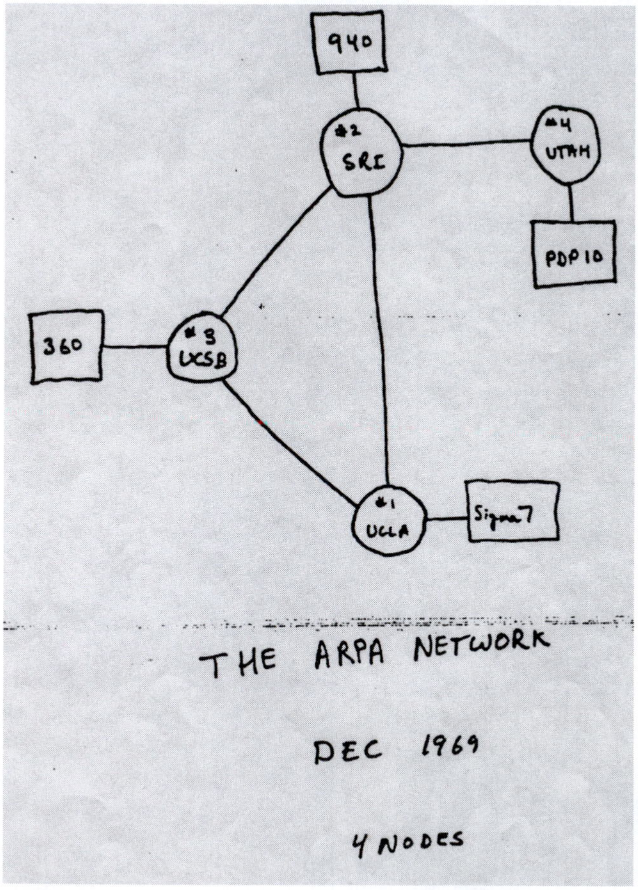

The Birth of the Internet Sketched in 1969, this crude diagram of the first four nodes of the Advanced Research Projects Agency Network (ARPANET) would lead to the explosive growth of the Internet in the 1990s and 2000s.

Multinationals and NGOs

Making it much easier to conduct business across national boundaries, communications advances helped stimulate an astonishing increase in the number of multinational corporations. In 1990, there were 3,000 multinationals worldwide. By 2003, the number had mushroomed to 63,000. With some 821,000 subsidiaries, the multinationals employed about 90 million people and accounted for perhaps one-fourth of the world's economic output.

Long a leader in the creation of multinationals, the United States was still home to many of the largest and wealthiest firms. By 2003, Wal-Mart was Mexico's largest employer, with 100,000 workers. But America now faced intense competition from

Overcoming the Boundary Between Capitalism and Communism United States retail giant Wal-Mart opens another store in the People's Republic of China, 2006.

Japan, Europe, and other nations. In 1962, nearly 60 percent of the top 500 multinationals were American; by 1999, the percentage had declined to 36.

Along with multinational business companies, private nongovernmental organizations—NGOs—also fostered globalization. Some NGOs, such as the International Red Cross, dated back to the nineteenth century. The World Economic Forum, which brought elite businessmen, politicians, and intellectuals together each year in Davos, Switzerland, was a product of the 1970s. So were the environmentalist Greenpeace and the humanitarian Doctors Without Borders. By the 2000s, there were more than 10,000 NGOs worldwide.

Expanding Trade

After international peace, the most basic necessity for globalization was the easy movement of goods, services, and capital across national boundaries. In the 1990s and 2000s, the United States and other nations, eager to support their multinational corporations and seize their share of the global market, moved aggressively to remove barriers to trade and investment. With the end of the cold war, America established economic relationships with the former republics of the USSR, the Eastern European countries of the Soviet bloc, the Socialist Republic of Vietnam, and the People's Republic of China. By 1996, Wal-Mart had a store in Beijing. Meanwhile, McDonald's had opened restaurants in Russia and several Eastern European nations.

To spur international trade and investment, nations also created regional economic alliances. Typically, these took the form of agreements in which member states guaranteed one another trading and investment privileges and lowered or

Making Economic Policy in a Global Age World leaders, including President George W. Bush (sixth from left, front row), meet in Washington, DC, in the midst of a developing economic crisis, November 2008.

abolished tariffs on imports and exports. In 1991, the member states of the European Economic Community, a pioneering regional trade alliance, signed the Maastricht Treaty drawing their economies together in a single vast unit, the European Union (EU), with its own currency, the euro. With a mere 6.4 percent of global population, the EU produced a third of the world's goods and more than a third of its trade.

The 1990s also witnessed the transformation of the international General Agreement on Tariffs and Trade (GATT). Another U.S. cold war creation, GATT had drawn together more than 100 nations. Its efforts to liberalize trade through agreements known as "rounds" culminated in 1993 when the Uruguay Round produced a dramatic victory for free-trade policies. The Uruguay Round also led to the rebirth of GATT as a new, more powerful global body, the World Trade Organization (WTO), whose decisions would be binding on member nations. The U.S. Senate approved American participation in the WTO, which opened in Geneva, Switzerland, in 1995.

Moving People

The movement of human beings was critical to globalization. Thanks to regional economic agreements and the end of the cold war, people could cross national borders more easily to provide needed labor. The United States remained a major destination. Between 1990 and 1994 alone, 4.5 million immigrants came to the United States. By 2000 the immigrant population had reached 26.3 million, about 11 percent of the national total population, the largest percentage since before World War II.

Short-term travel also facilitated globalization by exposing people to other nations and cultures. Low-cost jet flights and improved living standards enabled

AMERICA AND THE WORLD

>> Globalization's Final Frontier

Pervasive on earth, globalization also reached into space. Like the United States and the Soviet Union during the cold war, more and more of the world's nations translated their hopes, ambitions, and fears into space programs. Like America, other countries found satellites an indispensable part of globalization: they were critical to communications and information-gathering, and, accordingly, essential to building economies, spying on enemies, and positioning soldiers. A secure military foothold in space might even assure survival on earth. As a result, outer space became globalization's final frontier.

Dozens of countries had space programs by the 2000s. Most of these nations had to use the facilities of a relative handful of nations with the sophisticated technology needed to launch satellites. Reflecting the gradual economic and political integration of Europe, 13 Western European nations, including France, Germany, and the United Kingdom, had formed the European Space Agency in 1975. By the end of the twentieth century, ESA was using the Ariane launch vehicle to send satellites and probes into space. By then, too, India, Israel, and Japan were launching satellites, and Brazil was attempting to develop a launch capability.

The People's Republic of China had the most ambitious of the newer space programs. Despite its still-developing economy and limited investment in science, the PRC was determined to rival the United States not only in the exploration of space but perhaps also in the development of space-based military capabilities. The Chinese space program had launched satellites in the 1970s, developed the commercially successful Changzheng ("Long March") launch vehicle in the 1980s, and then begun a manned space program in the 1990s. In October 2003, the PRC became the third nation to put a man in space when the vehicle Shenzhou ("Sacred Vessel"), based on old Soviet technology, successfully carried an astronaut on a 21-hour flight. "This gives China a seat at the table," a European admitted.

Meanwhile, the original, cold war space powers struggled. The Russians, inheriting the remnants of the Soviet space program in the 1990s, could barely afford to keep it going. Their space station, Mir, was chronically unsafe. Desperate for money, the Russians auctioned memorabilia from past space voyages and signed up wealthy civilians as the first space tourists.

For most Americans, space no longer seemed exciting or important. Now that the Soviet Union was gone, NASA faced even leaner budgets. In February 2003, the shocking explosion of the space shuttle *Columbia*—the second tragic destruction of a shuttle—left Americans unsure about the safety and value of the space program.

As on earth, the United States pursued friendly collaboration with other countries. After partnering with the Soviets on space flights in the 1970s, the American

continued

>> **AMERICA AND THE WORLD** *continued*

space program joined Canada, Japan, Russia, and other nations in an often troubled effort to build the International Space Station in the 1990s.

The United States also unilaterally pursued its own interests in space. In the 2000s, President George W. Bush, like Ronald Reagan before him, favored the development of a space-based system to defend the United States against missile attack. Warily eying the PRC, policy makers feared an assault on American satellites and potential space weaponry. "The U.S. is an attractive candidate for a 'Space Pearl Harbor,'" a national committee warned in 2000. The globalization of space, like the globalization of the world, was both exhilarating and frightening.

Americans and others to vacation and study around the world. By the 1990s, tourism was possibly the largest single global industry. Study abroad increased nearly 10 percent a year.

The Politics of a New Economy

Globalization combined with ongoing technological change to create a new, information-centered American economy. This transformation produced a record economic boom in the 1990s; it also produced new insecurity and inequality. Faced with this situation, the political system offered generally conservative solutions emphasizing individual responsibility and limited government at the beginning of the new century. Despite unrest over immigration and trade, American leaders remained firmly committed to globalization.

> **[A]ll of us know that the problem with the new global economy is that it is both more rewarding and more destructive.**
>
> PRESIDENT BILL CLINTON, June 1999

The Information Economy

As deindustrialization continued, the nature of the postindustrial economy became clearer at the close of the twentieth century. By the 1990s, factories employed fewer production workers than in 1955; meanwhile, the service sector accounted for about 70 percent of the nation's economic activity. The rise of services using sophisticated communications, computing, and biotechnology encouraged the belief that the creation, organization, and distribution of information would define the twenty-first-century economy.

In the 1990s and 2000s, innovations in electronics continued to transform communications. More and more Americans carried pagers and cellular telephones. High-speed fiber-optic cables and satellite dishes expanded the power and reach of telephone and television systems. These developments spurred the spread of computing. By 1999 more than half of the nation's households had at least one computer. The development of computing and communications also spurred the hope that Americans would process information instead of raw materials, and produce knowledge instead of steel.

Advances in genetics and medical technology further sparked hopes for an information-centered economy. In the last decades of the twentieth century, scientists had made rapid advances in understanding animal and human genomes.

Corporations soon began applying this genetic knowledge to agriculture, medicine, and other fields. The result was biotechnology—the use of organisms and their products to alter human health and the environment. By the end of the 1990s, about one-third of the U.S. corn, cotton, and soybean crops were products of genetic engineering. By then, too, the U.S. Food and Drug Administration had approved more than 125 genetically engineered drugs for the treatment of cancer and other diseases.

Computing played a key role in the development of biotechnology. Drawing on computers and statistical techniques, researchers pioneered bioinformatics, the application of information science and technology to biological problems. Computers also drove the rapid development of medical technologies, including magnetic resonance imaging and computed tomography.

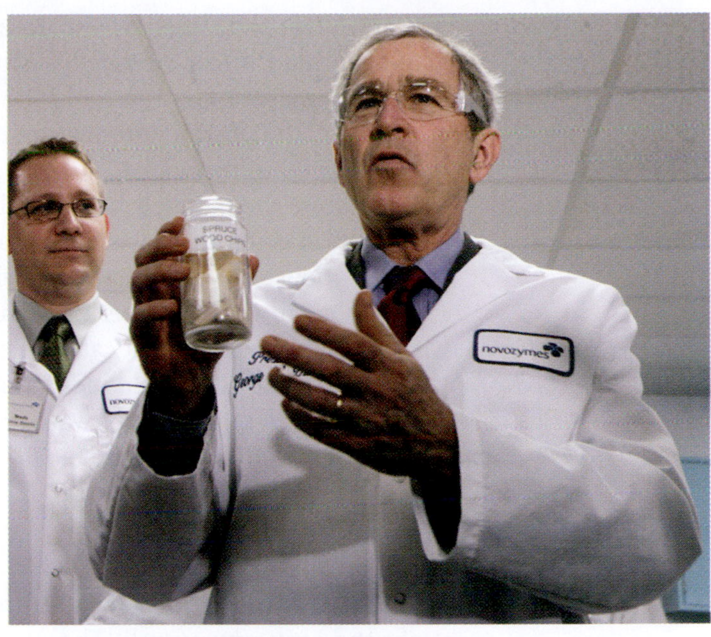

The Promise of Biotechnology President Bush touts the merits of bioengineered fuel for automobiles.

A Second Economic Revolution?

In fundamental respects, the information and industrial economies were quite different. Manual, blue-collar labor tended the machines of smokestack America; white-collar, well-educated labor tended the computers of information America. The industrial economy had eaten up fossil fuels, minerals, and other exhaustible resources and produced substantial pollution; the information economy promised less damage to the earth.

In some ways, however, the rise of the information economy repeated the Industrial Revolution. As in the late 1800s and early 1900s, technological change pushed new corporations to the forefront of American capitalism: software firms such as Microsoft and Oracle; hardware firms such as Dell and Intel; e-commerce pioneers such as Amazon.com and eBay; and the search engine giant Google.

Like the Industrial Revolution, the information revolution spurred a wave of corporate consolidation. The ABC television network, already merged with Capital Cities Communications in the 1980s, was taken over by Walt Disney in 1995. That year, media giant Time Warner, the product of a merger in 1989, bought out Turner Broadcasting. Then, in a sign of the growing importance of the Internet, Time Warner merged with Internet service provider America Online in 2000.

The information revolution also paralleled the Industrial Revolution by producing a new, hugely wealthy elite. The most famous of this new group of multibillionaires was Bill Gates, the cofounder of Microsoft, who became the richest American since John D. Rockefeller, the cofounder of Standard Oil, nearly a century before.

Just as the appearance of trains, planes, and machines stimulated the imagination of artists and intellectuals in the nineteenth and twentieth centuries, so did the appearance of computers at the end of the twentieth century and the beginning of the twenty-first. Digital technology made it easier than ever before to copy and manipulate text, images, and sounds, a development that encouraged collage and undermined linear narratives. More broadly, some thinkers believed a new, postmodern culture was replacing the modern culture inspired by industrialism. Hard to define, the postmodern culture embraced a more skeptical view of accepted truths and dominant ideologies.

Despite the parallels between the industrial and information revolutions, the information economy was still immature. Machine tools, railroads, and electricity had greatly boosted workers' productivity in the industrial era. Computers, the Internet, and biotechnology had yet to do the same in the 2000s. Moreover, most service positions required little education, used limited technology, and paid less than the best blue-collar jobs of the old industrial economy. By the 2000s, the biggest employer in America was neither a software company nor a car manufacturer, but rather a low-wage retail store, Wal-Mart.

Boom and Insecurity

For most of the 1990s, globalization and the information revolution seemed to benefit the economy overall. The productivity of American workers and the vitality of the service sector produced economic growth for nearly the entire decade, a record. Because of global competition, corporate cost cutting, and low oil prices, inflation was negligible. Interest rates were low; unemployment rose early in the decade but then dropped off to record lows. Driven by excitement about information-related companies, the stock market reached one record high after another. After passing 3,000 for the first time ever in 1991, the Dow Jones industrial average soared past 11,000 in 1999. As memories of the 1987 market crash faded, many Americans no longer felt the need to live with less. Symbolically, Congress repealed the federal 55-mile-per-hour speed limit for interstate highways in 1995, and big gas-guzzling sport-utility vehicles became popular.

Despite new SUVs, speed limits, and stock records, many Americans faced new economic challenges in the 1990s and 2000s. Employers, confronting global competition, reduced their labor forces aggressively. Traditionally, white-collar workers had enjoyed more job security than blue-collar workers. But corporate downsizing now affected both groups. In the 2000s, American multinationals outsourced white- as well as blue-collar jobs overseas. Even positions in computing and customer service migrated to the United Kingdom, the Philippines, and India, where English was spoken and wages were lower. Outsourcing jolted Americans who believed that college degrees and corporate employment guaranteed middle-class status. "This has been a very nasty journey," admitted an unemployed stockbroker. "You mourn your lifestyle. You mourn your identity."

A cartoonist lampoons life in the age of outsourcing: no American seems to be doing the work anymore.

The increasing costs of health care also troubled Americans. By the 1990s, the United States was spending a greater proportion of its

gross domestic product on health care than were other developed nations. Nevertheless, 43 million Americans did not have health insurance in 2003. The United States, almost alone among developed nations, had no national health insurance plan for its citizens. As employers cut costs, they decreased medical benefits for employees. The need for costly medical care would only increase as Americans' life expectancy continued to rise and the huge baby boom generation aged.

Americans feared, too, that they could not afford retirement. With the aging of the baby boom generation, there were more Americans over 65 and eligible for Social Security benefits than ever before (see Map 31–2). Many people believed there would not be enough money to pay the baby boomers' pensions in the twenty-first century. Private employers, meanwhile, reduced pension benefits for many retirees.

The Return of Inequality

The insecurities of many working- and middle-class Americans reflected a trend toward economic inequality. Allowing for inflation, the average weekly earnings of American workers in 1998 were less than in 1970. The decline of manufacturing meant the loss of relatively high-paying jobs. Employers were determined to hold down the growth of wages and salaries in the 1990s. Workers, facing the threats of downsizing and outsourcing, were reluctant to demand big wage increases, as were labor unions, which continued to have difficulty persuading workers to organize.

To stay even, Americans borrowed and worked more than before. Many families now had both parents in the paid workforce. In 1960, only a fifth of women with children under six held paying jobs; in 1995, two-thirds of such women worked for pay. Partly because many Americans now held two and even three jobs, people put in much more time at work. In 1960, Americans worked less—1,795 hours a year—

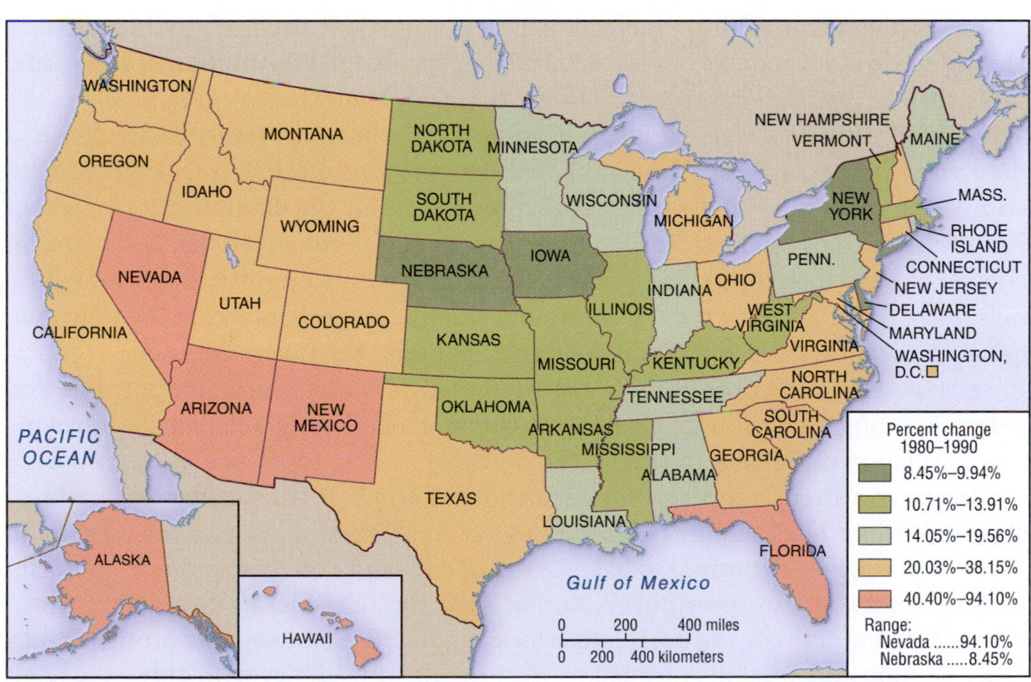

Map 31–2 Aging in America The increase in the percentage of the U.S. population aged 65 and over from 1980 to 1990 helped fuel worries about health care and Social Security.

than their counterparts in Britain, France, Germany, and Japan. By 1997–1998, they worked more—1,966 hours a year. Not surprisingly, more Americans told pollsters that they felt rushed.

Meanwhile, the wealthy fared exceptionally well in the transition to a globalized information economy. By 1949, the richest 1 percent of American households had seen its share of the nation's wealth dwindle to 20 percent. By 1997, the top 1 percent's share had zoomed up to 40 percent, nearly back to the record heights of the 1920s. In 2000, the richest 400 Americans had an average annual income of $174,000,000, almost quadruple their earnings only eight years earlier.

Several factors spurred the rebirth of great fortunes. The boom of the 1990s, fed by the information revolution, rewarded Bill Gates and other wealthy men and women with vast profits on their stocks and bonds. Tax cuts allowed the rich to keep more of their wealth. A change in public attitudes also benefited the rich. In the 1990s, observers noted the emergence of a "winner-take-all" culture in which it was acceptable for those at the top of companies and professions to earn far more money than ordinary workers.

At the start of the new century, the United States, the richest country in the world, was also the country with the largest gap between rich and poor. Many observers wondered whether strong social class differences, which had decreased in the mid-twentieth century, would once again define the nation and limit democracy.

The Power of Conservatism

Faced with troubling economic change, Americans had relatively little faith in the political system after the upheavals of the 1960s and 1970s. In 1994 only 19 percent of the people felt they could trust government. Politicians, Americans believed, were out of touch with ordinary citizens. Partly as a result, most voters did not favor a return to liberalism, with its faith in activist government. Instead, politics seldom strayed far from the conservative trail blazed by the Reagan Revolution of the 1980s. Nevertheless, national politics was closely, intensely contested.

In 1988, Reagan's vice president, George H. W. Bush of Texas, easily defeated the rather colorless liberal Democratic nominee, Governor Michael Dukakis of Massachusetts, to become the nation's 41st president. But the Republicans' hopes of continuing the conservative Reagan Revolution faded as voters left the Democrats in control of both the House and Senate. Squabbling with Congress, Bush vetoed 40 bills and even closed down the government briefly rather than accept the new budget authorization needed to fund federal operations. Yet Bush also made compromises that alienated conservatives. He supported new environmental controls and federal funding for education. In order to cut the federal budget deficit, he broke his firm campaign pledge not to raise taxes.

Running a tired campaign for reelection in 1992, Bush faced a surprisingly strong third-party challenge from the pugnacious Texas billionaire businessman, H. Ross Perot, who promised to balance the budget and end the "gridlock" in Washington. But it was Governor Bill Clinton of Arkansas, a moderate "New Democrat," who seemed to embody the best chance for change. Bush's broken tax promise and a weak economy doomed his campaign. Winning the presidency with only 43 percent of the popular vote, Clinton had a chance to partner with the Democratic-controlled Congress to push government back toward liberalism. But when the president proposed a liberal solution to the nation's health care crisis in 1993, Congress rejected the plan as too expensive and too intrusive in doctors' business and patients' lives. A year later, the Democrats lost control of Congress.

Fighting for his political future, Clinton catered to moderates and conservatives. "The era of big government is over," he declared. Through budget cuts and tax increases, he managed to end the budget deficit. The president accepted a bill limiting the federal government's authority to impose costly regulations and requirements, known as unfunded mandates, on the states. In 1996, he signed a welfare bill that significantly reduced federal support for the poor, especially children. To discourage dependence on government handouts, the bill limited welfare recipients to five years of assistance over their lifetime and required heads of households on welfare to find work within two years. Many Democrats and liberals angrily claimed that the president had embraced the conservative ideology of individual responsibility and betrayed the poor.

To keep the economy booming, Clinton blended liberal and conservative financial policies. In 1995, the White House and Congress pleased liberals by revising the Credit Reinvestment Act, originally passed during the Carter administration in 1977, to encourage banks to offer "subprime" mortgages—home loans to low-income Americans who would not traditionally qualify for such financing. Clinton also endorsed the conservative goal of easing federal regulation of the financial industry. In 1999, the president signed the Financial Services Modernization Act (also known as the Gramm-Leach-Bliley Act), which effectively repealed the Glass-Steagall Act of 1933, a New Deal measure preventing institutions from engaging in insurance and investment banking along with commercial banking. Now commercial banks, investment banks, and insurance companies would be free to compete for one another's business. Democrats went along with the new financial act in part because Republicans agreed to revise the Credit Reinvestment Act again to make it easier for low-income Americans to get the credit to buy houses. In the short run, subprime mortgages and deregulation helped sustain both the economic boom and President Clinton. But in little more than a decade, these actions would become much more controversial.

Thanks to his move to the right and the continuing economic boom, Clinton easily beat the Republican presidential nominee, longtime senator Bob Dole of Nebraska, in 1996. But Clinton's second term nearly collapsed in scandal over his real estate dealings and his adulterous affairs. In 1998, the House of Representatives voted two articles of impeachment charging the president with perjury and obstruction of justice. Only the second president to go on trial in the Senate, Clinton remained popular nonetheless. Most Americans seemed willing to separate the private and public lives of the president and wanted to keep him in office, particularly when his policies seemed to bring prosperity. Reflecting popular opinion, the Senate voted to acquit Clinton on both articles of impeachment.

Although Clinton had charted a moderate course between liberalism and conservatism, his scandal-ridden presidency did not guarantee Democratic success. In one of the closest elections in history, his vice president, Al Gore of Tennessee, lost to Governor George W. Bush of Texas, the son of the first President Bush, in 2000. Although Gore won the popular ballot by 550,000 votes, Bush appeared to capture a narrow majority of the Electoral College on election night. But it took the intervention of the Supreme Court to halt a controversial recount of Florida's vote and thereby make him the 43rd president.

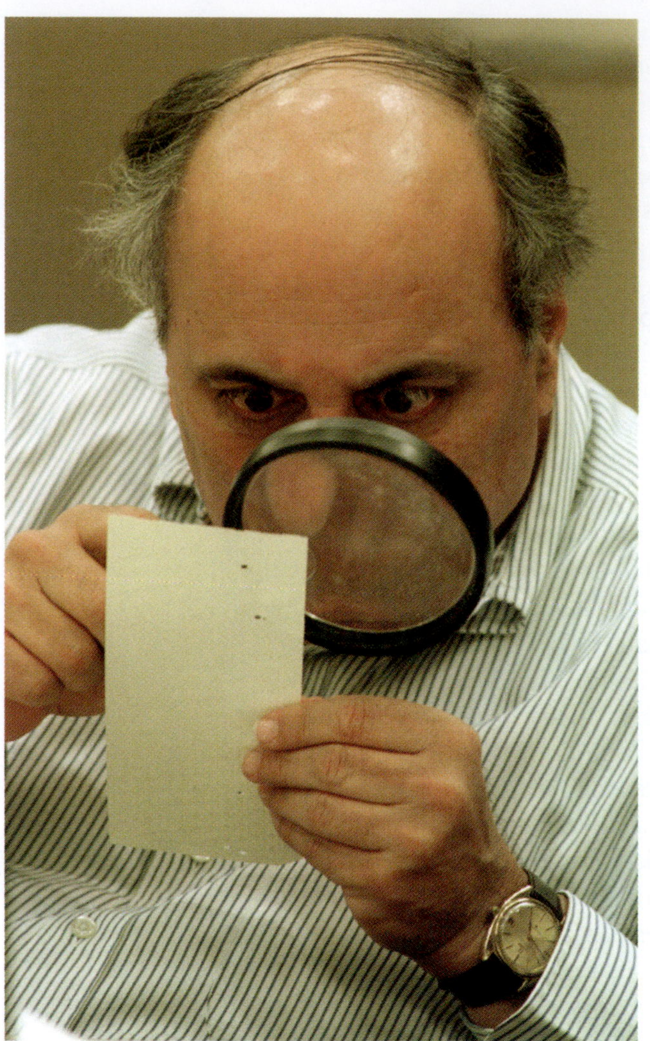

The Disputed Presidential Election of 2000 A judge tries to decide how to count a voter's ballot in Broward County in the crucial state of Florida.

Influenced by Reagan's success, the younger Bush was more conservative than his father. In his first term, "Bush 43" pushed successfully for tax cuts to stimulate the economy. Reflecting conservative opposition to government intervention, his administration weakened regulatory oversight of the financial industry. But Bush also accepted a quintessentially liberal initiative, an expensive drug benefit program for retired Americans.

In 2004, Bush faced another liberal Democrat, Senator John Kerry of Massachusetts, who tried to capitalize on worries over outsourcing and economic change. Yet Bush prevailed with 50.7 percent of the popular vote and a solid electoral majority. Buoyed by his victory, the president vowed to spend his "political capital" on conservative initiatives, including a reform of the Social Security system. His plans went nowhere, particularly after the Democrats won control of both houses of Congress in 2006. Thanks to Bush's tax cuts, drug plan, and military expenditures, the federal government ran a budget deficit again—another disappointment to conservatives, who yearned for smaller, less expensive government.

Contesting Globalization

Divided over many issues, Republican and Democratic leaders generally agreed with big businessmen that globalization represented a triumph for American institutions and values, including capitalism, free trade, and democracy. Even though the United States faced tough international economic competition, American political and corporate elites thought the nation was still better off than in a divided world without free trade. Some multinational executives did not see their interests as completely identical with those of the government. "I'm an internationalist first and a nationalist second," Ted Turner declared. But multinationals still depended on a powerful U.S. government to protect their investments around the globe.

In contrast, many middle- and working-class Americans did question whether globalization made their lives better. In the mid-1990s, the presence of between 2 and 4 million illegal migrants from Mexico angered many American citizens, particularly in Texas and California. Their argument was familiar: these illegal aliens drove down wages and took jobs from native-born Americans who paid higher taxes to provide the tax-evading migrants with education, health care, and welfare benefits. Supposedly, Spanish would rival English, immigrant cultures would dilute Anglo culture, and whites would lose political power. In response to such fears in 1994, California voters passed Proposition 187, a referendum denying illegal aliens access to public education and other benefits. Two years later, Congress appropriated more resources to stop the flow of illegal immigrants.

Three Presidents From left, George H. W. Bush ("Bush 41"), his son, George W. Bush ("Bush 43"), and 42nd president Bill Clinton.

The anti-immigrant movement did not get much further than that. Business generally welcomed immigration because it provided needed workers. Calculating the rapid growth of the Hispanic population, political leaders thought twice about antagonizing an increasingly powerful group of voters. Many native-born Americans, themselves the descendants of immigrants, believed immigration would help the economy and invigorate the dominant culture.

International trade provoked a more complex battle. The U.S. government, faced with the rapid-fire appearance of regional economic alliances, moved to create its own economic bloc. In 1992, the United States joined with Canada and Mexico to announce the North American Free Trade Agreement (NAFTA), which established the world's largest and richest low-tariff trading zone, to promote commerce among the three countries. Fearing more lost jobs at home, organized labor opposed the agreement. So did many environmentalists, who believed corporations would get around U.S. environmental laws by moving factory operations to Mexico. Third-party candidate H. Ross Perot capitalized on popular opposition to NAFTA. But the leadership of both major parties favored the agreement. In 1993, the Senate ratified NAFTA.

Combating Illegal Immigration A U.S. Border Patrol agent takes down the details of a group of illegal immigrants from Mexico arrested in the Altar Valley, Arizona, in 2008.

Opposition to globalization flared again at a meeting of the WTO in Seattle, Washington, in 1999. Labor unions, environmentalists, consumer activists, women's groups, and other organizations staged parades, meetings, and street theater. Demonstrators charged that the WTO served corporations and developed nations, damaged the environment, allowed AIDS to spread, and destroyed indigenous cultures. "The allegedly inevitable force of globalization has met the immovable object of grass-roots democracy," exulted one of the protestors. Fears of protest and terrorism led to cancellation of the WTO meetings scheduled for 2001.

Nevertheless, globalization was hard to contest. It would take more than isolated protests to alter the impact of new technologies; change the behavior of multinationals, trade blocs, and governments; and divert, let alone halt, the worldwide movement of people, ideas, goods, and capital in the twenty-first century.

A Changing People

Globalization was one of several forces reshaping American society and culture at the turn of the twenty-first century. As Latinos became the largest "minority" group, the United States headed rapidly toward the time when people of color, rather than whites, would make up a majority of the nation's population. As the experience of African Americans underscored, race and rights remained divisive issues. Concern about rights also spurred "culture wars" over family and sexual values and the status of women and homosexuals. In general, these struggles moved American society in a liberal rather than a conservative direction: the changing population became more tolerant of diversity and more willing to extend rights to disadvantaged groups.

A Diverse Society of Color

The racial and ethnic composition of the United States changed rapidly at the turn of the twenty-first century. In 2001, Americans of Hispanic or Latino origin outnumbered African Americans and became the largest minority group. Thanks to a strong job market, the Hispanic and Latino population had spread well beyond its traditional concentrations in south Florida and the rim of states from Texas to California. Mexican immigrants, for instance, came to stay in a host of small Midwestern towns and cities where semiskilled and unskilled jobs paid 10 and 15 times more than jobs in Mexico. At the edge of Kendallville, Indiana, a billboard beckoned to new Mexican arrivals, "Estamos Occupando"—We are hiring. By 2004, nonwhites made up one-quarter of the population. Americans of Hispanic or Latino origin, both white and nonwhite, numbered about 40 million—almost 14 percent of the nation's population. Expecting the number of Hispanics and Asians to triple in the next 50 years, the Census Bureau predicted that the United States would become a diverse society of color, with a nonwhite majority.

> **White men are an endangered species. I absolutely believe that, . . . what with affirmative action and everything.**
>
> HELEN CHENOWETH, Republican congresswoman, Idaho, January, 1996

As the population changed, the concept of race became more complicated. Many Americans had thought of race as largely a divide between black and white. But the growth of the Hispanic or Latino population confounded this simple division. Latinos and Latinas were conscious of their own distinctive histories. "White means mostly privilege and black means overcoming obstacles, a history of civil rights," explained Patria Rodriguez in 2003. "As a Latina, I can't try to claim one of these."

Like Tiger Woods, many Americans felt that mixed racial background was a basic and distinctive part of their identity. In response, the Census Bureau let people choose more than one race to describe themselves in 2000. Hispanics, epitomizing the complications of race, were allowed to identify themselves both as Hispanic and as members of any race. "It's a reminder," said a population expert, "that we will

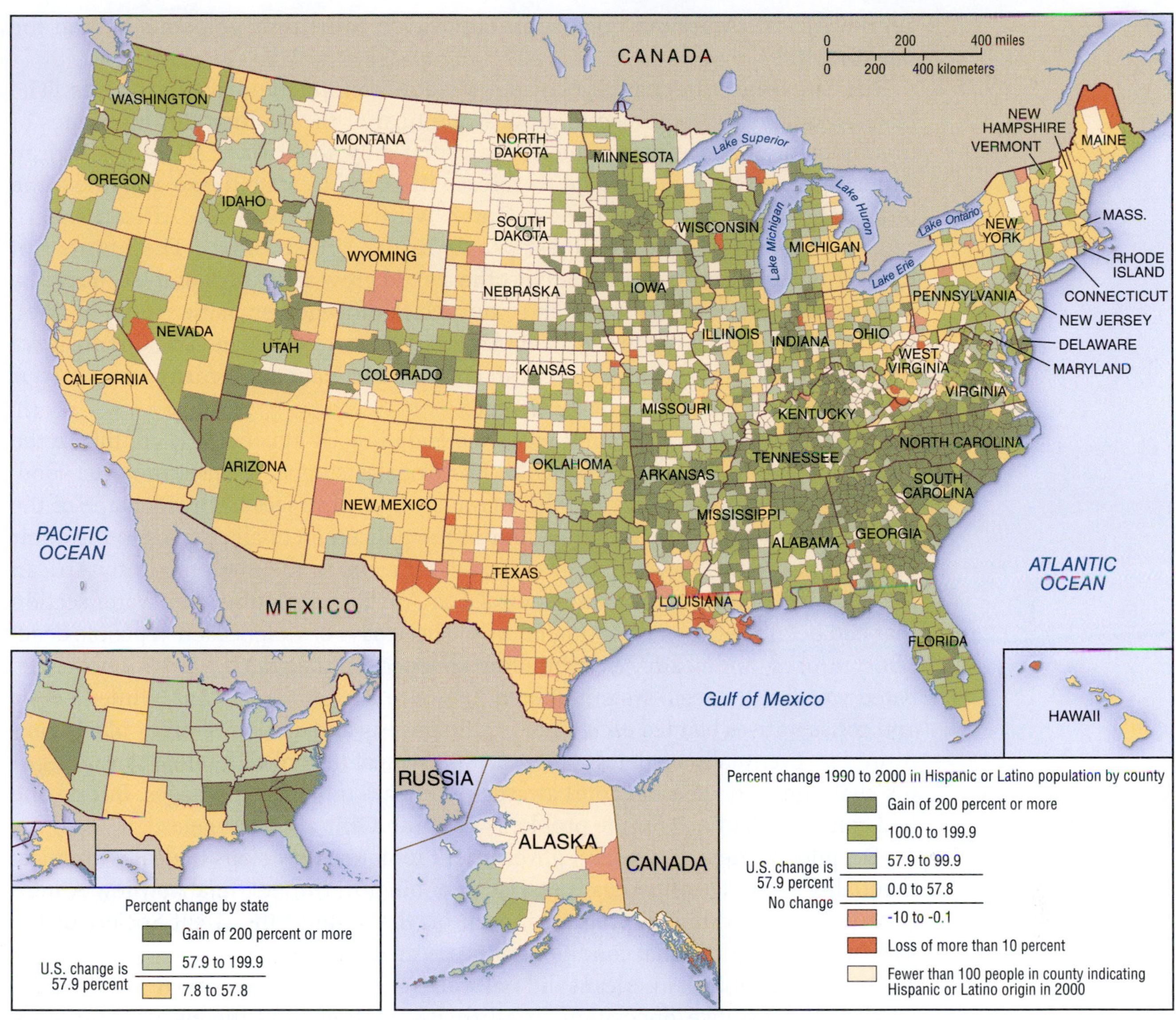

Map 31–3 The Growing Population of Americans of Hispanic or Latino Origin: Percent Change, 1990–2000
Thanks to a strong job market nationwide, the Hispanic and Latino population increased dramatically across the country. *Data Sources: U.S. Census Bureau, Census 2000 Redistricting Data (PL 94-171) Summary File and 1990 Census.*

increasingly, as Americans, need to find new ways of categorizing people and talking about their differences."

African Americans in the Post–Civil Rights Era

As Americans thought about the future, the African American experience was a reminder that issues of race and rights remained volatile and unresolved. By the 2000s, half a century after *Brown v. Board of Education,* southern schools were largely desegregated. But thanks to white flight from inner cities, northern schools were in many cases more segregated than ever. Despite continuing inequities, African Americans had made notable gains since *Brown.* In 1957, only 18 percent of black adults had graduated from high school. By 2002, 79 percent had graduated.

Yet the African American graduation rate lagged 10 percentage points behind the rate for whites.

African Americans had also made notable economic and political gains. The black middle class continued to grow at the turn of the century. But high rates of unemployment and imprisonment meant that only about six of every ten African American men were in the paid workforce in 2002. Despite the wealth and fame of talk show host and entrepreneur Oprah Winfrey, relatively few African Americans ranked among the wealthiest people in the United States. The number of high-profile African American public officials did grow at the turn of the century. By 1992, there were already more than 10,000 black officeholders nationwide. In 2001, Colin Powell became the first African American secretary of state, and Condoleezza Rice became the first African American (and female) national security advisor. Four years later, Rice became secretary of state.

These and other firsts did not mean the end of racial injustice and conflict in the United States. In 1991, white police in Los Angeles stopped a black motorist, Rodney King, for drunk driving and then savagely beat him. Despite a videotape of the beating, an all-white jury acquitted four of the policemen of all charges in the affair on April 29, 1992. The stunning verdict set off a riot in the predominantly African American community of South Central Los Angeles, including the Watts section that had been the center of rioting in 1965. Three days of violence left 51 people dead, 1,800 injured, and nearly 3,700 buildings burned. In the aftermath, Americans debated whether the legal system offered justice to African Americans, while liberals and conservatives blamed each other for the poverty and despair of many black communities. Eventually a federal court convicted two of the police for depriving King of his civil rights and another court awarded him $3.8 million in damages. But no one had concrete solutions for the problems of South Central Los Angeles.

Despite the riots, the federal government took few new steps to deal with racial inequality. In an age of popular pessimism about government, relatively few Americans believed that liberal programs, even on the scale of the Great Society of the 1960s, could secure equal conditions for African Americans.

At the same time, Americans did not want to undo the achievements of the past. Despite conservative opposition to affirmative action, this means of promoting equal opportunity in education and employment remained legal. In *Gratz v. Bollinger* in 2003, the Supreme Court, reflecting popular uneasiness with racial quotas and statistical formulas for diversity, struck down a "mechanical" point system used by the University of Michigan automatically to advantage minority applicants to its undergraduate program. But in *Grutter v. Bollinger,* the court endorsed Michigan's affirmative action program for law school admissions.

Culture Wars

Concerns about rights also drove a cluster of controversies, known as "culture wars," centering on changes in the family, marriage, gender, and sexuality. By the turn of the century, the ongoing transformation of the American family had become unmistakable. In the 1950s, two out of three families had a parent staying at home full-time; in 2000, with so many mothers in the workforce, less than one family in four had a stay-at-home parent. The supposedly "traditional" nuclear family of father, mother, and children no longer predominated in American households. Married

couples with children, 40 percent of all households as late as 1970, made up only 25 percent by 1996 (see Table 31–1). That year, 27 percent of families with children contained one parent, usually a mother, rather than two.

A number of factors led to these changes. Americans were marrying later, having fewer children, and having them later in life. The divorce rate doubled from 1960 to 1990. In the 1990s about half of all marriages were ending in divorce. As women's wages gradually rose, more women could afford to live alone or to head families by themselves.

Many conservatives and Republicans blamed these developments on the nation's alleged moral decline. In their view, the counterculture of the 1960s, liberals, the media, feminists, and gays had undermined the nation's "family values." "It is a cultural war, as critical to the kind of nation we will one day be as was the cold war itself," thundered the conservative commentator Patrick Buchanan in a speech to the Republican National Convention in 1992.

To defend the family, some conservatives argued that single mothers should receive fewer welfare benefits and that divorce should be made more difficult. In response, liberals claimed that the family was not dying but simply adapting to change as it always had. The different forms of the family, like social diversity in general, could be viewed as a good thing.

Whatever the merits of the liberal argument, conservatives found the battle for "family values" almost impossible to win. In 1992, George H. W. Bush's vice president, Dan Quayle, attacked the TV sitcom *Murphy Brown* for its positive portrayal of a career woman's decision to have a child out of wedlock. The show stayed on the air; Quayle and Bush lost their reelection bid. A decade later, a Federal Communications Commission crackdown on graphic and ostensibly obscene radio "shock jocks" such as Howard Stern led some radio networks and stations to drop controversial programming, but the business continued pretty much as before and Stern drew more listeners than ever. Hollywood movies and television programs continued to become more explicit.

Women in the Postfeminist Era

As the *Murphy Brown* controversy suggested, women, so often a focal point for fears about social change, were at the center of the culture wars. Women's position in American society had changed dramatically since the 1960s. The percentage of adult

 **Table 31–1** The Changing American Family, 1960–2006*

Year	Households	Families	Married-Couple Families	Single-Parent Families	One-Person Households
1960	52,799	44,905	23,358	3,332	6,917
1970	63,401	51,456	25,541	3,271	10,851
1980	80,776	58,426	24,961	6,061	18,296
1990	93,347	66,090	24,537	7,752	22,999
1996	99,627	69,594	24,920	9,284	24,900

Source: U.S. Census Bureau website, http://www.census.gov/population/socdemo/hhfam/rep86/96hh4.txt, http://www.bls.census.gov/population/socdemoc/hhfam/rep96/96hh1.txt and /96fml.txt.

*Numbers given in thousands.

women in the workforce rose, as did the percentage of women in high-paying white-collar jobs. Women were more visible in politics. After the 1992 elections, a record 53 women held seats in Congress. Bill Clinton selected and the Senate confirmed the first female attorney general, Janet Reno, in 1993, and the first female secretary of state, Madeleine Albright, in 1997.

Yet there was a sense of stagnation in the new century. In 2002, women earned on average 77.5 percent as much as men—little better than 10 years before. Women were still more likely than men to live in poverty. Bill Clinton's adulterous affairs dramatized women's insistence that men "just don't get it" about relationships between the sexes. Nearly half of women believed the women's movement had made their lives better, but the movement was now less visible and less vocal. Just as the 2000s were part of the "post–civil rights era," so they were part of the "postfeminist era."

Still, conservatives could not turn back the clock. Forced to raise troops without a draft, the military, one of the last and most intensely masculine preserves, needed female volunteers. In 1994, the Department of Defense rescinded the "Risk Rule" that kept women out of units in which they could be harmed or captured. As more women entered the military, the armed services repeatedly had to deal with charges of harassment. In 2000, the army even admitted that its highest-ranking woman general had been sexually harassed by a male general.

Conservatives also tried to limit women's access to abortion. At the grassroots level, the Right to Life movement picketed abortion clinics and tried to discourage pregnant women from having abortions. Some radicals resorted to violence, including the murder of clinic workers. Meanwhile, both presidents Bush opposed abortion and named antiabortion judges to the federal courts.

In spite of the protests and political maneuvers, the right and practice of abortion continued in the new century. In *Planned Parenthood v. Casey* in 1992, the Supreme Court narrowly voted to uphold much of a Pennsylvania law limiting access to abortions. But the Court also declared that a woman's right to choose an abortion was "a component of liberty we cannot renounce." As president, Clinton chose proabortion justices and vetoed antiabortion legislation.

Winning Gay and Lesbian Rights

Homosexuality was yet one more front in the culture wars. Although most Americans believed businesses should not discriminate on the basis of sexual preference, a majority in the 1990s still believed that homosexuality was morally wrong. Every year, there were hundreds of documented instances of violence against gays and lesbians.

As homosexuals pressed for equal rights, evangelical Christians and conservatives fought back. In 1992 Colorado voters passed a state referendum forbidding communities to pass laws protecting gay rights, but the state supreme court declared the referendum unconstitutional. In 1996, Congress passed the Defense of Marriage Act, which denied federal benefits to same-sex couples and allowed states to refuse to recognize same-sex marriages from other states.

The military was another battle zone. Officially barred from serving, homosexuals had long concealed their sexual orientation in order to remain in the military. Then, in 1992, a federal court ordered the navy to reinstate an openly gay petty officer who had been discharged. Campaigning for president that year,

Clinton promised to lift the ban on gays in the armed services. But in the White House, he compromised by instituting a "don't ask, don't tell" policy. The military would no longer ask recruits whether they were gay, and gays and lesbians would continue to conceal their sexual orientation.

The Spread of Same-Sex Marriage In June 2008, a ruling by the California State Supreme Court allowed same-sex couples, including this one, to marry.

Nevertheless, the tide seemed to turn. As AIDS spread more slowly among the gay population and heterosexuals contracted the disease, Americans were less likely to consider it "gay cancer" or God's punishment of homosexuals. Meanwhile, gays became a more accepted presence in society. More television shows positively depicted homosexuality. Openly gay men and women served in Congress. Many businesses, including Disneyland, welcomed gay customers. Leading corporations, including Ford and General Motors, began providing benefits to the partners of gay employees.

In the new century, Americans, especially younger ones, increasingly accepted the legitimacy of gay relationships. In *Lawrence v. Texas* in 2003, the U.S. Supreme Court struck down state antisodomy laws and effectively legalized gay sexual behavior. Invoking gays' "right to liberty," the majority declared, "The state cannot demean their existence or control their destiny by making their private sexual conduct a crime."

After *Lawrence,* there was new support for legalizing same-sex marriage. In 2004, the mayor of San Francisco, flouting state law, issued marriage licenses to same-sex couples. Strongly liberal Massachusetts became the first state to legalize same-sex marriages, and couples flocked to be married. Despite the support of conservatives and George W. Bush, a constitutional amendment banning gay marriage failed to pass that year. In 2008, the California Supreme Court overturned a state ban on same-sex marriage. But in November, a majority of California voters passed a referendum imposing a ban. The struggle over gay rights would continue.

The various battles over family values did little to alter the direction of social change in the United States. After a decade of the culture wars, Americans seemed willing to balance conservative economic policy with more liberal social values.

America in the Post–Cold War World

With the end of the cold war, America's role in the world, so plainly fixed for nearly half a century, suddenly became unclear. In 1991, the American-led victory in the Persian Gulf War suggested that the United States might serve as an active international police officer in a "New World Order." Nevertheless, Americans remained reluctant about intervention in crises abroad in the 1990s. But then the terrorist attacks of September 11, 2001, forced the United States into an ongoing global war on terror.

The New World Order

As the cold war ended, some Republicans called for a less internationalist foreign policy. Echoing conservatives of the 1940s and 1950s, they insisted that the United States should no longer provide financial aid and military protection to other countries. American soldiers, they felt, should risk their lives to protect the United States, not other countries. In contrast, a broad range of internationalists in both the Democratic and Republican parties believed the United States could protect itself and advance its political and economic interests only by remaining active in world affairs.

> You guys want to start a fight in my backyard, I got something for you.
>
> STAFF SGT. DAVID SAFSTROM, 82nd Airborne Division, on how he felt after 9/11

The most powerful internationalist was President George H. W. Bush. A naval aviator in World War II, the elder Bush believed that American isolationism had encouraged fascist aggression and world war in the 1930s and 1940s. So, Bush argued, the United States had to maintain its overseas commitments. With the help of other powerful countries, America should use foreign aid, military strength, NATO, and the United Nations to maintain a stable international system, a "New World Order." Bush wanted "a world in which democracy is the norm, in which private enterprise, free trade, and prosperity enrich every nation—a world in which the rule of law prevails." Much like Woodrow Wilson and Harry Truman before him, Bush mixed idealism and self-interest: a free world would be good both for other nations and for the United States. But only American power and leadership could preserve that world.

The New World Order was a broad, vague concept. Internationalists had a hard time explaining just what overseas commitments America needed to make. Critics noted a tension between Bush's call for order and his support for democracy. Was the United States supposed to protect antidemocratic countries in the name of international stability?

There was also a tension between Bush's commitment to international cooperation and the long-standing tendency for the United States to act alone in its own hemisphere. While the president spoke of the New World Order, he intervened unilaterally in the Central American nation of Panama in 1989. Bush had grown frustrated with General Manuel Noriega, the Panamanian leader who engaged in drug sales to the United States and other illegal activities. After Noriega thwarted democratic elections, Bush dispatched American troops, who captured Noriega and sent him to the United States for prosecution on drug charges in 1989. Bush's unilateral action, condemned by other Latin American countries, contradicted his rhetoric about international collaboration in the post–cold war world.

Finally, the New World Order, like the containment of Communism, could be expensive in lives and money. It was unclear whether Americans, mindful of the costs of the Vietnam War, would endorse armed intervention abroad. With the end of the cold war, many people also wanted a "peace dividend" of savings on foreign aid and military expenditures that could be spent on domestic needs.

The Persian Gulf War

The test of the New World Order came soon enough. On August 2, 1990, Iraq, led by President Saddam Hussein, overran Kuwait, its oil-rich but defenseless neighbor to the south. Entrenched in Kuwait, Iraq threatened its much larger western neighbor, oil-producing Saudi Arabia. Hussein's actions clearly jeopardized America's oil supply and its Saudi Arabian ally. The Kuwaiti invasion also obviously challenged Bush's calls for a stable global system of free and free-trading nations.

Comparing Hussein to Adolf Hitler, Bush created an international coalition opposing Iraq. By the end of 1990 over half a million U.S. troops had joined with forces from 36 nations in Operation Desert Shield to protect Saudi Arabia (see Map 31–4). Meanwhile, the Bush administration persuaded the United Nations to authorize military action if the Iraqis did not withdraw by January 15, 1991. The president also obtained congressional approval for the use of force.

When Hussein refused to pull back by the deadline, Operation Desert Shield became Operation Desert Storm. As television audiences around the world watched live CNN coverage, coalition missiles and planes struck Iraq on the night of January 17. Unable to contest the coalition's air power, Hussein launched Scud missile attacks against America's ally, Israel, hundreds of miles away. The missiles did little damage and failed to provoke Israeli retaliation that might have split the coalition. Instead, ground forces led by U.S. General Norman Schwarzkopf swept into Kuwait, devastated the Iraqi army, and pushed into Iraq in just 100 hours. Fearing accusations of cruelty, Bush called a halt before the invasion reached the Iraqi capital of Baghdad and toppled Hussein.

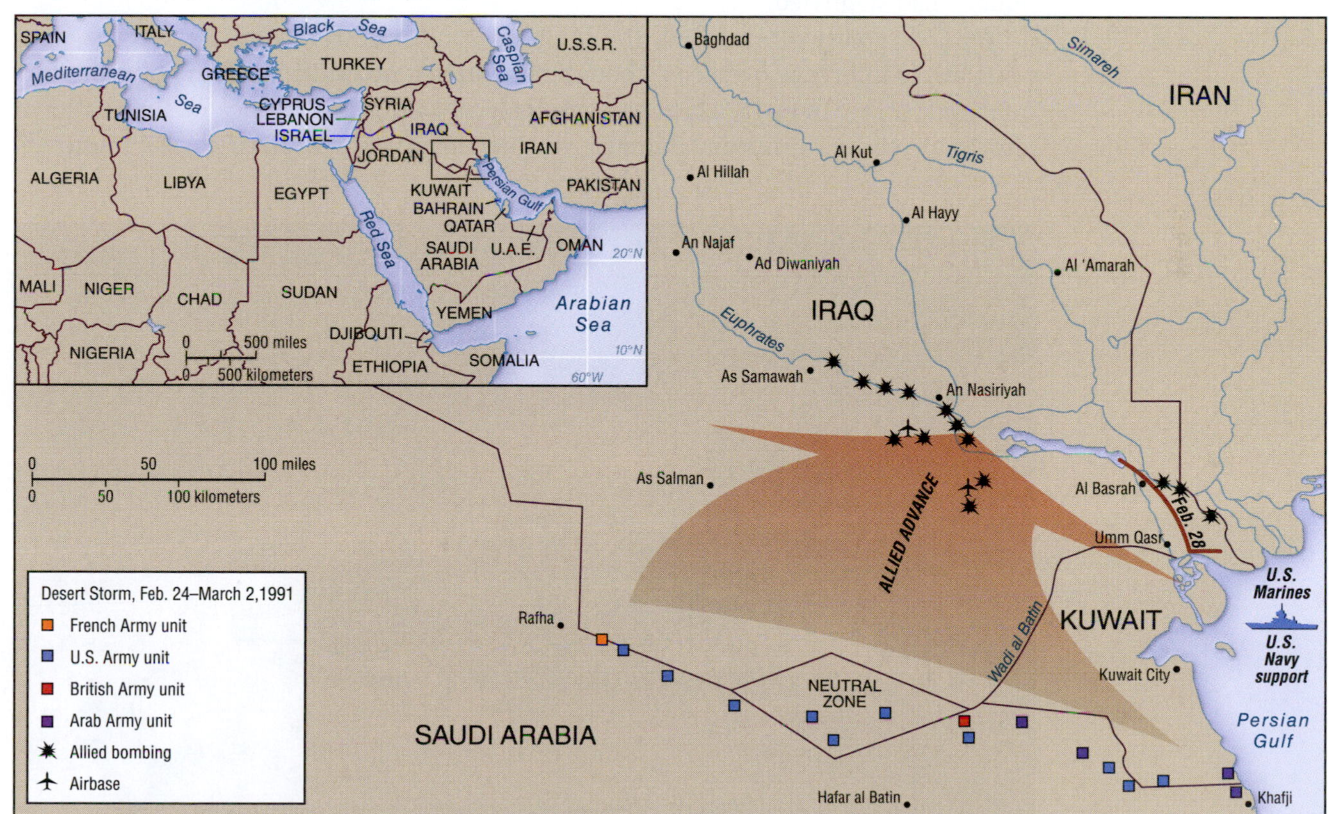

Map 31–4 The Persian Gulf War Operation Desert Storm, the allied attack on the forces of Iraq, tested President George H. W. Bush's vision of a "New World Order" in the oil-rich heart of the Middle East. *Mark C. Carnes et al,* Mapping America's Past *(New York: Henry Holt and Co., 1996), p. 267;* Hammond Atlas of the Twentieth Century *(New York: Times Books, 1996), p. 166.*

The Persian Gulf War seemed like a great victory for the United States and the New World Order. American technology appeared to work perfectly. Coalition forces suffered only about 220 battle deaths while killing thousands of Iraqis. American leadership and American power had halted aggression and restored freedom abroad. As Bush's popularity soared, the New World Order seemed like a practical reality.

Americans' euphoria did not last. Studies showed that U.S. weapons had not worked quite so well. As many as a quarter of Gulf War veterans suffered major health problems caused by exposure to chemical pesticides and, ironically, ingestion of pills intended to protect them from Iraqi chemical weapons. Despite the devastation of his forces, Saddam Hussein held on to power and ruthlessly repressed the Shiite and Kurdish populations. Despite the massive war effort, he would remain a threat to his neighbors and to American interests into the new century. The goals of the New World Order had not been fully achieved after all.

Retreating from the New World Order

In the years after the Persian Gulf War, the United States retreated from Bush's vision. Unwilling to maintain cold war spending levels, the nation cut troops, closed bases, and canceled weapons, including Reagan's Strategic Defense Initiative. The Central Intelligence Agency and other intelligence operations struggled with tight budgets, low morale, and public criticism. The federal government's foreign aid budget also stagnated.

As U.S. power diminished, the Vietnam syndrome returned: Americans were reluctant to intervene overseas when the nation had no critical military or economic interest at stake. In 1992, a civil war among local warlords complicated international efforts to relieve famine in Somalia, on the eastern horn of Africa. As hundreds

The Power Behind the "New World Order" American soldiers on a sophisticated M1 A1 Abrams tank, in the surreal glow of Kuwaiti oil fields burned by retreating Iraqi forces in March 1991.

of thousands of Somalis died, President Bush ordered 1,800 marines to serve in a United Nations force protecting the relief efforts. After Clinton took office in 1993, a warlord's forces massacred 32 U.S. troops in the capital city, Mogadishu. Clinton temporarily increased American forces in Somalia, but only on the condition that they all would be withdrawn in 1994. The chastened president directed that future U.S. involvement in peacekeeping operations would require a threat to international peace and security, or a benefit to "U.S. interests."

The United States showed a similar reluctance to intervene in the violence following the collapse of Communist rule in Yugoslavia. As this Eastern European country broke apart in the early 1990s, three ethnic groups—Serbs, Croats, and Muslim Slavs—fought a bitter civil war in the newly independent province of Bosnia-Herzegovina. The remnants of the old Yugoslavia, under the harsh leadership of Slobodan Milosevic, aided the Serbs in carrying out "ethnic cleansing," the forcible expulsion of Muslims and Croats from their homes. Faced with the worst mass brutality in Europe since World War II, Bush and Clinton were unwilling to risk American lives. Under intense pressure to stop the slaughter, Clinton allowed U.S. planes and missiles, operating in conjunction with NATO, to attack Serb forces in 1994. Backed by this devastating assault, the United States brokered a peace agreement in 1995. Clinton committed 20,000 troops to a peacekeeping force, even though most Americans opposed the move.

Yugoslavia posed a challenge again when the Milosevic regime attacked ethnic Albanians in the region of Kosovo. Humiliated by its inability to negotiate an end to the suffering in Kosovo, the Clinton administration finally supported a NATO air offensive against the Yugoslavian government in March 1999. The 78-day war that ended in June killed 2,000–5,000 people, badly damaged Yugoslavia's infrastructure, and forced Milosevic to accept a multinational peacekeeping force. NATO suffered no casualties, because Clinton and other leaders were unwilling to risk them. There was no longer any talk about a U.S.-led New World Order.

Al Qaeda and 9/11

As Americans shied away from international commitment, a mortal threat to the United States took shape. In February 1993 an explosive-laden truck blew up in an underground garage beneath the twin towers of New York City's giant office complex, the World Trade Center. Six people were killed and more than a thousand injured in the first major international terrorist incident inside the United States. Investigators traced the attack to followers of a radical Islamist spiritual leader from Egypt, Sheikh Omar Abdel-Rahman, who lived in New Jersey. Rahman and over a dozen associates were convicted for the bombing and other plots.

Surprisingly, most Americans paid little attention to terrorism in the aftermath of the attack. U.S. authorities generally ignored the plotters' connections to a terrorist organization, Al Qaeda, led by a wealthy Saudi Arabian exile, Osama bin Laden. A veteran of the resistance to the Soviet invasion of Afghanistan, bin Laden had gradually made Al Qaeda—Arabic for "base" or "foundation"—into an anti-Western movement dedicated to restoring the supposedly lost glory of Islam. The terrorist financier particularly hated the United States, for its support of Israel and its military presence in the Middle East.

Operating out of Sudan and then Afghanistan, Al Qaeda supported Muslim fighters in Bosnia and warlords in Somalia. In 1995 and 1996, the organization was

Osama bin Laden The terrorist leader sits for an interview at a secret location two months after the 9/11 attacks.

involved in deadly terrorist attacks on U.S. soldiers in Saudi Arabia. In 1996, bin Laden declared jihad—holy war—on the United States.

Although Clinton declared terrorism "the enemy of our generation," Americans paid little attention. Al Qaeda attacks continued. In 1998, almost simultaneous truck bombs at U.S. embassies in Kenya and Tanzania killed at least 224, including 12 Americans, and wounded 5,000. Blaming bin Laden, the Clinton administration unsuccessfully authorized his assassination and launched missile attacks on Al Qaeda facilities in Sudan and Afghanistan. In 2000, Al Qaeda members slammed an explosive-laden motorboat into the side of the U.S. destroyer *Cole* in the Yemeni port of Aden. Although 17 American sailors died, the president and his advisers did not retaliate against bin Laden (Map 31–5) .

Despite warnings, Clinton's successor, George W. Bush, paid little attention to Al Qaeda. Then, on the morning of September 11, 2001, the most ambitious Al Qaeda plot took place in a clear blue, morning sky. Nineteen Middle Eastern members of bin Laden's organization successfully passed through security at East Coast airports and boarded four passenger jets. In flight, the terrorists, brandishing box cutters and Mace or pepper spray, overwhelmed flight attendants and passengers, killed or wounded the pilots, took the controls, and redirected the flights. At 8:46 A.M., American 11 sped into the North Tower of the World Trade Center; 17 minutes later, United 175 hit the Trade Center's South Tower. At 9:37, American 77 struck the west wall of the Pentagon, outside Washington, DC. Aboard United 93, apparently headed toward Washington, too, there were sounds of struggle, a voice shouted, "Allah is the Greatest," and the jet crashed into an empty field in Shanksville, Pennsylvania, at 10:03. By then, the North Tower of the World Trade Center had collapsed in a cloud of smoke and debris. The South Tower followed at 10:28.

All told, the tragedy, which became known as "9/11," killed the 19 hijackers, 40 people in the crash at Shanksville, 184 at the Pentagon, and 2,751 at the World Trade Center. More Americans died on 9/11 than had died in the Japanese attack at Pearl Harbor on December 7, 1941. Only the Civil War battles of Antietam on September 17, 1862, and Cold Harbor on June 3, 1864, had been deadlier days in the nation's history. America's place in the post–cold war world had suddenly come into focus. "Terrorism against our nation will not stand," Bush vowed. A decade after the end of the cold war, the United States had begun the war on terror.

The War on Terror

In the days after 9/11, stunned Americans felt that the attacks had "changed everything." Much of national life stayed the same, but the catastrophe did funda-

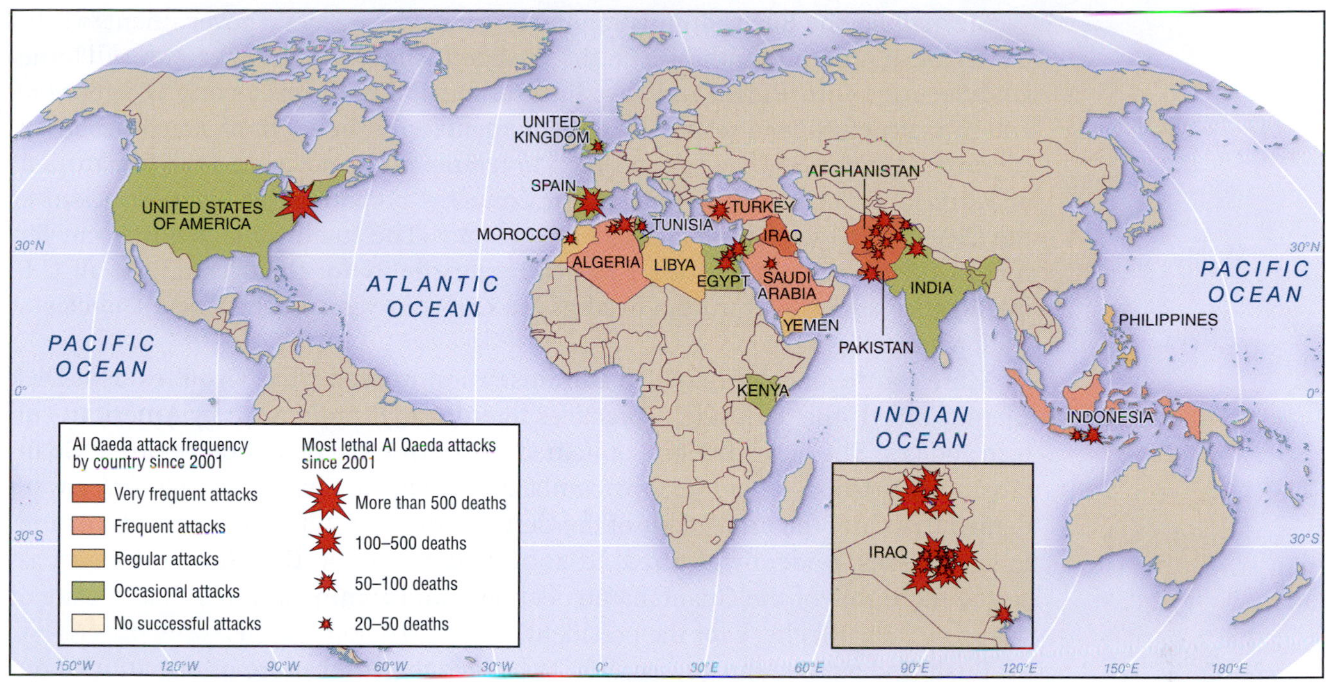

Map 31-5 The Global Reach of Al Qaeda

mentally reshape American foreign and security policy. Vowing privately on 9/11 "to kick some ass," President Bush declared publicly that evening, "We will make no distinction between the terrorists who committed these acts and those who harbor them." The United States demanded that the Taliban regime in Afghanistan, which protected bin Laden, turn over the terrorist. When the Taliban refused, Bush promised they would "pay the price." In October, U.S. and other NATO forces attacked Afghanistan. After American and British air strikes against Al Qaeda and Taliban targets, U.S., British, and Australian troops invaded the country to hunt down bin Laden, destroy his training camps, and drive out the Taliban.

Afghanistan, weak and impoverished, fell quickly, as the Taliban surrendered the capital, Kabul, in November and fled their stronghold Kandahar in December. Yet bin Laden and many of his men escaped in the remote, rugged, mountainous terrain to continue their fight along the border with Pakistan. So U.S. and NATO forces remained to protect the fragile new government and keep hunting bin Laden.

New York, September 11, 2001 As the North Tower of the World Trade Center burns in the background after being hit by a hijacked jet airliner, a second hijacked plane roars toward a fiery collision with the South Tower. Within hours, both towers would collapse, killing thousands.

Meanwhile, the Bush administration reorganized the federal government to combat terror. Within a month of 9/11, the president chose the first Director of Homeland Security, Tom Ridge, and gave him responsibility for protecting U.S. borders and infrastructure, and responding to emergencies in the event of a terrorist strike. In 2002, Congress elevated the position to cabinet rank and created the Department of Homeland Security. Two years later, Congress responded to harsh criticism of the CIA and FBI for failing to detect the 9/11 plot. The Intelligence Reform and Terrorism Prevention Act of 2004 stripped responsibility for the oversight of all U.S. intelligence agencies from the head of the CIA and vested it in a new Director of National Intelligence.

More controversially, the Bush administration worked what Vice President Dick Cheney called "the dark side"—practices traditionally condemned by American culture and law. The government maintained a controversial detention center at Guantánamo Bay, Cuba, where "enemy combatants" captured in the war on terror were denied trials and the protections of the Geneva Convention for prisoners of war and, in some cases, evidently tortured. In 2006 and 2008, the U.S. Supreme Court asserted the rights of the Guantánamo detainees and reminded Bush that "a state of war is not a blank check for the president."

Bush also wanted the government to be able to gather more information about its own citizens. In October, 2001, Congress hastily passed the USA Patriot Act—an acronym for the "Uniting and Strengthening America by Providing Appropriate Tools Required to Intercept and Obstruct Terrorism Act of 2001." This measure made it easier for the federal government to spy on Americans. The Patriot Act also allowed the attorney general to imprison indefinitely, without trial, noncitizens considered threats to national security.

Opponents condemned the Patriot Act as an unlawful and unequaled deprivation of civil liberties. In 2004, a federal judge declared part of the measure an unconstitutional infringement on First Amendment rights. Despite the controversy, the Bush administration pushed successfully for renewal and expansion of the act.

Bush also reconsidered the use of American military power. In the past, presidents had rejected preemptive, peacetime attacks on other nations. But Bush believed that terrorism presented "a threat without precedent." As 9/11 demonstrated, enemies did not need "great armies and great industrial capabilities to endanger the American people and our nation." So the president threatened to strike before a war began and even before a threat emerged in the first place. Bush further broke with cold war presidents, including his father, by calling for the United States to act alone when necessary rather than through alliances and the United Nations.

The Bush Doctrine of preemption and unilateral action risked isolating the United States in the world and making it seem selfish, dangerous, and illegitimate. Yet Bush, confident of American power and virtue, was willing to go it alone. "That's OK with me," he said. "We are America."

The Iraq War

The president knew where to apply his new doctrine. It was not enough to go after terrorist organizations, Bush said in his State of the Union address in January 2002. The United States must also "prevent regimes that sponsor terror from threatening America or our friends and allies with weapons of mass destruction."

AMERICAN LANDSCAPE

>> Gitmo, "The Least Worst Place"

From the camera eye of a satellite miles above, Guantánamo Bay stood out from the rest of eastern Cuba. The inlet was a horseshoe of brown and grey terrain amid the lush green of the island and the bright blue of the Atlantic. To the administration of George W. Bush, Guantánamo Bay was a grey area, too: one of the few places on earth that was American and yet not American, a drab anomaly perfect for one of the most controversial phases of the war on terror.

Guantánamo Bay, some 520 miles from Miami, Florida, had been an anomaly for more than a century. After the Spanish-American War of 1898, the U.S. government had taken the spot for a naval base: the inlet made a perfect harbor; the hills blocked off the rest of the island. The Cuban-American Treaty of 1903, modified in 1934, effectively gave America perpetual control over the base. For the bargain price of less than $4,000 a year, the United States could keep the facility until both Washington and Cuba agreed to end the arrangement.

Even when Fidel Castro came to power in 1959, the U.S. base remained at Guantánamo Bay, like a capitalist shard stuck in the side of the new Communist regime. Castro objected to the base and refused to cash all but one of America's annual checks, but he did not try to drive out the United States either. So Guantánamo Bay, or "Gitmo," as Americans called it, remained the oldest U.S. overseas naval base and the only one in a Communist country.

Nevertheless, Gitmo became less and less valuable over the years. As the cold war ended and the United States closed down many military bases, there was no real need for a naval installation so close to the U.S. mainland. The number of American military personnel assigned to Gitmo dwindled.

Then the war on terror began. The Bush administration needed to put captured Taliban fighters and other "enemy combatants" somewhere safe. It was too risky to leave detainees in unstable Afghanistan or Iraq; but it was also too risky to bring them to the United States, where courts, Congress, and public opinion could interfere in their imprisonment. So, the Bush administration looked, in the words of Secretary of Defense Donald Rumsfeld, for "the least worst place" to hold those captured in the war on terror.

Rumsfeld and his colleagues found it at Guantánamo Bay. The U.S. military controlled the base, but U.S. civil law did not apply. Gitmo, with its grey, pebbly beaches, was the perfect grey area for an administration determined to find its way around the law to prosecute the war on terror. Before 2001 was over, detainees began to arrive from Afghanistan. By the end of 2008, some 775 people had been incarcerated at Gitmo. To accommodate them, the U.S. government built up the base. There were soon no fewer than seven separate prison facilities; one of them, known only as "Camp 7," remained secret. Thousands of American personnel streamed in to run Gitmo.

For a time, the base provided the Bush administration with just the freedom it wanted and needed. CIA, FBI, and military interrogators, apparently copying Chinese Communist techniques from the 1950s, tortured some prisoners. According to detainees, their captors used sleep deprivation and beatings; they also mocked detainees' religious practices by defacing the Qur'an or flushing it down the toilet. Deprived of the

continued

>> **AMERICAN LANDSCAPE** *continued*

rights of captured military prisoners under the Geneva Convention, the detainees were also deprived of the right to trial—a feature of justice back in the United States. These conditions took a heavy toll on the prisoners: an unknown number committed suicide.

As details of life at Gitmo leaked out, critics of the Bush administration denied that the base was any sort of grey area at all. They argued that the laws of the United States should apply to the prisoners at the base: they deserved the protections of the Geneva Convention and the right to trial. More broadly, they saw Gitmo as proof that the war on terror, like other wars, had eroded due process, human rights, and other features of democracy, all in the name of battling for democracy. Even the lord chancellor of the United Kingdom—a U.S. ally—called the base a "shocking affront to democracy" in 2006.

Even though the U.S. Supreme Court seemed to agree, in its rulings of 2006 and 2008, Gitmo remained open—a swath of grey amid all the green and blue. ●

The Fall of Saddam Hussein As the coalition invasion overthrew the Iraqi regime, jubilant Iraqis pulled down statues of Saddam Hussein, like this one, in the spring of 2003.

The president identified Iran, Iraq, and North Korea as an "an axis of evil," potentially able to arm terrorists with nuclear, chemical, or biological weapons to threaten the United States directly.

Iraq was the focus of Bush's attention. In recent years, Saddam Hussein had plotted the assassination of the president's father and seemingly resumed attempts to gain weapons of mass destruction (WMD). In the Bush administration's view, a U.S. missile strike and United Nations economic sanctions and weapons inspections had not deterred Hussein, who had forced the inspectors to withdraw in 1998. After 9/11, Bush shared the view of key advisors that Hussein still had WMD and supported Al Qaeda. Further, some administration members argued that the replacement of Hussein with a democratic regime would encourage the spread of democracy around the Middle East and make Israel safer.

As the Bush administration moved toward confrontation with Iraq, nearly all of America's European allies, as well as Russia, China, and Middle Eastern countries, opposed a unilateral U.S. war. The United States did assemble a "coalition of the willing," but it was far smaller than the coalition assembled by the president's father 12 years earlier. Only Great Britain, Australia, and Poland joined the U.S. in committing troops.

On the night of March 19, 2003, Operation Iraqi Freedom began with a hail of Tomahawk cruise missiles aimed at Baghdad in an unsuccessful attempt to kill Hussein. To the surprise of many observers, the rest of the attack went almost flawlessly. On March 21, some 1,300 bombs and missiles rained down on Baghdad in a display of "shock and awe" meant to demoralize the Iraqi leadership. Meanwhile, coalition ground forces moved into Iraq, with the British striking south to seize the port city of Basra and the United States moving east to occupy Baghdad. American technology, particularly highly accurate missiles and smart bombs, worked quite well. The Iraqi army offered little resistance, as many of its soldiers simply disappeared into the civilian population. Hussein disappeared, too. By mid-April, his statues were toppling.

Swift and short, the war with Iraq seemed to be everything that the Bush administration had hoped. Only 138 U.S. soldiers had died. Standing before a huge banner declaring "Mission Accomplished" aboard an aircraft carrier on May 1, the president jubilantly announced, "Major combat operations in Iraq have ended." The United States seemed well on the way to winning the war on terror and reshaping the Middle East.

America in Crisis

By the 2000s, a new America, "a nation transformed," seemed to have taken shape. The twenty-first-century United States was a globalized, information-based, diverse nation, socially liberal and politically conservative. But the transformation of America was far from over. The costly war on terror dragged on without victory in either Afghanistan or Iraq. In 2008, financial catastrophe, gradually developing for several years, engulfed the economy. Along with the strain of the war on terror, the frightening economic downturn created a national crisis. Long-standing monuments of American capitalism teetered on the brink of collapse. So did the conservative policies that had shaped American governance for nearly two generations. Against this troubling backdrop, Americans used the presidential election to point their country in a new direction.

Iraq and Afghanistan in Turmoil

The jubilant announcement of "Mission Accomplished" soon gave way to sober realities in Iraq during 2003. There was looting in many communities. Despite an intensive search, no weapons of mass destruction could be found. It was difficult to restart the economy and train new Iraqi police and defense forces. Rather than embrace their liberators, many Iraqis resented the Americans. Worst of all, a violent insurgency, perhaps orchestrated by Saddam Hussein, tried to destabilize Iraq and drive out the United States.

Although U.S. forces captured Hussein in December 2003, the conflict went badly. Unable to prove that Hussein's regime had had ties to Al Qaeda before 9/11, the Bush administration faced charges of fighting an expensive, needless war and weakening the hunt for bin Laden in Afghanistan. Bush was further embarrassed by the brutal execution of Hussein and revelations of the humiliation and torture of Iraqis at a U.S. prison in Abu Ghraib. Although the Bush administration handed over sovereignty to a new Iraqi government, chosen by the United States, in 2004, more than 100,000 American troops remained.

Those forces now confronted "Al Qaeda in Iraq," a new terrorist group pledging allegiance to bin Laden, and also a sectarian civil war between Shiites and Sunnis. The insurgents' use of IEDs—improvised explosive devices—took a heavy toll on American troops. By the end of 2006, 3,000 U.S. soldiers had died and Iraq remained in turmoil.

Facing failure, the Bush administration responded with a controversial "surge," a temporary increase in troop strength to 130,000, in 2007. By mid-2008, the surge, along with changes in Iraqi politics, succeeded in decreasing the violence. But more than 4,000 U.S. soldiers and uncounted Iraqis had died, the Iraqi economy still struggled, and the Iraqi government was not truly democratic. American public opinion had largely turned against the war.

Meanwhile, the conflict in Afghanistan had worsened. As the United States focused resources and attention on Iraq, the Taliban, aided by foreign fighters, had gradually regained strength and the pro–United States government had lost power. Osama bin Laden remained at large, most likely somewhere along the mountainous border with Pakistan. Calling the situation "precarious and urgent," U.S. military leaders admitted they did not have enough troops to commit to Afghanistan. But the United States did prosecute the war more aggressively by striking into Pakistan. The American death toll climbed to a record of more than 100 in 2007 and passed 100 again in 2008. By then, over 600 U.S. soldiers had died since 2001 in what was becoming one of America's longest wars. Uncounted thousands of Afghans had died as well.

In addition to lives and money, the wars in Afghanistan and Iraq cost the United States popularity and influence around the globe. Sympathetic to Americans in the months after 9/11, many people no longer supported U.S. military action in the Middle East. The tragic toll of civilian deaths and the use of torture proved particularly costly for America's standing in the world. Critics argued that the U.S. government's callous mistreatment of Middle Easterners was winning converts for Al Qaeda and terrorism. At the same time, as the situation in Afghanistan underscored, the United States had seriously depleted its military power. When Russia invaded neighboring Georgia, a U.S. ally, in the summer of 2008, there was nothing the Bush administration could do to change the course of events. The United States no longer seemed like an unstoppable superpower or an unflagging champion of democracy.

The Economy in Jeopardy

In retrospect, the economic boom of the 1990s and 2000s looked a lot like the boom of the 1920s. In both periods, optimistic American consumers, buoyed by good times, borrowed money and bought houses and cars. Investors borrowed money, too, to buy stocks. All that buying spurred the economy and drove the stock market to record heights. But eventually all that borrowing reached its limits: new credit ran out, and many Americans found themselves unable to meet their debts. In both periods, too, business leaders and government officials paid too little attention to dangerous financial practices until it was too late.

Inflating the Housing Bubble In 2002, President George W. Bush encourages mortgage lenders to make it easier for Americans to buy homes.

By the early 2000s, the housing industry was developing a classic "bubble," an inflation of prices based on air and delusion, not reality. As Americans—some of them aided by subprime mortgages—bought houses in record numbers, the nation began to believe that homes were great investments whose value would just keep on increasing. Acting on this belief, some people bought houses they could not really afford and many people used houses as collateral for loans. In the process, banks made loans they should not have made. Moreover, financial institutions intentionally or unintentionally obscured the reality of bad mortgage loans by folding those loans into complex, risky new financial instruments, known as Collateralized Debt Obligations (CDOs), that they sold around the world. As a result, firms in the United States and abroad were vulnerable to trouble in housing but did not understand the danger.

The trouble began in 2005, when U.S. house prices stagnated and then began to fall the next year. As the housing bubble burst, many home owners discovered they were not as wealthy as they thought they were. Some of them, particularly those with subprime loans, had trouble making their payments; foreclosures—banks' repossession of homes for unpaid mortgages—began to increase. The consequences rippled outward: the home-construction industry suffered; it became harder for consumers to get credit.

The most dramatic consequences befell financial institutions. In the spring of 2008, the New York investment bank Bear Stearns, deeply involved in subprime mortgage loans and other risky practices, nearly collapsed despite help from the federal government. Only a takeover by banking giant JPMorgan Chase saved the

Crash Distraught traders at the Chicago Mercantile Exchange watch the stock market plunge, October 2008.

firm from bankruptcy. In the summer, the nation's largest mortgage lender, IndyMac Bank, failed; in line with New Deal legislation, the federal government stepped in to guarantee depositors' money. Then, Washington had to take over two key private corporations that bought and sold mortgages from banks—the Federal National Mortgage Association, known as "Fannie Mae," and the Federal Home Loan Mortgage Corporation, known as "Freddie Mac."

As these events unfolded, other developments joined to threaten not only the United States but the global economy as well. The cause of globalized free trade suffered when the World Trade Organization's round of trade talks held in Doha, Qatar, collapsed in failure. Oil prices, driven by rising demand from the rapidly growing economies of China and India, surged to record levels. High oil prices drove up the price of other goods, including food, and spurred inflation. Rising oil prices also hurt the auto industry, particularly the Big Three U.S. automakers—Chrysler, Ford, and General Motors—whose gas-guzzling SUVs became suddenly hard to sell. Although felt worldwide, these events particularly hurt the United States, which saw the value of the dollar decline around the globe. All these developments eroded the confidence of American consumers, particularly those who had run up big balances on their credit cards. The Dow Jones Industrial Average, which had reached a record high over 14,000 in October 2007, had declined into the 11,000s in early September 2008.

Despite these ominous trends, most people were still unprepared when disaster struck in mid-September. In a matter of days, the U.S. financial industry nearly collapsed: Lehman Brothers, another investment firm caught up in the subprime debacle, went bankrupt—the most valuable American corporation ever to fail; the Bank of America bought Merrill Lynch, still another near-bankrupt victim of dubious mortgage and other financial practices; and AIG, an insurance giant heavily involved in CDOs, headed toward collapse as well until the Federal Reserve effectively bought the company.

Meanwhile, U.S. and foreign stock markets buckled. The Dow Jones lost more than 4 percent of its value on September 15, and then another 4 percent two days later. As government officials and financial leaders around the world scrambled to save banks, keep the financial system operating, and prop up the stock markets, Americans worried whether the world faced a repeat of the great crash of 1929. At the end of the month, a panicked Congress approved the Emergency Economic Stabilization Act of 2008, an extraordinary financial package, worth as much as $700 billion, to try to bail out the U.S. financial industry, ensure the availability of credit to borrowers, and save the nation from depression.

The Presidential Election of 2008

As the economy reeled, Americans went about choosing the 44th president of the United States. Even before the financial meltdown, the election was proving a milestone in American history. Democratic senator Hillary Clinton of New York, the wife of Bill Clinton, seemed likely to become the first woman major-party presidential candidate. But Clinton's campaign, which emphasized her "experience" and her original support for the Iraq War, met unexpectedly tough resistance from the younger, first-term senator Barack Obama of Illinois. The son of a black Kenyan father and a white American mother, Obama, like Tiger Woods, evoked a more diverse, globalized nation. In contrast to Clinton, he ran on a platform of "change" for America and an end to the Iraq War. Narrowly defeating Clinton in an epic primary battle, Obama became the first African American major-party presidential nominee.

Obama's Republican opponent, Senator John McCain of Arizona, seemed much more a candidate of the status quo. The second-oldest major-party nominee in American history, the 72-year-old McCain was a generation older than the 47-year-old Obama. But the Republican, drawing attention away from his support of Bush administration policies, presented himself as a tough-minded, independent "maverick" with the courage to chart a new political course. The surprise selection of Alaska's reform governor Sarah Palin as the second female major-party candidate for the vice presidency underscored McCain's commitment to change.

The intensification of the economic crisis in October mortally wounded the Republican cause. Saddled with the unpopular wars and weak economy of the Bush administration, McCain seemed old and uncertain. Meanwhile, many voters were impressed by Obama's cool performance during the crisis, including his three televised debates with McCain. On election day in November, a majority of the electorate did what had seemed unthinkable even after the civil rights movement of the 1960s: they made an African American the president of the United States. Moreover, Obama won a clear victory, with 52.8 percent of the popular vote, the highest percentage in 20 years, and 365 electoral votes. Americans had seemingly given the Democrat his mandate for "change."

He would need it. Even before the celebration of Obama's history-making victory ended, the economic crisis deepened. In mid-November, the stock market lurched down again, dropping below the 8,000 mark. Despite the Emergency Economic Stabilization Act, financial institutions were still in peril and loans were still scarce. With the collapse of vehicle sales, the Big Three domestic automakers, so long the backbone of the American economy, headed toward bankruptcy. Unemployment rose and consumer spending fell. As the world economy slowed, oil prices did come down and inflation abated.

"Change We Can Believe In" Democratic nominee Barack Obama campaigns for the presidency in 2008.

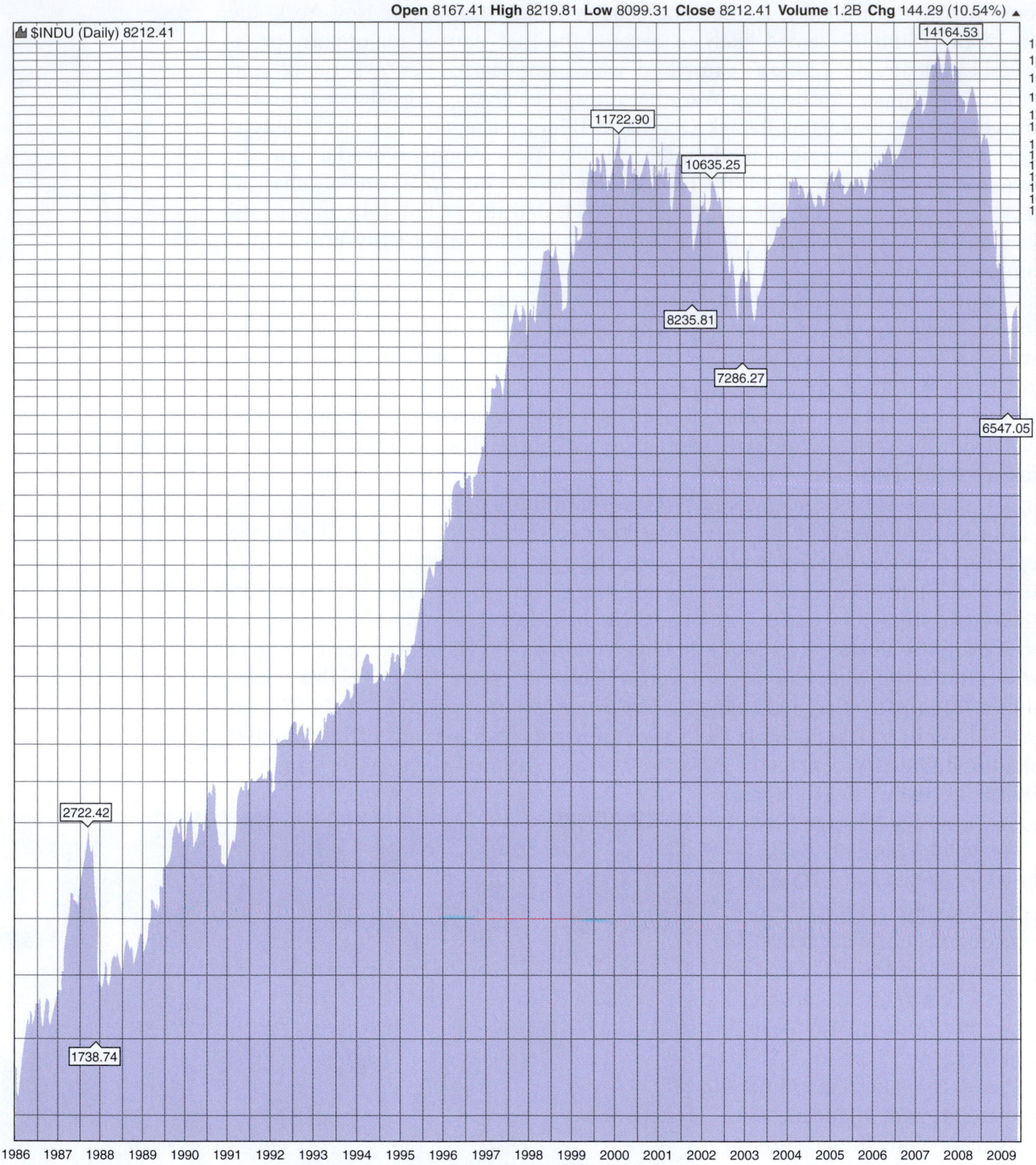

Open 8167.41 **High** 8219.81 **Low** 8099.31 **Close** 8212.41 **Volume** 1.2B **Chg** 144.29 (10.54%) ▲

$INDU (Daily) 8212.41

14164.53
11722.90
10635.25
8235.81
7286.27
6547.05
2722.42
1738.74

Figure 31–1 Dow Jones Industrial Average, 1986 to 2008 *Source: $INDU (Dow Jones Industrial Average) INDX, May 1, 2009. ©StockCharts.com.*

But now economists began to worry about the chances for deflation, the kind of long-term catastrophic decline in prices that intensified the Great Depression.

Conclusion

Whatever the outcome of the great crisis of 2008, the United States had reached the end of one era and the beginning of another. In the generation from the triumphal end of the cold war to the fearful collapse of the economic boom, the United States had effectively completed its long-term transformation into a globalized, information-based, racially diverse nation. The crisis seemed unlikely to change that basic reality. If anything, the demise or restructuring of old industrial giants such as General Motors would only reinforce the postindustrial identity of the United States.

Much else was already changing. The conservatism that had shaped American politics and government since the age of Ronald Reagan in the 1980s was in retreat. In the midst of the economic meltdown in the fall of 2008, the government and the people had spurned conservative ideology and accepted the kinds of dramatic government intervention reminiscent of the liberal New Deal of the 1930s and Great Society of the 1960s. The American people had turned as well to a president who called for change and embodied the social transformation of a globalized nation.

Much else about America's identity had become uncertain. Amid worldwide economic crisis, the nature of global ties could change. As the United States struggled with declining economic and military power and the war on terror, the nation's relationship to the world was at another crossroads. As Americans grappled with the prospect of economic recession or even depression, their attitude toward social and cultural diversity could change.

And so the American people prepared to move forward. "America, we have come so far. We have seen so much," Obama declared the night of his election. "But there's so much more to do."

Further Readings

Rajiv Chandresekaran, *Imperial Life in the Emerald City: Inside Iraq's Green Zone* (2006). A sensitive study of the U.S. occupation of Iraq in 2003–2004.

Steve Coll, *The Bin Ladens: An Arabian Family in the American Century* (2008). Engaging investigation of the origins of Al Qaeda's leader.

Stephanie Coontz, *The Way We Really Are: Coming to Terms with America's Changing Families* (1997). Details strains on family life.

Alfred A. Eckes Jr. and Thomas W. Zeiler, *Globalization and the American Century* (2003). Places the different aspects of globalization in long-term perspective.

National Commission on Terrorist Attacks Upon the United States, *The 9/11 Commission Report*, "Authorized Edition" (2004). This politically important document gains much of its power from its detailed, evenhanded unraveling of the events leading to the September 11 attack.

Kevin Phillips, *Wealth and Democracy: A Political History of the American Rich* (2002). A political scientist's passionate exploration of economic inequality and its political consequences.

Who, What?

Ted Turner 1036
George H. W. Bush ("Bush 41") 1044
Bill Clinton 1044
George W. Bush ("Bush 43") 1045
Saddam Hussein 1054
Osama bin Laden 1057
NGOs 1037
World Trade Organization 1038
Biotechnology 1040
Information economy 1040
Subprime mortgages 1045
"Family values" 1051
New World Order 1054
Bush Doctrine 1060

>> Timeline >>

▼ 1987
Intermediate-Range Nuclear Forces Treaty

▼ 1988
George H. W. Bush elected president

▼ 1989
Collapse of Communist regimes in Eastern Europe
Invasion of Panama

▼ 1990
Partial shutdown of federal government

▼ 1991
Persian Gulf War
Collapse of the Soviet Union
Dow Jones Industrial Average over 3,000 for first time

▼ 1992
Los Angeles riot after first Rodney King verdict
U.S. troops sent to Somalia
Bill Clinton elected president

▼ 1993
Terrorist truck bombing of World Trade Center, New York City
Ratification of North American Free Trade Agreement (NAFTA)

▼ 1994
End of "Risk Rule" for women soldiers

▼ 1995
Peace treaty in Bosnia-Herzegovina civil war
Opening of World Trade Organization

▼ 1996
Federal welfare reform
First Wal-Mart in People's Republic of China
Reelection of Bill Clinton as president

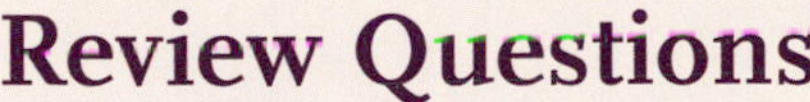

Review Questions

1. What set apart the globalization of the 1990s and 2000s from earlier linkages between the United States and the world?
2. What were the main features of the postindustrial political economy? Why were Americans anxious about the economy even though it was relatively strong?
3. Why did conservatives enjoy mixed political success in the 1990s and 2000s?
4. How did the foreign and security policies of the two presidents Bush differ? Which was more successful?
5. Did globalization, the information economy, and struggles for rights make it easier or harder for ordinary Americans to control their lives?

For further review materials and resource information, please visit www.oup.com/us/ofthepeople

▼ 1998

Terrorist truck bombings of U.S. embassies in Kenya and Tanzania

▼ 1999

Acquittal of Bill Clinton in Senate impeachment trial

NATO air war against Yugoslavia

Dow Jones Industrial Average over 10,000 for first time

▼ 2000

Terrorist attack on destroyer *Cole*

▼ 2001

George W. Bush declared president

9/11 attacks

Invasion of Afghanistan

▼ 2002

Creation of Department of Homeland Security

▼ 2003

U.S. Supreme Court gay rights ruling, *Lawrence v. Texas*

"Operation Iraqi Freedom," Coalition invasion of Iraq

▼ 2004

George W. Bush reelected

▼ 2007

U.S. military "surge" in Iraq

▼ 2008

Collapse of Doha world trade talks

U.S. financial crisis

Barack Obama elected president

Appendix A

Historical Documents

The Declaration of Independence

When in the course of human events, it becomes necessary for one people to dissolve the political bands which have connected them with another, and to assume, among the powers of the earth, the separate and equal station to which the Laws of Nature and of Nature's God entitle them, a decent respect to the opinions of mankind requires that they should declare the causes which impel them to the separation.

We hold these truths to be self-evident, that all men are created equal, that they are endowed by their Creator with certain unalienable Rights, that among these are life, liberty and the pursuit of happiness. That to secure these rights, governments are instituted among men, deriving their just powers from the consent of the governed; that whenever any form of government becomes destructive of these ends, it is the right of the people to alter or to abolish it, and to institute new Government, laying its foundation on such principles and organizing its powers in such form, as to them shall seem most likely to effect their safety and happiness. Prudence, indeed, will dictate that Governments long established should not be changed for light and transient causes; and, accordingly, all experience hath shown, that mankind are more disposed to suffer, while evils are sufferable, than to right themselves by abolishing the forms to which they are accustomed. But when a long train of abuses and usurpations, pursuing invariably the same object evinces a design to reduce them under absolute despotism, it is their right, it is their duty, to throw off such government, and to provide new guards for their future security. Such has been the patient sufferance of these colonies; and such is now the necessity which constrains them to alter their former systems of government. The history of the present King of Great Britain is a history of repeated injuries and usurpations, all having in direct object the establishment of an absolute tyranny over these States. To prove this, let facts be submitted to a candid world:

He has refused his assent to laws, the most wholesome and necessary for the public good.

He has forbidden his governors to pass laws of immediate and pressing importance, unless suspended in their operation till his assent should be obtained; and, when so suspended, he has utterly neglected to attend to them.

He has refused to pass other laws for the accommodation of large districts of people, unless those people would relinquish the right of representation in the legislature, a right inestimable to them and formidable to tyrants only.

He has called together legislative bodies at places unusual, uncomfortable, and distant from the depository of their public records, for the sole purpose of fatiguing them into compliance with his measures.

He has dissolved representative houses repeatedly, for opposing with manly firmness his invasions on the rights of the people.

He has refused for a long time, after such dissolutions, to cause others to be elected; whereby the legislative powers, incapable of annihilation, have returned to the People at large for their exercise; the State remaining in the mean time exposed to all the dangers of invasion from without, and convulsions within.

He has endeavored to prevent the population of these States; for that purpose obstructing the laws for naturalization of foreigners; refusing to pass others to encourage their migrations hither, and raising the conditions of new appropriations of lands.

He has obstructed the administration of justice, by refusing his assent to laws for establishing judiciary powers.

He has made judges dependent on his will alone, for the tenure of their offices, and the amount and payment of their salaries.

He has erected a multitude of new offices, and sent hither swarms of officers to harass our people, and eat out their substance.

He has kept among us, in times of peace, standing armies without the consent of our legislatures.

He has affected to render the Military independent of, and superior to, the civil power.

He has combined with others to subject us to a jurisdiction foreign to our constitution and unacknowledged by our laws; giving his assent to their acts of pretended legislation:

For quartering large bodies of armed troops among us;

For protecting them, by a mock trial, from punishment for any murders which they should commit on the inhabitants of these States;

For cutting off our trade with all parts of the world;

For imposing taxes on us without our Consent;

For depriving us, in many cases, of the benefits of Trial by Jury;

For transporting us beyond Seas to be tried for pretended offences;

For abolishing the free System of English Laws in a neighbouring Province, establishing therein an Arbitrary government, and enlarging its Boundaries so as to render it at once an example and fit instrument for introducing the same absolute rule into these colonies;

For taking away our charters, abolishing our most valuable laws, and altering fundamentally the forms of our governments;

For suspending our own legislatures, and declaring themselves invested with power to legislate for us in all cases whatsoever.

He has abdicated government here, by declaring us out of his protection and waging war against us.

He has plundered our seas, ravaged our coasts, burnt our towns, and destroyed the lives of our people.

He is at this time transporting large armies of foreign mercenaries to complete the works of death, desolation and tyranny, already begun with circumstances of cruelty and perfidy scarcely paralleled in the most barbarous ages, and totally unworthy the head of a civilized nation.

He has constrained our fellow citizens taken captive on the high seas to bear arms against their country, to become the executioners of their friends and brethren, or to fall themselves by their hands.

He has excited domestic insurrections amongst us, and has endeavored to bring on the inhabitants of our frontiers, the merciless Indian savages, whose known rule of warfare, is an undistinguished destruction of all ages, sexes and conditions.

In every stage of these oppressions we have petitioned for redress in the most humble terms; our repeated petitions have been answered only by repeated injury. A prince whose character is thus marked by every act which may define a tyrant, is unfit to be the ruler of a free people.

Nor have we been wanting in attentions to our British brethren. We have warned them from time to time of attempts by their legislature to extend an unwarrantable jurisdiction over us. We have reminded them of the circumstances of our emigration and settlement here. We have appealed to their native justice and magnanimity, and we have conjured them by the ties of our common kindred to disavow these usurpations, which, would inevitably interrupt our connections and correspondence. They, too, have been deaf to the voice of justice and of consanguinity. We must, therefore, acquiesce in the necessity, which denounces our separation, and hold them, as we hold the rest of mankind, enemies in war, in peace friends.

We, therefore, the representatives of the United States of America, in general Congress, assembled, appealing to the Supreme Judge of the world for the rectitude of our intentions, do, in the name, and by the authority of the good people of these colonies, solemnly publish and declare, that these united colonies are, and of right ought to be free and independent states; that they are absolved from all allegiance to the British Crown, and that all political connection between them and the state of Great Britain, is and ought to be totally dissolved; and that, as free and independent states, they have full power to levy war, conclude peace, contract alliances, establish commerce, and to do all other acts and things which independent states may of right do. And for the support of this declaration, with a firm reliance on the protection of Divine Providence, we mutually pledge to each other our lives, our fortunes and our sacred honor.

The Constitution of the United States of America

We the People of the United States, in Order to form a more perfect Union, establish Justice, insure domestic Tranquility, provide for the common defence, promote the general Welfare, and secure the Blessings of Liberty to ourselves and our Posterity, do ordain and establish this Constitution for the United States of America.

Article I

Section 1

All legislative Powers herein granted shall be vested in a Congress of the United States, which shall consist of a Senate and House of Representatives.

Section 2

The House of Representatives shall be composed of Members chosen every second Year by the People of the several States, and the Electors in each State shall have the Qualifications requisite for Electors of the most numerous Branch of the State Legislature.

No Person shall be a Representative who shall not have attained to the Age of twenty five Years, and been seven Years a Citizen of the United States, and who shall not, when elected, be an Inhabitant of that State in which he shall be chosen.

Representatives and direct Taxes shall be apportioned among the several States which may be included within this Union, according to their respective Numbers, which shall be determined by adding to the whole Number of free Persons, including those bound to Service for a Term of Years, and excluding Indians not taxed, three fifths of all other Persons. The actual Enumeration shall be made within three Years after the first Meeting of the Congress of the United States, and within every subsequent Term of ten Years, in such Manner as they shall by Law direct. The Number of Representatives shall not exceed one for every thirty Thousand, but each State shall have at Least one Representative; and until such enumeration shall be made, the State of New Hampshire shall be entitled to choose three, Massachusetts eight, Rhode-Island and Providence Plantations one, Connecticut five, New York six, New Jersey four, Pennsylvania eight, Delaware one, Maryland six, Virginia ten, North Carolina five, South Carolina five, and Georgia three.

When vacancies happen in the Representation from any State, the Executive Authority thereof shall issue Writs of Election to fill such Vacancies.

The House of Representatives shall choose their Speaker and other Officers; and shall have the sole Power of Impeachment.

Section 3

The Senate of the United States shall be composed of two Senators from each State, chosen by the Legislature thereof for six Years; and each Senator shall have one Vote.

Immediately after they shall be assembled in Consequence of the first Election, they shall be divided as equally as may be into three Classes. The Seats of the Senators of the first Class shall be vacated at the Expiration of the second Year, of the second Class at the Expiration of the fourth Year, and of the third Class at the Expiration of the sixth Year, so that one third may be chosen every second Year; and if Vacancies happen by Resignation, or otherwise, during the Recess of the Legislature of any State, the Executive thereof may make temporary Appointments until the next Meeting of the Legislature, which shall then fill such Vacancies.

No Person shall be a Senator who shall not have attained to the Age of thirty Years, and been nine Years a Citizen of the United States, and who shall not, when elected, be an Inhabitant of that State for which he shall be chosen.

The Vice President of the United States shall be President of the Senate, but shall have no Vote, unless they be equally divided.

The Senate shall choose their other Officers, and also a President pro tempore, in the Absence of the Vice President, or when he shall exercise the Office of President of the United States.

The Senate shall have the sole Power to try all Impeachments. When sitting for that Purpose, they shall be on Oath or Affirmation. When the President of the United States is tried, the Chief Justice shall preside: And no Person shall be convicted without the Concurrence of two thirds of the Members present.

Judgment in Cases of Impeachment shall not extend further than to removal from Office, and disqualification to hold and enjoy any Office of honor, Trust or Profit under the United States: but the Party convicted shall nevertheless be liable and subject to Indictment, Trial, Judgment and Punishment, according to Law.

Section 4

The Times, Places and Manner of holding Elections for Senators and Representatives, shall be prescribed in each State by the Legislature thereof; but the Congress may at any time by Law make or alter such Regulations, except as to the Places of chusing Senators.

The Congress shall assemble at least once in every Year, and such Meeting shall be on the first Monday in December, unless they shall by Law appoint a different Day.

Section 5

Each House shall be the Judge of the Elections, Returns and Qualifications of its own Members, and a Majority of each shall constitute a Quorum to do Business; but a smaller Number may adjourn from day to day, and may be authorized to compel the Attendance of absent Members, in such Manner, and under such Penalties as each House may provide.

Each House may determine the Rules of its Proceedings, punish its Members for disorderly Behaviour, and, with the Concurrence of two thirds, expel a Member.

Each House shall keep a Journal of its Proceedings, and from time to time publish the same, excepting such Parts as may in their Judgment require Secrecy; and the Yeas and Nays of the Members of either House on any question shall, at the Desire of one fifth of those Present, be entered on the Journal.

Neither House, during the Session of Congress, shall, without the Consent of the other, adjourn for more than three days, nor to any other Place than that in which the two Houses shall be sitting.

Section 6

The Senators and Representatives shall receive a Compensation for their Services, to be ascertained by Law, and paid out of the Treasury of the United States. They shall in all Cases, except Treason, Felony and Breach of the Peace, be privileged from Arrest during their Attendance at the Session of their respective Houses, and in going to and returning from the same; and for any Speech or Debate in either House, they shall not be questioned in any other Place.

No Senator or Representative shall, during the Time for which he was elected, be appointed to any civil Office under the Authority of the United States, which shall have been created, or the Emoluments whereof shall have been increased during such time; and no Person holding any Office under the United States, shall be a Member of either House during his Continuance in Office.

Section 7

All Bills for raising Revenue shall originate in the House of Representatives; but the Senate may propose or concur with Amendments as on other Bills.

Every Bill which shall have passed the House of Representatives and the Senate, shall, before it become a Law, be presented to the President of the United States: If he approve he shall sign it, but if not he shall return it, with his Objections to that House in which it shall have originated, who shall enter the Objections at large on their Journal, and proceed to reconsider it. If after such Reconsideration two thirds of that House shall agree to pass the Bill, it shall be sent, together with the Objections, to the other House, by which it shall likewise be reconsidered, and if approved by two thirds of that House, it shall become a Law. But in all such Cases the Votes of both Houses shall be determined by yeas and Nays, and the Names of the Persons voting for and against the Bill shall be entered on the Journal of each House respectively. If any Bill shall not be returned by the President within ten Days (Sundays excepted) after it shall have been presented to him, the Same shall be a Law, in like Manner as if he had signed it, unless the Congress by their Adjournment prevent its Return, in which Case it shall not be a Law.

Every Order, Resolution, or Vote to which the Concurrence of the Senate and House of Representatives may be necessary (except on a question of Adjournment) shall be presented to the President of the United States; and before the Same shall take Effect, shall be approved by him, or being disapproved by him, shall be repassed by two thirds of the Senate and House of Representatives, according to the Rules and Limitations prescribed in the Case of a Bill.

Section 8

The Congress shall have Power

To lay and collect Taxes, Duties, Imposts and Excises, to pay the Debts and provide for the common Defence and general Welfare of the United States; but all Duties, Imposts and Excises shall be uniform throughout the United States;

To borrow Money on the credit of the United States;

To regulate Commerce with foreign Nations, and among the several States, and with the Indian Tribes;

To establish an uniform Rule of Naturalization, and uniform Laws on the subject of Bankruptcies throughout the United States;

To coin Money, regulate the Value thereof, and of foreign Coin, and fix the Standard of Weights and Measures;

To provide for the Punishment of counterfeiting the Securities and current Coin of the United States;

To establish Post Offices and post Roads;

To promote the Progress of Science and useful Arts, by securing for limited Times to Authors and Inventors the exclusive Right to their respective Writings and Discoveries;

To constitute Tribunals inferior to the supreme Court;

To define and punish Piracies and Felonies committed on the high Seas, and Offences against the Law of Nations;

To declare War, grant Letters of Marque and Reprisal, and make Rules concerning Captures on Land and Water;

To raise and support Armies, but no Appropriation of Money to that Use shall be for a longer Term than two Years;

To provide and maintain a Navy;

To make Rules for the Government and Regulation of the land and naval Forces;

To provide for calling forth the Militia to execute the Laws of the Union, suppress Insurrections and repel Invasions;

To provide for organizing, arming, and disciplining the Militia, and for governing such Part of them as may be employed in the Service of the United States, reserving to the States respectively, the Appointment of the Officers, and the Authority of training the Militia according to the discipline prescribed by Congress;

To exercise exclusive Legislation in all Cases whatsoever, over such District (not exceeding ten Miles square) as may, by Cession of particular States, and the Acceptance of Congress, become the Seat of the Government of the United States, and to exercise like Authority over all Places purchased by the Consent of the Legislature of the State in which the Same shall be, for the Erection of Forts, Magazines, Arsenals, dock-Yards, and other needful Buildings;—And

To make all Laws which shall be necessary and proper for carrying into Execution the foregoing Powers, and all other Powers vested by this Constitution in the Government of the United States, or in any Department or Officer thereof.

Section 9

The Migration or Importation of such Persons as any of the States now existing shall think proper to admit, shall not be prohibited by the Congress prior to the Year one thousand eight hundred and eight, but a Tax or duty may be imposed on such Importation, not exceeding ten dollars for each Person.

The Privilege of the Writ of Habeas Corpus shall not be suspended, unless when in Cases of Rebellion or Invasion the public Safety may require it.

No Bill of Attainder or ex post facto Law shall be passed.

No Capitation, or other direct, Tax shall be laid, unless in Proportion to the Census or enumeration herein before directed to be taken.

No Tax or Duty shall be laid on Articles exported from any State.

No Preference shall be given by any Regulation of Commerce or Revenue to the Ports of one State over those of another; nor shall Vessels bound to, or from, one State, be obliged to enter, clear, or pay Duties in another.

No Money shall be drawn from the Treasury, but in Consequence of Appropriations made by Law; and a regular Statement and Account of the Receipts and Expenditures of all public Money shall be published from time to time.

No Title of Nobility shall be granted by the United States: And no Person holding any Office of Profit or Trust under them, shall, without the Consent of the Congress, accept of any present, Emolument, Office, or Title, of any kind whatever, from any King, Prince, or foreign State.

Section 10

No State shall enter into any Treaty, Alliance, or Confederation; grant Letters of Marque and Reprisal; coin Money; emit Bills of Credit; make any Thing but gold and silver Coin a Tender in Payment of Debts; pass any Bill of Attainder, ex post facto Law, or Law impairing the Obligation of Contracts, or grant any Title of Nobility.

No State shall, without the Consent of the Congress, lay any Imposts or Duties on Imports or Exports, except what may be absolutely necessary for executing it's inspection Laws: and the net Produce of all Duties and Imposts, laid by any State on Imports or Exports, shall be for the Use of the Treasury of the United States; and all such Laws shall be subject to the Revision and Control of the Congress.

No State shall, without the Consent of Congress, lay any Duty of Tonnage, keep Troops, or Ships of War in time of Peace, enter into any Agreement or Compact with another State, or with a foreign Power, or engage in War, unless actually invaded, or in such imminent Danger as will not admit of delay.

Article II

Section 1

The executive Power shall be vested in a President of the United States of America. He shall hold his Office during the Term of four Years, and, together with the Vice President, chosen for the same Term, be elected, as follows:

Each State shall appoint, in such Manner as the Legislature thereof may direct, a Number of Electors, equal to the whole Number of Senators and Representatives to which the State may be entitled in the Congress: but no Senator or Representative, or Person holding an Office of Trust or Profit under the United States, shall be appointed an Elector.

The Electors shall meet in their respective States, and vote by Ballot for two Persons, of whom one at least shall not be an Inhabitant of the same State with themselves. And they shall make a List of all the Persons voted for, and of the Number of Votes for each; which List they shall sign and certify, and transmit sealed to the Seat of the Government of the United States, directed to the President of the Senate. The President of the Senate shall, in the Presence of the Senate and House of Representatives, open all the Certificates, and the Votes shall then be counted. The Person having the greatest Number of Votes shall be the President, if such Number be a Majority of the whole Number of Electors appointed; and if there be more than one who have such Majority, and have an equal Number of Votes, then the House of Representatives shall immediately choose by Ballot one of them for President; and if no Person have a Majority, then from the five highest on the List the said House shall in like Manner choose the President. But in choosing the President, the Votes shall be taken by States, the Representation from each State having one Vote; A quorum for this purpose shall consist of a Member or Members from two thirds of the States, and a Majority of all the States shall be necessary to a Choice. In every Case, after the Choice of the President, the Person having the greatest Number of Votes of the Electors shall be the Vice President. But if there should remain two or more who have equal Votes, the Senate shall choose from them by Ballot the Vice President.

The Congress may determine the Time of choosing the Electors, and the Day on which they shall give their Votes; which Day shall be the same throughout the United States.

No Person except a natural born Citizen, or a Citizen of the United States, at the time of the Adoption of this Constitution, shall be eligible to the Office of President; neither shall any Person be eligible to that Office who shall not have attained to the Age of thirty five Years, and been fourteen Years a Resident within the United States.

In Case of the Removal of the President from Office, or of his Death, Resignation, or Inability to discharge the Powers and Duties of the said Office, the Same shall devolve on the Vice President, and the Congress may by Law provide for the Case of Removal, Death, Resignation or Inability, both of the President and Vice President, declaring what Officer shall then act as President, and such Officer shall act accordingly, until the Disability be removed, or a President shall be elected.

The President shall, at stated Times, receive for his Services, a Compensation, which shall neither be increased nor diminished during the Period for which he shall have been elected, and he shall not receive within that Period any other Emolument from the United States, or any of them.

Before he enter on the Execution of his Office, he shall take the following Oath or Affirmation:—"I do solemnly swear (or affirm) that I will faithfully execute the Office of President of the United States, and will to the best of my Ability, preserve, protect and defend the Constitution of the United States."

Section 2

The President shall be Commander in Chief of the Army and Navy of the United States, and of the Militia of the several States, when called into the actual Service of the United States; he may require the Opinion, in writing, of the principal Officer in each of the executive Departments, upon any Subject relating to the Duties of their respective Offices, and he shall have Power to grant Reprieves and Pardons for Offences against the United States, except in Cases of Impeachment.

He shall have Power, by and with the Advice and Consent of the Senate, to make Treaties, provided two thirds of the Senators present concur; and he shall nominate, and by and with the Advice and Consent of the Senate, shall appoint Ambassadors, other public Ministers and Consuls, Judges of the supreme Court, and all other Officers of the United States, whose Appointments are not herein otherwise provided for, and which shall be established by Law: but the Congress may by Law vest the Appointment of such inferior Officers, as they think proper, in the President alone, in the Courts of Law, or in the Heads of Departments.

The President shall have Power to fill up all Vacancies that may happen during the Recess of the Senate, by granting Commissions which shall expire at the End of their next Session.

Section 3

He shall from time to time give to the Congress Information of the State of the Union, and recommend to their Consideration such Measures as he shall judge necessary and expedient; he may, on extraordinary Occasions, convene both Houses, or either of them, and in Case of Disagreement between them, with Respect to the Time of Adjournment, he may adjourn them to such Time as he shall think proper; he shall receive Ambassadors and other public Ministers; he shall take Care that the Laws be faithfully executed, and shall Commission all the Officers of the United States.

Section 4

The President, Vice President and all civil Officers of the United States, shall be removed from Office on Impeachment for, and Conviction of, Treason, Bribery, or other high Crimes and Misdemeanors.

Article III

Section 1

The judicial Power of the United States shall be vested in one supreme Court, and in such inferior Courts as the Congress may from time to time ordain and establish. The Judges, both of the supreme and inferior Courts, shall hold their Offices during good Behaviour, and shall, at stated Times, receive for their Services a Compensation, which shall not be diminished during their Continuance in Office.

Section 2

The judicial Power shall extend to all Cases, in Law and Equity, arising under this Constitution, the Laws of the United States, and Treaties made, or which shall be made, under their Authority;—to all Cases affecting Ambassadors, other public Ministers and Consuls;—to all Cases of admiralty and maritime Jurisdiction;—to Controversies to which the United States shall be a Party;—to Controversies between two or more States;—between a State and Citizens of another State;—between Citizens of different States;—between Citizens of the same State claiming Lands under Grants of different States, and between a State, or the Citizens thereof, and foreign States, Citizens or Subjects.

In all Cases affecting Ambassadors, other public Ministers and Consuls, and those in which a State shall be Party, the supreme Court shall have original Jurisdiction. In all the other Cases before mentioned, the supreme Court shall have appellate Jurisdiction, both as to Law and Fact, with such Exceptions, and under such Regulations as the Congress shall make.

The Trial of all Crimes, except in Cases of Impeachment, shall be by Jury; and such Trial shall be held in the State where the said Crimes shall have been committed; but when not committed within any State, the Trial shall be at such Place or Places as the Congress may by Law have directed.

Section 3

Treason against the United States, shall consist only in levying War against them, or in adhering to their Enemies, giving them Aid and Comfort. No Person shall be convicted of Treason unless on the Testimony of two Witnesses to the same overt Act, or on Confession in open Court.

The Congress shall have Power to declare the Punishment of Treason, but no Attainder of Treason shall work Corruption of Blood, or Forfeiture except during the Life of the Person attainted.

Article IV

Section 1

Full Faith and Credit shall be given in each State to the public Acts, Records, and judicial Proceedings of every other State. And the Congress may by general Laws prescribe the Manner in which such Acts, Records and Proceedings shall be proved, and the Effect thereof.

Section 2

The Citizens of each State shall be entitled to all Privileges and Immunities of Citizens in the several States.

A Person charged in any State with Treason, Felony, or other Crime, who shall flee from Justice, and be found in another State, shall on Demand of the executive Authority of the State from which he fled, be delivered up, to be removed to the State having Jurisdiction of the Crime.

No Person held to Service or Labour in one State, under the Laws thereof, escaping into another, shall, in Consequence of any Law or Regulation therein, be discharged from such Service or Labour, but shall be delivered up on Claim of the Party to whom such Service or Labour may be due.

Section 3

New States may be admitted by the Congress into this Union; but no new State shall be formed or erected within the Jurisdiction of any other State; nor any State be formed by the Junction of two or more States, or Parts of States, without the Consent of the Legislatures of the States concerned as well as of the Congress.

The Congress shall have Power to dispose of and make all needful Rules and Regulations respecting the Territory or other Property belonging to the United States; and nothing in this Constitution shall be so construed as to Prejudice any Claims of the United States, or of any particular State.

Section 4

The United States shall guarantee to every State in this Union a Republican Form of Government, and shall protect each of them against Invasion; and on Application of the Legislature, or of the Executive (when the Legislature cannot be convened), against domestic Violence.

Article V

The Congress, whenever two thirds of both Houses shall deem it necessary, shall propose Amendments to this Constitution, or, on the Application of the Legislatures of two thirds of the several States, shall call a Convention for proposing Amendments, which, in either Case, shall be valid to all Intents and Purposes, as Part of this Constitution, when ratified by the Legislatures of three fourths of the several States, or by Conventions in three fourths thereof, as the one or the other Mode of Ratification may be proposed by the Congress; Provided that no Amendment which may be made prior to the Year One thousand eight hundred and eight shall in any Manner affect the first and fourth Clauses in the Ninth Section of the first Article; and that no State, without its Consent, shall be deprived of its equal Suffrage in the Senate.

Article VI

All Debts contracted and Engagements entered into, before the Adoption of this Constitution, shall be as valid against the United States under this Constitution, as under the Confederation.

This Constitution, and the Laws of the United States which shall be made in Pursuance thereof; and all Treaties made, or which shall be made, under the Authority of the United States, shall be the supreme Law of the Land; and the Judges in every State shall be bound thereby, any Thing in the Constitution or Laws of any State to the Contrary notwithstanding.

The Senators and Representatives before mentioned, and the Members of the several State Legislatures, and all executive and judicial Officers, both of the United States and of the several States, shall be bound by Oath or Affirmation, to support this Constitution; but no religious Test shall ever be required as a Qualification to any Office or public Trust under the United States.

Article VII

The Ratification of the Conventions of nine States, shall be sufficient for the Establishment of this Constitution between the States so ratifying the Same.

The Word, "the," being interlined between the seventh and eighth Lines of the first Page, the Word "Thirty" being partly written on an Erazure in the fifteenth Line of the first Page, The Words "is tried" being interlined between the thirty second and thirty third Lines of the first Page and the Word "the" being interlined between the forty third and forty fourth Lines of the second Page.

Attest William Jackson Secretary

Done in Convention by the Unanimous Consent of the States present the Seventeenth Day of September in the Year of our Lord one thousand seven hundred and Eighty seven and of the Independence of the United States of America the Twelfth In witness whereof We have hereunto subscribed our Names,

G°. Washington
Presidt and deputy from Virginia

Delaware
Geo: Read
Gunning Bedford jun
John Dickinson
Richard Bassett
Jaco: Broom

Maryland
James McHenry
Dan of St Thos. Jenifer
Danl. Carroll

Virginia
John Blair
James Madison Jr.

North Carolina
Wm. Blount
Richd. Dobbs Spaight
Hu Williamson

South Carolina
J. Rutledge
Charles Cotesworth Pinckney
Charles Pinckney
Pierce Butler

Georgia
William Few
Abr Baldwin

New Hampshire
John Langdon
Nicholas Gilman

Massachusetts
Nathaniel Gorham
Rufus King

Connecticut
Wm. Saml. Johnson
Roger Sherman

New York
Alexander Hamilton

New Jersey
Wil: Livingston
David Brearley
Wm. Paterson
Jona: Dayton

Pennsylvania
B Franklin
Thomas Mifflin
Robt. Morris
Geo. Clymer
Thos. FitzSimons
Jared Ingersoll
James Wilson
Gouv Morris

Articles

In addition to, and Amendment of the Constitution of the United States of America, proposed by Congress, and ratified by the Legislatures of the several States, pursuant to the fifth Article of the original Constitution.

(The first ten amendments to the U.S. Constitution were ratified December 15, 1791, and form what is known as the "Bill of Rights.")

AMENDMENT I

Congress shall make no law respecting an establishment of religion, or prohibiting the free exercise thereof; or abridging the freedom of speech, or of the press; or the right of the people peaceably to assemble, and to petition the Government for a redress of grievances.

AMENDMENT II

A well regulated Militia, being necessary to the security of a free State, the right of the people to keep and bear Arms, shall not be infringed.

AMENDMENT III

No Soldier shall, in time of peace be quartered in any house, without the consent of the Owner, nor in time of war, but in a manner to be prescribed by law.

AMENDMENT IV

The right of the people to be secure in their persons, houses, papers, and effects, against unreasonable searches and seizures, shall not be violated, and no Warrants shall issue, but upon probable cause, supported by Oath or affirmation, and particularly describing the place to be searched, and the persons or things to be seized.

AMENDMENT V

No person shall be held to answer for a capital, or otherwise infamous crime, unless on a presentment or indictment of a Grand Jury, except in cases arising in the land or naval forces, or in the Militia, when in actual service in time of War or public danger; nor shall any person be subject for the same offence to be twice put in jeopardy of life or limb; nor shall be compelled in any criminal case to be a witness against himself, nor be deprived of life, liberty, or property, without due process of law; nor shall private property be taken for public use, without just compensation.

AMENDMENT VI

In all criminal prosecutions, the accused shall enjoy the right to a speedy and public trial, by an impartial jury of the State and district wherein the crime shall have been committed, which district shall have been previously ascertained by law, and to be informed of the nature and cause of the accusation; to be confronted with the witnesses against him; to have compulsory process for obtaining witnesses in his favor, and to have the Assistance of Counsel for his defence.

AMENDMENT VII

In Suits at common law, where the value in controversy shall exceed twenty dollars, the right of trial by jury shall be preserved, and no fact tried by a jury, shall be otherwise re-examined in any Court of the United States, than according to the rules of the common law.

AMENDMENT VIII

Excessive bail shall not be required, nor excessive fines imposed, nor cruel and unusual punishments inflicted.

AMENDMENT IX

The enumeration in the Constitution, of certain rights, shall not be construed to deny or disparage others retained by the people.

AMENDMENT X

The powers not delegated to the United States by the Constitution, nor prohibited by it to the States, are reserved to the States respectively, or to the people.

AMENDMENT XI

Passed by Congress March 4, 1794. Ratified February 7, 1795.

Note: Article III, Section 2, of the Constitution was modified by Amendment XI.

The Judicial power of the United States shall not be construed to extend to any suit in law or equity, commenced or prosecuted against one of the United States by Citizens of another State, or by Citizens or Subjects of any Foreign State.

AMENDMENT XII

Passed by Congress December 9, 1803. Ratified June 15, 1804.

Note: A portion of Article II, Section 1, of the Constitution was superceded by the Twelfth Amendment.

The Electors shall meet in their respective states and vote by ballot for President and Vice-President, one of whom, at least, shall not be an inhabitant of the same state with themselves; they shall name in their ballots the person voted for as President, and in distinct ballots the person voted for as Vice-President, and they shall make distinct lists of all persons voted for as President, and of all persons voted for as Vice-President, and of the number of votes for each, which lists they shall sign and certify, and transmit sealed to the seat of the government of the United States, directed to the President of the Senate;—the President of the Senate shall, in the presence of the Senate and House of Representatives, open all the certificates and the votes shall then be counted;—The person having the greatest number of votes for President, shall be the President, if such number be a majority of the whole number of Electors appointed; and if no person have such majority, then from the persons having the highest numbers not exceeding three on the list of those voted for as President, the House of Representatives shall choose immediately, by ballot, the President. But in choosing the President, the votes shall be taken by states, the representation from each state having one vote; a quorum for this purpose shall consist of a member or members from two-thirds of the states, and a majority of all the states shall be necessary to a choice. [And if the House of Representatives shall not choose a President whenever the right of choice shall devolve upon them, before the fourth day of March next following, then the Vice-President shall act as President, as in case of the death or other constitutional disability of the President.—]* The person having the greatest number of votes as Vice-President, shall be the Vice-President, if such number be a majority of the whole number of Electors appointed, and if no person have a majority, then from the two highest numbers on the list, the Senate shall choose the Vice-President; a quorum for the purpose shall consist of two-thirds of the whole number of Senators, and a majority of the whole number shall be necessary to a choice. But no person constitutionally ineligible to the office of President shall be eligible to that of Vice-President of the United States.

*Superceded by Section 3 of the Twentieth Amendment.

AMENDMENT XIII

Passed by Congress January 31, 1865. Ratified December 6, 1865.

Note: A portion of Article IV, Section 2, of the Constitution was superceded by the Thirteenth Amendment.

Section 1.

Neither slavery nor involuntary servitude, except as a punishment for crime whereof the party shall have been duly convicted, shall exist within the United States, or any place subject to their jurisdiction.

Section 2.

Congress shall have power to enforce this article by appropriate legislation.

AMENDMENT XIV
Passed by Congress June 13, 1866. Ratified July 9, 1868.

Note: Article I, Section 2, of the Constitution was modified by Section 2 of the Fourteenth Amendment.

Section 1

All persons born or naturalized in the United States, and subject to the jurisdiction thereof, are citizens of the United States and of the State wherein they reside. No State shall make or enforce any law which shall abridge the privileges or immunities of citizens of the United States; nor shall any State deprive any person of life, liberty, or property, without due process of law; nor deny to any person within its jurisdiction the equal protection of the laws.

Section 2

Representatives shall be apportioned among the several States according to their respective numbers, counting the whole number of persons in each State, excluding Indians not taxed. But when the right to vote at any election for the choice of electors for President and Vice-President of the United States, Representatives in Congress, the Executive and Judicial officers of a State, or the members of the Legislature thereof, is denied to any of the male inhabitants of such State, being twenty-one years of age,* and citizens of the United States, or in any way abridged, except for participation in rebellion, or other crime, the basis of representation therein shall be reduced in the proportion which the number of such male citizens shall bear to the whole number of male citizens twenty-one years of age in such State.

Section 3

No person shall be a Senator or Representative in Congress, or elector of President and Vice-President, or hold any office, civil or military, under the United States, or under any State, who, having previously taken an oath, as a member of Congress, or as an officer of the United States, or as a member of any State legislature, or as an executive or judicial officer of any State, to support the Constitution of the United States, shall have engaged in insurrection or rebellion against the same, or given aid or comfort to the enemies thereof. But Congress may by a vote of two-thirds of each House, remove such disability.

Section 4

The validity of the public debt of the United States, authorized by law, including debts incurred for payment of pensions and bounties for services in suppressing insurrection or rebellion, shall not be questioned. But neither the United States nor any State shall assume or pay any debt or obligation incurred in aid of insurrection or rebellion against the United States, or any claim for the loss or emancipation of any slave; but all such debts, obligations and claims shall be held illegal and void.

Section 5

The Congress shall have the power to enforce, by appropriate legislation, the provisions of this article.

*Changed by Section 1 of the Twenty-sixth Amendment.

AMENDMENT XV

Passed by Congress February 26, 1869. Ratified February 3, 1870.

Section 1.

The right of citizens of the United States to vote shall not be denied or abridged by the United States or by any State on account of race, color, or previous condition of servitude.

Section 2

The Congress shall have the power to enforce this article by appropriate legislation.

AMENDMENT XVI

Passed by Congress July 2, 1909. Ratified February 3, 1913.

Note: Article I, Section 9, of the Constitution was modified by Amendment XVI.

The Congress shall have power to lay and collect taxes on incomes, from whatever source derived, without apportionment among the several States, and without regard to any census or enumeration.

AMENDMENT XVII

Passed by Congress May 13, 1912. Ratified April 8, 1913.

Note: Article I, Section 3, of the Constitution was modified by the Seventeenth Amendment.

The Senate of the United States shall be composed of two Senators from each State, elected by the people thereof, for six years; and each Senator shall have one vote. The electors in each State shall have the qualifications requisite for electors of the most numerous branch of the State legislatures.

When vacancies happen in the representation of any State in the Senate, the executive authority of such State shall issue writs of election to fill such vacancies: *Provided,* That the legislature of any State may empower the executive thereof to make temporary appointments until the people fill the vacancies by election as the legislature may direct.

This amendment shall not be so construed as to affect the election or term of any Senator chosen before it becomes valid as part of the Constitution.

AMENDMENT XVIII

Passed by Congress December 18, 1917. Ratified January 16, 1919. Repealed by Amendment XXI.

Section 1

After one year from the ratification of this article the manufacture, sale, or transportation of intoxicating liquors within, the importation thereof into, or the exportation thereof from the United States and all territory subject to the jurisdiction thereof for beverage purposes is hereby prohibited.

Section 2

The Congress and the several States shall have concurrent power to enforce this article by appropriate legislation.

Section 3

This article shall be inoperative unless it shall have been ratified as an amendment to the Constitution by the legislatures of the several States, as provided in the Constitution, within seven years from the date of the submission hereof to the States by the Congress.

AMENDMENT XIX

Passed by Congress June 4, 1919. Ratified August 18, 1920.

The right of citizens of the United States to vote shall not be denied or abridged by the United States or by any State on account of sex.

Congress shall have power to enforce this article by appropriate legislation.

AMENDMENT XX

Passed by Congress March 2, 1932. Ratified January 23, 1933.

Note: Article I, Section 4, of the Constitution was modified by Section 2 of this amendment. In addition, a portion of the Twelfth Amendment was superceded by Section 3.

Section 1

The terms of the President and the Vice President shall end at noon on the 20th day of January, and the terms of Senators and Representatives at noon on the 3d day of January, of the years in which such terms would have ended if this article had not been ratified; and the terms of their successors shall then begin.

Section 2

The Congress shall assemble at least once in every year, and such meeting shall begin at noon on the 3d day of January, unless they shall by law appoint a different day.

Section 3

If, at the time fixed for the beginning of the term of the President, the President elect shall have died, the Vice President elect shall become President. If a President shall not have been chosen before the time fixed for the beginning of his term, or if the President elect shall have failed to qualify, then the Vice President elect shall act as President until a President shall have qualified; and the Congress may by law provide for the case wherein neither a President elect nor a Vice President shall have qualified, declaring who shall then act as President, or the manner in which one who is to act shall be selected, and such person shall act accordingly until a President or Vice President shall have qualified.

Section 4

The Congress may by law provide for the case of the death of any of the persons from whom the House of Representatives may choose a President whenever the right of choice shall have devolved upon them, and for the case of the death of any of the persons from whom the Senate may choose a Vice President whenever the right of choice shall have devolved upon them.

Section 5

Sections 1 and 2 shall take effect on the 15th day of October following the ratification of this article.

Section 6

This article shall be inoperative unless it shall have been ratified as an amendment to the Constitution by the legislatures of three-fourths of the several States within seven years from the date of its submission.

AMENDMENT XXI

Passed by Congress February 20, 1933. Ratified December 5, 1933.

Section 1

The eighteenth article of amendment to the Constitution of the United States is hereby repealed.

Section 2

The transportation or importation into any State, Territory, or Possession of the United States for delivery or use therein of intoxicating liquors, in violation of the laws thereof, is hereby prohibited.

Section 3

This article shall be inoperative unless it shall have been ratified as an amendment to the Constitution by conventions in the several States, as provided in the Constitution, within seven years from the date of the submission hereof to the States by the Congress.

AMENDMENT XXII

Passed by Congress March 21, 1947. Ratified February 27, 1951.

Section 1

No person shall be elected to the office of the President more than twice, and no person who has held the office of President, or acted as President, for more than two years of a term to which some other person was elected President shall be elected to the office of President more than once. But this Article shall not apply to any person holding the office of President when this Article was proposed by Congress, and shall not prevent any person who may be holding the office of President, or acting as President, during the term within which this Article becomes operative from holding the office of President or acting as President during the remainder of such term.

Section 2

This article shall be inoperative unless it shall have been ratified as an amendment to the Constitution by the legislatures of three-fourths of the several States within seven years from the date of its submission to the States by the Congress.

AMENDMENT XXIII

Passed by Congress June 16, 1960. Ratified March 29, 1961.

Section 1

The District constituting the seat of Government of the United States shall appoint in such manner as Congress may direct:

A number of electors of President and Vice President equal to the whole number of Senators and Representatives in Congress to which the District would be entitled if it were a State, but in no event more than the least populous State; they shall be in addition to those appointed by the States, but they shall be considered, for the purposes of the election of President and Vice President, to be electors appointed by a State; and they shall meet in the District and perform such duties as provided by the twelfth article of amendment.

Section 2

The Congress shall have power to enforce this article by appropriate legislation.

AMENDMENT XXIV

Passed by Congress August 27, 1962. Ratified January 23, 1964.

Section 1

The right of citizens of the United States to vote in any primary or other election for President or Vice President, for electors for President or Vice President, or for Senator or Representative in Congress, shall not be denied or abridged by the United States or any State by reason of failure to pay poll tax or other tax.

Section 2

The Congress shall have power to enforce this article by appropriate legislation.

AMENDMENT XXV

Passed by Congress July 6, 1965. Ratified February 10, 1967.

Note: Article II, Section 1, of the Constitution was affected by the Twenty-fifth Amendment.

Section 1

In case of the removal of the President from office or of his death or resignation, the Vice President shall become President.

Section 2

Whenever there is a vacancy in the office of the Vice President, the President shall nominate a Vice President who shall take office upon confirmation by a majority vote of both Houses of Congress.

Section 3

Whenever the President transmits to the President pro tempore of the Senate and the Speaker of the House of Representatives his written declaration that he is unable to discharge the powers and duties of his office, and until he transmits to them a written declaration to the contrary, such powers and duties shall be discharged by the Vice President as Acting President.

Section 4

Whenever the Vice President and a majority of either the principal officers of the executive departments or of such other body as Congress may by law provide, transmit to the President pro tempore of the Senate and the Speaker of the House of Representatives their written declaration that the President is unable to discharge the powers and duties of his office, the Vice President shall immediately assume the powers and duties of the office as Acting President.

Thereafter, when the President transmits to the President pro tempore of the Senate and the Speaker of the House of Representatives his written declaration that no inability exists, he shall resume the powers and duties of his office unless the Vice President and a majority of either the principal officers of the executive department or of such other body as Congress may by law provide, transmit within four days to the President pro tempore of the Senate and the Speaker of the House of Representatives their written declaration that the President is unable to discharge the powers and duties of his office. Thereupon Congress shall decide the issue, assembling within forty-eight hours for that purpose if not in session. If the Congress, within twenty-one days after receipt of the latter written declaration, or, if Congress is not in session, within twenty-one days after Congress is required to assemble, determines by two-thirds vote of both Houses that the President is unable to discharge the powers and duties of his office, the Vice President shall continue to discharge the same as Acting President; otherwise, the President shall resume the powers and duties of his office.

AMENDMENT XXVI

Passed by Congress March 23, 1971. Ratified July 1, 1971.

Note: Amendment XIV, Section 2, of the Constitution was modified by Section 1 of the Twenty-sixth Amendment.

Section 1

The right of citizens of the United States, who are eighteen years of age or older, to vote shall not be denied or abridged by the United States or by any State on account of age.

Section 2

The Congress shall have power to enforce this article by appropriate legislation.

AMENDMENT XXVII

Originally proposed Sept. 25, 1789. Ratified May 7, 1992.

No law, varying the compensation for the services of the Senators and Representatives, shall take effect, until an election of representatives shall have intervened.

Lincoln's Gettysburg Address

Four score and seven years ago our fathers brought forth on this continent, a new nation, conceived in Liberty, and dedicated to the proposition that all men are created equal.

Now we are engaged in a great civil war, testing whether that nation, or any nation so conceived and so dedicated, can long endure. We are met on a great battle-field of that war. We have come to dedicate a portion of that field, as a final resting place for those who here gave their lives that that nation might live. It is altogether fitting and proper that we should do this.

But, in a larger sense, we can not dedicate—we can not consecrate—we can not hallow—this ground. The brave men, living and dead, who struggled here, have consecrated it, far above our poor power to add or detract. The world will little note, nor long remember what we say here, but it can never forget what they did here. It is for us the living, rather, to be dedicated here to the unfinished work which they who fought here have thus far so nobly advanced. It is rather for us to be here dedicated to the great task remaining before us—that from these honored dead we take increased devotion to that cause for which they gave the last full measure of devotion—that we here highly resolve that these dead shall not have died in vain—that this nation, under God, shall have a new birth of freedom—and that government of the people, by the people, for the people, shall not perish from the earth.

Appendix B

Historical Facts and Data

U.S. Presidents and Vice Presidents

Table App B–1 Presidents and Vice Presidents

	President	Vice President	Political Party	Term
1	George Washington	John Adams	No Party Designation	1789–1797
2	John Adams	Thomas Jefferson	Federalist	1797–1801
3	Thomas Jefferson	Aaron Burr George Clinton	Democratic Republican	1801–1809
4	James Madison	George Clinton Elbridge Gerry	Democratic Republican	1809–1817
5	James Monroe	Daniel D. Tompkins	Democratic Republican	1817–1825
6	John Quincy Adams	John C. Calhoun	Democratic Republican	1825–1829
7	Andrew Jackson	John C. Calhoun Martin Van Buren	Democratic	1829–1837
8	Martin Van Buren	Richard M. Johnson	Democratic	1837–1841
9	William Henry Harrison	John Tyler	Whig	1841
10	John Tyler	None	Whig	1841–1845
11	James Knox Polk	George M. Dallas	Democratic	1845–1849
12	Zachary Taylor	Millard Fillmore	Whig	1849–1850
13	Millard Fillmore	None	Whig	1850–1853
14	Franklin Pierce	William R. King	Democratic	1853–1857
15	James Buchanan	John C. Breckinridge	Democratic	1857–1861
16	Abraham Lincoln	Hannibal Hamlin Andrew Johnson	Union	1861–1865
17	Andrew Johnson	None	Union	1865–1869
18	Ulysses Simpson Grant	Schuyler Colfax Henry Wilson	Republican	1869–1877
19	Rutherford Birchard Hayes	William A. Wheeler	Republican	1877–1881
20	James Abram Garfield	Chester Alan Arthur	Republican	1881
21	Chester Alan Arthur	None	Republican	1881–1885
22	Stephen Grover Cleveland	Thomas Hendricks	Democratic	1885–1889
23	Benjamin Harrison	Levi P. Morton	Republican	1889–1893
24	Stephen Grover Cleveland	Adlai E. Stevenson	Democratic	1893–1897
25	William McKinley	Garret A. Hobart Theodore Roosevelt	Republican	1897–1901
26	Theodore Roosevelt	Charles W. Fairbanks	Republican	1901–1909
27	William Howard Taft	James S. Sherman	Republican	1909–1913
28	Woodrow Wilson	Thomas R. Marshall	Democratic	1913–1921

continued

 **Table App B–1** Presidents and Vice Presidents (cont.)

	President	Vice President	Political Party	Term
29	Warren Gamaliel Harding	Calvin Coolidge	Republican	1921–1923
30	Calvin Coolidge	Charles G. Dawes	Republican	1923–1929
31	Herbert Clark Hoover	Charles Curtis	Republican	1929–1933
32	Franklin Delano Roosevelt	John Nance Garner Henry A. Wallace Harry S. Truman	Democratic	1933–1945
33	Harry S. Truman	Alben W. Barkley	Democratic	1945–1953
34	Dwight David Eisenhower	Richard Milhous Nixon	Republican	1953–1961
35	John Fitzgerald Kennedy	Lyndon Baines Johnson	Democratic	1961–1963
36	Lyndon Baines Johnson	Hubert Horatio Humphrey	Democratic	1963–1969
37	Richard Milhous Nixon	Spiro T. Agnew Gerald Rudolph Ford	Republican	1969–1974
38	Gerald Rudolph Ford	Nelson Rockefeller	Republican	1974–1977
39	James Earl Carter Jr.	Walter Mondale	Democratic	1977–1981
40	Ronald Wilson Reagan	George Herbert Walker Bush	Republican	1981–1989
41	George Herbert Walker Bush	J. Danforth Quayle	Republican	1989–1993
42	William Jefferson Clinton	Albert Gore Jr.	Democratic	1993–2001
43	George Walker Bush	Richard Cheney	Republican	2001–2008
44	Barack Hussein Obama	Joseph Biden	Democratic	2008–

Admission of States into the Union

Table App B–2 Admission of States into the Union

	State	Date of Admission		State	Date of Admission
1	Delaware	December 7, 1787	26	Michigan	January 26, 1837
2	Pennsylvania	December 12, 1787	27	Florida	March 3, 1845
3	New Jersey	December 18, 1787	28	Texas	December 29, 1845
4	Georgia	January 2, 1788	29	Iowa	December 28, 1846
5	Connecticut	January 9, 1788	30	Wisconsin	May 29, 1848
6	Massachusetts	February 6, 1788	31	California	September 9, 1850
7	Maryland	April 28, 1788	32	Minnesota	May 11, 1858
8	South Carolina	May 23, 1788	33	Oregon	February 14, 1859
9	New Hampshire	June 21, 1788	34	Kansas	January 29, 1861
10	Virginia	June 25, 1788	35	West Virginia	June 20, 1863
11	New York	July 26, 1788	36	Nevada	October 31, 1864
12	North Carolina	November 21, 1789	37	Nebraska	March 1, 1867
13	Rhode Island	May 29, 1790	38	Colorado	August 1, 1876
14	Vermont	March 4, 1791	39	North Dakota	November 2, 1889
15	Kentucky	June 1, 1792	40	South Dakota	November 2, 1889
16	Tennessee	June 1, 1796	41	Montana	November 8, 1889
17	Ohio	March 1, 1803	42	Washington	November 11, 1889
18	Louisiana	April 30, 1812	43	Idaho	July 3, 1890
19	Indiana	December 11, 1816	44	Wyoming	July 10, 1890
20	Mississippi	December 10, 1817	45	Utah	January 4, 1896
21	Illinois	December 3, 1818	46	Oklahoma	November 16, 1907
22	Alabama	December 14, 1819	47	New Mexico	January 6, 1912
23	Maine	March 15, 1820	48	Arizona	February 14, 1912
24	Missouri	August 10, 1821	49	Alaska	January 3, 1959
25	Arkansas	June 15, 1836	50	Hawaii	August 21, 1959

Glossary

Antinomianism The belief that moral law was not binding on true Christians. The opposite of Arminianism, antinomianism held that good works would not count in the afterlife. Justification, or entrance to heaven, was by faith alone. See Calvinism.

Arminianism Religious doctrine developed by the Dutch theologian Jacobus Arminius that argued that men and women had free will and suggested that hence they would earn their way into heaven by good works.

Armistice A cessation of hostilities by agreement among the opposing sides; a cease-fire.

Associationalism President Herbert Hoover's preferred method of responding to the Depression. Rather than have the government directly involve itself in the economy, Hoover hoped to use the government to encourage associations of businessmen to cooperate voluntarily to meet the crisis.

Autarky At the height of the world depression, industrial powers sought to isolate their economies within self-contained spheres, generally governed by national (or imperial) economic planning. Japan's Co-Prosperity Sphere, the Soviet Union, and the British Empire each comprised a more or less closed economic unit.

Benevolent Empire The loosely affiliated network of charitable reform associations that emerged (especially in urban areas) in response to the widespread revivalism of the early nineteenth century.

Berdache In Indian societies, a man who dressed and adopted the mannerisms of women and had sex only with other men. In Native American culture, the *berdache,* half man and half woman, symbolized cosmic harmony.

Budget deficit The failure of tax revenues to pay for annual federal spending on military, welfare, and other programs. The resulting budget deficits forced Washington to borrow money to cover its costs. The growing budget deficits were controversial, in part because the government's borrowing increased both its long-term debt and the amount of money it had to spend each year to pay for the interest on loans.

Busing The controversial court-ordered practice of sending children by bus to public schools outside their neighborhoods in order to promote racial integration in the schools.

Calvinism Religious doctrine developed by the theologian John Calvin that argued that God alone determines who will receive salvation and, hence, men and women cannot earn their own salvation or even be certain about their final destinies.

Carpetbagger A derogatory term referring to northern whites who moved to the South after the Civil War. Stereotyped as corrupt and unprincipled, "carpetbaggers" were in fact a diverse group motivated by a variety of interests and beliefs.

Charter colony Settlement established by a trading company or other group of private entrepreneurs who received from the king a grant of land and the right to govern it. The charter colonies included Virginia, Plymouth, Massachusetts Bay, Rhode Island, and Connecticut.

City busting As late as the 1930s, President Roosevelt and most Americans regarded attacking civilians from the air as an atrocity, but during World War II cities became a primary target for U.S. warplanes. The inaccuracy of bombing, combined with racism and the belief that Japanese and German actions justified retaliation, led American air commanders to follow a policy of systematically destroying urban areas, particularly in Japan.

Communist Member of the Communist Party or follower of the doctrines of Karl Marx. The term (or accusation) was applied more broadly in the twentieth century to brand labor unionists, progressives, civil rights workers, and other reformers as agents of a foreign ideology.

Communitarians Individuals who supported and/or took up residence in separate communities created to embody improved plans of social, religious, and/or economic life.

Commutation The controversial policy of allowing potential draftees to pay for a replacement to serve in the army. The policy was adopted by both the Union and Confederate governments during the Civil War, and in both cases opposition to commutation was so intense that the policy was abandoned.

Consent One of the key principles of liberalism, which held that people could not be subject to laws to which they had not given their consent. This principle is reflected in both the Declaration of Independence and the preamble to the Constitution, which begins with the famous words "We the people of the United States, in order to form a more perfect union."

Constitutionalism A loose body of thought that developed in Britain and the colonies and was used by the colonists to justify the Revolution by claiming that it was in accord with the principles of the British Constitution. Constitutionalism had two main elements. One was the rule of law, and the other the principle of *consent,* that one cannot be subject to laws or taxation except by duly elected representatives. Both were rights that had been won through struggle with the monarch. Constitutionalism also refers to the tendency in American politics, particularly in the early nineteenth century, to transpose all political questions into constitutional ones.

Consumer revolution A slow and steady increase over the course of the eighteenth century in the demand for, and purchase of, consumer goods. The consumer revolution of the eighteenth century was closely related to the Industrial Revolution.

Consumerism An ideology that defined the purchase of goods and services as both an expression of individual identity and essential to the national economy. Increasingly powerful by the 1920s and dominant by the 1950s, consumerism urged people to find happiness in the pursuit of leisure and pleasure more than in the work ethic.

Containment The basic U.S. strategy for fighting the cold war. As used by diplomat George Kennan in a 1947 magazine essay, "containment" referred to the combination of diplomatic, economic, and military programs necessary to hold back Soviet expansionism after World War II.

Contraband of war In its general sense, contraband of war was property seized from an enemy. But early in the Civil War the term was applied to slaves running to Union lines as a way of preventing owners from reclaiming them. The policy effectively nullified the fugitive slave clause of the U.S. Constitution. It was a first critical step in a process that would lead to a federal emancipation policy the following year.

Cooperationists Those southerners who opposed immediate secession after the election of Abraham Lincoln in 1860. Cooperationists argued instead that secessionists should wait to see if the new president was willing to "cooperate" with the South's demands.

Copperhead A northerner who sympathized with the South during the Civil War.

Deindustrialization The reverse of industrialization, as factory shutdowns decreased the size of the manufacturing sector. Plant closings began to plague the American economy in the 1970s, prompting fears that the nation would lose its industrial base.

Democratic Republicans One of the two parties to make up the first American party system. Following the fiscal and political views of Jefferson and Madison, Democratic Republicans generally advocated a weak federal government and opposed federal intervention in the economy of the nation.

Détente This French term for the relaxation of tensions was used to describe the central foreign policy innovation of the Nixon administration—a new, less confrontational relationship with Communism. In addition to opening a dialogue with the People's Republic of China, Nixon sought a more stable, less confrontational relationship with the Soviet Union.

Diffusion The controversial theory that the problem of slavery would be resolved if the slave economy was allowed to expand, or "diffuse," into the western territories. Southerners developed this theory as early as the 1800s in response to northerners who hoped to restrict slavery's expansion.

Disfranchisement The act of depriving a person or group of voting rights. In the nineteenth century the right to vote was popularly known as the franchise. The Fourteenth Amendment of the Constitution affirmed the right of adult male citizens to vote, but state-imposed restrictions and taxes deprived large numbers of Americans—particularly African Americans—of the vote from the 1890s until the passage of the Voting Rights Act of 1964.

Domestic patriarchy The practice of defining the family by the husband and father, and wives and children as his domestic dependents. Upon marriage a wife's property became her husband's, and children owed obedience and labor to the family until they reached adulthood. In combination with an exclusive male suffrage, domestic patriarchy described the political as well as the social system that prevailed among free Americans until the twentieth century.

Downsizing American corporations' layoffs of both blue- and white-collar workers in an attempt to become more efficient and competitive. Downsizing was one of the factors that made Americans uneasy about the economy in the 1990s, despite the impressive surge in the stock market.

Dust Bowl Across much of the Great Plains, decades of wasteful farming practices combined with several years of drought in the early 1930s to produce a series of massive dust storms that blew the topsoil across hundreds of miles. The area in Texas and Oklahoma affected by these storms became known as the Dust Bowl.

E-commerce Short for "electronic commerce," this was the term for the Internet-based buying and selling that was one of the key hopes for the computer-driven postindustrial economy. The promise of e-commerce was still unfulfilled by the start of the twenty-first century.

Encomienda A system of labor developed by the Spanish in the New World in which Spanish settlers (*encomenderos*) compelled groups of Native Americans to work for them. The *encomendero* owned neither the land nor the Indians who worked for him, but had the unlimited right to compel a particular group of Indians to work for him. This system was unique to the New World; nothing precisely like it had existed in Europe or elsewhere.

"Establishment" The elite of mainly Ivy League–educated, Anglo-Saxon, Protestant, male, liberal northeasterners that supposedly dominated Wall Street and Washington after World War II. The Establishment's support for corporations, activist government, and containment engendered hostility from opposite poles of the political spectrum—from conservatives and Republicans like Richard Nixon at one end and from the New Left and the Movement at the other. Although many of the post–World War II leaders of the United States did tend to share common origins and ideologies, this elite was never as powerful, self-conscious, or unified as its opponents believed.

Eugenics The practice of attempting to solve social problems through the control of human reproduction. Drawing on the authority of evolutionary biology, eugenists enjoyed considerable influence in the United States, especially on issues of corrections and public health, from the turn of the century through World War II. Applications of this pseudoscience included the identification of "born" criminals by physical characteristics and "better baby" contests at county fairs.

Federalists One of the two political parties to make up the first American party system. Following the fiscal and political policies proposed by Alexander Hamilton, Federalists generally advocated the importance of a strong federal government, including federal intervention in the economy of the new nation.

Feminism An ideology insisting on the fundamental equality of women and men. The feminists of the 1960s differed over how to achieve that equality: while liberal feminists mostly demanded equal rights for women in the workplace and in politics, radical feminists more thoroughly condemned the capitalist system and male oppression and demanded equality in both private and public life.

Feudalism A social and political system that developed in Europe in the Middle Ages under which powerful lords offered less powerful noblemen protection in return for their loyalty. Feudalism also included the economic system of *manorialism,* under which dependent serfs worked on the manors controlled by those lords.

Fire-eaters Militant southerners who pushed for secession in the 1850s.

Flexible response The defense doctrine of the Kennedy and Johnson administrations. Abandoning the Eisenhower administration's heavy emphasis on nuclear weapons, flexible response stressed the buildup of the nation's conventional and special forces so that the president had a range of military options in response to Communist aggression.

Front Early twentieth-century mechanized wars were fought along a battle line or "front" separating opposing sides. By World War II, tactical innovations—blitzkrieg, parachute troops, gliders, and amphibious landings—complicated warfare by breaking through, disrupting, or bypassing the front. The front thus became a more fluid boundary than the fortified trench lines of World War I. The term also acquired a political meaning, particularly for labor and the left. A coalition of parties supporting (or opposing) an agreed-upon line could be called a "popular front."

Gentility A term without precise meaning that represented all that was polite, civilized, refined, and fashionable. It was everything that vulgarity was not. Because the term had no precise meaning, it was always subject to negotiation, striving, and anxiety as Americans, beginning in the eighteenth century, tried to show others that they were genteel through their manners, their appearance, and their styles of life.

Glass ceiling The invisible barrier of discrimination that prevented female white-collar workers from rising to top executive positions in corporations.

Greenbackers Those who advocated currency inflation by keeping the type of money printed during the Civil War, known as "greenbacks," in circulation.

Gridlock The political traffic jam that tied up the federal government in the late 1980s and the 1990s. Gridlock developed from the inability of either major party to control both the presidency and Congress for any extended period of time. More fundamentally, gridlock reflected the inability of any party or president to win a popular mandate for a bold legislative program.

Horizontal integration More commonly known as "monopoly." An industry was "horizontally integrated" when a single company took control of virtually the entire market for a specific product. John D. Rockefeller's Standard Oil came close to doing this.

Humanism A Renaissance intellectual movement that focused on the intellectual and artistic achievements of humankind. Under the patronage of Queen Isabel, Spain became a center of European humanism.

Immediatism The variant antislavery sentiment that demanded immediate (as opposed to gradual) personal and federal action against the institution of slavery. This approach was most closely associated with William Lloyd Garrison and is dated from the publication of Garrison's newspaper, *The Liberator,* in January 1831.

Imperialism A process of extending dominion over territories beyond the national boundaries of a state. In the eighteenth century, Britain extended imperial control over North America through settlement, but in the 1890s, imperial influence was generally exercised through indirect rule. Subject peoples generally retained some local autonomy while the imperial power controlled commerce and defense. Few Americans went to the Philippines as settlers, but many passed through as tourists, missionaries, traders, and soldiers.

Individualism The social and political philosophy celebrating the central importance of the individual human being in society. Insisting on the rights of the individual in relationship to the group, individualism was one of the intellectual bases of capitalism and democracy. The resurgent individualism of the 1920s, with its emphasis on each American's freedom and fulfillment, was a critical element of the decade's emergent consumerism and Republican dominance.

Industrious revolution Beginning in the late seventeenth century in western Europe and extending to the North American colonies in the eighteenth century, a fundamental change in the way people worked, as they worked harder and organized their households to produce goods that could be sold, so they could have money to pay for the new consumer goods they wanted.

Initiative, recall, and referendum First proposed by the People's Party's Omaha Platform (1892), along with the direct election of senators and the secret ballot, as measures to subject corporate capitalism to democratic controls. Progressives, chiefly in western and midwestern states, favored them as a check on the power of state officials. The *initiative* allows legislation to be proposed by petition. The *recall* allows voters to remove public officials, and the *referendum* places new laws or constitutional amendments on the ballot for the direct approval of the voters.

Interest group An association whose members organize to exert political pressure on officials or the public. Unlike political parties, whose platforms and slates cover nearly every issue and office, an interest group focuses on a narrower list of concerns reflecting the shared outlook of its members. With the decline of popular politics around the turn of the twentieth century, business, religious, agricultural, women's, professional, neighborhood, and reform associations created a new form of political participation.

Isolationist Between World War I and World War II, the United States refused to join the League of Nations, scaled back its military commitments abroad, and sought to maintain its independence of action in foreign affairs. These policies were called isolationist, although some historians prefer the term "independent internationalist," in recognition of the United States' continuing global influence. In the late 1930s, isolationists favored policies aimed at distancing the United States from European affairs and building a national defense based on air power and hemispheric security.

Joint-stock company A form of business organization that was a forerunner to the modern corporation. The joint-stock company was used to raise both capital and labor for New World ventures. Shareholders contributed either capital or their labor for a period of years.

Judicial nationalism The use of the judiciary to assert the primacy of the national government over state and local government and the legal principle of contract over principles of local custom.

Keynesian economics The theory, named after the English economist John Maynard Keynes, that advocated the use of "countercyclical" fiscal policy. This meant that during good times the government should pay down the debt, so that during bad times, it could afford to stimulate the economy with deficit spending.

Liberalism A body of political thought that traces its origins to John Locke and whose chief principles are consent, freedom of conscience, and property. Liberalism held that people could not be governed except by their own consent and that the purpose of government was to protect people as well as their property.

Linked economic development A form of economic development that ties together a variety of enterprises so that development in one stimulates development in others, for example, those that provide raw materials, parts, or transportation.

Manifest destiny A term first coined in 1845 by journalist John O'Sullivan to express the belief, widespread among antebellum Americans, that the United States was destined to expand across the North American continent to the Pacific and had an irrefutable right to the lands absorbed in this expansion. This belief was frequently justified on the grounds of claims to political and racial superiority.

Market revolution The term used to designate the period of the early nineteenth century, roughly 1815–1830, during which internal dependence on cash markets and wages became widespread.

Mass production A system of efficient, high-volume manufacturing based on division of labor into repetitive tasks, simplification, and standardization of parts, increasing use of specialized machinery, and careful supervision. Emerging since the nineteenth century, mass production reached a critical stage of development with Henry Ford's introduction of the moving assembly line at his Highland Park automobile factory. Mass production drove the prosperity of the 1920s and helped make consumerism possible.

Massive resistance The rallying cry of southern segregationists who pledged to oppose the integration of the schools ordered by the Supreme Court in *Brown v. Board of Education* in 1954. The tactics of massive resistance included legislation, demonstrations, and violence.

Massive retaliation The defense doctrine of the Eisenhower administration which promised "instant, massive retaliation" with nuclear weapons in response to Soviet aggression.

McCarthyism The hunt for Communist subversion in the United States in the first years of the cold war. Democrats, in particular, used the term, a reference to the sometimes disreputable tactics of Republican Senator Joseph R. McCarthy of Wisconsin, in order to question the legitimacy of the conservative anti-Communist crusade.

Mercantilism An economic theory developed in early-modern Europe to explain and guide the growth of European nation-states. Its goal was to strengthen the state by making the economy serve its interests. According to the theory of mercantilism, the world's wealth, measured in gold and silver, was fixed; that is, it could never be increased. As a result, each nation's chief economic objective must be to secure as much of the world's wealth as possible. One nation's gain was necessarily another's loss. Colonies played an important part in the theory of mercantilism. Their role was to serve as sources of raw materials and as markets for manufactured goods for the mother country alone.

Middle ground The region between European and Indian settlements in North America that was neither fully European nor fully Indian, but rather a new world created out of two different traditions. The middle ground came into being every time Europeans and Indians met, needed each other, and could not (or would not) achieve what they wanted through use of force.

Millennialism A strain of Protestant belief that holds that history will end with the thousand-year reign of Christ (the millennium). Some Americans saw the Great Awakening, the French and Indian War, and the Revolution as signs that the millennium was about to begin in America, and this belief infused Revolutionary thought with an element of optimism. Millennialism was also one aspect of a broad drive for social perfection in nineteenth-century America.

Modernization The process by which developing countries in the third world were to become more like the United States—i.e., capitalist, independent, and anti-Communist. Confidence about the prospects for modernization was one of the cornerstones of liberal foreign policy in the 1960s.

Moral suasion The strategy of using persuasion (as opposed to legal coercion) to convince individuals to alter their behavior. In the antebellum years, moral suasion generally implied an appeal to religious values.

Mutual aid societies Organizations through which people of relatively meager means pooled their resources for emergencies. Usually, individuals paid small amounts in dues and were able to borrow large amounts in times of need. In the early nineteenth century, mutual aid societies were especially common among workers in free African American communities.

National Republicans Over the first 20 years of the nineteenth century, the Republican Party gradually abandoned its Jeffersonian animosity toward an activist federal government and industrial development and became a strong proponent of both of these positions. Embodied in the American system, these new views were fully captured in the party's designation of itself as National Republicans by 1824.

Nativism A bias against anyone not born in the United States and in favor of native-born Americans. This attitude assumes the superior culture and political virtue of white Americans of Anglo-Saxon descent, or of individuals assumed to have that lineage. During the period 1820–1850, Irish immigrants became the particular targets of nativist attitudes.

New Left The radical student movement that emerged in opposition to the new liberalism in the 1960s. The New Left condemned the cold war and corporate power and called for the creation of a true "participatory democracy" in the United States. Placing its faith in the radical potential of young, middle-class students, the New Left differed from the "old left" of the late nineteenth and early twentieth centuries, which believed workers would lead the way to socialism.

Patriotism Love of country. Ways of declaring and displaying national devotion underwent a change from the nineteenth to the twentieth centuries. Whereas politicians were once unblushingly called patriotic, after World War I the title was appropriated to describe the sacrifices of war veterans. Patriotic spectacle in the form of public oration and electoral rallies gave way to military-style commemorations of Armistice Day and the nation's martial heritage.

Political virtue In the political thought of the early republic, the personal qualities required in citizens if the republic was to survive.

Polygyny Taking more than one wife. Indian tribes such as the Huron practiced polygyny, and hence they did not object when French traders who already had wives in Europe took Indian women as additional wives.

Popular sovereignty A solution to the slavery controversy espoused by leading northern Democrats in the 1850s. It held that the inhabitants of western territories should be free to decide for themselves whether or not they wanted to have slavery. In principle, popular sovereignty would prevent Congress from either enforcing or restricting slavery's expansion into the western territories.

Postindustrial economy The service- and computer-based economy that was succeeding the industrial economy, which had been dominated by manufacturing, at the end of the twentieth century.

Principle of judicial review The principle of law that recognizes in the judiciary the power to review and rule on the constitutionality of laws. First established in *Marbury v. Madison* (1803) under Chief Justice John Marshall.

Producers ideology The belief that all those who lived by producing goods shared a common political identity in opposition to those who lived off financial speculation, rent, or interest.

Proprietary colony Colony established by a royal grant to an individual or family. The proprietary colonies included Maryland, New York, New Jersey, Pennsylvania, and the Carolinas.

Public opinion Not quite democracy or consent, public opinion was a way of understanding the influence of the citizenry on political calculations. It emerged in the eighteenth century, when it was defined as a crucial source of a government's legitimacy. It was associated with the emergence of a press and a literate public free to discuss, and to question, government policy. In the twentieth century, Freudian psychology and the new mass media encouraged a view of the public as both fickle and powerful. Whereas the popular will (a nineteenth-century concept) was steady and rooted in national traditions, public opinion was variable and based on attitudes that could be aroused or manipulated by advertising.

Realism A major artistic movement of the late nineteenth century that embraced writers, painters, critics, and photographers. Realists strove to avoid sentimentality and to depict life "realistically."

Reconversion The economic and social transition from the war effort to peacetime. Americans feared that reconversion might bring a return to the depression conditions of the 1930s.

Re-export trade Marine trade between two foreign ports, with an intermediate stop in a port of the ship's home nation. United States shippers commonly engaged in the re-export trade during the European wars of the late eighteenth and early nineteenth centuries, when England and France tried to prevent each other from shipping or receiving goods. United States shippers claimed that the intermediate stop in the United States made their cargoes neutral.

Republicanism A set of doctrines rooted in classical antiquity that held that power is always grasping and dangerous and presents a threat to liberty. Republicanism supplied constitutionalism with a motive by explaining how a balanced constitution could be transformed into a tyranny as grasping men used their power to encroach on the liberty of citizens. In addition, republicanism held that people achieved fulfillment only through participation in public life, as citizens in a republic. Republicanism required the individual to display *virtue* by sacrificing his (or her) private interest for the good of the republic.

***Requerimiento* (the Requirement)** A document issued by the Spanish Crown in 1513 in order to clarify the legal bases for the enslavement of hostile Indians. Each *conquistador* was required to read a copy of the *Requerimiento* to each group of Indians he encountered. The *Requerimiento* promised friendship to all Indians who accepted Christianity, but threatened war and enslavement for all those who resisted.

Safety-valve theory An argument commonly made in the nineteenth century that the abundance of western land spared the United States from the social upheavals common to capitalist societies in Europe. In theory, as long as eastern workers had the option of migrating west and becoming independent farmers, they could not be subject to European levels of exploitation. Thus the West was said to provide a "safety-valve" against the pressures caused by capitalist development.

Scalawag A derogatory term referring to southern whites who sympathized with the Republicans during Reconstruction.

Second-wave feminism The reborn women's movement of the 1960s and 1970s that reinterpreted the first wave of nineteenth- and early twentieth-century feminists' insistence on civil rights and called for full economic, reproductive, and political equality.

Separation of powers One of the chief innovations of the Constitution and a distinguishing mark of the American form of democracy, in which the executive, legislative, and judicial branches of government are separated so that they can check and balance each other.

Slave power In the 1850s northern Republicans explained the continued economic and political strength of slavery by claiming that a "slave power" had taken control of the federal government and used its authority to keep slavery alive artificially.

Slave society A society in which slavery is central to the economy and political structure, in contrast to a *society with slaves,* in which the presence of slaves does not alter the fundamental structures of the society.

Slavery A system of extreme social inequality distinguished by the definition of a human being as property, or chattel, and thus, in principle, totally subordinated to the slave owner.

Social Darwinism Darwin's theory of natural selection transferred from biological evolution to human history. Social Darwinists argued that some individuals and groups, particularly racial groups, were better able to survive in the "race of life."

Stagflation The unusual combination of stagnant growth and high inflation that plagued the American economy in the 1970s.

Strict constructionism The view that the Constitution has a fixed, explicit meaning which can be altered only through formal amendment. Loose constructionism is the view that the Constitution is a broad framework within which various interpretations and applications are possible without formal amendment.

Suburbanization The spread of suburban housing developments and, more broadly, of the suburban ideal.

Supply-side economics The controversial theory, associated with economist Arthur Laffer, that drove "Reaganomics," the conservative economic policy of the Reagan administration. In contrast to liberal economic theory, supply-side economics emphasized that producers—the "supply side" of the economic equation—drove economic growth, rather than consumers—the "demand side." To encourage producers to invest more in new production, Laffer and other supply-siders called for massive tax cuts.

Tariff A tax on goods moving across an international boundary. Because the Constitution allows tariffs only on imports, as a political issue the tariff question has chiefly concerned the protection of domestic manufacturing from foreign competition. Industries producing mainly for American consumers have preferred a higher tariff, while farmers and industries aimed at global markets have typically favored reduced tariffs. Prior to the Civil War, the tariff was a symbol of diverging political economies in North and South. The North advocated high tariffs to protect growing domestic manufacturing ("protective tariffs"), and the South opposed high tariffs on the grounds that they increased the cost of imported manufactured goods.

Taylorism A method for maximizing industrial efficiency by systematically reducing the time and motion involved in each step of the production process. The "scientific" system was designed by Frederick Taylor and explained in his book *The Principles of Scientific Management* (1911).

Universalism Enlightenment belief that all people are by their nature essentially the same.

Vertical integration The practice of taking control of every aspect of the production, distribution, and sale of a commodity. For example, Andrew Carnegie vertically integrated his steel operations by purchasing the mines that produced the ore, the railroads that carried the ore to the steel mills, the mills themselves, and the distribution system that carried the finished steel to consumers.

Virtual representation British doctrine that said that all Britons, even those who did not vote, were represented by Parliament, if not "actually," by representatives they had chosen, then "virtually," because each member of parliament was supposed to act on behalf of the entire realm, not only his constituents or even those who had voted for him.

Voluntarism A style of political activism that took place largely outside of electoral politics. Voluntarism emerged in the nineteenth century, particularly among those Americans who were not allowed to vote. Thus women formed voluntary associations that pressed for social and political reforms, even though women were excluded from electoral politics.

Waltham system Named after the system used in early textile mills in Waltham, Massachusetts, the term refers to the practice of bringing all elements of production together in a single factory setting with the application of non-human-powered machinery.

Watergate The name of the Washington, DC, office and condominium complex where five men with ties to the presidential campaign of Richard Nixon were caught breaking into the headquarters of the Democratic National Committee in June 1972. "Watergate" became the catchall term for the wide range of illegal practices of Nixon and his followers that were uncovered in the aftermath of the break-in.

Whig Party The political party founded by Henry Clay in the mid-1830s. The name derived from the seventeenth- and eighteenth-century British antimonarchical position and was intended to suggest that the Jacksonian Democrats (and Jackson in particular) sought despotic powers. In many ways the heirs of National Republicans, the Whigs supported economic expansion, but they also believed in a strong federal government to control the dynamism of the market. The Whig Party attracted many moral reformers.

Whitewater With its echo of Richard Nixon's "Watergate" scandals in the 1970s, "Whitewater" became the catchall term for the scandals that plagued Bill Clinton's presidency in the 1990s. The term came from the name of a real estate development company in Arkansas. Clinton and his wife Hillary supposedly had corrupt dealings with the Whitewater Development Corporation in the 1970s and 1980s that they purportedly attempted to cover up in the 1990s.

Women's rights movement The antebellum organizing efforts of women on their own behalf, in the attempt to secure a broad range of social, civic, and political rights. This movement is generally dated from the convention of Seneca Falls in 1848. Only after the Civil War would women's rights activism begin to confine its efforts to suffrage.

Photo Credits

Chapter 1: Benson Latin American Collection, University of Texas, Austin, 2, 32; The London Art Archive/Alamy, 3; The Granger Collection, 7; Cahokia Mounds State Historic Site. Photo by Art Grossman, 8; Courtesy of the Trustees of the British Museum, 15; J. Dallet/ agefotostock, 16; Image copyright ©The Metropolitan Museum of Art/ Art Resource, NY, 17; Pierpont Morgan Library/ Art Resource, NY, 20; The Granger Collection, 29; Newberry Library, Chicago/Superstock, 31; The Granger Collection, 33; The Granger Collection, 34; National Museum, Damascus, Syria/Gianni Dagli Orti/The Art Archive, 35.

Chapter 2: Service Historique de la Marine, Vincennes, France/The Bridgeman Art Library, 38, 61; The Bridgeman Art Library, 39; National Anthropological Library, Smithsonian Institution, 43; University of Pennsylvania Museum, object NA9143, image #12972, 47; Wolfgang Kaehler, 48; Pilgrim Hall Museum, Plymouth, MA, 56; The Bridgeman Art Library, 58; Courtesy of the Trustees of The British Museum 59; Service Historique de la Marine, Vincennes, France/ The Bridgeman Art Library, 62; The British Museum/The Art Archive, 63; The Gilcrease Museum,Tulsa OK, 65.

Chapter 3: The Granger Collection, 68, 98; Borough of King's Lynn and West Norfolk, 69; Preservation Virginia, 71; University of Oxford/Ashmolean Museum of Art and Archaeology, 74; Marilyn Angel Wynn/ Nativestock.com, 75; Ira Block/National Geographic Stock/Getty Images, 75; Private Collection/Getty Images, 76; Pierre Dan, Histoire de Barbarie et de ses Corsaires, Paris, 1637, 80; Courtesy of Lester Walker, 92.

Chapter 4: Pennsylvania Academy of the Fine Arts, Philadelphia/The Bridgeman Art Library, 102, 110; Illustration by Walter Rane, 103; Private Collection/ The Bridgeman Art Library, 105; Museum of the City of New York/ The Bridgeman Art Library, 108; Collection of the New-York Historical Society, neg#81885d, 109; North Carolina State Archives, Division of Archives and History, 111; Plymouth County Commissioners, Plymouth Court House, Plymouth, MA/Dublin Seminar for New England Folklife, Concord, MA, 120; North Wind Picture Archives, 121; Springfield Library, Springfield, MA, 126; Museum of the City of New York/The Bridgeman Art Library, 127; ©President and Fellows Harvard University, Peabody Museum, 99-12-10/53121, 132; Kevin Fleming/Corbis, 134; Giraudon/The Bridgeman Art Library, 136; Chuck Place/ Place Photography, 137.

Chapter 5: Private Collection/The Bridgeman Art Library, 140, 154; Private Collection/ The Bridgeman Art Library, 141; Stowage of the British Slave Ship Brooks under the Regulated Slave Trade Act of 1788/Library of Congress, 147; The Granger Collection, 149; © Royal Geographical Society, 156; Virginia Historical Society, 157; Gibbes Museum, Gift of Mr. Joseph E. Jenkins ©Image Gibbes Museum of Art/Carolina Art Association, 1968.005.0001, 159; Library Company of Philadelphia, 160; Collection of the New-York Historical Society, neg#81577d, 155; Museum of Fine Arts, Boston. Bequest of Buckminster Brown, MD, 95.1359, 162; American Antiquarian Society, 173.

Chapter 6: The Granger Collection, 176, 204; Owned by Kate S. Rowland/Mrs. John Carrere; photography courtesy of Barbara M. Jones/ Mrs. Warner E. Jones. Frontispiece from A Narrative of the Captivity of Mrs. Johnson (Bowie, Md.: Heritage Books, Inc., 1990), 177; Courtesy of Dartmouth College Library, Rauner Specials Collections Library, 177; Washington University, St. Louis, MO/The Bridgeman Art Library, 184; The Granger Collection, 185; Albany Institute of History and Art, Purchase, 1993.44, 186; Hulton Archive/Getty Images, 187; Hulton Archive/Getty Images, 191; The Granger Collection, 193; Vereinigte Ostindische Compagnie bond, 194; The Granger Collection, 198; The Granger Collection, 200; The Manhattan Rare Book Company, 202; MPI/Gerry Images, 206; Division of Military History, National Museum of American History/Smithsonian Institution, 209.

Chapter 7: Reunion des Musees Nationaux/Art Resource, NY, 212, 231; The Granger Collection, 213; Bettmann/Corbis, 218; Library of Congress, 219; Yale University Art Gallery/Art Resource, NY, 221; James Nesterwitz/Alamy Images, 222; Division of Military History, National Museum of American History/Smithsonian Institution, 223; Erich Lessing/Art Resource, NY, 225; The Granger Collection, 226; American Numismatic Association, 235; The Granger Collection, 238; National Gallery of Canada, Ottawa, 242; The Granger Collection, 248; The Colonial Williamsburg Foundation, 251.

Chapter 8: The Granger Collection, 254, 259; Library Company of Philadelphia, 255; The Colonial Williamsburg Foundation. Gift of the Lasser Family, 256; The Granger Collection, 261; Edward Lawler, Jr., 264; American Antiquarian Society, 266; Maritime Museum of the Atlantic, 272; The Granger Collection, 281; The Granger Collection, 286; The Granger Collection, 287.

Chapter 9: Collection of the New-York Historical Society/The Bridgeman Art Library, 290, 301; The Granger Collection, 291; General Records of the U. S. government, National Archives, 295; American Antiquarian Society, 297; Peter Harholdt/Corbis, 305; Central Library Birmingham, West Midlands, UK/The Bridgeman Art Library, 308; The Granger Collection, 310; American Museum of Textile History, 311; National Portrait Gallery, Smithsonian Institution/Art Resource, NY, 317; The Granger Collection, 320; Franklin Institute, Philadelphia, PA, 323.

Chapter 10: Chicago History Museum/The Bridgeman Art Library, 328, 249; National Portrait Gallery, Smithsonian Institution/Art Resource, NY, 329; Chicago History Museum/ The Bridgeman Art Library, 333; Rare Books and Special Collections, Cornell University, 333; The Granger Collection, 334; Duke University Rare Book, Manuscript and Special Collections Library, 335; Dinodia Images/Alamy, 338; Image ©The Metropolitan Museum of art, New York/Art Resource, NY, 339; Collection of the New-York Historical Society, acc. 1953.251, 340; Wilberforce House, Hull City Museums and Art Galleries, UK/ The Bridgeman Art Library, 341; Library of Virginia, 342; Chicago History Museum/The Bridgeman Art Library, 344; The Granger Collection, 355; Photographs and Prints Division, Schomburg Center for Research in Black Culture, The New York Public Library, Astor, Lenox and Tilden Foundations, 358.

Chapter 11: St. Louis Art Museum/The Bridgeman Art Library, 362, 368; Bentley Historical Library, University of Michigan, 363; The Granger Collection, 366; The Granger Collection, 372; The Granger Collection, 373; Department of Political History, National Museum of American History, Smithsonian Institution, 378; picturehistory.com, 379; Library of Congress, 382; Bettmann/Corbis, 384; Woolrac Museum, Oklahoma/The Bridgeman Art Library, 386; The Granger Collection, 388; American Numismatic Association, 391.

Chapter 12: Geoffrey Clements/Corbis, 398, 409; The Granger Collection, 399; The Granger Collection, 402; Denver Public

Library, Western History Collection, 404; The Granger Collection, 405; Hawaiian Mission Children's Society Library, 406; Newberry Library, Chicago, 410; Lane County Historical Museum, 415; The Granger Collection, 417; Library of Congress, 419; The Granger Collection, 425; Brown Brothers, 427.

Chapter 13: Private Collection/ The Bridgeman Art Library, 432, 448; Smithsonian American Art Museum, Washington, DC/ Art Resource, NY, 433; The Granger Collection, 436; The Granger Collection, 438; The Amon Carter Museum, Ft. Worth, TX, 1983.156., 441; Courtesy of The Witte Museum, San Antonio, Texas, 443; The Palace of the Governors, New Mexico History Museum, 448; Smithsonian American Art Museum, Washington, DC/ Art Resource, NY, 451; The Bridgeman Art Library, 453; The Granger Collection, 454; Courtesy Special Collections, The University of Texas at Arlington, 458; Hulton Archive/Getty Images, 459.

Chapter 14: North Wind Picture Archives, 464, 482; Image ©The Metropolitan Museum of art, New York/Art Resource, NY, 465; Collection of the New-York Historical Society/The Bridgeman Art Library, 468; Seaver Center, Natural History Museum of Los Angeles, 473; Andrew McKiney/Dorling Kindersley/DK Images, 473; Bettmann/Corbis, 474; Bettmann/Corbis, 475; The Granger Collection, 476; Library of Congress, 479; The Granger Collection, 489; Abraham Lincoln Presidential Library and Museum, 489; Kansas State Capitol Building, 491.

Chapter 15: The Granger Collection, 496, 511; The Granger Collection, 497; Terwilliger Associates, 500; The Granger Collection, 503; Seventh Regiment Fund, Inc., 507; Rare Books and Special Collections, Library of Congress, 515; The Granger Collection, 516; Library of Congress, 519; The Granger Collection, 520; Harper's Weekly, 521; Courtesy of the National Archives and Record Administration, 522; Indiana State Museum, 524; The Granger Collection, 526; Culver Pictures/The Art Archive, 531; The Granger Collection, 533; Culver Pictures/The Art Archive, 535.

Chapter 16: Louis Psihoyos/ Sciencefaction.com, 538, 541; Library of Congress, 539; Photographs and Prints Division, Schomburg Center for Research in Black Culture, The New York Public Library, Astor, Lenox and Tilden Foundations, 543; Library of Congress, 544; Library of Congress, Rare Book and Special Collections, 549; Library of Congress, 550; Library of Congress, 554; Bettmann/Corbis, 558; The New York Times, May 27, 1868, 558; Bettmann/Corbis, 559; Library of Congress, 560; National Portrait Gallery, Smithsonian Institution/Art Resource, NY, 562; The Granger Collection, 564.

Chapter 17: The Granger Collection, 570, 580; The Granger Collection, 571; Bettmann/Corbis, 574; Princeton University Library, Rare Books and Special Collections, 576; Bettmann/Corbis, 577; Bettmann/Corbis, 581; Asheville Convention & Visitors Bureau, 584; The Granger Collection, 587; Bettmann/Corbis, 588; Bettmann/Corbis, 590; The Granger Collection, 593; Corbis, 595; Library of Congress, 595.

Chapter 18: The Granger Collection, 602, 610; Bettmann/Corbis, 603; Library of Congress, 607; The Granger Collection, 608; The Granger Collection, 616; Library of Congress, 618; The Granger Collection, 621; Library of Congress, 622; Chicago History Museum, 623; The Granger Collection, 626; Thomas Eakins, Swimming, 1885, Oil on canvas, 27 3/8 × 36 3/8 inches. The Amon Carter Museum, 1990.19.1, 627; The Granger Collection, 629.

Chapter 19: Kansas State Historical Society, 632, 656; Nebraska State Historical Society, 633; The Granger Collection, 637; Bettmann/Corbis, 639; Charles Guiteau Collection, Georgetown University Library, Special Collections, 641; The Granger Collection, 642; Bancroft Library, University of California, 647; Image ©The Metropolitan Museum of art, New York/Art Resource, NY, 649; Library of Congress, 650; The Granger Collection, 653; The Granger Collection, 654.

Chapter 20: The Granger Collection, 660, 667; The Granger Collection, 661; John W. Hartman Center for Sales, Advertising and Marketing, Duke University, 664; Berry-Hill Galleries, New York, 672; McKinley Memorial Library, 673; The Granger Collection, 675; The Granger Collection, 676; The Granger Collection, 676; Yale Divinity School, 681; United States Naval History Center, 683; Library of Congress, 686.

Chapter 21: Mt. Holyoke College Art Museum, 692, 715;; History of Medicine Collection/National Library of Medicine, 693; The Woodrow Wilson Presidential Library and Museum In Staunton, VA, 695; Photo by Carol Highsmith, courtesy Woodrow Wilson House, A National Trust Historic Site, 695; Hulton Archive/Getty Images, 701; The Art Archive, 702; Library of Congress, 703; Library of Congress, 706; The Verdict Magazine, 3/20/1899, 707; Chicago History Museum, 710; The Granger Collection, 713; William Howard Taft National Historic Site, 720; Corbis, 720.

Chapter 22: Courtesy of the Pennsylvania State Archives, 726, 739; Brown Brothers, 727; Hulton Archive/Getty Images, 732; Library of Congress, 734; Hudson Library and Historical Society, 735; Bettmann/Corbis, 736; The Granger Collection, 737; Getty Images, 741; The Granger Collection, 742; Allposters.com, 745; Burl Burlingame/Pacific Monograph, 746; Australian War Museum/ The Art Archive, 749; Capt. Jackson/Time & Life Pictures/Getty Images, 751; United States Naval History Center, 752; Digital Image © The Modern of Modern Art/Scala/ Art Resource, NY. ©Estate of Ben Shahn, Licensed by VAGA, NY, 754.

Chapter 23: Courtesy Craig F. Starr Gallery, New York, 758, 765; Hulton Archive/Getty Images, 759; Hulton Archive/Getty Images, 761; The Advertising Archive, 767; The Granger Collection, 769; Courtesy of Indiana University Press, Archives of Traditional Music, 772; The Granger Collection, 773; Hulton Archive/Getty Images, 776; Hulton Archive/ Getty Images, 777; Title Insurance and Trust/ C. C. Pierce Photograph Collection, Special Collections, University of Southern California Libraries, 778; Michael Ochs Archives/Getty Images, 780; The Granger Collection, 783; United States Naval History Center, 785; Swarthmore Library of Peace, 786; The New York Times/Redux, 786.

Chapter 24: Bettmann/Corbis, 790; Bettmann/Corbis, 791, 797; FPG/Hulton Archive/Getty Images, 794; Hulton Archive/ Getty Images, 795; Bettmann/Corbis, 799; Hulton Archive/Getty Images, 802; United States Forest Service, 803; Popperfoto/Getty Images, 804; Farm Security Administration Collection/Library of Congress, 806; Corbis, 807; Bernard Hoffman/Time & Life Pictures/ Getty Images, 808; Topfoto/The Image Works, 817; Photo courtesy WheatonArts, 819.

Chapter 25: Bettmann/Corbis, 822, 830; William Shrout/Time & Life Pictures/Getty Images, 827; William Shrout/Time & Life Pictures/Getty Images, 829; Courtesy National Park Service Museum Management Program and Tuskegee Airmen National Historic Site, TUA131, 833; United States Naval History Center, 835; Bettmann/Corbis, 839; Minnesota Historical Society/Corbis, 844; The Jack Iwata Collection, The Japanese American National Museum, 846; United States Naval History Center, 849; Bettmann/Corbis, 851; The Granger Collection, 854; Courtesy of Eden Camp Museum, Yorkshire/Dorling Kindersley/DK Images, 855.

Chapter 26: The Everett Collection, 858, 862; Bettmann/Corbis, 859; Art of Time Magazine/National Portrait Gallery, Smithsonian Institution, 865; The Daily Mail, 1946, 866; O. Oxley/Saudi Aramco World/PADIA, 867; SwimInk2.LLC/Corbis, 869; Courtesy Harry S. Truman Library, Independence, Missouri, 871; The Granger Collection, 876; Early Office Museum, hhpt:// www.earlyofficemuseum.com, 877; Hulton Archive/Getty Images, 879; Courtesy Harry S. Truman Library, Independence, Missouri,

882; Special Collections, Oregon State University Library, 883; Special Collections, Oregon State University Library, 887.

Chapter 27: Guy Gillette/Time & Life Pictures/Getty Images, 890, 897; Courtesy Time Inc., 891; Hagley Museum and Library, Better Living Magazine, 1972.341, 893; Time & Life Pictures/Getty Images, 894; Time & Life Pictures/Getty Images, 896; John W. Hartman Center for Sales, Advertising and Marketing, Duke University, 899; The Everett Collection, 899; Bettmann/Corbis, 904; AP Images, 906; Bettmann/Corbis, 908; Louis Armstrong House Museum, 909; AP Images, 910; Bettmann/Corbis, 914; AP Images, 917; Bettmann/Corbis, 918; A 1957 Herblock Cartoon, copyright by The Herblock Foundation, 919.

Chapter 28: Bettmann/Corbis, 922, 930; Courtesy Fred Downs, 923; Jack Moebes/Corbis, 925; Bettmann/Corbis, 927; David J. and Janice Frent Collection/Corbis, 927; Bettmann/Corbis, 928; Hulton-Deutsch Collection/Corbis, 931; Ralph Crane/Time & Life Pictures/Getty Images, 934; Francis Miller/Time & Life Pictures/Getty Images, 937; Tom Polumbaum/Newseum Collection, 940; Bruce Davidson/Magnum Photos, 941; Philip Jones Griffith/Magnum Photos, 945; AP Images, 946; AP Images, 949; Magnum Photos, 954; Jack Kightlinger/Corbis, 955; AP Images, 956.

Chapter 29: Elliott Landy/Corbis, 960, 983; AP Images, 961; Bettmann/Corbis, 964; Dow Archives, Chemical Heritage Foundation Archives, 965; Bettmann/Corbis, 967; Rauchwetter/dpa/Corbis, 969; AP Images, 970; Tim Page/Corbis, 971; John Sotomayer/The New York Times/Redux, 973; Bettmann/Corbis, 975; Bettmann/Corbis, 984; Bettmann/Corbis, 987; Gerald R. Ford Presidential Museum, Grand Rapids, Michigan, 988; Bettmann/Corbis, 990; Bettmann/Corbis, 992; www.jofreeman.com, 993.

Chapter 30: Stephen Ferry/Getty Images, 996, 1029; Courtesy Linda Chavez, 997; AFP/Getty Images, 1000; AP Images, 1000; AP Images, 1002; Dirck Halstead/Getty Images, 1004; Roger Ressmeyer/Corbis, 1007; Lee Frey/Hulton Archive/Getty Images, 1009; Time & Life Pictures/Getty Images, 1010; Diana Walker/Time & Life Pictures/Getty Images, 1012; Peter Jordan/Time & Life Pictures/Getty Images, 1013; AP Images, 1015; Ronald Reagan Library, 1016; Bettmann/Corbis, 1022.

Chapter 31: Cancan Chu/Getty Images, 1032, 1037; David Cannon/Allsport/Getty Images, 1033; Courtesy of The Computer History Museum, 1036; Tolga Adanall/MCT/Landov, 1038; Collection International Institute of Social History, Amsterdam, 1039; Charles Dharapak/AP Images, 1041; Fran@CartoonStock.com, 1042; Robert King/Newsmakers/Getty Images, 1046; Paul J. Richards/AFP/Getty Images, 1047; Reuters, 1047; Justin Sullivan/Getty Images, 1053; Peter Turnley/Corbis, 1056; Reuters/Corbis, 1058; AP Images, 1059; Reuters, 1061; AP Images, 1062; Ric Feld/AP Images, 1065; John Gress/Reuters/Landov, 1066; Jeff Haynes/Reuters/Landov, 1067.

Index

B

C

D

E

G

S

X

Y

Z